**RANDOM HOUSE
WEBSTER'S**

STUDENT notebook DICTIONARY

3rd Ed.

A

A, a (ā) *n.* the first letter of the English alphabet.

a (ə; *when stressed* ā) *adj. or indef. art. before initial consonant sounds.* **1.** one. **2.** any; any one.

a- a prefix indicating: **1.** not. **2.** without.

AA Alcoholics Anonymous.

A.A. Associate of Arts.

aard/vark/ (ärd/värk/) *n.* an African ant-eating mammal.

AARP, American Association of Retired Persons.

A.B. Bachelor of Arts.

A.B.A. American Bar Association.

a·back/ (ə bak/) *adv.* —*Idiom.* **taken aback,** disconcerted.

ab/a·cus (ab/ə kəs) *n.* a counting device using rows of sliding beads.

a·baft/ (ə baft/) *prep. Naut.* **1.** behind. —*adv.* **2.** at the stern.

ab/a·lo/ne (ab/ə lō/nē) *n.* an edible mollusk having a shell lined with mother-of-pearl.

a·ban/don (ə ban/dən) *v.t.* **1.** to leave completely. **2.** to give up. —*n.* **3.** a surrender to natural impulses. —**a·ban/don·ment,** *n.*

a·ban/doned *adj.* **1.** forsaken or deserted. **2.** unrestrained or uninhibited.

a·base/ (ə bās/) *v.t.,* **abased, abasing.** to humiliate or degrade. —**a·base/ment,** *n.*

a·bashed/ (ə basht/) *adj.* embarrassed.

a·bate/ (ə bāt/) *v.t., v.i.,* **abated, abating.** to make or become less intense. —**a·bate/ment,** *n.*

ab/at·toir/ (ab/ə twär/, ab/ə twär/) *n.* a slaughterhouse.

ab/bess (ab/is) *n.* a woman who is head of a convent.

ab/bey (ab/ē) *n.* a monastery or convent.

ab/bot (ab/ət) *n.* a man who is head of a monastery.

abbr. abbreviation.

ab·bre/vi·ate/ (ə brē/vē āt/) *v.t.,* **-ated, -ating.** to shorten. —**ab·bre/vi·a/tion,** *n.*

ABCs *n.* (*used with a pl. v.*) **1.** the alphabet. **2.** the basics. Also, **ABC's.**

ab/di·cate/ (ab/di kāt/) *v.t., v.i.,* **-cated, -cating.** to give up (power or office). —**ab/di·ca/tion,** *n.*

ab·do/men (ab/də mən) *n.* the part of the body between the thorax and the pelvis; belly. —**ab·dom/i·nal** (ab dom/ə nl) *adj.*

ab·dom/i·nals *n.pl.* the muscles of the abdomen. Also, **abs.**

ab·duct/ (ab dukt/) *v.t.* to kidnap. —**ab·duc/tion,** *n.* —**ab·duc/tor,** *n.*

a·beam/ (ə bēm/) *adv. Naut.* across a ship.

a·bed/ (ə bed/) *adv.* in bed.

ab/er·ra/tion (ab/ə rā/shən) *n.* **1.** deviation from what is usual or normal. **2.** mental unsoundness. —**ab·er/rant** (ə ber/ənt, ab/ər-) *adj.*

a·bet/ (ə bet/) *v.t.,* **abetted, abetting.** to encourage in wrongdoing. —**a·bet/tor, a·bet/ter,** *n.*

a·bey/ance (ə bā/əns) *n.* in abeyance, temporarily inactive.

ab·hor/ (ab hôr/) *v.t.,* **-horred, -horring.** to loathe. —**ab·hor/rence,** *n.* —**ab·hor/rent,** *adj.*

a·bide/ (ə bīd/) *v.,* **abode** (ə bōd/) or **abided, abiding.** —*v.t.* **1.** to tolerate. —*v.i.* **2.** to remain. **3.** to reside. **4. abide by, a.** to comply with. **b.** to keep, as a promise.

a·bid/ing *adj.* steadfast; lasting.

a·bil/i·ty (ə bil/i tē) *n., pl.* **-ties. 1.** the power to do something. **2.** competence.

ab/ject (ab/jekt, ab jekt/) *adj.* **1.** wretched. **2.** despicable. **3.** servile. —**ab/ject·ly,** *adv.*

ab·jure/ (ab jŏŏr/) *v.t.,* **-jured, -juring.** to repudiate or renounce. —**ab/ju·ra/tion,** *n.*

a·blaze/ (ə blāz/) *adj.* **1.** on fire. **2.** gleaming. **3.** excited.

a/ble (ā/bəl) *adj.,* **abler, ablest. 1.** having sufficient power or qualification. **2.** competent. —**a/bly,** *adv.*

-able a suffix indicating: **1.** able to be. **2.** tending to.

a/ble-bod/ied *adj.* physically fit.

ab·lu/tions (ə blŏŏ/shənz) *n.pl.* the washing of one's body, esp. as a ritual.

ab/ne·gate/ (ab/ni gāt/) *v.t.,* **-gated, -gating.** to renounce. —**ab/ne·ga/tion,** *n.*

ab·nor/mal (ab nôr/məl) *adj.* not normal; not usual or typical. —**ab/-**

nor·mal/i·ty (-mal/i tē) *n.* —**ab·nor/mal·ly,** *adv.*

a·board/ (ə bôrd/) *adv.* **1.** on a ship, train, etc. —*prep.* **2.** on.

a·bode/ (ə bōd/) *n.* a dwelling.

a·bol/ish (ə bol/ish) *v.t.* to do away with.

ab/o·li/tion (ab/ə lish/ən) *n.* **1.** an abolishing or being abolished. **2.** (*sometimes cap.*) the end of slavery in the U.S. —**ab/o·li/tion·ist,** *n.*

A/-bomb/ (ā/bom/) *n.* the atomic bomb.

a·bom/i·na·ble (ə bom/ə nə bəl) *adj.* **1.** very bad. **2.** detestable. —**a·bom/i·na·bly,** *adv.*

a·bom/i·nate/ (-nāt/) *v.t.,* **-nated, -nating.** to hate or detest. —**a·bom/i·na/tion,** *n.*

ab/o·rig/i·nal (ab/ə rij/ə nl) *adj.* **1.** having existed in a place from the beginning. —*n.* **2.** an aborigine.

ab/o·rig/i·ne (-rij/ə nē) *n.* an original inhabitant of a land.

a·bort/ (ə bôrt/) *v.i., v.t.* **1.** to undergo or cause abortion. **2.** to end prematurely. —**a·bor/tive,** *adj.*

a·bor/tion *n.* the induced or spontaneous expulsion of a fetus before it is viable.

a·bound/ (ə bound/) *v.i.* **1.** to exist in large quantities. **2.** abound in, to be well supplied with.

a·bout/ (ə bout/) *prep.* **1.** concerning. **2.** near or around. **3.** on every side of. **4.** on the verge of. —*adv.* **5.** approximately. **6.** almost. **7.** nearby. **8.** on all sides. **9.** in the opposite direction. —**Usage.** Both ON and ABOUT mean "concerning." ON and ABOUT is used when the information given is general and not too technical: *a novel* ABOUT *the Civil War.* ON is used when the information is particular, as by being scholarly or technical: *an important article* ON *the Civil War.*

a·bout/-face/ *n.* a reversal of position.

a·bove/ (ə buv/) *adv.* **1.** in or to a higher place. **2.** overhead. **3.** earlier in a text. —*prep.* **4.** over. **5.** higher or greater than. **6.** beyond the reach or level of. —*adj.* **7.** preceding. —*Idiom.* **8.** above all, most importantly.

a·bove/board/ *adv., adj.* without deception.

ab/ra·ca·dab/ra (ab/rə kə dab/rə) *n.* a word used in magic.

a·brade/ (ə brād/) *v.t., v.i.,* **abraded, abrading.** to scrape or rub away.

a·bra/sion (ə brā/zhən) *n.* **1.** a wearing or rubbing away. **2.** a scraped area on the skin.

a·bra/sive (ə brā/siv, -ziv) *adj.* **1.** tending to wear down. **2.** harsh. —*n.* **3.** material used to grind or smooth. —**a·bra/sive·ly,** *adv.*

a·breast/ (ə brest/) *adv.* **1.** side by side. **2.** abreast of, **a.** level with. **b.** informed or aware of.

a·bridge/ *v.t.,* **abridged, abridging.** to shorten. —**a·bridg/ment,** *n.*

a·broad/ (ə brôd/) *adv.* **1.** away from one's own country. **2.** over a large area.

ab/ro·gate/ (ab/rə gāt/) *v.t.,* **-gated, -gating.** to abolish or repeal. —**ab/ro·ga/tion,** *n.*

ab·rupt/ (ə brupt/) *adj.* **1.** sudden. **2.** curt. **3.** steep. —**ab·rupt/ly,** *adv.* —**ab·rupt/ness,** *n.*

ab/scess (ab/ses) *n.* an infected, pus-filled place on the body.

ab·scond/ (ab skond/) *v.i.* to depart suddenly and secretly.

ab/sent *adj.* (-sənt) **1.** not present. **2.** lacking. **3.** preoccupied. —*v.t.* (ab sent/) **4.** to keep (oneself) away. —**ab/sence,** *n.*

ab/sen·tee/ (ab/sən tē/) *n.* a person who is absent.

absentee bal/lot a ballot mailed by a voter who cannot come to the polls.

ab/sent-mind/ed *adj.* preoccupied; forgetful. —**ab/sent-mind/ed·ly,** *adv.* —**ab/sent-mind/ed·ness,** *n.*

ab/sinthe (ab/sinth) *n.* a bitter green liqueur.

ab/so·lute/ (ab/sə lŏŏt/) *adj.* **1.** complete; perfect. **2.** unrestricted. **3.** definite. **4.** pure. —**ab/so·lute/ly,** *adv.*

absolute pitch/ the ability to identify the pitch of a tone.

absolute ze/ro the temperature (−273.16° C or −459.69° F) at which molecular activity ceases.

ab·solve/ (ab zolv/) *v.t.,* **-solved, -solving. 1.** to declare free from guilt. **2.** to release from a duty. —**ab/so·lu/tion** (-sə lŏŏ/shən) *n.*

ab·sorb/ (ab sôrb/, -zôrb/) *v.t.* **1.** to take in or soak up. **2.** to occupy com-

pletely; fascinate. —**ab·sorb/ing,** *adj.* —**ab·sorb/ent·cy,** *n.*

ab·sorb/ent, *adj.* **1.** capable of absorbing. —*n.* **2.** a substance that absorbs. —**ab·sorb/en·cy,** *n.*

ab·sorp/tion (-sôrp/shən, -zôrp/-) *n.* **1.** an absorbing or being absorbed. **2.** mental preoccupation.

ab·stain/ (ab stān/) *v.i.* to refrain. **2.** to refrain from casting one's vote. —**ab·sten/tion** (-sten/shən) *n.*

ab·ste/mi·ous (ab stē/mē əs) *adj.* moderate in eating, drinking, etc.

ab/sti·nence (ab/stə nəns) *n.* an abstaining, as from food, alcohol, or sexual activity. —**ab/sti·nent,** *adj.*

ab/stract *adj.* (ab strakt/, ab/strakt) **1.** considered apart from specific objects. **2.** theoretical. **3.** (of art) not representing natural objects or forms. —*n.* (ab/strakt) **4.** a summary. **5.** an abstract idea. —*v.t.* (ab strakt/) **6.** to remove. **7.** to summarize. —**ab·strac/tion,** *n.*

ab·stract/ed *adj.* preoccupied; absent-minded.

ab·struse/ (ab strŏŏs/) *adj.* hard to understand.

ab·surd/ (ab sûrd/, -zûrd/) *adj.* contrary to common sense; ridiculous. —**ab·surd/ly,** *adv.* —**ab·surd/i·ty,** *n.*

a·bun/dance (ə bun/dəns) *n.* a plentiful supply. —**a·bun/dant,** *adj.* —**a·bun/dant·ly,** *adv.*

a·buse/ *v.,* **abused, abusing.** *n.* —*v.t.* (ə byŏŏz/) **1.** to use wrongly. **2.** to treat badly. **3.** to insult. —*n.* (ə byŏŏs/) **4.** wrong use. **5.** mistreatment. **6.** insulting language. —**a·bu/sive,** *adj.* —**a·bu/sive·ness,** *n.*

a·but/ (ə but/) *v.i., v.t.,* **abutted, abutting.** to be adjacent (to); border (on).

a·bys/mal (ə biz/məl) *adj.* **1.** extremely bad. **2.** very deep.

a·byss/ (ə bis/) *n.* **1.** a very deep chasm. **2.** hell.

Ab/ys·sin/i·an (ab/ə sin/ē ən) *adj.* **1.** from ancient Ethiopia. —*n.* **2.** type of cat.

AC 1. air conditioning. **2.** Also, **ac., a.c., A.C.** alternating current.

a·ca/cia (ə kā/shə) *n.* a small tree or shrub with yellow flowers.

ac/a·dem/ic (ak/ə dem/ik) *adj.* **1.** of a school, college, etc. **2.** theoretical. —*n.* **3.** a college teacher. —**ac/a·dem/i·cal·ly,** *adv.*

a·cad/e·my (ə kad/ə mē) *n., pl.* **-mies. 1.** a private secondary school. **2.** a school for specialized study. **3.** a society of scholars, artists, etc.

a·can/thus (ə kan/thəs) *n.* a Mediterranean plant having spiny leaves.

a/ cap·pel/la (ä/ kə pel/ə) *adv., adj. Music.* without instrumental accompaniment.

ac·cede/ (ak sēd/) *v.* **-ceded, -ceding. accede to, 1.** to agree to. **2.** to assume (an office or title).

ac·cel/er·ate/ (ak sel/ə rāt/) *v.,* **-ated, -ating.** —*v.t.* **1.** to increase the speed of. —*v.i.* **2.** to speed up; hasten. —**ac·cel/er·a/tion,** *n.*

ac·cel/er·a/tor *n.* a pedal that controls a vehicle's speed.

ac/cent (ak/sent) *n.* **1.** emphasis on a syllable or word. **2.** a distinctive way of pronouncing. **3.** a mark showing stress or vowel quality. —*v.t.* **4.** to emphasize.

ac·cen/tu·ate/ (ak sen/chŏŏ āt/) *v.t.,* **-ated, -ating.** to stress or emphasize. —**ac·cen/tu·a/tion,** *n.*

ac·cept/ (ak sept/) *v.t.* **1.** to receive willingly. **2.** to answer yes to (an invitation, offer, etc.). **3.** to agree to. **4.** to admit formally, as to a college. **5.** to regard as true. —**ac·cept/a·bil/i·ty,** *n.* —**ac·cept/a·ble,** *adj.* —**ac·cept/a·bly,** *adv.* —**ac·cept/ance,** *n.*

—**ac·cept/ed,** *adj.* —**Usage.** Because of similarity in pronunciation, ACCEPT and EXCEPT are sometimes confused in writing. ACCEPT is a verb meaning "to receive willingly": *Please accept my gift.* EXCEPT is usually a preposition meaning "other than": *Everybody came except you.* When EXCEPT is used as a verb, it means "to leave out": *Some students were excepted from taking the exam.*

ac/cess (ak/ses) *n.* **1.** the right to enter or use. **2.** a means of approach. —*v.t.* **3.** to gain access to. **4.** to gain access to (data, files, etc.) in a computer.

ac·ces/si·ble (-ses/ə bəl) *adj.* easy to reach or use. —**ac·ces/si·bil/i·ty,** *n.*

ac·ces/sion (-sesh/ən) *n.* **1.** the attainment of a rank, an office, etc. **2.** something added.

ac·ces/so·ry (-ses/ə rē) *n., pl.* **-ries. 1.** something added for convenience, decoration, etc. **2.** a person who has knowledge of or helps another commit a felony.

ac/ci·dent (ak/si dənt) *n.* **1.** an unexpected event, esp. one resulting in damage. **2.** chance. —**ac/ci·den/tal,** *adj.* —**ac/ci·den/tal·ly,** *adv.*

ac/ci·dent-prone/ *adj.* inclined to have accidents.

ac·claim/ (ə klām/) *v.t.* to greet with enthusiastic approval. —*n.* **2.** enthusiastic approval. —**ac/cla·ma/tion** (ak/lə mā/shən) *n.*

ac·cli/mate/ (ak/lə māt/, ə klī/mit) *v.t., v.i.,* **-ated, -ating.** to accustom or become accustomed to new conditions. Also, **ac·cli/ma·tize/.**

ac·cliv/i·ty (ə kliv/i tē) *n., pl.* **-ties.** an upward slope.

ac/co·lade/ (ak/ə lād/, -läd/) *n.* **1.** an award. **2.** high praise.

ac·com/mo·date/ (ə kom/ə dāt/) *v.t.,* **-dated, -dating. 1.** to supply with something needed. **2.** to do a favor for. **3.** to provide with lodging, food, etc. **4.** to adapt.

ac·com/mo·dat/ing *adj.* helpful; obliging.

ac·com/mo·da/tion *n.* **1.** the act of accommodating. **2.** **accommodations,** lodgings.

ac·com/pa·ni·ment (ə kum/pə nimənt, ə kump/ni-) *n.* **1.** something added, as for decoration. **2.** a musical part supporting the main part.

ac·com/pa·ny *v.t.,* **-nied, -nying. 1.** to go or be with. **2.** to provide musical support for (a soloist). —**ac·com/pa·nist,** *n.*

ac·com/plice (ə kom/plis) *n.* a partner in crime.

ac·com/plish (ə kom/plish) *v.t.* to complete successfully.

ac·com/plished *adj.* highly skilled.

ac·com/plish·ment *n.* **1.** successful completion. **2.** an achievement. **3.** an acquired skill.

ac·cord/ (ə kôrd/) *v.i.* **1.** to agree; be in harmony. —*v.t.* **2.** to cause to agree. **3.** to grant. —*n.* **4.** agreement. —*Idiom.* **5. of one's own accord,** voluntarily. —**ac·cord/ance,** *n.* —**ac·cord/ant,** *adj.*

ac·cord/ing·ly *adv.* therefore.

according to *prep.* **1.** in keeping with. **2.** as stated by.

ac·cor/di·on (ə kôr/dē ən) *n.* **1.** a portable musical instrument with a keyboard and bellows. —*adj.* **2.** having folds like an accordion bellows.

ac·cost/ (ə kôst/) *v.t.* **1.** to approach and speak to. **2.** to confront.

ac·count/ (ə kount/) *n.* **1.** a report or narration. **2.** importance. **3.** a sum of money deposited in a bank. **4.** a credit arrangement. **5.** a record of business transactions. —*v.* **6. account for,** to explain the reason for. —*Idiom.* **7. on account of,** because of. **8. on no account,** absolutely not. **9. take into account,** to consider.

ac·count/a·ble *adj.* responsible.

ac·count/ant *n.* a person trained in accounting.

ac·count/ing *n.* the organization and maintenance of financial records.

ac·cou/ter·ments (ə kŏŏ/trəmənts, -tər-) *n.pl.* personal clothing or equipment. Also, **ac·cou/tre·ments.**

ac·cred/it (ə kred/it) *v.t.* **1.** to certify as meeting requirements. **2.** to attribute. —**ac·cred/i·ta/tion,** *n.*

ac·cre/tion (ə krē/shən) *n.* **1.** an increase by growth or addition. **2.** an addition.

ac·crue/ (ə krŏŏ/) *v.i.,* **-crued, -cruing.** to be added as a periodic gain, as interest on money. —**ac·cru/al,** *n.*

ac·cul/tur·a/tion (ə kul/chə rā/shən) *n.* the adoption of the cultural traits of another group.

ac·cu/mu·late/ (ə kyŏŏ/myə lāt/) *v.t., v.i.,* **-lated, -lating.** to gather; collect. **2.** to increase in quantity. —**ac·cu/mu·la/tion,** *n.* —**ac·cu/mu·la·tive** (-lā tiv) *adj.*

ac/cu·rate (ak/yər it) *adj.* exact; correct. —**ac/cu·rate·ly,** *adv.* —**ac/cu·ra·cy,** *n.*

ac·curs/ed (ə kûr/sid, ə kûrst/) *adj.* **1.** under a curse. **2.** hateful.

ac·cuse/ (ə kyŏŏz/) *v.t.,* **-cused, -cusing. 1.** to blame. **2.** to charge with an offense. —**ac/cu·sa/tion** (ak/yŏŏ zā/shən) *n.* —**ac·cus/a·to/ry,** *adj.* —**ac·cus/er,** *n.*

ac·cused/ *n.* a person charged with a crime.

ac·cus/tom (ə kus/təm) *v.t.* to make familiar by use.

ac·cus/tomed *adj.* usual; habitual.

ace (ās) *n., v.,* **aced, acing.** —*n.* **1.** a playing card with one spot. **2.** an expert. —*v.t.* **3.** to do very well on.

a·cer/bic (ə sûr/bik) *adj.* **1.** sharp, as in manner. **2.** sour. —**a·cer/bi·ty,** *n.*

a·ce/ta·min/o·phen (ə sē/tə min/ə fən) *n.* a crystalline substance used to reduce pain or fever.

ac/e·tate/ (as/i tāt/) *n.* **1.** a salt or ester of acetic acid. **2.** a synthetic fiber derived from cellulose.

a·ce/tic (ə sē/tik) *adj.* **1.** of or producing vinegar.

acetic ac/id *n.* a sharp-tasting acid found in vinegar.

ac/e·tone/ (as/i tōn/) *n.* a flammable liquid used as a solvent.

a·cet/y·lene/ (ə set/l ēn/) *n.* a gas used in welding, etc.

ache (āk) *v.,* **ached, aching,** *n.* —*v.i.* **1.** to suffer a continuous dull pain. **2.** to yearn. —*n.* **3.** a continuous dull pain.

a·chieve/ (ə chēv/) *v.t.,* **achieved, achieving. 1.** to accomplish; bring about. —**a·chieve/ment,** *n.*

A·chil/les heel/ (ə kil/ēz) a vulnerable spot.

ac/id (as/id) *n.* **1.** a chemical that can react with a base to form a salt. **2.** a sour substance. —*adj.* **3.** of acids. **4.** sour or sharp. —**a·cid/ic,** *adj.* —**a·cid/i·ty,** *n.*

ac/id rain/ *n.* rain containing chemicals from pollution.

ac·knowl/edge (ak nol/ij) *v.t.,* **-edged, -edging. 1.** to admit. **2.** to show recognition of. **3.** to show appreciation for. **4.** to make known the receipt of. —**ac·knowl/edg·ment,** *n.*

ac/me (ak/mē) *n.* the highest point.

ac/ne (ak/nē) *n.* a skin disorder characterized by pimples.

ac/o·lyte/ (ak/ə līt/) *n.* **1.** an altar attendant. **2.** a follower.

ac/o·nite/ (ak/ə nīt/) *n.* a poisonous plant with irregular flowers.

a/corn (ā/kôrn, ā/kərn) *n.* the nut of the oak tree.

a·cous/tic (ə kŏŏ/stik) *adj.* of sound or hearing. —**a·cous/ti·cal·ly,** *adv.*

a·cous/tics *n.* **1.** (*used with a sing. v.*) the science of sound. **2.** (*used with a pl. v.*) the qualities of a space that affect sound.

ac·quaint/ (ə kwānt/) *v.t.* to make known or familiar.

ac·quaint/ance *n.* **1.** a person one knows casually. **2.** personal knowledge.

ac/qui·esce/ (ak/wē es/) *v.i.,* **-esced, -escing.** to agree or comply without protest. —**ac/qui·es/cence,** *n.* —**ac/qui·es/cent,** *adj.*

ac·quire/ (ə kwīr/) *v.t.,* **-quired, -quiring.** to get; obtain.

ac/qui·si/tion (ak/wə zish/ən n.) **1.** an acquiring. **2.** something acquired.

ac·quis/i·tive (ə kwiz/i tiv) *adj.* eager to acquire things. —**ac·quis/i·tive·ness,** *n.*

ac·quit/ (ə kwit/) *v.t.,* **-quitted, -quitting. 1.** to declare free of blame or guilt. **2.** to behave or conduct (oneself). —**ac·quit/tal,** *n.*

a/cre (ā/kər) *n.* a unit of land measurement (1/640 sq. mi. or 43,560 sq. ft.). —**a/cre·age,** *n.*

ac/rid (ak/rid) *adj.* sharp; biting.

ac/ri·mo/ny (ak/rə mō/nē) *n.* bitterness of manner or speech.

ac/ro·bat/ (ak/rə bat/) *n.* a performer on the trapeze, tightrope, etc. —**ac/ro·bat/ic,** *adj.*

ac/ro·bat/ics *n.* (*used with a pl. v.*) **1.** an acrobat's feats. **2.** any feats requiring agility.

ac/ro·nym (ak/rə nim) *n.* a word formed from successive initials or groups of letters, as NATO or UNICEF.

ac/ro·pho/bi·a (ak/rə fō/bē ə) *n.* a fear of heights.

a·cross/ (ə krôs/) *prep.* **1.** from one side to the other of. **2.** on the other side of. —*adv.* **3.** from one side to another.

across/-the-board/ *adj.* applying to all members or categories.

a·cryl/ic (ə kril/ik) *n.* a chemical substance used to make textile fibers and paints.

act (akt) *n.* **1.** something done. **2.** a law or decree. **3.** a division of a play or opera. —*v.i.* **4.** to do something. **5.** to behave. **6.** to pretend. **7.** to perform in a play, movie, etc.

act/ing *adj.* substitute.

ac·tin/i·um (ak tin/ē əm) *n.* a radioactive, silver-white metallic element.

ac′tion (ak′shən) *n.* **1.** the process of doing something. **2.** something done. **3.** behavior. **4.** combat. **5.** a lawsuit.

ac′tion·a·ble *adj.* providing grounds for a lawsuit.

ac′ti·vate′ (ak′tə vāt′) *v.t.*, **-vated, -vating.** to make active; start. —**ac′ti·va′tion,** *n.*

ac′tive (ak′tiv) *adj.* **1.** doing something. **2.** energetic. **3.** currently in progress. —**ac′tive·ly,** *adv.*

ac′tiv·ism *n.* vigorous action in pursuit of social or political goals. —**ac′tiv·ist,** *n.*

ac·tiv′i·ty (ak tiv′i tē) *n., pl.* **-ties. 1.** the state or quality of being active. **2.** a specific occupation or pursuit.

ac′tor (ak′tər) *n.* a person who performs in plays or movies. —**ac′tress,** *n.fem.*

ac′tu·al (ak′chōō al) *adj.* existing in reality. —**ac′tu·al′i·ty** (-al′i tē) *n.*

ac′tu·ar′y (ak′chōō er′ē) *n., pl.* **-aries.** a person who calculates insurance rates and risks. —**ac′tu·ar′i·al,** *adj.*

ac′tu·ate′ (ak′chōō āt′) *v.t.*, **-ated, -ating.** to put into action.

a·cu′i·ty (ə kyōō′i tē) *n.* sharpness of perception.

a·cu′men (ə kyōō′mən) *n.* mental keenness.

ac′u·punc′ture (ak′yōō pungk′-chər) *n.* the Chinese art of healing by inserting needles into the skin. —**ac′u·punc′tur·ist,** *n.*

a·cute′ (ə kyōōt′) *adj.* **1.** sharp; pointed. **2.** severe. **3.** keen. **4.** (of an angle) less than 90 degrees. —**a·cute′ly,** *adv.* —**a·cute′ness,** *n.*

ad (ad) an advertisement.

A.D. anno Domini: in the year of our Lord.

ad′age (ad′ij) *n.* a proverb.

a·da′gio (ə dä′jō, -zhē ō′) *adj., adv. Music.* slow.

ad′a·mant (ad′ə mənt) *adj.* unyielding.

Ad′am's ap′ple (ad′əmz) *n.* the projection of thyroid cartilage in front of the neck.

a·dapt′ (ə dapt′) *v.t.* **1.** to make suitable to requirements or conditions. —*v.i.* **2.** to adjust oneself to new conditions, environment, etc.

a·dapt′a·ble *adj.* able to adjust easily to new conditions. —**a·dapt′a·bil′i·ty,** *n.*

ad′ap·ta′tion (ad′ap tā′shən) *n.* **1.** an adapting or being adapted. **2.** the result of adapting.

a·dapt′er *n.* **1.** a connector for parts of different size or design. **2.** a device for adapting a tool or machine to a new use. Also, **a·dap′tor.**

add (ad) *v.t.* **1.** to join so as to increase. **2.** to find the sum of. **3.** to say further. —*v.i.* **4.** to be an addition. **5. add up,** to seem reasonable. **6. ~ up to,** to amount to.

ad′dend (ad′end, ə dend′) *n.* a number to be added to another.

ad·den′dum (ə den′dəm) *n., pl.* **-da** (-də). **1.** an addition. **2.** an appendix to a book.

ad′der (ad′ər) *n.* a small venomous snake.

ad′dict *n.* (ad′ikt) **1.** a person who is dependent on a substance, as a drug. —*v.t.* (ə dikt′) **2.** to make dependent on a drug. —**ad·dic′tion,** *n.* —**ad·dic′tive,** *adj.*

ad·di′tion (ə dish′ən) *n.* **1.** the act of adding. **2.** anything added. —*Idiom.* **3. in addition to,** besides. —**ad·di′tion·al,** *adj.* —**ad·di′tion·al·ly,** *adv.*

ad′di·tive (ad′i tiv) *n.* an added ingredient.

ad′dle (ad′l) *v.t.*, **-dled, -dling.** to confuse.

ad·dress′ (ə dres′) *n.* **1.** the place where one lives or where mail may be delivered. **2.** a formal speech. —*v.t.* **3.** to write an address on. **4.** to speak to. **5.** to apply (oneself) to a task. —**ad′dress·ee′** (ad′re sē′) *n.*

ad·duce′ (ə dōōs′, ə dyōōs′) *v.t.*, **-duced, -ducing.** to present or cite as evidence.

ad′e·noids (ad′n oidz′) *n.pl.* growths of tissue between the nose and the throat.

a·dept′ *adj.* (ə dept′) **1.** skilled. —*n.* (ad′ ept, ə dept′) **2.** expert.

ad′e·quate (ad′i kwit) *adj.* **1.** sufficient. **2.** just good enough. —**ad′e·quate·ly,** *adv.* —**ad′e·qua·cy,** *n.*

ADHD, attention deficit hyperactivity disorder.

ad·here′ (ad hēr′) *v.i.*, **-hered, -hering. 1.** to stick or cling. **2.** to be

faithful or loyal. —**ad·her′ence,** *n.* —**ad·her′ent,** *n., adj.* —**ad·he′sion** (-hē′zhən) *n.*

ad·he′sive (ad hē′siv, -ziv) *adj.* **1.** coated with a sticky substance. **2.** sticky. —*n.* **3.** a sticky substance.

ad hoc (ad hok′, hōk′) *adj., adv.* for a specified purpose.

ad hom′i·nem (hom′ə nəm, -nem′) *adj.* attacking an opponent personally instead of answering an argument.

a·dieu′ (ə dōō′, ə dyōō′) *interj., n. French.* good-by; farewell.

ad in′fi·ni′tum (ad in′fə nī′təm) *adv.* endlessly.

ad′i·pose′ (ad′ə pōs′) *adj.* fatty.

adj. adjective.

ad·ja′cent (ə jā′sənt) *adj.* lying near; adjoining.

ad′jec·tive (aj′ik tiv) *n.* a word describing a noun or pronoun. —**ad′-jec·ti′val** (-tī′vəl) *adj.*

ad·join′ (ə join′) *v.t.* to be next to.

ad·journ′ (ə jûrn′) *v.t., v.i.* to suspend (a proceeding) to a future time or place. —**ad·journ′ment,** *n.*

ad·judge′ (ə juj′) *v.t.*, **-judged, -judging. 1.** to decree or decide. **2.** to award judicially.

ad·ju′di·cate′ (ə jōō′di kāt′) *v.t.*, **-cated, -cating.** to settle (a dispute) judicially. —**ad·ju′di·ca′tion,** *n.*

ad′junct (aj′ungkt) *n.* **1.** something added but not essential. **2.** an assistant. **3.** a person teaching at a college without full status.

ad·jure′ (ə jōōr′) *v.t.*, **-jured, -juring.** to request or command solemnly.

ad·just′ (ə just′) *v.t.* **1.** to change slightly to make fit; adapt. **2.** to regulate. —*v.i.* **3.** to adapt oneself. —**ad·just′a·ble,** *adj.* —**ad·just′er,** **ad·jus′tor,** *n.* —**ad·just′ment,** *n.*

ad′ju·tant (aj′ə tənt) *n.* an assistant to a commanding officer.

ad-lib′ (ad lib′) *v.*, **-libbed, -libbing,** *adj.* —*v.t., v.i.* **1.** to improvise (speech, music, etc.). —*adj.* **2.** improvised. —**ad lib′,** *n., adv.*

Adm. admiral.

ad·min′is·ter (ad min′ə stər) *v.t.* **1.** to manage or direct. **2.** to give.

ad·min′is·tra′tion (ə strā′shən) *n.* **1.** the management of an office or business. **2.** the act of dispensing. **3.** the executive branch of a government. —**ad·min′is·tra′tive,** *adj.*

ad·min′is·tra′tor *n.* a manager.

ad′mi·ra·ble (ad′mər ə bəl), *adj.* worthy of admiration.

ad′mi·ral (ad′mər əl) *n.* a high-ranking navy officer.

ad·mire′ (ad mī°r′) *v.t.* **1.** to regard with pleasure or approval. **2.** to respect. —**ad′mi·ra′tion** (-mə rā′shən) *n.* —**ad·mir′er,** *n.* —**ad·mir′-ing·ly,** *adv.*

ad·mis′si·ble (ad mis′ə bəl) *adj.* able to be admitted or allowed.

ad·mis′sion (-mish′ən) *n.* **1.** the act of admitting. **2.** permission to enter. **3.** an entrance price. **4.** a confession or acknowledgment.

ad·mit′ (-mit′) *v.t.*, **-mitted, -mitting. 1.** to allow to enter. **2.** to permit. **3.** to confess or acknowledge. —**ad·mit′tance,** *n.*

ad·mit′ted·ly *adv.* as must be acknowledged.

ad·mon′ish (ad mon′ish) *v.t.* **1.** to advise against something. **2.** to reprove mildly. —**ad′mo·ni′tion** (ad′mə nish′ən) *n.* —**ad·mon′i·to′ry,** *adj.*

ad nau′se·am (ad nô′zē əm) *adv.* to a sickening degree.

a·do′ (ə dōō′) *n.* fuss; bother.

a·do′be (ə dō′bē) *n.* sun-dried brick.

ad′o·les′cence (ad′l es′əns) *n.* the period between childhood and adulthood. —**ad′o·les′cent,** *adj., n.*

a·dopt′ (ə dopt′) *v.t.* **1.** to accept as one's own. **2.** to become the legal parent of (the child of another). —**a·dop′tion,** *n.* —**a·dop′tive,** *adj.*

a·dore′ (ə dôr′) *v.t.*, **adored, adoring. 1.** to love greatly. **2.** to worship. **3.** to like very much. —**a·dor′a·ble,** *adj.* —**a·dor·a′tion** (ad′ə rā′shən) *n.*

a·dorn′ (ə dôrn′) *v.t.* to decorate with ornaments. —**a·dorn′ment,** *n.*

a·dre′nal (ə drēn′l) *adj.* of a pair of glands near the kidneys.

a·dren′al·in (ə drenʹl in) *n.* a hormone that stimulates the central nervous system.

a·drift′ (ə drift′) *adv., adj.* **1.** floating without anchor. **2.** without direction.

a·droit′ (ə droit′) *adj.* expert; deft. —**a·droit′ly,** *adv.* —**a·droit′ness,** *n.*

ad·sorb′ (ad sôrb′, -zôrb′) *v.t.* to hold (a gas, liquid, etc.) on a surface in a condensed layer.

ad′u·la′tion (aj′ə lā′shən) *n.* excessive praise.

a·dult′ (ə dult′) *adj.* **1.** full-grown; mature. **2.** of, befitting, or for adults. —*n.* **3.** a full-grown person.

a·dul′ter·ate′ *v.t.*, **-ated, -ating.** to make impure. —**a·dul′ter·a′tion,** *n.* —**a·dul′ter·ant,** *n.*

a·dul′ter·y *n., pl.* **-teries.** marital infidelity. —**a·dul′ter·er,** *n.* —**a·dul′ter·ess,** *n.* —**a·dul′ter·ous,** *adj.*

adv. 1. adverb. **2.** advertisement.

ad va lo′rem (ad və lôr′əm) *adj.* fixed at a percentage of the value.

ad·vance′ (ad vans′) *v.*, **-vanced, -vancing.** —*v.t.* **1.** to move forward. **2.** to propose. **3.** to raise in rank, price, etc. **4.** to supply beforehand. —*v.i.* **5.** to go forward. **6.** to rise in rank or status. —*n.* **7.** a forward move. **8.** a promotion. **9.** an increase. **10.** a loan. **11.** a friendly gesture. —*adj.* **12.** early. —*Idiom.* **13. in advance,** beforehand. —**ad·vance′ment,** *n.*

ad·vanced′ *adj.* **1.** ahead in knowledge, skill, etc. **2.** far along, as in age. **3.** progressive.

ad·van′tage (ad van′tij) *n.* **1.** a circumstance or condition favorable to success. **2.** a benefit or gain. —*Idiom.* **3. take advantage of, a.** to make use of. **b.** to impose upon by exploiting a weakness. —**ad′-van·ta′geous** (-tā′jəs) *adj.*

ad′vent (ad′vent) *n.* **1.** an arrival. **2. Advent,** the season beginning four Sundays before Christmas.

ad′ven·ti′tious (ad′vən tish′əs) *adj.* accidental.

ad·ven′ture (ad ven′chər) *n., v.,* **-tured, -turing. 1.** a risky undertaking. **2.** an exciting experience. —**ad·ven′tur·er,** *n.* —**ad·ven′tur·ous,** *adj.*

ad′verb (ad′vûrb) *n.* a word modifying a verb, adjective, or other adverb. —**ad·ver′bi·al,** *adj.*

ad′ver·sar′y (ad′vər ser′ē) *n., pl.* **-saries.** an opponent.

ad·verse′ (ad vûrs′) *adj.* opposing; unfavorable. —**ad·verse′ly,** *adv.*

ad·ver′si·ty (-vûr′si tē) *n., pl.* **-ties.** misfortune.

ad′ver·tise′ (ad′vər tīz′) *v.*, **-tised, -tising.** —*v.t.* **1.** to describe or praise publicly. **2.** to call public attention to. —*v.i.* **3.** to seek or offer goods or services in the news media. —**ad′ver·tis′er,** *n.* —**ad′ver·tise′ment,** *n.* —**ad′ver·tis′ing,** *n.*

ad·vice′ (ad vīs′) *n.* a recommendation concerning action.

ad·vis′a·ble (ad vī′zə bəl) *adj.* wise or prudent. —**ad·vis′a·bil′i·ty,** *n.*

ad·vise′ (ad vīz′) *v.t.*, **-vised, -vising. 1.** to give advice to. **2.** to recommend. **3.** to give information to. —**ad·vis′er, ad·vi′sor,** *n.*

ad·vis′ed·ly *adv.* deliberately.

ad·vi′so·ry *adj.* **1.** giving advice. —*n.* **2.** a report on existing or predicted conditions.

ad′vo·cate′ *v.*, **-cated, -cating,** *n.* —*v.t.* (ad′və kāt′) **1.** to urge or support by argument; recommend. —*n.* (-kit) **2.** a supporter of a cause. —**ad′vo·ca·cy** (-kə sē) *n.*

adz (adz) *n.* an axlike tool.

ae′gis (ē′jis) *n.* sponsorship.

ae′on (ē′ən, ē′on) *n.* an eon.

aer′ate (âr′āt) *v.t.*, **-ated, -ating.** to expose to or supply with air.

aer′i·al (âr′ē əl) *adj.* **1.** of or like the air. **2.** frequenting or growing in the air. —*n.* **3.** a radio or television antenna.

aer′ie (âr′ē, ēr′ē) *n., pl.* **-ies.** an eagle's nest.

aer·o′bic (â rō′bik) *adj.* **1.** needing oxygen to live. **2.** of aerobics.

aer·o′bics *n.pl.* exercises designed to strengthen the heart and lungs.

aer′o·dy·nam′ics (âr′ō dī nam′iks) *n.* the study of the action of air against solids. —**aer′o·dy·nam′ic,** *adj.*

aer′o·nau′tics *n.* the science of flight. —**aer′o·nau′ti·cal,** *adj.*

aer′o·plane′ (âr′ə plān′) *n. Brit.* an airplane.

aer′o·sol′ (âr′ə sôl′) *n.* **1.** liquid particles distributed through a gas. **2.** a spray of such liquid.

aer′o·space′ (âr′ō spās′) *n.* **1.** the earth's atmosphere and the space beyond. —*adj.* **2.** of missiles, spacecraft, etc., used in aerospace.

aes·thet′ic (es thet′ik) *adj.* **1.** of or appreciating beauty. **2.** artistic. —**aes′thete** (-thēt) *n.*

aes·thet′ics *n.* the branch of philosophy dealing with beauty.

a·far′ (ə fär′) *adv.* at a distance.

af·fa·ble (af′ə bəl) *adj.* warm and friendly. —**af′fa·bil′i·ty,** *n.*

af·fair′ (ə fâr′) *n.* **1.** anything requiring action; matter. **2.** affairs, business or public matters. **3.** a private concern. **4.** a sexual relationship. **5.** an incident causing public scandal. **6.** a social event.

af·fect′[1] (ə fekt′) *v.t.* to produce an effect on; act on; move.
—**Usage.** Because of similarity in pronunciation, AFFECT and EFFECT are sometimes confused in writing. The verb AFFECT means "to act on" or "to move": *His words affected the crowd so deeply that many wept.* The verb EFFECT means "to bring about, accomplish": *The new taxes effected many changes in people's lives.* The noun EFFECT means "result, consequence": *the tragic effect of the hurricane.*

af·fect′[2] (ə fekt′) *v.t.* **1.** to pretend. **2.** to assume pretentiously.

af′fec·ta′tion (af′ek tā′shən) *n.* **1.** pretense. **2.** artificiality of manner or appearance.

af·fect′ed (ə fek′tid) *adj.* **1.** full of affectation. **2.** assumed artificially. —**af·fect′ed·ly,** *adv.*

af·fec′tion (ə fek′shən) *n.* love; liking.

af·fec′tion·ate *adj.* fondly tender; loving. —**af·fec′tion·ate·ly,** *adv.*

af·fi′ance (ə fī′əns) *v.t.*, **-anced, -ancing.** to betroth.

af′fi·da′vit (af′i dā′vit) *n.* a written statement under oath.

af·fil′i·ate′ *v.*, **-ated, -ating,** *n.* —*v.t.* (ə fil′ē āt′) **1.** to associate or connect. —*v.i.* **2.** to associate oneself; unite. —*n.* (-ē it) **3.** an associate. —**af·fil′i·a′tion,** *n.*

af·fin′i·ty (ə fin′i tē) *n., pl.* **-ties. 1.** an attraction. **2.** a close similarity.

af·firm′ (ə fûrm′) *v.t.* **1.** to declare formally. **2.** to confirm. —*v.i.* **3.** to state something solemnly. —**af·fir·ma′tion** (af′ər mā′shən) *n.*

af·firm′a·tive *adj.* saying yes; affirming.

affirm′ative ac′tion *n.* a policy to increase opportunities for women and minorities.

af·fix′ *v.t.* (ə fiks′) **1.** to add on; attach. —*n.* (af′iks) **2.** an added part.

af·flict′ (ə flikt′) *v.t.* to distress physically or mentally. —**af·flic′tion,** *n.*

af′flu·ent (af′lōō ənt) *adj.* rich; abundant. —**af′flu·ence,** *n.*

af·ford′ (ə fôrd′) *v.t.* **1.** to have resources enough for. **2.** to provide.

af·fray′ (ə frā′) *n.* a public fight.

af·front′ (ə frunt′) *n.* **1.** an insult. —*v.t.* **2.** to offend.

af′ghan (af′gan) *n.* a knitted blanket.

a·field′ (ə fēld′) *adv.* **1.** at a distance. **2.** off the mark.

a·fire′ (ə fī°r′) *adv., adj.* on fire.

a·flame′ (ə flām′) *adv., adj.* in flames.

AFL-CIO American Federation of Labor and Congress of Industrial Organizations.

a·float′ (ə flōt′) *adv., adj.* **1.** floating. **2.** at sea. **3.** out of debt.

a·foot′ (ə fōōt′) *adv., adj.* **1.** in progress. **2.** on foot.

a·fore′said′ (ə fôr′sed′) *adj.* mentioned before. Also, **a·fore′men′-tioned** (-men′shənd).

a·fraid′ (ə frād′) *adj.* **1.** frightened. **2.** regretful.

a·fresh′ (ə fresh′) *adj.* anew.

Af′ri·can *adj.* **1.** of Africa. —*n.* **2.** a native of Africa.

Af′ri·can-A·mer′i·can *n.* **1.** a black American of African descent. —*adj.* **2.** of African-Americans.

Af′rican vi′olet *n.* a hairy-leaved African houseplant with purple, pink, or white flowers.

Af′ri·kaans′ (af′ri käns′, -känz′) *n.* a language of South Africa, derived from Dutch.

Af′ri·ka′ner (-kä′nər, -kan′ər) *n.* a white South African who speaks Afrikaans.

Af′ro (af′rō) *n., pl.* **-ros.** a full, bushy hairstyle.

aft (aft) *adv. Naut.* at or toward the stern.

af′ter (af′tər) *prep.* **1.** behind. **2.** about. **3.** later than. **4.** in imitation of. **5.** behind. **6.** later.

af′ter·birth′ *n.* the placenta expelled from the uterus after childbirth.

af′ter·care′ *n.* the care of a recovering patient.

af′ter·ef·fect′ *n.* a delayed or secondary effect.

af′ter·glow′ *n.* **1.** a glow after sunset. **2.** a pleasant memory.

af′ter·life′ *n.* life after death.

af′ter·math′ *n.* consequences.

af′ter·noon′ *n.* the period between noon and evening.

af′ter·taste′ *n.* a taste remaining in the mouth.

af′ter·thought′ *n.* a later thought. Also, **af′ter·wards.**

a·gain′ (ə gen′) *adv.* **1.** once more. **2.** besides.

a·gainst′ (ə genst′) *prep.* **1.** opposed to. **2.** in or into contact with.

a·gape′ (ə gāp′) *adv., adj.* wide open.

a′gar (ä′gär) *n.* a gel made from seaweed and used as a food thickener.

ag′ate (ag′it) *n.* a kind of quartz with colored bands.

a·ga′ve (ə gä′vē) *n.* a thick-leaved desert plant.

age (āj) *n., v.,* **aged, aging** or **ageing.** —*n.* **1.** the length of time in existence. **2.** a period of human life. **3.** a historical or geological period. **4.** the later part of life. —*v.i., v.t.* **5.** to grow or cause to grow old. **6.** to mature, as wine. —*Idiom.* **7. of age,** having reached adulthood.

ag′ed *adj.* **1.** (ā′jid) having lived long. **2.** (ājd) matured. —*n.pl.* (ā′jid) **3.** elderly people.

age′ism *n.* discrimination because of age.

age′less *adj.* **1.** apparently not aging. **2.** not outdated.

a′gen·cy (ā′jən sē) *n., pl.* **-cies. 1.** the function or office of an agent. **2.** a government bureau. **3.** the means of doing something.

a·gen′da (ə jen′də) *n.* a list of matters to be dealt with.

a′gent (ā′jənt) *n.* **1.** one acting for another. **2.** a means. **3.** an official.

ag·glom′er·a′tion (ə glom′ə rā′shən) *n.* a mass of varied parts.

ag·gran′dize (ə gran′dīz, ag′rən-dīz′) *v.t.*, **-dized, -dizing. 1.** to make great or greater in power, honor, etc. **2.** to make (something) seem greater. —**ag·gran′dize·ment** (-diz mənt) *n.*

ag′gra·vate′ (ag′rə vāt′) *v.t.*, **-vated, -vating. 1.** to make worse. **2.** to annoy. —**ag′gra·va′tion,** *n.* —**Usage.** In formal speech and writing, the meaning "to annoy" (*Stop aggravating me!*) is sometimes criticized and is used less often than the meaning "to make worse" (*His insulting words aggravated the tense situation*).

ag′gre·gate′ (ag′rə git) *v.*, **-gated, -gating.** —*adj.* (ag′ri git) **1.** total. —*n.* (-git) **2.** a mass. —*v.t., v.i.* (-gāt′) **3.** to gather into a mass.

ag·gres′sion (ə gresh′ən) *n.* **1.** a hostile act; attack. **2.** hostile behavior. —**ag·gres′sor,** *n.*

ag·gres′sive (ə gres′iv) *adj.* **1.** hostile. **2.** vigorously energetic.

ag·grieve′ (ə grēv′) *v.t.*, **-grieved, -grieving.** to wrong severely.

a·ghast′ (ə gast′) *adj.* horrified.

ag′ile (aj′əl) *adj.* quick; nimble. —**a·gil′i·ty** (ə jil′i tē) *n.*

ag′i·ta (aj′i ta) *n.* **1.** indigestion. **2.** anxiety.

ag′i·tate′ (aj′i tāt′) *v.*, **-tated, -tating.** —*v.t.* **1.** to shake. **2.** to disturb; excite. —*v.i.* **3.** to try to arouse public feeling. —**ag′i·ta′tion,** *n.* —**ag′i·ta′tor,** *n.*

a·glow′ (ə glō′) *adj., adv.* glowing.

ag·nos′tic (ag nos′tik) *n.* a person who believes that the existence of God is unknown and unknowable. —**ag·nos′ti·cism** (-tə siz′əm) *n.*

a·go′ (ə gō′) *adj., adv.* in the past.

a·gog′ (ə gog′) *adj.* eagerly excited.

ag′o·nize′ (ag′ə nīz′) *v.i.*, **-nized, -nizing.** to suffer or cause to suffer pain or anguish.

ag′o·ny (-nē) *n., pl.* **-nies.** intense pain or suffering.

ag′o·ra·pho′bi·a (ag′ər ə fō′bē ə) *n.* a fear of open spaces.

a·grar′i·an (ə grär′ē ən) *adj.* of the land.

a·gree′ (ə grē′) *v.i.*, **agreed, agreeing. 1.** to consent or promise. **2.** to have a similar opinion. **3.** to arrive at an understanding. **4.** to be beneficial.

a·gree′a·ble *adj.* **1.** pleasant. **2.** willing. —**a·gree′a·bly,** *adv.*

a·gree′ment *n.* **1.** harmony. **2.** an arrangement acceptable to all.

ag′ri·busi′ness (ag′rə biz′nis) *n.* the large-scale business of growing, processing, and distributing farm products.

ag′ri·cul′ture *n.* farming. —**ag′ri·cul′tur·al,** *adj.*

a·gron′o·my (ə gron′ə mē) *n.* the science of farm management.

a•ground′ (ə ground′) *adv., adj.* (of a ship) on or onto the shore.

a′gue (ā′gyōō) *n.* chills and fever, esp. when associated with malaria.

ah (ä) *interj.* (an exclamation of pain, surprise, or satisfaction)

a•head′ (ə hed′) *adv.* **1.** in or at the front. **2.** forward. **3.** into or for the future.

a•hoy′ (ə hoi′) *interj. Naut.* (hey there!)

aid (ād) *v.t., v.i.* **1.** to help. —*n.* **2.** help; assistance.

aide (ād) *n.* an assistant.

aide-de-camp (ād′də kamp′) *n., pl.* **aides-de-camp.** a military assistant.

AIDS (ādz) *n.* acquired immune deficiency syndrome: a disease making one increasingly susceptible to infections and other diseases.

ail *v.t.* **1.** to trouble. —*v.i.* **2.** to be sick.

ai′ler•on′ (ā′lə ron′) *n.* a flap on an airplane wing.

ail′ment *n.* an illness.

aim (ām) *v.t.* **1.** to point or direct at a target. —*v.i.* **2.** to direct a gun, punch, etc. **3.** to intend. **4.** to direct one's efforts. —*n.* **5.** the act of aiming. **6.** a target. **7.** a purpose. —**aim′less,** *adj.*

ain′t (ānt) *Nonstandard or Dial.* am not; are not; is not.

—*Usage.* AIN'T is more common in uneducated speech, though it occurs in the informal speech of the educated: *I ain't going. He ain't so young anymore.* The question form "Ain't I...?" is sometimes substituted for "Aren't I...?", which is usually considered to be ungrammatical. AIN'T also occurs in some humorous or set phrases, and it is sometimes used to give emphasis: *Ain't it the truth! It just ain't so!*

air (âr) *n.* **1.** the mixture of gases forming the earth's atmosphere. **2.** appearance; manner. **3.** a tune. —*v.t.* **4.** to expose to air. **5.** to broadcast. —*Idiom.* **6. in the air,** current. **7. off the air,** not broadcast. **8. on the air,** broadcasting. **9. up in the air,** not decided.

air′ bag′ *n.* a bag that inflates automatically to protect passengers in a car collision.

air′borne′ (-bôrn) *adj.* carried by air; flying.

air′brush′ *n.* **1.** an atomizer for spraying paint or other liquid. —*v.t.* **2.** to paint with an airbrush.

air′ condi′tioning *n.* a system for controlling the temperature and humidity of air. —**air′-condi′-tioned,** *adj.*

air′craft′ *n.* a vehicle or vehicles for flight.

air′field′ *n.* a ground area on which airplanes land and take off.

air′ force′ *n.* the military branch that carries out air operations.

air′lift′ *n.* **1.** major transport of supplies by aircraft in an emergency. —*v.t.* **2.** to move by airlift.

air′line′ *n.* an air transport company.

air′lin′er *n.* a large passenger airplane operated by an airline.

air′ lock′ *n.* an airtight compartment allowing passage between spaces that have different pressure.

air′mail′ *n.* **1.** the system of sending mail by airplane. **2.** mail sent by airplane. —*v.t.* **3.** to send by airplane. Also, **air′ mail′.**

air′plane′ *n.* a powered heavier-than-air craft with fixed wings.

air′port′ *n.* a place where aircraft pick up passengers and cargo.

air′ raid′ *n.* an attack by aircraft.

air′ship′ *n.* a lighter-than-air aircraft.

air′space′ *n.* the space above a nation, city, etc., over which it has control.

air′tight′ *adj.* **1.** impermeable to air. **2.** having no weak points.

air′waves′ *n.pl.* the medium of radio and television broadcasting.

air′y *adj.,* **-ier, -iest. 1.** of or like air. **2.** delicate. **3.** well ventilated. **4.** light; lively. —**air′i•ly,** *adv.*

aisle (īl) *n.* a passage between seats or shelves.

a•jar′ (ə jär′) *adj., adv.* partly open.

AK Alaska.

a.k.a. also known as.

a•kim′bo (ə kim′bō) *adj., adv.* with hands on hips.

a•kin′ (ə kin′) *adj.* alike.

AL Alabama.

à la or **a la** (ä′ lä, ä′ lə) *prep.* in the manner or style of.

Ala. Alabama.

al′a•bas′ter (al′ə bas′tər) *n.* a translucent white gypsum.

à la carte (ä′ lə kärt′) *adv., adj.*

with each dish on a menu separately priced.

a•lac′ri•ty (ə lak′ri tē) *n.* cheerful readiness.

à la mode (ä′ lə mōd′) *adv., adj.* **1.** in the fashion. **2.** with ice cream.

a•larm′ (ə lärm′) *n.* **1.** sudden fear caused by danger. **2.** a warning signal. —*v.t.* **3.** to fill with fear.

alarm′ clock′ *n.* a clock with a device to awaken a sleeper.

a•larm′ist *n.* a person who alarms others unnecessarily.

a•las′ (ə las′) *interj.* (an expression of dismay)

al′ba•tross′ (al′bə trôs′) *n.* **1.** a large white sea bird. **2.** a burden.

al•be′it (ôl bē′it) *conj.* although.

al•bi′no (al bī′nō) *n., pl.* **-nos.** a person or animal lacking in pigmentation in the skin or hair.

al′bum (al′bəm) *n.* a blank book for pictures, stamps, etc. **2.** a collection of recordings.

al•bu′men (al byōō′mən) *n.* egg white.

al•bu′min *n.* a water-soluble protein found in egg white, milk, blood, etc.

al′che•my (al′kə mē) *n.* medieval chemistry. —**al′che•mist,** *n.*

al′co•hol′ (al′kə hôl′) *n.* **1.** a colorless flammable liquid produced by fermentation. **2.** an intoxicating liquor containing alcohol.

al′co•hol′ic *adj.* **1.** of or containing alcohol. —*n.* **2.** a person addicted to alcohol. —**al′co•hol•ism,** *n.*

al′cove (al′kōv) *n.* a recessed space.

al′der (ôl′dər) *n.* a small tree of the birch family.

al′der•man (ôl′dər mən) *n., pl.* **-men.** a city official.

ale (āl) *n.* a kind of beer.

a•lert′ (ə lûrt′) *adj.* **1.** observant. **2.** vigilant. —*n.* **3.** a warning or alarm. —*v.t.* **4.** to warn. —**a•lert′ly,** *adv.* —**a•lert′ness,** *n.*

ale′wife′ (āl′wīf′) *n., pl.* **-wives.** a shadlike North American fish.

al•fal′fa (al fal′fə) *n.* a clover-like forage plant.

al•fres′co (al fres′kō) *adv., adj.* in the open air. Also, **al fres′co.**

al′gae (al′jē) *n.pl., sing.* **-ga** (-gə) one-celled water plants.

al′ge•bra (al′jə brə) *n.* a branch of mathematics using symbols rather than specific numbers. —**al′ge•bra′ic** (-jə brā′ik) *adj.*

ALGOL (al′gol) *n.* a computer language using mathematical symbols.

al′go•rithm (al′gə rith′əm) *n.* a set of rules or steps to solve mathematical problems, program a computer, etc. —**al′go•rith′mic,** *adj.*

a′li•as (ā′lē əs) *adv.* **1.** otherwise known as. —*n.* **2.** an assumed name.

al′i•bi′ (al′ə bī′) *n.* **1.** the defense by an accused person of having been elsewhere when a crime was committed. **2.** an excuse.

al′ien (āl′yən) *n.* **1.** a foreign-born resident. **2.** a creature from outer space. —*adj.* **3.** foreign.

al′ien•ate′ (-yə nāt′) *v.t.,* **-ated, -ating.** to cause to become unfriendly or hostile. —**al′ien•a′tion,** *n.*

a•light′ (ə līt′) *v.i.* **1.** to dismount. **2.** to descend to perch or sit.

a•light′² (ə līt′) *adv., adj.* lighted up.

a•lign′ (ə līn′) *v.t.* **1.** to bring into line. **2.** to ally (oneself) with a group or cause. —**a•lign′ment,** *n.*

a•like′ (ə līk′) *adv.* **1.** similarly. —*adj.* **2.** similar.

al′i•men′ta•ry (al′ə men′tə rē) *adj.* of or for nourishment.

alimen′tary canal′ *n.* a tube in the body through which food passes.

al′i•mo′ny (al′ə mō′nē) *n.* money paid for the support of a spouse after separation or divorce.

a•live′ (ə līv′) *adj.* **1.** living. **2.** active. **3.** lively. **4.** teeming.

al′ka•li′ (al′kə lī′) *n.* a chemical that neutralizes acids. —**al′ka•line′,** *adj.*

al′ka•loid′ (-loid′) *n.* a bitter, nitrogen-containing compound in plants.

all (ôl) *adj.* **1.** the whole amount or number of. —*pron.* **2.** the whole quantity; everything. —*n.* **3.** one's whole energy or property. —*adv.* **4.** entirely. —*Idiom.* **5. all but,** almost. **6. all in all,** everything considered. **7. at all,** to any degree or in any way.

Al′lah (al′ə, ä′lə) *n.* the Muslim name for God.

all′-around′ *adj.* versatile.

al•lay′ (ə lā′) *v.t.* to quiet or lessen.

al•lege′ (ə lej′) *v.t.,* **-leged, -leging.** to state without proof. —**al′le•ga′tion** (al′i gā′shən) *n.*

al•leged′ *adj.* **1.** declared to be so, but without proof. **2.** supposed. —**al•leg′ed•ly** (-lej/id-) *adv.*

al•le′giance (ə lē′jəns) *n.* loyalty to a government, group, cause, etc.

al′le•go′ry (al′ə gôr′ē) *n., pl.* **-ries.** a story in which characters and actions are symbols for ideas. —**al′le•gor′i•cal,** *adj.*

al•le′gro (ə lā′grō, ə leg′rō) *adv. Music.* fast.

al′le•lu′ia (al′ə lōō′yə) *interj.* hallelujah.

al′ler•gen (al′ər jən) *n.* a substance that causes an allergic reaction.

al•ler′gic (ə lûr′jik) *adj.* **1.** caused by an allergy. **2.** having an allergy. **3.** *Informal.* having a dislike.

al′ler•gist (-jist) *n.* a doctor who treats allergies.

al′ler•gy (-jē) *n., pl.* **-gies. 1.** a physical sensitivity to a substance. **2.** *Informal.* a strong dislike.

al•le′vi•ate′ (ə lē′vē āt′) *v.t.,* **-ated, -ating.** to lessen or relieve (pain). —**al•le′vi•a′tion,** *n.*

al′ley (al′ē) *n., pl.* **-leys.** a narrow street.

al′ley cat′ *n.* a domestic cat of unknown parentage.

al•li′ance (ə lī′əns) *n.* **1.** a formal union for mutual benefit. **2.** a close relationship.

al•lied′ (ə līd′, al′īd) *adj.* **1.** joined by common cause. **2.** related.

al′li•ga′tor (al′i gā′tər) *n.* a broad-snouted type of crocodile.

all′-in•clu′sive *adj.* comprehensive.

al•lit′er•a′tion (ə lit′ə rā′shən) *n.* repetition of the same sound at the beginning of two or more words.

al′lo•cate′ (al′ə kāt′) *v.t.,* **-cated, -cating.** to set apart for a special purpose. —**al′lo•ca′tion,** *n.*

al•lot′ (ə lot′) *v.t.,* **-lotted, -lotting.** to divide; distribute as a portion. —**al•lot′ment,** *n.*

all′-out′ *adj.* total; unrestricted.

al•low′ (ə lou′) *v.t.* **1.** to permit. **2.** to give. **3.** to concede. —*v.i.* **4.** to permit as a possibility. **5. allow for,** to make provision for. —**al•low′a•ble,** *adj.*

al•low′ance (ə lou′əns) *n.* **1.** an amount granted. **2.** a sum of money given regularly, as for expenses. —*Idiom.* **3. make allowance for,** to excuse.

al′loy *n.* (al′oi) **1.** a mixture of metals. —*v.t.* (ə loi′) **2.** to mix (metals).

all′ right′ *adj.* **1.** yes. **2.** satisfactorily. **3.** certainly. —*adj.* **4.** safe; sound. **5.** acceptable; satisfactory.

—*Usage.* The spelling ALRIGHT is used in informal writing. However, the phrase ALL RIGHT is preferred in formal, edited writing.

All′ Saints′ Day′ *n.* a Christian festival Nov. 1 in honor of the saints.

all′spice′ *n.* a sharp, fragrant spice from a tropical American tree.

all′-star′ *adj.* consisting of star performers.

all′-time′ *adj.* never equaled or surpassed.

al•lude′ (ə lōōd′) *v.i.,* **-luded, -luding.** to refer to casually or indirectly.

al•lure′ (ə lōōr′) *n., v.,* **-lured, -luring.** —*n.* **1.** fascination. —*v.t.* **2.** to attract; tempt. —**al•lure′ment,** *n.* —**al•lur′ing,** *adj.*

al•lu′sion (ə lōō′zhən) *n.* a casual or indirect reference.

al•lu′vi•um (ə lōō′vē əm) *n.* sediment deposited by flowing water. —**al•lu′vi•al,** *adj.*

al•ly′ *v.,* **-lied, -lying,** *n., pl.* **-lies.** —*v.t., v.i.* (ə lī′) **1.** to unite or become united in an alliance. —*n.* (al′ī) **2.** a person, nation, etc., bound to another, as by a treaty.

al′ma ma′ter (äl′mə mä′tər; al′mə mä′tər) *n.* one's school or college.

al′ma•nac′ (ôl′mə nak′) *n.* an annual publication containing statistical information, meteorological data, etc.

al•might′y (ôl mī′tē) *adj.* **1.** having unlimited power. —*n.* **2. the Almighty,** God.

al′mond (ä′mənd) *n.* the oval-shaped edible nut of a tree of the rose family.

al′most (ôl′mōst, ôl mōst′) *adv.* nearly.

alms (ämz) *n.pl.* money or food given to the poor.

al′oe (al′ō) *n.* a plant with fleshy leaves.

a•loft′ (ə lôft′) *adv., adj.* high up.

a•lo′ha (ə lō′ə, ä lō′hä) *n., interj.* **1.** hello. **2.** farewell.

a•lone′ (ə lōn′) *adj., adv.* **1.** apart from others. **2.** without another person. **3.** only.

a•long′ (ə lông′) *prep.* **1.** through the length of. —*adv.* **2.** parallel in the same direction. **3.** onward. **4.** in company; together.

a•long′side′ *adv.* **1.** to one's side. —*prep.* **2.** beside.

a•loof′ (ə lōōf′) *adj.* **1.** reserved in feeling or manner. —*adv.* **2.** at a distance. —**a•loof′ness,** *n.*

a•lot′ (ə lot′) *n.* LOT (def. 4).

—*Usage.* The spelling ALOT, though fairly common in informal writing, is usually considered an error. The two-word spelling A LOT is the accepted form: *He has a lot of money. I like her a lot.* A LOT is itself considered informal; in formal speech or writing, the phrases "a great number," "a great amount," or "a great deal" are usually substituted for A LOT.

a•loud′ (ə loud′) *adv.* in a voice that can be heard.

al•pac′a (al pak′ə) *n.* a South American mammal related to the llama and having soft silky wool.

al′pha (al′fə) *n.* the first letter of the Greek alphabet.

al′pha•bet′ (al′fə bet′, -bit) *n.* the letters of a language in order. —**al′pha•bet′i•cal,** *adj.* —**al′pha•bet•ize′,** *v.t.*

al′pha•nu•mer′ic *adj.* using both letters and numbers. —**al′pha•nu•mer′i•cal•ly,** *adv.*

al′pine (al′pīn, -pin) *adj.* growing or found in high mountains.

al•read′y (ôl red′ē) *adv.* **1.** prior to a certain time. **2.** so soon.

al•right′ (ôl rīt′) *adv., adj.* ALL RIGHT.

—*Usage.* See ALL RIGHT.

al′so (ôl′sō) *adv.* in addition.

alt. **1.** alternate. **2.** altitude. **3.** alto.

al′tar (ôl′tər) *n.* a table used for religious rites.

al′ter *v.t., v.i.* to make or become different. —**al′ter•a′tion,** *n.*

al′ter•ca′tion (ôl′tər kā′shən) *n.* an angry dispute.

al′ter e′go *n.* **1.** the other side of one's personality. **2.** a close friend.

al′ter•nate′ *v.,* **-nated, -nating,** *adj., n.* —*v.i., v.i.* (-nāt′) **1.** to occur or cause to occur in turns. —*adj.* (-nit) **2.** being every second one. —*n.* (-nit) **3.** a substitute. —**al′ter•na′tion,** *n.*

al′ternating cur′rent *n.* an electric current that regularly reverses its direction.

al•ter′na•tive (-tûr′nə tiv) *n.* **1.** another possible choice. —*adj.* **2.** offering a choice.

al′ter•na′tor (-tər nā′tər) *n.* a generator of alternating current.

al•though′ (ôl thō′) *conj.* even though.

al•tim′e•ter (al tim′i tər, al′tə mē′tər) *n.* a device for measuring altitude.

al′ti•tude′ (al′ti tōōd′, -tyōōd′) *n.* the height of a thing above a reference point, as sea level.

al′to (al′tō) *n., pl.* **-tos. 1.** the lowest female singing voice. **2.** a singer with this voice. —*adj.* **3.** of this pitch.

al′to•geth′er (ôl′tə geth′ər) *adv.* entirely.

al′tru•ism′ (al′trōō iz′əm) *n.* unselfish concern for others. —**al′tru•ist,** *n.* —**al′tru•is′tic,** *adj.*

al′um (al′əm) *n.* an astringent substance containing aluminum and potassium.

a•lu′mi•num (ə lōō′mə nəm) *n.* a light, silvery metal. Also, *Brit.,* **al′u•min′i•um** (al′yə min′ē əm).

a•lum′na (ə lum′nə) *n., pl.* **-nae** (-nē) a female graduate.

a•lum′nus (-nəs) *n., pl.* **-ni** (-nī). a male graduate.

al′ways (ôl′wāz, -wēz) *adv.* **1.** all the time. **2.** every time.

Alz′hei′mer's disease′ (älts′hī′-mərz, ôlts′-) *n.* a disease marked by increasing memory loss and mental deterioration, usu. in old age.

am (am; *unstressed* əm, m) *v.* 1st pers. sing. pres. indic. of **be.**

a.m. the period before noon. Also, **A.M.**

A.M.A. American Medical Association.

a•mal′gam (ə mal′gəm) *n.* a mixture, esp. one with mercury.

a•mal′ga•mate′ (-gə māt′) *v.t., v.i.,* **-mated, -mating.** to combine. —**a•mal′ga•ma′tion,** *n.*

am′a•nu•en′sis (ə man′yōō en′sis) *n., pl.* **-ses** (-sēz). a secretary.

am′a•ranth′ (am′ə ranth′) *n.* a plant with showy flowers.

am′a•ret′to (am′ə ret′ō, ä′mə-) *n.* an almond-flavored liqueur.

am′a•ryl′lis (am′ə ril′is) *n.* a plant with large red or pink lilylike flowers.

a•mass′ (ə mas′) *v.t.* to collect.

am′a•teur′ (am′ə chōōr′, -chər, -tər) *n.* a nonprofessional artist, athlete, etc. —**am′a•teur′ish,** *adj.* —**am′a•teur•ism,** *n.*

am′a•to′ry (am′ə tôr′ē) *adj.* of love.

a•maze′ (ə māz′) *v.t.,* amazed, amazing. to astonish greatly. —**a•maze′ment,** *n.*

am′a•zon′ (am′ə zon′, -zən) *n.* **1.** a female warrior of Greek legend. **2.** a tall, powerful woman.

am•bas′sa•dor (am bas′ə dər, -dôr′) *n.* a diplomat of the highest rank.

am′ber (am′bər) *n.* **1.** a yellowish brown fossil resin. **2.** yellowish brown.

am′ber•gris′ (-grēs′) *n.* a secretion of the sperm whale, used in perfumes.

am′bi•dex′trous (am′bi dek′strəs) *adj.* using both hands equally well.

am′bi•ence (am′bē əns) *n.* surroundings; atmosphere. Also, **am′bi•ance.** —**am′bi•ent,** *adj.*

am•big′u•ous (am big′yōō əs) *adj.* **1.** uncertain. **2.** having several possible interpretations. —**am•bi•gu′i•ty,** *n.*

am•bi′tion (-bish′ən) *n.* **1.** a desire for success, power, etc. **2.** the object so desired. —**am•bi′tious,** *adj.*

am•biv′a•lent (-biv′ə lənt) *adj.* with conflicting feelings. —**am•biv′a•lence,** *n.*

am′ble (am′bəl) *v.,* **-bled, -bling,** *n.* —*v.i.* **1.** to go at an easy pace. —*n.* **2.** a slow, easy pace.

am•bro′sia (am brō′zhə) *n.* the food of the Greek gods.

am′bu•lance (am′byə ləns) *n.* a vehicle for transporting the sick or wounded.

am′bu•la•to′ry (-lə tôr′ē) *adj.* able to walk.

am′bush (-bōōsh) *n.* **1.** concealment for a surprise attack. **2.** a place of such concealment. **3.** an attack from concealment. —*v.t., v.i.* **4.** to attack from ambush.

a•me′ba (ə mē′bə) *n., pl.* **-bas** or **-bae** (-bē). a microscopic one-celled animal. Also, **a•moe′ba.**

a•mel′io•rate′ (ə mēl′yə rāt′) *v.t., v.i.,* **-rated, -rating.** to improve. —**a•mel′io•ra′tion,** *n.*

a′men′ (ā′men′, ä′men′) *interj.* (so be it!)

a•me′na•ble (ə mē′nə bəl, ə men′ə-) *adj.* willing; agreeable.

a•mend′ (ə mend′) *v.t.* **1.** to modify (a bill, law, etc.). **2.** to improve. **3.** to correct. —*Idiom.* **4. make amends,** to compensate, as for an injury, loss, etc.

a•mend′ment *n.* a change in a formal text, as a law.

a•men′i•ty (ə men′i tē) *n., pl.* **-ties.** a feature that provides comfort or pleasure.

Am′er•a′sian (am′ə rā′zhən) *n.* a person of mixed American and Asian descent.

A•mer′i•can *adj.* **1.** of the U.S. or its inhabitants. **2.** of N or S America. —*n.* **3.** a citizen of the U.S. **4.** a native of the Western Hemisphere.

Amer′ican In′dian *n.* a member of the indigenous peoples of N or S America.

Amer′ican Sign′ Lan′guage *n.* a visual-gesture language used by deaf people in the U.S. and English-speaking parts of Canada.

am′e•thyst (am′ə thist) *n.* a violet quartz used in jewelry.

a′mi•a•ble (ā′mē ə bəl) *adj.* pleasantly kind or friendly. —**a′mi•a•bil′i•ty,** *n.* —**a′mi•a•bly,** *adv.*

am′i•ca•ble (am′i kə bəl) *adj.* friendly. —**am′i•ca•bly,** *adv.*

a•mid′ (ə mid′) *prep.* among. Also, **a•midst′.**

a•mid′ships′ *adv.* in or toward the middle part of a ship. Also, **amid′ship′.**

a•mi′go (ə mē′gō, ä mē′-) *n., pl.* **-gos.** *Spanish.* a male friend.

a•mi′no ac′id (ə mē′nō, am′ə nō) *n.* a type of organic compound from which proteins are made.

a•miss′ (ə mis′) *adv.* **1.** wrongly. **2.** wrong.

am′i•ty (am′i tē) *n.* friendship.

am′me•ter (am′mē′tər) *n.* an instrument for measuring amperes.

am·mo′nia (ə mōn′yə) *n.* **1.** a colorless, pungent, water-soluble gas. **2.** this gas dissolved in water.

am·mu·ni′tion (am′yə nish′ən) *n.* bullets or shells fired by guns.

am·ne′sia (am nē′zhə) *n.* loss of memory. —**am·ne′si·ac′** (-zhē ak′) *adj., n.*

am′nes·ty (am′nə stē) *n.* a general pardon for political crimes.

am·ni·o·cen·te′sis (am′nē ō sen tē′sis) *n., pl.* **-ses** (-sēz). a procedure in which fluid is withdrawn from the uterus of a pregnant woman for genetic diagnosis of the fetus.

a·mok′ (ə muk′, ə mok′) *adv.* amuck.

a·mong′ (ə mung′) *prep.* **1.** in the midst of. **2.** in the group of. **3.** for each of. Also, **a·mongst′.**

——**Usage.** Traditionally, BETWEEN is used to show relationship involving two people or things (*to decide between tea and coffee*), while AMONG expresses more than two (*The four brothers quarrelled among themselves*). BETWEEN, however, is also used to express relationship of persons or things considered individually, no matter how many: *Between holding public office, teaching, and raising a family, she has little free time.*

a·mor′al (ā môr′əl) *adj.* indifferent to moral standards. —**a′mo·ral′i·ty** (ā′mə ral′i tē) *n.*

am′o·rous (am′ər əs) *adj.* inclined to or expressing sexual love.

a·mor′phous (ə môr′fəs) *adj.* **1.** formless. **2.** indeterminate.

am′or·tize′ (am′ər tīz′, ə môr′tīz) *v.t.,* **-tized, -tizing.** to pay off gradually. —**am′or·ti·za′tion,** *n.*

a·mount′ (ə mount′) *n.* **1.** the sum total. **2.** quantity. —*v.i.* **3.** amount **to, a.** to add up to. **b.** to be equal to.

——**Usage.** AMOUNT refers to quantity that cannot be counted (*the amount of energy*), while NUMBER refers to things that can be counted (*a number of days*).

a·mour′ (ə mŏŏr′) *n.* a love affair.

a·mour-pro′pre (A MŎŎR PRŌ′PRə) *n.* French. self-esteem.

am′per·age (am′pər ij, am pēr′-) *n.* the strength of an electric current.

am′pere (am′pēr) *n.* a unit measuring electric current.

am′per·sand′ (am′pər sand′) *n.* a sign (&) meaning "and."

am·phet′a·mine (am fet′ə mēn′, -min) *n.* a drug that stimulates the central nervous system.

am·phib′i·an (-fib′ē ən) *n.* **1.** an animal living both in water and on land. —*adj.* **2.** Also, **am·phib′i·ous,** operating on land or water.

am′phi·the′a·ter (am′fə thē′ə tər, -thē′-) *n.* a theater with seats arranged in tiers around an open area.

am′ple (am′pəl) *adj.,* **-pler, -plest. 1.** sufficient. **2.** abundant. —**am′ply,** *adv.*

am′pli·fy′ (am′plə fī′) *v.t.,* **-fied, -fying.** to make larger, stronger, or louder. —**am′pli·fi·ca′tion,** *n.* —**am′pli·fi′er,** *n.*

am′pli·tude′ (-tōōd′, -tyōōd′) *n.* **1.** extent. **2.** abundance.

am′pule (am′pyŏŏl, -pŏŏl) *n.* a sealed glass or plastic vial containing a solution for hypodermic injection. Also, **am′pul, am′poule.**

am′pu·tate′ (am′pyŏŏ tāt′) *v.t.,* **-tated, -tating.** to cut off (a limb) by surgery. —**am′pu·ta′tion.** —**am′pu·tee′,** *n.*

a·muck′ (ə muk′) *adv.* —*Idiom.* **run** *or* **go amuck,** to be out of control.

am′u·let (am′yə lit) *n.* a charm worn to protect against evil.

a·muse′ (ə myŏŏz′) *v.t.,* amused, amusing. **1.** to occupy pleasantly. **2.** to cause to laugh. —**a·muse′ment,** *n.*

amuse′ment park′ *n.* a park with recreational rides.

an (ən; *when stressed an*) *adj. or indef. art. before initial vowel sounds.* See **a.**

a·nach′ro·nism (ə nak′rə niz′əm) *n.* a thing that belongs to a time period other than that in which it is placed. —**a·nach′ro·nis′tic,** *adj.*

an′a·con′da (an′ə kon′də) *n.* a very large South American snake.

an′a·gram (an′ə gram′) *n.* a word formed from the rearranged letters of another.

a′nal (ā′nəl) *adj.* of the anus.

an·al·ge′sic (an′əl jē′zik) *n.* a drug that relieves pain.

an′a·log comput′er (an′ə lôg′) *n.* a computer that represents data by measurable quantities rather than numbers.

an′a·logue′ (an′l ôg′) *n.* something analogous to something else. Also, **an′a·log′.**

a·nal′o·gy (ə nal′ə jē) *n., pl.* **-gies.** a similarity in some respects. —**a·nal′o·gous** (-gəs) *adj.*

a·nal′y·sis (ə nal′ih sis) *n., pl.* **-ses** (-sēz′). **1.** the separation of an entity into parts for close examination. **2.** psychoanalysis. —**an′a·lyst** (an′l ist) *n.* —**an′a·lyt′ic, an′a·lyt′i·cal,** *adj.*

an′a·lyze′ (an′l īz′) *v.t.,* **-lyzed, -lyzing. 1.** to subject to analysis. **2.** to psychoanalyze.

an′ar·chy (an′ər kē) *n.* **1.** a state of society without laws or government. **2.** chaos. —**an′ar·chism,** *n.* —**an′ar·chist,** *n.*

a·nath′e·ma (ə nath′ə mə) *n.* **1.** a solemn curse. **2.** a thing or person detested.

a·nat′o·my (ə nat′ə mē) *n., pl.* **-mies. 1.** the structure of an animal or plant. **2.** the science dealing with such structure. —**an′a·tom′i·cal** (an′ə tom′i kəl) *adj.*

an′ces·tor (an′ses tər) *n.* a person from whom one is descended. —**an·ces′tral,** *adj.* —**an′ces·try,** *n.*

an′chor (ang′kər) *n.* **1.** a heavy device lowered from a ship to keep it in place. **2.** the main broadcaster who coordinates a TV or radio newscast. —*v.t.* **3.** to fasten by an anchor. **4.** to serve as anchor for (a newscast).

an′chor·age (-ij) *n.* a place for anchoring ships.

an′cho·rite (ang′kə rīt′) *n.* a hermit.

an′chor·man′ *or* **an′chor·wom′an** *or* **an′chor·per′son,** *n., pl.* **-men.** a person who anchors a program of news, sports, etc.

an′cho·vy (an′chō vē) *n., pl.* **-vies.** a small, strongly flavored fish.

an′cient (ān′shənt) *adj.* **1.** of times long past. **2.** very old.

an′cil·lar′y (an′sə ler′ē) *adj.* **1.** subordinate. **2.** helping.

and (and; *unstressed* ənd, ən, n) *conj.* **1.** with; also. **2.** plus. **3.** *Informal.* (used in place of **to** in infinitive): *Try and stop me.*

an·dan′te (än dän′tā) *adv. Music.* at moderate speed.

and′i′ron (and′ī′ərn) *n.* one of a pair of metal supports for logs in a fireplace.

an′dro·gen (an′drə jən) *n.* a male sex hormone, as testosterone.

an·drog′y·nous (an droj′ə nəs) *adj.* having both masculine and feminine characteristics.

an′droid (an′droid) *n.* an automaton in human form.

an′ec·dote′ (an′ik dōt′) *n.* a short true story.

a·ne′mi·a (ə nē′mē ə) *n.* an inadequate supply of hemoglobin in the red blood cells. —**a·ne′mic,** *adj.*

a·nem′o·ne′ (ə nem′ə nē′) *n.* a plant with white, purple, or red flowers.

an′es·the′sia (an′əs thē′zhə) *n.* insensibility to pain. —**an·es′the·tist** (ə nes′thi-) *n.*

an′es·the·si·ol′o·gy (-zē ol′ə jē) *n.* the science of giving anesthetics. —**an′es·the·si·ol′o·gist,** *n.*

an′es·thet′ic (-thet′ik) *n.* **1.** a substance that causes anesthesia. —*adj.* **2.** of or causing anesthesia.

an′eu·rysm (an′yə riz′əm) *n.* a permanent pouch formed in a weakened artery wall. Also, **an′eu·rism.**

a·new′ (ə nōō′, ə nyōō′) *adv.* **1.** again. **2.** in a new way.

an′gel (ān′jəl) *n.* **1.** a spiritual being who is a messenger of God. **2.** a very kind and helpful person. —**an·gel′ic,** *adj.*

an′gel food′ cake′ *n.* a light, spongy cake made with egg whites.

an′ger (ang′gər) *n.* **1.** strong displeasure; outrage. —*v.t.* **2.** to make angry.

an·gi′na pec′to·ris (an jī′nə pek′tə ris) *n.* chest pain caused by inadequate blood flow to the heart.

an′gi·o·plas′ty (an′jē ə plas′tē) *n., pl.* **-ties.** the surgical repair of a blood vessel, using a balloon-tipped catheter to unclog it.

an′gle¹ (ang′gəl) *n., v.,* **-gled, -gling.** —*n.* **1.** the space between converging lines or surfaces. **2.** a point of view. —*v.t., v.i.* **3.** to move or bend at an angle. **4.** to write from a certain viewpoint.

an′gle² (ang′gəl) *v.i.,* **-gled, -gling. 1.** to fish with a hook on a line. **2.** to try for something by artful means. —**an′gler,** *n.*

An′gle (ang′gəl) *n.* a member of a Germanic people who migrated to England in the 5th century A.D.

An′gle·worm′ *n.* a worm used as bait in fishing.

An′gli·can (ang′gli kən) *adj.* **1.** of the Church of England. —*n.* **2.** a member of this church.

An′gli·cism (-siz′əm) *n.* an English word in another language.

An′gli·cize′ (-sīz′) *v.t., v.i.,* **-cized, -cizing.** to make or become English in form or character.

An′glo-Sax′on (ang′glō sak′sən) *n.* **1.** a person of English descent. **2.** an inhabitant of England before 1066. —*adj.* **3.** of Anglo-Saxons.

An·go′ra (ang gôr′ə) *n.* **1.** a cat, goat, or rabbit with long, silky hair. **2. angora,** yarn or fabric from an Angora goat or rabbit.

an′gry (ang′grē) *adj.,* **-grier, -griest. 1.** full of anger. **2.** inflamed. —**an′gri·ly,** *adv.*

angst (ängkst) *n.* a feeling of dread or anxiety.

ang′strom (ang′strəm) *n.* (*often cap.*) a unit of length equal to one ten millionth of a millimeter.

an′guish (ang′gwish) *n.* extreme pain or grief.

an′gu·lar (ang′gyə lər) *adj.* **1.** having angles. **2.** measured by an angle. **3.** lean and bony. —**an·gu·lar′i·ty,** *n.*

an′i·line (an′l in) *n.* an oily liquid used in dyes, plastics, etc.

an′i·mad·ver′sion (an′ə mad vûr′zhən) *n.* criticism. —**an′i·mad·vert′,** *v.i.*

an′i·mal (an′ə məl) *n.* **1.** a living thing that can move voluntarily. **2.** a beast. —*adj.* **3.** of animals.

an′i·mal′cule (an′ə mal′kyōōl) *n.* a very tiny animal.

an′i·mate′ *v.,* **-mated, -mating,** *adj.* —*v.t.* (-māt′) **1.** to give life to. **2.** to make lively. —*adj.* (-mit) **3.** alive.

an′i·ma′tion *n.* **1.** liveliness. **2.** an animated cartoon.

an′i·me′ (an′ə mā′) *n.* a Japanese style of animation, marked by highly stylized art and sexuality and violence.

an′i·mism (-miz′əm) *n.* the belief that animals and natural objects have souls.

an′i·mos′i·ty (an′ə mos′i tē) *n.* strong dislike or hostility.

an′i·mus (-məs) *n.* strong dislike; animosity.

an′ise (an′is) *n.* a plant yielding an aromatic seed (**an′i·seed′**) used in cooking.

an′kle (ang′kəl) *n.* the joint between the foot and the leg.

an′kle·bone′ *n.* the uppermost of the tarsal bones.

an′klet (-klit) *n.* **1.** a short, ankle-length sock. **2.** an ornament for the ankle.

an′nals (an′lz) *n.pl.* a historical record of events.

an·neal′ (ə nēl′) *v.t.* to toughen or temper (metal or glass).

an′ne·lid (an′l id) *n.* a segmented worm.

an·nex′ *v.t.* (ə neks′) **1.** to attach to something larger. —*n.* (an′ eks) **2.** a thing annexed. **3.** an attached building. —**an′nex·a′tion,** *n.*

an·ni′hi·late′ (ə nī′ə lāt′) *v.t.,* **-lated, -lating.** to destroy completely. —**an·ni′hi·la′tion,** *n.*

an′ni·ver′sa·ry (an′ə vûr′sə rē) *n., pl.* **-ries.** the yearly recurrence of the date of a past event.

an′no·tate′ (an′ə tāt′) *v.t.,* **-tated, -tating.** to supply (a text) with notes. —**an′no·ta′tion,** *n.*

an·nounce′ (ə nouns′) *v.t.,* **-nounced, -nouncing.** to make known publicly. —**an·nounce′ment,** *n.* —**an·nounc′er,** *n.*

an·noy′ (ə noi′) *v.t.* to irritate or trouble. —**an·noy′ance,** *n.*

an′nu·al (an′yōō əl) *adj.* **1.** yearly. **2.** (of a plant) living only one season. —*n.* **3.** an annual plant. **4.** a yearbook. —**an′nu·al·ly,** *adv.*

an·nu′i·ty *n., pl.* **-ties.** the income from an investment, paid yearly.

an·nul′ (ə nul′) *v.t.,* **-nulled, -nulling.** to declare void. —**an·nul′ment,** *n.*

an′nu·lar (an′yə lər) *adj.* ring-shaped.

An·nun·ci·a′tion (ə nun′sē ā′shən) *n.* the announcement by the angel Gabriel to the Virgin Mary that she would become the mother of Christ (celebrated March 25).

an′ode (an′ōd) *n.* **1.** an electrode with a positive charge. **2.** the negative terminal of a battery.

an′o·dyne′ (an′ə dīn′) *n.* something that relieves pain.

a·noint′ (ə noint′) *v.t.* to put oil on, as in a religious consecration.

a·nom′a·ly (ə nom′ə lē) *n., pl.* **-lies.** something irregular or abnormal. —**a·nom′a·lous,** *adj.*

a·non′ (ə non′) *adv. Archaic.* soon.

anon. anonymous.

a·non′y·mous (ə non′ə məs) *adj.* of unknown or undisclosed origin. —**an′o·nym′i·ty** (ə nim′i tē) *n.* —**a·non′y·mous·ly,** *adv.*

an′o·rak′ (an′ə rak′) *n.* a hooded jacket; parka.

an′o·rex′i·a (an′ə rek′sē ə) *n.* an eating disorder marked by excessive dieting. Also, **anorexia ner·vo′sa** (nûr vō′sə). —**an′o·rex′ic,** *adj., n.*

an·oth′er (ə nuth′ər) *adj.* **1.** additional. **2.** different. —*n.* **3.** one more. **4.** a different one.

an′swer (an′sər) *n.* **1.** a reply, as to a question. **2.** a solution to a problem. —*v.i.* **3.** to speak, write, or act in response. **4.** to be responsible. **5.** to be satisfactory. **6.** to conform. —*v.t.* **7.** to reply to. **8.** to fulfill. **9.** to correspond to.

an′swer·a·ble *adj.* **1.** able to be answered. **2.** responsible.

an′swering machine′ *n.* a device that answers telephone calls with a recorded message and records messages from callers.

ant (ant) *n.* a common small insect that lives in organized groups.

ant·ac′id (ant as′id) *n.* a medicine to counteract acids.

an·tag′o·nism (an tag′ə niz′əm) *n.* hostility. —**an·tag′o·nis′tic,** *adj.*

an·tag′o·nist (an tag′ə nist) *n.* **1.** an opponent. **2.** (*in literature*) the opponent of the hero or protagonist.

an·tag′o·nize′ (an tag′ə nīz′) *v.t.,* **-nized, -nizing.** to cause to become hostile.

ant·arc′tic (ant ärk′tik, -är′tik) *adj.* (*often cap.*) of or at the South Pole.

ante- a prefix indicating: **1.** happening before. **2.** in front of.

ant′eat′er *n.* a tropical American mammal having a long snout and feeding on ants and termites.

an·te·bel′lum (an′tē bel′əm) *adj.* before a war, esp. the American Civil War.

an·te·ced′ent (an′tə sēd′nt) *adj.* **1.** prior. —*n.* **2.** anything that precedes. **3.** a word or phrase referred to by a pronoun.

an′te·date′ (an′ti dāt′) *v.t.,* **-dated, -dating. 1.** to be of earlier date than. **2.** to predate.

an·te·di·lu′vi·an (an′tē di lōō′vē ən) *adj.* before the Biblical Flood.

an′te·lope′ (an′tl ōp′) *n.* a deerlike animal.

an·te me·rid′i·em (an′tē mə rid′ē əm) *adj.* before noon.

an·ten′na (an ten′ə) *n., pl.* antennae (-nē) *for* **1.** **1.** a feeler on the head of an insect. **2.** wires for transmitting radio waves, TV pictures, etc.

an·te′ri·or (an tēr′ē ər) *adj.* **1.** earlier. **2.** situated in front of.

an′te·room′ (an′tē rōōm′, -rŏŏm′) *n.* a room serving as an entrance to the main room.

an′them (an′thəm) *n.* a patriotic or sacred hymn.

an′ther (an′thər) *n.* the pollen-bearing part of a stamen.

an·thol′o·gy (an thol′ə jē) *n., pl.* **-gies.** a collection of writings.

an′thra·cite′ (an′thrə sīt′) *n.* hard coal.

an′thrax (an′thraks) *n.* a disease of cattle and sheep that is transmittable to humans.

an·thro·po·cen′tric (an′thrə pō sen′trik) *adj.* viewing everything in terms of human experience.

an′thro·poid′ (an′thrə poid′) *adj.* resembling a human or an ape.

an·thro·pol′o·gy (-pol′ə jē) *n.* the study of the origins, development, customs, etc., of humans. —**an′thro·pol′o·gist,** *n.*

an·thro·po·mor′phic (-pə môr′fik) *adj.* ascribing human qualities to a nonhuman thing or being. —**an·thro·po·mor′phism** (-fiz əm) *n.*

anti- a prefix indicating: **1.** against or opposed to. **2.** acting against.

an′ti·bi·ot′ic (an′ti bī ot′ik) *n.* a substance used to kill bacteria.

an′ti·bod′y *n., pl.* **-bodies.** a substance produced by the body that destroys bacteria and viruses.

an′tic (an′tik) *n.* **1.** a playful prank or a ridiculous act or gesture. —*adj.* **2.** ludicrous.

an·tic′i·pate′ (an tis′ə pāt′) *v.t.,* **-pated, -pating. 1.** to expect and prepare for. **2.** to look forward to. **3.** to forestall. —**an·tic′i·pa′tion,** *n.*

an·ti·cli′max (an′tē klī′maks, an′tī-) *n.* a disappointing or undramatic outcome.

an′ti·co·ag′u·lant (an′tē kō ag′yə lant, an′tī-) *n.* a substance that prevents coagulation of blood.

an′ti·de·pres′sant (an′tē di pres′ant, an′tī-) *n.* a drug for relieving depression.

an′ti·dote′ (an′ti dōt′) *n.* a medicine that counteracts poison.

an′ti·freeze′ (an′ti frēz′, an′tē-) *n.* a liquid used in an engine's radiator to prevent the cooling fluid from freezing.

an′ti·gen (an′ti jən) *n.* a substance that stimulates the production of antibodies.

an′ti·his′ta·mine′ (an′tē his′tə mēn′, -min) *n.* a substance used against allergic reactions.

an′ti·mat′ter (an′tē mat′ər, an′tī-) *n.* matter with charges opposite to those of common particles.

an′ti·mo′ny (an′tə mō′nē) *n.* a brittle white metallic element.

an′ti·ox′i·dant (an′tē ok′si dənt, an′tī-) *n.* an organic substance counteracting oxidation damage in animal tissues.

an′ti·pas′to (an′ti pä′stō) *n., pl.* **-pastos, -pasti** (-pä′stē). an Italian appetizer.

an·tip′a·thy (an tip′ə thē) *n.* dislike; aversion.

an′ti·per′spi·rant (an′ti pûr′spər ənt) *n.* an astringent product for reducing perspiration.

an·tip′o·des (an tip′ə dēz′) *n.pl.* places opposite each other on the globe.

an′ti·quar′i·an (an′ti kwâr′ē ən) *adj.* **1.** relating to antiquities. —*n.* **2.** an antiquary.

an′ti·quar′y (-kwer′ē) *n., pl.* **-ries.** a collector of antiquities.

an′ti·quat′ed (-kwā′tid) *adj.* old or obsolete.

an·tique′ (an tēk′) *adj.* **1.** old or old-fashioned. —*n.* **2.** a valuable old object.

an·tiq′ui·ty (-tik′wi tē) *n.* **1.** ancient times. **2.** antiquities, things from ancient times.

an′ti-Sem′ite (an′tē sem′īt, an′tī-) *n.* a person hostile to Jews. —**an′ti-Se·mit′ic** (-sə mit′ik) *adj.* —**an′ti-Sem′i·tism** (-sem′ tiz′əm) *n.*

an′ti·sep′tic (an′tə sep′tik) *adj.* **1.** destroying certain germs. —*n.* **2.** an antiseptic substance.

an′ti·so′cial (an′tē sō′shəl, an′tī-) *adj.* **1.** not associating with others in a friendly way. **2.** hostile to society.

an·tith′e·sis (an tith′ə sis) *n., pl.* **-ses. 1.** contrast. **2.** the direct opposite.

an′ti·tox′in (an′ti tok′sin) *n.* a substance counteracting germ-produced poisons in the body.

an′ti·trust′ (an′tē trust′, an′tī-) *adj.* opposing or intended to restrain business trusts or monopolies.

ant′ler (ant′lər) *n.* one of the horns on an animal of the deer family.

an′to·nym (an′tə nim′) *n.* a word of opposite meaning.

a′nus (ā′nəs) *n.* the opening at the lower end of the alimentary canal.

an′vil (an′vil) *n.* an iron block on which hot metals are hammered into shape.

anx·i′e·ty (ang zī′i tē) *n.* mental distress caused by fear. —**anx′ious** (angk′shəs) *adj.* —**anx′ious·ly,** *adv.*

an′y (en′ē) *adj.* **1.** one or more. **2.** some. **3.** every. —*pron.* **4.** any person, thing, etc. —*adv.* **5.** at all. —**Usage.** See SOME.

an′y·bod′y *pron.* any person.

an′y·how′ *adv.* in any way, case, etc. Also, **an′y·way′.**

an′y·one′ *pron.* anybody.

an′y·place′ *adv.* anywhere.

an′y·thing′ *pron.* any thing whatever.

an′y·time′ *adv.* at any time.

an′y·where′ *adv.* **1.** in, at, or to any place. —*Idiom.* **2. get anywhere,** to succeed.

A′ one′ (ā′ wun′) *adj.* excellent. Also, **A′ 1′, A′-1′.**

a·or′ta (ā ôr′tə) *n., pl.* **-tas, -tae** (-tē). the main artery from the heart.

a·pace′ (ə pās′) *adv.* quickly.

a·part′ (ə pärt′) *adv.* **1.** into pieces. **2.** separately. **3.** aside.

a·part′heid (-hāt, -hīt) *n.* (formerly, in South Africa) separation of and discrimination against blacks.

a·part′ment (-mənt) *n.* a set of rooms used as a residence.

ap′a·thy (ap′ə thē) *n.* lack of emotion or interest. —**ap′a·thet′ic** (-thet′ik) *adj.*

ape (āp) *n., v.,* aped, aping. —*n.* **1.**

a large, tailless monkeylike animal. —v.t. **2.** to imitate stupidly.

a·pé·ri·tif (ə per′i tēf′) n. liquor served before a meal.

ap′er·ture (ap′ər chər) n. an opening.

a′pex (ā′peks) n. the tip; summit.

a·pha·sia (ə fā′zhə) n. loss of the ability to speak or to understand language. —**a·pha′sic** (-zik) adj.

a·phe′li·on (ə fē′lē ən, ap hē′-) n. the point farthest from the sun in the orbit of a planet or comet.

a′phid (ā′fid, af′id) n. a tiny insect that sucks sap from plants.

aph′o·rism (af′ə riz′əm) n. a brief maxim.

aph′ro·dis·i·ac′ (af′rə dēz′ē ak′, -diz′ē ak′) adj. **1.** arousing sexual desire. —n. **2.** an aphrodisiac food, drug, etc.

a′pi·ar′y (ā′pē er′ē) n., pl. -ries. a place where bees are kept.

a·piece′ (ə pēs′) adv. for each.

a·plen′ty (ə plen′tē) adj., adv. in generous amounts.

a·plomb′ (ə plom′, ə plum′) n. poise; self-possession.

a·poc′a·lypse (ə pok′ə lips) n. **1.** a prophesy of a violent upheaval in which evil is defeated. **2. Apocalypse,** the last book of the New Testament. —**a·poc·a·lyp′tic,** adj.

A·poc′ry·pha (ə pok′rə fə) n. the Old Testament books not found in Jewish or Protestant scriptures.

a·poc′ry·phal adj. not verified; of doubtful authenticity.

ap′o·gee′ (ap′ə jē′) n. **1.** the remotest point of the orbit of the moon or a satellite. **2.** the highest point.

a·po·lit′i·cal (ā′pə lit′i kəl) adj. not interested in politics.

a·pol′o·gist (ə pol′ə jist) n. a person who defends a faith, idea, etc.

a·pol′o·gize v.i. -gized, -gizing. to offer an apology.

a·pol′o·gy n., pl. -gies. **1.** a statement of regret for one's act. **2.** a stated defense. —**a·pol·o·get′ic** (-jet′ik) adj.

ap′o·plex′y (ap′ə plek′sē) n. the sudden loss of bodily functions due to the bursting of a blood vessel. —**ap·o·plec′tic** (-plek′tik) adj.

a·pos′tate (ə pos′tāt, -tit) n. a deserter of one's faith, cause, etc. —**a·pos′ta·sy** (-tə sē) n.

a′ pos·te·ri·o′ri (ā′ pos·te′rē ôr′ī, -ôr′ē) adj. **1.** from particular instances to a general principle. **2.** based on observation or experiment.

a·pos′tle (ə pos′əl) n. **1.** a disciple sent by Jesus to preach the gospel. **2.** a moral reformer. —**ap′os·tol′ic** (ap′ə stol′ik) adj.

a·pos′tro·phe (ə pos′trə fē) n. a sign (′) indicating an omitted letter, the possessive, or certain plurals.

a·poth′e·car′y (ə poth′ə ker′ē) n., pl. -ries. a pharmacist.

a·poth′e·o′sis (ə poth′ē ō′sis, ap′-ə thē′ə sis) n., pl. -ses (-sēz). **1.** the ideal example. **2.** elevation to the rank of a god.

ap·pall′ (ə pôl′) v.t. to fill with dismay. —**ap·pall′ing,** adj.

ap′pa·ra′tus (ap′ə rat′əs, -rā′təs) n. equipment for a specific task.

ap·par′el (ə par′əl) n. clothing.

ap·par′ent (ə par′ənt, ə pâr′-) adj. **1.** obvious. **2.** seeming but not real. —**ap·par′ent·ly,** adv.

ap′pa·ri′tion (ap′ə rish′ən) n. a ghost.

ap·peal′ (ə pēl′) n. **1.** a call for aid, mercy, etc. **2.** a request for a review of a court verdict. **3.** attractiveness. —v.i. **4.** to make an earnest plea. **5.** to be attractive.

ap·pear′ (ə pēr′) v.i. **1.** to come into sight. **2.** to come before the public. **3.** to seem.

ap·pear′ance (-əns) n. **1.** the act of appearing. **2.** outward look.

ap·pease′ (ə pēz′) v.t., -peased, -peasing. **1.** to pacify; soothe. **2.** to yield to the demands of. —**ap·pease′ment,** n.

ap·pel′lant (ə pel′ənt) n. one who appeals.

ap·pel′late (ə pel′it) adj. (of a court) dealing with appeals.

ap′pel·la′tion (ap′ə lā′shən) n. a name or title.

ap·pend′ (ə pend′) v.t. to add or attach.

ap·pend′age (ə pen′dij) n. an attached part.

ap′pen·dec′to·my (ap′ən dek′tə-mē) n., pl. -mies. removal of the appendix.

ap·pen′di·ci′tis (ə pen′də sī′tis) n. inflammation of the appendix.

ap·pen′dix (ə pen′diks) n., pl.

-dixes, -dices (-də sēz′). **1.** a supplement. **2.** a closed tube attached to the large intestine.

ap′per·tain′ (ap′ər tān′) v.i. to belong or pertain.

ap′pe·tite′ (ap′i tīt′) n. a desire, esp. for food.

ap′pe·tiz′er (-tī′zər) n. a portion of food or drink served before a meal to stimulate the appetite. —**ap′pe·tiz′ing,** adj.

ap·plaud′ (ə plôd′) v.i., v.t. **1.** to clap the hands in approval or praise (of). **2.** to praise.

ap′ple (ap′əl) n. a round fruit with firm, white flesh.

ap′ple·jack′ n. brandy made from fermented cider.

ap′ple·sauce′ n. apples stewed to a pulp.

ap·pli′ance (ə plī′əns) n. a device or instrument.

ap′pli·ca·ble (ap′li kə bəl) adj. relevant; appropriate.

ap′pli·cant (-kənt) n. a person who applies, as for a job.

ap′pli·ca′tion (-kā′shən) n. **1.** the act of applying. **2.** the use to which something is put. **3.** a form filled out by an applicant. **4.** relevance. **5.** a request. **6.** persistent attention. **7.** Also, **applica′tion pro′gram.** a computer program used for a specific kind of task.

ap′pli·ca′tor n. a device for applying a substance, as medication.

ap′pli·qué′ (ap′li kā′) n., v., -quéd, -quéing. —n. **1.** a cutout design of one material applied to another. —v.t. **2.** to decorate with appliqué.

ap·ply′ (ə plī′) v., -plied, -plying. —v.i. **1.** to make a formal request, as for a job. **2.** to be relevant. —v.t. **3.** to put to use. **4.** to assign to a purpose. **5.** to spread on. **6.** to employ (oneself) diligently.

ap·point′ (ə point′) v.t. **1.** to choose or assign officially. **2.** to fix or set. —**ap·point·ee′,** n. —**ap·point′ive,** adj.

ap·point′ment n. **1.** the act of appointing. **2.** a prearranged meeting. **3.** a position to which a person is appointed.

ap·por′tion (ə pôr′shən) v.t. to divide into shares. —**ap·por′tion·ment,** n.

ap′po·site (ap′ə zit) adj. suitable.

ap·praise′ (ə prāz′) v.t., -praised, -praising. to estimate the value or quality of. —**ap·prais′al,** n. —**ap·prais′er,** n.

ap·pre′ci·a·ble (ə prē′shē ə bəl) adj. noticeable; considerable.

ap·pre′ci·ate′ (-shē āt′) v., -ated, -ating. —v.t. **1.** to be grateful for. **2.** to value highly. —v.i. **3.** to increase in value. —**ap·pre′cia·tive** (-shə-tiv) adj.

ap·pre′ci·a′tion n. **1.** gratitude. **2.** recognition, esp. of aesthetic quality. **3.** increase in value, as of property.

ap′pre·hend′ (ap′ri hend′) v.t. **1.** to take into custody. **2.** to understand.

ap′pre·hen′sion (-hen′shən) n. **1.** anxiety. **2.** the act of understanding. **3.** the act of arresting.

ap′pre·hen′sive (-siv) adj. worried.

ap·pren′tice (ə pren′tis) n., v., -ticed, -ticing. —n. **1.** a person learning a trade. —v.t., v.i. **2.** to employ or serve as an apprentice. —**ap·pren′tice·ship′,** n.

ap·prise′ (ə prīz′) v.t., -prised, -prising. to notify. Also, **ap·prize′.**

ap·proach′ (ə prōch′) v.t. **1.** to come nearer to. **2.** to begin work on. **3.** to make a proposal to. —v.i. **4.** to come nearer. —n. **5.** a coming near. **6.** a means of access. **7.** a method.

ap′pro·ba′tion (ap′rə bā′shən) n. approval.

ap·pro′pri·ate adj., v., -ated, -ating. —adj. (ə prō′prē it) **1.** suitable; proper. —v.t. (-prē āt′) **2.** to take possession of. **3.** to designate for a use. —**ap·pro′pri·ate·ly,** adv. —**ap·pro′pri·ate·ness,** n.

ap·pro′pri·a′tion n. **1.** the act of appropriating. **2.** money authorized to be paid from public funds.

ap·prov′al (ə prōō′vəl) n. **1.** the act of approving. **2.** permission. —Idiom. **3. on approval,** subject to rejection if not satisfactory.

ap·prove′ (ə prōōv′) v.t., -proved, -proving. —v.t. **1.** to think or speak well of. **2.** to consent to. —v.i. **3.** to confirm formally. —v.i. **4.** to have a favorable view.

ap·prox′i·mate adj., v., -mated, -mating. —adj. (ə prok′sə mit) **1.** nearly exact. **2.** similar. —v.t. (-māt′) **3.** to be about the same as.

—**ap·prox′i·mate′ly,** adv. —**ap·prox′i·ma′tion,** n.

ap·pur′te·nance (ə pûr′tn əns) n. something subordinate to something else.

Apr. April.

a′pri·cot′ (ap′ri kot, ā′pri-) n. a small peachlike fruit.

A′pril (ā′prəl) n. the fourth month of the year.

a′ pri·o′ri (ā′ prē ôr′ī, -ôr′ē) adj. **1.** from a general law to a particular instance. **2.** existing in the mind independent of experience.

a′pron (ā′prən) n. a protective garment for the front of one's clothes.

ap′ro·pos′ (ap′rə pō′) adj. **1.** at the right time. **2.** by the way —adj. **3.** appropriate and timely. —Idiom. **4. apropos of,** with reference to.

apse (aps) n. a vaulted recess in a church.

apt (apt) adj. **1.** prone; disposed. **2.** likely. **3.** being quick to learn. **4.** suited to the occasion. —**apt′ly,** adv. —**apt′ness,** n.

apt. apartment.

ap′ti·tude′ (ap′ti tōōd′, -tyōōd′) n. **1.** skill; talent. **2.** quickness in learning.

Aq′ua·lung′ Trademark. an underwater breathing device.

aq·ua·ma·rine′ n. **1.** a light greenish blue. **2.** a gemstone of this color.

a·quar′i·um (ə kwâr′ē əm) n., pl. -iums, -ia (-ē ə). a place for exhibiting aquatic animals and plants.

a·quat′ic (ə kwat′ik, ə kwot′-) adj. of or living in water.

aq′ue·duct′ (ak′wi dukt′) n. an artificial channel for conducting water from a distance.

a′que·ous (ā′kwē əs, ak′wē-) adj. of or like water.

a′queous hu′mor n. the fluid between the cornea and the lens of the eye.

aq′ui·fer (ak′wə fər) n. rock, gravel, or sand containing groundwater.

aq′ui·line′ (ak′wə līn′, -lin) adj. (of a nose) curved like a beak.

AR Arkansas.

Ar·ab (ar′əb) n. **1.** a member of an Arabic-speaking people. **2.** a member of a Semitic people inhabiting Arabia, SW Asia, and N Africa.

Ar′a·bic (ar′ə bik) n. **1.** a Semitic language spoken chiefly in SW Asia and N Africa. —adj. **2.** of Arabic, Arabia, or Arabs.

Ar′abic nu′meral n. any of the numerals 0, 1, 2, 3, 4, 5, 6, 7, 8, or 9.

ar′a·ble (ar′ə bəl) adj. (of land) capable of producing crops.

a·rach′nid (ə rak′nid) n. a small eight-legged animal, as the spider.

ar′bit·er (är′bi tər) n. a person empowered to decide or judge.

ar′bi·trage′ (-träzh′) n. the simultaneous sale of the same security in different markets to profit from unequal prices. —**ar′bi·trag′er,** n.

ar′bi·trar′y (är′bi trer′ē) adj. **1.** based on random choice. **2.** capricious. **3.** despotic. —**ar′bi·trar′i·ly,** adv.

ar′bi·trate′ (-trāt′) v., -trated, -trating. —v.t. **1.** to settle as, or submit to, an arbitrator. —v.i. **2.** to act as arbitrator. —**ar′bi·tra′tion,** n.

ar′bi·tra′tor n. a person empowered to settle a dispute.

ar′bor (är′bər) n. a place shaded by vines or trees.

ar·bo′re·al (är bôr′ē əl) adj. of or living in trees.

ar·bo·re′tum (är′bə rē′təm) n., pl. -tums, -ta (-tə). a parklike area with different kinds of trees for study or display.

ar·bu′tus (är byōō′təs) n. an evergreen shrub with red berries. **2.** a creeping plant with fragrant white or pink flowers.

arc (ärk) n. **1.** part of a circle. **2.** a luminous current between two electric conductors.

ar·cade′ (är kād′) n. **1.** a row of archways. **2.** a covered passage with stores.

ar·cane′ (är kān′) adj. mysterious.

arch¹ (ärch) n. **1.** a curved structure spanning an opening. —v.i., v.t. **2.** to form (into) an arch.

arch² (ärch) adj. consciously playful. —**arch′ly,** adv.

ar′chae·ol′o·gy (är′kē ol′ə jē) n. the study of past cultures through objects or their remains. Also, **ar′che·ol′o·gy.** —**ar′chae·o·log′i·cal** (-ə loj′i kəl) adj. —**ar′chae·ol′o·gist,** n.

ar·cha′ic (är kā′ik) adj. belonging to an earlier period; ancient.

arch′an′gel (ärk′ān′jəl) n. a chief angel.

arch′bish′op (ärch′bish′əp) n. a bishop of the highest rank.

arch′dea′con (ärch′dē′kən) n. a member of the clergy ranking next below a bishop.

arch′di·o·cese (ärch dī′ə sis, -sēz′, -sēs′) n. the diocese of an archbishop. —**arch′di·oc′e·san** (-os′ə-sən) adj.

arch′duke′ n. a prince of the former ruling house of Austria.

arch′en′e·my n., pl. -mies. a chief enemy.

arch′er (är′chər) n. one who shoots a bow and arrow. —**arch′er·y,** n.

ar′che·type′ (är′ki tīp′) n. an original pattern or model.

ar′chi·pel′a·go′ (är′kə pel′ə gō′) n., pl. -gos, -goes. **1.** a large group of islands. **2.** the body of water surrounding such a group.

ar′chi·tect′ (är′ki tekt′) n. a person who designs buildings.

ar′chi·tec′ture (-tek′chər) n. **1.** the profession of designing buildings. **2.** the style or design of a building. —**ar′chi·tec′tur·al,** adj. —**ar′chi·tec′tur·al·ly,** adv.

ar′chives (är′kīvz) n.pl. **1.** historical documents. **2.** a place for such documents.

arch′way′ (ärch′wā′) n. an entrance covered by an arch.

arc′tic (ärk′tik, är′tik) adj. **1.** (often cap.) of or at the North Pole. **2.** extremely cold.

ar′dent (är′dnt) adj. passionate; zealous. —**ar′dent·ly,** adv.

ar′dor (är′dər) n. intensity of feeling; enthusiasm.

ar′du·ous (är′jōō əs) adj. very difficult.

are (är; unstressed ər) v. pres. indic. pl. of **be.**

ar·e·a (âr′ē ə) n. **1.** the extent of a surface. **2.** a region. **3.** scope.

ar′ea code′ n. a three-digit number used in long-distance telephone dialing.

a·re′na (ə rē′nə) n. **1.** a space used for sports or other entertainments. **2.** a field of activity.

aren′t (ärnt, är′ənt) contraction of **are not.**

ar′got (är′gət, -gō) n. a special vocabulary used by a particular group of people.

ar·gu·a·ble (är′gyōō ə bəl) adj. **1.** doubtful; questionable. **2.** capable of being supported by persuasive argument; possible.

ar·gu·a·bly (är′gyōō ə blē) adv. as can be supported by persuasive argument.

ar·gue (är′gyōō) v., -gued, -guing. —v.i. **1.** to present reasons for or against something. **2.** to dispute. —v.t. **3.** to give reasons for or against. **4.** to persuade. —**ar′gu·ment,** n. —**ar′gu·men·ta′tion,** n.

ar′gu·men·ta·tive (-men′tə tiv) adj. fond of argument.

ar′gyle (är′gīl) n. (often cap.) a diamond-shaped knitting pattern, as of socks.

a′ri·a (är′ē ə) n. an operatic solo.

-arian a suffix indicating: **1.** one connected with. **2.** one supporting or practicing.

ar·id (ar′id) adj. dry. —**a·rid′i·ty** (ə rid′i tē) n.

a·right′ (ə rīt′) adv. rightly.

a·rise′ (ə rīz′) v.i., arose (ə rōz′), arisen (ə riz′ən), arising. **1.** to come into being. **2.** to get up. **3.** to move upward.

ar·is·toc·ra·cy (ar′ə stok′rə sē) n., pl. -cies. **1.** the nobility. **2.** a state governed by the nobility. —**a·ris′to·crat′** (ə ris′tə krat′) n. —**a·ris′to·crat′ic,** adj.

a·rith′me·tic n. (ə rith′mə tik) n. computation by numbers. —**ar′ith·met′i·cal** (ar′ith met′i kəl) adj. —**ar′ith·met′i·cal·ly,** adv.

Ariz. Arizona.

ark (ärk) n. Archaic. a large ship.

Ark. Arkansas.

arm¹ (ärm) n. **1.** an upper limb of the human body. **2.** an armlike part. **3.** a projecting support at the side of a chair, sofa, etc. —Idiom. **4.** at arm's length, at a distance.

arm² (ärm) n. **1.** a weapon. **2.** a branch of the military. —v.t. **3.** to equip with weapons. —v.i. **4.** to prepare for war. —Idiom. **5. up in arms,** indignant.

ar·ma′da (är mä′də) n. a fleet of warships.

ar′ma·dil′lo (är′mə dil′ō) n. a burrowing mammal covered with bony plates.

ar′ma·ged′don (är′mə ged′n) n. a crucial or final conflict.

ar′ma·ment (är′mə mənt) n. **1.** military weapons. **2.** equipping for war.

arm′ can′dy n. Slang. an attractive person who accompanies someone.

arm′chair′ n. a chair with supports for the arms.

armed′ for′ces n.pl. military, naval, and air forces.

ar′mi·stice (är′mə stis) n. a truce.

ar′mor (är′mər) n. a protective metal covering, as against weapons.

ar′mor·y (är′mə rē) n., pl. -ries. a storage place for weapons.

arm′pit′ n. the hollow under the arm at the shoulder.

ar′my (är′mē) n., pl. -mies. **1.** a military force for land combat. **2.** a large group.

a·ro′ma (ə rō′mə) n. a pleasant odor. —**ar·o·mat′ic** (ar′ə mat′ik) adj.

a·ro′ma·ther′a·py n. the use of fragrances to alter a person's mood.

a·rose′ (ə rōz′) v. pt. of **arise.**

a·round′ (ə round′) adv. **1.** on all sides. **2.** in a circle. **3.** nearby. —prep. **4.** on all sides of. **5.** near. **6.** approximately.

a·rouse′ (ə rouz′) v.t., aroused, arousing. **1.** to awaken. **2.** to excite. —**a·rous′al,** n.

ar·peg′gi·o (är pej′ē ō′, -pej′ō) n. the sounding of the notes in a chord in rapid succession.

ar·raign′ (ə rān′) v.t. **1.** to bring before a court. **2.** to accuse. —**ar·raign′ment,** n.

ar·range′ (ə rānj′) v.t., -ranged, -ranging. **1.** to put in order. **2.** to plan or prepare. **3.** to adapt. —**ar·range′ment,** n.

ar·rant (ar′ənt) adj. downright.

ar·ray′ (ə rā′) v.t. **1.** to arrange in order. **2.** to clothe. —n. **3.** an arrangement, as for battle. **4.** an impressive group. **5.** fine clothes.

ar·rears′ (ə rērz′) n.pl. **1.** the state of being late in repaying a debt. **2.** an overdue debt.

ar·rest′ (ə rest′) v.t. **1.** to take (a person) into legal custody. **2.** to stop or check. **3.** to catch and hold. —n. **4.** the taking of a person into legal custody. **5.** a stopping or being stopped.

ar·rest′ing adj. attracting attention; engaging.

ar·rive′ (ə rīv′) v.i., -rived, -riving. **1.** to reach one's destination. **2.** to come. **3.** to achieve success.

ar′ro·gant (ar′ə gənt) adj. insolently proud. —**ar′ro·gance,** n.

ar′ro·gate′ (-gāt′) v.t., -gated, -gating. to claim or appropriate without right. —**ar′ro·ga′tion,** n.

ar′row (ar′ō) n. **1.** a pointed stick shot by a bow. **2.** a figure with a wedge-shaped end.

ar′row·head′ n. the pointed tip of an arrow.

ar′row·root′ n. the edible starch from the root of a tropical plant.

ar·roy′o (ə roi′ō) n., pl. -os. a steep, dry gulch that fills with water after a heavy rain.

ar′se·nal (är′sə nl) n. a military storehouse or factory.

ar′se·nic (är′sə nik) n. a grayish white element forming poisonous compounds.

ar′son (är′sən) n. the intentional and illegal burning of a structure.

art (ärt) n. **1.** the production of something beautiful or extraordinary. **2.** paintings, drawings, sculptures, etc. **3.** skill; ability. **4. arts,** subjects other than the sciences. —**art′ful,** adj.

art dec′o (dek′ō) n. (often caps.) 1920s decorative art with geometric designs.

ar·te′ri·o·scle·ro′sis (är tēr′ē ō-sklə rō′sis) n. hardening of the arteries.

ar′ter·y (är′tə rē) n., pl. -ries. **1.** a blood vessel carrying blood from the heart. **2.** a main highway. —**ar·te′ri·al** (-tēr′ē əl) adj.

ar·thri′tis (är thrī′tis) n. inflammation of one or more joints. —**ar·thrit′ic** (-thrit′ik) adj.

ar′thro·pod′ (är′thrə pod′) n. an invertebrate with a segmented body and jointed legs, including insects, spiders, and crustaceans.

ar′ti·choke′ (är′ti chōk′) n. a thistlelike plant with an edible flower head.

ar′ti·cle (är′ti kəl) n. **1.** a factual published piece of writing. **2.** a particular thing; item. **3.** the words a, an, or the.

ar·tic′u·late adj., v., -lated, -lating. —adj. (är tik′yə lit) **1.** clear. **2.** able to express one's thoughts clearly. **3.** jointed. —*v.t.* (-lāt′) **4.** to pronounce clearly. **5.** to give clarity to. **6.** to unite by joints. —*v.i.* **7.** to speak clearly. **8.** to form a joint. —**ar·tic′u·la′tion,** *n.*

ar′ti·fact′ (är′tə fakt′) *n.* an object made by humans, esp. one belonging to an earlier time.

ar′ti·fice (är′tə fis) *n.* **1.** a clever trick. **2.** cleverness. **3.** trickery.

ar·ti·fi′cial (-tə fish′əl) *adj.* **1.** made by humans. **2.** not genuine. **3.** not natural; forced. —**ar·ti·fi·cial·ly,** *adv.* —**ar′ti·fi′ci·al′i·ty** (-fish′ē al′i-tē) *n.*

ar′tifi′cial life′ *n.* the simulation of any aspect of life, as through computers or biochemistry.

artifi′cial respira′tion *n.* the forcing of air into and out of the lungs of a nonbreathing person.

ar·til′ler·y (är til′ə rē) *n.* big guns.

ar′ti·san (är′tə zən) *n.* a person skilled in a practical art.

art′ist (är′tist) *n.* a practitioner of one of the fine arts. —**ar·tis′tic,** *adj.* —**art′ist·ry,** *n.*

art′less *adj.* natural.

art′y *adj.,* **-ier, -iest.** *Informal.* self-consciously artistic.

as (az; *unstressed* əz) *adv.* **1.** to the same extent. **2.** for example. —*conj.* **3.** to the same degree. **4.** in the same manner that. **5.** while. **6.** because. —*pron.* **7.** that. —*Idiom.* **8. as for** *or* **to,** with respect to. **9. as if** *or* **though,** as it would be if. **10. as is,** the way it appears. **11. as well,** in addition.

ASAP (ā′es′ā′pē′, ā′sap) **1.** as soon as possible. **2.** without delay. Also, **A.S.A.P., a.s.a.p.**

as·bes′tos (as bes′təs, az-) *n.* a fibrous mineral formerly used in fireproofing.

as·cend′ (ə send′) *v.i.* to climb; move upward.

as·cend′an·cy *n.* domination; power. —**as·cend′ant,** *adj., n.*

As·cen′sion (ə sen′shən) *n.* the bodily passing of Christ to heaven.

as·cent′ (ə sent′) *n.* **1.** the act of ascending. **2.** an upward slope.

as′cer·tain (as′ər tān′) *v.t.* to find out.

as·cet′ic (ə set′ik) *adj.* **1.** not allowing oneself luxuries or pleasures. —*n.* **2.** a person who is ascetic. —**as·cet′i·cism** (-ə siz′əm) *n.*

ASCII (as′kē) *n.* American Standard Code for Information Interchange: a standardized code for computer storage and transmission.

as·cor′bic ac′id (ə skôr′bik) *n.* vitamin C.

as′cot (as′kət, -kot) *n.* a tie or scarf with broad ends.

as·cribe′ (ə skrīb′) *v.t.,* **-cribed, -cribing.** to credit to a cause or source; attribute. —**as·crip′tion** (-skrip′shən) *n.*

a·sep′sis (ā sep′sis, ə sep′-) *n.* the absence of certain harmful bacteria. —**a·sep′tic** (-tik) *adj.*

a·sex′u·al (ā sek′shōō əl) *adj.* **1.** without sex; sexless. **2.** having no sex organs.

ash¹ (ash) *n., pl.* **ashes.** the powdery residue of burned matter.

ash² (ash) *n.* a tree having tough, straight-grained wood.

a·shamed′ (ə shāmd′) *adj.* feeling shame.

ash′en (ash′ən) *adj.* **1.** extremely pale. **2.** ash-colored.

a·shore′ (ə shôr′) *adv., adj.* on or to shore.

ash′tray′ *n.* a small dish for tobacco ashes.

A′sian (ā′zhən) *adj.* **1.** of Asia. —*n.* **2.** a native of Asia.

a·side′ (ə sīd′) *adv.* **1.** on or to one side. **2.** away from a present group or area or from one's thoughts. **3.** in reserve. —*n.* **4.** words spoken so as not to be heard by certain people. —*Idiom.* **5. aside from,** except for.

as′i·nine′ (as′ə nīn′) *adj.* silly.

ask (ask) *v.t.* **1.** to address a question to. **2.** to request information about. **3.** to request or request of. **4.** to invite. —*v.i.* **5.** to inquire. **6.** to make a request.

a·skance′ (ə skans′) *adv.* **1.** with a side glance. **2.** skeptically.

a·skew′ (ə skyōō′) *adv., adj.* crooked(ly).

a·sleep′ (ə slēp′) *adj., adv.* sleeping.

a·so′cial (ā sō′shəl) *adj.* **1.** not sociable. **2.** selfish.

asp (asp) *n.* a small poisonous snake.

as·par′a·gus (ə spar′ə gəs) *n.* a

plant of the lily family having edible shoots.

as·par′tame (ə spär′tām, as′pər-tām′) *n.* a low-calorie sugar substitute.

as′pect (as′pekt) *n.* **1.** appearance to the mind or eye. **2.** part; feature. **3.** the direction faced.

as′pen (as′pən) *n.* a kind of poplar.

as·per′i·ty (ə sper′i tē) *n.* **1.** sharpness. **2.** roughness.

as·per′sion (ə spûr′zhən, -shən) *n.* a derogatory remark.

as′phalt (as′fôlt) *n.* a hard black material used for pavements.

as·phyx′i·ate′ (as fik′sē āt′) *v.t., v.i.,* **-ated, -ating.** to suffocate. —**as·phyx′i·a′tion,** *n.*

as′pic (as′pik) *n.* a jelly made from meat, fish, or vegetable stock.

as′pi·ra′tion *n.* **1.** a strong desire to achieve an objective. **2.** the removal of a fluid from a body cavity with a syringe. **3.** the act of inhaling a foreign body.

as·pire′ (ə spī⁻r′) *v.i.,* **-pired, -piring.** to long, aim, or seek for. —**as·pir′ant,** *n.*

as′pi·rin (as′pər in, -prin) *n.* a derivative of salicylic acid used to reduce pain and fever.

ass (as) *n.* **1.** a donkey. **2.** a foolish person.

as·sail′ (ə sāl′) *v.t.* to attack violently. —**as·sail′ant,** *n.*

as·sas′si·nate′ (ə sas′ə nāt′) *v.t.,* **-nated, -nating. 1.** to kill a prominent person, usu. for political motives. **2.** to destroy viciously. —**as·sas′sin,** *n.* —**as·sas′si·na′tion,** *n.*

as·sault′ (ə sôlt′) *n.* **1.** a violent attack. —*v.t.* **2.** to attack violently.

as·say′ (a sā′) *v.t.* **1.** to analyze or evaluate. —*n.* **2.** an analysis of the composition of a substance. —**as·say′er,** *n.*

as·sem′blage (ə sem′blij) *n.* **1.** a group. **2.** an assembling.

as·sem′ble (ə sem′bəl) *v.* **-bled, -bling.** —*v.i.* **1.** to come together. —*v.t.* **2.** to bring or put together.

as·sem′bly *n., pl.* **-blies. 1.** a group gathered together. **2.** a legislative body. **3.** the putting together of parts.

as·sem′bly·man *or* **-wom′an,** *n., pl.* **-men** *or* **-wom·en.** a member of a legislative assembly.

as·sent′ (ə sent′) *v.i.* **1.** to agree. —*n.* **2.** agreement.

as·sert′ (ə sûrt′) *v.t.* **1.** to declare to be true. **2.** to defend, as rights or claims. —*Idiom.* **3. assert oneself,** to claim one's rights insistently. —**as·ser′tion,** *n.* —**as·ser′tive,** *adj.* —**as·ser′tive·ly,** *adv.* —**as·ser′tive·ness,** *n.*

as·sess′ (ə ses′) *v.t.* **1.** to estimate the value of. **2.** to determine the amount of. **3.** to impose a charge on. **4.** to judge the nature of. —**as·sess′ment,** *n.* —**as·ses′sor,** *n.*

as′set (as′et) *n.* **1.** property having monetary value. **2.** a useful quality.

as·sid′u·ous (ə sij′ōō əs) *adj.* persistent; diligent. —**as·sid′u·ous·ly,** *adv.* —**as′si·du′i·ty,** *n.*

as·sign′ (ə sīn′) *v.t.* **1.** to allot. **2.** to give as a task. **3.** to appoint. **4.** to ascribe. —**as·sign′a·ble,** *adj.* —**as·sign·ee′,** *n.* —**as·sign′ment,** *n.*

as′sig·na′tion (as′ig nā′shən) *n.* an appointment; rendezvous.

as·sim′i·late′ (ə sim′ə lāt′) *v.t., v.i.,* **-lated, -lating.** to absorb or become absorbed into the body, a group, the mind, etc. —**as·sim′i·la′tion,** *n.*

as·sist′ (ə sist′) *v.t., v.i.* to help; aid. —**as·sist′ance,** *n.* —**as·sist′ant,** *n., adj.*

assist′ed liv′ing *n.* housing for the elderly or infirm in which meals, medical care, and other assistance is available to residents.

assn. association.

as·so′ci·ate′ *v.,* **-ated, -ating,** *n., adj.* —*v.t.* (ə sō′shē āt′, -sē-) **1.** to join together; combine. **2.** to connect in the mind. —*v.i.* **3.** to join together as partners, colleagues, etc. —*n.* (-it) **4.** a partner; colleague. —*adj.* (-it) **5.** allied. —**as·so′ci·a′tion,** *n.*

as′so·nance (as′ə nəns) *n.* similarity of sound in words or syllables. —**as′so·nant,** *adj.*

as·sort′ed (ə sôr′tid) *adj.* of various kinds.

as·sort′ment *n.* a mixed collection.

asst. assistant.

as·suage′ (ə swāj′) *v.t.,* **-suaged, -suaging.** to lessen (pain, grief, etc.).

as·sume′ (ə sōōm′) *v.t.,* **-sumed, -suming. 1.** to accept without

proof. **2.** to take upon oneself. **3.** to pretend to be.

as·sump′tion (ə sump′shən) *n.* **1.** the act of assuming. **2.** an unverified belief.

as·sure′ (ə shŏŏr′) *v.t.,* **-sured, -suring. 1.** to declare positively to; promise. **2.** to make certain. —**as·sur′ance,** *n.* —**as·sured′,** *adj., n.*

as′ter (as′tər) *n.* a flower with many petals around a yellow center disk.

as′ter·isk (as′tə risk) *n.* a star (*) symbol used in writing as a reference mark.

—**Pronunciation.** The word AS-TERISK is pronounced (as′tə risk). Note that the final syllable is pronounced (-risk) with the (s) before the (k). Both (as′tə riks) and (as′tə-rik) are considered nonstandard pronunciations.

a·stern′ (ə stûrn′) *adv., adj. Naut.* toward or at the rear.

as′ter·oid′ (as′tə roid′) *n.* any of the small solid bodies revolving around the sun.

asth′ma (az′mə) *n.* a chronic respiratory disorder causing difficulty in breathing. —**asth·mat′ic** (az mat′ik) *adj., n.*

a·stig′ma·tism (ə stig′mə tiz′əm) *n.* an eye defect in which light rays do not focus on a single point. —**as′tig·mat′ic** (as′tig mat′ik) *adj.*

a·stir′ (ə stûr′) *adj., adv.* moving.

as·ton′ish (ə ston′ish) *v.t.* to surprise greatly; amaze. —**as·ton′ish·ing,** *adj.* —**as·ton′ish·ment,** *n.*

as·tound′ (ə stound′) *v.t.* to overwhelm with amazement.

as′tral (as′trəl) *adj.* of the stars.

a·stray′ (ə strā′) *adj., adv.* straying.

a·stride′ (ə strīd′) *adv.* **1.** with a leg on either side. **2.** with legs apart. —*prep.* **3.** with a leg on each side of. **4.** on both sides of.

as·trin′gent (ə strin′jənt) *adj.* **1.** causing constriction of skin tissue. **2.** harsh. —*n.* **3.** an astringent substance.

as·trol′o·gy (ə strol′ə jē) *n.* the study of the assumed influence of the stars on human affairs. —**as′tro·log′i·cal** (as′trə loj′i kəl) *adj.* —**as·trol′o·ger,** *n.*

as′tro·naut′ (as′trə nôt′) *n.* a person trained for space travel.

as′tro·nau′tics *n.* the science and technology of space travel. —**as′tro·nau′tic, as′tro·nau′ti·cal,** *adj.*

as′tro·nom′i·cal (-nom′i kəl) *adj.* **1.** of astronomy. **2.** enormous. —**as′tro·nom′i·cal·ly,** *adv.*

as·tron′o·my (ə stron′ə mē) *n.* the study of all the celestial bodies. —**as·tron′o·mer,** *n.*

as′tro·phys′ics (as′trō fiz′iks) *n.* the branch of astronomy dealing with the physical properties of celestial bodies. —**as′tro·phys′i·cist,** *n.*

as·tute′ (ə stōōt′, ə styōōt′) *adj.* keenly perceptive; clever. —**as·tute′ly,** *adv.* —**as·tute′ness,** *n.*

a·sun′der (ə sun′dər) *adv.* apart.

a·sy′lum (ə sī′ləm) *n.* **1.** an institution for the care of ill or needy persons. **2.** a place of refuge.

a·sym′me·try (ā sim′i trē) *n.* a lack of symmetry. —**a′sym·met′ric** (ā′sə me′trik), **a′sym·met′ri·cal,** *adj.*

at (at; *unstressed* ət, it) *prep.* **1.** (used to indicate a point in space or time). **2.** (used to indicate amount, degree, or rate). **3.** (used to indicate an objective). **4.** (used to indicate a condition). **5.** (used to indicate a cause).

at′a·vism (at′ə viz′əm) *n.* the reappearance of remote ancestral traits. —**at′a·vis′tic** (-vis′tik) *adj.*

ate (āt; *Brit.* et) *v.* pt. of **eat.**

at·el·ier′ (at′l yā′) *n.* a studio, esp. of an artist.

a′the·ism (ā′thē iz′əm) *n.* the belief that there is no God. —**a′the·ist,** *n.* —**a′the·is′tic** (-is′tik) *adj.*

ath′lete (ath′lēt) *n.* a person trained or gifted in sports or physical exercises. —**ath·let′ic** (-let′ik) *adj.* —**ath·let′ics,** *n.*

—**Pronunciation.** The word ATH-LETE is normally pronounced as a two-syllable word: (ath′lēt). Similarly, ATHLETIC has only three syllables: (ath let′ik). Pronunciations of these words that add an extra syllable, with a weak vowel sound inserted between the (th) and the (l) are not considered standard.

ath′lete's foot′ *n.* ringworm of the feet.

athlet′ic shoe′ *n.* a shoe for exercise or sport; sneaker.

at′las (at′ləs) *n.* a book of maps.

ATM automated-teller machine: a machine that provides certain bank

services when an electronic card is inserted.

at′mos·phere′ (at′məs fēr′) *n.* **1.** the air surrounding the earth. **2.** a pervading mood. —**at′mos·pher′ic** (-fer′ik) *adj.*

at′oll (at′ôl) *n.* a ring-shaped coral island.

at′om (at′əm) *n.* **1.** the smallest unit of an element having the properties of that element. **2.** something extremely small.

atom′ic bomb′ *n.* a bomb whose force is derived from the nuclear fission of certain atoms, causing the conversion of some mass to energy (**atomic energy**). Also, **a′tom bomb**.

at′om·iz′er (at′ə mī′zər) *n.* a device for making liquids into a fine spray.

a·ton′al (ā tōn′l) *adj.* lacking tonality. —**a′to·nal′i·ty** (-nal′i tē) *n.*

a·tone′ (ə tōn′) *v.i.,* **atoned, atoning.** to make amends for a wrong. —**a·tone′ment,** *n.*

a·top′ (ə top′) *adj., adv.* **1.** on or at the top. —*prep.* **2.** on the top of.

a′tri·um (ā′trē əm) *n., pl.* **atria, atriums. 1.** an enclosed court in a building. **2.** either of two upper chambers of the heart.

a·tro′cious (ə trō′shəs) *adj.* **1.** very bad. **2.** wicked. —**a·troc′i·ty** (ə tros′i tē) *n.*

at′ro·phy (at′rə fē) *n., v.,* **-phied, -phying.** —*n.* **1.** a wasting away of a body part. —*v.t., v.i.* **2.** to cause or undergo atrophy.

at′ro·pine′ (at′rə pēn′) *n.* a poisonous alkaloid of belladonna.

at·tach′ (ə tach′) *v.t.* **1.** to fasten or join. **2.** to bind by emotion. **3.** to take by legal authority.

at′ta·ché′ (at′ə shā′) *n.* an embassy official.

at·tach′ment (ə tach′mənt) *n.* **1.** an attaching or being attached. **2.** something fastened on. **3.** an emotional tie.

at·tack′ (ə tak′) *v.t.* **1.** to set against in a violent or hostile way. **2.** to set to work on vigorously. —*v.i.* **3.** to make an attack. —*n.* **4.** the act of attacking. **5.** the onset of illness. —**at·tack′er,** *n.*

at·tain′ (ə tān′) *v.t.* **1.** to achieve or accomplish. —**at·tain′a·ble,** *adj.* —**at·tain′ment,** *n.*

at·tempt′ (ə tempt′) *v.t.* **1.** to make an effort to accomplish. —*n.* **2.** an effort to accomplish something.

at·tend′ (ə tend′) *v.t.* **1.** to be present at. **2.** to go with. **3.** to take care of. —*v.i.* **4.** to be present. **5.** to take charge. **6.** to pay attention. —**at·tend′ance,** *n.* —**at·tend′ant,** *n., adj.*

at·ten′tion (ə ten′shən) *n.* **1.** the act of concentrating the mind on something. **2.** consideration; care. —**at·ten′tive** (-tiv) *adj.* —**at·ten′tive·ly,** *adv.* —**at·ten′tive·ness,** *n.*

at·ten′u·ate′ (-yōō āt′) *v.t., v.i.,* **-ated, -ating.** to make or become weak or thin. —**at·ten′u·a′tion,** *n.*

at·test′ (ə test′) *v.t.* **1.** to certify as true, genuine, etc. **2.** to give proof of. —*v.i.* **3.** to testify. —**at′tes·ta′tion** (at′e stā′shən) *n.*

at′tic (at′ik) *n.* a room directly under the roof.

at·tire′ (ə tī⁻r′) *v.,* **-tired, -tiring,** *n.* —*v.t.* **1.** to dress; adorn. —*n.* **2.** clothes.

at′ti·tude′ (at′i tōōd′, -tyōōd′) *n.* **1.** manner or feeling with regard to a person or thing. **2.** a position of the body.

attn. attention.

at·tor′ney (ə tûr′nē) *n.* a lawyer.

attor′ney gen′eral *n., pl.* **attorneys general, attorney generals.** the chief law officer of a country or state.

at·tract′ (ə trakt′) *v.t.* **1.** to draw by a physical force. **2.** to draw by appealing to the senses or by arousing the interest of.

at·trac′tion *n.* **1.** the act or power of attracting. **2.** an attractive quality. **3.** one that attracts.

at·trac′tive (-tiv) *adj.* having the power to attract. **2.** pleasing. **3.** arousing interest. —**at·trac′tive·ly,** *adv.* —**at·trac′tive·ness,** *n.*

at·trib·ute′ *v.,* **-uted, -uting.** —*v.t.* (ə trib′yōōt′) **1.** to regard as caused by or belonging to. —*n.* (at′rə byōōt′) **2.** a special quality or characteristic. —**at′tri·bu′tion,** *n.*

at·tri′tion (ə trish′ən) *n.* a wearing away.

at·tune′ (ə tōōn′, ə tyōōn′) *v.t.,* **-tuned, -tuning.** to bring into accord or harmony.

atty. attorney.

ATV *n.* all-terrain vehicle: a small

motor vehicle with treads or wheels for nonroad travel.

a·typ′i·cal (ā tip′i kəl) *adj.* not typical; irregular. —**a·typ′i·cal·ly,** *adv.*

au′burn (ô′bərn) *n.* a reddish brown.

auc′tion (ôk′shən) *n.* **1.** the sale of goods to the highest bidders. —*v.t.* **2.** to sell by auction. —**auc′tion·eer′,** *n.*

au·da′cious (ô dā′shəs) *adj.* bold; daring. —**au·dac′i·ty** (-das′i tē) *n.*

au′di·ble (ô′də bəl) *adj.* capable of being heard. —**au·di·bil′i·ty,** *n.* —**au′di·bly,** *adv.*

au′di·ence (ô′dē əns) *n.* **1.** a group of hearers or spectators. **2.** a formal hearing or interview.

au′di·o′ (ô′dē ō′) *adj.* **1.** of sound reception or reproduction. —*n.* **2.** the audible part of TV.

au′dio book′ *n.* an audio recording of a book.

au′di·ol′o·gy (-ol′ə jē) *n.* the study and treatment of hearing disorders. —**au′di·ol′o·gist,** *n.*

au′di·om′e·ter (-om′i tər) *n.* an instrument for testing hearing.

au′di·o·tape′ (ô′dē ō-) *n.* a magnetic tape for recording sound.

au′di·o·vis′u·al *adj.* using films, TV, and recordings, as for education.

au′dit (ô′dit) *n.* **1.** an official examination of financial records. —*v.t.* **2.** to conduct an audit of.

au·di′tion (ô dish′ən) *n.* **1.** a trial performance. —*v.t., v.i.* **2.** to give an audition (to).

au′di·to′ri·um (-tôr′ē əm) *n.* a large room for an audience.

au′di·to′ry *adj.* of hearing.

Aug. August.

au′ger (ô′gər) *n.* a tool for boring holes.

aught¹ (ôt) *n.* anything whatever.

aught² (ôt) *n.* a cipher (0); zero.

aug·ment′ (ôg ment′) *v.t.* to increase. —**aug′men·ta′tion,** *n.*

au′gur (ô′gər) *v.t.* **1.** to predict. **2.** to be a sign. —**au′gu·ry** (-gyə-) *n.*

Au′gust (ô′gəst) *n.* the eighth month of the year.

au·gust′ (ô gust′) *adj.* majestic.

au jus (ō zhōōs′) *adj.* (of meat) served in the natural juices.

auk (ôk) *n.* a northern diving bird.

auld′ lang syne′ (ôld′ lang zīn′) *n.* fondly remembered times.

aunt (ant, änt) *n.* **1.** the sister of a parent. **2.** the wife of an uncle.

au pair′ *n.* a young foreign visitor who does household tasks or cares for children in exchange for room and board.

au′ra (ôr′ə) *n.* **1.** an atmosphere, quality, etc. **2.** a radiance coming from the body.

au′ral (ôr′əl) *adj.* of or by hearing.

au′re·ole′ (ôr′ē ōl′) *n.* a halo.

au′ re·voir′ (ō′ rə vwär′) *interj. French.* good-by.

au′ri·cle (ôr′i kəl) *n.* **1.** the outer part of the ear. **2.** a chamber in the heart. —**au·ric′u·lar** (ô rik′yə lər) *adj.*

au·ror′a (ə rôr′ə) *n.* a display of bands of light in the night sky.

aus·pi′cious (ô spish′əs) *adj.* **1.** promising success. **2.** fortunate. —**aus·pi′cious·ly,** *adv.*

aus·tere′ (ô stēr′) *adj.* **1.** severe, as in manner. **2.** severely simple or plain. —**aus·ter′i·ty** (-ster′i tē) *n.*

Aus·tral′ian (ô strāl′yən) *adj.* **1.** of Australia. —*n.* **2.** a native of Australia.

Aus′tri·an (ô′strē ən) *adj.* **1.** of Austria or its inhabitants. —*n.* **2.** a native of Austria.

au·then′tic (ô then′tik) *adj.* genuine; real. —**au·then′ti·cal·ly,** *adv.* —**au·then′ti·cate′,** *v.t.* —**au·then·tic′i·ty** (-tis′i tē) *n.*

au′thor (ô′thər) *n.* a writer or creator. —**au′thor·ship′,** *n.*

au·thor′i·tar′i·an (ə thôr′i târ′ē-ən) *adj.* requiring total obedience.

au·thor′i·ta′tive (-tā′tiv) *adj.* **1.** having authority. **2.** accepted as true.

au·thor′i·ty *n., pl.* **-ties. 1.** the right to order or decide. **2.** one with such a right. **3.** a respected source of information.

au′thor·ize′ (ô′thə rīz′) *v.t.,* **-ized, -izing. 1.** to give authority to. **2.** to give permission for. —**auth′or·i·za′tion,** *n.*

au′tism (ô′tiz əm) *n.* a disorder characterized by extreme self-absorption and detachment from one's environment. —**au·tis′tic** (ô-tis′tik) *adj.*

au′to (ô′tō) *n.* automobile.

auto- a prefix meaning self or same.

au·to·bi·og·ra·phy (ô′tō bī og′rə fē) n., pl. **-phies.** the story of one's own life.

au·toc·ra·cy (ô tok′rə sē) n., pl. **-cies.** government in which one person has unlimited power. —**au′to·crat**′ (ô′tə krat′) n. —**au′to·crat′ic,** adj.

au·to·di·dact (ô′tō dī′dakt) n. a self-taught person.

au·to·graph (ô′tə graf′) n. **1.** a signature. —v.t. **2.** to write one's signature on.

au·to·im·mune (ô′tō i myōōn′) adj. of or relating to the body's immune response to its own components.

au·to·mat (ô′tə mat′) n. a restaurant with coin-operated service.

au·to·mate (-māt′) v.t., v.i., **-mated, -mating.** to operate by or undergo automation.

au·to·mat·ic (-mat′ik) adj. **1.** able to operate without human intervention. **2.** involuntary. **3.** done without thinking. —**au′to·mat′i·cal·ly,** adv.

au·to·mat′ic pi′lot n. an electronic control system for piloting aircraft.

au·to·ma·tion (-mā′shən) n. the use of automatic devices to control mechanical processes.

au·tom·a·ton (ô tom′ə ton′) n. a robot.

au·to·mo·bile (ô′tə mə bēl′) n. a four-wheeled passenger vehicle with an internal-combustion engine.

au·ton·o·my (ô ton′ə mē) n. self-government.

au·top·sy (ô′top sē) n., pl. **-sies.** an examination of a corpse for causes of death.

au·tumn (ô′təm) n. the season before winter; fall. —**au·tum′nal** (ô tum′nl) adj.

aux·il·ia·ry (ôg zil′yə rē) adj., n., pl. **-ries.** —adj. **1.** helping. **2.** additional. **3.** secondary. —n. **4.** an auxiliary person, thing, or group. **5.** a verb preceding other verbs to express tense, voice, etc.

a·vail (ə vāl′) v.t., v.i. **1.** to be of use, value, or advantage (to). —**Idiom. 2.** avail oneself of, to make use of. —n. **3.** use; help.

a·vail·a·ble (ə vāl′ə bəl) adj. ready for use; accessible. —**a·vail′a·bil′i·ty,** n.

av·a·lanche (av′ə lanch′) n. a large mass of falling snow, ice, etc.

a·vant-garde (ə vänt′gärd′, av′änt-) adj. **1.** progressive, esp. in the arts. —n. **2.** the advance group in a field, esp. in the arts.

av·a·rice (av′ər is) n. greed. —**av′a·ri′cious** (-rish′əs) adj.

ave. avenue.

a·venge (ə venj′) v.t., **avenged, avenging.** to take vengeance for. —**a·veng′er,** n.

av·e·nue (av′ə nyōō′) n. **1.** a broad street. **2.** an approach.

a·ver (ə vûr′) v.t., **averred, averring.** to declare to be true; assert confidently.

av·er·age (av′ər ij) n., adj., v., **-aged, -aging.** —n. **1.** a value arrived at by adding a series of quantities and dividing by the number of quantities in the series. **2.** a usual amount or level. —adj. **3.** of or like an average. **4.** common. —v.t. **5.** to find the average of. —v.i **6.** to amount to an average.

a·verse (ə vûrs′) adj. unwilling.

a·ver·sion (ə vûr′zhən) n. strong dislike.

a·vert (ə vûrt′) v.t. **1.** to turn away. **2.** to prevent.

a′vi·ar′y (ā′vē er′ē) n., pl. **-aries.** a place in which birds are kept.

a′vi·a′tion (ā′vē ā′shən) n. the production or operation of aircraft. —**a′vi·a′tor,** n.

av·id (av′id) adj. eager; greedy. —**a·vid′i·ty,** n. —**av′id·ly,** adv.

av·o·ca·do (av′ə kä′dō, ä′və-) n., pl. **-dos.** a pear-shaped tropical fruit with light-green pulp.

av·o·ca′tion (av′ə kā′shən) n. a hobby.

a·void (ə void′) v.t. to keep away from. —**a·void′a·ble,** adj. —**a·void′ance,** n.

av′oir·du·pois′ (av′ər də poiz′) n. a system of weights based on 16-ounce pounds.

a·vow (ə vou′) v.t. to declare. —**a·vow′al,** n. —**a·vowed′,** adj.

a·vun·cu·lar (ə vung′kyə lər) adj. of or like an uncle.

a·wait (ə wāt′) v.t. to wait for.

a·wake (ə wāk′) v., **awoke** (ə wōk′) or **awaked, awaking,** adj. —v.t., v.i. **1.** to rouse or emerge from sleep. —adj. **2.** not asleep; alert.

a·wak·en (ə wā′kən) v.t., v.i. to waken. —**a·wak′en·ing,** n., adj.

a·ward (ə wôrd′) v.t. **1.** to give as deserved or merited. **2.** to give by the decision of a court. —n. **3.** something awarded.

a·ware (ə wâr′) adj. having knowledge or realization; conscious. —**a·ware′ness,** n.

a·wash (ə wosh′) adj. flooded.

a·way (ə wā′) adv. **1.** from this or that place. **2.** to or at a distance. **3.** out of one's possession. **4.** out of existence. **5.** persistently. —adj. **6.** absent. **7.** distant.

awe (ô) n., v., **awed, awing.** —n. **1.** respectful fear and wonder. —v.t. **2.** to fill with awe.

awe·some (ô′səm) adj. **1.** inspiring or characterized by awe. **2.** Slang. very impressive.

awe·struck (-struk′) adj. filled with awe.

aw·ful (ô′fəl) adj. **1.** very bad or unpleasant. **2.** inspiring fear.

aw·ful·ly adv. **1.** very badly. In formal. very.

a·while (ə hwīl′) adv. for a short time.

—**Usage.** The adverb AWHILE is always spelled as one word: We rested awhile. A WHILE is a noun phrase (an article and a noun) and is used after a preposition: We rested for a while.

awk·ward (ôk′wərd) adj. **1.** lacking skill; clumsy. **2.** hard to use or deal with. **3.** inconvenient. **4.** embarrassing. —**awk′ward·ly,** adv. —**awk′ward·ness,** n.

awl (ôl) n. a pointed tool for making holes.

awn·ing (ô′ning) n. a rooflike shelter, as of canvas.

AWOL (pronounced as initials or ā′wôl) adj., adv. absent without leave.

a·wry (ə rī′) adv., adj. **1.** crooked. **2.** wrong.

ax (aks) n. a small chopping tool. Also, **axe.**

ax·i·om (ak′sē əm) n. an accepted truth. —**ax′i·o·mat′ic** (-ə mat′ik) adj.

ax·is (ak′sis) n., pl. **axes** (ak′sēz). the line about which something turns. —**ax′i·al,** adj.

ax·le (ak′səl) n. a shaft on which a wheel rotates.

a′ya·tol′lah (ä′yə tō′lə) n. a senior Islamic religious leader.

aye (ī) adv., n. yes.

a·zal′ea (ə zāl′yə) n. a shrub with variously colored funnel-shaped flowers.

az·ure (azh′ər) n. a sky-blue.

B

B, b (bē) n. the second letter of the English alphabet.

B.A. Bachelor of Arts.

bab·ble (bab′əl) v.i., **-bled, -bling. 1.** to talk indistinctly or foolishly. **2.** (of a stream) to murmur. —n. **3.** babbling speech or sound.

babe (bāb) n. **1.** a baby. **2.** a naive person.

ba·bel (bā′bəl) n. noisy confusion.

ba·boon (ba bōōn′, bə-) n. a large monkey of Africa and Arabia.

ba·bush·ka (bə bōōsh′kə) n. a woman's head scarf.

ba·by (bā′bē) n., pl. **-bies,** v., **-bied, -bying.** —n. **1.** an infant. **2.** a childish person. —v.t. **3.** to pamper. —**ba′by·ish,** adj.

ba′by boom′ n. a period of increase in the rate of births, esp. that following World War II. —**ba′by boom′er,** n.

ba′by's-breath′ n. a tall plant with many small white or pink flowers.

ba·by-sit (bā′bē sit′) v., **-sat** (-sat′) **-sitting.** —v.i. **1.** to care for a child while the parents are away. —v.t. **2.** to baby-sit for (a child). —**ba′by-sit′ter,** n.

bac·ca·lau·re·ate (bak′ə lôr′ē it) n. **1.** a bachelor's degree. **2.** a religious service for a graduating class.

bac·cha·nal (bak′ə nal′) n. an occasion of drunken revelry. —**bac′cha·na′li·an** (-nā′lē ən) adj.

bach·e·lor (bach′ə lər) n. **1.** an unmarried man. **2.** a person holding a degree from a 4-year college. —**bach′e·lor·hood,** n.

bach′elor's-but′ton n. a kind of plant with round flowers, esp. the cornflower.

ba·cil·lus (bə sil′əs) n., pl. **-cilli**

back (bak) n. **1.** the rear part of the human and animal body. **2.** the rear of an object or structure. **3.** the spine. —v.t. **4.** to sponsor. **5.** to cause to move backward. **6.** to bet in favor of. **7.** to furnish or form a back. —v.i. **8.** to move backward. **9. back down,** to abandon a claim or argument. **10. ~ off,** to retreat. **11. ~ out,** to fail to keep a commitment. —adj. **12.** situated in the rear. **13.** of a past time. **14.** overdue. —adv. **15.** at or toward the rear. **16.** toward the original point or condition. **17.** in return. —**Idiom. 18. behind one's back,** without one's knowledge. —**back′er,** n. —**back′ing,** n.

back′board′ n. in basketball, a vertical board behind the basket.

back′bone′ n. **1.** a connected series of bones down the back; spine. **2.** strength of character.

back·break′ing adj. demanding great effort.

back′drop′ n. **1.** the curtain at the back of a stage. **2.** the background of an event; setting.

back·fire′ v.i., **-fired, -firing. 1.** (of an engine) to make an explosive sound because of a wrongly timed ignition. **2.** to bring a result opposite to that planned. —n. **3.** an explosive ignition in an engine.

back·gam·mon (-gam′ən) n. a board game for two persons.

back′ground′ n. **1.** the back part of a picture. **2.** the causes of an event or condition. **3.** a person's origin, education, experience, etc.

back′hand′ n. in tennis and other sports, a stroke made with the back of the hand facing the direction of movement. —v.t. **2.** to hit with a backhand.

back·hand′ed adj. **1.** performed with the back of the hand forward. **2.** said in a sarcastic way; insincere.

back′lash′ n. a strong negative reaction.

back′log′ n. an accumulation.

back′pack′ n. **1.** a pack for supplies, carried on one's back. —v.i. **2.** to travel using a backpack.

back′-ped′al v.i., **-pedaled, -pedaling. 1.** to slow a bicycle by pressing backward on the pedals. **2.** to retreat from a previous stand.

back′side′ n. the buttocks.

back′slide′ v.i., **-slid** (-slid′) **-slid** or **-slidden, -sliding.** to fall back into bad habits.

back′stage′ adv. **1.** in the theater wings or dressing rooms. —adj. **2.** of the area behind the stage.

back′stroke′ n. a swimming stroke done while lying on one's back.

back′ talk′ n. impertinent replies.

back′track′ v.i. **1.** to retreat. **2.** to change one's opinion.

back′up′ n. **1.** a person or thing that supports or reinforces another. **2.** an accumulation caused by a stoppage. **3.** an alternate kept in reserve. **4.** a copy of a computer file kept in case the original is lost.

back′ward (-wərd) adv. **1.** toward the rear. **2.** with the back foremost. **3.** in the reverse of the usual way. **4.** toward the past. —adj. **5.** directed toward the back or past. **6.** behind in development. **7.** reversed. —**Idiom. 8. bend over backward,** to exert oneself. Also, **back′wards.**

back′wa′ter n. a place that is backward or stagnant.

back′woods′ n.pl. wooded or unsettled districts.

ba·con (bā′kən) n. **1.** salted or smoked meat from a hog. —**Idiom. 2. bring home the bacon,** to earn a living.

bac·te·ri·a (bak tēr′ē ə) n.pl., sing. **-um** (-əm) any group of one-celled organisms, involved in fermentation, infectious disease, etc. —**bac·te′ri·al,** adj.

bac·te·ri·ol·o·gy (-ol′ə jē) n. the study of bacteria. —**bac·te′ri·o·log′i·cal** (-ə loj′i kəl) adj. —**bac·te′ri·ol′o·gist,** n.

bad (bad) adj., **worse** (wûrs) **worst** (wûrst) —adj. **1.** not good. **2.** a bad thing, condition, or quality. —**bad′ly,** adv. —**bad′ness,** n.

—**Usage.** The adjective BAD, meaning "unpleasant, unattractive, unfavorable, spoiled, etc.," is the usual form after such verbs as sound, smell, look, feel, and taste: The music sounds bad. Are you feeling bad? The water tasted bad. BAD as an adverb appears mainly in informal situations: He wanted to win pretty bad.

bad′ blood′ n. hostility.

badge (baj) n. an emblem or insignia worn as a sign of membership, authority, etc.

badg·er (baj′ər) n. **1.** a burrowing, flesh-eating mammal. —v.t. **2.** to pester.

bad·i·nage (bad′n äzh′) n. playful banter.

bad·min·ton (bad′min tn) n. a game in which a shuttlecock is hit over a net with light rackets.

bad′-mouth′ (-mouth′, -mouth′) v.t. to criticize. Also, **bad′mouth′.**

baf·fle (baf′əl) v., **-fled, -fling.** —v.t. **1.** to bewilder. **2.** to frustrate. —n. **3.** an obstruction. —**baf′fle·ment,** n.

bag (bag) n., v., **bagged, bagging.** —n. **1.** a sack or container of flexible material. **2.** a purse. —v.i. **3.** to bulge. **4.** to hang loosely. —v.t. **5.** to put into a bag. **6.** to kill or catch. —**bag′gy,** adj. —**bag′gi·ness,** n.

bag·a·telle (bag′ə tel′) n. something of little value.

ba·gel (bā′gəl) n. a hard ringshaped bread roll.

bag·gage (bag′ij) n. trunks, suitcases, etc., for travel.

bag′pipe′ n. (often pl.) a musical instrument with a windbag and two or more pipes. —**bag′pip′er,** n.

bail (bāl) n. **1.** money given as security that an accused person will return for trial. **2.** the state of release following the payment of security. —v.t. **3.** to obtain the release of (an arrested person) by providing bail.

bail v.t., v.i. **1.** to dip (water) out of a boat. **2. bail out,** to make a parachute jump.

bail·iff (bā′lif) n. a public officer who keeps order in a courtroom.

bail·i·wick (bā′lə wik′) n. a person's area of authority, skill, etc.

bail′out′ n. a rescue from financial problems.

bait (bāt) n. **1.** food used as a lure in fishing or hunting. **2.** anything that lures. —v.t. **3.** to prepare (a hook or trap) with bait. **4.** to torment.

baize (bāz) n. a soft feltlike fabric.

bake (bāk) v., **baked, bak·ing.** —v.t. **1.** to cook by dry heat, as in an oven. **2.** to harden by heat. —v.i. **3.** to prepare food by baking it. **4.** to become baked.

bak′er's doz′en n. a dozen plus one; 13.

bak·er·y n., pl. **-eries.** a place for baking; baker's shop.

bak′ing pow′der n. a white powder used as a leavening agent.

bak′ing so′da n. sodium bicarbonate, a white powder used as an antacid and in baking.

bal·a·lai·ka (bal′ə lī′kə) n. a Russian stringed instrument with a triangular body.

bal·ance (bal′əns) n., v., **-anced, -ancing.** —n. **1.** a state of even distribution of weight or amount. **2.** an instrument for weighing. **3.** steadiness, as of the body. **4.** the difference between debits and credits. **5.** the remainder. —v.t. **6.** to bring to or hold in a state of balance. **7.** to be equal to. **8.** to add up the two sides of (an account) and determine the difference. **9.** to counteract. —v.i. **10.** to be equal. **11.** to be in a state of balance. **12.** to be in a state in which debits equal credits.

bal′ance sheet′ n. a statement showing the financial position of a business on a certain date.

bal·co·ny (bal′kə nē) n., pl. **-nies. 1.** a railed platform projecting from the wall of a building. **2.** the upper floor of seats in a theater.

bald (bôld) adj. **1.** lacking hair on the scalp. **2.** plain; undisguised.

bal·der·dash (bôl′dər dash′) n. nonsense.

bale (bāl) n., v., **baled, baling.** —n. **1.** a large bundle, esp. one compressed and bound. —v.t. **2.** to make into bales.

bale·ful adj. evil; menacing. —**bale′ful·ly,** adv.

balk (bôk) v.i. **1.** to stop or stop short. —v.t. **2.** to hinder; thwart. **3.** to refuse firmly. —n. **4.** a hindrance. —**balk′y,** adj.

ball (bôl) n. **1.** a round or roundish object. **2.** a game played with a ball. —v.t., v.i. **3.** to make or form into a ball.

ball (bôl) n. **1.** a large formal party for dancing. **2.** Informal. a very good time.

bal·lad (bal′əd) n. **1.** a narrative folk song or poem. **2.** a slow, romantic song.

bal·last (bal′əst) n. **1.** heavy material carried to ensure stability. —v.t. **2.** to furnish with ballast.

ball′ bear′ing n. **1.** a bearing in which a moving part turns on steel balls. **2.** one of these balls.

bal·le·ri·na (bal′ə rē′nə) n. a female ballet dancer.

bal·let (ba lā′) n. **1.** a dance form having intricate, formalized movements. **2.** a theatrical performance of such dancing.

bal·lis′tic mis′sile n. a guided missile that completes its trajectory in free fall.

bal·lis′tics n. the study of the motion of projectiles.

bal·loon (bə lōōn′) n. **1.** a bag filled with a gas lighter than air. —v.i. **2.** to go up in a balloon. **3.** to increase rapidly. —**bal·loon′ist,** n.

bal·lot (bal′ət) n., v., **-loted, -loting.** —n. **1.** a piece of paper or the like used in voting. **2.** the method or act of voting. **3.** the right to vote. —v.i. **4.** to vote by ballot.

ball′park′ n. a stadium for baseball games.

ball′point pen′ n. a pen that has a small ball bearing as a point.

ball′room′ n. a large room for dancing.

bal·ly·hoo (bal′ē hōō′) n. Informal. exaggerated publicity.

balm (bäm) n. **1.** anything that heals or soothes pain. **2.** an aromatic ointment or fragrance.

balm′y adj., **-ier, -iest. 1.** mild; refreshing. **2.** fragrant.

bal·sa (bôl′sə, bäl′-) n. a tropical tree with light wood.

bal·sam (bôl′səm) n. **1.** a fragrant substance given off by certain trees. **2.** any of these trees. **3.** an aromatic ointment. —**bal·sam′ic** (bôl sam′ik) adj.

bal′us·ter (bal′ə stər) n. a pillarlike support for a railing.

bal′us·trade′ (-ə strād′) n. a series of balusters supporting a railing.

bam·boo′ (bam bōō′) n., pl. **-boos.** a treelike tropical grass having a hollow woody stem.

bam·boo′zle (bam bōō′zəl) v.t., **-zled, -zling.** Informal. to trick.

ban (ban) v., **banned, banning.** —v.t. **1.** to prohibit. —n. **2.** a prohibition.

ba·nal (bə nal′, -näl′, bān′l) adj. commonplace; uninteresting. —**ba·nal′i·ty,** n.

ba·nan·a (bə nan′ə) n. the yellow, finger-shaped fruit of a tropical tree.

band (band) n. **1.** a strip of material for binding. **2.** a stripe. **3.** a range of frequencies, as in radio. —v.t. **4.** to mark with bands.

band (band) n. **1.** a company of persons acting together. **2.** a group of musicians. —v.t., v.i **3.** to unite.

band·age (ban′dij) n., v., **-aged, -aging.** —n. **1.** a strip of cloth for binding a wound. —v.t **2.** to bind with a bandage.

Band′-Aid′ Trademark. a small adhesive bandage with a gauze center.

ban·dan′na (ban dan′ə) n. a colored handkerchief worn on the head. Also, **ban·dan′a.**

ban·dit (ban′dit) n. a robber; outlaw.

band′stand′ n. the platform on which a band performs.

band′wag′on n. —**Idiom. jump on the bandwagon,** to join a cause or movement that appears popular and successful.

ban·dy (ban′dē) v., **-died, -dying,** adj. —v.t. **1.** to exchange (words) back and forth rapidly. —adj. **2.** (of legs) bent outward. —**ban′dy-leg′ged** (-leg′id, -legd′) adj.

bane (bān) n. a thing causing ruin.

bane·ful adj. destructive.

bang (bang) n. **1.** a sudden loud noise. —v.t. **2.** to make a loud noise. —v.i **3.** to strike noisily.

bang (bang) n. Often, **bangs.** a fringe of hair across the forehead.

ban·gle (bang′gəl) n. a rigid bracelet.

bang′-up′ adj. Informal. excellent.

ban·ish (ban′ish) v.t. **1.** to exile. **2.** to drive or put away. —**ban′ish·ment,** n.

ban′is·ter (ban′ə stər) n. a handrail, esp. on a staircase.

ban·jo (ban′jō) n., pl. **-jos, -joes.** a stringed musical instrument with a circular body. —**ban′jo·ist,** n.

bank (bangk) n. **1.** a slope bordering a stream. **2.** a pile; heap. —v.t. **3.** to border with or make into a bank. **4.** to cover (a fire) to make it burn slowly. —*v.i.* **5.** to slope upward.

bank² (bangk) *n.* **1.** an institution for receiving, lending, or safeguarding money. **2.** a store of something, as blood, for future use. —*v.i., v.t.* **3.** to deposit in a bank. **4.** **bank on,** to rely on. —**bank′er,** *n.* —**bank′ing,** *n.*

bank′roll′ *n.* **1.** money possessed. —*v.t.* **2.** to pay for; fund.

bank′rupt (-rupt) *adj.* **1.** unable to pay one's debts. **2.** lacking. —*n.* **3.** one who is bankrupt. —*v.t.* **4.** to make bankrupt. —**bank′rupt·cy,** *n.*

ban′ner (ban′ər) *n.* **1.** a flag. —*adj.* **2.** excellent.

banns (banz) *n.pl.* notice of intended marriage. Also, **bans.**

ban′quet (bang′kwit) *n.* **1.** a lavish meal. **2.** a ceremonious public dinner. —*v.t.* **3.** to entertain with a banquet.

ban′shee (ban′shē) *n.* a female spirit of folklore whose wailing means a loved one is about to die.

ban′tam (ban′təm) *n.* **1.** a breed of small domestic fowl. —*adj.* **2.** tiny.

ban′ter (ban′tər) *n.* **1.** good-natured teasing. —*v.i.* **2.** to use banter.

Ban′tu (ban′tōō) *n., pl.* **-tu, -tus. 1.** a family of languages spoken in Africa. **2.** a member of a Bantu-speaking people.

ban′yan (ban′yən) *n.* an East Indian fig tree that grows new trunks from its branches.

bap′tism (bap′tiz əm) *n.* an immersion in or application of water as a rite of purification and admission to the Christian Church. —**bap·tis′mal,** *adj.*

Bap′tist (-tist) *n.* a member of a Protestant denomination that baptizes believers by immersion.

bap·tize′ (bap tīz′, bap′tīz) *v.t.,* **-tized, -tizing.** to administer baptism to.

bar (bär) *n., v.,* **barred, barring,** *prep.* —*n.* **1.** a long, evenly shaped piece, esp. of wood or metal. **2.** a band; stripe. **3.** a long ridge in shallow waters. **4.** an obstruction; hindrance. **5.** a place where liquor is served. **6.** the legal profession or its members. **7.** a line marking the division between two measures of music. —*v.t.* **8.** to provide or fasten with a bar. **9.** to block; hinder. —*prep.* **10.** except for. —**barred,** *adj.*

barb (bärb) *n.* **1.** a point projecting backward. **2.** a nasty remark.

bar·bar′i·an (bär bâr′ē ən) *n.* **1.** a savage or uncivilized person. —*adj.* **2.** uncivilized. —**bar·bar′ic,** *adj.* —**bar·bar·i·cal·ly,** *adv.*

bar′ba·rism (-bə riz′əm) *n.* **1.** an uncivilized condition. **2.** a barbarous act.

bar·bar′i·ty (-bär′i tē) *n.* savage cruelty.

bar′ba·rous (-bər əs) *adj.* **1.** wild. **2.** savagely cruel. **3.** harsh.

bar′be·cue′ (bär′bi kyōō′) *n., v.,* **-cued, -cuing.** —*n.* **1.** meat or poultry roasted over an open fire. **2.** an outdoor meal at which foods are so cooked. —*v.t.* **3.** to cook over an open fire. Also, **bar′be·que′.**

barbed′ wire′ *n.* strands of wire twisted together with barbs at short intervals.

bar′ber (bär′bər) *n.* a person who gives haircuts, shaves, etc. —*v.t.* **2.** to shave or cut the hair of.

bar·bi′tu·rate (bär bich′ər it, bär′bi tŏor′it, -tyŏor′-) *n.* a sedative drug.

bar′ code′ *n.* a series of lines of different widths placed on an item for identification by a computer scanner.

bard (bärd) *n.* a poet. —**bard′ic,** *adj.*

bare (bâr) *adj.,* **barer, barest,** *v.,* **bared, baring.** —*adj.* **1.** uncovered; unclothed. **2.** unfurnished. **3.** plain. **4.** scarcely sufficient. —*v.t.* **5.** to reveal.

bare′back′ *adv., adj.* without a saddle.

bare′faced′ *adj.* **1.** undisguised. **2.** shameless.

bare′foot′ *adj., adv.* with the feet bare.

bare′ly *adv.* no more than; only just.

bar′gain (bär′gən) *n.* **1.** an agreement. **2.** something bought cheaply. —*v.i.* **3.** to discuss or arrive at an agreement. **4.** **bargain on** or **for,** to expect.

barge (bärj) *n., v.,* **barged, barging.** —*n.* **1.** an unpowered vessel for freight. —*v.t.* **2.** to carry by barge.

—*v.i.* **3.** to move clumsily. **4.** **barge in,** to intrude.

bar′i·tone′ (bar′i tōn′) *n.* **1.** a male voice or part between tenor and bass. **2.** a baritone singer, instrument, etc.

bar′i·um (bâr′ē əm, bar′-) *n.* an active metallic element.

bark¹ (bärk) *n.* **1.** the short, sharp cry of a dog. **2.** a short, sharp sound. —*v.i.* **3.** to sound a bark. **4.** to speak sharply. —*v.t.* **5.** to utter gruffly.

bark² (bärk) *n.* **1.** the external covering of woody plants. —*v.t.* **2.** to scrape the skin of. **3.** to strip the bark from.

bark′er (bär′kər) *n.* a person who stands at the entrance to a show and shouts out its attractions.

bar′ley (bär′lē) *n.* an edible cereal plant.

bar mitz′vah (bär mits′və) *n.* a religious ceremony admitting a boy to the Jewish community as an adult.

barn (bärn) *n.* a farm building for storing hay, grain, etc., and for housing animals.

bar′na·cle (bär′nə kəl) *n.* a type of shellfish that clings to ship bottoms and timber.

barn′storm′ *v.i., v.t.* to tour (rural areas) giving speeches or performing plays.

barn′yard′ *n.* a fenced area next to a barn.

ba·rom′e·ter (bə rom′i tər) *n.* **1.** an instrument for measuring atmospheric pressure. **2.** anything that indicates changes. —**bar·o·met′ric** (bar′ə me′trik) *adj.*

bar′on (bar′ən) *n.* a member of the lowest rank of the nobility. —**ba·ro′ni·al** (bə rō′ nē əl) *adj.*

bar′on·et (-ə nit, -net′) *n.* a member of a British hereditary order of honor. —**bar′on·et·cy,** *n.*

Ba·roque′ (bə rōk′) *adj.* **1.** of an architectural style of the 17th to mid-18th century, marked by elaborate ornamentation and grotesque effects. **2.** of the musical period extending roughly from 1600 to 1750.

bar′racks (bar′əks) *n.* (*used with a sing. or pl. v.*) a building for lodging soldiers.

bar′ra·cu′da (bar′ə kōō′də) *n.* a long, predatory marine fish.

bar·rage′ (bə räzh′) *n.* **1.** concentrated artillery fire. **2.** an overwhelming quantity.

bar′rel (bar′əl) *n., v.,* **-reled, -reling.** —*n.* **1.** a cylindrical wooden vessel with bulging sides. **2.** the quantity held in such a vessel. **3.** the tube-like part of a gun. —*v.i.* **4.** to travel very fast.

bar′ren (bar′ən) *adj.* **1.** sterile; unfruitful. **2.** dull. —**bar′ren·ness,** *n.*

bar·rette′ (bə ret′) *n.* a clasp for the hair.

bar′ri·cade′ (bar′i kād′, bar′i kād′) *n., v.,* **-caded, -cading.** —*n.* **1.** a defensive barrier. —*v.t.* **2.** to block or defend with a barricade.

bar′ri·er (bar′ē ər) *n.* anything that obstructs or limits entrance or access.

bar′ring (bär′ing) *prep.* excepting.

bar′ris·ter (bar′ə stər) *n.* in Britain, a trial lawyer.

bar′row (bar′ō) *n.* **1.** a wheelbarrow. **2.** an artificial mound.

bar′tend′er (bär′-) *n.* a person who mixes and serves drinks at a bar.

bar′ter (bär′tər) *v.t.* **1.** to trade by exchange of goods rather than money. —*n.* **2.** the act of bartering.

ba′sal (bā′səl, -zəl) *adj.* of or at the base.

ba·salt′ (bə sôlt′, bā′sôlt) *n.* the dark, hard rock from a volcano. —**ba·sal′tic,** *adj.*

base¹ (bās) *n., v.,* **based, basing.** —*n.* **1.** the bottom or foundation of something. **2.** a fundamental principle. **3.** a starting point. **4.** a military headquarters or supply installation. **5.** a chemical compound that unites with an acid to form a salt. —*v.t.* **6.** to form a base for. **7.** to establish. —*Idiom.* **8.** **off base,** badly mistaken.

base² (bās) *adj.,* **baser, basest. 1.** deserving contempt; despicable. **2.** inferior.

base′ball′ *n.* **1.** a ball game involving the batting of a ball, played by two teams on a diamond-shaped field. **2.** the ball used.

base′board′ *n.* the board forming the foot of an inside wall.

base′less *adj.* having no foundation; unfounded.

base′line′ *n.* **1.** the line between the bases on a baseball diamond. **2.**

---

the line at each end of a tennis court. **3.** a basic standard or level; guideline. Also, **base′ line′.**

base′ment *n.* the story of a building below the ground floor.

bash (bash) *v.t.* **1.** to strike violently. **2.** to attack with blows or words. —*n.* **3.** a hard blow. **4.** a lively party.

bash′ful *adj.* shy; easily embarrassed.

ba′sic (bā′sik) *adj.* **1.** forming a base or basis; fundamental. —*n.* **2.** **basics,** essential ingredients, procedures, etc. —**ba′si·cal·ly,** *adv.*

BASIC (bā′sik) *n.* a computer programming language using English words, punctuation, and algebraic notation.

bas′il (baz′əl, bā′zəl) *n.* an aromatic mintlike herb used in cooking.

ba·sil′i·ca (bə sil′i kə) *n.* an early Christian church with an apse at one end.

ba′sin (bā′sən) *n.* **1.** a round open container for liquids. **2.** an area drained by a river.

ba′sis (bā′sis) *n., pl.* **-ses** (-sēz). **1.** a foundation. **2.** a fundamental principle. **3.** the main ingredient.

bask (bask) *v.i.* **1.** to lie in pleasant warmth. **2.** to take pleasure in.

bas′ket (bas′kit) *n.* a container woven of straw, strips of wood, etc.

bas′ket·ball′ *n.* **1.** a game played by two teams who score points by tossing a ball through a goal on the opponents' side of the court. **2.** the ball used.

bas·ma′ti (bäs mä′tē) *n.* a variety of long-grain rice.

bas′-re·lief′ (bä′ri lēf′) *n.* a sculpture in which the figures are raised slightly.

bass¹ (bäs) *n.* **1.** the lowest pitch in music. **2.** the lowest male singing voice. **3.** a singer with this voice. —*adj.* **4.** of the lowest pitch.

bass² (bas) *n., pl.* **basses, bass.** any of numerous edible, spiny fishes.

bas′set hound′ (bas′it) *n.* a short-legged hound with a long body and long, drooping ears.

bas′si·net′ (bas′ə net′) *n.* a hooded basket, used as a baby's cradle.

bas·soon′ (ba sōon′, bə-) *n.* a large woodwind instrument of low range.

bas′tard (bas′tərd) *n.* **1.** an illegitimate child. **2.** a mean, unpleasant person. —*adj.* **3.** illegitimate in birth. **4.** not genuine; false. —**bas′tard·i·za′tion,** *n.* —**bas′tard·ize′,** *v.t.*

baste¹ (bāst) *v.t.,* **basted, basting.** to sew with long, loose, temporary stitches.

baste² (bāst) *v.t.,* **basted, basting.** to moisten (meat, poultry, etc.) while cooking.

bas′tion (bas′chən) *n.* **1.** the projecting part of a fortified place. **2.** a fortified place. **3.** anything seen as protecting some quality, condition, etc.

bat¹ (bat) *n., v.,* **batted, batting.** —*n.* **1.** the wooden club used in certain games to strike the ball. **2.** a heavy stick or club. **3.** a blow, as with a bat. —*v.t.* **4.** to hit with a bat. —*v.i.* **5.** to take one's turn as a batter.

bat² (bat) *n.* a nocturnal flying mammal.

bat³ (bat) *v.t.,* **batted, batting. 1.** to blink; flutter. —*Idiom.* **2.** **not bat an eye,** to show no emotion.

batch (bach) *n.* a quantity produced at one time or taken together.

bat′ed (bā′tid) *adj.* —*Idiom.* **with bated breath,** in a state of suspenseful anticipation.

bath (bath) *n., pl.* **baths. 1.** a washing of the entire body. **2.** the water used.

bathe (bāth) *v.,* **bathed, bathing.** —*v.i.* **1.** to take a bath. **2.** to swim for pleasure. —*v.t.* **3.** to immerse in water or other liquid. **4.** to give a bath to. **5.** to apply water or other liquid to. —**bath′er,** *n.*

bath′ing suit′ *n.* a garment worn for swimming; swimsuit.

ba′thos (bā′thos, -thōs) *n.* a change in tone from the important to the trivial. **2.** sentimentality; triteness. —**ba·thet′ic** (bə thet′ik) *adj.*

bath′robe′ *n.* a loose robe worn to and from the bath.

bath′room′ *n.* a room with a bathtub or shower and usu. a sink and toilet.

bath′tub′ *n.* a tub to bathe in.

ba·tik′ (bə tēk′) *n.* cloth that has

---

been waxed so that some parts resist dye.

ba·tiste′ (bə tēst′, ba-) *n.* a fine, sheer fabric.

bat mitz′vah (bät mits′və) *n.* a religious ceremony admitting a girl to the Jewish community as an adult.

ba·ton′ (bə ton′, ba-) *n.* **1.** a wand with which a conductor directs an orchestra. **2.** a staff serving as a mark of office.

bat·tal′ion (bə tal′yən) *n.* a military unit of at least three companies.

bat′ten (bat′n) *n.* **1.** a strip of wood holding something in place. —*v.t.* **2.** to fasten with this.

bat′ter¹ (bat′ər) *v.t.* **1.** to beat repeatedly. **2.** to subject (a person) to repeated abuse. **3.** to damage by rough usage.

bat′ter² (bat′ər) *n.* a mixture of flour, milk, and eggs.

bat′ter³ (bat′ər) *n.* a player whose turn it is to bat.

bat′tering ram′ *n.* a heavy beam for beating down walls, gates, etc.

bat′ter·y *n., pl.* **-teries.** a cell or cells for producing electricity. **2.** a group of artillery pieces. **3.** any group or series of similar or related things. **4.** an unlawful attack on a person by beating or wounding.

bat′tle (bat′l) *n., v.,* **-tled, -tling.** —*n.* **1.** a hostile encounter. —*v.t., v.i.* **2.** to fight.

bat′tle·field′ *n.* **1.** the ground on which a battle is fought. **2.** an area of conflict.

bat′tle·ment *n.* a low wall on a tower with spaces for shooting.

bat′tle·ship′ *n.* a heavily armed warship.

bat′ty (bat′ē) *adj.,* **-tier, -tiest.** *Slang.* crazy or eccentric.

bau′ble (bô′bəl) *n.* a cheap, showy trinket.

baud (bôd) *n.* a unit used to measure the speed of data transfer on a computer.

baux′ite (bôk′sīt, bō′zīt) *n.* the principal ore of aluminum.

bawd′y (bô′dē) *adj.,* **-ier, -iest.** indecent.

bawl (bôl) *v.i.* **1.** to cry lustily. —*v.t.* **2.** to shout out. —*n.* **3.** a loud shout.

bay¹ (bā) *n.* a wide inlet of the sea.

bay² (bā) *n.* **1.** a compartment or recess in a building. **2.** a compartment, as in an aircraft or ship.

bay³ (bā) *n.* **1.** a deep, prolonged howl. **2.** the stand made by a hunted animal or person. —*v.i.* **3.** to howl.

bay⁴ (bā) *n.* the laurel.

bay⁵ (bā) *n.* **1.** a reddish brown horse or other animal. **2.** a reddish brown.

bay′ber′ry *n., pl.* **-ries.** a fragrant shrub with waxy berries.

bay′ leaf′ *n.* the dried leaf of the laurel, used in cooking.

bay′o·net (bā′ə net′, bā′ə nit) *n., v.,* **-neted, -neting.** —*n.* **1.** a dagger attached to the muzzle of a gun. —*v.t.* **2.** to kill or wound with a bayonet.

bay′ou (bī′ōō) *n., pl.* **bayous.** a marshy arm of a lake, river, etc.

ba·zaar′ (bə zär′) *n.* **1.** a marketplace. **2.** a sale to benefit a charity.

ba·zoo′ka (bə zōō′kə) *n.* a portable weapon that fires an armor-piercing missile.

BB (bē′bē′) *n., pl.* **BB's.** small metal shot fired from an air rifle (**BB gun**).

B.C. before Christ.

B.C.E. before the Common (or Christian) Era.

be (bē; *unstressed* bē, bi) *v.* and *auxiliary v., pres. sing. 1st pers.* **am,** *2nd* **are,** *3rd* **is,** *pres. pl.* **are;** *past sing. 1st pers.* **was,** *2nd* **were,** *3rd* **was,** *past pl.* **were;** *pres. subj.* **be;** *past subj. sing. 1st, 2nd,* and *3rd pers.* **were;** *past subj. pl.* **were;** *past part.* **been;** *pres. part.* **be·ing.** —*v.i.* **1.** to exist or live. **2.** to occur. **3.** to occupy a certain place. **4.** to continue as before. **5.** (used to connect the subject with its predicate adjective or nominative). **6.** (used to form interrogative or imperative sentences). —*auxiliary verb.* **7.** (used with other verbs to form progressive tenses, the passive voice, etc.)

beach (bēch) *n.* **1.** an expanse of sand or pebbles along a shore. —*v.t.* **2.** to run or pull onto a beach.

beach′comb′er *n.* a person who gathers various objects on a beach.

beach′head′ *n.* the area that is the first objective of an invading army landing on a beach.

---

bea′con (bē′kən) *n.* a signal, as a light or fire.

bead (bēd) *n.* **1.** a small ball of glass, pearl, etc., designed to be strung. **2.** **beads,** a necklace of beads. **3.** any small globular body. —*v.t.* **4.** to ornament with beads. —*v.i.* **5.** to form in beads.

bea′gle (bē′gəl) *n.* a small hound with drooping ears.

beak (bēk) *n.* **1.** the bill of a bird. **2.** any similar projecting part.

beak′er *n.* **1.** a large drinking cup. **2.** a glass container with a pouring lip, used in a laboratory.

beam (bēm) *n.* **1.** a long piece of metal or wood that supports a structure or a machine. **2.** the breadth of a ship. **3.** a ray of light or other radiation. **4.** a radio signal. —*v.i.* **5.** to emit beams. **6.** to smile radiantly.

bean (bēn) *n.* **1.** the edible seed or pod of plants of the legume family. **2.** a plant producing beans. **3.** any other beanlike seed or plant. —*Idiom.* **4.** **spill the beans,** *Informal.* to reveal a secret.

bean′ count′er *n. Informal.* a person who makes judgments on the basis of numerical calculations.

bear¹ (bâr) *v.,* **bore** (bôr), **borne** (bôrn), **bearing.** —*v.t.* **1.** to support. **2.** to carry. **3.** to undergo; endure. **4.** to give birth to. —*v.i.* **5.** to go in a direction. **6.** **bear on,** to be relevant to. **7.** ~ **out,** to confirm. **8.** ~ **with,** to be patient with.

bear² (bâr) *n.* **1.** a large, stocky, omnivorous mammal. **2.** a clumsy or rude person. **3.** a person who believes that stock prices will fall. —*adj.* **4.** marked by falling prices, esp. of stocks.

beard (bērd) *n.* **1.** hair growing on the lower part of a man's face. **2.** a similar growth on an animal or plant. —*v.t.* **3.** to confront boldly.

bear′ hug′ *n.* a tight embrace.

bear′ing *n.* **1.** the manner in which one conducts or carries oneself. **2.** reference or relation. **3.** the support and guide for a rotating or sliding shaft, pivot, or wheel. **4.** **bearings,** position; direction.

beast (bēst) *n.* **1.** an animal. **2.** a coarse or inhuman person.

beast′ly *adj.,* **-lier, -liest. 1.** brutish. **2.** nasty.

beast′ of bur′den *n.* an animal used for carrying heavy loads.

beat (bēt) *v.,* **beat, beaten** or **beat, beating.** —*v.t.* **1.** to strike repeatedly. **2.** to dash against. **3.** to mark (time) in music. **4.** to flap. **5.** to stir vigorously. **6.** to defeat. —*v.i.* **7.** to pound. **8.** to throb. —*n.* **9.** a blow. **10.** the sound of a blow. **11.** one's regular path. **12.** musical rhythm.

be·a·tif′ic (bē′ə tif′ik) *adj.* blissful.

be·at′i·tude′ (bē at′i tōōd′, -tyōōd′) *n.* **1.** blessedness. **2.** (*often cap.*) any of the declarations of blessedness made by Jesus (Matthew 5).

beat′nik (bēt′nik) *n.* a disillusioned, unconventional person, esp. of the 1950s.

beau (bō) *n., pl.* **beaus, beaux.** a suitor.

beau′te·ous (byōō′tē əs) *adj.* beautiful.

beau·ti′cian (-tish′ən) *n.* a person who works in a beauty parlor.

beau′ti·ful (-tə fəl) *adj.* **1.** having beauty; delighting the senses or mind. **2.** wonderful.

beau′ti·fy′ (-fī′) *v.t.,* **-fied, -fying.** to make beautiful.

beau′ty *n., pl.* **-ties. 1.** the quality that gives intense pleasure to the sight or other senses. **2.** a beautiful thing or person.

beau′ty par′lor *n.* an establishment where women go for haircuts, manicures, etc.

bea′ver (bē′vər) *n.* a large amphibious rodent with sharp teeth and a flattened tail.

be·cause′ (bi kôz′, -koz′, -kuz′) *conj.* **1.** for the reason that. —*Idiom.* **2.** **because of,** on account of.

beck (bek) *n.* **1.** a beckoning gesture. —*Idiom.* **2.** **at someone's beck and call,** subject to someone's demands.

beck′on (-ən) *v.t., v.i.* to summon by a gesture.

be·cloud′ (bi kloud′) *v.t.* **1.** to darken with clouds. **2.** to make confused.

be·come′ (bi kum′) *v.,* **became** (-kām′) **become, becoming.** —*v.i.* **1.** to come, change, or grow to be. —*v.t.* **2.** to suit. —*Idiom.* **3.** **become of,** to happen to.

be·com′ing *adj.* **1.** attractive. **2.** suitable.

bed (bed) n. **1.** a piece of furniture on which a person sleeps. **2.** an area of ground on which plants are grown. **3.** the bottom of a lake, river, etc. **4.** a base.

bed′bug′ n. a wingless, bloodsucking insect.

bed′ding n. blankets, sheets, etc., for a bed.

be·dev′il (bi dev′əl) v.t., **-iled, -il·ing. 1.** to torment maliciously. **2.** to confuse; confound.

bed′fel′low n. **1.** a person sharing one's bed. **2.** an ally.

bed′lam (bed′ləm) n. a scene of loud confusion.

Bed′ou·in (bed′ōō in) n. a member of a tent-dwelling Arab people living in the desert.

bed′pan′ n. a shallow pan used as a toilet for a bedridden person.

be·drag′gled (bi drag′əld) adj. soiled and wet.

bed·rid′den (-rid′n) adj. confined to bed by illness.

bed′rock′ n. **1.** continuous solid rock under soil. **2.** any firm foundation.

bed′room′ n. a room for sleeping.

bed′sore′ n. a skin ulcer caused by long confinement in bed.

bed′spread′ n. a decorative cover for a bed.

bed′stead′ (-sted′, -stid) n. a frame for a bed.

bed′time′ n. the time a person goes to bed.

bee (bē) n. **1.** a four-winged, honey-producing insect. **2.** a social gathering for work or competition.

beech (bēch) n. a tree with smooth gray bark and small edible nuts (beech′nuts′).

beef (bēf) n., pl. **beeves** (bēvz) for **1; beefs** for **4,** v. —n. **1.** an adult cow, steer, or bull raised for its meat. **2.** its meat. **3.** Informal. muscular strength. **4.** Slang. a complaint. —v.i. **5.** Slang. to complain. **6. beef up,** to strengthen.

bee′hive′ n. **1.** a shelter for bees. **2.** a busy place.

bee′keep′er n. a person who raises bees.

bee′line′ n. a direct course.

been (bin) v. pp. of **be.**

beep (bēp) n. **1.** a short tone, usu. high in pitch, as from an electronic device. —v.i. **2.** to make a beep.

beep′er n. a small electronic device whose signal notifies the person carrying it of a message.

beer (bēr) n. a fermented beverage made from malt and hops.

beet (bēt) n. a plant with an edible red or white root.

bee·tle¹ (bēt′l) n. an insect with hard, horny forewings.

bee·tle² (bēt′l) adj., v., **-tled, -tling.** —adj. **1.** projecting; overhanging. —v.i. **2.** to project or overhang.

bee′tle-browed′ adj. **1.** having heavy projecting eyebrows. **2.** scowling.

be·fall′ (bi fôl′) v.t., v.i., **-fell, -fallen, -falling.** to happen (to).

be·fit′ (bi fit′) v.t., **-fitted, -fitting.** to be appropriate for.

be·fore′ (bi fôr′) adv. **1.** in front. **2.** earlier. —prep. **3.** in front of. **4.** previously to. **5.** in preference to. —conj. **6.** earlier than.

be·fore′hand′ adv. in advance; ahead of time.

be·friend′ (bi frend′) v.t. to act as a friend to.

be·fud′dle (bi fud′l) v.t., **-dled, -dling.** to confuse thoroughly.

beg (beg) v.t., v.i., **begged, begging. 1.** to ask for (charity). **2.** to ask humbly. **3. beg off,** to ask release from an obligation.

be·gan′ (bi gan′) v. pt. of **begin.**

be·get′ (bi get′) v.t., **begot** (bi got′), **begotten** or **begot, begetting. 1.** to be the father of. **2.** to cause.

beg′gar (beg′ər) n. **1.** a person who lives by begging. **2.** a very poor person. —v.t. **3.** to reduce to poverty.

beg′gar·ly adj. **1.** inadequate. **2.** mean.

be·gin′ (bi gin′) v.t., v.i., **be·gan, be·gun, be·gin·ning. 1.** to perform the first part of (something). **2.** to come or bring into existence.

be·gin′ner (bi gin′ər) n. a person who is just starting to learn something.

be·gin′ning n. **1.** the time or place at which anything starts. **2.** origin.

be·gone′ (bi gôn′) interj. depart!

be·gon′ia (bi gōn′yə) n. a plant with bright flowers and waxy leaves.

be·grudge′ (bi gruj′) v.t.,

-grudged, -grudging. 1. to envy the good fortune or pleasure of. **2.** to give or allow reluctantly.

be·guile′ (bi gīl′) v.t., **-guiled, -guiling. 1.** to deceive. **2.** to charm or delight.

be·gun′ (bi gun′) v. pp. of **begin.**

be·half′ (bi haf′) n. **1.** interest; support. —Idiom. **2. in** or **on behalf of,** as a representative of.

be·have′ (bi hāv′) v.i., **-haved, -having. 1.** to act or react in a certain way. **2.** to act properly. —v.t. **3.** to conduct (oneself) in a proper manner.

be·hav′ior (-yər) n. a way of behaving.

be·head′ (bi hed′) v.t. to cut off the head of.

be·he·moth (bi hē′məth) n. any huge or extremely powerful creature or thing.

be·hest′ (bi hest′) n. **1.** a command. **2.** an earnest request.

be·hind′ (bi hīnd′) prep. **1.** at or toward the rear of. **2.** later than. **3.** in the state of making less progress than. **4.** supporting. **5.** hidden by. —adv. **6.** at or toward the rear. **7.** in arrears. **8.** slow; late. —n. **9.** Informal. the buttocks.

be·hold′ (bi hōld′) v., **-held, -holding,** interj. —v.t. **1.** to look at; see. —interj. **2.** look! —**be·hold′er,** n.

be·hold′en adj. obliged.

be·hoove′ (bi hōōv′) v.t., **-hooved, -hooving.** to be necessary or proper for.

beige (bāzh) n. a light brown.

be′ing (bē′ing) n. **1.** existence. **2.** a living person or thing.

be·la′bor (bi lā′bər) v.t. to discuss or explain excessively.

be·lat′ed (bi lā′tid) adj. late.

bel′ can′to (bel′ kän′tō, -kän′-) n. a smooth, flowing style of operatic singing.

belch (belch) v.i., v.t. **1.** to expel (gas) from the stomach. **2.** to gush forth. —n. **3.** an act of belching.

be·lea′guer (bi lē′gər) v.t. to beset, as with difficulties.

bel′fry (bel′frē) n., pl. **-fries.** a bell tower.

Bel·gian (bel′jən) adj. **1.** of Belgium or its inhabitants. —n. **2.** a native of Belgium.

be·lie′ (bi lī′) v.t., **-lied, -lying. 1.** to misrepresent. **2.** to show to be false.

be·lief′ (bi lēf′) n. **1.** something believed. **2.** confidence; trust. **3.** a religious faith.

be·lieve′ (bi lēv′) v., **-lieved, -lieving.** —v.t. **1.** to accept as true or as speaking the truth. **2.** to think; suppose. —v.i. **3.** to accept the truth of something. —**be·liev′a·ble,** adj.

be·liev′er n. a person who believes, esp. one who has religious faith.

be·lit′tle (bi lit′l) v.t., **-littled, -littling.** to view or represent as less important.

bell (bel) n. a hollow, cup-shaped metal instrument producing a ringing sound when struck. —v.t. **2.** to put a bell on. —v.i. **3.** to have the shape of a bell.

bel′la·don′na (bel′ə don′ə) n. **1.** a poisonous plant having black berries and purplish red flowers. **2.** the drug obtained from this.

belle (bel) n. a beautiful woman.

bell′hop′ n. a person who carries luggage and runs errands in a hotel.

bel′li·cose′ (bel′i kōs′) adj. eager to fight.

bel·lig′er·ent (bə lij′ər ənt) adj. **1.** aggressively hostile. —n. **2.** a nation at war. —**bel·lig′er·ence, n.** —**bel·lig′er·ent·ly,** adv.

bell′ jar′ n. a bell-shaped glass cover, used in laboratories to contain gases or a vacuum.

bel′low (bel′ō) v.i. **1.** to make the loud, deep sound of a bull. —v.t. **2.** to utter in a loud, deep voice. —n. **3.** an act or sound of bellowing.

bel′lows (bel′ōz, -əz) n. (used with a sing. or pl. v.) a device for producing a strong current of air, consisting of a chamber that can be expanded and contracted.

bell′ pep′per n. a mild, bell-shaped pepper.

bell′weth′er (bel′weth′ər) n. **1.** one that leads or marks a trend. **2.** a male sheep wearing a bell and leading a flock.

bel′ly (bel′ē) n., pl. **-lies,** v., **-lied, -lying.** —n. **1.** the abdomen. **2.** the stomach. **3.** a rounded part. —v.t., v.i. **4.** to swell out.

bel′ly·ache′ n., v., **-ached, -aching.** —n.

1. a pain in the abdomen. —v.i. **2.** Informal. to complain.

be·long′ (bi lông′) v.i. **1.** to be properly placed. **2.** to be suitable. **3. belong to, a.** to be the property of. **b.** to be part of. **c.** to be a member of.

be·long′ings n.pl. one's personal possessions.

be·lov′ed (bi luv′id, -luvd′) adj. **1.** greatly loved. —n. **2.** a person who is beloved.

be·low′ (bi lō′) adv. **1.** in or toward a lower place. **2.** in a lower rank or grade. **3.** later in a text. —prep. **4.** lower down than.

belt (belt) n. **1.** an encircling band, esp. for the waist. **2.** an endless band to transmit motion or carry objects. **3.** a region. **4.** Slang. a hard blow. —v.t. **5.** to put a belt around. **6.** Slang. to hit hard. —Idiom. **7. below the belt,** unfairly.

belt′way′ n. a highway around the perimeter of an urban area.

be·moan′ (bi mōn′) v.t. to express grief over.

be·mused′ (bi myōōzd′) adj. **1.** bewildered. **2.** lost in thought.

bench (bench) n. **1.** a long, hard seat. **2.** a work table. **3.** a judge's seat. **4.** judges collectively. **5.** the seat on which team members sit while not playing in a game.

bench′mark′ n. a standard against which others can be measured.

bend (bend) v., **bent, bending,** n. —v.t. **1.** to curve. **2.** to shape into a curve. **3.** to guide in a certain direction. —v.i. **4.** to become curved. **5.** to turn or incline. —n. **6.** the act of bending. **7.** something bent.

be·neath′ (bi nēth′) adv. **1.** in or to a lower position; below. —prep. **2.** below; under. **3.** below the level or dignity of.

ben′e·dic′tion (ben′i dik′shən) n. a spoken blessing.

ben′e·fac′tor (-fak′tər) n. a person who gives financial or other help.

be·nef′i·cent (bə nef′ə sənt) adj. doing good. —**be·nef′i·cence, n.**

ben′e·fi′cial (ben′ə fish′əl) adj. having a helpful effect. —**ben′e·fi′cial·ly,** adv.

ben′e·fi′ci·ar·y (-fish′ē er′ē, -fish′ə rē) n., pl. **-aries.** a person who receives benefits or funds.

ben′e·fit (-fit) n., v., **-fited, -fiting.** —n. **1.** something helpful or advantageous. **2.** money from insurance, a public agency, etc. **3.** entertainment for a worthy cause. —v.t. **4.** to do good to. —v.i. **5.** to gain an advantage.

be·nev′o·lent (bə nev′ə lənt) adj. kind and charitable. —**be·nev′o·lence, n.**

be·night′ed (bi nī′tid) adj. intellectually or morally ignorant.

be·nign′ (bi nīn′) adj. **1.** kind. **2.** favorable. **3.** not malignant. —**be·nign′ly,** adv.

be·nig′nant (-nig′nənt) adj. **1.** kind. **2.** beneficial.

bent (bent) adj. **1.** curved. **2.** determined. —n. **3.** a natural talent.

be·numb′ (bi num′) v.t. **1.** to make numb. **2.** to make inactive.

ben′zene (ben′zēn, ben zēn′) n. a flammable liquid, used as a solvent.

ben′zine (-zēn) n. a colorless, flammable liquid used in cleaning and dyeing.

be·queath′ (bi kwēth′, -kwēth′) v.t. **1.** to give (property or money) in a will. **2.** to hand down.

be·quest′ (bi kwest′) n. **1.** a bequeathing. **2.** something bequeathed.

be·rate′ (bi rāt′) v.t., **-rated, -rating.** to scold.

be·reaved′ (bi rēvd′) adj. suffering a loved one's death. —**be·reave′, v.t.** —**be·reave′ment,** n.

be·reft′ (-reft′) adj. deprived.

be·ret′ (bə rā′) n. a soft, visorless cap.

ber′i·ber′i (ber′ē ber′ē) n. a disease caused by lack of vitamin B₁.

berm (bûrm) n. **1.** the shoulder of a road. **2.** a mound of snow or dirt.

ber′ry (ber′ē) n., pl. **-ries,** v., **-ried, -rying.** —n. **1.** a small, juicy, stoneless fruit. —v.i. **2.** to gather berries.

ber·serk′ (bər sûrk′, -zûrk′) adj. —Idiom. **go berserk,** to become violently enraged.

berth (bûrth) n. **1.** a sleeping space on a ship or train. **2.** a place for a ship to dock. —v.t. **3.** to provide with a berth. —Idiom. **4. give a wide berth to,** to keep a distance from.

ber′yl (ber′əl) n. a mineral, varieties of which are the gems emerald and aquamarine.

be·seech′ (bi sēch′) v.t., v.i.,

-sought, -seeching. to implore; beg (for).

be·set′ (bi set′) v.t., **-set, -setting. 1.** to attack on all sides. **2.** to surround.

be·side′ (bi sīd′) prep. **1.** at the side of. **2.** compared with. **3.** apart from. —Idiom. **4. beside oneself,** distraught.

be·sides′ adv. **1.** moreover; furthermore. **2.** in addition. —prep. **3.** in addition to. **4.** other than.

be·siege′ (bi sēj′) v.t., **-sieged, -sieging. 1.** to lay siege to. **2.** to crowd around.

be·smirch′ (bi smûrch′) v.t. to soil.

be·sot′ted (bi sot′id) adj. infatuated.

be·speak′ (bi spēk′) v.t., **-spoke** (-spōk′), **-spoken** or **-spoke, -speaking. 1.** to reserve. **2.** to show.

best (best) adj. **1.** of highest quality. **2.** most suitable. —adv. **3.** most excellently. **4.** in or to the highest degree. —n. **5.** someone or something that is best. —v.t. **6.** to defeat. —Idiom. **7. get the best of, a.** to gain the advantage over. **b.** to defeat. **8. make the best of,** to accept.

bes′tial (bes′chəl, bēs′-) adj. **1.** beastlike. **2.** brutal.

be·stir′ (bi stûr′) v.t., **-stirred, -stirring.** to rouse to action.

best′ man′ n. the chief attendant of the bridegroom.

be·stow′ (bi stō′) v.t. to present as a gift.

bet (bet) v., **bet** or **betted, betting,** n. —v.t. **1.** to risk or pledge (something, esp. money) on the outcome of a future event. —v.i. **2.** to make a bet. —n. **3.** a pledge made in betting. **4.** a thing pledged.

be′ta (bā′tə) n. the second letter of the Greek alphabet.

be′tel nut′ (bēt′l) the seed of a palm, often chewed in the tropics.

bête′ noire′ (bāt′ nwär′, bet′) n. a dreaded person or thing.

be·tide′ (bi tīd′) v.t., v.i., **-tided, -tiding.** to happen (to).

be·to′ken (bi tō′kən) v.t. to be a sign of.

be·tray′ (bi trā′) v.t. **1.** to deliver or reveal to an enemy by treachery. **2.** to be disloyal to. **3.** to reveal unintentionally. —**be·tray′er, n.**

be·troth′ (bi trōth′, -trôth′) v.t. to promise to marry. —**be·troth′al, n.** —**be·trothed′,** adj., n.

bet′ter (bet′ər) adj. **1.** of superior quality. **2.** preferable. **3.** greater. **4.** improved in health. —adv. **5.** in a more excellent manner. **6.** more completely. —v.t. **7.** to improve. **8.** to surpass. —n. **9.** something preferable. **10. betters.** those superior to oneself. —Idiom. **11. get the better of,** to prevail against.

be·tween′ (bi twēn′) prep. **1.** in the space separating. **2.** intermediate to. **3.** connecting. **4.** by the combined effort of. —adv. **5.** in the intervening space or time.

—Usage. Between you and I, though occasionally heard in the speech of educated persons, is not the commonly accepted form. Since the pronouns are objects of the preposition BETWEEN, the correct form is between you and me. See also AMONG.

be·twixt′ (bi twikst′) prep., adv. between.

bev′el (bev′əl) n., v., **-eled, -eling.** —n. **1.** a sloping edge. —v.t. **2.** to cut at a bevel. —v.i. **3.** to slant at a bevel.

bev′er·age (bev′ər ij) n. any drink.

bev′y (bev′ē) n., pl. **bevies. 1.** a flock of birds. **2.** a large group.

be·wail′ (bi wāl′) v.t. to lament.

be·ware′ (bi wâr′) v.i., v.t., **-wared, -waring.** to be cautious (of).

be·wil′der (bi wil′dər) v.t. to confuse. —**be·wil′der·ment, n.**

be·witch′ (bi wich′) v.t. **1.** to put under a magic spell. **2.** to charm.

be·yond′ (bē ond′) prep. **1.** on the farther side of. **2.** farther, more, or later on. —adv. **3.** farther on.

bi- a prefix meaning twice or two.

bi·an′nu·al (bī an′yōō əl) adj. occurring twice a year. —**bi·an′nu·al·ly,** adv.

bi′as (bī′əs) n. **1.** a diagonal line running across a woven fabric. **2.** prejudice. —adv. **3.** in a diagonal manner. —v.t. **4.** to prejudice.

bi·ath′lon (bī ath′lon) n. an athletic contest comprising two consecutive events.

bib (bib) n. a covering tied under the chin to protect the clothing while eating.

Bi′ble (bī′bəl) n. the sacred writings

of the Christian or the Jewish religion. —**Bib·li·cal, bib·li·cal** (bib′li kəl).

bib′li·og′ra·phy (bib′lē og′rə fē) n., pl. **-phies.** a list of writings on a subject or by an author.

bib′u·lous (bib′yə ləs) adj. fond of or addicted to alcohol.

bi·cam′er·al (bī kam′ər əl) adj. composed of two legislative bodies.

bi·car′bo·nate of so′da (bī-kär′bə nit, -nāt′) baking soda.

bi·cen·ten′ni·al n. a 200th anniversary. Also, **bi′cen·ten′a·ry.**

bi′ceps (-seps) n. a muscle of the upper arm.

bick′er (bik′ər) v.i. to quarrel about trivial things.

bi·cus′pid n. a tooth having two cusps or points.

bi′cy·cle (bī′si kəl) n., v., **-cled, -cling.** —n. a two-wheeled vehicle propelled by pedals. —v.i. to ride a bicycle. —**bi′cy·clist,** n.

bid (bid) v., **bade** (bad, bād) or **bid, bidden** or **bid, bidding,** n. —v.t. **1.** to command. **2.** to say as a greeting. **3.** to offer (a sum) as the price one will charge or pay. **4.** (in card games) to enter a bid of. —v.i. **5.** to make a bid. —n. **6.** the act of bidding. **7.** (in card games) a statement of the number of tricks a player expects to win. **8.** an offer of a price. **9.** an attempt.

bid′der n. a person who bids.

bide (bīd) v.i., **bided, biding.** —Idiom. **bide one's time,** to wait for a favorable opportunity.

bi·det′ (bē dā′) n. a low tub for bathing the genital area.

bi·en′ni·al (bī en′ē əl) adj. occurring every two years. —**bi·en′ni·al·ly,** adv.

bier (bēr) n. a stand for a coffin.

bi·fo′cal (bī fō′kəl, bī′fō′-) adj. **1.** having two focuses. **2.** (of an eyeglass lens) having separate areas for near and far vision. —n. **3. bifocals.** eyeglasses with bifocal lenses.

big (big) adj., **bigger, biggest. 1.** large in size, amount, etc. **2.** important.

big′a·my (big′ə mē) n., pl. **-mies.** the crime of marrying again while legally married. —**big′a·mist,** n.

big′ bang′ the′ory n. the theory that the universe began with an explosion of a dense mass of matter and is still expanding.

big′horn′ (big′hôrn′) n. a wild sheep of the Rocky Mountains with large, curving horns.

bight (bīt) n. **1.** a loop of rope. **2.** a deep bend in a coast; bay.

big′ot (big′ət) n. an intolerant person. —**big′ot·ed,** adj. —**big′ot·ry,** n.

bike (bīk) n., v., **biked, biking.** —n. **1.** a bicycle or motorcycle. —v.i. **2.** to ride a bike. —**bik′er,** n.

bi·ki′ni (bi kē′nē) n. **1.** a very brief two-piece bathing suit for women. **2.** a very brief bathing suit for men.

bi·lat′er·al (bī lat′ər əl) adj. on or affecting two sides.

bile (bīl) n. **1.** a digestive secretion of the liver. **2.** ill temper.

bilge (bilj) n. **1.** the lowest inner part of a ship's hull. **2.** water collected in bilges. **3.** Slang. foolish talk.

bi·lin′gual (bī ling′gwəl) adj. speaking or expressed in two languages.

bil′ious (bil′yəs) adj. **1.** of bile. **2.** suffering from liver trouble. **3.** irritable.

bilk (bilk) v.t. to cheat; defraud.

bill¹ (bil) n. **1.** an account of money owed. **2.** a piece of paper money. **3.** a draft of a proposed law. **4.** a poster. —v.t. **5.** to charge.

bill² (bil) n. the horny part of a bird's jaw.

bill′board′ n. a large outdoor advertising display panel.

bil′let (bil′it) n., v., **-leted, -leting.** —n. **1.** lodging for a soldier. —v.t. **2.** to provide lodging for.

bil·let-doux′ (bil′ā dōō′) n., pl. **billets-doux** (-dōōz′). a love letter.

bill′fold′ n. a wallet.

bil′liards (bil′yərdz) n. a game played with hard balls driven by a cue on a table.

bil′lings·gate′ (bil′ingz gāt′) n. coarse, abusive language.

bil′lion (bil′yən) n. a number represented in the U.S. by 1 followed by 9 zeros, and in Great Britain by 1 followed by 12 zeros.

bil′lion·aire′ (-âr′) n. a person whose assets are worth a billion dollars or more.

bill′ of sale′ n. a document transferring personal property from seller to buyer.

bil·low (bil'ō) n. **1.** a great wave or surge. —v.i. **2.** to swell out.

bil·ly goat n. a male goat.

bim·bo (bim'bō) n., pl. **-bos, -boes**. *Slang.* an attractive but stupid young woman.

bi·month·ly (bī munth'lē) adv., adj. every two months.

bin (bin) n. a box for storing grain, coal, etc.

bi·na·ry (bī'nə rē) adj. **1.** involving two parts, choices, etc. **2.** of a numerical system in which each place of a number is expressed as 0 or 1.

bind (bīnd) v.t., **bound, binding. 1.** to tie or encircle with a band. **2.** to bandage. **3.** to unite. **4.** to fasten (a book) in its cover. **5.** to obligate.

bind·ing n. **1.** something that binds. —adj. **2.** obligatory.

binge (binj) n., v., **binged, binging.** —n. **1.** a bout of excessive indulgence, as in eating. —v.i. **2.** to go on a binge.

bin·go (bing'gō) n. a game of chance using cards with numbered squares.

bin·na·cle (bin'ə kəl) n. a stand for a ship's compass.

bin·oc·u·lars (bə nok'yə lərz, bī-) n.pl. an instrument with two lenses that makes objects in the distance appear larger.

bio- a prefix meaning life or living organisms.

bi·o·chem·is·try (bī'ō kem'ə strē) n. the chemistry of living matter. —bi'o·chem'ist, n.

bi·o·de·grad·a·ble adj. capable of decaying and being absorbed harmlessly into the environment.

bi·o·di·ver·si·ty n. diversity of plant and animal species in an environment.

bi·o·eth·ics n. the study of the ethical implications of medical or biological procedures.

bi·og·ra·phy (bī og'rə fē) n., pl. **-phies.** a written account of a person's life. —bi·og'ra·pher, n. —bi·o·graph'i·cal (-ə graf'i kəl) adj.

bi·o·haz·ard n. anything used in or produced in biological research that poses a health hazard.

biolog·ical clock n. a natural mechanism regulating bodily cycles.

biolog·ical war·fare n. the use of toxic organisms as weapons.

bi·ol·o·gy (bī ol'ə jē) n. the scientific study of living organisms. —bi·o·log'i·cal (-ə loj'i kəl) adj. —bi·ol'o·gist, n.

bi·on·ics (bī on'iks) n. the srudy of electronic devices that function like living organisms. —bi·on'ic, adj.

bi·op·sy (bī'op sē) n., pl. **-sies.** the removal of a piece of living tissue for diagnostic study.

bi·o·rhythm (bī'ō-) n. a natural, periodic bodily cycle, as sleeping and waking.

bi·o·sphere (bī'ə-) n. the part of the earth's surface and atmosphere that supports life.

bi·o·tech·nol·o·gy (bī'ō-) n. the use of living organisms in making products or to manage the environment.

bi·par·ti·san (bī pär'tə zən) adj. representing two parties.

bi·par·tite (-pär'tīt) adj. **1.** having two parts. **2.** shared by two; joint.

bi·ped (-ped) n. a two-footed animal. —adj. **2.** having two feet.

birch (bûrch) n. a tree with smooth light bark.

bird (bûrd) n. an egg-laying vertebrate with feathers and wings.

bird's-eye (bûrdz'ī') adj. seen from above.

bi·ret·ta (bə ret'ə) n., pl. **-tas.** a stiff square cap worn by clergy.

birth (bûrth) n. **1.** an act or instance of being born. **2.** the act of bringing forth offspring. **3.** descent.

birth' control n. the prevention of unwanted pregnancy.

birth'mark' n. a blemish on the skin at birth.

birth'rate' n. the number of births in a given time and place.

birth'right' n. a hereditary right.

bis·cuit (bis'kit) n. a small, soft, raised bread.

bi·sect' (bī sekt') v.t. **1.** to cut into two parts. —v.i. **2.** to split into two parts.

bi·sex·u·al adj. **1.** sexually responsive to both sexes. —n. **2.** a bisexual person. —bi·sex'u·al·i·ty, n.

bish·op (bish'əp) n. **1.** a clergyman who supervises a number of local churches or a diocese. **2.** a chess piece that moves diagonally.

bish·op·ric (-rik) n. the diocese or office of a bishop.

bis·muth (biz'məth) n. a grayish white metallic element used in making alloys and in medicine.

bi·son (bī'sən) n., pl. **bisons, bison.** a North American buffalo having high, humped shoulders.

bisque (bisk) n. a thick cream soup.

bis·tro (bis'trō, bē'strō) n. a small restaurant or café.

bit¹ (bit) n. **1.** the mouthpiece of a bridle. **2.** a part of a tool that drills or bores or grips when twisted.

bit² (bit) n. **1.** a small piece or quantity. **2.** a short time.

bit³ (bit) n. a single, basic unit of computer information.

bitch (bich) n. **1.** a female dog. **2.** *Slang.* a malicious, unpleasant woman. —v.i. **3.** *Slang.* to complain.

bite (bīt) v., **bit, bitten** or **bit, biting,** n. —v.t. **1.** to cut or grip with the teeth. **2.** to sting. —v.i. **3.** to attack with the jaws. **4.** (of fish) to take bait. **5.** to take a firm hold. —n. **6.** the act of biting. **7.** a wound from biting. **8.** a sting. **9.** a morsel of food. **10.** a small meal.

bit·ing adj. **1.** sharp; harsh. **2.** severely critical.

bit·ter (bit'ər) adj. **1.** having a harsh taste. **2.** hard to bear. **3.** causing sharp pain. **4.** intensely hostile or resentful. —bit'ter·ly, adv. —bit'ter·ness, n.

bit·tern (bit'ərn) n. a type of wading bird.

bit·ter·sweet' adj. **1.** tasting both bitter and sweet. **2.** being both painful and pleasant.

bi·tu·men (bī tōo'mən, -tyōo'-) n. asphalt or an asphaltlike substance.

bitu·minous coal n. soft coal.

bi·valve n. a mollusk with two shells hinged together.

biv·ou·ac (biv'ōo ak') n., v., **-acked, -acking.** —n. **1.** a temporary resting or assembly place for troops. —v.i. **2.** to assemble in a bivouac.

bi·week·ly (bī-) adv., adj. **1.** every two weeks. **2.** twice a week.

bi·zarre' (bī zär') adj. strange.

blab (blab) v., **blabbed, blabbing.** —v.i. **1.** to talk idly. —v.t. **2.** to reveal (secrets).

black (blak) adj. **1.** lacking brightness or color. **2.** having dark skin color. **3.** without light. **4.** gloomy. **5.** wicked. —n. **6.** the color opposite to white. **7.** a member of a dark-skinned people, esp. of Africa or African ancestry. **8.** black clothing. —v.t., v.i. **9.** to make or become black. **10. black out,** to lose consciousness. —*Idiom.* **11. in the black,** earning a profit.

black'-and-blue' adj. discolored, as by bruising.

black'ball' n. **1.** an adverse vote. —v.t. **2.** to exclude; banish.

black'ber·ry n., pl. **-ries.** the dark purple fruit of certain brambles.

black'bird' n. a black-feathered American bird.

black'board' n. a smooth, dark board for writing on with chalk.

black'en v.t. **1.** to make black. **2.** to defame. —v.i. **3.** to grow black.

black' eye' n. discoloration of the skin around the eye.

black'-eyed' Su'san (sōo'zən) n. a plant having yellow, daisylike flowers with a dark center.

black'guard (blag'ärd, -ərd) n. a despicable person.

black'head' n. a small, dark fatty mass in a skin follicle.

black' hole' n. an area in outer space whose great density prevents the escape of light.

black'jack' n. **1.** a short, flexible, leather-covered club. **2.** a game of cards; twenty-one.

black'list' n. **1.** a list of persons in disfavor. —v.t. **2.** to put on a blacklist.

black' mag'ic n. sorcery.

black'mail' n. **1.** payment demanded from a person by threats to disclose damaging information. —v.t. **2.** to subject (a person) to blackmail. —black'mail'er, n.

black' mar'ket n. the buying and selling of goods in violation of rationing, price controls, etc.

black'out' n. **1.** the extinguishing or concealment of lights. **2.** a brief loss of consciousness.

black' sheep' n. a person who causes embarrassment or shame to his or her family.

black'smith' n. a person who shoes horses or forges iron objects.

black'thorn' n. a thorny shrub with plumlike fruit.

black'top' n., v., **-topped, -topping.** —n. **1.** a bituminous paving substance, as asphalt. —v.t. **2.** to pave with blacktop.

black' wid'ow n. a poisonous spider.

blad·der (blad'ər) n. **1.** a sac in the body that holds urine. **2.** an inflatable bag.

blade (blād) n. **1.** the flat cutting part of a knife, sword, etc. **2.** a leaf, esp. of grass. **3.** the thin, flat part of something.

blame (blām) v., **blamed, blaming,** n. —v.t. **1.** to hold responsible. **2.** to find fault with. —n. **3.** condemnation. **4.** responsibility for a fault. —blame'less, adj.

blanch (blanch) v.t. **1.** to whiten. **2.** to boil (food) briefly. —v.i. **3.** to turn pale.

bland (bland) adj. **1.** gentle; mild. **2.** not highly seasoned. **3.** dull.

blan·dish·ment (blan'dish mənt) n. coaxing or flattering words.

blank (blangk) adj. **1.** not written or printed on. **2.** without interest or expression. —n. **3.** a place or space where something is lacking. **4.** a printed form containing such spaces. **5.** a cartridge lacking a bullet. —blank'ness, n.

blan·ket (blang'kit) n. **1.** a warm bed covering. **2.** any extended covering. —v.t. **3.** to cover.

blare (blâr) v., **blared, blaring,** n. —v.i. **1.** to sound loudly. —n. **2.** a loud, raucous noise.

blar·ney (blär'nē) n. flattery.

bla·sé (blä zā') adj. bored.

blas·phe·my (blas'fə mē) n., pl. **-mies.** irreverent speech or action concerning sacred things. —blas·pheme', v.t., v.i. —blas·phe·mous, adj.

blast (blast) n. **1.** a gust of wind. **2.** a loud trumpet tone. **3.** an explosion. **4.** *Slang.* a very good time. —v.i. **5.** to explode. **6.** to produce a loud sound. —v.t. **7.** to blow. **8.** to destroy. —*Idiom.* **9. (at) full blast,** with full volume or speed.

blast' fur'nace n. a forced-air furnace for smelting iron ore.

blast'off' n. the launching of a rocket, spacecraft, etc.

bla·tant (blāt'nt) adj. very obvious. —bla·tan·cy, n. —bla·tant·ly, adv.

blaze¹ (blāz) n., v., **blazed, blazing.** —n. **1.** a bright fire. **2.** a bright, hot glow. **3.** a vivid display. **4.** an outburst. —v.i. **5.** to burn or shine brightly.

blaze² (blāz) n., v., **blazed, blazing.** —n. **1.** a mark made on a tree to indicate a trail. **2.** a white spot on an animal's face. —v.t. **3.** to mark with blazes.

blaz·er n. a solid-color or striped sports jacket.

bla·zon (blā'zən) v.t. **1.** to proclaim. **2.** to adorn.

bldg. building.

bleach (blēch) v.t., v.i. **1.** to make or become whiter. —n. **2.** a bleaching agent.

bleach·ers n.pl. tiers of spectators' seats.

bleak (blēk) adj. **1.** bare. **2.** cold and raw. **3.** dreary; depressing. —bleak'ly, adv. —bleak'ness, n.

blear·y (blēr'ē) adj. (of the eyesight) blurred or dimmed.

bleat (blēt) n. **1.** the cry of a sheep or goat. —v.i. **2.** to make such a cry.

bleed (blēd) v., **bled** (bled) **bleeding.** —v.i. **1.** to lose blood. **2.** to leak fluid. **3.** to run, as a dye. —v.t. **4.** to cause to lose blood. **5.** to drain fluid from. **6.** to extort money from.

bleep (blēp) v.t. to delete (sound, esp. speech) from a broadcast.

blem·ish (blem'ish) v.t. **1.** to spoil the perfection of. —n. **2.** a defect.

blend (blend) v.t. **1.** to mix smoothly so that the parts are no longer distinct. **2.** to mix, as tea or coffee, to produce a desired flavor. —v.i. **3.** to fit harmoniously. **4.** to have no visible separation. —n. **5.** something made by blending.

blend·er n. an electric appliance that purées or mixes food.

bless (bles) v.t., **blessed** or **blest, blessing. 1.** to make holy. **2.** to request divine favor on. **3.** to make happy.

blew (blōo) v. pt. of **blow.**

blight (blīt) n. **1.** a plant disease. **2.** a harmful influence. —v.t. **3.** to cause to wither. **4.** to ruin.

blimp (blimp) n. a small nonrigid airship.

blind (blīnd) adj. **1.** unable to see. **2.** uncontrolled. **3.** not based on reason or judgment. **4.** hidden. **5.** having no outlets. **6.** not easily seen. **7.** a window covering. **8.** a decoy or disguise. —blind'ly, adv. —blind'ness, n.

blind' date' n. an arranged date between two strangers.

blind'fold' v.t. **1.** to cover the eyes. —n. **2.** a covering over the eyes. —adj. **3.** with covered eyes.

blind'side' v.t., **-sided, -siding.** to hit someone unawares.

blink (blingk) v.i. **1.** to open and close the eyes rapidly. **2. blink at,** to ignore. **3.** the act of blinking. **4.** a gleam. —*Idiom.* **5. on the blink,** not working properly.

blink'er n. a flashing light.

blintz (blints) n. a thin pancake folded around a filling.

blip (blip) n. a spot of light on a radar screen.

bliss (blis) n. supreme happiness. —bliss'ful, adj.

blis·ter (blis'tər) n. **1.** a swelling on the skin containing watery liquid. —v.t. **2.** to raise blisters on.

blithe (blīth, blīth) adj. lighthearted; carefree. —blithe'ly, adv.

blitz (blits) n. **1.** a sudden and overwhelming military attack. **2.** any swift, vigorous attack. —v.t. **3.** to attack with a blitz.

bliz·zard (bliz'ərd) n. a severe snowstorm with high wind.

bloat (blōt) v.t. **1.** to expand or distend. —v.i. **2.** to become swollen.

blob (blob) n. **1.** a small lump or drop. **2.** a shapeless mass.

bloc (blok) n. a group, as of nations or legislators, united for a common purpose.

block (blok) n. **1.** a solid mass of wood, stone, etc. **2.** a quantity taken as a unit. **3.** an obstacle. **4.** an obstruction in a physical or mental process. **5.** a frame enclosing a pulley. **6.** a city section enclosed by intersecting streets or the length of one side of such a section. —v.t. **7.** to obstruct. **8. block out,** to outline roughly.

block·ade' (blo kād') n., v., **-aded, -ading.** —n. **1.** the closing off of a place by armed force. **2.** any obstruction. —v.t. **3.** to subject to a blockade.

block·age n. an obstruction.

block'bust'er n. a highly successful movie, novel, etc.

block'head' n. a stupid person.

block'house' n. a defensive military structure.

blond (blond) adj. **1.** having light-colored hair, skin, etc. **2.** light-colored. —n. **3.** a blond person.

blood (blud) n. **1.** the red fluid that circulates through the heart, veins, and arteries of animals. **2.** life. **3.** temperament. **4.** bloodshed. **5.** descent. **6.** kinship.

blood' count' n. the number of red and white blood cells in a specific volume of blood.

blood'cur'dling adj. causing terror.

blood' group' n. any of the classes into which human blood can be divided. Also called **blood' type'.**

blood'hound' n. a large dog with an acute sense of smell.

blood'mo·bile' (-mə bēl') n. a truck with equipment for receiving blood donations.

blood' pres'sure n. the pressure of the blood against the inner walls of the blood vessels.

blood'shed' n. killing or wounding.

blood'shot' adj. (of the eyes) red from dilated veins.

blood'stream' n. the blood flowing through the circulatory system.

blood'suck'er n. **1.** any creature that sucks blood. **2.** a person who extorts money.

blood'thirst'y adj. eager to shed blood.

blood' ves'sel n. an artery, vein, or capillary.

bloom (blōom) n. **1.** a flower. **2.** the state of flowering. **3.** a healthy glow. —v.i. **4.** to bear flowers. **5.** to flourish. —bloom'ing, adj.

bloom·ers (blōo'mərz) n.pl. short loose trousers formerly worn as underwear by women.

bloop·er (blōo'pər) n. an embarrassing mistake.

blos·som (blos'əm) n. **1.** a flower. —v.i. **2.** to produce blossoms. **3.** to develop.

blot (blot) n., v., **blotted, blotting.** —n. **1.** a spot or stain. —v.t. **2.** to spot or stain. **3.** to dry with absorb-

ent material. —v.i. **4.** to become blotted. **5. blot out,** to destroy.

blotch (bloch) n. **1.** a large spot. **2.** a skin blemish. —v.t. **3.** to mark with blotches. —blotch'y, adj.

blot·ter n. a piece of paper for blotting.

blouse (blous, blouz) n. a loose garment covering the upper body.

blow¹ (blō) n. **1.** a sudden, hard stroke. **2.** a sudden shock, calamity, etc.

blow² (blō) v., **blew, blown, blowing,** n. —v.i. **1.** (of the wind or air) to be in motion. **2.** to move along, carried by the wind. **3.** to produce a current of air. **4.** to give out sound by blowing or being blown. **5.** (of a fuse, tire, etc.) to be destroyed. —v.t. **6.** to drive by a current of air. **7.** to shape (glass, smoke, etc.) with a current of air. **8.** to cause to sound by blowing. **9.** to cause to explode. **10.** to melt (a fuse). **11.** *Informal.* to squander (money). **12.** *Informal.* to bungle. **13. blow over,** to subside. **14. ~ up, a.** to explode. **b.** to lose one's temper. —n. **15.** a blast of air or wind. —*Idiom.* **16. blow off steam,** to release tension.

blow'-by-blow' adj. detailed.

blow'-dry' v.t., **-dried, -dry·ing.** to dry or style (hair) with warm air from a hand-held appliance (**blow' dry'er**).

blow'out' n. a sudden rupture of a tire.

blow'pipe' n. a tube through which air or gas is forced.

blow'torch' n. a device producing a hot flame.

blow'up' n. **1.** an explosion. **2.** a violent outburst of temper. **3.** a photographic enlargement.

blowz·y (blou'zē) adj., **-i·er, -i·est.** disheveled. Also, **blows·y.**

blub·ber (blub'ər) n. **1.** the fat of whales. —v.i. **2.** to weep noisily.

bludg·eon (bluj'ən) n. **1.** a heavy club. —v.t. **2.** to strike with a bludgeon.

blue (blōo) n., adj., **bluer, bluest,** v., **blued, bluing** or **blueing.** —n. **1.** the color of a clear sky. —adj. **2.** of skin) discolored as by cold. **3.** depressed or unhappy. **4.** indecent. —v.t. **5.** to make blue. —*Idiom.* **6. out of the blue,** unexpectedly.

blue'ber·ry n., pl. **-ries.** the edible, usu. bluish, berry of certain shrubs.

blue'bird' n. a small blue North American songbird.

blue' blood' n. an aristocrat.

blue' cheese' n. a kind of strong-flavored cheese streaked with bluish mold.

blue' chip' n. a high-priced stock issued by a company known for its financial strength and the regular payment of dividends.

blue'-col'lar adj. of or designating manual laborers.

blue'jay' n. a crested jay with a bright blue back and gray breast.

blue' jeans' n.pl. trousers of blue denim.

blue' law' n. any law forbidding certain practices, as doing business, on Sunday.

blue'nose' n. a puritanical person.

blue'print' n. **1.** a white-on-blue photographic print of an architectural drawing. **2.** a plan of action.

blue' rib'bon n. the highest award.

blues n.pl. **1.** depression. **2.** a melancholy kind of jazz.

blue'stock'ing n. a woman with intellectual or interests.

bluff¹ (bluf) adj. **1.** good-naturedly frank. —n. **2.** a steep cliff or hill.

bluff² (bluf) v.t., v.i. **1.** to mislead (someone) by a show of confidence. —n. **2.** the act of bluffing. **3.** one who bluffs. —*Idiom.* **4. call someone's bluff,** to challenge someone to carry out a threat.

blu'ing n. a bleaching agent.

blun·der (blun'dər) n. **1.** a mistake. —v.i. **2.** to make a mistake. **3.** to move clumsily.

blun·der·buss' (-bus') n. **1.** a short musket that scatters shot at close range. **2.** an insensitive person.

blunt (blunt) adj. **1.** having a dull edge or point. **2.** abrupt in manner. —v.t., v.i. **3.** to make or become blunt. —blunt'ly, adv.

blur (blûr) v., **blurred, blurring,** n. —v.t., v.i. **1.** to make or become indistinct. —n. **2.** a smudge. **3.** a blurred condition or thing. —blur'ry, adj.

blurb (blûrb) n. a brief advertisement.

blurt (blûrt) v.t. to utter suddenly or tactlessly.

blush (blush) v.i. **1.** to redden. **2.** to feel embarrassment. —n. **3.** a reddening. **4.** a reddish tinge.

blush′er n. a cosmetic used to color the cheeks.

blus′ter (blus′tər) v.i. **1.** to blow stormily. **2.** to talk in an aggressive, swaggering manner. —n. **3.** boisterous noise and violence. **4.** noisy, empty threats.

blvd. boulevard.

bo′a (bō′ə) n. **1.** a large snake that crushes its prey. **2.** a long scarf of silk or feathers.

boar (bôr) n. a male swine.

board (bôrd) n. **1.** a thin flat piece of timber or stiff material. **2.** an official controlling body. **3.** daily meals provided for a fixed price. —v.t. **4.** to cover with boards. **5.** to enter (a ship, train, etc.). —v.i. **6.** to take one's meals for a fixed price. —Idiom. **7. on board**, on or in a ship, plane, etc. —board′er, n.

board′ing·house′ n. a house where one can get room and board for payment.

board′walk′ n. a wooden walk along a beach.

boast (bōst) v.i. **1.** to speak with excessive pride; brag. —v.t. **2.** to speak of with excessive pride. **3.** to be proud to own. —n. **4.** a thing boasted (of). **5.** bragging.

boat (bōt) n. **1.** a vessel for transport by water. —v.i. **2.** to go or move in a boat. —Idiom. **3. in the same boat**, in a similar difficult situation. —boat′ing, n.

boat′house′ (bōt′hous′) n., pl. -houses (-hou′ziz). a shed for sheltering boats at the water's edge.

boat′man (bōt′mən) n., pl. -men. a person who sails, rents, or works on boats.

boat′swain (bō′sən) n. a ship's officer in charge of deck work.

bob¹ (bob) n., v., **bobbed**, **bobbing.** —n. **1.** a short, jerky motion. —v.t., v.i. **2.** to move quickly down and up.

bob² (bob) n., v., **bobbed**, **bobbing.** —n. **1.** a short haircut. —v.t. **2.** to cut short.

bob′bin (bob′in) n. a reel or spool for thread.

bob′by pin n. a flat metal hairpin.

bob′cat′ n., pl. -cats, -cat. a North American lynx.

bob′o·link′ (-ə lingk′) n. a meadow-dwelling songbird.

bob′sled′ n., v., **-sledded, -sledding.** —n. **1.** a long sled with two pairs of runners and a steering mechanism. —v.i. **2.** to ride on a bobsled.

bob′tail′ n. **1.** a short tail. **2.** an animal with such a tail.

bob′white′ n. a North American quail.

bode (bōd) v.t., v.i., **boded, boding.** to be a sign of.

bo·de′ga (bō dā′gə) n. (esp. among Spanish-speaking Americans) a grocery store.

bod′ice (bod′is) n. the top part of a dress.

bod′y (bod′ē) n., pl. **bodies. 1.** the physical structure and substance of an animal. **2.** the torso. **3.** a corpse. **4.** the main or central part of a thing. **5.** a separate physical mass, as of land or water. **6.** a group regarded as a unit. **7.** substance; density.

bod′y·guard′ n. a person employed to protect someone.

bo′dy lang′uage n. communication through gestures or attitudes.

bo′dy pierc′ing n. the piercing of a body part, as the navel, to insert an ornamental ring or stud.

bod′y pol′itic n. a people forming a political body under a government.

bog (bog) n., v., **bogged, bogging.** —n. **1.** swampy ground. —v. **2. bog down**, to sink in or as if in a bog. —bog′gy, adj.

bog′gle (bog′əl) v., **-gled, -gling.** —v.t., v.i. to bewilder or be bewildered.

bo′gus (bō′gəs) adj. fake.

bo′gy (bō′gē, bōog′ē, bōō′gē) n., pl. **-gies.** anything that frightens. Also, **bo′gey, bo′gie.**

bo·he′mi·an (bō hē′mē ən) n. **1.** one who leads an unconventional life. —adj. **2.** unconventional.

boil¹ (boil) v.i. **1.** to bubble up and change into a gas as the result of heating. **2.** to be very angry. —v.t. **3.** to cause to boil. **4.** to cook in boiling liquid. —n. **5.** the act or state of boiling.

boil² (boil) n. an inflamed sore.

boil′ing point′ n. the temperature

at which a liquid boils, equal to 212°F (100°C) for water at sea level.

bois′ter·ous (boi′stər əs) adj. rough; noisy.

bok′ choy′ (bok′ choy′) n. an Asian plant whose leaves are used as a vegetable. Also, **bok′-choy′.**

bold (bōld) adj. **1.** courageous and daring. **2.** vivid; prominent. —bold′ly, adv.

bo·le′ro (bə lâr′ō, bō-) n., pl. -ros. **1.** a lively Spanish dance. **2.** a waist-length, open jacket.

boll (bōl) n. a rounded seed pod of a plant.

boll′ wee′vil n. a beetle that attacks bolls of cotton.

bo·lo′gna (bə lō′nē) n. a beef and pork sausage.

bol′ster (bōl′stər) n. **1.** a long pillow. —v.t. **2.** to support.

bolt (bōlt) n. **1.** a bar fastening a door. **2.** a similar part in a lock. **3.** a threaded metal pin. **4.** a sudden flight. **5.** a roll of cloth. **6.** a thunderbolt. —v.t. **7.** to fasten with a bolt. **8.** to swallow hurriedly. —v.i. **9.** to move or leave suddenly.

bomb (bom) n. **1.** a case filled with explosive material and set off by a detonating device or by impact. **2.** Slang. a total failure. —v.t. **3.** to attack with bombs. —v.i. **4.** Slang. to fail totally. —bomb′proof′, adj.

bom·bard′ (bom bärd′) v.t. **1.** to attack with artillery or bombs. **2.** to attack with questions, suggestions, etc. **3.** to direct particles or radiation against. —bom′bar·dier′ (-bər dēr′) n. —bom·bard′ment, n.

bom′bast (bom′bast) n. pompous words. —bom·bas′tic, adj.

bomb′er (bom′ər) n. **1.** an airplane that drops bombs. **2.** a person who drops or sets bombs.

bomb′shell′ n. something or someone having a sensational effect.

bo′na fide′ (bō′nə fīd′) adj. **1.** made or done in good faith. **2.** genuine.

bo·nan′za (bə nan′zə) n. **1.** a rich mass of ore. **2.** a source of riches.

bon′bon′ (bon′bon′) n. a piece of candy.

bond (bond) n. **1.** something that binds, confines, or unites. **2.** a written contractual obligation. **3.** an interest-bearing certificate of debt due to be paid to an individual. **4.** a put on or under bond. **5.** to connect.

bond′age (bon′dij) n. slavery.

bonds′man n., pl. **-men.** a person who gives surety for another.

bone (bōn) n., v., **boned, boning.** —n. **1.** one of the structures composing the skeleton. **2.** the hard substance forming it. —v.t. **3.** to remove the bones of. —Idiom. **4. to have a bone to pick with**, to have a reason to reproach. **5. make no bones about**, to speak openly about. —bon′y, adj.

bone′ chi′na n. a fine, white china.

bone′-dry′ adj. very dry.

bon′er (bō′nər) n. Slang. a stupid mistake.

bon′fire′ (bon′-) n. a large outdoor fire.

bon′go (bong′gō) n., pl. **-gos, -goes.** a small hand drum.

bon·jour′ (bôN zhōōr′) interj. French. hello.

bon′kers (bong′kərz) adj. Slang. crazy.

bon mot (bôN mō′) n., pl. **bons mots** (bôN mōz′). a witty comment.

bon′net (bon′it) n. a hat with strings tied under the chin.

bo·no′bo (bə nō′bō) n., pl. **-bos.** a kind of small chimpanzee.

bon′sai (bon sī′, bōn-) n., pl. **-sai.** a dwarf tree or shrub.

bo′nus (bō′nəs) n. something given or paid beyond what is due.

boo (bōō) interj. (an exclamation used to frighten or express contempt.)

boo′-boo′ n. Slang. **1.** a stupid mistake. **2.** a minor injury.

boo′by (bōō′bē) n., pl. **-bies.** Informal. a fool. Also, **boob.**

boo′by prize′ n. a prize given to the worst player in a contest.

boo′by trap′ n. a trap set for an unsuspecting person.

book (bōōk) n. **1.** printed or blank sheets bound together. **2.** a long literary work or a division of one. **3.** books, accounts. —v.t. **4.** to reserve. **5.** to enter in a book. **6.** to enter a charge against (an arrested person).

book′bind′ing (bōōk′bīn′ding) n. **1.** the process of binding books. —book′bind′er, n.

book′case′ n. a set of shelves for books.

book′end′ n. a support for holding up a row of books.

book′ie n. a bookmaker.

book′ing n. an engagement of a professional entertainer.

book′ish adj. fond of reading.

book′keep′ing n. the system of keeping records of business transactions. —book′keep′er, n.

book′let (-lit) n. a pamphlet.

book′mak′er n. a person whose business is taking bets.

book′mark′ n. something used to mark one's place in a book.

book′store′ (bōōk′stôr′) n. a store where books are sold. Also, **book′shop.**

book′worm′ n. a person who likes to read.

boom¹ (bōōm) v.i. **1.** to make a loud hollow sound. **2.** to flourish vigorously. —n. **3.** a loud hollow sound. **4.** rapid economic development.

boom² (bōōm) n. **1.** a long pole on a ship's mast, used to extend a sail. **2.** a floating chain, cable, etc., used to block navigation. **3.** a beam on a derrick, used to support objects to be lifted.

boom′er·ang′ (bōō′mə rang′) n. **1.** a curved piece of wood that returns when thrown. —v.i. **2.** to cause harm to the originator.

boon¹ (bōōn) n. a benefit.

boon² (bōōn) adj. **boon companion,** a jolly, pleasant companion.

boon′docks′ n.pl. **1.** a backwoods. **2.** a remote rural area.

boon′dog′gle (-dog′əl) n. Informal. useless work paid for with public money.

boor (bōōr) n. an unmannerly, rude person. —boor′ish, adj.

boost (bōōst) v.t. **1.** to lift by pushing. **2.** to aid by speaking well of. **3.** to increase. —n. **4.** an upward push. **5.** an act or comment that helps someone. **6.** an increase. —boost′er, n.

boot (bōōt) n. **1.** a covering for the foot and leg. **2.** a kick. —v.t. **3.** to kick. —Idiom. **4. to boot,** in addition.

booth (bōōth) n. **1.** a light structure for the sale or display of goods. **2.** a small compartment.

boot′leg′ n., v., **-legged, -legging.** adj. —n. **1.** something, esp. liquor, that is made or sold illegally. —v.t., v.i. **2.** to deal in (liquor or other goods) illegally. —adj. **3.** made or sold illegally. —boot′leg′ger, n.

boot′less adj. futile; useless.

boo′ty (bōō′tē) n. loot.

booze (bōōz) n., v., **boozed, boozing.** Informal. —n. **1.** liquor. —v.i. **2.** to drink liquor excessively.

bo′rax (bôr′aks) n. a white crystalline substance used as a cleanser, in glassmaking, etc.

Bor·deaux′ (bôr dō′) n., pl. **-deaux** (-dōz′). a type of wine produced in the region around Bordeaux in SW France.

bor·del′lo (bôr del′ō) n. a brothel.

bor′der (bôr′dər) n. **1.** an edge or boundary. **2.** the dividing line between one country, state, etc., and another. **3.** an ornamental design around an edge. —v.t. **4.** to make a border around. **5.** to form a border to. **6.** to adjoin. **7. border on,** a. to come close to being. **b.** to be next to.

bor′der·line′ n. **1.** a boundary. —adj. **2.** not definite.

bore¹ (bôr) v., **bored, boring.** —v.t. **1.** to drill into. **2.** to make (a hole) by drilling or digging. —v.i. **3.** to make a hole. —n. **4.** a bored hole. **5.** the inside diameter of a hole or cylinder.

bore² (bôr) v., **bored, boring.** —v.t. **1.** to weary by dullness. —n. **2.** a dull person or thing. —bore′dom, n.

bo′ric ac′id (bôr′ik) n. a white powder, used in solution as an antiseptic.

born (bôrn) adj. **1.** brought forth by birth. **2.** having a certain quality from birth.

born′-a·gain′ adj. recommitted to faith through an intense religious experience.

bor′ough (bûr′ō, bur′ō) n. **1.** a small incorporated town. **2.** one of the five divisions of New York City.

bor′row (bor′ō) v.t., v.i. **1.** to take or obtain on loan. **2.** to appropriate. —Usage. Do not confuse BORROW and LEND. Think of BORROW as "take," while LEND is "give." So you can *borrow* something you don't have, and you can *lend* something you do have.

borscht (bôrsht) n. a beet soup.

bos′om (bōōz′əm, bōō′zəm) n. **1.** the breast. **2. bosom friend,** a very close friend.

boss (bôs) n. **1.** an employer. **2.** a politician who controls the party organization. **3.** a person who is in charge. —v.t. **4.** to control; manage. **5.** to order about. —boss′y, adj.

bot (bot) n. a piece of software that can execute commands without user intervention.

bot′a·ny (bot′n ē) n. the science that deals with plant life. —bo·tan′i·cal (bə tan′i kəl) adj. —bot′a·nist, n.

botch (boch) v.t. **1.** to bungle. **2.** to patch clumsily. —n. **3.** a poor piece of work.

both (bōth) adj., pron. **1.** one and the other; the two. —conj. **2.** (used before words or phrases joined by and to indicate that each of the joined elements is included).

both′er (both′ər) v.t., v.i. **1.** to annoy (someone). **2.** to trouble or inconvenience (oneself). —n. **3.** trouble. —both′er·some (-səm) adj. causing annoyance or worry.

bot′tle (bot′l) n., v., **-tled, -tling.** —n. **1.** a narrow-necked glass or plastic container for liquids. —v.t. **2.** to put into a bottle.

bot′tle·neck′ n. **1.** a narrow passage. **2.** a place at which progress is obstructed.

bot′tom (bot′əm) n. **1.** the lowest part. **2.** the underside. **3.** the ground under a body of water. **4.** the seat of a chair. **5.** Informal. the buttocks. —adj. **6.** lowest. —v. **7. bottom out,** to reach the lowest level. —Idiom. **8. at bottom,** fundamentally.

bot′tom·less adj. **1.** without bottom. **2.** without limit.

bot′tom line′ n. **1.** the line of a financial statement that shows profit and loss. **2.** the final outcome.

bot′u·lism′ (boch′ə liz′əm) n. a sometimes fatal disease caused by eating spoiled foods.

bou·doir′ (bōō′dwär, -dwôr) n. a woman's bedroom or private room.

bouf·fant′ (bōō fänt′) adj. puffed out, as a hairdo.

bou·gain·vil·le·a (bōō′gən vil′ē ə, -vil′yə) n., pl. **-as.** a climbing shrub having small brightly colored flowers.

bough (bou) n. a branch of a tree.

bouil·la·baisse′ (bōō′yə bäs′, bōōl′-) n. a fish stew.

bouil′lon (bōōl′yon, -yən, bōō′-) n. a clear broth.

boul′der (bōl′dər) n. a large rock.

boul′e·vard′ (bōōl′ə värd′) n. a broad avenue.

bounce (bouns) v., **bounced, bouncing,** n. —v.i. **1.** to strike a surface and rebound. **2.** to move in a lively manner. **3.** (of a check) to be refused because of insufficient funds in the account. —v.t. **4.** to cause to bounce. —n. **5.** a bound or rebound. **6.** a sudden leap. **7.** liveliness. —bounc′y, adj.

bounc′er n. a person employed to eject disorderly patrons from a bar, nightclub, etc.

bounc′ing adj. healthy.

bound¹ (bound) v. **1.** pt. and pp. of **bind.** —adj. **2.** tied. **3.** made into a book. **4.** obligated. **5.** certain.

bound² (bound) v.i. **1.** to move by leaps. —n. **2.** a jump or bounce.

bound³ (bound) n. **1. bounds,** boundary. —v.t. **2.** to limit. **3.** to form the boundary of. —Idiom. **4. out of bounds,** beyond the permitted limits.

bound⁴ (bound) adj. going.

bound′a·ry (boun′də rē, -drē) n., pl. **-ries.** something marking limits.

bound′less adj. unlimited.

boun′te·ous (boun′tē əs) adj. generous. Also, **boun′ti·ful.**

boun′ty n., pl. **-ties. 1.** generosity. **2.** a generous gift. **3.** a reward.

bou·quet′ (bō kā′, bōō-) n. **1.** a bunch of flowers. **2.** an aroma.

bour′bon (bûr′bən) n. corn whiskey.

bour·geois′ (bōōr zhwä′) n., pl. **-geois,** adj. —n. **1.** a member of the middle class. **2.** a person who is overly concerned with respectability.

bour·geoi·sie′ (-zē′) n. the middle class.

bout (bout) n. **1.** a contest. **2.** a period; spell.

bou·tique′ (bōō tēk′) n. a small shop with fashionable items.

bo′vine (bō′vīn, -vēn) adj. **1.** of or resembling an ox or cow. **2.** dull.

bo′vine spon′gi·form encepha-

lop′athy (spun′jə fôrm′ en sef′ə-lop′ə thē), n. a fatal dementia of cattle. Also called **mad cow disease.**

bow¹ (bou) v.i. **1.** to bend the body or head, as in respect or greeting. **2.** to submit. —v.t. **3.** to bend (the body or head). **4.** to subdue. —n. **5.** a bending of the body or head in respect, greeting, etc. —Idiom. **6. take a bow,** to stand up to receive applause.

bow² (bō) n. **1.** a strip of bent wood for shooting arrows. **2.** a bend or curve. **3.** a looped knot. **4.** a rod strung with horsehairs, for playing the violin, cello, etc. —v.t., v.i. **5.** to bend; curve.

bow³ (bou) n. the forward end of a ship or boat.

bowd′ler·ize′ (bōd′lə rīz′, boud′-) v.t., **-ized, -izing.** to expurgate (a written work) in a prudish manner.

bow′el (bou′əl, boul) n. **1.** the intestine. Also, **bow′els. 2.** bowels, the innermost parts.

bow′er (bou′ər) n. a leafy shelter.

bow′ie knife′ (bō′ē, bōō′ē) n. a heavy knife with a long, single-edged blade.

bowl¹ (bōl) n. **1.** a deep, round dish. **2.** a rounded, hollow part. **3.** a stadium.

bowl² (bōl) n. **1.** a delivery of the ball in bowling. —v.i. **2.** to play at bowling. **3.** to move along smoothly and rapidly. —v.t. **4.** to roll (a ball) in bowling. **5. bowl over,** to surprise greatly.

bow′leg′ged (bō′leg′id) adj. having legs curved outward.

bow′man (bō′mən) n., pl. **-men.** an archer.

box (boks) n. **1.** a container or case, usu. having a lid. **2.** a compartment. **3.** a blow with the fist. **4.** Also, **box′wood′.** an evergreen tree or shrub. —v.t. **5.** to put into a box. —v.i. **6.** to fight with the fists. —box′er, n. —box′ing, n.

box′car′ n. a railroad freight car that is completely enclosed.

box′ of′fice n. an office at which tickets for a performance are sold.

boy (boi) n. a male child. —boy′hood, n. —boy′ish, adj.

boy′cott (-kot) v.t. **1.** to refuse to deal with or buy from. —n. **2.** the act of boycotting.

boy′friend′ n. **1.** a male sweetheart or lover. **2.** a male friend.

boy′sen·ber′ry (boi′zən ber′ē) n., pl. **-ries.** a blackberrylike fruit with a flavor similar to that of raspberries.

bra (brä) n. a woman's undergarment for supporting the breasts.

brace (brās) n., v., **braced, bracing.** —n. **1.** a device that holds parts together or in place. **2.** anything that stiffens or steadies. **3.** a character, {or}, used to connect words or lines to be considered together. **4. braces,** a device for straightening the teeth. **5.** a pair. —v.t. **6.** to fasten or strengthen with a brace. **7.** to steady (oneself).

brace′let (brās′lit) n. an ornamental band for the wrist.

brack′et (brak′it) n. **1.** a supporting piece projecting from a wall. **2.** either of two marks, [or], for enclosing parenthetical words. —v.t. **3.** to place within brackets.

brack′ish (brak′ish) adj. salty.

brad (brad) n. a small wire nail.

brag (brag) v.i., v.t., **bragged, bragging.** to boast.

brag·ga·do·ci·o (brag′ə dō′shē ō′) n., pl. **-os. 1.** empty boasting. **2.** a braggart.

brag′gart (-ərt) n. a person who brags a lot.

braid (brād) v.t. **1.** to weave together three or more strands of. —n. **2.** something braided.

Braille (brāl) n. a system of writing for the blind, using combinations of raised dots.

brain (brān) n. **1.** the part of the central nervous system enclosed in the skull of vertebrates. **2.** Sometimes, **brains.** intelligence. —v.t. **3.** to smash the skull of.

brain′ death′ n. the complete ending of brain function: used as a legal definition of death. —brain′-dead′, adj.

brain′ drain′ n. the loss of trained professional personnel to another company, nation, etc.

brain′storm′ n. a sudden idea.

brain'wash' *v.t.* to subject to brainwashing.

brain' wave' *n.* Usu., brain waves. electrical impulses given off by the brain.

braise (brāz) *v.t.*, braised, braising. to cook slowly in a small amount of liquid in a closed container.

brake (brāk) *n., v.*, braked, braking. —*n.* 1. a device for stopping a vehicle. —*v.t., v.i.* 2. to slow or stop with a brake.

bram'ble (bram'bəl) *n.* a prickly shrub.

bran (bran) *n.* the partly ground husk of grain.

branch (branch) *n.* 1. a division of the stem of a tree or shrub. 2. a local office or store of a large organization. 3. a section of a body or system. 4. a division of a family. —*v.i.* 5. to put out or divide into branches. 6. branch off, to divide into separate parts. 7. branch out, to expand or extend.

brand (brand) *n.* 1. kind or make. 2. a mark of ownership made by burning. 3. a burning piece of wood. 4. a mark of disgrace. —*v.t.* 5. to mark with a brand. 6. to put a mark of disgrace on.

brand'ish (bran'dish) *v.t.* to wave or flourish.

brand'-new' (bran'-, brand'-) *adj.* extremely new.

bran'dy (bran'dē) *n., pl.* -dies. a spirit distilled from wine.

brash (brash) *adj.* 1. impudent; tactless. 2. rash; impetuous.

brass (bras) *n.* 1. an alloy of copper and zinc. 2. the brass instruments of a band or orchestra. 3. high-ranking officials. 4. bold impudence. —**brass'y,** *adj.*

bras·siere' (brə zēr') *n.* a bra.

brass tacks *n.pl.* basic facts.

brat (brat) *n.* a spoiled or rude child.

brat'wurst' (brat'wûrst, -vŏorst', brät'-) *n.* a kind of pork sausage.

bra·va'do (brə vä'dō) *n.* boasting; swaggering.

brave (brāv) *adj.*, braver, bravest, *n., v.*, braved, braving. —*adj.* 1. courageous. —*n.* 2. a North American Indian warrior. —*v.t.* 3. to meet courageously. 4. to defy. —**brave'ly,** *adv.*

bra'vo (brä'vō, brä vō') *interj.* well done!

brawl (brôl) *n.* 1. a noisy quarrel. —*v.i.* 2. to quarrel noisily.

brawn (brôn) *n.* 1. muscles. 2. muscular strength. —**brawn'y,** *adj.*

bray (brā) *n.* 1. a harsh cry, as of a donkey. —*v.i.* 2. to sound a bray.

bra'zen (brā'zən) *adj.* 1. of or like brass. 2. shameless; impudent.

bra'zier (brā'zhər) *n.* a metal stand for holding burning coals.

Bra·zil' nut' (brə zil') *n.* the three-sided edible seed of a South American tree.

breach (brēch) *n.* 1. a gap. 2. a violation, as of a law. 3. a severance of friendly relations. —*v.t.* 4. to make a breach in.

bread (bred) *n.* 1. a baked food made of dough. 2. livelihood. —*v.t.* 3. to cover with breadcrumbs.

bread'crumb' *n.* a crumb of bread.

breadth (bredth, bretth) *n.* 1. width. 2. extent.

bread'win'ner *n.* a person who earns a livelihood to support dependents.

break (brāk) *v.*, broke (brōk) broken, breaking. —*v.t.* 1. to split into pieces. 2. to make useless. 3. to fracture. 4. to fail to keep (a promise, law, etc.) 5. to reveal, as news. 6. to ruin financially. 7. to wear down the spirit of. —*v.i.* 8. to split into fragments. 9. to become useless. 10. to become disconnected. 11. to interrupt an activity. 12. break down, to cease to function. 13. ~ out, a. to begin abruptly. b. to become visible. c. to escape. —*n.* 14. an opening made by breaking. 15. the act of breaking. 16. an interruption. 17. a brief rest. 18. an abrupt change. 19. an opportunity. —**break'a·ble,** *adj.* —**break'age,** *n.*

break'down' *n.* 1. a mechanical failure. 2. a mental or physical collapse. 3. an analysis.

break'er *n.* a wave breaking on land.

break'fast (brek'fəst) *n.* 1. the first meal of the day. —*v.i.* 2. to eat breakfast.

break'-in' (brāk'-) *n.* illegal forcible entry into a home, office, etc.

break'neck' *adj.* reckless or dangerous.

break'through' *n.* an important discovery.

break'up' *n.* 1. a separation or scattering of the parts of something. 2. the ending of a personal relationship.

break'wa'ter *n.* a barrier that breaks the force of waves.

breast (brest) *n.* 1. the chest. 2. a milk-producing gland on a woman's body. —*v.t.* 3. to meet or oppose boldly.

breast'bone' *n.* the sternum.

breast'-feed' *v.t.*, -fed, -feed·ing. to nurse (a baby) at the breast.

breast'stroke' *n.* a swimming stroke in which the arms are swept to the sides while the legs kick outward.

breath (breth) *n.* 1. the air taken into the lungs and then let out. 2. the act of breathing. 3. life. 4. a slight breeze. —*Idiom.* 5. out of breath, gasping for breath. 6. under one's breath, in a whisper. —**breath'less,** *adj.*

breathe (brēth) *v.*, breathed, breathing. —*v.t.* 1. to take (air) into the lungs and let it out again. 2. to whisper. —*v.i.* 3. to inhale and exhale. 4. to live.

breath'er (brē'thər) *n.* a pause for rest.

breath'tak'ing (breth'-) *adj.* astonishingly beautiful or exciting.

breech'es (brich'iz) *n.pl.* trousers.

breed (brēd) *v.*, bred (bred), breeding, *n.* —*v.t.* 1. to produce (offspring). 2. to give rise to. 3. to bring up. 4. to raise (animals). —*v.i.* 5. to produce offspring. 6. to be produced. —*n.* 7. a stock; strain. 8. sort or kind.

breed'ing *n.* 1. ancestry. 2. training. 3. manners.

breeze (brēz) *n.* a light current of air.

breeze'way' *n.* an open-sided roofed passageway joining two buildings.

breth·ren (breth'rin) *n.pl.* 1. fellow members. 2. *Old use.* brothers.

bre·vi·ar·y (brē'vē er'ē, brev'ē-) *n., pl.* -aries. a book of daily prayers and readings.

brev'i·ty (brev'i tē) *n.* shortness.

brew (brōō) *v.t.* 1. to make (beer) by boiling and fermenting the ingredients. 2. to prepare (tea or coffee) by boiling and steeping. 3. to bring about. —*v.i.* 4. to make beer. 5. to begin to form. —*n.* 6. a brewed beverage. —**brew'er·y,** *n.*

bri'ar (brī'ər) *n.* a brier.

bribe (brīb) *n., v.*, bribed, bribing. —*n.* 1. anything given to persuade or influence. —*v.t.* 2. to give or influence by a bribe. —**brib'er·y,** *n.*

bric-a-brac (brik'ə brak') *n.* trinkets.

brick (brik) *n.* 1. a building block of baked clay. —*v.t.* 2. to pave or build with brick.

brick'bat' *n.* 1. a fragment of brick. 2. a caustic criticism.

brid'al (brīd'l) *adj.* of or for a bride or a wedding.

bride (brīd) *n.* a woman newly married or about to be married.

bride'groom' *n.* a man newly married or about to be married.

brides'maid' *n.* a bride's wedding attendant.

bridge¹ (brij) *n., v.*, bridged, bridging. —*n.* 1. a structure spanning a river, road, etc. 2. a raised platform from which a ship is navigated. 3. the bony ridge of the nose. 4. an artificial replacement for a missing tooth. —*v.t.* 5. to make a bridge or passage over.

bridge² (brij) *n.* a card game for two pairs of players.

bridge'head' *n.* a military position held on a hostile river shore.

bridge'work' *n.* a dental bridge.

bri'dle (brīd'l) *n., v.*, -dled, -dling. —*n.* 1. the head harness of a horse. 2. anything that restrains. —*v.t.* 3. to put a bridle on. 4. to restrain.

bri'dle path' *n.* a wide path for riding horses.

brief (brēf) *adj.* 1. short. 2. concise. —*n.* 3. a summary. 4. a concise statement of the facts of a legal case. 5. briefs, close-fitting legless underpants. —*v.t.* 6. to make a summary of. 7. to instruct by a brief. —**brief'ly,** *adv.*

brief'case' *n.* a flat case for carrying papers.

bri'er (brī'ər) *n.* a prickly plant.

brig (brig) *n.* 1. a two-masted square-rigged ship. 2. a military prison.

bri·gade' (bri gād') *n.* a military unit forming part of a division. 2. a group organized for a specific purpose.

brig'a·dier' (brig'ə dēr') *n.* an army officer ranking between a colonel and a major general. Also, **brig'adier gen'eral.**

brig'and (brig'ənd) *n.* a bandit.

bright (brīt) *adj.* 1. giving out much light. 2. brilliant. 3. intelligent. 4. cheerful; lively. —**bright'en,** *v.i., v.t.* —**bright'ly,** *adv.* —**bright'ness,** *n.*

bril'liant (bril'yənt) *adj.* 1. shining brightly. 2. outstanding. 3. highly intelligent. —**bril'liance,** *n.*

brim (brim) *n., v.*, brimmed, brimming. —*n.* 1. the upper edge; rim. —*v.i., v.t.* 2. to fill or be full to the brim. —**brim'ful,** *adj.*

brim'stone' *n.* sulfur.

brin'dled *adj.* gray or brown with darker streaks.

brine (brīn) *n.* 1. salt water. 2. the sea. —**brin'y,** *adj.*

bring (bring) *v.t.*, brought (brôt), bringing. 1. to carry. 2. to cause to come. 3. to cause to occur. 4. bring about, to cause. 5. ~ forth, to produce. 6. ~ off, to accomplish. 7. ~ up, a. to rear, as a child. b. to mention. c. to vomit.

brink (bringk) *n.* 1. the edge of a steep place. 2. any extreme edge.

bri·quette' (bri ket') *n.* a small block of charcoal. Also, **bri·quet'.**

brisk (brisk) *adj.* 1. lively. 2. stimulating. —**brisk'ly,** *adv.*

bris'ket (bris'kit) *n.* the meat from an animal's breast.

bris'tle (bris'əl) *n., v.*, -tled, -tling. —*n.* 1. a short, stiff, coarse hair. —*v.i.* 2. to raise bristles, as in anger. 3. to show indignation. 4. to be thickly filled.

britch'es (brich'iz) *n.* (*used with a pl. v.*) breeches.

Brit'ish (brit'ish) *adj.* of Great Britain or its inhabitants.

Brit'ish ther'mal u'nit. the amount of heat needed to raise the temperature of 1 lb. (0.4 kg) of water 1°F. *Abbr.:* Btu, BTU

Brit'on (brit'n) *n.* a native of Great Britain.

brit'tle (brit'l) *adj.* hard but breaking easily.

broach (brōch) *v.t.* 1. to mention for the first time. 2. to pierce.

broad (brôd) *adj.* 1. large from side to side; wide. 2. having great extent. 3. not limited. 4. tolerant. 5. general. 6. plain or clear. —**broad'ly,** *adv.*

broad'cast' *v.*, -cast or -casted, -casting, *n.* —*v.t., v.i.* 1. to send (programs) by radio or television. 2. to scatter. —*n.* 3. something broadcast. 4. a radio or television program. —**broad'cast'er,** *n.*

broad'cloth' *n.* fine cotton material.

broad'en *v.i., v.t.* to make wider.

broad' jump' *n.* long jump.

broad'loom' *n.* any carpet woven on a wide loom.

broad'-mind'ed *adj.* tolerant.

broad'side' *n., adv., v.*, -sided, -siding. —*n.* 1. the simultaneous firing of all guns on one side of a warship. 2. a verbal attack. —*adv.* 3. directly on the side. —*v.t.* 4. to hit broadside.

broad'-spec'trum *adj.* (of antibiotics) effective against a wide range of organisms.

bro·cade' (brō kād') *n.* a woven fabric with a raised design.

broc'co·li (brok'ə lē) *n.* a green plant with edible flower heads.

bro·chure' (brō shŏor') *n.* a pamphlet; booklet.

brogue (brōg) *n.* an Irish accent.

broil (broil) *v.t., v.i.* to cook by direct heat. —**broil'er,** *n.*

broke (brōk) *v.* 1. pt. of break. —*adj.* 2. without money.

bro'ken (brō'kən) *v.* 1. pp. of break. —*adj.* 2. fragmented or fractured. 3. not functioning. 4. interrupted. 5. violated. 6. imperfectly spoken.

bro'ken-heart'ed *adj.* sorrowing deeply.

bro'ker *n.* an agent who buys and sells for a fee.

bro'mide (brō'mīd, -mid) *n.* 1. a chemical compound used as a sedative. 2. a trite saying.

bro'mine (brō'mēn, -min) *n.* a reddish, toxic liquid element.

bron'chi·al (brong'kē əl) *adj.* of the bronchi, the two branches of the windpipe.

bron·chi'tis (-kī'tis) *n.* an inflammation of the lining of the bronchial tubes.

bron'co (brong'kō) *n., pl.* -cos. a wild pony or small horse of the western U.S.

bron·to·saur (bron'tə sôr') or **bron·to·sau'rus** (-sôr'əs) *n., pl.* -saurs or -sauruses, -sauri (-sôr'ī). a huge herbivorous dinosaur.

bronze (bronz) *n.* 1. an alloy of copper and tin. 2. a brownish color.

brooch (brōch) *n.* an ornamental clasp or pin.

brood (brōōd) *n.* 1. young born or hatched at one time. —*v.i.* 2. to sit on eggs to be hatched. 3. to think in a troubled or morbid way.

brook¹ (brŏok) *n.* a small natural stream of fresh water.

brook² (brŏok) *v.t.* to bear; tolerate.

broom (brōōm, brŏom) *n.* 1. a long-handled sweeping implement. 2. a shrub bearing yellow flowers.

broom'stick' *n.* the handle of a broom.

bros. brothers.

broth (brôth) *n.* a thin soup made by simmering meat, fish, etc.

broth'el (broth'əl) *n.* a house where women work as prostitutes.

broth'er (bruth'ər) *n.* 1. a male child of the same parents as another person. 2. a male in the same group as another. 3. a male member of a religious order. —**broth'er·ly,** *adv.*

broth'er·hood' *n.* 1. the condition or quality of being a brother or brothers. 2. fellowship. 3. those engaged in a given trade.

broth'er-in-law' *n., pl.* brothers-in-law. 1. one's husband's or wife's brother. 2. one's sister's husband.

brought (brôt) *v.* pt. and pp. of bring.

brou·ha·ha' (brōō'hä hä') *n., pl.* -has. an uproar.

brow (brou) *n.* 1. an eyebrow. 2. the forehead. 3. the edge of a steep place.

brow'beat' *v.t.*, -beat, -beaten, -beating. to intimidate.

brown (broun) *n.* 1. a dark reddish or yellowish color. —*v.t., v.i.* 2. to make or become brown.

brown'-bag' *v.t.*, -bagged, -bagging. to bring (one's lunch) to work or school.

brown'ie (brou'nē) *n.* a small, chewy chocolate cake.

brown'out' *n.* a reduction of electric power to prevent a blackout.

brown' stud'y *n.* deep thought.

browse (brouz) *v.t., v.i.*, browsed, browsing. 1. to graze or feed (on). 2. to look through casually.

brows'er (brou'zər) *n.* 1. one that browses. 2. a computer program that allows users to read World Wide Web documents.

bru'in (brōō'in) *n.* a bear.

bruise (brōōz) *v.*, bruised, bruising, *n.* —*v.t.* 1. to injure without breaking the skin. —*n.* 2. an injury due to bruising.

bruis'er *n. Informal.* a strong, tough man.

brunch (brunch) *n.* a meal that serves as both breakfast and lunch.

bru·nette' (brōō net') *n.* a woman with dark hair and, often, dark skin and eyes.

brunt (brunt) *n.* the main force or impact.

brush (brush) *n.* 1. an instrument with bristles. 2. a bushy tail. 3. a close encounter. 4. a light touch. 5. dense bushes, shrubs, etc. —*v.t.* 6. to sweep, paint, etc., with a brush. 7. to touch lightly. 8. brush off, to reject bluntly. 9. ~ up on, to review, as a skill.

brush'-off' *n.* a blunt rejection.

brusque (brusk) *adj.* abrupt in speech or manner. —**brusque'ly,** *adv.*

Brus'sels sprouts' (brus'əlz) *n.* a kind of cabbage with small heads.

bru'tal (brōōt'l) *adj.* 1. cruel. 2. severe. —**bru·tal'i·ty,** *n.*

bru'tal·ize' (brōōt'l īz') *v.t.*, -ized, -izing. 1. to make brutal. 2. to treat brutally.

brute (brōōt) *n.* 1. a beast. 2. a brutal person. —*adj.* 3. animallike. 4. irrational. 5. savage; cruel. —**brut'ish,** *adj.*

B.S. Bachelor of Science.

Btu British thermal unit. Also, **BTU.**

bu. bushel.

bub'ble (bub'əl) *n., v.*, -bled, -bling. —*n.* 1. a transparent ball of gas, usu. in a liquid. —*v.i.* 2. to form or produce bubbles. —**bub'bly,** *adj.*

buc'ca·neer' (buk'ə nēr') *n.* a pirate.

buck¹ (buk) *n.* the male of the deer, rabbit, goat, etc.

buck² (buk) *v.i.* 1. (of a horse) to leap with arched back. 2. to resist something obstinately. —*v.t.* 3. to throw (a rider) by bucking. 4. to resist obstinately.

buck³ (buk) *n.* —*Idiom.* pass the buck, to shift responsibility.

buck'et (buk'it) *n.* 1. a deep, open-topped container; pail. —*Idiom.* 2. drop in the bucket, a small, inadequate amount.

buck'le (buk'əl) *n., v.*, -led, -ling. —*n.* 1. a clasp for two loose ends. —*v.t., v.i.* 2. to fasten with a buckle. 3. to bend. 4. buckle down, to set to work.

buck'ler *n.* a shield.

buck'ram (buk'rəm) *n.* a stiff cotton fabric.

buck'shot' *n.* large lead shot.

buck'skin' *n.* a strong, soft leather.

buck'tooth' *n., pl.* -teeth. a projecting front tooth.

buck'wheat' *n.* a plant with edible triangular seeds.

bu·col'ic (byōō kol'ik) *adj.* of or suggesting an idyllic rural life.

bud (bud) *n., v.*, budded, budding. —*n.* 1. a small bulge on a plant stem from which leaves or flowers develop. —*v.i.* 2. to put forth buds. 3. to begin to develop.

bud'dy (bud'ē) *n., pl.* -dies. *Informal.* a friend; comrade.

budge (buj) *v.t., v.i.*, budged, budging. to move slightly.

budg'et (buj'it) *n.* 1. an estimate of expected income and expenses. —*v.t.* 2. to allot (money, time, etc.).

buff (buf) *n.* 1. a soft, thick, light-yellow leather. 2. a yellowish brown. 3. an enthusiast. —*adj.* 4. made or colored like buff. —*v.t.* 5. to polish with a buffer.

buf'fa·lo' (buf'ə lō') *n., pl.* -loes, -los, -lo. any of several large, wild oxen, as the bison or the water buffalo.

buff'er¹ *n.* 1. anything used for absorbing shock. —*v.t.* 2. to act as a buffer to.

buff'er² *n.* a leather-covered polishing device.

buf·fet¹ (buf'it) *n.* 1. a blow or violent shock. —*v.t.* 2. to strike repeatedly.

buf·fet² (bə fā', bŏo-) *n.* 1. a cabinet for china, glassware, etc. 2. a meal where guests serve themselves.

buf·foon' (bə fōōn') *n.* a clown.

bug (bug) *n., v.*, bugged, bugging. —*n.* 1. an insect. 2. a microorganism. 3. a defect or imperfection. 4. a hidden microphone. —*v.t.* 5. to install a secret listening device in. 6. *Informal.* to annoy.

bug'bear' *n.* any source, real or imaginary, of fright or fear. Also, **bug'a·boo'** (bug'ə bōō').

bug'gy (bug'ē) *n., pl.* -gies. a carriage.

bu'gle (byōō'gəl) *n., v.*, -gled, -gling. —*n.* 1. a brass wind instrument without valves. —*v.i.* 2. to sound a bugle.

build (bild) *v.*, built, building, *n.* —*v.t.* 1. to construct. 2. to form. 3. to establish. —*v.i.* 4. to increase in intensity, tempo, etc. —*n.* 5. bodily shape. —**build'er,** *n.*

build'ing *n.* a structure with a roof and walls.

build'up' *n. Informal.* 1. a steady increase. 2. publicity.

built'-in' *adj.* 1. built as part of a structure. 2. an inseparable part of.

built'-up' *adj.* 1. made bigger or higher by adding something. 2. filled in with buildings.

bulb (bulb) *n.* 1. a swollen, underground stem with fleshy leaves, as in the onion or daffodil. 2. any round, enlarged part. 3. an incandescent lamp or its glass housing.

bulge (bulj) *n., v.*, bulged, bulging. —*n.* 1. a rounded projection. —*v.i.* 2. to swell out. —**bulg'y,** *adj.*

bul'gur (bul'gər) *n.* wheat, used in parboiled, cracked, and dried form.

bu·lim·i·a (byōō lim'ē ə, -lē'mē ə, bōō-) *n.* a disorder marked by eating binges followed by self-induced vomiting.

bulk (bulk) *n.* 1. size, esp. when great. 2. the main mass. —*v.i.* 3. to increase in size or importance. —**bulk'y,** *adj.*

bulk'head' *n.* a wall-like partition in a ship.

bull¹ (bŏol) *n.* 1. the male of a bovine animal or of certain other animals, as the elephant, whale, and moose. 2. a person who believes that stock prices will rise. —*adj.* 3. male. 4. marked by rising prices, esp. of stocks.

bull² (bool) *n.* an official document from the pope.

bull³ (bool) *n.* lies; nonsense.

bull'dog' *n.* a breed of short-haired, muscular dog.

bull'doz'er *n.* a powerful earth-moving tractor.

bul'let (bool'it) *n.* a small projectile for firing from small guns.

bul'le·tin (bool'i tn, -tin) *n.* **1.** a brief public statement, esp. late news. **2.** a periodical publication.

bull'fight' *n.* a traditional spectacle in which a bull is fought and killed by a matador. —**bull'fight'er,** *n.*

bull'finch' *n.* a songbird, the male of which has a rosy breast.

bull'frog' *n.* a large frog with a deep voice.

bull'head'ed *adj.* stubborn.

bull'horn' *n.* a megaphone.

bul'lion (bool'yan) *n.* gold or silver in bars.

bull'ock (bool'ak) *n.* a castrated bull.

bull'pen' *n.* the place where relief pitchers warm up.

bull's'-eye' *n.* the center of a target.

bul'ly (bool'ē) *n., pl.* **-lies,** *v.,* **-lied, -lying.** —*n.* **1.** an overbearing person who intimidates weaker people. —*v.t.* **2.** to intimidate.

bul'rush' (bool'rush') *n.* a tall, rushlike plant.

bul'wark (bool'wark, -wôrk) *n.* **1.** a defense wall. **2.** a protection.

bum (bum) *n. Informal.* **1.** a tramp or hobo. **2.** a loafer or idler. —*v.t.* **3.** *Informal.* to borrow without planning to return. —*adj.* **4.** of poor quality.

bum'ble (bum'bal) *v.,* **-bled, -bling.** —*v.i.* **1.** to blunder. —*v.t.* **2.** to bungle or botch.

bum'ble·bee' *n.* a large, hairy bee.

bum'mer (bum'ar) *n. Slang.* any unpleasant experience.

bump (bump) *v.t., v.i.* **1.** to strike or collide (with). **2.** to bounce along. —*n.* **3.** a collision; blow. **4.** a swelling from a blow. **5.** a small area higher than the surrounding surface. —**bump'y,** *adj.*

bump'er *n.* **1.** a guard for protecting the front or rear of an automobile in a collision. —*adj.* **2.** unusually abundant.

bump'kin *n.* an awkward, simple person from a rural area.

bun (bun) *n.* a kind of bread roll.

bunch (bunch) *n.* **1.** a cluster. **2.** a group. —*v.t., v.i.* **3.** to gather into a group.

bun'dle (bun'dl) *n., v.,* **-dled, -dling.** —*n.* **1.** several things loosely bound together. **2.** a package. —*v.t.* **3.** to wrap in a bundle. **4. bundle up,** to dress warmly.

bun'ga·low' (bung'ga lō') *n.* a small house.

bun'gee cord' (bun'jē) an elasticized cord with a hook at each end, used as a fastener.

bun'gle (bung'gal) *v.,* **-gled, -gling,** *n.* —*v.t., v.i.* **1.** to do badly. —*n.* **2.** something bungled.

bun'ion (bun'yan) *n.* an inflamed swelling at the base of the big toe.

bunk¹ (bungk) *n.* a built-in bed.

bunk² (bungk) *n.* bunkum.

bunk'er (bung'kar) *n.* **1.** a large bin. **2.** an underground refuge.

bun'kum (bung'kam) *n.* nonsense. Also, **bunk.**

bun'ny (bun'ē) *n., pl.* **-nies.** a rabbit.

Bun'sen burn'er (bun'san) *n.* a gas burner used in chemical laboratories.

bunt (bunt) *v.t., v.i.* to push or tap (something) forward.

bun'ting¹ (bun'ting) *n.* fabric for flags, signals, etc.

bun'ting² (bun'ting) *n.* a small, seed-eating songbird.

buoy (boo'ē, boi) *n.* **1.** an anchored floating marker. —*v.t.* **2.** to keep afloat. **3.** to mark with a buoy. **4.** to sustain or encourage.

buoy'ant (boi'ant, boo'yant) *adj.* **1.** able to float. **2.** cheerful. —**buoy'an·cy,** *n.*

bur (bûr) *n.* a prickly seed case.

bur'den (bûr'dn) *n.* **1.** a load. **2.** something borne with difficulty. —*v.t.* **3.** to load heavily or oppressively. —**bur'den·some,** *adj.*

bur'dock (bûr'dok) *n.* a broad-leaved weed having prickly burs.

bu'reau (byoor'ō) *n., pl.* **-eaus, -eaux.** **1.** a chest of drawers. **2.** a government department.

bu·reauc'ra·cy (byoo rok'ra sē) *n., pl.* **-cies.** **1.** government by a rigid hierarchy of officials. **2.** a group of officials. **3.** excessive administrative routine. —**bur'eau·crat',** *n.* —**bur'eau·crat'ic,** *adj.*

bur'geon (bûr'jan) *v.i.* **1.** to grow quickly. **2.** to begin to grow.

burg'er (bûr'gar) *n.* a hamburger.

bur'glar (bûr'glar) *n.* a thief who breaks and enters. —**bur'glar·ize',** *v.t., v.i.* —**bur'gla·ry,** *n.*

Bur'gun·dy (bûr'gan dē) *n., pl.* **-dies.** (*often l.c.*) a type of red or white wine orig. produced in Burgundy, in central France.

bur'i·al (ber'ē al) *n.* the act of burying.

bur'lap (bûr'lap) *n.* a coarse fabric of hemp or jute.

bur·lesque' (bar lesk') *n., v.,* **-lesqued, -lesquing.** —*n.* **1.** a parody. **2.** a bawdy stage show. —*v.t., v.i.* **3.** to mock by burlesque.

bur'ly (bûr'lē) *adj.,* **-lier, -liest.** **1.** of great bodily size. **2.** sturdy.

burn (bûrn) *v.,* **burned** or **burnt, burning,** *n.* —*v.i.* **1.** to be on fire. **2.** to give off light. **3.** to be hot. **4.** to be injured, damaged, or destroyed by fire or heat. **5.** to feel strong emotion. —*v.t.* **6.** to damage or destroy by fire. **7.** to use as fuel. **8.** to cause a stinging sensation in. **9.** **burn out,** to exhaust or become exhausted. —*n.* **10.** an injury caused by burning.

bur'nish (bûr'nish) *v.t.* to polish by friction.

bur·noose' (bar noos') *n.* a hooded cloak worn by Arabs.

burn'out' *n.* **1.** the point at which a rocket engine stops because it runs out of fuel. **2.** fatigue and frustration from too much work and stress.

burp (bûrp) *n.* **1.** a belch. —*v.i.* **2.** to belch. —*v.t.* **3.** to cause (a baby) to belch.

burr (bûr) *n.* a bur.

bur'ro (bûr'ō, boor'ō, bur'ō) *n., pl.* **-ros.** a donkey.

bur'row (bûr'ō, bur'ō) *n.* **1.** an animal's hole in the ground. —*v.i.* **2.** to dig or hide in a burrow. **3.** to proceed by digging. —*v.t.* **4.** to dig a burrow into. **5.** to make by burrowing.

bur'sa (bûr'sa) *n., pl.* **-sae** (-sē) **-sas.** a sac containing fluid, as between a tendon and a bone.

bur'sar (bûr'sar, -sär) *n.* a treasurer, esp. of a college.

bur·si'tis (bar sī'tis) *n.* inflammation of a bursa in a joint.

burst (bûrst) *v.,* **burst, bursting,** *n.* —*v.i.* **1.** to break open or issue forth violently. **2.** to rupture. —*v.t.* **3.** to cause to burst. —*n.* **4.** an act or result of bursting. **5.** a sudden display of activity or emotion.

bur'y (ber'ē) *v.t.,* **buried, burying. 1.** to put in the ground and cover with earth. **2.** to put (a dead body) in the ground or a tomb or the sea. **3.** to conceal. **4.** to involve (oneself) deeply.

bus (bus) *n., pl.* **buses, busses,** *v.,* **bused** or **bussed, busing** or **bussing.** —*n.* **1.** a large motor vehicle for many passengers. —*v.t.* **2.** to move by bus. —*v.i.* **3.** to travel by bus.

bus'boy' *n.* a waiter's helper.

bush (boosh) *n.* **1.** a low plant with many branches. **2.** land covered by bushes. —**Idiom. 3. beat around the bush,** to avoid talking about something directly.

bushed *adj. Informal.* exhausted.

bush'el (boosh'al) *n.* a unit of four pecks.

bush' league' *n.* a secondary baseball league.

busi'ness (biz'nis) *n.* **1.** an occupation, profession, or trade. **2.** a profit-seeking enterprise. **3.** patronage. **4.** affair; matter.

busi'ness·like' *adj.* practical and efficient.

busi'ness·man' or **-wo'man' -per'son,** *n., pl.* **-men** or **-wo·men** or **-per·sons.** a person engaged in business.

bus'ing (bus'ing) *n.* the moving of pupils by bus to achieve racially balanced classes. Also, **bus'sing.**

bust¹ (bust) *n.* **1.** a sculpture of the head and shoulders. **2.** a woman's bosom.

bust² (bust) *Informal.* —*v.i.* **1.** to burst or break. **2.** to go bankrupt. —*v.t.* **3.** to break. **4.** to arrest. **5.** to hit. —*n.* **6.** a failure. **7.** an arrest.

bus'tle (bus'al) *v.,* **-tled, -tling,** *n.* —*v.i.* **1.** to move or act energetically. —*n.* **2.** energetic activity.

bus'y (biz'ē) *adj.,* **-ier, -iest,** *v.,* **-ied, -ing.** —*adj.* **1.** actively employed. **2.** full of activity. —*v.t.* **3.** to make or keep busy.

bus'y·bod'y *n., pl.* **-bodies.** one who meddles in others' affairs.

but (but; *unstressed* bat) *conj.* **1.** on the contrary. **2.** except. **3.** and yet. —*prep.* **4.** other than. —*adv.* **5.** only.

bu'tane (byoo'tān) *n.* a colorless gas used as fuel.

butch (booch) *adj. Slang.* **1.** (of a woman) having traits usu. associated with men. **2.** (of a man) having exaggerated masculine traits.

butch'er (booch'ar) *n.* **1.** a dealer in meat. **2.** a person who slaughters or dresses animals for food. —*v.t.* **3.** to slaughter or dress (animals). **4.** to kill brutally. **5.** to bungle. —**butch'er·y,** *n.*

but'ler (but'lar) *n.* the chief male servant in a household.

butt¹ (but) *n.* **1.** the thicker or blunter end of anything. **2.** an unused end of something. **3.** *Slang.* the buttocks.

butt² (but) *n.* **1.** an object of ridicule. —*v.t., v.i.* **2.** to place or be placed end to end.

butt³ (but) *v.t., v.i.* **1.** to strike with the head or horns. **2. butt in,** to intrude.

but'ter (but'ar) *n.* **1.** the solid fatty part of milk. —*v.t.* **2.** to put butter on. **3. butter up,** to flatter.

but'ter·cup' *n.* a plant with yellow cup-shaped flowers.

but'ter·fin'gers *n., pl.* **-gers.** a clumsy person.

but'ter·fly' *n., pl.* **-flies.** an insect with broad, colorful wings.

but'ter·milk' *n.* the liquid remaining after butter has been separated from milk.

but'ter·nut' *n.* the edible oily nut of a tree of the walnut family.

but'ter·scotch' *n.* a kind of taffy.

but'tock (but'ak) *n.* either of the two fleshy rounded parts forming the rump of the human body.

but'ton (but'n) *n.* **1.** a disk or knob for fastening. **2.** a buttonlike object. —*v.t., v.i.* **3.** to fasten or be fastened with a button.

but'ton-down' *adj.* **1.** (of a collar) having buttonholes for attaching it to a shirt. **2.** conventional.

but'ton·hole' *n., v.,* **-holed, -holing.** —*n.* **1.** the slit through which a button is passed. —*v.t.* **2.** to approach and keep talking to.

but'tress (bu'tris) *n.* **1.** a projecting support built into or against a wall. **2.** any support. —*v.t.* **3.** to support.

bux'om (buk'sam) *adj.* (of a woman) full-bosomed.

buy (bī) *v.,* **bought** (bôt), **buying,** *n.* —*v.t.* **1.** to acquire by payment. **2. buy off,** to bribe. —*n.* **3.** a bargain.

buy'back' *n.* a repurchase by a company of its own stock.

buy'out' *n.* the purchase of a majority of shares in a company.

buzz (buz) *n.* **1.** a low humming sound. —*v.i.* **2.** to make a low humming sound.

buz'zard (buz'ard) *n.* a large carnivorous bird.

buzz'word' *n. Informal.* a word or phrase that has come into fashion in a particular profession.

by (bī) *prep.* **1.** near to. **2.** through. **3.** not later than. **4.** past. **5.** by way of. —*adv.* **6.** during. **7.** near. **8.** past.

by'-elec'tion *n.* a special election to fill a vacancy.

by'gone' *adj.* **1.** past. —*n.* **2.** something in the past.

by'law' *n.* a rule governing matters within a corporation.

by'line' *n.* a line, as in a newspaper, giving the writer's name.

BYOB bring your own booze/beer/bottle.

by'pass' *n.* **1.** a route going around a city or obstruction. **2.** a surgical procedure to provide passage around a diseased or blocked organ. —*v.t.* **3.** to avoid by means of a bypass.

by'play' *n.* action or speech aside from the main action.

by'-prod'uct *n.* a secondary product.

by'road' *n.* a side road; byway.

by'stand'er *n.* a person present but not involved.

byte (bīt) *n.* a unit of computer information, larger than a bit.

by'way' *n.* a little-used road.

by'word' *n.* **1.** a favorite word or phrase. **2.** a person regarded as the embodiment of some quality.

Byz'an·tine' (biz'an tēn', -tīn') *adj.* (*sometimes l.c.*) **1.** complex; intricate. **2.** marked by intrigue.

C

C, c (sē) *n.* the third letter of the English alphabet.

C Celsius, Centigrade.

c. 1. centimeter. **2.** century. **3.** copyright.

CA California.

ca. circa.

cab (kab) *n.* **1.** a taxicab. **2.** the part of a locomotive, truck, etc., where the driver sits.

ca·bal' (ka bal') *n.* a small group of secret plotters.

cab·a·na' (ka ban'a, -ban'ya) *n.* a small shelter at a beach or pool.

cab'a·ret' (kab'a rā') *n.* a restaurant providing entertainment.

cab'bage (kab'ij) *n.* a vegetable with a dense round head of leaves.

cab'in (kab'in) *n.* **1.** a small house. **2.** a room in a ship or plane.

cab'i·net (kab'a nit) *n.* **1.** a chief executive's advisory council. **2.** a cupboard with shelves or drawers.

ca'ble (kā'bal) *n., v.,* **-bled, -bling.** —*n.* **1.** a heavy, strong rope of fiber or metal wires. **2.** an insulated bundle of electrical wires. **3.** cable TV. **4.** a cablegram. —*v.t., v.i.* **5.** to send a cablegram (to).

ca'ble·gram' *n.* a telegram sent by underwater wires.

ca'ble TV' *n.* a system of distributing television programs to subscribers over coaxial cables.

ca·boo'dle (ka bood'l) *n. Informal.* the lot, pack, or crowd.

ca·boose' (ka boos') *n.* a car for the crew at the rear of a train.

ca·ca'o (ka kā'ō, -kä'ō) *n.* **-caos.** a tropical tree yielding cocoa.

cache (kash) *n., v.,* **cached, caching.** —*n.* **1.** a hiding place for treasure, food, etc. **2.** anything hidden in a cache. —*v.t.* **3.** to hide.

ca·chet' (ka shā') *n.* **1.** an official seal. **2.** superior status; prestige.

cack'le (kak'al) *v.,* **-led, -ling,** *n.* —*v.i.* **1.** to utter a shrill, broken cry, as of a hen. —*n.* **2.** the act or sound of cackling.

ca·coph'o·ny (ka kof'a nē) *n.* harsh, discordant sound.

cac'tus (kak'tas) *n., pl.* **-tuses, -ti** (-tī). a leafless, spiny desert plant.

cad (kad) *n.* a dishonorable man.

ca·dav'er (ka dav'ar) *n.* a corpse.

cad'die (kad'ē) *n., v.,* **-died, -dying.** —*n.* **1.** a person who carries a golfer's clubs. —*v.i.* **2.** to work as a caddie. Also, **cad'dy.**

ca'dence (kād'ns) *n.* **1.** rhythmic flow, as of sounds. **2.** the rise and fall of the voice.

ca·det' (ka det') *n.* a student at a military academy.

cadge (kaj) *v.t., v.i.,* **cadged, cadging.** to obtain (a thing) by begging.

cad'mi·um (kad'mē am) *n.* a white metallic element used in plating.

ca'dre (kä'drä, kad'rē) *n.* a highly trained group in an organization.

ca·du'ce·us (ka doo'sē as, -dyoo'-) *n., pl.* **-ce·i** (-sē ī'). a winged staff with two entwined snakes, used as a symbol of the medical profession.

Cae·sar'e·an (si zâr'ē an) *n.* a Cesarean.

ca·fé' (ka fā') *n.* a small informal restaurant.

caf·e·te'ri·a (kaf'i tēr'ē a) *n.* a self-service restaurant.

caf'feine (ka fēn') *n.* a stimulant found in coffee, tea, etc.

caf'tan (kaf'tan) *n.* a long wide-sleeved garment.

cage (kāj) *n., v.,* **caged, caging.** —*n.* **1.** a barred box or room. —*v.t.* **2.** to put in a cage.

cag'ey *adj.,* **-ier, -iest.** shrewd; cautious. Also, **cag'i·ly,** *adv.*

cais'son (kā'son, -san) *n.* **1.** a two-wheeled ammunition wagon. **2.** a watertight chamber for underwater construction.

ca·jole' (ka jōl') *v.t., v.i.,* **-joled, -joling.** to coax.

Ca'jun (kā'jan) *n.* a Louisianan of Nova Scotia-French origin.

cake (kāk) *n., v.,* **caked, caking.** —*n.* **1.** a sweet, baked breadlike food. **2.** a flat hard mass. —*v.t., v.i.* **3.** to form into a compact mass. —**Idiom. 4. piece of cake,** something that can be done easily.

Cal. California. Also, **Calif.**

cal. 1. caliber. **2.** calorie.

cal'a·bash' (kal'a bash') *n.* a kind of gourd.

cal·a·ma'ri (kal'a mär'ē, kä'la-) *n.* cooked squid.

cal'a·mine' (kal'a mīn') *n.* a pink powder containing zinc oxide, used in skin lotions.

ca·lam'i·ty (ka lam'i tē) *n., pl.* **-ties.** a disaster. —**ca·lam'i·tous,** *adj.*

cal'ci·fy' (kal'sa fī') *v.t., v.i.,* **-fied, -fying.** to harden by the deposit of calcium salts.

cal'ci·mine' (-mīn') *n., v.,* **-mined, -mining.** —*n.* **1.** a type of paint for walls, ceilings, etc. —*v.t.* **2.** to cover with calcimine.

cal'cite (kal'sīt) *n.* a mineral, calcium carbonate, that is a major constituent of limestone, marble, and chalk.

cal'ci·um (kal'sē am) *n.* a white metallic element.

cal'cu·late' (kal'kya lāt') *v.t.,* **-lated, -lating. 1.** to determine by using mathematics. **2.** to estimate. —**cal'cu·la'tion,** *n.*

cal'cu·lat'ing *adj.* shrewd.

cal'cu·la'tor *n.* a small electronic or mechanical device for making mathematical calculations.

cal'cu·lus (kal'kya las) *n.* a method of calculation by a system of algebraic notations.

cal'dron (kôl'dran) *n.* a cauldron.

cal'en·dar (kal'an dar) *n.* **1.** a table of the days, weeks, and months in a year. **2.** a list of events.

cal'en·der (kal'an dar) *n.* **1.** a press with rotating cylinders for paper, cloth, etc. —*v.t.* **2.** to press in such a machine.

calf¹ (kaf) *n., pl.* **calves.** the young of the cow and certain other mammals, as the elephant, whale, etc.

calf² (kaf) *n., pl.* **calves.** the back part of the leg below the knee.

cal'i·ber (kal'a bar) *n.* **1.** the diameter of a circular section. **2.** the diameter of a gun bore. **3.** degree of ability. Also, **cal'i·bre.**

cal'i·brate' (-brāt') *v.t.,* **-brated, -brating.** to mark (an instrument) for measuring purposes. —**cal'i·bra'tion,** *n.*

cal'i·co' (kal'i kō') *n., pl.* **-coes, -cos.** **1.** a printed cotton cloth. —*adj.* **2.** having blotches of a different color.

cal'i·pers (kal'a parz) *n.pl.* an instrument for measuring, consisting of two adjustable legs.

ca'liph (kā'lif) *n.* a former title for an Islamic religious and civil ruler.

cal'is·then'ics (kal'as then'iks) *n.pl.* physical exercises.

calk (kôk) *v.t., n.* caulk.

call (kôl) *v.t.* **1.** to cry out loudly. **2.** to summon; invite. **3.** to telephone. **4.** to name. **5.** to waken. —*v.i.* **6.** to speak loudly. **7.** to make a brief visit. **8.** (of a bird) to utter a characteristic cry. **9. call off,** to cancel. —*n.* **10.** a cry or shout. **11.** a summons. **12.** a brief visit. **13.** a need; demand. —**call'er,** *n.*

cal·lig'ra·phy (ka lig'ra fē) *n.* beautiful handwriting.

call'ing *n.* a vocation or profession.

cal'lous (kal'as) *adj.* insensitive.

cal'low (kal'ō) *adj.* immature.

cal'lus (kal'as) *n.* a hardened part of the skin.

calm (käm) *adj.* **1.** not excited; tranquil. **2.** still; not windy. —*n.* **3.** freedom from disturbance. **4.** absence of wind. **5.** serenity. —*v.t., v.i.* **6.** to make or become calm. —**calm'ly,** *adv.*

ca·lor'ic (ka lôr'ik) *adj.* **1.** of heat or calories. **2.** high in calories.

cal'o·rie (kal'a rē) *n.* a unit used to express heat and the energy value of food.

ca·lum'ni·ate' (ka lum'nē āt') *v.t.,* **-ated, -ating.** to slander. —**cal'um·ny** (kal'am nē) *n.*

calve (kav, käv) *v.i., v.t.* **calved, calving.** to give birth to (a calf).

Cal'vin·ism (kal'va niz'am) *n.* the doctrines of John Calvin, emphasizing predestination. —**Cal'vin·ist,** *n., adj.*

ca·lyp'so (ka lip'sō) *n.* a musical style of the West Indies.

ca'lyx (kā'liks) *n., pl.* **calyxes, calyces** (kal'a sēz', kā'la-). the small leaflike parts around the petals of a flower.

cam (kam) *n.* a machine part that gives a rocking motion to another part.

ca'ma·ra·de·rie (kä'ma rä'da rē) *n.* comradeship; fellowship.

cam'ber (kam'bar) *v.t., v.i.* **1.** to curve upward in the middle. —*n.* **2.** a slight upward curve.

cam/bric (kām/brik) *n.* a thin cotton or linen fabric.

cam/cord/er (kam/kôr/dər) *n.* a hand-held television camera that has a VCR.

came (kām) *v.* pt. of **come.**

cam/el (kam/əl) *n.* a large humped mammal living in the desert.

ca·mel/lia (kə mēl/yə) *n.* a shrub with glossy leaves and roselike flowers.

cam/e·o/ (kam/ē ō/) *n., pl.* **-eos. 1.** a gem with a head carved in a raised design. **2.** a brief appearance by a famous person in a film or play.

cam/er·a (kam/ər ə) *n.* **1.** a device for making photographs. —*Idiom.* **2. in camera,** privately.

cam/i·sole/ (kam/ə sōl/) *n.* a woman's sleeveless undershirt.

cam/o·mile/ (kam/ə mīl/) *n.* chamomile.

cam/ou·flage/ (kam/ə fläzh/) *n., v.,* **-flaged, -flaging.** —*n.* **1.** deceptive covering. —*v.t.* **2.** to disguise.

camp¹ (kamp) *n.* **1.** a place for temporary lodging, esp. in tents, for soldiers or vacationers. **2.** a faction. —*v.i.* **3.** to form or live in a camp. —**camp/er,** *n.*

camp² (kamp) *n.* **1.** something that amuses by being overdone or tasteless. —*adj.* **2.** Also, **camp/y.** amusing as camp.

cam·paign/ (kam pān/) *n.* **1.** a military operation. **2.** a course of organized activity in pursuit of a goal, as political office, sales, etc. —*v.i.* **3.** to engage in a campaign.

cam/pa·ni·le (kam/pə nē/lē, -nēl/) *n., pl.* **-niles, -nili** (-nē/lē). a bell tower.

cam/phor (kam/fər) *n.* a white crystalline substance used as a moth repellent, medicine, etc.

camp/site *n.* a place for camping.

cam/pus (kam/pəs) *n.* the grounds of a school, college, etc.

cam/shaft/ *n.* an engine shaft fitted with cams.

can¹ (kan; *unstressed* kən) *auxiliary v., pres.* **can;** *past* **could.** to be able or know how to.

can² (kan) *v.,* **canned, canning.** —*n.* **1.** a sealed metal container for food, beverages, etc. **2.** a container for garbage. —*v.t.* **3.** to put in an airtight metal or glass container.

Ca·na/di·an (kə nā/dē ən) *adj.* **1.** of Canada or its inhabitants. —*n.* **2.** a citizen of Canada.

ca·nal/ (kə nal/) *n.* **1.** an artificial waterway. **2.** a tube for food, air, etc., in an animal or plant.

can/a·pé (kan/ə pē, -pā/) *n.* a cracker or piece of bread topped with meat, fish, etc., and served as an appetizer.

ca·nard/ (kə närd/) *n.* a usu. derogatory rumor.

ca·nar/y (kə nâr/ē) *n., pl.* **-ies.** a yellow finch bred as a cage bird.

ca·nas/ta (kə nas/tə) *n.* a type of rummy played with two decks of cards.

can/cel (kan/səl) *v.t.,* **-celed, -celing. 1.** to make void. **2.** to call off. **3.** to cross out. —**can/cel·la/tion,** *n.*

can/cer (kan/sər) *n.* a malignant growth that tends to spread. —**can/cer·ous,** *adj.*

can·de·la/brum (kan/dl ä/brəm) *n., pl.* **-bra** (-brə). a branched candlestick. Also, **can/de·la/bra, pl. -bras.**

can/did (kan/did) *adj.* **1.** frank or honest. **2.** unposed, as a photograph. —**can/did·ly,** *adv.*

can/di·da (kan/di də) *n.* a disease-causing fungus.

can/di·date/ (kan/di dāt/, -dit) *n.* one seeking to be elected or chosen. —**can/di·da·cy,** *n.*

can/dle (kan/dl) *n.* a wax cylinder with a wick for burning.

can/dor (kan/dər) *n.* frankness.

can/dy (kan/dē) *n., pl.* **-dies,** *v.,* **-died, -dying.** —*n.* **1.** a sweet food made from sugar and flavoring. —*v.t.* **2.** to cook with sugar or syrup.

cane (kān) *n., v.,* **caned, caning.** —*n.* **1.** a stick used for support in walking. **2.** a long, woody stem. **3.** a rod used for beating. —*v.t.* **4.** to beat with a cane.

cane/brake/ *n.* a thicket of canes.

ca/nine (kā/nīn) *adj.* **1.** of dogs. —*n.* **2.** an animal of the dog family. **3.** one of the four pointed teeth next to the incisors.

can/is·ter (kan/ə stər) *n.* a small box or can.

can/ker (kang/kər) *n.* an ulcerous sore, esp. in the mouth. —**can/ker·ous,** *adj.*

can/na·bis (kan/ə bis) *n.* the hemp plant.

canned (kand) *adj.* **1.** preserved in cans or sealed jars. **2.** *Informal.* recorded.

can/ner·y *n., pl.* **-ies.** a factory where foods are canned.

can/ni·bal (kan/ə bəl) *n.* **1.** a person who eats human flesh. **2.** an animal that eats its own kind.

can/ni·bal·ize/ *v.t., v.i.,* **-ized, -izing.** to take from one thing, as a part from a machine, for use in another.

can·nol/i (kə nō/lē) *n.* a pastry shell filled with sweetened ricotta cheese.

can/non (kan/ən) *n.* a large mounted gun.

can/non·ade/ (-ə nād/) *n.* a long burst of cannon fire.

can/not (kan/ot, ka not/, kə-) *v.* a form of can not.

can/ny (kan/ē) *adj.,* **-nier, -niest. 1.** careful. **2.** shrewd.

ca·noe/ (kə nō̄/) *n.* a slender, light boat propelled by paddles.

can/on¹ (kan/ən) *n.* **1.** a rule enacted by a church body. **2.** a group of writings accepted as authentic.

can/on² (kan/ən) *n.* a member of the clergy of a cathedral.

can/on·ize/ *v.t.,* **-ized, -izing.** to declare officially as a saint.

can/o·py (kan/ə pē) *n., pl.* **-pies. 1.** a covering hung over a bed, throne, etc. **2.** an awning stretching from a doorway to a curb.

cant (kant) *n.* **1.** insincere statements of a pious nature. **2.** the vocabulary of a particular group.

can't (kant) a contraction of **cannot.**

can·ta·bi·le/ (kän tä/bi lā/, -bē) *adj., adv. Music.* songlike and flowing.

can·ta/ta (kən tä/tə) *n.* a choral composition.

can·teen/ (kan tēn/) *n.* **1.** a small container for carrying water. **2.** a cafeteria or entertainment place for military personnel.

can/ter (kan/tər) *n.* **1.** an easy gallop. —*v.i.* **2.** to go at this pace.

can/ti·cle (kan/ti kəl) *n.* a hymn.

can/ti·le/ver (kan/tl ē/vər) *n.* a structure supported at one end only.

can/to (kan/tō) *n., pl.* **-tos.** a section of a long poem.

can/ton (kan/tn, kan ton/) *n.* a small district in Switzerland.

can/tor (kan/tər) *n.* a synagogue official who sings certain prayers.

can/vas (kan/vəs) *n.* **1.** a heavy, coarse cloth used for sails, tents, etc. **2.** a painting on canvas.

can/vas·back/ *n., pl.* **-backs, -back.** a wild duck with a whitish or grayish back.

can/vass (kan/vəs) *v.t., v.i.* **1.** to solicit votes, opinions, etc., from a group. —*n.* **2.** a soliciting of votes, opinions, etc. —**can/vass·er,** *n.*

can/yon (kan/yən) *n.* a deep, narrow valley.

cap (kap) *n., v.,* **capped, capping.** —*n.* **1.** a tight-fitting hat with a visor. **2.** a cover. **3.** a maximum limit. —*v.t.* **4.** to cover. **5.** to outdo.

cap. 1. capacity. **2.** capital(ize). **3.** capital letter.

ca/pa·ble (kā/pə bəl) *adj.* able; qualified. —**ca/pa·bil/i·ty,** *n.*

ca·pa/cious (kə pā/shəs) *adj.* roomy.

ca·pac/i·tor (kə pas/i tər) *n.* a device for collecting and holding an electrical charge.

ca·pac/i·ty *n., pl.* **-ties. 1.** the ability to contain. **2.** volume. **3.** the ability to do. **4.** a function.

cape (kāp) *n.* **1.** a sleeveless coat. **2.** a projecting point of land.

ca/per¹ (kā/pər) *v.i.* **1.** to leap playfully. —*n.* **2.** a playful leap. **3.** a prank.

ca/per² (kā/pər) *n.* the pickled flower bud of a shrub, used as seasoning.

cap/il·lar/y (kap/ə ler/ē) *n., pl.* **-laries.** a tiny blood vessel or thin tube.

cap/i·tal (kap/i tl) *n.* **1.** a city in which the seat of government is located. **2.** a letter different from and larger than its corresponding lower-case letter. **3.** money available for business use. —*adj.* **4.** important or chief. **5.** excellent. **6.** uppercase. **7.** punishable by death.

cap/ital gain/ *n.* profit from the sale of an asset.

cap/ital goods/ *n.pl.* machines for the production of goods.

cap/i·tal·ism *n.* an economic system in which industry is privately owned. —**cap/i·tal·ist,** *n.*

cap/i·tal·ize/ *v.t.,* **-ized, -izing. 1.** to put in capital letters. **2.** to use as capital. **3. capitalize on,** to take advantage of.

cap/i·tal·ly *adv.* excellently.

cap/ital pun/ishment *n.* punishment by death.

Cap/i·tol (kap/i tl) *n.* **1.** the building in Washington, D.C., in which the U.S. Congress meets. **2.** (*often l.c.*) the building used by a state legislature.

ca·pit/u·late/ (kə pich/ə lāt/) *v.i.,* **-lated, -lating.** to surrender or yield.

cap/let (kap/lit) *n.* an oval pill, coated for easy swallowing.

ca/pon (kā/pon, -pən) *n.* a castrated rooster.

cap/puc·ci/no (kap/ə chē/nō) *n.* espresso coffee with foaming steamed milk.

ca·price/ (kə prēs/) *n.* a whim.

Capri/ pants/ *n.* women's fitted pants that end above the ankle.

cap/size (kap/sīz) *v.t., v.i.,* **-sized, -sizing.** to overturn; upset.

cap/stan (kap/stən, -stan) *n.* a device for winding in cables, ropes, etc.

cap/sule (kap/səl) *n.* **1.** a gelatin case enclosing medicine. **2.** a cabin in a spacecraft. **3.** a small sealed container. —**cap/su·lar,** *adj.*

capt. captain.

cap/tain (kap/tən) *n.* **1.** an officer below major or rear admiral. **2.** a ship's master. **3.** the leader of a sports team. —**cap/tain·cy,** *n.*

cap/tion (kap/shən) *n.* an explanation for a picture.

cap/tious (kap/shəs) *adj.* faultfinding, esp. about trivial matters.

cap/ti·vate/ (kap/tə vāt/) *v.t.,* **-vated, -vating.** to charm.

cap/tive (-tiv) *n.* **1.** a prisoner. —*adj.* **2.** unable to escape. —**cap·tiv/i·ty,** *n.*

cap/ture (-chər) *v.,* **-tured, -turing,** *n.* —*v.t.* **1.** to take prisoner. **2.** to record in lasting form. —*n.* **3.** the act of capturing. —**cap/tor,** *n.*

car (kär) *n.* **1.** an automobile. **2.** the cage of an elevator.

ca·rafe/ (kə raf/) *n.* a wide-mouthed bottle for wine, water, etc.

car/a·mel (kar/ə məl, kär/məl) *n.* a confection made of burnt sugar.

car/at (kar/ət) *n.* a unit of weight for gems. **2.** a karat.

car/a·van/ (kar/ə van/) *n.* a group traveling together.

car/a·way/ (kar/ə wā/) *n.* an herb with spicy seeds, used in cooking.

car/bide (kär/bīd) *n.* a carbon compound.

car/bine (kär/bēn, -bīn) *n.* a short rifle.

car/bo·hy/drate (kär/bō hī/drāt, -bə-) *n.* an organic compound group including starches and sugars.

car·bol/ic ac/id (kär bol/ik) *n.* a brown germicidal liquid.

car/bon (kär/bən) *n.* a nonmetallic element occurring as diamonds, charcoal, etc., and present in all living matter. —**car·bon·if/er·ous,** *adj.*

carbon 14 *n.* radiocarbon.

car/bon·ate/ (kär/bə nāt/) *v.t.,* **-ated, -ating.** to charge with carbon dioxide.

car/bon diox/ide *n.* a chemical compound of carbon and oxygen: a gas produced esp. by animal respiration.

car/bon monox/ide *n.* a chemical compound of carbon and oxygen: a poisonous gas produced esp. by automobile engines.

car/bon pa/per *n.* paper coated with a carbon pigment, used to make copies.

Car/bo·run/dum (kär/bə run/dəm) *Trademark.* an abrasive of carbon, silicon, etc.

car/bun·cle (kär/bung kəl) *n.* a painful sore under the skin.

car/bu·re/tor (kär/bə rā/tər, -byə-) *n.* a device that mixes fuel and air in an engine.

car/cass (kär/kəs) *n.* the dead body of an animal.

car·cin/o·gen (kär sin/ə jən) *n.* a cancer-producing substance. —**car/cin·o·gen/ic** (-sə nə jen/ik) *adj.*

car·ci·no/ma (kär/sə nō/mə) *n., pl.* **-mas, -mata.** a malignant tumor.

card¹ (kärd) *n.* **1.** a piece of stiff paper or plastic containing information. **2.** a folded piece of stiff paper printed with a greeting. **3.** a thin piece of cardboard used in playing various games. —*v.t.* **4.** to ask for proof of age.

card² (kärd) *n.* **1.** a comb for wool, flax, etc. —*v.t.* **2.** to dress (wool or flax) with a card.

card/board/ *n.* **1.** thin, stiff pasteboard. —*adj.* **2.** flimsy.

car/di·ac/ (kär/dē ak/) *adj.* of the heart.

car/diac arrest/ *n.* abrupt stopping of the heartbeat.

car/di·gan (kär/di gən) *n.* a sweater that buttons down the front.

car/di·nal (kär/dn l) *adj.* **1.** main; chief. **2.** (of numbers) used to express quantities or positions in series, e.g., 3, 15, 45. —*n.* **3.** a red songbird. **4.** a deep red. **5.** a high official of the Roman Catholic Church.

car/dinal num/ber *n.* any of the numbers that express amount, as *one, two, three.*

cardio- a prefix meaning heart.

car/di·o·graph/ (kär/dē ə graf/) *n.* an electrocardiograph. —**car/di·o·gram/,** *n.*

car/di·ol/o·gy (-ol/ə jē) *n.* the study of the heart and its functions.

car/di·o·pul/mo·nar/y *adj.* of the heart and lungs.

car/di·o·vas/cu·lar *adj.* of the heart and blood vessels.

card/sharp/ *n.* a person who cheats at card games. Also, **card/shark/.**

care (kâr) *n., v.,* **cared, caring.** —*n.* **1.** worry. **2.** caution. **3.** serious attention. **4.** protection. —*v.i.* **5.** to be concerned. **6.** to make provision. —*v.t.* **7.** to feel concern about. —**care/free/,** *adj.*

ca·reen/ (kə rēn/) *v.i., v.t.* to lean or cause to lean to one side.

ca·reer/ (kə rēr/) *n.* **1.** a profession followed as one's lifework. **2.** one's course through life. —*v.i.* **3.** to speed.

care/ful *adj.* **1.** cautious. **2.** done with accuracy. —**care/ful·ly,** *adv.*

care/giv/er *n.* a person who cares for a child or an invalid.

care/less *adj.* **1.** not paying attention. **2.** not accurate. **3.** unconcerned.

ca·ress/ (kə res/) *n.* **1.** a light touch expressing affection. —*v.t.* **2.** to stroke lightly and affectionately.

car/et (kar/it) *n.* a mark (^) indicating where something is to be inserted.

care/tak/er (kâr/-) *n.* **1.** a person who looks after a building, estate, etc. **2.** a caregiver.

care/worn/ *adj.* showing signs of worry.

car/fare/ (kär/fâr/) *n.* the cost of a ride.

car/go (kär/gō) *n., pl.* **-goes, -gos.** goods carried by vessel; freight.

car/i·bou/ (kar/ə bōō/) *n.* the North American reindeer.

car/i·ca·ture (kar/i kə chər) *n., v.,* **-tured, -turing.** —*n.* **1.** a mocking, exaggerated portrait. —*v.t.* **2.** to make a caricature of.

car/ies (kâr/ēz) *n., pl.* **-ies.** tooth decay.

car/il·lon/ (kar/ə lon/, -lən) *n.* a set of bells in a tower.

car/jack/ing (kär/jak/ing) *n.* the forcible theft of a car from its driver. —**car/jack/er,** *n.*

car/mine (-min) *n.* a crimson or purplish red.

car/nage (-nij) *n.* great slaughter.

car/nal (-nl) *adj.* of the body.

car·na/tion (kär nā/shən) *n.* a cultivated fragrant flower.

car·nel/ian (kär nel/yən) *n.* a reddish variety of chalcedony used in jewelry.

car/ni·val (kär/nə vəl) *n.* **1.** an amusement fair. **2.** the festival before Lent.

car/ni·vore/ (-vôr/) *n.* a flesh-eating mammal. —**car·niv/o·rous** (-niv/ə rəs) *adj.*

car/ob (kar/əb) *n.* the pulp from the long pods of a Mediterranean tree, used as a chocolate substitute.

car/ol (kar/əl) *n.* **1.** a Christmas hymn. —*v.i.* **2.** to sing joyously. —**car/ol·er,** *n.*

car/om (kar/əm) *v.t.* **1.** to hit and rebound. —*n.* **2.** a hit and rebound.

ca·rot/id (kə rot/id) *n.* either of two large arteries in the neck.

ca·rouse/ (kə rouz/) *v.i.,* **-roused, -rousing.** to take part in a noisy or drunken gathering.

carp¹ (kärp) *v.i.* to find fault.

carp² (kärp) *n.* a large fresh-water fish.

car/pal (kär/pəl) *adj.* **1.** of the carpus. —*n.* **2.** a wrist bone.

car/pal tun/nel syn/drome *n.* chronic wrist and hand pain associated esp. with repetitive movements, as at a keyboard.

car/pel (kär/pəl) *n.* a seed-bearing leaf.

car/pen·ter (-pən tər) *n.* a person who builds or repairs wooden structures. —**car/pen·try,** *n.*

car/pet (-pit) *n.* **1.** a fabric covering for floors. **2.** any covering like a carpet. —*v.t.* **3.** to cover with a carpet. —*Idiom.* **4. call on the carpet,** to reprimand.

car/pool/ *n.* **1.** an arrangement by automobile owners who take turns driving their cars to a destination, as to work. —*v.i.* **2.** to take part in a carpool.

car/port/ *n.* a roof that provides shelter for a car.

car/pus (kär/pəs) *n., pl.* **-pi** (pī). **1.** the wrist. **2.** the wrist bones as a group.

car/rel (kar/əl) *n.* a small study space in a library. Also, **car/rell.**

car/riage (-ij) *n.* **1.** a wheeled vehicle. **2.** a movable part for carrying something. **3.** posture.

car/rier pig/eon *n.* a homing pigeon.

car/ri·on (kar/ē ən) *n.* dead flesh.

car/rot (kar/ət) *n.* an orange root vegetable.

car/ry (kar/ē) *v.t.,* **-ried, -rying. 1.** to transport. **2.** to support; bear the weight of. **3.** to serve as a medium for the transmission of. **4.** to win a majority of votes in. **5.** to have as a consequence. **6.** to have in stock. **7. carry on, a.** to manage. **b.** to persevere. **c.** to be disruptive. **8. ~ out,** to accomplish.

car/ry-out/ *adj., n.* takeout.

car/sick/ *adj.* nauseated and dizzy from car travel.

cart (kärt) *n.* a small wagon.

carte/ blanche/ (kärt/ blänch/, blänsh/) *n.* authority to do as one thinks best.

car·tel/ (kär tel/) *n.* a syndicate controlling prices and production.

Car·te/sian coor/dinates (kär tē/zhən) *n.pl.* a system of coordinates for locating a point on a plane by its distance from each of two intersecting lines.

car/ti·lage (kär/tl ij) *n.* a firm, elastic type of body tissue.

car·tog/ra·phy (kär tog/rə fē) *n.* the production of maps.

car/ton (kär/tn) *n.* a cardboard box.

car·toon/ (kär tōōn/) *n.* **1.** a comic drawing. **2.** a sketch for a painting. —**car·toon/ist,** *n.*

car/tridge (kär/trij) *n.* **1.** a case containing a bullet and explosive for a gun. **2.** a compact case, as for film.

cart/wheel/ *n.* **1.** a sideways handspring. —*v.i.* **2.** to roll forward end over end.

carve (kärv) *v.,* **carved, carving.** —*v.t.* **1.** to cut in order to form a shape or design. **2.** to cut into slices, as meat. —*v.i.* **3.** to form designs by carving. **4.** to carve meat. —**carv/er,** *n.*

car/y·at/id (kar/ē at/id) *n., pl.* **-ids, -i·des** (-i dēz/). a sculptured female figure used as a column.

ca·sa/ba (kə sä/bə) *n., pl.* **-bas.** a melon with a yellow rind.

cas·cade/ (kas käd/) *n.* **1.** a waterfall. **2.** anything falling like a waterfall. —*v.i.* **3.** to fall in a cascade.

case¹ (kās) *n.* **1.** an example. **2.** the state of things. **3.** a matter requiring investigation. **4.** a statement of arguments. **5.** a patient or client. **6.** a lawsuit. **7.** a category in the inflection of nouns, adjectives, and pronouns. —*Idiom.* **8. in any case,** anyhow. **9. in case,** if. **10. in case of,** in the event of.

case² (kās) *n., v.,* **cased, casing.** —*n.* **1.** a container. —*v.t.* **2.** to put in a case.

ca/sein (kā/sēn) *n.* a protein derived from milk.

case/ment (kās/mənt) *n.* a window opening on side hinges.

cash (kash) *n.* **1.** money in the form of coins or banknotes. —*v.t.* **2.** to give or get cash for (a check, money order, etc.).

cash/ew (kash/ōō, kə shōō/) *n.* a small curved nut.

cash·ier/ (ka shēr/) *n.* a person employed to collect money for purchases, as in a store.

cashier's/ check/ *n.* a check drawn by a bank on its own funds and signed by its cashier.

cash′mere (kazh′mēr, kash′-) *n.* a soft wool fabric.

cas′ing (kā′sing) *n.* **1.** an outer covering. **2.** a framework, as of a door.

ca·si′no (kə sē′nō) *n., pl.* **-nos.** a place for gambling.

cask (kask) *n.* a barrel for liquids.

cas′ket (kas′kit) *n.* a coffin.

cas·sa′va (kə sä′və) *n.* a tropical plant with starchy roots.

cas′se·role (kas′ə rōl′) *n.* **1.** a covered baking dish. **2.** food baked in such a dish.

cas·sette′ (kə set′) *n.* a compact case for film or recording tape.

cas′sock (kas′ək) *n.* a long, close-fitting garment worn by the clergy.

cast (kast) *v.,* **cast, casting,** —*v.t.* **1.** to throw. **2.** to send forth. **3.** to deposit (a ballot or vote). **4.** to form (an object) by pouring into a mold. **5.** to choose (actors) for (a play). —*n.* **6.** the act of throwing. **7.** something made in a mold. **8.** the actors in a play. **9.** a rigid surgical dressing. **10.** a hue; shade.

cas′ta·net′ (kas′tə net′) *n.* one of a pair of wooden shells held in the palm and clicked together to accompany dancing.

cast′a·way *n.* a shipwrecked person.

caste (kast) *n.* a rigid system of social divisions.

cast′er *n.* a small swivel-mounted wheel. Also, **cast′or.**

cas′ti·gate (kas′ti gāt′) *v.t.,* **-gated, -gating.** to scold severely.

cast i′ron *n.* a hard, brittle alloy of carbon, iron, and silicon.

cas′tle (kas′əl) *n.* **1.** a royal or noble residence, usu. fortified. **2.** the rook in chess.

cas′tor oil (kas′tər) *n.* a strongly laxative oil.

cas′trate (kas′trāt) *v.t.,* **-trated, -trating.** to remove the testicles of.

cas·u·al (kazh′ōō əl) *adj.* **1.** accidental; not planned. **2.** not caring. **3.** informal.

cas′u·al·ty *n., pl.* **-ties.** a person injured or killed in an accident or in a war.

cas′u·ist·ry (kazh′ōō ə strē) *n.* overly subtle argument.

cat (kat) *n.* **1.** a small, furry domestic animal. —*Idiom.* **2. let the cat out of the bag,** to reveal a secret. —**cat′like′,** *adj.*

cat′a·clysm′ (kat′ə kliz′əm) *n.* a violent upheaval or disaster. —**cat′a·clys′mic,** *adj.*

cat′a·comb′ (-kōm′) *n.* an underground cemetery.

cat′a·logue (kat′l ôg′) *n., v.,* **-logued, -loguing.** —*n.* **1.** an organized list. **2.** a book or brochure containing descriptive information about items, courses, artworks, etc. —*v.t., v.i.* **3.** to make a catalogue (of). Also, **cat′a·log′.**

ca·tal′pa (kə tal′pə) *n.* a tree with bell-shaped white flowers.

cat′a·lyst (kat′l ist) *n.* **1.** a substance causing a chemical reaction without itself being affected. **2.** anything precipitating an event.

cat′a·ma·ran′ (kat′ə mə ran′) *n.* a two-hulled boat.

cat′a·mount′ *n.* a wild cat, as the cougar.

cat′a·pult′ (-pult′, -pŏŏlt′) *n.* **1.** a device for hurling or launching (stones). —*v.t., v.i.* **2.** to hurl or be hurled from in this way.

cat′a·ract′ (-rakt′) *n.* **1.** a waterfall. **2.** an opaque area in the lens of the eye.

ca·tarrh′ (kə tär′) *n.* an inflammation of a mucous membrane, esp. of the respiratory tract.

ca·tas′tro·phe (kə tas′trə fē) *n.* a sudden great disaster. —**cat′a·stroph′ic** (kat′ə strof′ik) *adj.*

cat′bird′ *n.* a songbird with a cat-like call.

cat′call′ *n.* a jeer.

catch (kach) *v.,* **caught, catching,** *n.* —*v.t.* **1.** to capture. **2.** to trap. **3.** to surprise. **4.** to be in time for. **5.** to get and hold. **5.** to be in time for. **6.** to get or contract, as an illness. —*v.i.* **7.** to become entangled. **8.** catch on, a. to become popular. b. to understand. **9.** — **up, a.** to overtake something moving. **b.** to do extra work so one is no longer behind. —*n.* **10.** the act of catching. **11.** anything that catches. **12.** something caught. **13.** a snag.

Catch-22 (katch′twen′tē tōō′) *n.* a frustrating situation in which one is trapped by contradictory conditions.

catch′ing *adj.* contagious.

catch′word′ *n.* a slogan.

catch′y *adj.,* **-ier, -iest.** memorable and pleasing.

cat′e·chism (kat′i kiz′əm) *n.* a set of questions and answers on the principles of a religion.

cat′e·gor′i·cal (-gôr′i kəl) *adj.* unconditional.

cat′e·go·ry (-gôr′ē) *n., pl.* **-ries.** a division; class. —**cat′e·go·rize′** (-gə rīz′) *v.t.*

ca′ter (kā′tər) *v.i.* **1.** to provide food and service for a party. **2.** to provide what is needed. —*v.t.* **3.** to provide food and service for. —**ca′ter·er,** *n.*

cat′er-cor′nered (kat′i-, kat′ē-, kat′ər-) *adj.* **1.** diagonal. —*adv.* **2.** diagonally.

cat′er·pil′lar (kat′ə pil′ər) *n.* the wormlike larva of a butterfly or moth.

cat′er·waul (kat′ər wôl′) *v.i.* **1.** to utter long wailing cries. —*n.* **2.** such a cry.

cat′fish′ *n.* a scaleless fresh-water fish.

cat′gut′ *n.* string made from animal intestines.

ca·thar′sis (kə thär′sis) *n.* **1.** the release of the emotions, as through art. **2.** purgation of the bowels.

ca·thar′tic *adj.* **1.** causing a catharsis. —*n.* **2.** a strong laxative.

ca·the′dral (kə thē′drəl) *n.* the main church of a diocese.

cath′e·ter (kath′i tər) *n.* a thin tube inserted into a body passage.

cath′ode (kath′ōd) *n.* **1.** an electrode with a negative charge. **2.** the positive terminal of a battery.

cath′ode ray *n.* a beam of electrons coming from a cathode.

cath′ode-ray′ tube′ *n.* a vacuum tube generating cathode rays directed at a screen, used to display images on a receiver or monitor. *Abbr.:* CRT.

cath′o·lic (kath′ə lik) *adj.* **1.** universal. **2.** broad-minded.

Cath′o·lic (kath′ə lik) *adj.* **1.** of the Roman Catholic Church. **2.** of any orthodox Christian church. **3.** of the Christian church as a whole. —*n.* **4.** a member of a Catholic church. —**Ca·thol′i·cism** (kə thol′ə siz′əm) *n.*

cat′kin (kat′kin) *n.* a spike of bunched, small petal-less flowers.

cat′nap′ *n., v.,* **-napped, -napping.** —*n.* **1.** a short, light sleep. —*v.i.* **2.** to sleep briefly.

cat′nip *n.* a plant with strong-smelling leaves attractive to cats.

cat′-o′-nine′-tails′ (kat′ə nīn′-) *n.,* a whip having nine knotted cords on a handle.

CAT′ scan′ (kat) *n.* an examination using x-rays at various angles to show a cross section of the body. **2.** an image so produced.

cat′s′-paw′ *n.* a person used by another to do unpleasant work.

cat′sup (kat′səp, kech′əp, kach′-) *n.* ketchup.

cat′tail′ *n.* a tall, spiky marsh plant.

cat′tle (kat′l) *n.* bovine animals, as cows and steers.

cat′ty (kat′ē) *adj.,* **-tier, -tiest.** slyly malicious.

cat′walk′ *n.* a high, narrow walkway.

Cau·ca′sian (kô kā′zhən) *adj.* **1.** of or characteristic of one of the racial divisions of humankind, marked by minimum skin pigmentation. —*n.* **2.** a Caucasian person.

cau′cus (kô′kəs) *n.* a political meeting.

caught (kôt) *v.* pt. and pp. of **catch.**

caul′dron (kôl′drən) *n.* a big kettle.

cau′li·flow′er (kô′lə flou′ər) *n.* a kind of cabbage with a head of white florets.

caulk (kôk) *v.t.* **1.** to fill the seams of to keep water or air out. —*n.* **2.** Also, **caulk′ing.** material used to caulk.

cause (kôz) *n., v.,* **caused, causing.** —*n.* **1.** a person or thing producing a result. **2.** a reason. **3.** an ideal or goal. —*v.t.* **4.** to bring about. —**caus′al,** *adj.* —**caus·al′i·ty,** *n.*

cause cé·lè·bre (kôz′ sə leb′) *n., pl.* **causes cé·lè·bres** (kôz′ sə leb′) a controversy attracting public attention.

cause′way′ *n.* a raised road across wet ground.

caus′tic (kô′stik) *adj.* **1.** corroding. **2.** sharply critical or sarcastic.

cau′ter·ize′ (kô′tə rīz′) *v.t.,* **-ized, -izing.** to burn (tissue) to stop bleeding or kill infection.

cau′tion (kô′shən) *n.* **1.** carefulness. **2.** a warning. —*v.t., v.i.* **3.** to warn. —**cau′tious,** *adj.*

cav′al·cade′ (kav′əl kād′) *n.* a procession, esp. on horseback.

cav·a·lier′ (kav′ə lēr′) *n.* **1.** a knight or horseman. **2.** a courtly gentleman. —*adj.* **3.** haughty; indifferent. **4.** casual.

cav′al·ry (kav′əl rē) *n., pl.* **-ries.** troops on horseback or in armored vehicles. —**cav′al·ry·man,** *n.*

cave (kāv) *n., v.,* **caved, caving.** —*n.* **1.** a hollow space in the earth. —*v.* **2. cave in, a.** to collapse or cause to collapse. **b.** to yield.

ca′ve·at′ (kav′ē ät′) *n.* a warning.

cave′ man′ *n.* **1.** a Stone Age cave dweller. **2.** a rough, brutal man.

cav′ern (kav′ərn) *n.* a large cave.

cav′i·ar′ (-ē är′) *n.* the roe of sturgeon, salmon, etc.

cav′il (-əl) *v.,* **-iled, -iling,** *n.* —*v.i.* **1.** to raise trivial objections. —*n.* **2.** a trivial objection.

cav′i·ty (-i tē) *n., pl.* **-ties. 1.** a hollow place. **2.** a decayed place in a tooth.

ca·vort′ (kə vôrt′) *v.i.* to prance.

caw (kô) *n.* **1.** the harsh call of a crow. —*v.i.* **2.** to make a caw.

cay·enne′ (kī en′) *n.* hot pepper.

CB citizens band: a private two-way radio.

cc. **1.** carbon copy. **2.** cubic centimeter.

CCU coronary-care unit.

CD **1.** certificate of deposit. **2.** Civil Defense. **3.** compact disc.

CD-ROM (sē′dē′rom′) *n.* a compact disc for storing digitized read-only data.

cease (sēs) *v.,* **ceased, ceasing,** *n.* —*v.i., v.t.* **1.** to stop; end. —*n.* **2.** a stopping. —**cease′less,** *adj.*

cease′-fire′ *n.* a truce.

ce′dar (sē′dər) *n.* an evergreen tree having fragrant wood.

cede (sēd) *v.t.,* **ceded, ceding. 1.** to yield or give up. **2.** to transfer by legal document.

ceil′ing (sē′ling) *n.* **1.** the overhead surface of a room. **2.** an upper limit.

cel′e·brate (sel′ə brāt′) *v.,* **-brated, -brating.** —*v.t.* **1.** to observe with festivities. **2.** to perform with appropriate rites. —*v.i.* **3.** to have a good time. —**cel′e·bra′tion,** *n.*

ce·leb′ri·ty (sə leb′ri tē) *n., pl.* **-ties. 1.** a famous person. **2.** fame.

ce·ler′i·ty (sə ler′i tē) *n.* speed.

cel′er·y (sel′ə rē) *n.* a plant with edible leaf stalks.

ce·les′tial (sə les′chəl) *adj.* of heaven or the sky.

cel′i·ba·cy (sel′ə bə sē) *n.* **1.** sexual abstinence. **2.** the state of being unmarried.

cell (sel) *n.* **1.** a small room. **2.** a microscopic biological structure containing nuclear material. **3.** a device for converting chemical energy into electricity. **4.** a unit of an organization. —**cel′lu·lar,** *adj.*

cel′lar (sel′ər) *n.* an underground room.

cel′lo (chel′ō) *n., pl.* **-los.** a large violinlike instrument. —**cel′list,** *n.*

cel′lo·phane′ (sel′ə fān′) *n.* transparent wrapping material.

cel′lular phone′ *n.* a mobile telephone. Also, **cell′ phone′.**

cel′lu·lite′ (sel′yə līt′, -lēt′) *n.* lumpy fat deposits, esp. in the thighs.

cel′lu·loid′ (-loid′) *n.* a tough flammable substance.

cel′lu·lose′ (-lōs′) *n.* a carbohydrate of plant origin.

Cel′si·us (sel′sē əs) *adj.* of a temperature scale in which water freezes at 0° and boils at 100°.

Celt (kelt, selt) *n.* a member of an ancient group of peoples inhabiting the British Isles and areas of W and central Europe.

Celt′ic *n.* **1.** a branch of the Indo-European language family, including Irish and Welsh. —*adj.* **2.** of the Celts or their languages.

ce·ment′ (si ment′) *n.* **1.** a clay-lime mixture that hardens into a stonelike mass. **2.** a binding material. —*v.t.* **3.** to unite by or cover with cement.

cem′e·ter′y (sem′i ter′ē) *n., pl.* **-ter·ies.** a burial ground.

cen′o·taph′ (sen′ə taf′) *n.* a monument for someone buried elsewhere.

Ce′no·zo′ic (sē′nə zō′ik) *adj.* of the present geologic era.

cen′ser (sen′sər) *n.* an incense burner, swung on a chain.

cen′sor (sen′sər) *n.* **1.** an official who examines books, films, etc., to eliminate anything objectionable.

—*v.t.* **2.** to act upon as a censor. —**cen′sor·ship′,** *n.*

cen·so′ri·ous (-sôr′ē əs) *adj.* severely critical.

cen′sure (-shər) *n., v.,* **-sured, -suring.** —*n.* **1.** strong disapproval. —*v.t.* **2.** to rebuke strongly.

cen′sus (sen′səs) *n.* an official count of inhabitants.

cent (sent) *n.* $\frac{1}{100}$ of a dollar; penny.

cent. century.

cen′taur (sen′tôr) *n.* a mythological creature that is half horse and half man.

cen·ten′ar·y (sen ten′ə rē, sen′tn-er′ē) *n., pl.* **-aries.** a 100th anniversary.

cen·ten′ni·al (-ten′ē əl) *n.* **1.** a 100th anniversary. —*adj.* **2.** of 100 years.

cen′ter (sen′tər) *n.* **1.** the middle point, part, or person. —*v.t., v.i.* **2.** to place or gather at the center. **3.** to concentrate. Also, **cen′tre.**

cen′ter·fold′ *n.* the facing pages in the center of a magazine.

cen′ter·piece′ *n.* a decoration for the center of a table.

cen′ti·grade′ (sen′ti grād′) *adj.* Celsius.

cen′ti·gram′ *n.* $\frac{1}{100}$ of a gram.

cen′ti·li′ter (-lē′tər) *n.* $\frac{1}{100}$ of a liter.

cen′ti·me′ter *n.* $\frac{1}{100}$ of a meter.

cen′ti·pede′ (-pēd′) *n.* an insect with many legs.

cen′tral (sen′trəl) *adj.* **1.** in, of, at, or forming the center. **2.** main; principal. —**cen′tral·ly,** *adv.*

cen′tral·ize′ *v.,* **-ized, -izing.** —*v.t.* **1.** to gather about a center. **2.** to bring under one control. —*v.i.* **3.** to come together at or form a center. —**cen′tral·i·za′tion,** *n.*

cen′tral nerv′ous sys′tem *n.* the brain and spinal cord.

cen·trif′u·gal (-trif′yə gəl, -ə gəl) *adj.* moving away from the center.

cen′tri·fuge′ (-fyōōj′) *n.* a high-speed rotating machine for separating substances.

cen·trip′e·tal (-trip′i tl) *adj.* moving toward the center.

cen′trist (sen′trist) *n.* a person with moderate political views.

cen′tu·ry (sen′chə rē) *n., pl.* **-ries.** a period of one hundred years.

CEO chief executive officer.

ce·phal′ic (sə fal′ik) *adj.* of or toward the head.

ce·ram′ic (sə ram′ik) *adj.* of clay and similar materials. —**ce·ram′ics,** *n.*

ce′re·al (sēr′ē əl) *n.* **1.** a grass plant yielding edible grain. **2.** a food made from such a grain.

cer′e·bel′lum (ser′ə bel′əm) *n.* the rear part of the brain, controlling movement and balance.

cer′e·bral (ser′ə brəl, sə rē′-) *adj.* **1.** of the brain. **2.** intellectual.

cere′bral pal′sy *n.* a condition marked by difficulty in coordinating movement, due to brain injury.

cer′e·brum (sə rē′brəm, ser′ə-) *n., pl.* **-brums, -bra** (-brə). the front part of the brain, controlling voluntary movement and conscious processes.

cer′e·mo′ny (ser′ə mō′nē) *n., pl.* **-nies.** a formal act or ritual. —**cer′e·mo′ni·al,** *adj., n.*

ce·rise′ (sə rēs′, -rēz′) *n.* a medium to deep red.

cer′tain (sûr′tn) *adj.* **1.** free from doubt; sure. **2.** destined. **3.** agreed upon. **4.** definite but unspecified. —**cer′tain·ly,** *adv.* —**cer′tain·ty,** *n.*

cer·tif′i·cate (sər tif′i kit) *n.* an official document affirming something.

certif′icate of depos′it *n.* a bank receipt for money deposited, showing the interest to be paid for a certain period.

cer′ti·fy′ (sûr′tə fī′) *v.t.,* **-fied, -fying. 1.** to attest as certain. **2.** to guarantee. **3.** to vouch for in writing. —**cer′ti·fi·ca′tion,** *n.*

cer′ti·tude′ (-tōōd′, -tyōōd′) *n.* sureness.

ce·ru′le·an (sə rōō′lē ən) *n.* a deep blue.

cer′vix (sûr′viks) *n., pl.* **cervixes, cervices** (sûr′və sēz′). a necklike part, esp. the lower end of the uterus. —**cer′vi·cal** (-vi kəl) *adj.*

Ce·sar′e·an (si zâr′ē ən) *n.* the delivery of a baby by cutting through the abdomen and uterus. Also, **Cesar′ean sec′tion, C-section, Cae·sar′e·an.**

ces·sa′tion (se sā′shən) *n.* a temporary or complete stopping.

ces′sion (sesh′ən) *n.* **1.** the act of ceding. **2.** something ceded.

cess′pool′ (ses′pōōl′) *n.* a receptacle for sewage from a house.

cf. compare.

cg. centigram.

ch. **1.** chapter. **2.** church.

Cha·blis′ (sha blē′) *n.* a dry white wine. Also, **cha·blis′.**

chad (chad) *n.* one of the small paper disks formed when holes are punched in punch cards, punch-card ballots, etc.

chafe (chāf) *v.,* **chafed, chafing.** —*v.t.* **1.** to wear away or make sore by rubbing. **2.** to warm by rubbing. **3.** to irritate. —*v.i.* **4.** to rub. **5.** to become irritated.

chaff (chaf) *n.* **1.** the husks of grain separated from the seeds. **2.** worthless matter.

chaf′ing dish′ (chā′fing) *n.* a device for cooking or warming food at the table.

cha·grin′ (shə grin′) *n.* **1.** embarrassment or humiliation. —*v.t.* **2.** to cause chagrin to.

chain (chān) *n.* **1.** a connected series of links. **2.** any connected series. **3.** a mountain range. —*v.t.* **4.** to fasten with a chain.

chain′ reac′tion *n.* a series of events, each causing the following.

chain′ saw′ *n.* a power saw with teeth set on an endless chain.

chair (châr) *n.* **1.** a seat, usu. with a back and four legs, for one person. **2.** a position of authority. **3.** a chairman, chairwoman, or chairperson. —*v.t.* **4.** to preside over.

chair′man or **-wom′an** or **-per′son,** *n., pl.* **-men** or **-women** or **-persons.** a presiding officer or head of a board or department.

chaise′ longue′ (shāz′ lông′) *n.* a chair with a long seat.

chal·ced′o·ny (kal sed′n ē, kal′si-dō′nē) *n., pl.* **-nies.** a translucent kind of quartz.

cha·let′ (sha lā′) *n.* a mountain house with wide eaves.

chal′ice (chal′is) *n.* a large goblet.

chalk (chôk) *n.* **1.** a soft, powdery white limestone. **2.** a piece of chalk, used to write on blackboards. —*v.t.* **3.** to mark with chalk. **4. chalk up,** to score or earn.

chal′lenge (chal′inj) *v.,* **-lenged, -lenging.** —*n.* **1.** a summons to engage in a contest. **2.** a demand for an explanation. **3.** a demanding task. **4.** a formal objection. —*v.t.* **5.** to issue a challenge to.

challenged *adj.* (as a euphemism) disabled, handicapped, or deficient (preceded by an adverb).

cham′ber (chām′bər) *n.* **1.** a room, esp. a bedroom. **2.** an assembly hall. **3.** a legislative body. **4. chambers,** a judge's office. **5.** an enclosed space.

cham′ber·lain (-lin) *n.* a high official of a royal court.

cham′ber·maid′ *n.* a maid who cleans hotel rooms.

cham′ber mu′sic *n.* music for performance by a small ensemble.

cha·me′le·on (kə mē′lē ən) *n.* a lizard that is able to change color.

cham′ois (sham′ē) *n.* **1.** a European antelope. **2.** the soft leather from its skin.

cham′o·mile′ (kam′ə mīl′, -mēl′) *n.* a plant whose flowers are used as a tea. Also, **cam′o·mile′.**

champ¹ (champ) *n. Informal.* a champion.

champ² (chomp, champ) *v.t., v.i.* to bite noisily.

cham·pagne′ (sham pān′) *n.* a sparkling white wine.

cham′pi·on (cham′pē ən) *n.* **1.** the best competitor. **2.** a supporter. —*v.t.* **3.** to support. —*adj.* **4.** best. —**cham′pi·on·ship′,** *n.*

chance (chans) *n., v.,* **chanced, chancing,** *adj.* —*n.* **1.** fate; luck. **2.** a possibility. **3.** an opportunity. **4.** a risk. —*v.i.* **5.** to occur by chance. —*v.t.* **6.** to risk. —*adj.* **7.** accidental. —*Idiom.* **8. by chance,** accidentally. **9. on the (off) chance,** relying on the (slight) possibility.

chan′cel (chan′səl) *n.* the space around the altar in a church.

chan′cel·ler·y (-sə lə rē, -səl rē) *n., pl.* **-leries.** the position or offices of a chancellor.

chan′cel·lor (-sə lər) *n.* **1.** a chief or high government official. **2.** a university head.

chan′cer·y (-sə rē) *n., pl.* **-ceries.** a high law court.

chan′cre (shang′kər) *n.* a lesion.

chanc′y (chan′sē) *adj.,* **-cier, -ciest.** risky; uncertain.

chan·de·lier′ (shan′dl ēr′) *n.* a decorative hanging lighting fixture.

chan′dler (chand′lər) *n.* a dealer in supplies for ships.

change (chānj) *v.,* **changed, chang-**

ing, *n.* —*v.t.* **1.** to make different. **2.** to exchange. —*v.i.* **3.** to become different. **4.** to transfer between means of transportation. **5.** to put on different clothes. —*n.* **6.** an alteration. **7.** a substitution. **8.** coins. —**change/a·ble,** *adj.*

change of life *n.* menopause.

change/o·ver *n.* a change from one system to another.

chan/nel (chan/l) *n., v.,* **-neled, -neling.** —*n.* **1.** the bed of a stream. **2.** a wide strait. **3.** a route. **4.** a frequency band used by radio or television. —*v.t.* **5.** to convey or direct in a channel.

chant (chant) *n.* **1.** a simple melody. **2.** a phrase repeated rhythmically. —*v.i.* **3.** to sing in a chant. **4.** to shout rhythmically.

chant/ey (shan/tē) *n., pl.* **-eys, -ies.** a sailors' song. Also, **chant/y.**

chan/ti·cleer/ (chan/ti klēr/) *n.* a rooster.

Cha/nu·kah (кнä/nə kə, hä/-) *n.* Hanukkah.

cha/os (kā/os) *n.* complete disorder. —**cha·ot/ic** (-ot/ik) *adj.*

chap¹ (chap) *v.i.,* **chapped, chapping.** (of the skin) to become rough and red.

chap² (chap) *n. Informal.* a fellow.

chap. chapter.

chap/el (chap/əl) *n.* a private or subordinate place of worship.

chap/er·on/ (shap/ə rōn/) *n., v.,* **-oned, -oning.** —*n.* **1.** an older person who accompanies younger persons at a social gathering. —*v.t., v.i.* **2.** to be a chaperon (for). Also, **chap/er·one/.**

chap/lain (chap/lin) *n.* a member of the clergy associated with a college, hospital, etc.

chap/let (chap/lit) *n.* a wreath for the head.

chaps (chaps, shaps) *n.pl.* leather leg protectors worn by cowboys.

chap/ter (chap/tər) *n.* **1.** a division of a book. **2.** a branch of an organization. **3.** the canons of a cathedral.

char (chär) *v.t., v.i.,* **charred, charring.** to burn slightly.

char/ac·ter (kar/ik tər) *n.* **1.** the qualities that form the individual nature of a person or thing. **2.** moral quality. **3.** reputation. **4.** a person in a novel, play, etc. **5.** a written or printed symbol.

char/ac·ter·is/tic (-tə ris/tik) *adj.* **1.** typical. —*n.* **2.** a special feature.

char/ac·ter·ize/ *v.t.,* **-ized, -izing. 1.** to be a characteristic of. **2.** to describe the character of. —**char/-ac·ter·i·za/tion,** *n.*

cha·rades/ (shə rādz/) *n.* a guessing game in which players act out a word or phrase.

char/coal/ *n.* a black material made by burning wood without air.

chard (chärd) *n.* a plant with edible leafy green stalks.

Char/don·nay/ (shär/dn ā/) *n.* a dry white wine.

charge (chärj) *v.,* **charged, charging,** *n.* —*v.t.* **1.** to ask as a price. **2.** to defer payment for. **3.** to attack by rushing violently at. **4.** to accuse. **5.** to command. **6.** to fill. **7.** to supply with electrical energy. —*v.i.* **8.** to rush violently. **9.** to require payment. —*n.* **10.** an expense or cost. **11.** an attack. **12.** a duty. **13.** a command. **14.** an accusation. —*Idiom.* **15.** in charge, in command. —**charge/a·ble,** *adj.*

charg/er *n.* a battle horse.

char/i·ot (char/ē ət) *n.* a horse-drawn two-wheeled vehicle of the ancient world. —**char/i·ot·eer/,** *n.*

cha·ris/ma (kə riz/mə) *n.* the power to charm and inspire people. —**char/is·mat/ic** (kar/iz mat/ik) *adj.*

char/i·ty (char/i tē) *n., pl.* **-ties. 1.** generosity toward the needy. **2.** a fund or institution that benefits the needy. **3.** kindness in judging others. —**char/i·ta·ble,** *adj.*

char/la·tan (shär/lə tn) *n.* a quack; fraud.

char/ley horse/ (chär/lē) *n.* a cramp or sore muscle, esp. in the leg.

charm (chärm) *n.* **1.** the power to attract. **2.** a magical object, verse, etc. **3.** a trinket on a bracelet or necklace. —*v.t., v.i.* **4.** to attract; enchant. —**charm/er,** *n.* —**charm/ing,** *adj.*

char/nel house/ (chär/nl) *n.* a place for dead bodies.

chart (chärt) *n.* **1.** a sheet displaying data in tabular form. **2.** a map. —*v.t.* **3.** to make a chart of.

char/ter *n.* **1.** a governmental document outlining the conditions under which a corporate body is or-

ganized. **2.** a temporary lease of a bus, aircraft, etc. —*v.t.* **3.** to establish by charter. **4.** to hire; lease.

char/ter mem/ber *n.* an original member of an organization.

char·treuse/ (shär trōz/) *n.* a yellowish green.

char/wom/an (chär/-) *n.* a woman who cleans offices, houses, etc.

char/y (châr/ē) *adj.,* **charier, chariest.** careful.

chase (chās) *v.,* **chased, chasing,** *n.* —*v.t.* **1.** to follow in order to seize. **2.** to drive away. —*n.* **3.** an instance of chasing.

chasm (kaz/əm) *n.* **1.** a deep cleft in the earth. **2.** any gap.

chas/sis (chas/ē, shas/ē) *n.* the frame, wheels, and motor of a vehicle.

chaste (chāst) *adj.,* **chaster, chastest. 1.** refraining from unlawful sexual activity. **2.** celibate. **3.** simple. —**chas/ti·ty** (chas/ti tē) *n.*

chas/ten (chā/sən) *v.t.* to discipline by punishing.

chas·tise/ (chas tīz/, chas/tīz) *v.t.,* **-tised, -tising. 1.** to punish; beat. **2.** to criticize severely.

chat (chat) *v.,* **chatted, chatting,** *n.* —*v.i.* **1.** to talk informally. —*n.* **2.** an informal conversation.

cha·teau/ (sha tō/) *n., pl.* **-teaux** (-tōz/). a stately residence.

chat/ room/ *n.* a branch of a computer system in which participants can have live discussions.

chat/tel (chat/l) *n.* a movable article of personal property.

chat/ter (chat/ər) *v.i.* **1.** to talk rapidly or foolishly. **2.** to click rapidly. —*n.* **3.** rapid or foolish talk.

chat/ty (chat/ē) *adj.,* **-tier, -tiest. 1.** given to chatting. **2.** having a friendly, informal style.

chauf/feur (shō/fər, shō fûr/) *n.* a hired driver.

chau/vin·ism/ (shō/və niz/əm) *n.* **1.** excessive patriotism. **2.** fanatic devotion to any group, cause, etc. —**chau/vin·ist** (-və nist) *n., adj.*

cheap (chēp) *adj.* **1.** inexpensive. **2.** shoddy. **3.** stingy. —**cheap/en,** *v.t., v.i.*

cheap/skate/ *n.* a stingy person.

cheat (chēt) *v.t.* **1.** to defraud; swindle. —*v.i.* **2.** to practice deceit. **3.** to violate rules. —*n.* **4.** a person who cheats. **5.** a fraud.

check (chek) *v.t.* **1.** to stop or restrain. **2.** to investigate; verify. **3.** to note with a mark. **4.** to leave or receive for temporary custody. —*v.i.* **5.** to make an inquiry. **6.** **check in,** to report one's arrival. **7.** **~ out,** to leave a hotel, hospital, etc., officially. —*n.* **8.** a stop; restraint. **9.** a written order for a bank to pay money. **10.** an inquiry. **11.** a mark (✓) to indicate approval, verification, etc. **12.** a restaurant bill. **13.** an identification tag. **14.** a square pattern. **15.** *Chess.* a direct attack on the king.

check/er *n.* **1.** a piece used in checkers. **2.** **checkers,** a game played on a checkerboard by two persons, each with 12 playing pieces.

check/er·board/ *n.* a board with 64 squares on which checkers is played.

check/ered *adj.* **1.** marked with squares. **2.** varied. **3.** dubious.

check/list/ *n.* a list of items for comparison, verification, etc.

check/mate/ (-māt/) *n., v.,* **-mated, -mating.** —*n.* **1.** *Chess.* an inescapable check. **2.** a defeat. —*v.t.* **3.** *Chess.* to put into inescapable check. **4.** to defeat.

check/out/ *n.* **1.** the act of leaving and paying for a hotel room. **2.** a counter where customers pay for purchases.

check/point/ *n.* a place where travelers are stopped for inspection.

check/up/ *n.* a physical examination.

ched/dar (ched/ər) *n.* a sharp cheese.

cheek (chēk) *n.* **1.** the soft side of the face. **2.** *Informal.* a cheerful lack of respect. —**cheek/i·ly,** *adv.* —**cheek/y,** *adj.*

cheer (chēr) *n.* **1.** a shout of support. **2.** gladness. —*v.t.* **3.** to shout encouragement to. **4.** to raise the spirits of. —*v.i.* **5.** to utter cheers. **6.** to become cheerful.

cheer/ful *adj.* **1.** full of cheer. **2.** pleasant and bright.

cheer/less *adj.* gloomy.

cheese (chēz) *n.* a food made from pressed milk curds.

cheese/burg/er *n.* a hamburger with melted cheese.

cheese/cloth/ *n.* a cotton fabric of loose weave.

chee/tah (chē/tə) *n.* a wild cat resembling the leopard.

chef (shef) *n.* a professional cook.

chem/i·cal (kem/i kəl) *adj.* **1.** of chemistry. —*n.* **2.** a substance produced by or used in chemistry. —**chem/i·cal·ly,** *adv.*

chem/ical war/fare *n.* warfare using chemicals as weapons.

che·mise/ (shə mēz/) *n.* a woman's shirtlike undergarment.

chem/is·try (kem/ə strē) *n.* **1.** the study of the composition and activity of substances. **2.** rapport. —**chem/ist,** *n.*

che/mo·ther/a·py (kē/mō ther/ə-pē) *n.* the treatment of disease, esp. cancer, with chemicals.

cheque (chek) *n. Brit.* a bank check.

cher/ish (cher/ish) *v.t.* to treat as dear.

cher/ry (cher/ē) *n., pl.* **-ries.** a small, pulpy red fruit of certain trees.

cher/ub (cher/əb) *n.* **1.** *pl.* **cherubim** (-ə bim) a celestial being. **2.** *pl.* **cherubs.** a chubby child with wings.

chess (ches) *n.* a board game for two players, each using 16 pieces.

chest (chest) *n.* **1.** the part of the body between the neck and the abdomen. **2.** a large box with a lid. **3.** a set of drawers for clothes.

chest/nut/ (ches/nut/) *n.* **1.** an edible nut. **2.** a reddish brown.

chev/i·ot (shev/ē ət) *n.* a sturdy, coarse woolen fabric.

chev/ron (shev/rən) *n.* a set of V-shaped stripes.

chew (chōō) *v.t., v.i.* to crush with the teeth.

chew/ing gum/ *n.* a flavored preparation for chewing.

chew/y *adj.,* **-ier, -iest.** not easily chewed.

chi (kī) *n., pl.* **chis.** the 22nd letter of the Greek alphabet.

Chi·an/ti (kē än/tē) *n.* a dry red wine of Italy.

chic (shēk) *adj.* stylish. —**Pronunciation.** The pronunciation (chik) for the word CHIC is considered nonstandard except when used jokingly.

chi·can/er·y (shi kā/nə rē, chi-) *n., pl.* **-ies. 1.** deception. **2.** a trick.

Chi·ca/no (chi kä/nō) *n., pl.* **-nos.** a Mexican-American.

chick (chik) *n.* **1.** a young chicken. **2.** *Slang: Usu. Offensive.* a young woman.

chick/a·dee/ (chik/ə dē/) *n.* a small gray bird with a dark cap.

chick/en (chik/ən) *n.* **1.** a common domestic fowl. **2.** *Slang.* a coward.

chick/en·pox/ *n.* a viral disease marked by the eruption of blisters.

chick/pea/ *n.* a legume with pea-like seeds.

chic/o·ry (-ə rē) *n., pl.* **-ries. 1.** a plant with toothed edible leaves. **2.** its root, ground and used with coffee.

chide (chīd) *v.t., v.i.,* **chided, chiding.** to scold.

chief (chēf) *n.* **1.** a leader. —*adj.* **2.** main; principal. —**chief/ly,** *adv.*

chief/tain (-tən) *n.* the chief of a clan or tribe.

chif·fon/ (shi fon/) *n.* a sheer silk or rayon fabric.

chif/fo·nier/ (shif/ə nēr/) *n.* a tall chest of drawers.

chig/ger (chig/ər) *n.* the larva of certain parasite mites.

chil/blains/ (chil/blānz/) *n.pl.* an inflammation caused by overexposure to the cold.

child (chīld) *n., pl.* **children** (chil/-drən). **1.** a boy or girl. **2.** a son or daughter. —**child/hood,** *n.* —**child/ish,** *adj.* —**child/less,** *adj.* —**child/like/,** *adj.*

child/bear/ing *n.* **1.** the act of bringing forth children. —*adj.* **2.** capable of or relating to the bearing of children.

child/birth *n.* an act or instance of bringing forth a child.

child/proof/ *adj.* designed to prevent children from being hurt.

chil/i (chil/ē) *n., pl.* **-ies. 1.** the pungent pod of a red pepper. **2.** a dish made with these peppers.

chill (chil) *n.* **1.** coldness. **2.** a cold feeling with shivering. —*adj.* **3.** cold. **4.** not cordial. —*v.t., v.i.* **5.** to make or become cold. —**chil/ly,** *adj.*

chime (chīm) *n., v.,* **chimed, chiming.** —*n.* **1.** a set of musical tubes, bells, etc. —*v.t.* **2.** to sound chimes. —*v.t.* **3.** to announce by chiming. **4. chime in,** to interrupt.

chi·me/ra (ki mēr/ə, kī-) *n.* **1.** (*often cap.*) a mythical monster with a

lion's head, goat's body, and serpent's tail. **2.** an illusion.

chi·mer/i·cal (-mer/i kəl, -mēr/-) *adj.* **1.** unreal; imaginary. **2.** wildly fanciful.

chim/ney (chim/nē) *n., pl.* **-neys.** a structure for carrying off smoke.

chim/pan·zee/ (chim/pan zē/, chim pan/zē) *n.* a large, intelligent African ape.

chin (chin) *n.* the part of the face below the mouth.

chi/na (chī/nə) *n.* **1.** porcelain or ceramic material. **2.** tableware made of this.

chin·chil/la (chin chil/ə) *n.* a small rodent valued for its fur.

Chi/nese/ (chī nēz/, -nēs/) *n., pl.* **-nese.** —*n.* **1.** a native of China. **2.** a language of China. —*adj.* **3.** of China, its people, or their language.

chink¹ (chingk) *n.* a crack, as in a wall.

chink² (chingk) *n.* **1.** a short, sharp ringing sound. —*v.i.* **2.** to make such a sound.

chi·nook/ (shi nŏŏk/, -nōōk/), *n., pl.* **-nook, -nooks.** a warm, dry wind that blows down the E slopes of the Rocky Mountains.

chintz (chints) *n.* a printed cotton fabric.

chintz/y *adj.,* **-ier, -iest.** cheap-looking.

chip (chip) *n., v.,* **chipped, chipping.** —*n.* **1.** a small, thin, flat piece, as of wood. **2.** a small piece of food. **3.** a flaw where something has broken off. **4.** a disk used in games. **5.** a tiny slice of semiconducting material carrying an electric charge. —*v.t.* **6.** to break a fragment from. —*v.i.* **7.** to break off in small bits. **8. chip in,** to contribute. —*Idiom.* **9. chip on one's shoulder,** a readiness to quarrel.

chip/munk (-mungk) *n.* a small, striped squirrel-like animal.

chip/per *adj. Informal.* lively.

chi·rop/o·dy (ki rop/ə dē, kī-) *n.* podiatry.

chi/ro·prac/tor (kī/rə prak/tər) *n.* one who treats pain by manipulating body structures.

chirp (chûrp) *n.* **1.** the short, sharp sound made by small birds. —*v.i.* **2.** to make such a sound. Also, **chir/rup** (cher/əp, chûr/-).

chis/el (chiz/əl) *n.* **1.** a tool with a broad cutting tip. —*v.t., v.i.* **2.** to cut with such a tool. **3.** *Informal.* to cheat.

chit/chat/ (chit/chat/) *n.* light talk.

chiv/al·ry (shiv/əl rē) *n.* **1.** qualities such as courtesy and courage. **2.** medieval knighthood. —**chiv/al·rous,** *adj.*

chive (chīv) *n.* an onionlike plant with slender leaves.

chlo/rine (klôr/ēn, -in) *n.* a green gaseous element. —**chlor/in·ate/** (-i nāt/) *v.t.*

chlo/ro·form/ (klôr/ə fôrm/) *n.* **1.** a colorless liquid whose gas causes unconsciousness. —*v.t.* **2.** to administer chloroform to.

chlo/ro·phyll (-fil) *n.* the green coloring matter of plants.

chock (chok) *n.* a wedge; block.

choc·o·hol/ic (chŏ/kə hô/lik, -hol/ik) *n.* a person who is excessively fond of chocolate.

choc/o·late (chô/kə lit) *n.* **1.** a product made from cacao seeds, usu. sweetened. **2.** a candy or beverage made from this. **3.** a dark brown.

choice (chois) *n.* **1.** the act of choosing. **2.** the right to choose. **3.** a person or thing chosen. —*adj.* **4.** excellent.

choir (kwīər) *n.* a group of singers, esp. in a church.

choke (chōk) *v.,* **choked, choking,** *n.* —*v.t.* **1.** to stop the breath of. **2.** to obstruct. —*v.i.* **3.** to be unable to breathe. **4.** to be obstructed. —*n.* **5.** the act of choking. **6.** a device that controls the flow of air in an automobile engine.

chol/er·a (kol/ər ə) *n.* a severe, contagious infection of the small intestine.

chol/er·ic (kol/ər ik) *adj.* easily irritated or angered.

cho·les/ter·ol/ (kə les/tə rôl/) *n.* a fatty, crystalline substance in animal products.

chomp (chomp) *v.t., v.i.* to chew noisily.

choose (chōōz) *v.t.,* **chose** (chōz), **chosen, choosing.** —*v.t.* **1.** to select from a number of things. **2.** to desire. —*v.i.* **3.** to make a choice.

choos/y *adj.,* **-ier, -iest.** hard to please; particular.

chop¹ (chop) *v.,* **chopped, chop-**

ping, *n.* —*v.t.* **1.** to cut with blows. **2.** to cut in pieces. —*n.* **3.** a sharp blow. **4.** a thick slice of meat with the rib.

chop² (chop) *n.* Usu., **chops,** the jaw.

chop/per *n.* **1.** a thing that chops. **2.** *Informal.* a helicopter.

chop/py *adj.,* **-pier, -piest. 1.** (of a body of water) forming short waves. **2.** uneven.

chop/sticks/ *n.pl.* sticks used in eating in some Asian countries.

cho/ral (kôr/əl) *adj.* of or for a chorus or choir.

cho·rale/ (kə ral/, -räl/) *n.* **1.** a type of hymn. **2.** a choir.

chord¹ (kôrd) *n.* a combination of notes sounded together.

chord² (kôrd) *n.* the line segment between two points on a curve.

chore (chôr) *n.* a routine job.

cho/re·og/ra·phy (kôr/ē og/rə fē) *n.* **1.** the art of composing dances. **2.** the movements composed for a dance, show, etc. —**cho/re·o·graph/** (-ə graf/) *v.t., v.i.* —**cho/re·og/ra·pher,** *n.*

chor/is·ter (kôr/ə stər) *n.* a singer in a choir.

chor/tle (chôr/tl) *v.,* **-tled, -tling,** *n.* —*v.i.* **1.** to chuckle gleefully. —*n.* **2.** a gleeful chuckle.

cho/rus (kôr/əs) *n.* **1.** a group of singers. **2.** a refrain. **3.** something said or sung by many people, birds, etc. —*v.t., v.i.* **4.** to sing or speak simultaneously.

chose (chōz) *v. pt. of* **choose.**

chow (chou) *n. Slang.* food.

chow/der (chou/dər) *n.* a thick soup of vegetables, clams, etc.

Christ (krīst) *n.* Jesus Christ; (in Christian belief) the Messiah.

chris/ten (kris/ən) *v.t.* **1.** to baptize; name. **2.** to name at baptism. —**chris/ten·ing,** *n.*

Chris/ten·dom (kris/ən dəm) *n.* all Christians.

Chris/tian (kris/chən) *adj.* **1.** of Jesus Christ, His teachings, etc. —*n.* **2.** a believer in Christianity.

Chris/ti·an/i·ty (-chē an/i tē) *n.* the religion based on the teachings of Jesus Christ.

Chris/tian Sci/ence *n.* a Scripture-based religion that emphasizes spiritual healing. —**Chris/tian Sci/entist,** *n.*

Christ/mas (kris/məs) *n.* an annual Christian festival honoring the birth of Jesus, celebrated on December 25.

chro·mat/ic (krō mat/ik, krə-) *adj.* **1.** of color. **2.** progressing by semitones.

chro/mi·um (krō/mē əm) *n.* a lustrous metallic element. Also, **chrome.**

chro/mo·some/ (krō/mə sōm/) *n.* the threadlike part of a cell that carries the genes.

chron/ic (kron/ik) *adj.* constant; long-lasting; habitual.

chron/i·cle (kron/i kəl) *n., v.,* **-cled, -cling.** —*n.* **1.** a record of events in order. —*v.t.* **2.** to record in a chronicle.

chrono- a prefix meaning time.

chro·nol/o·gy (krə nol/ə jē) *n., pl.* **-gies.** an arrangement of things in the order in which they occurred. —**chron/o·log/i·cal** (kron/l oj/i kəl) *adj.*

chro·nom/e·ter (krə nom/i tər) *n.* a very precise clock.

chrys/a·lis (kris/ə lis) *n.* the pupa of a moth or butterfly.

chry·san/the·mum (kri san/thə-məm) *n.* a plant that produces colorful flowers in the autumn.

chub/by *adj.,* **-bier, -biest.** plump.

chuck¹ (chuk) *v.t.* **1.** to toss. **2.** to pat lightly. —*n.* **3.** a light pat.

chuck² (chuk) *n.* the cut of beef between the neck and the shoulder blade.

chuck/le (chuk/əl) *v.,* **-led, -ling,** *n.* —*v.i.* **1.** to laugh softly. —*n.* **2.** a soft laugh.

chum (chum) *n.* a close friend. —**chum/my,** *adj.*

chump (chump) *n. Informal.* a fool.

chunk (chungk) *n.* a thick piece.

chunk/y *adj.,* **-ier, -iest. 1.** thick or stout; stocky. **2.** full of chunks.

church (chûrch) *n.* **1.** a place of Christian worship. **2.** a religious service. **3.** (*sometimes cap.*) a Christian denomination.

Church/ of Je/sus Christ/ of Lat/ter-day Saints/ *n.* a denomination founded in the U.S. in 1830 and based on a sacred book believed to have been written by a prophet called Mormon.

churl (chûrl) n. **1.** a rude person. **2.** a peasant. —**churl′ish,** adj.

churl′ish (chûr′lish) adj. boorish.

churn (chûrn) n. **1.** a container in which cream or milk is beaten to make butter. —v.t. **2.** to agitate (cream or milk) or make (butter) in a churn. **3.** to shake briskly. —v.i. **4.** to move or shake in agitation.

chute (shōōt) n. a sloping slide.

chut′ney (chut′nē) n. an East Indian relish.

chutz′pah (кнōōt′spə, hōōt′-) n. Slang. nerve; gall. Also, **chutz′pa.**

CIA Central Intelligence Agency.

ci·ca′da (si kā′də) n. a large insect with a shrill call.

-cide a suffix indicating: **1.** a killer. **2.** the act of killing.

ci′der (sī′dər) n. apple juice.

ci·gar′ (si gär′) n. a roll of tobacco leaves for smoking.

cig′a·rette′ (sig′ə ret′) n. tobacco rolled in paper for smoking.

cil′i·a (sil′ē ə) n.pl., sing. **-i·um** (-ē əm). the short, hairlike organelles on the surface of certain cells.

cinch (sinch) n. **1.** a strap for securing a saddle. **2.** Informal. a sure or easy thing.

cin′der (sin′dər) n. a partially burned piece; ash.

cin′e·ma (sin′ə mə) n. **1.** motion pictures. **2.** a movie theater.

cin′e·ma·tog′ra·phy (-tog′rə fē) n. the art or technique of motion-picture photography.

cin′na·mon (sin′ə mən) n. a brown spice from the bark of an Asian tree.

ci′pher (sī′fər) n. **1.** the symbol (0) for zero. **2.** secret writing.

cir′ca (sûr′kə) prep. approximately.

cir′cle (sûr′kəl) n., v., **-cled, -cling.** —n. **1.** a closed plane curve with all points at a uniform distance from its center. **2.** a range; scope. **3.** a group of friends or associates. —v.t. **4.** to enclose in a circle. **5.** to revolve around. —v.i **6.** to move in a circle.

cir′cuit (-kit) n. **1.** a line or route around an area or object. **2.** a tour, esp. in connection with duties. **3.** an electrical path. —**cir′cuit·ry,** n.

cir′cuit break′er n. a device that interrupts an electrical circuit to prevent excessive current.

cir·cu′i·tous (sər kyōō′i təs) adj. roundabout. —**cir·cu′i·tous·ly,** adv.

cir′cu·lar (-kyə lər) adj. **1.** of or in a circle. —n. **2.** a letter or advertisement for general circulation.

cir′cu·late′ (-lāt′) v.i., **-lated, -lating.** —v.i. **1.** to move around. **2.** to distribute. —**cir′cu·la·to′ry** (-lə tôr′ē) adj.

circum- a prefix indicating around or about.

cir′cum·cise′ (sûr′kəm sīz′) v.t., **-cised, -cising.** to remove the foreskin of. —**cir′cum·ci′sion** (-sizh′ən) n.

cir·cum′fer·ence (sər kum′fər əns) n. the outer boundary of a circle.

cir′cum·flex′ (sûr′kəm fleks′) n. a kind of diacritical mark (^).

cir′cum·lo·cu′tion (-lō kyōō′shən) n. a roundabout expression.

cir′cum·nav′i·gate′ v.t., **-gated, -gating.** to sail around.

cir′cum·scribe′ v.t., **-scribed, -scribing. 1.** to encircle. **2.** to confine.

cir′cum·spect′ (-spekt′) adj. cautious; watchful. —**cir′cum·spec′tion** (-spek′shən) n.

cir′cum·stance′ (-stans′) n. **1.** a condition accompanying or affecting a fact or event. **2.** Usu., **circumstances,** the existing conditions. **3. circumstances,** a person's condition with respect to material welfare. **4.** ceremony.

cir′cum·stan′tial (-stan′shəl) adj. **1.** of or from circumstances. **2.** incidental.

cir′cumstan′tial ev′idence n. proof of facts offered as evidence from which other facts are to be inferred.

cir′cum·vent′ (-vent′) v.t. to outwit or evade. —**cir′cum·ven′tion,** n.

cir′cus (sûr′kəs) n. a show with animals, acrobats, etc.

cir·rho′sis (si rō′sis) n. a chronic liver disease.

cir′rus (sir′əs) n. a fleecy cloud.

cis′tern (sis′tərn) n. a water tank.

cit′a·del (sit′ə dl, -ə del′) n. a fortress.

cite (sīt) v.t., **cited, citing. 1.** to quote as an authority or example. **2.** to summon to appear in court. **3.** to commend. —**ci·ta′tion,** n.

cit′i·zen (sit′ə zən, -sən) n. a native

or naturalized inhabitant of a country. —**cit′i·zen·ship′,** n.

cit′ric ac′id (si′trik) n. a white powder found in citrus fruits.

cit′ron (si′trən) n. a lemonlike fruit.

cit′ro·nel′la (si′trə nel′ə) n. a pungent oil that repels insects.

cit′rus (si′trəs) n. a fruit such as the orange, lemon, etc.

cit′y (sit′ē) n., pl. **-ies.** a large town.

civ′ic (siv′ik) adj. of a city or citizens.

civ′ics n. the study of civic affairs.

civ′il (-al) adj. **1.** of citizens. **2.** civilized. **3.** polite. —**ci·vil′i·ty** (-vil′i-tē) n.

ci·vil′ian (si vil′yən) n. **1.** a person not on active duty with the military, police, etc. —adj. **2.** of such persons.

civ′i·li·za′tion (siv′ə lə zā′shən) n. **1.** the act or process of civilizing. **2.** the culture of a people or period. **3.** civilized conditions.

civ′i·lize (-līz′) v.t., **-lized, -lizing.** to bring out of a savage state.

civ′il lib′erty n. a fundamental right guaranteed by law.

civ′il rights′ n.pl. the rights of all people to freedom and equality.

civ′il ser′vant n. an employee of the civil service.

civ′il serv′ice n. the branches of governmental administration outside the armed services.

civ′il war′ n. a war between citizens of the same country.

cl. centiliter.

claim (klām) v.t. **1.** to demand as one's right, property, etc. **2.** to assert. —n. **3.** a demand. **4.** an assertion. **5.** something claimed. —**claim′ant,** n.

clair·voy′ant (klâr voi′ənt), adj. **1.** seeing beyond physical vision. —n. **2.** a person who has the ability to see beyond physical vision. —**clair·voy′ance,** n.

clam (klam) n. a hard-shelled, edible bivalve mollusk.

clam′ber (klam′bər, klam′ər) v.t., v.i. to climb awkwardly.

clam′my adj., **-mier, -miest.** cold and damp. —**clam′mi·ness,** n.

clam′or (klam′ər) n. **1.** a loud outcry or noise. —v.i. **2.** to raise a clamor. —**clam′or·ous,** adj.

clamp (klamp) n. **1.** a device for holding objects together. —v.t. **2.** to fasten with a clamp.

clan (klan) n. a group of related families.

clan·des′tine (klan des′tin) adj. done in secret.

clang (klang) v.i., v.t. **1.** to ring harshly. —n. **2.** Also, **clang′or.** a harsh ring.

clank (klangk) n. **1.** a sharp, hard, nonvibrating sound. —v.i., v.t. **2.** to make or cause to make such a sound.

clap (klap) v., **clapped, clapping,** n. —v.t. **1.** to hit together, as hands. —v.i. **2.** to applaud. —n. **3.** the act or sound of clapping.

clap′board (klab′ərd) n. overlapping boards on exterior walls.

clap′per n. the tongue of a bell.

clap′trap′ (klap′-) n. insincere speech.

clar′et (klar′it) n. a dry red wine.

clar′i·fy′ (klar′ə fī′) v.t., v.i., **-fied, -fying.** to make or become clear. —**clar′i·fi·ca′tion,** n.

clar′i·net′ (-ə net′) n. a single-reed woodwind instrument.

clar′i·on (-ē ən) adj. clear and shrill.

clar′i·ty (-i tē) n. clearness.

clash (klash) v.i. **1.** to conflict. **2.** to collide loudly. —v.t. **3.** to strike with a loud sound. —n. **4.** a collision. **5.** a conflict.

clasp (klasp) n. **1.** a fastening device. **2.** a firm grasp. **3.** a hug. —v.t. **4.** to fasten. **5.** to grasp with the hand. **6.** to hug.

class (klas) n. **1.** a group of similar persons or things. **2.** social rank. **3.** a group of students. **4.** a division. **5.** Informal. elegance, grace, or dignity. —v.t. **6.** to classify.

class′ action′ n. a lawsuit on behalf of persons with a complaint in common.

clas′sic (klas′ik) adj. Also, **clas′si·cal. 1.** of the finest type. **2.** serving as a standard. **3.** in the Greek or Roman manner. —n. **4.** an author, book, etc. of acknowledged excellence. —**clas′si·cism′** (klas′ə-siz′əm) n.

clas′si·fied′ (klas′ə fīd′) adj. limited to authorized persons.

clas′si·fy′ v.t., **-fied, -fying.** to arrange in classes. —**clas′si·fi·ca′tion,** n.

class′mate′ n. a member of the same class at school or college.

class′room′ n. a room in which classes are held.

class′y adj., **-ier, -iest.** Informal. stylish; elegant.

clat′ter (klat′ər) v.t., v.i. **1.** to make or cause to make a rattling sound. —n. **2.** such a sound.

clause (klôz) n. **1.** a part of a sentence with its own subject and predicate. **2.** a part of a document.

claus′tro·pho′bi·a (klô′strə fō′-bē ə) n. a fear of being in closed places. —**claus′tro·pho′bic,** adj.

clav′i·chord′ (klav′i kôrd′) n. an early keyboard instrument.

clav′i·cle (klav′i kəl) n. the slender bone connecting the scapula and the sternum.

claw (klô) n. **1.** a sharp, curved nail on an animal's paw. —v.t. **2.** to tear or scratch roughly.

clay (klā) n. a soft earthy material, flexible when wet, used in making bricks, pottery, etc.

clean (klēn) adj. **1.** free from dirt or foreign matter. **2.** pure. —adv. **3.** completely. —v.t., v.i. **4.** to make or become clean. **5. clean up, a.** to tidy up. **b.** to finish. **c.** to make a large profit. —**clean′er,** n.

clean·ly (klen′lē) adj. **1.** keeping or kept clean. —adv. **2.** in a clean manner. —**clean′li·ness,** n.

cleanse (klenz) v.t., **cleansed, cleansing.** to clean or purify. —**cleans′er,** n.

clear (klēr) adj. **1.** transparent. **2.** easily seen, heard, or understood. **3.** evident. **4.** unobstructed. **5.** free of obligations. **6.** blameless. —adv. **7.** in a clear manner. —v.t., v.i. **8.** to make or become clear. **9.** to pay in full. **10.** to pass beyond. **11. clear out, a.** to remove the contents of. **b.** to go away quickly. **12. clear up,** to explain. —**clear′ly,** adv.

clear′ance n. **1.** the space between two objects. **2.** an authorization. **3.** Also called **clear′ance sale′.** the sale of goods at very low prices to make room for new merchandise.

clear′-cut′ adj. **1.** having clear outlines. **2.** definite.

clear′ing n. a treeless space, as in a forest.

cleat (klēt) n. a metal piece fastened to a surface to give support or prevent slipping.

cleav′age (klē′vij) n. **1.** a split or division. **2.** the space between a woman's breasts.

cleave[1] (klēv) v.t., v.i., **cleft** (kleft) or **cleaved, cleaving.** to split or divide.

cleave[2] (klēv) v.i., **cleaved, cleaving. 1.** to cling. **2.** to remain faithful.

cleav′er n. a heavy knife.

clef (klef) n. a sign on a musical staff that indicates pitch.

cleft (kleft) n. a split.

cleft′ lip′ n. a birth defect in which there is a vertical fissure in the upper lip.

cleft′ pal′ate n. a birth defect in which there is a fissure in the roof of the mouth.

clem′a·tis (klem′ə tis) n. a climbing vine having showy flowers.

clem′ent (klem′ənt) adj. **1.** merciful. **2.** (of the weather) mild. —**clem′en·cy,** n.

clench (klench) v.t. to close tightly.

cler′gy (klûr′jē) n., pl. **-gies.** the body of ordained persons in a religious denomination. —**cler′-gy·man,** n. —**cler′gy·wom·an,** n. fem.

cler′ic (kler′ik) n. a member of the clergy.

cler′i·cal adj. **1.** of clerks. **2.** of the clergy.

clerk (klûrk) n. **1.** a person who does office tasks, keeps records, etc. **2.** a salesperson in a store.

clev′er (klev′ər) adj. bright, witty, or creative. —**clev′er·ly,** adv.

clew (klōō) n. a ball of yarn, thread, etc.

cli·ché′ (klē shā′) n. a trite expression.

click (klik) n. **1.** a slight, sharp sound. —v.i. **2.** to make a click. **3.** Informal. to succeed. —v.t. **4.** to cause to click.

clicks′-and-mor′tar adj. of a company that does business on the Internet and in traditional stores.

cli′ent (klī′ənt) n. **1.** a person who uses the services of a professional. **2.** a customer.

cli·en·tele′ (klī′ən tel′) n. clients.

cliff (klif) n. a high, steep rock face.

cliff′-hang′er n. a suspenseful situation.

cli·mac′ter·ic (klī mak′tər ik) n. a period of decreasing reproductive capacity.

cli′mate (klī′mit) n. the prevailing weather conditions of an area. —**cli·mat′ic** (-mat′ik) adj.

cli′max (klī′maks) n. **1.** the highest point. **2.** a decisive moment in a plot. **3.** an orgasm. —**cli·mac′tic** (-mak′tik) adj.

climb (klīm) v.i. **1.** to move upward or toward the top. —v.t. **2.** to get to the top of. —n. **3.** an ascent made by climbing.

clinch (klinch) v.t. **1.** to settle (a matter) decisively. **2.** to fasten (a nail) by bending the point. —n. **3.** the act of clinching. —**clinch′er,** n.

cling (kling) v.i., **clung** (klung), **clinging.** to hold firmly to a person, idea, etc.

clin′ic (klin′ik) n. a place for the medical treatment of outpatients.

clink (klingk) v.i., v.t. **1.** to make a light, ringing sound. —n. **2.** such a sound.

clink′er (kling′kər) n. a fused stony mass, esp. in a furnace.

clip (klip) v., **clipped, clipping,** n. —v.t. **1.** to cut or cut off with short snips. **2.** Informal. to hit sharply. —n. **3.** an act of clipping. **4.** a clasp. **5.** a cartridge holder.

clip′per (klip′ər) n. **1.** a cutting device. **2.** a fast sailing ship.

clique (klēk) n. a small, exclusive group.

clit′o·ris (klit′ər is) n., pl. **clitorises** or **clitorides** (kli tôr′i dēz′). the erectile organ of the vulva.

cloak (klōk) n. **1.** a loose outer garment. —v.t. **2.** to cover with a cloak. **3.** to conceal.

cloak′-and-dag′ger adj. of espionage or intrigue.

clob′ber (klob′ər) v.t. Informal. **1.** to batter. **2.** to defeat decisively.

clock (klok) n. a device for telling time.

clock′wise′ adv., adj. in the direction that clock hands turn.

clock′work′ n. **1.** the mechanism of a clock. —**Idiom. 2. like clockwork,** with perfect regularity.

clod (klod) n. a piece of earth.

clog (klog) v., **clogged, clogging,** n. —v.t. **1.** to obstruct. —n. **2.** anything that obstructs. **3.** a shoe with a thick rubber or wooden sole.

clois′ter (kloi′stər) n. **1.** a covered walk. **2.** a monastery or nunnery.

clone (klōn) n., v., **cloned, cloning.** —n. **1.** an organism created by asexual reproduction. **2.** Informal. a duplicate. —v.i., v.t. **3.** to grow or cause to grow as a clone.

close, v., closed, closing, adj., closer, closest, adv. —v.t. (klōz) **1.** to shut or obstruct. **2.** to bring to an end. **3.** to bring together. —v.i. **4.** to become closed. **5.** to reach an agreement. **6. close down,** to terminate the operation of. **7. ~ in on,** to approach stealthily. —adj. (klōs) **8.** near. **9.** intimate. **10.** compact. **11.** lacking fresh air. **12.** secretive. **13.** nearly equal. —adv. (klōs) **14.** in a close manner. **15.** near. —n. (klōz) **16.** the end. —**close′ly,** adv.

close′ call′ (klōs) n. a narrow escape.

closed′-cap′tioned adj. broadcast with captions visible only with a decoding device.

closed′ shop′ n. a place where workers must belong to a union.

close′out′ (klōz′-) n. a sale on goods at greatly reduced prices.

clos′et (kloz′it) n. **1.** a small room or cabinet for clothes, utensils, etc. —adj. **2.** secret. —v.t. **3.** to shut up in a private room for a talk.

close′up′ (klōs′-) n. a photograph taken at close range.

clo′sure n. **1.** closing or being closed. **2.** a conclusion. **3.** something that closes.

clot (klot) n., v., **clotted, clotting.** —n. **1.** a mass, esp. of dried blood. —v.i., v.t. **2.** to form a clot.

cloth (klôth) n. **1.** a fabric of woven or knitted threads. **2.** a piece of such a fabric. **3. the cloth,** the clergy. —adj. **4.** made of cloth.

clothe (klōth) v.t., **clothed** or **clad** (klad) **clothing.** to dress or cover.

clothes (klōz, klōthz) n.pl. garments; apparel. Also, **cloth′ing.**

cloud (kloud) n. **1.** a visible mass of water or ice in the air. **2.** a mass of smoke or dust. **3.** anything causing gloom. —v.t. **4.** to cover with clouds or gloom. —v.i. **5.** to become cloudy. —**Idiom. 6. under a cloud,** in disgrace.

cloud′burst′ n. a sudden and very heavy rainfall.

cloud′ nine′ n. Informal. a state of perfect happiness.

clout (klout) n. **1.** a blow with the hand. **2.** Informal. influence. —v.t. **3.** to hit with the hand.

clove[1] (klōv) n. a tropical spice.

clove[2] (klōv) n. a section of a plant bulb, as of garlic.

clo′ver (klō′vər) n. a plant with three-part leaves and dense flower heads.

clown (kloun) n. **1.** a comic performer. **2.** a prankster. **3.** a fool. —v.i. **4.** to act like a clown. —**clown′ish,** adj.

cloy (kloi) v.t., v.i. to weary by excess, as of sweetness.

club (klub) n., v., **clubbed, clubbing.** —n. **1.** a heavy stick or bat. **2.** an organized group. **3. clubs,** a suit of playing cards. —v.t. **4.** to beat with a club. —v.i **5.** to unite.

club′foot′ n. a deformed foot.

club′ so′da n. soda water.

cluck (kluk) n. **1.** the call of a hen. —v.i. **2.** to utter such a call.

clue (klōō) n. a guide in solving a problem, mystery, etc.

clump (klump) n. **1.** a cluster. **2.** a mass. —v.i. **3.** to walk heavily. **4.** to gather into clumps.

clum′sy (klum′zē) adj., **-sier, -siest.** awkward. —**clum′si·ly,** adv.

clung (klung) v. pt. and pp. of **cling.**

clus′ter (klus′tər) n. **1.** a group; bunch. —v.i., v.t. **2.** to gather into or form a cluster.

clutch (kluch) v.t. **1.** to grasp tightly. —n. **2.** a tight grip. **3. clutches,** control. **4.** a device for engaging or disengaging machinery.

clut′ter (klut′ər) v.t. **1.** to litter with things in a disorderly way. —n. **2.** things scattered in disorder.

cm centimeter.

CO 1. Colorado. **2.** Commanding Officer.

co- a prefix indicating: **1.** together. **2.** joint.

Co. 1. Company. **2.** County.

c/o care of.

coach (kōch) n. **1.** an enclosed carriage, bus, etc. **2.** an athletic trainer or a private tutor. **3.** the least expensive class of air travel. —v.t. **4.** to instruct.

co·ag′u·late′ (kō ag′yə lāt′) v.i., v.t., **-lated, -lating.** to thicken or clot.

coal (kōl) n. a black mineral burned as fuel.

co·a·lesce′ (kō′ə les′) v.i., **-lesced, -lescing.** to unite or grow together.

co·a′li′tion (-lish′ən) n. an alliance.

coarse (kôrs) adj., coarser, coarsest. **1.** composed of large particles. **2.** rough. **3.** vulgar. —**coarse′ly,** adv. —**coars′en,** v.t., v.i.

coast (kōst) n. **1.** the seashore. —v.i. **2.** to drift easily. —**coast′al,** adj.

coast′er n. a small dish or mat for placing under a glass.

coast′ guard′ n. the military service that enforces maritime laws, saves lives at sea, etc.

coat (kōt) n. **1.** an outer garment. **2.** a covering, as fur or bark. **3.** a layer of anything that covers. —v.t. **4.** to cover with a coat.

coat′ing n. an outer layer.

coat′ of arms′ n. the emblems, motto, etc., of one's family.

co·au′thor (kō ô′thər, kō′ô′-) n. **1.** one of two or more joint authors. —v.t. **2.** to be a coauthor of.

coax (kōks) v.t., v.i. to urge by persuasion, flattery, etc.

co·ax′i·al (kō ak′sē əl) adj. having a common axis, as coaxial cables for simultaneous long-distance transmission of television signals.

cob (kob) n. a corncob.

co′balt (kō′bôlt) n. **1.** a silvery metallic element. **2.** a deep blue.

cob′ble (kob′əl) v.t., **-bled, -bling. 1.** to mend (shoes). **2.** to put together clumsily. —**cob′bler,** n.

COBOL (kō′bôl) n. a computer language for writing programs to process large files.

co′bra (kō′brə) n. a poisonous snake of India and Africa.

cob′web′ (kob′-) n. a spider web.

co·caine′ (kō kān′, kō′kān) n. a narcotic drug obtained from a South American shrub.

coc′cyx (kok′siks) n., pl. **coc·cy′ges** (kok sī′jēz, kok′si jēz′). a triangular bone at the bottom of the spinal column; tailbone. —**coc·cyg′e·al** (-sij′ē əl) adj.

cock[1] (kok) n. **1.** a rooster. **2.** a male bird. **3.** a valve. **4.** the hammer in a gun. —v.t. **5.** to set the cock of (a gun).

cock² (kok) *v.t.* to turn up or to one side.

cock•ade′ (ko kād′) *n.* a rosette worn on the hat as a sign of rank.

cock′a•too′ (kok′ə tōō′, kok′ə tōō′) *n.* a crested parrot.

cock′eyed′ *adj.* **1.** tilted to one side. **2.** ridiculous.

cock′le (kok′əl) *n.* **1.** a mollusk with heart-shaped valves. —*Idiom.* **2. cockles of one's heart,** the place of one's deepest feelings.

cock′ney (-nē) *n.* **1.** a resident of the East End of London. **2.** the dialect of such persons.

cock′pit′ *n.* a place for a pilot.

cock′roach′ *n.* a rapid crawling insect with a flat body.

cock′tail′ *n.* a drink containing chilled liquors and flavoring.

cock′y *adj.,* **-ier, -iest.** arrogant; conceited. —**cock′i•ness,** *n.*

co′coa (kō′kō) *n.* **1.** the powdered seeds of cacao. **2.** a beverage made from this. **3.** a shade of brown.

co′co•nut′ (kō′kə nut′, -nət) *n.* the large, hard-shelled seed of the **co′co** palm.

co•coon′ (kə kōōn′) *n.* the silky covering spun by insect larvae.

cod (kod) *n.* an edible N Atlantic fish.

C.O.D. cash, or collect, on delivery.

co′da (kō′də) *n.* the final passage of a musical movement.

cod′dle (kod′l) *v.t.,* **-dled, -dling. 1.** to pamper. **2.** to cook in water just below the boiling point.

code (kōd) *n.* **1.** a system of laws or rules. **2.** a system of signals or secret words. —*v.t.* **3.** to put into code.

co′deine (kō′dēn) *n.* a drug derived from opium, used to relieve pain.

codg′er (koj′ər) *n.* an eccentric elderly man.

cod′i•cil (kod′ə səl) *n.* a supplement to a will.

cod′i•fy′ (kod′ə fī′, kō′də-) *v.t.,* **-fied, -fying.** to organize into a formal code. —**cod′i•fi•ca′tion,** *n.*

co′ed′ (kō′ed′, -ed′) *adj.* **1.** serving both men and women; coeducational. —*n.* **2.** a female student, esp. in a coeducational school.

co•ed•u•ca′tion *n.* education of both sexes in the same classes. —**co•ed•u•ca′tion•al,** *adj.*

co•ef•fi′cient (kō′ə fish′ənt) *n.* a number by which another is multiplied.

co•erce′ (kō ûrs′) *v.t.,* **-erced, -ercing.** to compel or bring about by force or threats. —**co•er′cion** (-ûr′shən) *n.* —**co•er′cive,** *adj.*

co•ex•ist′ *v.i.* **1.** to exist at the same time. **2.** to exist together peacefully. —**co•ex•ist′ence,** *n.*

cof′fee (kô′fē) *n.* a beverage made from the roasted and ground seeds of a tropical tree.

cof′fer (kô′fər) *n.* **1.** a box for valuables. **2. coffers,** the treasury of an organization.

cof′fin (kô′fin) *n.* a box for a corpse.

cog (kog) *n.* a tooth on a wheel (**cog′wheel′**), connecting with another such wheel.

co′gent (kō′jənt) *adj.* convincing. —**co′gen•cy,** *n.* —**co′gent•ly,** *adv.*

cog′i•tate′ (koj′i tāt′) *v.i., v.t.,* **-tated, -tating.** to think deeply (about). —**cog′i•ta′tion,** *n.*

co′gnac (kōn′yak) *n.* brandy.

cog′nate (kog′nāt) *adj.* related or similar. —*n.* **2.** a related word.

cog•ni′tion (-nish′ən) *n.* **1.** the act or process of knowing. **2.** something known.

cog′ni•zance (-nə zəns) *n.* awareness. —**cog′ni•zant,** *adj.*

cog•no′men (kog nō′mən) *n.* a family name; surname.

co•gno•scen′ti (kon′yə shen′tē, kog′nə-), *n.pl., sing.* **-te** (-tā, -tē). those having superior knowledge of a particular field.

co•hab′it (kō hab′it) *v.i.* to live together, esp. as husband and wife, without being married. —**co•hab′i•ta′tion,** *n.*

co•here′ (kō hēr′) *v.i.,* **-hered, -hering.** to stick together.

co•her′ent (-hēr′ənt, -her′-) *adj.* logically connected. —**co•her′ence,** *n.*

co•he′sion (-hē′zhən) *n.* the act or state of cohering, uniting, or sticking together.

co•he′sive (kō hē′siv) *adj.* **1.** causing to cohere. **2.** tending to unify.

co′hort (kō′hôrt) *n.* **1.** a companion. **2.** a group, esp. of soldiers.

coif′fure′ (kwä fyŏŏr′) *n.* a hairstyle.

coil (koil) *v.t., v.i.* **1.** to wind in

rings. —*n.* **2.** a series of spirals or rings. **3.** one such ring.

coin (koin) *n.* **1.** a piece of metal used as money. —*v.t.* **2.** to make metal into money. **3.** to invent (a word). —**coin′age,** *n.*

co•in•cide′ (kō′in sīd′) *v.i.,* **-cided, -ciding. 1.** to occur at the same time, place, etc. **2.** to match.

co′i•tus (kō′i təs) *n.* sexual intercourse. —**co′i•tal,** *adj.*

coke¹ (kōk) *n.* the solid carbon produced from coal.

coke² (kōk) *n. Slang.* cocaine.

Col. 1. Colonel. **2.** Colorado.

co′la (kō′lə) *n.* a soft drink containing an extract from kola nuts.

col′an•der (kul′ən dər, kol′-) *n.* a perforated container for draining foods.

cold (kōld) *adj.* **1.** having a low temperature. **2.** not affectionate or cordial. —*n.* **3.** the absence of heat. **4.** a common illness marked by sneezing, coughing, etc. —*Idiom.* **5. out in the cold,** neglected. —**cold′ly,** *adv.*

cold′-blood′ed *adj.* **1.** having blood at the same temperature as the environment. **2.** without feeling.

cold′ cream′ *n.* a preparation for cleansing or soothing the skin.

cold′ feet′ *n. Informal.* a lack of courage.

cold′ shoul′der *n.* a deliberate show of indifference.

cold′ tur′key *Informal.* —*n.* **1.** abrupt withdrawal from an addictive substance. —*adv.* **2.** impromptu.

cold′ war′ *n.* rivalry between nations just short of armed conflict.

cole′slaw′ (kōl′slô′) *n.* a salad of sliced raw cabbage.

col′ic (kol′ik) *n.* acute pain in the abdomen. —**col′ick•y,** *adj.*

col•i•se′um (kol′i sē′əm) *n.* a large stadium.

co•li′tis (kə lī′tis, kō-) *n.* inflammation of the colon.

col•lab′o•rate′ (kə lab′ə rāt′) *v.i.,* **-rated, -rating. 1.** to work with another. **2.** to cooperate with the enemy. —**col•lab′o•ra′tion,** *n.* —**col•lab′o•ra′tor,** *n.*

col•lage′ (kə läzh′) *n.* a work of art made by pasting various materials on a surface.

col•lapse′ (kə laps′) *v.,* **-lapsed, -lapsing,** *n.* —*v.i.* **1.** to fall in or together. **2.** to fail abruptly. —*v.t.* **3.** to cause to collapse. —*n.* **4.** a falling in or down. **5.** a sudden failure. —**col•laps′i•ble,** *adj.*

col′lar (kol′ər) *n.* **1.** the part of a garment around the neck. —*v.t.* **2.** to seize by the collar.

col′lar•bone′ *n.* the clavicle.

col•lat′er•al (kə lat′ər əl) *n.* **1.** security pledged on loan. —*adj.* **2.** additional. **3.** secondary.

col′league (kol′ēg) *n.* a fellow worker.

col•lect′ (kə lekt′) *v.t.* **1.** to gather together. **2.** to take payment of. —*v.i.* **3.** to accumulate. —*adj., adv.* **4.** payable on delivery. —**col•lec′tion,** *n.* —**col•lec′tor,** *n.*

col•lect′i•ble *n.* **1.** an object collected. —*adj.* **2.** able to be collected.

col•lec′tive *adj.* **1.** combined. **2.** of a group.

collec′tive bar′gaining *n.* negotiation between a union and employer.

col′lege (kol′ij) *n.* a degree-granting school of higher learning. —**col•le′giate** (kə lē′jit) *adj.*

col•lide′ (kə līd′) *v.i.,* **-lided, -liding. 1.** to strike one another violently; crash. **2.** to conflict.

col′lie (kol′ē) *n.* a kind of large, long-haired dog.

col′lier (kol′yər) *n.* a coal miner.

col•li′sion (kə lizh′ən) *n.* **1.** a crash. **2.** a conflict.

col′lo•cate′ (kol′ə kāt′) *v.t.,* **-cated, -cating.** to arrange in proper order. —**col′lo•ca′tion,** *n.*

col•lo′qui•al (kə lō′kwē əl) *adj.* appropriate to casual rather than formal speech or writing.

col•lo′qui•um (-kwē əm) *n., pl.* **-quiums, -quia** (-kwē ə) a conference of experts in a field.

col′lo•quy (kol′ə kwē) *n., pl.* **-quies.** a discussion.

col•lu′sion (kə lōō′zhən) *n.* a conspiracy for illegal purposes.

Colo. Colorado.

co•logne′ (kə lōn′) *n.* a mildly perfumed liquid.

co′lon¹ (kō′lən) *n.* a punctuation mark (:).

co′lon² (kō′lən) *n.* the lower part of the large intestine.

colo′nel (kûr′nl) *n.* a military officer ranking below a general.

co•lo′ni•al•ism (kə lō′nē ə liz′əm) *n.* the policy of extending national authority over foreign territories.

col′on•nade′ (kol′ə nād′) *n.* a series of columns.

col′o•ny (kol′ə nē) *n., pl.* **-nies. 1.** a group of people settling in another land. **2.** a territory subject to an outside ruling power. **3.** a community. —**co•lo′ni•al** (kə lō′nē əl) *adj., n.* —**col′o•nist,** *n.* —**col′o•nize′,** *v.t., v.i.*

col′o•phon′ (kol′ə fon′) *n.* a publisher's or printer's emblem.

col′or (kul′ər) *n.* **1.** the quality of an object with respect to the light reflected by it. **2.** pigment. **3.** complexion. **4.** a vivid quality. **5. colors,** a flag. —*v.t.* **6.** to apply color to. **7.** to give a special character to. Also, *Brit.,* **col′our.** —**col′or•ing,** *n.*

col′o•ra•tu′ra (kul′ər ə tōōr′ə, -tyōōr′ə, kol′-) *n.* a soprano specializing in music containing ornamental trills.

col′or-blind′ *adj.* **1.** unable to distinguish certain colors. **2.** without racial bias.

col′or•ful *adj.* **1.** full of color. **2.** vivid; interesting.

col′or•less *adj.* **1.** without color. **2.** drab.

co•los′sal (kə los′əl) *adj.* huge.

co•los′sus (-los′əs) *n.* **1.** a huge statue. **2.** anything huge.

colt (kōlt) *n.* a young male horse.

col•um•bine′ (kol′əm bīn′) *n.* a plant with flowers having white to blue sepals.

col′umn (kol′əm) *n.* **1.** an upright shaft or support. **2.** a long area of print. **3.** a regular journalistic piece. **4.** a long group of troops, ships, etc.

col′um•nist (-əm nist) *n.* a journalist who writes a regular column.

com- a prefix indicating: **1.** with or together. **2.** completely.

co′ma (kō′mə) *n.* a state of prolonged unconsciousness. —**com′a•tose′** (-tōs′) *adj.*

comb (kōm) *n.* **1.** a toothed object for straightening hair. **2.** the growth on a cock's head. —*v.t.* **3.** to tidy with a comb. **4.** to search.

com•bat′ *v.,* **-bated, -bating,** *n.* —*v.t., v.i.* (kəm bat′, kom′bat) **1.** to fight (against). —*n.* (kom′bat) **2.** battle. —**com•bat′ant,** *n.* —**com•bat′ive,** *adj.*

com•bi•na′tion (kom′bə nā′shən) *n.* **1.** the act of combining. **2.** a mixture. **3.** an alliance. **4.** the set of figures dialed to operate a lock.

com•bine′ *v.,* **-bined, -bining,** —*v.t., v.i.* (kəm bīn′) **1.** to unite; join. —*n.* (kom′bīn) **2.** a combination of persons for a common interest. **3.** a machine that cuts and threshes grain.

com′bo (kom′bō) *n., pl.* **-bos.** *Informal.* a small jazz band.

com•bus′ti•ble (kəm bus′tə bəl) *adj.* **1.** capable of burning. —*n.* **2.** a combustible substance.

com•bus′tion (-chən) *n.* **1.** the act or process of burning. **2.** the process in which substances combine with oxygen and produce heat.

come (kum) *v.i.,* **came, come, coming. 1.** to move toward someone or something. **2.** to arrive. **3.** to occur. **4. come about,** to happen. **5. ~ across** or **upon,** to encounter by chance. **6. ~ around** or **round, a.** to revive. **b.** to change one's opinion. **7. ~ into,** to acquire or inherit. **8. ~ through, a.** to endure successfully. **b.** to fulfill requirements. **9. ~ up with,** to produce.

come′back′ *n.* **1.** a return to a former, higher status. **2.** a retort.

co•me′di•an (kə mē′dē ən) *n.* a humorous actor or performer.

com′e•dy (kom′i dē) *n., pl.* **-dies.** a humorous play, movie, etc.

come′ly (kum′lē) *adj.,* **-lier, -liest.** attractive. —**come′li•ness,** *n.*

com′er (kum′ər) *n.* one likely to have great success.

com′et (kom′it) *n.* a small bright celestial body with a tail of dust and gas.

come′up′pance (-up′əns) *n.* deserved punishment.

com′fort (kum′fərt) *v.t.* **1.** to console or soothe. —*n.* **2.** consolation. **3.** a person or thing giving consolation. **4.** a state of ease and satisfaction.

com′fort•er *n.* **1.** one who comforts. **2.** a warm quilt.

com′ic (kom′ik) *adj.* **1.** of comedy. **2.** Also, **com′i•cal.** funny. —*n.* **3.** a comedian. **4. comics,** comic strips.

com′ic strip′ *n.* a sequence of drawings relating a comic story.

com′ma (kom′ə) *n.* a punctuation mark (,).

com•mand′ (kə mand′) *v.t.* **1.** to order. **2.** to control. —*v.i.* **3.** to have authority. —*n.* **4.** an order. **5.** control. **6.** expertise. **7.** troops, a ship, etc., under a commander.

com′man•dant′ (kom′ən dant′, -dänt′) *n.* a commanding officer.

com•man•deer′ (-dēr′) *v.t.* to seize for official use.

com•mand′er *n.* **1.** a person who commands. **2.** a naval officer below a captain.

com•mand′ment *n.* a command.

com•man′do (kə man′dō) *n., pl.* **-dos, -does.** a member of a military unit trained for surprise raids.

com•mem′o•rate′ (kə mem′ə rāt′) *v.t.,* **-rated, -rating.** to honor the memory of. —**com•mem′o•ra′tion,** *n.* —**com•mem′o•ra′tive** (-rə tiv) *adj.*

com•mence′ (kə mens′) *v.i., v.t.,* **-menced, -mencing.** to start.

com•mence′ment *n.* **1.** a beginning. **2.** the ceremony of awarding degrees or diplomas at a school.

com•mend′ (kə mend′) *v.t.* **1.** to recommend. **2.** to entrust. **3.** to praise. —**com•mend′a•ble,** *adj.* —**com′men•da′tion** (kom′ən dā′-shən) *n.* —**com•mend′a•to′ry,** *adj.*

com•men′su•rate (-men′sha rit, -sə-) *adj.* **1.** of the same size. **2.** corresponding in size or degree.

com′ment (kom′ent) *n.* **1.** a remark. **2.** an interpretation. —*v.i.* **3.** to make remarks.

com′men•tar′y (-ən ter′ē) *n., pl.* **-taries.** explanatory comments.

com′men•ta′tor (-tā′tər) *n.* a person who discusses news or other topics on radio or television.

com′merce (kom′ərs) *n.* trade.

com•mer′cial (kə mûr′shəl) *adj.* **1.** of or in commerce. —*n.* **2.** a radio or television advertisement.

com•mer′cial•ize′ *v.t.,* **-ized, -izing.** to treat as a business.

com•min′gle (kə ming′gəl) *v.t., v.i.,* **-gled, -gling.** to blend.

com•mis′er•ate′ (kə miz′ə rāt′) *v.i.,* **-ated, -ating.** to sympathize.

com′mis•sar′y (kom′ə ser′ē) *n., pl.* **-ies.** a store selling food and supplies on a military post.

com•mis′sion (kə mish′ən) *n.* **1.** the act of committing. **2.** an order or document granting authority, esp. one granted to military officers. **3.** authority granted for an action. **4.** a group of persons with a special task. **5.** a sum paid to an agent, salesperson, etc. —*v.t.* **6.** to give a commission to. **7.** to authorize. **8.** to put into service.

commis′sioned of′ficer *n.* a military officer holding rank by commission.

com•mis′sion•er *n.* a government official in charge of a department.

com•mit′ (kə mit′) *v.t.,* **-mitted, -mitting. 1.** to give in trust or charge. **2.** to do. **3.** to obligate. —**com•mit′ment,** *n.*

com•mit′tee *n.* a group assigned to investigate or act on a matter.

com•mode′ (kə mōd′) *n.* **1.** a chest of drawers. **2.** a stand with a washbasin. **3.** a toilet.

com•mo′di•ous (kə mō′dē əs) *adj.* roomy.

com•mod′i•ty (kə mod′i tē) *n., pl.* **-ties. 1.** an article of trade. **2.** any unprocessed good.

com′mo•dore′ (kom′ə dôr′) *n.* an officer below a rear admiral.

com′mon (kom′ən) *adj.* **1.** belonging to or shared by all. **2.** widespread. **3.** ordinary. **4.** vulgar. **5.** *n.* an area of public land. —*Idiom.* **6. in common,** shared equally. —**com′mon•ly,** *adv.*

com′mon denom′inator *n.* **1.** a number that is a multiple of all the denominators of a set of fractions. **2.** a shared characteristic, belief, etc.

com′mon•er *n.* one of the common people.

com′mon law′ *n.* the system of law based on custom and court decisions.

com′mon•place′ *adj.* **1.** ordinary; trite. —*n.* **2.** such a remark.

com′mons *n.* **1. Commons,** the elective house of certain legislatures. **2.** a large dining room, as in a college.

com′mon sense′ *n.* sound practical judgment. —**com′mon•sense′,** *adj.*

com′mon•weal′ (-wēl′) *n.* the common welfare.

com′mon•wealth′ (-welth′) *n.* **1.** a state. **2.** the people of a state.

com•mo′tion (kə mō′shən) *n.* disturbance.

com•mu′nal (kə myōōn′l, kom′yə-nl) *adj.* of or belonging to a community.

com•mune′¹ (kə myōōn′) *v.i.,* **-muned, -muning.** to talk together.

com′mune² (kom′yōōn) *n.* a small community with shared property.

com•mu′ni•ca•ble (-ni kə bəl) *adj.* capable of being communicated.

com•mu′ni•cate′ *v.,* **-cated, -cating.** —*v.t.* **1.** to make known. **2.** to transmit. —*v.i.* **3.** to exchange thoughts, information, etc.

com•mu′ni•ca′tion *n.* **1.** the act of communicating. **2.** something communicated, as a letter.

com•mu′ni•ca′tive (-kā′tiv, -kə-) *adj.* inclined to communicate.

com•mun′ion (kə myōōn′yən) *n.* **1.** an act of sharing. **2.** a group with the same religion. **3.** Holy Communion.

com•mu•ni•qué′ (kə myōō′ni kā′) *n.* an official bulletin.

com′mu•nism (kom′yə niz′əm) *n.* **1.** a social system based on the collective ownership of property. **2. Communism,** a political doctrine advocating this. —**com′mu•nist** (-nist) *n., adj.*

com•mu′ni•ty (kə myōō′ni tē) *n., pl.* **-ties.** a group of people having common interests or living in one locality.

com•mute′ (kə myōōt′) *v.,* **-muted, -muting.** —*v.i.* **1.** to travel regularly between home and work. —*v.t.* **2.** to reduce (a punishment). —*n.* **3.** a trip made by commuting. —**com•mut′er,** *n.*

com•pact′ *adj.* (kəm pakt′, kom′pakt) **1.** packed together. **2.** small. —*v.t.* (kəm pakt′) **3.** to pack tightly together. —*n.* (kom′pakt) **4.** a small cosmetic case. **5.** an agreement.

com′pact disc′ *n.* an optical disc on which music, data, or images are digitally recorded. Also, **CD.**

com•pac′tor (kəm pak′tər, kom′pak-) *n.* an appliance that compresses trash into small bundles.

com•pan′ion (kəm pan′yən) *n.* **1.** an associate. **2.** a person in a close relationship with another. **3.** a mate for something. —**com•pan′ion•a•ble,** *adj.* —**com•pan′ion•ship′,** *n.*

com′pa•ny (kum′pə nē) *n., pl.* **-nies. 1.** a business organization. **2.** companionship. **3.** guests. **4.** a basic unit of troops. —*Idiom.* **5. part company,** to cease association.

com•par′a•tive (kəm par′ə tiv) *adj.* **1.** of or based on comparison. **2.** relative. **3.** designating the intermediate degree of comparison of adjectives and adverbs.

com•pare′ (kəm pâr′) *v.,* **-pared, -paring.** —*v.t.* **1.** to examine for similarities. **2.** to liken. —*v.i.* **3.** to be worthy of comparison. **4.** to make comparisons. —**com′pa•ra•ble** (kom′pər ə bəl) *adj.*

com•par′i•son *n.* **1.** a comparing or being compared. **2.** a likening.

com•part′ment (kəm pärt′mənt) *n.* a separate room, space, etc. —**com•part•men′tal•ize′,** *v.t.*

com′pass (kum′pəs) *n.* **1.** an instrument for determining direction. **2.** extent. **3.** a tool for drawing circles.

com•pas′sion (kəm pash′ən) *n.* sympathy. —**com•pas′sion•ate,** *adj.* —**com•pas′sion•ate•ly,** *adv.*

com•pat′i•ble (kəm pat′ə bəl) *adj.* able to exist or work together. —**com•pat′i•bil′i•ty,** *n.*

com•pa′tri•ot (kəm pā′trē ət) *n.* a person from one's own country.

com•pel′ (kəm pel′) *v.t.,* **-pelled, -pelling.** to force.

com•pel′ling *adj.* **1.** forceful. **2.** demanding attention.

com•pen′di•um (-dē əm) *n., pl.* **-diums, -dia** (-dē ə). a summary.

com′pen•sate′ (kom′pən sāt′) *v.t.,* **-sated, -sating. 1.** to counterbalance; offset. **2.** to pay. —**com′pen•sa′tion,** *n.*

com•pete′ (kəm pēt′) *v.i.,* **-peted, -peting.** to take part in a contest.

com′pe•tent (kom′pi tənt) *adj.* **1.** having suitable ability for some purpose. **2.** adequate. **3.** legally qualified. —**com′pe•tence, com′pe•ten•cy,** *n.*

com•pe•ti′tion (kom′pi tish′ən) *n.* **1.** the act of competing. **2.** contest. **3.** rivalry. —**com•pet′i•tive** (kəm-pet′i tiv) *adj.* —**com•pet′i•tor,** *n.*

com•pile′ (kəm pīl′) *v.t.,* **-piled, -piling. 1.** to put together (material from various sources) into a book, list, etc. **2.** to gather together. **—com·pil′er,** *n.* **—com′pi·la′tion** (kom′pə lā′shən) *n.*

com·pla′cen·cy (kəm plā′sən sē) *n., pl.* **-cies.** a feeling of quiet pleasure or security. Also, **com·pla′cence.** **—com·pla′cent,** *adj.*

com·plain′ (kəm plān′) *v.i.* **1.** to express pain, dissatisfaction, etc. **2.** to accuse formally in a law court. **—com·plain′er,** *n.*

com·plain′ant *n.* one who makes a complaint, as in a legal action.

com·plaint′ *n.* **1.** an expression of pain, discontent, etc. **2.** a cause of pain, discontent, etc. **3.** a formal accusation in a law court.

com·plai′sant (kəm plā′sənt) *adj.* inclined to please.

com′ple·ment *n.* (kom′plə mənt) **1.** that which completes. **2.** the amount that completes. **—v.t.** (-ment) **3.** to form a complement to. **—com′ple·men′ta·ry,** *adj.*

com·plete′ (kəm plēt′) *adj., v.,* **-pleted, -pleting.** **—adj. 1.** entire. **2.** finished. **3.** thorough. **4.** to make complete. **—com·plete′ly,** *adv.* **—com·ple′tion,** *n.*

com·plex′ *adj.* (kəm pleks′, kom′-pleks) **1.** having many parts; intricate. **—n.** (kom′pleks) **2.** an assemblage of related parts. **3.** a group of buildings. **4.** a group of feelings that influences behavior. **—com·plex′i·ty,** *n.*

com·plex′ion (kəm plek′shən) *n.* the color of the skin.

com′pli·ca′ted (kom′pli kā′tid) *adj.* complex or difficult. **—com′pli·cate′,** *v.t.*

com·plic′i·ty (kəm plis′i tē) *n., pl.* **-ties.** partnership in guilt.

com′pli·ment *n.* (kom′plə mənt) **1.** an expression of praise. **—v.t.** (-ment) **2.** to pay a compliment to.

com′pli·men′ta·ry *adj.* **1.** praising. **2.** given free.

com·ply′ (kəm plī′) *v.i.,* **-plied, -plying.** to conform. **—com·pli′-ance,** *n.* **—com·pli′ant,** *adj.*

com·po′nent (kəm pō′nənt) *n.* **1.** a part of a whole. **—adj. 2.** serving as part of something larger.

com·port′ (kəm pôrt′) *v.t.* to conduct (oneself); behave.

com·pose′ (kəm pōz′) *v.t.,* **-posed, -posing. 1.** to make by combining. **2.** to constitute. **3.** to calm. **4.** to create (a musical work). **—com′-po·si′tion** (kom′pə zish′ən) *n.*

com·posed′ *adj.* calm.

com·pos′er *n.* a writer, esp. of music.

com·pos′ite (kəm poz′it) *adj.* made of many parts.

com′post (kom′pōst) *n.* a decaying mixture of organic matter.

com·po′sure (kəm pō′zhər) *n.* calmness.

com′pote (kom′pōt) *n.* stewed fruit in syrup.

com′pound *adj.* (kom′pound) **1.** having two or more parts, functions, etc. **—n.** (kom′pound) **2.** something made by combining parts. **3.** an enclosure with buildings. **—v.t.** (kəm pound′) **4.** to combine. **5.** to make worse by adding to.

com′pound in′terest *n.* interest paid on both the principal and the accrued interest.

com′pre·hend′ (kom′pri hend′) *v.t.* **1.** to understand. **2.** to include. **—com′pre·hen′si·ble,** *adj.* **—com′-pre·hen′sion,** *n.*

com′pre·hen′sive (-hen′siv) *adj.* including much or all.

com·press′ *v.t.* (kəm pres′) **1.** to press together into less space. **2.** to shorten. **—n.** (kom′pres) **3.** a pad applied to an injured or inflamed part of the body. **—com·pres′sion,** *n.* **—com·pres′sor,** *n.*

com·prise′ (kəm prīz′) *v.t.,* **-prised, -prising. 1.** to consist of. **2.** to include.

com′pro·mise′ (kom′prə mīz′) *n., v.,* **-mised, -mising. —n. 1.** an agreement reached by mutual concessions. **2.** something intermediate. **—v.t. 3.** to settle by compromise. **4.** to make vulnerable. **—v.i. 5.** to make a compromise.

comp′ time′ (komp) *n.* time off from work granted to an employee in place of overtime pay.

comp·trol′ler (kən trō′lər) *n.* a government or corporate officer in charge of finances; controller.

com·pul′sion (kəm pul′shən) *n.* **1.** the act of compelling or the state of being compelled. **2.** an irresistible impulse.

com·pul′sive *adj.* due to or acting on inner compulsion.

com·punc′tion (kəm pungk′shən) *n.* regret.

com·pute′ (kəm pyōōt′) *v.,* **-puted, -puting. —v.i. 1.** to calculate. **—v.t. 2.** to determine by arithmetical calculation. **—com′pu·ta′tion** (kom′-) *n.*

com·put′er *n.* a programmable electronic apparatus for processing data at high speed.

com·pu′ter·ize′ *v.t.,* **-ized, -izing. 1.** to process or store by computer. **2.** to automate by computer.

com′rade (kom′rad) *n.* a companion or associate.

con[1] (kon) *adv.* **1.** against. **—n. 2.** the argument or vote against something.

con[2] (kon) *adj., v.,* **conned, conning. —adj. 1.** involving abuse of trust. **—v.t. 2.** to cheat.

con·cave′ (kon kāv′) *adj.* curved inward.

con·ceal′ (kən sēl′) *v.t.* to hide or keep secret. **—con·ceal′ment,** *n.*

con·cede′ (kən sēd′) *v.,* **-ceded, -ceding. —v.t. 1.** to acknowledge as true. **2.** to grant. **3.** to make a concession.

con·ceit′ (kən sēt′) *n.* **1.** excess self-esteem. **2.** a fanciful idea. **—con·ceit′ed,** *adj.*

con·ceive′ (kən sēv′) *v.,* **-ceived, -ceiving. —v.t. 1.** to form (a plan or idea). **2.** to imagine. **3.** to become pregnant with. **—v.i. 4.** to think. **5.** to become pregnant. **—con·ceiv′-a·ble,** *adj.*

con′cen·trate′ (kon′sən trāt′) *v.,* **-trated, -trating,** *n.* **—v.t. 1.** to direct toward one point. **2.** to intensify. **—v.i. 3.** to give one's full attention. **—n. 4.** a concentrated product. **—con′cen·tra′tion,** *n.*

concentra′tion camp′ *n.* a guarded compound for the confinement of political prisoners, minorities, etc.

con·cen′tric (kən sen′trik) *adj.* having the same center.

con′cept (kon′sept) *n.* a general idea.

con·cep′tion (kən sep′shən) *n.* **1.** the act of conceiving or the state of being conceived. **2.** an idea.

con·cep′tu·a·lize′ (-chōō ə līz′) *v.,* **-lized, -lizing. —v.t. 1.** to form a concept of. **—v.i. 2.** to think in concepts.

con·cern′ (kən sûrn′) *v.t.* **1.** to relate to. **2.** to involve. **3.** to trouble. **—n. 4.** something that relates to or affects a person. **5.** anxiety.

con·cerned′ *adj.* **1.** interested or affected. **2.** troubled; anxious.

con·cern′ing *prep.* about.

con′cert (kon′sûrt) *n.* **1.** a musical performance. **2.** accord. **—Idiom. 3.** in concert, jointly.

con·cert′ed (kən sûr′tid) *adj.* **1.** planned together. **2.** performed together or in cooperation.

con′cer·ti′na (kon′sər tē′nə) *n.* a small accordion.

con·cer′to (kən cher′tō) *n., pl.* **-tos** or **-ti** (-tē). a musical piece for solo instrument and orchestra.

con·ces′sion (kən sesh′ən) *n.* **1.** the act of conceding. **2.** the thing or point conceded.

conch (kongk, konch) *n.* a marine mollusk with a spiral shell.

con·cil′i·ate′ (kən sil′ē āt′) *v.t.,* **-ated, -ating. 1.** to overcome the distrust of; win over. **2.** to reconcile. **—con·cil′i·a′tion,** *n.* **—con·cil′i·a·to′ry** (-ə tôr′ē) *adj.*

con·cise′ (kən sīs′) *adj.* brief; succinct. **—con·cise′ly,** *adv.*

con′clave (kon′klāv) *n.* a private meeting.

con·clude′ (kən klōōd′) *v.,* **-cluded, -cluding. —v.t. 1.** to finish. **2.** to settle. **3.** to deduce. **—v.i. 4.** to end. **—con·clu′sive,** *adj.*

con·clu′sion (-klōō′zhən) *n.* **1.** the end. **2.** a result. **3.** a deduction. **4.** a final decision.

con·coct′ (kon kokt′, kən-) *v.t.* **1.** to make by combining ingredients. **2.** to devise. **—con·coc′tion,** *n.*

con·com′i·tant (kon kom′i tənt, kən-) *adj.* **1.** accompanying. **—n. 2.** anything concomitant.

con′cord (kon′kôrd, kong′-) *n.* **1.** agreement. **2.** peace.

con·cord′ance (kon kôr′dns, kən-) *n.* **1.** concord. **2.** an index of the key words of a book.

con·cor′dat (kon kôr′dat) *n.* an official agreement.

con′course (kon′kôrs, kong′-) *n.* a large open space for crowds.

con′crete *adj., n., v.,* **-creted, -creting. —adj.** (kon krēt′, kon krēt′) **1.** constituting an actual thing; real.

2. made of concrete. **—n.** (kon′krēt) **3.** a building material of cement and hard matter. **—v.t.** (kon krēt′) **4.** to cover with concrete.

con·cu′bine (kong′kyə bīn′) *n.* **1.** a woman living with but not married to a man, esp. a woman regarded as subservient. **2.** a secondary wife.

con·cu′pis·cent (-kyōō′pi sənt) *adj.* lustful. **—con·cu′pis·cence,** *n.*

con·cur′ (kən kûr′) *v.i.,* **-curred, -curring. 1.** to agree. **2.** to occur at the same time. **—con·cur′rence,** *n.* **—con·cur′rent,** *adj.*

con·cus′sion (kən kush′ən) *n.* an injury to the brain from a blow, fall, etc.

con·demn′ (kən dem′) *v.t.* **1.** to express strong disapproval of. **2.** to pronounce guilty. **3.** to pronounce unfit for use. **—con′dem·na′tion** (kon′dem nā′shən, -dəm-) *n.*

con·dense′ (kən dens′) *v.,* **-densed, -densing. —v.t. 1.** to make more dense or compact. **2.** to reduce from gas or vapor to liquid. **—v.i. 3.** to become condensed. **—con′den·sa′tion** (kon′dən sā′shən) *n.*

condensed′ milk′ *n.* thick, sweetened milk.

con′de·scend′ (kon′də send′) *v.i.* to act as if one is doing something that is beneath one's dignity. **—con′de·scen′sion,** *n.*

con′di·ment (kon′də mənt) *n.* a seasoning.

con·di′tion (kən dish′ən) *n.* **1.** a state of being. **2.** a restricting circumstance; prerequisite. **—v.t. 3.** to put in a proper state. **4.** to accustom. **—con·di′tion·al,** *adj.*

con·di′tion·er *n.* something that conditions, as a preparation applied to the hair or skin.

con·dole′ (kən dōl′) *v.i.,* **-doled, -doling.** to express sympathy. **—con·do′lence,** *n.*

con′dom (kon′dəm, kun′-) *n.* a contraceptive device worn over the penis.

con′do·min′i·um (kon′də min′ē-əm) *n.* an apartment house in which each unit is individually owned. Also, *Informal.* **con′do** (-dō).

con·done′ (kən dōn′) *v.t.,* **-doned, -doning.** to disregard or overlook.

con′dor (kon′dər, -dôr) *n.* a kind of vulture.

con·du′cive (kən dōō′siv, -dyōō′-) *adj.* tending to produce.

con′duct *n.* (kon′dukt) **1.** behavior. **2.** management. **—v.t.** (kən dukt′) **3.** to behave (oneself). **4.** to manage. **5.** to lead or carry. **6.** to direct, as an orchestra. **7.** to transmit. **—con·duc′tion,** *n.*

con·duc′tor (kən duk′tər) *n.* **1.** a guide. **2.** a person who conducts an orchestra or chorus. **3.** an official on a train. **4.** a substance that conveys electricity, heat, etc.

con′duit (kon′dwit) *n.* a pipe for water or other fluid.

cone (kōn) *n.* **1.** a form tapering from a round base to a single point. **2.** the fruit of the fir, pine, etc.

con·fec′tion (kən fek′shən) *n.* candy or another sweet preparation. **—con·fec′tion·er,** *n.* **—con·fec′tion·er′y,** *n.*

con·fed′er·a·cy (kən fed′ər ə sē) *n., pl.* **-cies. 1.** a league. **2. the Confederacy,** the eleven states that seceded from the U.S. in 1860–61.

con·fed′er·ate *adj.* (kən fed′ər it) **1.** in league. **2.** of the Confederacy. **—n.** (-ər it) **3.** an ally. **4.** an accomplice. **5. Confederate,** a supporter of the Confederacy. **—con·fed′er·a′tion,** *n.*

con·fer′ (kən fûr′) *v.,* **-ferred, -ferring. —v.t. 1.** to bestow. **—v.i. 2.** to consult. **—con·fer′ment,** *n.*

con′fer·ence (kon′fər əns) *n.* a meeting for discussion.

con·fess′ (kən fes′) *v.t., v.i.* **1.** to admit or acknowledge. **2.** to declare (one's sins) to a priest. **—con·fes′sion,** *n.*

con·fes′sed·ly (-id lē) *adv.* by confession; admittedly.

con·fes′sion·al *adj.* **1.** characteristic of confession. **—n. 2.** a place in a church set apart for confession.

con·fes′sor *n.* **1.** one who confesses. **2.** one who hears confessions.

con·fet′ti (kən fet′ē) *n.* bits of colored paper thrown at festive events.

con′fi·dant′ or **con′fi·dante′** (kon′fi dant′, -dänt′) *n.* a person to whom secrets are told.

con·fide′ (kən fīd′) *v.,* **-fided, -fiding. —v.t. 1.** to tell in secret. **2.** to**

entrust. **3. confide in,** to discuss private matters with.

con′fi·dence (kon′fi dəns) *n.* **1.** full trust. **2.** assurance. **3.** a secret communication. **—con′fi·dent,** *adj.*

con′fi·den′tial (-den′shəl) *adj.* **1.** secret or private. **2.** entrusted with secrets. **—con′fi·den′tial·ly,** *adv.*

con·fig′u·ra′tion (kən fig′yə rā′-shən) *n.* shape; external form.

con·fine′ *v.,* **-fined, -fining,** *n.* **—v.t.** (kən fīn′) **1.** to keep within bounds. **2.** to shut or lock up. **—n. 3.** confines, (kon′fīnz) a boundary.

con·fined′ *adj.* restricted.

con·fine′ment *n.* **1.** imprisonment. **2.** childbirth.

con·firm′ (kən fûrm′) *v.t.* **1.** to make definite. **2.** to make valid. **3.** to administer confirmation to.

con′fir·ma′tion (kon′fər-) *n.* **1.** a confirming or being confirmed. **2.** a ceremony of admission to membership in a church.

con·firmed′ *adj.* **1.** made definite. **2.** habitual.

con′fis·cate′ (kon′fə skāt′) *v.t.,* **-cated, -cating.** to seize by authority. **—con′fis·ca′tion,** *n.*

con′fla·gra′tion (kon′flə grā′shən) *n.* a fierce fire.

con·flict′ *v.i.* (kən flikt′) **1.** to clash; disagree. **—n.** (kon′flikt) **2.** a fight. **3.** a disagreement.

con′flu·ence (kon′flōō əns) *n.* an act or place of flowing together. **—con′flu·ent,** *adj.*

con·form′ (kən fôrm′) *v.i.* **1.** to comply. **2.** to act in accord with prevailing custom. **3.** to be similar. **—v.t. 4.** to make similar. **5.** to bring into accord. **—con·form′ist,** *n.* **—con·form′i·ty,** *n.*

con·found′ (kon found′) *v.t.* **1.** to confuse. **2.** to astonish.

con·found′ed *adj.* bewildered.

con·front′ (kən frunt′) *v.t.* **1.** to face in a hostile way. **2.** to stand or come in front of. **—con′fron·ta′-tion** (kon′frun tā′shən) *n.* **—con′-fron·ta′tion·al,** *adj.*

con·fuse′ (kən fyōōz′) *v.t.,* **-fused, -fusing. 1.** to bewilder. **2.** to make unclear. **3.** to throw into disorder. **—con·fu′sion,** *n.*

con·fute′ (-fyōōt′) *v.t.,* **-futed, -futing.** to prove wrong.

con·geal′ (kən jēl′) *v.t., v.i.* to make or become solid or thick.

con·gen′ial (kən jēn′yəl) *adj.* **1.** agreeable in nature. **2.** suited in tastes, temperament, etc. **—con·ge′ni·al′i·ty** (-jē′nē al′i tē) *n.*

con·gen′i·tal (kən jen′i tl) *adj.* present from birth. **—con·gen′i·tal·ly,** *adv.*

con·gest′ (kən jest′) *v.t.* **1.** to fill to excess; clog. **2.** to make (a body part) abnormally full of blood or other fluid. **—con·ges′tion,** *n.*

con·glom′er·ate *n., adj., v.,* **-ated, -ating. —n.** (kən glom′ər it) **1.** something composed of heterogeneous elements. **2.** a company owning a variety of other companies. **—adj. 3.** mixed. **—v.t.** (-ə rāt′) **4.** to gather into a coherent mass. **—con·glom′er·a′tion,** *n.*

con·grat′u·late′ (kən grach′ə lāt′) *v.t.,* **-lated, -lating.** to express pleasure to (a person) for an accomplishment or good fortune. **—con·grat′u·la′tions,** *n.pl.*

con′gre·gate′ (kong′gri gāt′) *v.i.,* **-gated, -gating.** to assemble. **—con′gre·ga′tion,** *n.* **—con′gre·ga′tion·al,** *adj.*

con′gre·ga′tion·al *adj.* **1.** of congregations. **2. Congregational,** denoting a church denomination in which each church acts independently.

con′gress (kong′gris) *n.* **1. Congress,** the national legislative body of the U.S. **2.** a formal meeting. **—con·gres′sion·al** (kəng gresh′ə-nl) *adj.*

con′gru·ent (kong′grōō ənt) *adj.* **1.** agreeing. **2.** (of geometric figures) being exactly the same size and shape. **—con′gru·ence,** *n.*

con·gru′i·ty (kən grōō′i tē) *n., pl.* **-ties.** agreement; harmony. **—con′-gru·ous** (kong′grōō əs) *adj.*

con′ic (kon′ik) *adj.* of or like a cone. Also, **con′i·cal.**

co′ni·fer (kō′nə fər, kon′ə-) *n.* an evergreen tree bearing cones. **—co·nif′er·ous** (-nif′ər əs) *adj.*

con·jec′ture (kən jek′chər) *n., v.,* **-tured, -turing. —n. 1.** a guess. **—v.t., v.i. 2.** to conclude from insufficient evidence; guess.

con·join′ (kən join′) *v.t., v.i.* to join together.

con′ju·gal (kon′jə gəl) *adj.* of marriage.

con′ju·gate′ (-gāt′) *v.t.,* **-gated,**

-gating. to give the inflected forms of (a verb). **—con′ju·ga′tion,** *n.*

con·junc′tion (kən jungk′shən) *n.* **1.** a union; combination. **2.** a word that joins words, phrases, clauses, or sentences.

con·junc′ti·vi′tis (kən jungk′tə vī′-tis) *n.* inflammation of the mucous membrane of the eye.

con·jure (kon′jər, kun′-) *v.,* **-jured, -juring. —v.t. 1.** to invoke or produce by magic. **—v.i. 2.** to practice magic. **—con′jur·er,** *n.*

conk (kongk) *Slang.* **—v.t. 1.** to strike on the head. **2. conk out. a.** to break down. **b.** to go to sleep. **—n. 3.** a blow on the head.

Conn. Connecticut.

con·nect′ (kə nekt′) *v.t., v.i.* **1.** to join together. **2.** to associate mentally. **—con·nec′tive,** *adj., n.*

con·nec′tion *n.* **1.** a connecting or being connected. **2.** anything that connects. **3.** relationship. **4.** a transfer by a passenger from one airplane, train, etc., to another.

con·nive′ (kə nīv′) *v.i.,* **-nived, -niving. 1.** to cooperate secretly; conspire. **2.** to give unspoken consent to. **—con·niv′ance,** *n.*

con′nois·seur′ (kon′ə sûr′) *n.* an expert judge in matters of taste.

con·note′ (kə nōt′) *v.t.,* **-noted, -noting.** to suggest in addition to the explicit meaning; imply. **—con′no·ta′tion** (kon′ə tā′shən) *n.*

con·nu′bi·al (kə nōō′bē əl, -nyōō′-) *adj.* matrimonial.

con′quer (kong′kər) *v.t.* **1.** to overcome by force. **2.** to win by effort. **—con′quer·or,** *n.* **—con′quest,** *n.*

con·quis′ta·dor′ (kong kwis′tə-dôr′, -kēs′-) *n., pl.* **conquis·ta·dors, conquis·ta·do′res** (-kēs′tə dôr′ēz, -āz). a 16th-century Spanish conqueror of the Americas.

con·san·guin′e·ous (kon′sang-gwin′ē əs) *adj.* related by birth. **—con′san·guin′i·ty,** *n.*

con′science (kon′shəns) *n.* one's sense of right and wrong.

con′sci·en′tious (-shē en′shəs, -sē-) *adj.* careful and hardworking.

conscien′tious objec′tor *n.* a person who refuses to serve in the military for moral reasons.

con′scious (kon′shəs) *adj.* **1.** aware of one's own existence, sensations, etc. **2.** having the mental faculties awake. **3.** intentional. **—con′-scious·ness,** *n.*

con′script *n.* (kon′skript) **1.** one drafted for military service. **—v.t.** (kən skript′) **2.** to draft for military service. **—con·scrip′tion,** *n.*

con′se·crate′ (kon′si krāt′) *v.t.,* **-crated, -crating. 1.** to make sacred. **2.** to dedicate to some purpose. **—con′se·cra′tion,** *n.*

con·sec′u·tive (kən sek′yə tiv) *adj.* following in uninterrupted order. **—con·sec′u·tive·ly,** *adv.*

con·sen′sus (kən sen′səs) *n.* general agreement.

con·sent′ (kən sent′) *v.i.* **1.** to agree to or comply with another's proposal. **—n. 2.** agreement.

con′se·quence′ (kon′si kwens′, -kwəns) *n.* **1.** a result. **2.** importance.

con′se·quent′ *adj.* following; resulting. **—con′se·quent·ly,** *adv.*

con′se·quen′tial (-kwen′shəl) *adj.* **1.** consequent. **2.** important.

con′ser·va′tion (kon′sər vā′shən) *n.* **1.** the act of conserving. **2.** the preservation of resources. **—con′-ser·va′tion·ist,** *n.*

con·serv′a·tive (kən sûr′və tiv) *adj.* **1.** in favor of preserving existing conditions. **2.** cautious. **3.** traditional. **—n. 4.** a conservative person. **—con·serv′a·tism,** *n.*

con·serv′a·to′ry (-tôr′ē) *n., pl.* **-ries. 1.** a school of music or drama. **2.** a greenhouse.

con·serve′ *v.,* **-served, -serving,** *n.* **—v.t.** (kən sûrv′) **1.** to prevent injury, decay, or loss of. **—n.** (kon′-sûrv) **2.** a kind of jam.

con·sid′er (kən sid′ər) *v.t.* **1.** to think about carefully. **2.** to believe or suppose. **3.** to respect. **—con·sid′er·ate,** *adj.*

con·sid′er·a·ble *adj.* important or sizable. **—con·sid′er·a·bly,** *adv.*

con·sid′er·a′tion (-ə rā′shən) *n.* **1.** careful thought. **2.** a fact kept in mind. **3.** regard. **4.** a payment.

con·sid′er·ing *prep.* in view of.

con·sign′ (kən sīn′) *v.t.* **1.** to deliver. **2.** to entrust. **3.** to ship (goods) for sale. **—con·sign′ment,** *n.*

con·sist′ (kən sist′) *v.* **1. consist in,** to be contained or inherent in. **2. consist of,** to be composed of.

con·sist′en·cy (-sis′tən sē) *n., pl.*

-cies. 1. degree of firmness or density. **2.** adherence to the same principles, behavior, etc.

con·sis′to·ry (kən sis′tə rē) *n., pl.* **-ries.** a church council.

con·sole′[1] (kən sōl′) *v.t.,* **-soled, -soling.** to comfort. **—con′so·la′tion,** *n.* **—con·sol′a·ble,** *adj.*

con·sole[2] (kon′sōl) *n.* a cabinet or unit containing controls.

con·sol′i·date′ (kən sol′i dāt′) *v.i.,* **-dated, -dating. 1.** to combine into a single whole. **2.** to make or become secure. **—con·sol′i·da′tion,** *n.*

con′som·mé′ (kon′sə mā′) *n.* a clear soup.

con′so·nant (kon′sə nənt) *n.* **1.** a letter other than a vowel or the sound it represents. **—adj. 2.** consistent.

con′sort *n.* (kon′sôrt) **1.** a spouse, esp. of a ruler. **—v.i.** (kən sôrt′) **2.** to associate.

con·sor′ti·um (kən sôr′shē əm, -tē-) *n., pl.* **-tia** (-shē ə, -tē ə). a combination, as of corporations, for carrying out a purpose.

con·spic′u·ous (kən spik′yŏŏ əs) *adj.* **1.** easily seen. **2.** attracting attention. **—con·spic′u·ous·ly,** *adv.*

con·spire′ (kən spīr′) *v.i.,* **-spired, -spiring.** to plan secretly, usu. to do something unlawful. **—con·spir′a·cy** (-spir′ə sē) *n.* **—con·spir′a·tor,** *n.*

con′sta·ble (kon′stə bəl) *n.* a police officer.

con·stab′u·lar′y (kən stab′yə ler′ē) *n., pl.* **-ies.** the police.

con′stant (kon′stənt) *adj.* **1.** not changing. **2.** uninterrupted. **3.** faithful. **—n. 4.** something unchanging. **—con′stan·cy,** *n.*

con′stel·la′tion (kon′stə lā′shən) *n.* a group of stars.

con′ster·na′tion (kon′stər nā′shən) *n.* sudden great dismay.

con′sti·pate′ (kon′stə pāt′) *v.t.,* **-pated, -pating.** to cause difficult evacuation of the bowels. **—con′sti·pa′tion,** *n.*

con·stit′u·ent (kən stich′ŏŏ ənt) *adj.* **1.** serving to make up something; component. **—n. 2.** an ingredient. **3.** a voter in a given district. **—con·stit′u·en·cy,** *n.*

con′sti·tute′ (kon′sti tŏŏt′, -tyŏŏt′) *v.t.,* **-tuted, -tuting. 1.** to compose or form. **2.** to establish.

con′sti·tu′tion (-tŏŏ′shən, -tyŏŏ′-) *n.* **1.** a system of governmental principles or the document embodying these principles. **2.** composition. **3.** physical condition. **—con′sti·tu′tion·al,** *adj.*

con·strain′ (kən strān′) *v.t.* **1.** to force or oblige. **2.** to restrict. **—con·strained′,** *adj.* **—con·straint′,** *n.*

con·strict′ (kən strikt′) *v.t.* to make narrow, as by squeezing. **—con·stric′tion,** *n.*

con·struct′ (kən strukt′) *v.t.* to build by putting parts together. **—con·struc′tion,** *n.*

con·struc′tive *adj.* **1.** helping to improve. **2.** of construction.

con·strue′ (kən strŏŏ′) *v.t.,* **-strued, -struing.** to interpret.

con′sul (kon′səl) *n.* an official appointed by a government to look after its business interests and its citizens in a foreign country. **—con′su·lar,** *adj.* **—con′su·late** (-sə lit) *n.*

con·sult′ (kən sult′) *v.t.* **1.** to ask information or advice of. **—v.i. 2.** to confer. **—con·sult′ant,** *n.* **—con′sul·ta′tion,** *n.*

con·sume′ (kən sŏŏm′) *v.t.,* **-sumed, -suming. 1.** to use up. **2.** to devour. **3.** to destroy. **4.** to engross.

con·sum′er *n.* a person who uses goods or services.

con′sum·mate′ *v.,* **-mated, -mating,** *adj.* **—v.t.** (kon′sə māt′) **1.** to make complete. **2.** to complete (a marriage) by sexual intercourse. **—adj.** (kən sum′it, kon′sə mit) **3.** perfect. **—con′sum·ma′tion,** *n.*

con·sump′tion (kən sump′shən) *n.* **1.** a consuming. **2.** the amount consumed. **3.** *Older Use.* tuberculosis. **—con·sump′tive,** *adj., n.*

cont. continued.

con′tact (kon′takt) *n.* **1.** a touching or meeting. **2.** close association. **3.** a person through whom one can gain access to information. **4.** an electrical connection. **—v.t. 5.** to put into contact. **6.** to communicate with. **—v.i. 7.** to enter into contact.

con′tact lens *n.* a corrective lens put directly on the eye.

con·ta′gion (kən tā′jən) *n.* **1.** the spread of disease by contact. **2.** a

disease spread by contact. **—con·ta′gious,** *adj.*

con·tain′ (kən tān′) *v.t.* **1.** to have within itself. **2.** to include. **3.** to limit. **—con·tain′er,** *n.*

con·tam′i·nate′ (kən tam′ə nāt′) *v.t.,* **-nated, -nating.** to pollute.

con·temn′ (kən tem′) *v.t.* to scorn.

con′tem·plate′ (kon′təm plāt′, -tem-) *v.,* **-plated, -plating. —v.t. 1.** to observe thoughtfully. **2.** to consider. **3.** to intend. **—v.i. 4.** to meditate. **—con′tem·pla′tion,** *n.*

con·tem′po·rar′y (kən tem′pə rer′ē) *adj., n., pl.* **-raries.** —*adj.* **1.** Also, **con·tem′po·ra′ne·ous** (-rā′nē əs). of the same age or date. **2.** of the present time. **—n. 3.** a person or thing of the same date or age as another.

con·tempt′ (kən tempt′) *n.* **1.** scorn. **2.** the state of being despised. **3.** open disrespect.

con·tempt′i·ble *adj.* deserving contempt.

con·temp′tu·ous *adj.* showing contempt.

con·tend′ (kən tend′) *v.i.* **1.** to compete. **—v.t. 2.** to assert.

con′tent[1] (kon′tent) *n.* **1.** Usu. **contents. a.** something contained. **b.** the subjects in a book, document, etc. **2.** meaning.

con·tent′[2] (kən tent′) *adj.* **1.** satisfied. **—v.t. 2.** to make content. **—n. 3.** Also, **con·tent′ment.** satisfaction.

con·ten′tion (-shən) *n.* **1.** conflict; dispute. **2.** something asserted in an argument. **—con·ten′tious,** *adj.*

con·ter′mi·nous (kən tûr′mə nəs) *adj.* **1.** having a common boundary. **2.** enclosed within the same boundaries. **—con·ter′mi·nous·ly,** *adv.*

con′test *n.* (kon′test) **1.** a competition. **2.** a struggle. **—v.t.** (kən test′) **3.** to compete for. **4.** to dispute. **—con·test′ant,** *n.*

con′text (kon′tekst) *n.* **1.** what comes before or follows a word or statement and influences its meaning. **2.** circumstances.

con·tig′u·ous (kən tig′yŏŏ əs) *adj.* **1.** touching. **2.** near.

con′ti·nence (kon′tn əns) *n.* **1.** self-restraint. **2.** the ability to control bodily discharges.

con′ti·nent (kon′tn ənt) *n.* **1.** one of the seven main land masses of the earth. **—adj. 2.** self-restrained. **3.** able to control bodily discharges.

con′ti·nen′tal (kon′ti nen′tl) *adj.* **1.** of a continent. **2. Continental,** European.

continen′tal divide′ *n.* a divide separating river systems that flow to opposite sides of a continent.

con′tinen′tal shelf′ *n.* the part of a continent submerged in relatively shallow sea.

con·tin′gen·cy (kən tin′jən sē) *n., pl.,* **-cies. 1.** dependence on chance. **2.** a chance event.

con·tin′gent *adj.* **1.** dependent on something else. **—n. 2.** a group that is part of a larger body.

con·tin′u·al (kən tin′yŏŏ əl) *adj.* recurring regularly or frequently. **—con·tin′u·al·ly,** *adv.*

—Usage. Use CONTINUAL for actions that occur over and over again (especially actions that are annoying): *The dog's continual barking was driving me crazy.* The word CONTINUOUS is used for actions that keep going and do not stop: *We had continuous electricity during the big storm.*

con·tin′ue *v.,* **-tinued, -tinuing. —v.i. 1.** to go on without interruption. **2.** to resume. **3.** to last. **4.** to remain in a state or place. **—v.t. 5.** to go on with. **6.** to extend.

con′ti·nu′i·ty (kon′tn ŏŏ′i tē, -tn yŏŏ′-) *n., pl.* **-ties. 1.** the state of being continuous. **2.** a continuous whole.

con·tin′u·ous (kən tin′yŏŏ əs) *adj.* going on without interruption. **—con·tin′u·ous·ly,** *adv.*

—Usage. See CONTINUAL.

con·tin′u·um (-yŏŏ əm) *n., pl.* **-tinua.** a continuous extent, series, or whole.

con·tort′ (kən tôrt′) *v.t., v.i.* to twist or become twisted out of shape. **—con·tor′tion,** *n.*

con·tor′tion·ist *n.* a person who performs feats involving contorted positions.

con′tour (kon′tŏŏr) *n.* the outline of a figure or body.

contra- a prefix meaning against, opposite, or opposing.

con′tra·band′ (kon′trə band′) *n.* goods imported or exported illegally.

con′tra·cep′tion (-sep′shən) *n.* the deliberate prevention of conception. **—con′tra·cep′tive,** *adj., n.*

con′tract *n.* (kon′trakt) **1.** a formal agreement. **—v.t.** (kən trakt′) **2.** to make shorter or smaller. **3.** to catch, as an illness. **4.** to incur, as a debt. **—v.i. 5.** to shrink. **6.** to enter into a formal agreement.

con′trac·tor (kon′trak tər) *n.* a person who performs work or supplies goods by contract.

con′tra·dict′ (kon′trə dikt′) *v.t.* **1.** to assert the contrary of. **2.** to imply a denial of. **—v.i. 3.** to utter a contrary statement. **—con′tra·dic′tion,** *n.* **—con′tra·dic′to·ry,** *adj.*

con·tral′to (kən tral′tō) *n., pl.* **-tos. 1.** the lowest female voice. **2.** a singer with this voice.

con·trap′tion (kən trap′shən) *n.* a strange machine; gadget.

con′tra·ry (kon′trer ē) *adj., n., pl.* **-ries. —adj. 1.** opposite. **2.** (also kən trâr′ē) stubbornly willful. **—n. 3.** something opposite. **—Idiom. 4. on the contrary,** in opposition to what has been said. **5. to the contrary,** to the opposite effect.

con·trast′ *v.t.* (kən trast′) **1.** to compare in order to show differences. **—v.i. 2.** to exhibit unlikeness when compared. **—n.** (kon′trast) **3.** unlikeness shown by comparing. **4.** something unlike.

con′tra·vene′ (kon′trə vēn′) *v.t.,* **-vened, -vening.** to oppose. **—con′tra·ven′tion** (-ven′shən) *n.*

con′tre·temps′ (kon′trə tän′) *n., pl.* **-temps.** an unfortunate happening.

con·trib′ute (kən trib′yŏŏt) *v.t., v.i.,* **-uted, -uting. 1.** to give (money, aid, etc.) together with others. **—Idiom. 2. contribute to,** to be a factor in. **—con′tri·bu′tion** (kon′trə byŏŏ′shən) *n.* **—con·trib′u·tor,** *n.* **—con·trib′u·to·ry,** *adj.*

con·trite′ (kən trīt′) *adj.* penitent. **—con·tri′tion** (-trish′ən) *n.*

con·trive′ (kən trīv′) *v.t.,* **-trived, -triving.** to plan or scheme.

con·trol′ (kən trōl′) *v.,* **-trolled, -trolling,** *n.* **—v.t. 1.** to have direction over. **2.** to restrain. **—n. 3.** the act or power of controlling. **4.** a restraint. **5.** a regulating device. **—con·trol′la·ble,** *adj.*

con·trol′ler *n.* **1.** an officer who superintends finances. **2.** a regulator.

con′tro·ver′sy (kon′trə vûr′sē) *n., pl.* **-sies. 1.** a prolonged public dispute. **2.** an argument. **—con′tro·ver′sial** (-vûr′shəl) *adj.*

con′tro·vert′ (kon′trə vûrt′, kon′trə vûrt′) *v.t.* to dispute; deny.

con′tu·ma′cious (kon′tŏŏ mā′shəs, -tyŏŏ-) *adj.* stubbornly disobedient.

con′tu·me·ly (kon′tŏŏ mə lē, -tyŏŏ-) *n., pl.* **-lies.** insulting or humiliating treatment or language.

con·tu′sion (kən tŏŏ′zhən, -tyŏŏ′-) *n.* a bruise.

co·nun′drum (kə nun′drəm) *n.* anything that puzzles.

con′ur·ba′tion (kon′ər bā′shən) *n.* a continuous group of towns or cities.

con′va·lesce′ (kon′və les′) *v.i.,* **-lesced, -lescing.** to recover from illness. **—con′va·les′cence,** *n.* **—con′va·les′cent,** *adj., n.*

con·vec′tion (kən vek′shən) *n.* the transfer of heat by the movement of the warm parts of a liquid or gas.

con·vene′ (kən vēn′) *v.i., v.t.,* **-vened, -vening.** to assemble.

con·ven′ient (-vēn′yənt) *adj.* **1.** suitable to the needs or purpose. **2.** at hand; accessible. **—con·ven′ience,** *n.*

con′vent (kon′vent, -vənt) *n.* a community of nuns or the building they occupy.

con·ven′tion (kən ven′shən) *n.* **1.** an assembly. **2.** an agreement. **3.** an accepted usage or custom.

con·ven′tion·al *adj.* conforming to accepted standards. **2.** ordinary.

con·verge′ (kən vûrj′) *v.i., v.t.,* **-verged, -verging.** to meet in a point.

con·ver′sant (kən vûr′sənt) *adj.* familiar.

con′ver·sa′tion (kon′vər sā′shən) *n.* informal oral communication between people or an instance of this. **—con′ver·sa′tion·al,** *adj.*

con·verse′[1] (kən vûrs′) *v.i.,* **-versed, -versing.** to talk informally with someone.

con′verse[2] *adj.* (kən vûrs′) **1.** opposite or contrary. **—n.** (kon′vûrs) **2.** something opposite or contrary.

con·ver′sion *n.* **1.** the act or process of converting or the state of be-

ing converted. **2.** change in form or function. **3.** change from one belief, viewpoint, etc., to another.

con·vert′ *v.t.* (kən vûrt′) **1.** to change into a different form. **2.** to persuade to different beliefs. **—v.i. 3.** to become converted. **—n.** (kon′vûrt) **4.** a converted person. **—con·vert′er,** *n.*

con·vert′i·ble *adj.* **1.** able to be converted. **—n. 2.** a car with a folding top.

con·vex′ (kon veks′) *adj.* curved outward. **—con·vex′i·ty,** *n.*

con·vey′ (kən vā′) *v.t.* **1.** to transport; transmit. **2.** to communicate. **—con·vey′or, con·vey′er** *n.*

con·vey′ance *n.* **1.** the act of conveying. **2.** a vehicle.

con·vict′ *v.t.* (kən vikt′) **1.** to find guilty. **—n.** (kon′vikt) **2.** a convicted person in prison.

con·vic′tion *n.* **1.** a convicting or being convicted. **2.** a firm belief.

con·vince′ (kən vins′) *v.t.,* **-vinced, -vincing.** to cause (a person) to believe something is true. **—con·vinc′ing,** *adj.*

con·viv′i·al (kən viv′ē əl) *adj.* sociable and festive. **—con·viv′i·al·i·ty** (-al′i tē) *n.*

con·voke′ (kən vōk′) *v.t.,* **-voked, -voking.** to call together. **—con′vo·ca′tion** (kon′və kā′shən) *n.*

con′vo·lut′ed (kon′və lŏŏ′tid) *adj.* **1.** twisted. **2.** complicated.

con′vo·lu′tion (kon′və lŏŏ′shən) *n.* a coil.

con′voy (kon′voi) *v.t.* **1.** to escort for protection. **—n. 2.** a group of ships or vehicles traveling together.

con·vulse′ (kən vuls′) *v.t.,* **-vulsed, -vulsing.** to cause to shake violently with laughter, pain, etc. **—con·vul′sive,** *adj.*

con·vul′sion *n.* **1.** a series of violent, involuntary muscular contractions. **2.** a violent disturbance.

co′ny (kō′nē, kun′ē) *n., pl.* **-nies.** a rabbit.

coo (kŏŏ) *v.,* **cooed, cooing,** *n.* **—v.i. 1.** to utter or imitate the soft murmuring sound of a dove. **—n. 2.** such a sound.

cook (kŏŏk) *v.t.* **1.** to prepare (food) by heating. **—v.i. 2.** to prepare food by heating. **3.** to undergo cooking. **—n. 4.** one who cooks.

cook′book′ *n.* a book with recipes and instructions for cooking.

cook′er·y *n.* the art of cooking.

cook′ie *n.* a small sweet cake.

cook′out′ *n.* an outdoor gathering at which food is cooked and eaten.

cool (kŏŏl) *adj.* **1.** moderately cold. **2.** calm. **3.** not enthusiastic. **4.** *Slang.* great; excellent. **—v.t., v.i. 5.** to make or become cool. **—cool′ly,** *adv.*

cool′ant *n.* a substance used to reduce the temperature of a system.

cool′er *n.* a container for keeping something cool.

coo′lie (kŏŏ′lē) *n.* an unskilled, poorly paid laborer, esp. formerly in the Far East.

coop (kŏŏp, kŏŏp) *n.* **1.** a cage for fowls. **—v.t. 2.** to keep in or as if in a coop.

coop′er *n.* a barrel maker.

co·op′er·ate′ (kō op′ə rāt′) *v.i.,* **-ated, -ating.** to work or act together. **—co·op′er·a′tion,** *n.*

co·op′er·a·tive (-ər ə tiv) *adj.* **1.** cooperating or willing to cooperate. **—n. 2.** an enterprise owned and operated by its members. **3.** Also, **co-op** (kō′op′). an apartment house jointly owned by its tenants.

co-opt′ (kō opt′) *v.t.* **1.** to choose as a fellow member. **2.** to win over into a larger group.

co·or′di·nate′ *v.,* **-nated, -nating,** *adj., n.* **—v.t.** (kō ôr′dn āt′) **1.** to place in order. **2.** to combine in harmonious relationship. **—adj.** (-dn it) **3.** of equal order or degree. **—n. 4.** a coordinate person or thing. **—co·or′di·na′tion,** *n.*

coot (kŏŏt) *n.* a kind of water bird.

cop (kop) *n. Informal.* a police officer.

co′pay′ (kō′pā′) *n.* a fixed amount paid by a patient to a health-care provider. Also, **co′pay′ment.**

cope[1] (kōp) *v.i.,* **coped, coping.** to deal with problems or duties.

cope[2] (kōp) *n.* a long cloak worn by the clergy.

cop′i·er (kop′ē ər) *n.* a machine for making copies.

co′pi′lot (kō′pī′lət) *n.* an aircraft pilot who is second in command.

cop′ing (kō′ping) *n.* the top layer of a wall.

co′pi·ous (kō′pē əs) *adj.* abundant.

cop′per (kop′ər) *n.* a soft reddish metallic element.

cop′per·head′ *n.* a poisonous snake with a copper-colored head.

copse (kops) *n.* a thicket of small trees or bushes. Also, **cop′pice.**

cop′u·late′ (kop′yə lāt′) *v.i.,* **-lated, -lating.** to have sexual intercourse. **—cop′u·la′tion,** *n.*

cop′y (kop′ē) *n., pl.* **-ies,** *v.,* **-ied, -ying. —n. 1.** a reproduction or imitation. **2.** a specimen of a book, magazine, etc. **3.** material to be printed. **—v.t., v.i. 4.** to make a copy (of). **5.** to imitate.

cop′y·cat′ *n.* an imitator.

cop′y·right′ *n.* **1.** exclusive control of a book, picture, etc. **—v.t. 2.** to secure the copyright on. **—adj. 3.** covered by copyright.

co·quette′ (kō ket′) *n.* a female flirt. **—co·quet′tish,** *adj.*

cor′al (kôr′əl) *n.* **1.** a substance formed of the skeletons of tiny marine animals. **2.** a yellowish pink.

cord (kôrd) *n.* **1.** a thin rope. **2.** a small, flexible, insulated electrical cable. **3.** 128 cu. ft. of firewood.

cor′dial (kôr′jəl) *adj.* **1.** hearty; friendly. **—n. 2.** a liqueur. **—cor·dial′i·ty** (-al′i tē, -jē al′-) *n.*

cord′ite (kôr′dīt) *n.* a smokeless explosive.

cord′less *adj.* (of an electrical appliance) having a self-contained power supply.

cor′don (kôr′dn) *n.* a line of police, soldiers, etc., guarding an area.

cor′do·van (kôr′də vən) *n.* a soft leather.

cor′du·roy′ (kôr′də roi′) *n.* a ribbed cotton fabric.

core (kôr) *n., v.,* **cored, coring. —n. 1.** the central part. **—v.t. 2.** to remove the core of.

co′ri·an·der (kôr′ē an′dər) *n.* an herb with pungent leaves and seeds.

cork (kôrk) *n.* **1.** the bark of a Mediterranean oak tree. **2.** a stopper of cork, rubber, etc. **—v.t. 3.** to close with a cork.

cork′screw′ *n.* a spiral, pointed instrument for removing corks.

cor′mo·rant (kôr′mər ənt) *n.* a diving seabird.

corn[1] (kôrn) *n.* **1.** a cereal plant bearing large ears with kernels. **2.** *Informal.* something trite. **—v.t. 3.** to preserve in brine.

corn[2] (kôrn) *n.* a horny growth, esp. on the toe.

corn′ bread′ *n.* a bread made with cornmeal.

corn′cob′ *n.* the core of an ear of corn that holds the grains.

cor′ne·a (kôr′nē ə) *n.* the transparent outer covering of the eye.

cor′ner (kôr′nər) *n.* **1.** the place or point where two lines or streets meet. **2.** a secluded place. **3.** a monopoly. **—v.t. 4.** to drive into a corner. **5.** to gain exclusive control of (a stock or commodity). **—Idiom. 6. cut corners,** to reduce cost, labor, etc.

cor′ner·stone′ *n.* **1.** a stone representing the starting place in the construction of a building. **2.** something essential.

cor·net′ (kôr net′) *n.* a wind instrument resembling the trumpet.

corn′flow′er *n.* a plant with small blue flowers.

cor′nice (kôr′nis) *n.* a horizontal projection at the top of a wall.

corn′meal′ *n.* meal from corn.

corn′starch′ *n.* a starchy flour from corn.

cor′nu·co′pi·a (kôr′nə kō′pē ə, -nyə-) *n.* a horn of plenty.

corn′y (kôr′nē) *adj.,* **-ier, -iest.** trite, sentimental, or old-fashioned.

co·rol′la (kə rol′ə, -rō′lə) *n.* the petals of a flower.

cor′ol·lar′y (kôr′ə ler′ē) *n., pl.* **-laries.** a logical deduction.

co·ro′na (kə rō′nə) *n., pl.* **-nas, -nae** (-nē). a circle of light.

cor′o·nar′y (kôr′ə ner′ē) *adj., n., pl.* **-naries. —adj. 1.** of the arteries supplying the heart with blood. **—n. 2.** a heart attack.

cor′o·na′tion (kôr′ə nā′shən) *n.* the act of crowning.

cor′o·ner (kôr′ə nər) *n.* an official who investigates suspicious deaths.

cor′o·net′ (kôr′ə net′) *n.* a small crown.

corp. corporation.

cor′po·ral′[1] (kôr′pər əl) *adj.* physical.

cor′po·ral[2] (kôr′pər əl) *n.* an officer ranking below a sergeant.

cor′po·ra′tion (-rā′shən) *n.* an association created by law and having the powers and liabilities of an individual. —**cor′po•rate** (-pər it, -prit) adj.

cor•po′re•al (kôr pôr′ē əl) adj. material; tangible.

corps (kôr) n., pl. **corps. 1.** a military unit. **2.** any group.

corpse (kôrps) n. a dead body.

cor′pu•lent (kôr′pyə lənt) adj. fat.

cor′pus (kôr′pəs) n., pl. **-pora** (-pər ə). **1.** a complete collection of writings. **2.** a body, esp. when dead.

cor′pus•cle (kôr′pə səl) n. a blood cell.

cor•ral′ (kə ral′) n., v., **-ralled, -ralling.** —n. **1.** a pen for livestock. —v.t. **2.** to keep in a corral. **3.** to corner or capture.

cor•rect′ (kə rekt′) v.t. **1.** to make right. **2.** to mark or remove errors. **3.** to rebuke or punish. —adj. **4.** right. —**cor•rec′tion,** n. —**cor•rec′tive,** adj., n.

cor′re•late′ (kôr′ə lāt′) v.t., **-lated, -lating.** to establish in orderly connection. —**cor′re•la′tion,** n.

cor′re•spond′ (kôr′ə spond′) v.i. **1.** to match or be similar. **2.** to communicate by letters. —**cor′re•spond′ence,** n.

cor′re•spond′ent n. **1.** a letter writer. **2.** a person employed by a newspaper, television network, etc., to report news from a distant place. —adj. **3.** similar.

cor′ri•dor (kôr′i dər) n. **1.** a long hallway. **2.** a strip of land forming an outlet through foreign territory. **3.** a densely populated region with major transportation routes.

cor•rob′o•rate′ (kə rob′ə rāt′) v.t., **-rated, -rating.** to confirm. —**cor•rob′o•ra′tion,** n. —**cor•rob′o•ra′tive** (-ə rā′tiv, -ər ə tiv) adj.

cor•rode′ (kə rōd′) v., **-roded, -roding.** —v.t. **1.** to eat or wear away gradually. —v.i. **2.** to become corroded. —**cor•ro′sion** (-rō′zhən) n. —**cor•ro′sive,** adj.

cor′ru•gate′ (kôr′ə gāt′) v., **-gated, -gating.** —v.t. **1.** to bend into grooves and ridges. —v.i. **2.** to become corrugated.

cor•rupt′ (kə rupt′) adj. **1.** dishonest. **2.** immoral. **3.** decayed. —v.t., v.i. **4.** to make or become corrupt. —**cor•rup′tion,** n.

cor•sage′ (kôr säzh′) n. a small bouquet to be worn.

cor′sair (kôr′sâr) n. a pirate.

cor′set (kôr′sit) n. an undergarment for shaping the body.

cor•tege′ (kôr tezh′) n. a procession.

cor′tex (kôr′teks) n. the outer covering of the brain or an organ.

cor′ti•sone′ (kôr′tə zōn′, -sōn′) n. a hormone used in treating autoimmune or inflammatory diseases.

cor′us•cate′ (kôr′ə skāt′, kor′-) v.i., **-cated, -cating.** to sparkle. —**cor′us•ca′tion,** n.

cor•vette′ (kôr vet′) n. a small, fast sailing vessel.

cos•met′ic (koz met′ik) n. **1.** a beautifying product. —adj. **2.** of cosmetics. **3.** superficial.

cos′mic (koz′mik) adj. **1.** of the cosmos. **2.** vast.

cos•mog′o•ny (-mog′ə nē) n., pl. **-nies.** a theory of the origin of the universe.

cos•mol′o•gy (-mol′ə jē) n. the study of the origin and structure of the universe.

cos′mo•pol′i•tan (koz′mə pol′i tn) adj. worldly.

cos′mos (-məs, -mōs) n. the ordered universe.

cost (kôst) n. **1.** the price paid for something. **2.** a loss or penalty. —v.t. **3.** to require the payment of. **4.** to result in the loss of. —**cost′ly,** adj.

cost′-ef•fec′tive adj. producing optimum results for the expenditure.

cost′ of liv′ing n. the average amount paid for basic necessities.

cos′tume (kos′tōōm, -tyōōm) n. historical or theatrical dress.

co′sy (kō′zē) adj., **-sier, -siest,** n., pl. **-sies.** cozy.

cot (kot) n. a light, portable bed.

cote (kōt) n. a shelter for pigeons, sheep, etc.

co•te′rie (kō′tə rē) n. a group of social acquaintances.

co•til′lion (kə til′yən) n. a formal ball.

cot′tage (kot′ij) n. a small house.

cot′tage cheese′ n. a soft, mild cheese made from skim-milk curds.

cot′ter (kot′ər) n. a pin fitting into a machinery opening.

cot′ton (kot′n) n. **1.** a soft white substance attached to the seeds of a

tropical plant. **2.** cloth or thread made of this substance.

cot′ton•mouth′ (-mouth′) n. a poisonous snake of southeastern U.S. swamps. Also, **wa′ter moc′casin.**

cot′ton•seed′ n. the seed of the cotton plant, yielding an oil (**cottonseed oil**) used in cooking and medicine.

cot′ton•wood′ n. a kind of poplar with cottony tufts on the seeds.

couch (kouch) n. a long piece of furniture for sitting or lying.

couch′ pota′to n. Informal. a person who watches a lot of television.

cou′gar (kōō′gər) n. a large American wildcat.

cough (kôf) v.i. **1.** to expel air from the lungs suddenly and loudly. —n. **2.** the act or sound of coughing.

cough′ drop′ n. a lozenge for relieving a cough, sore throat, etc.

could (kŏŏd; unstressed kəd) auxiliary v. **1.** pt. of **can¹. 2.** (used to express politeness or doubt).

cou•lomb′ (kōō lom′, -lōm′) n. a unit of electricity.

coun′cil (koun′səl) n. a deliberative or advisory body. —**coun′cil•or, coun′cil•lor,** n.

coun′sel (koun′səl) n., v., **-seled, -seling.** —n. **1.** advice. **2.** consultation. **3.** a lawyer. —v.t. **4.** to advise. —**coun′sel•or, coun′sel•lor,** n.

count¹ (kount) v. **1.** to find the total number of. **2.** to name the numbers up to. **3.** to consider. —v.i. **4.** to name the numbers in order. **5.** to be important. **6.** count on, to rely on. —n. **7.** the act of counting. **8.** the total. **9.** an item in an indictment.

count² (kount) n. a nobleman.

count′down′ n. a backward counting to zero, indicating the start of a scheduled event.

coun′te•nance (koun′tn əns) n., v., **-nanced, -nancing.** —n. **1.** the face. **2.** facial expression. —v.t. **3.** to approve.

count′er¹ (-tər) n. **1.** a table on which goods can be shown, business transacted, etc. **2.** a small object used to keep account in games. —Idiom. **3.** over the counter, (of medicines) without requiring a prescription. **4.** under the counter, in a secretive manner.

count′er² (-tər) adv. **1.** in the opposite direction. —adj. **2.** opposite. —n. **3.** something opposite to something else. —v.t., v.i. **4.** to oppose.

counter- a prefix indicating: **1.** opposite. **2.** against. **3.** in response to.

coun′ter•act′ v.t. to act in opposition to.

coun′ter•at•tack′ n. **1.** an attack made in response to another attack. —v.t., v.i. **2.** to make a counterattack (against).

coun′ter•bal′ance n., v., **-anced, -ancing.** —n. (koun′tər bal′əns) **1.** a weight or influence balancing another. —v.t., v.i. (koun′tər bal′əns) **2.** to act as a counterbalance (to).

coun′ter•clock′wise′ adv., adj. in a direction opposite to the movement of clock hands.

coun′ter•cul′ture n. those opposed to a prevailing culture.

coun′ter•feit′ (-fit) adj. **1.** fake. —n. **2.** a fraudulent imitation. —v.t., v.i. **3.** to make a counterfeit (of). **4.** to feign.

coun′ter•in•tel′li•gence n. activity thwarting espionage by an enemy power.

coun′ter•mand′ (-mand′) v.t. to cancel (an order).

coun′ter•part′ n. a person or thing corresponding to another.

coun′ter•point′ n. a method of combining melodies.

coun′ter•pro•duc′tive adj. giving results contrary to those intended.

coun′ter•sign′ n. **1.** a secret sign. —v.t. **2.** to sign (a document) to confirm the signature of another person.

coun′ter•ten′or n. a male singer whose voice range is that of a female alto.

count′ess (koun′tis) n. **1.** the wife of a count or earl. **2.** a woman equal in rank to a count or earl.

count′less adj. too many to count.

coun′try (kun′trē) n., pl. **-tries. 1.** a nation or its land or people. **2.** areas with fields, farms, forests, etc., and few buildings or people.

coun′try•side′ n. a rural area.

coun′ty (koun′tē) n., pl. **-ties.** a political unit within a state.

coup (kōō) n., pl. **coups.** a daring and successful act.

coup′ d'é•tat′ (kōō′ dā tä′) n., pl. **coups d'état** (-dā täz′, -tä′). an overthrow of a government by force.

coupe (kōōp) n. a small, two-door car. Also, **cou•pé′** (kōō pā′).

cou′ple (kup′əl) n., v., **-pled, -pling.** —n. **1.** a combination of two of a kind. **2.** a grouping of two persons. —v.t., v.i. **3.** to join or unite. —**cou′pling,** n.

—Usage. Do not confuse PAIR and COUPLE. Both words have the meaning "a group of two" but are used differently. PAIR is used when two things come as a set, with one not usually used without the other: *a pair of gloves* or when there is one item that has two parts, as in *a pair of scissors.* COUPLE is used for things of the same kind that happen to be two in number: *a couple of books.*

cou′plet (kup′lit) n. a pair of rhyming lines.

cou′pon (kōō′pon, kyōō′-) n. a certificate entitling the holder to a gift or discount.

cour′age (kûr′ij, kur′-) n. bravery. —**cou•ra′geous** (kə rā′jəs) adj.

cour′i•er (kûr′ē ər) n. a messenger.

course (kôrs) n., v., **coursed, coursing.** —n. **1.** a path, route, or channel. **2.** a direction taken. **3.** a manner of proceeding. **4.** a series of lessons. **5.** one part of a meal. —v.i. **6.** to run or move swiftly. —Idiom. **7.** in due course, in the proper order of events. **8.** of course, certainly.

cours′er, n. a swift horse.

court (kôrt) n. **1.** a place where justice is administered. **2.** an open space enclosed by buildings or walls. **3.** a sovereign's residence and retinue. **4.** an assembly held by a sovereign. **5.** homage or attention. **6.** a level area for certain games. —v.t. **7.** to seek to win the favor of. **8.** to woo. **9.** to act in a way that causes.

cour′te•ous (kûr′tē əs) adj. polite.

cour′te•san (kôr′tə zən) n. a prostitute with noble or wealthy clients.

cour′te•sy (kûr′tə sē) n., pl. **-sies. 1.** polite behavior. **2.** a courteous act.

cour′ti•er (kôr′tē ər) n. an attendant at a royal court.

court′ly adj. polite or elegant.

court′-mar′tial n., pl. **courts-martial,** v., **-tialed, -tialing.** —n. **1.** a military court. —v.t. **2.** to try by court-martial.

cous′in (kuz′ən) n. the child of one's uncle or aunt.

cou•tu′ri•er (kōō tŏŏr′ē ər, -ē ā′) n. a designer of fashionable clothes.

cove (kōv) n. a recess in a shoreline.

cov′en (kuv′ən, kō′vən) n. an assembly of witches.

cov′e•nant (kuv′ə nənt) n. a solemn agreement; oath or pact.

cov′er (kuv′ər) v.t. **1.** to place something over or upon. **2.** to hide from view. **3.** to deal with. **4.** to protect. **5.** to travel over. **6.** to meet or offset. —v.i. **7.** to substitute for someone. **8.** to provide an alibi. —n. **9.** something that covers. **10.** protection. **11.** an assumed identity. —Idiom. **12.** take cover, to seek shelter. **13.** under cover, secretly.

cov′er•age (-ij) n. **1.** protection by insurance. **2.** the reporting of news.

cov′er•let (-lit) n. a quilt.

cov′ert (kō′vərt) adj. **1.** secret. —n. **2.** a thicket giving shelter to animals. —**cov′ert•ly,** adv.

cov′er-up′ n. concealment of illegal activity, a blunder, etc.

cov′et (kuv′it) v.t., v.i. to desire (another's property) eagerly or wrongfully. —**cov′et•ous,** adj.

cov′ey (kuv′ē) n., pl. **-eys.** a small flock.

cow¹ (kou) n. the female of a bovine or other large animal, as the whale.

cow² (kou) v.t. to intimidate.

cow′ard (kou′ərd) n. one who lacks courage. —**cow′ard•ice** (-ər dis) n.

cow′boy′ or **cow′girl′** n. a cattle herder.

cow′er (kou′ər) v.i. to crouch in fear.

cowl (koul) n. a hooded garment or the hood itself.

cow′lick′ n. a tuft of hair growing in a different direction from the rest of the hair.

cowl′ing n. a metal housing for an aircraft engine.

cow′slip′ n. a plant with fragrant yellow flowers.

cox′swain (kok′sən) n. a person who steers a boat or racing shell.

coy (koi) adj. pretending to be shy or embarrassed. —**coy′ly,** adv. —**coy′ness,** n.

coy•o•te (kī ō′tē) n. a wild animal related to the wolf.

coz′en (kuz′ən) v.t., v.i. to cheat or deceive.

co′zy (kō′zē) adj., **-zier, -ziest.** —adj. **1.** snugly warm and comfortable. —n. **2.** a knitted or padded cover for keeping a teapot or coffeepot warm. —**co′zi•ly,** adv. —**co′zi•ness,** n.

CPA certified public accountant.

CPI consumer price index.

CPR cardiopulmonary resuscitation: a form of lifesaving.

CPU central processing unit: the key component of a computer system.

crab (krab) n. a crustacean with a broad flat body and four pairs of legs.

crab′ ap′ple n. a small tart apple.

crab′by adj., **-bier, -biest.** grouchy.

crack (krak) v.i. **1.** to make a sudden, sharp sound. **2.** to break without separating. **3.** (of the voice) to break abruptly. —v.t. **4.** to cause to make a sudden, sharp sound. **5.** to cause to break without separating. **6.** to strike forcefully. **7. crack down,** to take severe measures. —n. **8.** a sudden, sharp sound. **9.** a break without the separation of parts. **10.** a slight opening. **11.** a sharp blow. **12.** a witty remark. **13.** Slang. a potent, smokable form of cocaine. —Idiom. **14. get cracking,** to hurry up.

crack′down′ n. a stern enforcement of regulations.

crack′er n. **1.** a crisp, thin biscuit. **2.** a firecracker.

crack′le (krak′əl) v., **-led, -ling.** —v.i. **1.** to make repeated, small sharp noises. —n. **2.** such a sound.

crack′pot′ n. a person with irrational ideas.

crack′up′ n. a mental breakdown.

cra′dle (krād′l) n., v., **-dled, -dling.** —n. **1.** a bed for a baby, usu. on rockers. —v.t. **2.** to place in a cradle. **3.** to hold protectively.

craft (kraft) n. **1.** a skill; skilled trade. **2.** cunning. **3.** vessels or aircraft.

craft′y adj., **-ier, -iest.** cunning.

crag (krag) n. a steep, rugged rock.

cram (kram) v., **crammed, cramming.** —v.t. **1.** to fill tightly; stuff. —v.i. **2.** to study hard for an examination.

cramp¹ (kramp) n. **1.** an involuntary muscular contraction. —v.t., v.i. **2.** to affect or be affected with a cramp.

cramp² (kramp) v.t. to restrict or hinder.

cramped (krampt) adj. confined.

cran′ber•ry (kran′ber′ē) n., pl. **-ries.** an edible sour red berry.

crane (krān) n., v., **craned, craning.** —n. **1.** a tall wading bird. **2.** a device for lifting heavy weights. —v.t., v.i. **3.** to stretch (the neck).

cra′ni•um (krā′nē əm) n., pl. **-niums, -nia** (-nē ə). the skull.

crank (krangk) n. **1.** a right-angled lever used to operate a machine. **2.** Informal. an ill-tempered person. **3.** a person with strange ideas. —v.t. **4.** to start by turning a crank.

crank′y (krang′kē) adj., **-ier, -iest.** ill-tempered. —**crank′i•ness,** n.

cran′ny (kran′ē) n., pl. **-nies.** a narrow opening.

crap (krap) n. Slang. **1.** worthless material. **2.** false or meaningless statements.

crape (krāp) n. crepe (defs. 1, 2).

crap′pie (krap′ē) n. a type of large sunfish.

craps (kraps) n. a dice game.

crash (krash) v.i. **1.** to make a loud, clattering noise. **2.** to fall with damage. **3.** to strike, collide, or break noisily. **4.** to collapse suddenly. **5.** (of a computer) to fail suddenly. —v.t. **6.** to cause to break violently and noisily. **7.** to cause (a vehicle) to crash. **8.** to enter (a party) without invitation. —n. **9.** an act or instance of crashing. **10.** a sudden loud noise. **11.** a collapse.

crass (kras) adj. insensitive; crude.

crate (krāt) n., v., **crated, crating.** —n. **1.** a wooden box for packing. —v.t. **2.** to put in a crate.

cra′ter n. a cup-shaped hole, as in a volcano or on the moon.

cra•vat′ (krə vat′) n. a necktie.

crave (krāv) v.t., **craved, craving.** to yearn or beg for.

cra′ven (krā′vən) adj. **1.** cowardly. —n. **2.** a coward.

crav′ing n. an intense yearning.

crawl (krôl) v.i. **1.** to move on hands and knees or with the belly close to the ground. **2.** to move slowly. —n. **3.** the act of crawling. **4.** a crawling pace. **5.** an overhand swimming stroke. —**crawl′er,** n.

cray′fish′ (krā′fish′) n. a crustacean resembling a lobster. Also, **craw′fish′** (krô′-).

cray′on (krā′on) n. a stick of colored wax for drawing.

craze (krāz) v., **crazed, crazing,** n. —v.t. **1.** to make or become insane. —n. **2.** a fad.

cra′zy (krā′zē) adj., **-zier, -ziest. 1.** insane. **2.** impractical.

creak (krēk) v.i. **1.** to squeak sharply. —n. **2.** a creaking sound.

cream (krēm) n. **1.** the fatty part of milk. **2.** a thick, smooth substance to put on the skin. **3.** the best part of anything. —v.t. **4.** to make with cream. **5.** to mix until creamy.

cream′er•y, n., pl. **-ies.** a place where dairy goods are produced.

cream′ of tar′tar n. a white powdery substance used in baking.

crease (krēs) n., v., **creased, creasing.** —n. **1.** a ridge produced by folding, striking, etc. **2.** a wrinkle. —v.t. **3.** to make creases in. —v.i. **4.** to become creased.

cre•ate′ (krē āt′) v.t., **-ated, -ating.** to cause to exist. —**cre•a′tion,** n. —**cre•a′tive,** adj. —**cre•a′tor,** n.

crea′ture (krē′chər) n. an animal or human being.

cre′dence (krēd′ns) n. belief.

cre•den′tials (kri den′shəlz) n. pl. documents providing evidence of identity, qualifications, etc.

cre•den′za (kri den′zə) n. a sideboard, esp. one without legs.

cred′i•ble (kred′ə bəl) adj. believable. —**cred′i•bil′i•ty,** n.

cred′it (kred′it) n. **1.** the belief that something is true. **2.** commendation for an accomplishment. **3.** a source of honor. **4.** permission to pay for goods later. **5.** a balance in a person's favor. —v.t. **6.** to believe. **7.** to give credit for or to.

cred′it•a•ble adj. worthy.

cred′it card′ n. a card entitling the holder to make purchases and pay for them later.

cred′i•tor n. a person to whom money is owed.

cred′it un′ion n. a cooperative group that makes loans to its members at low interest rates.

cred′u•lous (krej′ə ləs) adj. willing to believe too readily. —**cre•du′li•ty** (krə dōō′li tē, -dyōō′-) n.

creed (krēd) n. a formal statement of beliefs.

creek (krēk, krik) n. **1.** a small stream. —Idiom. **2. up the creek,** in trouble.

creel (krēl) n. a wickerwork basket for carrying fish.

creep (krēp) v., **crept** (krept) or **creeped, creeping,** n. —v.i. **1.** to move slowly with the body close to the ground. **2.** to move slowly or stealthily. **3.** (of a plant) to grow along the ground, a wall, etc. —n. **4.** Slang. an obnoxious person. **5. the creeps,** a sensation of anxiety or disgust.

creep′y adj., **-ier, -iest.** having or causing a sensation of horror.

cre′mate (krē′māt) v.t., **-mated, -mating.** to burn (a dead body) to ashes. —**cre•ma′tion,** n. —**cre′ma•to′ry,** n.

Cre′ole (krē′ōl) n. **1.** one of French and Spanish blood born in Louisiana. **2.** creole, pidgin that has become the native language of a group.

cre′o•sote′ (krē′ə sōt′) n. an oily liquid from coal and wood tar, used as a wood preservative and an antiseptic.

crepe (krāp; for 3 also krep) n. **1.** a light crinkled fabric. **2.** Also, **crepe′ pa′per.** thin, wrinkled paper used for decorating. **3.** a thin, light pancake.

cre•scen′do (kri shen′dō) n., pl. **-dos.** a gradual increase in loudness.

cres′cent (kres′ənt) n. **1.** the shape of the moon in its first or last quarter. **2.** an object having this shape.

cress (kres) n. a plant with pungent leaves, eaten in salads.

crest (krest) n. **1.** the top of a hill. **2.** the highest point. **3.** a tuft on the head of a bird or animal. **4.** the foamy top of a wave. **5.** the point of highest flood. **6.** a heraldic device. —v.i. **7.** to form or rise to a crest.

crest·fal·len *adj.* discouraged or depressed.

cre·tin (krēt′n) *n.* a boorish person.

cre·tonne (kri ton′) *n.* a heavy printed cotton fabric.

cre·vasse (krə vas′) *n.* a deep cleft, esp. in a glacier.

crev·ice (krev′is) *n.* a crack forming an opening.

crew (krōō) *n.* a group of persons working together, as on a ship.

crew·cut *n.* a haircut in which the hair is very closely cropped.

crib (krib) *n., v.,* **cribbed, cribbing.** —*n.* **1.** a child's bed with enclosed sides. **2.** a bin for storing grain. **3.** a manger. **4.** *Informal.* notes or translation used dishonestly by students taking an exam. —*v.t.* **5.** to put in a crib. **6.** *Informal.* to use a crib.

crib·bage (krib′ij) *n.* a card game using a score-board with pegs.

crick (krik) *n.* a muscle spasm.

crick·et (krik′it) *n.* **1.** a leaping insect that makes a chirping sound. **2.** an outdoor ball game, popular in Britain, played by two teams with bats, balls, and wickets.

cri·er (krī′ər) *n.* one who makes announcements.

crime (krīm) *n.* an unlawful act.

crim·i·nal (krim′ə nl) *adj.* **1.** guilty of crime. **2.** dealing with crime or its punishment. —*n.* **3.** a person convicted of a crime. —**crim′i·nal·ly,** *adv.*

crimp (krimp) *v.t.* **1.** to make wavy. —*n.* **2.** a crimped form. —*Idiom.* **3.** put a crimp in, to hinder.

crim·son (krim′zən) *n.* a deep red.

cringe (krinj) *v.i.,* **cringed, cringing.** to shrink in fear or embarrassment.

crin·kle (kring′kəl) *v.,* **-kled, -kling,** *n.* —*v.t., v.i.* **1.** to wrinkle. **2.** to rustle. —*n.* **3.** a wrinkle. **4.** a rustling sound. —**crin′kly,** *adj.*

crin·o·line (krin′l in) *n.* **1.** a stiff, coarse fabric. **2.** a petticoat.

crip·ple (krip′əl) *n., v.,* **-pled, -pling.** —*n.* **1.** *Sometimes Offensive.* a lame or disabled person or animal. —*v.t.* **2.** to disable.

cri·sis (krī′sis) *n., pl.* **-ses** (-sēz). a decisive stage or point.

crisp (krisp) *adj.* **1.** brittle. **2.** firm and fresh. **3.** brisk and decided. **4.** bracing. —*v.t., v.i.* **5.** to make or become crisp. —**crisp′ness,** *n.*

criss·cross (kris′krôs′) *adj.* **1.** marked with crossed lines. —*n.* **2.** a crisscross pattern. —*v.t.* **3.** to move back and forth over. **4.** to mark with crossed lines.

cri·te·ri·on (krī tēr′ē ən) *n., pl.* **-teria** (-tēr′ē ə). a standard for judgment.

crit·ic (krit′ik) *n.* **1.** a person who judges art or literature. **2.** a person who tends to make harsh judgments.

crit·i·cal *adj.* **1.** severe in judgment. **2.** involving criticism. **3.** crucial.

crit·i·cism *n.* **1.** faultfinding. **2.** the art of judging the merits of anything.

crit·i·cize (-sīz′) *v.i., v.t.,* **-cized, -cizing.** **1.** to discuss as a critic. **2.** to find fault (with).

cri·tique (kri tēk′) *n., v.,* **-tiqued, -tiquing.** —*n.* **1.** an article evaluating a work. —*v.t.* **2.** to analyze critically.

crit′ter (krit′ər) *n. Dial.* a creature.

croak (krōk) *v.i.* **1.** to utter a hoarse cry, as that of a frog. —*n.* **2.** such a sound.

cro·chet′ (krō shā′) *v.i.* to form thread into designs with a hooked needle.

crock (krok) *n.* an earthen jar.

croc·o·dile′ (krok′ə dīl′) *n.* a large aquatic reptile with long, powerful jaws and tail.

cro·cus (krō′kəs) *n.* a small bulbous plant blooming in early spring.

crois·sant′ (*Fr.* krwä sän′; *Eng.* krə sänt′) *n.* a crescent-shaped pastry.

crone (krōn) *n.* a witchlike old woman.

cro·ny (krō′nē) *n., pl.* **-nies.** a close friend.

crook (krŏŏk) *n.* **1.** a hooked stick. **2.** a bend. **3.** a dishonest person. —*v.t., v.i.* **4.** to bend; curve.

croon (krōōn) *v.i., v.t.* to sing softly.

crop (krop) *n., v.,* **cropped, cropping.** —*n.* **1.** the cultivated produce from the soil. **2.** a short whip. **3.** a pouch in the gullet of a bird. —*v.t.* **4.** to remove the ends of. **5.** to cut short. **6. crop up,** to appear.

cro·quet′ (krō kā′) *n.* a lawn game played with wooden balls and mallets.

cro·quette′ (krō ket′) *n.* a fried or baked piece of chopped food.

cro·sier (krō′zhər) *n.* the staff of a bishop.

cross (krôs) *n.* **1.** a structure whose basic form has an upright with a transverse piece. **2.** the emblem of Christianity. **3.** a figure resembling a cross. **4.** a mixture of breeds. —*v.t.* **5.** to put, lie, or pass across. **6.** to oppose or frustrate. **7.** to mark (out). **8.** to mix (breeds). **9.** to make the sign of the cross over. —*v.i.* **10.** to intersect. **11.** to move or extend from one side to another. **12. cross off** or **out,** to cancel, as by drawing a line through. —*adj.* **13.** lying crosswise. **14.** angry. —*Idiom.* **15. cross one's mind,** to occur to one. **16. cross one's path,** to meet.

cross′bow′ (-bō′) *n.* a weapon consisting of a bow fixed on a stock like that of a rifle.

cross′breed′ *v.,* **crossbred, crossbreeding,** *n.* —*v.t., v.i.* **1.** to hybridize. —*n.* **2.** a hybrid.

cross′-coun′try *adj.* **1.** proceeding over fields, through woods, etc., rather than on a road or track. **2.** from one end of a country to the other. —*n.* **3.** the sport of cross-country racing.

cross′-ex·am′ine *v.t.,* **cross-examined, cross-examining.** to examine closely, as an opposing witness. —**cross′-ex·am′in·a′tion,** *n.*

cross′-eye′ *n.* a condition in which one or both eyes turn inward. —**cross′-eyed′,** *adj.*

cross′ fire′ *n.* lines of gunfire crossing one another.

cross′hatch′ *v.t.* to shade with intersecting parallel lines. —**cross′hatch′ing,** *n.*

cross′-pur′pose *n.* **1.** a contrary purpose. —*Idiom.* **2. at cross-purposes,** in a way that involves mutual misunderstanding.

cross′ ref′erence *n.* a reference to another part of a book.

cross′ sec′tion *n.* **1.** a section made by cutting across something. **2.** a representative sample of a whole.

cross′walk′ *n.* a place where people can cross the street.

cross′word puz′zle *n.* a puzzle in which words determined from numbered clues are fitted into a pattern of squares.

crotch (kroch) *n.* a place where something divides, as the human body between the legs.

crotch′et (kroch′it) *n.* an odd fancy or whim.

crotch′et·y *adj.* grumpy.

crouch (krouch) *v.i.* **1.** to stoop low with the knees bent. —*n.* **2.** the act of crouching.

croup (krōōp) *n.* an inflammation of the throat causing coughing and difficult breathing.

crou·pi·er (krōō′pē ər, -pē ā′) *n.* an attendant who handles bets and money at a gambling table.

crou·ton (krōō′ton) *n.* a small cube of toasted bread.

crow[1] (krō) *n.* **1.** a large bird with black feathers. —*Idiom.* **2. as the crow flies,** in a straight line. **3. eat crow,** to admit a mistake.

crow[2] (krō) *v.i.* **1.** to utter the cry of a rooster. **2.** to boast. **3.** to utter a cry of pleasure. —*n.* **4.** the cry of a rooster. **5.** a cry of pleasure.

crow′bar′ *n.* an iron bar for prying something open.

crowd (kroud) *n.* **1.** a large group. —*v.i.* **2.** to press forward. —*v.t.* **3.** to cram. **4.** to push.

crown (kroun) *n.* **1.** an ornate ceremonial headgear worn by a monarch. **2.** the power of a sovereign. **3.** the top. —*v.t.* **4.** to place a crown on. **5.** to honor. **6.** to be at the top of.

crow's′-feet′ *n.pl.* tiny wrinkles at the outer corner of the eye.

CRT cathode-ray tube.

cru·cial (krōō′shəl) *adj.* vitally important.

cru·ci·ble (krōō′sə bəl) *n.* **1.** a vessel for heating substances to high temperatures. **2.** a severe trial.

cru·ci·fix (krōō′sə fiks) *n.* a cross with a figure of Jesus crucified.

cru·ci·fy′ (-fī′) *v.t.,* **-fied, -fying.** **1.** to put to death on a cross. **2.** to persecute. —**cru′ci·fix′ion,** *n.*

crude (krōōd) *adj.,* **cruder, crudest,** *n.* —*adj.* **1.** in a raw or unrefined state. **2.** unfinished; rough. **3.** vulgar. —*n.* **4.** unrefined petroleum.

cru·di·tés′ (krōō′di tā′) *n.pl.* cut-up raw vegetables served with a dip.

cru·el (krōō′əl) *adj.* willfully causing pain. —**cru′el·ly,** *adv.* —**cru′el·ty,** *n.*

cru·et (krōō′it) *n.* a stoppered bottle for vinegar, oil, etc.

cruise (krōōz) *v.,* **cruised, cruising,** *n.* —*v.i.* **1.** to sail or fly at a moderate speed. **2.** to travel for pleasure. —*n.* **3.** a pleasure voyage on a ship.

cruis·er *n.* **1.** a kind of warship. **2.** a small pleasure boat.

crul·ler (krul′ər) *n.* a twisted oblong doughnut.

crumb (krum) *n.* a small bit of bread, cookie, etc.

crum·ble (krum′bəl) *v.t., v.i.,* **-bled, -bling.** to break into small fragments.

crum·my (krum′ē) *adj.,* **-mier, -miest.** *Informal.* **1.** shabby. **2.** worthless. **3.** miserable.

crum·ple (krum′pəl) *v.,* **-pled, -pling.** —*v.t.* **1.** to crush into wrinkles. —*v.i.* **2.** to become crushed into wrinkles. **3.** to collapse.

crunch (krunch) *v.t.* **1.** to chew or crush noisily. —*n.* **2.** an act or sound of crunching. **3.** a critical situation.

cru·sade′ (krōō sād′) *n., v.,* **-saded, -sading.** —*n.* **1.** a medieval Christian expedition to recover the Holy Land from the Muslims. **2.** a campaign for a cause. —*v.i.* **3.** to engage in a crusade. —**cru·sad′er,** *n.*

crush (krush) *v.t.* **1.** to bruise or break by pressing. **2.** to pound into fragments. **3.** to suppress completely. —*v.i.* **4.** to become crushed. —*n.* **5.** a dense crowd. **6.** an infatuation.

crust (krust) *n.* **1.** a hard outer layer, as of bread. —*v.t., v.i.* **2.** to cover or become covered with a crust. —**crust′y,** *adj.*

crus·ta·cean (kru stā′shən) *n.* a sea animal having a hard shell, as the lobster, shrimp, etc.

crutch (kruch) *n.* **1.** a stick with a crosspiece under the armpit for support in walking. **2.** any aid or prop.

crux (kruks) *n., pl.* **cruxes, cruces** (krōō′sēz). the vital point.

cry (krī) *v.,* **cried, crying,** *n., pl.* **cries.** —*v.i.* **1.** to make sounds of grief or suffering. **2.** to weep. **3.** to shout. **4.** (of an animal) to make a characteristic sound. —*v.t.* **5.** to utter loudly. —*n.* **6.** a shout or scream. **7.** a fit of weeping. **8.** an animal's call. **9.** an appeal. —*Idiom.* **10.** a **far cry,** completely different.

cry′o·gen′ics (krī′ə jen′iks) *n.* the study of extremely low temperatures. —**cry′o·gen′ic,** *adj.*

crypt (kript) *n.* an underground chamber, esp. for burial.

cryp′tic *adj.* mysterious.

crys′tal (kris′tl) *n.* **1.** a clear transparent mineral. **2.** a body with symmetrical plane faces. **3.** fine glass. —**crys′tal·line** (-in, -īn′) *adj.*

crys′tal·lize′ *v.i., v.t.,* **-lized, -lizing.** **1.** to form or cause to form into crystals. **2.** to assume or cause to assume a definite form. —**crys′tal·li·za′tion,** *n.*

C′-sec′tion *n.* a Cesarean.

CST Central Standard Time.

CT Connecticut.

ct. 1. carat. **2.** cent. **3.** count.

cu. cubic.

cub (kub) *n.* a young fox, bear, etc.

cub′by·hole′ (kub′ē-) *n.* a small enclosed space.

cube (kyōōb) *n., v.,* **cubed, cubing.** —*n.* **1.** a solid bounded by six equal sides. **2.** *Math.* the third power of a quantity. —*v.t.* **3.** to cut into cubes. **4.** *Math.* to raise to the third power. —**cu′bic,** *adj.*

cu·bi·cle (kyōō′bi kəl) *n.* a small room.

cub′ism *n.* an artistic style marked by the reduction of natural forms to geometric shapes. —**cub′ist,** *adj., n.*

cuck′old (kuk′əld) *n.* the husband of an unfaithful wife.

cuck′oo (kōō′kōō, kŏŏk′ōō) *n.* a slim, stout-billed, long-tailed bird.

cu′cum·ber (kyōō′kum bər) *n.* a fleshy, green-skinned cylindrical fruit.

cud (kud) *n.* the food that a cow returns to its mouth from its stomach for further chewing.

cud·dle (kud′l) *v.,* **-dled, -dling.** —*v.t.* **1.** to hug tenderly. —*v.i.* **2.** to lie close. —*n.* **3.** a hug. —**cud′dly,** *adj.*

cudg′el (kuj′əl) *n.,* **-eled, -eling.** —*n.* **1.** a short thick stick. —*v.t.* **2.** to beat with a cudgel.

cue[1] (kyōō) *n.* (esp. on stage) something that signals speech or action.

cue[2] (kyōō) *n.* a rod used to strike the ball in billiards, pool, etc.

cuff[1] (kuf) *n.* **1.** a fold at the end of a sleeve or pants leg. —*Idiom.* **2. off the cuff,** impromptu.

cuff[2] (kuf) *v.t.* **1.** to slap. —*n.* **2.** a slap.

cui·sine′ (kwi zēn′) *n.* cookery.

cul-de-sac (kul′də sak′, -sak′, kōōl′-) *n., pl.* **culs-de-sac** or **cul-de-sacs.** a street closed at one end.

cu′li·nar′y (kyōō′lə ner′ē, kul′ə-) *adj.* of cooking.

cull (kul) *v.t.* to select the best parts of.

cul′mi·nate′ (kul′mə nāt′) *v.i., v.t.,* **-nated, -nating.** to reach the highest point. —**cul′mi·na′tion,** *n.*

cul′pa·ble (kul′pə bəl) *adj.* deserving blame. —**cul·pa·bil′i·ty,** *n.*

cul′prit (kul′prit) *n.* a person guilty of an offense.

cult (kult) *n.* **1.** a religious sect or system. —*adj.* **2.** popular with a particular group.

cul′ti·vate (kul′tə vāt′) *v.t.,* **-vated, -vating.** **1.** to prepare and care for (land). **2.** to develop the possibilities of. —**cul′ti·va′tion,** *n.*

cul′ti·vat′ed *adj.* **1.** prepared for raising crops. **2.** cultured.

cul′ture (kul′chər) *n.* **1.** artistic and intellectual pursuits. **2.** development of the mind. **3.** a state or form of civilization. **4.** the growth of bacteria for study. **5.** the raising of plants or animals.

cul′ture shock′ *n.* the distress of persons exposed to a new culture.

cul′vert (kul′vərt) *n.* a drain under a road, sidewalk, etc.

cum′ber·some (kum′bər səm) *adj.* clumsy or bulky.

cum′mer·bund (kum′ər bund′) *n.* a wide sash worn at the waist.

cu′mu·la·tive (kyōō′myə lə tiv) *adj.* increasing by successive additions.

cu′mu·lus (kyōō′myə ləs) *n., pl.* **-li.** a puffy, rounded cloud.

cu·ne·i·form′ (kyōō nē′ə fôrm′) *adj.* composed of wedge-shaped elements, as some ancient writing.

cun′ning (kun′ing) *adj.* **1.** clever. **2.** sly. —*n.* **3.** skill. **4.** craftiness.

cup (kup) *n., v.,* **cupped, cupping.** —*n.* **1.** a small open drinking vessel, usu. with a handle. —*v.t.* **2.** to form into a cup.

cup′board (kub′ərd) *n.* a closet with shelves for dishes, food, etc.

Cu′pid (kyōō′pid) *n.* the Roman god of carnal love.

cu·pid′i·ty (-pid′i tē) *n.* greed.

cu·po·la (kyōō′pə lə) *n.* a light, rounded structure on a roof.

cur (kûr) *n.* a mongrel dog.

cu′rate (kyōōr′it) *n.* a member of the clergy assisting a rector or vicar.

cu·ra′tor (kyōō rā′tər, kyōōr′ā-) *n.* a person in charge of a museum, art collection, etc.

curb (kûrb) *n.* **1.** a strap for restraining a horse. **2.** a restraint. **3.** the edge of a sidewalk. —*v.t.* **4.** to control.

curd (kûrd) *n.* a substance formed when milk coagulates, used in making cheese.

cur·dle (kûr′dl) *v.t., v.i.,* **-dled, -dling.** to change into curds; congeal.

cure (kyōōr) *n., v.,* **cured, curing.** —*n.* **1.** a remedy. **2.** restoration to health. —*v.t.* **3.** to restore to health. **4.** to preserve (meat, fish, etc.).

cu′ri·o′ (kyōōr′ē ō′) *n., pl.* **-rios.** an unusual valuable article.

cu·ri·os′i·ty (kyōōr′ē os′i tē) *n., pl.* **-ties. 1.** the desire to know about anything. **2.** a rare thing.

cu′ri·ous (-əs) *adj.* **1.** eager to know. **2.** prying. **3.** strange.

curl (kûrl) *v.t.* **1.** to form into ringlets. **2.** to coil. —*v.i.* **3.** to grow or form in ringlets. —*n.* **4.** a ringlet. —**curl′er,** *n.* —**curl′y,** *adj., n.*

cur′lew (kûr′lōō) *n.* a shorebird with a long curved bill.

curl′i·cue′ (kûr′li kyōō′) *n.* an ornamental curl.

cur·mudg′eon (kər muj′ən) *n.* a bad-tempered, difficult person.

cur′rant (kûr′ənt) *n.* **1.** a small seedless raisin. **2.** a small, edible sour berry.

cur′ren·cy (kûr′ən sē) *n., pl.* **-cies. 1.** the money in use in a country. **2.** general acceptance.

cur′rent (kûr′ənt) *adj.* **1.** present. **2.** generally accepted. —*n.* **3.** a flowing. **4.** water, air, etc., moving in one direction. **5.** the movement of electricity.

cur·ric′u·lum (kə rik′yə ləm) *n., pl.* **-lums, -la** (-lə). a course of study.

cur′ry[1] (kûr′ē, kur′ē) *n., pl.* **-ries,** *v.,* **-ried, -rying.** —*n.* **1.** an East Indian hot dish or powder (**curry powder**). —*v.t.* **2.** to prepare with curry.

cur′ry[2] (kûr′ē, kur′ē) *v.t.,* **-ried, -rying. 1.** to rub and comb (a horse). —*Idiom.* **2. curry favor,** to seek to advance oneself through flattery.

cur′ry·comb′ *n.* a wire brush for a horse.

curse (kûrs) *n., v.,* **cursed** or **curst, cursing.** —*n.* **1.** a wish that evil or misfortune befall someone or something. **2.** a great evil or misfortune. **3.** a profane or obscene word. —*v.t.* **4.** to wish evil upon. **5.** to swear at. **6.** to afflict with evil. —*v.i.* **7.** to swear profanely.

cur′sive (kûr′siv) *adj.* (of handwriting) in flowing strokes with letters joined together.

cur′sor (-sər) *n.* a movable symbol on a computer screen to indicate where data may be input.

cur′so·ry *adj.* hasty and superficial.

curt (kûrt) *adj.* rudely abrupt.

cur·tail′ (kər tāl′) *v.t.* to cut short or reduce. —**cur·tail′ment,** *n.*

cur′tain (kûr′tn) *n.* **1.** a piece of fabric hung to adorn, conceal, etc. —*v.t.* **2.** to cover with curtains.

curt′sy (kûrt′sē) *n., pl.* **-sies,** *v.,* **-sied, -sying.** —*n.* **1.** a respectful bow by women, made by bending the knees. —*v.i.* **2.** to make a curtsy.

cur′va·ture (kûr′və chər) *n.* **1.** a curved condition. **2.** the degree of curving.

curve (kûrv) *n., v.,* **curved, curving.** —*n.* **1.** a continuously bending line. —*v.i., v.t.* **2.** to bend or move in a curve.

cush·ion (kŏŏsh′ən) *n.* **1.** a soft pad or pillow. **2.** something to absorb shocks. —*v.t.* **3.** to lessen the effects of. **4.** to provide with a cushion.

cush′y (kŏŏsh′ē) *adj.* **-ier, -iest.** *Informal.* easy and profitable.

cusp (kusp) *n.* a point.

cus′pid (kus′pid) *n.* one of the canine teeth in humans.

cus·pi·dor′ (-pi dôr′) *n.* a large bowl for spit from chewing tobacco.

cus′tard (kus′tərd) *n.* a cooked dish of eggs and milk.

cus·to′di·an *n.* **1.** a person who has custody. **2.** the caretaker of property.

cus′to·dy (-tə dē) *n., pl.* **-dies. 1.** guardianship and care. **2.** imprisonment. —**cus·to′di·al** (kə stō′dē əl) *adj.*

cus′tom (kus′təm) *n.* **1.** a usual practice. **2.** habits or usages collectively. **3. customs, a.** duties on imports and exports. **b.** the agency collecting these. —*adj.* **4.** made for the individual.

cus′tom·ar′y *adj.* usual; habitual.

cus′tom·er *n.* a person who purchases something from another.

cus′tom·ize′ *v.t.,* **-ized, -izing.** to make to individual specifications.

cut (kut) *v.,* **cut, cutting,** *n.* —*v.t.* **1.** to divide, sever, or penetrate with a sharp instrument. **2.** to harvest. **3.** to trim. **4.** to shorten or reduce. **5.** to dilute. **6.** to ignore. **7.** to absent oneself from. —*v.i.* **8.** to move or cross. **9. cut in, a.** to push oneself or a vehicle between others. **b.** to interrupt. —*n.* **10.** the act of cutting. **11.** the result of cutting. **12.** a straight passage. **13.** a share. **14.** a reduction. —*Idiom.* **15.** a **cut above,** superior to. **16. cut out for,** fitted for.

cut′-and-dried′ *adj.* routine.

cu·ta′ne·ous (kyōō tā′nē əs) *adj.* of the skin.

cut′back′ *n.* a reduction.

cute (kyōōt) *adj.,* **cuter, cutest.** attractive or pretty in a dainty way.

cu′ti·cle (kyōō′ti kəl) *n.* the hardened skin around a fingernail or toenail.

cut′lass (kut′ləs) *n.* a short curved sword.

cut′ler·y (-lə rē) *n.* knives, forks, and spoons collectively.

cut′let (-lit) *n.* a slice of meat for frying or broiling.

cut′off′ *n.* **1.** a point beyond which something is no longer effective or possible. **2.** a road that leaves another to make a shortcut.

cut′-rate′ *adj.* offered at reduced prices.

cut′ter *n.* **1.** one that cuts. **2.** a single-masted sailing ship.

cut′throat′ *n.* **1.** a murderer. —*adj.* **2.** ruthless.

cut′tle·fish′ (kut′l fish′) *n., pl.* **-fish, -fishes.** a marine mollusk with ten arms and a hard internal shell (**cut′tle·bone′**).

cy′a·nide′ (sī′ə nīd′) *n.* a highly

poisonous compound of sodium or potassium.

cyber- a prefix meaning computer.

cy/ber·net/ics (sī/bər net/iks) *n.* the study of control and communications systems in living beings and machines.

cy/ber·space/ *n.* **1.** the realm of electronic communication. **2.** virtual reality.

cy/cle (sī/kəl) *n., v.,* **-cled, -cling.** —*n.* **1.** a recurring series. **2.** a recurring period of time in which certain events repeat themselves in the same order. **3.** a bicycle, motorcycle, etc. —*v.i.* **4.** to ride a bicycle. **5.** to move in cycles.

cy/clone (sī/klōn) *n.* a violent weather system with circular wind motion. —**cy·clon/ic** (-klon/ik) *adj.*

cy/clo·tron/ (-tron/) *n.* a device used in splitting atoms.

cyg/net (sig/nit) *n.* a young swan.

cyl/in·der (sil/in dər) *n.* **1.** a round elongated solid with ends that are equal parallel circles. **2.** a machine part or opening in this form. —**cy·lin/dri·cal,** *adj.*

cym/bal (sim/bəl) *n.* a percussion instrument consisting of a concave brass plate that produces a sharp ringing sound when struck.

cyn/ic (sin/ik) *n.* a person who believes only selfishness motivates human action. —**cyn/i·cal,** *adj.* —**cyn/i·cism** (-ə siz/əm) *n.*

cy/no·sure/ (sī/nə shŏŏr/) *n.* the center of attention.

cy/press (sī/prəs) *n.* an evergreen tree with dark green, scalelike leaves.

cyst (sist) *n.* an abnormal sac in or on the body, containing fluid or soft matter. —**cys/tic,** *adj.*

cys/tic fi·bro/sis (sis/tik fī brō/sis) *n.* a hereditary disease marked by breathing difficulties and the growth of excess fibrous tissue.

czar (zär) *n.* the former emperor of Russia. Also, **tsar.**

Czech (chek) *n.* a native or language of the Czech Republic.

D

D, d (dē) *n.* the fourth letter of the English alphabet.

d. 1. date. **2.** deceased. **3.** degree. **4.** diameter. **5.** dose.

D.A. District Attorney.

dab (dab) *v.t., v.i.,* **dabbed, dabbing. 1.** to apply by light strokes. —*n.* **2.** a small quantity.

dab/ble (dab/əl) *v.i.,* **-bled, -bling. 1.** to play in water. **2.** to work at anything in a superficial manner.

dachs/hund/ (däks/hŏŏnt/, -hŏŏnd/) *n.* a small dog with short legs and a long body.

Da/·cron (dā/kron, dak/ron) *Trademark.* a strong synthetic fabric.

dad (dad) *n. Informal.* father.

dad/dy (dad/ē) *n., pl.* **-dies.** *Informal.* father.

dad/dy-long/legs/ or **dad/dy long/legs/** *n., pl.* **-longlegs.** a spiderlike arachnid with long, slender legs.

daf/fo·dil (daf/ə dil) *n.* a plant with trumpet-shaped yellow flowers.

daft (daft) *adj.* **1.** crazy. **2.** foolish.

dag/ger (dag/ər) *n.* a short, pointed two-edged weapon.

dahl/ia (dal/yə, däl/-) *n.* a showy cultivated flowering plant.

dai/ly (dā/lē) *adj.* of or occurring each day.

dain/ty (dān/tē) *adj.,* **-tier, -tiest,** *n., pl.* **-ties.** —*adj.* **1.** delicate. **2.** fastidious. —*n.* **3.** a delicacy. —**dain/ti·ly,** *adv.*

dair/y (dâr/ē) *n., pl.* **-ies.** a place for making or selling milk, butter, etc.

da/is (dā/is) *n.* a raised platform.

dai/sy (dā/zē) *n., pl.* **-sies.** a flower with a yellow center and white petals.

dale (dāl) *n.* a valley.

dal/ly (dal/ē) *v.i.,* **-lied, -lying. 1.** to waste time. **2.** to flirt. —**dal/li·ance,** *n.*

Dal·ma/tian (dal mā/shən) *n.* a large white-and-black dog.

dam¹ (dam) *n., v.,* **dammed, damming.** —*n.* **1.** a barrier to obstruct the flow of water. —*v.t.* **2.** to stop up.

dam² (dam) *n.* a female parent of a four-footed domestic animal.

dam/age (dam/ij) *n., v.,* **-aged, -aging.** —*n.* **1.** injury or harm. **2.**

damages, payment for loss or injury. —*v.t.* **3.** to cause damage to.

dam/ask (dam/əsk) *n.* a reversible fabric with a figured pattern.

dame (dām) *n.* **1. Dame,** in Britain, an official title of honor for a woman. **2.** *Slang: Sometimes Offensive.* a woman.

damn (dam) *v.t.* **1.** to declare to be bad. **2.** to condemn to hell. —**dam/na·ble** (-nə bəl) *adj.* —**dam·na/tion,** *n.*

damp (damp) *adj.* **1.** moist. —*n.* **2.** moisture. —*v.t.* Also, **damp•en. 3.** to moisten. **4.** to discourage. **5.** to deaden. —**damp/ness,** *n.*

damp/er *n.* **1.** a control for air or smoke currents, as in a fireplace. **2.** a discouraging influence.

dam/sel (dam/zəl) *n.* a maiden.

dam/son (dam/zən, -sən) *n.* a small purple plum.

dance (dans) *v.,* **danced, dancing,** *n.* —*v.i.* **1.** to move the feet and body rhythmically to music. **2.** to leap or skip. —*n.* **3.** a pattern of motions performed to music. **4.** the art of dancing. **5.** a gathering for dancing. —**danc/er,** *n.*

dan/de·li/on (dan/dl ī/an) *n.* a weedy plant with yellow flowers.

dan/der (-dər) *n.* **1.** loose skin scales shed from various animals. **2.** *Informal.* temper.

dan/dle (dan/dl) *v.t.,* **-dled, -dling.** to move a (child) lightly up and down.

dan/druff (-drəf) *n.* scales of dry skin on the scalp.

dan/dy (dan/dē) *n., pl.* **-dies,** *adj.,* **-dier, -diest.** —*n.* **1.** a man who is excessively concerned about his clothes. —*adj.* **2.** fine.

Dane (dān) *n.* a native of Denmark.

dan/ger (dān/jər) *n.* **1.** likelihood of harm. **2.** an instance of this. —**dan/ger·ous,** *adj.*

dan/gle (dang/gəl) *v.,* **-gled, -gling.** —*v.i.* **1.** to hang loosely. —*v.t.* **2.** to cause to hang loosely.

Dan/ish (dā/nish) *adj.* **1.** of Denmark. —*n.* **2.** the language of the Danes. **3.** (*sometimes l.c.*) a filled pastry.

dank (dangk) *adj.* unpleasantly damp. —**dank/ness,** *n.*

dap/per (dap/ər) *adj.* neat and well-dressed.

dap/ple (dap/əl) *adj., v.,* **-pled, -pling,** *n.* —*adj.* **1.** marked with spots of dark and light. —*v.t.* **2.** to mark with spots of light and dark. —*n.* **3.** an animal with a dappled coat.

dare (dâr) *v.,* **dared, daring,** *n.* —*v.i.* **1.** to have the courage for something. —*v.t.* **2.** to have the boldness to try. **3.** to challenge (someone) to do something. —*n.* **4.** a challenge.

dare/dev/il *n.* **1.** a recklessly daring person. —*adj.* **2.** recklessly daring.

dar/ing *adj.* **1.** courageous. —*n.* **2.** adventurous courage.

dark (därk) *adj.* **1.** having little or no light. **2.** blackish. **3.** not pale or fair. **4.** gloomy. —*n.* **5.** the absence of light. **6.** night. —**dark/en,** *v.t., v.i.* —**dark/ly,** *adv.* —**dark/ness,** *n.*

Dark/ Ag/es the Middle Ages from A.D. 476 to about 1000.

dark/ horse/ *n.* an unexpected winner.

dark/room/ *n.* a darkened place for developing photographs.

dar/ling (där/ling) *n.* **1.** a loved one. **2.** a favorite. —*adj.* **3.** very dear. **4.** charming.

darn (därn) *v.t.* **1.** to mend by weaving stitches across a hole. —*n.* **2.** a darned place.

dart (därt) *n.* **1.** a slender pointed missile. **2. darts,** a game in which darts are thrown at a target. **3.** a tapered seam. —*v.i.* **4.** to move swiftly.

dash (dash) *v.t.* **1.** to strike or throw violently against something. **2.** to frustrate. **3. dash off, a.** to hurry away. **b.** to do something quickly. —*n.* **4.** a small quantity. **5.** a hasty movement. **6.** a punctuation mark (-) noting an abrupt break or pause. **7.** a short race.

dash/board/ *n.* the instrument panel on a motor vehicle.

dash/ing *adj.* **1.** lively. **2.** stylish.

das/tard (das/tərd) *n.* a coward.

da/ta (dā/tə, dat/ə) *n.pl., sing.* **da•tum** (dā/təm, dat/əm). facts or items of information.

da/ta·base/ *n.* a collection of data, esp. one accessible by computer.

da/ta proc/essing *n.* the high-speed handling of information by computer.

date¹ (dāt) *n., v.,* **dated, dating.**

—*n.* **1.** a particular month, day, and year. **2.** an inscription on a writing, coin, etc., that shows the time of writing, casting, etc. **3.** a social engagement arranged beforehand. **4.** the period to which any event belongs. **5.** a person with whom one has a date. —*v.i.* **6.** to belong to a particular period. **7.** to go out on dates. —*v.t.* **8.** to mark with a date. **9.** to show the age of. **10.** to go out on a date with.

date² (dāt) *n.* the fleshy, edible fruit of the date palm.

dat/ed *adj.* **1.** having or showing a date. **2.** out-of-date.

da/tive (dā/tiv) *adj.* denoting a grammatical case that indicates the indirect object of a verb.

daub (dôb) *v.t., v.i.* **1.** to smear or paint clumsily. —*n.* **2.** something daubed on.

daugh/ter (dô/tər) *n.* a female child.

daugh/ter-in-law *n., pl.* **daughters-in-law.** the wife of one's son.

daunt (dônt, dänt) *v.t.* to intimidate or discourage.

daunt/less *adj.* bold; fearless.

dav/en·port/ (dav/ən pôrt/) *n.* a large sofa.

dav/it (dav/it, dā/vit) *n.* a crane used for raising and lowering boats and anchors on a ship.

daw/dle (dôd/l) *v.,* **-dled, -dling.** —*v.i.* **1.** to waste time; idle. **2.** to walk slowly and aimlessly. —*v.t.* **3.** to waste (time) by trifling. —**daw/dler,** *n.*

dawn (dôn) *n.* **1.** the break of day. **2.** the beginning of anything. —*v.i.* **3.** to begin to grow light. **4.** to become apparent.

day (dā) *n.* **1.** the period of light between two nights. **2.** a period of 24 hours. **3.** the part of a day given to work. **4.** a period of existence or influence. —*Idiom.* **5. call it a day,** to stop working for the rest of the day. **6. day in, day out,** every day.

day/break/ *n.* the first appearance of daylight; dawn.

day/ care/ *n.* supervised daytime care for young children or the elderly, usu. at a center outside the home. —**day/-care/,** *adj.*

day/dream/ *n.* **1.** pleasant idle thoughts indulged in while awake. —*v.i.* **2.** to have daydreams. —**day/dream/er,** *n.*

day/light/ *n.* **1.** the period of light during a day. **2.** public knowledge. **3.** dawn.

day/light-sav/ing time *n.* time one hour later than standard time, usu. used in the summer. Also, **day/light-sav/ing time.**

day/time/ *n.* the time between sunrise and sunset.

day/-to-day/ *adj.* **1.** daily. **2.** routine.

daze (dāz) *v.,* **dazed, dazing,** *n.* —*v.t.* **1.** to cause to feel stunned or overwhelmed. —*n.* **2.** a dazed state.

daz/zle (daz/əl) *v.t.,* **-zled, -zling. 1.** to overpower by intense light. **2.** to impress by splendor.

dba doing business as.

DC 1. direct current. **2.** District of Columbia.

D.D. Doctor of Divinity.

D.D.S. 1. Doctor of Dental Science. **2.** Doctor of Dental Surgery.

Dec. December.

de·cade (dek/ād) *n.* a ten-year period.

dec/a·dence (dek/ə dəns, di kād/ns) *n.* **1.** moral deterioration. **2.** excessive self-indulgence. **3.** a falling into decay. —**dec/a·dent,** *adj.*

de·caf/fein·at/ed (dē kaf/ə nā/tad) *adj.* having the caffeine removed.

dec/a·gon/ *n.* a polygon with 10 angles and 10 sides.

dec/a·he/dron (dek/ə hē/drən) *n., pl.* **-drons, -dra** (-drə). a solid figure with ten faces.

de/cal (dē/kal, di kal/) *n.* a design on specially prepared paper for transfer to wood, metal, etc.

Dec/a·logue/ (dek/ə lôg/) *n.* the Ten Commandments.

de·camp/ (di kamp/) *v.i.* to depart, esp. secretly.

de·cant/ (di kant/) *v.t.* to pour (liquid) into another container, leaving the sediment behind.

de·cant/er *n.* an ornamental bottle for wine, brandy, etc.

de·cap/i·tate/ (di kap/i tāt/) *v.t.,* **-tated, -tating.** to behead.

de·cath/lon (di kath/lon) *n.* an athletic contest of ten track-and-field events.

de·cay/ (di kā/) *v.i.* **1.** to decline in quality, health, etc. **2.** to rot. —*n.* **3.** decomposition. **4.** a gradual decline.

refusing to respond. —**deaf/en,** *v.t.* —**deaf/ness,** *n.*

deaf/-mute/ *n. Often Offensive.* a person who is unable to hear or speak.

deal (dēl) *v.,* **dealt, dealing,** *n.* —*v.i.* **1.** to be concerned. **2.** to take action regarding someone or something. **3.** to do business. **4.** to distribute. —*v.t.* **5.** to distribute. **6.** a bargain. **7.** a secret agreement. **8.** an undefined quantity.

deal/er *n.* **1.** a person who deals. **2.** a merchant or trader.

dean (dēn) *n.* **1.** an official in a university or college. **2.** the head of a cathedral.

dear (dēr) *adj.* **1.** much loved. **2.** expensive. —*n.* **3.** a beloved one. **4.** a kind or generous person. —**dear/ly,** *adv.*

dearth (dûrth) *n.* scarcity.

death (deth) *n.* **1.** the act of dying or the state of being dead. **2.** extinction; destruction. —**death/ly,** *adj., adv.*

death/bed/ *n.* **1.** the bed on which a person dies. **2.** the last hours before death.

death/less *adj.* not subject to death.

de·ba/cle (də bä/kəl, -bak/əl, dā-) *n.* **1.** a disaster. **2.** a general rout.

de·bar/ (di bär/) *v.t.,* **-barred, -barring.** to shut out or exclude.

de·bark/ (di bärk/) *v.t., v.i.* to disembark. —**de/bar·ka/tion,** *n.*

de·base/ (di bās/) *v.t.,* **-based, -basing.** to reduce in quality or value.

de·bate/ (di bāt/) *n., v.,* **-bated, -bating.** —*n.* **1.** a discussion involving opposing viewpoints. —*v.i., v.t.* **2.** to discuss (a matter) by giving opposing viewpoints. —**de·bat/a·ble,** *adj.*

de·bauch/ (di bôch/) *v.t.* to corrupt; seduce. —**de·bauch/er·y,** *n.*

de·ben/ture (di ben/chər) *n.* a short-term, negotiable, interest-producing note representing debt.

de·bil/i·tate/ (di bil/i tāt/) *v.t.,* **-tated, -tating.** to make weak.

de·bil/i·ty *n., pl.* **-ties.** weakness.

deb/it (deb/it) *n.* **1.** a recorded item of debt. —*v.t.* **2.** to charge (a person or account) with a debt. **3.** to enter as a debit in an account.

deb/o·nair/ (deb/ə nâr/) *adj.* **1.** suave; worldly. **2.** carefree.

de·brief/ (dē brēf/) *v.t.* to question in order to gather information about a completed mission.

de·bris/ (də brē/, dā/brē) *n.* the remains of anything destroyed or broken; rubbish.

debt (det) *n.* **1.** something owed. **2.** a state of owing. —**debt/or,** *n.*

de·bug/ (dē bug/) *v.t.,* **-bugged, -bugging. 1.** to remove defects or errors from (a computer program). **2.** to remove electronic bugs from (a room or building).

de·bunk/ (di bungk/) *v.t.* to expose as false.

de·but/ (dā byōō/, di-, dā/byōō) *n.* **1.** a first public appearance, as of a performer. **2.** a formal introduction of a young woman into society. —*v.i.* **3.** to make a debut. —*v.t.* **4.** to introduce to the public.

deb/u·tante/ (deb/yŏŏ tänt/) *n.* a young woman making a debut into society.

—*n.* **1.** a particular month, day, and year. **2.** an inscription on a writing, coin, etc., that shows the time of writing, casting, etc. **3.** a social engagement arranged beforehand. **4.** the period to which any event belongs. **5.** a person with whom one has a date. —*v.i.* **6.** to belong to a particular period. **7.** to go out on dates. —*v.t.* **8.** to mark with a date. **9.** to show the age of. **10.** to go out on a date with.

de·cease/ (di sēs/) *n., v.,* **-ceased, -ceasing.** —*n.* **1.** death. —*v.i.* **2.** to die. —**de·ceased/,** *adj.*

de·ceit/ (di sēt/) *n.* **1.** the act or process of deceiving. **2.** a trick.

de·ceit/ful *adj.* **1.** given to deceiving. **2.** misleading. —**de·ceit/ful·ly,** *adv.*

de·ceive/ (di sēv/) *v.t., v.i.,* **-ceived, -ceiving.** to cause to believe something that is false; trick.

de·cel/er·ate/ (dē sel/ə rāt/) *v.t., v.i.,* **-ated, -ating.** to slow down.

De·cem/ber (di sem/bər) *n.* the twelfth month of the year.

de/cen·cy (dē/sən sē) *n., pl.* **-cies. 1.** the state or quality of being decent. **2.** courtesy; propriety.

de/cent (dē/sənt) *adj.* **1.** conforming to accepted standards of propriety. **2.** respectable. **3.** adequate. **4.** kind. —**de/cent·ly,** *adv.*

de·cen/tral·ize/ (dē sen/trə līz/) *v.t.,* **-ized, -izing.** to end central control of.

de·cep/tion (di sep/shən) *n.* **1.** the act of deceiving. **2.** a trick. —**de·cep/tive,** *adj.*

dec/i·bel/ (des/ə bel, -bəl) *n.* a unit for expressing intensity of sound.

de·cide/ (di sīd/) *v.,* **-cided, -ciding.** —*v.t.* **1.** to solve (a dispute). **2.** to make up one's mind about. —*v.i.* **3.** to come to a decision.

de·cid/ed *adj.* **1.** unquestionable; certain. **2.** determined. —**de·cid/ed·ly,** *adv.*

de·cid/u·ous (di sij/ōō əs) *adj.* shedding the leaves annually.

dec/i·mal (des/ə məl) *adj.* **1.** of tenths or the number ten. **2.** proceeding by tens. —*n.* **3.** a fraction whose denominator is some power of 10, usu. indicated by a dot (**decimal point**) before the numerator.

dec/i·mate/ (des/ə māt/) *v.t.,* **-mated, -mating.** to destroy much of.

de·ci/pher (di sī/fər) *v.t.* to make out the meaning of. —**de·ci/pher·a·ble,** *adj.*

de·ci/sion (di sizh/ən) *n.* **1.** the act of deciding or of making up one's mind. **2.** something decided. **3.** a judgment. **4.** determination.

de·ci/sive (-sī/siv) *adj.* **1.** having the power to decide. **2.** displaying firmness. **3.** definite. —**de·ci/sive·ly,** *adv.* —**de·ci/sive·ness,** *n.*

deck (dek) *n.* **1.** a floor of a ship. **2.** a porch. **3.** a pack of playing cards. —*v.t.* **4.** to clothe in something festive.

de·claim/ (di klām/) *v.t., v.i.* to speak loudly and rhetorically.

dec/la·ma/tion (dek/lə mā/shən) *n.* oratorical speech.

de·clar/a·tive (di klâr/ə tiv) *adj.* serving to state or explain.

de·clare/ (di klâr/) *v.t.,* **-clared, -claring. 1.** to make known publicly. **2.** to state emphatically. **3.** to indicate. —**dec/la·ra/tion** (dek/lə rā/shən) *n.*

de·clen/sion (di klen/shən) *n.* the inflection of nouns, pronouns, and adjectives.

de·cline/ (di klīn/) *v.,* **-clined, -clining,** *n.* —*v.t.* **1.** to refuse courteously. **2.** to cause to slope downward. **3.** to inflect (a noun, pronoun, or adjective). —*v.i.* **4.** to express courteous refusal. **5.** to lose strength. —*n.* **6.** a downward slope. **7.** a deterioration.

de·code/ (dē kōd/) *v.t.,* **-coded, -coding.** to translate from code.

de·com·mis/sion *v.t.* to retire (a vessel) from active service.

de·com·pose/ (-kəm pōz/) *v.t., v.i.,* **-posed, -posing. 1.** to separate into constituent parts. **2.** to rot. —**de/com·po·si/tion,** *n.*

de·con·ges/tant (dē/kən jes/tənt) *adj.* **1.** relieving congestion of the upper respiratory tract. —*n.* **2.** a decongestant agent.

de·con·tam/i·nate/ (-nāt/) *v.t.,* **-nated, -nating.** to make safe by removing or neutralizing harmful contaminants.

dé·cor/ (dā kôr/, di-) *n.* a style of decoration, as of a room. Also, **de·cor/.**

dec/o·rate/ (dek/ə rāt/) *v.t.,* **-rated, -rating. 1.** to make attractive by adding something ornamental. **2.** to design the interior of, as a room. **3.** to confer an honor on. —**dec/o·ra/tion,** *n.* —**dec/o·ra·tive** (-ər ə tiv) *adj.* —**dec/o·ra·tor,** *n.*

dec/o·rous *adj.* proper; dignified.

de·co/rum (di kôr/əm) *n.* correctness of behavior.

de·coy/ *n.* (dē/koi, di koi/) **1.** a person or animal who lures another into danger. **2.** anything used as a lure. —v.t. (di koi', dē'koi) **3.** to lure by a decoy.

de·crease' v., -creased, -creasing. n. —v.i., v.t. (di krēs') **1.** to lessen, as in size or quantity. —n. (dē'krēs, di krēs') **2.** the act or process of decreasing. **3.** the amount by which something is decreased.

de·cree' (di krē') n., v., -creed, -creeing. —n. **1.** a formal order. —v.t., v.i. **2.** to order by decree.

de·crep'it (di krep'it) adj. old and feeble. —de·crep'i·tude', n.

de·cre·scen'do (dē'kri shen'dō, dā'-) adj., adv. Music. gradually decreasing in loudness.

de·crim·i·nal·ize' (dē krim'ə nl īz') v.t., -ized, -izing. to remove criminal penalties for. —de·crim'i·nal·i·za'tion, n.

de·cry' (di krī') v.t., -cried, -crying. to denounce publicly.

ded'i·cate' (ded'i kāt') v.t., -cated, -cating. **1.** to set apart. **2.** to devote to some purpose, cause, or person. —ded'i·ca'tion, n.

de·duce' (di dōōs', -dyōōs') v.t., -duced, -ducing. to arrive at (a conclusion) by reasoning; infer.

de·duct' (di dukt') v.t. to subtract.

de·duct'i·ble adj. **1.** able to be deducted. —n. **2.** the amount a person must pay on each claim made on an insurance policy.

de·duc'tion n. **1.** the act of deducting. **2.** something deducted. **3.** the act of deducing. **4.** something deduced. —de·duc'tive, adj.

deed (dēd) n. **1.** something done; an act. **2.** a document transferring property from one person to another. —v.t. **3.** to transfer by deed.

dee'jay (dē'jā') n. a disc jockey.

deem (dēm) v.t. to think; estimate.

deep (dēp) adj. **1.** extending far down or in. **2.** difficult to understand. **3.** intense. **4.** involved. **5.** dark. **6.** obscure. **7.** low in pitch. —n. **8.** a deep part. —adv. **9.** at great depth. —deep'en, v.t., v.i. —deep'ly, adv.

deep'-freeze' v., -froze, -frozen, -freezing, —v.t. **1.** to freeze (food) quickly. —n. **2.** a refrigerator that deep-freezes.

deep'-fry' v.t., -fried, -frying. to cook in boiling fat deep enough to cover food. —deep'-fry'er, n.

deep'-seat'ed adj. firmly implanted.

deep' space' n. space beyond the solar system.

deer (dēr) n., pl. **deer.** a hoofed, ruminant animal, the male of which usually has antlers.

de·face' (di fās') v.t., -faced, -facing. to spoil the appearance of.

de fac'to (dē fak'tō, dā) adv. **1.** in fact. —adj. **2.** actually existing, esp. without legal authority.

de·fame' (di fām') v.t., -famed, -faming. to attack the reputation of; slander or libel. —def'a·ma'tion (def'ə mā'shən) n. —de·fam'a·to'ry (-fam'ə tôr'ē) adj.

de·fault' (di fôlt') n. **1.** failure to act or to appear; neglect. —v.i. **2.** to fail to meet an obligation. —v.t. **3.** to lose by default.

de·feat' (di fēt') v.t. **1.** to overcome in a contest. **2.** to frustrate. —n. **3.** the act of defeating or the state of being defeated.

de·feat'ist n. one who accepts defeat too easily. —de·feat'ism, n.

def'e·cate' (def'i kāt') v.i., -cated, -cating. to discharge feces from the bowels. —def'e·ca'tion, n.

de·fect' (n. dē'fekt, di fekt') n. **1.** a fault; imperfection. —v.i. (di fekt') **2.** to desert a cause, country, etc. —de·fec'tive, adj.

de·fec'tion n. desertion of a cause, country, etc.

de·fend' (di fend') v.t. **1.** to protect against attack. **2.** to uphold by argument. **3.** to serve as attorney for (a defendant). —de·fend'er, n.

de·fend'ant n. a person accused of a crime or sued in court.

de·fense' n. **1.** resistance to attack. **2.** something that defends. **3.** arguments defending against an accusation. —de·fense'less, adj.

defense' mech'anism n. an unconscious process that protects a person from painful ideas.

de·fen'sive adj. **1.** intended for defense. **2.** sensitive to criticism. —n. **3.** an attitude of defense.

de·fer'[1] (di fûr') v., -ferred, -ferring. —v.t. **1.** to postpone. —v.i. **2.** to put off action. —de·fer'ment, n.

de·fer'[2] (di fûr') v.i., -ferred, -ferring. to yield respectfully to a person's wishes or opinion.

def'er·ence (def'ər əns) n. polite

respect. —def'er·en'tial (-ə ren'shəl) adj.

de·fi'ance (di fī'əns) n. **1.** bold resistance to authority. **2.** contempt. —de·fi'ant, adj. —de·fi'ant·ly, adv.

de·fi'cien·cy (di fish'ən sē) n., pl. -cies. **1.** lack. **2.** the amount lacked.

de·fi'cient adj. **1.** lacking something; defective. **2.** inadequate.

def'i·cit (def'ə sit) n. the amount by which a total falls short of the required amount.

de·file' (di fīl') v.t., -filed, -filing. to make foul or dirty.

de·fine' (di fīn') v.t., -fined, -fining. **1.** to state the meaning of (a word, phrase, etc.). **2.** to specify. **3.** to mark the limits of.

def'i·nite (def'ə nit) adj. **1.** clearly defined. **2.** having fixed limits. **3.** positive. —def'i·nite·ly, adv.

def'i·ni'tion n. **1.** the act of making definite or clear. **2.** the formal statement of the meaning of a word, phrase, etc. **3.** the condition of being definite.

de·fin'i·tive (di fin'i tiv) adj. **1.** most reliable. **2.** serving to define. **3.** conclusive. —de·fin'i·tive·ly, adv.

de·flate' (di flāt') v.t., -flated, -flating. **1.** to release air or gas from. **2.** to reduce in importance or size. **3.** to reduce (currency, prices, etc.) from an inflated condition. —de·fla'tion, n.

de·flect' (di flekt') v.t., v.i. to turn from a course. —de·flec'tion, n.

de·fo'li·ate' (dē fō'lē āt') v.t., -ated, -ating. **1.** to strip of leaves. **2.** to clear of vegetation. —de·fo'li·a'tion, n. —de·fo'li·ant (-ənt) n.

de·for'est (di fôr'ist) v.t. to clear of trees. —de·for'es·ta'tion, n.

de·form' v.t. to mar the natural form, shape, or beauty of. —de·form'i·ty, n.

de·fraud' v.t. to deprive of by fraud. —de·fraud'er, n.

de·fray' v.t. to pay all or part of.

de·frost' v.t. **1.** to remove the frost or ice from. **2.** to thaw. —v.i. **3.** to become free of frost. **4.** to thaw.

deft (deft) adj. quick and skillful.

de·funct' (di fungkt') adj. no longer in existence.

de·fuse' (dē fyōōz') v.t., -fused, -fusing. **1.** to remove the detonating fuse from. **2.** to make less dangerous or tense.

de·fy' (di fī') v.t., -fied, -fying. **1.** to resist boldly. **2.** to challenge to do something.

de·gen'er·ate' v., -ated, -ating, adj., n. —v.t. (di jen'ə rāt') **1.** to decline physically, mentally, or morally. —adj. (-ər it) **2.** having declined physically, mentally, or morally. —n. (-ər it) **3.** a person who has declined, esp. morally.

de·grade' (di grād') v.t., -graded, -grading. to lower in dignity, quality, or status. —deg'ra·da'tion (deg'ri dā'shən) n.

de·gree' (di grē') n. **1.** any of a series of steps or stages in a process. **2.** the 360th part of a circle. **3.** a unit of measure for temperature. **4.** an academic title conferred by a college or university on completion of a course of study.

de·hu'man·ize' (dē hyōō'mə nīz'; often -yōō'-) v.t., -ized, -izing. to deprive of human qualities.

de·hu·mid'i·fi'er n. a device for removing moisture from the air. —de·hu·mid'i·fy, v.t.

de·hy'drate' v., -drated, -drating. —v.t. **1.** to remove water from. —v.i. **2.** to lose fluids or water. —de·hy·dra'tion, n.

de·i·fy (dē'ə fī') v.t., -fied, -fying. to make a god of.

deign (dān) v.t., v.i. to condescend (to do or grant).

de'ism (dē'iz əm) n. belief in a god's existence based on reason rather than on divine revelation. —de'ist, n.

de'i·ty (dē'i tē) n., pl. -ties. a god or goddess.

dé'jà vu' (dā'zhä vōō', n.) a feeling of having lived through the present moment before.

de·ject'ed (di jek'tid) adj. in low spirits. —de·jec'tion, n.

de ju're (di jōōr'ē, dā jōōr'ā) adv., adj. by right or according to law.

Del. Delaware.

de·lay' (di lā') v.t. **1.** to postpone. **2.** to hinder. —v.i. **3.** to linger. —n. **4.** the act of delaying. **5.** an instance of being delayed.

de·lec'ta·ble (di lek'tə bəl) adj. delightful or delicious.

del'e·gate n., v., -gated, -gating. —n. (del'i git, -gāt') **1.** a person

designated to represent another. —v.t. (-gāt') **2.** to send or appoint as a delegate. **3.** to give (powers) to another as agent.

del'e·ga'tion n. **1.** a group of delegates. **2.** a delegating or being delegated.

de·lete' (di lēt') v.t., -leted, -leting. to strike out (something written). —de·le'tion, n.

del'e·te'ri·ous (del'i tēr'ē əs) adj. harmful.

del'i (del'ē) n. a delicatessen.

de·lib'er·ate adj., v., -ated, -ating. —adj. (di lib'ər it) **1.** intentional. **2.** slow and careful. —v.i. (-ə rāt') **3.** to think carefully. **4.** to confer. —de·lib'er·a'tion, n. —de·lib'er·ate·ly, adv.

del'i·ca·cy (del'i kə sē) n., pl. -cies. **1.** the quality or state of being delicate. **2.** something delightful, esp. a choice food.

del'i·cate (-kit) adj. **1.** fine in texture, quality, etc. **2.** fragile. **3.** precise in action. **4.** keenly sensitive. —del'i·cate·ly, adv.

del'i·ca·tes'sen (del'i kə tes'ən) n. a store that sells prepared foods.

de·li'cious (di lish'əs) adj. highly pleasing, esp. to taste.

de·light' (di līt') n. **1.** a high degree of pleasure; joy. —v.t. **2.** to give delight to. —v.i. **3.** to have or take great pleasure. —de·light'ed, adj. —de·light'ful, adj.

de·lim'it (di lim'it) v.t. to fix the limits of. —de·lim'i·ta'tion, n.

de·lin'e·ate' (di lin'ē āt') v.t., -ated, -ating. **1.** to outline. **2.** to describe.

de·lin'quent (di ling'kwənt) adj. **1.** neglectful of an obligation. **2.** guilty of an offense. —n. **3.** a person who is delinquent. —de·lin'quen·cy, n.

de·lir'i·um (di lēr'ē əm) n. a temporary mental disorder marked by excitement, hallucinations, etc. —de·lir'i·ous, adj.

de·liv'er (di liv'ər) v.t. **1.** to carry and turn over (letters, goods, etc.) to someone. **2.** to hand over. **3.** to utter. **4.** to direct. **5.** to set free. **6.** to assist at the birth of. —v.i. **7.** to give birth. **8.** to do something.

de·liv'er·ance n. rescue.

de·liv'er·y n. **1.** the delivering of something. **2.** a giving up. **3.** one's manner while speaking. **4.** the act of striking or throwing. **5.** childbirth. **6.** something delivered.

dell (del) n. a small, wooded valley.

del·phin'i·um (del fin'ē əm) n., pl. -iums, -ia (-ē ə). a tall blue garden flower.

del'ta (del'tə) n. **1.** the fourth letter of the Greek alphabet. **2.** a triangular plain between the branches of the mouth of a river.

de·lude' (di lōōd') v.t., -luded, -luding. to mislead or deceive.

del'uge (del'yōōj) n., v., -uged, -uging. —n. **1.** a great flood. **2.** anything that overwhelms. —v.t. **3.** to flood. **4.** to overwhelm.

de·lu'sion (di lōō'zhən) n. a false opinion or conception.

de·luxe' (də luks') adj. of finest quality.

delve (delv) v.i., delved, delving. to search carefully for information.

Dem. 1. Democrat. **2.** Democratic.

dem'a·gogue' (dem'ə gog') n. an orator or leader who gains power by arousing people's emotions and prejudices. —dem'a·gogu'er·y, n.

de·mand' (di mand') v.t. **1.** to claim as a right. **2.** to require. **3.** to ask for in an urgent or peremptory manner. —v.i. **4.** to ask. —n. **5.** a claim. **6.** an urgent requirement. **7.** consumers' desire for a product.

de·mar'cate (di mär'kāt, dē'mär-kāt') v.t., -cated, -cating. to set the limits of. —de'mar·ca'tion, n.

de·mean' (di mēn') v.t. to lower in standing.

de·mean'or n. conduct; behavior.

de·ment'ed (di men'tid) adj. **1.** crazy. **2.** affected with dementia.

de·men'tia (-sha, -shē ə) n. severe mental impairment.

de·mer'it (di mer'it) n. a mark against a person for misconduct.

demi- a prefix indicating half.

dem'i·god' (dem'ē god') n. one partly divine and partly human.

de·mil'i·ta·rize' (dē mil'i tə rīz') v.t., -rized, -rizing. to remove from military control. —de·mil'i·ta·ri·za'tion, n.

de·mise' (di mīz') n. death.

dem'i·tasse' (dem'i tas', -täs') n. a small coffee cup.

dem'o (dem'ō) n., pl. -os. a product displayed or offered for trial.

de·mo'bi·lize' (dē mō'bə līz') v.t., -lized, -lizing. to disband (troops).

de·moc'ra·cy (di mok'rə sē) n., pl. -cies. **1.** government in which the people hold supreme power, usu. through their elected representatives. **2.** a state having such government. **3.** social equality.

dem'o·crat' n. **1.** a supporter of democracy. **2. Democrat,** a member of the Democratic Party.

dem'o·crat'ic adj. **1.** of or advocating democracy. **2. Democratic,** of the Democratic Party, one of two major political parties in the U.S.

dem'o·graph'ics (dem'ə graf'iks) n.pl. the statistical data of a human population, as those showing age, income, etc.

de·mol'ish (di mol'ish) v.t. to destroy. —dem'o·li'tion (dem'ə-lish'ən) n.

de'mon (dē'mən) n. **1.** an evil spirit. **2.** a cruel person.

de·mon'ic (də mon'ik) adj. **1.** inspired as if by a demon. **2.** like a demon.

dem'on·strate' (dem'ən strāt') v., -strated, -strating. —v.t. **1.** to describe or explain. **2.** to prove. **3.** to display. —v.i. **4.** to parade or picket in support or opposition. —de·mon'stra·ble (di mon'strə bəl) adj. —dem'on·stra'tion, n. —dem'on·stra'tor, n.

de·mon'stra·tive (də mon'strə tiv) adj. **1.** showing one's feelings openly. **2.** showing. **3.** proving.

de·mor'al·ize' (di mor'ə līz') v.t., -ized, -izing. to destroy the confidence of.

de·mote' (di mōt') v.t., -moted, -moting. to reduce the rank or position of. —de·mo'tion, n.

de·mur' (di mûr') v.i., -murred, -murring. to raise objections. —de·mur'ral, n.

de·mure' (di myoor') adj. shy and modest. —de·mure'ly, adv.

den (den) n. **1.** the lair of a wild animal. **2.** a room at home for relaxing.

de·na'ture v.t., -tured, -turing. **1.** to change the natural character of. **2.** to make (alcohol) undrinkable.

de·ni'al (di nī'əl) n. **1.** a statement that something is not true. **2.** refusal to believe a doctrine. **3.** the refusal to grant a request.

den'im (den'əm) n. **1.** a heavy cotton fabric. **2. denims,** trousers of this.

den'i·zen (den'ə zən) n. an inhabitant.

de·nom'i·nate' (di nom'ə nāt') v.t., -nated, -nating. to give a name to.

de·nom'i·na'tion n. **1.** a particular religious body. **2.** a grade in a series of values. **3.** a class or kind of persons or things.

de·nom'i·na'tor n. **1.** the lower term in a fraction. **2.** something held in common.

de·note' (di nōt') v.t., -noted, -noting. **1.** to indicate. **2.** to mean.

de'noue·ment' (dā'nōō mäN') n. the final resolution of a plot or story. Also, **dé'noue·ment'.**

de·nounce' (di nouns') v.t., -nounced, -nouncing. **1.** to speak against publicly. **2.** to inform against.

dense (dens) adj., denser, densest. **1.** having the parts crowded together; compact. **2.** stupid. **3.** opaque. —dense'ly, adv.

den'si·ty n. **1.** the state or quality of being dense. **2.** stupidity. **3.** the average number per unit of area.

dent (dent) n. **1.** a small depression in a surface. **2.** a slight effect. —v.t., v.i. **3.** to make a dent in or to become dented.

den'tal (den'tl) adj. of the teeth or dentistry.

den'tal floss' n. a thread used to clean between the teeth.

den'ti·frice (-tə fris) n. a substance for cleaning the teeth.

den'tin (-tn, -tin) n. the hard tissue forming the major part of a tooth.

den'tist n. a person trained in the prevention and treatment of tooth and gum diseases. —den'-tist·ry, n.

den'ture (-chər, -choor) n. an artificial replacement for teeth.

de·nude' (di nōōd', -nyōōd') v.t., -nuded, -nuding. to strip bare.

de·nun'ci·a'tion (di nun'sē ā'-shən) n. **1.** a condemnation. **2.** an accusation.

de·ny' (di nī') v.t., -nied, -nying. **1.**

to declare that (a statement) is not true. **2.** to refuse to agree to or give. **3.** to disown.

de·o'dor·ant (dē ō'dər ənt) n. a substance for destroying odors.

de·o'dor·ize' v.t., -ized, -izing. to get rid of odor. —de·o'dor·iz'er, n.

de·part' (di pärt') v.i. to go away; leave. —de·par'ture, n.

de·part'ment n. a part or division of an organization. —de·part·men'tal, adj.

de·pend' (di pend') v.i. **1.** to rely. **2.** to be determined by something else. —de·pend'ence, n. —de·pend'ent, adj., n.

de·pend'a·ble adj. able to be depended on. —de·pend·a·bil'i·ty, n.

de·pict' (di pikt') v.t. to represent in a picture or in words. —de·pic'tion, n.

de·pil'a·to'ry (di pil'ə tôr'ē) adj., n., pl. -ries. —adj. **1.** capable of removing hair. —n. **2.** a depilatory agent.

de·plete' (di plēt') v.t., -pleted, -pleting. to reduce by using up.

de·plore' v.t. (-plôr' -plōr'), -plored, -ploring. **1.** to regret. **2.** to disapprove of. —de·plor'a·ble, adj.

de·ploy' (-ploi') v.t. to place strategically. —de·ploy'ment, n.

de·po·lit'i·cize' (dē'pə lit'ə sīz') v.t., -cized, -cizing. to remove from the realm of politics.

de·pop'u·late' (dē pop'yə lāt') v.t., -lated, -lating. to reduce the population of. —de·pop'u·la'tion, n.

de·port' (di pôrt') v.t. **1.** to expel from a country. **2.** to behave (oneself).

de·por·ta'tion (dē'pôr tā'shən) n. the lawful expulsion of a person from a country.

de·port'ment n. conduct.

de·pose' (di pōz') v.t., -posed, -posing. **1.** to remove from office. **2.** to testify under oath.

de·pos'it (di poz'it) v.t. **1.** to place in a bank account. **2.** to put down. **3.** to lay down by a natural process. **4.** to give as security. —n. **5.** money placed in a bank account. **6.** sediment. **7.** anything given as security.

dep'o·si'tion (dep'ə zish'ən) n. **1.** written testimony under oath. **2.** removal from an office. **3.** something deposited.

de·pos'i·to'ry (di poz'i tôr'ē) n., pl. -ries. a place where something is deposited for safekeeping.

de'pot (dē'pō; Mil. or Brit. dep'ō) n. **1.** a railroad or bus station. **2.** a storage place.

de·prave' (di prāv') v.t., -praved, -praving. to corrupt morally. —de·praved', adj. —de·prav'i·ty (-prav'i tē) n.

dep're·cate' (dep'ri kāt') v.t., -cated, -cating. **1.** to express disapproval of. **2.** to belittle. —dep're·ca·to·ry, adj.

de·pre'ci·ate' (di prē'shē āt') v.t., -ated, -ating. —v.t. **1.** to lessen the value of. **2.** to belittle. —v.i. **3.** to decline in value.

dep're·da'tion (dep'ri dā'shən) n. plundering.

de·press' (di pres') v.t. **1.** to make sad. **2.** to press down. **3.** to lower in amount or value. —de·pressed', adj.

de·pres'sion n. **1.** a depressing or being depressed. **2.** an area lower than the surrounding one. **3.** sadness or gloom. **4.** a period of decline in business activity and employment. —de·pres'sive, adj.

de·prive' (-prīv') v.t., -prived, -priving. to keep from possessing or enjoying something. —dep'ri·va'tion (dep'rə vā'shən) n.

dept. 1. department. **2.** deputy.

depth (depth) n. **1.** a measurement taken downward or inward through an object. **2.** deepness. **3.** intensity. **4.** Often, **depths,** a deep or inner part. —Idiom. **5. in depth,** thoroughly.

dep'u·ta'tion (dep'yə tā'shən) n. a group of people sent to represent others.

dep'u·ty (-tē) n., pl. -ties. a person authorized to act as a representative. —dep'u·tize' (-tīz') v.t.

de·rail' (dē rāl') v.t. **1.** to cause (a train) to run off the rails. **2.** to deflect from a purpose. —v.i. **3.** to become derailed.

de·range' (di rānj') v.t., -ranged, -ranging. **1.** to throw into disorder. **2.** to make insane.

der'by (dûr'bē; Brit. där'-) n., pl. -bies. **1.** a stiff hat with a rounded crown. **2.** a race.

de·reg′u·late (dē reg′yə lāt′) v.t., -lated, -lating. to free of regulation.

der′e·lict (der′ə likt) adj. 1. abandoned. 2. neglectful of duty. —n. 3. anything abandoned. 4. a person who lacks a home or means of support.

der′e·lic′tion n. 1. deliberate neglect. 2. an abandoning or being abandoned.

de·ride′ (di rīd′) v.t., -rided, -riding. to ridicule. —**de·ri′sion** (-rizh′ən) n. —**de·ri′sive** (-rī′siv) adj.

de·riv′a·tive (di riv′ə tiv) adj. 1. not original. —n. 2. something derived.

de·rive′ (di rīv′) v., -rived, -riving. —v.t. 1. to obtain from a source. 2. to obtain by reasoning. —v.i. 3. to originate. —**der′i·va′tion** (der′ə vā′shən) n.

der′ma·ti′tis (dûr′mə tī′tis) n. inflammation of the skin.

der′ma·tol′o·gy (-tol′ə jē) n. the branch of medicine dealing with treatment of the skin.

de·rog′a·to·ry (di rog′ə tôr′ē) adj. disparaging; belittling.

der′rick (der′ik) n. 1. a boom for lifting heavy cargo. 2. the towerlike framework over an oil well.

der·ri·ère′ (der′ē âr′) n. the buttocks.

de·scend′ (di send′) v.i. 1. to go or move down. 2. to slope downward. —**de·scent′**, n.

de·scend′ant n. a person descended from a specific ancestor; offspring.

de·scribe′ (di skrīb′) v.t., -scribed, -scribing. 1. to tell in words what (a person or thing) is like. 2. to draw the outline of. —**de·scrip′tion**, n. —**de·scrip′tive**, adj.

de·scry′ (di skrī′) v.t., -scried, -scrying. 1. to notice. 2. to detect.

des′e·crate (des′i krāt′) v.t., -crated, -crating. to treat (something sacred) with irreverence; profane. —**des′e·cra′tion**, n.

de·seg′re·gate v.t., v.i., -gated, -gating. to eliminate racial segregation in (schools, housing, etc.).

de·sen′si·tize v.t., -tized, -tizing. to make less sensitive.

des′ert¹ (dez′ərt) n. a very dry, often sandy, region.

de·sert² (di zûrt′) v.t., v.i. 1. to leave or run away from (a person, duty, etc.). 2. (of military personnel) to leave (service) without permission or intention to return. —**de·sert′er**, n. —**de·ser′tion**, n.

de·sert³ (di zûrt′) n. Often, **deserts.** due reward or punishment.

de·serve′ (di zûrv′) v.t., v.i., -served, -serving. to be worthy of (reward, punishment, etc.); merit.

des′ic·cate (des′i kāt′) v.t., v.i., -cated, -cating. to dry up.

de·sid′er·a′tum (di sid′ə rā′təm, -rä′-, -zid′-) n., pl. -ta (-tə). something wanted.

de·sign′ (di zīn′) v.t. 1. to prepare the preliminary plans for. 2. to plan and fashion skillfully. 3. to form in the mind. —v.i. 4. to make sketches or plans. 5. to plan an object, work of art, etc. —n. 6. a sketch or plan. 7. the organization of elements in an object. 8. an ornamental pattern. 9. purpose. —**de·sign′er**, n.

des′ig·nate (dez′ig nāt′) v., -nated, -nating. adj. —v.t. 1. to specify. 2. to name. 3. to select. —adj. (dez′ig nit) 4. selected for an office but not yet installed. —**des′ig·na′tion**, n.

des′ignated driv′er n. a person who does not drink alcohol at a gathering in order to drive companions home safely.

de·sign′ing adj. scheming.

de·sir′a·ble adj. 1. pleasing. 2. arousing desire. 3. advisable.

de·sire′ (di zīʳr′) v., -sired, -siring, n. —v.t. 1. to wish or long for. 2. to ask for. —n. 3. a longing. 4. a request. 5. something desired. 6. sexual urge.

de·sist′ (di zist′, -sist′) v.i. to cease.

desk (desk) n. 1. a table for writing. 2. a section of an organization, as a newspaper office.

desk′top pub′lishing n. the design and production of publications using a microcomputer.

des′o·late (des′ə lit) adj. 1. deserted; uninhabited. 2. lonely. 3. dismal. —**des′o·la′tion**, n.

de·spair′ (di spâr′) n. 1. hopelessness or a cause of hopelessness. —v.i. 2. to lose hope.

des′per·a′do (des′pə rä′dō, -rä′-) n., pl. -does, -dos. a reckless outlaw.

des′per·ate (des′pər it) adj. 1. reckless from despair. 2. having an urgent need or desire. 3. extreme. —**des′per·a′tion**, n.

des′pi·ca·ble (des′pi kə bəl, di-spik′ə-) adj. contemptible.

de·spise′ (di spīz′) v.t., -spised, -spising. to scorn or hate.

de·spite′ (di spīt′) prep. in spite of.

de·spoil′ (di spoil′) v.t. to rob or plunder.

de·spond′ent (di spon′dənt) adj. in low spirits; dejected. —**de·spond′en·cy** n.

des′pot (des′pət, -pot) n. a tyrant. —**des·pot′ic**, adj.

des·sert′ (di zûrt′) n. a usu. sweet food served as the final course of a meal.

des′ti·na′tion (des′tə nā′shən). the place to which a person or thing travels or is sent.

des′tine (-tin) v.t., -tined, -tining. 1. to set apart for a purpose. 2. to determine beforehand.

des′ti·ny n., pl. -nies. 1. fate. 2. the predetermined course of events.

des′ti·tute (-tōōt′, -tyōōt′) adj. 1. very poor. 2. deprived or lacking.

de·stroy′ (di stroi′) v.t. 1. to demolish. 2. to put an end to. 3. to kill. 4. to make useless.

de·stroy′er n. 1. one that destroys. 2. a fast warship.

de·struct′ (di strukt′) v.i. to be destroyed automatically.

de·struc′tion n. 1. a destroying or being destroyed. 2. a cause or means of destroying. —**de·struc′tive**, adj.

des′ue·tude′ (des′wi tōōd′, -tyōōd′) n. the state of being no longer used.

des′ul·to·ry (des′əl tôr′ē) adj. 1. lacking in consistency or order. 2. random. —**des′ul·to·ri·ly**, adv.

de·tach′ (di tach′) v.t. to unfasten and separate. —**de·tach′a·ble**, adj.

de·tached′ adj. 1. not attached. 2. impartial. 3. not involved.

de·tach′ment n. 1. a detaching or being detached. 2. aloofness. 3. impartiality.

de·tail′ (di tāl′, dē′tāl) n. 1. an individual or minute part. 2. such parts collectively. 3. troops or a group selected for special duty. —v.t. 4. to relate in detail. 5. to assign for a particular duty. —Idiom. 6. **in detail,** item by item.

de·tain′ (di tān′) v.t. 1. to delay. 2. to keep in custody.

de·tect′ (di tekt′) v.t. to discover or notice. —**de·tec′tion,** n. —**de·tec′tor,** n.

de·tec′tive n. one who investigates crimes, obtains evidence, etc.

dé·tente′ (dā tänt′) n. a relaxing of tensions, esp. between nations.

de·ten′tion (di ten′shən) n. 1. the keeping of a person in custody. 2. the keeping of a student after school hours as punishment.

de·ter′ (di tûr′) v.t., -terred, -terring. 1. to discourage or restrain from acting. 2. to prevent. —**de·ter′rence,** n. —**de·ter′rent,** adj., n.

de·ter′gent (di tûr′jənt) n. a cleansing agent.

de·te′ri·o·rate (di tēr′ē ə rāt′) v.t., v.i., -rated, -rating. to make or become worse. —**de·te′ri·o·ra′tion,** n.

de·ter′mi·na′tion (-nā′shən) n. 1. the process of coming to a decision. 2. firmness of purpose.

de·ter′mine (-min) v., -mined, -mining. —v.t. 1. to settle or resolve (a dispute, question, etc.). 2. to conclude, as after observation. 3. to decide upon. —v.i. 4. to decide.

de·ter′mined adj. 1. full of determination. 2. decided; settled.

de·ter′rence (di tûr′əns) n. discouragement, as of crime or military aggression. —**de·ter′rent,** adj., n.

de·test′ (di test′) v.t. to dislike intensely. —**de·test′a·ble,** adj.

de·throne′ (dē thrōn′) v.t., -throned, -throning. to remove from a throne.

det′o·nate (det′n āt′) v.i., v.t., -nated, -nating. to explode. —**det′o·na′tion,** n.

de′tour (dē′tŏōr, di tŏōr′) n. 1. a roundabout course or route. —v.i., v.t. 2. to make or cause to make a detour.

de′tox n., v., -toxed, -toxing. Informal. —n. 1. detoxification. —v.t. (dē toks′) 2. to detoxify.

de·tox′i·fy v.t., -fied, -fying. to rid of the effects of alcohol or drug use. —**de·tox′i·fi·ca′tion,** n.

de·tract′ (di trakt′) v. detract from,

to take away a part, as from quality or reputation.

det′ri·ment (de′trə mənt) n. 1. damage or loss. 2. a cause of damage or loss. —**det′ri·men′tal,** adj.

de·tri′tus (di trī′təs) n. 1. rock particles worn away from a mass. 2. debris.

deuce (dōōs, dyōōs) n. 1. a card or die with two pips. 2. a tie score.

dev′as·tate′ (dev′ə stāt′) v.t., -tated, -tating. 1. to cause great destruction to. 2. to overwhelm. —**dev′as·ta′tion,** n.

de·vel′op (di vel′əp) v.t. 1. to make more advanced, effective, or usable. 2. to cause to grow. 3. to bring into being. 4. to elaborate in detail. 5. to treat (film) so as to make images visible. —v.i. 6. to become more advanced, mature, etc. 7. to come gradually into existence or operation. —**de·vel′op·ment,** n. —**de·vel′op·er,** n.

de·vi′ant (dē′vē ənt) adj. deviating from an accepted norm. —n. 2. a deviant person or thing.

de′vi·ate′ (dē′vē āt′) v.i., -ated, -ating. to turn aside from a course, standard, or topic. —**de′vi·a′tion,** n.

de·vice′ (di vīs′) n. 1. a thing made or used for a specific purpose. 2. a scheme. 3. a slogan or emblem.

dev′il (dev′əl) n. 1. **the Devil,** Satan. 2. an evil spirit or person. 3. a mischievous person. —**dev′il·ish,** adj. —**dev′il·try,** n.

dev′il's ad′vocate n. a person who takes an opposing view for the sake of argument.

dev′il's food′ cake′ n. a rich chocolate cake.

de′vi·ous (dē′vē əs) adj. 1. roundabout. 2. not straightforward.

de·vise′ (di vīz′) v.t., -vised, -vising. 1. to plan or contrive. 2. to bequeath (property) by will.

de·void′ (di void′) adj. totally lacking.

de·volve′ (di volv′) v.t., v.i., -volved, -volving. to pass or be passed on from one to another.

de·vote′ (di vōt′) v.t., -voted, -voting. to apply to a certain pursuit, cause, etc. 2. to dedicate.

de·vot′ed adj. zealous in loyalty or affection.

dev·o·tee′ (dev′ə tē′) n. a person who is greatly devoted to something.

de·vo′tion (di vō′shən) n. 1. great love or loyalty. 2. profound dedication. 3. **devotions,** prayers.

de·vour′ (di vour′) v.t. 1. to eat up hungrily. 2. to take in eagerly with the senses or intellect.

de·vout′ (di vout′) adj. 1. devoted to divine worship; pious. 2. earnest.

dew (dōō, dyōō) n. atmospheric moisture condensed in droplets at night and deposited in small drops on a cool surface. —**dew′y,** adj.

dew′ point′ n. the temperature at which dew begins to form.

dex·ter′i·ty (dek ster′i tē) n. skill. —**dex′ter·ous** (-əs, -strəs) adj.

dex′trose (dek′strōs) n. a type of sugar.

di·a·be·tes (dī′ə bē′tis, -tēz) n. a disease characterized by high levels of glucose in the blood. —**di′a·bet′ic** (-bet′ik) adj., n.

di·a·bol′ic (dī′ə bol′ik) adj. devilish. Also, **di′a·bol′i·cal.**

di′a·crit′ic (dī′ə krit′ik) n. Also called **di′a·crit′i·cal mark.** a mark added to a letter to give it a particular phonetic value.

di′a·dem′ (dī′ə dem′) n. a crown.

di′ag·nose′ (dī′əg nōs′, -nōz′) v.t., v.i., -nosed, -nosing. to make a diagnosis (of).

di′ag·no′sis n. 1. the process of identifying a disease or condition by medical examination. 2. the decision reached. —**di′ag·nos′tic** (-nos′tik) adj.

di·ag′o·nal (dī ag′ə nl) adj. 1. extending from one corner to the opposite one. —n. 2. a line extending from one corner to the opposite corner. —**di·ag′o·nal·ly,** adv.

di′a·gram′ (dī′ə gram′) n., v., -gramed, -graming. —n. 1. a drawing, chart, or plan that outlines and explains something. —v.t. 2. to make a diagram of.

di′al (dī′əl, dīl) n., v., dialed, dialing. —n. 1. the numbered face on a watch or clock. 2. a similar face or plate with a movable pointer. 3. a movable disk on a telephone. —v.t. 4. to select or contact by using a dial.

di′a·lect′ (dī′ə lekt′) n. pronunciation or words peculiar to an area.

di′a·lec′tic (dī′ə lek′tik) n. 1. Also **di′a·lec′ti·cal.** of the nature of logical argumentation. —n. 2. Often **di′a·lec′tics.** the art or practice of debate or conversation by which the truth of a theory or opinion is arrived at logically.

di′a·logue′ (dī′ə lôg′) n. a conversation between two or more people. Also, **di′a·log′.**

di·al′y·sis (dī al′ə sis) n. the removal of waste products from the blood of someone with kidney disease.

di·am′e·ter (dī am′i tər) n. a straight line through the center of a circle.

di′a·met′ri·cal (dī′ə me′tri kəl) adj. being in direct opposition. —**di′a·met′ri·cal·ly,** adv.

di′a·mond (dī′mənd, dī′ə-) n. 1. a very hard, brilliant, precious stone. 2. a figure having four equal sides and two acute and two obtuse angles. 3. **diamonds,** a suit of playing cards marked with such shapes. 4. a baseball field.

dia′mond·back′ n. a rattlesnake with diamond-shaped markings.

di′a·per (dī′pər, dī′ə pər) n. 1. a piece of absorbent material worn as underpants by a baby. —v.t. 2. to put a diaper on.

di·aph′a·nous (dī af′ə nəs) adj. very sheer and light.

di′a·phragm′ (dī′ə fram′) n. 1. the muscle between the chest and the abdomen. 2. a vibrating disk, as in a telephone. 3. a contraceptive device that fits over the cervix.

di′ar·rhe′a (dī′ə rē′ə) n. a disorder characterized by frequent and fluid bowel movements.

di′a·ry (dī′ə rē) n., pl. -ries. 1. a daily record of events. 2. a book for recording these. —**di′a·rist,** n.

di·a·ton′ic (dī′ə ton′ik) adj. of a major or minor musical scale containing five whole notes and two semitones.

di′a·tribe′ (-trīb′) n. a bitter, abusive denunciation.

dib′ble (dib′əl) n. a pointed instrument for making holes in soil.

dice (dīs) n.pl., sing. **die,** v., diced, dicing. —n. 1. small cubes, marked on each side with one to six spots, used in games. 2. a game played with these. —v.t. 3. to cut into small cubes. —v.i. 4. to play at dice.

dick′ey (dik′sē) adj., -ier, -iest. risky.

di·chot′o·my (dī kot′ə mē) n., pl. -mies. division into two parts.

dick′er (dik′ər) v.i. to bargain.

di·cot′y·le′don (dī kot′l ēd′n, dī′kot l-) n. a plant having two embryonic seed leaves.

dic′tate (dik′tāt) v., -tated, -tating, n. —v.t., v.i. 1. to say or read aloud (something) to be written down or recorded. 2. to command. —n. 3. a command. —**dic·ta′tion,** n.

dic′ta·tor n. an absolute ruler. —**dic·ta·to′ri·al** (-tə tôr′ē əl) adj. —**dic·ta′tor·ship′,** n.

dic′tion (dik′shən) n. style of speaking or writing.

dic′tion·ar′y (dik′shə ner′ē) n., pl. -aries. a book that lists the words of a language with their meanings and other information.

dic′tum (dik′təm) n., pl. -ta, -tums. an authoritative declaration.

did (did) v. pt. of **do.**

di·dac′tic (dī dak′tik) adj. intended for instruction.

did′n′t (did′nt) a contraction of **did not.**

die¹ (dī) v.i., died, dying. 1. to cease to live. 2. to cease to function. 3. to lose force; fade.

die² (dī) n., pl. **dies** for 1; **dice** for 2. 1. a device that cuts or shapes material. 2. sing. of **dice.**

die′hard′ n. a person who stubbornly resists change.

di·er′e·sis (dī er′ə sis) n., pl. -ses. a sign (¨) placed over the second of two vowels, indicating it is pronounced separately, as in Noël.

die′sel (dē′zəl, -səl) n. a vehicle powered by a diesel engine.

die′sel en′gine n. an internal-combustion engine in which fuel oil is ignited by the heat of compressed air.

di′et¹ (dī′it) n. 1. the food one usu. eats. 2. a particular selection of food, as for health. —v.i., v.t. 3. to go or put on a diet.

di′et² (dī′it) n. a legislative body.

di′e·tet′ic (-tet′ik) adj. 1. of diet. 2. suitable for special diets. —n. 3. **dietetics,** the science of nutrition and food preparation.

di′e·ti′tian (dī′i tish′ən) n. a per-

son who is trained in nutrition and dietetics. Also, **di′e·ti′cian.**

dif′fer (dif′ər) v.i. 1. to be unlike. 2. to disagree.

dif′fer·ence (dif′ər əns, dif′rəns) n. 1. the state or degree of being different. 2. a disagreement. 3. the amount separating two quantities.

dif′fer·ent (dif′-) adj. 1. not alike. 2. distinct. 3. various. 4. not ordinary. —**dif′fer·ent·ly,** adv.

—Usage. DIFFERENT FROM is more common today in introducing a phrase, but DIFFERENT THAN is also used: *New York speech is different from/than that of Chicago.* DIFFERENT THAN is usually used when a clause follows, especially when the word "from" would create an awkward sentence: *The stream followed a different course than the map showed.*

dif′fer·en′ti·ate (-en′shē āt′) v., -ated, -ating. —v.t. 1. to distinguish. 2. to perceive the difference in. —v.i. 3. to become unlike. 4. to make a distinction. —**dif′fer·en′ti·a′tion,** n.

dif′fi·cult (dif′i kult′, -kəlt) adj. 1. requiring special effort or skill. 2. hard to do or understand. 3. hard to deal with.

dif′fi·cul′ty n., pl. -ties. 1. the condition of being difficult. 2. a difficult situation. 3. trouble. 4. a disagreement.

dif′fi·dent (-dənt) adj. timid; shy.

dif·frac′tion (di frak′shən) n. a breaking up of light rays, producing a spectrum.

dif·fuse′ v., -fused, -fusing, adj. —v.t., v.i. (di fyōōz′) 1. to spread or scatter. —adj. (-fyōōs′) 2. wordy. 3. spread or scattered.

dig (dig) v., dug (dug) or **digged,** digging, n. —v.i. 1. to break up and move earth. 2. to make one's way by digging. —v.t. 3. to break up, turn over, or loosen (earth). 4. to uncover by removing earth. 5. to form by removing material. —n. 6. a thrust. 7. a cutting remark. 8. an excavation. —**dig′ger,** n.

dig′e·ra′ti (dij′ə rä′tē, -rä′-) n.pl. people skilled with or knowledgeable about computers.

di·gest′ v.t. (di jest′) 1. to dissolve (food) in the stomach for absorption by the body. 2. to absorb mentally. —n. (dī′jest) 3. a collection or summary. —**di·ges′tion,** n. —**di·gest′ive,** adj.

dig′it (dij′it) n. 1. a finger or toe. 2. any Arabic numeral from 0 to 9.

dig′it·al (-l) adj. of, using, or expressing data in numerals.

dig′i·tal·is (-tal′is, -tā′lis) n. a medicine derived from foxglove leaves, used to stimulate the heart.

dig′i·tize′ (-tīz′) v.t., -tized, -tizing. to convert (data) to digital form.

dig′ni·fied′ (dig′nə fīd′) adj. marked by dignity; stately.

dig′ni·fy′ v.t., -fied, -fying. to give honor or dignity to.

dig′ni·tar′y (-ter′ē) n., pl. -ries. a high-ranking person.

dig′ni·ty n., pl. -ties. 1. formal or serious conduct or manner. 2. worthiness. 3. high rank, title, etc.

di·gress′ (di gres′, dī-) v.i. to wander from the main topic, argument, etc. —**di·gres′sion,** n.

dike (dīk) n. a long wall or bank built to prevent flooding.

di·lap′i·dat′ed (di lap′i dā′tid) adj. ruined or decayed. —**di·lap′i·da′tion,** n.

di·late′ (dī lāt′) v.t., v.i., -lated, -lating. to make or become wider. —**di·la′tion,** n.

dil′a·to·ry (dil′ə tôr′ē) adj. delaying; tardy. —**dil′a·to·ri·ness,** n.

di·lem′ma (di lem′ə) n. a situation requiring a choice between equally unpleasant alternatives.

dil′et·tante′ (dil′i tänt′, dil′i tänt′) n. a person who dabbles in an activity or subject for amusement.

dil′i·gence (dil′i jəns) n. earnest effort. —**dil′i·gent,** adj.

dill (dil) n. an herb with aromatic seeds and leaves.

dil′ly-dal′ly (dil′ē dal′ē) v.i., -lied, -lallying. to waste time, esp. by indecision.

di·lute′ (di lōōt′, dī-) v.t., -luted, -luting. 1. to make (a liquid) thinner or weaker, as by adding water. 2. to reduce the strength of. —**di·lu′tion,** n.

dim (dim) adj., dimmer, dimmest, v., dimmed, dimming. —adj. 1. not bright. 2. indistinct. —v.t., v.i. 3. to make or become dim. —**dim′ly,** adv.

dime (dīm) n. a ten-cent coin.

di·men′sion (di men′shən, dī-) n. a

1. extension in a given direction. **2.** dimensions, measurement in length, width, and thickness. **—di·men'sion·al,** adj.

di·min'ish (di min'ish) v.t., v.i. to make or become smaller, less, or less important.

di·min'u·en'do (di min'yōō en'dō) adj., adv. Music. gradually reducing in loudness.

di·min'u·tive (di min'ya tiv) adj. **1.** tiny. **—n. 2.** a word denoting smallness, familiarity, or affection.

dim'i·ty (dim'i tē) n., pl. **-ties.** a thin cotton fabric.

dim'ple (dim'pal) n. a small natural hollow, esp. in the cheek.

dim'wit' n. Slang. a stupid person. **—dim'wit'ted,** adj.

din (din) n., v., **dinned, dinning. —n. 1.** a loud, confused noise. **—v.t. 2.** to assail with a din.

dine (dīn) v.i., **dined, dining.** to eat dinner.

din'er n. **1.** a person who dines. **2.** a railroad dining car. **3.** a restaurant resembling this.

di·nette' (-net') n. a small area or alcove for dining.

din'ghy (ding'gē) n., pl. **-ghies.** a small boat.

din'gy (din'jē) adj., **-gier, -giest.** of a dark, dull, or dirty color.

din'ner (din'ər) n. the main meal of the day.

di'no·saur' (dī'nə sôr') n. any of various extinct, prehistoric reptiles.

dint (dint) n. **1.** force. **2.** a dent.

di'o·cese' (dī'ə sis, -sēz', -sēs') n. a district under a bishop. **—di·oc'e·san** (-os'ə sən) adj., n.

di'o·ram'a (dī'ə ram'ə, -rä'mə) n. a miniature three-dimensional scene against a painted background.

di·ox'ide (dī ok'sīd, -sid) n. an oxide with two atoms of oxygen.

di·ox'in (-ok'sin) n. a toxic byproduct of pesticide manufacture.

dip (dip) v., **dipped, dipping.** **—v.t. 1.** to plunge briefly into a liquid. **2.** to bail or scoop. **—v.i. 3.** to go under water and emerge quickly. **4.** to drop suddenly. **5.** to slope down. **—n. 6.** the act of dipping. **7.** a downward slope. **8.** a substance into which something is dipped. **9.** a brief swim.

diph·the'ri·a (dif thēr'ē ə, dip-) n. an infectious disease marked by high fever and breathing difficulty.

diph'thong (dif'thông, dip'-) n. a gliding speech sound containing two vowels.

di·plo'ma (di plō'mə) n. a document conferring a degree or certifying the successful completion of a course of study.

di·plo'ma·cy (-sē) n., pl. **-cies. 1.** the conduct of international relations. **2.** skill in negotiation. **—dip'lo·mat'** (dip'lə mat') n.

dip'lo·mat'ic adj. **1.** of diplomacy. **2.** tactful.

dip'so·ma'ni·a (dip'sə mā'nē ə, -sō-) n. an irresistible craving for alcohol. **—dip'so·ma'ni·ac,** n.

dip'ter·ous (dip'tər əs) adj. having two wings or two winglike parts.

dire (dī''r) adj., **direr, direst.** dreadful; ominous.

di·rect' (di rekt', dī-) v.t. **1.** to manage or guide. **2.** to command. **3.** to serve as director of. **4.** to show (a person) the way or how to do something. **5.** to address. **—adj. 6.** proceeding in a straight line. **7.** without intermediary agents or conditions. **8.** straightforward. **—di·rect'ly,** adv. **—di·rect'ness,** n.

direct' cur'rent n. an electric current flowing continuously in one direction.

di·rec'tion n. **1.** an act of directing. **2.** the line along which a thing faces or moves. **3.** supervision. **—di·rec'tion·al,** adj.

di·rec'tive n. an authoritative order or instruction.

di·rec'tor n. **1.** one that directs. **2.** one of the persons chosen to govern the affairs of a company. **3.** the person who guides the performers in a play or film.

di·rec'to·ry n., pl. **-ries.** a list of names, locations, telephone numbers, etc.

dirge (dûrj) n. a song or poem commemorating the dead.

dir'i·gi·ble (dir'i jə bəl, di rij'ə-) n. a self-propelled, lighter-than-air aircraft; airship.

dirk (dûrk) n. a dagger.

dirt (dûrt) n. **1.** any foul or filthy substance. **2.** soil. **3.** obscene words. **4.** gossip.

dirt'y adj., **-ier, -iest,** v., **-ied, -ying. —adj. 1.** soiled or soiling. **2.** vile. **3.** obscene. **4.** unpleasant. **—v.t., v.i. 5.** to make or become dirty. **—dirt'i·ness,** n.

dis (dis) v., **dissed, dissing** v. Slang. **—v.t. 1.** to show disrespect for. **2.** to disparage. **—n. 3.** disparagement or criticism.

dis- a prefix indicating: **1.** reversal. **2.** negation or lack. **3.** removal.

dis·a'ble (-ā'bal) v.t., **-bled, -bling.** to make unable or unfit. **—dis'a·bil'i·ty,** n.

dis·a'bled adj. handicapped; incapacitated.

dis·a·buse' (-byōōz') v.t., **-bused, -busing.** to free from deception.

dis'ad·van'tage n. an unfavorable condition; handicap.

dis'ad·van'taged adj. lacking economic and social opportunity.

dis·af·fect' v.t. to make discontented.

dis'a·gree' v.i., **-greed, -greeing. 1.** to differ in opinion. **2.** to fail to agree. **3.** to quarrel. **—dis'a·gree'ment,** n.

dis'a·gree'a·ble adj. unpleasant; grouchy.

dis'al·low' v.t. to refuse to allow.

dis'ap·pear' v.i. **1.** to cease to be seen. **2.** to cease to exist. **—dis'ap·pear'ance,** n.

dis'ap·point' v.t. to fail to fulfill the hopes of. **—dis'ap·point'ment,** n.

dis'ap·pro·ba'tion n. disapproval.

dis'ap·prove' v., **-proved, -proving. —v.t. 1.** to think (something) wrong. **2.** to withhold approval from. **—v.i. 3.** to have an unfavorable opinion. **—dis'ap·prov'al,** n.

dis·arm' v.t. **1.** to deprive of weapons. **2.** to make less hostile.

dis·ar·range' v.t., **-ranged, -ranging.** to disturb the arrangement of.

dis·ar·ray' n. lack of order.

dis·as·so'ci·ate (-āt') v.t., v.i. **-ated, -ating.** to dissociate.

dis·as'ter (di zas'tər) n. an event that occurs suddenly and causes great damage. **—dis·as'trous,** adj.

dis·a·vow' (dis'a vou') v.t. to deny knowledge of or responsibility for. **—dis'a·vow'al,** n.

dis·band' v.t. to break up (an organization).

dis·bar' v.t., **-barred, -barring.** to expel from the legal profession.

dis·be·lieve' v.t., v.i., **-lieved, -lieving.** to refuse or be unable to believe. **—dis'be·lief',** n.

dis·burse' (dis bûrs') v.t., **-bursed, -bursing.** to pay out.

disc (disk) n. **1.** a disk. **2.** a phonograph record.

dis·card' v.t. to cast aside. **—n.** (dis'kärd) **2.** the act of discarding. **3.** something discarded.

dis·cern' (di sûrn', -zûrn') v.t., v.i. to perceive by the sight or the mind. **—dis·cern'i·ble,** adj. **—dis·cern'ment,** n.

dis·cern'ing adj. showing good judgment and understanding.

dis·charge' v., **-charged, -charging,** n. **—v.t.** (dis chärj') **1.** to remove the contents of. **2.** to send or pour forth. **3.** to shoot (a gun). **4.** to fulfill the requirements of (a duty). **5.** to dismiss from employment. **6.** to pay (a debt). **—v.i. 7.** to get rid of a burden. **8.** to pour forth. **9.** to go off, as a gun. **—n.** (dis'chärj) **10.** the act of discharging. **11.** something discharged.

dis·ci'ple (di sī'pal) n. a follower.

dis'ci·pline (dis'ə plin) n., v., **-plined, -plining. —n. 1.** training to act in accordance with rules. **2.** behavior in accord with rules of conduct. **3.** a branch of learning. **4.** punishment. **—v.t. 5.** to train by instruction and exercise. **6.** to bring under control. **7.** to punish. **—dis'ci·pli·nar'y,** adj.

disc' jockey' n. a person who plays and comments on recorded music on a radio program.

dis·claim' v.t. to disown.

dis·close' v.t., **-closed, -closing.** to reveal. **—dis·clo'sure,** n.

dis'co (dis'kō) n., pl. **-cos. 1.** a discotheque. **2.** a style of popular music having a heavy rhythmic beat.

dis·col'or v.t., v.i. to change color. **—dis·col'or·a'tion,** n.

dis'com·bob'u·late' (dis'kəm bob'yə lāt') v.t., **-lated, -lating.** to confuse or disconcert.

dis·com'fit (dis kum'fit) v.t. **1.** to confuse; disconcert. **2.** to frustrate. **—dis·com'fi·ture,** n.

dis·com'fort n. **1.** lack of comfort. **2.** anything disturbing to comfort.

dis'com·mode' (dis'kə mōd') v.t., **-moded, -moding.** to cause inconvenience to.

dis'com·pose' v.t., **-posed, -posing. 1.** to upset the order of. **2.** to disturb the composure of.

dis'con·cert' (dis'kan sûrt') v.t. to disturb the self-possession of; perturb.

dis'con·nect' v.t. to break the connection of.

dis'con'so·late (dis kon'sə lit) adj. sad; gloomy. **—dis·con'so·late·ly,** adv.

dis'con·tent' (-kan tent') adj. Also **dis'con·tent'ed. 1.** not contented. **—n. 2.** lack of contentment.

dis'con·tin'ue v., **-tinued, -tinuing. —v.t. 1.** to put an end to; stop. **—v.i. 2.** to come to an end.

dis'cord n. **1.** lack of harmony. **2.** difference of opinion. **3.** any harsh noise. **—dis·cord'ant,** adj.

dis'co·theque' (dis'kə tek', dis'kə tek') n. a nightclub for dancing.

dis'count v.t. (dis'kount, dis·kount') **1.** to deduct an amount from. **2.** to sell at a reduced price. **3.** to disregard. **—n.** (dis'kount) **4.** an act of discounting. **5.** an amount deducted.

dis·cour'age v.t., **-aged, -aging. 1.** to deprive of courage or confidence. **2.** to hinder.

dis·course n., v., **-coursed, -coursing. —n.** (dis'kôrs) **1.** a conversation. **2.** a formal discussion of a subject. **—v.i.** (dis kôrs') **3.** to talk. **4.** to treat a subject formally.

dis·cour'te·sy n., pl. **-sies. 1.** rudeness. **2.** an impolite act. **—dis·cour'te·ous,** adj.

dis·cov'er v.t. to obtain sight or knowledge of. **—dis·cov'er·er,** n. **—dis·cov'er·y,** n.

—**Usage.** Do not confuse DISCOVER and INVENT, two words that deal with something new. DISCOVER is used when the object is an idea or place that existed before, but few people or no one knew about it. In the sentence *Columbus discovered the New World,* the New World clearly existed and was known to the people living there, but not to Columbus and the people of his time. INVENT is used when the object is a device or thing built. In the sentence *Edison invented the light bulb,* the light bulb did not exist before Edison invented it, and it was not known by anyone.

dis·cred'it v.t. **1.** to injure the reputation of. **2.** to disbelieve. **—n. 3.** loss or lack of belief. **4.** disgrace.

dis·creet' (di skrēt') adj. cautious in conduct or speech; prudent. **—dis·creet'ly,** adv.

dis·crep'an·cy (di skrep'ən sē) n., pl. **-cies.** a difference; inconsistency.

dis·crete' (di skrēt') adj. separate.

dis·cre'tion (di skresh'ən) n. **1.** the freedom to decide something. **2.** the quality of being discreet.

dis·crim'i·nate' (di skrim'ə nāt') v.i., **-nated, -nating. 1.** to show partiality. **2.** to note a difference. **—dis·crim'i·na'tion,** n.

dis·crim'i·nat'ing adj. having good taste or judgment.

dis·cur'sive (dis kûr'siv) adj. rambling from one subject to another.

dis'cus (dis'kəs) n. a disk for throwing in athletic competition.

dis·cuss' (di skus') v.t. to consider or examine by argument, comment, etc. **—dis·cus'sion,** n.

dis·dain' (dis dān', di stān') v.t. to scorn. **—dis·dain'ful,** adj.

dis·ease' (di zēz') n. an abnormal condition; an illness. **—dis·eased',** adj.

dis'em·bark' (dis'em bärk') v.i. to leave an airplane or ship. **—dis'em·bar·ka'tion,** n.

dis'en·chant' v.t. to free from enchantment or illusion.

dis'en·gage' v.t., **-gaged, -gaging. —v.t. 1.** to separate; disconnect. **—v.i. 2.** to become disengaged.

dis·fa'vor n. displeasure; dislike.

dis·fig'ure v.t., **-ured, -uring.** to spoil the appearance of. **—dis·fig'ure·ment,** n.

dis·fran'chise or **dis·en·fran'chise** v.t., **-chised, -chising.** to deprive of a right, esp. the right to vote.

dis·gorge' (dis gôrj') v.t., **-gorged, -gorging. 1.** to eject; throw up.

dis·grace' n., v., **-graced, -gracing. —n. 1.** loss of respect or honor. **2.** a person or thing that causes loss of respect or honor. **—v.t. 3.** to bring shame upon. **—dis·grace'ful,** adj.

dis·grun'tle (dis grun'tl) v.t., **-tled, -tling.** to make discontented or resentful.

dis·guise' (dis gīz', di skīz') v., **-guised, -guising,** n. **—v.t. 1.** to conceal the true identity or character of. **—n. 2.** something that disguises.

dis·gust' (dis gust', di skust') v.t. **1.** to cause loathing or nausea in. **—n. 2.** a strong loathing. **—dis·gust'ed,** adj. **—dis·gust'ing,** adj.

dish (dish) n. **1.** an open, shallow container for holding food. **2.** a particular article of food.

dis·ha·bille' (dis'ə bēl', -bē') n. the state of being partially dressed.

dis·heart'en v.t. to discourage.

dis·hon'est adj. not honest.

dis·hon'or n. **1.** lack or loss of honor; disgrace. **—v.t. 2.** to disgrace. **—dis·hon'or·a·ble,** adj.

dish'wash'er n. a person or machine that washes dishes.

dis·il·lu'sion v.t. to free from pleasing but false beliefs.

dis·in·cline' v.t., **-clined, -clining.** to make unwilling or reluctant.

dis'in·fect' v.t. to cleanse in order to destroy disease germs. **—dis'in·fect'ant,** n., adj.

dis'in·for·ma'tion n. deliberately misleading information.

dis·in·gen'u·ous adj. insincere.

dis'in·her'it v.t. to deprive of an inheritance.

dis·in'te·grate' v.i., **-grated, -grating.** to break into parts. **—dis·in'te·gra'tion,** n.

dis·in·ter' v.t., **-terred, -terring.** to unearth; dig up.

dis·in'ter·est'ed adj. not partial or biased.

—**Usage.** Do not confuse DISINTERESTED and UNINTERESTED. DISINTERESTED means "able to act fairly; not partial or biased," while UNINTERESTED means "not taking an interest."

dis·joint'ed adj. disconnected; incoherent.

disk (disk) n. **1.** a thin, flat, circular plate. **2.** a plate for storing electronic data. **3.** a roundish, flat anatomical part, as in the spine. **4.** a phonograph record.

disk' drive', n. a device on a computer that enables the user to read data from or store data on a disk.

disk·ette' n. a floppy disk.

dis·like' v., **-liked, -liking,** n. **—v.t. 1.** to regard with displeasure. **—n. 2.** a feeling of not liking.

dis'lo·cate' (dis'lō kāt', dis lō'kāt) v.t., **-cated, -cating. 1.** to put out of place or order. **2.** to put out of joint, as a limb.

dis·lodge' v.t., **-lodged, -lodging.** to force out of place.

dis·loy'al adj. not loyal; faithless.

dis'mal (diz'məl) adj. **1.** gloomy. **2.** very bad. **—dis'mal·ly,** adv.

dis·man'tle v.t., **-tled, -tling. 1.** to take away equipment from. **2.** to take apart.

dis·may' (dis mā') v.t. **1.** to surprise and discourage. **—n. 2.** surprise and discouragement.

dis·mem'ber v.t. **1.** to remove the limbs of. **2.** to divide into parts.

dis·miss' (dis mis') v.t. **1.** to direct or allow to go. **2.** to discharge from service. **3.** to reject. **—dis·mis'sal,** n.

dis·mount' v.i. to get down, as from a horse or a bicycle.

dis'o·be'di·ent adj. not obedient. **—dis'o·be'di·ence,** n.

dis'o·bey' v.t., v.i. to neglect or refuse to obey.

dis·or'der n. **1.** lack of order; confusion. **2.** an illness. **—v.t. 3.** to create disorder in. **—dis·or'der·ly,** adj.

dis·or'gan·ize' v.t., **-ized, -izing.** to destroy the orderly system or arrangement of. **—dis·or'gan·i·za'tion,** n.

dis·o'ri·ent' v.t. **1.** to cause to lose one's way. **2.** to confuse mentally.

dis·own' v.t. to refuse to acknowledge as belonging to oneself.

dis·par'age (di spar'ij) v.t., **-aged, -aging.** to speak slightingly of.

dis'par·ate (dis'pər it, di spar'-) adj. different. **—dis·par'i·ty,** n.

dis·pas'sion·ate adj. impartial; calm. **—dis·pas'sion·ate·ly,** adv.

dis·patch' v.t. **1.** to send off. **2.** to dispose of (a matter) quickly. **3.** to kill. **—n. 4.** the act of sending off. **5.** execution. **6.** speedy action. **7.** a message or report sent quickly.

dis·pel' (di spel') v.t., **-pelled, -pelling.** to drive off; scatter.

dis·pen'sa·ry (di spen'sə rē) n., pl. **-ries.** a place where medicine is dispensed.

dis'pen·sa'tion (dis'pan sā'shən, -pen-) n. **1.** an act of dispensing. **2.** the divine ordering of the world's affairs. **3.** an official exemption from a law or obligation.

dis·pense' (di spens') v.t., **-pensed, -pensing. 1.** to distribute; administer. **2.** to make up and distribute (medicines). **3.** dispense with, to do without. **—dis·pens'er,** n.

dis·perse' (di spûrs') v., **-persed, -persing. —v.t. 1.** to scatter. **2.** to dispel. **—v.i. 3.** to become scattered. **—dis·per'sal,** n.

dis·pir'it·ed adj. downhearted.

dis·place' v.t., **-placed, -placing. 1.** to put out of the usual place. **2.** to take the place of. **—dis·place'ment,** n.

dis·play' (di splā') v.t. **1.** to show or exhibit. **—n. 2.** an act or instance of displaying.

dis·please' v.t., v.i., **-pleased, -pleasing.** to annoy or offend. **—dis·pleas'ure** (-plezh'ər) n.

dis·pose' v.t., v.i., **-posed, -posing. 1.** to place or arrange. **2.** to make willing to do something. **3.** dispose of, **a.** to settle. **b.** to get rid of. **—dis·pos'a·ble,** adj., n. **—dis·pos'al,** n.

dis'po·si'tion (dis'pə zish'ən) n. **1.** one's mental outlook. **2.** tendency. **3.** arrangement. **4.** final settlement of a matter.

dis'pos·sess' v.t. to put (a person) out of possession. **—dis'pos·ses'sion,** n.

dis'pro·por'tion n. lack of proportion. **—dis'pro·por'tion·ate,** adj.

dis·prove' v.t., **-proved, -proving.** to prove to be false.

dis·pute' (di spyōōt') v., **-puted, -puting,** n. **—v.i. 1.** to engage in argument. **2.** to quarrel. **—v.t. 3.** to argue about or against. **4.** to fight about. **—n. 5.** an argument; quarrel. **—dis·put'a·ble,** adj. **—dis'pu·ta'tion,** n.

dis·qual'i·fy' v.t., **-fied, -fying.** to make ineligible. **—dis·qual'i·fi·ca'tion,** n.

dis·qui'et n. **1.** anxiety; uneasiness. **—v.t. 2.** to cause disquiet to.

dis're·gard' v.t. to ignore. **—n. 2.** neglect.

dis're·pair' n. the condition of needing repair.

dis·rep'u·ta·ble, adj.

dis're·pute' n. bad repute; disfavor. **—dis·rep'u·ta·ble,** adj.

dis're·spect' n. lack of respect. **—dis're·spect'ful,** adj.

dis·robe' v.t., v.i., **-robed, -robing.** to undress.

dis·rupt' (dis rupt') v.t. **1.** to break up. **2.** to disturb. **—dis·rup'tion,** n. **—dis·rup'tive,** adj.

dis'sat·is·fac'tion n. **1.** lack of satisfaction. **2.** a cause or feeling of displeasure. **—dis·sat'is·fy',** v.t.

dis·sect' (di sekt', dī-) v.t. **1.** to cut apart for examination. **2.** to analyze in detail. **—dis·sec'tion,** n.

dis·sem'ble (di sem'bal) v.t., v.i., **-bled, -bling.** to conceal (motives or thoughts). **—dis·sem'bler,** n.

dis·sem'i·nate' (di sem'ə nāt') v.t., **-nated, -nating.** to spread widely.

dis·sen'sion (di sen'shan) n. strong disagreement; discord.

dis·sent' (di sent') v.i. **1.** to differ in opinion or sentiment. **—n. 2.** a difference of opinion.

dis'ser·ta'tion (dis'ər tā'shən) n. a formal essay or thesis.

dis·serv'ice n. harm or injury.

dis'si·dent (dis'i dant) n. **1.** a person who dissents from established opinions. **2.** dissenting, as in opinion. **—dis'si·dence,** n.

dis·sim'i·lar adj. not similar. **—dis·sim'i·lar'i·ty** (-lar'i tē) n.

dis·sim'u·late' (dis sim'yə lāt') v.t., v.i., **-lated, -lating.** to dissemble.

dis'si·pate' (dis'ə pāt') v., **-pated, -pating. —v.t. 1.** to scatter. **2.** to use wastefully. **—v.i. 3.** to become scattered. **4.** to indulge in dissolute behavior. **—dis'si·pa'tion,** n.

dis·so'ci·ate' (di sō'shē āt', -sē-) v.t., v.i., **-ated, -ating.** to break the association of.

dis'so·lute' (dis'ə lōōt') adj. lacking moral restraint.

dis·solve' (di zolv') v., **-solved, -solving. —v.t. 1.** to make a solution of. **2.** to melt. **3.** to break (a tie). **4.** to dismiss (an assembly). **—v.i. 5.** to become dissolved. **6.** to disappear gradually. **7.** to break down emotionally. **—dis'so·lu'tion** (dis'ə lōō'shən) n.

dis'so·nance (dis'ə nəns) n. inharmonious sound; discord.

dis·suade' (di swād') v.t., **-suaded, -suading.** to persuade against.

dist. 1. distance. **2.** district.

dis'taff (dis'taf) adj. **1.** of women. **—n. 2.** a staff for holding wool, flax, etc., in spinning.

dis'tance (dis'təns) n. **1.** the space

between two things, points, etc. **2.** remoteness. **3.** a distant region. **4.** aloofness.

dis·tant adj. **1.** far off in space or time; remote. **2.** reserved or aloof. —**dis′tant·ly**, adv.

dis·taste′ n. dislike; aversion. —**dis·taste′ful**, adj.

dis·tem′per (dis tem′pər) n. an infectious disease of dogs and cats.

dis·tend′ (di stend′) v.t., v.i. to swell. —**dis·ten′tion**, n.

dis·till′ (di stil′) v.t., v.i. **1.** to subject to or undergo distillation. **2.** to fall in drops. —**dis·till′er·y**, n.

dis′til·la′tion n. **1.** the process of heating, evaporating, and condensing a liquid. **2.** the purification of a substance by such a method.

dis·tinct′ (di stingkt′) adj. **1.** different in nature or quality. **2.** clear. **3.** separate. —**dis·tinct′ly**, adv.

dis·tinc′tion n. **1.** an act or instance of distinguishing. **2.** the recognizing of differences. **3.** a distinguishing quality. **4.** a special honor. —**dis·tinc′tive**, adj.

dis·tin′guish (di sting′gwish) v.t. **1.** to mark off as different. **2.** to recognize as distinct. **3.** to perceive clearly. **4.** to make prominent.

dis·tin′guished adj. **1.** characterized by distinction. **2.** dignified or elegant.

dis·tort′ (di stôrt′) v.t. **1.** to twist out of shape. **2.** to give a false meaning to.

dis·tract′ (di strakt′) v.t. to divert the attention of.

dis·trac′tion n. **1.** a distracting or being distracted. **2.** mental distress. **3.** a person or thing that prevents concentration. **4.** something that amuses.

dis·traught′ (di strôt′) adj. crazed with anxiety; deeply agitated.

dis·tress′ (di stres′) n. **1.** anxiety, pain, or sorrow. —v.t. **2.** to afflict with anxiety, pain, or sorrow.

dis·trib′ute (di strib′yŏŏt) v.t., -uted, -uting. **1.** to divide and give out in shares. **2.** to spread over a space. —**dis′tri·bu′tion**, n. —**dis·trib′u·tor**, n.

dis′trict (dis′trikt) n. **1.** a political division. **2.** a region.

dis′trict attor′ney an attorney for the government within a given district.

dis·trust′ v.t. **1.** to have no trust in. —n. **2.** lack of trust; suspicion.

dis·turb′ (di stûrb′) v.t. **1.** to interrupt the rest or peace of. **2.** to put out of order. **3.** to trouble. —**dis·turb′ance**, n.

dis·use′ (dis yŏŏs′) n. the state of not being used.

ditch (dich) n. **1.** a long, narrow channel in the ground. —v.t. **2.** to crash-land on water and abandon (an aircraft). **3.** Slang. to get rid of.

dith′er (dith′ər) n. **1.** flustered excitement or fear. —v.i. **2.** to be indecisive.

dit′to (dit′ō) n., pl. -tos, adv. —n. **1.** the above or the same (used in accounts, lists, etc.). —adv. **2.** as stated before.

dit′to mark′ n. a mark (″) used as a sign for ditto.

dit′ty (dit′ē) n., pl. -ties. a simple song.

di·u·ret′ic (dī′ə ret′ik) adj. **1.** causing more urine to be excreted. —n. **2.** a diuretic medicine.

di·ur′nal (dī ûr′nl) adj. **1.** occurring each day. **2.** of or active in the daytime.

div. 1. dividend. **2.** division. **3.** divorced.

di′va (dē′və, -vä) n. a principal female singer in an opera.

di′van (di van′) n. a sofa or couch.

dive (dīv) v., dived or dove (dōv), dived, diving, n. —v.i. **1.** to plunge headfirst into water. **2.** to plunge, fall, or descend through the air. **3.** to rush. —n. **4.** an act of diving. **5.** a sudden decline. —**div′er**, n.

di·verge′ (di vûrj′, dī-) v.i., -verged, -verging. **1.** to move or extend in different directions from a point. **2.** to differ, as in opinion. **3.** to deviate, as from a path. —**di·ver′gence**, n. —**di·ver′gent**, adj.

di·vers (dī′vərz) adj. various.

di·verse′ (di vûrs′, dī-) adj. of different kinds.

di·ver′si·fy v., -fied, -fying. —v.t. **1.** to vary. —v.i. **2.** to become diversified.

di·ver′sion n. **1.** the act of turning aside. **2.** a distraction.

di·ver′si·ty n. difference or variety.

di·vert′ (di vûrt′, dī-) v.t. **1.** to turn aside, as from a course. **2.** to distract. **3.** to amuse.

di·vest′ (di vest′, dī-) v.t. **1.** to strip of clothing, ornament, etc. **2.** to deprive, as of property rights.

di·vide′ (di vīd′) v., -vided, -viding, n. —v.t. **1.** to separate into parts, sections, etc. **2.** to cut off. **3.** to separate into equal parts by mathematical division. —v.i. **4.** to become divided. **5.** to diverge. **6.** to perform mathematical division. —n. **7.** a ridge separating drainage basins. —**di·vid′er**, n.

div′i·dend (div′i dend′) n. **1.** a number to be divided. **2.** a sum paid to shareholders out of company earnings. **3.** a bonus.

di·vine′ (di vīn′) adj., n., v., -vined, -vining. —adj. **1.** of, from, or like God or a god. **2.** devoted to God or a god. **3.** Informal. extremely good. —n. **4.** a theologian or cleric. —v.t. **5.** to prophesy. **6.** to perceive by intuition. —**di·vine′ly**, adv.

divin′ing rod′ n. a forked stick for finding underground water.

di·vin′i·ty (-vin′i tē) n., pl. -ties. **1.** the quality of being divine. **2.** a divine being.

di·vi′sion (di vizh′ən) n. **1.** the act or result of dividing. **2.** the arithmetic operation of finding how many times one number is contained in another. **3.** something that divides. **4.** a section. **5.** disagreement. **6.** a major unit of the army or navy. —**di·vis′i·ble**, adj.

di·vi′sive (-vī′siv) adj. creating dissension.

di·vi′sor (-vī′zər) n. a number by which another number is divided.

di·vorce′ (di vôrs′) n., v., -vorced, -vorcing. —n. **1.** legal dissolution of a marriage. **2.** total separation. —v.t. **3.** to separate by divorce. —v.i. **4.** to get a divorce.

di·vor·cee′ (-sē′) n. a divorced woman.

div′ot (div′ət) n. a piece of turf gouged out by the stroke of a golf club.

di·vulge′ (di vulj′, dī-) v.t., -vulged, -vulging. to disclose or reveal.

Dix′ie (dik′sē) n. the southern states of the U.S., esp. those that joined the Confederacy.

Dix′ie·land′ n. a style of jazz marked by accented four-four rhythm and improvisation.

diz′zy (diz′ē) adj., -zier, -ziest. **1.** having a sensation of whirling and a tendency to fall. **2.** confused. **3.** Informal. foolish; silly. —**diz′zi·ly**, adv.

D.J. (dē′jā′) disc jockey. Also, **DJ, dee′jay.**

DNA deoxyribonucleic acid, the substance that carries genes along its strands.

do¹ (dŏŏ; unstressed dŏŏ, də) v., did, done, doing, n. —v.t. **1.** to perform (an act). **2.** to execute (an amount of work). **3.** to accomplish. **4.** to be the cause of (good, harm, etc.). **5.** to deal with. **6.** to exert. **7.** to render. **8.** to suffice for. —v.i. **9.** to act. **10.** to proceed. **11.** to be enough. —auxiliary v. **12.** (used to ask questions, to make negative statements, to add emphasis, and to avoid repetition). **13. do away with,** to abolish. **14.** ~ **in,** a. to kill. b. to exhaust. **15.** ~ **out of,** Informal. to cheat. —n. **16.** Informal. a social gathering.

do² (dō) n. the musical syllable used for the first note of a scale.

DOA dead on arrival.

Do′ber·man pin′scher (dō′bər mən pin′shər) n. a large dog with a short, usu. black or brown coat.

do′cent (dō′sənt) n. a lecturer or guide, esp. in a museum.

doc′ile (dos′əl) adj. readily trained; submissive.

dock¹ (dok) n. **1.** a wharf. **2.** a waterway between two piers for receiving a ship while in port. **3.** a platform for loading trucks, freight cars, etc. —v.t. **4.** to bring (a ship) into a dock. **5.** to join (a space vehicle) with another spacecraft. —v.i. **6.** to come into a dock. **7.** (of two space vehicles) to join together.

dock² (dok) v.t. **1.** to cut off the end of. **2.** to deduct from (wages).

dock³ (dok) n. the place in a courtroom where a prisoner is placed during trial.

dock′et (dok′it) n. **1.** a list of court cases. **2.** a list of business to be transacted.

doc′tor (dok′tər) n. **1.** a person licensed to practice medicine. **2.** a person who has a doctor's degree. —v.t. **3.** to treat medically. **4.** to tamper with.

doc′tor·ate (-it) n. a doctor's degree.

doc′tor's degree′ n. the highest degree awarded by universities.

doc′tri·naire′ (-trə nâr′) adj. adhering stubbornly to a doctrine.

doc′trine (-trin) n. **1.** a particular principle of a religion or government. **2.** a body of teachings. —**doc′tri·nal**, adj.

doc′u·ment n. (-mənt) **1.** a paper giving information. **2.** a computer data file. —v.t. (-ment′) **3.** to support by documents.

doc′u·men′ta·ry (-men′tə rē) adj., n., pl. -ries. —adj. **1.** of or derived from documents. **2.** depicting an actual event, life story, etc. —n. **3.** a documentary film.

dod′der (dod′ər) v.i. to totter.

dodge (doj) v., dodged, dodging, n. —v.t. **1.** to avoid by a quick movement or strategy. —v.i. **2.** to move suddenly. —n. **3.** a quick, evasive movement. **4.** a trick. —**dodg′er**, n.

do′do (dō′dō) n., pl. -dos, -does. a large, extinct flightless bird.

doe (dō) n. the female of the deer, rabbit, etc.

does (duz) v. third pers. sing. pres. indic. of **do.**

does′n't (duz′ənt) contraction of does not.

doff (dof) v.t. to remove, as one's hat.

dog (dôg) n., v., dogged, dogging. —n. **1.** a domesticated carnivore. **2.** any animal belonging to the same family, as the wolf, fox, etc. —v.t. **3.** to follow closely.

dog′-ear′ n. a folded-down corner of a book page. —**dog′-eared′**, adj.

dog′ged (dô′gid) adj. persistent.

dog′ger·el (dô′gər əl) n. trivial poetry.

dog′house′ n. **1.** a shelter for a dog. —Idiom. **2. in the doghouse,** in disfavor.

dog′ma (-mə) n. a system of principles or beliefs, as of a church.

dog·mat′ic (-mat′ik) adj. **1.** of dogma. **2.** arrogantly asserting opinions. —**dog′ma·tism′**, n.

dog′wood′ n. a tree with white or pink blossoms.

doi′ly (doi′lē) n., pl. -lies. a small ornamental mat.

Dol′by (dōl′bē) Trademark. a system for reducing the high-frequency noise in a tape recording.

dol′drums (dōl′drəmz, dol′-) n.pl. **1.** a belt of calm and light winds near the equator. **2.** a state of inactivity. **3.** a dull, depressed mood.

dole (dōl) n., v., doled, doling. —n. **1.** an allotment of money or food given to the needy. —v.t. **2.** to distribute in charity. **3.** to give out in small quantities.

dole′ful adj. sorrowful; gloomy.

doll (dol) n. **1.** a toy representing a baby or other human being. **2.** an attractive or nice person.

dol′lar (dol′ər) n. the basic monetary unit in the U.S. and certain other countries.

dol′lop (dol′əp) n. a lump or blob of some soft substance.

dol′ly (dol′ē) n., pl. -lies. **1.** a low cart for moving heavy loads. **2.** a movable platform for a movie or TV camera.

dol′or·ous (dō′lər əs, dol′ər-) adj. full of or causing pain or sorrow.

dol′phin (dol′fin) n. a marine mammal having a beaklike snout.

dolt (dōlt) n. a stupid person. —**dolt′ish**, adj.

-dom a suffix indicating: **1.** domain. **2.** rank or station. **3.** general condition.

do·main′ (dō mān′) n. **1.** a field of action, thought, influence, etc. **2.** the area governed by a single ruler or government.

dome (dōm) n. **1.** a rounded ceiling or roof. **2.** anything shaped like this.

do·mes′tic (də mes′tik) adj. **1.** of the home. **2.** of one's own country. —n. **3.** a servant. —**do′mes·tic′i·ty** (dō′me stis′i tē) n.

do·mes′ti·cate′ (-kāt′) v.t., -cated, -cating. **1.** to train (an animal) to live with humans. **2.** to accustom to household life.

domes′tic part′ner n. either member of an unmarried cohabiting couple.

domes′tic vi′olence n. acts of violence against a member of one's immediate family.

dom′i·cile (dom′ə sīl′, -səl, dō′mə-) n. a house or home.

dom′i·nant adj. ruling or controlling. —**dom′i·nance**, n.

dom′i·nate′ (dom′ə nāt′) v., -nated, -nating. —v.t. **1.** to rule over. **2.** to be the major influence in. **3.** to tower above. —v.i. **4.** to exercise power. **5.** to occupy a commanding position. —**dom′i·na′tion**, n.

dom′i·neer′ (dom′ə nēr′) v.i. to act in a way that forces others to behave; bully.

do·min′ion (də min′yən) n. **1.** authority to govern. **2.** the territory governed.

dom′i·no′ (dom′ə nō′) n., pl. -noes. **1.** a small, flat block marked with dots. **2. dominoes,** a game played with dominoes.

don (don) v.t., donned, donning. to put on.

do′nate (dō′nāt, dō nāt′) v.t., v.i., -nated, -nating. to contribute or give. —**do·na′tion**, n.

don′key (dong′kē, dông′-, dung′-) n. a long-eared domesticated animal related to the horse.

don′ny·brook′ (don′ē brŏŏk′) n. (often cap.) a brawl.

do′nor (dō′nər) n. one who donates.

doo′dle (dŏŏd′l) v.i., v.t., -dled, -dling. to draw or scribble idly.

doom (dŏŏm) n. **1.** adverse fate. **2.** ruin or death. **3.** an unfavorable judgment. —v.t. **4.** to destine to an adverse fate.

dooms′day′ n. the day of the Last Judgment.

door (dôr) n. **1.** a movable barrier for opening and closing an entrance, cabinet, etc. **2.** a doorway.

door′step′ n. a step in front of a door.

door′way′ n. the entrance to a building, room, etc.

dope (dōp) n., v., doped, doping. —n. **1.** Slang. a narcotic. **2.** Slang. information. **3.** Informal. a stupid person. —v.t. **4.** Slang. to drug.

dop′ey adj., -ier, -iest. Informal. **1.** stupid. **2.** sluggish or confused, as from drug use. Also, **dop′y.**

dor′mant (dôr′mənt) adj. **1.** temporarily inactive. **2.** undeveloped. —**dor′man·cy**, n.

dor′mer (dôr′mər) n. a vertical window in a projection built from a sloping roof.

dor′mi·to′ry (dôr′mi tôr′ē) n., pl. -ries. **1.** a building, as at a college, containing rooms for residents. **2.** communal sleeping quarters.

dor′mouse′ (dôr′mous′) n., pl. -mice. a small bushy-tailed rodent.

dor′sal (dôr′səl) adj. of or on the back.

do′ry (dôr′ē) n., pl. -ries. a flat-bottomed rowboat.

DOS (dôs) n. a disk operating system for microcomputers.

dose (dōs) n., v., dosed, dosing. —n. **1.** the amount of medicine taken at one time. —v.t. **2.** to give a dose of medicine to.

dos′si·er (dos′ē ā′) n. a file of documents containing detailed information.

dot (dot) n., v., dotted, dotting. —n. **1.** a small, roundish mark. **2.** the shorter signal in Morse code. **3.** a period, esp. as used in an Internet address. —v.t. **4.** to mark with dots.

do′tage (dō′tij) n. a decline of mental faculties in old age.

dote (dōt) v., doted, doting. **dote on,** to be excessively fond of.

dou′ble (dub′əl) adj., n., v., -bled, -bling. —adj. **1.** twice as large, as many, etc. **2.** composed of two like parts. **3.** suitable for two. **4.** folded in two. —n. **5.** a double quantity. **6.** a duplicate. **7. doubles,** a game between two pairs of players. —v.t. **8.** to make double. **9.** to bend or fold with one part over the other. **10.** to repeat. —v.i. **11.** to become double. **12.** to turn back. **13.** to serve in two capacities.

dou′ble bass′ (bās) n. the lowest-pitched instrument of the violin family.

doub′le-cross′ v.t. to cheat.

doub′le-dig′it adj. involving two-digit numbers.

dou′ble en·ten′dre (än tän′drə, -tänd′) n., pl. dou′ble en·ten′dres (än tän′drəz, -tändz′). a word or expression with two meanings, one of which is usually indecent.

dou′ble-head′er n. two games played on the same day in immediate succession.

dou′ble play′ n. a baseball play in which two players are put out.

dou′ble stand′ard n. any set of principles applied differently to one group than to another.

dou′ble take′ n. a delayed response, as to something not immediately recognized.

doub′le-talk′ n. speech that means something different from its apparent meaning.

doubt (dout) v.t. **1.** to be uncertain and undecided about. **2.** to distrust. —v.i. **3.** to be uncertain. —n. **4.** a feeling of uncertainty and indecision. **5.** distrust or suspicion.

doubt′ful adj. **1.** feeling doubt. **2.** causing doubt or suspicion.

douche (dŏŏsh) n., v., douched, douching. —n. **1.** a jet of liquid applied to a body part or cavity. —v.t., v.i. **2.** to apply a douche (to).

dough (dō) n. a mixture of flour, liquid, etc., for baking into bread, pastry, etc.

dough′nut (dō′nət, -nut′) n. a ringlike cake of fried, sweet dough.

dour (dŏŏr, douⁿr, dou′ər) adj. sullen; gloomy.

douse (dous) v.t., doused, dousing. **1.** to throw water on. **2.** to extinguish. **3.** to plunge into water.

dove¹ (duv) n. a bird of the pigeon family.

dove² (dōv) v. a pt. of dive.

dove′cote′ (-kōt′) n. a structure for housing tame pigeons.

dove′tail′ n. **1.** a wedge-shaped joint that interlocks two pieces of wood. —v.t., v.i. **2.** to join by means of a dovetail. **3.** to fit together harmoniously.

dow·a′ger (dou′ə jər) n. **1.** a titled or wealthy widow. **2.** a dignified elderly woman.

dow′dy (dou′dē) adj., -dier, -diest. not stylish.

dow′el (dou′əl) n. a wooden or metal pin fitting into a hole to hold two pieces of wood or stone together.

dow′er (dou′ər) n. a widow's share of her husband's property.

down¹ (doun) adv. **1.** to, at, or in a lower place or state. **2.** to a lower value or rate. **3.** to a lesser pitch or volume. **4.** from an earlier to a later time. **5.** from a greater to a lesser strength, amount, etc. **6.** in cash at the time of purchase. —prep. **7.** in a descending direction on or along. —adj. **8.** directed downward. **9.** being at a low position. **10.** depressed. —v.t. **11.** to knock, throw, or bring down. —Idiom. **12. down cold** or **pat,** learned perfectly. **13. down on,** hostile to.

down² (doun) n. the soft feathers of birds.

down′cast′ adj. dejected.

down′er n. Informal. **1.** a depressing experience. **2.** a sedative drug.

down′fall′ n. **1.** ruin. **2.** something causing ruin.

down′grade′ v., -graded, -grading, n. —v.t. **1.** to reduce in rank, importance, etc. —n. **2.** a downward slope.

down′heart′ed adj. dejected.

down′hill′ adv. (doun′hil′; adj. -hil′) adv. **1.** down a slope. **2.** into a worse condition. —adj. **3.** going downward. **4.** free of obstacles.

down′ pay′ment n. an amount given as partial payment when something is purchased.

down′play′ v.t. to minimize.

down′pour′ n. a heavy rain.

down′right′ adj. **1.** thorough. —adv. **2.** completely.

down′scale′ adj. of or for people at the lower end of the economic scale.

down′size′ v.t., -sized, -sizing. to reduce in size or number.

down′stage′ adv., adj. at or toward the front of the stage.

down′stairs′ (adv. -stârz′; adj. -stârz′) adv., adj. to or on a lower floor.

down′stream′ adv., adj. in the direction of the current of a stream.

Down′ syn′drome n. a genetic disorder characterized by mental retardation, a wide, flattened skull, and slanting eyes. Also, **Down′s syn′drome.**

down′-to-earth′ adj. practical.

down′trod′den adj. oppressed.

down′turn′ n. a downward trend.

down′ward, adv. **1.** Also, **down′wards.** to a lower level or condition. —adj. **2.** moving down.

down′wind′ (-wind′) adv., adj. in the direction toward which the wind is blowing.

down′y adj., -ier, -iest. like soft feathers.

dow′ry (dou′rē) n., pl. -ries. the property that a bride brings to her husband at marriage.

dowse (dous) v.i., **dowsed, dowsing.** to search for underground water using a divining rod.

dox·ol·o·gy (dok sol′ə jē) n., pl. **-gies.** a hymn praising God.

doz. dozen.

doze (dōz) v., **dozed, dozing,** n. —v.i. **1.** to sleep lightly. —n. **2.** a light sleep.

doz·en (duz′ən) n., pl. **dozen, dozens.** a group of 12.

Dr. 1. Doctor. **2.** Drive.

drab (drab) adj., **-ber, -best.** dull; uninteresting.

draft (draft) n. **1.** a drawing or sketch. **2.** a rough preliminary form of any writing. **3.** a current of air. **4.** selection for military service, an athletic team, etc. **5.** a written order for payment. **6.** the act of pulling loads on the load pulled. **7.** beer drawn from a cask. **8.** a drink or dose. —v.t. **9.** to sketch. **10.** to compose. **11.** to select by draft.

draft·ee′ n. a person who has been drafted, as for military service.

drafts′man n. a person employed in making mechanical drawings.

draft′y adj., **-ier, -iest.** letting in currents of air.

drag (drag) v., **dragged, dragging,** n. —v.t. **1.** to pull slowly and with effort; haul. **2.** to search (the bottom of a body of water). —v.i. **3.** to be drawn along. **4.** to trail on the ground. **5.** to move slowly and with effort. —n. **6.** any device for searching the bottom of a body of water. **7.** a hindrance. **8.** Slang. a bore. **9.** a puff on a cigarette, pipe, etc. **10.** Slang. clothing characteristically worn by the opposite sex.

drag′net′ n. **1.** a fishing net drawn along the bottom of a stream. **2.** a system for catching a criminal.

drag′on (drag′ən) n. a mythical reptile able to breath out fire.

drag′on·fly′ n., pl. **-flies.** an insect with a long, narrow body and four gauzy wings.

dra·goon′ (drə gōōn′) n. **1.** a heavily armed mounted soldier. —v.t. **2.** to force; coerce.

drag′ race′ n. a race with cars accelerating from a standstill.

drain (drān) v.t. **1.** to draw off (a liquid) gradually. **2.** to empty by drawing off liquid. **3.** to exhaust or use up gradually. —v.i. **4.** to flow off or empty gradually. —n. **5.** a channel or pipe for draining. **6.** a continuous outflow. —**drain′age,** n.

drake (drāk) n. a male duck.

dram (dram) n. an apothecaries′ weight, equal to ⅛ ounce.

dra′ma (drä′mə, dram′ə) n. **1.** a play for acting on the stage. **2.** a vivid series of events. **3.** dramatic quality.

dra·mat′ic (drə mat′ik) adj. **1.** of plays or the theater. **2.** highly vivid or compelling.

dra·mat′ics n. **1.** (used with a sing. v.) the performance of plays. **2.** (used with a pl. v.) exaggerated conduct or emotion.

dram′a·tist (dram′ə tist, drä′mə-) n. a writer of plays.

dram′a·tize′ v.t., **-tized, -tizing. 1.** to put into a form suitable for acting. **2.** to express vividly.

drank (drangk) v. pt. of **drink.**

drape (drāp) v., **draped, draping,** n. —v.t. **1.** to cover or hang loosely with fabric. **2.** to arrange in folds. —n. **3.** a long, heavy curtain. —**dra′per·y,** n.

dras′tic (dras′tik) adj. having a violent or harsh effect.

draught (draft) n. Brit. a draft.

draw (drô) v., **drew** (drōō), **drawn, drawing,** n. —v.t. **1.** to cause to move in a particular direction by pulling. **2.** to pull down, over, or out. **3.** to attract. **4.** to sketch. **5.** to take in, as a breath. **6.** to deduce. **7.** to stretch. **8.** to choose or have assigned to one at random. —v.i. **9.** to exert a pulling or attracting force. **10.** to move or pass. **11.** to take out a weapon. **12. draw on,** to make use of as a source. **13. ~ out, a.** to pull out. **b.** to prolong. **c.** to persuade to speak. —n. **14.** the act or result of drawing. **15.** something that attracts. **16.** something drawn. **17.** a contest that ends in a tie.

draw′back′ n. a disadvantage.

draw′bridge′ n. a bridge that can be raised.

draw′er (drôr for 1, 2; drô′ər for 3) n. **1.** a sliding, lidless box, as in a desk or bureau. **2. drawers,** underpants. **3.** a person who draws.

draw′ing n. **1.** a picture drawn with pencil or crayon. **2.** a lottery.

drawl (drôl) v.t., v.i. **1.** to speak slowly. —n. **2.** a drawled utterance.

drawn (drôn) adj. tense; haggard.

dray (drā) n. a low, strong cart without fixed sides.

dread (dred) v.t. **1.** to fear greatly. —n. **2.** great fear. —adj. **3.** feared.

dread′ful adj. **1.** causing dread. **2.** extremely bad.

dread′ful·ly adv. very.

dread′locks′ n. a hairstyle of many long, ropelike pieces.

dream (drēm) n. **1.** a series of images or thoughts passing through the mind during sleep. **2.** a daydream. **3.** a goal. **4.** something of unreal beauty. —v.i. **5.** to have a dream. —v.t. **6.** to see imagine in a dream. **7.** to imagine as possible.

dream′ team′ n. a group of highly skilled experts.

drear′y adj., **-ier, -iest. 1.** gloomy; sad. **2.** boring. —**drear′i·ly,** adv.

dredge¹ (drej) n., v., **dredged, dredging.** —n. **1.** a machine for scooping up mud. —v.t. **2.** to remove with a dredge.

dredge² (drej) v.t., **dredged, dredging.** to coat (food) with flour.

dregs (dregz) n.pl. **1.** the matter that settles to the bottom of a liquid. **2.** the least valuable part of anything.

drench (drench) v.t. to soak.

dress (dres) n. **1.** a woman′s garment consisting of bodice and skirt in one piece. **2.** clothing. —v.t. **3.** to clothe. **4.** to decorate. **5.** to prepare for cooking or for use. **6.** to treat (wounds). —v.i. **7.** to put on one′s clothes. **8. dress down, a.** to scold. **b.** to dress informally. **9. ~ up, a.** to put on one′s best clothing. **b.** to dress in costume.

dres·sage′ (drə säzh′, dre-) n. the art of training a horse in obedience and precision of movement.

dress′ cir′cle n. the first gallery of seats in a theater.

dress′er¹ n. a chest of drawers.

dress′er² n. a person employed to dress others.

dress′ing n. **1.** a sauce, as for a salad. **2.** a stuffing, as for a fowl. **3.** material to dress a wound.

dress′ rehears′al n. a final rehearsal with costumes.

dress′y adj., **-ier, -iest.** fancy or formal.

drew (drōō) v. pt. of **draw.**

drib′ble (drib′əl) v., **-bled, -bling,** n. —v.i., v.t. **1.** to fall or let fall in drops. **2.** to advance (a ball or puck) by bouncing it or pushing it. —n. **3.** a trickle or drop.

dri′er (drī′ər) n. a dryer.

drift (drift) n. **1.** an act or instance of being carried along by currents of water or air. **2.** a deviation from a set course. **3.** a tendency. **4.** something piled up by wind. —v.i. **5.** to be carried along by currents. **6.** to wander aimlessly. **7.** to be driven into heaps, as snow. —v.t. **8.** to cause to drift.

drift′er n. a person who moves frequently from one place or job to another.

drill¹ (dril) n. **1.** a shaftlike tool for making holes. **2.** any strict, methodical exercise. —v.t., v.i. **3.** to pierce with a drill. **4.** to perform or make perform training drills.

drill² (dril) n. **1.** a furrow for seeds. **2.** a machine for sowing seeds.

drill³ (dril) n. a strong twilled cotton fabric.

drink (dringk) v., **drank** (drangk), **drunk** (drungk), **drinking,** n. —v.t. **1.** to swallow (a liquid). —v.i. **2.** to swallow a liquid. **3.** to consume alcoholic drinks, esp. to excess. —n. **4.** any liquid for drinking. **5.** alcoholic liquors.

drip (drip) v., **dripped, dripping,** n. —v.i., v.t. **1.** to fall or let fall in drops. —n. **2.** the act or sound of dripping. **3.** liquid that drips.

drive (drīv) v., **drove** (drōv), **driven, driving,** n. —v.t. **1.** to send or expel by force. **2.** to force in or down. **3.** to convey in a vehicle. **4.** to cause and guide the movement of. **5.** to urge. —v.i. **6.** to cause and guide the movement of a vehicle or animal. **7.** to travel in a vehicle. **8.** to strive toward a goal. **9. drive at,** to intend to convey. —n. **10.** a trip in a vehicle. **11.** an inner urge. **12.** a strong effort toward a goal. **13.** energy. **14.** a road for vehicles. **15.** a military offensive.

drive′-by′ adj., n., pl. **drive-bys.** —adj. **1.** occurring while driving past a person. **2.** casual; offhand. —n. **3.** a drive-by shooting.

drive′-in′ n. a facility or business

that may be used without getting out of one′s car.

driv′el (driv′əl) n. foolish talk.

drive′way′ n. a road on private property.

driz′zle (driz′əl) v., **-zled, -zling,** —v.i. **1.** to rain in fine drops. —n. **2.** a very light rain.

droll (drōl) adj. amusing in an odd way.

drom·e·dar·y (drom′i der′ē, drum′-) n., pl. **-daries.** a single-humped camel.

drone¹ (drōn) n. **1.** the male of the honeybee. **2.** a lazy person.

drone² (drōn) v., **droned, droning.** —v.i. **1.** to make a deep humming sound. **2.** to speak in a dull, monotonous tone. —n. **3.** a deep humming sound.

drool (drōōl) v.i. **1.** to water at the mouth; salivate. —n. **2.** saliva dripping from the mouth.

droop (drōōp) v.i. **1.** to sink, bend, or hang down. **2.** to lose spirit or courage. —n. **3.** a drooping.

drop (drop) n., v., **dropped, dropping.** —n. **1.** a small, rounded mass of liquid. **2.** a small quantity. **3. drops,** liquid medicine given in drops. **4.** an act of falling. **5.** the distance of a fall. **6.** a steep descent. **7.** a decline in amount, value, etc. —v.i. **8.** to fall in drops. **9.** to fall lower or backward. **10.** to sink. —v.t. **11.** to let fall in drops. **12.** to let or cause to fall. **13.** to reduce in value, quality, etc. **14.** to leave out; omit. **15.** to remove or dismiss. **16. drop in,** to pay a casual visit. **17. ~ off,** to fall asleep. **b.** to decline. **18. ~ out,** to withdraw.

drop′ kick′ n. a kick made by dropping a ball to the ground and kicking it as it starts to bounce up.

drop′out′ n. a person who withdraws, esp. a student who leaves school before graduation.

drop′per n. a small tube with a squeezable bulb for drawing in a liquid and expelling it in drops.

dross (drôs) n. waste matter.

drought (drout) n. a long period of dry weather.

drove (drōv) v. **1.** pt. of **drive.** —n. **2.** a group of driven cattle. **3.** Usu. **droves.** a large crowd.

drown (droun) v.i. **1.** to die by suffocation in liquid. —v.t. **2.** to kill by suffocation in liquid. **3.** to flood. **4. drown out,** to overpower, as by a louder sound.

drow′sy (drou′zē) adj., **-sier, -siest.** sleepy.

drub (drub) v.t., **drubbed, drubbing. 1.** to beat. **2.** to defeat.

drudge (druj) n., v., **drudged, drudging.** —n. **1.** a person who does dull or menial work. —v.i. **2.** to do such work. —**drudg′er·y,** n.

drug (drug) n., v., **drugged, drugging.** —n. **1.** a chemical substance used in medicine. **2.** a narcotic. —v.t. **3.** to add or give a drug to.

drug′gist n. a person licensed to prepare and sell drugs and medicines; pharmacist.

drug′store′ n. a store that sells medicines, toiletries, etc.

Dru·id (drōō′id) n. (often l.c.) a member of a pre-Christian, Celtic religious order. —**Dru′id·ism,** n.

drum (drum) n., v., **drummed, drumming.** —n. **1.** a percussion instrument consisting of a round frame covered with a tightly stretched membrane that is struck to produce a sound. **2.** any cylindrical object. **3.** the eardrum. —v.i. **4.** to beat a drum. **5.** to tap one′s fingers rhythmically. —v.t. **6.** to perform by beating a drum. **7. drum up,** to get by vigorous effort.

drum′ ma′jor n. the leader of a marching band.

drum′ majorette′ n. a majorette.

drum′stick′ n. **1.** a stick for beating a drum. **2.** the leg of a cooked fowl.

drunk (drungk) adj. **1.** having one′s mental and physical powers impaired by alcoholic drink. —n. **2.** a drunk person. —v. **3.** pp. of **drink.**

drunk′ard (drung′kərd) n. a person who is habitually drunk.

drunk′en (drung′kən) adj. **1.** intoxicated. **2.** caused or marked by intoxication.

dry (drī) adj., **drier, driest,** v., **dried, drying.** —adj. **1.** not wet. **2.** without rain. **3.** empty of or not yielding liquid. **4.** thirsty. **5.** dull; uninteresting. **6.** not expressing emotion. **7.** not allowing the sale of alcoholic beverages. **8.** (of wine) not sweet. —v.t., v.i. **9.** to make or become dry. —**dry′ly, dri′ly** adv.

dry′ad (drī′əd, -ad) n. (often cap.) (in Greek myth) a wood nymph.

dry′-clean′ v.t. to clean (clothing) with solvents. —**dry′-clean′er,** n.

drive′way′ n. a road on private property.

dry′er n. a machine for drying.

dry′ ice′ n. solid carbon dioxide, used esp. as a refrigerant.

dry′ run′ n. a rehearsal or trial.

DST daylight-saving time.

du′al (dōō′əl, dyōō′-) adj. twofold.

dub¹ (dub) v.t., **dubbed, dubbing.** to name formally.

dub² (dub) v.t., **dubbed, dubbing.** to furnish (a film or tape) with a new sound track.

du′bi·ous (dōō′bē əs) adj. doubtful.

du′cal (dōō′kəl, dyōō′-) adj. of dukes.

duch′ess (duch′is) n. **1.** a duke′s wife. **2.** a woman equal in rank to a duke.

duch′y (duch′ē) n., pl. **duchies.** the territory of a duke or duchess.

duck¹ (duk) n. a web-footed swimming bird with a broad, flat bill.

duck² (duk) v.i., v.t. **1.** to lower or bend (the head or body) suddenly. **2.** to evade. **3.** to plunge under water.

duck³ (duk) n. a heavy cotton fabric.

duck′ling n. a young duck.

duct (dukt) n. any tube, canal, pipe, etc., by which liquid or air is conveyed. —**duct′less,** adj.

duc′tile (duk′tl, -til) adj. **1.** (of metal) readily drawn out into wire. **2.** capable of being shaped.

duct′ tape′ (duk, dukt) n. a strongly adhesive cloth tape.

dud (dud) n. a failure.

dude (dōōd, dyōōd) n. **1.** a man excessively concerned with his clothes. **2.** Slang. a fellow; guy.

dudg′eon (duj′ən) n. anger.

due (dōō, dyōō) adj. **1.** owing or owed. **2.** proper. **3.** adequate. **4.** expected. —n. **5.** something owed or naturally belonging to someone. **6. dues,** a regular fee for membership. —adv. **7.** directly or exactly.

du′el (dōō′əl, dyōō′-) n., v., **-eled, -eling.** —n. **1.** a planned combat between two persons. —v.t., v.i. **2.** to fight in a duel. —**du′el·ist,** n.

du·et′ (dōō et′, dyōō-) n. a musical composition for two performers.

duf′fel bag′ (duf′əl) n. a large, cylindrical bag.

dug (dug) v. a pt. and pp. of **dig.**

dug′out′ n. **1.** a boat made by hollowing out a log. **2.** a roofed structure where baseball players sit when not on the field. **3.** a rough shelter dug in the ground.

duke (dōōk, dyōōk) n. a nobleman ranking immediately below a prince. —**duke′dom,** n.

dul′cet (dul′sit) adj. melodious.

dul′ci·mer (dul′sə mər) n. a musical instrument with metal strings that are struck with light hammers.

dull (dul) adj. **1.** not sharp. **2.** not bright. **3.** boring; tedious. **4.** stupid. **5.** not lively. —v.t., v.i. **6.** to make or become dull.

dull′ard (-ərd) n. a stupid person.

du′ly (dōō′lē, dyōō′-) adv. **1.** properly. **2.** punctually.

dumb (dum) adj. **1.** silly or stupid. **2.** lacking the power of speech. **3.** silent.

dumb′bell′ n. **1.** a bar with weighted ends, used for exercising. **2.** Slang. a stupid person.

dumb·found′ (dum found′, dum′-found′) v.t. to astonish.

dumb′wait′er n. a small elevator for moving food, garbage, etc.

dum′my n., pl. **-mies,** adj. —n. **1.** an imitation or copy. **2.** a model of the human figure, used for displaying clothes. **3.** Informal. a stupid person. —adj. **4.** counterfeit.

dump (dump) v.t. **1.** to drop in a heap. **2.** to unload. **3.** to discard or dismiss. —n. **4.** a place where garbage is deposited. **5.** Informal. a dilapidated, dirty place.

dump′ling (-ling) n. **1.** a mass of boiled dough. **2.** a wrapping of dough enclosing a filling.

dump′y adj., **-ier, -iest.** short and stout.

dun¹ (dun) v., **dunned, dunning,** —v.t. **1.** to make repeated demands upon for the payment of a debt. —n. **2.** a demand for payment.

dun² (dun) adj. a dull grayish brown.

dunce (duns) n. a stupid person.

dune (dōōn, dyōōn) n. a sand hill formed by the wind.

dung (dung) n. manure.

dun′ga·rees′ (dung′gə rēz′) n.pl. overalls or trousers of blue denim.

dun′geon (dun′jən) n. a strong underground prison.

dunk (dungk) v.t. **1.** to dip in a beverage before eating. **2.** to submerge briefly in liquid.

du′o (dōō′ō, dyōō′ō) n. **1.** a duet. **2.** a couple or pair.

du′o·de′num (dōō′ə dē′nəm, dyōō′-; dōō od′n əm, dyōō-) n. the upper part of the small intestine.

dupe (dōōp, dyōōp) n., v., **duped, duping.** —n. **1.** a person who is easily fooled. —v.t. **2.** to deceive.

du′plex (dōō′pleks, dyōō′-) n. **1.** an apartment with two floors. **2.** a house for two families.

du′pli·cate adj., n., v., **-cated, -cating.** —adj. (dōō′pli kit) **1.** exactly like something else. **2.** double. —n. (-kit) **3.** an exact copy. —v.t. (-kāt′) **4.** to make an exact copy of. **5.** to repeat.

du·plic′i·ty (dōō plis′i tē, dyōō-) n., pl. **-ties.** deceitfulness.

du′ra·ble (dōōr′ə bəl, dyōōr′-) adj. lasting. —**du′ra·bil′i·ty,** n.

du·ra′tion (dōō rā′shən, dyōō-) n. the length of time something continues.

du·ress′ (dōō res′, dyōō-, door′is, dyoor′-) n. the use of force.

dur′ing (dōōr′ing, dyōōr′-) prep. **1.** throughout **2.** at some point in the course of.

du′rum (dōōr′əm, dyōōr′-) n. a wheat yielding flour used in pasta.

dusk (dusk) n. twilight.

dust (dust) n. **1.** fine particles of earth or other matter. —v.t. **2.** to wipe the dust from. **3.** to sprinkle with powder or dust. —v.i. **4.** to wipe dust from furniture, woodwork, etc. —**dust′y,** adj.

Dutch (duch) adj. **1.** of the Netherlands, its inhabitants, or their language. —n. **2.** the language of the Netherlands and N and W Belgium. **3.** the people of the Netherlands.

Dutch′ door′ n. a door that is horizontally divided so that each half can be opened separately.

Dutch′ ov′en n. a heavy pot with a close-fitting lid.

Dutch′ treat′ n. a meal or entertainment for which each person pays his or her own way.

Dutch′ un′cle n. a mentor who criticizes very frankly.

du′te·ous (dōō′tē əs, dyōō′-) adj. dutiful; obedient.

du′ti·ful adj. performing the duties expected of one.

du′ty (dōō′tē, dyōō′-) n., pl. **-ties. 1.** moral or legal obligation. **2.** action required by one′s position or occupation. **3.** a tax on imports and exports.

DVD an optical disc that can store a very large amount of digital data, as text, music, or images.

dwarf (dwôrf) n. **1.** a person, animal, or plant of abnormally small size. —adj. **2.** of small size. —v.t. **3.** to cause to seem small by comparison. **4.** to stunt.

dweeb (dwēb) n. Slang. a nerd; wimp.

dwell (dwel) v.i., **dwelt** or **dwelled, dwelling. 1.** to live or stay as a resident. **2. dwell on,** to think, speak, or write about at length. —**dwell′ing,** n.

dwin′dle (dwin′dl) v.i., v.t., **-dled, -dling.** to make or become less.

dye (dī) n., v., **dyed, dyeing.** —n. **1.** a substance used to color cloth, hair, etc. —v.t. **2.** to color with a dye.

dyed′-in-the-wool′ adj. complete.

dyke (dīk) n. **1.** a dike. **2.** Slang: Usu. Disparaging and Offensive. (a term used to refer to a female homosexual.)

dy·nam′ic (dī nam′ik) adj. **1.** forceful; energetic. **2.** of force or energy.

dy′na·mite′ (dī′nə mīt′) n., v., **-mited, -miting.** —n. **1.** a powerful explosive made of nitroglycerin. —v.t. **2.** to blow up with dynamite.

dy′na·mo′ (-mō′) n., pl. **-mos. 1.** a machine for generating electricity. **2.** an energetic, forceful person.

dy′nas·ty (dī′nə stē) n., pl. **-ties.** a line of rulers from the same family.

dys- a prefix meaning ill or bad.

dys′en·ter′y (dis′ən ter′ē) n. an infectious disease of the intestines.

dys·func′tion n. impairment of function or malfunctioning.

dys·lex′i·a (dis lek′sē ə) n. a learning disorder causing abnormal difficulty in reading and spelling. —**dys·lex′ic,** adj., n.

dys·pep′sia (dis pep′shə, -sē ə) n. indigestion.

dz. dozen.

E

E, e (ē) *n.* the fifth letter of the English alphabet.

E 1. east, eastern. 2. English.

ea. each.

each (ēch) *adj., pron.* 1. every one of two or more. —*adv.* 2. to, from, or for each.

ea·ger (ē′gər) *adj.* full of desire or enthusiasm. —**ea′ger·ness,** *n.*

ea·gle (ē′gəl) *n.* a large bird of prey.

ea·gle-eyed *adj.* having unusually sharp eyesight.

ea·glet (ē′glit) *n.* a young eagle.

ear[1] (ēr) *n.* 1. the organ of hearing. 2. the external part of this. 3. the sense of hearing. 4. attention. 5. an ear-shaped part. —*Idiom.* 6. **be all ears,** to listen intently. 7. **play it by ear,** to improvise.

ear[2] (ēr) *n.* the seed-bearing part of a cereal plant, as corn.

ear′drum′ *n.* a thin membrane in the ear that vibrates when struck by sound waves.

earl (ûrl) *n.* a nobleman ranking below a marquis. —**earl′dom,** *n.*

ear′lobe′ or **ear′ lobe′** *n.* the soft lower part of the external ear.

ear·ly (ûr′lē) *adj.,* -lier, -liest, *adj.* 1. in or during the first part of a period of time or series of events. 2. before the expected time.

ear′mark′ *v.t.* to set aside for a particular purpose.

ear′muffs′ *n.pl.* warm connected coverings for the ears.

earn (ûrn) *v.t.* 1. to gain in return for labor or by one's merit. 2. to produce as interest or profit.

ear′nest (ûr′nist) *adj.* 1. serious. 2. showing sincerity of feeling.

earn′ings *n.pl.* wages or profits.

ear′phone′ (ēr′fōn′) *n.* a sound receiver that fits on the ear.

ear′ring′ (ēr′ring′, ēr′ing) *n.* an ornament worn on the earlobe.

ear′shot′ *n.* range of hearing.

ear′split′ting *adj.* extremely loud or shrill.

earth (ûrth) *n.* 1. (*often cap.*) the planet third in order from the sun. 2. the surface of the earth; ground. 3. soil and dirt.

earth′en *adj.* made of clay or earth.

earth′en·ware′ *n.* pottery made of baked clay.

earth′ly *adj.,* -lier, -liest. 1. of the earth, as opposed to heaven. 2. conceivable.

earth′quake′ *n.* a series of vibrations of the earth's surface.

earth′shak′ing *adj.* significantly affecting something basic.

earth′work′ *n.* a fortification formed of earth.

earth′worm′ *n.* a worm that burrows in the soil.

earth′y *adj.,* -ier, -iest. 1. of earth or soil. 2. coarse; unrefined.

ease (ēz) *n., v.,* eased, easing. —*n.* 1. freedom from pain, trouble, anxiety, effort, etc. —*v.t.* 2. to free from care or pain. 3. to make less difficult. —*v.i.* 4. to become less difficult or painful.

ea′sel (ē′zəl) *n.* a support stand, as for a painting.

ease′ment *n.* a right by one property owner to use the land of another for a specific purpose.

east (ēst) *n.* 1. a cardinal point of the compass, the direction in which the sun rises. 2. **the East,** a region in this direction. —*adj.* 3. toward, in, or from the east. —*east′ern, adj.* —*east′ern·er, n.* —*east′ward, adv., adj.*

East′er (ē′stər) *n.* a festival celebrating Christ's resurrection.

east′er·ly *adj., adv.* toward or blowing from the east.

East′ern Hem′isphere *n.* the part of the globe east of the Atlantic, including Asia, Africa, Australia, and Europe.

eas′y (ē′zē) *adj.,* easier, easiest, *adv.* 1. not difficult. 2. free from pain, worry, or care. 3. not forced or hurried. —*adv.* 4. in an easy way. —*eas′i·ly, adv.*

eas′y-go′ing *adj.* casual; relaxed.

eat (ēt) *v.,* ate (āt), eating, eaten. —*v.t.* 1. to take into the mouth and swallow. 2. to wear away or dissolve. —*v.i.* 3. to have a meal.

eat′ing disor′der *n.* a disorder characterized by severe disturbances in eating habits.

eaves (ēvz) *n.pl.* the overhanging lower edge of a roof.

eaves′drop′ *v.i.,* -dropped, -dropping. to listen secretly.

ebb (eb) *n.* 1. the flowing back of the tide as the water returns to the sea. 2. a decline. —*v.i.* 3. to flow back. 4. to decline.

eb′on·y (eb′ə nē) *n., pl.* -ies. 1. a hard black wood from trees of Africa and Asia. 2. a deep black.

eBook (ē′book′) *n.* a portable electronic device used to download and read books or magazines that are in digital form. Also, **e-book.**

e·bul′lient (i bul′yənt, i bool′-) *adj.* full of enthusiasm and high spirits.

ec·cen′tric (ik sen′trik) *adj.* 1. unconventional. 2. not having the same center. 3. not placed in the center. 4. not circular, as an orbit. —*n.* 5. an unconventional person. —*ec′cen·tric′i·ty* (-tris′i tē) *n.*

ec·cle′si·as′tic (i klē′zē as′tik) *n.* a member of the clergy. —*adj.* 2. Also, **ec·cle′si·as′ti·cal.** of a church or the clergy.

ech′e·lon (esh′ə lon′) *n.* a level of command or rank.

ech′o (ek′ō) *n., pl.* echoes, *v.,* echoed, echoing. —*n.* 1. a repetition of sound caused by the reflection of sound waves. 2. an imitation. —*v.i.* 3. to be repeated by an echo. —*v.t.* 4. to repeat in imitation.

é·clair′ (ā klâr′) *n.* a cream- or custard-filled pastry.

é·clat′ (ā klä′) *n.* 1. brilliance of success or reputation. 2. acclaim.

ec·lec′tic (i klek′tik) *adj.* chosen from various sources.

e·clipse′ (i klips′) *n., v.,* eclipsed, eclipsing. —*n.* 1. the blocking of the light of one heavenly body by another. 2. loss of splendor or status. —*v.t.* 3. to obscure.

e·clip′tic (i klip′tik) *n.* the apparent annual path of the sun.

e′co·cide′ (ek′ə sīd′, ē′kə-) *n.* the destruction of large areas of the natural environment.

e·col′o·gy (i kol′ə jē) *n.* the study of the relationship between organisms and the environment. —*e·col′o·gist, n.*

ec′o·nom′i·cal (ek′ə nom′i kəl, ē′kə-) *adj.* avoiding waste; thrifty.

ec′o·nom′ics *n.* 1. the science of the production, distribution, and use of goods and services. 2. (*used with a pl. v.*) financial considerations. —*ec′o·nom′ic, adj.* —*e·con′o·mist* (i kon′ə mist) *n.*

e·con′o·mize′ (i kon′ə mīz′) *v.i.,* -mized, -mizing. to be thrifty.

e·con′o·my *n., pl.* -mies. 1. thrifty management. 2. the management of the resources of an area. 3. the prosperity or earnings of a place. 4. the efficient use of something.

ec′o·sys′tem (ek′ō sis′təm, ē′kō-) *n.* a system formed by the interaction of a group of organisms with its environment.

ec′ru (ek′roo) *n.* a light brown; beige. Also, **éc·ru** (ā′kroo).

ec′sta·sy (ek′stə sē) *n., pl.* -sies. 1. intense delight. 2. an overpowering emotion. —*ec·stat′ic* (ek stat′ik) *adj.*

ec′u·men′i·cal (ek′yoo men′i kəl) *adj.* 1. universal. 2. pertaining to or fostering worldwide Christian unity.

ec′ze·ma (ek′sə mə, eg′zə-, ig zē′-) *n.* a skin disease causing itching and scaling.

E′dam (ē′dəm) *n.* a mild yellow Dutch cheese produced in a round shape.

ed′dy (ed′ē) *n., pl.* -dies, *v.,* -died, -dying. —*n.* 1. a current running counter to the main current. —*v.t., v.i.* 2. to whirl in eddies.

e′del·weiss′ (ād′l vīs′, -wīs′) *n.* a small, flowering Alpine plant.

e·de′ma (i dē′mə) *n.* abnormal retention of fluid in body tissue.

E′den (ēd′n) *n.* the garden where Adam and Eve first lived; paradise.

edge (ej) *n., v.,* edged, edging. —*n.* 1. the line at which something ends. 2. a verge. 3. the thin, sharp side of a blade. 4. sharpness. —*v.t.* 5. to border. —*v.i.* 6. to move gradually. —**edge′wise′,** *adv.*

edg′y *adj.,* -ier, -iest. nervous or tense.

ed′i·ble (ed′ə bəl) *adj.* fit to be eaten. —*ed′i·bil′i·ty, n.*

e′dict (ē′dikt) *n.* an official decree.

ed′i·fice (ed′ə fis) *n.* a large building.

ed′i·fy′ *v.t.,* -fied, -fying. to instruct and improve. —*ed′i·fi·ca′tion, n.*

ed′it (ed′it) *v.t.* 1. to prepare (a manuscript) for publication. 2. to

revise or correct. 3. to prepare (film or tape) by arranging sections.

e·di′tion (i dish′ən) *n.* 1. the form in which a literary work is published. 2. the number of copies printed at one time. 3. a version of something.

ed′i·to′ri·al (ed′i tôr′ē əl) *n.* 1. an article in a periodical presenting the opinion of the publishers or editors. —*adj.* 2. of an editor or editing. 3. of or resembling an editorial. —*ed′i·to′ri·al·ize′, v.i.*

ed′u·cate′ (ej′ŏŏ kāt′) *v.t.,* -cated, -cating. 1. to develop the mind and abilities of. 2. to provide with training or information. —*ed′u·ca′tion, n.* —*ed′u·ca′tion·al, adj.*

EEG electroencephalogram.

eel (ēl) *n.* a snakelike fish.

e′er (âr) *adv. Poetic.* ever.

ee′rie (ēr′ē) *adj.,* -rier, -riest. strange and mysterious; unsettling. —*ee′ri·ly, adv.*

ef·face′ (i fās′) *v.t.,* -faced, -facing. 1. to wipe out. 2. to make inconspicuous. —*ef·face′ment, n.*

ef·fect′ (i fekt′) *n.* 1. a result; consequence. 2. the power to produce results. 3. operation. 4. an impression. 5. **effects,** personal property. —*v.t.* 6. to accomplish or produce. —*Usage.* See AFFECT.

ef·fec′tive *adj.* 1. producing the intended results. 2. in operation. 3. striking. —*ef·fec′tive·ness, n.*

ef·fec′tive·ly *adv.* 1. in an effective way. 2. for all practical purposes.

ef·fec′tu·al (-chŏŏ əl) *adj.* producing an intended effect.

ef·fem′i·nate (i fem′ə nit) *adj.* (of a man) having traits usu. considered feminine.

ef′fer·vesce′ (ef′ər ves′) *v.i.,* -vesced, -vescing. 1. to give off bubbles of gas. 2. to show liveliness. —*ef′fer·ves′cence, n.* —*ef′fer·ves′cent, adj.*

ef·fete′ (i fēt′) *adj.* 1. decadent. 2. worn out.

ef′fi·ca′cious (ef′i kā′shəs) *adj.* producing the desired result. —*ef′fi·ca·cy* (-kə sē) *n.*

ef·fi′cient (i fish′ənt) *adj.* acting effectively without waste of time or effort. —*ef·fi′cien·cy, n.*

ef′fi·gy (ef′i jē) *n., pl.* -gies. an image of a person, esp. someone disliked.

ef·flu′ent (ef′lŏŏ ənt) *adj.* 1. flowing out. —*n.* 2. something that flows out.

ef·flu′vi·um (i flŏŏ′vē əm) *n., pl.* -via (-vē ə), -vi·ums. an often disagreeable vapor or odor.

ef′fort (ef′ərt) *n.* 1. exertion of energy. 2. something achieved by exertion.

ef·fron′ter·y (i frun′tə rē) *n., pl.* -teries. impudence.

ef·ful′gent (i ful′jənt) *adj.* shining brilliantly. —*ef·ful′gence, n.*

ef·fu′sion (i fyŏŏ′zhən) *n.* 1. the act or result of pouring forth. 2. an unrestrained expression. —*ef·fu′sive, adj.*

e.g. for example.

e·gal′i·tar′i·an (i gal′i târ′ē ən) *adj.* asserting or resulting from belief in the equality of all people.

egg[1] (eg) *n.* 1. the roundish reproductive body produced by the female of certain animals. 2. a female reproductive cell; ovum.

egg[2] (eg) *v.* egg on, to urge on.

egg′head′ *n. Informal.* an intellectual.

egg′nog′ *n.* a drink containing eggs, milk, sugar, and usu. rum.

egg′plant′ *n.* a dark-purple vegetable.

egg′ roll′ *n.* a casing of egg dough rolled around minced meat, vegetables, etc., and fried.

egg′shell′ *n.* the shell of a bird's egg.

eg′lan·tine′ (eg′lan tīn′, -tēn′) *n.* the sweetbrier.

e′go (ē′gō) *n.* the self.

e′go·cen′tric (-sen′trik) *adj.* self-centered.

e′go·ism *n.* self-centeredness. —*e′go·ist, n.*

e′go·tism *n.* 1. conceit. 2. selfishness. —*e′go·tist, n.* —*e′go·tis′tic, e′go·tis′ti·cal, adj.*

e·gre′gious (i grē′jəs) *adj.* extraordinarily bad; flagrant.

e′gress (ē′gres) *n.* an exit.

e′gret (ē′grit) *n.* a kind of heron.

E·gyp′tian (i jip′shən) *adj.* 1. of Egypt or its inhabitants. —*n.* 2. a native of Egypt.

eh (ā, e) *interj.* (an exclamation of surprise or doubt.)

ei′der·down′ (ī′dər doun′) *n.* 1. down from the female **eider duck,** a northern sea duck. 2. a quilt filled with eiderdown.

eight (āt) *n., adj.* seven plus one. —**eighth,** *adj., n.*

eight′ball′ *n.* 1. (in pool) a black ball bearing the number eight. —*Idiom.* 2. **behind the eightball,** in a difficult situation.

eight′een′ (ā′tēn′) *n., adj.* ten plus eight. —**eight·eenth′,** *adj., n.*

eight′y *n., adj.* ten times eight. —**eight′i·eth,** *adj., n.*

ein·stein′i·um (īn stī′nē əm) *n.* a synthetic, radioactive metallic element.

ei′ther (ē′thər, ī′thər) *adj., pron.* 1. one or the other of two. 2. each of two. —*conj.* 3. (used with or to indicate a choice.) —*adv.* 4. as well. —*Pronunciation.* The pronunciations (ē′thər) for the word EITHER and (nē′thər) for the word NEITHER, with the vowel of *see,* are the usual ones in American English. The pronunciations (ī′thər) and (nī′thər) with the vowel of *sigh,* occur occasionally in the U.S., chiefly in the speech of the educated and in standard broadcasting English. Since the 19th century, the (ī) has been the more common pronunciation in standard British speech.

e·jac′u·late′ (i jak′yə lāt′) *v.t., v.i.,* -lated, -lating. 1. to eject (semen). 2. to exclaim. —*e·jac′u·la′tion, n.*

e·ject′ (i jekt′) *v.t.* to drive or force out.

eke (ēk) *v.,* eked, eking. **eke out,** 1. to supplement. 2. to make (a living) with difficulty.

e·lab′o·rate *adj., v.,* -rated, -rating. —*adj.* (i lab′ər it) 1. worked out in great detail. 2. ornate. —*v.t.* (-ə rāt′) 3. to work out in great detail. —*v.i.* 4. to expand.

é·lan′ (ā län′, ā län′) *n.* dash or vivacity.

e·lapse′ (i laps′) *v.i.,* elapsed, elapsing. to slip or slip by.

e·las′tic (i las′tik) *adj.* 1. able to return to its original length or shape after being stretched. 2. adaptable. 3. springy. —*n.* 4. elastic material.

e·late′ (i lāt′) *v.t.,* elated, elating. to make extremely happy. —*e·la′tion, n.*

el′bow (el′bō) *n.* 1. the joint between the upper arm and the forearm. —*v.t.* 2. to push aside with one's elbow.

el′bow grease′ *n.* hard work.

el′bow·room′ *n.* space to move or work freely.

eld′er[1] (el′dər) *adj.* older. —*n.* 2. an older person.

eld′er[2] (el′dər) *n.* a small tree bearing clusters of red, black, or yellow **el′der·ber′ries.**

eld′er·ly *adj.* approaching old age.

eld′est (el′dist) *adj.* oldest.

e·lect′ (i lekt′) *v.t.* 1. to select by vote. 2. to choose. —*adj.* 3. chosen.

e·lec′tion *n.* 1. the act of electing. 2. the fact of being elected.

e·lec′tion·eer′ *v.i.* to work for a candidate in an election.

e·lec′tive *adj.* 1. chosen by election. 2. empowered to elect. 3. optional. —*n.* 4. an elective academic course.

e·lec′tor·al col′lege (-tər əl) *n.* a body of special voters (**electors**) chosen to elect the president and vice-president of U.S.

e·lec′tor·ate (-tər it) *n.* a body of voters.

e·lec′tric (i lek′trik) *adj.* 1. Also, **e·lec′tri·cal.** pertaining to electricity. 2. exciting. —*e·lec′tri·cal·ly, adv.*

e·lec′tri′cian (i lek trish′ən, ē′lek-) *n.* a person who installs or repairs electrical systems.

e·lec′tric′i·ty (-tris′i tē) *n.* 1. a fundamental form of energy occurring in matter and having effects such as light, heat, etc. 2. electric current.

e·lec′tri·fy′ (-trə fī′) *v.t.,* -fied, -fying. 1. to charge with electricity. 2. to supply with or equip for use of electric power. 3. to thrill. —*e·lec′tri·fi·ca′tion, n.*

e·lec′tro·car′di·o·gram′ (i lek′trō kär′dē ə gram′) *n.* a graphic record of heart action produced by an electrocardiograph.

e·lec′tro·car′di·o·graph′ *n.* an instrument that records heart movements.

e·lec′tro·cute′ (i lek′trə kyōōt′) *v.t.,* -cuted, -cuting. to kill by electricity.

e·lec′trode (i lek′trōd) *n.* a conductor through which an electric current enters or exits a nonmetallic portion of a circuit.

e·lec′tro·en·ceph′a·lo·gram′ (i lek′trō en sef′ə lə gram′) *n.* the graphic record produced by an electroencephalograph.

e·lec′tro·en·ceph′a·lo·graph′ *n.* an instrument for measuring and recording the electric activity of the brain.

e·lec·trol′o·gist (i lek trol′ə jist) *n.* a person trained in electrolysis for removing unwanted hair.

e·lec·trol′y·sis (-ə sis) *n.* 1. the passage of an electric current through an electrolyte. 2. the destruction of hair roots by electric current.

e·lec′tro·lyte′ (-trə līt′) *n.* a substance that conducts electricity when melted or dissolved.

e·lec′tro·mag′net (i lek′trō-) *n.* a device with an iron or steel core that is magnetized by electric current in a surrounding coil. —*e·lec′tro·mag·net′ic, adj.*

e·lec′tron (i lek′tron) *n.* a particle containing a negative electric charge.

electron′ic mail′ *n.* e-mail.

e·lec·tron′ics *n.* the science dealing with the development of devices and systems involving the flow of electrons. —*e·lec·tron′ic, adj.* —*e·lec·tron′i·cal·ly, adv.*

el′e·gant (el′i gənt) *adj.* 1. tastefully luxurious. 2. dignified. 3. of superior quality. —*el′e·gance, n.*

el′e·gy (el′i jē) *n., pl.* -gies. a mournful or melancholy poem. —*el·e·gi′ac* (-jī′ak) *adj.*

el′e·ment (el′ə mənt) *n.* 1. a part of a whole. 2. a substance that cannot be broken down chemically. 3. a natural environment. 4. **elements, a.** the basic principles. **b.** atmospheric forces. **c.** the bread and wine of the Eucharist.

el′e·men′ta·ry (-tə rē) *adj.* dealing with the simplest or basic aspects of something.

elemen′tary school′ *n.* a school giving instruction in basic subjects in six or eight grades.

el′e·phant (el′ə fənt) *n.* a very large mammal with a long trunk and large tusks.

el′e·phan′tine (el′ə fan′tēn, -tīn) *adj.* 1. huge. 2. clumsy.

el′e·vate′ (el′ə vāt′) *v.t.,* -vated, -vating. to raise to a higher place or status.

el′e·va′tion *n.* 1. an elevating or being elevated. 2. the height to which something is elevated. 3. altitude.

el′e·va′tor *n.* 1. a moving platform or cage for lifting or lowering. 2. a building for storing grain.

e·lev′en (i lev′ən) *n., adj.* ten plus one. —**e·lev′enth,** *adj., n.*

elf (elf) *n., pl.* **elves.** a tiny, mischievous being in folklore.

e·lic′it (i lis′it) *v.t.* to draw forth.

e·lide′ (i līd′) *v.t.,* -lided, -liding. to omit (a vowel, consonant, etc.) in pronunciation.

el′i·gi·ble (el′i jə bəl) *adj.* 1. being a worthy choice. 2. qualified to be chosen. —*el′i·gi·bil′i·ty, n.*

e·lim′i·nate′ (i lim′ə nāt′) *v.t.,* -nated, -nating. 1. to get rid of. 2. to leave out.

e·lite′ (i lēt′, ā lēt′) *n.* 1. (*often used with a pl. v.*) the choice, best, or most powerful of a group, class, etc. —*adj.* 2. of the best or most select.

e·lit′ism *n.* the practice of or belief in rule by an elite. —*e·lit′ist, adj.*

e·lix′ir (i lik′sər) *n.* 1. a sweetened solution used as a flavoring in medicine. 2. a preparation believed capable of prolonging life.

elk (elk) *n.* a large deer.

el·lipse′ (i lips′) *n.* a closed plane curve shaped like an oval.

el·lip′sis (i lip′sis) *n., pl.* -ses. the omission of a word or phrase.

el·lip′ti·cal (-ti kəl) *adj.* 1. having the form of an ellipse. 2. of or marked by ellipsis. —*el·lip′ti·cal·ly, adv.*

elm (elm) *n.* a large shade tree.

el′o·cu′tion (el′ə kyōō′shən) *n.* the art of public speaking.

e·lon′gate (i lông′gāt) *v.i., v.t.,* -gated, -gating. to lengthen. —*e·lon·ga′tion, n.*

e·lope′ (i lōp′) *v.i.,* eloped, eloping. to run off secretly to be married. —*e·lope′ment, n.*

el′o·quent (el′ə kwənt) *adj.* skilled in fluent, forceful speaking. —*el′o·quence, n.*

else (els) *adj.* 1. different. 2. additional. —*adv.* 3. otherwise.

else•where′ *adv.* in or to another place.

e•lu′ci•date′ (i lōō′si dāt′) *v.t., v.i.,* **-dated, -dating**. to make clear by explaining. —**e•lu′ci•da′tion,** *n.*

e•lude′ (i lōōd′) *v.t.,* **eluded, eluding. 1.** to skillfully escape detection or capture by. **2.** to escape the memory or understanding of. —**e•lu′sive,** *adj.*
—Usage. See ESCAPE.

E•ly′si•um (i lizh′ē əm, i liz′-) *n.* (in Greek mythology) the abode of the blessed after death. —**E•ly′sian** (i lizh′ən), *adj.*

e•ma′ci•ate′ (i mā′shē āt′) *v.t.,* **-ated, -ating**. to make abnormally thin. —**e•ma′ci•a′tion,** *n.*

e′•mail′ or **e•mail′** or **E•mail′** (ē′māl′) *n.* **1.** a system for sending messages between computers. **2.** a message sent by e-mail. —*v.t.* **3.** to send a message to by e-mail.

em′a•nate′ (i lizh′ē əm) *v.t.,* **-nated, -nating**. to flow out or issue forth.

e•man′ci•pate′ (i man′sə pāt′) *v.t.,* **-pated, -pating**. to free from restraint; liberate. —**e•man′ci•pa′tion,** *n.*

e•mas′cu•late′ (i mas′kyə lāt′) *v.t.,* **-lated, -lating. 1.** to castrate. **2.** to weaken. —**e•mas′cu•la′tion,** *n.*

em•balm′ (em bäm′) *v.t.* to treat (a dead body) with chemicals to preserve it. —**em•balm′•er,** *n.*

em•bank′ment (em bank′mənt) *n.* a bank or mound to hold back water, carry a roadway, etc.

em•bar′go (em bär′gō) *n., pl.* **-goes**. a government order restricting movement of ships or goods.

em•bark′ (em bärk′) *v.i.* **1.** to board a ship or aircraft. **2.** to begin an enterprise. —**em′bar•ka′tion,** *n.*

em•bar′rass (en bar′əs) *v.t.* to make self-conscious or ashamed. —**em•bar′rass•ment,** *n.*

em′bas•sy (em′bə sē) *n., pl.* **-sies. 1.** an ambassador's headquarters. **2.** an ambassador and staff.

em•bat′tled (em bat′ld) *adj.* prepared for or engaged in conflict.

em•bed′ (em bed′) *v.t., v.i.,* **-bedded, -bedding**. to fix or be fixed into a surrounding mass.

em•bel′lish (em bel′ish) *v.t.* **1.** to beautify with ornamentation. **2.** to enhance by adding detail. —**em•bel′lish•ment,** *n.*

em′ber (em′bər) *n.* a live coal.

em•bez′zle (em bez′əl) *v.t.,* **-zled, -zling**. to steal (money entrusted to one). —**em•bez′zle•ment,** *n.*

em•bit′ter *v.t.* to cause to feel bitterness.

em•bla′zon (em blā′zən) *v.t.* to decorate, as with heraldic devices.

em′blem (em′bləm) *n.* **1.** a symbol. **2.** a figure identifying something.

em•bod′y *v.t.,* **-ied, -ying**. to put in concrete form; exemplify. —**em•bod′i•ment,** *n.*

em′bo•lism (em′bə liz′əm) *n.* the closing off of a blood vessel.

em•boss′ (em bôs′) *v.t.* to decorate with a raised design.

em•brace′ *v.,* **-braced, -bracing,** —*v.t.* **1.** to hug. **2.** to accept willingly. **3.** to include. —*n.* **4.** a hug.

em•broi′der (en broi′dər) *v.t., v.i.* **1.** to decorate with needlework. **2.** to add fictitious details to (a story). —**em•broi′der•y,** *n.*

em•broil′ *v.t.* to involve in conflict.

em′bry•o′ (em′brē ō′) *n., pl.* **-bryos**. an organism in the first stages of development. —**em′bry•on′ic,** *adj.*

em•cee′ (em′sē′) *n., v.,* **-ceed, -ceeing**. —*n.* **1.** a master of ceremonies. —*v.i., v.i.* **2.** to serve or direct as master of ceremonies.

e•mend′ (i mend′) *v.t.* to change (a text) by correcting.

em′er•ald (em′ər əld) *n.* **1.** a precious green gem. **2.** a clear, deep green.

e•merge′ (i mûrj′) *v.i.,* **emerged, emerging. 1.** to come into existence. **2.** to come into view. —**e•mer′gence,** *n.*

e•mer′gen•cy (i mûr′jən sē) *n., pl.* **-cies**. an urgent situation requiring immediate action.

e•mer′i•tus (i mer′i təs) *adj.* retired from professional duty but retaining one's title.

em′er•y (em′ə rē) *n.* a mineral used for grinding and polishing.

e•met′ic (i met′ik) *n.* a medicine that causes vomiting.

em′i•grate (em′i grāt′) *v.i.,* **-grated, -grating**. to leave one country to settle in another. —**em′i•grant** (-grənt) *n., adj.* —**em′i•gra′tion,** *n.*

é′mi•gré′ (em′i grā′) *n.* a person who emigrates, esp. one who flees for political reasons.

em′i•nence (em′ə nəns) *n.* high rank or place. —**em′i•nent,** *adj.*

em′inent domain′ *n.* the power of the state to take private property for public use.

em′is•sar′y (em′ə ser′ē) *n., pl.* **-saries**. an agent sent on a mission.

e•mit′ (i mit′) *v.t.,* **emitted, emitting**. to send forth. —**e•mis′sion,** *n.*

e•mol′lient (i mol′yənt) *adj.* **1.** softening; soothing. —*n.* **2.** an emollient substance.

e•mol′u•ment (i mol′yə mənt) *n.* a salary.

e•mote′ (i mōt′) *v.i.,* **emoted, emoting**. to show emotion in or as if in acting.

e•mo′tion (i mō′shən) *n.* a strong feeling. —**e•mo′tion•al,** *adj.*

em′pa•thy (em′pə thē) *n.* identification with the feelings of another. —**em′pa•thize′,** *v.i.*

em′per•or (em′pər ər) *n.* the male ruler of an empire.

em′pha•sis (em′fə sis) *n., pl.* **-ses**. special stress or importance. —**em•phat′ic** (-fat′ik) *adj.* —**em•phat′i•cal•ly,** *adv.* —**em′pha•size′,** *v.t.*

em′phy•se′ma (em′fə sē′mə) *n.* a chronic lung disease.

em′pire (em′pīʳ) *n.* **1.** a group of nations under one powerful ruler. **2.** a powerful enterprise controlled by one person or group.

em•pir′i•cal (em pir′i kəl) *adj.* drawing on experience or observation.

em•ploy′ (em ploi′) *v.t.* **1.** to engage the services of; hire. **2.** to make use of. —*n.* **3.** employment; service. —**em•ploy′ee,** *n.* —**em•ploy′er,** *n.*

em•ploy′ment *n.* **1.** an employing or being employed. **2.** an occupation.

em•po′ri•um (em pôr′ē əm) *n.* a large store.

em•pow′er *v.t.* **1.** to give power or authority to. **2.** to enable. —**em•pow′er•ment,** *n.*

em′press (em′pris) *n.* **1.** the female ruler of an empire. **2.** the wife of an emperor.

emp′ty (emp′tē) *adj.,* **-tier, -tiest,** *v.,* **-tied, -tying.** —*adj.* **1.** containing nothing. **2.** vacant. **3.** lacking force. —*v.t., v.i* **4.** to make or become empty. **5.** to discharge.

emp′ty nest′ syn′drome *n.* a depressed state felt by some parents after their children have grown up and left home.

EMT emergency medical technician.

e′mu (ē′myōō) *n.* a large, flightless Australian bird.

em′u•late′ (em′yə lāt′) *v.t.,* **-lated, -lating**. to imitate in an effort to equal or surpass.

e•mul′si•fy′ (i mul′sə fī′) *v.t., v.i.,* **-fied, -fying**. to make into or form an emulsion.

e•mul′sion (-shən) *n.* **1.** a milklike mixture of liquids. **2.** a photosensitive coating on film.

en- a prefix meaning: **1.** to put into or on. **2.** to cover or surround with. **3.** to make or cause to be.

en•a′ble (en ā′bəl) *v.t.,* **-bled, -bling. 1.** to make able. **2.** to make possible.

en•act′ *v.t.* **1.** to make into law. **2.** to act the part of. —**en•act′ment,** *n.*

en•am′el (i nam′əl) *n., v.,* **-eled, -eling.** —*n.* **1.** a glassy coating fused to metal, pottery, etc. **2.** a paint that dries to a glossy surface. **3.** the surface of the teeth. —*v.t.* **4.** to apply enamel to.

en•am′or (i nam′ər) *v.t.* to fill with love.

en•camp′ *v.t., v.i.* to settle in a camp. —**en•camp′ment,** *n.*

en•cap′su•late′ (en kap′sə lāt′) *v.t.,* **-lated, -lating**. to summarize or condense.

en•case′ (en kās′) *v.t.* **-cased, -casing**. to enclose in or as if in a case.

en•ceph′a•li′tis (en sef′ə lī′tis) *n.* inflammation of the brain.

en•chant′ (en chant′) *v.t.* to bewitch; charm. —**en•chant′ment,** *n.*

en′chi•la′da (en′chə lä′də) *n.* a tortilla rolled around a filling, usu. with a chili-flavored sauce.

en•cir′cle *v.t.,* **-cled, -cling**. to surround.

encl. 1. enclosed. **2.** enclosure.

en′clave (en′klāv, än′-) *n.* a small area surrounded by foreign territory.

en•close′ (en klōz′) *v.t.,* **-closed, -closing. 1.** to shut in on all sides. **2.** to surround, as with a fence. **3.**

to put in an envelope along with something else. —**en•clo′sure,** *n.*

en•code′ *v.t.,* **-coded, -coding**. to convert into code.

en•co′mi•um (en kō′mē əm) *n., pl.* **-miums, -mia**. formal words of praise.

en•com′pass (en kum′pəs) *v.t.* **1.** to encircle; surround. **2.** to include.

en′core (äng′kôr, än′-) *n.* **1.** a demand by an audience for a repetition of a song, the performance of an additional piece, etc. **2.** a performance in response to an encore.

en•coun′ter (en koun′tər) *v.t.* **1.** to meet unexpectedly. —*n.* **2.** an unexpected meeting. **3.** a battle.

en•cour′age (en kûr′ij, -kur′-) *v.t.,* **-aged, -aging. 1.** to inspire with courage or confidence. **2.** to stimulate. —**en•cour′age•ment,** *n.*

en•croach′ (en krōch′) *v.i.* to trespass on the property or rights of another.

en•cum′ber (en kum′bər) *v.t.* **1.** to hinder. **2.** to burden. —**en•cum′brance,** *n.*

en•cyc′li•cal (en sik′li kəl) *n.* a letter from the pope to all bishops.

en•cy′clo•pe′di•a (en sī′klə pē′dē ə) *n.* a book with information on all branches of knowledge or on all aspects of one branch. —**en•cy′clo•pe′dic,** *adj.*

end (end) *n.* **1.** the last part. **2.** a point that indicates the limit of something. **3.** the farthest part or point of something. **4.** a purpose. **5.** an outcome. **6.** destruction. —*v.t., v.i.* **7.** to bring or come to an end. —*Idiom.* **8. make ends meet,** to keep one's expenses within one's income. —**end′less,** *adj.*

en•dan′ger (en dān′jər) *v.t.* **1.** to expose to danger. **2.** to threaten with extinction.

en•dear′ (en dēr′) *v.t.* to make beloved.

en•deav′or (en dev′ər) *v.i.* **1.** to make an earnest effort. —*n.* **2.** an attempt.

en•dem′ic (en dem′ik) *adj.* belonging to a particular people or place.

end′ing *n.* a concluding part.

en′dive (en′dīv, än dēv′) *n.* a plant with curly leaves used in salad. **2.** Also called **Belgian endive.** a plant with a narrow head of whitish, edible leaves.

en′do•crine (en′də krin, -krīn′) *adj.* **1.** secreting internally into the blood or lymph. **2.** of glands that secrete hormones directly into the blood or lymph.

en′do•cri•nol′o•gy (en′dō krə-nol′ə jē), *n.* the study of the endocrine glands. —**en′do•cri•nol′o•gist,** *n.*

en•dorse′ (en dôrs′) *v.t.,* **-dorsed, -dorsing. 1.** to express approval or support of. **2.** to sign one's name on the back of (a check).

en•dow′ (en dou′) *v.t.* **1.** to provide with a permanent source of income. **2.** to equip.

en•dure′ (en door′, -dyoor′) *v.,* **-dured, -during.** —*v.t.* **1.** to hold up under (pain or hardship) without yielding. **2.** to tolerate. —*v.i.* **3.** to last. —**en•dur′ance,** *n.*

en′e•ma (en′ə mə) *n.* liquid injected into the rectum.

en′e•my (en′ə mē) *n., pl.* **-mies**. a person who is hostile and wishes or tries to harm another.

en′er•gize′ (en′ər jīz′) *v.t.,* **-gized, -gizing**. to give energy to.

en′er•gy (-jē) *n., pl.* **-gies. 1.** the capacity for vigorous activity. **2.** the capacity to do work. **3.** a source of usable power, as oil. —**en•er•get′ic** (-jet′ik) *adj.*

en′er•vate′ (en′ər vāt′) *v.t.,* **-vated, -vating**. to deprive of strength.

en•fee′ble (en fē′bəl) *v.t.,* **-bled, -bling**. to weaken.

en•fold′ *v.t.* **1.** to wrap up. **2.** to hug.

en•force′ *v.t.,* **-forced, -forcing. 1.** to compel obedience to. **2.** to obtain by force. —**en•force′ment,** *n.* —**en•forc′er,** *n.*

en•fran′chise *v.t.,* **-chised, -chising**. to grant voting rights to.

en•gage′ (en gāj′) *v.,* **-gaged, -gaging.** —*v.t.* **1.** to occupy the attention of. **2.** to employ. **3.** to attract and hold. **4.** to bind by a pledge, esp. a pledge to marry. **5.** to enter into conflict with. **6.** to cause (gears) to become interlocked. —*v.i.* **7.** to be involved. **8.** to assume an obligation. **9.** to enter into conflict. **10.** to interlock. —**en•gaged′,** *adj.*

en•gage′ment *n.* **1.** the act of engaging or the state of being en-

gaged. **2.** an appointment. **3.** an agreement to marry. **4.** a battle.

en•gen′der *v.t.* to cause.

en′gine (en′jən) *n.* **1.** a machine for converting energy into force and motion. **2.** a locomotive.

en′gi•neer′ (en′jə nēr′) *n.* **1.** a person trained in engineering. **2.** an engine operator. —*v.t.* **3.** to contrive; bring about.

en′gi•neer′ing *n.* the practical application of science and mathematics, as in the design of systems and structures.

Eng′lish (ing′glish; often -lish) *n.* **1.** the language of England, the U.S., Australia, New Zealand, etc. **2.** the people of England. —*adj.* **3.** of England, its inhabitants, or their language.

Eng′lish horn′ *n.* a woodwind instrument lower in pitch than the oboe.

en•gorge′ *v.t., v.i.,* **-gorged, -gorging. 1.** to swallow greedily. **2.** to fill or congest, esp. with blood. —**en•gorge′ment,** *n.*

en•grave′ *v.t.,* **-graved, -graving. 1.** to cut (letters or a design) into a hard surface. **2.** to ornament by such cutting. —**en•grav′er,** *n.* —**en•grav′ing,** *n.*

en•gross′ (en grōs′) *v.t.* to occupy completely. —**en•gross′ing,** *adj.*

en•gulf′ *v.t.* **1.** to swallow up. **2.** to overwhelm.

en•hance′ (en hans′) *v.t.,* **-hanced, -hancing. 1.** to intensify. **2.** to improve.

e•nig′ma (ə nig′mə) *n.* a puzzling person, event, or situation. —**en′ig•mat′ic,** *adj.*

en•join′ *v.t.* to direct or order.

en•joy′ *v.t.* **1.** to take pleasure in. **2.** to have the use of. —**en•joy′a•ble,** *adj.* —**en•joy′ment,** *n.*

en•large′ *v.t., v.i.,* **-larged, -larging**. to make or grow larger. —**en•large′ment,** *n.*

en•light′en (en līt′n) *v.t.* **1.** to give understanding to. **2.** to free of ignorance. —**en•light′en•ment,** *n.*

en•list′ *v.i., v.t.* **1.** to enroll for military service. **2.** to secure for a cause. —**en•list′ment,** *n.*

en•liv′en (en līʹvən) *v.t.* to make active or lively.

en masse′ (än mas′, äN) *adv.* in a mass; all together.

en•mesh′ *v.t.* to entangle.

en′mi•ty (en′mi tē) *n., pl.* **-ties**. hatred.

en•nui′ (än wē′) *n.* boredom.

e•nor′mi•ty (i nôr′mi tē) *n., pl.* **-ties. 1.** great wickedness. **2.** an outrageous crime; atrocity.

e•nor′mous (-məs) *adj.* huge.

e•nough′ (i nuf′) *adj.* **1.** sufficient for a purpose. —*n.* **2.** an adequate amount. —*adv.* **3.** sufficiently.

en•quire′ (en kwīʳ′) *v.i., v.t.,* **-quired, -quiring**. to inquire. —**en•quir′y,** *n.*

en•rage′ *v.t.,* **-raged, -raging**. to make very angry.

en•rap′ture (en rap′chər) *v.t.,* **-tured, -turing**. to delight.

en•rich′ *v.t.* **1.** to make rich. **2.** to improve. —**en•rich′ment,** *n.*

en•roll′ *v.t., v.i.* to accept as or become a member. —**en•roll′ment,** *n.*

en route′ (än rōōt′) *adv.* on the way.

en•sconce′ (en skons′) *v.t.,* **-sconced, -sconcing**. to settle securely or snugly.

en•sem′ble (än säm′bəl) *n.* **1.** all the parts of a thing taken together. **2.** a group performing together. **3.** an outfit.

en•shrine′ *v.t.,* **-shrined, -shrining. 1.** to put in a shrine. **2.** to cherish as sacred.

en•shroud′ *v.t.* to conceal.

en′sign (en′sīn; *Mil.* -sən) *n.* **1.** a military flag. **2.** the lowest commissioned naval officer.

en•slave′ *v.t.,* **-slaved, -slaving**. to make a slave of.

en•snare′ *v.t.,* **-snared, -snaring**. to capture in a snare; entrap.

en•sue′ (en sōō′) *v.i., v.i.,* **-sued, -suing**. to follow in order or as a result.

en•sure′ (en shoor′) *v.t.,* **-sured, -suring**. to make certain; secure.

en•tail′ (en tāl′) *v.t.* to cause or involve by necessity or as a consequence.

en•tan′gle *v.t.,* **-gled, -gling. 1.** to make tangled. **2.** to involve in difficulties or complications.

en•tente′ (än tänt′) *n.* an international agreement on a common policy.

en′ter (en′tər) *v.t.* **1.** to come or go in or into. **2.** to begin. **3.** to be-

come involved in. **4.** to put on a list. —*v.i.* **5.** to come or go in.

en′ter•i′tis (en′tə rī′tis) *n.* inflammation of the intestines.

en′ter•prise′ (en′tər prīz′) *n.* **1.** a project, esp. one requiring boldness or originality. **2.** adventurous spirit. **3.** a business firm.

en′ter•pris′ing *adj.* showing imagination and initiative.

en′ter•tain′ (en′tər tān′) *v.t.* **1.** to amuse. **2.** to treat as a guest. **3.** to have in one's mind. —**en′ter•tain′er,** *n.* —**en′ter•tain′ment,** *n.*

en•thrall′ (en thrôl′) *v.t.* **1.** to captivate. **2.** to enslave.

en•throne′ *v.t.,* **-throned, -throning**. to place on or as if on a throne. —**en•throne′ment,** *n.*

en•thuse′ (en thōōz′) *v.,* **-thused, -thusing.** —*v.i.* **1.** to show enthusiasm. —*v.t.* **2.** to fill with enthusiasm.

en•thu′si•asm (-thōō′zē az′əm) *n.* lively, absorbing interest. —**en•thu′si•ast′,** *n.* —**en•thu′si•as′tic,** *adj.*

en•tice′ (en tīs′) *v.t.,* **-ticed, -ticing**. to lead on by exciting hope or desire; allure. —**en•tice′ment,** *n.* —**en•tic′ing•ly,** *adv.*

en•tire′ (en tīʳr′) *adj.* whole or complete. —**en•tire′ly,** *adv.* —**en•tire′ty,** *n.*

en•ti′tle *v.t.,* **-tled, -tling. 1.** to give a right to. **2.** to give a title to.

en′ti•ty (en′ti tē) *n., pl.* **-ties**. something that exists as a separate thing.

en•tomb′ *v.t.* **1.** to place in a tomb.

en′to•mol′o•gy (en′tə mol′ə jē) *n.* the study of insects. —**en′to•mol′o•gist,** *n.*

en′tou•rage′ (än′tōō räzh′) *n.* a group of attendants.

en′tr′acte′ (än trakt′, äN-) *n.* **1.** the interval between two acts of a play or opera. **2.** a performance during such an interval.

en′trails (en′trālz, -trəlz) *n.pl.* the inner organs, esp. the intestines.

en′trance¹ (-trəns) *n.* **1.** the act of entering. **2.** a place for entering. **3.** the right to enter.

en•trance′² (-trans′) *v.t.,* **-tranced, -trancing**. to fill with delight.

en′trant (en′trənt) *n.* a person who enters a competition or a contest.

en•trap′ *v.t.,* **-trapped, -trapping**. to catch in or as if in a trap.

en•treat′ (en trēt′) *v.t., v.i.* to ask earnestly. —**en•treat′y,** *n.*

en′tree (än′trā) *n.* **1.** the main course of a meal. **2.** access.

en•trench′ *v.t.* to establish firmly.

en′tre•pre•neur′ (än′trə prə nûr′) *n.* a person who organizes a business, esp. one involving risk. —**en′tre•pre•neur′i•al,** *adj.*

en′tro•py (en′trə pē) *n.* **1.** a measure of the energy in a system that is not available for conversion into mechanical work. **2.** the tendency toward disorder in any system.

en•trust′ *v.t.* to give to as a trust.

en′try (en′trē) *n., pl.* **-tries. 1.** a place of entrance. **2.** permission or right to enter. **3.** the act of entering. **4.** an item entered in a list or contest.

en•twine′ *v.t.,* **-twined, -twining**. to twine around or together.

e•nu′mer•ate′ (i nōō′mə rāt′, i nyōō′-) *v.t.,* **-ated, -ating**. to name one by one; list. —**e•nu′mer•a′tion,** *n.*

e•nun′ci•ate′ (i nun′sē āt′) *v.t.,* **-ated, -ating. 1.** to pronounce. **2.** to state clearly.

en′u•re′sis (en′yə rē′sis) *n.* bedwetting.

en•vel′op (en vel′əp) *v.t.* **1.** to wrap up. **2.** to surround.

en′ve•lope′ (en′və lōp′, än′-) *n.* a flat paper container, as for a letter.

en•vi′ron•ment (en vī′rən mənt, -vī′ərn-) *n.* **1.** surroundings. **2.** the external factors, as air, water, etc., affecting an organism. —**en•vi′ron•men′tal** (-men′tl) *adj.* —**en•vi′ron•men′tal•ist,** *n.*

en•vi′rons *n.pl.* the surrounding districts, as of a city.

en•vis′age (en viz′ij) *v.t.,* **-aged, -aging**. to form a mental picture of. Also, **en•vi′sion.**

en′voy (en′voi, än′-) *n.* **1.** a diplomatic representative. **2.** a messenger.

en′vy (en′vē) *n., pl.* **-vies,** *v.,* **-vied, -vying.** —*n.* **1.** discontent at another's possessions or success. **2.** an object of envy. —*v.t.* **3.** to regard with envy. —**en′vi•ous,** *adj.*

en′zyme (en′zīm) *n.* a protein formed in living cells and capable of producing chemical changes in other substances.

e/on (ē′ən, ē′on) *n.* a long period of time.

EPA Environmental Protection Agency.

ep/au·let/ (ep/ə let′, -lit) *n.* an ornamental shoulder piece on a uniform. Also, **ep/au·lette/**.

e·phem/er·al (i fem/ər əl) *adj.* lasting a very short time.

ep/ic (ep/ik) *n.* **1.** a long poem or story describing heroic deeds. —*adj.* **2.** of or like an epic.

ep/i·cen/ter (ep/ə sen/tər) *n.* a point directly above the center of an earthquake.

ep/i·cure/ (ep/i kyŏŏr′) *n.* a person with refined taste in food and drink. —**ep/i·cu·re/an,** *adj.*

ep/i·dem/ic (ep/i dem/ik) *adj.* **1.** affecting many persons at once. —*n.* **2.** an epidemic disease.

ep/i·der/mis *n.* the outer layer of skin.

ep/i·glot/tis (-glot/is) *n., pl.* -glottises, -glottides (-glot/i dēz′). a flap of cartilage that covers the windpipe during swallowing.

ep/i·gram/ (ep/i gram′) *n.* a short witty saying.

ep/i·lep/sy (ep/ə lep/sē) *n.* a nervous disorder usu. marked by convulsions. —**ep/i·lep/tic,** *adj., n.*

ep/i·logue/ (ep/ə lôg′) *n.* a concluding part or speech.

e·piph/a·ny (i pif/ə nē) *n.* **1.** Epiphany, a festival commemorating the Wise Men's visit to Christ, celebrated on January 6. **2.** an appearance. **3.** a sudden realization.

e·pis/co·pal (-pəl) *adj.* **1.** governed by bishops. **2.** Episcopal, of the Anglican or Protestant Episcopal Church.

ep/i·sode/ (ep/ə sōd′) *n.* an incident in a series of events. —**ep/i·sod/ic** (-sod/ik) *adj.*

e·pis/tle (i pis/əl) *n.* a letter.

ep/i·taph/ (ep/i taf′) *n.* an inscription on a tomb.

ep/i·thet/ (ep/ə thet′) *n.* a descriptive term.

e·pit/o·me (i pit/ə mē) *n.* **1.** a perfect example. **2.** a summary. —**e·pit/o·mize/,** *v.t.*

ep/och (ep/ək) *n.* a distinctive period of time. —**ep/och·al,** *adj.*

ep·ox/y (i pok/sē) *n., pl.* -ies. a tough synthetic resin used in glue.

ep/si·lon (ep/sə lon′, -lən, ep si/lən) *n.* the fifth letter of the Greek alphabet.

Ep/som salts/ (ep/səm) *n.pl.* salts used esp. as a cathartic.

eq/ua·ble (ek/wə bəl) *adj.* **1.** free from many changes. **2.** calm.

e/qual (ē/kwəl) *adj., n., v.,* **equaled, equaling.** —*adj.* **1.** alike in amount, rank, value, size, etc. **2.** the same in operation or effect. **3.** having adequate means or ability. —*n.* **4.** one that is equal. —*v.t.* **5.** to be or become equal to. **6.** to do something equal to. —**e·qual/i·ty,** *n.* —**e/qual·ize/,** *v.t.*

e/qual sign/ *n.* a symbol (=) indicating equality between the terms it separates. Also, **e/quals sign/.**

e/qua·nim/i·ty (ē/kwə nim/i tē) *n.* calmness.

e·quate/ (i kwāt′) *v.t.,* **equated, equating.** to make or consider as equivalent.

e·qua/tion (i kwā/zhən) *n.* **1.** an equating or being equated. **2.** an expression of the equality of two quantities.

e·qua/tor (-tər) *n.* an imaginary circle around the earth midway between the North Pole and the South Pole. —**e/qua·to/ri·al,** *adj.*

e·ques/tri·an (i kwes/trē ən) *adj.* **1.** of horseback riding or riders. —*n.* **2.** a person who rides horses.

e/qui·dis/tant (ē/kwi dis/tənt) *adj.* equally distant.

e/qui·lat/er·al (ē/kwi lat/ər əl) *adj.* having all the sides equal.

e/qui·lib/ri·um (-lib/rē əm) *n., pl.* -riums, -ria. a state of balance between opposing forces, powers, or influences.

e/quine (ē/kwīn) *adj.* of horses.

e/qui·nox/ (ē/kwə noks′) *n.* one of the times when day and night are of equal length.

e·quip/ (i kwip′) *v.t.,* **equipped, equipping.** to provide with what is needed.

e·quip/ment *n.* **1.** an equipping or being equipped. **2.** the articles needed for a specific activity.

eq/ui·ta·ble (ek/wi tə bəl) *adj.* fair and impartial.

eq/ui·ty *n., pl.* -ties. **1.** fairness. **2.**

the value of a property beyond any amounts owed on it.

e·quiv/a·lent (i kwiv/ə lənt) *adj.* **1.** equal in value, meaning, effect, etc. —*n.* **2.** something equivalent. —**e·quiv/a·lence,** *n.*

e·quiv/o·cal (i kwiv/ə kəl) *adj.* **1.** ambiguous. **2.** questionable.

e·quiv/o·cate/ (-kāt′) *v.i.,* -cated, -cating. to express oneself ambiguously. —**e·quiv/o·ca/tion,** *n.*

e/ra (ēr/ə, er/ə) *n.* a period of history.

ERA 1. Also, **era.** earned run average. **2.** Equal Rights Amendment.

e·rad/i·cate/ (i rad/i kāt′) *v.t.,* -cated, -cating. to remove completely.

e·rase/ (i rās′) *v.t.,* erased, erasing. **1.** to rub out. **2.** to eliminate. —**e·ras/a·ble,** *adj.* —**e·ras/er,** *n.*

e·ra/sure (-zhər) *n.* **1.** an act of erasing. **2.** a place where something has been erased.

ere (âr) *prep., conj. Archaic.* before.

e·rect/ (i rekt′) *adj.* **1.** upright. —*v.t.* **2.** to build. **3.** to set up.

e·rec/tile (i rek/tl, -til, -tīl) *adj.* capable of being distended with blood and becoming rigid.

e·rec/tion (-shən) *n.* **1.** something erected. **2.** a distended and rigid state of an organ, as the penis.

erg (ûrg) *n.* a unit of work or energy.

er/go (ûr/gō, er/gō) *conj., adv.* therefore.

er/go·nom/ics (ûr/gə nom/iks) *n.* an applied science that coordinates workplace design and equipment with workers' needs.

er/mine (ûr/min) *n.* **1.** a kind of weasel. **2.** its white winter fur.

e·rode/ (i rōd′) *v.,* eroded, eroding. —*v.t.* **1.** to wear away. —*v.i.* **2.** to become worn away. —**e·ro/sion,** *n.*

e·rog/e·nous (i roj/ə nəs) *adj.* sensitive to sexual stimulation.

e·rot/ic (i rot/ik) *adj.* **1.** of sexual love. **2.** arousing sexual desire. —**e·rot/i·cism** (-ə siz/əm) *n.*

e·rot/i·ca (-i kə) *n.pl.* erotic literature and art.

err (ûr, er) *v.i.* **1.** to be mistaken. **2.** to sin.

er/rand (er/ənd) *n.* a short trip for a specific purpose.

er/rant (er/ənt) *adj.* **1.** straying from the proper course. **2.** wandering.

er·rat/ic (i rat/ik) *adj.* irregular or unpredictable.

er·ra/tum (i rä/təm, i rat/əm) *n., pl.* -ta. an error in printing or writing.

er·ro/ne·ous (ə rō/nē əs, e rō/-) *adj.* incorrect.

er/ror (er/ər) *n.* **1.** a mistake. **2.** being wrong.

er·satz/ (er zäts′) *adj.* serving as a substitute; artificial.

erst/while/ *adj.* former.

ERT estrogen replacement therapy.

er/u·dite/ (er/yŏŏ dīt′) *adj.* learned.

e·rupt/ (i rupt′) *v.i.* **1.** to burst forth. **2.** (of a volcano, geyser, etc.) to eject matter. —**e·rup/tion,** *n.*

e·ryth/ro·cyte/ (i rith/rə sīt′) *n.* a red blood cell.

es/ca·late/ (es/kə lāt′) *v.i., v.t.,* -lated, -lating. to increase in intensity, amount, size, etc.

es/ca·la/tor *n.* a continuously moving stairway.

es/ca·pade/ (es/kə pād′) *n.* a reckless adventure.

es·cape/ (i skāp′) *v.,* -caped, -caping, *n.* —*v.i.* **1.** to get away. **2.** to avoid a danger. **3.** to get out of a container. —*v.t.* **4.** to get away from. **5.** to succeed in avoiding. **6.** to elude. —*n.* **7.** an act or means of escaping. **8.** avoidance of reality. **9.** leakage, as of gas. —**es·cap/ee,** *n.*

   —**Usage.** ESCAPE, ELUDE, EVADE mean to keep away from something. To ESCAPE is to manage to keep away from danger, pursuit, observation, etc.: *to escape punishment.* To ELUDE is to slip through an apparently tight net, and implies using skill or cleverness: *The fox eluded the hounds.* To EVADE is to turn aside from or go out of reach of a person or thing, usually by moving or directing attention elsewhere: *We evaded the traffic jam by taking an alternate route.*

es·cape/ment (i skāp/mənt) *n.* the part of a clock that measures beats and controls the speed of the wheels.

es·cap/ism *n.* an attempt to forget reality through fantasy. —**es·cap/ist,** *n., adj.*

es/ca·role/ (es/kə rōl′) *n.* a broad-leaved endive.

es·carp/ment (i skärp/mənt) *n.* a long clifflike ridge.

es·chew/ (es chōō′) *v.t.* to avoid.

es/cort *n.* (es/kôrt) **1.** someone accompanying another for protection or courtesy. **2.** a man accompanying a woman in public. —*v.t.* (i-skôrt′) **3.** to accompany as an escort.

es·cutch/eon (i skuch/ən) *n.* a shield with a coat of arms.

Es/ki·mo/ (es/kə mō′) *n.* **1.** a member of a people living in regions from Greenland through Canada and Alaska to NE Siberia. **2.** the languages spoken by the Eskimos.

ESL English as a second language.

e·soph/a·gus (i sof/ə gəs) *n., pl.* -gi (-jī′). a tube connecting the throat and the stomach.

ESP extrasensory perception.

esp. especially.

es/pa·drille/ (es/pə dril′) *n.* a flat shoe with a cloth upper and a rope sole.

es·pe/cial (i spesh/əl) *adj.* special. —**es·pe/cial·ly,** *adv.*

Es/pe·ran/to (es/pə rän/tō, -ran/-) *n.* an artificial language based on major European languages.

es/pi·o·nage/ (es/pē ə näzh′, -nij) *n.* the act or practice of spying.

es/pla·nade/ (es/plə näd′, -näd′) *n.* an open level space for public walks.

es·pouse/ (i spouz′, i spous′) *v.t.,* -poused, -pousing. **1.** to adopt or support, as a cause. **2.** to marry. —**es·pous/al,** *n.*

es·pres/so (e spres/ō) *n.* a strong coffee made by forcing hot water through finely ground coffee beans.

es·prit/ de corps/ (e sprē′ də kôr′) *n.* a sense of unity and common purpose.

es·py/ (i spī′) *v.t.,* -pied, -pying. to catch sight of.

es·quire/ (es/kwī′r) *n.* a title of respect, applied chiefly to lawyers. *Abbr.:* Esq.

es/say *n.* (es/ā) **1.** a short literary composition on a particular subject. **2.** an attempt. —*v.t.* (e sā′) **3.** to try.

es/say·ist *n.* a writer of essays.

es/sence (es/əns) *n.* **1.** the basic, real nature of a thing. **2.** a concentrated form of a substance. **3.** a perfume.

es·sen/tial (ə sen/shəl) *adj.* **1.** absolutely necessary. —*n.* **2.** something basic or necessary.

es·sen/tial·ly *adv.* basically.

EST Eastern Standard Time.

est. 1. established. **2.** estimate. **3.** estimated.

es·tab/lish (i stab/lish) *v.t.* **1.** to bring into being. **2.** to settle, as in a position. **3.** to cause to be accepted. **4.** to prove.

es·tab/lish·ment *n.* **1.** an establishing or being established. **2.** an institution or business. **3. the Establishment,** the group controlling government and social institutions.

es·tate/ (i stāt′) *n.* **1.** a piece of landed property. **2.** a person's possessions or property, esp. that of a deceased person.

es·teem/ (i stēm′) *v.t.* **1.** to regard with respect or admiration. —*n.* **2.** respect or admiration.

es/ter (es/tər) *n.* a chemical compound produced by the reaction between an acid and an alcohol.

es/thete *n.* an aesthete.

es/ti·ma·ble (es/tə mə bəl) *adj.* worthy of high regard.

es/ti·mate/ *v.,* -mated, -mating, *n.* —*v.t.* (es/tə māt′) **1.** to form an approximate judgment regarding the amount, worth, etc., of. —*v.i.* **2.** to make an estimate. —*n.* (-mit) **3.** an approximate judgment or calculation. **4.** a statement of the approximate cost. —**es/ti·ma/tion,** *n.*

es·trange/ (i strānj′) *v.t.,* -tranged, -tranging. to make unfriendly.

es/tro·gen (es/trə jən) *n.* any of several female sex hormones.

es/trus (es/trəs) *n.* a period of sexual receptivity in female mammals. —**es/trous,** *adj.*

es/tu·ar/y (es/chŏŏ er/ē) *n., pl.* -aries. the part of a river at which the current meets the sea tides.

e/ta (ā/tə) *n., pl.* -tas. the seventh letter of the Greek alphabet.

ETA estimated time of arrival.

et al. (et al′, äl′, ôl′) and others.

et cet/er·a (et set/ər ə, se/trə) *adv.* and others, esp. of the same sort. *Abbr.:* etc.

etch (ech) *v.t.* to cut a design into (metal) with acid. —**etch/ing,** *n.*

e·ter/nal (i tûr/nl) *adj.* **1.** without beginning or end; existing always. **2.** not subject to change. —**e·ter/nal·ly,** *adv.*

e·ter/ni·ty (-ni tē) *n.* **1.** infinite time. **2.** eternal existence.

eth/ane (eth/ān) *n.* a colorless, odorless, flammable gas used chiefly as a fuel.

e/ther (ē/thər) *n.* **1.** a colorless liquid used as a solvent and formerly as an anesthetic. **2.** the upper part of space.

e·the/re·al (i thēr/ē əl) *adj.* **1.** light or airy. **2.** heavenly.

eth/ics (eth/iks) *n.* **1.** a system of moral principles. **2.** the branch of philosophy dealing with right and wrong. —**eth/i·cal,** *adj.*

eth/nic (eth/nik) *adj.* **1.** of a group sharing a common culture. —*n.* **2.** a member of an ethnic group.

eth/nic cleans/ing *n.* the elimination of an ethnic group from a society, as by genocide or forced emigration.

eth·nic/i·ty (-nis/i tē) *n.* ethnic traits or association.

eth·nol/o·gy (eth nol/ə jē) *n.* a branch of anthropology dealing with cultural comparisons.

e·thol/o·gy (ē thol/ə jē) *n.* the scientific study of animal behavior.

e/thos (ē/thos, eth/ōs) *n.* the distinguishing character or spirit of a person, group, or culture.

eth/yl (eth/əl) *n.* a fluid used in gasoline.

et/i·quette (et/i kit, -ket′) *n.* conventions of social behavior.

et seq. and the following.

é/tude (ā/tŏŏd, ā/tyŏŏd) *n.* a musical composition played to improve technique and for its artistic merit.

et/y·mol/o·gy (et/ə mol/ə jē) *n., pl.* -gies. the history of a word's origin and development.

eu- a prefix meaning good.

eu/ca·lyp/tus (yōō/kə lip/təs) *n., pl.* -ti. an evergreen tree with strongsmelling leaves.

Eu/cha·rist (yōō/kə rist) *n.* Holy Communion.

eu·gen/ics (yōō jen/iks) *n.* a science concerned with improving the genetic traits of the human race.

eu/lo·gy (yōō/lə jē) *n., pl.* -gies. spoken or written praise of a person, esp. of someone who has died. —**eu/lo·gize/,** *v.t.*

eu/nuch (yōō/nək) *n.* a castrated man.

eu/phe·mism (yōō/fə miz/əm) *n.* the substitution of a mild expression for one thought to be offensive. —**eu/phe·mis/tic,** *adj.*

eu/pho·ny (yōō/fə nē) *n., pl.* -nies. pleasantness of sound, esp. a pleasing combination of words. —**eu·pho/ni·ous** (-fō/nē əs) *adj.*

eu·pho/ri·a (yōō fôr/ē ə) *n.* a strong feeling of happiness or well-being. —**eu·phor/ic,** *adj.*

Eur·a/sian (yŏŏ rā/zhən) *adj.* **1.** of or originating in both Europe and Asia, or in the two considered as one continent.

eu·re/ka (yŏŏ rē/kə) *interj.* (an exclamation of triumph at a discovery.)

eu/ro (yŏŏr/ō, yûr/-) *n., pl.* -ros. the official common currency of most W European countries.

Eu/ro·pe/an (yŏŏr/ə pē/ən) *adj.* **1.** of Europe or its inhabitants. —*n.* **2.** a native of Europe.

Eu·sta/chian tube (yōō stā/shən) *n.* (often *l.c.*) a canal between the middle ear and the pharynx.

eu/tha·na/sia (yōō/thə nā/zhə) *n.* painless killing of a person or animal suffering from an incurable disease.

e·vac/u·ate/ (i vak/yōō āt′) *v.t.,* -ated, -ating. **1.** to make empty. **2.** to remove (persons or things) from (a place), esp. for safety. —**e·vac/u·a/tion,** *n.*

e·vade/ (i vād′) *v.t., v.i.,* evaded, evading. to avoid or escape, esp. by cleverness. —**e·va/sion,** *n.* —**e·va/sive,** *adj.*

   —**Usage.** See ESCAPE.

e·val/u·ate/ (i val/yōō āt′) *v.t.,* -ated, -ating. to determine the value, quality, or importance of. —**e·val/u·a/tion,** *n.*

ev/a·nes/cent (ev/ə nes/ənt) *adj.* fading away.

ev/an·gel/i·cal (ē/van jel/i kəl, ev/-ən-) *adj.* **1.** of or in keeping with the Gospels. **2.** of those Christian churches that stress the authority of the Scriptures. **3.** marked by zeal.

e·van/ge·list (i van/jə list) *n.* **1.** a

preacher of the Christian gospel. **2. Evangelist,** one of the writers of the four Gospels. —**e·van/ge·lism,** *n.* —**e·van/ge·lize/,** *v.t., v.i.*

e·vap/o·rate/ (i vap/ə rāt′) *v.,* -rated, -rating. —*v.i.* **1.** to change into vapor. **2.** to disappear. —*v.t.* **3.** to convert into vapor.

eve (ēv) *n.* the evening or day before an event or holiday.

e/ven (ē/vən) *adj.* **1.** level. **2.** smooth. **3.** uniform. **4.** equal in quantity. **5.** divisible by two. **6.** calm. —*adv.* **7.** still; yet. **8.** (used to suggest an extreme case). **9.** indeed. —*v.t., v.i.* **10.** to make or become even.

e/ven·hand/ed *adj.* impartial; fair.

eve/ning (ēv/ning) *n.* the latter part of the day and early part of the night.

eve/ning star/ *n.* a bright planet, esp. Venus, visible around sunset.

e·vent/ (i vent′) *n.* something that happens, esp. something important. —**e·vent/ful,** *adj.*

e·ven/tu·al (i ven/chōō əl) *adj.* happening at an indefinite future time. —**e·ven/tu·al·ly,** *adv.*

e·ven/tu·al/i·ty *n., pl.* -ties. a possible event or circumstance.

ev/er (ev/ər) *adv.* **1.** at any time. **2.** at all times. **3.** in any possible case.

ev/er·glade/ *n.* a tract of low, swampy land.

ev/er·green/ *adj.* **1.** having green leaves all year. —*n.* **2.** an evergreen plant.

ev/er·last/ing *adj.* lasting forever.

eve/ry (ev/rē) *adj.* **1.** each one in a group. **2.** all possible.

eve/ry·bod/y (-bod/ē, -bud/ē) *pron.* every person.

eve/ry·day/ *adj.* **1.** of or for ordinary days. **2.** ordinary.

eve/ry·one/ *pron.* everybody.

eve/ry·thing/ *pron.* all things.

eve/ry·where/ *adv.* in every place.

e·vict/ (i vikt′) *v.t.* to expel (a tenant) from property by legal means. —**e·vic/tion,** *n.*

ev/i·dence (ev/i dəns) *n., v.,* -denced, -dencing. —*n.* **1.** something establishing a fact as true. **2.** something presented in a law court to support a case. —*v.t.* **3.** to show clearly.

ev/i·dent *adj.* clear to the sight or mind. —**ev/i·dent·ly** (ev/i dənt lē, ev/i dent/lē) *adv.*

e/vil (ē/vəl) *adj.* **1.** wicked. **2.** harmful. **3.** unfortunate.

e/vil·do/er *n.* a person who does wrong.

e/vil eye/ *n.* a look thought capable of inflicting harm.

e·vince/ (i vins′) *v.t.,* evinced, evincing. to make evident.

e·vis/cer·ate/ (i vis/ə rāt′) *v.t.,* -ated, -ating. **1.** to remove the entrails of. **2.** to deprive of vital parts.

e·voke/ (i vōk′) *v.t.,* evoked, evoking. **1.** to call up (memories, feelings, etc.). **2.** to draw forth. —**ev/o·ca/tion** (ev/ə kā/shən) *n.* —**e·voc/a·tive** (i vok/-) *adj.*

e·volve/ (i volv′) *v.t., v.i.,* evolved, evolving. to develop gradually.

ewe (yōō) *n.* a female sheep.

ew/er (yōō/ər) *n.* a wide-mouthed pitcher.

ex- a prefix meaning: **1.** out of or from, **2.** utterly or thoroughly. **3.** former.

ex. example.

ex·ac/er·bate/ (ig zas/ər bāt′, eksas/-) *v.t.,* -bated, -bating. to make more severe or violent.

ex·act/ (ig zakt′) *adj.* **1.** precise; accurate. —*v.t.* **2.** to demand; require.

ex·act/ing *adj.* **1.** severe in making demands. **2.** requiring close attention.

ex·ag/ger·ate/ (ig zaj/ə rāt′) *v.t.,* -ated, -ating. to make seem larger, better, etc., than is really true.

ex·alt/ (ig zôlt′) *v.t.* **1.** to raise in rank, power, etc. **2.** to praise. —**ex/al·ta/tion,** *n.*

ex·am/ (ig zam′) *n. Informal.* an examination.

ex·am/i·na/tion *n.* **1.** an examining or being examined. **2.** a test of knowledge or qualifications.

ex·am/ine (-in) *v.t.,* -ined, -ining. **1.** to inspect carefully. **2.** to test the knowledge or qualifications of.

ex·am/ple (ig zam/pəl) *n.* **1.** one of a number of things that shows what others of the same kind are like. **2.** a person or thing worthy of being imitated. **3.** a fact illustrating a rule or method.

ex·as/per·ate/ (ig zas/pə rāt′) *v.t.,* -ated, -ating. to irritate or provoke greatly.

ex·ca·vate' (eks'kə vāt') v.t., -vated, -vating. 1. to make a hole in. 2. to dig out (earth, sand, etc.) 3. to expose by digging. —**ex·ca·va'tion**, n. —**ex'ca·va'tor**, n.

ex·ceed' (ik sēd') v.t. 1. to go beyond the limits of. 2. to be superior to.

ex·ceed'ing·ly adv. extremely.

ex·cel' (ik sel') v.i., v.t., -celled, -celling. to be superior (to); surpass (others).

ex'cel·lence (ek'sə ləns) n. the fact or state of excelling.

Ex'cel·len·cy (ek'sə lən sē) n., pl. -cies. a title of honor given to certain high officials.

ex'cel·lent adj. remarkably good.

ex·cel'si·or (ik sel'sē ər, ek-) n. fine wood shavings.

ex·cept'¹ (ik sept') prep. 1. not including; but. —conj. 2. with the exception that; only.
—**Usage.** See ACCEPT.

ex·cept'² (ik sept') v.t. to leave out. —v.i. 2. to object.

ex·cep'tion·a·ble adj. liable to exception.

ex·cep'tion·al adj. unusual, esp. superior.

ex'cerpt n. (ek'sûrpt) 1. a passage or quotation, as from a book. —v.t. (ik sûrpt', ek'sûrpt) 2. to take (an excerpt) from a book, film, etc.

ex·cess' (ik ses') n. 1. the amount by which one thing exceeds another. 2. a surplus. —adj. (ek'ses) 3. being more than necessary, usual, or desirable.

ex·ces'sive adj. too much.

ex·change' (iks chānj') v., -changed, -changing. —v.t. 1. to give or receive in place of something else. —n. 2. an act of exchanging. 3. something exchanged. 4. a place where commodities or securities are exchanged. 5. a central office.

ex·cheq'uer (iks chek'ər) n. a treasury, as of a nation.

ex·cise'¹ (ek'sīz) n. a tax on certain goods.

ex·cise'² (ik sīz') v.t., -cised, -cising. to remove by cutting.

ex·cite' (ik sīt') v.t., -cited, -citing. 1. to stir up the feelings of. 2. to arouse (feelings). 3. to stir to action. —**ex·cit'a·ble**, adj. —**ex·cite'ment**, n.

ex·claim' (ik sklām') v.i., v.t. to cry out. —**ex·cla·ma'tion** (ek'sklə mā'shən) n.

ex·clude' (ik sklood') v.t., -cluded, -cluding. 1. to shut or keep out. 2. to omit. —**ex·clu'sion**, n.

ex·clu'sive (ik sklōo'siv) adj. 1. excluding others. 2. single or sole. 3. expensive or fashionable.

ex·com·mu'ni·cate' (eks'kə myōo'ni kāt') v.t., -cated, -cating. to cut off from communion or membership of a church. —**ex'com·mu'ni·ca'tion**, n.

ex·co'ri·ate' (ik skôr'ē āt') v.t., -ated, -ating. to denounce.

ex'cre·ment (ek'skrə mənt) n. bodily waste.

ex·cres'cence (ik skres'əns) n. an abnormal outgrowth. —**ex·cres'cent**, adj.

ex·crete' (ik skrēt') v.t., -creted, -creting. to eliminate (waste) from the body. —**ex·cre'tion**, n.

ex·cru'ci·at'ing (ik skrōo'shē ā'ting) adj. 1. causing intense suffering. 2. intense or extreme.

ex'cul·pate' (ek'skul pāt', ik skul'pāt) v.t., -pated, -pating. to free of blame. —**ex'cul·pa'tion**, n.

ex·cur'sion (ik skûr'zhən) n. a short trip.

ex·cuse' v., -cused, -cusing, n. —v.t. (ik skyōoz') 1. to pardon or forgive. 2. to be a justification of. 3. to release from an obligation. —n. (ik skyōos') 4. a reason for excusing or being excused.

ex'e·crate' (ek'si krāt') v.t., -crated, -crating. 1. to detest utterly. 2. to denounce.

ex'e·cute' (ek'si kyōot') v.t., -cuted, -cuting. 1. to accomplish. 2. to perform; do. 3. to put to death according to law. —**ex'e·cu'tion**, n. —**ex'e·cu'tion·er**, n.

ex·ec'u·tive (ig zek'yə tiv) n. 1. a person with administrative or managerial power in an organization. —adj. 2. of or having such power.

ex·ec'u·tor (-tər) n. a person named to carry out a will.

ex·ec'u·trix' (-triks) n. a woman named to carry out a will.

ex'e·ge'sis (ek'si jē'sis) n., pl. -ses (-sēz) a critical explanation or interpretation, esp. of Scripture.

ex·em'plar (ig zem'plər, -plär) n. a model or pattern.

ex·em'pla·ry (-plə rē) adj. worthy of imitation.

ex·em'pli·fy' (-plə fī') v.t., -fied, -fying. to serve as an example of.

ex·empt' (ig zempt') v.t. 1. to free from an obligation. —adj. 2. not subject to an obligation. —**ex·emp'tion**, n.

ex'er·cise' (ek'sər sīz') n., v., -cised, -cising. —n. 1. physical or mental exertion to increase skill or strength. 2. a putting into action or use. 3. **exercises**, a traditional ceremony. —v.t. 4. to put through exercises. 5. to put into action. —v.i. 6. to take bodily exercise.

ex·ert' (ig zûrt') v.t. 1. to put forth. 2. to put in force. 3. to put (oneself) into vigorous effort. —**ex·er'tion**, n.

ex·hale' (eks hāl') v.i., v.t., -haled, -haling. to breathe out.

ex·haust' (ig zôst') v.t. 1. to use up completely. 2. to tire out. —n. 3. the steam or gases ejected from an engine. —**ex·haus'tion**, n.

ex·haus'tive adj. thorough.

ex·hib'it (ig zib'it) v.t. 1. to show; display for public view. —n. 2. an act of exhibiting. 3. something exhibited. —**ex'hi·bi'tion** (ek'sə bish'ən) n. —**ex·hib'i·tor**, n.

ex·hib'i·tion·ism (-bish'ə niz'əm) n. a desire or tendency to display oneself. —**ex'hi·bi'tion·ist**, n.

ex·hil'a·rate' (ig zil'ə rāt') v.t., -rated, -rating. 1. to make lively. 2. to make joyful. —**ex·hil'a·ra'tion**, n.

ex·hort' (ig zôrt') v.t., v.i. to advise or urge earnestly. —**ex'hor·ta'tion** (eg'zôr tā'shən) n.

ex·hume' (ig zōom', -zyōom') v.t., -humed, -huming. to dig up (a dead body).

ex'i·gen·cy (ek'si jən sē) n., pl. -cies. 1. a state of urgency. 2. **exigencies**, things needed urgently. —**ex'i·gent**, adj.

ex'ile (eg'zīl, ek'sīl) n., v., -iled, -iling. —n. 1. enforced absence from one's country. 2. an exiled person. —v.t. 3. to send into exile.

ex·ist' (ig zist') v.i. 1. to be. 2. to live. 3. to continue to be or live. —**ex·ist'ence**, n. —**ex·ist'ent**, adj.

ex'is·ten'tial (eg'zi sten'shəl, ek'-) adj. of existence.

ex'is·ten'tial·ism n. a philosophy that stresses personal liberty and responsibility. —**ex'is·ten'tial·ist**, n., adj.

ex'it (eg'zit, ek'sit) n. 1. a way out. 2. a departure, as that of an actor from the stage. —v.i., v.t 3. to leave.

exo- a prefix meaning outside.

ex'o·crine (ek'sə krin, -krīn') adj. 1. secreting externally through a duct. 2. of glands that secrete externally through a duct.

ex'o·dus (ek'sə dəs) n. 1. a mass departure or emigration. 2. **Exodus**, the departure of the Israelites from Egypt under Moses.

ex' of·fi·ci·o' (eks' ə fish'ē ō') adv., adj. because of one's office.

ex·on'er·ate' (ig zon'ə rāt') v.t., -ated, -ating. to clear of blame.

ex·or'bi·tant (ig zôr'bi tənt) adj. excessive, esp. in cost.

ex'or·cise' (ek'sôr sīz', -sər-) v.t., -cised, -cising. 1. to expel (an evil spirit) by prayer. 2. to free (a person or place) of evil spirits. —**ex'or·cism**, n. —**ex'or·cist**, n.

ex'o·sphere' (ek'sō sfēr') n. the highest region of the atmosphere.

ex·ot'ic (ig zot'ik) adj. 1. foreign. 2. strikingly unusual.

ex·pand' (ik spand') v.t., v.i. to increase in size, scope, or extent; spread out. —**ex·pan'sion**, n.

ex·panse' (ik spans') n. a broad, unbroken space.

ex·pan'sive (ik span'siv) adj. 1. extensive; wide. 2. warm and cordial.

ex·pa'ti·ate' (ik spā'shē āt') v.i., -ated, -ating. to talk or write at length.

ex·pa'tri·ate' v., -ated, -ating, n. —adj. —v.t., -ated, -ating (-āt') 1. to banish; exile. 2. to withdraw (oneself) from residence in one's native country. —n. (-it) 3. an expatriated person. —adj. (-it) 4. dwelling in a foreign land.

ex·pect' (ik spekt') v.t. 1. to look for as likely to happen or arrive; look forward to. 2. to consider as due or proper. —**ex·pect'an·cy**, n. —**ex·pect'ant**, adj.

ex'pec·ta'tion n. 1. the act or state of expecting. 2. something expected.

ex·pec'to·rate' (-rāt') v.i., v.t., -rated, -rating. to spit, esp. to

cough and spit up mucus. —**ex·pec'to·rant**, n.

ex·pe'di·ent (ik spē'dē ənt) adj. 1. fit or suitable for a purpose. 2. marked by self-interest. —n. 3. a handy means to an end. —**ex·pe'di·en·cy**, n.

ex'pe·dite' (ek'spi dīt') v.t., -dited, -diting. to speed up.

ex'pe·di'tion (ek'spi dish'ən) n. 1. a journey for a specific purpose. 2. a group on such a journey.

ex'pe·di'tious adj. prompt.

ex·pel' (ik spel') v.t., -pelled, -pelling. to drive or force away.

ex·pend' (ik spend') v.t. 1. to use up. 2. to spend. —**ex·pend'i·ture**, n.

ex·pend'a·ble adj. available for spending. 2. capable of being sacrificed if necessary.

ex·pense' (ik spens') n. 1. cost. 2. a cause of spending. 3. **expenses**, charges incurred through business. —**Idiom.** 4. **at the expense of**, at the sacrifice of.

ex·pen'sive adj. costing much.

ex·pe'ri·ence (ik spēr'ē əns) n., v., -enced, -encing. —n. 1. something lived through. 2. observation of events as they occur. 3. knowledge gained from such things. —v.t. 4. to have experience of.

ex·pe'ri·enced adj. wise or skillful through experience.

ex·per'i·ment (ik sper'ə mənt) n. 1. an act or operation to discover something unknown or to test a supposition, principle, etc. —v.i. (-ment') 2. to conduct an experiment. —**ex·per'i·men'tal** (-men'tl) adj. —**ex·per'i·men·ta'tion**, n.

ex'pert n. (eks'pûrt) 1. a person with special skill in a particular field. —adj. (ek'spûrt; also ik spûrt') 2. skilled. —**ex·pert'ly**, adv.

ex'per·tise' (ek'spər tēz') n. expert skill or knowledge.

ex'pi·ate' (ek'spē āt') v.t., -ated, -ating. to make amends for. —**ex'pi·a'tion**, n.

ex·pire' (ik spī°r') v.i., -pired, -piring. 1. to come to an end. 2. to die. 3. to breathe out.

ex·plain' (ik splān') v.t. 1. to make clear. 2. to account for. —v.i. 3. to give an explanation. —**ex'pla·na'tion**, n. —**ex·plan'a·to·ry** (ik splan'-) adj.

ex'ple·tive (ek'spli tiv) n. an often profane exclamation.

ex'pli·cate' (-kāt') v.t., -cated, -cating. to explain in detail.

ex·plic'it (ik splis'it) adj. fully and clearly expressed.

ex·plode' (ik splōd') v., -ploded, -ploding. —v.i. 1. to burst suddenly, noisily, and violently. 2. to burst forth violently or emotionally. —v.t. 3. to cause to explode. —**ex·plo'sion**, n. —**ex·plo'sive**, adj., n.

ex·ploit'¹ (eks'ploit) n. a notable deed.

ex·ploit'² (ik sploit') v.t. to use, esp. selfishly or for profit. —**ex'ploi·ta'tion**, n. —**ex·ploit'a·tive**, n.

ex·plore' (ik splôr') v., -plored, -ploring. —v.t. 1. to travel through (an area) to learn about it. 2. to examine. —v.i. 3. to engage in exploring. —**ex'plo·ra'tion** (ek'splə rā'shən) n. —**ex·plor'a·to·ry**, adj. —**ex·plor'er**, n.

ex·po'nent (ik spō'nənt or, esp. for 2, ek'spō nənt) n. 1. a person who promotes an idea, cause, etc. 2. Math. a symbol placed to the upper right of another to indicate the power to which the latter is to be raised.

ex·port' v.t. (ik spôrt') 1. to send to other countries. —n. (ek'spôrt) 2. something exported.

ex·pose' (ik spōz') v.t., -posed, -posing. 1. to lay open, as to danger. 2. to reveal. 3. to allow light to reach (film).

ex'po·sé' (ek'spō zā') n. exposure of wrongdoing.

ex'po·si'tion (ek'spə zish'ən) n. 1. a large public exhibition. 2. the act of explaining. 3. an explanation.

ex·pos'i·to·ry (ik spoz'i tôr'ē) adj. serving to expound or explain.

ex' post' fac'to (eks' pōst' fak'tō) adj. made or done after the fact; retroactive.

ex·pos'tu·late' (ik spos'chə lāt') v.i., -lated, -lating. to protest or to remonstrate.

ex·po'sure (-spō'zhər) n. 1. an exposing or being exposed. 2. the action of exposing film to the light. 3. position with regard to weather or direction.

ex·pound' (ik spound') v.t. to explain in detail.

ex·press' (ik spres') v.t. 1. to put into words. 2. to make known, as feelings or thoughts. 3. to squeeze out. —adj. 4. clearly stated. 5. moving fast, with few stops, as a train. —n. 6. an express train.

ex·pres'sion n. 1. the act of expressing. 2. a word or phrase. 3. a look or intonation that expresses feeling.

ex·pres'sion·ism n. (often cap.) a style in art, literature, etc., stressing the subjective element in experience and the symbolic aspects of objects. —**ex·pres'sion·ist**, n., adj. —**ex·pres'sion·is'tic**, adj.

ex·pres'sive (ik spres'iv) adj. 1. meaningful. 2. serving to express.

ex·press'way' n. a road for high-speed traffic.

ex·pro'pri·ate' (eks prō'prē āt') v.t., -ated, -ating. to take for public use.

ex·pul'sion (ik spul'shən) n. the act of driving out or the state of being driven out.

ex·punge' (ik spunj') v.t., -punged, -punging. to wipe out; obliterate.

ex'pur·gate' (ek'spər gāt') v.t., -gated, -gating. to remove objectionable parts from.

ex'qui·site (ik skwiz'it, ek'skwi zit) adj. delicately beautiful.

ex'tant (ek'stənt, ik stant') adj. still existing.

ex·tem'po·ra'ne·ous (ik stem'pə rā'nē əs) adj. done, spoken, or performed without preparation. —**ex·tem'po·re** (ik stem'pə rē) adv.

ex·tend' (ik stend') v.t. 1. to stretch or draw out. 2. to make longer or larger. 3. to offer. —**ex·ten'sion**, n.

ex·tend'ed fam'ily n. a family comprising a married couple, their children, and close relatives.

ex·ten'sive (-siv) adj. far-reaching.

ex·tent' (ik stent') n. the space or degree to which a thing extends; scope.

ex·ten'u·ate' (ik sten'yōo āt') v.t., -ated, -ating. to make seem less serious.

ex·te'ri·or (ik stēr'ē ər) adj. 1. being on the outer side or the outside. —n. 2. an exterior surface.

ex·ter'mi·nate' (ik stûr'mə nāt') v.t., -nated, -nating. to get rid of by destroying. —**ex·ter'mi·na'tion**, n. —**ex·ter'mi·na'tor**, n.

ex·ter'nal (ik stûr'nl) adj. 1. outer. 2. acting from without. 3. superficial.

ex·tinct' (ik stingkt') adj. 1. no longer existing. 2. no longer active. —**ex·tinc'tion**, n.

ex·tin'guish (ik sting'gwish) v.t. 1. to put out, as a fire. 2. to wipe out. —**ex·tin'guish·er**, n.

ex'tir·pate' (ek'stər pāt') v.t., -pated, -pating. to destroy totally.

ex·tol' (ik stōl') v.t., -tolled, -tolling. to praise highly.

ex·tort' (ik stôrt') v.t. to get (money, information, etc.) by force or threat. —**ex·tor'tion**, n.

ex·tor'tion·ate (ik stôr'shə nit) adj. excessive.

ex'tra (ek'strə) adj. 1. more than is usual, expected, or necessary; additional. —n. 2. an additional feature or expense. —adv. 3. in excess of what is usual.

extra- a prefix meaning outside or beyond.

ex·tract' v.t. (ik strakt') 1. to pull or draw out with effort. 2. to copy out, as from a book. 3. to obtain by pressure, distillation, or use of chemicals. —n. (ek'strakt) 4. something extracted. 5. an excerpt. —**ex·trac'tion**, n.

ex'tra·cur·ric'u·lar (ek'strə kə rik'yə lər) adj. outside a regular curriculum.

ex'tra·dite' (ek'strə dīt') v.t., -dited, -diting. to deliver (a fugitive or criminal) to another state. —**ex'tra·di'tion** (-dish'ən) n.

ex'tra·le'gal adj. beyond the authority of law.

ex'tra·mu'ral (-myōor'əl) adj. involving members of more than one school.

ex·tra'ne·ous (ik strā'nē əs) adj. not essential.

ex·traor'di·nar'y (ik strôr'dn er'ē, ek'strə ôr'-) adj. unusual or remarkable. —**ex·traor'di·nar'i·ly**, adv.

ex·trap'o·late' (ik strap'ə lāt') v.t., v.i., -lated, -lating. to infer (an unknown) from something known. —**ex·trap'o·la'tion**, n.

ex'tra·sen'so·ry (ek'strə sen'sə rē) adj. beyond one's physical senses.

ex'tra·ter·res'tri·al adj. 1. being

or from outside the earth's limits. —n. 2. an extraterrestrial being.

ex·trav'a·gant (ik strav'ə gənt) adj. 1. spending more than is necessary or wise. 2. excessive. —**ex·trav'a·gance**, n.

ex·trav'a·gan'za (-gan'zə) n. a lavish production.

ex·treme' (ik strēm') adj. 1. going well beyond the moderate or ordinary. 2. outermost. 3. very great or intense. —n. 4. one of two things that are complete opposites. 5. an extreme degree, act, or condition. —**ex·treme'ly**, adv.

ex·trem'ism n. a tendency to take extreme measures, esp. in politics.

ex·trem'i·ty (ik strem'i tē) n., pl. -ties. 1. the farthest part. 2. an arm or leg. 3. a condition of extreme need, danger, etc.

ex'tri·cate' (ek'stri kāt') v.t., -cated, -cating. to disentangle.

ex·trin'sic (ik strin'sik, -zik) adj. not inherent or essential. 2. being or coming from without; external.

ex'tro·vert' (ek'strə vûrt') n. an outgoing person. —**ex'tro·ver'sion**, n. —**ex'tro·vert'ed**, adj.

ex·trude' (ik strōod') v.t., -truded, -truding. to force or press out.

ex·u'ber·ant (ig zōo'bər ənt) adj. 1. uninhibitedly enthusiastic. 2. abundant. —**ex·u'ber·ance**, n.

ex·ude' (ig zōod' ik sōod') v.i., v.t., -uded, -uding. 1. to ooze or cause to ooze out. 2. to radiate.

ex·ult' (ig zult') v.i. to rejoice triumphantly. —**ex·ult'ant**, adj. —**ex'ul·ta'tion**, n.

eye (ī) n., v., eyed, eying or eyeing. —n. 1. the organ of sight. 2. sight; vision. 3. an attentive look. 4. something like an eye. —v.t. 5. to look at.

eye'ball' n. 1. the globe of the eye. —v.t. 2. Informal. to examine.

eye'brow' n. the ridge and line of short hairs over the eye.

eye'ful (ī'fool) n., pl. -fuls. 1. a thorough view. 2. Informal. an attractive person.

eye'glass'es n.pl. a pair of corrective lenses in a frame.

eye'lash' n. one of the short hairs at the edge of the eyelid.

eye'let (ī'lit) n. a small hole, as for a lace.

eye'lid' n. the movable skin covering the eye.

eye'o'pen·er n. something that causes sudden enlightenment.

eye'sight' n. 1. the power or act of seeing. 2. one's range of vision.

eye'sore' n. something unpleasant to look at.

eye'tooth' n. a canine tooth in the upper jaw.

eye'wash' n. 1. a soothing solution for the eyes. 2. nonsense.

eye'wit'ness n. a person who has seen an event and can give an account of it.

ey'rie (âr'ē, ēr'ē) n., pl. -ries. the lofty nest of a bird of prey; aerie.

F

F, f (ef) n. the sixth letter of the English alphabet.

F 1. Fahrenheit. 2. female.

f. 1. feet. 2. female. 3. folio. 4. foot. 5. franc.

FAA Federal Aviation Administration.

fa'ble (fā'bəl) n. a short tale used to teach a moral.

fab'ric (fab'rik) n. 1. a cloth made by weaving or knitting fibers. 2. framework.

fab'ri·cate' (-ri kāt') v.t., -cated, -cating. 1. to construct. 2. to invent; make up.

fab'u·lous (fab'yə ləs) adj. 1. almost impossible to believe. 2. marvelous.

fa·cade' (fə säd') n. 1. the front of a building. 2. outward appearance.

face (fās) n., v., faced, facing. —n. 1. the front part of the head. 2. an expression on the face. 3. outward appearance. 4. a grimace. 5. the surface. 6. the most important side; front. —v.t. 7. to look toward. 8. to confront directly or bravely. 9. to put a facing on. —v.i. 10. to turn or be turned. 11. to have the face in a certain direction. 12. **face up to,** a. to admit. b. to meet courageously. —**Idiom.** 13. **face to face,** a. opposite one another. b. confronting one another. 14. **to one's face,** in one's presence.

face'less adj. lacking identity.

face′-lift′ *n.* **1.** surgery to eliminate facial sagging and wrinkles. **2.** renovation to improve the appearance of a building.

face′-sav′ing *adj.* saving one's prestige or dignity.

fac′et (fas′it) *n.* **1.** one of the surfaces of a cut gem. **2.** an aspect.

fa•ce′tious (fə se′shəs) *adj.* not meant to be taken seriously.

face′ val′ue (fas′ val′yoo for 1; fas′ val′yoo for 2) *n.* **1.** the value printed on the face of a stock, bond, etc. **2.** apparent value.

fa′cial (fā′shəl) *adj.* **1.** of or for the face. —*n.* **2.** a treatment to beautify the face.

fac′ile (fas′il) *adj.* **1.** easily done. **2.** superficial.

fa•cil′i•tate (fə sil′i tāt′) *v.t.,* **-tated, -tating.** to make easier. —**fa•cil′i•ta′tion,** *n.* —**fa•cil′i•ta′tor,** *n.*

fa•cil′i•ty (-i tē) *n., pl.* **-ties. 1.** something designed or installed for a specific purpose. **2.** ease.

fac′ing (fā′sing) *n.* **1.** a decorative or protective outer layer. **2.** a lining applied along an edge of a garment.

fac•sim′i•le (fak sim′ə lē) *n.* **1.** an exact copy. **2.** a fax.

fact (fakt) *n.* **1.** something known to exist or to have happened. **2.** something known to be true. —**fac′tu•al,** *adj.*

fac′tion (fak′shən) *n.* **1.** a group within a larger group. **2.** dissension. —**fac′tion•al,** *adj.*

fac′tious (-shəs) *adj.* causing strife.

fac′tor (fak′tər) *n.* **1.** one of the elements contributing to a result. **2.** one of two numbers multiplied.

fac′to•ry (fak′tə rē) *n., pl.* **-ries.** a place where goods are manufactured.

fac′ul•ty (fak′əl tē) *n., pl.* **-ties. 1.** a special ability. **2.** one of the powers of the mind or body. **3.** the teaching staff of a school.

fad (fad) *n.* a temporary fashion.

fade (fād) *v.,* **faded, fading.** —*v.i.* **1.** to lose freshness, color, or vitality. **2.** to disappear gradually. —*v.t.* **3.** to cause to fade.

fag¹ (fag) *n.,* **fagged, fagging.** —*n.* **1.** *Slang.* a cigarette. **2.** a drudge. —*v.t.* **3.** to exhaust.

fag² (fag) *n. Slang: Usu. Disparaging and Offensive.* (a term used to refer to a male homosexual.)

fag′ot (fag′ət) *n.* a bundle of sticks bound together and used as fuel.

Fahr′en•heit′ (far′ən hīt′) *adj.* of a temperature scale in which water freezes at 32° and boils at 212°.

fail (fāl) *v.i.* **1.** to be unsuccessful. **2.** to weaken. **3.** to stop functioning. **4.** to die away. **5.** to become bankrupt. —*v.t.* **6.** to be unsuccessful in the performance of. **7.** to be of no help to. —**fail′ure,** *n.*

fail′ing *n.* **1.** a defect or fault. —*prep.* **2.** in the absence of.

faille (fīl, fāl) *n.* a ribbed fabric of silk or rayon.

fail′-safe′ *adj.* ensured against failure of a mechanical system, nuclear reactor, etc.

faint (fānt) *adj.* **1.** lacking brightness or clarity. **2.** feeling weak or dizzy. —*v.i.* **3.** to lose consciousness briefly.

faint′heart′ed *adj.* lacking courage.

fair¹ (fâr) *adj.* **1.** free from bias or injustice. **2.** proper under the rules. **3.** moderately good or large. **4.** (of the weather) fine. **5.** having light-colored skin and hair. **6.** attractive. **7.** likely; promising. —**fair′ly,** *adv.* —**fair′ness,** *n.*

fair² (fâr) *n.* **1.** a usu. competitive exhibition, as of farm products. **2.** an exhibition and sale of goods.

fair′ shake′ *n.* a just and equal opportunity or treatment.

fair′y (fâr′ē) *n., pl.* **fairies. 1.** a tiny supernatural being. **2.** *Slang: Disparaging and Offensive.* (a contemptuous term used to refer to a male homosexual.)

fair′y•land′ *n.* the imaginary realm of fairies.

fair′y tale′ *n.* **1.** a story, usu. for children, about magical creatures. **2.** an improbable story.

faith (fāth) *n.* **1.** confidence or trust. **2.** religious belief. **3.** loyalty.

faith′ful *adj.* **1.** steady in allegiance or affection. **2.** reliable. **3.** true to fact or standard.

fa•ji′tas (fä hē′təz, fə-) *n. (used with a sing. or pl. v.)* thin strips of marinated and grilled meat, served with tortillas.

fake (fāk) *v.,* **faked, faking,** *n., adj.*

—*v.t.* **1.** to make an imitation of to mislead others. —*v.t.* **2.** to pretend. —*n.* **3.** an imitation intended to be passed off as genuine. **4.** one who fakes. —*adj.* **5.** not genuine.

fa•kir′ (fə kēr′) *n.* a Muslim or Hindu ascetic or mendicant considered to be a wonder-worker.

fal′con (fôl′kən, fal′-) *n.* a swift bird of prey.

fall (fôl) *v.,* **fell** (fel) **fallen, falling,** *n.* —*v.i.* **1.** to come down suddenly to a lower position; drop. **2.** to decline. **3.** to lose position. **4.** to be overthrown. **5.** to pass into a specified condition. **6.** to die in combat. **7. fall back on,** to have recourse to. **8. ~ out,** to quarrel. **9. ~ through,** to fail. —*n.* **10.** an act or instance of falling. **11.** autumn. **12.** surrender or capture, as of a city.

fall′guy′ *n. Slang.* **1.** an easy victim. **2.** a scapegoat.

fal′li•ble (fal′ə bəl) *adj.* liable to be mistaken. —**fal/li•bil′i•ty,** *n.*

fall′ing-out′ *n., pl.* **fallings-out, falling-outs.** a quarrel.

fal•lo′pi•an (or **Fal•lo′pi•an) tube′** (fə lō′pē ən) *n.* either of a pair of long ducts in the female abdomen that transport ova from the ovary to the uterus.

fall′out′ *n.* **1.** radioactive particles carried by the air. **2.** an incidental outcome or product.

fal′low (fal′ō) *adj.* (of land) plowed and left unseeded for a season.

fal′low deer′ *n.* a Eurasian deer with a yellowish coat.

false (fôls) *adj.,* **falser, falsest. 1.** not true or correct. **2.** not loyal. **3.** deceptive. **4.** not genuine. —**fal′si•fy,** *v.t.*

false′hood *n.* a lie.

fal•set′to (fôl set′ō) *n., pl.* **-tos.** an artificially high-pitched voice.

fal′ter (fôl′tər) *v.i.* **1.** to hesitate or waver. **2.** to speak hesitantly. **3.** to move unsteadily.

fame (fām) *n.* widespread reputation; renown. —**famed,** *adj.*

fa•mil′iar (fə mil′yər) *adj.* **1.** commonly known or seen. **2.** well-acquainted. **3.** intimate. **4.** too personal. —**fa•mil/i•ar′i•ty** (-ē ar′i tē, -yar′-) *n.* —**fa•mil′iar•ize′,** *v.t.*

fam′i•ly (fam′ə lē, fam′lē) *n., pl.* **-lies. 1.** parents and their children as a group. **2.** a group of persons descended from a common ancestor. **3.** a set of relatives. **4.** a group of related things or individuals. —**fa•mil′ial** (fə mil′yəl) *adj.*

fam′ily leave′ *n.* an unpaid leave of absence from work in order to take care of a baby or an ailing family member.

fam′ily tree′ *n.* a genealogical chart of a family.

fam′ine (fam′in) *n.* extreme scarcity of food.

fam′ish (fam′ish) *v.t., v.i.* to suffer or cause to suffer extreme hunger.

fa′mous (fā′məs) *adj.* widely known; renowned.

fa′mous•ly *adv.* very well.

fan¹ (fan) *n., v.,* **fanned, fanning.** —*n.* **1.** a device, either waved in the hand or operated electrically, that produces a current of air. **2.** something resembling a fan. —*v.t.* **3.** to cause air to blow upon. **4.** to spread out from a central point.

fan² (fan) *n.* an enthusiastic devotee.

fa•nat′ic (fə nat′ik) *n.* **1.** a person who is excessively devoted to a cause. —*adj.* **2.** excessively devoted to a cause. —**fa•nat′i•cal,** *adj.* —**fa•nat′i•cism** (-ə siz′əm) *n.*

fan′ci•er (fan′sē ər) *n.* a person with a special interest in something, as in breeding animals.

fan′ci•ful *adj.* **1.** imaginary or unreal. **2.** imaginative or inventive.

fan′cy (fan′sē) *n., pl.* **-cies,** *adj.,* **-cier, -ciest,** *v.,* **-cied, -cying.** —*n.* **1.** imagination. **2.** the thing imagined. **3.** a whim. **4.** a liking. —*adj.* **5.** of high quality. **6.** decorative. —*v.t.* **7.** to imagine. **8.** to believe without question. **9.** to crave.

fan′cy-free′ *adj.* free from emotional ties, esp. love.

fan′fare′ *n.* **1.** a flourish played on trumpets. **2.** a showy display.

fang (fang) *n.* a long, sharp tooth.

fan′ny *n., pl.* **-nies.** *Informal.* the buttocks.

fan•ta′sia (fan tā′zhə) *n.* a fanciful musical work.

fan′ta•size′ (-tə sīz′) *v.,* **-sized, -sizing.** —*v.i.* **1.** to have fanciful

ideas. —*v.t.* **2.** to create in one's daydreams.

fan•tas′tic (-tas′tik) *adj.* **1.** wonderful and strange. **2.** excellent.

fan′ta•sy (-tə sē, -zē) *n., pl.* **-sies. 1.** imagination. **2.** a daydream or illusion. **3.** a fantasia.

FAQ (fak, ef′ā′kyoo′) *n., pl.* **FAQs, FAQ's.** *Computers.* frequently asked questions: a document that introduces newcomers to a topic.

far (fär) *adv., adj.,* **farther, farthest.** —*adv.* **1.** at or to a great distance or remote point. —*adj.* **2.** distant. —*Idiom.* **3. by far,** very much. **4. far and away,** without doubt. **5. far and wide,** everywhere. **6. so far,** up to a certain point.

far′a•way′ (fär′ə wā′) *adj.* **1.** distant. **2.** preoccupied; dreamy.

farce (färs) *n.* **1.** light comedy. **2.** a foolish or ridiculous display; pretense. —**far′ci•cal,** *adj.*

fare (fâr) *n., v.,* **fared, faring.** —*n.* **1.** the price charged a passenger for travel. **2.** a paying passenger. **3.** food. —*v.i.* **4.** to get along.

fare′well′ (fâr′wel′) *interj.* **1.** goodbye. —*n.* **2.** good wishes at parting. **3.** a departure. —*adj.* **4.** final.

far′-fetched′ *adj.* not reasonable or probable.

far′-flung′ *adj.* **1.** extending over a great distance. **2.** widely distributed.

fa•ri′na (fə rē′nə) *n.* flour or grain cooked as a cereal.

farm (färm) *n.* **1.** a tract of land on which crops and livestock are raised. —*v.t.* **2.** to cultivate (land). —*v.i.* **3.** to operate a farm. **4. farm out,** to assign (work) to another. —**farm′er,** *n.* —**farm′ing,** *n.*

farm′yard′ *n.* an enclosed area surrounded by farm buildings.

far′-off′ *adj.* distant.

far•ra′go (fə rä′gō, -rā′-) *n., pl.* **-goes.** a confused mixture.

far′-reach′ing *adj.* extending far in influence or effect.

far′row (far′ō) *n.* **1.** a litter of pigs. —*v.i.* **2.** to give birth to young pigs.

far′sight′ed (-sī′tid, -sī′-) *adj.* **1.** seeing distant objects best. **2.** planning for the future.

far′ther (fär′thər) *adv., compar. of* **far. 1.** at or to a greater distance or extent. —*adj., compar. of* **far. 2.** more distant. **3.** additional.

—**Usage.** FARTHER is used to indicate physical distance: *Is it much farther to the hotel?* FURTHER is used to refer to additional time, amount, or abstract ideas: *I would rather not talk about this further.* But both FARTHER and FURTHER are often used for distance of any kind: *Here is the solution; look no farther/further. His study of the novel reaches farther/further than any earlier one.*

far′thest (-thist) *adv., superl. of* **far. 1.** at or to the greatest distance. —*adj., superl. of* **far. 2.** most distant.

FBI Federal Bureau of Investigation.

FCC Federal Communications Commission.

FDA Food and Drug Administration.

FDIC Federal Deposit Insurance Corporation.

fas′ci•nate′ (fas′ə nāt′) *v.t.,* **-nated, -nating. 1.** to attract and hold, as by a unique power or a special quality. **2.** to arouse the interest of. —**fas′ci•na′tion,** *n.*

fas′cism (fash′iz əm) *n.* a dictatorship emphasizing aggressive nationalism, militarism, and racism. —**fas′cist,** *n., adj.* —**fa•scis′tic,** *adj.*

fash′ion (fash′ən) *n.* **1.** a prevailing style. **2.** manner. —*v.t.* **3.** to give shape to; make.

fash′ion•a•ble *adj.* in or using the latest style. —**fash′ion•a•bly,** *adv.*

fast¹ (fast) *adj.* **1.** acting or moving with speed. **2.** done in little time. **3.** (of a timepiece) ahead of the correct time. **4.** firmly fixed or held. —*adv.* **5.** quickly. **6.** firmly; tightly.

fast² (fast) *v.i.* **1.** to go without food or certain kinds of food. —*n.* **2.** the act of fasting. **3.** the period of fasting.

fas′ten (fas′ən) *v.t.* **1.** to fix or attach firmly or securely. —*v.i.* **2.** to become fastened. —**fas′ten•er,** *n.*

fast′-food′ *adj.* specializing in food that is prepared and served quickly.

Feb. February.

Feb•ru•ar′y (feb′roo er′ē, feb′yoo-) *n., pl.* **-aries.** the second month of the year.

—**Pronunciation.** The second pronunciation for FEBRUARY shown above, with the first (r) replaced by (y), occurs because neighboring sounds that are alike tend to become different. This word also conforms to the pattern (-yoo er′ē) by analogy with the pronunciation of

events are determined by fate. —**fa′tal•ist,** *n.*

fa•tal′i•ty (fā tal′i tē, fə-) *n., pl.* **-ties.** a death caused by a disaster.

fate (fāt) *n.* **1.** the power believed to control events; destiny. **2.** something that happens unavoidably.

fat′ed *adj.* subject to fate; destined.

fate′ful *adj.* having important or disastrous consequences.

fa′ther (fä′thər) *n.* **1.** a male parent. **2.** a founder. **3.** a title for a priest. **4. Father,** God. —*v.t.* **5.** to beget. —**fa′ther•hood,** *n.* —**fa′ther•ly,** *adj.*

fa′ther-in-law′ *n., pl.* **fathers-in-law.** the father of one's spouse.

fa′ther•land′ *n.* **1.** one's native country. **2.** the land of one's ancestors.

fath′om (fath′əm) *n.* **1.** a unit of nautical measure equal to 6 feet (1.8 m). —*v.t.* **2.** to understand.

fa•tigue′ (fə tēg′) *n., v.,* **-tigued, -tiguing.** —*n.* **1.** weariness from exertion. **2.** the weakening of material from repeated stress. **3.** nonmilitary labor by military personnel. —*v.t., v.i.* **4.** to weary with exertion.

fat′ty ac′id *n.* an organic acid found in animal and vegetable fats.

fat′u•ous (fach′oo əs) *adj.* foolish or silly.

fau′cet (fô′sit) *n.* a device for controlling the flow of liquid from a pipe; tap.

fault (fôlt) *n.* **1.** a defect or flaw. **2.** responsibility for something wrong. **3.** an error. **4.** a fracture in a body of rock. —*Idiom.* **5. at fault,** blameworthy. —**faul′ty,** *adj.*

faun (fôn) *n.* an ancient Roman deity, part man and part goat.

fau′na (fô′nə) *n., pl.* **-nas, -nae** (-nē). the animals or animal life of a particular region or period.

faux pas′ (fō pä′) *n.* an embarrassing social error.

fa′vor (fā′vər) *n.* **1.** a kind act. **2.** approval. **3.** preferential treatment. —*v.t.* **4.** to regard with favor. **5.** to prefer. **6.** to show favor to. **7.** to be favorable to. **8.** to resemble. —*Idiom.* **9. in favor of, a.** in support of. **b.** to the advantage of.

fa′vor•a•ble *adj.* **1.** showing approval. **2.** pleasing. **3.** advantageous.

fa′vor•ite *n.* **1.** a person or thing preferred. **2.** the one most likely to win. —*adj.* **3.** preferred.

fa′vor•it•ism (-ə tiz′əm) *n.* preference shown toward certain persons.

fawn¹ (fôn) *n.* a young deer.

fawn² (fôn) *v.i.* to try to win favor by being servile.

fax (faks) *n.* **1.** a method or device for sending documents by telephone. **2.** an item sent in this way. —*v.t.* **3.** to send by fax.

faze (fāz) *v.t.,* **fazed, fazing.** to cause to be disconcerted.

the first month of the year, *January.* Although the pronunciation of FEBRUARY with (y) is often criticized, both pronunciations are used by educated speakers and are considered standard.

fe′ces (fē′sēz) *n.pl.* excrement.

feck′less (fek′lis) *adj.* **1.** incompetent. **2.** irresponsible and lazy.

fe′cund (fē′kund) *adj.* fertile.

fed. **1.** federal. **2.** federated. **3.** federation.

fed′er•al (fed′ər əl) *adj.* of a system in which states unite under a central government distinct from the individual governments of the separate states.

fed′er•ate′ (fed′ə rāt′) *v.t., v.i.,* **-ated, -ating.** to unite under a central authority.

fe•do′ra (fi dôr′ə) *n.* a soft felt hat with a curved brim.

fee (fē) *n.* a sum charged, as for professional services.

fee′ble (fē′bəl) *adj.,* **-bler, -blest. 1.** weak. **2.** ineffective.

feed (fēd) *v.,* **fed** (fed) **feeding,** *n.* —*v.t.* **1.** to give food to. **2.** to provide as food. **3.** to supply for growth or operation. —*v.i.* **4.** (esp. of animals) to eat. —*n.* **5.** food for livestock. —**feed′er,** *n.*

feed′back′ *n.* a reaction or response.

feel (fēl) *v.,* **felt** (felt) **feeling,** *n.* —*v.t.* **1.** to perceive or examine by touch. **2.** to be conscious of. **3.** to have a physical sensation of. —*v.i.* **4.** to have perception by touch. **5.** to have a sensation of being. —*n.* **6.** a quality that is perceived by touching. **7.** the sense of touch.

feel′er *n.* **1.** a proposal or remark designed to elicit reaction. **2.** an organ of touch, as an antenna.

feign (fān) *v.t.* to pretend.

feint (fānt) *n.* **1.** a deceptive move. —*v.i., v.t.* **2.** to make or deceive with a feint.

feist′y (fī′stē) *adj.,* **-ier, -iest. 1.** lively. **2.** ready to argue or fight.

fe•lic′i•tate′ (fə lis′i tāt′) *v.t.,* **-tated, -tating.** to congratulate.

fe•lic′i•tous (-təs) *adj.* **1.** well chosen for an occasion. **2.** enjoyable.

fe•lic′i•ty *n., pl.* **-ties. 1.** happiness. **2.** a capacity for skill or grace.

fe′line (fē′līn) *adj.* **1.** of or like cats. —*n.* **2.** an animal of the cat family.

fell (fel) *v.t.* to cut or strike down.

fel′low (fel′ō) *n.* **1.** a man. **2.** a companion. **3.** an equal. **4.** a graduate student who receives a stipend. **5.** a member of a learned or professional group.

fel′low•ship′ *n.* **1.** companionship. **2.** the position or stipend of an academic fellow.

fel′on (fel′ən) *n.* a person who has committed a felony.

fel′o•ny *n., pl.* **-nies.** a serious crime, as burglary or murder. —**fe•lo′ni•ous** (fə lō′nē əs) *adj.*

felt (felt) *v.* **1.** pt. and pp. of **feel.** —*n.* **2.** a fabric made by pressing fibers together. —*adj.* **3.** of felt.

fem. 1. female. **2.** feminine.

fe′male (fē′māl) *adj.* **1.** belonging to the sex that conceives and bears young. —*n.* **2.** a female person or animal.

fem′i•nine (fem′ə nin) *adj.* of, like, or suitable for women. —**fem′i•nin′i•ty,** *n.*

fem′i•nism (-i niz′əm) *n.* support of social, political, and economic rights for women equal to those of men. —**fem′i•nist,** *adj., n.*

fe′mur (fē′mər) *n.* the thighbone.

fen (fen) *n.* swampy ground.

fence (fens) *n., v.,* **fenced, fencing.** —*n.* **1.** a barrier around an open area, used to prevent entrance or mark a boundary. **2.** a person who receives and disposes of stolen goods. —*v.t.* **3.** to enclose or separate with a fence. **4.** to sell to a fence. —*v.i.* **5.** to practice the sport of fencing. **6.** to try to avoid giving direct answers. —*Idiom.* **7. on the fence,** undecided.

fenc′ing *n.* **1.** the sport of fighting with foils. **2.** fences or material for fences.

fend (fend) *v.* **1. fend off,** to ward off. **2. fend for,** to try to manage.

fend′er *n.* a metal part mounted over the wheel of a vehicle.

fen′nel (fen′l) *n.* a plant with seeds used for flavoring.

fe′ral (fēr′əl, fer′-) *adj.* in a wild state; not tamed.

fer′ment *v.i., v.t.* (fər ment′) **1.** to undergo or cause to undergo fermentation. —*n.* (fûr′ment) **2.** a substance causing fermentation. **3.** agitation; excitement.

fer/men·ta/tion *n.* a chemical change caused by an organic substance, as yeast, mold, or bacteria, producing effervescence and heat.

fern (fûrn) *n.* a nonflowering plant with feathery leaves.

fe·ro/cious (fə rō/shəs) *adj.* savagely fierce or cruel. **—fe·roc/i·ty** (fə ros/i tē) *n.*

fer/ret (fer/it) *n.* **1.** a kind of weasel. **—v.t. 2.** to search out and bring to light.

fer/ric (fer/ik) *adj.* of or containing iron.

Fer/ris wheel/ (fer/is) *n.* an amusement ride consisting of a large upright wheel with seats suspended from its rim.

fer/rous (fer/əs) *adj.* of or containing iron.

fer/ry (fer/ē) *n., pl.* **-ries,** *v.,* **-ried, -rying. —n. 1.** a boat used for transporting persons or things across a river, bay, etc. **2.** a place where ferries operate. **—v.t. 3.** to carry over a fixed route in a boat. **—v.i. 4.** to go in a ferry.

fer/tile (fûr/tl) *adj.* **1.** producing abundantly. **2.** able to bear young. **3.** capable of developing.

fer/ti·lize/ *v.t.,* **-lized, -lizing. 1.** to render (an egg) capable of development through union with a sperm. **2.** to enrich, as soil. **—fer/ti·li·za/tion,** *n.* **—fer/ti·liz/er,** *n.*

fer/vent (fûr/vənt) *adj.* having or showing intensity of feeling; ardent. **—fer/ven·cy,** *n.*

fer/vid (-vid) *adj.* **1.** vehement; impassioned. **2.** very hot.

fes/ter (fes/tər) *v.i.* **1.** to form pus. **2.** to rankle, as bitterness.

fes/ti·val (fes/tə vəl) *n.* **1.** a time of celebration. **2.** a program of cultural events or entertainment.

fes/tive *adj.* **1.** of or suitable for a feast or festival. **2.** joyous.

fes·tiv/i·ty (-tiv/i tē) *n., pl.* **-ties.** a festive celebration.

fes·toon/ (fe stōōn/) *n.* **1.** a chain of foliage hung between two points. **—v.t. 2.** to decorate with or as if with festoons.

fet/a (fet/ə) *n.* a white, brine-cured cheese usu. made from sheep's or goat's milk.

fetch (fech) *v.t.* **1.** to go and bring back. **2.** to cause to come. **3.** to sell for.

fetch/ing *adj.* charming.

fete (fāt, fet) *n., v.,* **feted, feting. —n. 1.** a festive celebration or entertainment. **2.** a religious festival. **—v.t. 3.** to honor with a fete.

fet/id (fet/id, fē/tid) *adj.* stinking.

fe/tish (fet/ish, fē/tish) *n.* **1.** an object believed to have magical power. **2.** something to which one is irrationally devoted. **—fet/ish·ism,** *n.*

fet/lock (fet/lok/) *n.* **1.** the part of a horse's leg behind the hoof. **2.** the tuft of hair on this part.

fet/ter (fet/ər) *n.* **1.** a chain or shackle put on the feet. **2.** fetters, anything that restrains. **—v.t. 3.** to put fetters on. **4.** to restrain.

fet/tle (fet/l) *n.* condition.

fe/tus (fē/təs) *n.* the young of an animal in the womb or egg. **—fe/tal,** *adj.*

feud (fyōōd) *n.* **1.** lasting hostility. **—v.i. 2.** to engage in a feud.

feu/dal·ism (fyōōd/l iz/əm) *n.* a social and economic system in medieval Europe by which land was held by vassals in exchange for military and other service given to overlords. **—feu/dal,** *adj.*

fe/ver (fē/vər) *n.* **1.** an abnormally high body temperature. **2.** intense nervous excitement. **—fe/ver·ish,** *adj.*

few (fyōō) *adj.* **1.** not many. **—n. 2.** a small number. **—pron. 3.** a small number of persons or things. **—Usage.** See LESS.

fey (fā) *adj.* **1.** strange; whimsical. **2.** supernatural; enchanted.

fez (fez) *n., pl.* **fezzes.** a flat-topped cone-shaped felt hat.

ff 1. folios. **2.** (and the) following (pages, verses, etc.).

fi·an·cé/ (fē/än sā/, fē än/sā) *n.* a man engaged to be married.

fi·an·cée/ *n.* a woman engaged to be married.

fi·as/co (fē as/kō) *n., pl.* **-cos, -coes.** a complete and humiliating failure.

fi/at (fē/ät, fī/ət) *n.* an authoritative order or decree.

fib (fib) *n., v.,* **fibbed, fibbing. —n. 1.** a mild lie. **—v.i. 2.** to tell a fib.

fi/ber (fī/bər) *n.* **1.** a fine threadlike piece, as of cotton. **2.** matter or

material formed of fibers. **3.** plant matter that is bulky and stimulates the action of the intestines. **4.** essential character, quality, or strength. **—fi/brous,** *adj.* **—fi/broid,** *adj.*

fi/ber·glass/ *n.* a material composed of fine glass fibers.

fi/ber op/tics *n.* the technology of sending light and images through glass or plastic fibers. **—fi/ber·op/tic,** *adj.*

fib/ril·la/tion (fib/rə lā/shən, fī/brə-) *n.* rapid and irregular contractions of the heart muscle.

fi·bro/sis (fī brō/sis) *n.* the development of excess fibrous connective tissue in an organ.

fib/u·la (fib/yə lə) *n., pl.* **-lae** (-lē) **-las.** the outer and thinner of the two bones extending from the knee to the ankle.

FICA (fī/kə, fē/-) Federal Insurance Contributions Act.

fick/le (fik/əl) *adj.* not constant.

fic/tion (fik/shən) *n.* **1.** the class of literature consisting of works of imaginative narration in prose form. **2.** works of this class, as novels or short stories. **3.** something made up. **—fic/tion·al,** *adj.*

fic·ti/tious (-tish/əs) *adj.* **1.** false. **2.** of or consisting of fiction.

fid/dle (fid/l) *n., v.,* **-dled, -dling. —n. 1.** a violin. **—v.i. 2.** to play the fiddle. **3.** to move the hands nervously.

fid/dle·sticks/ *interj.* (an exclamation of impatience, disbelief, etc.).

fi·del/i·ty (fi del/i tē, fī-) *n., pl.* **-ties. 1.** faithfulness. **2.** accuracy.

fidg/et (fij/it) *v.i.* **1.** to move about restlessly. **—n. 2.** fidgets, restlessness.

fi·du/ci·ar/y (-shē er/ē) *adj., n., pl.* **-ies. —adj. 1.** held or given in trust. **—n. 2.** a person who holds something in trust for another.

field (fēld) *n.* **1.** a piece of open ground, as for cultivation. **2.** an area where sports are played. **3.** an area of activity or interest. **4.** an area rich in a natural resource. **5.** all the competitors in a contest.

field/ day/ *n.* **1.** a day devoted to outdoor sports or contests. **2.** a chance for unrestricted enjoyment.

fiend (fēnd) *n.* **1.** an evil spirit. **2.** a cruel person. **3.** *Informal.* an addict. **—fiend/ish,** *adj.*

fierce (fērs) *adj.,* **fiercer, fiercest. 1.** wild and savage. **2.** violent. **3.** eager or intense. **—fierce/ly,** *adv.*

fier/y (fī°r/ē, fī/ə rē) *adj.,* **-ier, -iest. 1.** of or like fire. **2.** ardent or passionate.

fi·es/ta (fē es/tə) *n.* a festival.

fife (fīf) *n.* a small high-pitched flute.

fif·teen/ (fif/tēn/) *n., adj.* ten plus five. **—fif·teenth/,** *adj., n.*

fifth (fifth) *adj.* **1.** next after the fourth. **—n. 2.** a fifth part or the fifth one of a series.

fifth/ col/umn *n.* a group of people who work for the enemy within a country at war.

fifth/ wheel/ *n.* one that is unnecessary or unwanted.

fif/ty (fif/tē) *n., adj.* ten times five. **—fif/ti·eth,** *adj., n.*

fig (fig) *n.* the pear-shaped fruit of a semitropical tree.

fig. 1. figurative. **2.** figure.

fight (fīt) *n., v.,* **fought, fighting. —n. 1.** a battle. **2.** a struggle. **3.** an angry argument. **—v.i. 4.** to engage in battle. **5.** to strive. **—v.t. 6.** to contend with in battle. **7.** to carry on. **—fight/er,** *n.*

fig/ment (fig/mənt) *n.* something imagined.

fig·ur·a·tive (-yər ə tiv) *adj.* of the nature of or involving a figure of speech; metaphorical. **—fig/ur·a·tive·ly,** *adv.*

fig/ure *n., v.,* **-ured, -uring. —n. 1.** a written symbol of a number. **2.** an amount or value. **3.** a written symbol other than a letter. **4.** the form or shape of something. **5.** a pattern. **—v.t. 6.** to calculate. **7.** *Informal.* to conclude or think. **8.** to work with numerical figures. **9.** to be or appear. **10.** figure on, to plan or count on. **11. ~ out,** to solve.

fig/ure·head/ *n.* **1.** a leader who has no real power. **2.** a carved figure on the bow of a ship.

fig/ure of speech/ *n.* an expression, as a metaphor, in which words are used in a nonliteral sense.

fig/ur·ine/ (-yə rēn/) *n.* a miniature statue.

fil/a·ment (fil/ə mənt) *n.* **1.** a very

fine thread. **2.** a threadlike conductor in a light bulb.

fil/bert (fil/bərt) *n.* a kind of hazelnut.

filch (filch) *v.t.* to steal.

file¹ (fīl) *n., v.,* **filed, filing. —n. 1.** a container in which papers are arranged in order. **2.** a collection of papers arranged in order. **3.** a collection of computer data stored by name. **4.** a line of persons or things. **—v.t. 5.** to arrange or keep in a file. **—v.i. 6.** to march in a line.

file² (fīl) *n., v.,* **filed, filing. —n. 1.** a metal tool having rough surfaces for smoothing metal, wood, etc. **—v.t. 2.** to smooth or reduce with a file.

fil/i·al (fil/ē əl) *adj.* of or befitting a son or daughter.

fil/i·bus/ter (fil/ə bus/tər) *n.* **1.** the use of long speeches to prevent or delay the adoption of legislation. **—v.i., v.t. 2.** to impede (legislation) by making long speeches.

fil/i·gree/ (-i grē/) *n.* delicate ornamental work of fine wires.

Fil·i·pi·no (fil/ə pē/nō) *n., pl.* **-nos.** a native of the Philippines.

fill (fil) *v.t.* **1.** to make full. **2.** to spread through completely. **3.** to occupy. **4.** to supply the requirements of. **5.** to stop up. **—v.i. 6.** to become full. **7. fill in, a.** to supply (missing information). **b.** to complete by adding detail. **c.** to act as a substitute. **8. ~ out, a.** to complete (a form) by supplying information. **b.** to become rounder and fuller. **—n. 9.** a full supply. **10.** material for building up the level of an area.

fil·let (fi lā/) *n.* **1.** a narrow strip, esp. of meat or fish. **—v.t. 2.** to cut (meat or fish) into a fillet.

fil/lip (fil/əp) *n.* something that excites.

fil/ly (fil/ē) *n., pl.* **-lies.** a young female horse.

film (film) *n.* **1.** a thin layer or coating. **2.** a thin sheet or strip with a photographically sensitive coating. **3.** a motion picture. **—v.t. 4.** to cover with a film. **5.** to make a film of. **—v.i. 6.** to become covered with a film. **—film/y,** *adj.*

film/strip/ *n.* a length of film containing still pictures for projecting on a screen.

fil/ter (fil/tər) *n.* **1.** a device or substance for straining the impurities out of liquid or gas. **2.** a screen that modifies light or sound waves. **—v.t., v.i. 3.** to remove by or pass through a filter. **—fil·tra/tion,** *n.*

filth (filth) *n.* **1.** disgusting dirt. **2.** obscenity. **—filth/y,** *adj.*

fin (fin) *n.* a winglike or paddlelike organ on aquatic animals.

fi·na·gle (fi nā/gəl) *v.i., v.t.,* **-gled, -gling.** to practice or obtain by trickery.

fi/nal (fīn/l) *adj.* **1.** last. **2.** conclusive. **—fi·nal/i·ty** (fī nal/i tē) *n.* **—fi/nal·ize/,** *v.t.*

fi·na/le (fi nä/lē) *n.* the concluding part of something.

fi/nance (fi nans/, fī/nans) *n., v.,* **-nanced, -nancing. —n. 1.** the management of funds. **2.** finances, monetary resources. **—v.t. 3.** to supply with money. **—fi·nan/cial,** *adj.*

fin/an·cier/ (fin/ən sēr/, fī/nən-) *n.* a person who manages large financial operations.

finch (finch) *n.* a small songbird with a short bill.

find (fīnd) *v.,* **found** (found) **finding.** *—v.t.* **1.** to come upon. **2.** to locate or obtain. **3.** to learn. **4.** to recover (something lost). **—v.i. 5.** (of a jury) to decide. **—n. 6.** something found; a discovery.

fine¹ (fīn) *adj.,* **finer, finest,** *adv.* **—adj. 1.** excellent. **2.** in small particles. **3.** delicate; very thin. **4.** highly skilled. **5.** refined. **—adv. 6.** very well.

fine² (fīn) *n., v.,* **fined, fining. —n. 1.** a sum of money exacted as a penalty. **—v.t. 2.** to subject to a fine.

fine/ art/ *n.* painting, sculpture, music, etc.

fin/er·y *n.* fine or showy clothing.

fi·nesse/ (fi ness/) *n.* **1.** delicacy or subtlety of performance or skill. **2.** tact in handling a situation.

fin/ger (fing/gər) *n.* **1.** any of the five parts extending from the end of the hand. **—v.t. 2.** to touch with the fingers. **—fin/ger·nail/,** *n.*

fin/ger·print/ *n.* **1.** an impression of the markings of the surface of the fingertip. **—v.t. 2.** to take or record the fingerprints of a person.

fin/ger·tip/ *n.* the tip of a finger.

fin/ick·y (fin/i kē) *adj.* excessively particular.

fi/nis (fin/is, fē nē/, fī/nis) *n.* the end.

fin/ish (fin/ish) *v.t.* **1.** to bring to an end. **2.** to come to the end of. **3.** to use completely. **4.** to destroy. **5.** to complete in detail. **6.** to put a coating on. **—v.i. 7.** to come to an end. **—n. 8.** the final part. **9.** something that completes a thing. **10.** a surface coating or treatment.

fi/nite (fī/nīt) *adj.* having bounds or limits. **—fi/nite·ly,** *adv.*

Finn (fin) *n.* a native of Finland.

Finn/ish (fin/ish) *adj.* **1.** of Finland, its inhabitants, or its people. **—n. 2.** the language of Finland.

fiord (fyôrd, fē ôrd/) *n.* a fjord.

fir (fûr) *n.* a cone-bearing evergreen tree of the pine family.

fire (fī°r) *n., v.,* **fired, firing. —n. 1.** the light, heat, and flame given off by something burning. **2.** a burning mass. **3.** a destructive burning. **4.** brilliance. **5.** anger or excitement. **—v.t. 6.** to set on fire. **7.** to fill with excitement. **8.** to shoot (a weapon). **9.** to bake in a kiln. **10.** to dismiss from a job. **—v.i. 11.** to catch fire. **12.** to discharge a weapon.

fire/arm/ *n.* a gun.

fire/bomb/ *n.* **1.** an incendiary bomb. **—v.t. 2.** to attack with firebombs.

fire/crack/er *n.* a small firework that makes a loud noise.

fire/fight/er *n.* a person who fights destructive fires.

fire/fly/ *n., pl.* **-flies.** a nocturnal beetle that produces light.

fire/place/ *n.* the part of a chimney that opens into a room and in which fuel is burned.

fire/plug/ *n.* a hydrant with water for fighting fires.

fire/proof/ *adj.* resistant to destruction by fire.

fire/trap/ *n.* a building likely to burn and difficult to escape from.

fire/works/ *n.pl.* devices ignited for a display of light or a loud noise.

firm¹ (fûrm) *adj.* **1.** not soft or yielding when pressed. **2.** securely fixed. **3.** resolute. **—v.t., v.i. 4.** to make or become firm.

firm² (fûrm) *n.* a business organization.

fir/ma·ment (fûr/mə mənt) *n.* the sky.

first (fûrst) *adj.* **1.** being before all others. **—adv. 2.** before all others. **3.** for the first time. **—n. 4.** the person or thing that is first. **5.** the winning rank in a competition.

first/ aid/ *n.* emergency treatment.

first/ class/ *n.* **1.** the highest class or grade. **2.** the most expensive class in travel. **3.** the class of mail sealed against inspection. **—first/-class/,** *adj.*

first/hand/ or **first/-hand/,** *adv.* from the first or original source.

first/-rate/ *adj.* **1.** of the highest quality. **—adv. 2.** very well.

fis/cal (fis/kəl) *adj.* of public revenues.

fish (fish) *n., pl.* **fish, fishes,** *v.* *—n.* **1.** a cold-blooded aquatic vertebrate having gills and fins. **—v.t. 2.** to try to catch fish in. **—v.i. 3.** to try to catch fish. **4.** to search carefully.

fisher·man *n.* a person who fishes.

fish/er·y *n.* a place where fish are caught.

fish/y *adj.,* **-ier, -iest.** like a fish, esp. in taste or smell. **2.** of questionable character; dubious. **—fish/i·ness,** *n.*

fis/sion (fish/ən) *n.* a splitting, esp. of the nucleus of an atom. **—fis/sion·a·ble,** *adj.*

fis/sure (fish/ər) *n.* a narrow opening.

fist (fist) *n.* a closed hand.

fist/ful (-fŏŏl) *n., pl.* **-fuls.** a handful.

fist/i·cuffs/ (-i kufs/) *n.pl.* a fight with the fists.

fit¹ (fit) *adj.,* **fitter, fittest,** *v.,* **fitted, fitting,** *n.* **—adj. 1.** suitable. **2.** proper. **3.** healthy. **—v.t. 4.** to be suitable or proper for. **5.** to be of the right size or shape for. **6.** to equip. **—v.i. 7.** to be suitable or proper. **8.** to be of the right size or shape. **—n. 9.** the manner in which a thing fits. **—fit/ness,** *n.*

fit² (fit) *n.* a sudden attack of illness or emotion.

fit/ful *adj.* irregular.

fit/ting *adj.* **1.** appropriate. **—n. 2.** the process of trying on clothes

that are being made or altered. **2.** anything provided as standard equipment.

five (fīv) *n., adj.* four plus one.

fix (fiks) *v.t.* **1.** to repair or mend. **2.** to make fast, steady, or definite. **3.** to direct or hold steadily. **4.** to establish.

fix·a/tion (fik sā/shən) *n.* an obsession.

fixed *adj.* not changing.

fix/ings *n.pl. Informal.* appropriate accompaniments.

fix/ture (-chər) *n.* **1.** something securely fixed in place. **2.** a person or thing that is firmly established.

fizz (fiz) *v.i.* **1.** to make a hissing sound; effervesce. **—n. 2.** a fizzing sound. **3.** an effervescent drink.

fiz/zle (fiz/əl) *v.,* **-zled, -zling,** *n.* **—v.i. 1.** to hiss weakly. **—n. 3.** a failure.

fjord (fyôrd, fē ôrd/) *n.* a narrow arm of the sea.

FL Florida.

fl. 1. (he or she) flourished. **2.** fluid.

Fla. Florida.

flab (flab) *n.* loose, excessive flesh.

flab/ber·gast/ (flab/ər gast/) *v.t.* to astound.

flab/by (flab/ē) *adj.,* **-bier, -biest.** not firm. **—flab/bi·ness,** *n.*

flac/cid (flak/sid, flas/id) *adj.* soft and limp.

flag¹ (flag) *n., v.,* **flagged, flagging. —n. 1.** a piece of cloth with distinctive colors or design that is used as a symbol. **2.** something used to attract attention. **—v.t. 3.** to place a flag on. **4.** to signal with a flag.

flag² (flag) *n.* a plant with long, sword-shaped leaves.

flag³ (flag) *v.i.,* **flagged, flagging.** to lose energy or interest.

flag/el·late/ (flaj/ə lāt/) *v.t.,* **-lated, -lating.** to whip; flog.

flag/on (flag/ən) *n.* a container for liquids, esp. one with a handle, spout, and cover.

fla/grant (flā/grənt) *adj.* shockingly noticeable.

flag/ship/ *n.* **1.** a ship carrying the commander of a fleet. **2.** the most important one of a group.

flail (flāl) *n.* **1.** an instrument for threshing grain. **—v.t., v.i. 2.** to strike or strike at, as with a flail.

flair (flâr) *n.* **1.** aptitude; talent. **2.** smartness of style or manner.

flak (flak) *n.* **1.** antiaircraft fire. **2.** critical or hostile reaction.

flake (flāk) *n., v.,* **flaked, flaking. —n. 1.** a small, thin piece. **—v.i. 2.** to peel off or form into flakes.

flak/y *adj.,* **-ier, -iest. 1.** of or like flakes. **2.** lying or coming off in flakes. **3.** *Slang.* eccentric; odd.

flam·boy/ant (flam boi/ənt) *adj.* showy; colorful.

flame (flām) *n., v.,* **flamed, flaming. —n. 1.** tongue-shaped burning gas or vapor. **—v.i. 2.** to burn with or glow like flames.

fla·men/co (flə meng/kō) *n.* a dance style of the Spanish gypsies.

fla·min/go (flə ming/gō) *n., pl.* **-gos, -goes.** a tall wading bird with pink feathers and long legs.

flam/ma·ble (flam/ə bəl) *adj.* easily set on fire. **—flam/ma·bil/i·ty,** *n.*

flange (flanj) *n.* a projecting rim.

flank (flangk) *n.* **1.** a side, esp. the side of the body between the ribs and hip. **—v.t. 2.** to stand or be placed at the side of.

flan/nel (flan/l) *n.* a soft wool or cotton fabric.

flap (flap) *v.,* **flapped, flapping,** *n.* **—v.i., v.t. 1.** to swing or cause to swing loosely and noisily. **2.** to move up and down. **—n. 3.** a flapping movement. **4.** something flat attached at one side and hanging loosely. **5.** *Informal.* a state of nervous excitement.

flare (flâr) *v.,* **flared, flaring,** *n.* **—v.i. 1.** to blaze with a sudden unsteady flame. **2.** to burst out into sudden anger. **3.** to spread outward. **—n. 4.** a signal fire. **5.** a sudden burst. **6.** an outward curve.

flare/up/ *n.* a sudden outburst or outbreak.

flash (flash) *n.* **1.** a sudden burst of light. **2.** a sudden, brief outburst. **3.** an instant. **4.** a brief news dispatch **—v.i. 5.** to break into sudden light. **6.** to appear suddenly. **7.** to move rapidly. **—v.t. 8.** to cause to flash. **9.** to show briefly. **10.** to display ostentatiously.

flash/back/ *n.* an earlier event inserted out of order in a story.

flash/bulb/ *n.* a bulb giving a burst of light for photography.

flash/light/ *n.* a portable battery powered light.

flash′y *adj.*, **-ier, -iest.** showy and tasteless.

flask (flask) *n.* a flat metal or glass bottle.

flat¹ (flat) *adj.*, **flatter, flattest,** *n.* —*adj.* **1.** level. **2.** horizontal. **3.** not thick. **4.** absolute. **5.** lacking flavor or effervescence. **6.** not shiny. **7.** *Music.* **a.** lowered a half tone in pitch. **b.** below an intended pitch. —*n.* **8.** something flat. **9.** a flat surface. **10.** *Music.* a sign indicating that a note is lowered a half tone. —*flat′ten,* *v.t., v.i.*

flat² (flat) *n.* an apartment.

flat′bed′ *n.* a truck with a trailer platform open on all sides.

flat′car′ *n.* a railroad car without sides or top.

flat′fish′ *n.* a fish with a broad, flat body, as a flounder.

flat′foot′ *n., pl.* **-feet** for 1b, **-foots** for 1a. **1. a.** a condition in which the arch of the foot is flattened. **b.** Usu. **flatfeet.** feet with flattened arches. **2.** *Slang.* a police officer.

flat′-out′ *adj. Informal.* **1.** using full speed, resources, etc. **2.** downright.

flat′ter (flat′ər) *v.t.* **1.** to praise insincerely or excessively. **2.** to show favorably. —**flat′ter•y,** *n.*

flat′u•lent (flach′ə lənt) *adj.* **1.** having an accumulation of gas in the intestines. **2.** inflated and empty; pompous. —**flat′u•lence,** *n.*

flat′ware′ *n.* table utensils.

flaunt (flônt) *v.t.* to display boldly.

fla′vor (flā′vər) *n.* **1.** the distinctive taste of something. —*v.t.* **2.** to give flavor to. —**fla′vor•ing,** *n.*

flaw (flô) *n.* a defect or weakness. —**flawed,** *adj.* —**flaw′less,** *adj.*

flax (flaks) *n.* a plant with blue flowers that is cultivated for its edible, oil-producing seeds and for its fiber, used for making linen. —**flax′en,** *adj.*

flay (flā) *v.t.* **1.** to strip the skin from. **2.** to criticize severely.

flea (flē) *n.* a small, bloodsucking, leaping insect.

flea′ mar′ket *n.* a market, often outdoors, where used articles, antiques, etc., are sold.

fleck (flek) *n.* **1.** a small bit or spot. —*v.t.* **2.** to mark with flecks.

fledg′ling (flej′ling) *n.* a young bird that has just grown flight feathers.

flee (flē) *v.i., v.t.,* **fled** (fled) **fleeing.** to run away (from).

fleece (flēs) *n., v.,* **fleeced, fleecing.** —*n.* **1.** the woolly covering of a sheep. —*v.t.* **2.** to swindle. —**fleec′y,** *adj.*

fleet¹ (flēt) *n.* an organized group of ships, aircraft, or road vehicles.

fleet² (flēt) *adj.* swift.

fleet′ing *adj.* temporary.

flesh (flesh) *n.* **1.** the muscle and fat of an animal body. **2.** the body. **3.** the soft part of a fruit or vegetable. —**flesh′y,** *adj.*

flesh′pot′ *n.* a place of unrestrained pleasure.

flew (flōō) *v.* a pt. of **fly.**

flex (fleks) *v.t., v.i.* **1.** to bend. **2.** to tighten (a muscle) by contraction.

flex′i•ble (-ə bəl) *adj.* **1.** capable of bending. **2.** adaptable.

flib′ber•ti•gib′bet (flib′ər tē jib′it) *n.* a flighty person.

flick (flik) *n.* **1.** a quick light blow or stroke. —*v.t.* **2.** to strike, remove, or operate with a flick.

flick′er *v.i.* **1.** to burn unsteadily. —*n.* **2.** a flickering light or movement. **3.** a brief occurrence.

fli′er (flī′ər) *n.* **1.** a pilot. **2.** a small circular. Also, **fly′er.**

flight (flīt) *n.* **1.** the act or power of flying. **2.** a trip in an airplane. **3.** a hasty departure. **4.** a series of steps.

flight′less *adj.* incapable of flying.

flight′y *adj.,* **-ier, -iest.** frivolous and irresponsible.

flim′sy (flim′zē) *adj.,* **-sier, -siest.** **1.** weak or thin. **2.** not convincing. —**flim′si•ness,** *n.*

flinch (flinch) *v.i.* to draw back; shrink; wince.

fling (fling) *v.,* **flung** (flung) **flinging,** *n.* —*v.t.* **1.** to throw with force, violence, or abandon. **2.** to involve (oneself) vigorously in an undertaking. **3.** to move with haste or violence. —*n.* **4.** an act of flinging. **5.** a short period of indulgence in pleasure.

flint (flint) *n.* a hard stone that strikes sparks. —**flint′y,** *adj.*

flip (flip) *v.,* **flipped, flipping,** *n., adj.,* **flipper, flippest.** —*v.t.* **1.** to turn over by tossing. **2.** to move with a sudden stroke. —*n.* **3.** such a movement. —*adj.* **4.** flippant.

flip′-flop′ *n.* **1.** a sudden reversal, as of opinion. **2.** a flat backless rubber shoe with a thong between the first two toes.

flip′pant (flip′ənt) *adj.* frivolously disrespectful or lacking in seriousness. —**flip′pan•cy,** *n.*

flip′per *n.* **1.** a broad flat limb, as of a seal, for swimming. **2.** a paddlelike rubber device worn on the foot as an aid in swimming.

flirt (flûrt) *v.i.* **1.** to act amorously without serious intentions. —*n.* **2.** a person who flirts. —**flir•ta′tion,** *n.* —**flir•ta′tious,** *adj.*

flit (flit) *v.i.,* **flitted, flitting.** to fly or move swiftly and lightly.

float (flōt) *v.i.* **1.** to rest or move gently on liquid, in the air, etc. —*v.t.* **2.** to cause to float. **3.** to issue (stocks, bonds, etc.) in order to raise money. —*n.* **4.** something that floats. **5.** a vehicle carrying a display in a parade. —**flo•ta′tion** (flō-tā′shən) *n.*

flock (flok) *n.* **1.** a group of animals, as sheep or birds. **2.** a large group of people. **3.** a church congregation. —*v.i.* **4.** to gather or go in a flock.

floe (flō) *n.* a sheet of floating ice.

flog (flog) *v.t.,* **flogged, flogging.** to beat with a whip or stick.

flood (flud) *n.* **1.** a great overflow of water, esp. over land that is usually dry. **2.** a great outpouring. —*v.t.* **3.** to cover with a flood. —*v.i.* **4.** to become flooded.

flood′light′ *n.* **1.** an artificial light that illuminates a large area. —*v.t.* **2.** to illuminate with a floodlight.

flood′ tide′ *n.* the inflow of the tide.

floor (flôr) *n.* **1.** the surface of a room on which one walks. **2.** a level in a building. **3.** the bottom surface, as of the ocean. **4.** the right to speak. —*v.t.* **5.** to furnish with a floor. **6.** to confound.

floor′ing *n.* floor covering.

flop (flop) *v.,* **flopped, flopping,** *n.* —*v.i.* **1.** to move or fall in a clumsy manner. **2.** to fail completely. —*n.* **3.** an act of flopping. **4.** a complete failure.

flop′py *adj.,* **-pier, -piest.** limp.

flop′py disk′ *n.* a thin plastic disk for storing computer data.

flo′ra (flôr′ə) *n., pl.* **floras, florae** (flôr′ē). the plants or plant life of a particular region or period.

flo′ral *adj.* of flowers.

flo′ret (flôr′it) *n.* a small flower.

flor′id (flôr′id) *adj.* **1.** reddish in color. **2.** excessively ornate.

flo′rist *n.* a person who sells flowers and plants.

floss (flôs) *n.* **1.** the silky fiber from certain plants. **2.** embroidery thread. **3.** dental floss. —*v.i., v.t.* **4.** to use or clean with dental floss.

flo•til′la (flō til′ə) *n.* a group of small ships.

flot′sam (flot′səm) *n.* wreckage of a ship and its cargo found floating on the water.

flounce¹ (flouns) *v.,* **flounced, flouncing,** *n.* —*v.i.* **1.** to go with exaggerated or impatient movements. —*n.* **2.** a flouncing movement.

flounce² (flouns) *n.* a ruffle.

floun′der¹ (floun′dər) *v.i.* to struggle clumsily.

floun′der² (floun′dər) *n.* a flat edible fish.

flour (flou′r, flou′ər) *n.* **1.** the finely ground meal of grain. —*v.t.* **2.** to cover with flour.

flour′ish (flûr′ish) *v.i.* **1.** to thrive or be successful. —*v.t.* **2.** to brandish. —*n.* **3.** a dramatic gesture. **4.** a decoration or embellishment. **5.** an elaborate musical passage.

flout (flout) *v.t., v.i.* to treat with or show scorn; scoff (at).

flow (flō) *v.i.* **1.** to move in a stream. **2.** to proceed smoothly. **3.** to hang loosely. —*n.* **4.** the act or rate of flowing. **5.** something that flows.

flow′ chart′ *n.* a chart showing the steps in a procedure or system.

flow′er (flou′ər) *n.* **1.** the blossom of a plant. **2.** the best part, product, or example. —*v.i.* **3.** to produce flowers. **4.** to develop fully. —**flow′er•y,** *adj.*

flow′er•pot′ *n.* a container in which to grow plants.

flown (flōn) *v.* a pp. of **FLY¹.**

flu (flōō) *n.* influenza.

flub (flub) *v.t., v.i.,* **flubbed, flubbing.** to botch or bungle.

fluc′tu•ate′ (fluk′chōō āt′) *v.i.,* **-ated, -ating.** to vary irregularly.

flue (flōō) *n.* a passage for smoke, air, or gas.

flu′ent (flōō′ənt) *adj.* spoken or able to speak with ease. —**flu′en•cy,** *n.*

fluff (fluf) *n.* **1.** light, downy particles. **2.** a soft, light mass. **3.** something light or frivolous. —*v.t.* **4.** to make or become fluffy. **5.** to make a mistake (in).

fluff′y *adj.,* **-ier, -iest.** **1.** of, like, or covered with fluff. **2.** light and airy. **3.** frivolous.

flu′id (flōō′id) *n.* **1.** a substance that flows. —*adj.* **2.** flowing. **3.** not rigid.

fluke¹ (flōōk) *n.* **1.** the barbed part of an anchor or a spear. **2.** either half of a whale's tail.

fluke² (flōōk) *n.* a lucky chance.

fluke³ (flōōk) *n.* a flounder.

flume (flōōm) *n.* **1.** a deep, narrow gorge containing a stream. **2.** an artificial channel for water.

flung (flung) *v.* pt. and pp. of **fling.**

flunk (flungk) *v.i., v.t.* to fail, esp. in a course or examination.

flun′ky *n., pl.* **-kies.** a person who does menial work.

fluo•res′cence (flōō res′əns, flô) *n.* the emission of visible light by a substance upon exposure to external radiation. —**fluo•res′cent,** *adj.*

fluores′cent lamp′ *n.* a tubular electric lamp in which light is produced by the fluorescence of phosphors coating the inside of the tube.

fluor′i•da′tion (flōōr′ə dā′shən, flôr′-) *n.* the addition of fluorides to drinking water to reduce tooth decay.

fluor′ide (-īd) *n.* a chemical compound containing fluorine.

fluor′ine (-ēn) *n.* a nonmetallic chemical element, a yellowish toxic gas.

flur′ry (flûr′ē) *n., pl.* **-ries.** **1.** a light shower of snow. **2.** a sudden commotion or excitement.

flush¹ (flush) *n.* **1.** a rosy glow; blush. **2.** a rushing flow of water. **3.** a sudden rise of emotion. **4.** a sensation of heat. —*v.t.* **5.** to wash out with a rush of water. —*v.i.* **6.** to become red in the face.

flush² (flush) *adj.* **1.** even with an adjoining surface. **2.** well supplied. **3.** even with the right or left margin of a page of type.

flus′ter (flus′tər) *v.t.* to confuse and agitate.

flute (flōōt) *n.* **1.** a wind instrument with a high range, consisting of a tube with fingerholes or keys. **2.** a decorative groove. —**flut′ist,** *n.*

flut′ter (flut′ər) *v.i.* **1.** to wave or flap about. **2.** to beat rapidly and irregularly, as the heart. **3.** to be agitated. —*n.* **4.** a fluttering movement. **5.** a state of nervous excitement. —**flut′ter•y,** *adj.*

flux (fluks) *n.* **1.** a flowing. **2.** continuous change. **3.** a substance added to metal to aid in fusion.

fly¹ (flī) *v.,* **flew** (flōō), **flown** (flōn), **flying,** *n., pl.* **flies.** —*v.i.* **1.** to move or be carried through the air, using wings or in an aircraft. **2.** to move swiftly. —*v.t.* **3.** to cause to move through the air or transport by air. **4.** to operate (an aircraft). —*n.* **5.** a flap that conceals fasteners in a garment opening. **6.** **flies,** the space above a theater stage.

fly² (flī) *n., pl.* **flies.** **1.** a winged insect. **2.** a fishhook designed to resemble an insect.

fly′-blown′ *adj.* tainted; spoiled.

fly′-by-night′ *adj.* not reliable or stable.

fly′er *n.* a flier.

fly′ing but′tress *n.* an arch projecting from and supporting a wall.

fly′ing col′ors *n.pl.* outstanding success.

fly′ing sau′cer *n.* a disk-shaped object reportedly seen flying at high speed and altitude.

fly′leaf′ *n., pl.* **-leaves.** a blank page in the front or back of a book.

fly′wheel′ *n.* a wheel that regulates the speed of machinery.

foal (fōl) *n.* **1.** a young horse or related mammal. —*v.i.* **2.** to give birth to a foal.

foam (fōm) *n.* **1.** a mass of tiny bubbles. **2.** a lightweight spongy material, as rubber or plastic. —*v.i.* **3.** to form foam.

foam′ rub′ber *n.* a spongy rubber used esp. in cushions.

fob¹ (fob) *n.* a watch chain or an ornament on such a chain.

fob² (fob) *v.t.,* **fobbed, fobbing. fob off,** to dispose of (something inferior) by trickery; palm off.

fo′cus (fō′kəs) *n., pl.* **-cuses, -ci** (-sī) *v.,* **-cused, -cusing.** —*n.* **1.** a central point, as of attention. **2.** a point at which rays meet. **3.** the adjustment of an optical device to produce a clear image. —*v.t.* **4.** to bring into focus. **5.** to concentrate. —*v.i.* **6.** to become focused. —**fo′cal,** *adj.*

fod′der (fod′ər) *n.* food for livestock.

foe (fō) *n.* an enemy.

fog (fog) *n., v.,* **fogged, fogging.** —*n.* **1.** thick mist. **2.** mental confusion. —*v.t., v.i.* **3.** to envelop or become enveloped with fog. —**fog′gy,** *adj.*

fo′gy (fō′gē) *n., pl.* **-gies.** an old-fashioned person.

foi′ble (foi′bal) *n.* a minor weakness in a person's character.

foil¹ (foil) *v.t.* to frustrate or thwart.

foil² (foil) *n.* **1.** metal in the form of very thin sheets. **2.** a person or thing that makes another seem better by contrast.

foil³ (foil) *n.* a thin, flexible fencing sword with a blunt point.

foist (foist) *v.t.* to get a person to accept, buy, etc. (something inferior or undesirable).

fold¹ (fōld) *v.t.* **1.** to bend (paper, cloth, etc.) over upon itself. **2.** to bring together and intertwine or cross. **3.** to enclose, wrap, or envelop. —*v.i.* **4.** to be folded. **5.** to fail, esp. to go out of business. —*n.* **6.** a folded part. **7.** a line or crease made by folding.

fold² (fōld) *n.* **1.** an enclosure for sheep. **2.** a group sharing common beliefs.

-fold a suffix meaning: **1.** having so many parts. **2.** times as many.

fold′er *n.* **1.** a folded cover for holding loose papers. **2.** a circular.

fo′li•age (fō′lē ij) *n.* leaves.

fo′lic ac′id (fō′lik, fol′ik) *n.* one of the B vitamins.

fo′li•o′ (fō′lē ō′) *n., pl.* **-ios.** **1.** a sheet of paper folded once to make two leaves, or four pages, of a book. **2.** a book having pages of the largest size. **3.** a page number.

folk (fōk) *n., pl.* **folk** or **folks.** **1.** people. **2.** an ethnic group. **3. folks,** *Informal.* one's relatives. —*adj.* **4.** of the common people.

folk′lore′ *n.* the traditional customs and beliefs of a people.

folk′ song′ *n.* a song originating among the common people or a song of similar character written by a known composer.

folk′sy *adj.,* **-sier, -siest.** friendly; informal.

fol′li•cle (fol′i kal) *n. Anatomy.* a small cavity, sac, or gland.

fol′low (fol′ō) *v.t.* **1.** to come or go after. **2.** to pursue. **3.** to conform to or obey. **4.** to keep up with and understand. —*v.i.* **5.** to come next after something else. **6.** to result.

fol′low•er *n.* a person who follows; a disciple.

fol′low•ing *n.* a group of admirers or disciples.

fol′low-through′ *n.* **1.** the last part of a motion, as after a ball has been struck. **2.** the act of continuing a plan, program, etc., to completion.

fol′ly (fol′ē) *n., pl.* **-lies.** foolishness or a foolish action or idea.

fo•ment′ (fō ment′) *v.t.* to foster or instigate.

fond (fond) *adj.* **1.** affectionate; loving. **2.** doting. **3.** cherished. **4. fond of,** having a liking or affection for. —**fond′ly,** *adv.*

fon′dant (fon′dənt) *n.* a creamy sugar paste used in candies.

fon′dle (fon′dl) *v.t.,* **-dled, -dling.** to caress.

font¹ (font) *n.* a basin for baptismal water in a church.

font² (font) *n. Printing.* a complete set of type in one style.

food (fōōd) *n.* a substance that is taken into the body to sustain life.

food′ chain′ *n. Ecol.* a series of organisms in which each member is fed upon by the one above it.

food′ proc′essor *n.* an appliance for chopping, shredding, or otherwise processing food.

fool (fōōl) *n.* **1.** a silly or stupid person. **2.** a court jester. —*v.t.* **3.** to trick. —*v.i.* **4.** to act like a fool. —**fool′ish,** *adj.*

fool′har′dy *adj.,* **-dier, -diest.** recklessly bold.

fool′proof′ *adj.* **1.** involving no risk or harm. **2.** never-failing.

fools′cap′ (fōōlz′kap′) *n.* a type of writing paper.

fool′s′ gold′ *n.* iron or copper pyrites.

fool′s′ par′adise *n.* a state of illusory happiness.

foot (fōōt) *n., pl.* **feet** (fēt) *v.* —*n.* **1.** the part of the leg on which the body stands. **2.** a part similar to a foot. **3.** a unit of length equal to 12 inches. **4.** the lowest part. **5.** a metrical unit in verse. —*v.t.* **6.** to pay. —*Idiom.* **7. on foot,** by walking or running. **8. under foot,** in the way.

foot′age (-ij) *n.* length or extent in feet.

foot′ball′ *n.* **1.** a game in which two opposing teams of 11 players defend goals at opposite ends of a field. **2.** the ball used. **3.** *Chiefly Brit.* rugby or soccer.

foot′hill′ *n.* a hill at the base of a mountain.

foot′hold′ *n.* **1.** a support for the feet. **2.** a firm basis for further progress.

foot′ing *n.* **1.** a support for the foot. **2.** a basis. **3.** stability.

foot′less *adj.* having no basis.

foot′lights′ *n.pl.* the lights at the front of a stage floor.

foot′lock′er *n.* a small trunk.

foot′loose′ *adj.* free to go or travel about.

foot′man *n.* a male servant.

foot′note′ *n.* a note printed at the bottom of a page.

foot′print′ *n.* a mark left by the foot.

foot′step′ *n.* the setting down of a foot or the sound of this.

foot′stool′ *n.* a low stool for resting the feet.

fop (fop) *n.* a man excessively concerned with his clothes.

for (fôr; *unstressed* fər) *prep.* **1.** with the purpose of. **2.** intended to benefit or be used by. **3.** as the price of. **4.** in favor of. **5.** appropriate to. **6.** on behalf of. **7.** during. —*conj.* **8.** because.

for′age (fôr′ij) *n., v.,* **-aged, -aging.** —*n.* **1.** food for horses or cattle. —*v.i.* **2.** to search about.

for′ay (fôr′ā) *n.* **1.** a quick raid. **2.** an attempt.

for•bear′ (fôr bâr′) *v.,* **-bore** (-bôr′), **-borne** (-bôrn′), **-bearing.** —*v.t.* **1.** to refrain from. —*v.i.* **2.** to be patient.

for•bid′ (fər bid′, fôr-) *v.t.,* **-bade** (-bad′) or **-bad,** **-bidden** or **-bid, -bidding.** **1.** to order (a person) not to do something. **2.** to prohibit (something). **3.** to prevent.

for•bid′ding *adj.* threatening or discouraging.

force (fôrs) *n., v.,* **forced, forcing.** —*n.* **1.** strength. **2.** violence. **3.** energy. **4.** power to influence or persuade. **5.** a body of military troops or police. —*v.t.* **6.** to compel to do something. **7.** to bring about or obtain by force. **8.** to break open. **9.** to cause (plants) to grow at an increased rate.

for′ceps (fôr′səps, -seps) *n.* a medical instrument for seizing and holding objects.

for′ci•ble (fôr′sə bal) *adj.* done by force. —**for′ci•bly,** *adv.*

ford (fôrd) *n.* **1.** a place where a body of water may be crossed by wading or driving. —*v.t.* **2.** to cross at a ford. —**ford′a•ble,** *adj.*

fore (fôr) *adj.* **1.** situated in front. **2.** first in place, time, order, or rank. —*adv.* **3.** forward. —*n.* **4.** the front.

fore- a prefix meaning: **1.** before. **2.** front. **3.** preceding. **4.** chief.

fore′arm′ *n.* the part of the arm between the elbow and the wrist.

fore′bear′ *n.* an ancestor.

fore′cast′ *v.,* **-cast, -casting,** *n.* —*v.t.* **1.** to predict (a future condition or happening). —*n.* **2.** a prediction.

fore′cas•tle (fōk′səl, fôr′kas′əl) *n.* the forward part of a ship's upper deck.

fore•close′ (-klōz′) *v.,* **-closed, -closing.** —*v.t.* **1.** to take possession of property and keep (a mortgage) from being redeemed because the debt is not being repaid. —*v.i.* **2.** to foreclose a mortgage. —**fore•clo′sure,** *n.*

fore′fa′ther *n.* an ancestor.

fore′fin′ger *n.* the finger next to the thumb.

fore′front′ *n.* **1.** the foremost part. **2.** the leading position.

fore•go′ing *adj.* previous.

fore′ground′ *n.* the part of a scene nearest to the viewer.

fore′hand′ *n.* **1.** in sports, a stroke made with the palm of the hand facing the direction of movement.

fore′head (fôr′id, fôr′hed′) *n.* the part of the face above the eyes.

for′eign (fôr′in) *adj.* **1.** of or from another country. **2.** not belonging to the place where found.

fore′man or **-wom′an** or **-per′son** *n.*, *pl.* **-men** or **-women** or **-persons.** the person in charge of a work crew or jury.

fore′most *adj.*, *adv.* first in place, rank, or importance.

fore′noon′ *n.* the period of day before noon.

fo·ren′sic (fə ren′sik) *adj.* of or used in courts of law or in public debate.

fore′play′ *n.* sexual stimulation leading to intercourse.

fore′run′ner *n.* a person or thing that precedes and foreshadows another.

fore·see′ *v.t.*, **-saw**, **-seen**, **-seeing.** to see or know in advance. —**fore′sight′**, *n.*

fore·shad′ow *v.t.* to show or indicate beforehand.

fore′skin′ *n.* the skin on the end of the penis.

for′est (fôr′ist) *n.* a large area of land covered with trees.

fore·stall′ *v.t.* to prevent or hinder by acting in advance.

for′est·a′tion (fôr′ə stā′shən) *n.* the planting of forests.

for′est rang′er *n.* an officer who supervises the care of public forests.

for′est·ry *n.* the science of planting and caring for forests.

fore·tell′ *v.t.*, **-told**, **-telling.** to tell of beforehand.

fore′thought′ *n.* careful thought and planning for the future.

for·ev′er (fôr ev′ər, fər-) *adv.* always.

fore·warn′ *v.t.* to warn in advance.

fore′word′ *n.* an introductory statement in a book.

for′feit (fôr′fit) *n.* **1.** something given up as a penalty. —*v.t.* **2.** to lose as a forfeit. —*adj.* **3.** forfeited.

for′fei·ture (-fi chər) *n.* **1.** a forfeiting. **2.** something forfeited.

for·gath′er *v.i.* to gather together.

for·gave′ (fər gāv′) *v.* pt. of **forgive.**

forge¹ (fôrj) *v.*, **forged**, **forging**, *n.* —*v.t.* **1.** to shape (metal) by heating and hammering. **2.** to fashion by concerted effort. **3.** to imitate fraudulently. —*n.* **4.** a furnace in which metal is heated before shaping. —**for′ger·y**, *n.*

forge² (fôrj) *v.i.*, **forged**, **forging.** to move ahead steadily.

for·get′ (fər get′) *v.*, **-got** (-got′), **-gotten**, **-getting.** —*v.t.* **1.** to be unable to remember. **2.** to stop thinking about. —*v.i.* **3.** to cease or fail to think of something. —**for·get′ta·ble**, *adj.*

for·get′ful *adj.* tending to forget.

for·get′-me-not′ *n.* a small plant with blue flowers.

for·give′ (fər giv′) *v.*, **-gave** (-gāv′), **-given**, **-giving.** —*v.t.* **1.** to grant pardon for or to. **2.** to cancel (a debt). **3.** to cease to feel angry at or for. —*v.i.* **4.** to grant pardon.

for·go′ (fôr gō′) *v.t.*, **-went** (-went′) **-gone** (-gôn′), **-going.** to do without.

fork (fôrk) *n.* **1.** a pronged instrument or tool. **2.** a point of division into branches or one of the branches. —*v.t.* **3.** to pierce, dig, or carry with a fork. —*v.i.* **4.** to divide into branches.

fork′lift′ *n.* a vehicle with two power-operated prongs for lifting heavy weights.

for·lorn′ (fôr lôrn′) *adj.* **1.** miserable. **2.** forsaken.

form (fôrm) *n.* **1.** shape. **2.** a mold. **3.** the way in which something appears or exists. **4.** a kind, type, or variety. **5.** a customary method of doing something. **6.** a document with blank spaces to be filled in. —*v.t.* **7.** to shape. **8.** to make or produce. **9.** to develop. —*v.i.* **10.** to take form or a particular form.

for′mal (fôr′məl) *adj.* **1.** following accepted custom or standard practice. **2.** marked by form or ceremony. **3.** precisely stated. —**for′mal·ize′**, *v.t.*

form·al′de·hyde′ (fôr mal′də hīd′, fər-) *n.* a toxic gas used as a disinfectant and preservative.

for·mal′i·ty (-mal′i tē) *n.*, *pl.* **-ties.** **1.** strict adherence to established rules. **2.** a formal act.

for′mat (fôr′mat) *n.*, *v.*, **-matted**, **-matting.** —*n.* **1.** the general style of a book, magazine, etc. **2.** the organization of something. **3.** the arrangement of data for computer input or output. —*v.t.* **4.** to provide a format for. **5.** to prepare (a computer disk) for use.

for·ma′tion (for mā′shən) *n.* **1.** the act of forming. **2.** the manner in which something is formed. **3.** something formed.

form′a·tive (fôr′mə tiv) *adj.* **1.** giving form. **2.** relating to formation and development.

for′mer (fôr′mər) *adj.* **1.** of an earlier time. **2.** being the first-mentioned. —**for′mer·ly**, *adv.*

for′mi·da·ble (fôr′mi də bəl) *adj.* **1.** causing fear or awe. **2.** very difficult. —**for′mi·da·bly**, *adv.*

form′ let′ter *n.* a standardized letter sent to many people.

for′mu·la (fôr′myə lə) *n.*, *pl.* **-las**, **-lae** (-lē′). **1.** a scientific description or mathematical rule expressed in figures and symbols. **2.** a set form of words. **3.** a milk mixture for a baby.

for′mu·late′ (fôr′myə lāt′) *v.t.*, **-lated**, **-lating.** **1.** to state systematically. **2.** to devise.

for′ni·cate′ (fôr′ni kāt′) *v.i.*, **-cated**, **-cating.** to have sexual intercourse with someone to whom one is not married. —**for′ni·ca′tion**, *n.*

for·sake′ (fôr sāk′) *v.t.*, **-sook** (-sŏŏk′), **-saken**, **-saking.** **1.** to abandon. **2.** to give up.

for·swear′ *v.*, **-swore**, **-sworn**, **-swearing.** —*v.t.* **1.** to renounce under oath. **2.** to deny under oath. —*v.i.* **3.** to commit perjury.

for·syth′i·a (fôr sith′ē ə, fər-) *n.* a shrub bearing yellow flowers in early spring.

fort (fôrt) *n.* a fortified place.

forte′ (fôrt, fôr′tā) *n.* a person's specialty.

for′te² (fôr′tā) *adv. Music.* loudly. —**Pronunciation.** In the noun sense (*She draws pretty well, but sculpture is really her forte*), the established, traditional pronunciation of FORTE is with one syllable: (fôrt). However, the two-syllable pronunciation (fôr′tā) which is correct for the adverb (a musical term borrowed from Italian), is increasingly heard for the noun as well.

forth (fôrth) *adv.* onward, outward, or forward.

forth′com′ing *adj.* **1.** about to appear. **2.** available.

forth′right′ *adj.* direct in manner or speech.

forth′with′ *adv.* at once.

for′ti·fy′ (fôr′tə fī′) *v.t.*, **-fied**, **-fying.** to strengthen or make more effective. —**for′ti·fi·ca′tion**, *n.*

for·tis′si·mo′ (fôr tis′ə mō′) *adv. Music.* very loudly.

for′ti·tude′ (fôr′ti tōōd′, -tyōōd′) *n.* **1.** strength and courage in facing danger or trouble.

fort′night′ *n.* two weeks.

FORTRAN (fôr′tran) *n.* a computer programming language used esp. for solving problems in science and engineering.

for′tress (fôr′tris) *n.* a fortified place.

for·tu′i·tous (fôr tōō′i təs, -tyōō′-) *adj.* **1.** happening by chance. **2.** lucky.

for′tu·nate (fôr′chə nit) *adj.* lucky.

for′tune *n.* **1.** wealth. **2.** chance; luck. **3.** fate; destiny.

for′tune-tell′er *n.* a person who claims to read the future.

for′ty (fôr′tē) *n.*, *adj.* ten times four. —**for′ti·eth**, *adj.*, *n.*

for′ty-nin′er (-nī′nər) *n.* a person participating in the 1849 California gold rush.

fo′rum (fôr′əm) *n.* a place or assembly for public discussion.

for′ward (fôr′wərd) *adv.* **1.** toward or to what is in front. **2.** into view. —*adj.* **3.** directed toward the front. **4.** advanced. **5.** bold. —*v.t.* **6.** to send on, as to a new address.

fos′sil (fos′əl) *n.* the preserved remains of an animal or plant. —**fos′sil·ize′**, *v.t.*, *v.i.*

fos′ter (fô′stər) *v.t.* **1.** to promote the growth of. **2.** to bring up (a child that is not own's one). —*adj.* **3.** giving or receiving parental care although not legally related.

foul (foul) *adj.* **1.** grossly offensive. **2.** filthy; dirty. **3.** clogged. **4.** entangled. **5.** stormy. **6.** contrary to the rules of a game. —*n.* **7.** a violation of the rules of a game. —*v.t.* **8.** to make foul. **9.** to clog or obstruct. **10.** to entangle. **11.** to disgrace. —*v.i.* **12.** to become foul. **13.** to commit a foul.

foul′-up′ *n.* a mix-up caused by inefficiency or stupidity.

found¹ (found) *v.* pt. and pp. of **find.**

found² (found) *v.t.* **1.** to establish. **2.** to provide a firm basis for.

foun·da′tion *n.* **1.** basis. **2.** the base on which a building rests. **3.** an institution endowed for the

public benefit. **4. a founding or being founded.

foun′der (foun′dər) *v.i.* **1.** to fill with water and sink. **2.** to fail completely. —*n.* **3.** a person who founds an institution.

found′ling *n.* an abandoned child.

found′ry (foun′drē) *n.*, *pl.* **-ries.** a place where molten metal is cast.

foun′tain (foun′tn) *n.* **1.** a spring of water. **2.** a source.

foun′tain·head′ *n.* a source.

four (fôr) *n.*, *adj.* three plus one. —**fourth**, *adj.*, *n.*

4 × 4 (fôr′bī fôr, fôr′bī fôr′) *n.* a vehicle having four wheels and a four-wheel drive. Also, **four-by-four.**

401(k) (fôr′ō′wun′kā′, fôr′-) *n.* a savings plan that allows employees to contribute a fixed amount or income to a retirement account.

four′-in-hand′ *n.* **1.** a necktie tied in a slipknot with the ends left hanging. **2.** a vehicle with four horses driven by one person.

four′-o′clock′ *n.* a plant with tubular flowers that open in the late afternoon.

four′post′er *n.* a bed with four corner posts.

four′score′ *adj.* eighty.

four′some (-səm) *n.* a group of four.

four′square′ *adj.* **1.** firm; forthright. —*adv.* **2.** firmly; frankly.

four′teen′ *n.*, *adj.* ten plus four. —**fourteenth′**, *adj.*, *n.*

fowl (foul) *n.* a bird, esp. a domestic hen, rooster, turkey, etc.

fox (foks) *n.* **1.** a carnivorous animal of the dog family. **2.** a crafty person. —*v.t.* **3.** to trick.

fox′glove′ *n.* a tall plant with bell-shaped purple flowers and leaves that yield digitalis.

fox′hole′ *n.* a small pit used for cover in battle.

fox′ trot′ *n.* a ballroom dance for couples.

fox′y *adj.*, **-ier**, **-iest.** slyly clever.

foy′er (foi′ər, foi′ā) *n.* a lobby or entrance hall.

Fr. **1.** Father. **2.** French. **3.** Friar.

fra′cas (frā′kəs, frak′əs) *n.* a disorderly disturbance.

frac′tion (frak′shən) *n.* **1.** a number expressed in the form *a/b*. **2.** a part of a whole. —**frac′tion·al**, *adj.*

frac′tious (frak′shəs) *adj.* **1.** rebellious. **2.** irritable.

frac′ture (frak′chər) *n.*, *v.*, **-tured**, **-turing.** —*n.* **1.** a break. —*v.t.*, *v.i.* **2.** to break or crack.

frag′ile (fraj′əl) *adj.* easily damaged. —**fra·gil′i·ty** (frə jil′i tē) *n.*

frag′ment *n.* (frag′mənt) **1.** a part broken off. **2.** an unfinished part. —*v.i.*, *v.t.* (frag′ment, frag ment′) **3.** to break into fragments.

fra′grance (frā′grəns) *n.* a pleasant scent. —**fra′grant**, *adj.*

frail (frāl) *adj.* **1.** not physically strong. **2.** easily broken.

frame (frām) *n.*, *v.*, **framed**, **framing.** —*n.* **1.** a decorative border. **2.** a rigid supporting structure. **3.** an enclosing case. **4.** a particular state. —*v.t.* **5.** to shape or devise. **6.** to put a frame around. **7.** to cause an innocent person to seem guilty.

frame′-up′ *n.* a fraudulent incrimination of an innocent person.

frame′work′ *n.* a skeletal supporting structure.

franc (frangk) *n.* the basic monetary unit of France, Belgium, Switzerland, and several other countries.

fran′chise (fran′chīz) *n.* **1.** the right to vote. **2.** the right to market a company's goods in a given area.

frank (frangk) *adj.* **1.** direct and honest in expression. —*n.* **2.** a mark indicating that a piece of mail may be sent postage free. —*v.t.* **3.** to mark (mail) with a frank.

frank′furt·er (frangk′fər tər) *n.* a cooked sausage.

frank′in·cense′ (frang′kin sens′) *n.* an aromatic resin used as incense.

fran′tic (fran′tik) *adj.* wild with emotion. —**fran′ti·cal·ly**, *adv.*

fra·ter′nal (frə tûr′nl) *adj.* of or befitting a brother. —**fra·ter′nal·ly**, *adv.*

fra·ter′ni·ty *n.*, *pl.* **-ties.** **1.** brotherhood. **2.** a society of male students in a college or university.

frat′er·nize′ (frat′ər nīz′) *v.i.*, **-nized**, **-nizing.** **1.** to associate in a friendly way. **2.** to associate cordially with members of a hostile or proscribed group.

frat′ri·cide′ (fra′tri sīd′, frā′-) *n.* **1.** the act of killing one's brother. **2.** a person who kills his or her brother.

fraud (frôd) *n.* **1.** deceit or trickery. **2.** a particular instance of deceit. **3.** a person who commits fraud. —**fraud′u·lent**, *adj.*

fraught (frôt) *adj.* filled.

fray¹ (frā) *n.* a noisy quarrel; fight.

fray² (frā) *v.t.*, *v.i.* **1.** to make or become worn so that there are loose threads at the edge. **2.** to make or become strained or upset.

fraz′zle (fraz′əl) *v.*, **-zled**, **-zling**, *n.* —*v.t.*, *v.i.* **1.** to make or become fatigued. **2.** to fray. —*n.* **3.** a state of fatigue.

freak (frēk) *n.* an abnormal phenomenon, person, or animal.

freck′le (frek′əl) *n.* a small brownish spot on the skin. —**freck′led**, *adj.*

free (frē) *adj.*, **freer**, **freest**, *adv.*, *v.*, **freed**, **freeing.** —*adj.* **1.** having personal rights or liberty. **2.** independent. **3.** not attached. **4.** not occupied or in use. **5.** provided without charge. —*adv.* **6.** without charge. —*v.t.* **7.** to make free. **8.** to disentangle. —**free′dom**, *n.*

free′boot′er *n.* a pirate.

free′-for-all′ *n.* a fight or contest open to all.

free′lance′ (-lans′) *adj.*, *n.*, *v.*, **-lanced**, **-lancing.** —*n.* **1.** Also, **free′lanc′er.** a person who sells services without working on a regular basis for any employer. —*v.i.* **2.** to work as a freelance. —*adj.* **3.** of or being a freelance.

free′load′ *v.i. Informal.* to take advantage of the generosity of others.

Free′ma′son *n.* a member of a secret fraternal association for mutual assistance and the promotion of brotherly love. —**Free′ma′son·ry**, *n.*

free′ rad′ical *n.* a molecule capable of multiplying rapidly and harming the immune system.

free′way′ *n.* a major highway.

freeze (frēz) *v.*, **froze** (frōz), **frozen**, **freezing**, *n.* —*v.i.* **1.** to become hardened into ice. **2.** to become hardened or stiffened because of loss of heat. **3.** to be at the degree of cold at which water turns to ice. **4.** to suffer the effects of intense cold or fear. **5.** to become temporarily inoperable. —*v.t.* **6.** to make into ice. **7.** to harden or stiffen by cold. **8.** to subject to freezing temperatures. **9.** to kill or damage by frost or cold. **10.** to fix (rents, prices, or wages) at a specific level. **11.** to make unnegotiable. —*n.* **12.** an act of freezing or the state of being frozen.

freight (frāt) *n.* **1.** transportation of goods or payment for such transportation. **2.** the goods transported. —*v.t.* **3.** to load with freight. **4.** to transport by freight.

freight′er *n.* a ship or aircraft carrying freight.

French (french) *adj.* **1.** of France, its inhabitants, or its language. —*n.* **2.** the language or people of France. —**French′man**, *n.*, *pl.* **-men.** —**French′wom′an**, *n.*, *pl.* **-wom′en.**

French′ door′ *n.* a door having long panes of glass.

French′ dress′ing *n.* **1.** a salad dressing of oil and vinegar. **2.** a creamy orange salad dressing.

French′ fries′ *n.pl.* strips of potato that have been deep-fried.

French′ horn′ *n.* a coiled brass wind instrument.

fre·net′ic (frə net′ik) *adj.* frantic or frenzied.

fren′zy (fren′zē) *n.*, *pl.* **-zies.** **1.** a state of extreme agitation or wild excitement. **2.** mental derangement. —**fren′zied**, *adj.*

fre′quen·cy (frē′kwən sē) *n.*, *pl.* **-cies.** **1.** the state of being frequent. **2.** rate of recurrence. **3.** *Physics.* the number of cycles per unit of time of a wave or oscillation.

fre′quent *adj.* (frē′kwənt) **1.** occurring often. —*v.t.* (fri kwent′) **2.** to visit often.

fres′co (fres′kō) *n.*, *pl.* **-coes, -cos.** a painting on a damp plaster surface.

fresh (fresh) *adj.* **1.** new. **2.** not salty, as water. **3.** not stale or spoiled. **4.** not preserved by canning or pickling. **5.** refreshing, as air. **6.** inexperienced. **7.** *Informal.* impudent. —**fresh′en**, *v.t.*, *v.i.*

fresh′et (fresh′it) *n.* a sudden flooding of a stream.

fresh′man *n.*, *pl.* **-men.** **1.** a first-year student. **2.** a beginner.

fresh′wa′ter *adj.* of or living in water that is not salty.

fret¹ (fret) *v.*, *n.*, **fretted**, **fretting.** —*v.i.*, *v.t.* **1.** to feel or cause to feel worry. —*n.* **2.** vexation. —**fret′ful**, *adj.*

fret² (fret) *n.* an angular design or intersecting bands.

fret³ (fret) *n.* a ridge across the strings of an instrument.

Freud′i·an (froi′dē ən) *adj.* **1.** of or relating to the psychoanalytic theories of Sigmund Freud. —*n.* **2.** a person, esp. a psychoanalyst, who follows Freud's theories.

Fri. Friday.

fri′a·ble (frī′ə bəl) *adj.* crumbly.

fri′ar (frī′ər) *n.* a member of a mendicant religious order. —**fri′ar·y**, *n.*

fric′as·see′ (frik′ə sē′) *n.* **1.** pieces of meat or fowl, stewed in a sauce. —*v.t.* **2.** to prepare as a fricassee.

fric′tion (frik′shən) *n.* **1.** surface resistance to motion. **2.** the rubbing of one surface against another. **3.** conflict, as between persons.

Fri′day (frī′dā, -dē) *n.* the sixth day of the week.

friend (frend) *n.* a person attached to another by affection or regard. —**friend′ly**, *adj.* —**friend′ship**, *n.*

frieze (frēz) *n.* a decorative band around a room or building.

frig′ate (frig′it) *n.* a small fast war ship.

fright (frīt) *n.* **1.** sudden and extreme fear. **2.** a shocking thing. —**fright′en**, *v.t.*, *v.i.*

fright′ful *adj.* **1.** causing fright; horrible. **2.** *Informal.* ugly; tasteless. **3.** *Informal.* very great. —**fright′ful·ly** *adv. Informal.* very.

frig′id (frij′id) *adj.* **1.** very cold. **2.** lacking warmth of feeling. **3.** (of a woman) sexually unresponsive. —**fri·gid′i·ty**, *n.*

frill (fril) *n.* **1.** a trimming, as lace gathered at one edge. **2.** an unnecessary feature; luxury. —**frill′y**, *adj.*

fringe (frinj) *n.*, *v.*, **fringed**, **fringing.** —*n.* **1.** a decorative border of hanging threads, cords, etc. **2.** an outer edge. **3.** something regarded as marginal or extreme. —*v.t.* **4.** to furnish with fringe.

frip′per·y (frip′ə rē) *n.*, *pl.* **-peries.** cheap finery.

frisk (frisk) *v.i.* **1.** to dance, leap, or skip playfully. —*v.t.* **2.** to search (a person) for a concealed weapon, drugs, etc.

frisk′y *adj.*, **-ier**, **-iest.** playful.

frit′ter¹ (frit′ər) *v.t.* to squander little by little.

frit′ter² (frit′ər) *n.* a small cake of fried batter, containing corn, apples, etc.

friv′o·lous (friv′ə ləs) *adj.* **1.** not serious or deserving serious notice. **2.** self-indulgent and carefree. —**fri·vol′i·ty** (fri vol′i tē) *n.*

frizz (friz) *v.i.*, *v.t.* **1.** to form into small curls. —*n.* **2.** something frizzed, as hair. —**friz′zy**, *adj.*

fro (frō) *adv.* from; back.

frock (frok) *n.* a dress.

frog (frog) *n.* **1.** a small, tailless amphibian with long hind legs. **2.** a slight hoarseness.

frol′ic (frol′ik) *n.*, *v.*, **-icked**, **-icking.** —*n.* **1.** fun; gaiety. —*v.i.* **2.** to frolic merrily. —**frol′ic·some**, *adj.*

from (frum, from; *unstressed* frəm) *prep.* **1.** having as a starting point. **2.** as removed, separated, or distinguished. **3.** having as a source, agent, or cause.

frond (frond) *n.* a large, finely divided leaf.

front (frunt) *n.* **1.** the part of something that faces forward. **2.** an area of activity. **3.** a pretense. **4.** a line of battle. **5.** land facing a road, river, etc. **6.** a person or thing serving as a cover or disguise. —*adj.* **7.** of or at the front. —*v.t.*, *v.i.* **8.** to face. **9.** to serve as a front (for). —*Idiom.* **10.** up front, *Informal.* **a.** before anything else. **b.** candid. —**fron′tal**, *adj.*

front′age (frun′tij) *n.* the front of a property.

front′ burn′er *n.* a condition of top priority.

fron·tier′ *n.* **1.** the border between countries. **2.** land that forms the outer edge of a country's settled regions. —**fron·tiers′man**, *n.*

fron′tis·piece′ (frun′tis pēs′, fron′-) *n.* a picture preceding a title page.

front′-run′ner *n.* a person who leads in a competition.

frost (frôst) *n.* **1.** a freezing condition. **2.** a cover of tiny ice particles. —*v.t.* **3.** to cover with frost or frosting.

frost′bite′ *n.* injury to a body part from prolonged exposure to cold.

frost′ing *n.* a sweet, creamy mixture for coating baked goods.

froth (frôth) *n.* **1.** foam. —*v.t.*, *v.i.* **2.** to cover with or give out foam.

fro′ward (frō′wərd, frō′ərd) *adj.* willfully contrary.

frown (froun) *v.i.* **1.** to contract the brow, as in displeasure. **2. frown on,** to view with disapproval. —*n.* **3.** a frowning look.

frowz′y (frou′zē) *adj.*, **-ier, -iest. 1.** dirty and untidy.

froze (frōz) *v.* pt. of **freeze.**

fro′zen *v.* **1.** pp. of **freeze.** —*adj.* **2.** turned into ice. **3.** very cold. **4.** preserved by freezing. **5.** fixed.

fruc′ti•fy (fruk′tə fī′, frook′-) *v.*, **-fied, -fying.** —*v.i.* **1.** to bear fruit. —*v.t.* **2.** to make productive. —**fruc′ti•fi•ca′tion,** *n.*

fruc′tose (-tōs) *n.* a very sweet sugar in honey and many fruits.

fru′gal (frōo′gəl) *adj.* thrifty.

fruit (frōot) *n.* **1.** the edible part of a plant developed from a flower. **2.** a product or result.

fruit′ful *adj.* productive; successful.

fru•i′tion (frōo ish′ən) *n.* attainment of something hoped or worked for.

fruit′less *adj.* not producing results or success.

frump (frump) *n.* a dowdy, drab woman. —**frump′y,** *adj.*

frus′trate (frus′trāt) *v.t.*, **-trated, -trating. 1.** to defeat (plans, efforts, etc.). **2.** to cause disappointment. —**frus•tra′tion,** *n.*

fry[1] (frī) *v.*, **fried, frying,** *n.*, *pl.* **fries.** —*v.t.* **1.** to cook in fat over direct heat. —*v.i.* **2.** to undergo frying. —*n.* **3.** something fried.

fry[2] (frī) *n.*, *pl.* **fry.** the young of fish.

ft. 1. feet. **2.** foot. **3.** fort.

FTC Federal Trade Commission.

fuch′sia (fyōo′shə) *n.* **1.** a plant with pink to purplish drooping flowers. **2.** a purplish red color.

fudge (fuj) *n.* a kind of soft candy.

fuel (fyōo′əl) *n.*, *v.*, **fueled, fueling.** —*n.* **1.** something, as coal, oil, etc., that can be burned to create heat or power. **2.** something that stimulates. —*v.t.* **3.** to supply with or take in fuel.

fu′gi•tive (fyōo′ji tiv) *n.* **1.** a person who flees. —*adj.* **2.** having run away. **3.** passing quickly.

fugue (fyōog) *n.* a musical composition in which themes are performed by different voices in turn.

-ful a suffix meaning: **1.** full of or characterized by. **2.** tending to or able to. **3.** as much as will fill.

ful′crum (fōol′krəm, ful′-) *n.*, *pl.* **-crums, -cra.** the support on which a lever turns.

ful•fill′ (fōol fil′) *v.t.* **1.** to carry out (a prophecy or promise). **2.** to perform (a task or duty). **3.** to satisfy (requirements, obligations, etc.). —**ful•fill′ment,** *n.*

full (fōol) *adj.* **1.** filled to the limit. **2.** complete. **3.** of maximum size, extent, degree, etc. **4.** well supplied. **5.** rounded in form. **6.** rich in sound. —*adv.* **7.** completely. **8.** exactly. —**ful′ly,** *adv.*

full′-blown′ *adj.* completely developed.

full′-bod′ied *adj.* of full strength, flavor, or richness.

full′-fledged′ *adj.* **1.** of full rank. **2.** fully developed.

full′-scale′ *adj.* **1.** having the exact size of an original. **2.** using all possible means.

ful′mi•nate′ (ful′mə nāt′) *v.i.*, **-nated, -nating. 1.** to explode loudly. **2.** to issue violent denunciations.

ful′some (fōol′səm, ful′-) *adj.* sickeningly excessive, as praise.

fum′ble (fum′bəl) *v.*, **-bled, -bling,** *n.* —*v.i.* **1.** to grope about clumsily. —*v.t.* **2.** to handle clumsily. —*n.* **3.** an act of fumbling.

fume (fyōom) *n.*, *v.*, **fumed, fuming.** —*n.* **1.** smoke or vapor, esp. of an irritating nature. —*v.i.* **2.** to emit fumes. **3.** to show anger. —*v.t.* **4.** to subject to fumes.

fu′mi•gate′ (fyōo′mi gāt′) *v.t.*, **-gated, -gating.** to disinfect with fumes. —**fu′mi•ga′tion,** *n.*

fun (fun) *n.* **1.** enjoyment or amusement. **2.** something that provides amusement. —*Idiom.* **3. make fun of,** to ridicule.

func′tion (fungk′shən) *n.* **1.** the kind of activity or purpose proper to a person or thing. **2.** a ceremonious public occasion. —*v.i.* **3.** to work. **4.** to perform a function.

func′tion•ar′y (-shə ner′ē) *n.*, *pl.* **-aries.** an official.

fund (fund) *n.* **1.** a sum of money for a specific purpose. **2.** a supply. —*v.t.* **3.** to provide money for.

fun′da•men′tal (fun′də men′tl)

adj. **1.** of or being a foundation or basis. **2.** essential. —*n.* **3.** a basic principle.

fun′da•men′tal•ist *n.* a person who believes in the literal interpretation of a religious text.

fu′ner•al (fyōo′nər əl) *n.* the ceremony prior to burial or cremation.

fu′neral direc′tor *n.* a person who arranges funerals.

fu•ne′re•al (-nēr′ē əl) *adj.* **1.** gloomy. **2.** of funerals.

fun′gus (fung′gəs) *n.*, *pl.* **fungi** (fun′jī). a plant of the group including mushrooms and molds.

funk (fungk) *n.* **1.** a state of fear. **2.** depression.

funk′y (fung′kē) *adj.*, **-ier, -iest. 1.** having an earthy, blues-based character, as jazz. *Slang.* offbeat.

fun′nel (fun′l) *n.*, *v.*, **-neled, -neling.** —*n.* **1.** a tube with a cone-shaped top for pouring a substance through a small opening. **2.** a smokestack. —*v.t.*, *v.i.* **3.** to pass through a funnel.

fun′ny (fun′ē) *adj.*, **-nier, -niest. 1.** causing laughter. **2.** strange; odd.

fun′ny bone′ *n.* the part of the elbow that tingles when hit.

fur (fûr) *n.*, *v.*, **furred, furring.** —*n.* **1.** the soft, thick hairy coat of a mammal. **2.** a garment made of fur. **3.** a coating like fur. —*v.t.*, *v.i.* **4.** to cover or become covered with fur. —**fur′ry,** *adj.*

fur′be•low′ (fûr′bə lō′) *n.* a bit of showy trimming.

fur′bish (fûr′bish) *v.t.* to restore to good condition.

fu′ri•ous (fyōor′ē əs) *adj.* **1.** very angry. **2.** violent; intense.

furl (fûrl) *v.t.* to roll tightly.

fur′long (fûr′lông) *n.* ⅛ of a mile (0.2 km) or 220 yards (201 m).

fur′lough (fûr′lō) *n.* **1.** a leave of absence, esp. in the military. —*v.t.* **2.** to give a furlough to.

fur′nace (fûr′nis) *n.* a structure in which heat is generated.

fur′nish (fûr′nish) *v.t.* **1.** to provide. **2.** to fit out with furniture.

fur′nish•ings *n.pl.* **1.** articles of furniture for a room. **2.** articles of dress.

fur′ni•ture (-ni chər) *n.* movable articles as tables, chairs, beds, etc., for furnishing a room.

fu′ror (fyōor′ôr, -ər) *n.* general excitement; uproar.

fur′ri•er (fûr′ē ər) *n.* a dealer in furs.

fur′row (fûr′ō) *n.* **1.** a narrow groove made by a plow. **2.** a wrinkle. —*v.t.* **3.** to make furrows in. —*v.i.* **4.** to become furrowed.

fur′ther (fûr′thər) *adv.* **1.** to or at a greater distance or extent. **2.** moreover. —*adj.* **3.** more distant or extended. **4.** more. —*v.t.* **5.** to promote. —**fur′ther•ance,** *n.*
—**Usage.** See **FARTHER.**

fur′ther•more′ *adv.* in addition; moreover; besides.

fur′ther•most′ *adj.* most distant.

fur′thest (-thist) *adj.*, *adv.* farthest.

fur′tive (-tiv) *adj.* **1.** stealthy. **2.** sly; shifty.

fu′ry (fyōor′ē) *n.*, *pl.* **-ries. 1.** violent passion, esp. anger. **2.** violence.

fuse[1] (fyōoz) *n.* a tube or cord of easily burnt material for igniting an explosive.

fuse[2] (fyōoz) *n.*, *v.*, **fused, fusing.** —*n.* **1.** a safety device that breaks an electrical connection when excessive current runs through it. —*v.t.*, *v.i.* **2.** to blend or unite by melting together. —**fu′si•ble,** *adj.*

fu′se•lage (fyōo′sə läzh′, -lij) *n.* the central structure of an airplane.

fu′sil•lade′ (fyōo′sə läd′, -läd′) *n.* **1.** a continuous discharge of guns. **2.** a general discharge of anything.

fuss (fus) *n.* **1.** needless or useless concern or activity. **2.** a complaint about something trivial. —*v.i.* **3.** to make a fuss. **4.** to complain about something trivial.

fus′tian (fus′chən) *n.* **1.** a stout fabric. **2.** inflated writing or speech.

fus′ty (fus′tē) *adj.*, **-tier, -tiest. 1.** moldy; musty. **2.** old-fashioned.

fu′tile (fyōot′l, fyōo′tīl) *adj.* incapable of producing a useful result. —**fu•til′i•ty** (-til′i tē) *n.*

fu′ton (fōo′ton) *n.* a cotton-covered quiltlike mattress placed on a low frame for sleeping or as seating.

fu′ture (fyōo′chər) *adj.* **1.** coming after the present time. **2.** of being a verb tense that refers to events or states in time to come. —*n.* **3.** future time. **4.** an event or condition in the future. **5. futures,** commodities bought and sold speculatively for future delivery.

fu′tur•is′tic *adj.* of the future.

fuzz (fuz) *n.* loose, light, fluffy matter.

fuzz′y *adj.*, **-ier, -iest. 1.** covered with fuzz. **2.** blurred. —**fuzz′i•ly,** *adv.* —**fuzz′i•ness,** *n.*

FYI for your information.

G

G, g (jē) *n.* the seventh letter of the English alphabet.

g 1. gram. **2.** gravity.

GA 1. Gamblers Anonymous. **2.** general of the army. **3.** Georgia.

Ga. Georgia.

gab (gab) *n.*, *v.*, **gabbed, gabbing.** *Informal.* —*n.* **1.** idle talk; chatter. —*v.i.* **2.** to chatter. —**gab′by,** *adj.*

gab′ar•dine′ (gab′ər dēn′) *n.* a twill fabric.

gab′ble (gab′əl) *n.*, *v.*, **-bled, -bling.** —*n.* **1.** rapid, unintelligible talk. —*v.i.* **2.** to speak rapidly and unintelligibly.

ga′ble (gā′bəl) *n.* the triangular part of an outside wall, enclosed by the edges of a ridged roof.

gad (gad) *v.*, **gadded, gadding. gad about,** to move restlessly from one place to another in search of pleasure. —**gad′a•bout′,** *n.*

gad′a•bout′ *n.* a person who moves from one social activity to another.

gad′fly′ *n.*, *pl.* **-flies. 1.** a fly that bites livestock. **2.** a person who annoys or stirs up others.

gadg′et (gaj′it) *n.* a small mechanical device. —**gadg′et•ry,** *n.*

Gael (gāl) *n.* a Gaelic-speaking inhabitant of Scotland or Ireland.

Gael′ic (gā′lik) *n.* **1.** Scottish Gaelic. **2.** Irish (def. 2). —*adj.* **3.** of the Gaels or Gaelic.

gaff (gaf) *n.* a hook for landing fish.

gaffe (gaf) *n.* a social blunder.

gaf′fer *n.* **1.** the chief electrician on a film or TV show. **2.** *Informal.* an old man.

gag[1] (gag) *v.*, **gagged, gagging,** *n.* —*v.t.* **1.** to stop up the mouth of (a person) to prevent speech. **2.** to restrain from free speech. —*v.i.* **3.** to retch or choke. —*n.* **4.** something that gags. **5.** any suppression of free speech.

gag[2] (gag) *n.*, *v.*, **gagged, gagging.** *Informal.* —*n.* **1.** a joke. —*v.i.* **2.** to tell jokes.

gage (gāj) *n.*, *v.t.*, **gaged, gaging.** gauge.

gag′gle (gag′əl) *n.* a flock of geese.

gai′e•ty (gā′i tē) *n.* merriment.

gai′ly (gā′lē) *adv.* merrily.

gain (gān) *v.t.* **1.** to get as a result of one's efforts. **2.** to acquire as an addition. **3.** to obtain as a profit. **4.** (of a timepiece) to run fast. —*v.i.* **5.** to get nearer. **6.** to improve. —*n.* **7.** profit or advantage. **8.** an increase.

gain′say′ (gān′sā′, gān sā′) *v.t.*, **-said, -saying.** to deny; contradict.

gait (gāt) *n.* a manner of walking or running.

gal (gal) *n. Informal: Sometimes Offensive.* a girl.

gal. gallon.

ga′la (gā′lə, gal′ə; *esp. Brit.* gä′lə) *adj.* **1.** festive. —*n.* **2.** a festive occasion.

gal′ax•y (gal′ək sē) *n.*, *pl.* **-axies. 1.** a very large system of stars. **2. the Galaxy,** the Milky Way. **3.** any large and brilliant group. —**ga•lac′tic** (gə lak′tik) *adj.*

gale (gāl) *n.* **1.** a strong wind. **2.** a noisy outburst, as of laughter.

gall[1] (gôl) *n.* **1.** impudence. **2.** bile. **3.** bitterness of spirit.

gall[2] (gôl) *v.t.* **1.** to make sore by rubbing. **2.** to irritate. —*n.* **3.** a sore made by rubbing. **4.** something irritating.

gal′lant (gal′ənt; *for 2 also* gə lant′, -länt′) *adj.* **1.** brave. **2.** attentive to women.

gall′blad′der *n.* a sac attached to the liver in which bile is stored.

gal′le•on (gal′ē ən, gal′yən) *n.* a large sailing ship of the 15th to 17th centuries.

gal′ler•y (gal′ə rē) *n.*, *pl.* **-eries. 1.** a balcony in a theater. **2.** a place for art exhibits. **3.** a corridor.

gal′ley (gal′ē) *n.* **1.** a ship propelled by many oars. **2.** a ship's kitchen.

gal′li•vant′ (gal′ə vant′) *v.i.* to travel about, seeking pleasure.

gal′lon (gal′ən) *n.* a unit of capacity equal to 4 quarts (3.7853 liters).

gal′lop (gal′əp) *v.i.* **1.** to run at full speed. —*n.* **2.** the fastest gait of a horse.

gal′lows (gal′ōz, -əz) *n.* a wooden frame for execution by hanging.

gall′stone′ *n.* a stony mass formed in the gallbladder.

ga•lore′ (gə lôr′) *adv.* in abundance.

ga•losh′es (gə losh′iz) *n.pl.* overshoes.

gal′va•nize′ (gal′və nīz′) *v.t.*, **-nized, -nizing. 1.** to stimulate by or as if by electric current. **2.** to coat with zinc.

gam′bit (gam′bit) *n.* a clever tactic used to gain an advantage.

gam′ble (gam′bəl) *v.*, **-bled, -bling,** *n.* —*v.i.* **1.** to play a game of chance for money. —*v.t.* **2.** to wager or risk. —*n.* **3.** anything involving risk or chance. —**gam′bler,** *n.*

gam′bol (gam′bəl) *v.*, **-boled, -boling,** *n.* —*v.i.* **1.** to skip about playfully. —*n.* **2.** a skipping about.

game[1] (gām) *n.* **1.** a pastime or amusement. **2.** a competitive activity involving skill and played according to rules. **3.** wild animals, hunted for sport. —*adj.* **4.** brave and willing. —**game′ly,** *adv.*

game[2] (gām) *adj.* lame.

game′ plan′ *n.* a carefully planned strategy or course of action.

gam′ete (gam′ēt) *n.* a mature reproductive cell that unites with another to form a new organism.

gam′in (gam′in) *n.* a street urchin.

gam′ma (gam′ə) *n.* the third letter of the Greek alphabet.

gam′ut (gam′ət) *n.* the full scale.

gam′y (gā′mē) *adj.*, **-ier, -iest.** having the strong flavor of game.

gan′der (gan′dər) *n.* **1.** a male goose. **2.** *Slang.* a look.

gang (gang) *n.* **1.** a group of people who associate or work together. **2.** a band of criminals. —*v.* **3. gang up on,** to attack as a group.

gan′gling (gang′gling) *adj.* awkwardly tall and thin.

gan′gli•on (gang′glē ən) *n.*, *pl.* **-glia, -glions.** a mass of connected nerve cells.

gang′plank′ *n.* a movable structure used for boarding or leaving a ship.

gan′grene (gang′grēn, gang grēn′) *n.* death of soft body tissue. —**gan′gre•nous** (-grə nəs) *adj.*

gang′sta rap′ (gang′stə) *n.* a type of rap music whose lyrics feature violence and sexual exploits.

gang′ster *n.* a member of a criminal gang.

gang′way′ *n.* (gang′wā′) **1.** a gangplank. **2.** a narrow passage. —*interj.* (gang′wā′) **3.** (make way!)

gan′try (gan′trē) *n.*, *pl.* **-tries. 1.** a spanning framework, as on a crane. **2.** a multilevel scaffolding used to erect rockets.

gaol (jāl) *n.*, *v.t. Brit.* jail.

gap (gap) *n.* **1.** an opening. **2.** a wide difference. **3.** a ravine.

gape (gāp, gap) *v.i.*, **gaped, gaping. 1.** to stare with open mouth, as in wonder. **2.** to open wide.

ga•rage′ (gə räzh′, -räj′) *n.* a place where motor vehicles are kept or repaired.

garb (gärb) *n.* **1.** clothing. —*v.t.* **2.** to clothe.

gar′bage (gär′bij) *n.* trash; refuse.

gar•ban′zo (gär bän′zō) *n.*, *pl.* **-zos.** the chickpea.

gar′ble (gär′bəl) *v.t.*, **-bled, -bling.** to distort or confuse.

gar′den (gär′dn) *n.* **1.** an area where flowers, vegetables, etc., are cultivated. —*v.i.* **2.** to tend a garden. —**gar′den•er,** *n.*

gar•de′nia (gär dē′nyə, -nē ə) *n.* a shrub with shiny leaves and fragrant white flowers.

gar′den-vari′ety *adj.* common.

gar•gan′tu•an (gär gan′chōo ən) *adj.* gigantic; colossal.

gar′gle (gär′gəl) *v.*, **-gled, -gling,** *n.* —*v.t.*, *v.i.* **1.** to rinse (the throat) with liquid kept in motion by the breath. —*n.* **2.** liquid for gargling.

gar′goyle (gär′goil) *n.* a grotesquely carved figure on a building.

gar′ish (gâr′ish, gar′-) *adj.* tastelessly showy. —**gar′ish•ly,** *adv.*

gar′land (gär′lənd) *n.* **1.** a wreath of flowers, leaves, etc. —*v.t.* **2.** to deck with garlands.

gar′lic (gär′lik) *n.* a plant with a pungent bulb used in cooking. —**gar′lick•y,** *adj.*

gar′ment (gär′mənt) *n.* an article of clothing.

gar′ner (gär′nər) *v.t.* to gather; acquire.

gar′net (gär′nit) *n.* a deep-red gem.

gar′nish (gär′nish) *v.t.* **1.** to add something ornamental to. **2.** to decorate (a food). —*n.* **3.** a decoration for food.

gar′nish•ee′ (gär′ni shē′) *v.t.*, **-eed, -eeing.** to take (money or property of a debtor) by legal authority pending settlement in court.

gar′ret (gar′it) *n.* an attic.

gar′ri•son (gar′ə sən) *n.* **1.** a body of troops defending a fort. **2.** a military post. —*v.t.* **3.** to station (troops) in a fort.

gar•rote′ (gə rot′, -rōt′) *n.*, *v.*, **-roted, -roting.** —*n.* **1.** a cord, wire, etc. used to strangle a person. —*v.t.* **2.** to strangle with a garrote.

gar′ru•lous (gar′ə ləs, gar′yə-) *adj.* very talkative. —**gar•ru′li•ty** (gə rōo′li tē) *n.*

gar′ter (gär′tər) *n.* a device for holding up a stocking.

gar′ter snake′ *n.* a common, harmless striped snake.

gas (gas) *n.*, *pl.* **gases,** *v.*, **gassed, gassing.** —*n.* **1.** a fluid substance that can expand indefinitely. **2.** any such fluid used as a fuel, anesthetic, etc. **3.** gasoline. **4.** intestinal gas. —*v.t.* **5.** to overcome or poison with gas.

gash (gash) *n.* **1.** a long deep cut. —*v.t.* **2.** to make a gash in.

gas′ket (gas′kit) *n.* a rubber or metal ring used to make a joint watertight.

gas′o•line′ (gas′ə lēn′, gas′ə lēn′) *n.* a flammable liquid from petroleum, used as motor fuel.

gasp (gasp) *n.* **1.** a sudden short intake of breath. —*v.i.* **2.** to breathe with effort. —*v.t.* **3.** to utter with gasps.

gas′tric (gas′trik) *adj.* of the stomach.

gas•tri′tis (ga strī′tis) *n.* inflammation of the stomach.

gas′tro•nom′i•cal (gas′trə nom′i-kəl) *adj.* of good eating. Also, **gas′tro•nom′ic.** —**gas•tron′o•my** (gä-stron′ə mē) *n.*

gate (gāt) *n.* **1.** a movable hinged barrier in a fence, wall, etc. **2.** any means of entrance.

gat′ed (gā′tid) *adj.* being a residential neighborhood protected by gates, guards, etc.

gate′way′ *n.* a passage or entrance.

gath′er (gath′ər) *v.t.* **1.** to bring together into one group or place. **2.** to harvest. **3.** to conclude. **4.** to collect. **5.** to draw (cloth) into folds by stitching. —*v.i.* **6.** to come together. —*n.* **7. gathers,** a fold or pucker. —**gath′er•ing,** *n.*

gauche (gōsh) *adj.* lacking social grace.

gaud′y (gô′dē) *adj.*, **-ier, -iest.** tastelessly showy. —**gaud′i•ly,** *adv.*

gauge (gāj) *v.*, **gauged, gauging,** *n.* —*v.t.* **1.** to estimate. **2.** to measure. —*n.* **3.** a standard of measure. **4.** a device for measuring. **5.** the distance between the two rails in a track.

gaunt (gônt) *adj.* extremely thin and bony; emaciated.

gaunt′let[1] (gônt′lit, gänt′-) *n.* **1.** a glove with a large cuff. —*Idiom.* **2. throw down the gauntlet,** to challenge someone.

gaunt′let[2] (gônt′lit, gänt′-) *n.* **1.** an ordeal. —*Idiom.* **2. run the gauntlet,** to suffer severe criticism or trouble.

gauze (gôz) *n.* a thin fabric.

gav′el (gav′əl) *n.* a small mallet used to signal for attention.

gawk (gôk) *v.i.* to stare stupidly.

gawk′y (gô′kē) *adj.*, **-ier, -iest.** awkward.

gay (gā) *adj.*, **gayer, gayest,** *n.* —*adj.* **1.** merry. **2.** bright. **3.** homosexual. —*n.* **4.** a homosexual person. —**gay′ly,** *adv.*

gaze (gāz) *v.*, **gazed, gazing,** *n.* —*v.i.* **1.** to look steadily. —*n.* **2.** a steady look.

ga•ze′bo (gə zā′bō, -zē′-) *n.*, *pl.* **-bos, -boes.** an open structure on a site with a pleasant view.

ga•zelle′ (gə zel′) *n.* a small antelope of Africa and Asia.

ga•zette′ (gə zet′) *n.* a newspaper.

gaz′et•teer′ (gaz′i tēr′) *n.* a geographical dictionary.

ga•zil′lion (gə zil′yən) *n. Informal.* an extremely large, indeterminate number.

gaz•pa′cho (gäz pä′chō) *n.* a Spanish chilled vegetable soup.

gear (gēr) *n.* **1.** a toothed wheel that engages with another toothed wheel in machinery. **2.** equipment. —*v.t.* **3.** to provide with or connect by gears. **4.** to adjust.

gear'shift' *n.* a gear-changing lever in an auto's transmission system.

geck'o (gek'ō) *n., pl.* **-os** or **-oes.** a small tropical lizard.

GED general equivalency diploma.

geek (gēk) *n. Slang.* **1.** a peculiar person, esp. one who is overly intellectual. **2.** a computer expert.

gee'zer (gē'zər) *n.* an odd or eccentric man, esp. an older one.

Gei'ger count'er (gī'gər) *n.* an instrument for measuring radioactivity.

gei'sha (gā'shə, gē'-) *n.* a Japanese woman trained to provide companionship for men.

gel (jel) *n., v.,* **gelled, gelling. —n. 1.** a jellylike or gluelike substance. **—v.i. 2.** to form a gel.

gel'a·tin (jel'ə tn) *n.* a substance made by boiling animal bones, used in jellies, glue, etc. **—ge·lat'i·nous** (jə lat'n əs) *adj.*

geld'ing (gel'ding) *n.* a castrated horse. **—geld,** *v.t.*

gel'id (jel'id) *adj.* icy.

gem (jem) *n.* **1.** a precious stone. **2.** something prized for its beauty or excellence.

Gen. General.

gen'darme (zhän'därm) *n.* a French police officer.

gen'der (jen'dər) *n.* **1.** the character of being male or female; sex. **2.** a set of grammatical categories applied to nouns, as masculine, feminine, or neuter.

gene (jēn) *n.* the biological unit that carries inherited traits.

ge·ne·al'o·gy (jē'nē ol'ə jē, -al'-, jen'ē-) *n., pl.* **-gies. 1.** an account of a person's ancestry. **2.** the study of family ancestries. **—ge'ne·a·log'i·cal** (-ə loj'i kəl) *adj.* **—ge'ne·al'o·gist,** *n.*

gen'er·al (jen'ər əl) *adj.* **1.** of, affecting, or including all in a group. **2.** not limited to one class, field, etc. **3.** not specific. **—n. 4.** an army officer of any of the five highest ranks. **—gen'er·al·ly,** *adv.*

gen'er·al'i·ty (-al'i tē) *n., pl.* **-ties.** a general statement.

gen'er·al·ize' *v.,* **-ized, -izing. —v.t. 1.** to form a general conclusion from. **—v.i. 2.** to form general principles, opinions, etc. **3.** to speak in general terms.

gen'eral practi'tioner *n.* a doctor whose practice is not limited to any specific branch of medicine.

gen'er·ate' (jen'ə rāt') *v.t.,* **-ated, -ating.** to bring into existence.

gen'er·a'tion *n.* **1.** all the people born at about the same time. **2.** the average period between the birth of parents and the birth of their offspring (about 30 years). **3.** a single step in natural descent. **4.** the act or process of generating.

Genera'tion X' (eks) *n.* the generation born in the U.S. after 1965.

Genera'tion Y' *n.* the generation born in the 1980s and 1990s, esp. in the U.S.

gen'er·a'tor *n.* a machine that converts mechanical energy into electricity.

ge·ner'ic (jə ner'ik) *adj.* **1.** of or applying to all members of a group, class, genus, etc. **2.** (of a product) not having a brand name. **—ge·ner'i·cal·ly,** *adv.*

gen'er·ous (jen'ər əs) *adj.* **1.** giving freely. **2.** abundant. **—gen'er·os'i·ty** (-ə ros'i tē) *n.*

gen'e·sis (-ə sis) *n.* a beginning.

ge·net'ics (jə net'iks) *n.* the branch of biology that deals with heredity. **—ge·net'ic,** *adj.*

gen., genl. general.

gen'ial (jēn'yəl, jē'nē əl) *adj.* pleasantly cheerful or friendly.

ge'nie (jē'nē) *n.* a spirit, often appearing in human form.

gen'i·ta'li·a (jen'i tā'lē ə, -tāl'yə) *n.pl.* the genitals.

gen'i·tals (-tlz) *n.pl.* the sexual organs.

gen'i·tive (jen'i tiv) *n.* **1.** the grammatical case indicating possession or origin. **—adj. 2.** of or relating to this case.

gen'i·to·u'ri·nar'y (jen'i tō-) *adj.* of the genital and urinary organs.

gen'ius (jēn'yəs) *n.* **1.** an exceptionally great natural ability. **2.** a person having such ability.

gen'o·cide' (jen'ə sīd') *n.* the planned extermination of a national or racial group.

gen're (zhän'rə) *n.* a class or category of artistic work.

gen·teel' (jen tēl') *adj.* affectedly refined and polite.

gen'tian (jen'shən) *n.* a plant with blue flowers.

gen'tile (jen'tīl) *adj.* **1.** (*often cap.*) not Jewish. **—n. 2.** a person who is not Jewish.

gen'tle (jen'tl) *adj.,* **-tler, -tlest. 1.** mild; kindly. **2.** not rough or severe; moderate.

gen'tle·man *n., pl.* **-men. 1.** a man who has good manners. **2.** a man of good family. **3.** (used as a polite term) any man.

gen'tri·fi·ca'tion (jen'trə fi kā'shən) *n.* the renovation of run-down urban neighborhoods by upper-income people, thus displacing lower-income families and small businesses. **—gen'tri·fy,** *v.t.*

gen'try *n.* wellborn people.

gen'u·flect' (-yōō flekt') *v.i.* to bend one knee in reverence.

gen'u·ine (-yōō in *or, sometimes,* -īn) *adj.* real; authentic. **—gen'u·ine·ly,** *adv.*

ge'nus (jē'nəs) *n., pl.* **genera, genuses. 1.** a biological group of similar animals or plants, usu. including several species. **2.** a kind.

geo- a prefix meaning earth.

ge'ode (jē'ōd) *n.* a hollow nodular stone often lined with crystals.

ge'o·des'ic dome' (jē'ə des'ik, -dē'sik) *n.* a dome with a framework of straight members that form a grid of polygonal faces.

ge·og'ra·phy (jē og'rə fē) *n.* **1.** the study of the earth's surface, climate, population, etc. **2.** the features and arrangement of a region. **—ge·og'ra·pher,** *n.* **—ge'o·graph'i·cal** (-ə graf'i kəl) *adj.*

ge·ol'o·gy (jē ol'ə jē) *n.* the science that deals with the earth's physical history and changes. **—ge·ol'o·gist,** *n.*

ge'o·mag·net'ic (jē'ō mag net'ik) *adj.* of the earth's magnetism.

ge'o·met'ric (-ə met'rik) *adj.* **1.** Also **ge'o·met'ri·cal.** of geometry or its principles. **2.** resembling the lines and figures used in geometry.

ge·om'e·try (jē om'i trē) *n.* the branch of mathematics dealing with points, lines, angles, and solids.

ge'o·phys'ics *n.* the branch of geology that deals with the physics of the earth and its atmosphere.

ge'o·pol'i·tics *n.* the study of the influence of physical geography on the politics of a state.

ge'o·sta'tion·ar'y *adj.* of an orbiting satellite traveling at the same speed as the earth so as to remain in the same spot over the earth.

ge'o·ther'mal *adj.* of the earth's internal heat.

ge·ra'ni·um (ji rā'nē əm) *n.* a garden plant with showy red, white, or pink flowers.

ger'bil (jûr'bəl) *n.* a small burrowing rodent, popular as a pet.

ger'i·at'rics (jer'ē a'triks, jēr'-) *n.* the branch of medicine dealing with the aged. **—ger'i·at'ric,** *adj.*

germ (jûrm) *n.* **1.** a microscopic disease-producing organism. **2.** a seed or origin from which something may develop.

Ger'man (jûr'mən) *n.* **1.** of Germany, its inhabitants, or their language. **—n. 2.** the language of Germany, Austria, and part of Switzerland. **3.** the people of Germany.

ger·mane' (jər mān') *adj.* relevant.

Ger'man mea'sles *n.* rubella.

Ger'man shep'herd *n.* a large dog with a thick, usu. gray or black-and-tan coat.

ger'mi·cide' (jûr'mə sīd') *n.* an agent that kills germs. **—ger'mi·cid'al,** *adj.*

ger'mi·nate' *v.i., v.t.,* **-nated, -nating.** to begin or cause to grow; sprout. **—ger'mi·na'tion,** *n.*

ger·on·tol'o·gy (jer'ən tol'ə jē, jēr'-) *n.* the study of aging and the problems and care of old people.

ger'ry·man'der (jer'ē man'dər) *v.t.* to divide (a state, county, etc.) into voting districts so as to give one group or area an unequal advantage.

ger'und (jer'ənd) *n.* the *-ing* form of an English verb when functioning as a noun.

ges·ta'tion (je stā'shən) *n.* the period of carrying young in the womb.

ges·tic'u·late' (je stik'yə lāt') *v.i.,* **-lated, -lating.** to make gestures.

ges'ture (jes'chər) *n., v.,* **-tured, -turing. —n. 1.** an expressive movement of the hand, body, head, etc. **2.** any act or communication demonstrating an attitude or emotion. **—v.i. 3.** to make expressive movements.

get (get) *v.,* **got** (got), **got** or **gotten, getting. —v.t. 1.** to obtain or receive. **2.** to fetch. **3.** to cause or cause to become, move, etc. **4.** to capture. **5.** to prepare, as a meal. **6.** to understand. **—v.i. 7.** to arrive at a place. **8.** to become. **9. get ahead,** to be successful. **10. ~ along,** to be on good terms. **11. ~ away with,** to escape detection or punishment. **12. ~ over,** to recover from. **13. ~ through, a.** to complete. **b.** to make oneself understood. **14. ~ together,** to meet.

get'a·way' *n.* **1.** an escape. **2.** a place for relaxing, a vacation, etc.

get'-up' *n. Informal.* an outfit.

gew'gaw (gyōō'gô, gōō'-) *n.* a gaudy ornament.

gey'ser (gī'zər, -sər) *n.* a hot spring that sends up water and steam.

ghast'ly (gast'lē) *adj.,* **-lier, -liest. 1.** horrible. **2.** deathly pale.

gher'kin (gûr'kin) *n.* **1.** a small cucumber. **2.** a small pickle.

ghet'to (get'ō) *n., pl.* **-tos, -toes.** a section in which mostly poor minorities live. **—ghet'to·ize,** *v.t.*

ghost (gōst) *n.* the disembodied spirit of a dead person imagined as haunting the living.

ghost'writ'er *n.* a person who writes for another person who is presumed to be the author. **—ghost'write',** *v.t., v.i.*

ghoul (gōōl) *n.* **1.** an evil spirit believed to rob graves, prey on corpses, etc. **2.** a person morbidly interested in misfortunes.

GI *n., pl.* **GIs** or **GI's.** an enlisted soldier.

gi'ant (jī'ənt) *n.* **1.** (in folklore) a being of superhuman size. **2.** a person of great size, achievement, etc. **—adj. 3.** huge.

gib'ber (jib'ər) *v.i.* to speak unintelligibly. **—gib'ber·ish,** *n.*

gib'bet (jib'it) *n.* a gallows.

gib'bon (gib'ən) *n.* a small, long-armed ape.

gibe (jīb) *v.,* **gibed, gibing,** *n.* **—v.t. 1.** to mock; jeer. **—n. 2.** a sarcastic remark.

gib'lets (jib'lits) *n.pl.* the heart, liver, and gizzard of a fowl.

gid'dy (gid'ē) *adj.,* **-dier, -diest. 1.** dizzy. **2.** frivolous.

gift (gift) *n.* **1.** something given. **2.** the act of giving. **3.** a talent.

gift'ed *adj.* **1.** talented. **2.** highly intelligent.

gig¹ (gig) *n.* a single engagement, as of jazz musicians.

gig² (gig) *n.* a light carriage drawn by one horse.

giga- a prefix used in units of measure equal to one billion.

gig'a·byte' (gig'ə bīt', jig'-), *n. Computers.* **1.** 2^{30} (1,073,741,824) bytes; 1024 megabytes. **2.** 10^9, or one billion (1,000,000,000), bytes; 1000 megabytes.

gi·gan'tic (jī gan'tik, ji-) *adj.* very large. **—gi·gan'ti·cal·ly,** *adv.*

gig'gle (gig'əl) *v.,* **-gled, -gling,** *n.* **—v.i. 1.** to laugh lightly in a silly way. **—n. 2.** a silly laugh.

gig'o·lo' (jig'ə lō') *n., pl.* **-los.** a man supported by his female lover.

Gi'la mon'ster (hē'lə) *n.* a large, venomous lizard.

gild (gild) *v.t.,* **gilded** or **gilt, gilding.** to coat with gold.

gill¹ (gil) *n.* the breathing organ of fish.

gill² (jil) *n.* a unit of liquid measure, ¼ pint (4 fluid ounces).

gilt (gilt) *n.* the gold used for gilding.

gilt'-edged' or **gilt'-edge'** *adj.* of the highest quality.

gim'crack' (jim'krak') *n.* a showy trifle.

gim'let (gim'lit) *n.* a small tool for boring holes.

gim'mick (gim'ik) *n.* a device or trick to attract attention.

gimp'y (gim'pē) *adj.,* **-ier, -iest.** *Slang.* limping or lame.

gin¹ (jin) *n.* **1.** an alcoholic liquor flavored with juniper berries. **2.** a card game.

gin² (jin) *n., v.,* **ginned, ginning. —n. 1.** a machine for separating cotton from its seeds. **2.** a trap. **—v.t. 3.** to put (cotton) through a gin.

gin'ger (jin'jər) *n.* a plant with a spicy root used in cooking.

gin'ger ale' *n.* a carbonated soft drink flavored with ginger.

gin'ger·bread' *n.* **1.** a cake flavored with ginger and molasses. **2.** elaborate architectural ornamentation.

gin'ger·ly *adj.* **1.** wary. **—adv. 2.** warily.

gin'ger·snap' *n.* a crisp cookie flavored with ginger.

ging'ham (ging'əm) *n.* a checked or striped cotton fabric.

gin'gi·vi'tis (jin'jə vī'tis) *n.* inflammation of the gums.

gink'go or **ging'ko** (ging'kō, jing'-) *n., pl.* **-goes** or **-koes.** a shade tree with fan-shaped leaves, native to China.

gin'seng (jin'seng) *n.* a plant with a root used medicinally.

gi·raffe' (jə raf') *n.* a tall, long-necked, spotted animal of Africa.

gird (gûrd) *v.t.,* **girt** or **girded, girding. 1.** to encircle. **2.** to prepare for action

gird'er *n.* a horizontal metal beam supporting a structure.

gir'dle *n., v.,* **-dled, -dling. —n. 1.** a light corset. **2.** anything that encircles. **—v.t. 3.** to encircle.

girl (gûrl) *n.* a female child. **—girl'hood',** *n.* **—girl'ish,** *adj.*

girl'friend' *n.* a frequent or favorite female companion or friend.

girth (gûrth) *n.* **1.** the measure around a body or object. **2.** a band that passes underneath a horse to hold a saddle in place.

gist (jist) *n.* the essential point or meaning of a matter.

give (giv) *v.,* **gave** (gāv), **given, giving,** *n.* **—v.t. 1.** to present. **2.** to hand to someone. **3.** to grant to someone. **4.** to utter. **5.** to provide. **6.** to yield. **—v.i. 7.** to make a gift. **8.** to yield under pressure. **9. give in,** to admit defeat. **10. ~ up, a.** to abandon hope or effort. **b.** to surrender. **—n. 11.** elasticity.

give'a·way' *n.* **1.** a revealing act, remark, etc. **2.** something given away.

giv'en *v.* **1.** pp. of **give.** **—adj. 2.** specified. **3.** inclined. **—n. 4.** an established fact or condition.

giz'zard (giz'ərd) *n.* the lower stomach of birds.

gla'cial (glā'shəl) *adj.* **1.** of glaciers or ice sheets. **2.** bitterly cold. **3.** moving very slowly.

gla'cier *n.* a great mass of ice moving very slowly.

glad (glad) *adj.,* **gladder, gladdest. 1.** pleased; happy; joyful. **2.** causing joy. **—glad'den,** *v.t.* **—glad'ness,** *n.*

glade (glād) *n.* an open space in a forest.

glad'i·a'tor (glad'ē ā'tər) *n.* (in ancient Rome) a swordsman fighting to the death for public entertainment.

glad'i·o'lus (-ō'ləs) *n., pl.* **-lus, -li** (-lī) **-luses.** a plant bearing tall spikes of flowers.

glad'ly *adv.* **1.** with pleasure. **2.** willingly.

glam'or·ize' (glam'ə rī') *v.t.,* **-ized, -izing.** to make glamorous.

glam'our (glam'ər) *n.* alluring charm and attractiveness. **—glam'or·ous,** *adj.*

glance (glans) *v.,* **glanced, glancing,** *n.* **—v.i. 1.** to look quickly or briefly. **2.** to strike a surface and bounce off. **—n. 3.** a quick look.

gland (gland) *n.* any organ or group of cells that secretes some substance.

glans (glanz) *n.* the head of the penis or the clitoris.

glare (glâr) *n., v.,* **glared, glaring. —n. 1.** a very harsh light. **2.** a fierce look. **—v.i. 3.** to shine with a harsh light. **4.** to stare fiercely.

glar'ing *adj.* **1.** dazzlingly bright. **2.** very obvious.

glass (glas) *n.* **1.** a hard, brittle, transparent substance. **2.** glasses, eyeglasses. **3.** a drinking container made of glass. **4.** anything made of glass. **—adj. 5.** of glass.

glass' ceil'ing *n.* a not generally acknowledged upper limit to professional advancement, esp. for women or minorities.

glass'ware' *n.* articles of glass.

glass'y *adj.,* **-ier, -iest. 1.** like glass. **2.** without expression; dull.

glau·co'ma (glô kō'mə, glou-) *n.* a condition of elevated fluid pressure within the eyeball, causing increasing loss of vision.

glaze (glāz) *v.,* **glazed, glazing,** *n.* **—v.t. 1.** to fit with glass. **2.** to put a smooth, glossy coating on. **—v.i. 3.** to become glazed or glassy. **—n. 4.** a smooth, glossy coating.

gla'zier (glā'zhər) *n.* a person who installs glass.

gleam (glēm) *n.* **1.** a beam of light or subdued or reflected light. **2.** a brief indication of a quality. **—v.i. 3.** to send forth a gleam.

glean (glēn) *v.t., v.i.* **1.** to gather (grain) left by the reapers. **2.** to collect (information) little by little.

glee (glē) *n.* open delight or pleasure. **—glee'ful,** *adj.*

glee' club' *n.* a singing group.

glen (glen) *n.* a narrow valley.

glib (glib) *adj.* speaking very readily but insincerely.

glide (glīd) *v.,* **glided, gliding,** *n.* **—v.i. 1.** to move smoothly. **—n. 2.** a gliding movement.

glid'er *n.* a motorless aircraft.

glim'mer (glim'ər) *n.* **1.** a faint unsteady light. **2.** a small amount. **—v.i. 3.** to shine or appear faintly. **—glim'mer·ing,** *n.*

glimpse (glimps) *n., v.,* **glimpsed, glimpsing. —n. 1.** a brief look. **—v.t. 2.** to catch a glimpse of. **—v.i. 3.** to look briefly.

glint (glint) *n.* **1.** a tiny, quick flash of light. **2.** a trace. **—v.i. 3.** to shine with a glint.

glis'ten (glis'ən) *v.i.* **1.** to sparkle. **—n. 2.** a glistening; sparkle.

glitch (glich) *n. Informal.* a defect.

glit'ter (glit'ər) *v.i.* **1.** to reflect light with a brilliant sparkle. **2.** to make a brilliant show. **—n. 3.** a sparkling light. **4.** showy brilliance. **5.** small glittering ornaments.

glitz'y (glit'sē) *adj.,* **-ier, -iest.** *Informal.* tastelessly showy.

gloam'ing (glō'ming) *n.* twilight.

gloat (glōt) *v.i.* to be maliciously triumphant.

glob (glob) *n.* a rounded lump or mass.

glo'bal warm'ing (glō'bəl) *n.* an increase in the average temperature of the earth's atmosphere that causes changes in climate.

globe (glōb) *n.* **1.** the planet Earth. **2.** a sphere with a map of the earth on it. **3.** anything shaped like a sphere. **—glob'al,** *adj.*

globe'trot'ter *n.* a person who travels regularly all over the world.

glob'ule (glob'yōōl) *n.* a small spherical body. **—glob'u·lar,** *adj.*

gloom (glōōm) *n.* **1.** darkness. **2.** a feeling of depression. **—gloom'y,** *adj.*

glo'ri·fy' (glôr'ə fī') *v.t.,* **-fied, -fying. 1.** to praise highly. **2.** to treat (something) as more splendid or excellent than it is.

glo'ry *n., pl.* **-ries,** *v.,* **-ried, -rying. —n. 1.** very great praise or honor. **2.** magnificence. **3.** a state of absolute happiness. **—v.i. 4.** to exult triumphantly. **—glo'ri·ous,** *adj.*

gloss¹ (glos) *n.* **1.** a shine on a surface. **—v.t. 2.** to put a gloss on. **3. gloss over,** to cover up, as a mistake. **—glos'sy,** *adj.*

gloss² (glos) *n.* an explanation of a word, usu. in the margin or between the lines of a text. **—v.t. 2.** to insert glosses on.

glos'sa·ry (glos'ə rē) *n., pl.* **-ries.** a list of difficult or specialized words with definitions.

glot'tis (glot'is) *n.* the opening at the upper part of the windpipe. **—glot'tal,** *adj.*

glove (gluv) *n., v.,* **gloved, gloving. —n. 1.** a covering for the hand with a separate piece for each finger. **—v.t. 2.** to cover with a glove. **—gloved,** *adj.*

glow (glō) *n.* **1.** a light sent out by a heated substance. **2.** brightness or warmth. **—v.i. 3.** to send out light and heat without flame. **4.** to show a bright, ruddy color. **5.** to show emotion or excitement.

glow'er (glou'ər) *v.i.* **1.** to stare with sullen dislike or anger. **—n. 2.** a look of sullen dislike or anger.

glow'worm' (glō'wûrm') *n.* a beetle that emits a greenish light.

glu'cose (glōō'kōs) *n.* a sugar found in fruits and honey.

glue (glōō) *n., v.,* **glued, gluing. —n. 1.** an adhesive substance obtained from gelatin. **—v.t. 2.** to attach with glue.

glum (glum) *adj.,* **glummer, glummest.** silently gloomy.

glut (glut) *v.,* **glutted, glutting,** *n.* **—v.t. 1.** to fill to excess. **2.** to flood (the market) with a particular item or service. **—n. 3.** an excess.

glu'ten (glōōt'n) *n.* a sticky component of flour.

glu'tin·ous *adj.* sticky.

glut'ton (glut'n) *n.* **1.** a greedy person. **2.** a person who is eager for something. **—glut'ton·ous,** *adj.*

glyc'er·in (glis'ər in) *n.* a colorless liquid made from fats, used as a sweetener and in lotions. Also, **gly′cer·ine.**

gly′co·gen (glī′kə jən, -jen′) *n.* a carbohydrate in animal tissues, changed into glucose when needed.

gnarled (närld) *adj.* twisted and misshapen.

gnash (nash) *v.t., v.i.* to grind (the teeth) together, as in rage.

gnat (nat) *n.* a kind of small fly.

gnaw (nô) *v.t.* **1.** to bite on persistently. **2.** to wear away. —*v.i.* **3.** to bite persistently. **4.** to cause distress. —**gnaw′ing,** *adj.*

gnome (nōm) *n.* a dwarf in fairy tales.

GNP gross national product.

gnu (nōō, nyōō) *n., pl.* **gnus, gnu.** an African antelope.

go (gō) *v., went** (went)**, gone** (gôn)**, going,** *pl.* **goes.** —*v.i.* **1.** to move; proceed. **2.** to depart. **3.** to function. **4.** to extend. **5.** to become. **6.** to make a certain sound. **7.** (of time) to pass. **8.** (of colors) to harmonize. **9. go after,** to try to get. **10. ~ around,** **a.** to be enough for all. **b.** to circulate. **11. ~ for, a.** to try for. **b.** to attack. **c.** to like very much. **12. ~ off, a.** to explode. **b.** to leave. **13. ~ over, a.** to review or examine. **b.** to succeed. **14. ~ through with,** to finish. **15. ~ under,** to fail or founder. —*n.* **16.** energy. **17.** an attempt. —*Idiom.* **18. let go, a.** to free. **b.** to cease to employ. **19. on the go,** very busy. **20. to go,** (of food) to be taken away and eaten elsewhere.

goad (gōd) *n.* **1.** a pointed stick for driving animals. **2.** anything that urges on. —*v.t.* **3.** to urge on.

goal (gōl) *n.* **1.** an aim. **2.** the end point or target in a race or game. **3.** a single score in various games.

goal′keep′er *n.* in soccer, hockey, etc.) the player whose chief duty is to prevent the opposition from scoring a goal.

goat (gōt) *n.* a horned mammal related to the sheep.

goat·ee′ (gō tē′) *n.* a pointed beard.

gob (gob) *n.* **1.** a mass. **2. gobs,** *Informal.* a large quantity.

gob′ble¹ (gob′əl) *v.t., v.i.,* **-bled, -bling.** to eat greedily.

gob′ble² (gob′əl) *v.,* **-bled, -bling** *n.* —*v.i.* **1.** to make the cry of a male turkey. —*n.* **2.** this cry.

gob′ble·de·gook′ (-də gŏŏk′) *n.* nonsense.

gob′bler *n.* a male turkey.

go′-be·tween′ *n.* an intermediary.

gob′let (gob′lit) *n.* a glass with a foot and stem.

gob′lin (gob′lin) *n.* an ugly, mischievous elf.

god (god) *n.* **1.** a superhuman being presiding over some part of human affairs. **2. God,** the creator and ruler of the universe in the Christian, Jewish, and Muslim religions. **3.** any person or object that is adored or admired.

god′child′ *n.* a child for whom a godparent serves as sponsor. —**god′daugh′ter,** *n.* —**god′son′,** *n.*

god′dess *n.* **1.** a female god. **2.** a woman admired for her beauty.

god′ly *adj.,* **-lier, -liest. 1.** devout. **2.** of God or gods.

god′par′ent *n.* a person who serves as sponsor of a child at baptism. —**god′fath′er,** *n.* —**god′moth′er,** *n.*

god′send′ *n.* anything unexpected but welcome.

goes (gōz) *v.* third pers. sing. pres. indic. of **go.**

go′fer (gō′fər) *n. Slang.* an employee whose main duty is running errands.

gog′gle (gog′əl) *n., v.,* **-gled, -gling.** —*n.* **1. goggles,** protective eyeglasses. —*v.i.* **2.** to stare with wide-open eyes.

goi′ter (goi′tər) *n.* an enlargement of the thyroid gland.

gold (gōld) *n.* **1.** a precious yellow metal. **2.** riches. **3.** a bright yellow.

gold′brick′ *Slang.* —*n.* **1.** Also, **gold′brick′er.** a person who shirks work. —*v.i.* **2.** to shirk work.

gold′en·rod′ *n.* a plant bearing clusters of small yellow flowers on long stalks.

gold′finch′ *n.* a yellow-feathered American finch.

gold′fish′ *n.* a small, gold-colored fish of the carp family.

golf (golf) *n.* a game in which clubs are used to hit a small ball into a series of holes. —**golf′er,** *n.*

go′nad (gō′nad, gon′ad) *n.* an ovary or testis. —**go·nad′al,** *adj.*

gon′do·la (gon′dl ə *or, esp. for 1,* gon dō′lə) *n.* **1.** a long, narrow boat used on the canals in Venice. **2.** a car suspended from a cable. —**gon′do·lier′** (-lēr′) *n.*

gon′er (gô′nər) *n. Informal.* one that is dead, lost, or past recovery.

gong (gông) *n.* a large bronze disk that gives a hollow sound when struck.

gon′or·rhe′a (gon′ə rē′ə) *n.* a venereal disease that causes a discharge from the genitals.

goo (gŏŏ) *n., pl.* **goos.** *Informal.* **1.** a thick or sticky substance. **2.** sentimentality.

good (gŏŏd) *adj.* **1.** morally excellent. **2.** of high or adequate quality. **3.** well-behaved. **4.** kind. **5.** valid. **6.** favorable. —*n.* **7.** profit or advantage. **8.** virtue. **9. goods,** possessions. —*Idiom.* **10. for a.** sure to repay. **b.** worth. **c.** useful for.

Good′ Fri′day *n.* the Friday before Easter, commemorating the Crucifixion of Christ.

good′ly *adj.,* **-lier, -liest.** numerous or abundant.

good′ Sa·mar′i·tan (sə mar′i tn) *n.* a person who helps those in need.

good′will′ *n.* friendly feelings or intentions.

good′y (gŏŏd′ē) *n., pl.* **-ies.** something pleasing to eat, as candy.

goof (gŏŏf) *Informal.* —*n.* **1.** a foolish or stupid person. **2.** a mistake. —*v.i.* **3.** to make a mistake. **4. goof off** or **around,** to waste time. —**goof′y,** *adj.*

goon (gŏŏn) *n. Slang.* **1.** a hired hoodlum. **2.** a stupid, foolish, or awkward person.

goose (gŏŏs) *n., pl.* **geese.** a web-footed water bird, larger than a duck. **2.** the female of this bird.

goose′ber′ry *n., pl.* **-ries.** a sour, edible green berry.

goose′ flesh′ *n.* the bristling of hair on the skin, as from cold or fear. Also, **goose pimples, goose bumps.**

G.O.P. Grand Old Party (epithet of the Republican Party).

go′pher (gō′fər) *n.* a burrowing rodent.

gore¹ (gôr) *n.* **1.** clotted blood. **2.** bloodshed. —**gor′y,** *adj.*

gore² (gôr) *v.t.,* **gored, goring.** to pierce with a horn.

gore³ (gôr) *n.* a triangular insert of cloth.

gorge (gôrj) *n., v.,* **gorged, gorging.** —*n.* **1.** a narrow rocky ravine. —*v.t., v.i.* **2.** to stuff (oneself) with food.

gor′geous (gôr′jəs) *adj.* **1.** splendid. **2.** very beautiful.

go·ril′la (gə ril′ə) *n.* a large African ape.

gos′ling (goz′ling) *n.* a young goose.

gos′pel (gos′pəl) *n.* **1.** the teachings of Jesus and the apostles. **2. Gospel,** any of the first four New Testament books. **3.** absolute truth.

gos′sa·mer (gos′ə mər) *n.* **1.** a filmy cobweb. **2.** something very light and delicate. —*adj.* **3.** like gossamer.

gos′sip (gos′əp) *n., v.,* **-siped, -siping.** —*n.* **1.** idle talk or rumor about others′ private affairs. **2.** a person who spreads gossip. —*v.i.* **3.** to spread gossip.

got (got) *v.* a pt. and pp. of **get.**

Goth′ic (goth′ik) *adj.* **1.** noting a style of medieval European architecture, marked by pointed arches. **2.** (*often l.c.*) noting a style of literature marked by gloomy settings and mysterious events.

got′ten *v.* a pp. of **get.**

Gou′da (gou′də, gŏŏ′-) *n.* a mild, yellowish Dutch cheese.

gouge (gouj) *n., v.,* **gouged, gouging.** —*n.* **1.** a chisel with a concave blade. **2.** a hole made by or as if by a gouge. —*v.t.* **3.** to dig out with a gouge. **4.** to swindle or overcharge.

gou′lash (gŏŏ′läsh, -lash) *n.* a stew of meat and vegetables, seasoned with paprika.

gourd (gôrd, gŏŏrd) *n.* **1.** the hard-shelled fruit of a vine related to the squash. **2.** a dipper made from a dried gourd shell.

gour·mand′ (gŏŏr mänd′, gŏŏr′-mənd) *n.* one who is fond of good eating, often to excess.

gour′met′ (gŏŏr mā′, gŏŏr′mā) *n.* a lover of fine food.

gout (gout) *n.* a painful disease of the joints. —**gout′y,** *adj.*

gov. **1.** government. **2.** governor.

gov·ern (guv′ərn) *v.t.* to rule by authority. **2.** to influence. **3.** to control.

gov′ern·ess *n.* a woman employed to teach children in their home.

gov′ern·ment (-ərn mənt, -ər-mənt) *n.* **1.** the system by which a state is governed. **2.** a governing body of persons. **3.** control; rule.

gov′er·nor (-ər nər, -ə nər) *n.* **1.** the head of a U.S. state. **2.** a person governing a colony, territory, etc. **3.** the head of an institution.

govt. government.

gown (goun) *n.* **1.** a woman's formal dress. **2.** a loose robe worn by judges, the clergy, etc.

G.P. General Practitioner.

grab (grab) *v.,* **grabbed, grabbing,** *n.* —*v.t.* **1.** to seize suddenly, eagerly, roughly, or forcibly. —*n.* **2.** the act of grabbing.

grace (grās) *n., v.,* **graced, gracing.** —*n.* **1.** beauty of form, manner, etc. **2.** goodwill. **3.** mercy. **4.** God's love or favor. **5.** a prayer of thanks said at mealtime. —*v.t.* **6.** to lend grace to. **7.** to favor or honor. —**grace′-ful,** *adj.*

gra′cious (grā′shəs) *adj.* **1.** kind or courteous. **2.** marked by good taste or luxury.

grack′le (grak′əl) *n.* a blackbird with iridescent black plumage.

gra·da′tion (grā dā′shən) *n.* **1.** a change taking place in a series of stages. **2.** a stage in such a series.

grade (grād) *n., v.,* **graded, grading.** —*n.* **1.** a degree in a scale, as of rank or quality. **2.** a category. **3.** a stage in a process. **4.** a division in a school. **5.** a mark showing the quality of a student's work. —*v.t.* **6.** to arrange in grades. **7.** to make level. **8.** to assign a grade to (a student's work). —*Idiom.* **9. make the grade,** to succeed.

grade′ cros′sing *n.* an intersection of a railroad track and a road.

grade′ school′ *n.* an elementary school.

grad′u·al (graj′ŏŏ əl) *adj.* changing, moving, etc., by degrees.

grad′u·ate *n., adj., v.,* **-ated, -ating.** —*n.* (-it) **1.** a person who has received an academic degree or diploma. —*adj.* (-it) **2.** having an academic degree or diploma. **3.** of academic study beyond the baccalaureate level. —*v.i.* (-āt′) **4.** to receive a diploma or degree. —*v.t.* **5.** to grant an academic diploma or degree to. **6.** to divide into or mark with degrees or other divisions.

graf·fi′ti (grə fē′tē) *n.pl., sing.* **graf-fito** (-tō). markings scrawled or painted on public surfaces.

graft¹ (graft) *n.* **1.** a bud or shoot of a plant inserted into another plant to form a new plant. **2.** living tissue transplanted to another part of the body or from one person to another. —*v.t., v.i.* **3.** to insert (a graft). **4.** to transplant (living tissue) as a graft.

graft² (graft) *n.* **1.** obtaining money or advantage dishonestly, as by political influence. **2.** the advantage obtained.

gra′ham (grā′əm, gram) *adj.* made of whole-wheat flour.

Grail (grāl) *n.* (in medieval legend) the cup or chalice used at the Last Supper of Christ with the apostles.

grain (grān) *n.* **1.** a small, hard seed of a cereal plant. **2.** any small, hard particle. **3.** a tiny amount. **4.** the pattern of wood fibers. —**grain′y,** *adj.*

gram (gram) *n.* a metric unit of weight equal to 1/1000 of a kilogram.

-gram a suffix meaning something written or drawn.

gram′mar (gram′ər) *n.* **1.** the features or constructions of a language as a whole. **2.** knowledge or usage of the preferred forms in speaking or writing. —**gram·mar′i·an** (grə mar′ē ən) *n.* —**gram·mat′i·cal** (grə mat′i kəl) *adj.* —**grat·i·fi·ca′tion,** *n.*

gran′a·ry (grā′nə rē, gran′ə-) *n., pl.* **-ries.** a storehouse for grain.

grand (grand) *adj.* **1.** large or impressive. **2.** of great importance. **3.** splendid. —*n.* **4.** a grand piano. **5.** *Informal.* a thousand dollars.

grand′child′ (gran′chīld′) *n.* a child of one's son or daughter. —**grand′daugh′ter,** *n.* —**grand′son′,** *n.*

gran·dee′ (gran dē′) *n.* a nobleman.

gran′deur (gran′jər, -jŏŏr) *n.* greatness; splendor.

gran·dil′o·quence (gran dil′ə-kwəns) *n.* lofty, often pompous speech. —**gran·dil′o·quent,** *adj.*

gran′di·ose′ (gran′dē ōs′) *adj.* grand or pompous.

grand′ ju′ry a jury designated to determine if a law has been violated and whether the evidence warrants prosecution.

grand′par′ent *n.* a parent of a parent. —**grand′fa′ther,** *n.* —**grand′moth′er,** *n.*

grand′ pian′o a piano with a horizontal case on three legs.

grand′stand′ (gran′-, grand′-) *n.* **1.** a main seating area, as of a stadium. —*v.i.* **2.** to conduct oneself to impress onlookers.

grange (grānj) *n.* a farmers′ organization.

gra·ni′ta (grə nē′tə) *n.* sweet granular ice flavored with fruit juice or wine

gran′ite (gran′it) *n.* a very hard, coarse-grained rock.

gra·no′la (grə nō′lə) *n.* a cereal of dried fruit, grains, nuts, etc.

grant (grant) *v.t.* **1.** to give; bestow. **2.** to admit to. —*n.* **3.** something granted, as a piece of land. —*Idiom.* **4. take for granted, a.** to accept as true. **b.** to fail to appreciate.

gran′u·late′ (gran′yə lāt′) *v.t., v.i.,* **-lated, -lating.** to form into granules or grains.

gran′ule (-yŏŏl) *n.* a small grain or particle.

grape (grāp) *n.* a smooth-skinned fruit that grows in clusters on a vine.

grape′fruit′ *n.* a large yellow citrus fruit.

grape′vine′ *n.* **1.** a vine on which grapes grow. **2.** a person-to-person route by which gossip spreads.

graph (graf) *n.* a diagram showing relations among things by dots, lines, etc.

-graph a suffix meaning: **1.** something written or drawn. **2.** an instrument that writes or records.

graph′ic *adj.* **1.** vivid. **2.** of writing, drawing, engraving, etc.

graph′ics *n.pl.* **1.** the arts of drawing, engraving, etc. **2.** drawings, charts, etc. **3.** a pictorial computer output.

graph′ite (-īt) *n.* a soft carbon.

graph·ol′o·gy (gra fol′ə jē) *n.* the study of handwriting.

-graphy a suffix meaning: **1.** the process or form of writing, printing, or describing. **2.** an art or science concerned with these.

grap′nel (grap′nl) *n.* a hooked device for grasping.

grap′ple (grap′əl) *n., v.,* **-pled, -pling.** —*n.* **1.** a hook for grasping; grapnel. **2.** a seizing. —*v.i.* **3.** to use a grapnel. **4.** to struggle. —*v.t.* **5.** to seize or hold.

grasp (grasp) *v.t.* **1.** to seize and hold. **2.** to understand. —*n.* **3.** the act of grasping. **4.** mastery.

grasp′ing *adj.* greedy.

grass (gras) *n.* **1.** a plant with jointed stems and bladelike leaves. **2.** grass-covered ground. —**grass′y,** *adj.*

grass′hop′per *n.* a leaping insect.

grass′land′ *n.* open grass-covered land; prairie.

grass′ roots′ *n.* ordinary citizens, as contrasted with the leadership or elite. —**grass′-roots′,** *adj.*

grate¹ (grāt) *n.* **1.** a frame of metal bars for holding burning fuel. **2.** a framework of crossed bars used as a guard or cover.

grate² (grāt) *v.i.* **1.** to have an irritating effect. **2.** to make a rough scraping sound. —*v.t.* **3.** to reduce to small particles by rubbing against a rough surface. **4.** to rub together with a harsh sound. **5.** to irritate.

grate′ful *adj.* **1.** thankful. **2.** expressing gratitude. —**grate′ful·ly,** *adv.*

grat′i·fy′ (grat′ə fī′) *v.t.,* **-fied, -fying. 1.** to please. **2.** to satisfy. —**grat′i·fi·ca′tion,** *n.*

gra′tis (grat′is, grä′tis) *adv., adj.* free of charge.

grat′i·tude′ (grat′i tŏŏd′, -tyŏŏd′) *n.* the quality or feeling of being grateful.

gra·tu′i·tous (grə tŏŏ′i təs, -tyŏŏ′-) *adj.* **1.** free of charge. **2.** being without reasonable cause.

gra·tu′i·ty *n., pl.* **-ties.** a tip.

grave¹ (grāv) *n.* a place of or an excavation for burial of a dead body.

grave² (grāv) *adj.,* **graver, gravest. 1.** serious or solemn. **2.** important.

grav′el (grav′əl) *n.* small stones.

grav′el·ly *adj.* **1.** made up of or like gravel. **2.** harsh-sounding.

grave′yard′ *n.* a cemetery.

grave′yard shift′ *n.* a work shift usu. beginning about midnight.

grav·i·ta′tion (grav′i tā′shən) *n.* the force of attraction between two bodies. —**grav·i·tate′,** *v.i.*

grav′i·ty *n., pl.* **-ties. 1.** the force attracting bodies to the earth's center. **2.** heaviness. **3.** seriousness.

gra′vy (grā′vē) *n., pl.* **-vies.** a sauce made from the juices of cooked meat.

gray (grā) *n.* **1.** a color between black and white. —*adj.* **2.** of this color. **3.** ambiguous. **4.** vaguely depressing.

gray′ mat′ter *n.* **1.** a reddish gray nerve tissue of the brain. **2.** *Informal.* brains.

graze¹ (grāz) *v.,* **grazed, grazing.** —*v.i.* **1.** to feed on grass. —*v.t.* **2.** to put (livestock) out to graze.

graze² (grāz) *v.t., v.i.,* **grazed, grazing.** to touch or rub (something) lightly in passing.

grease *n., v.,* **greased, greasing.** —*n.* (grēs) **1.** animal fat. **2.** any fatty or oily matter. —*v.t.* (grēs, grēz) **3.** to put grease on or in. —**greas′y,** *adj.*

great (grāt) *adj.* **1.** very large in size, number, intensity, etc. **2.** excellent. **3.** famous. **4.** important. —**great′ly,** *adv.*

Great′ Dane′ *n.* a kind of very large and powerful dog.

grebe (grēb) *n.* a kind of diving bird.

greed (grēd) *n.* excessive desire, esp. for wealth. —**greed′i·ly,** *adv.* —**greed′y,** *adj.*

Greek (grēk) *adj.* **1.** of Greece, its inhabitants, or its language. —*n.* **2.** a native of Greece. **3.** the language of Greece.

green (grēn) *adj.* **1.** of the color of growing foliage. **2.** unripe. **3.** inexperienced. —*n.* **4.** the color between blue and yellow. **5. greens,** the edible leaves of certain plants. **6.** grassy land.

green′back′ *n.* a U.S. legal-tender note.

green′belt′ *n.* an area of open land surrounding a community.

green′er·y *n.* plants.

green′horn′ *n.* an inexperienced person.

green′house′ *n.* a glass building where plants are grown.

green′house effect′ *n.* heating of the atmosphere resulting from the absorption by certain gases of solar radiation.

green′room′ *n.* a lounge in a theater for use by performers.

green′ thumb′ *n.* an exceptional skill in growing plants.

greet (grēt) *v.t.* **1.** to address on meeting. **2.** to receive. **3.** to show itself to. —**greet′ing,** *n.*

gre·gar′i·ous (gri gâr′ē əs) *adj.* fond of the company of others.

grem′lin (grem′lin) *n.* an imaginary mischievous being blamed for disruptions in any activity.

gre·nade′ (gri nād′) *n.* a small explosive thrown by hand.

gren′a·dier′ (gren′ə dēr′) *n.* a member of a British infantry regiment.

grew (grŏŏ) *v.* pt. of **grow.**

grey (grā) *adj. Chiefly Brit.* gray.

grey′hound′ *n.* a slender swift dog.

grid (grid) *n.* **1.** a grating of crossed bars. **2.** a network of crossed lines as on a map, chart, etc. **3.** a system of electrical distribution.

grid′dle (grid′l) *n.* a shallow frying pan.

grid′i′ron *n.* **1.** a grill. **2.** a football field.

grid′lock′ *n.* a complete stoppage of movement in all directions due to traffic blocking intersections.

grief (grēf) *n.* deep sorrow.

griev′ance (grē′vəns) *n.* **1.** a wrong. **2.** a complaint against a wrong.

grieve (grēv) *v.i., v.t.,* **grieved, grieving.** to feel or cause to feel sorrow.

griev′ous *adj.* **1.** causing grief. **2.** very serious.

grif′fin (grif′in) *n.* a fabled monster with the head and wings of an eagle and the body of a lion.

grill (gril) *n.* **1.** a utensil topped by a metal framework for cooking food over direct heat. —*v.t.* **2.** to broil on a grill. **3.** to question severely and persistently.

grille (gril) *n.* an ornamental metal barrier.

grim (grim) *adj.,* **grimmer, grimmest. 1.** stern. **2.** having a harsh or forbidding air. —**grim′ly,** *adv.*

grim·ace (grim′əs, gri mās′) *n., v.,* **-maced, -macing.** —*n.* **1.** a facial expression indicating pain, disapproval, etc. —*v.i.* **2.** to make grimaces.

grime (grīm) *n.* dirt adhering to a surface.

grin (grin) *v.,* **grinned, grinning,** *n.* —*v.i.* **1.** to smile openly and broadly. —*n.* **2.** a broad smile.

grind (grīnd) *v.,* **ground** (ground) **grinding,** *n.* —*v.t.* **1.** to wear, crush, or sharpen by friction. **2.** to reduce to particles. **3.** to rub together harshly, as the teeth. **4.** to operate by turning a crank. **5.** the act or sound of grinding. **6.** a grade of fineness. **7.** *Informal.* dreary, uninteresting work.

grind′stone′ *n.* a rotating stone wheel for sharpening, shaping, etc.

grip (grip) *n., v.,* **gripped, gripping.** —*n.* **1.** a firm grasp. **2.** control. **3.** a handclasp. **4.** a handle. **5.** mental hold. —*v.t.* **6.** to grasp. **7.** to hold the attention of. **8.** to take firm hold. —*Idiom.* **9.** **come to grips with,** to face and cope with.

gripe (grīp) *v.,* **griped, griping,** *n.* —*v.i.* **1.** *Informal.* to complain. —*v.t.* **2.** to produce pain in the bowels of. **3.** to annoy. —*n.* **4.** *Informal.* a complaint. —**grip′er,** *n.*

gris′ly (griz′lē) *adj.,* **-lier, -liest.** gruesome.

grist (grist) *n.* grain to be ground.

gris′tle (gris′əl) *n.* cartilage in meat.

grit (grit) *n., v.,* **gritted, gritting.** —*n.* **1.** hard, abrasive particles. **2.** firmness of character. —*v.t.* **3.** to clamp (the teeth) together.

grits (grits) *n.pl.* ground hominy.

griz′zly (griz′lē) *adj.,* **-zlier, -zliest.** gray, as hair or fur.

griz′zly bear′ *n.* a large North American brown bear with coarse, gray-tipped fur.

groan (grōn) *n.* **1.** a low moan of pain, grief, disapproval, etc. —*v.i., v.t.* **2.** to utter (with) a groan.

gro′cer (grō′sər) *n.* the owner of a store that sells food and household articles.

gro′cer·y *n., pl.* **-ies. 1.** a store selling food and household articles. **2.** Usu., **groceries.** food bought at such a store.

grog (grog) *n.* **1.** a mixture of rum and water. **2.** any alcoholic drink.

grog′gy *adj.,* **-gier, -giest.** dazed and weakened.

groin (groin) *n.* the fold where the thigh joins the abdomen.

grom′met (grom′it, grum′-) *n.* a metal eyelet.

groom (grōōm, grŏŏm) *n.* **1.** a bridegroom. **2.** a person who takes care of horses. —*v.t.* **3.** to make neat. **4.** to clean and brush (an animal). **5.** to prepare for a position.

groove (grōōv) *n., v.,* **grooved, grooving.** —*n.* **1.** a long, narrow cut in a surface. —*v.t.* **2.** to cut a groove in.

grope (grōp) *v.,* **groped, groping.** —*v.i.* **1.** to feel about blindly or uncertainly. —*v.t.* **2.** to seek (one's way) by groping.

gros′beak′ (grōs′bēk′) *n.* a finch with a thick, conical bill.

gross (grōs) *adj.* **1.** without deductions. **2.** flagrant; extreme. **3.** disgusting. **4.** very fat or large. —*n.* **5.** the total amount before deductions. **6.** twelve dozen.

gross′ na′tional prod′uct *n.* the total monetary value of all goods and services produced in a country during one year.

gro·tesque′ (grō tesk′) *adj.* fantastically ugly or absurd.

grot′to (grot′ō) *n., pl.* **-tos, -toes.** a cave.

grouch (grouch) *n.* **1.** an ill-tempered person. —*v.i.* **2.** to be sulky. —**grouch′y,** *adj.*

ground (ground) *n.* **1.** the earth's solid surface. **2.** earth or soil. **3.** **grounds,** the land surrounding a building. **4.** Usu., **grounds,** the basis for a belief. **5.** **grounds,** coffee dregs. **6.** of or on ground. —*v.t.* **7.** to place on a foundation. **8.** to teach the basics to. **9.** to cause (a ship) to run aground. **10.** to restrict (an aircraft or pilot) to the ground. **11.** *Informal.* to restrict the social activities of. —*Idiom.* **12.** **gain (or lose) ground,** to advance (or fail to advance).

ground′hog′ *n.* a stocky North American burrowing rodent; woodchuck.

ground′less *adj.* without rational basis.

ground′ rules′ *n.pl.* the basic rules of conduct in a given situation.

ground′swell′ *n.* a surge of feelings, esp. among the general public.

ground′work′ *n.* the basis of a project.

group (grōōp) *n.* **1.** a number of persons, animals, or things considered together. —*v.t., v.i.* **2.** to form into a group.

group′er (grōō′pər) *n., pl.* **-ers, -er.** a large warm-water sea bass.

group′ie *n., pl.* **-ies.** a young fan of a rock group or a celebrity.

grouse[1] (grous) *n.* a game bird with a short bill and feathered legs.

grouse[2] (grous) *v.i.,* **groused, grousing.** to complain.

grout (grout) *n.* a thin, coarse mortar used to fill crevices.

grove (grōv) *n.* a small wood or orchard.

grov′el (grov′əl, gruv′-) *v.i.,* **-eled, -eling.** to humble oneself.

grow (grō) *v.,* **grew** (grōō) **grown, growing.** —*v.i.* **1.** to increase in size; develop. **2.** to become. —*v.t.* **3.** to cause or allow to grow; cultivate. **4.** grow on, to become gradually more liked by. **5.** ~ **up,** to become mature. —**grow′er,** *n.*

growl (groul) *n.* **1.** a deep guttural sound, as of anger or hostility. —*v.i., v.t.* **2.** to utter a growl.

grown (grōn) *adj.* **1.** arrived at full growth. —*v.* **2.** pp. of **grow.**

grown′up′ *n.* an adult. —**grown′-up′,** *adj.*

growth (grōth) *n.* **1.** the act of growing. **2.** a size or stage of development. **3.** something that has grown. **4.** a tumor.

grub (grub) *n., v.,* **grubbed, grubbing.** —*n.* **1.** the thick-bodied larva of certain insects. **2.** *Slang.* food. —*v.t.* **3.** to uproot. —*v.i.* **4.** to search by digging. **5.** to work hard.

grub′by *adj.,* **-bier, -biest.** dirty.

grudge (gruj) *n., v.,* **grudged, grudging.** —*n.* **1.** a feeling of ill will. —*v.t.* **2.** to give reluctantly. **3.** to resent the good fortune of. —**grudg′ing·ly,** *adv.*

gru′el (grōō′əl) *n.* a thin cooked cereal.

gru′el·ing (grōō′ə ling, grōō′ling) *adj.* exhausting; arduous.

grue′some (grōō′səm) *adj.* causing horror and repugnance.

gruff (gruf) *adj.* **1.** low and hoarse. **2.** brusque or surly.

grum′ble (grum′bəl) *v.,* **-bled, -bling.** —*v.i.* **1.** to mutter in discontent. —*v.t.* **2.** to utter by grumbling. —*n.* **3.** a complaint.

grump′y (grum′pē) *adj.,* **-ier, -iest.** bad-tempered.

grunge (grunj) *n. Slang.* **1.** dirt; filth. **2.** a style or fashion marked by unkempt clothing, derived from a movement in rock music characterized by aggressive, nihilistic songs. —**grun′gy,** *adj.*

grunt (grunt) *v.i., v.t.* **1.** to utter (with) the deep, guttural sound of a hog. —*n.* **2.** such a sound.

gryph′on (grif′ən) *n.* a griffin.

gua′no (gwä′nō) *n.* a manure from the excrement of sea birds.

guar′an·tee′ (gar′ən tē′) *n., v.,* **-teed, -teeing.** —*n.* **1.** an assurance that something is of specified quality or content. **2.** something offered as security that an obligation will be fulfilled. **3.** something assuring a particular outcome. —*v.t.* **4.** to make or give a guarantee. **5.** to promise.

guar′an·tor′ (-tôr′) *n.* a person who guarantees.

guard (gärd) *v.t.* **1.** to watch over. **2.** to keep safe from harm. —*v.i.* **3.** to take precautions. —*n.* **4.** a person who guards. **5.** a close watch. **6.** a device that prevents injury, loss, etc.

guard′ed *adj.* **1.** cautious; prudent. **2.** protected or restrained.

guard′i·an *n.* **1.** a person who guards or protects. **2.** a person legally entrusted with the care of another.

gua′va (gwä′və) *n.* the large yellow fruit of a tropical tree.

gu·ber·na·to′ri·al (gōō′bər nə tôr′ē əl, gyōō′-) *adj.* of a governor or the office of a governor.

guer·ril′la (gə ril′ə) *n.* a member of a band of soldiers that harasses the enemy.

guess (ges) *v.t., v.i.* **1.** to form an opinion about (something) without complete evidence. **2.** to be correct in such an opinion. —*n.* **3.** the act of guessing. **4.** an opinion reached by guessing.

guess′work′ *n.* **1.** a guessing. **2.** conclusions drawn from guesses.

guest (gest) *n.* **1.** a person who spends time at another's home. **2.** a customer at a hotel, restaurant, etc.

guf·faw′ (gu fô′, gə-) *n.* **1.** a burst of loud laughter. —*v.i.* **2.** to laugh loudly.

guid′ance (gīd′ns) *n.* **1.** an act or instance of guiding. **2.** advice or counseling.

guide (gīd) *v.,* **guided, guiding,** *n.* —*v.t.* **1.** to show the way. **2.** to lead or direct in any action. —*n.* **3.** one that guides.

guide′book′ *n.* a book of directions and information, as for tourists.

guid′ed mis′sile *n.* a radio-controlled aerial missile.

guide′line′ *n.* any guide or indication of a future course of action.

guild (gild) *n.* **1.** an organization of people having a common interest. **2.** a medieval association of merchants or artisans.

guile (gīl) *n.* deceitful cunning.

guil·lo·tine (gil′ə tēn′, gē′ə-) *n.* a machine for beheading people.

guilt (gilt) *n.* **1.** the fact of having committed an offense. **2.** a feeling of responsibility or regret for having done something wrong.

guin′ea fowl′ (gin′ē) *n.* a gray-speckled domesticated fowl.

guin′ea pig′ *n.* **1.** a tailless rodent raised as a pet and for use in laboratories. **2.** the subject of any experiment.

guise (gīz) *n.* outward appearance.

gui·tar′ (gi tär′) *n.* a musical instrument usu. having six strings that are plucked. —**gui·tar′ist,** *n.*

gulch (gulch) *n.* a deep, narrow ravine marking the course of a stream.

gulf (gulf) *n.* **1.** a large arm of the sea partly enclosed by land. **2.** an abyss. **3.** any wide gap.

gull[1] (gul) *n.* a long-winged sea bird, usu. white with gray or black wings and back.

gull[2] (gul) *v.t.* **1.** to trick or cheat. —*n.* **2.** a person who is easily deceived. —**gul′li·ble,** *adj.*

gul′let (gul′it) *n.* the esophagus or the throat.

gul′li·ble (gul′ə bəl) *adj.* easily deceived. —**gul·li·bil′i·ty,** *n.*

gul′ly (gul′ē) *n., pl.* **-lies.** a deep channel cut by running water.

gulp (gulp) *v.t.* **1.** to swallow greedily. —*v.i.* **2.** to gasp, as if swallowing large amounts of a liquid. —*n.* **3.** the act of gulping.

gum[1] (gum) *n., v.,* **gummed, gumming.** —*n.* **1.** a sticky substance exuded from certain trees. **2.** chewing gum. —*v.t.* **3.** to smear, stick together, or clog with gum.

gum[2] (gum) *n.* Often, **gums.** the firm, fleshy tissue around the teeth.

gum′bo (gum′bō) *n., pl.* **-bos.** a soup thickened with okra.

gum′drop′ *n.* a small chewy candy.

gump′tion (gump′shən) *n.* **1.** initiative; resourcefulness. **2.** courage.

gum′shoe′ *n., pl.* **-shoes. 1.** *Slang.* a detective. **2.** a rubber overshoe.

gun (gun) *n., v.,* **gunned, gunning.** —*n.* **1.** a weapon that shoots missiles from a metal tube by the force of an explosive. **2.** any device for shooting or ejecting something under pressure. —*v.t.* **3.** to shoot with a gun. **4.** to cause (an engine) to speed up quickly. —*Idiom.* **5.** **under the gun,** under pressure.

gun′fire′ *n.* the firing of guns.

gung′-ho′ (gung′hō′) *adj. Informal.* thoroughly enthusiastic and loyal.

gunk (gungk) *n. Slang.* any sticky or greasy matter.

gun′man *n., pl.* **-men.** an armed criminal.

gun′ny *n., pl.* **-nies.** a strong coarse material used for sacks.

gun′point′ *n.* —*Idiom.* **at gunpoint,** under threat of being shot.

gun′pow′der *n.* an explosive mixture used in guns and for blasting.

gun′shot′ *n.* a shot fired from a gun.

gun′smith′ *n.* a person who makes or repairs firearms.

gun′wale (gun′l) *n.* the upper edge of the side of a vessel.

gup′py (gup′ē) *n., pl.* **-pies.** a small fish often kept in aquariums.

gur′gle (gûr′gəl) *v.,* **-gled, -gling,** *n.* —*v.i.* **1.** to flow irregularly and noisily. —*n.* **2.** the sound of this.

gur′ney (gûr′nē) *n.* a wheeled table for transporting patients.

gu′ru (gŏŏr′ōō, gŏŏ rōō′) *n.* **1.** any person who teaches or advises. **2.** a Hindu spiritual teacher.

gush (gush) *v.i.* **1.** to flow out suddenly and forcibly. **2.** to talk effusively. —*n.* **3.** a sudden flow.

gush′er *n.* a flowing oil well.

gus′set (gus′it) *n.* a triangular piece of material inserted to improve fit or to reinforce.

gus′sy (gus′ē) *v.,* **-sied, -sying.** *Informal.* **gussy up,** to dress up or decorate in a showy manner.

gust (gust) *n.* **1.** a sudden blast of wind. **2.** an outburst of emotion. —**gust′y,** *adj.*

gus′ta·to′ry (gus′tə tôr′ē) *adj.* of taste.

gus′to (gus′tō) *n.* hearty enjoyment.

gut (gut) *n., v.,* **gutted, gutting.** —*n.* **1.** the intestine. **2.** **guts, a.** the bowels. **b.** courage. —*v.t.* **3.** to remove the guts of. **4.** to destroy the interior of, as a building. —*adj.* **5. a.** basic. **b.** based on instincts.

guts′y *adj.,* **-ier, -iest.** daring or courageous.

gut′ter (gut′ər) *n.* a channel for leading off rainwater.

gut′tur·al (gut′ər əl) *adj.* of or pronounced in the throat.

guy[1] (gī) *n.* **1.** a man or boy. **2.** **guys,** people.

guy[2] (gī) *n.* a rope or cable used to steady an object.

guz′zle (guz′əl) *v.i., v.t.,* **-zled, -zling.** to drink or eat greedily. —**guz′zler,** *n.*

gym·na′si·um (jim nā′zē əm) *n., pl.* **-siums, -sia.** a room or building for physical exercise.

gym′nast (jim′nəst, -nast) *n.* a person trained in gymnastics.

gym·nas′tics (-nas′tiks) *n.pl.* physical exercises that demonstrate strength, balance, or agility.

gy′ne·col·o·gy (gī′ni kol′ə jē) *n.* the branch of medicine dealing with the health of women, esp. of the reproductive system. —**gy′ne·col·o·gist,** *n.*

gyp (jip) *v.t., v.i.,* **gypped, gypping.** *Informal.* to cheat.

gyp′sum (jip′səm) *n.* a chalk-like mineral.

Gyp′sy (jip′sē) *n., pl.* **-sies.** a member of a wandering people.

gy′rate (jī′rāt, jī rāt′) *v.i.,* **-rated, -rating.** to move in a circle or spiral. —**gy·ra′tion,** *n.*

gy′ro·scope′ (jī′rə skōp′) *n.* a rotating wheel mounted so its axis can turn in all directions, used to maintain equilibrium and determine direction.

H

H, h (āch) *n.* the eighth letter of the English alphabet.

ha′be·as cor′pus (hā′bē əs kôr′pəs) *n.* a writ requiring that an arrested person be brought before a court to determine whether he or she has been detained legally.

hab′er·dash′er·y (hab′ər dash′ə rē) *n., pl.* **-eries.** a shop selling men's shirts, ties, socks, etc. —**hab′er·dash′er,** *n.*

hab′it (hab′it) *n.* **1.** a pattern of behavior. **2.** customary practice. **3.** a monk's or nun's garb. **4.** addiction.

hab′it·a·ble (hab′i tə bəl) *adj.* able to be lived in.

hab′i·tat′ (-tat′) *n.* the natural environment of a plant or animal.

hab′i·ta′tion *n.* a dwelling.

ha·bit·u·al (hə bich′ōō əl) *adj.* **1.** fixed by habit. **2.** common or usual. —**ha·bit′u·al·ly,** *adv.*

ha·bit′u·ate′ (hə bich′ōō āt′) *v.t.,* **-ated, -ating.** to accustom.

ha·bit·u·é′ (-ōō ā′) *n.* a regular visitor to a place.

ha·ci·en·da (hä′sē en′də) *n., pl.* **-das.** (in Spanish America) a large estate or ranch. **2.** the house on such an estate.

hack[1] (hak) *v.t.* **1.** to cut roughly. —*v.i.* **2.** to cough dryly. —*n.* **3.** a cut or notch. **4.** a dry cough.

hack[2] (hak) *n.* **1.** a writer who does routine work. **2.** a horse or vehicle for hire. —*v.i.* **3.** to drive a taxi. **4.** to work as a hack. —*adj.* **5.** routine.

hack′er *n. Slang.* **1.** a skilled computer enthusiast. **2.** a computer user who tries to gain unauthorized access to systems.

hack′les (hak′əlz) *n.pl.* **1.** the hair that can bristle on the back of an animal's neck. —*Idiom.* **2.** **with one's hackles up,** angry.

hack′ney (-nē) *n., pl.* **-neys.** a horse or carriage for hire.

hack′neyed *adj.* trite.

hack′saw′ *n.* a saw for cutting metal.

had′dock (had′ək) *n.* a N Atlantic food fish of the cod family.

Ha′des (hā′dēz) *n.* **1.** the Greek god of the underworld. **2.** hell.

haft (haft) *n.* a handle.

hag (hag) *n.* an ugly old woman.

hag′gard (hag′ərd) *adj.* appearing gaunt, wasted, or exhausted.

hag′gle (hag′əl) *v.i.,* **-gled, -gling.** to argue about price.

hai′ku (hī′kōō) *n., pl.* **-ku.** a Japanese poem consisting of 3 lines of 5, 7, and 5 syllables, respectively.

hail[1] (hāl) *v.t.* **1.** to greet. **2.** to call out or signal to. —*n.* **3.** a call or greeting.

hail[2] (hāl) *n.* **1.** ice pellets falling in a shower. **2.** a shower of anything. —*v.i.* **3.** to fall like hail.

hail′stone′ *n.* a pellet of hail.

hair (hâr) *n.* **1.** a fine threadlike structure on the human head, the body of a mammal, etc. **2.** a mass of such structures. —**hair′less,** *adj.* —**hair′y,** *adj.*

hair′breadth′ *n.* a very small space or distance. Also, **hairs′breadth′,** *n.*

hair′cut′ *n.* **1.** the act of cutting hair. **2.** a hairstyle.

hair′do′ (-dōō′) *n., pl.* **-dos.** a hairstyle.

hair′dress′er *n.* a person who cuts or arranges hair.

hair′piece′ *n.* a toupee or wig.

hair′pin′ *n.* **1.** a U-shaped pin for fastening up the hair. —*adj.* **2.** sharply curved back, as in a U shape.

hair′-rais′ing *adj.* terrifying.

hair′spray′ *n.* a liquid spray for holding the hair in place.

hair′style′ *n.* a way of arranging the hair. —**hair′styl′ist,** *n.*

hair′-trig′ger *adj.* easily set off.

hake (hāk) *n.* a codlike marine food fish.

hal′cy·on (hal′sē ən) *adj.* peaceful; happy; carefree.

hale (hāl) *adj.* healthy.

half (haf) *n., pl.* **halves,** *adj., adv.* —*n.* **1.** one of two equal parts. —*adj.* **2.** being a half. **3.** incomplete. —*adv.* **4.** partly.

half′-baked′ *adj.* **1.** not sufficiently planned or prepared. **2.** foolish.

half′ broth′er *n.* a brother related through one parent only.

half′-cocked′ *adj.* ill-prepared.

half′-heart′ed *adj.* unenthusiastic.

half′-life′ *n., pl.* **-lives.** the time required for one half of the atoms of a radioactive substance to decay.

half′ note′ *n.* a musical note equal in time value to half a whole note.

half′ sis′ter *n.* a sister related through one parent only.

half′-truth′ *n.* a deceptive statement that is only partly true.

half′way′ (-wā′, -wā′) *adv.* **1.** to the midpoint. **2.** partially or almost. —*adj.* **3.** midway. **4.** partial or inadequate.

half′way house′ *n.* a residence for persons released from a hospital, prison, etc.

half′-wit′ *n.* a foolish person.

hal′i·but (hal′ə bət, hol′-) *n.* a kind of large edible flounder.

hal·i·to′sis (hal′i tō′sis) *n.* bad breath.

hall (hôl) *n.* **1.** a corridor. **2.** an entrance room of a house or building. **3.** a large public room.

hal·le·lu′jah (hal′ə lōō′yə) *interj.* **1.** Praise ye the Lord! **2.** an exclamation of joy.

hall′mark′ (hôl′-) *n.* **1.** any mark or indication of genuineness or quality. **2.** any distinguishing characteristic.

hal′low (hal′ō) *v.t.* to make or honor as holy.

Hal′low·een′ or **Hal′low·e′en** (hal′ə wēn′, -ō en′, hol′-) *n.* the evening of October 31; the eve of All Saints' Day.

hal·lu·ci·na′tion (hə lōō′sə nā′shən) *n.* an experience of seeing or hearing something that does not exist outside the mind. **2.** an illusion. —**hal·lu′ci·nate′,** *v.i.*

hal·lu′ci·no·gen (-nə jən) *n.* a substance producing hallucinations.

hall′way′ *n.* a corridor.

ha′lo (hā′lō) *n., pl.* **-los, -loes.** a circle of light around the head of a holy personage in a picture.

halt[1] (hôlt) *v.i., v.t.* **1.** to stop or cause to stop. —*n.* **2.** a stop.

halt[2] (hôlt) *v.i.* **1.** to falter or hesitate. —*adj.* **2.** lame.

hal′ter (hôl′tər) *n.* **1.** a strap for

leading or restraining a horse. **2.** a noose. **3.** a woman's top, tied behind the neck and back.

halve (hav) *v.t.,* **halved, halving. 1.** to divide into two equal parts. **2.** to reduce to half.

hal/yard (hal/yərd) *n.* a line for hoisting a sail or flag.

ham[1] (ham) *n.* **1.** a cut of meat from the rear thigh of a hog. **2.** the back of the human thigh.

ham[2] (ham) *n., v.,* **hammed, hamming.** —*n.* **1.** a performer who overacts. **2.** an amateur radio operator. —*v.i., v.t.* **3.** to overact.

ham•burg•er (ham/bûr/gər) *n.* a patty of ground beef or a sandwich of this.

ham/let (ham/lit) *n.* a small village.

ham/mer (ham/ər) *n.* **1.** a tool with a head set crosswise on a handle, used for driving nails, beating metal, etc. **2.** something resembling this. —*v.t., v.i.* **3.** to beat with a hammer. **4.** to strike repeatedly.

ham/mock (ham/ək) *n.* a hanging bed of canvas or cord.

ham/per[1] (ham/pər) *v.t.* to hold back; impede.

ham/per[2] (ham/pər) *n.* a large covered basket.

ham/ster (ham/stər) *n.* a shorttailed rodent often kept as a pet.

ham/string *n., v.,* **-strung, -stringing.** —*n.* **1.** a tendon behind the knee. —*v.t.* **2.** to disable by cutting the hamstring. **3.** to make powerless or ineffective.

hand (hand) *n.* **1.** the end part of the arm. **2.** anything resembling a hand in shape or function. **3.** a manual worker or crew member. **4.** means; agency. **5.** assistance. **6.** side or direction. **7.** a round of applause. **8.** a pledge of marriage. **9.** the cards held by a player. —*v.t.* **10.** to give or pass by hand. **11. hand down,** to deliver or transmit. **12. ~ out,** to distribute. —*Idiom.* **13.** at hand, near. **14. hand in hand,** close together. **15. hands down,** effortlessly. **16. on hand,** available.

hand/bag/ *n.* a woman's purse.

hand/ball/ *n.* a game in which players strike a ball against a wall with the hand.

hand/bill/ *n.* a small printed notice, usu. distributed by hand.

hand/book/ *n.* a guide or reference book; manual.

hand/clasp/ *n.* a handshake.

hand/cuff/ *n.* **1.** a metal ring, linked to another by a chain, that can be locked around a prisoner's wrist. —*v.t.* **2.** to put handcuffs on.

hand/ful (-fŏŏl) *n., pl.* **-fuls. 1.** the amount a hand can hold. **2.** *Informal.* a difficult person or thing.

hand/gun/ *n.* a firearm that can be held and fired with one hand.

hand/i•cap/ (han/dē kap/) *n., v.,* **-capped, -capping.** —*n.* **1.** a disadvantage. **2.** a physical or mental disability. —*v.t.* **3.** to place at a disadvantage.

hand/i•craft/ *n.* **1.** manual skill. **2.** products requiring such skill.

hand/i•work/ *n.* **1.** work done by hand. **2.** the work of a particular person.

hand/ker•chief (hang/kər chif, -chēf/) *n.* a small cloth for wiping the nose, eyes, etc.

han/dle (han/dl) *n., v.,* **-dled, -dling.** —*n.* **1.** a part by which a thing is grasped or held by the hand. —*v.t.* **2.** to touch or pick up with the hands. **3.** to manage or control. **4.** to deal in.

hand/made/ *adj.* made by hand.

hand/out/ *n.* **1.** something given to a needy person. **2.** printed material distributed to a group. **3.** anything given away for nothing.

hand/shake/ *n.* a gripping and shaking of each other's hand in greeting or agreement.

hands/-off/ *adj.* not intervening.

hand/some (han/səm) *adj.* **1.** good-looking. **2.** generous.

hands/-on/ *adj.* involving active personal participation.

hand/spring/ *n.* a complete flipping of the body, landing first on the hands, then on the feet.

hand/-to-mouth/ *adj.* providing barely enough to survive.

hand/writ/ing *n.* **1.** writing done by hand. **2.** a style of such writing. —**hand/writ/ten** (-rit/n).

hand/y (han/dē) *adj.,* **-ier, -iest. 1.** within easy reach. **2.** easily used. **3.** skillful with the hands.

han/dy•man/ *n., pl.* **-men.** a person hired to do small jobs, as repairs.

hang (hang) *v.,* **hung** (hung) or **hanged, hanging.** —*v.t.* **1.** to at-

tach (a thing) so that it is supported from above with the lower part moving freely. **2.** to execute by suspending from a rope around the neck. **3.** to attach to a wall. **4.** to let (one's head) droop. —*v.i.* **5.** to be suspended so as to swing freely. **6.** to suffer death by hanging. **7.** to incline downward. **8.** to drape, as a garment. —*n.* **9.** the way a thing hangs.

hang/ar (hang/ər) *n.* a shelter for housing aircraft.

hang/dog/ *adj.* abject.

hang/ glid/ing *n.* the sport of soaring through the air while harnessed to a kitelike glider (**hang/ glid/er**).

hang/man *n.* a person who hangs condemned criminals.

hang/nail/ *n.* a small piece of loose skin around a fingernail.

hang/o/ver *n.* a sick feeling from drinking too much alcohol.

hang/up/ *n. Slang.* a preoccupation or psychological block.

hank (hangk) *n.* a coil or loop of yarn, thread, hair, etc.

han/ker (hang/kər) *v.i.* to have a longing.

hank/y-pank/y *n. Informal.* **1.** mischief. **2.** illicit sexual relations.

han/som (han/səm) *n.* a two-wheeled covered cab.

Ha/nuk•kah (кнä/nə kə, hä/-) *n.* a Jewish festival commemorating the rededication of the Temple in Jerusalem.

hap/haz/ard (hap haz/ərd) *adj.* having no plan or order; random.

hap/less *adj.* unfortunate.

hap/pen (hap/ən) *v.i.* **1.** to take place; occur. **2.** to discover by chance. —**hap/pen•ing,** *n.*

hap/pen•stance/ (-stans/) *n.* a chance happening or event.

hap/py (hap/ē) *adj.,* **-pier, -piest. 1.** pleased or delighted. **2.** pleasing. **3.** bringing good luck; fortunate.

ha/ra•ki/ri (här/ə kēr/ē) *n.* Japanese ritual suicide by cutting the abdomen.

ha•rangue/ (hə rang/) *n., v.,* **-rangued, -ranguing.** —*n.* **1.** a long, passionate speech. —*v.t.* **2.** to address in a harangue.

ha•rass/ (hə ras/, har/əs) *v.t.* **1.** to disturb persistently. **2.** to attack repeatedly. —**har•ass/ment,** *n.*
——**Pronunciation.** HARASS has traditionally been pronounced (har/əs). A newer pronunciation, (hə ras/), which has developed in North American but not British English, is sometimes criticized. However, it is now the more common pronunciation among younger educated U.S. speakers.

har/bin•ger (här/bin jər) *n.* one that heralds the approach of something.

har/bor (här/bər) *n.* **1.** a sheltered part of a body of water where ships can anchor. **2.** a place of shelter. —*v.t.* **3.** to give shelter to.

hard (härd) *adj.* **1.** firm to the touch; not soft. **2.** difficult. **3.** harsh; severe. **4.** (of water) containing mineral salts that interfere with the action of soap. **5.** (of drugs) addictive. **6.** (of drinks) containing much alcohol. —*Idiom.* **7. hard up,** *Informal.* needing money. —*adv.* **8.** with great energy. —**hard/en,** *v.t., v.i.* —**hard/ness,** *n.*

hard/-bit/ten *adj.* tough; stubborn.

hard/-boiled/ *adj.* **1.** (of an egg) boiled long enough for the yolk and white to solidify. **2.** not sentimental; tough.

hard/ ci/der *n.* fermented cider.

hard/ cop/y *n.* computer output printed on paper.

hard/-core/ *adj.* **1.** uncompromising. **2.** (of pornography) explicit. **3.** persistent or chronic.

hard/ disk/ *n.* a rigid computer disk for storing programs and large amounts of data.

hard/ drive/ *n.* a disk drive containing a hard disk.

hard/hat/ *n.* **1.** a protective helmet worn by construction workers. **2.** a construction worker.

hard/head/ed *adj.* **1.** practical; realistic; shrewd. **2.** obstinate; willful.

hard/heart/ed *adj.* unfeeling.

hard/-line/ or **hard/line/** *adj.* uncompromising, as in politics.

hard/ly *adv.* barely or scarcely.

hard/-nosed/ *adj. Informal.* practical and shrewd.

hard/ship *n.* suffering or need.

hard/tack/ *n.* a hard biscuit.

hard/ware/ *n.* **1.** metalware, as tools, locks, etc. **2.** the electronic devices of a computer system.

hard/wood/ *n.* the hard, compact wood of various trees.

har/dy (här/dē) *adj.,* **-dier, -diest.** sturdy; strong.

hare (hâr) *n.* a mammal related to but larger than the rabbit.

hare/brained/ *adj.* foolish.

hare/lip/ *n. Offensive.* a split upper lip; cleft lip.

har/em (hâr/əm, har/-) *n.* **1.** the women's section of a Muslim house. **2.** the women in a Muslim household.

hark (härk) *v.i.* **1.** to listen. **2. hark back,** to recollect a previous event or topic.

har/le•quin (här/lə kwin, -kin) *n.* a character in comic theater, usu. masked and dressed in multicolored, diamond-patterned tights.

har/lot (här/lət) *n.* a prostitute.

harm (härm) *n.* **1.** injury or damage. —*v.t.* **2.** to cause harm to. —**harm/ful,** *adj.* —**harm/less,** *adj.*

har•mon/i•ca (här mon/i kə) *n.* a wind instrument played by exhaling and inhaling through metal reeds.

har/mo•ny (här/mə nē) *n., pl.* **-nies. 1.** agreement. **2.** a pleasing arrangement of parts. **3.** the combination of tones blended into pleasing chords. —**har/mo•nize,** *v.t., v.i.* —**har•mon/i•ous** (-mō/nē əs) *adj.*

har/ness (här/nis) *n.* **1.** the straps and bands by which a horse is controlled. —*v.t.* **2.** to put a harness on. **3.** to control and make use of.

harp (härp) *n.* **1.** a musical instrument with strings stretched on a triangular frame. —*v.i.* **2.** to play the harp. **3. harp on,** to repeat tediously. —**harp/ist,** *n.*

har•poon/ (här pōōn/) *n.* **1.** a spearlike missile attached to a rope, used in hunting whales. —*v.t.* **2.** to strike with a harpoon.

harp/si•chord/ (härp/si kôrd/) *n.* a keyboard instrument in which the strings are plucked by quill points connected with the keys. —**harp/si•chord/ist,** *n.*

har/ri•dan (har/i dn) *n.* a scolding, vicious woman.

har/ri•er (har/ē ər) *n.* a kind of hunting dog.

har/row (har/ō) *n.* **1.** an implement for leveling or breaking up plowed land. —*v.t.* **2.** to draw a harrow over. **3.** to disturb painfully.

har/row•ing *adj.* very distressing.

har/ry (har/ē) *v.t.,* **-ried, -rying.** to harass.

harsh (härsh) *adj.* **1.** rough or unpleasant to the senses. **2.** severe; cruel.

har/vest (här/vist) *n.* **1.** the gathering of crops. **2.** the season when crops are gathered. **3.** a yield of one season. **4.** the result of something. —*v.t., v.i.* **5.** to gather or reap. —**har/vest•er,** *n.*

has (haz; *unstressed* həz, əz) *v.* third pers. sing. pres. indic. of **have.**

has/-been/ *n.* a person or thing that is no longer effective, successful, etc.

hash[1] (hash) *n.* **1.** chopped meat and potatoes browned together. **2.** a mess. —*v.t.* **3.** to chop. **4.** to discuss thoroughly.

hash[2] (hash) *n. Slang.* hashish.

hash/ish (hash/ēsh, hä shēsh/) *n.* a narcotic made from Indian hemp.

hasn't (haz/ənt) contraction of **has not.**

hasp (hasp) *n.* a clasp for a door or lid.

has/sle (has/əl) *n., v.,* **-sled, -sling.** *Informal.* —*n.* **1.** a disorderly dispute. **2.** a troublesome situation. —*v.i.* **3.** to quarrel. —*v.t.* **5.** to bother or harass.

has/sock (has/ək) *n.* a cushion used as a footstool.

haste (hāst) *n.* **1.** hurry. **2.** quick or rash action. —**hast/y,** *adj.* —**hast/i•ness,** *n.*

has/ten (hā/sən) *v.i., v.t.* to hurry.

hat (hat) *n.* a shaped covering for the head.

hatch[1] (hach) *v.t.* **1.** to bring forth (young) from the egg. **2.** to plot. —*v.i.* **3.** to emerge from an egg. —**hatch/er•y,** *n.*

hatch[2] (hach) *n.* **1.** an opening in the floor, a ship's deck, etc. **2.** the cover for such an opening.

hatch/et (hach/it) *n.* a small ax.

hatch/et job/ *n.* a maliciously destructive critique.

hatch/way/ *n.* an opening in a ship's deck.

hate (hāt) *v.,* **hated, hating.** —*v.t.* **1.** to dislike intensely. —*v.i.* **2.**

to feel hatred. —*n.* **3.** intense dislike. **4.** the object of hatred.

hate/ful *adj.* arousing or deserving hate. —**hate/ful•ly,** *adv.*

haugh/ty (hô/tē) *adj.,* **-tier, -tiest.** disdainfully proud; arrogant.

haul (hôl) *v.t., v.i.* **1.** to pull with force. **2.** to transport. —*n.* **3.** an act of hauling. **4.** the load hauled. **5.** the distance over which something is hauled.

haunch (hônch, hänch) *n.* **1.** the hip. **2.** the leg and loin of an animal.

haunt (hônt, hänt) *v.t.* **1.** to visit or appear to frequently as a ghost. **2.** to recur persistently in the mind of. **3.** to visit often. —*n.* **4.** a place frequently visited. —**haunt/ed,** *adj.*

haunt/ing *adj.* lingering in the mind.

haute/ cou•ture/ (ōt/ kōō tōōr/) high fashion.

haute/ cui•sine/ (ōt/ kwi zēn/) gourmet cooking.

have (hav; *unstressed* həv, əv;) *v.,* **had, having.** —*v.t.* **1.** to possess; hold. **2.** to get. **3.** to experience. **4.** to give birth to. **5.** to cause to or cause to be. **6.** to engage in. **7.** to permit. **8.** to outwit. —*auxiliary verb.* **9.** (used with a past participle to form perfect tenses). **10.** (used with an infinitive to express obligation). —*Idiom.* **11. have it in for,** to wish harm to. **12. have it out,** to reach an understanding through discussion or fighting.
——**Usage.** See OF.

ha/ven (hā/vən) *n.* **1.** a harbor. **2.** a place of shelter.

have/-not/ *n.* Usu., **have-nots.** a poor individual or group.

haven't (hav/ənt) contraction of **have not.**

hav/er•sack/ (hav/ər sak/) *n.* a single-strapped shoulder bag for carrying supplies.

hav/oc (hav/ək) *n.* great destruction.

Haw. Hawaii.

hawk[1] (hôk) *n.* **1.** a bird of prey. **2.** a person who advocates war.

hawk[2] (hôk) *v.t.* to offer for sale by calling aloud in public. —**hawk/er,** *n.*

haw/ser (hô/zər, -sər) *n.* a heavy rope.

haw/thorn/ (hô/thôrn/) *n.* a small tree with thorns and red berries.

hay (hā) *n.* grass cut and dried for fodder.

hay/ fe/ver *n.* inflammation of the eyes and respiratory tract, caused by pollen.

hay/stack/ *n.* a stack of hay built up in the open air.

hay/wire/ *adj.* out of order.

haz/ard (haz/ərd) *n.* **1.** something causing danger. —*v.t.* **2.** to venture or risk. —**haz/ard•ous,** *adj.*

haze[1] (hāz) *n.* **1.** a fine mist. **2.** vagueness. —**ha/zy,** *adj.*

haze[2] (hāz) *v.t.,* **hazed, hazing.** to subject to humiliating tricks.

ha/zel (hā/zəl) *n.* **1.** a tree or shrub bearing small edible nuts. **2.** a light golden- or greenish-brown.

ha/zel•nut/ *n.* the nut of the hazel; filbert.

H/-bomb/ *n.* the hydrogen bomb.

HDTV high-definition television.

he (hē; *unstressed* ē) *pron.* **1.** the male last mentioned. —*n.* **2.** a male.

head (hed) *n.* **1.** the upper part of the body, containing the skull with mouth, eyes, ears, nose, and brain. **2.** the mind. **3.** the top part of anything. **4.** a leader or chief. **5.** froth at the top of a liquid. **6.** the source of a river. —*adj.* **7.** leading or main. **8.** situated at the top or front. —*v.t.* **9.** to lead. **10.** to be the chief of. —*v.i.* **11.** to move in a certain direction. **12. head off,** to intercept. —*Idiom.* **13. come to a head,** to reach a crisis. **14. keep (or lose) one's head,** to keep (or lose) one's self-control. **15. over one's head,** beyond one's ability to understand.

head/ache/ *n.* **1.** a pain in the upper part of the head. **2.** an annoying person, situation, etc.

head/band/ *n.* a band worn around the head.

head/dress *n.* a covering or decoration for the head.

head/first/ *adv.* **1.** with the head in front. **2.** rashly.

head/ing *n.* **1.** something that serves as a head, top, or front. **2.** a title of a page, chapter, etc.

head/land (-lənd) *n.* a promontory extending into a body of water.

head/light/ *n.* a light with a reflector on the front of a vehicle.

head/line/ *n.* a heading in a newspaper.

head/long/ *adv.* **1.** headfirst. **2.** rashly. —*adj.* **3.** rash. **4.** done with the head foremost.

head/-on/ *adj., adv.* with the head or front foremost.

head/phone/ *n.* Usu., **head/phones.** a device worn over the ears for listening to a radio, audiotape, etc.

head/quar/ters *n.* a center of command or operations.

head/stone/ *n.* a stone marker at the head of a grave.

head/strong/ *adj.* willful.

head/way/ *n.* progress.

head/y *adj.,* **-ier, -iest. 1.** giddy; dizzy. **2.** intoxicating; exciting.

heal (hēl) *v.t.* **1.** to restore to health. —*v.i.* **2.** to get well. —**heal/er,** *n.*

health (helth) *n.* **1.** the general condition of the body or mind. **2.** soundness of body or mind. —**health/ful,** *adj.* —**health/y,** *adj.*

heap (hēp) *n.* **1.** a group of things lying one on another; pile. —*v.t., v.i.* **2.** to pile or become piled.

hear (hēr) *v.,* **heard** (hûrd) **hearing.** —*v.t.* **1.** to perceive by the ear. **2.** to listen to. **3.** to receive a report of. —*v.i.* **4.** to be able to perceive sound. **5.** to receive information.

heark/en (här/kən) *v.i.* to listen.

hear/say/ *n.* rumor.

hearse (hûrs) *n.* a vehicle used to carry a coffin.

heart (härt) *n.* **1.** the organ keeping the blood in circulation. **2.** the seat of life or emotion. **3.** compassion. **4.** the vital part. **5. hearts,** a suit of playing cards with heart-shaped figures. —*Idiom.* **6. at heart,** basically. **7. by heart,** from memory.

heart/ache/ *n.* grief.

heart/ attack/ *n.* any sudden insufficiency of oxygen supply to the heart that results in heart muscle damage.

heart/break/ *n.* great sorrow or anguish. —**heart/bro/ken,** *adj.*

heart/burn/ *n.* a burning sensation in the stomach and esophagus.

heart/en *v.t.* to encourage.

heart/felt/ *adj.* deeply felt.

hearth (härth) *n.* **1.** the floor of a fireplace. **2.** the fireside.

heart/land/ *n.* any central or vital area, as of a state or country.

heart/less *adj.* lacking compassion.

heart/-rend/ing *adj.* causing or expressing intense grief.

heart/sick/ *adj.* extremely sad.

heart/strings/ *n.pl.* the strongest feelings.

heart/-to-heart/ *adj.* sincere and intimate.

heart/y *adj.,* **-ier, -iest. 1.** warmhearted. **2.** genuine. **3.** vigorous. **4.** substantial. —**heart/i•ly,** *adv.*

heat (hēt) *n.* **1.** the condition or quality of being hot. **2.** the sensation of hotness. **3.** energy that causes a rise in temperature, expansion, etc. **4.** intensity of feeling. —*v.t., v.i.* **5.** to make or become excited. **6.** to make or become hot.

heat/ed *adj.* excited or angry. —**heat/ed•ly,** *adv.*

heath (hēth) *n.* **1.** an area of open, uncultivated land. **2.** any shrub common on such land.

hea/then (hē/thən) *n.* **1.** one who does not believe in an established religion; pagan. —*adj.* **2.** pagan.

heat/ light/ning *n.* lightning too distant for thunder to be heard.

heat/stroke/ *n.* headache, fever, etc., caused by too much heat.

heave (hēv) *v.,* **heaved, heaving,** *n.* —*v.t.* **1.** to lift with effort. **2.** to lift and throw with effort. —*v.i.* **3.** to rise and fall rhythmically. **4.** to retch. —*n.* **5.** an act of heaving.

heav/en (hev/ən) *n.* **1.** the abode of God, the angels, and the spirits of the righteous dead. **2.** Usu., **heavens.** the sky. **3.** a place or state of bliss.

heav/y (hev/ē) *adj.,* **-ier, -iest. 1.** of great weight, amount, size, force, or intensity. **2.** serious. **3.** intense. **4.** clumsy. —**heav/i•ly,** *adv.*

heav/y-du/ty *adj.* made for hard use.

heav/y-hand/ed *adj.* tactless.

heav/y-heart/ed *adj.* preoccupied with sorrow or worry.

heav/y-set/ *adj.* large in body.

He•bra/ic (hi brā/ik) *adj.* of the Hebrews or their culture.

He/brew (hē/brōō) *n.* **1.** a member of a group of Semitic peoples of ancient Palestine. **2.** their language, now the national language of Israel. —*adj.* **3.** of the Hebrews or their language.

heck′le (hek′əl) *v.t.*, **-led, -ling.** to harass (a speaker) with comments or questions.

hec′tare (hek′târ) *n.* a unit of area equal to 10,000 square meters (2.47 acres).

hec′tic *adj.* marked by confusion, excitement, or hurried activity.

hec′tor (-tər) *v.t.* **1.** to harass by bullying. —*v.i.* **2.** to be a bully.

hedge (hej) *n.*, *v.*, **hedged, hedging.** —*n.* **1.** a dense row of bushes or small trees forming a boundary. **2.** an act or means of hedging. —*v.t.* **3.** to surround with a hedge. **4.** to offset a possible loss by counterbalancing—(one's bets, investments, etc.). —*v.i.* **5.** to avoid a direct answer or commitment.

hedge′hog′ *n.* a small spiny mammal.

he′don·ist (hēd′n ist) *n.* a person who lives for pleasure. —**he′don·ism,** *n.*

heed (hēd) *v.t., v.i.* **1.** to give careful attention (to). —*n.* **2.** careful attention. —**heed′ful,** *adj.* —**heed′less,** *adj.*

heel¹ (hēl) *n.* **1.** the back part of the foot below the ankle. **2.** the part of a shoe, sock, etc., covering this. —*v.t.* **3.** to furnish (shoes) with heels. —*v.i.* **4.** (of a dog) to follow at one's heels on command. —*Idiom.* **5.** **down at heel,** dressed shabbily. **6. kick up one's heels,** to have a lively time. **7. on the heels of,** closely following.

heel² (hēl) *v.i., v.t.* to lean or cause to lean to one side.

heel³ (hēl) *n.* a dishonorable person.

heft (heft) *n.* **1.** heaviness. **2.** importance. —*v.t.* **3.** to test for weight by lifting.

hef′ty *adj.*, **-tier, -tiest. 1.** heavy. **2.** large.

he·gem′o·ny (hi jem′ə nē, hej′ə mō′-) *n., pl.* **-nies.** domination.

heif′er (hef′ər) *n.* a young cow that has not calved.

height (hīt) *n.* **1.** extent upward. **2.** the distance between the highest and lowest points. **3.** the highest point. —**height′en,** *v.t., v.i.*

Heim′lich maneu′ver (hīm′lik) *n.* a procedure to aid a choking person by applying sudden pressure to the upper abdomen.

hei′nous (hā′nəs) *adj.* evil.

heir (âr) *n.* a person who inherits or who has a right to inherit the property, title, etc., of another.

heir′ess *n.* a female heir.

heir′loom′ *n.* a family possession handed down from one generation to another.

heist (hīst) *Slang.* —*n.* **1.** a robbery. —*v.t.* **2.** to rob.

held (held) *v.* pt. and pp. of **hold.**

hel′i·cop′ter (hel′i kop′tər, hē′li-) *n.* an aircraft lifted by blades that rotate on a horizontal axis.

he′li·o·cen′tric (hē′lē ō sen′trik) *adj.* having the sun as a center.

he′li·um (hē′lē əm) *n.* a light, colorless gas.

he′lix (hē′liks) *n., pl.* **hel′i·ces** (hel′ə sēz′), **helixes.** a spiral.

hell (hel) *n.* **1.** the place of punishment of the wicked after death. **2.** any place or state of misery. —**hell′ish,** *adj.*

hell′bent′ (hel′ə bôr′) *adj.* recklessly determined.

hel′le·bore′ (hel′ə bôr′) *n.* a poisonous plant of the buttercup or lily family.

Hel·len′ic (he len′ik, -lē′nik) *adj.* Greek.

hel·lo′ (he lō′, hə-, hel′ō) *interj.* an exclamation of greeting.

helm (helm) *n.* **1.** a device by which a ship is steered. **2.** the place of control.

hel′met (hel′mit) *n.* a protective, rigid head covering.

hel′ot (hel′ət, hē′lət) *n.* a slave.

help (help) *v.t.* **1.** to provide what is necessary to accomplish something. **2.** to make easier. **3.** to be useful to. **4.** to serve (a customer). —*v.i.* **5.** to give aid. —*n.* **6.** aid; relief. **7.** a helping person or thing. —**help′er,** *n.* —**help′ful,** *adj.*

help′ing *n.* a portion of food served.

help′less *adj.* **1.** unable to help oneself. **2.** powerless.

help′mate′ *n.* a companion and helper.

hel′ter-skel′ter (hel′tər skel′tər) *adv.* in disorderly haste.

hem (hem) *v.*, **hemmed, hemming,** *n.* —*v.t.* **1.** to fold back and sew down the edge of (cloth, a gar-

ment, etc.). **2. hem in,** to confine and restrict. —*n.* **3.** an edge made by hemming.

he′ma·tol′o·gy (-tol′ə jē) *n.* the study of the blood. —**he′ma·to·log′ic** (-tl oj′ik), **he′ma·to·log′i·cal,** *adj.* —**he′ma·tol′o·gist,** *n.*

hem′i·sphere′ (hem′i sfēr′) *n.* **1.** one of the halves of the earth. **2.** a half of a sphere.

hem′lock (hem′lok′) *n.* **1.** a cone-bearing tree of the pine family. **2.** a poisonous plant of the parsley family.

he′mo·glo′bin (hē′mə glō′bin, hem′ə-) *n.* an oxygen-carrying compound in red blood cells.

he′mo·phil′i·a (hē′mə fil′ē ə) *n.* a genetic disorder marked by excessive bleeding. —**he′mo·phil′i·ac′,** *n.*

hem′or·rhage (hem′ər ij) *n., v.*, **-rhaged, -rhaging.** —*n.* **1.** a discharge of blood. —*v.i.* **2.** to bleed profusely.

hem′or·rhoid′ (hem′ə roid′) *n.* Usu., **hemorrhoids.** a painful dilation of blood vessels in the anus.

hemp (hemp) *n.* **1.** a plant with tough fibers used for making rope. **2.** an intoxicating drug made from the hemp plant.

hen (hen) *n.* a female bird.

hence (hens) *adv.* **1.** therefore. **2.** from this time. **3.** from this place.

hence′forth′ (hens′fôrth′, hens′fôrth′) *adv.* from now on.

hench′man (hench′mən) *n., pl.* **-men.** a trusted supporter.

hen′na (hen′ə) *n.* a reddish dye.

hep′a·rin (hep′ə rin) *n.* an anticoagulant found esp. in the liver.

hep′a·ti′tis (hep′ə tī′tis) *n.* inflammation of the liver.

hep·tath′lon (hep tath′lən, -lon) *n.* an athletic contest comprising seven track-and-field events.

her (hûr; *unstressed* hər, ər) *pron.* **1.** the objective case of **she.** —*adj.* **2.** a form of the possessive case of **she.**

her′ald (her′əld) *n.* **1.** a messenger or forerunner. **2.** one that proclaims. —*v.t.* **3.** to proclaim. **4.** to usher in.

her′ald·ry *n.* the art of devising and describing coats of arms, tracing genealogies, etc. —**he·ral′dic** (he ral′dik, hə-) *adj.*

herb (ûrb; *esp. Brit.* hûrb) *n.* **1.** a flowering plant with a nonwoody stem. **2.** such a plant used in medicine or cooking. —**herb′al,** *adj.*

her·ba′ceous (hûr bā′shəs, ûr-) **1.** herblike. **2.** (of plants) not woody.

herb′age (ûr′bij, hûr′-) *n.* nonwoody plants.

herb′i·cide′ (hûr′bə sīd′, ûr′-) *n.* a substance for killing plants, esp. weeds. —**her′bi·cid′al,** *adj.*

her·biv′o·rous (hûr biv′ər əs, ûr-) *adj.* feeding on plants. —**her′bi·vore′** (hûr′bə vôr′, ûr′-) *n.*

herd (hûrd) *n.* **1.** a number of animals feeding or moving together. —*v.i., v.t.* **2.** to move or gather as a herd.

here (hēr) *adv.* **1.** in, at, or to this place. **2.** in the present. —*n.* **3.** this place or point.

here′a·bout′ or **here′a·bouts′** *adv.* in this neighborhood.

here·aft′er *adv.* **1.** from now on. **2.** a life after death. **3.** the future.

here·by′ *adv.* by means of this.

he·red′i·tar′y (hə red′i ter′ē) *adj.* **1.** passing from parents to offspring; inherited. **2.** holding rights, a title, etc., by inheritance.

he·red′i·ty *n.* the passing on of traits from parents to offspring.

here·in′ *adv.* in this place.

her′e·sy (her′ə sē) *n., pl.* **-sies. 1.** a religious opinion contrary to accepted doctrine. **2.** any belief contrary to established beliefs or customs. —**her′e·tic** (her′i tik) *n.*

here′to·fore′ *adv.* before now.

here′with′ *adv.* along with or by means of this.

her′it·a·ble (her′i tə bəl) *adj.* capable of being inherited.

her′it·age (her′i tij) *n.* **1.** something passed on by inheritance. **2.** traditions and history.

her·maph′ro·dite′ (hûr maf′rə dīt′) *n.* an animal or plant with reproductive organs of both sexes.

her·met′ic (hûr met′ik) *adj.* airtight. Also, **her·met′i·cal.**

her′mit (hûr′mit) *n.* a person living apart from others.

her′mit·age (-mi tij) *n.* a hermit's dwelling.

her′ni·a (hûr′nē ə) *n.* the protru-

sion of an organ or tissue through the surrounding wall.

he·ro (hēr′ō) *n., pl.* **-roes. 1.** a man admired for brave deeds, noble qualities, etc. **2.** the main male character in a story, play, etc. —**her′o·ism** (her′ō iz′əm) *n.*

he·ro′ic (hi rō′ik) *adj.* **1.** brave, daring, or noble. **2.** dealing with the deeds of heroes.

her′o·in (her′ō in) *n.* a narcotic and addictive drug derived from morphine.

her′o·ine (her′ō in) *n.* **1.** a woman admired for brave deeds, noble qualities, etc. **2.** the main female character in a story, play, etc.

her′on (her′ən) *n.* a long-legged wading bird.

her′pes (hûr′pēz) *n.* a viral disease characterized by blisters on the skin or mucous membranes.

her′ring (her′ing) *n.* a food fish of the N Atlantic.

her′ring·bone′ *n.* **1.** a pattern of slanting lines in adjoining vertical rows. **2.** a fabric with this pattern.

hers (hûrz) *pron.* a possessive form of **she,** used as a predicate adjective. **2.** that or those belonging to her.

her·self′ *pron.* a reflexive or intensive form of **her.**

hertz (hûrts) *n., pl.* **hertz.** a unit of frequency equal to one cycle per second.

hes′i·tate′ (hez′i tāt′) *v.i.*, **-tated, -tating. 1.** to wait to act or speak because of fear, doubt, or reluctance. **2.** to pause. —**hes′i·tant** (-tənt) *adj.* —**hes′i·ta′tion, hes′i·tan·cy,** *n.*

het′er·o·dox′ (het′ər ə doks′) *adj.* not in accordance with established doctrine.

het′er·o·ge′ne·ous (-jē′nē əs) *adj.* composed of people or things of different kinds.

het′er·o·sex′u·al *adj.* **1.** sexually attracted to the opposite sex. —*n.* **2.** a heterosexual person. —**het′er·o·sex′u·al′i·ty,** *n.*

heu·ris′tic (hyŏ ris′tik; *often* yŏŏ-) *adj.* encouraging a person to learn or understand by experimentation or trial-and-error methods.

hew (hyŏŏ; *often* yŏŏ) *v.*, **hewed, hewed** or **hewn, hewing.** —*v.t.* **1.** to chop or cut with an ax, sword, etc. **2.** to make by cutting.

hex (heks) *v.t.* **1.** to cast a spell on. **2.** to bring bad luck to. —*n.* **3.** a spell or charm.

hex′a·gon′ (hek′sə gon′, -gən) *n.* a six-sided polygon. —**hex·ag′o·nal** (hek sag′ə nl) *adj.*

hex·am′e·ter (hek sam′i tər) *n.* a verse of six feet.

hey′day′ (hā′dā′) *n.* the time of greatest success, popularity, etc.

hgt. height.

hgwy. highway.

HI Hawaii.

hi·a′tus (hī ā′təs) *n., pl.* **-tuses, -tus.** a break or interruption.

hi·ba′chi (hi bä′chē) *n.* a small brazier covered with a grill.

hi′ber·nate′ (hī′bər nāt′) *v.i.*, **-nated, -nating.** to spend the winter in a dormant state. —**hi′ber·na′tion,** *n.*

hi·bis′cus (hī bis′kəs, hi-) *n.* a plant with large, showy flowers.

hic′cup (hik′up, -əp) *n.* a sudden involuntary drawing in of breath with a "hic" sound. —*v.i.* **2.** to make the sound of a hiccup. Also, **hic′cough.**

hick (hik) *n.* a provincial, unsophisticated person.

hick′o·ry (hik′ə rē) *n., pl.* **-ries.** a N American tree of the walnut family, bearing an edible nut.

hide¹ (hīd) *v.*, **hid** (hid) **hidden** or **hid, hiding,** *n.* —*v.t.* **1.** to conceal from sight. **2.** to keep secret. —*v.i.* **3.** to conceal oneself.

hide² (hīd) *n.* an animal's skin.

hide′a·way *n.* a private retreat.

hide′bound′ *adj.* narrow and rigid in opinion.

hid′e·ous (hid′ē əs) *adj.* very ugly.

hide′out′ *n.* a safe place to hide, esp. from the law.

hi′er·ar′chy (hī′ə rär′kē) *n., pl.* **-chies.** any system in which one person or thing is ranked one above another.

hi′er·o·glyph′ic (hī′ər ə glif′ik, hī′rə-) *n.* **1.** of picture writing, as among the ancient Egyptians. —*n.* **2.** a hieroglyphic symbol.

hi·fi′ (hī′fī′) *n.* high fidelity.

high (hī) *adj.*, **-er, -est. 1.** lofty; tall. **2.** having a certain height. **3.** far above the ground. **4.** greater than normal. **5.** above others in rank. **6.**

elevated in pitch. **7.** *Informal.* under the influence of alcohol or drugs. —*adv.* **8.** at or to a high place, rank, etc. —*n.* **9.** a high point or level. **10.** an atmospheric system of high pressure. **11.** a state of euphoria.

high′brow′ *n.* **1.** a cultured or intellectual person. —*adj.* **2.** typical of a highbrow.

high′ fidel′ity *n.* sound reproduction with little distortion of the original.

high′-flown′ *adj.* pretentious.

high′ fre′quency *n.* the range of radio frequencies between 3 and 30 megahertz.

high′-hand′ed *adj.* arrogant.

high′lands (-ləndz) *n.* a hilly area.

high′light′ *v.t.* **1.** to emphasize. **2.** to create highlights in. —*n.* **3.** an important event, scene, etc. **4.** an area of contrasting brightness.

high′ly *adv.* very; extremely.

high′-mind′ed *adj.* having or showing noble principles.

high′ness (-nis) *n.* **1.** the quality or state of being high. **2. Highness,** a title given to royalty.

high′-pres′sure *adj., v.*, **-sured, -suring.** —*adj.* **1.** having a pressure above the normal. **2.** stressful. **3.** aggressive. —*v.t.* **4.** to persuade aggressively.

high′rise′ *adj.* **1.** (of a building) having many stories. —*n.* **2.** a tall building.

high′road′ *n.* **1.** an honorable course. **2.** an easy course. **3.** *Chiefly Brit.* a highway.

high′ school′ *n.* a school consisting of grades 9 through 12.

high′ seas′ *n.* the open ocean.

high′-spir′it·ed *adj.* lively.

high′-strung′ *adj.* highly sensitive or nervous.

high′-tech′ *n.* **1.** technology using highly sophisticated and advanced equipment and techniques. —*adj.* **2.** using or suggesting high-tech.

high′-ten′sion *adj.* of relatively high voltage.

high′way′ *n.* a main road.

high′way′man *n., pl.* **-men.** a highway robber.

hi′jack′ (hī′jak′) *v.t.* to seize (a plane, truck, etc.) by force.

hike (hīk) *v.*, **hiked, hiking,** *n.* —*v.i.* **1.** to walk a long distance, esp. through rural areas. —*n.* **2.** a long walk. —**hik′er,** *n.*

hi·lar′i·ous (hi lâr′ē əs, -lar′-) *adj.* **1.** very funny. **2.** noisily merry. —**hi·lar′i·ty,** *n.*

hill (hil) *n.* **1.** a raised part of the earth's surface, smaller than a mountain. **2.** a heap or mound. —**hill′y,** *adj.*

hill′ock (-ək) *n.* a small hill.

hilt (hilt) *n.* the handle of a sword or tool.

him (him) *pron.* the objective case of **he.**

him·self′ (him self′; *medially often* im-) *pron.* the reflexive or emphatic form of **him.**

hind¹ (hīnd) *adj.* situated in the rear.

hind² (hīnd) *n.* the female red deer.

hin′der (hin′dər) *v.t.* to cause delay or difficulty in. —**hin′drance,** *n.*

hind′most′ (hīnd′-) *adj.* nearest the rear.

hind′sight′ *n.* keen understanding of an event after it has occurred.

Hin′du·ism (hin′dŏŏ iz′əm) *n.* the major religion of India. —**Hin′du,** *n., adj.*

hinge (hinj) *n., v.*, **hinged, hinging.** —*n.* **1.** a jointed device on which a door, lid, etc., moves. —*v.t., v.i.* **2.** to attach or be attached by a hinge. **3. hinge on,** to depend on.

hint (hint) *n.* **1.** an indirect suggestion. —*v.t., v.i.* **2.** to give a hint.

hin′ter·land′ (hin′tər land′) *n.* an area remote from cities.

hip¹ (hip) *n.* the projecting part on each side of the body below the waist.

hip² (hip) *adj.*, **-per, -pest.** *Slang.* familiar with the latest styles or ideas.

hip′-hop′ *n. Slang.* the popular culture of usu. black urban youth as characterized by rap music.

hip′pie (hip′ē) *n.* a young person of the 1960s who rejected conventional social values.

hip′po (hip′ō) *n., pl.* **-pos.** a hippopotamus.

hip′po·drome′ (hip′ə drōm′) *n.* an arena for equestrian events.

hip′po·pot′a·mus (hip′ə pot′ə məs) *n., pl.* **-muses, -mi** (-mī′). a large African river mammal with short legs and a thick skin.

hire (hī³r) *v.*, **hired, hiring,** *n.* —*v.t.* **1.** to engage the services of (a person) or the use of (a thing) for a set price. —*n.* **2.** the act of hiring or the condition of being hired.

hire′ling (-ling) *n.* a person who works only for pay.

hir′sute (hûr′sŏŏt, hûr sŏŏt′) *adj.* hairy. —**hir′sute·ness,** *n.*

his (hiz; *unstressed* iz) *pron.* **1.** the possessive form of **he.** **2.** that or those belonging to him.

His·pan′ic (hi span′ik) *n.* **1.** a person of Spanish or Latin-American descent. —*adj.* **2.** of Spain or Hispanics.

hiss (his) *v.i.* **1.** to make a prolonged s sound. **2.** to express disapproval in this way. —*n.* **3.** a hissing sound.

his·tor′ic (hi stôr′ik) *adj.* well-known in history.

his′to·ry (his′tə rē, -trē) *n., pl.* **-ries. 1.** the knowledge, study, or record of past events. **2.** a pattern of events determining the future. —**his·to′ri·an** (hi stôr′ē ən) *n.*

his′tri·on′ics (his′trē on′iks) *n.pl.* overly dramatic behavior or speech. —**his′tri·on′ic,** *adj.*

hit (hit) *v.*, **hit, hitting,** *n.* —*v.t.* **1.** to deal a blow to. **2.** to collide with. **3.** to reach with a missile, weapon, etc. **4.** to have a marked effect on. **5.** to come upon. —*v.i.* **6.** to strike. **7.** to come into collision. **8.** to come to light. —*n.* **9.** a collision. **10.** a blow. **11.** a success.

hitch (hich) *v.t.* **1.** to fasten by a hook, rope, etc. **2.** to raise jerkily. —*v.i.* **3.** to become fastened. **4.** to move jerkily. —*n.* **5.** a fastening or knot. **6.** an obstruction or problem. **7.** a jerk or pull.

hitch′hike′ *v.i., v.t.*, **-hiked, -hiking.** to travel by begging a ride from a stranger.

hith′er (hith′ər) *adv.* to this place.

hith′er·to′ *adv.* until now.

HIV human immunodeficiency virus, the cause of AIDS.

hive (hīv) *n.* **1.** a shelter for bees. **2.** the bees living in a hive.

hives (hīvz) *n.pl.* an eruption of itchy swellings on the skin.

HMO *pl.* **HMOs, HMO's.** health maintenance organization: a health-care plan that provides services to subscribers.

H.M.S. Her (or His) Majesty's Ship.

hoard (hôrd) *n.* **1.** a supply that is hidden for future use. —*v.t., v.i.* **2.** to accumulate a hoard (of). —**hoard′er,** *n.*

hoar′frost′ (hôr′frôst′) *n.* a cover of tiny ice particles.

hoarse (hôrs) *adj.* having a low and harsh voice.

hoar′y (hôr′ē) *adj.* **1.** white with age. **2.** old.

hoax (hōks) *n.* **1.** something intended to deceive. —*v.t.* **2.** to deceive; trick.

hob′ble (hob′əl) *v.*, **-bled, -bling.** —*v.i.* **1.** to limp. —*v.t.* **2.** to cause to limp. **3.** to fasten together the legs of (a horse, mule, etc.) to prevent free movement. **4.** to impede.

hob′by (hob′ē) *n., pl.* **-bies.** an activity pursued for pleasure rather than money.

hob′by·horse′ *n.* **1.** a stick with a horse's head, ridden by children. **2.** a favorite idea or project.

hob′gob′lin *n.* something causing superstitious fear.

hob′nob′ (-nob′) *v.i.*, **-nobbed, -nobbing.** to associate on friendly terms.

ho′bo (hō′bō) *n., pl.* **-bos, -boes.** a tramp; vagrant.

hock¹ (hok) *n.* the joint in the hind leg of a horse, cow, etc.

hock² (hok) *v.t.* **1.** to pawn. —*n.* **2.** the state of being held as security. **3.** the condition of owing.

hock′ey (hok′ē) *n.* a game played on a field or on ice with bent clubs (**hockey sticks**) and a ball or disk.

ho′cus-po′cus (hō′kəs pō′kəs) *n.* meaningless words used in magic tricks.

hod (hod) *n.* **1.** a trough for carrying mortar, bricks, etc. **2.** a coal scuttle.

hodge′podge′ (hoj′poj′) *n.* a mixture; jumble.

hoe (hō) *n., v.*, **hoed, hoeing.** —*n.* **1.** a tool for breaking the soil and weeding. —*v.t., v.i.* **2.** to dig or weed with a hoe.

hog (hog) *n., v.*, **hogged, hogging.** —*n.* **1.** a domesticated swine. **2.** a greedy or filthy person. —*v.t.* **3.** to take more than one's share of. —**hog′gish,** *adj.*

hogs′head′ *n.* a large cask.

hog′tie′ *v.t.*, **-tied, -tying. 1.** to tie

(an animal) with all four feet together. **2.** to hamper; thwart.

hog′wash′ n. nonsense; bunk.

hog′-wild′ adj. wildly enthusiastic.

hoi′ pol·loi′ (hoi′ pə loi′) n. the common people; the masses.

hoist (hoist) v.t. **1.** to lift, esp. by machine. —n. **2.** a hoisting apparatus. **3.** the act of lifting.

hok′ey (hō′kē) adj., **-ier, -iest. 1.** overly sentimental. **2.** obviously contrived. —**hok′i·ness,** n.

hold (hōld) v., **held** (held) **holding,** n. —v.t. **1.** to have in the hand. **2.** to support. **3.** to possess or occupy. **4.** to keep in a specified condition. **5.** to contain. **6.** to restrain or detain. **7.** to regard. **8.** to believe. —v.i. **9.** to remain in a specified condition. **10.** to remain valid. **11. hold forth,** to speak at length. **12. ~ out,** **a.** to offer. **b.** to last. **c.** to refuse to yield. **13. ~ up, a.** to delay. **b.** to rob at gunpoint. —n. **14.** a grasp. **15.** a means of exerting influence. **16.** a cargo space below a ship's deck. —**hold′er,** n.

hold′ing n. **1.** a section of leased land, esp. for farming. **2. holdings,** legally owned property.

hold′out′ n. one who refuses to take part, give in, etc.

hold′up′ n. **1.** a delay. **2.** a robbery at gunpoint.

hole (hōl) n., v., **holed, holing.** —n. **1.** an opening or gap. **2.** a hollow place. **3.** the burrow of an animal. **4.** an unpleasant situation.

hol·i·day (hol′i dā′) n. **1.** a day on which business is suspended to commemorate a person or event. **2.** a holy day. —adj. **3.** festive.

ho′li·ness (hō′lē nis) n. the quality or state of being holy.

ho·lis′tic (hō lis′tik) adj. of or using therapies that consider the body and the mind as an integrated whole.

hol·lan·daise (hol′an dāz′) n. a sauce of egg yolks, butter, and seasonings.

hol′low (hol′ō) adj. **1.** empty. **2.** sunken. **3.** dull. **4.** meaningless; insincere. —n. **5.** a hole. **6.** a valley. —v.t., v.i. **7.** to make or become hollow.

hol′ly (hol′ē) n., pl. **-lies.** a shrub with glossy leaves and red berries.

hol′ly·hock′ (-hok′, -hôk′) n. a tall plant with showy, colored flowers.

hol′o·caust′ (hol′ə kôst′, hō′lə-) n. **1.** a great destruction, esp. by fire. **2. the Holocaust,** the slaughter of European Jews by the Nazis.

ho′lo·gram′ (hol′ə gram′, hō′lə-) n. a three-dimensional image made by a laser.

ho·log′ra·phy (hə log′rə fē) n. the technique of making holograms.

hol′ster (hōl′stər) n. a case for a pistol, worn on the body.

ho′ly (hō′lē) adj., **-lier, -liest. 1.** recognized or revered as sacred. **2.** dedicated to God.

Ho′ly Commun′ion n. a Christian sacrament in which the Last Supper of Jesus is commemorated with consecrated bread and wine.

Ho′ly Ghost′ n. the Holy Spirit.

Ho′ly Spir′it n. the third person of the Trinity. Also, **Holy Ghost.**

hom′age (hom′ij, om′-) n. reverence or respect.

home (hōm) n., adj., adv., v., **homed, homing.** —n. **1.** a place of residence. **2.** an institution for people needing special care. **3.** one's native place or country. —adj. **4.** of one's home. —adv. **5.** to or at home. —v.i. **6.** to go home or toward a specified point.

home′land′ n. one's native land.

home′less adj. lacking a home.

home′ly adj., **-lier, -liest. 1.** plain; not beautiful. **2.** simple.

home′made′ adj. made at home or at the place where it is sold.

home′mak′er n. a person who manages a home.

home′ of′fice n. **1.** the main office of a company. **2.** work or office space set up in a person's home and used regularly and exclusively for business.

ho′me·op′a·thy (hō′mē op′ə thē) n. a method of treating disease with small doses of drugs that in a healthy person would cause symptoms like those of the disease. —**ho′me·o·path′ic** (-ə path′ik) adj.

home′ page′ n. the initial page of a Web site.

home′sick′ adj. longing for home.

home′spun′ n. **1.** plain; simple. —n. **2.** cloth made at home.

home′stead (-sted, -stid) n. a dwelling with its land and buildings.

home′stretch′ n. the last part of a racetrack, endeavor, etc.

hom′ey adj., **-ier, -iest.** cozy.

hom′i·cide (hom′ə sīd′, hō′mə-) n. the killing of one person by another. —**hom′i·cid′al,** adj.

hom′i·ly (hom′ə lē) n., pl. **-lies.** a sermon. —**hom′i·let′ic** (-let′ik) adj.

hom′ing pi′geon (hō′ming) n. a pigeon trained to carry messages and return home.

hom′i·ny (hom′ə nē) n. hulled corn from which the bran and germ have been removed.

homo- a prefix meaning same.

ho′mo·ge′ne·ous (hō′mə jē′nē əs) adj. **1.** composed of parts that are all of the same kind. **2.** of the same kind. —**ho′mo·ge·ne′i·ty** (-ji nē′ə tē) n.

ho·mog′e·nize′ (hə moj′ə nīz′, hō-) v.t., **-nized, -nizing. 1.** to make homogeneous. **2.** to treat (milk) so that the fat is evenly distributed.

hom′o·graph′ (hom′ə graf′, hō′mə-) n. a word spelled the same as another but having a different meaning.

hom′o·nym′ (hom′ə nim) n. a word that is like another in sound, but not in meaning.

ho·ri·zon′tal (hôr′ə zon′tl) adj. parallel to level ground.

hom′o·pho′bi·a (hō′mə fō′bē ə) n. a hatred of homosexuals.

Ho′mo sa′pi·ens (hō′mō sā′pē·ənz) n. the species to which human beings belong.

ho′mo·sex′u·al (hō′mə sek′shōō·əl) adj. **1.** sexually attracted to persons of the same sex. —n. **2.** a homosexual person. —**ho′mo·sex′u·al′i·ty** (-al′i tē) n.

Hon. 1. Honorable. **2.** Honorary.

hon′cho (hon′chō) n., pl. **-chos.** Slang. an important person.

hone (hōn) v.t., **honed, honing.** to sharpen to a fine edge.

hon′est (on′ist) adj. **1.** honorable or trustworthy. **2.** gained fairly. **3.** sincere. **4.** truthful. —**hon′est·ly,** adv. —**hon′es·ty,** n.

hon′ey (hun′ē) n. a sweet fluid produced by bees from nectar.

hon′ey·comb′ n. **1.** a wax structure built by bees to store honey. **2.** anything resembling such a structure.

hon′ey·dew′ mel′on n. a melon with a pale greenish rind and light green flesh.

hon′ey·moon′ n. a vacation taken by a newly married couple.

hon′ey·suck′le n. a shrub bearing fragrant tubular flowers.

honk (hongk) n. **1.** the cry of a goose. **2.** any similar sound. —v.i., v.t. **3.** to make or cause to make such a sound.

hon′or (on′ər) n. **1.** honesty in one's beliefs and action. **2.** high respect or public esteem. **3.** a token of this. —v.t. **4.** to hold in high respect. **5.** to show regard for. **6.** to confer an honor on. **7.** to accept as valid.

hon′or·a·ble adj. **1.** showing principles of honor. **2.** worthy of honor.

hon′o·rar′i·um (on′ə rär′ē əm) n., pl. **-iums, -ia** (-ē ə). a payment for professional services for which a price is not set.

hon′or·ar′y (-rer′ē) adj. given for honor only.

hood[1] (hōōd) n. **1.** a flexible covering for the head and neck. **2.** something resembling this. **3.** the part of an automobile body that covers the engine. —**hood′ed,** adj.

hood[2] (hōōd) n. a hoodlum.

hood′lum (hōōd′ləm, hōōd′-) n. a young thug or ruffian.

hood′wink′ (hōōd′wingk′) v.t. to deceive.

hoof (hōōf, hōōf) n., pl. **hoofs, hooves** (hōōvz, hōōvz). the horny covering of an animal's foot. —**hoofed,** adj.

hook (hōōk) n. **1.** a curved piece of metal for catching, pulling, etc. **2.** something having a sharp curve. —v.t. **3.** to seize, fasten, or hold with a hook. —v.i. **4.** to curve or bend like a hook. —Idiom. **5.** off the hook, released from a difficulty.

hook′er n. Slang. a prostitute.

hook′up′ n. a connection of parts or apparatus into a circuit, network, machine, or system.

hoo′li·gan (hōō′li gən) n. a hoodlum.

hoop (hōōp, hōōp) n. a rigid circular band of metal or wood.

hoop′la (hōōp′lä) n. Informal. excitement.

hoo·ray′ (hōō rā′) interj., n. hurrah.

hoot (hōōt) v.i. **1.** to shout in scorn.

2. to utter the cry of an owl. —n. **3.** an owl's cry. **4.** a scornful shout.

hop[1] (hop) v., **hopped, hopping.** —v.i. **1.** to make a short, bouncing leap. **2.** to leap on one foot. **3.** to make a short, quick trip. —v.t. **4.** to jump over. **5.** to board (a vehicle). —n. **6.** a short leap, esp. on one foot. **7.** a short trip, esp. by air. **8.** Informal. a dance.

hop[2] (hop) n. **1.** a twining plant of the hemp family. **2. hops,** its dried ripe cones, used in brewing, medicine, etc.

hope (hōp) n., v., **hoped, hoping.** —n. **1.** the feeling that something desired is possible. **2.** a person or thing giving cause for hope. **3.** something hoped for. —v.t. **4.** to look forward to with desire and confidence. —v.i. **5.** to have hope. —**hope′ful,** adj.

hop′per (hop′ər) n. a bin in which material is stored temporarily.

horde (hôrd) n. a crowd.

hore′hound′ (hōr′hound′) n. an herb containing a bitter juice.

ho·ri·zon′ (hə rī′zən) n. the apparent line between earth and sky.

hor′i·zon′tal (hôr′ə zon′tl) adj. parallel to level ground.

hor′mone (hôr′mōn) n. a secretion of an endocrine gland that affects the functions of specific organs, tissues, etc.

horn (hôrn) n. **1.** a hard pointed growth on the heads of cattle, goats, etc. **2.** a hornlike part. **3.** a brass wind instrument. **4.** a device that sounds a warning.

hor′net (hôr′nit) n. a large wasp.

horn′pipe′ n. a lively jiglike dance.

hor′o·scope′ (hôr′ə skōp′) n. a chart of the heavens used in astrology to predict events in a person's life.

hor·ren′dous (hə ren′dəs) adj. dreadful; horrible.

hor′ri·ble (hôr′ə bəl) adj. **1.** causing horror. **2.** very unpleasant.

hor′rid (-id) adj. extremely unpleasant.

hor′ror (hôr′ər) n. **1.** intense fear and loathing. **2.** anything causing such a feeling. **3.** a strong aversion. —**hor′ri·fy′,** v.t.

hors-d'oeuvre′ (ôr dûrv′) n., pl. **hors-d'oeuvres** (ôr dûrv′, -dûrvz′). a small portion of food served before a meal.

horse (hôrs) n. **1.** a large four-footed animal domesticated for pulling loads and riding. **2.** a frame with legs on which something is mounted.

horse′back′ n. **1.** the back of a horse. —adv. **2.** on horseback.

horse′man or **horse′wo′man** n., pl. **-men** or **-women.** a person skilled in riding a horse.

horse′play′ n. rough play.

horse′pow′er n. a unit of power equal to 550 foot-pounds per second.

horse′rad′ish n. a cultivated plant with a pungent root.

horse′ sense′ n. common sense.

horse′shoe′ n. **1.** a U-shaped iron plate nailed to a horse's hoof. **2. something U-shaped. 3. horseshoes,** a game in which horseshoes are tossed.

hors′y adj., **-ier, -iest. 1.** of or like a horse. **2.** dealing with or fond of horses.

hor′ti·cul′ture (hôr′ti kul′chər) n. the art of cultivating gardens.

ho·san′na (hō zan′ə) interj. an exclamation praising God.

hose (hōz) n., v., **hosed, hosing.** —n. **1.** a flexible tube for conveying liquid. **2.** stockings. —v.t. **3.** to spray with a hose.

ho′sier·y (hō′zhə rē) n. stockings.

hos′pice (hos′pis) n. a facility for supportive care of the dying.

hos′pi·ta·ble (hos′pi tə bəl, ho·spit′ə-) adj. **1.** treating guests warmly and generously. **2.** favorably receptive.

hos′pi·tal (hos′pi tl) n. an institution for treatment of the sick and injured.

hos′pi·tal′i·ty (-tal′i tē) n., pl. **-ties.** the warm reception of guests or strangers.

hos′pi·tal·ize′ v.t., **-ized, -izing.** to place in a hospital for care. —**hos′pi·tal·i·za′tion,** n.

host[1] (hōst) n. **1.** a person who entertains guests. **2.** a moderator for a television or radio program. —v.t., v.i. **3.** to act as host to.

host[2] (hōst) n. a great number.

Host (hōst) n. the bread consecrated in the celebration of the Eucharist.

hos′tage (hos′tij) n. a person given or held as security.

hos′tel (hos′tl) n. an inexpensive lodging for young travelers.

hos′tile (hos′til, esp. Brit. -tīl) adj. **1.** opposed; unfriendly. **2.** of enemies. —**hos·til′i·ty** (ho stil′i tē) n.

hot (hot) adj., **hotter, hottest. 1.** having a high temperature. **2.** feeling great heat. **3.** peppery. **4.** showing intense feeling. **5.** Informal. currently popular. **6.** Slang. recently stolen.

hot′bed′ n. **1.** a glass-covered, heated bed of earth for growing plants. **2.** a place where something thrives and spreads.

hot′-blood′ed adj. **1.** excitable. **2.** passionate.

hot′ cake′ n. a pancake.

hot′ dog′ n. a frankfurter.

hos·tel′ (ho tel′) n. a building offering food and lodging to travelers.

hot′ flash′ n. a sudden, brief feeling of heat experienced by some menopausal women.

hot′head′ n. an impetuous or short-tempered person. —**hot′head′ed,** adj.

hot′house′ n. a greenhouse.

hot′ line′ n. a direct telephone line for immediate communications of major importance.

hot′ plate′ n. a portable electrical appliance for cooking.

hot′ pota′to n. Informal. an unpleasant or risky situation or issue.

hot′ rod′ n. Slang. a car with an engine built for increased speed. —**hot′ rod′der,** n.

hot′shot′ n. Slang. a skillful and often vain person.

hot′ tub′ n. a large wooden tub of hot water big enough for several persons.

hot′ wa′ter n. Informal. trouble.

hound (hound) n. **1.** any of several breeds of hunting dog. —v.t. **2.** to hunt or track. **3.** to harass.

hour (ou³r, ou′ər) n. **1.** a period of 60 minutes. **2.** any specific time of day. —**hour′ly,** adj., adv.

hour′glass′ n. a device for measuring time by the draining of sand from the top part to the bottom part of a glass container.

house n., v., **housed, housing.** —n. (hous) **1.** a building in which people live. **2.** a building for any special purpose. **3.** a legislative or deliberative body. **4.** a commercial firm. **5.** a family or dynasty. —v.t. (houz) **6.** to provide with shelter or space for work or storage.

house′break′er n. a person who breaks into another's house with the intent to steal.

house′bro′ken adj. (of an animal) trained to excrete outdoors or to behave appropriately indoors.

house′fly′ n., pl. **-flies.** a medium-sized fly.

house′hold′ n. **1.** the people of a house. **2.** a home and its related affairs. —adj. **3.** domestic.

house′hus′band n. a married man who stays at home to manage the household.

house′keep′er n. a person who manages a house. —**house′keep′ing,** n.

house′plant′ n. an ornamental plant grown indoors.

house′warm′ing n. a party to celebrate a new home.

house′wife′ n., pl. **-wives.** a married woman who stays at home to manage the household.

house′work′ n. the work done in housekeeping.

hous′ing (hou′zing) n. **1.** any lodging or dwelling place. **2.** houses collectively. **3.** anything that protects.

HOV high-occupancy vehicle: a bus, van, or car with two or more passengers.

hov′el (huv′əl, hov′-) n. a small, mean dwelling.

hov′er (huv′ər, hov′-) v.i. **1.** to hang suspended in air. **2.** to wait nearby.

Hov′er·craft Trademark. a vehicle that can skim over water on a cushion of air.

how (hou) adv. **1.** in what way? **2.** to what extent or degree? **3.** in what state or condition? —conj. **4.** the way in which.

how·ev′er conj. **1.** nevertheless. —adj. **2.** to whatever extent. —conj. **3.** in whatever manner or state.

how′itz·er (hou′it sər) n. a short-barreled cannon.

howl (houl) v.i. **1.** to utter the loud, long, mournful cry of a wolf, dog, etc. **2.** to utter a similar cry. —n. **3.** the cry of the wolf, dog, etc. **4.** any similar cry.

how·so·ev′er adv. however.

hoy′den (hoid′n) n. a tomboy.

HP horsepower.

HQ headquarters.

H.S. High School.

ht. height.

HTML HyperText Markup Language: a set of standards, a variety of SGML, used to tag the elements of a hypertext document on the World Wide Web.

hub (hub) n. **1.** the central part of a wheel. **2.** a center of activity.

hub′bub (hub′ub) n. an uproar.

hu′bris (hyōō′bris, hōō′-) n. excessive pride.

huck′le·ber′ry (huk′əl ber′ē) n., pl. **-ries.** the dark blue, edible berry of a shrub of the heath family.

huck′ster (huk′stər) n. **1.** a peddler. **2.** an aggressive seller or promoter.

HUD (hud) Department of Housing and Urban Development.

hud′dle (hud′l) v., **-dled, -dling,** n. —v.i., v.i. **1.** to crowd together closely. —n. **2.** a closely gathered group or heap.

hue (hyōō) n. a color.

huff (huf) n. **1.** a fit of sulking anger. —v.i. **2.** to breathe heavily.

hug (hug) v., **hugged, hugging,** n. —v.t. **1.** to clasp in the arms affectionately. **2.** to stay close to. —n. **3.** a tight clasp with the arms.

huge (hyōōj; often yōōj) adj., **huger, hugest.** very large in size or extent.

Hu′gue·not′ (hyōō′gə not′; often yōō′-) n. a French Protestant in the 16th and 17th centuries.

hu′la (hōō′lə) n. a Hawaiian dance.

hulk (hulk) n. **1.** the body of an old ship. **2.** a bulky person or thing.

hulk′ing adj. heavy and clumsy.

hull[1] (hul) n. **1.** the outer covering of a seed or fruit. —v.t. **2.** to remove the hull of.

hull[2] (hul) n. the hollow lower part of a ship.

hul′la·ba·loo′ (hul′ə bə lōō′) n., pl. **-loos.** Informal. an uproar.

hum (hum) v., **hummed, humming,** n. —v.i. **1.** to make a low droning sound. **2.** to sing with closed lips. **3.** to be busy or active. —n. **4.** the act or sound of humming.

hu′man (hyōō′mən) adj. **1.** of or like people. —n. **2.** Also, **human being.** a person.

hu·mane′ (-mān′) adj. compassionate and sympathetic toward others. —**hu·mane′ly,** adv.

hu′man·ism n. a system of thought focusing on human interests, values, and dignity. —**hu′man·ist,** n., adj.

hu·man′i·tar′i·an (-man′i târ′ē·ən) adj. **1.** having concern for the welfare of people. —n. **2.** a person who promotes human welfare.

hu·man′i·ty n., pl. **-ties. 1.** the human race. **2.** the state or quality of being human. **3. the humanities,** literature, philosophy, art, etc., as distinguished from the sciences.

hu′man·ize′ (-mə nīz′) v.t., v.i., **-ized, -izing.** to make or become human or humane.

hu′man·kind′ n. the human race.

hu′man·ly adv. by human means.

hum′ble (hum′bal, um′-) adj., **-bler, -blest,** v., **-bled, -bling.** —adj. **1.** not proud. **2.** low in rank, condition, etc. —v.t. **3.** to lower in status or condition. —**hum′ble·ness,** n. —**hum′bly,** adv.

hum′bug′ n. **1.** an impostor. **2.** something intended to deceive.

hum′drum′ adj. dull.

hu′mid (hyōō′mid) adj. moist. —**hu·mid′i·fy,** n.

hu·mid′i·fy′ v.t., **-fied, -fying.** to make humid. —**hu·mid′i·fi′er,** n.

hu′mi·dor′ (-mi dôr′) n. a container to keep tobacco moist.

hu·mil′i·ate′ (hyōō mil′ē āt′) v.t., **-ated, -ating.** to harm the pride or self-respect of. —**hu·mil′i·a′tion,** n.

hu·mil′i·ty n. the quality or state of being humble.

hum′ming·bird′ n. a tiny colorful bird with wings that beat rapidly.

hum′mock (hum′ək) n. a very small hill.

hu·mon′gous (hyōō mung′gəs, -mong′-) adj. Slang. huge.

hu′mor (hyōō′mər) n. **1.** the quality of being amusing or comical. **2.** the ability to perceive this. **3.** a mood. **4.** a whim. —v.t. **5.** to indulge. —**hu′mor·ist,** n. —**hu′mor·ous,** adj.

hump (hump) n. **1.** a rounded protruding part on the back. —v.t. **2.** to raise (the back) in a hump.

hump′back′ n. **1.** a back with a

hump. 2. a hunchback. **3.** a kind of whale.

hu′mus (hyōō′məs) *n.* the dark organic material in soils, produced by decomposing matter.

hunch (hunch) *v.t.* **1.** to push out or up in a hump. —*n.* **2.** an intuitive feeling.

hun′dred (hun′drid) *n., adj.* ten times ten. —**hun′dredth,** *adj.*

hung (hung) *v.* a pt. and pp. of **hang.**

Hun·gar′i·an (hung går′ē ən) *adj.* **1.** of Hungary, its inhabitants, or its language. —*n.* **2.** a native of Hungary. **3.** the language of Hungary.

hun′ger (hung′gər) *n.* **1.** a need or desire for food. **2.** a strong desire. —*v.i.* **3.** to be hungry. **4.** to have a strong desire.

hun′gry *adj.,* **-grier, -griest. 1.** having a desire or need for food. **2.** desiring.

hunk (hungk) *n.* **1.** a large piece. **2.** *Slang.* a handsome, muscular man.

hun′ker (hung′kər) *v.i.* to squat on one's heels.

hunt (hunt) *v.t.* **1.** to chase to catch or kill. **2.** to search for. —*v.i.* **3.** to kill wild animals. —*n.* **4.** the act of hunting. **5.** a search. —**hunt′er,** *n.*

hur′dle (hûr′dl) *n., v.,* **-dled, -dling.** —*n.* **1.** a barrier over which runners or horses leap in a race. **2.** an obstacle. —*v.t.* **3.** to leap over.

hurl (hûrl) *v.t.* to throw with great force.

hurl′y-burl′y (hûr′lē bûr′lē) *n.* noisy disorder and confusion.

hur·rah′ (hə rä′, -rô′) *interj., n.* an exclamation of joy, triumph, etc.

hur′ri·cane′ (hûr′i kān′, hur′-) *n.* a violent tropical storm.

hur′ry (hûr′ē, hur′ē) *v.,* **-ried, -rying,** *n., pl.* **-ries.** —*v.i.* **1.** to move or act with haste. —*v.t.* **2.** to cause to move or act with haste; rush. —*n.* **3.** a state of urgency. **4.** hurried movement. —**hur′ried·ly,** *adv.*

hurt (hûrt) *v.,* **hurt, hurting,** *n.* —*v.t.* **1.** to cause injury, harm, or pain to. —*v.i.* **2.** to feel pain. **3.** to cause pain, damage, or distress. —*n.* **4.** injury or damage.

hur′tle (hûr′tl) *v.i., v.t.,* **-tled, -tling.** to move or fling violently.

hus′band (huz′bənd) *n.* **1.** a married man. —*v.t.* **2.** to manage prudently.

hus′band·ry *n.* the cultivation of crops and the raising of livestock.

hush (hush) *interj.* **1.** a command to be silent. —*v.t., v.i.* **2.** to make or become silent. —*n.* **3.** silence.

husk (husk) *n.* **1.** the dry covering of seeds. —*v.t.* **2.** to remove the husk from.

husk′y¹ *adj.,* **-ier, -iest. 1.** big and strong. **2.** (of the voice) hoarse.

husk′y² *n., pl.* **-ies.** (*sometimes cap.*) a sturdy sled dog of arctic regions.

hus′sy (hus′ē, huz′ē) *n., pl.* **-sies.** a disreputable woman.

hus′tle (hus′əl) *v.,* **-tled, -tling,** *n.* —*v.i.* **1.** to proceed or work energetically. **2.** to push. —*v.t.* **3.** to force or push roughly. **4.** to urge. —*n.* **5.** energetic activity. —**hus′tler,** *n.*

hut (hut) *n.* a small or humble dwelling.

hutch (huch) *n.* **1.** a pen for small animals. **2.** a chestlike cabinet with open shelves above.

hwy. highway.

hy′a·cinth (hī′ə sinth) *n.* a plant with a cylindrical cluster of fragrant flowers.

hy′brid (hī′brid) *n.* **1.** the offspring of two plants or animals of different breeds, species, etc. **2.** anything made by combining different elements.

hy′brid·ize *v.i., v.t.,* **-ized, -izing.** to produce or cause to produce hybrids.

hy·dran′gea (hī drān′jə) *n.* a shrub with large white, pink, or blue flower clusters.

hy′drant (hī′drənt) *n.* an upright pipe with an outlet for drawing water from a water main.

hy·drau′lic (hī drô′lik) *adj.* **1.** of or operated by liquid under pressure. **2.** of hydraulics.

hy·drau′lics *n.* the science of moving liquids.

hydro- a prefix meaning: **1.** water. **2.** hydrogen.

hy′dro·car′bon (hī′drə kär′bən) *n.* a compound containing only hydrogen and carbon.

hy′dro·ceph′a·lus (-sef′ə ləs) *n.* an abnormal accumulation of fluid inside the skull. Also, **-ceph′a·ly.** —**hy′dro·ce·phal′ic** (hī′drō sə fal′ik), *adj., n.*

hy′dro·e·lec′tric (hī′drō-) *adj.* pertaining to electricity derived from the energy of falling water. —**hy′dro·e·lec·tric′i·ty,** *n.*

hy′dro·foil′ *n.* a boat with a structure that lifts the hull out of water when traveling at high speed.

hy′dro·gen (-jən) *n.* a colorless, odorless, flammable gas, the lightest of the elements.

hy′dro·gen·ate′ (hī′drə jə nāt′, hī-droj′ə-) *v.t., adj.* **-ated, -ating.** to combine with or treat with hydrogen.

hy′drogen bomb′ *n.* a powerful bomb that derives its explosive energy from the fusion of hydrogen isotopes.

hy′drogen perox′ide *n.* a liquid used as an antiseptic and a bleach.

hy′dro·pho′bi·a (hī′drə fō′bē ə) *n.* **1.** a fear of water. **2.** rabies.

hy′dro·plane′ *n.* **1.** an airplane that lands on water. **2.** a light, high-speed motorboat that planes along the surface of the water.

hy′dro·pon′ics (-pon′iks) *n.* the cultivation of plants in liquids rather than in soil. —**hy′dro·pon′ic,** *adj.*

hy′dro·ther′a·py *n.* the use of water to treat disease or injury.

hy·e′na (hī ē′nə) *n.* a carnivorous mammal of Africa and Asia.

hy′giene (hī′jēn) *n.* a condition or practice conducive to health. —**hy′gi·en′ic** (-jē en′ik, -jen′-, -jē′-nik) *adj.* —**hy·gien′ist** (-jē′nist, -jen′ist) *n.*

hy·grom′e·ter (hī grom′i tər) *n.* an instrument for measuring humidity.

hy′men (hī′mən) *n.* a fold of mucous membrane partly closing the vagina in a virgin.

hymn (him) *n.* a song of praise.

hym′nal (him′nl) *n.* a book of hymns. Also, **hymn′book′.**

hype (hīp) *v.,* **hyped, hyping,** *n. Informal.* —*v.t.* **1.** to create interest in by flamboyant methods. —*n.* **2.** exaggerated promotion.

hyper- a prefix meaning over, above, or excessive.

hy′per·ac′tive (hī′pər-) *adj.* unusually active.

hy′per·bo·le (hī pûr′bə lē) *n.* obvious exaggeration.

hy′per·crit′i·cal (hī′pər-) *adj.* excessively critical.

hy′per·gly·ce′mi·a (-glī sē′mē ə) *n.* an abnormally high level of glucose in the blood.

hy′per·ten′sion *n.* high blood pressure.

hy′per·text′ *n.* computerized data in which pieces of text, pictures, etc., are linked so that a user can move from one object to another.

hy′per·ven′ti·la′tion *n.* prolonged rapid or deep breathing. —**hy′per·ven′ti·late′,** *v.i.*

hy′phen (hī′fən) *n.* a short line (-) connecting parts or syllables of a word. —**hy′phen·ate′,** *v.t.*

hyp·no′sis (hip nō′sis) *n., pl.* **-ses** (-sēz). an artificially produced sleeplike state in which a person obeys suggestions. —**hyp·not′ic** (-not′ik) *adj.* —**hyp′no·tism′** (-nə-tiz′əm) *n.* —**hyp′no·tist,** *n.* —**hyp′-no·tize′,** *v.t.*

hy′po (hī′pō) *n., pl.* **-pos.** a hypodermic needle or injection.

hypo- a prefix meaning under.

hy′po·al′ler·gen′ic *adj.* designed to minimize the chance of an allergic reaction.

hy′po·chon′dri·a (hī′pə kon′drē ə) *n.* an excessive preoccupation with one's health. —**hy′po·chon′dri·ac′,** *n., adj.*

hy·poc′ri·sy (hi pok′rə sē) *n., pl.* **-sies.** the false professing of qualities such as virtue, piety, etc.

hyp′o·crite (hip′ə krit) *n.* a person given to hypocrisy. —**hyp′o·crit′i·cal,** *adj.*

hy′po·der′mic (hī′pə dûr′mik) *adj.* **1.** introduced under the skin, as a needle. —*n.* **2.** a syringe and needle for hypodermic injections.

hy′po·gly·ce′mi·a (hī′pō glī sē′-mē ə) *n.* an abnormally low level of glucose in the blood.

hy·pot′e·nuse (hī pot′n ōōs′, -yōōs′) *n.* the side of a right triangle opposite the right angle.

hy′po·ther′mi·a (hī′pə thûr′mē ə) *n.* a body temperature that is below normal.

hy·poth′e·sis (hī poth′ə sis, hi-) *n., pl.* **-ses** (-sēz). a proposition set forth as an explanation of something, often as the basis for further investigation. —**hy′po·thet′i·cal** (-pə thet′i kəl) *adj.*

hys′sop (his′əp) *n.* a fragrant plant of the mint family.

hys′ter·ec′to·my (his′tə rek′tə mē) *n., pl.* **-mies.** surgical removal of the uterus.

hys·te′ri·a (hi ster′ē ə, -stēr′-) *n.* an uncontrollable emotional outburst. —**hys·ter′i·cal** (-ster′-) *adj.* —**hys·ter′i·cal·ly,** *adv.*

hys·ter′ics (-ster′iks) *n.pl.* a fit of hysteria.

Hz hertz.

I

I, i (ī) *n.* the ninth letter of the English alphabet.

I (ī) *pron.* the subject form of the singular pronoun used by a person speaking about himself or herself.

IA or **Ia.** Iowa.

-iatrics a suffix meaning medical care or treatment.

-iatry a suffix meaning healing or medical practice.

i′bex (ī′beks) *n., pl.* **i′bex·es, ib′i·ces′** (ib′ə sēz′, ī′bə-), **ibex.** a wild goat with backward-curving horns.

ibid. (ib′id) ibidem.

i′bi·dem (ib′i dəm, i bī′dəm) *adv.* in the same book, chapter, etc., previously cited.

i′bis (ī′bis) *n.* a large wading bird.

-ible a variant of *-able.*

i′bu·pro′fen (ī′byōō prō′fən) *n.* an anti-inflammatory drug.

-ic¹ an adjective suffix meaning: of or pertaining to; like or characteristic of; containing or made of.

-ic² a noun suffix meaning: person having; agent or drug; follower.

ICC Interstate Commerce Commission.

ice (īs) *n., v.,* **iced, icing.** —*n.* **1.** frozen water. **2.** a frozen dessert. —*v.t.* **3.** to freeze. **4.** to cool with ice. **5.** to cover with icing. —*v.i.* **6.** to change to or become coated with ice.

ice′berg′ (-bûrg) *n.* a large mass of ice floating at sea.

ice′box′ *n.* an insulated food chest cooled by ice.

ice′ cream′ *n.* a frozen dessert made with cream and flavorings.

ice′ skate′ *n.* a shoe with a metal blade for skating on ice. —**ice-skate,** *v.i.*

ich′thy·ol′o·gy (ik′thē ol′ə jē) *n.* the study of fishes.

i′ci·cle (ī′si kəl) *n.* a hanging, tapering mass of ice.

ic′ing *n.* a sweet mixture for covering cakes, cookies, etc.

i′con (ī′kon) *n.* **1.** a sacred image. **2.** a symbol. **3.** a small graphic on a computer screen.

i·con′o·clast′ (-ə klast′) *n.* a person who attacks cherished beliefs. —**i·con′o·clas′tic,** *adj.*

-ics a suffix meaning: **1.** art, science, or field. **2.** activities of a certain kind.

ICU intensive care unit.

id (id) *n.* the unconscious, instinctive part of the psyche.

ID (ī′dē′) *n., pl.* **IDs, ID's.** a document, card, or other means of identification.

ID or **Id.** Idaho.

i·de′a (ī dē′ə, ī dē′ə′) *n.* **1.** a conception or plan formed in the mind. **2.** an opinion. **3.** a purpose.

i·de′al (ī dē′əl, ī dēl′) *n.* **1.** a conception or standard of perfection. **2.** a person or thing regarded as perfect. —*adj.* **3.** regarded as perfect. —**i·de′al·ize′,** *v.t.*

i·de′al·ism′ *n.* belief in or behavior according to one's ideals. —**i·de′al·ist,** *n.*

i·den′ti·cal (ī den′ti kəl, i den′-) *adj.* the same. —**i·den′ti·cal·ly,** *adv.*

i·den′ti·fy′ (-fī) *v.t.,* **-fied, -fying.** **1.** to recognize as being a particular person or thing. **2.** to associate closely. —**i·den′ti·fi·ca′tion,** *n.*

i·den′ti·ty (-tē) *n., pl.* **-ties. 1.** the fact or state of remaining the same. **2.** the sense of self.

i′de·ol′o·gy (ī′dē ol′ə jē, id′ē-) *n., pl.* **-gies.** the beliefs that guide a person, institution, or group. —**i′de·o·log′i·cal,** *adj.*

id′i·om (id′ē əm) *n.* **1.** a phrase whose meaning cannot be predicted from the usual meanings of the words. **2.** the manner of expression characteristic of a certain language. —**id′i·o·mat′ic,** *adj.*

id′i·o·syn′cra·sy (-sing′krə sē) *n., pl.* **-sies.** a habit or mannerism peculiar to an individual. —**id′i·o·syn·crat′ic,** *adj.*

id′i·ot (id′ē ət) *n.* a very stupid person. —**id′i·ot′ic** (-ot′ik) *adj.* —**id′i·ot′i·cal·ly,** *adv.*

i′dle (īd′l) *adj., v.,* **idled, idling.** —*adj.* **1.** not active. **2.** worthless. **3.** lazy. —*v.i.* **4.** to do nothing. **5.** (of an engine) to operate at a low speed. —*v.t.* **6.** to pass (time) doing nothing. —**i′dler,** *n.* —**i′dly,** *adv.*

i′dol (īd′l) *n.* **1.** a person or thing that is worshiped. **2.** an image representing a god. —**i′dol·ize′,** *v.t.*

i·dol′a·try (ī dol′ə trē) *n., pl.* **-tries. 1.** the worship of idols. **2.** excessive admiration. —**i·dol′a·ter,** *n.*

i′dyll (īd′l) *n.* **1.** a scene of charming peace and simplicity. **2.** a literary work describing such a scene. Also, **i′dyl.** —**i·dyl′lic** (ī dil′ik) *adj.*

i.e. that is.

if (if) *conj.* **1.** in case that. **2.** even though. **3.** whether.

if′fy *adj.,* **-fier, -fiest.** *Informal.* not resolved; indefinite.

ig′loo (ig′lōō) *n., pl.* **-loos.** a hut built of snow blocks.

ig′ne·ous (ig′nē əs) *adj.* **1.** produced under intense heat. **2.** of fire.

ig·nite′ (ig nīt′) *v.,* **-nited, -niting.** —*v.t., v.i.* to set on or catch fire. —**ig·ni′tion** (-nish′ən) *n.*

ig·no′ble (ig nō′bəl) *adj.* not noble in character.

ig′no·min′i·ous (ig′nə min′ē əs) *adj.* **1.** disgraceful. **2.** contemptible. —**ig′no·min′y,** *n.*

ig′no·ra′mus (-rā′məs, -ram′əs) *n.* an ignorant person.

ig′no·rant (ig′nər ənt) *adj.* **1.** lacking in knowledge or education. **2.** unaware. —**ig′no·rance,** *n.*

ig·nore′ (ig nôr′) *v.t.,* **-nored, -noring.** to take no notice of.

i·gua′na (i gwä′nə) *n.* a large tropical lizard.

IL Illinois.

il- a prefix equivalent to *in-*.

ilk (ilk) *n.* family or kind.

ill (il) *adj.* **1.** sick. **2.** evil. **3.** hostile; unkind. **4.** unfavorable. —*n.* **5.** trouble. **6.** evil. **7.** sickness. —*adv.* **8.** badly or poorly. **9.** with difficulty.

Ill. Illinois.

ill′-bred′ *adj.* rude.

il·le′gal (i lē′gəl) *adj.* against the law.

il·leg′i·ble (-lej′ə bəl) *adj.* hard to read.

il·le·git′i·mate (il′i jit′ə mit) *adj.* **1.** unlawful. **2.** born to parents who are not married to each other. —**il′le·git′i·ma·cy** (-mə sē) *n.*

ill′-fat′ed *adj.* **1.** destined to a bad fate. **2.** bringing bad luck.

il·lib′er·al *adj.* **1.** narrow-minded; bigoted. **2.** not generous.

il·lic′it *adj.* unlawful; not allowed.

il·lim′it·a·ble (i lim′i tə bəl) *adj.* boundless.

il·lit′er·ate (i lit′ər it) *adj.* **1.** unable to read and write. —*n.* **2.** an illiterate person. —**il·lit′er·a·cy,** *n.*

ill′-man′nered *adj.* having bad manners.

ill′ness *n.* **1.** the state of being ill. **2.** a particular ailment; sickness.

il·log′i·cal (i loj′i kəl) *adj.* not logical. —**il·log′i·cal·ly,** *adv.*

ill′-starred′ *adj.* unlucky; ill-fated.

ill′-treat′ *v.t.* to treat badly or cruelly. —**ill′-treat′ment,** *n.*

il·lu′mi·nate′ (i lōō′mə nāt′) *v.t.,* **-nated, -nating. 1.** to supply with light. **2.** to make clear. —**il·lu′mi·na′tion,** *n.*

illus. **1.** illustrated. **2.** illustration.

ill′-use′ *v.,* **ill-used, ill-using.** —*v.t.* (il′yōōz′) **1.** to treat badly or unjustly. —*n.* (-yōōs′) **2.** bad or unjust treatment.

il·lu′sion (i lōō′zhən) *n.* **1.** a false belief. **2.** something that creates a false impression of reality. —**il·lu′-so·ry** (-sə rē, -zə-) *adj.*

il′lus·trate′ (il′ə strāt′, i lus′trāt) *v.t.,* **-trated, -trating. 1.** to furnish (a book or article) with pictures. **2.** to make clear by examples. —**il′lus·tra′tion,** *n.* —**il′lus·tra′tor,** *n.*

il·lus′tri·ous (i lus′trē əs) *adj.* distinguished.

ill′ will′ *n.* hostile feeling.

im- a suffix equivalent to *in-.*

im′age (im′ij) *n.* **1.** a likeness. **2.** a picture in the mind. **3.** an optical picture of a thing as produced by reflection in a mirror or through a lens. **4.** a general or public perception; reputation.

im′age·ry *n., pl.* **-ries. 1.** mental images collectively. **2.** the use of figures of speech.

im·ag′i·nar′y (i maj′ə ner′ē) *adj.* existing only in the imagination.

im·ag′i·na′tion (-nā′shən) *n.* **1.** the act or faculty of imagining. **2.** the ability to form mental images. **3.** creativity. —**im·ag′i·na·tive** (-nə tiv) *adj.*

im·ag′ine (i maj′in) *v.t., v.i.,* **-ined, -ining. 1.** to form mental images (of). **2.** to think. **3.** to suppose or guess. —**im·ag′i·na·ble,** *adj.*

i·mam′ (i mäm′) *n.* a Muslim religious leader.

im·bal′ance (im bal′əns) *n.* lack of balance.

im′be·cile (im′bə sil) *n.* a stupid person.

im·bibe′ (im bīb′) *v.t.,* **-bibed, -bibing. 1.** to drink. **2.** to receive into the mind.

im·bro′glio (im brōl′yō) *n., pl.* **-glios.** a complicated situation.

im·bue′ (im byōō′) *v.t.,* **-bued, -buing. 1.** to inspire. **2.** to saturate.

im′i·tate′ (im′i tāt′) *v.t.,* **-tated, -tating. 1.** to copy. **2.** to follow as a model or example. —**im′i·ta′tive,** *adj.* —**im′i·ta′tion,** *n.*

im·mac′u·late (i mak′yə lit) *adj.* **1.** spotlessly clean. **2.** free from blemish or error.

im′ma·nent (im′ə nənt) *adj.* remaining within; inherent. —**im′ma·nence,** *n.*

im′ma·te′ri·al (im′ə tēr′ē əl) *adj.* **1.** unimportant. **2.** not physical.

im′ma·ture′ *adj.* not mature.

im·meas′ur·a·ble *adj.* limitless.

im·me′di·ate (i mē′dē it) *adj.* **1.** occurring without delay. **2.** nearest, with nothing in between. **3.** of the present time. —**im·me′di·a·cy** (-ə sē) *n.*

im′me·mo′ri·al *adj.* beyond memory, record, or knowledge.

im·mense′ (i mens′) *adj.* vast. —**im·men′si·ty,** *n.*

im·merse′ (i mûrs′) *v.t.,* **-mersed, -mersing. 1.** to plunge into liquid. **2.** to involve deeply. —**im·mer′-sion,** *n.*

im′mi·grant (im′i grənt) *n.* a person who immigrates.

im′mi·grate′ (-grāt′) *v.i.,* **-grated, -grating.** to come to a foreign country as a permanent resident. —**im′mi·gra′tion,** *n.*

im′mi·nent (im′ə nənt) *adj.* about to happen. —**im′mi·nence,** *n.*

im·mo′bile (i mō′bəl, -bēl) *adj.* **1.** incapable of moving or being moved. **2.** not moving. —**im′mo·bil′i·ty,** *n.* —**im·mo′bi·lize′,** *v.t.*

im·mod′er·ate (-it) *adj.* excessive.

im·mod′est *adj.* not modest.

im′mo·late′ (im′ə lāt′) *v.t.,* **-lated, -lating. 1.** to kill as a sacrifice. **2.** to destroy by fire. —**im′mo·la′tion,** *n.*

im·mor′al *adj.* morally wrong. —**im′mo·ral′i·ty,** *n.*

im·mor′tal *adj.* **1.** living forever. **2.** remembered forever. —*n.* **3.** an immortal being. —**im′mor·tal′i·ty,** *n.* —**im·mor′tal·ize′,** *v.t.*

im·mov′a·ble *adj.* **1.** fixed; stationary. **2.** unyielding.

im·mune′ (i myōōn′) *adj.* **1.** protected from a disease or infection. **2.** exempt. —**im·mu′ni·ty,** *n.* —**im′mu·ni·za′tion,** *n.* —**im′mu·nize′,** *v.t.*

immune′ sys′tem *n.* the network of cells and tissues that protects the body from disease.

im′mu·nol′o·gy (-nol′ə jē) *n.* the branch of science dealing with the immune system.

im·mure′ (i myŏŏr′) *v.t.,* **-mured, -muring.** to enclose within walls.

im·mu′ta·ble *adj.* unchangeable.

imp (imp) *n.* **1.** a little demon. **2.** a mischievous child. —**imp′ish,** *adj.*

im′pact *n.* (im′pakt) **1.** a collision. **2.** effect. —*v.t., v.i.* (im pakt′) **3.** to make contact (with) forcefully. **4.** to have an effect (on).

im·pact′ed *adj.* (of a tooth) wedged too tightly in its socket to erupt properly.

im·pair′ (im pâr′) *v.t.* to damage; weaken. —**im·pair′ment,** *n.*

im·pale′ *v.t.,* **-paled, -paling.** to pierce with something pointed.

im·pal′pa·ble *adj.* **1.** incapable of being felt by touch. **2.** difficult for the mind to grasp.

im·pan′el *v.t.,* **-eled, -eling. 1.** to enter on a list for jury duty. **2.** to select (a jury) from a panel.

im·part′ *v.t.* **1.** to make known. **2.** to give.

im·par′tial *adj.* not biased. —**im·par′ti·al′i·ty** (-shē al′i tē) *n.*

im·pass′a·ble *adj.* not able to be passed through.

im′passe (im′pas, im pas′) *n.* a position from which there is no escape.

im·pas′sioned *adj.* filled with intense feeling.

im·pas′sive *adj.* showing or feeling no emotion. —**im·pas′sive·ly,** *adv.*

im·pa′tience *n.* lack of patience. —**im·pa′tient,** *adj.*

im·peach′ (im pēch′) *v.t.* to charge (a public official) with misconduct in office. —**im·peach′ment,** *n.*

im·pec′ca·ble (im pek′ə bəl) *adj.* faultless; flawless. —**im·pec′ca·bly,** *adv.*

im·pe·cu′ni·ous (im′pi kyōō′nē əs) *adj.* having no money.

im·pede′ (im pēd′) *v.t.,* **-peded, -peding.** to hinder.

im·ped′i·ment (im ped′ə mənt) *n.* **1.** a hindrance. **2.** a speech defect.

im·pel′ *v.t.,* **-pelled, -pelling.** to drive or urge forward.

im·pend′ *v.i.* to be about to happen.

im·pen′e·tra·ble *adj.* **1.** not able to be penetrated or entered. **2.** not able to be understood. —**im·pen′e·tra·bil′i·ty,** *n.*

im·per′a·tive (im per′ə tiv) *adj.* **1.** absolutely necessary. **2.** expressing a command.

im′per·cep′ti·ble *adj.* very slight.

im·per′fect *adj.* **1.** having a defect. **2.** not complete. **3.** designating a verb tense indicating a continuing or repeated action or a state in the past. —**im′per·fec′tion,** *n.* —**im·per′fect·ly,** *adv.*

im·pe′ri·al (im pēr′ē əl) *adj.* of an empire.

im·pe′ri·al·ism′ *n.* the policy of extending the rule of a nation over other peoples. —**im·pe′ri·al·ist,** *n., adj.*

im·per′il *v.t.,* **-iled, -iling.** to endanger.

im·pe′ri·ous (im pēr′ē əs) *adj.* domineering.

im·per′ish·a·ble *adj.* not subject to decay.

im·per′me·a·ble *adj.* not able to be penetrated by liquid. —**im·per′me·a·bil′i·ty,** *n.*

im·per′son·al *adj.* not referring to a particular person.

im·per′son·ate′ *v.t.,* **-ated, -ating.** to assume the character or appearance of. —**im·per′son·a′tion,** *n.* —**im·per′son·a′tor,** *n.*

im·per′ti·nence *n.* **1.** the act of being impertinent. **2.** an impertinent utterance.

im·per′ti·nent *adj.* **1.** disrespectful. **2.** not relevant. —**im·per′ti·nent·ly,** *adv.*

im′per·turb′a·ble *adj.* incapable of being upset or excited; calm.

im·per′vi·ous (im pûr′vē əs) *adj.* **1.** not allowing penetration. **2.** incapable of being affected.

im·pe·ti′go (im′pi tī′gō) *n.* a contagious skin infection.

im·pet′u·ous (im pech′ōō əs) *adj.* rash or hasty. —**im·pet′u·os′i·ty** (-os′i tē) *n.*

im′pe·tus (im′pi təs) *n.* a driving or moving force.

im·pi′e·ty *n., pl.* **-ties. 1.** a lack of reverence. **2.** an impious act.

im·pinge′ (im pinj′) *v.i.,* **-pinged, -pinging. 1.** to encroach or infringe. **2.** to strike.

im′pi·ous (im′pē əs, im pī′-) *adj.* **1.** not reverent; irreligious. **2.** disrespectful.

im·pla′ca·ble (im plak′ə bəl) *adj.* not to be appeased or pacified.

im·plant′ *v.t.* (im plant′) **1.** to establish or plant firmly. **2.** to insert (a tissue, organ, etc.) into the body. —*n.* (im′plant′) **3.** a device or material used to repair or replace a body part.

im·plaus′i·ble *adj.* causing disbelief. —**im·plau′si·bil′i·ty,** *n.*

im′ple·ment *n.* (im′plə mənt) **1.** an instrument or tool. —*v.t.* (-ment′, -mənt) **2.** to put into effect. —**im′ple·men·ta′tion,** *n.*

im′pli·cate′ (im′pli kāt′) *v.t.,* **-cated, -cating.** to show to be involved.

im′pli·ca′tion *n.* **1.** an implying or being implied. **2.** something implied. **3.** an implicating or being implicated.

im·plic′it (im plis′it) *adj.* **1.** implied; not explicit. **2.** unquestioning; absolute.

im·plode′ (im plōd′) *v.i.,* *v.t.,* **-ploded, -ploding.** to burst inward. —**im·plo′sion,** *n.*

im·plore′ (im plôr′) *v.t.,* **-plored, -ploring.** to urge or beg.

im·ply′ (im plī′) *v.t.,* **-plied, -plying.** to indicate or suggest without stating directly.

im′po·lite′ *adj.* rude.

im·pol′i·tic *adj.* not wise or prudent.

im·pon′der·a·ble *adj.* incapable of being precisely measured or evaluated.

im·port′ *v.t.* (im pôrt′) **1.** to bring in from another country. **2.** to mean or signify. —*n.* (im′pôrt) **3.** anything imported. **4.** importance or significance. **5.** meaning. —**im′por·ta′tion,** *n.* —**im·port′er,** *n.*

im·por′tant (im pôr′tnt) *adj.* **1.** of much significance. **2.** having authority or distinction. —**im·por′tance,** *n.*

im′por·tune′ (im′pôr tōōn′, -tyōōn′, im pôr′chən) *v.t.,* *v.i.,* **-tuned, -tuning.** to urge or beg persistently. —**im·por′tu·nate,** *adj.*

im·pose′ *v.t.,* **-posed, -posing. 1.** to set as an obligation. **2.** to thrust upon others. **3. impose on,** to take unfair advantage of. —**im′po·si′tion** (-pə zish′ən) *n.*

im·pos′ing *adj.* impressive.

im·pos′si·ble *adj.* **1.** not capable of being or happening. **2.** not able to be done. —**im·pos′si·bil′i·ty,** *n.*

im′post (im′pōst) *n.* a tax or duty.

im·pos′tor (im pos′tər) *n.* a person who pretends to be someone else. Also, **im·pos′ter.**

im′po·tent (im′pə tənt) *adj.* **1.** lacking power or force. **2.** (of a male) unable to attain or sustain an erection. —**im′po·tence,** *n.*

im·pound′ *v.t.* to seize and hold in legal custody.

im·pov′er·ish (im pov′ər ish, -pov′rish) *v.t.* **1.** to make poor. **2.** to exhaust the strength of.

im·prac′ti·ca·ble (im prak′ti kə·bəl) *adj.* incapable of being put into practice or use.

im·prac′ti·cal *adj.* **1.** not practical or useful. **2.** not able to deal with practical matters.

im′pre·ca′tion (-pri kā′shən) *n.* a curse.

im′pre·cise′ *adj.* vague; not exact.

im·preg′na·ble (im preg′nə bəl) *adj.* strong enough to resist attack.

im·preg′nate (-nāt) *v.t.,* **-nated, -nating. 1.** to make pregnant. **2.** to permeate. —**im′preg·na′tion,** *n.*

im′pre·sa′ri·o (im′prə sär′ē ō′, -sâr′-) *n., pl.* **-os.** a person who organizes or manages public entertainments, as operas.

im·press′[1] *v.t.* (im pres′) **1.** to affect strongly; influence. **2.** to fix in the mind. **3.** to produce (a mark) by pressure. —*n.* (im′pres) **4.** the act of impressing. **5.** a mark made by pressure.

im·press′[2] (im pres′) *v.t.* **1.** to force into public service. **2.** to take for public use.

im·pres′sion (im presh′ən) *n.* **1.** a strong effect on the mind or feelings. **2.** a vague awareness. **3.** a mark produced by pressure.

im·pres′sion·a·ble *adj.* easily influenced, esp. emotionally.

im·pres′sion·ism *n.* (*often cap.*) a style of 19th-century painting characterized by short brush strokes to represent the effect of light on objects. —**im·pres′sion·ist,** *n.* —**im·pres′sion·is′tic,** *adj.*

im·pres′sive *adj.* causing admiration or respect.

im′pri·ma′tur (im′pri mä′tər, -mā′-) *n.* sanction; approval.

im′print *n.* a mark made by pressure.

im·pris′on *v.t.* to put in prison. —**im·pris′on·ment,** *n.*

im·prob′a·ble *adj.* not likely to be true or to happen. —**im·prob′a·bil′i·ty,** *n.*

im·promp′tu (im promp′tōō, -tyōō) *adj., adv.* without preparation.

im·prop′er *adj.* not right, suitable, or proper. —**im′pro·pri′e·ty** (im′prə prī′i tē) *n.* —**im·prop′er·ly,** *adv.*

im·prove′ *v.t.,* *v.i.,* **-proved, -proving.** to make or become better. —**im·prove′ment,** *n.*

im·prov′i·dent *adj.* not providing for the future. —**im·prov′i·dence,** *n.* —**im·prov′i·dent·ly,** *adv.*

im′pro·vise′ (im′prə vīz′) *v.t.,* *v.i.,* **-vised, -vising. 1.** to perform or deliver at short notice. **2.** to make from whatever is available. —**im·prov′i·sa′tion** (-prov′ə zā′shən) *n.*

im·pru′dent *adj.* not prudent; unwise.

im′pu·dent (im′pyə dənt) *adj.* impertinent; disrespectful. —**im′pu·dence,** *n.*

im·pugn′ (im pyōōn′) *v.t.* to cast doubt on.

im′pulse (im′puls) *n.* **1.** a sudden inclination to do something. **2.** a driving force. —**im·pul′sive,** *adj.*

im·pu′ni·ty (im pyōō′ni tē) *n.* exemption from punishment.

im·pure′ *adj.* not pure. —**im·pu′ri·ty,** *n.*

im·pute′ (im pyōōt′) *v.t.,* **-puted, -puting.** to attribute (esp. a fault) to someone.

in (in) *prep.* **1.** included within a place. **2.** during. **3.** into. —*adv.* **4.** in or into some place, position, etc. **5.** on the inside. —*adj.* **6.** fashionable. **7.** being in power. —*Idiom.* **8. in for,** certain to experience. **9. in that,** because.

IN Indiana.

in- a prefix meaning not or lacking.

in. inch.

in ab·sen′tia (in ab sen′shə, -shē ə) *Latin.* in absence.

in·ac′ti·vate′ (in ak′tə vāt′) *v.t.,* **-vated, -vating.** to make inactive.

in′ad·vert′ent (in′əd vûr′tnt) *adj.* unintentional. —**in′ad·vert′ent·ly,** *adv.*

in·al′ien·a·ble *adj.* not to be taken away or transferred.

in·am·o·ra′ta (in am′ə rä′tə, in′am-) *n.* a female lover.

in·ane′ (i nān′) *adj.* silly; ridiculous. —**in·an′i·ty** (i nan′i tē) *n.*

in·ar·tic′u·late (-lit) *adj.* **1.** lacking the ability to express oneself clearly. **2.** not fully expressed.

in′as·much′ as′ *conj.* **1.** seeing that; since. **2.** to such a degree as.

in·au′gu·rate′ (in ô′gyə rāt′) *v.t.,* **-rated, -rating. 1.** to begin formally. **2.** to admit to office formally. —**in·au′gu·ral,** *adj., n.* —**in·au′gu·ra′tion,** *n.*

in′board′ *adj., adv.* located inside a hull or aircraft.

in′born′ *adj.* present at birth.

in′bound′ *adj.* inward bound.

in′breed′ *v.t.* to produce by breeding closely related individuals. —**in′breed′ing,** *n.* —**in′bred′,** *adj.*

inc. 1. incomplete. **2.** incorporated. **3.** increase.

in′can·des′cence (in′kən des′əns) *n.* the glow caused by intense heat.

in′can·ta′tion (in′kan tā′shən) *n.* the chanting of words as a magic spell.

in′ca·pac′i·tate′ (in′kə pas′i tāt′) *v.t.,* **-tated, -tating.** to make unfit or unable. —**in′ca·pac′i·ty,** *n.*

in·car′cer·ate′ (in kär′sə rāt′) *v.t.,* **-ated, -ating.** to imprison.

in·car′nate (in kär′nit, -nāt) *adj.* given a bodily form; personified.

in′cen′di·ar′y (in sen′dē er′ē) *adj., n., pl.* **-aries.** —*adj.* **1.** of or causing fires. **2.** arousing strife. —*n.* **3.** a person who maliciously sets fires.

in·cense′[1] (in′sens) *n.* a substance giving a sweet odor when burned.

in·cense′[2] (in sens′) *v.t.,* **-censed, -censing.** to make angry.

in·cen′tive (in sen′tiv) *n.* something that incites to action.

in·cep′tion (in sep′shən) *n.* beginning.

in·ces′sant (in ses′ənt) *adj.* not ceasing. —**in·ces′sant·ly,** *adv.*

in′cest (in′sest) *n.* sexual relations between close relatives. —**in·ces′tu·ous** (-ses′chōō əs) *adj.*

inch (inch) *n.* **1.** a unit of length, $\frac{1}{12}$ foot. —*v.t.,* *v.i.* **2.** to move by small degrees.

in·cho′ate (in kō′it) *adj.* just begun; not fully developed.

inch′worm′ *n.* a moth larva that moves in a looping motion.

in′ci·dence (in′si dəns) *n.* the rate at which a thing occurs.

in′ci·dent *n.* **1.** an occurrence or event. —*adj.* **2.** likely to happen. —**in′ci·den′tal** (-dn′tl) *adj., n.* —**in′ci·den′tal·ly,** *adv.*

in·cin′er·ate′ (in sin′ə rāt′) *v.i.,* **-ated, -ating.** to burn to ashes. —**in·cin′er·a′tor,** *n.*

in·cip′i·ent (in sip′ē ənt) *adj.* beginning to exist.

in·cise′ (in sīz′) *v.t.,* **-cised, -cising.** to cut into; engrave. —**in·ci′sion,** *n.*

in·ci′sive (-sī′siv) *adj.* **1.** cutting. **2.** mentally sharp.

in·ci′sor (in sī′zər) *n.* a front tooth used for cutting.

in·cite′ (in sīt′) *v.t.,* **-cited, -citing.** to urge to action. —**in·cite′ment,** *n.*

incl. including.

in·cline′ *v.,* **-clined, -clining.** —*v.i.* (in klīn′) **1.** to lean; bend. **2.** to have a tendency or preference. —*n.* (in′klīn) **3.** a slanted surface.

in·clude′ (in klōōd′) *v.t.,* **-cluded, -cluding. 1.** to contain as part of a whole. **2.** to put into a group. —**in·clu′sion** (-klōō′zhən) *n.* —**in·clu′sive** (-siv) *adj.*

in·cog′ni·to (in′kog nē′tō, in kog′ni tō′) *adj., adv.* with one's identity hidden.

in′come (in′kum) *n.* money received as wages, interest, etc.

in′com′ing *adj.* coming in.

in′com·mu′ni·ca′do (in′kə myōō′ni kä′dō) *adv., adj.* without means of communicating.

in·com′pa·ra·ble *adj.* **1.** beyond comparison. **2.** unequaled.

in′con·sid′er·ate *adj.* thoughtless.

in·con′ti·nent *adj.* **1.** unable to control discharges of urine or feces. **2.** lacking in moderation. —**in·con′ti·nence,** *n.*

in·cor′po·rate′ (-pə rāt′) *v.,* **-rated, -rating.** —*v.t.* **1.** to form into a corporation. **2.** to include as a part. —*v.i.* **3.** to form a corporation.

in′cor·po′re·al *adj.* not material.

in′cor·ri′gi·ble (in kôr′i jə bəl, -kor′-) *adj.* not able to be reformed.

in·crease′ *v.,* **-creased, -creasing.** —*v.t.,* *v.i.* (in krēs′) **1.** to make or become greater. —*n.* (in′krēs) **2.** the act or process of increasing. **3.** a growth or addition. —**in·creas′ing·ly,** *adv.*

in·cred′i·ble *adj.* unbelievable; amazing. —**in·cred′i·bly,** *adv.*

in·cred′u·lous *adj.* **1.** unbelieving. **2.** showing disbelief.

in′cre·ment (in′krə mənt, ing′-) *n.* an addition; increase. —**in′cre·men′tal** (-men′tl) *adj.*

in·crim′i·nate′ (in krim′ə nāt′) *v.t.,* **-nated, -nating.** to accuse of or indicate involvement in a crime. —**in·crim′i·na′tion,** *n.*

in′cu·bate′ (in′kyə bāt′, ing′-) *v.t.,* *v.i.,* **-bated, -bating.** to hatch (eggs) by warmth. —**in′cu·ba′tion,** *n.*

in′cu·ba′tor *n.* **1.** an apparatus for hatching eggs. **2.** an apparatus for warming premature infants.

in′cul·cate′ (in kul′kāt, in′kul kāt′) *v.t.,* **-cated, -cating.** to implant (habits) by repeated urging.

in·cum′bent (in kum′bənt) *adj.* **1.** currently holding an office. **2.** obligatory. —*n.* **3.** the holder of an office.

in·cur′ (in kûr′) *v.t.,* **-curred, -curring. 1.** to come into or acquire. **2.** to bring upon oneself.

in·cur′sion (in kûr′zhən, -shən) *n.* a hostile invasion; raid.

Ind. Indiana.

in·debt′ed *adj.* **1.** owing money. **2.** obligated for favors received.

in′de·ci′pher·a·ble *adj.* not able to be read or deciphered.

in′de·ci′sion *n.* the inability to decide. —**in′de·ci′sive,** *adj.*

in·deed′ (in dēd′) *adv.* **1.** in fact; truly. —*interj.* **2.** an exclamation of surprise or skepticism.

in′de·fat′i·ga·ble (in′di fat′i gə·bəl) *adj.* untiring.

in·del′i·ble (in del′ə bəl) *adj.* incapable of being removed or erased.

in·dem′ni·fy′ (in dem′nə fī′) *v.t.,* **-fied, -fying.** to compensate for or insure against damage or loss. —**in·dem′ni·ty,** *n.*

in·dent′ (in dent′) *v.t.* to set in from the margin.

in·den′ture (in den′chər) *n., v.,* **-tured, -turing.** —*n.* **1.** a contract binding a person to service. **2.** to bind by indenture.

in′de·pend′ent *adj.* **1.** free. **2.** not controlled by or dependent on others. —**in′de·pend′ence,** *n.*

in′-depth′ *adj.* intensive; thorough.

in′de·struct′i·ble *adj.* incapable of being destroyed.

in′dex (in′deks) *n., pl.* **-dexes, -dices** (-də sēz′) *v.* —*n.* **1.** (in a book) an alphabetical list of names, topics, etc., with page references. **2.** an indication. **3.** a number expressing a property or ratio, as of economic growth. —*v.t.* **4.** to provide with or enter in an index.

In′di·an *n.* **1.** an American Indian. **2.** any of the languages of the American Indians. **3.** a native of the Republic of India. —*adj.* **4.** of the American Indians or their languages. **5.** of India or S Asia.

In′dian sum′mer *n.* a period of mild, dry weather in late fall.

in′di·cate′ (in′di kāt′) *v.t.,* **-cated, -cating. 1.** to be a sign of. **2.** to point to. —**in′di·ca′tion,** *n.* —**in′di·ca′tor,** *n.*

in·dic′a·tive (-dik′ə tive) *adj.* **1.** pointing out. **2.** designating the verb mood used for ordinary statements and questions.

in·dict′ (in dīt′) *v.t.* to charge with a crime. —**in·dict′ment,** *n.*

in·dif′fer·ent *adj.* **1.** without interest or concern. **2.** not very good. —**in·dif′fer·ence,** *n.*

in·dig′e·nous (in dij′ə nəs) *adj.* native.

in′di·gent (in′di jənt) *adj.* needy; destitute. —**in′di·gence,** *n.*

in′di·ges′tion *n.* discomfort caused by difficulty in digesting food.

in′dig·na′tion (in′dig nā′shən) *n.* anger aroused by something unjust or offensive. —**in·dig′nant,** *adj.*

in·dig′ni·ty *n., pl.* **-ties.** an injury to a person's dignity; humiliation.

in′di·go (in′di gō′) *n., pl.* **-gos, -goes.** a deep blue color or dye.

in·dis·crim′i·nate (in′di skrim′ə nit) *adj.* **1.** lacking in care, judgment, etc. **2.** between together.

in′dis·posed′ *adj.* **1.** mildly ill. **2.** unwilling. —**in′dis·po·si′tion,** *n.*

in′dis·sol′u·ble (in′di sol′yə bəl) *adj.* unable to be dissolved, decomposed, undone, or destroyed.

in′di·vid′u·al (in′də vij′ōō əl) *adj.* **1.** single; particular. **2.** of, characteristic of, or for one person or thing only. —*n.* **3.** a single person, animal, or thing. —**in′di·vid′u·al′i·ty** (-al′i tē) *n.* —**in′di·vid′u·al·ly,** *adv.*

in′di·vid′u·al·ist *n.* a person who is very independent.

in·doc′tri·nate′ (in dok′trə nāt′) *v.t.,* **-nated, -nating.** to instruct in a doctrine or idea. —**in·doc′tri·na′tion,** *n.*

In′do-Eu·ro′pe·an (in′dō yōōr′ə·pē′ən) *n.* **1.** a family of languages spoken or formerly spoken in Europe and SW, central, and S Asia. —*adj.* **2.** of Indo-European.

in′do·lent (in′dl ənt) *adj.* lazy. —**in′do·lence,** *n.*

in·dom′i·ta·ble (in dom′i tə bəl) *adj.* incapable of being dominated.

in′door′ *adj.* located or used inside a building.

in·doors′ *adv.* in or into a building.

in·du′bi·ta·ble (in dōō′bi tə bəl, -dyōō′-) *adj.* not to be doubted.

in·duce′ (in dōōs′, -dyōōs′) *v.t.,* **-duced, -ducing. 1.** to persuade; influence. **2.** to cause; bring about. —**in·duce′ment,** *n.*

in·duct′ (in dukt′) *v.t.* to install in an office, military service, etc.

in·duc′tion *n.* **1.** reasoning from particular facts. **2.** an inducting or being inducted.

in·dulge′ (in dulj′) *v.t.,* **-dulged, -dulging. 1.** to yield to (desires, feelings, etc.). **2.** to yield to the wishes (of oneself or another). —**in·dul′gence,** *n.* —**in·dul′gent,** *adj.*

in·dus′tri·al *adj.* **1.** of, used in, or resulting from industry. **2.** having many industries.

in·dus′tri·al·ist *n.* the owner or manager of an industrial plant.

in·dus′tri·al·ize′ *v.t.,* **-ized, -izing.** —*v.t.* **1.** to introduce industry into. —*v.i.* **2.** to become industrial.

in·dus′tri·ous *adj.* hard-working.

in′dus·try (in′də strē) *n., pl.* **-tries. 1.** manufacture or production of goods. **2.** any general business activity. **3.** diligent work.

in·e′bri·ate′ *v.,* **-ated, -ating,** *n.* —*v.t.* (in ē′brē āt′) **1.** to make drunk. —*n.* (-it) **2.** a drunken person.

in·ef′fa·ble (in ef′ə bəl) *adj.* not able to be expressed in words.

in′ef·fec′tu·al *adj.* producing no effect.

in·ept′ (in ept′, i nept′) *adj.* **1.** incompetent. **2.** unsuitable. **3.** foolish. —**in·ept′i·tude′,** *n.*

in·eq′ui·ty *n., pl.* **-ties.** unfairness.

in·ert′ (in ûrt′, i nûrt′) *adj.* **1.** having no inherent power to move, resist, or act. **2.** slow-moving. **3.** having little or no ability to react chemically. —**in·er′tia,** *n.*

in·ev′i·ta·ble (in ev′i tə bəl) *adj.* not able to be avoided. —**in·ev′i·ta·bil′i·ty,** *n.* —**in·ev′i·ta·bly,** *adv.*

in·ex′o·ra·ble (in ek′sər ə bəl) *adj.* **1.** unyielding; relentless. **2.** not to be persuaded. —**in·ex′o·ra·bly,** *adv.*

in·ex′pert (in eks′pûrt, in′ik spûrt′) *adj.* unskilled.

in′ex·pli′ca·ble (in ek′spli kə bəl, in′ik splik′ə-) *adj.* incapable of being explained.

in′ex·tri′ca·ble (in ek′stri kə bəl, in′ik strik′ə-) *adj.* **1.** from which one cannot escape. **2.** incapable of being disentangled or loosed.

in·fal′li·ble (in fal′ə bəl) *adj.* never failing or making mistakes.

in′fa·mous (in′fə məs) *adj.* having or causing an evil reputation.

in′fa·my *n., pl.* **-mies. 1.** a very bad

reputation as the result of an outrageous act. **2.** an infamous act.

in′fant (in′fənt) *n.* a child during the earliest period of its life. —**in′fan·cy,** *n.* —**in′fan·tile** (-fan tīl′) *adj.*

in′fan·try (in′fan trē) *n., pl.* -**tries.** the branch of an army composed of soldiers who fight on foot. —**in′fan·try·man,** *n.*

in′farct′ (in′ färkt′, in färkt′) *n.* an area of dead or dying tissue, as in the heart. Also, **in·farc′tion.**

in·fat′u·ate′ (in fach′ŏŏ āt′) *v.t.,* -**ated, -ating.** to inspire with a foolish love or admiration. —**in·fat′u·a′tion,** *n.*

in·fect′ (in fekt′) *v.t.* to affect or contaminate with disease or germs. —**in·fec′tion,** *n.*

in·fec′tious *adj.* causing or communicable by infection.

in·fer′ (in fûr′) *v.t.,* -**ferred, -ferring.** to conclude by reasoning or from facts; deduce. —**in·fer′ence,** *n.*

in·fe′ri·or (in fēr′ē ər) *adj.* **1.** lower in rank, importance, quality, value, or position. —*n.* **2.** a person inferior to others. —**in·fe′ri·or′i·ty** (-ôr′i tē) *n.*

in·fer′nal (in fûr′nl) *adj.* hellish; diabolical. **2.** of hell.

in·fer′no (-nō) *n., pl.* -**nos. 1.** a place of intense heat. **2.** hell.

in·fest′ (in fest′) *v.t.* to overrun in a troublesome manner. —**in′fes·ta′tion,** *n.*

in′fi·del (in′fi dl, -del′) *n.* a person who does not believe in a religion.

in′field′ *n.* the area of a baseball field inside the base lines. —**in′field′er,** *n.*

in′fight′ing *n.* conflict within a group.

in·fil′trate (in fil′trāt, in′fil trāt′) *v.t., v.i.,* -**trated, -trating.** to move into (an organization, enemy area, etc.) gradually and without being noticed. —**in′fil·tra′tion,** *n.*

in′fi·nite (in′fə nit) *adj.* **1.** so great that it cannot be measured. **2.** endless. —*n.* **3.** something infinite. —**in·fin′i·ty** (in fin′i tē) *n.*

in′fin·i·tes′i·mal (in′fin i tes′ə məl) *adj.* exceedingly small.

in·fin′i·tive (in fin′i tiv) *n.* a verb form not indicating person, number, or tense, usu. preceded by *to* in English.

in·firm′ (-fûrm′) *adj.* feeble; weak. —**in·fir′mi·ty,** *n.*

in·fir′ma·ry (-fûr′mə rē) *n., pl.* -**ries.** a place for the care of the sick and injured.

in·flame′ *v.t., v.i.,* -**flamed, -flaming. 1.** to kindle or excite (passions, desires, etc.). **2.** to affect or become affected with inflammation.

in·flam′ma·ble (-flam′ə bəl) *adj.* **1.** capable of being set on fire. **2.** easily aroused to passion or anger.

in′flam·ma′tion (-flə mā′shən) *n.* redness, swelling, and fever in an area of the body in response to an infection or injury.

in·flam′ma·to′ry (-tô′rē) *adj.* **1.** tending to arouse anger, passion, etc. **2.** of or caused by inflammation.

in·flate′ (in flāt′) *v.,* -**flated, -flating.** —*v.t.* **1.** to fill with air or gas so as to expand. **2.** to increase unduly, as prices. —*v.i.* **3.** to become inflated.

in·fla′tion (-shən) *n.* **1.** a steady rise in prices resulting in a loss of the value of money. **2.** an inflating or being inflated.

in·flect′ *v.t.* **1.** to change the pitch of (the voice). **2.** to change the form of (a word) by inflection.

in·flict′ *v.t.* to cause (anything unwelcome) to be suffered.

in′flow′ *n.* **1.** a flowing in. **2.** something that flows in.

in′flu·ence (in′flōō əns) *n., v.,* -**enced, -encing.** —*n.* **1.** the power to affect another. **2.** something that does this. —*v.t.* **3.** to affect or alter. —**in′flu·en′tial** (-en′shəl) *adj.*

in′flu·en′za (-en′zə) *n.* a contagious viral disease with respiratory symptoms and fever.

in′flux′ *n.* a flowing or coming in.

in′fo·mer′cial (in′fō mûr′shəl) *n.* a program-length television commercial designed to appear to be standard programming.

in·form′ (in fôrm′) *v.t.* **1.** to supply with information. —*v.i.* **2.** to give incriminating evidence about someone. —**in·form′ant,** *n.* —**in·form′er,** *n.* —**in·form′a·tive,** *adj.*

in′for·ma′tion (-fər mā′shən) *n.* knowledge given or received concerning particular facts. —**in′for·ma′tion·al,** *adj.*

in′for·ma′tion su′perhighway *n.*

a large-scale communications network linking computers, television sets, etc.

in′fo·tain′ment (in′fō tān′mənt) *n.* broadcasting or publishing that treats factual matter in an entertaining way, as by dramatizing real events.

in′fra (in′frə) *adv.* below, esp. in a text.

in·frac′tion (in frak′shən) *n.* a violation.

in′fra·red′ *adj.* of or using invisible radiation wavelengths that are just longer than red in the visible spectrum.

in′fra·struc′ture *n.* **1.** the basic framework of a system or organization. **2.** basic facilities, as transportation.

in·fringe′ (in frinj′) *v.,* -**fringed, -fringing.** —*v.t.* **1.** to violate. —*v.i.* **2.** to trespass or encroach on.

in·fu′ri·ate (in fyŏŏr′ē āt′) *v.t.,* -**ated, -ating.** to make very angry.

in·fuse′ (in fyōōz′) *v.t.,* -**fused, -fusing. 1.** to put into as if by pouring. **2.** to fill with something. **3.** to soak (as tea or herbs) to extract the flavor. —**in·fu′sion,** *n.*

in·gen′ious (in jēn′yəs) *adj.* cleverly inventive. —**in′ge·nu′i·ty** (in′jə nōō′i tē, -nyōō′-) *n.*

in′ge·nue′ (an′zhə nōō′) *n.* an artless, innocent young woman or such a role in a play.

in·gen′u·ous (in jen′yōō əs) *adj.* free from deceit; innocent.

in·gest′ (in jest′) *v.t.* to take into the body, as food or liquid.

in′got (ing′gət) *n.* a mass of metal cast in a form.

in·grained′ *adj.* fixed firmly in a surface or a person's character.

in′grate *n.* an ungrateful person.

in·gra′ti·ate′ (in grā′shē āt′) *v.t.,* -**ated, -ating.** to get (oneself) into someone's favor, esp. to gain an advantage.

in·gre′di·ent (in grē′dē ənt) *n.* an element or part of a mixture.

in′gress (in′gres) *n.* the act of entering. **2.** the right to enter.

in·hab′it (in hab′it) *v.t.* to live in. —**in·hab′it·ant,** *n.*

in′ha·la′tor (in′hə lā′tər) *n.* an apparatus to help one inhale anesthetics, medicine, etc. **2.** a respirator.

in·hale′ (in hāl′) *v.t., v.i.,* -**haled, -haling.** to breathe in. —**in′ha·la′tion,** *n.*

in·hal′er *n.* **1.** an inhalator. **2.** a person who inhales.

in·here′ (in hēr′) *v.i.,* -**hered, -hering.** to be an inseparable part or element. —**in·her′ent** (-hēr′ənt, -her′-) *adj.*

in·her′it (in her′it) *v.t., v.i.* **1.** to receive (property, a title, etc.) by succession or will, esp. from someone who has died. **2.** to receive (a characteristic) from one's parents. —**in·her′it·ance,** *n.*

in·hib′it (in hib′it) *v.t.* to restrain or hinder. —**in′hi·bi′tion,** *n.*

in′house′ (*adj.* in′hous′; *adv.* -hous′) *adj., adv.* using an organization's own staff or resources.

in·hu′man *adj.* **1.** brutal; very cruel. **2.** not human. —**in′hu·man′i·ty,** *n.*

in·im′i·cal (i nim′i kəl) *adj.* hostile.

in·im′i·ta·ble (i nim′i tə bəl) *adj.* not able to be imitated.

in·iq′ui·ty (i nik′wi tē) *n., pl.* -**ties. 1.** great injustice. **2.** a wicked act.

in·i′tial (i nish′əl) *adj., n., v.,* -**tialed, -tialing.** —*adj.* **1.** of or occurring at the beginning. —*n.* **2.** the first letter of a word or a proper name. —*v.t.* **3.** to sign with initials. —**in·i′tial·ly,** *adv.*

in·i′ti·ate′ (i nish′ē āt′) *v.t.,* -**ated, -ating. 1.** to begin. **2.** to instruct in some subject. **3.** to admit into membership. —**in·i′ti·a′tion,** *n.*

in·i′ti·a·tive (i nish′ē ə tiv, i nish′ə-) *n.* **1.** an introductory step. **2.** readiness and ability to take action.

in·ject′ (in jekt′) *v.t.* **1.** to force (a fluid), as into tissue. **2.** to introduce (a remark), as into a conversation. —**in·jec′tion,** *n.*

in·junc′tion (in jungk′shən) *n.* a court order.

in′jure (in′jər) *v.t.,* -**jured, -juring. 1.** to cause harm to. **2.** to treat unjustly. —**in·ju′ri·ous** (-jŏŏr′ē əs) *adj.* —**in′ju·ry,** *n.*

ink (ingk) *n.* **1.** a colored writing fluid. —*v.t.* **2.** to mark with ink. —**ink′y,** *adj.*

ink′ling (ingk′ling) *n.* a slight suggestion.

in′land (*adj.* in′lənd; *adv.* -land′, -lənd) *adj.* **1.** of or in the interior of

a region. —*adv.* **2.** of or toward an inland area.

in′-law′ *n.* a relative by marriage.

in·lay′ *v.,* -**laid, -laying,** *n.* —*v.t.* (in′lā′, in′lā′) **1.** to insert (pieces of wood, ivory, etc.) in a surface. —*n.* (in′lā′) **2.** an inlaid design.

in′let (-let, -lit) *n.* a narrow bay.

in′line skate′ *n.* a roller skate with four wheels in a straight line.

in′mate′ *n.* a person confined in a prison, hospital, etc.

in me·mo′ri·am (in mə môr′ē əm) *prep.* in memory (of).

in′most′ *adj.* farthest within. Also, **in′ner·most′.**

inn *n.* **1.** a hotel. **2.** a tavern.

in·nards (in′ərdz) *n.pl.* the internal parts.

in·nate′ (i nāt′, in′āt) *adj.* existing in one from birth.

in′ner (in′ər) *adj.* **1.** being farther within. **2.** internal.

in′ner cit′y *n.* a central part of a city.

in′ning (in′ing) *n. Baseball.* one round of play for both teams.

in′no·cence (in′ə səns) *n.* **1.** freedom from guilt or evil. **2.** lack of worldly knowledge. —**in′no·cent,** *adj., n.*

in·noc′u·ous (i nok′yŏŏ əs) *adj.* harmless.

in′no·vate′ (in′ə vāt′) *v.i., v.t.,* -**vated, -vating.** to bring in (something new). —**in′no·va′tion,** *n.* —**in′no·va′tor,** *n.* —**in′no·va′tive,** *adj.*

in′nu·en′do (in′yŏŏ en′dō) *n., pl.* -**dos, -does.** an indirect, usu. disparaging, remark.

in·nu′mer·a·ble *adj.* too numerous to be counted.

in·oc′u·late′ (in nok′yə lāt′) *v.t.,* -**lated, -lating.** to inject a vaccine into (a person or animal) to protect against a disease. —**in·oc′u·la′tion,** *n.*

in·or′di·nate (in ôr′dn it) *adj.* excessive. —**in·or′di·nate·ly,** *adv.*

in·pa′tient *n.* a patient who stays in a hospital while receiving treatment.

in′put′ *n., v.,* -**putted** or -**put, -putting.** —*n.* **1.** something that is put in. **2.** data put into a computer. —*v.t.* **3.** to enter (data) into a computer.

in′quest *n.* a judicial inquiry, esp. one into a death.

in·quire′ (in kwīr′) *v.i.,* -**quired, -quiring.** to seek information by questioning; investigate. —**in·quir′y** (in kwīr′ē, in′kwə rē) *n.*

in′qui·si′tion (in′kwə zish′ən, ing′-) *n.* **1.** an official investigation. **2.** harsh and prolonged questioning. —**in·quis′i·tor,** *n.*

in·quis′i·tive (-kwiz′i tiv) *adj.* very curious.

in′road′ *n.* **1.** an intrusion on someone's territory or rights. **2.** a hostile attack.

in·sane′ (in sān′) *adj.* **1.** mentally deranged. **2.** very foolish. —**in·san′i·ty** (-san′i tē) *n.*

in·sa′tia·ble (in sā′shə bəl, -shē ə-) *adj.* incapable of being satisfied.

in·scribe′ (in skrīb′) *v.t.,* -**scribed, -scribing.** to write or engrave. —**in·scrip′tion** (-skrip′shən) *n.*

in·scru′ta·ble (in skrŏŏ′tə bəl) *adj.* not easily understood; mysterious. —**in·scru′ta·bil′i·ty,** *n.*

in′sect (in′sekt) *n.* a small six-legged creature having a body divided into three parts.

in·sec′ti·cide′ (-sek′tə sīd′) *n.* a substance used for killing insects.

in·sem′i·nate′ (in sem′ə nāt′) *v.t.,* -**nated, -nating.** to insert semen into. —**in·sem′i·na′tion,** *n.*

in·sen′sate (in sen′sāt, -sit) *adj.* without feeling or sensitivity.

in·sen′si·ble *adj.* **1.** incapable of feeling or perceiving. **2.** unaware; unconscious. —**in·sen′si·bil′i·ty,** *n.*

in·sert′ *v.t.* (in sûrt′) **1.** to put or place in. —*n.* (in′sûrt) **2.** something inserted. —**in·ser′tion,** *n.*

in′shore′ *adj.* **1.** on or close to the shore. —*adv.* **2.** toward the shore.

in′side′ (in′sīd′, in′sīd′) *n.* **1.** the inner part or side. —*adj.* **2.** inner. —*adv.* **3.** in or into the inner part. —*prep.* **4.** on or to the inside of.

in·sid′er *n.* a person who has influence, esp. one privy to confidential information.

in·sid′i·ous (in sid′ē əs) *adj.* proceeding harmfully without being noticed.

in′sight′ *n.* understanding of the true nature of something.

in·sig′ni·a (in sig′nē ə) *n., pl.* -**nia**

or -**nias.** a badge or other symbol of rank, honor, etc.

in·sin′u·ate′ (in sin′yŏŏ āt′) *v.t.,* -**ated, -ating. 1.** to hint slyly. **2.** to instill or insert subtly or artfully. —**in·sin′u·a′tion,** *n.*

in·sip′id (in sip′id) *adj.* lacking interest or color; dull.

in·sist′ (in sist′) *v.i.* **1.** to be firm or persistent. —*v.t.* **2.** to assert emphatically. —**in·sist′ence,** *n.* —**in·sist′ent,** *adj.*

in′so·far′ *adv.* to such an extent.

in′sole′ *n.* **1.** the inner sole of a shoe. **2.** a removable sole put into a shoe for comfort.

in′so·lent (in′sə lənt) *adj.* disrespectful. —**in′so·lence,** *n.*

in·sol′vent *adj.* unable to pay one's debts. —**in·sol′ven·cy,** *n.*

in·som′ni·a (in som′nē ə) *n.* sleeplessness. —**in·som′ni·ac′,** *n., adj.*

in′so·much′ *adv.* **1.** to such a degree (that). **2.** inasmuch (as).

in·sou′ci·ant (in sōō′sē ənt) *adj.* free from care.

in·spect′ (in spekt′) *v.t.* to look over carefully or officially. —**in·spec′tion,** *n.*

in·spec′tor *n.* **1.** a person who inspects. **2.** a police official.

in·spire′ (in spīr′) *v.t.,* -**spired, -spiring. 1.** to animate. **2.** to arouse (a feeling, thought, etc.). **3.** to prompt to action. —**in′spi·ra′tion** (in′spə rā′shən) *n.* —**in·spi·ra′tion·al,** *adj.*

Inst. 1. Institute. **2.** Institution.

in·stall′ (in stôl′) *v.t.* **1.** to put in position for use. **2.** to establish. **3.** to place (a person) in office formally. —**in′stal·la′tion,** *n.*

in·stall′ment *n.* a division, as of a payment or story.

install′ment plan′ *n.* a system for paying for an item in installments.

in′stance (in′stəns) *n., v.,* -**stanced, -stancing. 1.** a particular case. **2.** an example. —*v.t.* **3.** to cite as an instance.

in′stant *n.* **1.** a moment. **2.** a particular moment. —*adj.* **3.** immediate. —**in′stant·ly,** *adv.*

in′stan·ta′ne·ous (-stən tā′nē əs) *adj.* occurring in an instant.

in·stead′ (in sted′) *adv.* as a substitute.

in′step′ *n.* the upper arch of the foot.

in′sti·gate′ (in′sti gāt′) *v.t.,* -**gated, -gating.** to incite or provoke to some action. —**in′sti·ga′tor,** *n.*

in·still′ *v.t.* to introduce slowly.

in′stinct (in′stingkt) *n.* **1.** a natural impulse. **2.** a natural tendency or talent. —**in·stinc′tive,** *adj.*

in′sti·tute′ (in′sti tōōt′, -tyōōt′) *v.,* -**tuted, -tuting.** —*v.t.* **1.** to establish. **2.** to start. —*n.* **3.** a society for promoting the arts, scientific research, etc.

in′sti·tu′tion *n.* **1.** an organization devoted to the promotion of a public cause. **2.** the building occupied by such an organization. **3.** an established tradition, rule, etc. **4.** a place for the care or confinement of people. —**in′sti·tu′tion·al,** *adj.* —**in′sti·tu′tion·al·ize′,** *v.t.*

in·struct′ (in strukt′) *v.t.* **1.** to teach. **2.** to direct; command. —**in·struc′tion,** *n.* —**in·struc′tive,** *adj.* —**in·struc′tor,** *n.*

in′stru·ment (in′strə mənt) *n.* **1.** a tool, esp. one for precision work. **2.** a device for producing music. **3.** a means; agent. **4.** a device for monitoring or controlling. **5.** a legal document. —**in′stru·men′tal** (-men′tl) *adj.*

in′su·lar (in′sə lər, ins′yə-) *adj.* **1.** of islands. **2.** narrow in viewpoint.

in′su·late′ (-lāt′) *v.t.,* -**lated, -lating. 1.** to cover with a material that prevents passage of heat, electricity, or sound. **2.** to place in an isolated situation. —**in′su·la′tion,** *n.* —**in′su·la′tor,** *n.*

in′su·lin (in′sə lin, ins′yə-) *n.* a hormone that regulates the body's absorption of sugar and other nutrients.

in·sult′ *v.t.* (in sult′) **1.** to treat with contemptuous rudeness. —*n.* (in′sult) **2.** a contemptuously rude remark or act.

in·su′per·a·ble (in sōō′pər ə bəl) *adj.* unable to be overcome.

in·sure′ *v.t.,* -**sured, -suring. 1.** to guarantee compensation for loss, damage, etc. **2.** to make certain. —**in·sur′ance,** *n.* —**in·sur′er,** *n.*

in·sur′gent (in sûr′jənt) *n.* **1.** a rebel. —*adj.* **2.** rebellious.

in′sur·rec′tion (in′sə rek′shən) *n.* an armed rebellion.

in·tact′ (in takt′) *adj.* undamaged.

in·tagl′io (in tal′yō, -tāl′-) *n., pl.* -**taglios, -tagli** (-tal′yē, -tāl′yē-). a design carved into rather than projecting from a surface.

in′take′ *n.* **1.** the point at which something is taken in. **2.** the act of taking in. **3.** a quantity taken in.

in′te·ger (in′ti jər) *n.* a whole number.

in′te·gral (in′ti grəl, in teg′rəl) *adj.* necessary to form a whole.

in′te·grate′ (in′ti grāt′) *v.,* -**grated, -grating.** —*v.t.* **1.** to bring together into a unified whole. **2.** to make (a school, neighborhood, etc.) available to all racial or ethnic groups. —**in′te·gra′tion,** *n.*

in·teg′ri·ty (in teg′ri tē) *n.* **1.** honesty. **2.** the state of being whole.

in·teg′u·ment (in teg′yə mənt) *n.* a skin, rind, etc.

in′tel·lect′ (in′tl ekt′) *n.* the mind's power of reasoning and understanding.

in′tel·lec′tu·al *adj.* **1.** appealing to or relying on the intellect. **2.** having a strong intellect. —*n.* **3.** a person who pursues intellectual interests.

in·tel′li·gence (in tel′i jəns) *n.* **1.** ability to learn, reason, and understand. **2.** information, esp. secret information about an enemy. **3.** an organization that gathers secret information.

in·tel′li·gent *adj.* having a high mental capacity.

in·tel′li·gi·ble (-jə bəl) *adj.* understandable. —**in·tel′li·gi·bil′i·ty,** *n.*

in·tend′ (in tend′) *v.t.* to have in mind as something to be done.

in·tend′ed *n. Informal.* the person one plans to marry.

in·tense′ (in tens′) *adj.* **1.** existing in a high or extreme degree. **2.** having strong feeling. —**in·ten′si·fy′,** *v.t., v.i.* —**in·ten′si·ty,** *n.*

in·ten′sive *adj.* thorough.

in·tent′ *n.* (in tent′) **1.** something intended. **2.** the act of intending. —*Idiom.* **3.** to or for all intents and purposes, practically speaking.

in·tent′ [2] (in tent′) *adj.* **1.** firmly fixed or directed. **2.** having the attention sharply focused. **3.** determined. —**in·tent′ly,** *adv.*

in·ten′tion *n.* **1.** purpose. **2.** meaning. —**in·ten′tion·al,** *adj.*

in·ter′ (in tûr′) *v.t.,* -**terred, -terring.** to bury (a body).

inter- a prefix meaning: **1.** between or among. **2.** reciprocally.

in′ter·act′ (in′tər akt′) *v.i.* to act upon one another. —**in′ter·ac′tion,** *n.* —**in′ter·ac′tive,** *adj.*

in′ter·breed′ *v.t., v.i.,* -**bred, -breeding.** to crossbreed (a plant or animal).

in′ter·cede′ (-sēd′) *v.i.,* -**ceded, -ceding.** to act or plead in behalf of one in trouble. —**in′ter·ces′sion,** *n.*

in′ter·cept′ (-sept′) *v.t.* to stop or interrupt the course or progress of.

in′ter·change′ *v.,* -**changed, -changing,** *n.* —*v.t.* (in′tər chānj′) **1.** to put each in the place of the other. **2.** to exchange. —*n.* (in′tər·chānj′) **3.** an act of interchanging. **4.** a highway intersection that allows vehicles to move without crossing the streams of traffic.

in′ter·con·ti·nen′tal *adj.* between or among continents.

in′ter·course′ *n.* **1.** dealings among individuals or nations. **2.** sexual relations; coitus.

in′ter·de·nom′i·na′tion·al *adj.* between or involving different religious denominations.

in′ter·de·pend′ent *adj.* mutually dependent. —**in′ter·de·pend′ence,** *n.*

in′ter·dict′ *n.* (in′tər dikt′) **1.** a decree that prohibits. —*v.t.* (in′tər dikt′) **2.** to prohibit officially. —**in′ter·dic′tion,** *n.*

in′ter·est (in′tər ist, -trist) *n.* **1.** a feeling of attention, curiosity, etc. **2.** the object of one's attention, curiosity, etc. **3.** a business, cause, etc., in which a person has a share. **4.** advantage. **5. a.** a sum charged for borrowing money. **b.** the rate for such charge. —*v.t.* **6.** to excite or hold the attention of.

in′ter·est·ing (-tər ə sting, -trə sting, -tə res′ting) *adj.* engaging the attention or curiosity.

in′ter·face′ *n., v.,* -**faced, -facing.** —*n.* (in′tər fās′) **1.** a common boundary. **2.** computer hardware or software that communicates information between entities. —*v.t., v.i.* (in′tər fās′, in′tər fās′) **3.** to interact or coordinate smoothly.

in′ter·fere′ (-fēr′) *v.i.,* -**fered, -fering. 1.** to hamper or obstruct ac-

tion. 2. to meddle. —**in·ter·fer·ence,** n.

in·ter·im (in'tər əm) n. 1. an intervening time. —adj. 2. temporary.

in·te·ri·or (in tēr'ē ər) adj. 1. inner. —n. 2. the inner part.

in·ter·ject' (in'tər jekt') v.t. to insert abruptly between other things.

in·ter·jec'tion (-jek'shən) n. 1. the act of interjecting. 2. something interjected. 3. an exclamation that expresses emotion, as indeed!

in·ter·lace' v.i., v.t., -laced, -lacing. to unite by weaving together.

in·ter·lock' v.i., v.t. to lock, join, or fit together closely.

in·ter·loc·u·tor (-lok'yə tər) n. a participant in a conversation.

in·ter·loc·u·to·ry (-tôr'ē) adj. Law. (of a decision or decree) not final.

in·ter·lop·er (-lō'pər) n. an intruder.

in·ter·lude' (-lōōd') n. 1. an intervening episode, period, or space. 2. something performed in this.

in·ter·mar'ry v.i., -ried, -rying. 1. to become connected by marriage. 2. to marry outside one's religion, ethnic group, etc. —**in'ter·mar'riage,** n.

in·ter·me·di·ar·y (-mē'dē er'ē) adj., n., pl. -aries. —adj. 1. being between; intermediate. —n. 2. an intermediate agent; mediator.

in·ter·me·di·ate (-it) adj. being or acting between two points, stages, etc.

in·ter·ment (in tûr'mənt) n. burial.

in·ter·mez'zo (in'tər met'sō, -med'zō) n., pl. -mezzos, -mezzi (-met'sē, -med'zē). a short musical composition, as between divisions of a longer work.

in·ter·mi·na·ble (in tûr'mə nə bəl) adj. seeming to be without end; endless. —**in·ter·mi·na·bly,** adv.

in·ter·mis·sion (in'tər mish'ən) n. an interval between periods of action, as between the acts in a play.

in·ter·mit·tent (-mit'nt) adj. alternately ceasing and starting again.

in·tern¹ (in'tûrn) n. 1. a recent medical school graduate serving under supervision in a hospital. 2. someone working as a trainee to gain experience. —v.i. 3. to serve as an intern. —**in'tern·ship,** n.

in·tern² (in tûrn') v.t. to confine within limits, as prisoners of war. —**in·tern'ment,** n.

in·ter·nal (in tûr'nl) adj. 1. inner. 2. not foreign; domestic.

inter'nal med'icine n. the diagnosis and nonsurgical treatment of diseases.

in·ter·na·tion·al adj. 1. among nations. 2. of many nations. —**in'ter·na'tion·al·ize,** v.t., v.i.

in·ter·na·tion·al·ize v.t., v.i., -ized, -izing. 1. to make international. 2. to bring under international control.

in·ter·ne·cine (-nē'sēn, -sīn, -nes'ēn, -nē'sin) adj. involving conflict within a group.

In·ter·net' n. a large computer network linking smaller networks worldwide.

in·tern·ist (in'tûr nist, in tûr'nist) n. a doctor specializing in internal medicine.

in·ter·per·son·al adj. between persons.

in·ter·plan·e·tar·y adj. between planets.

in·ter·play n. reciprocal relationship or action.

in·ter·po·late (in tûr'pə lāt') v.t., -lated, -lating. to insert to alter or clarify meaning.

in·ter·pose' v.t., v.i., -posed, -posing. 1. to place or come between (other things). 2. to intervene.

in·ter·pret (in tûr'prit) v.t. 1. to explain the meaning of. 2. to translate. —**in·ter·pre·ta'tion,** n. —**in·ter'pret·er,** n.

in·ter·ra·cial adj. of, for, or between persons of different races.

in·ter·re·lat·ed adj. closely associated.

in·ter·ro·gate' (in ter'ə gāt') v.t., v.i., -gated, -gating. to question, esp. formally. —**in·ter'ro·ga'tion,** n. —**in·ter'rog·a·tive** (-ter'ə rog'ə tiv) adj. —**in·ter'ro·ga'tor,** n.

in·ter·rupt' (in'tə rupt') v.t. 1. to break the continuity of. 2. to stop (a person) in the midst of something. —v.i. 3. to interfere with action or speech. —**in'ter·rup'tion,** n.

in·ter·scho·las'tic adj. existing or occurring between schools.

in·ter·sect' (-sekt') v.t. to divide by crossing; cross.

in·ter·sec'tion n. 1. a place where roads meet. 2. an intersecting.

in·ter·sperse' (-spûrs') v.t., -spersed, -spersing. to scatter here and there.

in·ter·state' adj. connecting or involving different states.

in·ter·stel·lar adj. situated or occurring between the stars.

in·ter'stice (in tûr'stis) n. a small space between things.

in·ter·twine' v.t., v.i., -twined, -twining. to unite by twining together.

in·ter·ur·ban adj. between cities.

in·ter·val (in'tər vəl) n. 1. an intervening period of time. 2. a space between things. 3. the difference in musical pitch between two tones.

in·ter·vene' (-vēn') v.i., -vened, -vening. 1. to come between disputing people. 2. to occur between other events or periods. —**in'ter·ven'tion** (-ven'shən) n.

in·ter·view' n. 1. a formal meeting to assess someone or to get information from someone. —v.t. 2. to have an interview with.

in·tes·tate (in tes'tāt, -tit) adj. not having made a will.

in·tes·tine (in tes'tin) n. the lower part of the alimentary canal. —**in·tes'ti·nal,** adj.

in·ti·mate¹ (in'tə mit) adj. 1. having a close personal relationship. 2. private or personal. —n. 3. an intimate friend. —**in'ti·ma·cy** (-mə sē) n.

in·ti·mate² (in'tə māt') v.t., -mated, -mating. to make known indirectly; imply. —**in'ti·ma'tion,** n.

in·tim·i·date (in tim'i dāt') v.t., -dated, -dating. 1. to make fearful. 2. to force into or deter from some action by causing fear. —**in·tim'i·da'tion,** n.

in·to (in'tōō; unstressed -tŏŏ, -tə) prep. 1. to the inside of. 2. toward or in the direction of. 3. to a particular action, circumstance, etc.

in·tone' v.t., -toned, -toning. 1. to use a particular spoken tone. 2. to chant.

in·tox·i·cate' (in tok'si kāt') v.t., -cated, -cating. 1. to make drunk. 2. to make extremely happy.

in·trac·ta·ble adj. hard to manage or deal with.

in·tra·mu·ral (in'trə myŏŏr'əl) adj. within one school.

in·tra·net' (in'trə net') n. a computer network with restricted access, as within a corporation, that uses Internet technology.

in·tran·si·gent (in tran'si jənt) adj. refusing to compromise. —**in·tran'si·gence,** n.

in·tran·si·tive (-tiv) adj. (of a verb) not taking a direct object.

in·tra·ve·nous (in'trə vē'nəs) adj. within or into a vein.

in·trep·id (in trep'id) adj. fearless.

in·tri·cate (in'tri kit) adj. very complicated. —**in'tri·ca·cy** (-kə sē) n.

in·trigue' (in trēg') v., -trigued, -triguing. —v.t. (in trēg') 1. to arouse the curiosity of. —v.i. 2. to plot craftily. —n. (in trēg', in'trēg) 3. a crafty design or plot.

in·tro·duce' (in'trə dōōs', -dyōōs') v.t., -duced, -ducing. 1. to make (a person) known to another. 2. to bring into notice or use. 3. to begin. —**in'tro·duc'tion** (-duk'shən) n. —**in'tro·duc'to·ry** (-duk'tə rē) adj.

in·tro·spec'tion (in'trə spek'shən) n. examination of one's own thoughts and motives. —**in'tro·spec'tive,** adj.

in·tro·vert' (-vûrt') n. a shy person concerned chiefly with inner thoughts or feelings. —**in'tro·ver'sion** (-vûr'zhən) n. —**in'tro·vert'ed,** adj.

in·trude' (in trōōd') v., -truded, -truding. —v.t. 1. to thrust in. —v.i. 2. to come in without welcome. —**in·tru'sion** (-trōō'zhən) n. —**in·tru'sive** (-siv) adj.

in·tu·i·tion (in'tōō ish'ən, -tyōō-) n. direct perception of truth, fact, etc., without reasoning. —**in·tu'i·tive** (-i tiv) adj. —**in·tu'i·tive·ly,** adv.

in·un·date (in'ən dāt', -un-) v.t., -dated, -dating. 1. to flood. 2. to overwhelm. —**in'un·da'tion,** n.

in·ure' (in yŏŏr', i nŏŏr') v.t., -ured, -uring. to toughen or accustom.

in·vade' (in vād') v.t., -vaded, -vading. 1. to enter as an enemy. 2. to enter and cause harm. —**in·vad'er,** n. —**in·va'sion** (-vā'zhən) n.

in·val·id¹ (in'və lid) n. 1. a sickly or infirm person. —adj. 2. unable to care for oneself due to illness or disability. 3. of or for invalids.

in·val·id² (in val'id) adj. without force or foundation; not valid.

in·val·i·date (in val'i dāt') v.t., -dated, -dating. to make invalid.

in·val·u·a·ble adj. priceless.

in·vec·tive (in vek'tiv) n. vehement denunciation or abuse.

in·veigh' (in vā') v.i. to attack violently with words.

in·vei·gle (in vā'gəl, -vē'-) v.t., -gled, -gling. to lure or entice.

in·vent' v.t. 1. to devise (something new). 2. to make up. —**in·ven'tion,** n. —**in·ven'tive,** adj. —**in·ven'tor,** n.

—**Usage.** See DISCOVER.

in·ven·to·ry (in'vən tôr'ē) n., pl. -tories. a list of stock or goods.

in·verse' (in vûrs', in'vûrs) adj. reversed in position or direction.

in·vert' (-vûrt') v.t. 1. to turn upside down. 2. to reverse in position, direction, or relationship. —**in·ver'sion,** n.

in·ver·te·brate adj. 1. without a backbone. —n. 2. an invertebrate animal.

in·vest' v.t. 1. to put (money) to use in hope of profit. 2. to give or devote (time, effort, etc.). 3. to give power or authority to. —**in·vest'ment,** n. —**in·ves'tor,** n.

in·ves·ti·gate' (in ves'ti gāt') v.t., v.i., -gated, -gating. to search or inquire (into) systematically. —**in·ves'ti·ga'tion,** n. —**in·ves'ti·ga'tive,** adj. —**in·ves'ti·ga'tor,** n.

in·vet·er·ate (in vet'ər it) adj. confirmed in habit, feeling, etc.

in·vid·i·ous (in vid'ē əs) adj. likely to cause ill will.

in·vig·or·ate' (in vig'ə rāt') v.t., -ated, -ating. to fill with energy.

in·vin·ci·ble (in vin'sə bəl) adj. unable to be conquered. —**in·vin'ci·bil'i·ty,** n.

in·vi·o·la·ble (in vī'ə lə bəl) adj. incapable of being violated or destroyed.

in·vi·o·late (-lit, -lāt') adj. free from violation, injury, or desecration.

in·vite' (-vīt') v.t., -vited, -viting. 1. to request the presence of. 2. to ask politely. 3. to act so as to bring on. 4. to attract. —**in'vi·ta'tion** (in'vi·tā'shən) n.

in·vit'ing adj. attractive or tempting.

in vi·tro (in vē'trō) adj. (of a biological entity or process) developed or maintained in a controlled nonliving environment, as a laboratory vessel.

in·vo·ca·tion (in'və kā'shən) n. a prayer for aid, guidance, etc.

in·voice (in'vois) n., v., -voiced, -voicing. —n. 1. an itemized bill with the prices of goods sent or services provided to a buyer. —v.t. 2. to present an invoice to or for.

in·voke' (in vōk') v.t., -voked, -voking. 1. to beg for. 2. to call on in prayer. 3. to cite as authoritative.

in·vol·un·tar·y adj. 1. unintentional. 2. without conscious control.

in·volve' (in volv') v.t., -volved, -volving. 1. to include as a necessary consequence. 2. to include within itself. 3. to bring into a troublesome matter. 4. to preoccupy. —**in·volve'ment,** n.

in·ward (in'wərd) adv. 1. Also, **in'wards.** toward the inside. —adj. 2. situated on or directed toward the inside. 3. mental or spiritual. —**in'ward·ly,** adv.

in'-your-face' adj. Informal. involving confrontation; defiant.

I/O input/output.

i·o·dine (ī'ə dīn', -din; in Chem. also -dēn') n. a nonmetallic element used in medicine and dyes.

i·on (ī'ən, ī'on) n. an electrically charged particle.

-ion a suffix meaning: action or process; result of action; state or condition.

i·on·ize (ī'ə nīz') v., -nized, -nizing. —v.t. 1. to separate or change into ions. 2. to produce ions in. —v.i. 3. to become ionized. —**i·on·i·za'tion,** n.

i·on·o·sphere (ī on'ə sfēr') n. the outermost region of the earth's atmosphere, consisting of ionized layers.

i·o·ta (ī ō'tə) n., pl. -tas. 1. a very small quantity. 2. the ninth letter of the Greek alphabet.

IOU n., pl. IOUs, IOU's. a written acknowledgment of a debt.

ip·so fac·to (ip'sō fak'tō) adv. by the fact itself.

IQ intelligence quotient.

IRA (pronounced as initials or ī'rə) individual retirement account.

I·ra·ni·an (i rā'nē ən, i rä'-) adj. 1. of Iran or its inhabitants. 2. of one of the two major branches of the Indo-Iranian languages. —n. 3. the Iranian languages. 4. a native of Iran.

I·ra·qi (i rak'ē, i rä'kē) adj., n., pl. -qis. 1. of Iraq or its people. —n. 2. a native of Iraq.

ire (ī°r) n. anger. —**i·rate'** (ī rāt', ī'rāt) adj.

ir·i·des·cence (ir'i des'əns) n. a display of lustrous colors like a rainbow. —**ir'i·des'cent,** adj.

i·ris (ī'ris) n. 1. the colored part of the eye. 2. a perennial plant with flowers having three upright petals.

I·rish (ī'rish) n. 1. the natives of Ireland. 2. the Celtic language of Ireland. —adj. 3. of Ireland, its inhabitants, or their language.

irk (ûrk) v.t. to irritate or annoy. —**irk'some,** adj.

i·ron (ī'ərn) n. 1. a hard gray metallic element, used for making tools, machinery, etc. 2. something made of iron. 3. an appliance with a flat metal bottom for pressing cloth. 4. irons, shackles. 5. of or like iron. —v.t., v.i. 6. to press with a heated iron.

i·ron·clad' adj. 1. iron-plated, as a ship. 2. very rigid or exacting.

i'ron cur'tain n. (formerly) a barrier between the Soviet bloc and other countries after World War II.

i·ro·ny (ī'rə nē, ī'ər-) n., pl. -nies. 1. the use of words to convey a meaning that is the opposite of the literal meaning. 2. an outcome contrary to expectations. —**i·ron'ic** (ī ron'ik) adj.

ir·ra·di·ate' (i rā'dē āt') v.t., -ated, -ating. 1. to shed rays of light upon. 2. to expose to radiation.

ir·ra·tion·al (i rash'ə nl) adj. lacking reason or judgment.

ir·rec·on·cil·a·ble (i rek'ən sī'lə bəl) adj. unable to be brought into agreement.

ir·re·deem·a·ble (ir'i dē'mə bəl) adj. not able to be redeemed.

ir·re·duc·i·ble (ir'i dōō'sə bəl, -dyōō'-) adj. not able to be reduced.

ir·ref·u·ta·ble (i ref'yə tə bəl) adj. impossible to refute.

ir·reg·u·lar (i reg'yə lər) adj. 1. not symmetrical. 2. not conforming to established rules.

ir·rel·e·vant (i rel'ə vənt) adj. not relevant or pertinent. —**ir·rel'e·vance,** n.

ir·re·li·gious (ir'i lij'əs) adj. 1. not practicing a religion. 2. hostile to religion.

ir·rep·a·ra·ble (i rep'ər ə bəl) adj. incapable of being made good or remedied.

ir·re·press·i·ble (ir'i pres'ə bəl) adj. incapable of being restrained.

ir·re·proach·a·ble (ir'i prō'chə bəl) adj. blameless.

ir·re·sist·i·ble (ir'i zis'tə bəl) adj. not able to be resisted.

ir·res·o·lute (i rez'ə lōōt') adj. undecided.

ir·re·spec·tive adj. without regard to.

ir·re·spon·si·ble (ir'i spon'sə bəl) adj. lacking a sense of responsibility. —**ir·re·spon'si·bly,** adv.

ir·re·triev·a·ble (ir'i trē'və bəl) adj. incapable of being recovered.

ir·rev·er·ent (i rev'ər ənt) adj. lacking reverence or respect.

ir·rev·o·ca·ble (i rev'ə kə bəl) adj. not to be revoked or recalled.

ir·ri·gate' (ir'i gāt') v.t., -gated, -gating. to supply with water by artificial means. —**ir'ri·ga'tion,** n.

ir·ri·ta·ble (ir'i tə bəl) adj. easily annoyed or angered. —**ir'ri·ta·bil'i·ty,** n.

ir·ri·tate' (-tāt') v.t., -tated, -tating. 1. to make annoyed or angry. 2. to make sore. —**ir'ri·tant** (-tnt) n. —**ir'ri·ta'tion,** n.

IRS Internal Revenue Service.

is (iz) v. third pers. sing. pres. indic. of **be.**

-ish a suffix meaning: 1. of or belonging to. 2. like or having characteristics of. 3. inclined to. 4. near or about. 5. somewhat.

Is·lam' (is läm', is lä'm, iz'-) n. the religion of the Muslims, as set forth in the Koran. —**Is·lam'ic,** adj.

is·land (ī'lənd) n. a body of land completely surrounded by water. —**is'land·er,** n.

isle (īl) n. an island, esp. a small one.

is·let (ī'lit) n. a tiny island.

ism (iz'əm) n. a distinctive doctrine, theory, or system.

-ism a suffix meaning: action or practice; condition; doctrine; distinctive feature or usage.

i·so·bar (ī'sə bär') n. a line on a map connecting the points at which barometric pressure is the same.

i·so·late (ī'sə lāt') v.t., -lated, -lating. to place or keep alone. —**i·so·la'tion,** n.

i·so·la·tion·ist n. a person opposed to a country's participation in world affairs.

i·so·met·rics n.pl. exercises in which one body part is tensed against another. —**i·so·met'ric,** adj.

i·sos·ce·les (ī sos'ə lēz') adj. (of a triangle) having two sides equal.

i·so·tope' (ī'sə tōp') n. one of two or more forms of a chemical element having the same atomic number but different atomic weights.

Is·rae·li (iz rā'lē) n., pl. -lis, -li, -li, adj. 1. a native or inhabitant of modern Israel. —adj. 2. of modern Israel or its inhabitants.

Is·ra·el·ite (-rē ə lit', -rä-) n. a member of the Hebrew people who inhabited ancient Israel.

is·sue (ish'ōō) v., -sued, -suing. n. —v.t. 1. to send out; discharge. 2. to publish. —v.i. 3. to go, pass, or flow out. 4. to be published. —n. 5. a sending out or putting forth. 6. something issued. 7. a point in question. 8. offspring. 9. a result. —**Idiom.** 10. at issue, being disputed. 11. take issue, to disagree. —**is'su·ance,** n.

isth·mus (is'məs) n. a strip of land surrounded by water and connecting two large land bodies.

it (it) pron. third pers. sing. neuter pronoun.

ital. italic.

I·tal·ian (i tal'yən) adj. 1. of Italy, its people, or its language. —n. 2. a native of Italy. 3. the language of Italy.

—**Pronunciation.** The pronunciation of ITALIAN with the beginning sound (ī), (pronounced like eye) is heard primarily from uneducated speakers. This pronunciation is sometimes used as a joke and sometimes as an insult, but is considered offensive in either case.

i·tal·ic (i tal'ik, ī tal'-) adj. of a printing type that slopes to the right.

itch (ich) v.i. 1. to feel a tingling irritation of the skin that causes a desire to scratch. —n. 2. an itching sensation. 3. a restless longing. —**itch'y,** adj.

i·tem (ī'təm) n. a separate article.

i·tem·ize v.t., -ized, -izing. to state by items; list. —**i·tem·i·za'tion,** n.

i·tin·er·ant (ī tin'ər ənt, i tin'-) adj. 1. traveling from place to place. —n. 2. a person who goes from place to place.

i·tin·er·ar·y (-ə rer'ē) n., pl. -aries. a detailed plan for a journey; route.

-itis a suffix meaning inflammation of a body part.

its (its) adj. the possessive form of **it.**

it's (its) a contraction of **it is.**

it·self' pron. a reflexive form of **it.**

IV (ī'vē') n., pl., IVs, IV's. an apparatus for intravenous delivery of medicines, nutrients, etc.

I've (īv) a contraction of **I have.**

i·vo·ry (ī'və rē, īv'rē) n., pl. -ries. 1. a hard white substance composing the tusks of the elephant, walrus, etc. 2. a yellowish white.

i'vory tow'er n. a place remote from worldly affairs.

i·vy (ī'vē) n., pl. -ies. a climbing vine with smooth, evergreen leaves. —**i'vied,** adj.

-ize a suffix meaning: 1. to engage in. 2. to treat in a certain way. 3. to become or form into. 4. to make or cause to be.

J

J, j (jā) n. the tenth letter of the English alphabet.

jab (jab) v., jabbed, jabbing, n. —v.t., v.i. 1. to poke or punch. —n. 2. a sharp, quick thrust or punch.

jab·ber (jab'ər) v.i., v.t. 1. to talk

rapidly or indistinctly. —*n.* **2.** such talk.

jack (jak) *n.* **1.** a device for lifting heavy objects short heights. **2.** a playing card with a picture of a soldier or servant. **3.** an electrical connecting device. —*v.t.* **4.** to raise with a jack.

jack′al (jak′əl) *n.* a wild dog.

jack′ass′ *n.* **1.** a male donkey. **2.** a fool.

jack′et (jak′it) *n.* **1.** a short coat. **2.** an outer covering.

jack′ham′mer *n.* a compressed-air portable drill for rock, concrete, etc.

jack′-in-the-box′ *n., pl.* **-boxes.** a toy consisting of a box from which a figure springs up when the lid is opened.

jack′knife′ *n., pl.* **-knives,** *v.,* **-knifed, -knifing.** —*n.* **1.** a large folding pocketknife. —*v.i., v.t.* **2.** (of a trailer truck) to have or cause to have the cab and trailer swivel into a V.

jack′pot′ *n.* the cumulative prize in a contest, lottery, etc.

jack′ rab′bit *n.* a large rabbit of W North America.

Ja·cuz′zi (jə kōō′zē) *Trademark.* a brand name for a type of whirlpool bath.

jade[1] (jād) *n.* a hard green stone, used for carvings and jewelry.

jade[2] (jād) *n.* **1.** a broken-down horse. **2.** a disreputable woman.

jad′ed *adj.* weary and bored.

jag′ged *adj.* having ragged notches.

jag′uar (jag′wär) *n.* a large, powerful cat of tropical America.

jai′ a·lai′ (hī′ lī′, hī′ ə lī′) *n.* a game played with basketlike rackets on a three-walled court.

jail (jāl) *n.* a prison. —*v.t.* **2.** to put in prison. —**jail′er,** *n.*

ja·la·pe′ño (hä′lə pān′yō) *n., pl.* **-ños.** a Mexican hot pepper.

ja·lop′y (jə lop′ē) *n., pl.* **-pies.** an old, decrepit automobile.

jam[1] (jam) *v.,* **jammed, jamming,** *n.* —*v.t.* **1.** to push into a space. **2.** to make unworkable. **3.** to interfere with (radio signals). —*v.i.* **4.** to become stuck or unworkable. —*n.* **5.** people or objects jammed together. **6.** *Informal.* a difficult situation.

jam[2] (jam) *n.* a preserve of crushed fruit with sugar.

jamb (jam) *n.* the side post of a door or window.

jam′bo·ree′ (jam′bə rē′) *n.* noisy merrymaking.

Jan. January.

jan′gle (jang′gəl) *v.,* **-gled, -gling,** *n.* —*v.i., v.t.* **1.** to make or cause a harsh metallic sound. —*n.* **2.** a harsh metallic sound.

jan′i·tor (jan′i tər) *n.* the caretaker of a building.

Jan′u·ar′y (jan′yōō er′ē) *n.* the first month of the year.

Jap′a·nese′ (jap′ə nēz′, -nēs′) *n., pl.* **-nese.** *adj.* —*n.* **1.** a native of Japan. **2.** the language of Japan. —*adj.* **3.** of Japan, its people, or their language.

jar[1] (jär) *n.* a broad-mouthed bottle.

jar[2] (jär) *v.t., v.i.,* **jarred, jarring. 1.** to jolt or shake. **2.** to have an unpleasant effect (on).

jar′gon (jär′gən, -gon) *n.* vocabulary meaningful only to a particular profession or group.

jas′mine (jaz′min, jas′-) *n.* a shrub with fragrant white or yellow flowers.

jas′per (jas′pər) *n.* a kind of quartz.

jaun′dice (jôn′dis, jän′-) *n.* a condition causing yellow discoloration of the skin, whites of the eyes, etc.

jaun′diced *adj.* **1.** affected with jaundice. **2.** envious and resentful.

jaunt (jônt, jänt) *n.* a short pleasure trip.

jaun′ty (jôn′tē, jän′-) *adj.,* **-tier, -tiest.** lively and cheerful. —**jaun′ti·ly,** *adv.*

ja′va (jä′və) *n.* **1.** *Slang.* coffee. **2. Java,** *Trademark.* a programming language used to create interactive Internet applications.

jave′lin (jav′lin, jav′ə-) *n.* a light spear.

jaw (jô) *n.* **1.** either of two bones forming the framework of the mouth. **2.** one of two or more parts that grip something. —*v.i.* **3.** *Slang.* to chat.

jaw′bone′ *n., v.,* **-boned, -boning.** —*n.* **1.** the bone of the jaw. —*v.t.* **2.** to influence by persuasion.

jay (jā) *n.* a noisy blue or gray songbird.

jay′walk′ *v.i.* to cross a street carelessly. —**jay′walk′er,** *n.*

jazz (jaz) *n.* **1.** popular music marked by strong rhythm and improvisation. **2.** *Slang.* insincere talk.

jazz′y *adj.,* **-ier, -iest. 1.** of or like jazz music. **2.** flashy.

J.D. Doctor of Jurisprudence; Doctor of Laws.

jeal′ous (jel′əs) *adj.* **1.** resentful and envious, as of another's success. **2.** watchful in guarding something. —**jeal′ous·y,** *n.*

jeans (jēnz) *n.pl.* trousers of twilled cotton.

Jeep (jēp) *Trademark.* a small rugged type of automobile.

jeer (jēr) *v.i., v.t.* **1.** to shout scornfully. —*n.* **2.** a scornful shout.

Je·ho′vah (ji hō′və) *n.* God.

je·june′ (ji jōōn′) *adj.* **1.** lacking interest or importance. **2.** lacking maturity; childish.

jell (jel) *v.i., v.t.* **1.** to become or cause to become jellylike in consistency. **2.** to become or cause to become clear.

jel′ly (jel′ē) *n., pl.* **-lies,** *v.,* **-lied, -lying.** —*n.* **1.** a sweet spread of fruit juice boiled down with sugar. **2.** any substance of such consistency. —*v.i., v.t.* **3.** to become or cause to become jellylike.

jel′ly·bean′ *n.* a small, beanshaped chewy candy.

jel′ly·fish′ *n.* **-fish, -fishes.** a stinging marine animal with a soft, jellylike body.

jel′ly roll′ *n.* a thin cake spread with jelly and rolled up.

jeop′ard·ize′ (jep′ər dīz′) *v.t.,* **-ized, -izing.** to expose to danger.

jer′e·mi′ad (jer′ə mī′əd, -ad) *n.* a prolonged lament; complaint.

jerk (jûrk) *n.* **1.** a quick, sharp pull. **2.** *Slang.* a stupid person. —*v.t., v.i.* **3.** to pull or move with a jerk. —**jerk′y,** *adj.*

jer′kin (jûr′kin) *n.* a close-fitting, usu. sleeveless jacket.

jerk′wa′ter *adj.* insignificant and remote.

jer′ry-built′ (jer′ē-) *adj.* flimsily made.

jer′sey (jûr′zē) *n.* **1.** a soft knitted fabric. **2.** a shirt of this.

jest (jest) *n.* **1.** a joke. —*v.i.* **2.** to joke or banter. —**jest′er,** *n.*

jet[1] (jet) *n., v.,* **jet·ted, jet·ting,** *adj.* —*n.* **1.** a stream of gas or liquid under pressure. **2.** Also, **jet plane.** a plane operated by jet propulsion. —*v.t., v.i.* **3.** to shoot (something) forth in a stream.

jet[2] (jet) *n.* a hard black stone.

jet′ lag′ *n.* fatigue after a jet flight to a different time zone.

jet′ propul′sion *n.* forward movement caused by a body's reaction to the expulsion of jets of gas from a rear vent. —**jet′-pro·pelled′,** *adj.*

jet′sam (jet′səm) *n.* goods thrown overboard to lighten a ship.

jet′ti·son (jet′ə sən, -zən) *v.t.* to cast (cargo) overboard.

jet′ty (jet′ē) *n., pl.* **-ties. 1.** a structure built into the water. **2.** a pier.

Jew (jōō) *n.* **1.** a member of a people who trace their descent from the biblical Israelites. **2.** a follower of Judaism. —**Jew′ish,** *adj.*

jew′el (jōō′əl) *n.* **1.** a precious stone; gem. **2.** a treasured person or thing.

jib (jib) *n.* a triangular sail set forward from a mast.

jibe[1] (jīb) *v.i.,* **jibed, jibing.** to be in harmony or accord.

jibe[2] (jīb) *v.i., v.t.,* **jibed, jibing.** to gibe.

jif′fy (jif′ē) *n., pl.* **-fies.** a short time.

jig (jig) *n., v.,* **jigged, jigging.** —*n.* **1.** a lively folk dance. —*v.i.* **2.** to dance a jig.

jig′ger (jig′ər) *n.* a measure of 1½ oz. (45 ml) for liquors.

jig′gle (jig′əl) *v.,* **-gled, -gling,** *v.,* *v.i.* **1.** to move with short, quick jerks. —*n.* **2.** the act of jiggling.

jig′saw′ *n.* a saw with a narrow vertical blade for cutting curves, patterns, etc.

jig′saw puz′zle *n.* a set of irregularly cut flat pieces that form a picture when fitted together.

jilt (jilt) *v.t.* to reject a (previously encouraged suitor).

Jim′ Crow′ (jim) *n. (sometimes l.c.)* a policy of discrimination against blacks. —**Jim′-Crow′,** *adj.*

jim′my (jim′ē) *n., pl.* **-mies,** *v.,* **-mied, -mying.** —*n.* **1.** a short crowbar. —*v.t.* **2.** to force open.

jim′son·weed′ (jim′sən wēd′) *n.* a coarse plant with poisonous leaves.

jin′gle (jing′gəl) *v.,* **-gled, -gling,** *n.* —*v.i., v.t.* **1.** to make or cause to make repeated clinking sounds. —*n.* **2.** a jingling sound. **3.** a very simple verse.

jin′go·ism (jing′gō iz′əm) *n.* chauvinism marked by an aggressive foreign policy. —**jin′go·is′tic,** *adj.*

jinx (jingks) *n.* **1.** a cause of bad luck. —*v.t.* **2.** to cause bad luck.

jit′ter·bug′ (jit′ər bug′) *n.* a jazz dance.

jit′ters *n.pl. Informal.* nervousness. —**jit′ter·y,** *adj.*

jive (jīv) *n., v.,* **jived, jiv·ing.** —*n.* **1.** swing music or early jazz. **2.** meaningless talk. —*v.t., v.i.* **3.** *Slang.* to fool or kid (someone).

job (job) *n.* **1.** a piece of work. **2.** employment. **3.** a task.

job′ ac′tion *n.* a work slowdown by employees to win demands.

job′ber *n.* a dealer in odd lots of merchandise.

job′ lot′ *n.* a large assortment of goods sold as a single unit.

jock (jok) *n. Informal.* **1.** an athlete. **2.** an enthusiast.

jock′ey (jok′ē) *n.* **1.** a person who rides horses in races. —*v.i.* **2.** to maneuver.

jo·cose′ (jō kōs′, jə-) *adj.* joking. Also, **joc′und** (jok′ənd, jō′kənd).

joc′u·lar (jok′yə lər) *adj.* joking. —**joc·u·lar′i·ty** (-lar′i tē) *n.*

jodh′purs (jod′pərz) *n.pl.* riding breeches.

jog (jog) *v.,* **jogged, jogging,** *n.* —*v.t.* **1.** to push or shake. **2.** to stir to activity. —*v.i.* **3.** to run at a slow, steady pace, esp. for exercise. —*n.* **4.** a nudge. **5.** a steady pace. **6.** a bend or turn.

joie de vi′vre (zhwad′ vē′vrᵃ) *n. French.* delight in being alive.

join (join) *v.t., v.i.* **1.** to put or come together. **2.** to become a member of (a group).

join′er *n.* an assembler of woodwork. —**join′er·y,** *n.*

joint (joint) *n.* **1.** the place at which two things join. **2.** the place where two bones fit together. **3.** *Slang.* a disreputable place. **4.** *Slang.* a marijuana cigarette. —*adj.* **5.** shared by, common to, or done by two or more. —*v.t.* **6.** to join or divide by a joint. —**Idiom. 7.** out of joint, **a.** dislocated. **b.** in disorder. —**joint′ly,** *adv.*

joist (joist) *n.* one of the parallel beams supporting a floor or ceiling.

joke (jōk) *n., v.,* **joked, jok·ing.** —*n.* **1.** an amusing remark, story, etc. **2.** an object of ridicule. —*v.i.* **3.** to make or tell jokes. —**jok′ing·ly,** *adv.*

jol′ly (jol′ē) *adj.,* **-lier, -liest,** *v.,* **-lied, -lying,** *adv.* —*adj.* **1.** in good spirits; merry. —*v.t.* **2.** to try to keep (someone) in good humor. —*adv.* **3.** *Brit. Informal.* very. —**jol′li·ness,** *jol′li·ty,* *n.*

jolt (jōlt) *v.t.* **1.** to shake roughly. **2.** to shock. —*v.i.* **3.** to move jerkily. —*n.* **4.** a shock.

jon′quil (jong′kwil, jon′-) *n.* a fragrant yellow or white narcissus.

josh (josh) *v.t., v.i.* to tease.

jos′tle (jos′əl) *v.t., v.i.,* **-tled, -tling.** to push or shove rudely.

jot (jot) *n., v.,* **jot·ted, jot·ting,** *n.* —*v.t.* **1.** to write down quickly or briefly. —*n.* **2.** a little bit.

jounce (jouns) *v.,* **jounced, jouncing,** *n.* —*v.i., v.t.* **1.** to move joltingly. —*n.* **2.** a jouncing movement.

jour′nal (jûr′nl) *n.* **1.** a daily record of events. **2.** a newspaper or periodical.

jour′nal·ese′ (-ēz′, -ēs′) *n.* a writing style typical of newspapers.

jour′nal·ism (-iz′əm) *n.* the occupation of writing, editing, and publishing or broadcasting news. —**jour′nal·ist,** *n.* —**jour′nal·is′tic,** *adj.*

jour′ney (jûr′nē) *n.* **1.** the act or course of traveling. —*v.i.* **2.** to travel.

jour′ney·man *n., pl.* **-men.** a skilled worker.

joust (joust) *n.* a combat between mounted knights.

jo′vi·al (jō′vē əl) *adj.* hearty and good-humored. —**jo′vi·al·i·ty** (-al′i tē) *n.*

jowl (joul) *n.* **1.** the lower jaw. **2.** flesh hanging from the lower jaw.

joy (joi) *n.* **1.** happiness; delight. **2.** a source of delight. —**joy′ful, joy′ous,** *adj.*

joy′ride′ *n.* a pleasure ride, esp. in a recklessly driven vehicle.

joy′stick′ *n.* **1.** *Informal.* the control stick of an airplane. **2.** a lever for controlling the action in a computer game.

JP Justice of the Peace.

Jr. junior. Also, **jr.**

ju′bi·lant (jōō′bə lənt) *adj.* showing great joy. —**ju′bi·la′tion** (-lā′shən) *n.*

ju′bi·lee′ (jōō′bə lē′) *n.* a celebration, esp. of an anniversary.

Ju′da·ism (-dē iz′əm, -də-) *n.* the religion of the Jewish people.

judge (juj) *n., v.,* **judged, judging.** —*n.* **1.** a public officer who hears and decides cases in a court of law. **2.** a person who decides who has won a contest. **3.** a person able to pass critical judgment. —*v.t.* **4.** to pass legal judgment on. **5.** to form an opinion about. —*v.i.* **6.** to act as a judge.

judg′ment (-mənt) *n.* **1.** a decision, as in a court of law. **2.** good sense. **3.** an opinion.

judg·men′tal (-men′tl) *adj.* making judgments, esp. on morality.

ju·di′cial (jōō dish′əl) *adj.* of justice, courts of law, or judges.

ju·di′ci·ar′y (-dish′ē er′ē, -dish′ə rē) *n., pl.* **-ies.** —*adj.* **1.** the legal branch of a government. **2.** the system of courts in a country. —*adj.* **3.** of judges.

ju·di′cious *adj.* wise; prudent.

ju′do (jōō′dō) *n.* a martial art based on jujitsu.

jug (jug) *n.* **1.** a container for liquid, having a handle and a narrow neck. **2.** *Slang.* a jail; prison.

jug′ger·naut′ (-mən nôt′) *n.* any overpowering, irresistible force.

jug′gle (jug′əl) *v.,* **-gled, -gling.** —*v.t.* **1.** to do tricks by tossing and catching (several objects) at once. **2.** to manage the requirements of (several activities) at once. —*v.i.* **3.** to juggle objects. —**jug′gler,** *n.*

jug′u·lar (jug′yə lər) *adj.* **1.** of the neck. —*n.* **2.** a large vein in the neck.

juice (jōōs) *n.* **1.** the liquid part of plants, esp. fruits and vegetables. **2.** the natural fluid of an animal body. —**juic′y,** *adj.*

juic′er *n.* an appliance for extracting juice from fruits and vegetables.

ju·jit′su (jōō jit′sōō) *n.* a Japanese method of self-defense without weapons.

ju′jube (jōō′jōōb, jōō′jōō bē′) *n.* a chewy fruity candy.

juke′box′ (jōōk′boks′) *n.* a coin-operated device for playing recorded music.

Jul. July.

ju′li·enne′ (jōō′lē en′) *adj.* (of vegetables) cut into thin strips.

Ju·ly′ (jōō lī′, jə-) *n.* the seventh month of the year.

jum′ble (jum′bəl) *v.,* **-bled, -bling,** *v.t., v.i.* **1.** to mix or be mixed in a confused mass. —*n.* **2.** a disordered mass.

jum′bo (jum′bō) *adj.* very large.

jump (jump) *v.i., v.t.* **1.** to spring or leap (over). **2.** to increase suddenly. —*n.* **3.** a spring; leap. **4.** a sudden rise in amount, price, etc. —**Idiom. 5. get** or **have the jump on,** to have an advantage over.

jump′er[1] *n.* **1.** one that jumps. **2.** one of a pair of electric cables for starting a dead car battery.

jump′er[2] *n.* a sleeveless dress worn over a shirt.

jump′-start′ *n.* **1.** the starting of a car engine with jumpers. —*v.t.* **2.** to give a jump-start to. **3.** to enliven or revive.

jump′suit′ *n.* a one-piece suit.

jump′y *adj.,* **-ier, -iest.** nervous.

Jun. June.

jun′co (jung′kō) *n., pl.* **-cos.** a small North American finch.

junc′tion (jungk′shən) *n.* **1.** a joining or being joined. **2.** a place where things meet.

junc′ture (-chər) *n.* **1.** a point of time. **2.** a crisis. **3.** a point at which two bodies are joined.

June (jōōn) *n.* the sixth month of the year.

jun′gle (jung′gəl) *n.* wild land overgrown with vegetation, esp. in the tropics.

jun′ior (jōōn′yər) *adj.* **1.** younger. **2.** of lower rank. —*n.* **3.** a third-year high school or college student.

jun′ior col′lege *n.* a two-year college.

jun′ior high′ school′ *n.* a school consisting of grades 7 through 9.

ju′ni·per (jōō′nə pər) *n.* an evergreen shrub or tree with berrylike cones.

junk[1] (jungk) *n.* **1.** old or discarded material. **2.** something worthless. —*v.t.* **3.** to discard.

junk[2] (jungk) *n.* a flat-bottomed Chinese ship.

jun′ket (jung′kit) *n.* **1.** a custard-like dessert. **2.** a pleasure trip, esp. one made by a government official at public expense.

junk′ food′ *n.* high-calorie food having little nutritional value.

junk′ie *n. Informal.* **1.** a drug addict. **2.** a person who craves or is enthusiastic about something.

junk′ mail′ *n.* unsolicited commercial material mailed in bulk.

jun′ta (hōōn′tə, jun′-, hun′-) *n.* a small group ruling a country, esp. after a seizure of power.

—**Pronunciation.** When the word JUNTA was borrowed into English from Spanish in the early 17th century, its pronunciation was thoroughly Anglicized to (jun′tə). During the 20th century, esp. in North America, the pronunciation (hōōn′tə), which comes from Spanish (hōōn′tä) has come into frequent use, probably through people's renewed awareness of the word's Spanish origins. A hybrid form, combining English and Spanish influence, (hun′tə) is also heard. Any of these pronunciations is perfectly standard.

Ju′pi·ter (jōō′pi tər) *n.* **1.** the largest planet in the solar system, fifth from the sun. **2.** the supreme deity of the ancient Romans.

Ju·ras′sic (jōō ras′ik) *adj.* of a period of the Mesozoic Era when dinosaurs lived.

ju′ris·dic′tion (jōōr′is dik′shən) *n.* power; authority; control.

ju′ris·pru′dence (-prōōd′ns) *n.* the science of law.

ju′rist *n.* an expert in law, as a judge.

ju′ror (jōōr′ər, -ôr) *n.* a member of a jury.

ju′ry (jōōr′ē) *n., pl.* **-ries.** a group of persons selected to make a decision, esp. in a law court.

just (just) *adj.* **1.** fair; right. **2.** lawful. **3.** true. —*adv.* **4.** exactly. **5.** simply. **6.** barely. **7.** only. **8.** very recently.

jus′tice (jus′tis) *n.* **1.** fairness; rightness. **2.** the administration of punishment or reward. **3.** a judge.

jus′tice of the peace′ *n.* a local public officer who performs marriages, tries minor cases, etc.

jus′ti·fy′ *v.t., v.i.,* **-fied, -fying. 1.** to show to be just, true, right, etc. **2.** to defend. —**jus′ti·fi·ca′tion,** *n.*

jut (jut) *v.i.,* **jutted, jutting.** to project; protrude.

jute (jōōt) *n.* a strong fiber made from certain East Indian plants.

ju′ve·nile (jōō′və nl, -nīl′) *adj.* **1.** young. **2.** immature. **3.** for young people. —*n.* **4.** a young person.

ju′venile delin′quency *n.* illegal or antisocial behavior by a minor. —**ju′venile delin′quent,** *n.*

jux′ta·pose′ (juk′stə pōz′, juk′stə pōz′) *v.t.,* **-posed, -posing.** to place close together, as for contrast. —**jux′ta·po·si′tion** (-pə zish′ən) *n.*

K

K, k (kā) *n.* the eleventh letter of the English alphabet.

K 1. karat. **2.** Kelvin. **3.** kilobyte. **4.** kilometer. **5.** thousand.

k 1. karat. **2.** kilogram.

ka·bu′ki (kə bōō′kē, kä′bōō kē′) *n.* a popular drama of Japan.

kai′ser (kī′zər) *n.* a German emperor.

kale (kāl) *n.* a cabbagelike plant with wrinkled leaves.

ka·lei′do·scope′ (kə lī′də skōp′) *n.* an optical device in which colored bits change patterns continually.

kan′ga·roo′ (kang′gə rōō′) *n., pl.* **-roos, -roo.** a leaping Australian marsupial with long, powerful hind legs.

kan′garoo court′ *n.* a self-appointed tribunal disregarding legal principles or human rights.

Kans. Kansas.

ka′o·lin (kā′ə lin) *n.* a fine white clay.

ka′pok (kā′pok) *n.* the silky down from the seeds of certain trees.

kap′pa (kap′ə) *n., pl.* **-pas.** the tenth letter of the Greek alphabet.

ka·put′ (kä pōōt′, -pōōt′, kə-) *adj. Informal.* ruined or broken.

ka·ra·o·ke (kar′ē ō′kē) *n.* singing along to music in which the original vocals have been eliminated.

kar′at (kar′ət) n. 1/24 part: a unit for measuring the purity of gold.

ka·ra′te (kə rä′tē) n. a Japanese method of self-defense.

kar′ma (kär′mə) n. (in Hinduism and Buddhism) fate as the result of one's actions in successive incarnations.

ka·ty·did (kā′tē did) n. a large green grasshopper.

kay′ak (kī′ak) n. an Eskimo canoe or a small boat resembling this.

ka·zoo′ (kə zōō′) n., pl. **-zoos.** a tubular musical toy that buzzes when one hums into it.

KB kilobyte.

kc kilocycle.

ke·bab′ (kə bob′) n. cubes of marinated meat, vegetables, etc., broiled on a skewer.

keel (kēl) n. 1. the central framing part in the bottom of a ship's hull. —v. 2. **keel over, a.** to capsize. **b.** to fall or cause to fall over.

keen[1] (kēn) adj. 1. sharp or piercing. 2. intelligent. 3. intense. 4. eager. —**keen′ly,** adv.

keen[2] n. a wailing lament. —v.t., v.i. 2. to wail in lament (for the dead).

keep (kēp) v., **kept** (kept) **keeping,** n. —v.t. 1. to retain in one's possession. 2. to cause to continue in a given position or state. 3. to take care of. 4. to prevent. 5. to obey or fulfill. —v.i. 6. to continue or go on. 7. to stay in good condition. —n. 8. board and lodging. 9. the strong inner portion of a castle. —**Idiom.** 10. **for keeps,** permanently. —**keep′er,** n.

keep′ing n. 1. conformity. 2. care.

keep′sake′ n. a souvenir.

keg (keg) n. a small barrel.

kelp (kelp) n. any large brown seaweed.

Kel′vin (kel′vin) adj. of or noting an absolute scale of temperature in which 0° equals −273.16° Celsius.

ken (ken) n. knowledge.

Ken. Kentucky.

ken′nel (ken′l) n. 1. a shelter for a dog or cat. 2. an establishment where dogs or cats are bred or boarded.

ken′te (ken′tā) n. a colorful Ghanaian fabric, often worn as a symbol of African-American pride.

kept (kept) v. pt. and pp. of **keep.**

ker′chief (kûr′chif, -chēf) n. a square scarf worn as a covering for the head or neck.

ker′nel (kûr′nl) n. the center part of a nut.

ker·o·sene′ (ker′ə sēn′) n. a type of oil used as fuel.

kes′trel (kes′trəl) n. a small falcon.

ketch′up (kech′əp, kach′-) n. a type of thick tomato sauce with spices.

ket′tle (ket′l) n. a metal container for boiling liquids.

ket′tle·drum′ n. a large drum with a round copper bottom.

key (kē) n. 1. a metal piece for moving the bolt of a lock. 2. something that explains or solves. 3. a lever pressed by the finger on a computer, piano, etc. 4. a system of related musical tones. —adj. 5. chief; essential. —v.t. 6. to regulate the pitch of. 7. **key up,** to excite or make nervous.

key′board′ n. 1. the row or set of keys on a piano, computer, etc. —v.t., v.i. 2. to insert (data) into a computer. —**key′board′er,** n.

key′note′ n. 1. the basic note of a scale. 2. the basic idea or theme.

key′stone′ n. the stone forming the summit of an arch.

kg kilogram.

khak′i (kak′ē, kä′kē) n. a dull yellowish brown.

kHz kilohertz.

kib·butz′ (ki bōōts′, -bōōts′) n., pl. **-butzim.** a collective farm in Israel.

kib′itz·er (kib′it sər) n. Informal. a person offering unwanted advice. —**kib′itz,** v.i.

kick (kik) v.t. 1. to strike with the foot. 2. Slang. to give up (a habit). —v.i. 3. to make a rapid thrust with the foot. 4. (of a gun) to recoil. —n. 5. the act of kicking. 6. Informal. a thrill.

kick′back′ n. a part of an income given, usu. secretly, to someone who made the income possible.

kick′off′ n. the kick that begins play in football or soccer. 2. the beginning of anything.

kick′stand′ n. the bar for holding a bicycle upright when not in use.

kid[1] (kid) n. 1. Informal. a child. 2. a young goat. 3. leather made from the skin of a young goat.

kid[2] (kid) v.t., v.i., **kidded, kidding.** Informal. to tease. —**kid′der,** n.

kid′nap (kid′nap) v.t., **-napped** or **-naped, -napping** or **-naping.** to carry off by force, esp. for ransom. —**kid′nap·per, kid′nap·er,** n.

kid′ney (kid′nē) n. one of a pair of organs that filter waste from the blood and secrete urine.

kid′ney bean′ n. a red-skinned dried bean.

kid′ney stone′ n. an abnormal stony mass formed in the kidney.

kill (kil) v.t. 1. to cause the death of. 2. to spend (time) unprofitably. —n. 3. a killing. 4. an animal killed.

kil′ler whale′ n. a large, predatory, black-and-white dolphin.

kill′ing n. 1. the act of one that kills. 2. a quick, large profit. —adj. 3. fatal. 4. exhausting.

kill′-joy′ n. a person who spoils others' pleasure.

kiln (kil, kiln) n. a large furnace for making bricks, firing pottery, etc.

ki′lo (kē′lō, kil′ō) n., pl. **-los.** 1. a kilogram. 2. a kilometer.

kilo- a prefix meaning thousand.

kil′o·byte′ (kil′ə bīt′) n. 1. 1024 bytes. 2. (loosely) 1000 bytes. Also, **kilo.**

kil′o·gram′ n. 1000 grams. Also, **kilo.**

kil′o·hertz′ n., pl. **-hertz.** a unit of frequency equal to 1000 cycles per second.

kil′o·li·ter (-lē′-), n. 1000 liters.

ki·lom·e·ter (ki lom′i tər, kil′ə-mē′-) n. 1000 meters.
  —**Pronunciation.** The first pronunciation of KILOMETER is something of a mystery. The usual pronunciation both for *units of measurement* starting with *kilo-* (kilobyte) and for *units of length* ending in *-meter* (centimeter) gives primary stress to the first syllable and secondary to the third *-me-.* Logically, KILOMETER should follow this pattern, and in fact has been pronounced (kil′ə mē′tər) since the early 1800s. However, another pronunciation of KILOMETER, with stress on the *-om-,* or second syllable, has been around for nearly as long. It is reinforced by words for *instruments* of measurement (rather than *units* of measurement) that also end in *-meter* (thermometer, barometer). Although criticized because it does not fit the expected pattern, the pronunciation (ki lom′i tar) is very common in American English and has gained popularity in Britain. Both pronunciations are used by educated speakers, including scientists.

kil′o·watt′ n. 1000 watts.

kilt (kilt) n. a pleated, knee-length tartan skirt worn by Scotsmen.

ki·mo′no (kə mō′nə, -nō) n., pl. **-nos.** a loose dressing gown.

kin (kin) n. relatives. Also, **kin′folk′.**

kind[1] (kīnd) adj. gentle; considerate. —**kind′ness,** n.

kind[2] (kīnd) n. 1. a class or group of animals, objects, etc. 2. variety; sort.

kin′der·gar′ten (kin′dər gär′tn, -dn) n. a class or school for young children.

kind′heart′ed (kīnd′-) adj. having or showing kindness.

kin′dle (kin′dl) v., **-dled, -dling.** —v.t. 1. to set fire to. 2. to excite. —v.i. 3. to begin to burn.

kin′dling n. material for starting a fire.

kind′ly (kīnd′lē) adj., **-lier, -liest,** adv. —adj. 1. kind. —adv. 2. in a kind manner. 3. favorably.

kin′dred (kin′drid) adj. 1. related; similar. —n. 2. one's relatives.

ki·net′ic (ki net′ik, kī-) adj. of motion.

king (king) n. 1. a male sovereign or ruler. 2. a man or thing supreme in its class. 3. a playing card bearing a picture of a king. 4. a chess piece. —**king′ly,** adj., adv.

king′dom (-dəm) n. 1. a state ruled by a king or queen. 2. one of the three divisions of natural objects.

king′fish′er n. a bright blue fish-eating bird.

king′-size′ adj. extra large.

kink (kingk) n. 1. a twist or curl. —v.i., v.t. 2. to curl or cause to curl. —**kink′y,** adj.

kin′ship n. 1. family relationship. 2. affinity; likeness.

ki·osk′ (kē′osk, kē osk′) n. a small open structure where newspapers, refreshments, etc., are sold.

kip′per (kip′ər) n. a salted, dried herring or salmon.

kis′met (kiz′mit, -met, kis′-) n. fate.

kiss (kis) v.t., v.i. 1. to touch with

the lips in affection, greeting, etc. —n. 2. the act of kissing.

kit (kit) n. 1. a set of supplies, tools, etc. 2. a set of materials or parts for assembly.

kitch′en (kich′ən) n. a place for cooking.

kite (kīt) n. 1. a light, paper-covered frame flown on a long string. 2. a type of hawk.

kith′ and kin′ (kith) n. friends and relatives.

kitsch (kich) n. something pretentious and shallow showing a lack of good taste.

kit′ten (kit′n) n. a young cat.

kit′ten·ish adj. playfully coy or cute.

kit′ty-cor′nered adj. catercornered. Also, **kit′ty-cor′ner.**

ki′wi (kē′wē) n. 1. a flightless bird of New Zealand. 2. an egg-sized brown fruit with edible green pulp.

KKK Ku Klux Klan.

Klee′nex (klē′neks) Trademark. a soft paper tissue.

klep′to·ma′ni·a (klep′tə mā′nē ə) n. an irresistible compulsion to steal. —**klep′to·ma′ni·ac′,** n.

klutz (kluts) n. Slang. a clumsy person. —**klutz′y,** adj.

km kilometer.

knack (nak) n. a special skill.

knap′sack′ (nap′sak′) n. a supply bag carried on one's back.

knave (nāv) n. a dishonest person.

knead (nēd) v.t. to work (dough) with the hands.

knee (nē) n. the joint in the middle part of the leg.

knee′cap′ n. the flat bone at the front of the knee.

knee′-jerk′ adj. Informal. reacting in an automatic, habitual way.

kneel (nēl) v.i., **knelt** (nelt) or **kneeled, kneeling.** to go down or rest on one's knees.

knell (nel) n. the slow, deep sound of a bell.

knelt (nelt) v. a pt. and pp. of **kneel.**

knew (nōō, nyōō) v. pt. of **know.**

knick′ers (nik′ərz) n.pl. loose-fitting short trousers gathered at the knee.

knick′knack′ (nik′nak′) n. a trinket.

knife (nīf) n., pl. **knives** (nīvz), v., **knifed, knif·ing.** —n. 1. a cutting instrument having a sharp blade in a handle. —v.t. 2. to stab with a knife.

knight (nīt) n. 1. (in the Middle Ages) a chivalrous soldier. 2. a man given a rank with the title "Sir." 3. a chess piece shaped like a horse's head. —v.t. 4. to name a man a knight. —**knight′hood,** n.

knit (nit) v., **knitted** or **knit, knitting,** n. —v.t. 1. to make (a fabric or garment) by interlocking loops of yarn with needles. 2. to join together firmly. —n. 3. a knitted garment.

knob (nob) n. a rounded projecting part forming a handle.

knock (nok) v.t. 1. to strike a sharp, sounding blow. 2. to make a pounding noise. —v.t. 3. to strike a sharp, sounding blow to. 4. to make by striking. 5. Informal. to criticize. 6. **knock off,** to stop. 7. **~ out,** to make unconscious. —n. 8. the act or sound of knocking. 9. a blow or thump. 10. Informal. criticism.

knock′-knee′ n. inward curvature of the legs at the knees.

knock′out′ n. 1. a boxing blow that knocks the opponent to the canvas. 2. Informal. one that is extremely attractive.

knoll (nōl) n. a small hill.

knot (not) n., v., **knotted, knotting.** —n. 1. an interlacing of a cord, rope, etc., drawn tight into a knob. 2. a cluster of persons or things. 3. a hard mass where a branch joins a tree trunk. 4. one nautical mile per hour. —v.t. 5. to form a knot in. —v.i. 6. to become tied or tangled. —**knot′ty,** adj.

know (nō) v., **knew** (nōō, nyōō) **known, knowing.** —v.t. 1. to understand, remember, or experience. —v.i. 2. to be aware. —**Idiom.** 3. **in the know,** having knowledge or information. —**know′a·ble,** adj.

know′-how′ n. Informal. skill.

know′ing adj. 1. having or revealing knowledge. 2. deliberate. —**know′ing·ly,** adv.

knowl′edge (nol′ij) n. 1. the fact or state of knowing. 2. understanding or information one has learned. 3. all that is known.

knowl′edge·a·ble (-i jə bəl) adj. well-informed.

knuck′le (nuk′əl) n., v., **-led, -ling.** —n. 1. a joint of a finger. —v. 2. **knuckle down,** to apply oneself earnestly. 3. **~ under,** to submit.

knuck′le·head′ n. Informal. a stupid, inept person.

ko·a′la (kō ä′lə) n. a gray, tree-dwelling Australian marsupial.

kohl·ra′bi (kōl rä′bē, -rab′ē) n., pl. **-bies.** a variety of cabbage.

koi (koi) n., pl. **kois, koi.** a colorful carp.

ko′la (kō′lə) n. a tropical African tree grown for its nuts, used to flavor soft drinks.

kook (kōōk) n. Slang. an eccentric person. —**kook′y,** adj.

Ko·ran′ (kə rän′, -ran′, kô-) n. the sacred scripture of Islam.

Ko·re′an (kə rē′an) n. 1. a native of Korea. 2. the language of this people. —adj. 3. of Korea, its people, or their language.

ko′sher (kō′shər) adj. permissible to eat according to Jewish law.

kow′tow′ (kou′tou′, -tou′, kō′-) v.i. to act in a servile manner.

kryp′ton (krip′ton) n. an inert gas.

KS Kansas.

ku′dos (kōō′dōz, -dōs, -dos, kyōō′-) n. honor; glory.

kum′quat (kum′kwot) n. a small, orange citrus fruit.

kung′ fu′ (kung′ fōō′, kōōng′) n. a Chinese technique of unarmed combat.

kvetch (kvech), Slang. —v.i. 1. to complain chronically. —n. 2. a person who kvetches.

KW kilowatt. Also, **kw.**

KY Kentucky. Also, **Ky.**

L

L, l (el) n. the twelfth letter of the English alphabet.

l. 1. left. 2. length. 3. line. 4. liter.

LA Louisiana. Also, **La.**

lab (lab) n. a laboratory.

la′bel (lā′bəl) n., v., **-beled, -beling.** —n. 1. a piece of paper or cloth attached to an object and giving information about it. —v.t. 2. to put a label on. 3. to describe as.

la·bi·a (lā′bē ə) n.pl., sing. **-bium.** the liplike folds of the vulva.

la·bi·al (lā′bē əl) adj. of the lips or labia.

la′bor (lā′bər) n. 1. bodily toil; work. 2. childbirth. 3. workers as a group. —v.i. 4. to work hard. 5. to move slowly and heavily. —v.t. 6. to emphasize excessively. Also, Brit. **la′bour.** —**la′bor·er,** n.

lab·o·ra·to·ry (lab′rə tôr′ē, lab′-ər ə-) n., pl. **-ries.** a place for scientific research and experiment.

la′bored adj. done with difficulty.

la·bo·ri·ous (lə bôr′ē əs) adj. involving much effort.

la′bor un′ion n. an organization of workers for mutual benefit, esp. by collective bargaining.

la·bur′num (lə bûr′nəm) n. a poisonous shrub with yellow flowers.

lab′y·rinth (lab′ə rinth) n. a complicated network of passages; maze. —**lab′y·rin′thine,** adj.

lace (lās) n., v., **laced, lacing.** —n. 1. a delicate netlike fabric. 2. a cord for tying; shoelace. —v.t. 3. to fasten with a lace. —**lac′y,** adj.

lac′er·ate′ (las′ə rāt′) v.t., **-ated, -ating.** to tear roughly; mangle. —**lac′er·a′tion,** n.

lach′ry·mal (lak′rə məl) adj. of or producing tears.

lach′ry·mose′ (-mōs′) adj. tearful.

lack (lak) n. 1. the state or fact of being without something. —v.t., v.i. 2. to be wanting or deficient (in).

lack·a·dai·si·cal (lak′ə dā′zi kəl) adj. listless; unenthusiastic.

lack′ey (lak′ē) n. a servile follower.

lack′lus′ter adj. dull.

la·con′ic (lə kon′ik) adj. using few words. —**la·con′i·cal·ly,** adv.

lac′quer (lak′ər) n. 1. a kind of varnish. —v.t. 2. to coat with lacquer.

la·crosse′ (lə krôs′) n. a game played with a ball that is carried in a net at the end of a stick.

lac′tate (lak′tāt) v.i., **-tated, -tating.** to secrete milk. —**lac·ta′tion,** n.

lac′tose (-tōs) n. a sugar-like crystalline substance in milk.

la·cu′na (lə kyōō′nə) n., pl. **-nae** (nē) **-nas.** a gap.

lad (lad) n. a boy.

lad′der (lad′ər) n. uprights with steps between for climbing.

lad′en (lād′n) adj. loaded heavily.

lad′ing (lā′ding) n. cargo; freight.

la′dle (lād′l) n., v., **-dled, -dling.** —n. 1. a large deep-bowled spoon. —v.t. 2. to serve with a ladle.

la′dy (lā′dē) n., pl. **-dies.** 1. a refined, polite woman. 2. **Lady,** a British title for a noblewoman.

la′dy·bug′ n. a small, spotted, brightly colored beetle. Also, **la′dy·bird′.**

la′dy·fin′ger n. a small, oblong sponge cake.

la′dy's-slip′per n. an orchid with a slipper-shaped flower lip.

lag (lag) v., **lagged, lagging,** n. —v.i. 1. to fall behind; move slowly or belatedly. —n. 2. an instance of lagging. 3. an interval.

la′ger (lä′gər, lô′-) n. a kind of light beer.

lag′gard (lag′ərd) n. 1. a person who lags. —adj. 2. moving slowly.

la·gniappe′ (lan yap′, lan′yap) n. a gratuity. Also, **la·gnappe′.**

la·goon′ (lə gōōn′) n. a saltwater lake or pond separated from the sea by sand dunes or bars.

laid′-back′ (lād′-) adj. Informal. relaxed; easygoing.

lair (lâr) n. a wild animal's den.

lais′sez faire′ (les′ā fâr′) n. a policy of non-interference in trade, others' affairs, etc. —**lais′sez-faire′,** adj.

la′i·ty (lā′i tē) n. laypersons.

lake (lāk) n. a large body of water enclosed by land.

lam (lam) n., v., **lammed, lamming.** Slang. —n. 1. a hasty escape. —v.i. 2. to escape; flee. —**Idiom.** 3. **on the lam,** hiding or fleeing from the police.

la′ma (lä′mə) n. a Tibetan or Mongolian Buddhist monk.

La·maze′ meth′od (lə mäz′) n. a method by which an expectant mother is prepared for natural birth by physical conditioning and breathing exercises.

lamb (lam) n. 1. a young sheep. 2. its flesh as food.

lam·baste′ (lam bāst′, -bast′) v.t., **-basted, -basting.** Informal. 1. to beat severely. 2. to reprimand harshly.

lamb′da (lam′də) n., pl. **-das.** the 11th letter of the Greek alphabet.

lam′bent (lam′bənt) adj. 1. glowing lightly. 2. (of wit) gently brilliant.

lame (lām) adj., **lamer, lamest,** v., **lamed, laming.** —adj. 1. crippled or stiff or sore. 3. inadequate. —v.t. 4. to make lame.

la·mé′ (la mā′, lä-) n. an ornamental fabric with metallic threads.

lame′ duck′ (lām) n. an elected official who is completing a term after the election of a successor.

la·ment′ (lə ment′) v.t., v.i. 1. to mourn; express grief (for). —n. 2. Also, **lam·en·ta′tion** (lam′ən tā′-shən), an expression of grief. —**la·ment′a·ble,** adj.

lam′i·nate′ (lam′ə nāt′) v.t., **-nated, -nating.** 1. to form into thin plates or layers. 2. to cover with layers. —n. 3. Also, **lam′i·nat·ed.** made of layers. —**lam′i·na′tion,** n.

lamp (lamp) n. a device producing artificial light.

lamp′black′ n. a pigment made from soot.

lam·poon′ (lam pōōn′) n. 1. a broad, harsh satire. —v.t. 2. to ridicule in a lampoon.

lam′prey (lam′prē) n. an eel-like fish.

lamp′shade′ n. a shade for screening the light of a lamp.

lance (lans) n., v., **lanced, lanc·ing.** —n. 1. a long spear. —v.t. 2. to open with a lancet.

lan′cet (lan′sit) n. a sharp-pointed surgical tool.

land (land) n. 1. the part of the earth's surface above water. 2. ground or soil. 3. country. —v.t., v.i. 4. to bring or come to land. 5. to fall to the earth or floor.

land′ed adj. 1. owning land. 2. consisting of land.

land′fall′ n. 1. a sighting of land after a voyage or flight. 2. the land sighted or reached.

land′fill′ n. 1. an area of land built up from refuse material. 2. material deposited in a landfill.

land′ing n. 1. the act of one that lands. 2. a place for landing persons and goods. 3. the level floor between flights of stairs.

land′la′dy n., pl. **-dies.** a woman who owns and leases property.

land′locked′ adj. 1. shut in by

land. **2.** having no access to the sea.

land/lord/ *n.* a person who owns and leases property.

land/lub/ber (-lub′ər) *n.* a person unused to the sea and ships.

land/mark/ *n.* **1.** a prominent object serving as a guide. **2.** a site of historical importance. **3.** an important event, achievement, etc.

land/mass/ *n.* a large area of land.

land/ mine/ *n.* an explosive charge hidden just under the surface of the ground and detonated by pressure.

land/scape/ (-skāp′) *n., v.,* **-scaped, -scaping.** —*n.* **1.** a broad view of natural scenery. **2.** a picture portraying such scenery. —*v.t.* **3.** to improve the appearance of (an area) by planting trees, shrubs, etc. —land/scap/er, *n.*

land/slide/ *n.* **1.** a fall of earth or rock. **2.** an overwhelming majority of votes in an election.

lane (lān) *n.* a narrow road.

lan/guage (lang′gwij) *n.* **1.** speech or writing. **2.** any means of communication.

lan/guid (lang′gwid) *adj.* moving slowly and weakly. —lan/guid•ly, *adv.*

lan/guish (-gwish) *v.i.* **1.** to be or become weak. **2.** to long; pine. —lan/guish•ing, *adj.*

lan/guor (-gar) *n.* lack of energy or interest. —lan/guor•ous, *adj.*

lank (langk) *adj.* **1.** Also, **lank/y.** thin. **2.** straight and limp.

lan/o•lin (lan′l in) *n.* a fat from wool, used in ointments and cosmetics.

lan/tern (lan′tərn) *n.* a lamp with a transparent or translucent protective case.

lan/yard (lan′yərd) *n.* a short rope.

lap (lap) *n.* the top part of the thighs of a seated person.

lap² (lap) *n.,v.,* **lapped, lapping.** —*n.* **1.** a circuit of a course in racing. **2.** a part of a journey. —*v.t.* **3.** to lay (something) partly over something underneath. **4.** to get a lap ahead of (a competitor). —*v.i.* **5.** to fold around something.

lap³ (lap) *v.t., v.i.,* **lapped, lapping.** **1.** (of water) to wash (against something) lightly. **2.** to take in (liquid) with the tongue.

la•pel/ (lə pel′) *n.* the folded-back part on the front of a coat.

lap/i•dar/y (lap′i der′ē) *n., pl.* **-ries.** one who cuts or polishes gems.

lap/is laz/u•li (lap′is laz′ōō lē, -lī′, laz′yōō-). **1.** a deep blue semiprecious gem. **2.** a sky-blue color.

lapse (laps) *n., v.,* **lapsed, lapsing.** —*n.* **1.** a slight error; slip of memory. **2.** an interval of time. —*v.i.* **3.** to fall from a previous standard. **4.** to come to an end. **5.** to fall, slip, or sink. **6.** to pass, as time.

lap/top/ *n.* a portable microcomputer.

lar/ce•ny (lär′sə nē) *n., pl.* **-nies.** theft. —lar/ce•nist, *n.*

larch (lärch) *n.* a deciduous tree of the pine family.

lard (lärd) *n.* **1.** pig fat used in cooking. —*v.t.* **2.** to put strips of fat in (lean meat) before cooking.

lard/er (lär′dər) *n.* a pantry.

large (lärj) *adj.,* **larger, largest. 1.** great in size or number. —*Idiom.* **2.** at large, **a.** at liberty. **b.** in general. —large/ness, *n.*

large/ly *adv.* mostly.

large/-scale/ *adj.* extensive.

lar•gess/ (lär jes′, lär′jis) *n.* generosity. Also, **lar•gesse/.**

lar/go (lär′gō) *adj., adv. Music.* slowly and with dignity.

lar/i•at (lar′ē ət) *n.* a long, noosed rope used to tether an animal.

lark (lärk) *n.* **1.** a kind of songbird. **2.** a carefree adventure.

lark/spur/ (-spûr′) *n.* a plant with blue or pink flowers on tall stalks.

lar/va (lär′və) *n., pl.* **-vae** (-vē). an insect between the egg and pupal stages. —lar/val, *adj.*

lar/yn•gi/tis (lar′ən jī′tis) *n.* inflammation of the larynx, often with a loss of voice.

lar/ynx (lar′ingks) *n., pl.* **laryn•ges** (lə rin′jēz), **larynxes.** the upper part of the windpipe containing the vocal cords. —la•ryn/ge•al (lə rin′jē-əl, lar′ən jē′əl) *adj.*

la•sa/gna (lə zän′yə, lä-) *n.* a baked dish of wide strips of pasta layered with cheese, tomato sauce, and meat or vegetables. Also, **la•sa/gne.**

las•civ/i•ous (lə siv′ē əs) *adj.* lewd.

la/ser (lā′zər) *n.* a device for amplifying light and focusing it into an intense beam.

lash (lash) *n.* **1.** the flexible part of a whip. **2.** a blow with a whip. **3.** an eyelash. —*v.t.* **4.** to strike with or as if with a lash. **5.** to bind. **6.** lash out, to speak out angrily.

lass (las) *n.* a girl.

las/si•tude (las′i tōōd′, -tyōōd′) *n.* weariness.

las/so (las′ō, la sōō′) *n., pl.* **-sos, -soes,** *v.,* **-soed, -soing.** —*n.* **1.** a lariat for catching horses or cattle. —*v.t.* **2.** to catch with a lasso.

last (last) *adj.* **1.** latest. **2.** final. —*adv.* **3.** most recently. **4.** finally. —*n.* **5.** that which is last. **6.** a footshaped form on which shoes are made. —*v.i.* **7.** to continue in time, force, etc. **8.** to remain in usable condition. —*Idiom.* **9.** at (long) last, finally.

last/ing *adj.* permanent; enduring.

Last/ Sup/per *n.* the supper of Jesus and His disciples on the eve of His Crucifixion.

lat. latitude.

latch (lach) *n.* **1.** a device for fastening a door or gate. —*v.t.* **2.** to fasten with a latch. **3.** latch onto, to attach oneself to.

late (lāt) *adj., adv., later, latest.* **1.** after the usual or proper time. **2.** being or lasting well along in time. **3.** recent. **4.** deceased.

late/ly *adv.* recently.

la/tent (lāt′nt) *adj.* hidden; dormant; undeveloped.

lat/er•al (lat′ər əl) *adj.* on or from the side. —lat/er•al•ly, *adv.*

la/tex (lā′teks) *n.* **1.** a milky liquid from certain plants. **2.** a synthetic version of this.

lath (lath) *n.* **1.** a thin wood strip. **2.** a material for backing plaster. —*v.t.* **3.** to cover with laths.

lathe (lāth) *n.* a machine for shaping wood, metal, etc., by turning it against a cutting tool.

lath/er (lath′ər) *n.* **1.** foam made with soap and water. **2.** foam formed from sweating. —*v.i., v.t.* **3.** to form or cover with lather.

Lat/in (lat′n) *n.* **1.** the language of ancient Rome. **2.** a member of any people speaking a Latin-based language. —*adj.* **3.** of the Latin language. **4.** of people speaking a Latin-based language. —*adj.*

La•ti/na (lə tē′nə, la-) *n., pl.* **-nas.** a Hispanic girl or woman.

La•ti/no (lə tē′nō, la-) *n., pl.* **-nos.** a Hispanic.

lat/i•tude/ (lat′i tōōd′, -tyōōd′) *n.* **1.** distance in degrees north or south of the equator. **2.** freedom to speak or act.

la•trine/ (lə trēn′) *n.* a communal toilet, esp. in a camp or barracks.

lat/ter (lat′ər) *adj.* **1.** being the second of two. **2.** near the end.

lat/tice (lat′is) *n.* a structure of criss-crossed strips.

laud (lôd) *v.t.* to praise. —laud/a•ble, *adj.* —laud/a•to/ry, *adj.*

laugh (laf) *v.i.* **1.** to express mirth audibly. **2.** laugh at, to ridicule. —*n.* **3.** an act or sound of laughing. —laugh/ter, *n.*

laugh/a•ble *adj.* ridiculous.

laugh/ing•stock/ *n.* an object of ridicule.

launch (lônch, länch) *v.t.* **1.** to set afloat or send off. **2.** to start. **3.** to throw. —*v.i.* **4.** to go into action. —*n.* **5.** a large open motorboat. —launch/er, *n.*

launch/ pad/ *n.* a platform for launching rockets.

laun/der (lôn′dər, län′-) *v.t., v.i.* to wash or wash and iron.

Laun/dro•mat/ (-drə mat′) *Trademark.* a self-service laundry with coin-operated machines.

laun/dry *n., pl.* **-dries. 1.** clothes to be washed. **2.** a place where clothes are laundered.

lau/re•ate (lôr′ē it) *n.* a person who has been honored.

lau/rel (lôr′əl) *n.* **1.** a small glossy evergreen tree. **2.** laurels, honor won.

la/va (lä′və, lav′ə) *n.* molten rock from a volcano.

lav/a•to/ry (lav′ə tôr′ē) *n., pl.* **-ries. 1.** a toilet facility. **2.** a washbowl.

lav/en•der (lav′ən dər) *n.* a fragrant shrub with purple flowers. **2.** a pale purple.

lav/ish (lav′ish) *adj.* **1.** extravagant. —*v.t.* **2.** to expend or give in great amounts.

law (lô) *n.* **1.** the rules established by a government under which people live. **2.** a rule that must be obeyed. **3.** a statement of what always occurs under certain conditions. —law/-abid/ing, *adj.* —law/break/er, *n.* —law/break/ing, *n., adj.*

law/ful *adj.* permitted by law.

law/less *adj.* **1.** without regard for the law. **2.** uncontrolled by law.

lawn¹ (lôn) *n.* grass-covered land that is kept mowed.

lawn² (lôn) *n.* a thin cotton or linen fabric.

law/suit/ *n.* a case brought before a court.

law/yer (lô′yər, loi′ər) *n.* a person trained and licensed to practice law.

lax (laks) *adj.* **1.** careless. **2.** slack.

lax/a•tive (lak′sə tiv) *adj.* **1.** helping to move the bowels. —*n.* **2.** a laxative agent.

lay¹ (lā) *v.,* **laid, laying,** *n.* —*v.t.* **1.** to place or put down, esp. on a flat surface. **2.** to place in proper position. **3.** to present for consideration. **4.** (of a hen) to produce (eggs). **5.** to attribute. **6.** pt. of **lie. 7. lay off, a.** to dismiss (an employee). **b.** *Informal.* to cease. —*n.* **8.** the position of something.
—**Usage.** Many speakers confuse the verbs LAY and LIE because both include the meaning "in a flat position." LAY means "to put down" or "to place, especially in a flat position." A general rule to remember is that if the word "put" or "place" can be substituted in a sentence, then LAY is the verb to use: *Lay* (= put, place) *the books on the table. She laid* (= put, placed) *the baby in the cradle.* But the verb LIE means "to be in a flat position" or "to be situated": *Lie down and rest a moment. The baby is lying down.* For many speakers, the problem comes in the past tense for these two verbs, because the past tense of LIE is *lay,* which looks like, but is not, the present tense of LAY: *The dog will want to lie in the shade; yesterday it lay in the grass.* Note that we can LAY an infant down in a crib; he or she will LIE there until picked up.

lay² (lā) *adj.* **1.** not ordained into the clergy. **2.** not a member of a profession.

lay/er *n.* **1.** one thickness of material. —*v.t.* **2.** to arrange in layers.

lay•ette/ (-et′) *n.* a complete outfit for a newborn baby.

lay/man or **lay/wom/an** or **lay/per/son,** *n., pl.* **-men** or **-wom•en** or **-per•sons. 1.** a person who is not a member of the clergy. **2.** a person who is not a member of a given profession.

lay/off/ *n.* the dismissal of employees.

lay/out/ *n.* **1.** an arrangement. **2.** a plan for printed matter.

laze (lāz) *v.i., v.t.,* **lazed, lazing.** to pass (time) idly.

la/zy (lā′zē) *adj.,* **-zier, -ziest. 1.** unwilling to work. **2.** slow-moving.

lb. *pl.* **lbs., lb.** pound.

l.c. lowercase.

lea (lē, lā) *n.* a meadow.

leach (lēch) *v.i.* **1.** to soak through or in. —*v.t.* **2.** to dissolve by soaking.

lead¹ (lēd) *v.,* **led** (led) **leading,** *n.* —*v.t.* **1.** to guide by going before or with. **2.** to influence. **3.** to pass (one's life). **4.** to be or go at the head of. —*v.i.* **5.** to be a route to a place. **6.** to be or go first. **7.** to result in. —*n.* **8.** the position in advance of others. **9.** the extent of such advance. **10.** a clue. **11.** the main part in a play. —lead/er, *n.* —lead/er•ship/, *n.*

lead² (led) *n.* **1.** a heavy gray metal. **2.** a plummet. **3.** graphite used in pencils. —lead/en, *adj.*

lead/ing ques/tion (lē′ding) *n.* a question worded to prompt the desired answer.

lead/ time/ (lēd) *n.* the time between the beginning of a process and the appearance of results.

leaf (lēf) *n., pl.* **leaves** (lēvz), *v.* —*n.* **1.** the flat green part on the stem of a plant. **2.** a thin sheet, as of paper or metal. —*v.* **3. leaf through,** to turn pages quickly. —leaf/y, *adj.*

leaf/let (-lit) *n.* **1.** a pamphlet. **2.** a small leaf.

league (lēg) *n., v.,* **leagued, leaguing.** —*n.* **1.** an alliance; pact. **2.** a group of sports teams organized for competition. **3.** a unit of distance, about three miles. —*v.t., v.i.* **4.** to unite in a league.

leak (lēk) *n.* **1.** an unintended hole or crack. **2.** a disclosure of secret information. —*v.i.* **3.** to pass in or out through a leak. —*v.t.* **4.** to let (fluid or light) enter or escape. **5.** to disclose. —leak/age, *n.* —leak/y, *adj.*

lean¹ (lēn) *v.,* **leaned** or **leant, lean-**

ing. —*v.i.* **1.** to bend from an upright position. **2.** to rest for support. **3.** to depend. **4.** to tend. —*v.t.* **5.** to cause to lean.

lean² (lēn) *adj.* **1.** not fat or rich. **2.** economical.

lean/-to/ *n., pl.* **lean-tos.** a structure with a single-sloped roof abutting a wall.

leap (lēp) *v.,* **leaped** or **leapt** (lept, lēpt) **leaping.** —*v.i.* **1.** to spring through the air; jump. **2.** to act quickly. —*v.t.* **3.** to jump over. **4.** to cause to leap. —*n.* **5.** a jump.

leap/frog/ *n., v.,* **-frogged, -frogging.** —*n.* **1.** a game in which players leap over each other's backs. —*v.t.* **2.** to jump over as in leapfrog.

leap/ year/ *n.* a year with February 29 as an extra day.

learn (lûrn) *v.t.* **1.** to acquire knowledge of or skill in. **2.** to commit to memory. **3.** to hear about. —*v.i.* **4.** to acquire knowledge or skill. —learn/er, *n.* —learn/ing, *n.*

learn/ed (lûr′nid) *adj.* scholarly.

learn/ing disabil/ity *n.* difficulty in reading, writing, etc., associated with impairment of the central nervous system.

lease (lēs) *n., v.,* **leased, leasing.** —*n.* **1.** a contract renting property for a certain time period. —*v.t.* **2.** to get by means of a lease.

leash (lēsh) *n.* **1.** a strap for controlling an animal. —*v.t.* **2.** to control by a leash.

least (lēst) *adj.* **1.** smallest in size, amount, etc. —*n.* **2.** the least amount, degree, etc. —*adv.* **3.** to the smallest extent, amount, etc. —*Idiom.* **4. at least, a.** at the lowest estimate. **b.** in any case. **5. not in the least,** not at all.

leath/er (leth′ər) *n.* material made from the skin of an animal, prepared by tanning. —leath/er•y, *adj.*

leath/er•neck/ *n. Informal.* a U.S. marine.

leave¹ (lēv) *v.,* **left** (left), **leaving.** —*v.i.* **1.** to go away from or depart from permanently. **2.** to let remain. **3.** to abandon. **4.** to give for use after one's death. —*v.i.* **5.** to go away. **6. leave off,** to stop; discontinue. **7. ~ out,** to omit.

leave² (lēv) *n.* **1.** permission to do something. **2.** Also, **leave/ of ab/sence.** permission to be absent or the time this permission lasts. —*Idiom.* **3. take one's leave,** to depart. **4. take leave of,** to part from.

leav/en (lev′ən) *n.* **1.** Also, **leav/en•ing.** a fermenting agent to raise dough. —*v.t.* **2.** to make dough rise with a leaven.

lech/er•ous (lech′ər əs) *adj.* lustful. —lech/er, *n.* —lech/er•y, *n.*

lec/tern (lek′tərn) *n.* a stand with a sloping top from which something is read.

lec/ture (lek′chər) *n., v.,* **-tured, -turing.** —*n.* **1.** an instructive speech. **2.** a lengthy reprimand. —*v.i.* **3.** to give a lecture. —*v.t.* **4.** to reprimand at length. —lec/tur•er, *n.*

ledge (lej) *n.* a narrow shelf.

ledg/er (lej′ər) *n.* an account book.

lee (lē) *n.* **1.** the side away from the wind. **2.** shelter. —*adj.* **3.** of or on the lee. —lee/ward, *adj., n.*

leech (lēch) *n.* a bloodsucking worm.

leek (lēk) *n.* a vegetable related to the onion.

leer (lēr) *n.* **1.** a sly or lustful glance. —*v.i.* **2.** to look with a leer.

leer/y (lēr′ē) *adj.,* **-ier, -iest.** wary.

lee/way/ *n.* **1.** extra time, space, etc. **2.** a degree of freedom of action.

left (left) *adj.* **1.** of or on the side that is toward the west when a person is facing north. —*n.* **2.** the left side. **3. the Left,** people favoring liberal reform or radical change. —left/-hand/, *adj.* —left/-hand/ed, *adj.*

left/ist *n.* (*sometimes cap.*) **1.** a member of the political Left. —*adj.* **2.** of the political Left.

left/ wing/ *n.* the liberal or radical element in an organization. —left/-wing/, *adj.*

leg (leg) *n.* **1.** one of the limbs supporting a body. **2.** any leglike part.

leg/a•cy (leg′ə sē) *n., pl.* **-cies.** anything bequeathed.

le/gal (lē′gəl) *adj.* of, permitted, or established by law. —le•gal/i•ty (-gal′i tē) *n.* —le/gal•ize/, *v.t.*

le/gal•ese/ (-gə lēz′, -lēs′) *n.* excessive legal jargon.

leg/a•tee/ (leg′ə tē′) *n.* a person who receives a legacy.

le•ga/tion (li gā′shən) *n.* **1.** a diplomatic minister and staff. **2.** the official headquarters of a diplomatic minister.

le•ga/to (lə gä′tō) *adj., adv. Music.* smooth and flowing; without breaks.

leg/end (lej′ənd) *n.* **1.** a story handed down by tradition. **2.** a person in such a story. **3.** a map key. —leg/end•ar/y, *adj.*

leg/er•de•main/ (lej′ər də mān′) *n.* sleight of hand.

leg/ging *n.* a covering for the leg.

leg/i•ble (lej′ə bəl) *adj.* easily read.

le/gion (lē′jən) *n.* **1.** a military unit. **2.** a great number. —le/gion•naire/, *n.*

leg/is•late/ (lej′is lāt′) *v.,* **-lated, -lating.** —*v.i.* **1.** to make laws. —*v.t.* **2.** to control by law. —leg/is•la/tion, *n.* —leg/is•la/tive, *adj.* —leg/is•la/tor, *n.*

leg/is•la/ture (-chər) *n.* a lawmaking body.

le•git/i•mate (li jit′ə mit) *adj.* **1.** lawful; valid. **2.** according to established rules. **3.** born of married parents. —le•git/i•ma•cy (-mə sē) *n.* —le•git/i•mize/, *v.t.*

leg/ume (leg′yōōm, li gyōōm′) *n.* **1.** any of a family of plants having pods that split open when dry, comprising beans, peas, etc. **2.** the pod or seed of such a plant.

lei (lā) *n.* a flower wreath for the neck.

lei/sure (lē′zhər, lezh′ər) *n.* **1.** time free from work or duty. —*adj.* **2.** unoccupied; having leisure.

lei/sure•ly *adj.* relaxed; unhurried.

leit/mo•tif/ (līt′mō tēf′) *n.* **1.** a recurring musical phrase in an opera. **2.** a dominant theme or underlying pattern in an artistic work.

lem/ming (lem′ing) *n.* a small arctic mouse-like rodent noted for periodic mass migrations and mass drownings.

lem/on (lem′ən) *n.* **1.** the yellowish acid fruit of a citrus tree. **2.** *Informal.* a person or thing that is defective.

lem/on•ade/ (-ə nād′) *n.* a beverage of lemon juice, sugar, and water.

le/mur (lē′mər) *n.* a small treedwelling monkeylike animal.

lend (lend) *v.,* **lent, lending.** —*v.t.* **1.** to give temporary use of. **2.** to allow the use of (money) on payment of interest. **3.** to give or impart.
—**Usage.** See BORROW.

length (lengkth, length) *n.* **1.** the size or extent from end to end. **2.** a piece of cloth, string, etc.). **3.** a large extent of something. —*Idiom.* **4. at length, a.** finally. **b.** in detail. —length/en, *v.t., v.i.* —length/wise/, *adv., adj.* —length/y, *adj.*

le/ni•ent (lē′nē ənt, lēn′yənt) *adj.* not severe; gentle. —le/ni•en•cy, *n.*

lens (lenz) *n., pl.* **lenses. 1.** a glass for changing the convergence of light rays, used in eyeglasses, telescopes, etc. **2.** a similar part of the eye.

Lent (lent) *n.* the season of penitence and fasting before Easter. —Lent/en, *adj.*

len/til (len′til, -tl) *n.* the edible seed of a pealike plant.

le•o•nine/ (lē′ə nīn′) *adj.* of or like the lion.

leop/ard (lep′ərd) *n.* a large animal of the cat family, usu. tawny with black spots.

le/o•tard/ (lē′ə tärd′) *n.* a tight, flexible, one-piece garment worn by acrobats, dancers, etc.

lep/er (lep′ər) *n.* a person afflicted with leprosy.

lep/re•chaun/ (lep′rə kôn′) *n.* an elf in Irish folklore.

lep/ro•sy (lep′rə sē) *n.* a contagious disease marked by skin ulcerations.

les/bi•an (lez′bē ən) *n.* **1.** a female homosexual. —*adj.* **2.** pertaining to female homosexuals.

lese majesty (lēz′ maj′əs tē) *n.* an offense against the dignity of a ruler. **2.** treason.

le/sion (lē′zhən) *n.* an area of diseased or injured tissue.

less (les) *adv.* **1.** to a smaller extent. —*adj.* **2.** smaller. **3.** lower in importance. —*n.* **4.** a smaller amount or quantity. —*prep.* **5.** minus. —less/en, *v.t., v.i.*
—**Usage.** FEWER is the comparative form of FEW. It is properly used before plural nouns that refer to individuals or things that can be counted (*fewer words; no fewer than 31 states*). LESS is the comparative form of LITTLE. It should modify

only singular mass nouns that refer to things that are abstract or cannot be counted (*less sugar; less doubt*). LESS may be used before plural nouns only when they involve measurements or mathematics (*less than $50; less than three miles*.)

les·see/ (le sē′) *n.* one granted a lease.

les′ser *adj.* a comparative of *little*.

les′son (les′ən) *n.* 1. something to be learned. 2. a chapter or exercise assigned to a student.

les′sor (les′ôr, le sôr′) *n.* a person who grants a lease.

lest (lest) *conj.* for fear that.

let (let) *v.t.,* **let, letting. 1.** to permit. 2. to rent out. 3. to cause to. 4. **let down,** to disappoint; fail. 5. ~ **off, a.** to release explosively. **b.** to release without punishment.

-let a suffix indicating: 1. small. 2. an article worn on.

let′down/ *n.* a disappointment.

le′thal (lē′thəl) *adj.* deadly.

leth′ar·gy (leth′ər jē) *n., pl.* **-gies.** lack of energy; drowsy dullness. —**le·thar′gic** (lə thar′jik) *adj.*

let′ter (let′ər) *n.* 1. a written communication. 2. a symbol that is part of an alphabet. 3. literal meaning. 4. letters, literature. —*v.t.* 5. to mark with letters.

let′tered *adj.* literate; learned.

let′ter·head/ *n.* 1. a printed heading on stationery. 2. paper with a letterhead.

let′ter-per′fect *adj.* precise in every detail.

let′tuce (let′is) *n.* a plant with large crisp leaves used in salad.

let′up/ *n.* cessation; pause; relief.

leu·ke′mi·a (lōō kē′mē ə) *n.* a cancerous disease of the bone marrow.

leu′ko·cyte (lōō′kə sīt′) *n.* a white blood cell.

lev·ee (lev′ē) *n.* a river embankment to prevent floods.

lev·el (lev′əl) *adj., n., v.,* **-eled, -eling.** —*adj.* 1. horizontal. 2. equal. 3. steady. 4. sensible. —*n.* 5. the horizontal line or plane in which something is located. 6. height. 7. a device for determining a horizontal plane. —*v.t.* 8. to make level or equal. 9. to knock down. —*v.i.* 10. to become level.

lev′el-head′ed *adj.* sensible.

lev′el play′ing field/ *n.* a state of equality; an equal opportunity.

lev′er (lev′ər, lē′vər) *n.* a bar moving on a fixed support to exert force.

lev′er·age (-ij) *n.* the means of achieving a purpose.

le·vi′a·than (li vī′ə thən) *n.* something of immense size or power.

Le′vi's (lē′vīz) *(used with a pl. v.) Trademark.* a brand of denim jeans.

lev′i·tate/ (-tāt′) *v.i., v.t.,* **-tated, -tating.** to rise or cause to rise into the air in apparent defiance of gravity. —**lev′i·ta′tion,** *n.*

lev′i·ty (lev′i tē) *n.* lack of seriousness.

lev′y (lev′ē) *v.,* **levied, levying,** *n., pl.* **levies.** —*v.t.* 1. to raise or collect a tax by authority. 2. to make (war). —*n.* 3. an act of levying. 4. something levied.

lewd (lōōd) *adj.* obscene; indecent.

lex′i·cog′ra·phy (lek′si kog′rə fē) *n.* the process of writing dictionaries.

lex′i·con (-kon′, -kən) *n.* a dictionary.

lg. 1. large. 2. long.

li·a·bil′i·ty (lī′ə bil′i tē) *n., pl.* **-ties.** 1. a debt. 2. a disadvantage. 3. the state of being liable.

li′a·ble *adj.* 1. subject to legal obligation or penalty. 2. likely.

li·ai′son (lē ā′zon, lē′ā zōn′) *n.* 1. a contact or connection maintained to ensure cooperation. 2. an illicit sexual relationship.

li′ar (lī′ər) *n.* one who tells lies.

li·ba′tion (lī bā′shən) *n.* 1. the pouring out of wine or oil to honor a deity. 2. the liquid poured. 3. an alcoholic drink.

li′bel (lī′bəl) *n., v.,* **-beled, -beling.** —*n.* 1. defamation falsely or unjustly in writing or print. —*v.t.* 2. to publish libel against. —**li′bel·ous,** *adj.*

lib′er·al (lib′ər əl, lib′rəl) *adj.* 1. favoring political reform and progressive government. 2. tolerant. 3. generous. 4. not strict. —*n.* 5. a person having liberal views. —**lib′er·al·ism,** *n.* —**lib′er·al′i·ty** (-ə ral′i tē) *n.* —**lib′er·al·ize/** *v.t., v.i.*

lib′eral arts/ *n.pl.* college courses comprising the arts, humanities, and natural and social sciences.

lib′er·ate/ (lib′ə rāt′) *v.t.,* **-ated, -ating.** to set free. —**lib′er·a′tion,** *n.* —**lib′er·a′tor,** *n.*

lib′er·tar′i·an (lib′ər târ′ē ən) *n.* a person who advocates liberty in thought or conduct.

lib′er·tine/ (-tēn′, -tin) *n.* an unrestrained and immoral person.

lib′er·ty *n., pl.* **-ties. 1.** freedom; independence. 2. liberties, impertinent freedom or familiarity.

li·bi′do (li bē′dō) *n., pl.* **-dos.** sexual desire.

li′brar·y (lī′brer′ē, -brə rē, -brē) *n., pl.* **-ries.** 1. a place to house a collection of books, magazines, etc. 2. a collection of books. —**li·brar′i·an,** *n.*

—**Pronunciation.** LIBRARY, with two barely separated *r*-sounds, demonstrates the tendency for neighboring sounds that are alike to become different, or for one of them to disappear altogether. This can lead to forms like the pronunciation (lī′ber ē) which is likely to be heard from less educated or very young speakers and is often criticized. However, (lī′brē) the third pronunciation shown above, is considered perfectly standard, even though one of the *r*-sounds has been dropped.

li·bret′to (li bret′ō) *n., pl.* **-brettos, -bretti** (-bret′ē). the text of an opera. —**li·bret′tist,** *n.*

li′cense (lī′səns) *n., v.,* **-censed, -censing.** —*n.* 1. an official permit to own, use, or do something. 2. deviation from rules, facts, etc. —*v.t.* 3. to grant a license to.

li·cen·see/ (-sən sē′) *n.* a person to whom a license is granted.

li·cen′tious (-sen′shəs) *adj.* sexually immoral.

li′chen (lī′kən) *n.* a crustlike plant on rocks, trees, etc.

lic′it (lis′it) *adj.* lawful.

lick (lik) *v.t.* 1. to pass the tongue over. 2. (of waves or flames) to touch lightly. 3. *Informal.* to beat or defeat. —*n.* 4. an act of licking. 5. a small amount.

lick′ing *n. Informal.* 1. a beating or thrashing. 2. a defeat or setback.

lic′o·rice (lik′ər ish, -ə ris) *n.* a plant root used in candy.

lid (lid) *n.* 1. a hinged or removable cover. 2. an eyelid.

lie¹ (lī) *n., v.,* **lied, lying.** —*n.* 1. a deliberately false statement. —*v.i.* 2. to tell a lie.

lie² (lī) *v.,* **lay** (lā), **lain** (lān), **lying,** *n.* —*v.i.* 1. to assume or have a reclining position. 2. to be or remain. —*n.* 3. a manner of lying. —**Usage.** See LAY.

lie′ detec′tor *n.* a device to detect lying in response to questions, by measuring changes in pulse, blood pressure, etc.; polygraph.

liege (lēj, lēzh) *n.* a feudal lord or king.

lien (lēn, lē′ən) *n.* the legal right to another's property until a debt is paid.

lieu (lōō) *n.* **in lieu of,** instead of.

lieu·ten′ant (lōō ten′ənt; in *Brit. use, except in the navy,* lef ten′ənt) *n.* 1. a commissioned officer in the army or navy. 2. an aide.

life (līf) *n., pl.* **lives** (līvz). 1. the quality that distinguishes animals and plants from inanimate things. 2. the period of being alive. 3. living things. 4. a manner of living. 5. animation. —**life′like/,** *adj.*

life′blood/ *n.* 1. the blood. 2. a vital element.

life′boat/ *n.* a boat for rescuing passengers from a sinking ship.

life′-care/ *adj.* (of a facility or community) designed to provide for the basic needs of elderly residents.

life′guard/ *n.* a person employed to protect swimmers, as at a beach.

life′long/ *adj.* lasting all of one's life.

life′ part′ner *n.* one member of a monogamous relationship.

life′ preserv′er *n.* a buoyant device to keep a person afloat.

lif′er *n.* a person serving a term of imprisonment for life.

life′sav′er *n.* a person or thing that saves one from death or difficulty. —**life′sav′ing,** *n.*

life′-size/ *adj.* of the actual size of a person, object, etc.

life′style/ *n.* a person's general pattern of living. Also, **life′-style/.**

life′-sup·port/ *adj.* of equipment or techniques that sustain or substitute for essential body functions.

life′time/ *n.* the duration of a person's life.

lift (lift) *v.t.* 1. to move upward. 2. to raise. 3. to remove, as a restriction. —*v.i.* 4. to go up. —*n.* 5. the act of lifting. 6. a ride given to a pedestrian. 7. a feeling of exaltation. 8. *Brit.* an elevator.

lift′-off/ *n.* the vertical ascent of a rocket.

lig′a·ment (lig′ə mənt) *n.* a band of tissue holding bones or organs together.

lig′a·ture (lig′ə chər, -chōōr′) *n.* 1. a surgical thread or wire for tying blood vessels. 2. two or more letters combined, as *fl.*

light¹ (līt) *n., adj., v.,* **lighted** or **lit** (lit), **lighting.** —*n.* 1. something that makes things visible or gives illumination. 2. daylight. 3. aspect. 4. enlightenment. —*adj.* 5. having light. 6. pale. —*v.t.* 8. to set burning. 9. to brighten. —*Idiom.* 10. **in light of,** considering. 11. **see the light, a.** to come into existence. **b.** to understand something.

light² (līt) *adj., adv.* 1. not heavy. 2. not serious. 3. (of food) easy to digest. 4. (of sleep or a sleeper) easily disturbed.

light³ (līt) *v.i.,* **lighted** or **lit** (lit), **lighting.** 1. to land; alight. 2. to happen upon.

light′en¹ *v.t., v.i.* to make or become less dark.

light′en² *v.t., v.i.* to make or become less heavy or burdensome.

light′er¹ *n.* something that lights.

light′er² *n.* a flat-bottomed barge.

light′-fin′gered *adj.* likely to steal.

light′-head′ed *adj.* dizzy and faint.

light′-heart′ed *adj.* cheerful.

light′house/ *n.* a tower displaying a beacon light to guide sailors.

light′ning (-ning) *n.* a flash of light in the sky caused by an electrical discharge.

light′ning bug/ *n.* a firefly.

light′ning rod/ *n.* a metal rod to divert lightning from a structure into the ground.

light′-year/ *n.* the distance that light travels in one year.

lig′ne·ous (lig′nē əs) *adj.* of the nature of or resembling wood.

lig′nite (lig′nīt) *n.* a kind of brown, wood-textured coal.

like¹ (līk) *adj.* 1. of the same form, kind, appearance, etc. —*prep.* 2. resembling. 3. in the manner of. 4. characteristic of. —*conj.* 5. *Informal.* as; as if. —*n.* 6. a similar person or thing; match. 7. **the like,** something similar.

like² (līk) *v.,* **liked, liking,** *n.* —*v.t.* 1. to find agreeable. 2. to wish for. —*v.i.* 3. to feel inclined. —*n.* 4. **likes,** the things a person likes. —**lik′a·ble, like′a·ble,** *adj.*

like′ly *adj.,* **-lier, -liest,** *adv.* —*adj.* 1. probable. 2. suitable. —*adv.* 3. probably. —*v.t.* to point out the similarity of.

like′ness *n.* 1. an image; picture. 2. the fact of being similar.

like′wise/ *adv.* 1. also. 2. in like manner.

li′lac (lī′lək, -läk, -lak) *n.* a shrub with fragrant purple or white flowers.

Lil′li·pu′tian (lil′i pyōō′shən) *adj.* 1. very small. 2. trivial.

lilt (lilt) *n.* a rhythmic cadence.

lil′y (lil′ē) *n., pl.* **-ies.** a plant with erect stems and large funnel-shaped flowers.

lil′y-liv′ered (-liv′ərd) *adj.* cowardly.

lil′y of the val′ley *n., pl.* **lilies of the valley.** a plant with a spike of white bell-shaped flowers.

li′ma bean/ (lī′mə) *n.* a broad, flat, edible bean.

limb (lim) *n.* 1. an arm, leg, or wing. 2. a branch of a tree.

lim′ber (lim′bər) *adj.* 1. flexible; supple. —*v.* 2. limber up, to make or become limber.

lim′bo¹ (lim′bō) *n., pl.* **-bos.** a place or state of oblivion.

lim′bo² (lim′bō) *n., pl.* **-bos.** a West Indian dance involving bending backward to pass under a horizontal bar.

lime¹ (līm) *n., v.,* **limed, liming.** —*n.* 1. a white powder used in mortar, plaster, fertilizer, etc. —*v.t.* 2. to treat with lime.

lime² (līm) *n.* the small, greenish, acid fruit of a tropical tree.

lime′light/ *n.* 1. fame. 2. a strong light formerly used on stage.

lim′er·ick (lim′ər ik) *n.* a humorous five-line rhymed verse.

lime′stone/ *n.* a rock consisting chiefly of powdered calcium.

lim′it (lim′it) *n.* 1. the farthest extent; boundary. —*v.t.* 2. to fix within limits. —**lim′i·ta′tion,** *n.*

lim′it·ed *adj.* 1. restricted 2. (of trains, buses, etc.) making few stops.

lim′o (lim′ō) *n., pl.* **-os.** *Informal.* a limousine.

lim′ou·sine/ (lim′ə zēn′, lim′ə zēn′) *n.* a luxurious automobile for several passengers.

limp¹ (limp) *v.i.* 1. to walk with a labored movement, as when lame. —*n.* 2. a lame movement.

limp² (limp) *adj.* not stiff or firm. —**limp′ly,** *adv.*

lim′pet (lim′pit) *n.* a small shellfish that sticks to rocks.

lim′pid (-pid) *adj.* clear or transparent. —**lim·pid′i·ty, lim′pid·ness,** *n.*

linch′pin/ (linch′-) *n.* 1. a pin inserted through the end of an axle to keep a wheel on. 2. a key person or thing that holds an organization or structure together.

lin′den (lin′dən) *n.* a tree with heart-shaped leaves and fragrant flowers.

line¹ (līn) *n., v.,* **lined, lining.** —*n.* 1. a long thin mark made on a surface. 2. a row. 3. a row of persons. 4. a course of action, thought, etc. 5. a boundary. 6. a string, cord, etc. 7. an occupation. —*v.t.* 8. to form a line. —*v.i.* 9. to mark with lines. —*Idiom.* 10. **draw the line,** to impose a limit. 11. **hold the line,** to maintain the status quo.

line² (līn) *v.t.,* **lined, lining.** to cover the inner side of.

lin′e·age (lin′ē ij) *n.* ancestry.

lin′e·al (-əl) *adj.* 1. being in a direct line. 2. linear.

lin′e·a·ment (-ə mənt) *n.* a feature, as of the face.

lin′e·ar (-ər) *adj.* 1. of or using lines. 2. involving measurement in one dimension only. 3. long and narrow.

line′man *n., pl.* **-men.** a worker who repairs telephone, telegraph, etc., wires.

lin′en (lin′ən) *n.* 1. fabric made from flax. 2. **linens,** bedding, tablecloths, etc., made of linen or cotton.

lin′er¹ (lī′nər) *n.* a ship or airplane on a regular route.

lin′er² (lī′nər) *n.* something serving as a lining.

line′-up/ *n.* 1. people in a line for inspection. 2. the arrangement of a sports team.

-ling a suffix meaning: 1. a person connected with. 2. little.

lin′ger (ling′gər) *v.i.* 1. to remain in a place. 2. to persist.

lin·ge·rie/ (län′zhə rā′, -jə-, lan′-zhə rē′) *n.* women's underwear.

lin′go (ling′gō) *n., pl.* **-goes.** *Informal.* jargon; unfamiliar language.

lin·gui′ni (-gwē′nē) *n.* a kind of slender, flat pasta.

lin′guist (-gwist) *n.* a person skilled in languages.

lin·guis′tics *n.* the science of language. —**lin·guis′tic,** *adj.*

lin′i·ment (lin′ə mənt) *n.* a liquid rubbed on the body to relieve muscular pain.

lin′ing (lī′ning) *n.* an inner covering, as in a coat.

link (lingk) *n.* 1. a section of a chain. 2. a bond. —*v.t., v.i.* 3. to unite. —**link′age,** *n.*

links *n.pl.* a golf course.

lin′net (lin′it) *n.* a small finch.

li·no′le·um (li nō′lē əm) *n.* a hard, washable floor covering.

lin′seed/ (lin′sēd′) *n.* the seed of flax.

lin′sey-wool′sey (lin′zē wōōl′zē) *n.* a fabric of linen and wool.

lint (lint) *n.* bits of thread.

lin′tel (lin′tl) *n.* a beam above a door or window.

li′on (lī′ən) *n.* a large tawny animal of the cat family, native to Africa and Asia.

li′on·ess *n.* a female lion.

li′on·heart′ed *adj.* brave.

li′on·ize/ *v.t.,* **-ized, -izing.** to treat as a celebrity.

lip (lip) *n.* 1. either of the fleshy edges forming the margin of the mouth. 2. a projecting edge. 3. *Slang.* impudent talk.

lip′o·suc′tion (lip′ə suk′shən, lī′pə-) *n.* surgical withdrawal of excess fat from under the skin.

lip′read′ing *n.* a method of understanding spoken words by interpreting a speaker's lip movements. —**lip′read′,** *v.t., v.i.*

lip′ serv′ice *n.* insincere profession of admiration, support, etc.

lip′stick/ *n.* a cosmetic for coloring the lips.

liq′ue·fy/ (lik′wə fī′) *v.t., v.i.,* **-fied, -fying.** to make or become liquid. —**liq′ue·fac′tion** (-fak′shən) *n.*

li·queur/ (li kûr′, -kyōōr′) *n.* a strong sweet alcoholic drink.

liq′uid (lik′wid) *n.* 1. a substance that flows, as water or oil. —*adj.* 2. of or being a liquid. 3. (of assets) in or convertible to cash.

liq′ui·date/ (-wi dāt′) *v.t.,* **-dated, -dating.** 1. to settle, as debts. 2. to convert (assets) into cash. 3. to dissolve (a business or estate). —**liq′ui·da′tion,** *n.*

liq′uor (lik′ər) *n.* 1. an alcoholic beverage. 2. a liquid.

lisle (līl) *n.* a fabric woven of strong linen or cotton thread.

lisp (lisp) *n.* 1. a speech defect in which *s* and *z* are pronounced like *th.* —*v.t., v.i.* 2. to speak with a lisp.

lis′some (lis′əm) *adj.* 1. lithe; supple. 2. agile. Also, **lis′som.**

list¹ (list) *n.* 1. a written series of words, names, etc. —*v.t.* 2. to make a list of.

list² (list) *n.* 1. a leaning to one side. —*v.i., v.t.* 2. to incline or cause to incline to one side.

lis′ten (lis′ən) *v.i.* to pay attention in order to hear. —**lis′ten·er,** *n.*

list′less (list′lis) *adj.* lacking energy.

list′ price/ *n.* the price at which something is sold to the public.

lit. 1. literally. 2. literature.

lit′a·ny (lit′n ē) *n., pl.* **-nies.** 1. a form of prayer with responses. 2. a prolonged account.

li′ter (lē′tər) *n.* a metric unit of liquid capacity, equal to 1.0567 U.S. quarts. Also, *Brit.,* **li′tre.**

lit′er·al (lit′ər əl) *adj.* in accordance with the strict meaning of a word or text.

lit′er·al-mind′ed *adj.* interpreting literally and without imagination.

lit′er·ar′y (-ə rer′ē) *adj.* of books and writings.

lit′er·ate (-ər it) *adj.* 1. able to read and write. 2. educated. —**lit′er·a·cy** (-ə sē) *n.*

lit′e·ra′ti (-ə rä′tē, -rā′-) *n.pl.* persons of literary attainments.

lit′er·a·ture (lit′ər ə chər, -chōōr′, li′trə-) *n.* 1. writing in prose or verse that is regarded as having lasting worth because of its excellence. 2. the writings dealing with a particular subject.

lithe (līth) *adj.* limber; supple.

li·thog′ra·phy (li thog′rə fē) *n.* printing from a stone or metal plate treated with a combination of substances that either absorb or repel ink. —**lith′o·graph,** *n.*

lit′i·gant (lit′i gənt) *n.* a person engaged in a lawsuit.

lit′i·gate/ (-gāt′) *v.t.,* **-gated, -gating.** —*v.i.* 1. to carry on a lawsuit. —*v.t.* 2. to make the subject of a lawsuit. —**lit′i·ga′tion,** *n.*

lit′mus pa′per (lit′məs) *n.* paper that turns red in acid and blue in alkaline.

lit′mus test/ *n.* the use of a single factor as a basis for judgment.

Litt. D. Doctor of Letters; Doctor of Literature.

lit′ter (lit′ər) *n.* 1. scattered objects, rubbish, etc. 2. the young born to an animal at one birth. 3. a stretcher for moving someone sick or injured. 4. bedding for animals. 5. material used to absorb animal waste. —*v.t.* 6. to strew (a place) with litter. 7. to scatter (objects) in disorder.

lit′ter·bug/ *n.* a person who litters public places with trash.

lit′tle (lit′l) *adj.,* **-tler, -tlest.** 1. small in size, amount, degree, etc. —*adv.* 2. not at all. —*n.* 3. a small amount.

lit′tor·al (lit′ər əl) *adj.* of the shore of a lake, sea, or ocean.

lit′ur·gy (lit′ər jē) *n., pl.* **-gies.** a form of public worship. —**li·tur′gi·cal** (li tûr′ji kəl) *adj.*

liv′able (liv′ə bəl) *adj.* suitable for living.

live¹ (liv) *v.,* **lived, living.** —*v.i.* 1. to be or remain alive. 2. to continue in existence, memory, etc. 3. to dwell. —*v.t.* 4. to pass or spend.

live² (līv) *adj.* 1. alive. 2. burning. 3. not exploded. 4. connected to electric power.

live′li·hood/ (līv′lē hōōd′) *n.* a means of supporting oneself.

live′long/ (liv′-) *adj.* entire; whole.

live/ly (līv/lē) adj., **-lier; -liest.** active; spirited.

liv/er (liv/ər) n. a large, vital abdominal organ that secretes bile.

liv/er·wurst/ (-wûrst/) n. liver sausage.

liv/er·y (liv/ə rē, liv/rē) n., pl. **-eries.** 1. a uniform worn by male servants. 2. the keeping of horses for hire.

live/stock/ (līv/stok/) n. domestic farm animals.

live/ wire/ (līv) n. Informal. an energetic, vivacious person.

liv/id (liv/id) adj. 1. furiously angry. 2. dull bluish gray.

liv/ing (liv/ing) adj. 1. being alive. 2. sufficient for living. —n. 3. the condition of one that lives. 4. livelihood.

liv/ing room/ n. a room for leisure activities, entertaining, etc.

liv/ing will/ n. a document directing that no extraordinary measures be taken to prolong the signer's life during a terminal illness.

liz/ard (liz/ərd) n. a four-legged reptile with a long tail.

lla/ma (lä/mə, yä/-) n. a woolly South American animal related to the camel.

LL.B. Bachelor of Laws.

LL.D. Doctor of Laws.

load (lōd) n. 1. anything carried at one time. 2. something that weighs down like a burden. —v.t. 3. to put a load on. 4. to oppress. 5. to put ammunition into (a firearm). —load/er, n.

loaf (lōf) n., pl. **loaves** (lōvz), v. —n. 1. a shaped mass of bread. —v. 2. to spend time idly. —loaf/er, n.

loam (lōm) n. loose fertile soil.

loan (lōn) n. 1. the act of lending. 2. something lent. —v.t., v.i. 3. to lend.

loan/ shark/ n. Informal. a person who lends money at exorbitant interest rates.

loan/word/ n. a word borrowed from another language.

loath (lōth, lōth) adj. reluctant.

loathe (lōth) v., **loathed, loathing.** to feel intense dislike for. —loath/some** (lōth/səm, lōth/-) adj.

lob (lob) v.t., **lobbed, lobbing.** to strike or hurl in a high curve.

lob/by n., pl. **-bies,** v., **-bied, -bying.** —n. 1. an entrance hall. 2. a group that tries to influence the votes of legislators. —v.i. 3. to try to influence legislation. —v.t. 4. to try to influence the votes of (legislators). —lob/by·ist, n.

lobe (lōb) n. a roundish projection.

lo·bot/o·my (lə bot/ə mē, lō-) n., pl. **-mies.** a surgical incision of the brain lobe to treat mental disorder. —lo·bot/o·mize/, v.t.

lob/ster (lob/stər) n. an edible marine shellfish with large claws.

lo/cal (lō/kəl) adj. 1. of or in a particular area. —n. 2. a local branch of a trade union. 3. a train that makes all stops. —lo/cal·ly, adv.

lo·cale/ (lō kal/, -käl/) n. a setting.

lo·cal/i·ty (-kal/i tē) n., pl. **-ties.** a place; area.

lo/cal·ize/ (-kə līz/) v.t., **-ized, -izing.** to confine to a particular place.

lo/cate (lō/kāt, lō kāt/) v., **-cated, -cating.** —v.t. 1. to find or establish the place of. —v.i. 2. to become settled.

lo·ca/tion n. 1. an act or instance of locating. 2. the place where something is.

loc. cit. (lok/ sit/) in the place cited.

lock (lok) n. 1. a device for fastening a door, lid, etc. 2. a chamber in a canal for moving vessels from one water level to another. —v.t. 3. to secure with a lock. 4. to shut in or out. 5. to join firmly.

lock² (lok) n. a curl of hair.

lock/er n. a chest, closet, etc., locked for safekeeping.

lock/et (-it) n. a small case for a keepsake, usu. worn on a necklace.

lock/jaw/ n. tetanus in which the jaws become tightly locked.

lock/out/ n. a business closure to force acceptance of an employer's terms of work.

lock/smith/ n. a person who makes or repairs locks.

lock/step/ n. 1. a way of marching in close file. 2. a rigidly inflexible pattern or process.

lock/up/ n. a jail.

lo/co (lō/kō) adj. Slang. crazy.

lo/co·mo/tion (lō/kə mō/shən) n. the act or power of moving about.

lo/co·mo/tive n. an engine that pulls railroad cars.

lo/co·weed/ (lō/kō-) n. a plant causing a disease in livestock.

lo/cust (lō/kəst) n. 1. a grasshopper migrating in swarms that consume vegetation. 2. a North American tree with white flowers.

lo·cu/tion (lō kyōō/shən) n. a word, phrase, or expression.

lode (lōd) n. a mineral deposit.

lode/star/ n. a guiding star.

lode/stone/ n. a magnetic stone.

lodge (loj) n., v., **lodged, lodging.** —n. 1. a temporary residence. 2. the meeting place of a fraternal organization. —v.i. 3. to live in a place temporarily. 4. to be fixed in a place. —v.t. 5. to furnish with temporary housing. —lodg/er, n.

lodg/ing n. 1. temporary housing. 2. lodgings, rooms.

loft (lôft) n. 1. a space under a sloping roof; attic. 2. an upper story of a warehouse.

loft/y adj., **-ier, -iest.** 1. tall. 2. exalted in rank or character. 3. haughty. —loft/i·ly, adv.

log (lôg) n., v., **logged, logging.** —n. 1. a section of the trunk or limb of a felled tree. 2. Also, **log/book/.** a record of events. —v.t. 3. to cut (trees) into logs. 4. to record in a log. —v.i. 5. to fell trees and cut out logs for timber. 6. **log in** or **on,** to gain access to a computer system. 7. ~ **off** or **out,** to end a session on a computer system. —log/ger, n.

lo/gan·ber/ry (lō/gən ber/ē) n., pl. **-ries.** a dark red tart berry.

log/a·rithm (lô/gə rith/əm) n. Math. the symbol of the number of times a number must be multiplied by itself to equal a given number.

loge (lōzh) n. the front section of the lowest balcony in a theater.

log/ger·head/ (lô/gər hed/, log/ər-) n. —Idiom. **at loggerheads,** in conflict.

log/ic (loj/ik) n. a science or method of reasoning. —lo·gi/cian n.

log/i·cal, adj. 1. according to the principles of logic. 2. reasonable. —log/i·cal·ly, adv.

lo·gis/tics (lō jis/tiks, lə-) n. the management of the details of an operation.

log/jam/ (lôg/-) n. 1. a pileup of logs, as in a river. 2. a blockage.

lo/go (lō/gō) n. a representation or symbol of a company name, trademark, etc. Also, **lo/go·type/.**

log/roll/ing n. the exchange of support or favors, esp. in politics.

lo/gy (lō/gē) adj., **-gier, -giest.** sluggish.

-logy a suffix meaning the study of.

loin (loin) n. the part of the body between the ribs and the hipbone.

loin/cloth/ n. a cloth worn around the loins or hips.

loi/ter (loi/tər) v.i. to linger aimlessly about a place.

loll (lol) v.i. 1. to recline in a lazy manner. 2. to hang loosely.

lol/li·pop/ (lol/ē pop/) n. hard candy on a stick.

lone (lōn) adj. solitary; sole.

lone/ly (lōn/lē) adj., **-lier, -liest.** 1. solitary. 2. having a depressing feeling of being alone. 3. isolated. —lone/li·ness, n.

lon/er n. a person who spends much time alone.

lone/some (-səm) adj. 1. depressed by being alone. 2. remote.

long¹ (lông) adj. 1. of great or specified length. —adv. 2. for a long time.

long² (lông) v.i. to have a strong desire.

lon·gev/i·ty (lon jev/i tē) n. 1. long life. 2. length of life.

long/hand/ (lông/-) n. ordinary handwriting.

lon/gi·tude/ (lon/ji tōōd/, -tyōōd/) n. distance east or west of a point on the earth's surface.

lon/gi·tu/di·nal (lon/ji tōōd/n l, -tyōōd/-) adj. 1. of longitude. 2. lengthwise.

long/ jump/ n. a jump for distance from a running start.

long/-lived/ (-līvd/, -livd/) adj. having a long life or duration.

long/-range/ adj. spanning a long distance or time.

long/shore/man n. a person who loads and unloads ships.

long/ shot/ n. a racehorse, team, etc., with little chance of winning.

2. an undertaking with little chance for success.

long/-term/ adj. involving a long time.

long/-wind/ed (-win/did) adj. continuing to speak for too long.

look (lŏŏk) v.i. 1. to turn the eyes toward something in order to see. 2. to seem. 3. **look after,** to care for. 4. ~ **down on,** to view with contempt. 5. ~ **forward to,** to anticipate happily. 6. ~ **into,** to investigate. 7. ~ **up,** to search for. 8. ~ **up to,** to admire. —n. 9. the act of looking. 10. appearance.

look/ing glass/ n. a mirror.

look/out/ n. 1. a watch. 2. a person for keeping watch. 3. a place for keeping watch.

loom¹ (lōōm) n. a device for weaving fabric.

loom² (lōōm) v.i. to come into view as large and indistinct.

loon (lōōn) n. a ducklike diving bird.

loon/y adj., **-ier, -iest.** Informal. 1. insane. 2. extremely foolish.

loop (lōōp) n. 1. a portion of a string, ribbon, etc., folded upon itself so as to leave an opening between the parts; anything shaped like this. —v.i., v.t. 2. to form (into) a loop.

loop/hole/ n. 1. a narrow opening in a wall. 2. a means of evading a rule without breaking it.

loose (lōōs) adj., **-er, -est,** v., **loosed, loosing.** —adj. 1. not firm or tight. 2. not confined. 3. not packed together. 4. not exact. —v.t. 5. to set free. 6. to shoot (missiles). —loos/en, v.t., v.i.

loot (lōōt) n. 1. plunder taken in war. 2. anything taken by dishonesty, force, etc. 3. Slang. money or gifts. —v.t. 4. to take (as) loot. —loot/er, n.

lop (lop) v.t., **lopped, lopping.** to cut off.

lope (lōp) v.i., **loped, loping.** to move or run with a long, easy stride.

lop/sid/ed adj. uneven.

lo·qua/cious (lō kwā/shəs) adj. talkative. —lo·quac/i·ty (-kwas/i tē) n.

lord (lôrd) n. 1. a master. 2. a British nobleman. 3. **Lord,** God or Jesus Christ. —v. 4. **lord it over,** to behave in a domineering manner toward. —lord/ly, adj. —lord/ship, n.

lore (lôr) n. learning.

lor/ry (lôr/ē) n., pl. **-ries.** Brit. a truck.

lose (lōōz) v., **lost** (lôst) **losing.** —v.t. 1. to fail to keep. 2. to misplace. 3. to be deprived of. 4. to fail to win. —v.i. 5. to suffer loss.

loss (lôs) n. 1. the act of losing. 2. disadvantage from losing. 3. the thing, person, or amount lost. —Idiom. **at a loss,** bewildered.

lost (lôst, lost) adj. 1. no longer to be found. —v. 2. pt. and pp. of **lose.**

lot (lot) n. 1. an object drawn to decide a question by chance. 2. allotted share; portion. 3. a piece of land. 4. Often, **lots.** Informal. a great number or amount. —Usage. See ALOT.

Lo·thar/i·o (lō thâr/ē ō/) n., pl. **-os.** (often l.c.) a man who obsessively seduces women.

lo/tion (lō/shən) n. liquid to rub on the skin.

lot/ter·y (lot/ə rē) n., pl. **-ies.** a sale of tickets on prizes to be awarded by means of a drawing.

lot/to (lot/ō) n. a game of chance similar to bingo.

lo/tus (lō/təs) n. 1. a water lily of Egypt and Asia. 2. a mythical fruit that causes forgetfulness.

loud (loud) adj. 1. easily heard. 2. noisy. 3. garish.

loud/mouth/ (-mouth/) n. a braggart; gossip.

loud/speak/er n. a device for increasing the volume of sound.

lounge (lounj) v., **lounged, lounging.** n. —v.i. 1. to pass time idly. 2. to loll. —n. 3. a kind of sofa. 4. a public room for socializing.

louse (lous) n., pl. **lice** (līs). 1. a bloodsucking insect. 2. a contemptible person.

lous/y (lou/zē) adj., **-ier, -iest.** 1. Informal. bad. 2. troubled with lice.

lout (lout) n. a clumsy ill-mannered person. —lout/ish, adj.

lou/ver (lōō/vər) n. one of a set of slanting, overlapping slats to admit air and light but shut out rain.

lov/a·ble (luv/ə bəl) adj. attracting love. Also, **love/a·ble.**

love (luv) n., v., **loved, loving.** —n. 1. tender, passionate affection. 2. strong personal liking. 3. a person toward whom love is felt. —v.t. 4. to have love (for). —lov/er, n. —lov/ing, adj.

love/lorn/ (-lôrn/) adj. deprived of love or a lover.

love/ly (luv/lē) adj., **-lier, -liest.** charming. —love/li·ness, n.

lov/ing cup/ n. a large two-handled drinking cup.

low¹ (lō) adj. 1. not high or tall. 2. below the normal level. 3. sad. 4. humble or inferior. 5. not loud. 6. vulgar. —adv. 7. in a low position. 8. in a quiet tone. —n. 9. a low point or level. 10. an area of low atmospheric pressure. —Idiom. 11. **lay low,** to overpower. 12. **lie low,** to hide oneself.

low² (lō) v.i. 1. (of cattle) to make a deep mooing sound. —n. 2. a deep mooing sound made by cattle.

low/brow/ n. 1. an uncultured person. —adj. 2. typical of a lowbrow.

low/down/ n. (lō/doun/) 1. the real and unadorned facts. —adj. (-doun/) 2. contemptible; mean.

low/er¹ (lō/ər) adj. 1. comparative of **low¹.** —v.t. 2. to reduce or diminish. 3. to make lower. —v.i. 4. to become lower. —adj. 5. under.

low/er² (lou/ər) v.i. 1. to be threatening. 2. to frown.

low/er·case/ (lō/ər-) adj. 1. (of a letter) of a form often different from and smaller than its corresponding capital letter. —n. 2. a lowercase letter.

low/ fre/quency n. a radio frequency between 30 and 300 kilohertz.

low/-key/ adj. understated.

low/life/ n., pl. **-lifes.** a disreputable or degenerate person.

low/ly adj., **-lier, -liest.** having a low rank; humble.

low/-mind/ed adj. coarse; vulgar.

low/ pro/file n. a deliberately inconspicuous manner.

lox (loks) n. smoked salmon.

loy/al (loi/əl) adj. faithful; steadfast. —loy/al·ly, adv. —loy/al·ty, n.

loz/enge (loz/inj) n. 1. a flavored candy, often medicated. 2. a diamond-shaped object.

LPN licensed practical nurse.

LSD lysergic acid diethylamide, a powerful psychedelic drug.

Lt. lieutenant.

Ltd. limited.

lu/bri·cant (lōō/bri kənt) n. a lubricating substance.

lu/bri·cate/ (-kāt/) v.t., **-cated, -cating.** to oil or grease, esp. to diminish friction.

lu/cid (lōō/sid) adj. 1. easily understood. 2. clear. 3. rational. —lu·cid/i·ty, n.

Lu/cite (lōō/sīt) Trademark. a transparent plastic.

luck (luk) n. 1. chance. 2. good fortune. —luck/less, adj.

luck/y adj., **-ier, -iest.** having or due to good luck. —luck/i·ly, adv.

lu/cra·tive (lōō/krə tiv) adj. profitable.

lu/cre (lōō/kər) n. gain or money.

lu/di·crous (lōō/di krəs) adj. ridiculous. —lu/di·crous·ly, adv.

lug¹ (lug) v.t., **lugged, lugging.** to pull or carry with effort.

lug² n. 1. a projecting handle. 2. Slang. an awkward, clumsy fellow.

luge (lōōzh) n., v., **luged, luging.** —n. 1. a small racing sled. —v.i. 2. to race on a luge.

lug/gage (lug/ij) n. suitcases, trunks, etc.; baggage.

lug/ nut/ n. a large nut, esp. for attaching a wheel to a vehicle.

lu·gu/bri·ous (lōō gōō/brē əs, -gyōō/-) adj. excessively mournful.

luke/warm/ (lōōk/-) adj. slightly warm.

lull (lul) v.t. 1. to soothe, esp. to put to sleep. 2. to give a false sense of security. —n. 3. a brief stillness.

lull/a·by/ (-ə bī/) n., pl. **-bies.** a song used to lull a child to sleep.

lum·ba/go (lum bā/gō) n. pain in the lower back.

lum/bar (lum/bər, -bär) adj. of or close to the loins.

lum/ber¹ (lum/bər) n. 1. timber made into boards, planks, etc. —v.i. 2. to cut and prepare timber.

lum/ber² (lum/bər) v.i. to move heavily.

lum/ber·jack/ n. a person who fells trees.

lum/ber·yard/ n. a yard where lumber is stored for sale.

lu/mi·nar/y (lōō/mə ner/ē) n., pl. **-ies.** 1. a celestial body. 2. a person who inspires many.

lu/mi·nes/cent (lōō/mə nes/ənt) adj. emitting light without heat. —lu/mi·nes/cence, n.

lu/mi·nous (-nəs) adj. 1. reflecting light; shining. 2. clear. —lu/mi·nos/i·ty (-nos/i tē) n.

lum/mox (lum/əks) n. Informal. a clumsy, stupid person.

lump (lump) n. 1. an irregular mass. 2. a swelling. —adj. 3. including many. —v.t. 4. to unite into one mass. —v.i. 5. to form a lump.

lu/na·cy (lōō/nə sē) n. insanity.

lu/nar (-nər) adj. 1. of or according to the moon. 2. crescent-shaped.

lu/na·tic (-tik) n. 1. an insane person. —adj. 2. for the insane. 3. crazy.

lunch (lunch) n. 1. Also, **lunch/eon** (lun/chən). a midday meal. —v.i. 2. to eat lunch.

lung (lung) n. either of the two saclike respiratory organs.

lunge (lunj) n., v., **lunged, lunging.** —n. 1. a sudden forward movement. —v.i. 2. to make a lunge.

lu/pine¹ (lōō/pin) n. a plant with tall, dense clusters of blue, pink, or white flowers.

lu/pine² (lōō/pīn) adj. of or resembling the wolf.

lu/pus (lōō/pəs) n. an autoimmune disease characterized by skin inflammation and joint pain.

lurch¹ (lûrch) n. 1. a sudden lean to one side. —v.i. 2. to stagger.

lurch² (lûrch) n. a difficult situation.

lure (lŏŏr) n., v., **lured, luring.** —n. 1. anything that entices or allures. —v.t. 2. to attract; entice.

lu/rid (lŏŏr/id) adj. 1. sensational; shocking. 2. glaringly lighted.

lurk (lûrk) v.i. to lie hidden.

lus/cious (lush/əs) adj. delicious.

lush (lush) adj. 1. tender and juicy. 2. abundant.

lust (lust) n. 1. strong sexual desire. 2. any strong desire. —v.i. 3. to have a strong desire. —lust/ful, adj.

lus/ter (lus/tər) n. gloss; radiance. Also, **lus/tre.** —lus/trous, adj.

lust/y adj., **-ier, -iest.** vigorous.

lute (lōōt) n. a stringed instrument having a long neck and a hollow, pear-shaped body. —lut/en·ist, n.

Lu/ther·an (lōō/thər ən) adj. 1. of a Protestant denomination following the doctrine of Martin Luther. —n. 2. a member of the Lutheran church. —Lu/ther·an·ism, n.

lux·u/ri·ant (lug zhŏŏr/ē ənt, luk shŏŏr/-) adj. richly abundant. —lux·u/ri·ance, n.

lux·u/ri·ate/ (-āt/) v.i., **-ated, -ating.** to delight in something.

lux·u/ry (luk/shə rē, lug/zhə-) n., pl. **-ries.** 1. choice and costly comforts or pleasures. 2. something enjoyable but not necessary. 3. an unusual pleasure allowed oneself. —lux·u/ri·ous (lug zhŏŏr/ē əs, luk shŏŏr/-) adj.

-ly a suffix meaning: in a specified manner; according to; to or from a specified direction, like or characteristic of; every.

ly·ce/um (lī sē/əm) n. a hall for public lectures, concerts, etc.

lye (lī) n. a white alkaline substance used for washing.

ly/ing-in/ adj. 1. of or for childbirth. —n. 2. childbirth.

Lyme/ disease/ (līm) n. a tick-transmitted disease characterized esp. by joint pains and fatigue.

lymph (limf) n. a yellowish fluid containing lymphocytes and fats that surrounds body cells and carries away their wastes. —lym·phat/ic (lim fat/ik) adj.

lym/pho·cyte/ (lim/fə sīt/) n. a kind of white blood cell helping to produce antibodies.

lynch (linch) v.t. to put to death without legal authority.

lynx (lingks) n., pl. **lynxes, lynx.** a kind of wildcat having a short tail and tufted ears.

lyre (lī²r) n. an ancient harplike instrument.

lyr/ic (lir/ik) adj. Also, **lyr/i·cal.** 1. (of poetry) having the form of a song expressing the writer's feelings. 2. of or writing such poetry. —n. 3. a lyric poem. 4. **lyrics,** the words for a song. —lyr/i·cism (-ə siz/m) n. —lyr/i·cist, n.

M

M, m (em) *n.* the thirteenth letter of the English alphabet.

ma (mä) *n. Informal.* mother.

MA Massachusetts.

M.A. Master of Arts.

ma'am (mam, mäm; *unstressed* məm) *n. Informal.* madam.

ma·ca·bre (mə kä′brə, -käb′) *adj.* gruesome.

mac·ad·am (mə kad′əm) *n.* a road-making material containing broken stones. **—mac·ad′am·ize′**, *v.t.*

mac·a·ro′ni (mak′ə rō′nē) *n.* tube-shaped pasta.

mac·a·roon′ (mak′ə rōōn′) *n.* an almond or coconut cookie.

ma·caw′ (mə kô′) *n.* a large, long-tailed parrot.

mace[1] (mās) *n.* **1.** a clublike armor-breaking weapon. **2.** a ceremonial staff.

mace[2] (mās) *n.* a spice made from the husk of the nutmeg.

Mace (mās) *n. Trademark.* a chemical spray for subduing attackers.

mac′er·ate′ (mas′ə rāt′) *v.t.*, **-ated, -ating.** to soften by steeping in liquid.

ma·che·te (mə shet′ē, -chet′ē) *n.* a heavy swordlike knife.

Mach·i·a·vel′li·an (mak′ē ə vel′ē-ən) *adj.* unscrupulously cunning.

mach′i·na′tion (mak′ə nā′shən) *n.* a cunning plan.

ma·chine′ (mə shēn′) *n.* **1.** a mechanical device. **2.** a group controlling a political party.

machine′ gun′ *n.* a firearm that shoots a continuous stream of bullets.

ma·chin′er·y *n.* machines or mechanical parts.

ma·chin′ist *n.* one who operates a powered tool, ship's engines, etc.

ma·chis′mo (mä chēz′mō) *n.* exaggerated masculinity.

Mach′ num′ber (mäk) *n.* the ratio of the speed of an object to the speed of sound.

ma′cho (mä′chō) *adj.* exaggeratedly virile.

mack′er·el (mak′ər əl) *n.* a N Atlantic food fish.

mack′i·naw′ (mak′ə nô′) *n.* a short, heavy, woolen coat.

mack′in·tosh′ (mak′in tosh′) *n.* a raincoat.

mac′ra·mé (mak′rə mā′) *n.* a decorative work of knotted cords.

macro- a prefix meaning large.

mac′ro·cosm (mak′rə koz′əm) *n.* the universe as a whole.

ma′cron (mā′kron, mak′ron) *n.* a horizontal line over a vowel to show it is long.

mac′u·la (mak′yə lə) *n., pl.* **-lae** (-lē) **-las. 1.** a spot, esp. on the skin. **2.** the point of sharpest vision on the retina.

mac′ular degenera′tion *n.* deterioration of the macula in the center of the retina, resulting in a loss of central vision.

mad (mad) *adj.,* **madder, maddest. 1.** insane. **2.** angry. **3.** violent. **—mad′den,** *v.t.*

mad′am (mad′əm) *n.* **1.** a female term of address. **2.** a woman in charge of a brothel.

mad·ame (mad′əm, mə dam′, -däm′, ma-), *n., pl.* **mes·dames** (mā-dam′, -däm′). (*often cap.*) a French title equivalent to Mrs.

mad′cap′ *adj.* impulsive; rash.

mad′ cow′ disease′ *n.* bovine spongiform encephalopathy.

made *v.* pt. of make.

mad·e·moi·selle′ (mad′ə mə zel′, mad′mwa-, mam zel′) *n., pl.* **mademoiselles, mesdemoiselles** (mā-də zel′, -zelz′, mād′mwa-). a French term of address for an unmarried woman.

mad′man′ or **mad′wom′an** *n., pl.* **-men** or **-wom·en.** an insane person.

Ma·don′na (mə don′ə) *n.* the Virgin Mary.

mad′ras (mad′rəs, mə dras′, -dräs′) *n.* a light cotton fabric.

mad′ri·gal (mad′ri gəl) *n.* an unaccompanied song for several voices.

mael′strom (māl′strəm) *n.* a whirlpool. **2.** a state of confusion.

mae′nad (mē′nad) *n.* a female worshiper of the Greek god Dionysus. **2.** a frenzied woman.

maes′tro (mī′strō) *n., pl.* **-tros.** a master, esp. of music.

Ma′fi·a (mä′fē ə, maf′ē ə) *n.* a se-cret society allegedly engaged in criminal activities.

ma′fi·o′so (mä′fē ō′sō, -sē) *n., pl.* **-si** (-sē) **-sos.** a member of the Mafia.

mag·a·zine′ (mag′ə zēn′) *n.* **1.** a periodical publication. **2.** a store-house for ammunition. **3.** a cartridge chamber, as in a rifle.

mag′got (mag′ət) *n.* the larva of a fly.

Ma′gi (mā′jī) *n.pl.* the three wise men who brought gifts to the infant Jesus.

mag′ic (maj′ik) *n.* **1.** the art of producing illusions or tricks. **2.** the use of techniques to exert control over the supernatural. **—adj.** Also, **mag′i·cal. 3.** used in or done by magic. **4.** enchanting. **—ma·gi′cian** (mə jish′ən) *n.*

mag·is·te′ri·al (maj′ə stēr′ē al) *adj.* masterlike; authoritative.

mag′is·trate′ (-strāt′, -strit) *n.* a civil public official.

mag′ma (mag′mə) *n.* molten rock.

mag·nan′i·mous (mag nan′ə məs) *adj.* generous; high-minded. **—mag′na·nim′i·ty** (-nə nim′i tē) *n.*

mag′nate (-nāt, -nit) *n.* a business leader.

mag·ne′sia (mag nē′zhə), *n.* a white tasteless substance used as an antacid and laxative.

mag·ne′si·um (-zē əm, -zhəm) *n.* a light, silvery metallic element.

mag′net (mag′nit) *n.* **1.** a metal body that attracts iron or steel. **2.** something or someone that attracts.

mag·net′ic (-net′ik) *adj.* **1.** of a magnet or magnetism. **2.** attractive.

magnet′ic field′ *n.* a region near a magnet, electric current, or moving charged particle in which a magnetic force acts.

mag′net·ism (mag′ni tiz′əm) *n.* **1.** the characteristic properties of magnets. **2.** the science of magnets. **3.** great personal charm. **—mag′net·ize′,** *v.t.*

mag′net·ite′ (mag′ni tīt′) *n.* a common black mineral.

mag·ne′to (mag nē′tō) *n., pl.* **-tos.** a small electric generator.

mag·nif′i·cent (mag nif′ə sənt) *adj.* **1.** splendid. **2.** noble. **—mag·nif′i·cence** *n.*

mag′ni·fy′ (mag′nə fī′) *v.t.,* **-fied, -fying. 1.** to increase the apparent or actual size of. **2.** to exaggerate. **—mag′ni·fi′er,** *n.*

mag′ni·tude′ (-ni tōōd′, -tyōōd′) *n.* size or extent.

mag·no′li·a (mag nōl′yə, -nō′lē ə) *n.* a tree with large fragrant flowers.

mag′num o′pus *n.* the chief work of a great writer, musician, etc.

mag′pie′ (mag′pī′) *n.* a noisy black-and-white bird that steals.

ma·ha·ra′jah (mä′hə rä′jə, -zhə) *n.* (formerly) a ruling prince in India.

ma·ha·ra′nee (-nē) *n.* **1.** the wife of a maharajah. **2.** (formerly) an Indian princess.

ma·hat′ma (mə hät′mə, -hat′-) *n.* (in India) a person revered for wisdom and saintliness.

mah′-jongg′ (mä′jông′, -zhông′) *n.* a Chinese game played with tiles.

ma·hog′a·ny (mə hog′ə nē) *n., pl.* **-nies.** a tropical American tree or its hard red-brown wood.

maid (mād) *n.* **1.** a female servant. **2.** an unmarried woman.

maid′en *n.* **1.** a young unmarried woman. **—adj. 2.** of maidens. **3.** unmarried. **4.** initial.

maid′en·hair′ *n.* a fern with finely divided fronds.

mail[1] (māl) *n.* **1.** letters, parcels, etc., delivered by a postal service. **2.** a system to deliver mail. **—v.t. 3.** to send by mail. **—mail′box′, —mail′ car′rier, —mail′man′,** *n.*

mail[2] (māl) *n.* flexible armor.

mail′lot′ (mä yō′, ma-) *n.* a one-piece bathing suit for women.

maim (mām) *v.t.* to injure so as to lose the use of a body part.

main (mān) *adj.* **1.** chief. **—n. 2.** a chief pipe or duct. **3.** strength. **4.** the ocean. **—main′ly,** *adv.*

main′frame′ *n.* a large computer, often the hub of a system.

main′land′ (-land′, -lənd) *n.* continental land rather than an island.

main′spring′ *n.* the chief spring of a mechanism.

main′stay′ *n.* a chief support.

main′stream′ *n.* the dominant course or trend.

main·tain′ (mān tān′) *v.t.* **1.** to support. **2.** to assert. **3.** to keep in order or condition. **—main′te·nance** (-tə nəns) *n.*

mai′tre d'hô·tel′ (mā′trə dō tel′) *n.* the head of a restaurant staff. Also, **mai′tre d′** (mā′tər dē′).

maize (māz) *n.* corn.

maj·es′ty (maj′ə stē) *n., pl.* **-ties. 1.** regal grandeur. **2.** a title of a sovereign. **—ma·jes′tic** (mə jes′tic) *adj.*

ma·jol′i·ca (mə jol′i kə, mə yol′-) *n.* a kind of pottery.

ma′jor (mā′jər) *n.* **1.** an army officer above a captain. **2.** a person of legal age. **—adj. 3.** larger or more important.

ma′jor·do′mo (-dō′mō) *n.* a steward.

ma′jor·ette′ (-jə ret′) *n.* a young woman who leads a marching band.

ma′jor gen′eral *n.* a military officer above a brigadier.

ma·jor′i·ty (mə jôr′i tē) *n., pl.* **-ties. 1.** a number larger than half of a total. **2.** full legal age.

make (māk) *v.,* **made** (mād) **making,** *n.* **—v.t. 1.** to create; form. **2.** to cause to be or exist. **3.** to prepare. **4.** to force. **5.** to appoint. **6.** to win or earn. **7.** to amount to. **8.** to reach. **9.** to act or behave. **10.** to cause to be as specified. **11. make over,** to alter. **12. — up, a.** to invent. **b.** to compensate. **c.** to settle. **d.** to reconcile. **—n. 13.** style. **14.** brand. **—Idiom. 15. make believe,** to pretend. **16. make it,** to achieve success.

make′-be·lieve′ *n.* **1.** a pretending that a fanciful thing is true. **—adj. 2.** imaginary.

make′shift′ *n.* **1.** a temporary substitute. **—adj. 2.** substitute

make′up′ *n.* **1.** cosmetics. **2.** organization; composition.

mal- a prefix meaning bad or ill.

mal′a·chite′ (mal′ə kīt′) *n.* a green mineral, an ore of copper.

mal·ad·just′ed *adj.* badly adjusted, esp. to social conditions.

mal·a·droit′ (mal′ə droit′) *adj.* awkward.

mal′a·dy (mal′ə dē) *n., pl.* **-dies.** an illness.

ma·laise′ (ma lāz′, -lez′, mə-) *n.* **1.** weakness. **2.** a vague uneasiness.

mal′a·mute′ (mal′ə myōōt′) *n.* an Alaskan breed of large dogs.

mal′a·prop·ism (mal′ə prop iz′-əm) *n.* a ludicrous misuse of similar words.

ma·lar′i·a (mə lâr′ē ə) *n.* a mosquito-borne disease. **—ma·lar′i·al,** *adj.*

ma·lar′key (mə lär′kē) *n. Slang.* nonsense.

mal·con·tent′ (mal′kən tent′) *n.* a dissatisfied person.

mal de mer′ (mal də meR′) *French.* seasickness.

male (māl) *adj.* **1.** of the sex that produces sperm. **—n. 2.** a male person or animal.

mal′e·dic′tion (mal′i dik′shən) *n.* a curse.

mal′e·fac′tor (mal′ə fak′tər) *n.* a criminal or evil doer.

ma·lev′o·lent (mə lev′ə lənt) *adj.* wishing evil. **—ma·lev′o·lence,** *n.*

mal·fea′sance (mal fē′zəns) *n.* misconduct in office.

mal·formed′ *adj.* badly formed. **—mal′for·ma′tion,** *n.*

mal′ice (mal′is) *n.* evil intent. **—ma·li′cious** (mə lish′shəs) *adj.*

ma·lign′ (mə līn′) *v.t.* to speak ill of. **—adj. 2.** evil.

ma·lig′nan·cy (mə lig′nən sē) *n., pl.* **-cies. 1.** a malignant state. **2.** a cancerous growth.

ma·lig′nant (-nənt) *adj.* **1.** causing harm or suffering. **2.** cancerous.

ma·lig′ni·ty (-ni tē) *n., pl.* **-ties. 1.** the state of being malignant. **2.** an instance of malignant feeling or behavior.

ma·lin′ger (mə ling′gər) *v.i.* feign sickness to avoid work. **—ma·lin′ger·er,** *n.*

mall (môl) *n.* **1.** a covered shopping center. **2.** a shaded walk.

mal′lard (mal′ərd) *n.* a wild duck.

mal′le·a·ble (mal′ē ə bəl) *adj.* **1.** that may be hammered or rolled into shape. **2.** readily influenced.

mal′let (mal′it) *n.* a wooden-headed hammer.

mal·nu·tri′tion *n.* bad nutrition.

mal′oc·clu′sion *n.* irregular contact between the upper and lower teeth.

mal·o′dor·ous *adj.* smelling bad.

mal·prac′tice *n.* improper professional behavior.

malt (môlt) *n.* a germinated grain used in liquor-making.

malt′ose (môl′tōs) *n.* a sugar formed by action of an enzyme on starch.

ma′ma (mä′mə, mə mä′) *n. Informal.* mother.

mam′mal (mam′əl) *n.* a vertebrate animal whose young are suckled.

mam′ma·ry (mam′ə rē) *adj.* of breasts.

mam′mo·gram′ (mam′ə gram′) *n.* an x-ray photograph of a breast, for detection of tumors.

mam′mon (mam′ən) *n.* material wealth.

mam′moth (mam′əth) *n.* **1.** a large extinct elephant. **—adj. 2.** huge.

man (man) *n., pl.* **men** (men) *v.,* **manned, manning. —n. 1.** an adult male person. **2.** the human race. **—v.t. 4.** to supply with a crew. **5.** to operate.

man′a·cle (man′ə kəl) *n., v.,* **-cled, -cling. —n. 1.** a handcuff. **—v.t. 2.** to handcuff.

man′age (man′ij) *v.,* **-aged, -aging. —v.t. 1.** to succeed in accomplishing. **2.** to supervise, direct, or control. **—v.i. 3.** to cope.

man′age·ment *n.* **1.** the act or process of managing. **2.** the persons in charge.

man′ag·er *n.* a person who manages a business, team, etc. **—man·a·ge′ri·al** (-i jēr′ē əl) *adj.*

ma·ña′na (mä nyä′nä) *n. Spanish.* tomorrow.

man′a·tee′ (man′ə tē′) *n.* a plant-eating aquatic mammal.

man·da′mus (man dā′məs) *n., pl.* **-mus·es.** *Law.* a writ from a superior court commanding that a thing be done.

man′da·rin (man′də rin) *n.* **1.** a public official in the Chinese Empire. **2. Mandarin,** a dialect of Chinese.

man′date (man′dāt) *n.* **1.** authority over territory granted to a nation. **2.** territory under such authority. **3.** an authorization to act granted by an electorate. **4.** a command.

man′da·to′ry (man′də tôr′ē) *adj.* officially required.

man·di′ble (man′də bəl) *n.* a bone comprising the lower jaw.

man′do·lin (man′dl in, man′dl in′) *n.* a stringed musical instrument.

man′drake (man′drāk, -drik) *n.* a narcotic plant whose root resembles a human form.

man′drel (man′drəl) *n.* a rod or axle in machinery.

mane (mān) *n.* the long hair at the neck of horses or lions.

ma·neu′ver (mə nōō′vər) *n.* **1.** a planned movement or procedure, esp. in war. **—v.i., v.t. 2.** to perform or cause to perform a maneuver. **3.** to position or manipulate skillfully. **—ma·neu′ver·a·ble,** *adj.*

man′ Fri′day *n., pl.* **men Friday.** a reliable male assistant.

man′ga·nese′ (mang′gə nēs′, -nēz′) *n.* a hard metallic element.

mange (mānj) *n.* a skin disease of animals. **—man′gy,** *adj.*

man′ger (mān′jər) *n.* a trough for feeding livestock.

man′gle (mang′gəl) *v.,* **-gled, -gling,** *n.* **—v.t. 1.** to disfigure, esp. by crushing. **2.** to bungle. **—n. 3.** a device with rollers for removing water in washing clothes.

man′go (mang′gō) *n., pl.* **-goes.** the fruit of a tropical tree.

man′grove (mang′grōv, man′-) *n.* a kind of tropical tree.

man′han′dle (man′han′dl) *v.t.,* **-dled, -dling.** to handle roughly.

man′hole′ *n.* an access hole to a sewer.

man′-hour′ *n.* the ideal amount of work done by a person in an hour.

man′hunt′ *n.* an intensive search for a fugitive.

ma′ni·a (mā′nē ə) *n.* **1.** great excitement. **2.** violent insanity.

ma′ni·ac′ (mā′nē ak′) *n.* a lunatic. **—ma·ni′a·cal** (mə nī′ə kəl) *adj.*

man′ic (man′ik) *adj.* irrationally excited or lively.

man′ic-depress′ive *adj.* suffering from a mental disorder in which enthusiasm alternates with depression.

man′i·cure′ (man′i kyoor′) *n., v.,* **-cured, -curing.** **1.** a cosmetic treatment of the fingernails. **—v.t. 2.** to give a manicure. **—man′i·cur′ist,** *n.*

man′i·fest′ (man′ə fest′) *adj.* **1.** evident. **—v.t. 2.** to show plainly. **—n. 3.** a list of cargo and passengers.

man′i·fes′to (-fes′tō) *n., pl.* **-toes.** a public declaration of intentions.

man′i·fold′ (man′ə fōld′) *adj.* **1.** of many kinds or parts. **—n. 2.** a pipe with many outlets.

man′i·kin (man′i kin) *n.* a model of the human body.

Ma·nil′a pa′per (mə nil′ə) *n.* a strong, yellowish brown paper.

man′ in the street′ *n.* an ordinary person.

ma·nip′u·late′ (mə nip′yə lāt′) *v.t.,* **-lat·ed, -lat·ing.** to manage or handle with skill or cunning. **—ma·nip′u·la′tion, —ma·nip′u·la′tive,** *adj.* **—ma·nip′u·la′tor,** *n.*

man′kind′ (man′kīnd′) *n.* the human race.

man′ly *adj.,* **-lier, -liest.** virile.

man′na (man′ə) *n.* divine food given to the Israelites.

man′ne·quin (man′i kin) *n.* a model for displaying clothes.

man′ner (man′ər) *n.* **1.** a way of doing or happening. **2. manners,** ways of behaving with reference to polite standards. **3.** sort.

man′ner·ism *n.* a peculiar way of doing something.

man′ner·ly *adj.* polite.

man′-of-war′ *n., pl.* **men-of-war.** a warship.

man′or (man′ər) *n.* a large estate.

man′pow′er *n.* power in terms of an available labor force.

man·qué′ (mäng kā′) *adj.* unfulfilled.

man′sard (man′särd) *n.* a roof with two slopes of different pitch on all sides.

manse (mans) *n.* a parson's house.

man′sion (man′shən) *n.* a large or stately house.

man′slaugh′ter *n.* the unlawful killing of a person without malice.

man′ta (man′tə, män′-) *n.* a huge ray with pectoral fins.

man′tel (man′tl) *n.* an ornamental structure around a fireplace.

man·til′la (man til′ə, -tē′ə) *n.* a lace head scarf for Spanish women.

man′tis (man′tis) *n.* a kind of carnivorous insect.

man·tis′sa (man tis′ə) *n.* the decimal part of a common logarithm.

man′tle (man′tl) *n., v.,* **-tled, -tling. —n. 1.** a loose cloak. **2.** something that covers. **—v.t. 3.** to envelop.

man′tra (man′trə, män′-) *n.* a Hindu or Buddhist sacred incantation.

man′u·al (man′yōō əl) *adj.* **1.** of or done with the hands or by human effort. **—n. 2.** a small instruction book. **—man′u·al·ly,** *adv.*

man′u·fac′ture (man′yə fak′chər) *n., v.,* **-tured, -turing. 1.** the making of goods, esp. in great quantity. **2.** something made. **3.** to make or fabricate.

man′u·mit′ (man′yə mit′) *v.t.,* **-mitted, -mitting.** to release from slavery. **—man′u·mis′sion,** *n.*

ma·nure′ (mə nōor′, -nyōor′) *n.* animal excrement used as fertilizer.

man′u·script′ (man′yə skript′) *n.* a handwritten or typed text.

man′y (men′ē) *adj.* **1.** comprising a large number; numerous. **—n. 2.** a large number of persons or things.

Mao′ism (mou′iz əm) *n.* the policies of the Chinese Communist leader Mao Zedong. **—Mao′ist,** *n., adj.*

map (map) *n., v.,* **mapped, mapping. —n. 1.** a flat representation of all or part of the earth. **—v.t. 2.** to show on a map. **3.** to plan.

ma′ple (mā′pəl) *n.* a broad-leaved tree grown for shade, ornament, sap, or timber.

mar (mär) *v.t.,* **marred, marring.** to damage or disfigure.

Mar. March.

ma·ra′ca (mə rä′kə, -rak′ə) *n.* a gourd-shaped rattle, used as a rhythm instrument.

mar′a·thon′ (mar′ə thon′, -thən) *n.* a long contest, esp. a foot race of 26 miles, 385 yards.

ma·raud′ (mə rôd′) *v.i., v.t.* to rove in quest of plunder. **—ma·raud′er,** *n.*

mar′ble (mär′bəl) *n.* **1.** a crystalline limestone used in sculpture and building. **2.** a small glass ball used in games. **—adj. 3.** of marble.

mar′bling *n.* an intermixture of fat with lean in meat.

march (märch) *v.i.* **1.** to walk with measured tread. **2.** to advance. **—v.t. 3.** to cause to march. **—n. 4.** the act of marching. **5.** the distance covered in a march. **6.** music for marching.

March (märch) *n.* the third month of the year.

mar′chion·ess (mär′shə nis, -nes′) *n.* **1.** the wife of a marquess. **2.** a woman of a rank equal to a marquess.

Mar′di Gras (mär′dē grä′, grä′) *n.* the Tuesday before Lent, often celebrated as a carnival.

mare (mâr) *n.* a female horse.

mare′s′-nest′ *n.* a complicated situation.

mar′ga·rine (mär′jər in) *n.* a butterlike product made from vegetable oils and water or milk.

mar′gin (mär′jin) *n.* **1.** an edge. **2.** the space around text on a page. **3.** an amount beyond what is necessary.

mar′gin·al *adj.* **1.** of or at a margin. **2.** barely acceptable.

mar′gi·na′li·a (-jə nā′lē ə) *n.pl.* marginal notes.

mar′gue·rite (mär′gə rēt′) *n.* a daisylike chrysanthemum.

mar′i·gold′ (mar′i gōld′) *n.* a common yellow- or orange-flowered plant.

ma·ri·jua′na (mar′ə wä′nə) *n.* a narcotic plant.

ma·rim′ba (mə rim′bə) *n.* a xylophone with chambers for resonance.

ma·ri′na (mə rē′nə) *n.* a docking area for small boats.

mar′i·nade′ (mar′ə nād′) *n.* a pungent liquid mixture for steeping food.

mar′i·nate′ *v.t.,* -nated, -nating. to season by steeping.

ma·rine′ (mə rēn′) *adj.* **1.** of the sea. —*n.* **2.** a member of the U.S. Marine Corps. **3.** a fleet of ships.

Marine′ Corps′ a military force trained for sea-launched assaults on land.

mar′i·ner (mar′ə nər) *n.* a sailor.

mar′i·o·nette′ (mar′ē·ə net′) *n.* a puppet on strings.

mar′i·tal (mar′i tl) *adj.* of marriage.

mar′i·time′ (mar′i tīm′) *adj.* of the sea or shipping.

mar′jo·ram (mär′jər əm) *n.* an aromatic herb used as seasoning.

mark (märk) *n.* **1.** a visible sign. **2.** an object aimed at. **3.** a rating; grade. **4.** a lasting effect. —*v.t.* **5.** to be a feature of. **6.** to put a mark on, as a grade or price. **7.** to pay attention to. —**mark′er,** *n.*

mark′down′ *n.* a price reduction.

marked (märkt) *adj.* **1.** conspicuous; striking. **2.** singled out for revenge. —**mark′ed·ly,** *adv.*

mar′ket (mär′kit) *n.* **1.** a place for selling and buying. **2.** a food store. **3.** demand for a commodity. —*v.t.* **4.** to sell or buy. —**mar′ket·a·ble,** *adj.*

mar′ket·place′ *n.* **1.** an open area where a market is held. **2.** the world of business, trade, and economics.

marks′man *n., pl.* -men. a person who shoots well. —**marks′man·ship′,** *n.*

mark′up′ *n.* a price increase by a retailer.

mar′lin (mär′lin) *n.* a large game fish.

mar′ma·lade′ (mär′mə lād′) *n.* a citrus fruit preserve.

mar′mo·set′ (mär′mə zet′, -set′) *n.* a small tropical American monkey.

mar′mot (mär′mət) *n.* a bushy-tailed rodent.

ma·roon′[1] (mə rōōn′) *n.* a dark brownish red.

ma·roon′[2] (mə rōōn′) *v.t.* **1.** to put ashore and abandon on a deserted island. **2.** to isolate without aid.

mar·quee′ (mär kē′) *n.* a projecting structure over an entrance. **2.** a large tent.

mar′que·try (mär′ki trē) *n.* inlaid work forming a pattern.

mar′quis (mär′kwis, mär kē′) *n.* a European nobleman ranking below a duke.

mar·quise′ (-kēz′) *n.* **1.** the wife of a marquis. **2.** a woman of a rank equal to a marquis.

mar′riage (mar′ij) *n.* **1.** a legal union of a man and woman. **2.** a wedding. —**mar′riage·a·ble,** *adj.*

mar′row (mar′ō) *n.* the soft inner tissue of bone.

mar′ry (mar′ē) *v.,* -ried, -rying. —*v.t.* **1.** to take as a husband or wife. **2.** to join in marriage. —*v.i.* **3.** to take a husband or wife.

Mars (märz) *n.* **1.** the planet fourth from the sun. **2.** the Roman god of war.

marsh (märsh) *n.* a tract of low, wet land. —**marsh′y,** *adj.*

mar′shal (mär′shəl) *n., v.,* -shaled, -shaling. —*n.* **1.** a federal officer. —*v.t.* **2.** to rally; organize.

marsh′ gas′ *n.* a decomposition product of organic matter.

marsh′mal′low (-mel′ō, -mal′ō) *n.* a soft candy made from gelatin.

marsh′ mar′igold *n.* a yellow-flowered plant of the buttercup family.

mar·su′pi·al (mär sōō′pē əl) *n.* an animal carrying its young in a pouch, as the kangaroo.

mart (märt) *n.* a market.

mar′ten (mär′tn) *n.* a small, American fur-bearing animal.

mar′tial (mär′shəl) *adj.* warlike.

mar′tial art′ *n.* any of various forms of East Asian self-defense or combat.

mar′tial law′ *n.* law imposed by military forces.

mar′tin (mär′tn) *n.* a bird of the swallow family.

mar′ti·net′ (mär′tn et′) *n.* a person who enforces strict discipline.

mar·ti′ni (mär tē′nē) *n.* a cocktail of gin and vermouth.

mar′tyr (mär′tər) *n.* **1.** a person who willingly dies for a belief. —*v.t.* **2.** to make a martyr of. —**mar′tyr·dom,** *n.*

mar′vel (mär′vəl) *n., v.,* -veled, -veling. —*n.* **1.** a wonderful or astonishing thing. —*v.i., v.t.* **2.** to wonder (at or about).

mar′vel·ous *adj.* **1.** superbly fine. **2.** arousing wonder or astonishment. —**mar′vel·ous·ly,** *adv.*

Marx′ism *n.* the system of thought developed by Karl Marx on which communism is based. —**Marx′ist,** *n., adj.*

mar′zi·pan′ (mär′zə pan′) *n.* a confection of almond paste and sugar.

mas·car′a (ma skar′ə) *n.* a cosmetic for eyelashes.

mas′cot (mas′kot, -kət) *n.* a person, animal, or thing bringing good luck.

mas′cu·line (mas′kyə lin) *adj.* of, like, or suitable for men. —**mas′cu·lin′i·ty,** *n.*

ma′ser (mā′zər) *n.* a device for producing electromagnetic waves.

mash (mash) *n.* **1.** a soft pulpy mass. —*v.t.* **2.** to crush into a soft pulpy mass. —**mash′er,** *n.*

mask (mask) *n.* **1.** a disguise or protection for the face. —*v.t.* **2.** to disguise or cover.

mas·och·ism (mas′ə kiz′əm, maz′-) *n.* pleasure in suffering. —**mas′och·ist,** *n.* —**mas′och·is′tic,** *adj.*

ma′son (mā′sən) *n.* a builder with stone, brick, etc. —**ma′son·ry,** *n.*

mas′quer·ade′ (mas′kə rād′) *n., v.,* -aded, -ading. —*n.* **1.** a disguise. **2.** a party at which guests wear a disguise. —*v.i.* **3.** to be disguised.

mass[1] (mas) *n.* **1.** a body of coherent matter. **2.** a quantity or size. **3.** weight. **4. the masses,** the common people. —*v.i., v.t.* **5.** to form into a mass. —*adj.* **6.** of or affecting the masses. **7.** done on a large scale.

mass[2] (mas) *n. (often cap.)* the celebration of the Eucharist.

Mass. Massachusetts.

mas′sa·cre (mas′ə kər) *n., v.,* -cred, -cring. —*n.* **1.** the killing of many people. —*v.t.* **2.** to slaughter.

mas·sage′ (mə säzh′, -säj′) *v.,* -saged, -saging. —*v.t.* **1.** to manipulate the body by rubbing or kneading. —*n.* **2.** such treatment.

mas·seur′ (mə sûr′, -sōōr′) *n.* a man who provides massage.

mas·seuse′ (mə sōōs′, -sōōz′) *n.* a woman who provides massage.

mas′sive (mas′iv) *adj.* large; heavy.

mass′ me′dia *n.pl.* the means of communication that reach great numbers of people.

mass′ noun′ *n.* a noun that refers to an indefinitely divisible substance or an abstract notion.

mass′ num′ber *n.* the number of nucleons in an atomic nucleus.

mass′-produce′ *v.t.,* -duced, -ducing. to produce in large quantities. —**mass′ produc′tion,** *n.*

mast (mast) *n.* an upright pole on a ship.

mas·tec′to·my (ma stek′tə mē) *n., pl.* -mies. the surgical removal of a breast.

mas′ter (mas′tər) *n.* **1.** a person in control. **2.** a male teacher. **3.** a skilled person. —*adj.* **4.** chief. —*v.t.* **5.** to conquer. **6.** to become an expert in.

mas′ter·ful *adj.* asserting power.

mas′ter·ly *adj.* highly skilled.

mas′ter·mind′ *n.* **1.** one who originates or oversees a plan. —*v.t.* **2.** to plan as a mastermind.

mas′ter of cer′emonies *n.* a person who conducts events.

mas′ter·piece′ *n.* a work of highest skill.

mas′ter's degree′ *n.* a degree awarded to a student who has completed at least one year of graduate study.

mas′ter ser′geant *n.* a noncommissioned officer of the highest rank.

mas′ter·stroke′ *n.* an extremely skillful action.

mas′ter·y *n.* **1.** command; grasp. **2.** dominance. **3.** expert skill.

mast′head′ *n.* a box in a newspaper, magazine, etc., giving names of owners and staff.

mas′ti·cate′ (mas′ti kāt′) *v.t.,* -cated, -cating. to chew.

mas′tiff (mas′tif) *n.* a powerful dog.

mas′to·don′ (mas′tə don′) *n.* a large extinct elephantlike mammal.

mas′toid (mas′toid) *n.* a protuberance of bone behind the ear.

mas′tur·bate′ (mas′tər bāt′) *v.i., v.t.,* -bated, -bating. to manually stimulate one's own genitals or the genitals of (another). —**mas′tur·ba′tion,** *n.*

mat (mat) *n., v.,* matted, matting. —*n.* **1.** a covering for a floor or other surface. **2.** material bordering a picture. **3.** a thick tangled mass. —*v.t., v.i.* **4.** to form into a mat.

mat′a·dor′ (mat′ə dôr′) *n.* a bullfighter.

match[1] (mach) *n.* **1.** a person or thing resembling or equaling another. **2.** a thing that goes well with another. **3.** a competition; contest. **4.** a marriage. —*v.t.* **5.** to equal. **6.** to fit together with. **7.** to arrange marriage for. —*v.i.* **8.** to go together well.

match[2] (mach) *n.* a stick chemically tipped to strike fire.

match′less *adj.* unequaled.

match′mak′er *n.* an arranger of marriages.

mate (māt) *n., v.,* mated, mating. —*n.* **1.** one of a pair. **2.** a husband or wife. **3.** an officer of a merchant ship. **4.** a companion. —*v.t., v.i.* **5.** to join; pair. **6.** to copulate.

ma·te′ri·al (mə tēr′ē əl) *n.* **1.** the substance of which a thing is made. **2.** fabric. —*adj.* **3.** physical. **4.** pertinent. —**ma·te′ri·al·ly,** *adv.*

ma·te′ri·al·ism *n.* **1.** devotion to material objects or wealth. **2.** the belief that all reality is material.

ma·te′ri·al·ize′ *v.i.,* -ized, -izing. **1.** to be realized; appear. **2.** to assume material form.

ma·te′ri·el′ (mə tēr′ē el′) *n.* supplies, esp. military.

ma·ter′ni·ty (mə tûr′ni tē) *n.* **1.** the state of being a mother. —*adj.* **2.** for pregnant women or new mothers. —**ma·ter′nal,** *adj.*

math′e·mat′ics (math′ə mat′iks) *n.* the science of numbers. —**math·e·mat′i·cal,** *adj.* —**math·e·ma·ti′cian** (-mə tish′ən) *n.*

mat·i·née′ (mat′n ā′) *n.* an afternoon performance.

mat′ins (mat′nz) *n.* morning prayers.

ma′tri·arch′ (mā′trē ärk′) *n.* the female head of a family or tribe. —**ma′tri·ar′chal,** *adj.*

ma′tri·ar′chy (-är′kē) *n., pl.* -chies. a form of social organization in which a female is head of the family.

mat′ri·cide′ (ma′tri sīd′, mā′-) *n.* **1.** the act of killing one's mother. **2.** a person who commits such an act. —**mat′ri·cid′al,** *adj.*

ma·tric·u·late (mə trik′yə lāt′) *v.i.,* -lated, -lating. to enroll as a student. —**ma·tric′u·la′tion,** *n.*

mat′ri·mo′ny (ma′trə mō′nē) *n.* marriage. —**mat′ri·mo′ni·al,** *adj.*

ma′trix (mā′triks, ma′-) *n., pl.* -trices (-tri sēz′), -trixes. **1.** a place or point where something originates. **2.** a mold; model.

ma′tron (mā′trən) *n.* **1.** a dignified married woman. **2.** a female institutional officer. —**ma′tron·ly,** *adj.*

matte (mat) *adj.* **1.** having a dull surface, without luster. —*n.* **2.** a dull surface or finish.

mat′ter (mat′ər) *n.* **1.** the substance of which a physical object consists. **2.** trouble. **3.** pus. **4.** a subject of concern or discussion. —*v.i.* **5.** to be of importance. —**Idiom. 6. as a matter of fact,** actually.

mat′ter-of-fact′ *adj.* adhering to fact; straightforward.

mat′ting (mat′ing) *n.* material for mats.

mat′tock (mat′ək) *n.* a digging tool.

mat′tress (ma′tris) *n.* a thick filled case for sleeping on.

ma·ture′ (mə tōōr′, -tyōōr′, -chōōr′) *adj.,* -turer, -turest, *v.,* -tured, -turing. —*adj.* **1.** grown or developed. **2.** adult in manner or thought. **3.** payable. —*v.i., v.t.* **4.** to become or make mature. —**ma·tu′ri·ty,** *n.*

mat′zo (mät′sə) *n., pl.* -zos. unleavened bread.

maud′lin (môd′lin) *adj.* weakly sentimental.

maul (môl) *v.t.* to injure by rough treatment.

maun′der (môn′dər) *v.i.* **1.** to talk in a rambling way. **2.** to wander.

mau·so·le′um (mô′sə lē′əm, -zə-) *n., pl.* -leums, -lea (-lē′ə). a tomb in the form of a building.

mauve (mōv, môv) *n.* a pale purple.

ma′ven (mā′vən) *n.* an expert.

mav′er·ick (mav′ər ik) *n.* **1.** a nonconformist. **2.** an unbranded animal.

maw (mô) *n.* the mouth, throat, or stomach of an animal.

mawk′ish (mô′kish) *adj.* sickeningly sentimental. —**mawk′ish·ly,** *adv.*

max·il′la (mak sil′ə) *n., pl.* maxillae (-sē) the upper jaw. —**max′il·lar′y** (-sa ler′ē) *adj.*

max′im (mak′sim) *n.* a proverb.

max′i·mum (mak′sə məm) *n.* **1.** the greatest degree or quantity. —*adj.* **2.** greatest possible.

may (mā) *aux. v., pres.* **may;** *past* **might** (mīt). (used to express possibility or permission.)

May (mā) *n.* the fifth month of the year.

may′be *adv.* it may be (that).

May′day′ *n.* an international radio distress call.

may′flow′er *n.* a plant that blossoms in May.

may′fly′ *n., pl.* -flies. an insect with large transparent forewings.

may′hem (mā′hem, -əm) *n.* **1.** the crime of willfully crippling or mutilating someone. **2.** random violence.

may′on·naise′ (mā′ə nāz′) *n.* a sauce made of egg yolks, oil, and vinegar. Also, *Informal.* **may′o.**

may′or (mā′ər) *n.* the chief officer of a city. —**may′or·al,** *adj.*

may′or·al·ty (mā′ər əl tē, mâr′əl-) *n., pl.* -ties. the office or tenure of a mayor.

maze (māz) *n.* a confusing arrangement of paths.

ma·zur′ka (mə zûr′kə,-zōōr′-) *n.* a lively Polish dance.

MD Maryland. Also, **Md.**

M.D. Doctor of Medicine.

me (mē) *pron.* the objective case of I.

ME Maine.

mead (mēd) *n.* a liquor of fermented honey.

mead′ow (med′ō) *n.* a tract of level grassland.

mead′ow·lark′ *n.* a North American songbird.

mea′ger (mē′gər) *adj.* poor; scanty.

meal[1] (mēl) *n.* the food served and eaten at one time.

meal[2] (mēl) *n.* coarse powder ground from the seeds of a grain.

meal′y-mouthed′ *adj.* avoiding candid speech.

mean[1] (mēn) *v.,* **meant** (ment) meaning. —*v.t.* **1.** to intend (to do or signify). **2.** to signify. —*v.i.* **3.** to have specified intentions.

mean[2] (mēn) *adj.* **1.** unkind; malicious. **2.** poor; shabby. —**mean′ly,** *adv.* —**mean′ness,** *n.*

mean[3] (mēn) *n.* **1.** means, a method for achieving a purpose. **2.** means, resources, esp. money. **3.** something midway between two extremes; average. —*adj.* **4.** middle. —**Idiom. 5. by all means,** certainly. **6. by no means,** not at all.

me·an′der (mē an′dər) *v.i.* to wander aimlessly.

mean′ing *n.* **1.** what is intended to be expressed. **2.** the aim or purpose. —**mean′ing·ful,** *adj.*

mean′time′ *n.* **1.** the time between. —*adv.* Also, **mean′while′. 2.** in the time between.

mea′sles (mē′zəlz) *n.* an infectious disease marked by small red spots.

mea′sly (mē′zlē) *adj.,* -slier, -sliest. *Informal.* miserably small.

meas′ure (mezh′ər) *v.,* -ured, -uring, *n.* —*v.t.* **1.** to ascertain the size of. —*v.i.* **2.** to be of a specified size. **3.** measure up, to reach the necessary standard. —*n.* **4.** the process of measuring. **5.** the dimensions of something. **6.** an instrument or system used in measuring. **7.** Usu., **measures,** an action to achieve an

end. —**Idiom. 8. for good measure,** as an extra. —**meas′ure·ment,** *n.*

meas′ured *adj.* careful; deliberate.

meat (mēt) *n.* **1.** the flesh of animals used as food. **2.** the edible part of a fruit, nut, etc. **3.** the essential part; gist.

meat′y *adj.,* -ier, -iest. **1.** like or full of meat. **2.** rich in content.

Mec′ca (mek′ə) *n.* **1.** the spiritual center of Islam. **2.** (*often l.c.*) a place that attracts many people.

me·chan′ic (mə kan′ik) *n.* a skilled worker with machinery.

me·chan′i·cal *adj.* of or operated by machinery.

me·chan′ics *n.* the science of motion and of the action of forces on bodies.

mech′an·ism (mek′ə niz′əm) *n.* **1.** the structure of a machine. **2.** a piece of machinery.

mech′a·nis′tic (-nis′tik) *adj.* of or like machinery.

mech′a·nize′ *v.t.,* -nized, -nizing. **1.** to make mechanical. **2.** to equip with machinery.

med′al (med′l) *n.* a badgelike metal object given for merit.

med′al·ist *n.* a medal winner.

me·dal′lion (mə dal′yən) *n.* a large medal or medallike ornament.

med′dle (med′l) *v.i.,* -dled, -dling. to interfere. —**med′dle·some,** *adj.*

me′di·a (mē′dē ə) *n.pl.* the means of mass communication.

me′di·al (mē′dē əl) *adj.* average.

me′di·an (mē′dē ən) *adj.* **1.** in the middle. —*n.* **2.** the middle number, point, etc.

me′di·ate′ (mē′dē āt′) *v.t., v.i.,* -ated, -ating. to settle or act as an intermediary. —**me′di·a′tor,** *n.*

med′ic (med′ik) *n. Informal.* a doctor or medical aide.

Med′i·caid′ (med′i kād′) *n.* government-supported medical care for low-income persons.

med′i·cal (med′i kəl) *adj.* of medicine. **2.** curative. —**med′i·cal·ly,** *adv.*

me·dic′a·ment (mə dik′ə mənt, med′i kə-) *n.* a healing substance.

Med′i·care′ (med′i kâr′) *n.* government-supported medical insurance for those 65 and older.

med′i·cate′ *v.t.,* -cated, -cating. to treat with medicine. —**med′i·ca′tion,** *n.*

me·dic′i·nal (mə dis′ə nl) *adj.* curative. —**me·dic′i·nal·ly,** *adv.*

med′i·cine (med′ə sin) *n.* **1.** a substance used in treating illness. **2.** the art of restoring physical health.

med′icine man′ *n.* among American Indians, a person believed to have magical powers.

me′di·e′val (mē′dē ē′vəl, mid ē′-) *adj.* of the Middle Ages. Also, **me′di·ae′val.**

me′di·o′cre (mē′dē ō′kər) *adj.* of ordinary or moderate quality. —**me′di·oc′ri·ty** (-ok′ri tē) *n.*

med′i·tate′ (med′i tāt′) *v.i.,* -tated, -tating. to think deeply. —**med′i·ta′tion,** *n.* —**med′i·ta′tive,** *adj.*

me′di·um (mē′dē əm) *n., pl.* -dia (-dē ə), except for 4, -diums, *adj.* —*n.* **1.** something intermediate or moderate. **2.** a means of doing or conveying something. **3.** a surrounding substance. **4.** a person believed able to communicate with the dead. **5.** a means of mass communication. —*adj.* **6.** intermediate.

med′ley (med′lē) *n.* a mixture.

me·dul′la (mə dul′ə) *n.* the soft, marrowlike center of an organ.

meek (mēk) *adj.* submissive.

meer′schaum (mēr′shəm, -shôm) *n.* a claylike mineral, used for tobacco pipes.

meet[1] (mēt) *v.,* **met** (met) meeting, *n., adj.* —*v.t.* **1.** to come upon. **2.** to come into contact with. **3.** to be introduced to. **4.** to pay or satisfy. —*v.i.* **5.** to come together. —*n.* **6.** a meeting of competitors for a sports contest. —*adj.* **7.** proper.

meet′ing *n.* **1.** a coming together. **2.** a gathering of persons.

mega- a prefix meaning: **1.** one million. **2.** large.

meg′a·hertz′ (meg′ə hûrts′) *n., pl.* -hertz. one million hertz.

meg′a·lo·ma′ni·a (meg′ə lō mā′nē ə) *n.* a delusion of greatness, riches, etc.

meg′a·lop′o·lis (meg′ə lop′ə lis) *n.* a very large urbanized area.

meg′a·phone′ (meg′ə fōn′) *n.* a cone-shaped device for magnifying sound.

meg′a·plex′ (-pleks′) *n.* a large building containing usu. more than a dozen movie theaters.

meg′a·ton′ *n.* an explosive force

equal to that of one million tons of TNT.

mei·o·sis (mī ō′sis) *n.* a part of the process of gamete formation.

mel·a·mine (mel′ə mēn′) *n.* a crystalline solid used in making resins.

mel·an·chol·i·a (mel′ən kō′lē ə) *n.* a severe form of depression.

mel·an·chol·y (mel′ən kol′ē) *n.* **1.** low spirits; depression. —*adj.* **2.** sad.

mé·lange (mā länzh′, -länj′) *n.* a mixture.

mel·a·nin (mel′ə nin) *n.* a pigment accounting for the dark color of skin, hair, etc.

mel·a·no·ma (-nō′mə) *n.* a darkly pigmented malignant skin tumor.

meld¹ (meld) *v.t., v.i.* to display (a combination of cards) for a score.

meld² (meld) *v.t., v.i.* to merge; blend. —*n.* **2.** a blend.

me·lee (mā′lā) *n.* a confused, general fight.

mel·io·rate (mēl′yə rāt′) *v.t., v.i., -rated, -rating.* to ameliorate.

mel·lif·lu·ous (mə lif′lōō əs) *adj.* soft and sweet in speech.

mel·low (mel′ō) *adj.* **1.** soft and rich. **2.** genial. —*v.t., v.i.* **3.** to make or become mellow.

me·lo·de·on (mə lō′dē ən) *n.* a reed organ.

me·lo·di·ous *adj.* tuneful.

mel·o·dra·ma (mel′ə drä′mə, -dram′ə) *n.* a play emphasizing theatrical effects and strong emotions.

mel·o·dra·mat·ic *adj.* **1.** of melodrama. **2.** overly emotional.

mel·o·dy (mel′ə dē) *n., pl. -dies.* an arrangement of musical sounds. —**me·lod′ic** (mə lod′ik) *adj.*

mel·on (mel′ən) *n.* an edible fruit of certain annual vines.

melt (melt) *v.t., v.i.* **1.** to make or become liquid, esp. by heat. **2.** to soften.

melt′down′ *n.* the melting of a nuclear reactor core.

melt′ing pot′ *n.* a locality in which a blending of peoples or cultures takes place.

mem·ber (mem′bər) *n.* **1.** a part of a structure. **2.** one belonging to an organization. —**mem′ber·ship′**, *n.*

mem·brane (mem′brān) *n.* a thin film of tissue in animals and plants.

me·men·to (mə men′tō) *n., pl. -tos, -toes.* something serving as a reminder.

mem·oir (mem′wär, -wôr) *n.* **1.** a record of events based on the writer's personal observation. **2.** **memoirs,** an autobiography.

mem·o·ra·bil·i·a (-ə bil′ē ə, -bil′yə) *n.pl.* souvenirs.

mem·o·ra·ble *adj.* worth remembering. —**mem′o·ra·bly,** *adv.*

mem·o·ran·dum (mem′ə ran′dəm) *n., pl. -dums, -da (-də).* a written statement or reminder. Also, **memo.**

me·mo·ri·al (mə môr′ē əl) *n.* **1.** something honoring the memory of a person or event. —*adj.* **2.** serving as a memorial.

mem·o·rize (mem′ə rīz′) *v.t., v.i., -rized, -rizing.* to commit to memory.

mem·o·ry *n., pl. -ries.* **1.** the faculty of remembering. **2.** something remembered. **3.** the length of time of recollection. **4.** the capacity of a computer to store data.

men·ace (men′is) *n., -v.t., v.i.* **1.** to threaten or be threatened. —*n.* **2.** something that threatens.

mé·nage (mā näzh′) *n.* a household.

me·nag·er·ie (mə naj′ə rē, -nazh′-) *n.* a collection of animals.

mend (mend) *v.t.* **1.** to repair. **2.** to improve. **3.** to heal. —*n.* **4.** a mended place. —**Idiom. 5. on the mend,** improving.

men·da·cious (men dā′shəs) *adj.* untruthful. —**men·dac′i·ty** (-das′i-tē) *n.*

men·di·cant (men′di kənt) *n.* a beggar.

men·ha·den (men hād′n) *n., pl. -den.* a herringlike Atlantic fish.

me·ni·al (mē′nē əl) *adj.* **1.** humble; servile. —*n.* **2.** a servant.

me·nin·ges (mi nin′jēz) *n.pl., sing.* **me·ninx** (mē′ningks). the three membranes covering the brain and spinal cord.

men·in·gi·tis (men′in jī′tis) *n.* an inflammation of the meninges.

men·o·pause (men′ə pôz′) *n.* the period of cessation of menstruation.

bolic candelabrum used during Hanukkah.

men·ses (men′sēz) *n.* (*used with a sing. or pl. v.*) the menstrual flow or period.

men·stru·a·tion (men′strōō ā′-shən) *n.* the monthly discharge of blood from the uterus. —**men′stru·al,** *adj.* —**men′stru·ate′,** *v.i.*

men·sur·a·ble (-shər ə bəl, -sər ə-bəl) *adj.* capable of being measured.

-ment a suffix meaning: **1.** an action or resulting state. **2.** a product. **3.** a means.

men·tal (men′tl) *adj.* of or in the mind. —**men′tal·ly,** *adv.*

men·tal·i·ty (-tal′i tē) *n., pl. -ties.* **1.** mental ability. **2.** a characteristic mental attitude.

men·thol (men′thôl, -thol) *n.* a colorless alcohol from peppermint oil. —**men′thol·at′ed** (-thə lā′tid) *adj.*

men·tion (men′shən) *v.t.* **1.** to speak or write about briefly. —*n.* **2.** a brief reference.

men·tor (men′tôr, -tər) *n.* an adviser.

men·u (men′yōō, mā′nyōō) *n.* a list of dishes that can be served.

me·ow (mē ou′, myou) *n.* **1.** the sound a cat makes. —*v.i.* **2.** to make such a sound.

mer·can·tile (mûr′kən tēl′, -tīl′, -til) *adj.* of or engaged in trade.

mer·ce·nar·y (mûr′sə ner′ē) *adj., n., pl. -naries.* —*adj.* **1.** acting only for profit. —*n.* **2.** a hired soldier.

mer·cer·ize (mûr′sə rīz′) *v.t., -ized, -izing.* to treat (cotton) for greater strength.

mer·chan·dise (n., v., -dised, -dis-ing. -z′) *n.* (mûr′chən dīz′, -dīs′) **1.** goods; wares. —*v.t., v.i.* (-dīz′) **2.** to buy and sell.

mer·chant (-chənt) *n.* a person who buys and sells goods.

mer·chant·man *n., pl. -men.* a trading ship.

mer·chant marine′ *n.* the ships of a nation that are used for trade.

mer·cu·ri·al (mər kyōōr′ē əl) *adj.* **1.** of mercury. **2.** unpredictable.

mer·cu·ry (mûr′kyə rē) *n.* **1.** a heavy metallic element. **2. Mercury,** the smallest planet, nearest to the sun. **3. Mercury,** the Roman messenger god.

mer·cy (mûr′sē) *n., pl. -cies.* **1.** pity; compassion. **2.** an act of compassion. —**mer′ci·ful,** *adj.*

mere (mēr) *adj.* being nothing more nor better than that specified. —**mere′ly,** *adv.*

mer·e·tri·cious (mer′i trish′əs) *adj.* falsely attractive.

merge (mûrj) *v.t., v.i., merged, merging.* to combine.

me·rid·i·an (mə rid′ē ən) *n.* a circle on the earth's surface passing through the poles.

me·ringue (mə rang′) *n.* egg whites beaten with sugar and browned in an oven.

me·ri·no (mə rē′nō) *n., pl. -nos.* **1.** a kind of sheep. **2.** soft wool.

mer·it (mer′it) *n.* **1.** worth. **2.** a commendable quality. —*v.t.* **3.** to deserve. —**mer′i·to′ri·ous** (-i tôr′-ē əs) *adj.*

mer·maid′ (mûr′mād′) *n.* an imaginary sea creature, half woman and half fish.

mer·man′ *n., pl. -men.* an imaginary sea creature, half man and half fish.

mer·ry (mer′ē) *adj., -rier, -riest.* joyous; cheerful. —**mer′ri·ly,** *adv.*

mer·ry-go-round′ *n.* a revolving amusement ride.

mer·ry·mak·ing *n.* festivity; revelry. —**mer′ry·ma·ker,** *n.*

me·sa (mā′sə) *n.* a high, steep-walled plateau.

mé·sal·li·ance (mā′zə lī′əns, -zal-yäNs′) *n.* a marriage with a social inferior.

mesh (mesh) *n.* **1.** a fabric of open texture. **2.** a network. **3.** the engagement of gear teeth. —*v.t., v.i.* **4.** to engage or become engaged, as gear teeth. **5.** to match; coordinate.

mes·mer·ize (mez′mə rīz′) *v.t., -ized, -izing.* to hypnotize. —**mes′-mer·ism** (-mə riz′əm) *n.*

Mes·o·lith·ic (mez′ə lith′ik, mes′-) *adj.* of a transitional period of the Stone Age.

mes·o·sphere′ (mez′ə sfēr′) *n.* an atmospheric region between the stratosphere and thermosphere.

Mes·o·zo·ic (mez′ə zō′ik) *adj.* of a geologic era occurring between 230 and 65 million years ago.

mes·quite′ (me skēt′, mes′kēt) *n.* a tree of the southwest U.S.

mess (mes) *n.* **1.** a dirty or disorderly condition. **2.** a group taking

meals together regularly. **3.** meals so taken. —*v.t.* **4.** to make dirty or untidy. **5.** to spoil; bungle. —**mess′y,** *adj.*

mes·sage (mes′ij) *n.* a communication.

mes·sen·ger (mes′ən jər) *n.* the bearer of a message.

Mes·si·ah (mi sī′ə) *n.* **1.** the expected deliverer of the Jews. **2.** (in Christian theology) Jesus Christ.

mes·ti·zo (me stē′zō) *n., pl. -zos, -zoes.* a person who is part-Spanish, part-Indian.

meta- a prefix meaning: **1.** after or beyond. **2.** behind. **3.** change.

me·tab·o·lism (mə tab′ə liz′əm) *n.* the biological processes of converting food into energy. —**met·a·bol′ic** (met′ə bol′ik) *adj.*

met·a·car·pus (met′ə kär′pəs) *n., pl. -pi.* the bones of the forelimb between the wrist and fingers. —**met·a·car′pal,** *adj., n.*

met·al (met′l) *n.* an elementary substance such as gold or copper. —**me·tal′lic** (mə tal′ik) *adj.* —**met′-al·ware′,** *n.*

met·al·lur·gy (met′l ûr′jē) *n.* the science of working with metals.

met·a·mor·phose (met′ə môr′fōz, -fōs) *v.i., v.t., -phosed, -phosing.* to transform.

met·a·mor·pho·sis (-fə sis) *n., pl. -ses (-sēz′).* a drastic change.

met·a·phor (met′ə fôr′, -fər) *n.* a figure of speech in which a word or phrase is applied to an object or concept it does not literally denote in order to suggest comparison with its basic meaning. —**met·a·phor′i·cal,** *adj.*

met·a·phys·ics (met′ə fiz′iks) *n.* a branch of philosophy concerned with the ultimate nature of reality. —**met·a·phys′i·cal,** *adj.*

me·tas·ta·size (mə tas′tə sīz′) *v.i., -sized, -sizing.* to spread from one to another part of the body. —**me·tas′ta·sis** (-sis) *n.*

met·a·tar·sus (met′ə tär′səs) *n., pl. -si.* the bones of the hind limb between the ankle and toes. —**met·a·tar′sal,** *adj., n.*

mete (mēt) *v.t., meted, meting.* to allot; distribute.

me·te·or (mē′tē ər, -ôr′) *n.* a small body of rock or metal passing through the earth's atmosphere.

me·te·or·ic (-ôr′ik) *adj.* **1.** of meteors. **2.** sudden and spectacular.

me·te·or·ite′ (-ə rīt′) *n.* a meteor reaching earth.

me·te·or·ol·o·gy (-ə rol′ə jē) *n.* the science of atmospheric phenomena, esp. weather. —**me·te·or·o·log′i·cal** (-ər ə loj′i kəl) *adj.* —**me·te·or·ol′o·gist,** *n.*

me·ter (mē′tər) *n.* **1.** a unit of length in the metric system, equal to 39.37 inches. **2.** the rhythmic element in music and poetry. **3.** a device for measuring flow. —*v.t.* **4.** to measure with a meter. Also, *Brit.,* **me′tre.**

meth·a·done′ (meth′ə dōn′) *n.* a synthetic narcotic used in treating heroin addiction.

meth·ane (meth′ān) *n.* a colorless, odorless, flammable gas.

meth·a·nol′ (meth′ə nôl′) *n.* a colorless liquid used as a solvent, fuel, etc.

meth·od (meth′əd) *n.* a system of doing something.

me·thod·i·cal (mə thod′i kəl) *adj.* **1.** done or acting in a systematic way. **2.** painstaking; deliberate. —**me·thod′i·cal·ly,** *adv.*

Meth·od·ist (meth′ə dist) *n.* a member of a Protestant denomination that developed out of the teachings of John Wesley. —**Meth′-od·ism,** *n.*

meth·od·ol·o·gy (-ə dol′ə jē) *n., pl. -gies.* a system of methods and principles.

meth·yl (meth′əl) *n.* a univalent group derived from methane.

meth·yl al·cohol *n.* methanol.

me·tic·u·lous (mə tik′yə ləs) *adj.* minutely careful.

mé·tier (mā′tyā) *n.* a field of activity in which one has special ability. Also, **me·tier.**

met·ric (me′trik) *adj.* of a decimal system of weights and measures, based on the meter and gram.

met·ro·nome (me′trə nōm′) *n.* a device for marking tempo.

me·trop·o·lis (mi trop′ə lis) *n.* a large, busy city.

met·ro·pol·i·tan (me′trə pol′i tn) *adj.* **1.** of or in a city. **2.** of cities and urban areas.

met·tle (met′l) *n.* **1.** spirit; fortitude. **2.** disposition.

mew (myōō) *n.* **1.** the cry of a cat. —*v.i.* **2.** to emit a mew.

mews (myōōz) *n.* a street with dwellings converted from stables.

Mex·i·can (mek′si kən) *adj.* **1.** of Mexico or its inhabitants. —*n.* **2.** a native of Mexico.

mez·za·nine (mez′ə nēn′, mez′ə-nēn′) *n.* a low story between two main floors; balcony.

mez·zo·so·pran·o (met′sō-, med′zō-) *n.* a voice between soprano and contralto in range.

M.F.A. Master of Fine Arts.

MI Michigan.

mi·as·ma (mī az′mə, mē-) *n., pl. -mata (-mə tə), -mas.* a vapor from decaying organic matter.

mi·ca (mī′kə) *n.* a shiny mineral occurring in thin layers.

Mich. Michigan.

micro- a prefix meaning very small.

mi·crobe (mī′krōb) *n.* a microorganism, esp. one causing disease.

mi·cro·brew·er·y (-, brōō′ə rē) *n., pl. -ies.* a small brewery usu. producing exotic or high quality beer.

mi′cro·chip′ *n.* a chip (def. 5).

mi·cro·com·put′er *n.* a compact computer with less capability than a minicomputer.

mi·cro·cosm (mī′krə koz′əm) *n.* a world in miniature.

mi·cro·fi′ber *n.* a very fine polyester fiber.

mi·cro·fiche (-fēsh′) *n.* a small sheet of microfilm.

mi·cro·film (mī′krə film′) *n.* **1.** a very small photograph of a page, document, etc. —*v.t.* **2.** to make a microfilm of.

mi·cro·man·age *v.t., -aged, -ag-ing.* to manage with excessive attention to minor details.

mi·crom·e·ter (mī krom′i tər) *n.* a device for measuring tiny distances.

mi·cron (mī′kron) *n.* the millionth part of a meter.

mi·cro·or·gan·ism (mī′krō-) *n.* a microscopic organism.

mi·cro·phone (mī′krə fōn′) *n.* an instrument for changing sound waves into electric impulses.

mi·cro·proc·es·sor (mī′krō pros′-es ər, -ə sər; *esp. Brit.* -prō′ses ər, -sə sər) *n.* a computer circuit that performs all the functions of a CPU.

mi·cro·scope (mī′krə skōp′) *n.* an instrument for inspecting minute objects.

mi·cro·scop·ic (-skop′ik) *adj.* **1.** of microscopes. **2.** extremely small.

mi·cro·sur·ger·y (mī′krō sûr′jə rē) *n.* surgery performed under magnification.

mi·cro·wave *n., v. -waved, -wav-ing.* —*n.* **1.** a short radio wave used in radar, cooking, etc. **2.** an oven that uses microwaves to cook food. —*v.t.* **3.** to cook in a microwave oven.

mid (mid) *adj.* **1.** middle. —*prep.* **2.** amid.

mid′day′ (-dā′, -dā′) *n.* noon.

mid·dle (mid′l) *adj.* **1.** equally distant from given limits. **2.** intermediate. —*n.* **3.** a middle part.

Mid′dle Ag′es *n.* a period of European history, about A.D. 476 to 1500.

mid′dle class′ *n.* the class of people intermediate between the poor and the wealthy.

Mid′dle East′ *n.* the area from Libya east to Afghanistan.

Mid′dle Eng′lish *n.* the English language of the period c1150–1475.

mid′dle·man′ *n.* a merchant who buys goods from the producer and resells them.

middle-of-the-road *adj.* moderate.

mid′dle school′ *n.* a school consisting of grades 5 or 6 through 8.

mid′dling *adj.* **1.** medium. **2.** mediocre.

midge (mij) *n.* a tiny fly.

midg′et (mij′it) *n.* a very small person or thing.

mid′land (-lənd) *n.* the interior of a country.

mid′night′ *n.* 12 o'clock at night.

mid′night sun′ *n.* the sun visible at midnight in summer in arctic and antarctic regions.

mid′point′ *n.* a point at or near the middle.

mid′riff (-rif) *n.* a part of the body between the chest and abdomen.

mid′ship·man *n., pl. -men.* a student training to be an officer in the U.S. Navy or Marine Corps.

midst (midst) *n.* the middle.

mid′sum′mer (-sum′ər, -sum′-) *n.* the middle of summer.

mid′term *n.* **1.** the halfway point of a school term. **2.** an examination given at midterm.

mid′way *adj., adv.* (mid′wā′) **1.** in the middle of the way or distance. —*n.* (-wā′) **2.** an area of games and sideshows, as at a carnival.

mid′wife′ *n., pl. -wives.* a woman who assists at childbirth.

mid′win′ter (-win′tər, -win′-) *n.* the middle of winter.

mien (mēn) *n.* demeanor; bearing.

miff (mif) *n.* a petty quarrel.

miffed (mift) *adj.* offended.

might¹ (mīt) *aux. v., pres. sing. and pl.* **might;** *past* **might.** **1.** pt. of **may.** **2.** (used to express possibility or obligation). **3.** (used in polite requests for permission).

might² (mīt) *n.* strength or force.

might′y *adj., -ier, -iest, adv.* —*adj.* **1.** powerful; huge. —*adv.* **2.** *Informal.* very. —**might′i·ness,** *n.*

mi·gnon·ette′ (min′yə net′) *n.* a plant with clusters of small flowers.

mi·graine (mī′grān) *n.* a severe headache, often with nausea.

mi·grate (-grāt) *v.i., -grated, -grat-ing.* to go from one region to another. —**mi·gra′tion,** *n.* —**mi′gra-to′ry** (-grə tôr′ē) *adj.* —**mi′grant,** *adj., n.*

mi·ka·do (mi kä′dō) *n., pl. -dos.* a title of the emperor of Japan.

mike (mīk) *n. Informal.* a microphone.

mil (mil) *n.* one thousandth of an inch.

milch (milch) *adj.* giving milk.

mild (mīld) *adj.* gentle; temperate.

mil·dew (mil′dōō′, -dyōō′) *n.* **1.** a discoloration caused by fungus. —*v.t., v.i.* **2.** to affect or become affected with mildew.

mile (mīl) *n.* a unit of distance, equal on land to 5280 ft.

mile′age (mī′lij) *n.* **1.** the miles traveled. **2.** an allowance for travel expenses.

mile′stone′ *n.* an important event.

mi·lieu′ (mil yōō′, mēl-; *Fr.* mē-lyœ′) *n., pl. -lieus, -lieux.* surroundings; environment.

mil′i·tant (mil′i tənt) *adj.* aggressive.

mil′i·ta·rism (-tə riz′əm) *n.* **1.** military spirit. **2.** domination by the military. —**mil′i·ta·rist,** *n.*

mil′i·ta·rize′ *v.t., -ized, -izing.* to equip with military weapons.

mil′i·tar·y (-ter′ē) *adj.* **1.** of armed forces, esp. on land. —*n.* **2.** armed forces or soldiers collectively.

mil′itary police′ *n.* soldiers who act as police within the army.

mil′i·tate′ (-tāt′) *v.i., -tated, -tat-ing.* to act (for or against).

mi·li′tia (mi lish′ə) *n.* an organization for emergency military service. —**mi·li′tia·man,** *n.*

milk (milk) *n.* **1.** a liquid secreted by female mammals to feed their young. —*v.t.* **2.** to draw milk from. —**milk′y,** *adj.*

milk′ glass′ *n.* an opaque white glass.

milk′man′ *n., pl. -men.* a man who sells or delivers milk.

milk′weed′ *n.* a plant with milky juice.

Milk′y Way′ *n.* the galaxy containing our solar system.

mill (mil) *n.* **1.** a place where manufacturing is done. **2.** a device for grinding. **3.** a place where grain is ground. **4.** one tenth of a cent. —*v.t.* **5.** to grind or treat with a mill. **6.** to groove the edges of (a coin). —*v.i.* **7.** to move about in confusion. —*n.*

mil·len·ni·um (mi len′ē əm) *n., pl. -niums, -nia (-nē ə).* **1.** a period of a thousand years. **2.** a thousandth anniversary.

mil′let (mil′it) *n.* a cereal grass.

milli- a prefix meaning thousand or thousandth.

mil′liard (mil′yərd, -yärd) *n. Brit.* one billion.

mil′li·gram′ (mil′i gram′) *n.* one thousandth of a gram.

mil′li·li′ter *n.* one thousandth of a liter.

mil′li·me′ter *n.* one thousandth of a meter.

mil′li·ner (mil′ə nər) *n.* a person who makes or sells women's hats. —**mil′li·ner′y,** *n.*

mil′lion (mil′yən) *n.* 1000 times 1000. —**mil′lionth,** *adj., n.*

mil·lion·aire′ (mil′yə nâr′) *n.* a person having a million dollars or more.

mill′race′ *n.* a channel for the current of water driving a mill wheel.

mill′stone′ *n.* **1.** a stone for grinding grain. **2.** a heavy mental or emotional burden.

mill′stream′ *n.* the stream in a millrace.

mill′wright′ *n.* a person who designs and installs mill machinery.

milque′toast′ (milk′tōst′) *n.* (*often cap.*) a timid person.

milt (milt) *n.* the sperm-containing secretion of male fish.

mime (mīm, mēm) *n.* **1.** expression by mute gestures; pantomime. **2.** an actor skilled in mime.

mim′e·o·graph′ (mim′ē ə graf′) *n.* **1.** a stencil device for duplicating. —*v.t.* **2.** to copy with a mimeograph.

mim′ic (mim′ik) *v.*, **-icked, -icking,** *n.* —*v.t.* **1.** to imitate the speech or actions of. —*n.* **2.** a person who mimics. —**mim′ic·ry,** *n.*

mi·mo′sa (mi mō′sə, -zə) *n.* a semitropical tree or shrub.

min′a·ret′ (min′ə ret′) *n.* a tower for calling Muslims to prayer.

min′a·to′ry (min′ə tôr′ē) *adj.* threatening.

mince (mins) *v.*, **minced, mincing.** —*v.t.* **1.** to chop fine. **2.** to moderate (words). —*v.i.* **3.** to speak or behave with affected elegance.

mince′meat′ *n.* a cooked mixture of chopped meat, raisins, spices, etc., used in pies.

mind (mīnd) *n.* **1.** the thinking part of a human or animal. **2.** intellectual power. **3.** opinion. **4.** inclination. **5.** memory. —*v.t.* **6.** to obey. **7.** to attend to or care for. **8.** to object to. —*v.i.* **9.** to obey. **10.** to attend. **11.** to object.

mind′ful *adj.* careful.

mind′less *adj.* **1.** heedless. **2.** requiring no intelligence.

mine[1] (mīn) *pron.* **1.** a possessive form of I. **2.** that or those belonging to me.

mine[2] (mīn) *n.* **1.** an excavation in the earth for resources. **2.** a stationary explosive device. **3.** an abundant source. —*v.t.* **4.** to extract from a mine. **5.** to dig in to extract resources. **6.** to place explosive mines in. —*v.i.* **7.** to work in a mine. —**min′er,** *n.*

min′er·al (min′ər əl) *n.* **1.** a natural inorganic substance. **2.** a substance obtained by mining. —*adj.* **3.** of minerals.

min′er·al′o·gy (-ə rol′ə jē, -ral′ə-) *n.* the science of minerals.

min′eral wa′ter *n.* water containing dissolved mineral salts or gases.

min′e·stro′ne (min′ə strō′nē) *n.* a thick vegetable soup.

mine′sweep′er *n.* a ship used to remove explosive mines.

min′gle (ming′gəl) *v.i., v.t.,* **-gled, -gling.** to mix or blend.

min′i (min′ē) *n.* a small version.

mini- a prefix meaning small.

min′i·a·ture (min′ē ə chər, min′ə-) *n.* **1.** a very small version or representation of something. **2.** a tiny painting. —*adj.* **3.** on a small scale. —**min′i·a·tur·ize′,** *v.t.*

min′i·bus′ *n.* a small bus.

min′i·com·put′er *n.* a computer with capabilities between those of a microcomputer and mainframe.

min′im (min′əm) *n.* the smallest unit of liquid measure.

min′i·mal·ism (-mə liz′əm) *n.* a spare and simple style.

min′i·mize′ (-mīz′) *v.t.,* **-mized, -mizing. 1.** to reduce to the minimum. **2.** to represent as being of minimum value or importance.

min′i·mum (-məm) *n.* **1.** the least possible quantity, degree, etc. —*adj.* **2.** Also, **min′i·mal** (-məl). lowest.

min′ion (min′yən) *n.* a servile follower.

min′is·ter (min′ə stər) *n.* **1.** a person authorized to conduct worship. **2.** a government representative abroad. **3.** the head of a governmental department. —*v.i.* **4.** to give care. —**min′is·te′ri·al** (-stēr′ē əl) *adj.* —**min′is·tra′tion,** *n.*

min′is·try (-ə strē) *n., pl.* **-tries. 1.** a religious calling. **2.** the clergy. **3.** the office of a department of government. **4.** a body of executive officials. **5.** the act of ministering.

min′i·van′ *n.* a small passenger van.

mink (mingk) *n.* a semiaquatic mammal or its soft brown fur.

Minn. Minnesota.

min′ne·sing′er (min′ə sing′ər) *n.* a lyric poet of medieval Germany.

min′now (min′ō) *n.* a tiny fish.

mi′nor (mī′nər) *adj.* **1.** lesser in size

or importance. **2.** under legal age. —*n.* **3.** a person under legal age.

mi·nor′i·ty (mi nôr′i tē, mī-) *n., pl.* **-ties. 1.** a number or part forming less than half of a whole. **2.** a group differing from the majority, as in race. **3.** the state or time of being under legal age.

min′strel (min′strəl) *n.* **1.** a medieval musician or singer. **2.** a white performer in blackface singing black American songs in a variety show.

mint[1] (mint) *n.* **1.** a place where money is coined. **2.** a huge sum. —*v.t.* **3.** to make coins.

mint[2] (mint) *n.* an aromatic herb.

min′u·et′ (min′yōō et′) *n.* a stately dance.

mi′nus (mī′nəs) *prep.* **1.** less. **2.** lacking. —*adj.* **3.** less than. **4.** involving subtraction.

mi·nus′cule (min′ə skyōōl, mi·nus′kyōōl) *adj.* tiny.

min·ute[1] (min′it) *n.* **1.** sixty seconds. **2. minutes,** a record of proceedings.

mi·nute[2] (mī nōōt′, -nyōōt′) *adj.* extremely small. —**mi·nute′ly,** *adv.*

mi·nu′ti·ae′ (mi nōō′shē ē′) *n.pl.* trifling matters.

mir′a·cle (mir′ə kəl) *n.* a supernatural act or effect. —**mi·rac′u·lous** (mi rak′yə ləs) *adj.*

mi·rage′ (mi räzh′) *n.* an atmospheric illusion in which images of far-distant objects are seen.

mire (mī[ə]r) *n., v.,* **mired, miring.** —*n.* **1.** a swamp. **2.** deep mud. —*v.i., v.t.* **3.** to sink or stick in or as if in mire.

mir′ror (mir′ər) *n.* **1.** a reflecting surface. —*v.t.* **2.** to reflect.

mirth (mûrth) *n.* gaiety and laughter. —**mirth′less,** *adj.*

mis- a prefix meaning: **1.** wrong. **2.** lack of.

mis′ad·ven′ture (mis′ad ven′chər) *n.* a misfortune; mishap.

mis′an·thrope′ (mis′ən thrōp′, miz′-) *n.* a hater of humanity. —**mis′an·throp′ic** (-throp′ik) *adj.*

mis′ap·ply′ *v.t.,* **-plied, -plying.** to use wrongly. —**mis′ap·pli·ca′tion,** *n.*

mis′ap·pre·hend′ *v.t.* to misunderstand. —**mis′ap·pre·hen′sion** (-hen′shən) *n.*

mis′ap·pro′pri·ate′ (-āt′) *v.t.,* **-ated, -ating.** to use wrongly as one's own.

mis′be·got′ten *adj.* ill-conceived.

mis′be·have′ *v.i.,* **-haved, -having.** to behave badly. —**mis′be·hav′ior,** *n.*

misc. miscellaneous.

mis·cal′cu·late′ *v.t.,* **-lated, -lating.** to judge badly.

mis·call′ *v.t.* to call by a wrong name.

mis·car′riage *n.* **1.** a premature birth resulting in death of the fetus. **2.** failure to attain the right result.

mis·car′ry (mis kar′ē; for 1 also mis′kar′ē) *v.i.,* **-ried, -rying. 1.** to give birth to a fetus before it is viable. **2.** to be unsuccessful.

mis·cast′ *v.t.* to cast in an unsuitable role.

mis′ce·ge·na′tion (mi sej′ə nā′shən, mis′i jə-) *n.* a sexual union between persons of different races.

mis′cel·la′ne·ous (mis′ə lā′nē əs) *adj.* unclassified; various.

mis′cel·la′ny (mis′ə lā′nē) *n., pl.* **-nies.** a collection of various items, esp. literary works.

mis·chance′ *n.* bad luck.

mis′chief (mis′chif) *n.* **1.** harm, trouble, or injury, caused willfully. **2.** annoying conduct or activity. —**mis′chie·vous** (mis′chə vəs) *adj.*
——**Pronunciation.** The word MIS-CHIEVOUS is pronounced with three syllables. The pronunciation (mis-chē′ē əs) with four syllables, is usually considered nonstandard. Note that although a spelling *mischievious,* which reflects this nonstandard pronunciation by including an extra *i* after the *v,* was occasionally seen between the 16th and 19th centuries, it is not considered a correct spelling today.

mis′ci·ble (mis′ə bəl) *adj.* capable of being mixed.

mis′con·ceive′ *v.t.,* **-ceived, -ceiving.** to misunderstand. —**mis′con·cep′tion,** *n.*

mis′con·duct *n.* improper or illegal conduct.

mis′con·strue′ (mis′kən strōō′) *v.t.,* **-strued, -struing.** to misinterpret.

mis′cre·ant (mis′krē ənt) *n.* a villain.

mis·deed′ *n.* an immoral deed.

mis′de·mean′or *n.* a minor offense.

mise-en-scène′ (mē zän sen′) *n., pl.* **mise-en-scènes** (-senz′). **1.** the placement of actors, scenery, and properties on stage. **2.** surroundings.

mi′ser (mī′zər) *n.* a hoarder of wealth. —**mi′ser·ly,** *adj.*

mis′er·a·ble (miz′ər ə bəl) *adj.* **1.** very unhappy. **2.** causing misery. **3.** contemptible; despicable.

mis′er·y *n., pl.* **-eries.** suffering or emotional distress.

mis·fire′ (mis fī[ə]r′) *v.t.,* **-fired, -firing.** to fail to fire.

mis·fit′ *n.* **1.** (mis′fit′) a maladjusted person. **2.** (mis fit′, mis′fit′) a poor fit.

mis·for′tune *n.* bad luck.

mis·giv′ing *n.* a doubt.

mis·guid′ed *adj.* mistaken; ill-informed.

mis·han′dle *v.t.,* **-dled, -dling. 1.** to handle roughly. **2.** to manage badly.

mis′hap (mis′hap, mis hap′) *n.* an unlucky accident.

mish′mash′ (mish′mäsh′, -mash′) *n.* a jumble; hodgepodge.

mis′in·form′ *v.t.* to give false information to. —**mis′in·for·ma′tion,** *n.*

mis′in·ter′pret *v.t.* to interpret wrongly.

mis·judge′ *v.t.,* **-judged, -judging.** to judge wrongly.

mis·lay′ *v.t.,* **-laid, -laying. 1.** to lay or place wrongly. **2.** to misplace.

mis·lead′ (-lēd′) *v.t.,* **-led, -leading. 1.** to lead in the wrong direction. **2.** to lead into error, as in conduct.

mis·man′age *v.t.,* **-aged, -aging.** to manage badly.

mis·match′ *v.t.* **1.** (mis mach′) to match unsuitably. —*n.* (mis mach′, mis′mach′) **2.** an unsuitable match.

mis·no′mer (mis nō′mər) *n.* a name applied wrongly.

mi·sog′a·my (mi sog′ə mē, mī-) *n.* hatred of marriage. —**mi·sog′a·mist,** *n.*

mi·sog′y·ny (mi soj′ə nē, mī-) *n.* hatred of women. —**mi·sog′y·nist,** *n.*

mis·place′ *v.t.,* **-placed, -placing. 1.** to lose temporarily. **2.** to place unwisely.

mis·print′ (mis′print′, mis print′) *n.* an error in printing.

mis·pri′sion (mis prizh′ən) *n.* a neglect or violation of official duty.

mis′pro·nounce′ *v.t.,* **-nounced, -nouncing.** to pronounce wrongly.

mis·quote′ *v.t.,* **-quoted, -quoting.** to quote incorrectly.

mis·read′ (-rēd′) *v.t.,* **-read** (red′) **-reading. 1.** to read wrongly. **2.** to misinterpret.

mis′rep·re·sent′ *v.t.* to represent incorrectly or falsely.

mis·rule′ *n., v.,* **-ruled, -ruling.** —*n.* **1.** bad or unwise rule. —*v.t.* **2.** to rule badly.

miss[1] (mis) *v.t.* **1.** to fail to hit, do, meet, catch, etc. **2.** to regret the absence of. **3.** to escape or avoid. —*v.i.* **4.** to fail to hit something. **5.** to fail. —*n.* **6.** a failure, esp. a failure to hit something.

miss[2] (mis) *n.* **1. Miss,** a title of respect for an unmarried woman. **2.** a girl.

Miss. Mississippi.

mis′sal (mis′əl) *n.* a book of prayers and rites for celebrating Mass.

mis·shap′en *adj.* deformed.

mis′sile (-əl; *esp. Brit.* -īl) *n.* an object thrown or shot.

mis′sion (mish′ən) *n.* **1.** a group sent abroad for specific work. **2.** a duty. **3.** an air operation against an enemy. **4.** a missionary post.

mis′sion·ar′y (-ə ner′ē) *n., pl.* **-aries,** *adj.* —*n.* **1.** a person sent to propagate religious faith. —*adj.* **2.** of religious missions.

mis′sive (mis′iv) *n.* a letter.

mis·spell′ *v.t.* to spell wrongly.

mis·spend′ *v.t.,* **-spent, -spending.** to squander.

mis·state′ *v.t.,* **-stated, -stating.** to state wrongly.

mis·step′ *n.* an error.

mist (mist) *n.* a light, thin fog. —**mist′y,** *adj.*

mis·take′ (mi stāk′) *n., v.,* **-took, -taken, -taking.** —*n.* **1.** an error in judgment, action, or belief. —*v.t.* **2.** to identify, understand, interpret, or regard wrongly.

mis·tak′en *adj.* wrong; incorrect; in error. —**mis·tak′en·ly,** *adv.*

Mis′ter (mis′tər) *n.* a title of address for a man. *Abbr.:* **Mr.**

mis′tle·toe′ (mis′əl tō′) *n.* a parasitic plant with waxy white berries.

mis·treat′ *v.t.* to treat badly. —**mis·treat′ment,** *n.*

mis′tress (mis′tris) *n.* **1.** a female in control. **2.** a woman who has a sexual relationship with a married man.

mis·tri′al *n.* a trial ended without a verdict.

mis·trust′ *n.* **1.** a lack of trust. —*v.t.* **2.** to regard with mistrust.

mis′un·der·stand′ *v.t., v.i.,* **-stood, -standing.** to understand wrongly. —**mis′un·der·stand′ing,** *n.*

mis·use′ *n., v.,* **-used, -using.** —*n.* (-yōōs′) **1.** improper use. —*v.t.* (-yōōz′) **2.** to use badly or wrongly. **3.** to abuse.

mite (mīt) *n.* **1.** a tiny parasitic insect. **2.** a small thing or bit.

mi′ter (mī′tər) *n.* **1.** a headdress worn by a bishop. **2.** a joint formed by pieces of wood that fit together at an angle. —*v.t.* **3.** to join with a miter. Also, *Brit.,* **mi′tre.**

mit′i·gate′ (mit′i gāt′) *v.t.,* **-gated, -gating.** to make less severe.

mi·to′sis (mī tō′sis) *n.* a method of cell division.

mitt (mit) *n.* a thick glove.

mit′ten (mit′n) *n.* a fingerless glove.

mix (miks) *v.t.* **1.** to put together; combine. —*v.i.* **2.** to associate. **3. mix up,** to confuse. —*n.* **4.** a mixture.

mixed′ num′ber *n.* a number consisting of a whole number and a fraction or decimal.

mix′ture (-chər) *n.* an act or product of mixing.

mix′-up′ *n.* a state of confusion.

miz′zen·mast′ (miz′ən mast′; *Naut.* -məst) *n.* the third mast from forward on a ship.

ml milliliter.

mm millimeter.

MN Minnesota.

mne·mon′ic (ni mon′ik) *adj.* **1.** aiding memory. —*n.* **2.** a mnemonic device.

MO 1. Also, **Mo.** Missouri. **2.** modus operandi.

moan (mōn) *n.* **1.** a low groan. —*v.i.* **2.** to utter moans.

moat (mōt) *n.* a deep, water-filled ditch around a castle.

mob (mob) *n., v.,* **mobbed, mobbing.** —*n.* **1.** a crowd, esp. a disorderly one. —*v.t.* **2.** to crowd in; crowd around.

mo′bile *adj.* (mō′bəl, -bēl) **1.** capable of moving or being moved. —*n.* (-bēl) **2.** a suspended artwork with parts that move in the breeze. —**mo·bil′i·ty,** *n.*

mo′bi·lize′ (mō′bə līz′) *v.t., v.i.,* **-lized, -lizing.** to make or become ready, as for war.

mob′ster (mob′stər) *n.* a member of a criminal mob.

moc′ca·sin (mok′ə sin, -zən) *n.* a soft shoe.

mo′cha (mō′kə) *n.* **1.** a kind of coffee. **2.** a flavoring made from coffee and chocolate.

mock (mok) *v.t.* **1.** to mimic or ridicule. —*n.* **2.** imitation.

mock′er·y *n., pl.* **-ies. 1.** ridicule; derision. **2.** a mocking travesty.

mock′ing·bird′ *n.* a songbird that imitates other birds.

mock′-up′ *n.* a model.

mode[1] (mōd) *n.* **1.** a method. **2.** a particular type or form.

mode[2] (mōd) *n.* fashion or style.

mod′el (mod′l) *n., adj., v.,* **-eled, -eling.** —*n.* **1.** a standard for imitation. **2.** a small-scale copy. **3.** a person paid to wear and display clothing. **4.** a person who poses for an artist. —*adj.* **5.** serving as a model. —*v.t.* **6.** to pattern after a model. **7.** to wear as a model. **8.** to form. —*v.i.* **9.** to work as a model.

mo′dem (mō′dəm, -dem) *n.* a device enabling transfer of data between computers via telephone lines.

mod′er·ate *adj., n., v.,* **-ated, -ating.** —*adj.* (mod′ər it) **1.** not extreme or excessive. —*n.* (-ər it) **2.** a person having moderate views. —*v.t., v.i.* (-ə rāt′) **3.** to make or become moderate. **4.** to preside over or act as a moderator.

mod′er·a′tor *n.* the director of a group discussion.

mod′ern (mod′ərn) *adj.* of present and recent time. —**mo·der′ni·ty**

(-dûr′ni tē) *n.* —**mod′ern·ize′,** *v.t., v.i.*

Mod′ern Eng′lish *n.* the English language since c1475.

mod′ern·ism *n.* **1.** modern character or tendencies. **2.** a modern usage. **3.** divergence from the past in the arts, occurring esp. in the 29th century.

mod′est (mod′ist) *adj.* **1.** humble in estimating oneself. **2.** simple; moderate. **3.** decent; moral. —**mod′est·ly,** *adv.* —**mod′es·ty,** *n.*

mod′i·cum (mod′i kəm) *n.* a small amount.

mod′i·fy (mod′ə fī′) *v.t.,* **-fied, -fying.** to alter or moderate. —**mod′i·fi·ca′tion,** *n.* —**mod′i·fi′er,** *n.*

mod′ish (mō′dish) *adj.* fashionable.

mo·diste′ (mō dēst′) *n.* a woman making fashionable women's attire.

mod′u·late′ (moj′ə lāt′) *v.t.,* **-lated, -lating. 1.** to adjust to a proper measure or proportion. **2.** to vary the amplitude, frequency, or intensity of. —**mod′u·la′tion,** *n.*

mod′ule (moj′ōōl) *n.* **1.** a building unit. **2.** a self-contained segment of a spacecraft. —**mod′u·lar,** *adj.*

mo′dus op·e·ran′di (mō′dəs op′-ə ran′dē, -dī) *n., pl.* **mo′di op′e·ran′di** (mō′dē, -dī). a method of operating.

mo′gul (mō′gəl) *n.* a powerful or influential person.

mo′hair′ (mō′hâr′) *n.* a fabric from the fleece of the Angora goat.

moil (moil) *v.i.* to labor.

moi·ré′ (mwä rā′, mô-) *n., pl.* **-rés.** a fabric, as silk, with a watery appearance.

moist (moist) *adj.* damp. —**mois′ten** (moi′sən) *v.t., v.i.*

mois′ture (-chər) *n.* dampness; small beads of water.

mois′tur·ize′ *v.t.,* **-ized, -izing.** to add moisture to. —**mois′tur·iz′er,** *n.*

mo′lar (mō′lər) *n.* a broad back tooth.

mo·las′ses (mə las′iz) *n.* a thick syrup produced in refining sugar.

mold[1] (mōld) *n.* **1.** a form for shaping molten or plastic material. **2.** something formed in a mold. **3.** distinctive character or type. —*v.t.* **4.** to form or shape.

mold[2] (mōld) *n.* **1.** a fungus growth on vegetable or animal matter. —*v.i.* **2.** to become covered with mold. —**mold′y,** *adj.*

mold′er *v.i.* to decay.

mold′ing *n.* a decorative strip of contoured material.

mole[1] (mōl) *n.* **1.** a burrowing mammal with fur. **2.** a spy who works from within an enemy intelligence agency.

mole[2] (mōl) *n.* a dark-colored spot on the skin.

mol′e·cule′ (mol′ə kyōōl′) *n.* the smallest physical unit of a chemical element or compound. —**mo·lec′u·lar** (mə lek′yə lər) *adj.*

mole′hill′ *n.* **1.** a small mound of earth raised by moles. **2.** something small and insignificant.

mole′skin′ *n.* **1.** the fur of a mole. **2.** a heavy cotton fabric.

mo·lest′ (mə lest′) *v.t.* **1.** to annoy or bother. **2.** to make indecent sexual advances to. —**mo·lest′er,** *n.*

moll (mol) *n. Slang.* the female companion of a gangster.

mol′li·fy′ (mol′ə fī′) *v.t.,* **-fied, -fying.** to appease in temper.

mol′lusk (mol′əsk) *n.* a hard-shelled invertebrate animal.

mol′ly·cod′dle (mol′ē kod′l) *v.t.,* **-dled, -dling.** to pamper.

molt (mōlt) *v.i.* to shed skin or feathers.

mol′ten (mōl′tən) *adj.* melted.

mom (mom) *n. Informal.* mother.

mo′ment (mō′mənt) *n.* **1.** a very short space of time. **2.** importance.

mo′men·tar′y (-mən ter′ē) *adj.* very brief. —**mo′men·tar′i·ly,** *adv.*

mo·men′tous (-men′təs) *adj.* important.

mo·men′tum (-təm) *n., pl.* **-ta** (-tə) **-tums.** force or speed of movement.

mom′my (mom′ē) *n., pl.* **-mies.** *Informal.* mother.

Mon. Monday.

mon′ad (mon′ad, mō′nad) *n.* a one-celled organism.

mon′arch (mon′ərk, -ärk) *n.* a hereditary sovereign.

mon′ar·chism *n.* advocacy of monarchy. —**mon′ar·chist,** *n.*

mon′ar·chy *n., pl.* **-chies. 1.** government by a monarch. **2.** a country governed by a monarch.

mon′as·ter′y (mon′ə ster′ē) *n., pl.* **-teries.** a residence of monks.

mo·nas'tic (mə nas'tik) *adj.* of or characteristic of monks or nuns. —mo·nas'ti·cism, *n.*

Mon'day (mun'dā, -dē) *n.* the second day of the week.

mon'e·tar'y (mon'i ter'ē, mun'-) *adj.* of money.

mon'ey (mun'ē) *n., pl.* **moneys, monies. 1.** pieces of metal or certificates used to buy and sell. **2.** wealth.

mon'eyed (-ēd) *adj.* wealthy.

mon'gol·ism (mong'gə liz'əm, mon'-) *n.* a former term for Down syndrome.

mon'goose (mong'gōōs, mon'-) *n., pl.* **-gooses.** a carnivorous animal of Asia.

mon'grel (mung'grəl, mong'-) *n.* **1.** an animal or plant resulting from the crossing of different breeds. —*adj.* **2.** of mixed breeds.

mon'i·ker (mon'i kər) *n. Slang.* a name. Also, **mon'ick·er.**

mon'ism (mon'iz əm, mō'niz əm) *n.* the theory that reality consists of a single element. —**mon'ist,** *n.* —**mo·nis'tic,** *adj.*

mo·ni'tion (mə nish'ən, mō-) *n.* a warning.

mon'i·tor (mon'i tər) *n.* **1.** a pupil who assists a teacher. **2.** a television or computer screen. —*v.t.* **3.** to check or watch continuously.

mon'i·to'ry (-tôr'ē) *adj.* warning.

monk (mungk) *n.* a male member of a religious order.

mon'key (mung'kē) *n.* **1.** a mammal strongly resembling a human being. —*v.i.* **2.** to trifle idly; fool.

mon'key busi'ness *n.* mischievous behavior.

mon'key wrench' *n.* a wrench with an adjustable jaw.

mono- a prefix meaning one.

mon'o·chrome (mon'ə krōm') *adj.* of one color.

mon'o·cle (mon'ə kəl) *n.* an eyeglass for one eye.

mon'o·clo'nal (mon'ə klōn'l) *adj.* pertaining to cell products derived from a single biological clone.

mon'o·cot'y·le·don (mon'ə kot'l-ēd'n) *n.* a plant having an embryo containing a single seed leaf.

mo·noc'u·lar (mə nok'yə lər) *adj.* **1.** having one eye. **2.** for the use of only one eye.

mon'o·dy (mon'ə dē) *n., pl.* **-dies.** a poem lamenting someone's death.

mo·nog'a·my (mə nog'ə mē) *n.* the practice of having one spouse at a time. —**mo·nog'a·mous,** *adj.* —**mo·nog'a·mist,** *n.*

mon'o·gram (mon'ə gram') *n.* a design made of one's initials.

mon'o·graph (mon'ə graf') *n.* a treatise on one subject.

mon'o·lith (-lith) *n.* **1.** a structure of a single block of stone. **2.** something having a solid, uniform, or inflexible quality. —**mon'o·lith'ic,** *adj.*

mon'o·logue' (-lôg') *n.* a talk by a single speaker. Also, **mon'o·log'.**

mon'o·ma'ni·a *n.* an obsessive zeal for or interest in a single thing. —**mon'o·ma'ni·ac,** *n.*

mon'o·nu'cle·o'sis (-nōō'klē ō'sis, -nyōō'-) *n.* a disease marked by fever, swelling of lymph nodes, etc.

mon'o·plane' *n.* an airplane with one wing on each side.

mo·nop'o·ly (mə nop'ə lē) *n., pl.* **-lies. 1.** exclusive control. **2.** a company having exclusive control over a commodity or service. **3.** a commodity or service so controlled. —**mo·nop'o·lize',** *v.t.*

mon'o·rail' (mon'ə rāl') *n.* **1.** a single rail serving as a track for wheeled vehicles. **2.** a car or train moving on such a rail.

mon'o·so'di·um glu'ta·mate' (mon'ə sō'dē əm glōō'tə māt') *n.* a white crystalline powder used to intensify the flavor of foods.

mon'o·syl'la·ble *n.* a word of one syllable. —**mon'o·syl·lab'ic,** *adj.*

mon'o·the·ism *n.* a doctrine or belief that there is only one God.

mon'o·tone' *n.* a single tone of unvarying pitch.

mo·not'o·ny (mə not'n ē) *n.* wearisome uniformity. —**mo·not'o·nous,** *adj.*

mon·sieur' (mə syœ') *n., pl.* **messieurs** (me syœ'). a French term of address for a man.

mon·si'gnor (mon sē'nyər, mon'-sē nyôr', mōn'-) *n., pl.* **-gnors, -gnori** (mon'sē nyôr'ē). a title of certain Roman Catholic priests.

mon·soon' (mon sōōn') *n.* a seasonal wind of S Asia.

mon'ster (mon'stər) *n.* **1.** an animal or plant of abnormal form. **2.** a wicked creature. **3.** anything huge.

mon'strance (mon'strəns) *n.* a receptacle used in churches for display of the consecrated Host.

mon·stros'i·ty (mon stros'i tē), *pl.* **-ties.** a grotesquely abnormal thing.

mon'strous (-strəs) *adj.* **1.** huge. **2.** frightful.

Mont. Montana.

mon·tage' (mon tāzh'; *Fr.* mŌN-tÄzh') *n.* a blending of elements from several pictures into one.

month (munth) *n.* any of twelve parts of a calendar year.

month'ly *adj., n., pl.* **-lies,** *adv.* —*adj.* **1.** occurring, appearing, etc., once a month. **2.** lasting for a month. —*n.* **3.** a periodical published once a month. —*adv.* **4.** once a month. **5.** by the month.

mon'u·ment (mon'yə mənt) *n.* a memorial structure.

mon'u·men'tal (-men'tl) *adj.* **1.** very great; significant. **2.** serving as a monument.

moo (mōō) *n.* **1.** the sound a cow makes. —*v.t.* **2.** to utter such a sound.

mooch (mōōch) *Slang.* —*v.i.* **1.** to borrow without intending to pay back. —*n.* **2.** Also, **mooch'er.** a person who mooches.

mood (mōōd) *n.* a frame of mind.

mood'y *adj.,* **-ier, -iest.** given to bad moods. —**mood'i·ly,** *adv.*

moon (mōōn) *n.* **1.** the earth's natural satellite. **2.** the natural satellite of any planet. —*v.i.* **3.** to behave dreamily.

moon'light' *n.* **1.** light from the moon. —*v.i.* **2.** to work at a second job after the principal one.

moon'shine' *n.* illegally made liquor. —**moon'shin'er,** *n.*

moon'stone' *n.* a pearly gem.

moon'struck' *adj.* **1.** mentally deranged. **2.** dreamily bemused.

moor¹ (mōōr) *n.* a tract of open peaty wasteland.

moor² (mōōr) *v.t., v.i.* to secure or be secured in place, as a ship.

moor'ing *n.* **1.** moorings, cables, anchors, etc., by which a ship is moored. **2.** a place where a ship is moored.

moose (mōōs) *n., pl.* **moose.** a large animal of the deer family.

moot (mōōt) *adj.* **1.** open to discussion or debate. **2.** of little practical value.

mop (mop) *n., v.,* **mopped, mopping.** —*n.* **1.** a piece of cloth, sponge, etc., fastened to a stick, for washing or dusting. —*v.t.* **2.** to clean with a mop.

mope (mōp) *v.i.,* **moped, moping.** to be in low spirits.

mo'ped' (mō'ped') *n.* a motorized bicycle.

mop'pet (mop'it) *n.* a child.

mo·raine' (mə rān') *n.* a mass of stone, sand, etc., left by a glacier.

mor'al (môr'əl) *adj.* **1.** of or concerned with right conduct. **2.** virtuous. —*n.* **3.** morals, principles of conduct. **4.** a moral lesson. —**mor'al·ist,** *n.* —**mor'al·is'tic,** *adj.* —**mor'al·ly,** *adv.*

mo·rale' (mə ral') *n.* spirits; mood.

mo·ral'i·ty (mə ral'i tē, mô-) *n.* **1.** conformity to rules of right conduct. **2.** moral quality.

mor'al·ize' (môr'ə līz') *v.i.,* **-ized, -izing.** to think or pronounce on moral questions.

mo·rass' (mə ras') *n.* a swamp.

mor'a·to'ri·um (môr'ə tôr'ē əm) *n., pl.* **-toria** (tôr'ē ə), **-toriums. 1.** legal permission to delay payment of debts. **2.** any temporary cessation.

mo'ray (môr'ā, mô rā') *n.* a tropical eel.

mor'bid (môr'bid) *adj.* **1.** unwholesomely gloomy. **2.** of disease. —**mor·bid'i·ty,** *adj.*

mor'dant (môr'dnt) *adj.* **1.** sarcastic; biting. **2.** burning; corrosive.

more (môr) *adj.* **1.** in greater amount or degree. **2.** additional. —*n.* **3.** an additional or greater quantity or degree. —*adv.* **4.** in or to a greater extent or degree. **5.** in addition.

mo·rel' (mə rel') *n.* a kind of edible mushroom.

more·o'ver *adv.* in addition to what has been said; besides.

mo'res (môr'āz, -ēz) *n.pl.* the social and moral customs of a group.

mor'ga·nat'ic (môr'gə nat'ik) *adj.* designating marriage between a royal person and a commoner.

morgue (môrg) *n.* a place where corpses are taken for identification.

mor'i·bund (môr'ə bund') *adj.* dying.

Mor·mon (môr'mən) *n.* the popular name given to a member of the Church of Jesus Christ of Latter-day Saints. —**Mor'mon·ism,** *n.*

morn (môrn) *n.* morning.

morn'ing *n.* **1.** the first part of the day. **2.** done or occurring in the morning.

morn'ing-glo'ry *n., pl.* **morning-glories.** a vine with funnel-shaped flowers.

morn'ing sick'ness *n.* nausea occurring esp. in the morning during the first months of pregnancy.

morn'ing star' *n.* a bright planet seen in the east immediately before sunrise.

mo·roc'co (mə rok'ō) *n.* a fine leather.

mo·ron (môr'on) *n.* a stupid person. —**mo·ron'ic** (mə ron'ik) *adj.*

mo·rose' (mə rōs') *adj.* gloomily ill-humored. —**mo·rose'ly,** *adv.*

mor'pheme (môr'fēm) *n.* a minimal grammatical unit.

mor'phine (môr'fēn) *n.* a narcotic found in opium.

morph'ing (-fing) *n.* the smooth transformation of one image into another by computer.

mor·phol'o·gy (môr fol'ə jē) *n.* **1.** the study of the form and structure of organisms. **2.** the study of word formation.

mor'row (môr'ō) *n. Poetic.* the next day.

Morse' code' (môrs) *n.* a telegraphic code of long and short signals.

mor'sel (môr'səl) *n.* a small amount.

mor'tal (môr'tl) *adj.* **1.** liable to death. **2.** causing death. **3.** extreme. —*n.* **4.** a human being.

mor·tal'i·ty (môr tal'i tē) *n., pl.* **-ties. 1.** mortal nature. **2.** the relative death rate.

mor'tar (môr'tər) *n.* **1.** a bowl in which drugs, foods, etc., are pulverized. **2.** a short cannon. **3.** material used to bind masonry.

mor'tar·board' *n.* an academic cap with a square, flat top and tassel.

mort'gage (môr'gij) *n., v.,* **-gaged, -gaging.** —*n.* **1.** a conditional transfer of property as security for debt. —*v.t.* **2.** to put a mortgage on.

mor·ti'cian (môr tish'ən) *n.* an undertaker.

mor'ti·fy' (môr'tə fī') *v.t.,* **-fied, -fying. 1.** to humiliate. **2.** to subdue (the body) by abstinence or pain.

mor'tise (môr'tis) *n.* a slot in wood for a tenon.

mor'tu·ar'y (môr'chōō er'ē) *n., pl.* **-aries.** a place where bodies are prepared for burial.

mo·sa'ic (mō zā'ik) *n.* a design made of small colored pieces of stone.

mo'sey (mō'zē) *v.i. Informal.* to stroll.

mosh (mosh) *v.i. Slang.* to engage in a form of frenzied dancing.

Mos'lem (moz'ləm, mos'-) *n., adj.* Muslim.

mosque (mosk) *n.* a Muslim place of prayer.

mos·qui'to (mə skē'tō) *n., pl.* **-toes, -tos.** a common biting insect.

moss (môs) *n.* a small, leafy-stemmed plant growing on rocks, moist ground, etc.

moss'back' *n. Informal.* a person having antiquated ideas.

most (mōst) *adj.* **1.** the greatest, as in number. **2.** the majority of. —*n.* **3.** the greatest amount or degree. —*adv.* **4.** to the greatest extent or degree.

most'ly *adv.* **1.** in most cases. **2.** in greater part.

mote (mōt) *n.* a small particle.

mo·tel' (mō tel') *n.* a roadside hotel for automobile travelers.

mo·tet' (mō tet') *n.* an unaccompanied polyphonic choral composition.

moth (môth) *n.* an insect, some of whose larvae eat cloth.

moth'ball' *n.* a ball of camphor, naphthalene, etc., for repelling moths.

moth'er (muth'ər) *n.* **1.** a female parent. **2.** the head of a group of nuns. **3.** a source. —*adj.* **4.** of, like, or being a mother. —*v.t.* **5.** to act as or like a mother to. —**moth'er·hood',** *n.* —**moth'er·ly,** *adj.*

moth'er-in-law' *n., pl.* **mothers-in-law.** the mother of one's spouse.

moth'er·land' *n.* one's native land. **2.** the land of one's ancestors.

moth'er-of-pearl' *n.* the inner layer of certain shells.

mo·tif' (mō tēf') *n.* a recurring subject or theme.

mo'tile (mōt'l, mō'til) *adj.* capable of moving spontaneously. —**mo·til'i·ty,** *n.*

mo'tion (mō'shən) *n.* **1.** the action or process of moving. **2.** a gesture. **3.** a formal proposal made in a meeting. —*v.t., v.i.* **4.** to direct by or make a motion.

mo'tion pic'ture *n.* **1.** a series of images projected so rapidly that things seem to move. **2.** a story in this form.

mo'ti·vate' (mō'tə vāt') *v.t.,* **-vated, -vating.** to give a motive to. —**mo'ti·va'tion,** *n.*

mo'tive (-tiv) *n.* a purpose; incentive.

mot'ley (mot'lē) *adj.* widely, often grotesquely, varied.

mo'tor (mō'tər) *n.* **1.** a small, powerful engine. —*adj.* **2.** of or causing motion. **3.** of or operated by a motor. **4.** of or for motor vehicles. —*v.i.* **5.** to travel by automobile.

mo'tor·bike' *n.* a small motorcycle.

mo'tor·boat' *n.* a boat run by a motor.

mo'tor·cade' (-kād') *n.* a procession of automobiles.

mo'tor·car' *n.* an automobile.

mo'tor·cy'cle *n.* a heavy motor-driven bicycle. —**mo'tor·cy'clist,** *n.*

mo'tor·ist *n.* an automobile driver.

mo'tor·ize' *v.t.,* **-ized, -izing.** to furnish with motors.

mo'tor·man *n., pl.* **-men.** a person who drives an electrically operated vehicle.

mot'tle (mot'l) *v.t.,* **-tled, -tling.** to mark with spots or blotches.

mot'to (mot'ō) *n., pl.* **-toes, -tos.** a phrase expressing one's guiding principle.

moue (mōō) *n., pl.* **moues** (mōō). a pouting grimace.

mould (mōld) *n., v.i. Brit.* mold.

mound (mound) *n.* a heap, as of earth; hill.

mount (mount) *v.t.* **1.** to go up; get up on. **2.** to organize and launch. **3.** to prepare for display. **4.** to fix in a setting. —*v.i.* **5.** to increase. **6.** to ascend or get up on something. —*n.* **7.** the act or manner of mounting. **8.** a horse for riding. **9.** a support, setting, etc. **10.** a mountain.

moun'tain (moun'tn) *n.* a lofty natural elevation on the earth's surface. —**moun'tain·ous,** *adj.*

moun'tain ash' *n.* a small tree of the rose family.

moun'tain bike' *n.* a sturdy bicycle designed for off-road use.

moun'tain·eer' *n.* a mountain climber. —**moun'tain·eer'ing,** *n.*

moun'tain lau'rel *n.* a shrub bearing rose or white flowers.

moun'tain li'on *n.* a cougar.

moun'te·bank' (moun'tə bangk') *n.* a charlatan.

mourn (môrn) *v.i., v.t.* to grieve (for); feel or express sorrow (for). —**mourn'er,** *n.* —**mourn'ful,** *adj.* —**mourn'ing,** *n.*

mouse (mous) *n., pl.* **mice** (mīs) *v.,* **moused, mousing.** —*n.* **1.** a small rodent. **2.** a palm-sized device used to select items on a computer screen. —*v.i.* **3.** to hunt for mice.

mouse' pota'to *n. Informal.* a person who spends leisure time at a computer, usu. on the Internet.

mousse (mōōs) *n.* **1.** a frothy dessert. **2.** a foamy preparation used to style hair.

mous·tache' (mus'tash, mə stash') *n.* a mustache.

mous'y (mou'sē, -zē) *adj.,* **-ier, -iest. 1.** drab. **2.** meek.

mouth *n., pl.* **mouths,** *v.* —*n.* (mouth) **1.** an opening through which an animal eats. **2.** any opening. —*v.t.* (mouth) **3.** to utter pompously or dishonestly. **4.** to form silently with the mouth. —**mouth'ful',** *n.*

mouth'or'gan *n.* a harmonica.

mouth'piece' *n.* **1.** a piece held in or to the mouth. **2.** a spokesperson.

mouth'wash' *n.* a solution for cleaning the mouth.

mouth'-wa'ter·ing *adj.* appetizing.

mou'ton (mōō'ton) *n.* a processed sheepskin.

move (mōōv) *v.,* **moved, moving,** *n.* —*v.i.* **1.** to change place or position. **2.** to change one's abode. **3.** to advance. **4.** to make a formal proposal in a meeting. —*v.t.* **5.** to cause to change place or position. **6.** to affect emotionally. —*n.* **7.** the act of moving. **8.** a purposeful action. —*Idiom.* **9.** on the move, **a.** active. **b.** going from place to place. **c.** advancing.

move'ment *n.* **1.** the act or process of moving. **2.** a trend in thought. **3.** the works of a mechanism. **4.** a main division of a piece of music.

mov'ie (mōō'vē) *n.* **1.** a motion picture. **2.** movies, **a.** the motion-picture industry. **b.** the showing of a motion picture.

mow (mō) *v.t.,* **mowed, mowed** or **mown, mowing. 1.** to cut down (grass, grain, etc.). **2.** mow down, to kill in great numbers. —**mow'er,** *n.*

moz'za·rel'la (mots'ə rel'ə, mōt'-) *n.* a mild, white, semisoft cheese.

MP 1. a member of Parliament. **2.** Military Police.

mph miles per hour.

Mr. (mis'tər) *pl.* **Messrs.** (mes'ərz). Mister; a title of address for a man.

MRI magnetic resonance imaging: a process of producing images of the body using a magnetic field and radio waves.

Mrs. (mis'iz, miz'iz) *pl.* **Mmes.** (mā-däm', -dam'). a title of address for a married woman.

MS 1. Also, **ms, ms.** manuscript. **2.** Mississippi. **3.** multiple sclerosis.

Ms. (miz) a title of address for a married or unmarried woman.

M.S. Master of Science.

MSG monosodium glutamate.

MT Montana.

mu (mōō, myōō) *n., pl.* **mus.** the 12th letter of the Greek alphabet.

much (much) *adj.* **1.** great in quantity or degree. —*n.* **2.** a great quantity. **3.** a great or notable thing. —*adv.* **4.** to a great extent or degree. **5.** generally.

mu'ci·lage (myōō'sə lij) *n.* a gummy adhesive.

muck (muk) *n.* **1.** dirt or mud. **2.** moist barn refuse. —**muck'y,** *adj.*

muck'rake' *v.i.,* **-raked, -raking.** to expose scandal. —**muck'rak'er,** *n.*

mu'cous (myōō'kəs) *adj.* **1.** secreting mucus. **2.** of or like mucus.

mu'cous mem'brane *n.* a membrane lining all body passages open to the air.

mu'cus (-kəs) *n.* the sticky secretion of a mucous membrane.

mud (mud) *n.* **1.** wet soft earth. **2.** malicious statements. —**mud'dy,** *adj., v.t.*

mud'dle (mud'l) *v.,* **-dled, -dling,** *n.* —*v.t.* **1.** to mix up; confuse. **2.** to act in a confused way. —*n.* **3.** a state of confusion.

mud'dle·head'ed *adj.* confused in one's thinking.

mud'sling'ing *n.* efforts to discredit an opponent by malicious remarks.

mu·ez'zin (myōō ez'in, mōō-) *n.* a crier who summons Muslims to prayer.

muff (muf) *n.* **1.** a tubular covering for the hands. —*v.t., v.i.* **2.** to handle or act clumsily.

muf'fin (muf'in) *n.* a small round bread.

muf'fle (muf'əl) *v.t.,* **-fled, -fling. 1.** to deaden (sound). **2.** to wrap in a scarf, cloak, etc.

muf'fler *n.* **1.** a device for deadening sound. **2.** a heavy neck scarf.

muf'ti (muf'tē) *n.* civilian dress.

mug (mug) *n., v.,* **mugged, mugging.** —*n.* **1.** a cup with a handle. **2.** *Slang.* the face. —*v.t.* **3.** to assault, usually with intent to rob. —**mug'ger,** *n.*

mug'gy *adj.,* **-gier, -giest.** hot and humid.

mug' shot' *n.* a photograph of the face of a criminal suspect.

mug'wump (mug'wump') *n.* a person who takes an independent position.

Mu·ham'mad (mōō ham'əd, -hä'-məd) *n.* the founder of Islam, A.D. 570–632.

muk'luk (muk'luk) *n.* a soft boot worn by Eskimos.

mu·lat'to (mə lat'ō, -lä'tō) *n., pl.* **-toes.** a person with mixed black and white ancestry.

mul'ber'ry (mul'ber'ē, -bə rē) *n., pl.* **-ries.** a tree bearing a dark-purple, berrylike fruit.

mulch (mulch) *n.* **1.** a loose covering of leaves, straw, etc., on plants. —*v.t.* **2.** to surround with mulch.

mulct (mulkt) *v.t.* **1.** to deprive of by trickery. **2.** to fine.

mule (myōōl) *n.* the offspring of a donkey and a mare.

mule′ deer′ *n.* a deer with large ears and a gray coat.

mu·le·teer′ (myōō′lə tēr′) *n.* a mule-driver.

mul·ish (myōō′lish) *adj.* stubborn.

mull[1] (mul) *v.t.* to think about carefully.

mull[2] (mul) *v.t.* to heat and spice (ale, wine, cidar, etc.).

mul′lein (mul′ən) *n.* a tall, woolly-leaved weed.

mul′let (mul′it) *n.* a common food fish.

mul·li·ga·taw′ny (-gə tô′nē) *n.* a curry-flavored soup.

mul′lion (mul′yən) *n.* a vertical member separating the lights of a window.

multi- a prefix meaning many.

mul′ti·cul′tur·al·ism (mul′tē kul′chər ə liz′əm, mul′tī-) *n.* the recognition of different cultural identities within a unified society.

mul′ti·far′i·ous (mul′tə fâr′ē əs) *adj.* many and varied.

mul′ti·me′di·a (mul′tē-, mul′tī-) *n.* the combined use of several media or mass media.

mul′ti·na′tion·al *n.* **1.** a corporation with operations in many countries. —*adj.* **2.** of several nations or multinationals.

mul′ti·ple (mul′tə pəl) *adj.* **1.** consisting of or involving many. —*n.* **2.** a number evenly divisible by a stated other number.

mul′tiple scler·o′sis *n.* a disease leading to neural and muscular impairments.

mul′ti·pli·cand′ (-pli kand′) *n.* a number to be multiplied by another.

mul′ti·plic′i·ty (-plis′i tē) *n., pl.* **-ties.** a great number or variety.

mul′ti·ply′ (mul′tə plī′) *v.t., v.i.,* **-plied, -plying. 1.** to increase in number or quantity. **2.** to add (a number) to itself a stated number of times. —**mul′ti·pli′er,** *n.* —**mul′ti·pli·ca′tion,** *n.*

mul′ti·tude′ (mul′ti tōōd′, -tyōōd′) *n.* a great number.

mul′ti·tu′di·nous *adj.* **1.** numerous. **2.** having many parts.

mum (mum) *adj.* silent.

mum′ble (mum′bəl) *v.,* **-bled, -bling,** *n.* —*v.t., v.i.* **1.** to speak quietly and unintelligibly. —*n.* **2.** a mumbling sound.

mum′ble·ty·peg′ (mum′bəl tē-peg′) *n.* a game in which a pocketknife is flipped so it sticks in the ground. Also, **mum′ble-the-peg′** (-thə-).

mum′bo jum′bo (mum′bō jum′bō) *n.* senseless language.

mum′mer (mum′ər) *n.* **1.** a person in a festive disguise. **2.** an actor.

mum′my (mum′ē) *n., pl.* **-mies.** a dead body preserved by the ancient Egyptians.

mumps (mumps) *n.* a disease marked by swelling of the salivary glands.

munch (munch) *v.i., v.t.* to chew steadily or vigorously.

mun·dane′ (mun dān′, mun′dān) *adj.* commonplace.

mu·nic′i·pal (myōō nis′ə pəl) *adj.* of a city.

mu·nic′i·pal′i·ty (-pal′i tē) *n., pl.* **-ties.** a self-governing city.

mu·nif′i·cent (myōō nif′ə sənt) *adj.* extremely generous. —**mu·nif′i·cence,** *n.* —**mu·nif′i·cent·ly,** *adv.*

mu·ni′tions (myōō nish′ənz) *n.pl.* weapons and ammunition.

mu′ral (myōōr′əl) *n.* a picture painted on a wall.

mur′der (mûr′dər) *n.* **1.** an unlawful intentional killing. —*v.t.* **2.** to kill unlawfully and deliberately. —**mur′der·er,** *n.* —**mur′der·ous,** *adj.*

murk′y *adj.,* **-ier, -iest.** dark and gloomy. —**murk′i·ness,** *n.*

mur′mur (mûr′mər) *n.* **1.** a low, continuous, indistinct sound. **2.** a complaint. —*v.i., v.t.* **3.** to make or express in a murmur.

mur′rain (mûr′in) *n.* a disease of cattle.

mus′ca·dine (mus′kə din, -dīn′) *n.* an American grape.

mus′cat (mus′kət, -kat) *n.* a sweet grape.

mus′cle (mus′əl) *n., v.,* **-cled, -cling.** —*n.* **1.** a bundle of fibers in the body that contract to produce motion. **2.** strength. —*v.i.* **3.** *Informal.*

to force one's way. —**mus′cu·lar** (-kyə lər) *adj.*

mus′cle·bound′ *adj.* having enlarged and inelastic muscles.

mus′cular dys′tro·phy (dis′trə fē) *n.* a hereditary disease marked by gradual wasting of muscles.

muse (myōōz) *v.i.,* **mused, musing.** to reflect quietly.

Muse (myōōz) *n.* **1.** one of nine Greek goddesses of the arts. **2.** muse, the inspiration motivating a poet, artist, etc.

mu·se′um (myōō zē′əm) *n.* a place for permanent public exhibits.

mush[1] (mush *or, esp. for 2, 3,* mōōsh) *n.* **1.** meal, esp. cornmeal, boiled in water or milk. **2.** a thick, soft mass. **3.** maudlin sentiment. —**mush′y,** *adj.*

mush[2] (mush) *v.i.* to travel over snow with a dog team and sled.

mush′room (mush′rōōm, -rŏŏm) *n.* **1.** a fleshy fungus, usu. umbrella-shaped, sometimes edible. —*v.i.* **2.** to grow quickly.

mu′sic (myōō′zik) *n.* **1.** the art of arranging sounds for effect by rhythm, melody, etc. **2.** the score of a musical composition.

mus′i·cal *adj.* **1.** of music. **2.** pleasant-sounding. **3.** fond of or skilled in music. —*n.* **4.** Also, **mus′ical com′edy.** a play with music.

mu′si·cale′ (-kal′) *n.* a social occasion featuring music.

mu·si′cian (-zish′ən) *n.* a person who performs or composes music.

mu′si·col′o·gy (-zi kol′ə jē) *n.* the scholarly study of music. —**mu′si·col′o·gist,** *n.*

mu′sic vid′eo *n.* a videotape featuring a dramatized rendition of a pop song.

musk (musk) *n.* an animal secretion, used in perfume. —**musk′y,** *adj.*

mus′keg (mus′keg) *n.* a bog.

mus′kel·lunge′ (mus′kə lunj′) *n., pl.* **-lung·es, -lunge.** a large fish of the pike family.

mus′ket (mus′kit) *n.* an early rifle.

mus′ket·eer′ *n.* a soldier armed with a musket.

musk′mel′on *n.* a sweet edible melon.

musk′ox′ *n., pl.* **-oxen.** a large mammal of arctic regions.

musk′rat′ *n.* a large aquatic American rodent.

Mus′lim (muz′lim, mŏŏz′-, mŏŏs′-) *n.* **1.** a follower of Islam. —*adj.* **2.** of or pertaining to Islam.

mus′lin (muz′lin) *n.* a plain-weave cotton fabric.

muss (mus) —*v.t.* **1.** to make messy. —*n.* **2.** disorder.

mus′sel (mus′əl) *n.* a bivalve mollusk, sometimes edible.

must (must) *aux. v.* **1.** (used to express obligation or necessity). **2.** (used to express strong probability or inevitability). —*n.* **3.** something necessary or required.

mus′tache (mus′tash, mə stash′) *n.* hair growing on the upper lip.

mus′tang (mus′tang) *n.* a small wild horse of the western U.S.

mus′tard (mus′tərd) *n.* a pungent yellow powder made from the seeds of the mustard plant.

mus′tard gas′ *n.* an irritating and poisonous liquid used in warfare.

mus′ter (mus′tər) *v.t., v.i.* **1.** to assemble, as troops; gather. —*n.* **2.** an assembly. —*Idiom.* **3. pass muster,** to be found acceptable.

mus′ty (mus′tē) *adj.,* **-tier, -tiest. 1.** stale-smelling. **2.** outdated.

mu′ta·ble (myōō′tə bəl) *adj.* subject to change. —**mu′ta·bil′i·ty,** *n.*

mu′tant (myōōt′nt) *n.* an organism resulting from mutation. —*adj.* **2.** resulting from mutation.

mu′tate (myōō′tāt) *v.i., v.t.,* **-tated, -tating.** to undergo or cause to undergo mutation.

mu·ta′tion *n.* **1.** a sudden change in a genetic characteristic. **2.** an individual or species characterized by such a change. **3.** a change.

mute (myōōt) *adj.,* **muter, mutest,** *n., v.,* **muted, muting.** —*adj.* **1.** silent. **2.** incapable of speech. —*n.* **3.** a person unable to utter words. **4.** a device for muffling a musical instrument. —*v.t.* **5.** to deaden the sound of.

mu′ti·late (myōōt′l āt′) *v.t.,* **-lated, -lating.** to injure by depriving of or harming a part. —**mu′ti·la′tion,** *n.*

mu′ti·ny (myōōt′n ē) *n., pl.* **-nies,** *v.,* **-nied, -nying.** —*n.* **1.** a military revolt against lawful authority. —*v.i.* **2.** to commit mutiny. —**mu′ti·neer′,** *n.* —**mu′ti·nous,** *adj.*

mutt (mut) *n. Slang.* a mongrel dog.

mut′ter (mut′ər) *v.i., v.t.* **1.** to speak low and indistinctly; grumble. —*n.* **2.** the act or sound of muttering.

mut′ton (mut′n) *n.* the flesh of sheep, used as food.

mut′ton·chops′ *n.pl.* side whiskers narrow at the temples and broad at the jawline.

mu′tu·al (myōō′chōō əl) *adj.* **1.** done, experienced, etc., by two or more in relation to each other. **2.** common; shared.

mu′tual fund′ *n.* **1.** an investment fund consisting of a diversified list of securities that is owned jointly by those who have bought shares in it. **2.** an investment company that manages such a fund.

muu′muu′ (mōō′mōō′) *n., pl.* **-muus.** a loose-fitting dress.

muz′zle (muz′əl) *n., v.,* **-zled, -zling.** —*n.* **1.** an animal's jaws. **2.** a cagelike device for an animal's jaws. **3.** the mouth of a firearm. —*v.t.* **4.** to put a muzzle on. **5.** to silence.

my (mī) *pron.* the possessive form of I used before a noun.

my·as·the′ni·a (mī′as thē′nē ə) *n.* muscle weakness. —**my·as·then′ic** (-then′ik) *adj.*

my·col′o·gy (mī kol′ə jē) *n.* the study of fungi. —**my·col′o·gist,** *n.*

my·e·li′tis (mī′ə lī′tis) *n.* **1.** inflammation of the spinal cord. **2.** inflammation of the bone marrow.

my′na (mī′nə) *n.* an Asiatic bird sometimes taught to talk.

my·o′pi·a (mī ō′pē ə) *n.* nearsightedness. —**my·op′ic** (-op′ik, -ō′pik) *adj.*

myr′i·ad (mir′ē əd) *n.* **1.** an indefinitely great number. —*adj.* **2.** consisting of a myriad.

myr′i·a·pod′ (mir′i ə pod′) *n.* a many-legged worm.

myrrh (mûr) *n.* an aromatic substance from certain plants.

myr′tle (mûr′tl) *n.* **1.** an evergreen shrub. **2.** a periwinkle[2].

my·self′ *pron., pl.* **ourselves. 1.** the reflexive form of **me.** **2.** an intensive form of I or **me.**

mys′ter·y (mis′tə rē) *n., pl.* **-teries. 1.** anything secret, unknown, or unexplained. **2.** obscurity. **3.** a secret rite. —**mys·te′ri·ous** (mi stēr′ē-əs) *adj.* —**mys·te′ri·ous·ly,** *adv.*

mys′tic (mis′tik) *adj.* Also, **mys′ti·cal. 1.** of mysticism. **2.** occult. —*n.* **3.** a believer in mysticism.

mys′ti·cism (-tə siz′əm) *n.* a doctrine of direct spiritual intuition of God, truth, etc.

mys′ti·fy′ *v.t.,* **-fied, -fying.** to bewilder purposely.

mys·tique′ (mi stēk′) *n.* an aura of mystery or power.

myth (mith) *n.* **1.** a legendary story, person, etc. **2.** a false popular belief. —**myth′i·cal,** *adj.*

my·thol′o·gy (mi thol′ə jē) *n., pl.* **-gies.** a body of myths. —**myth′o·log′i·cal** (mith′ə loj′i kəl) *adj.*

N

N, n (en) *n.* the fourteenth letter of the English alphabet.

N north, northern.

nab (nab) *v.t.,* **nabbed, nabbing.** *Informal.* to seize; arrest.

na′bob (nā′bob) *n.* a wealthy, influential, or powerful person.

na′cre (nā′kər) *n.* mother-of-pearl.

na′dir (nā′dər, -dēr) *n.* **1.** the lowest point. **2.** the point on a celestial sphere directly below a given point.

nag[1] (nag) *v.,* **nagged, nagging,** *n.* —*v.t.* **1.** to annoy or scold constantly. —*n.* **2.** a person who nags.

nag[2] (nag) *n.* an old horse.

nai′ad (nā′ad, -əd, nī′-) *n.* a water nymph.

nail (nāl) *n.* **1.** a slender piece of metal for holding pieces of wood together. **2.** a horny plate at the end of fingers and toes. —*v.t.* **3.** to fasten with nails. **4.** *Informal.* to secure or seize.

na·ive′ (nä ēv′) *adj.* **1.** simple. **2.** lacking experience. Also, **na·ïve′.**

na·ive·té′ (nä ēv tā′) *n.* artless simplicity. Also, **na·ïve·té′.**

na′ked (nā′kid) *adj.* **1.** without clothing or covering. **2.** (of the eye) unassisted in seeing. **3.** plain.

name (nām) *n., v.,* **named, naming.** —*n.* **1.** the word or words by which a person, place, or thing is designated. **2.** a reputation. **3.** on

behalf or with the authority of. —*v.t.* **4.** to give a name to. **5.** to specify. **6.** to appoint.

name′less *adj.* **1.** having no name. **2.** not referred to by name.

name′ly *adv.* that is to say.

name′sake′ *n.* a person having the same name as another.

nan′ny (nan′ē) *n., pl.* **-nies.** a person employed to take care of a child.

nan′ny goat′ *n.* a female goat.

nan′o·sec′ond (nan′ə sek′ənd, nā′-nə-) *n.* one billionth of a second.

nap[1] (nap) *n., v.,* **napped, napping.** —*n.* **1.** a brief period of sleep. —*v.i.* **2.** to sleep for a short time.

nap[2] (nap) *n.* the short, fuzzy fibers on the surface of cloth.

na′palm (nā′päm) *n.* **1.** a highly incendiary jellylike substance used in bombs, flamethrowers, etc. —*v.t.* **2.** to attack with napalm.

nape (nāp, nap) *n.* the back of the neck.

naph′tha (naf′thə, nap′-) *n.* a petroleum derivative.

naph′tha·lene′ (-lēn′) *n.* a white crystalline substance used in mothballs and some dyes.

nap′kin (nap′kin) *n.* a piece of cloth or paper used while eating to wipe the lips or fingers.

nar′cis·sism (när′sə siz′em) *n.* an excessive admiration of oneself. —**nar′cis·sis′tic** (-sis′tik) *adj.*

nar·cis′sus (när sis′əs) *n.* a bulb plant that blooms in the spring.

nar·co′sis (när kō′sis) *n.* a state of drowsiness or stupor.

nar·cot′ic (-kot′ik) *adj.* **1.** sleep-inducing. —*n.* **2.** a substance that dulls pain, induces sleep, etc. **3.** an addictive drug, esp. an illegal one.

nar′rate (nar′āt, na rāt′) *v.t.,* **-rated, -rating.** to tell or relate (a story, event, etc.). —**nar·ra′tion,** *n.*

nar′ra·tive (-ə tiv) *n.* **1.** a story or account of events. —*adj.* **2.** that narrates. **3.** of narration.

nar′row (nar′ō) *adj.* **1.** not broad or wide. **2.** literal or strict in interpreting rules, laws, etc. **3.** minute. —*v.i., v.t.* **4.** to make or become narrow. —*n.* **5.** a narrow place, thing, etc.

nar′row-mind′ed *adj.* unwilling to accept new ideas.

nar′whal (när′wəl) *n.* a small arctic whale.

NASA (nas′ə) *n.* National Aeronautics and Space Administration.

na′sal (nā′zəl) *adj.* **1.** of noses. **2.** spoken through the nose. —*n.* **3.** a nasal sound. —**na′sal·ly,** *adv.*

nas′cent (nas′ənt, nā′sənt) *adj.* beginning to exist or develop.

na·stur′tium (nə stûr′shəm, na-) *n.* a garden plant with yellow, orange, or red flowers.

nas′ty (nas′tē) *adj.,* **-tier, -tiest. 1.** spiteful or mean. **2.** objectionable. —**nas′ti·ly,** *adv.*

na′tal (nāt′l) *adj.* of a person's birth.

na′tion (nā′shən) *n.* **1.** a population living in one territory under the same government. **2.** people related by traditions or ancestry. —**na′tion·al** (nash′ə nl) *adj., n.*

na′tion·al·ism (nash′ə nl iz′əm) *n.* devotion to one's nation. —**na′tion·al·ist,** *n., adj.*

na′tion·al′i·ty (nash′ə nal′i tē) *n., pl.* **-ties. 1.** the condition of being a member of a particular nation. **2.** a nation or people.

na′tion·al·ize′ *v.t.,* **-ized, -izing.** to bring under national control.

na′tion·wide′ (nā′shən-) *adj., adv.* extending across an entire nation.

na′tive (nā′tiv) *adj.* **1.** belonging to by birth, nationality, or nature. **2.** of natives. **3.** being the place of origin of a person or thing. —*n.* **4.** a person, animal, or plant native to a region.

Na′tive Amer′ican *n., adj.* American Indian.

na·tiv′i·ty (nə tiv′i tē) *n., pl.* **-ties.** a birth.

NATO (nā′tō) *n.* North Atlantic Treaty Organization.

nat′ty (nat′ē) *adj.,* **-tier, -tiest.** neat; trim.

nat′u·ral (nach′ər əl) *adj.* **1.** of, existing in, or formed by nature. **2.** to be expected in circumstances. **3.** without affectation. **4.** *Music.* neither sharp nor flat. —**nat′u·ral·ly,** *adv.* —**nat′u·ral·ness,** *n.*

nat′ural child′birth *n.* childbirth without the use of any drugs.

nat′ural gas′ *n.* a mixture of gaseous hydrocarbons that accumulate in porous sedimentary rocks.

nat′ural his′tory *n.* the study of natural objects.

nat′u·ral·ism (-ər ə liz′əm) *n.* the artistic or literary style that represents objects or events as they occur in nature or real life. —**nat′u·ral·is′tic,** *adj.*

nat′u·ral·ist *n.* **1.** a student of nature. **2.** an adherent of naturalism.

nat′u·ral·ize′ *v.t.,* **-ized, -izing. 1.** to confer citizenship upon. **2.** to introduce to a region.

nat′ural re′source *n.* a source of wealth occurring in nature.

nat′ural selec′tion *n.* the process by which life forms having traits that enable them to adapt to the environment survive in greater numbers.

na′ture (nā′chər) *n.* **1.** the natural world as it exists without human beings. **2.** the universe. **3.** a person's character. **4.** a kind or sort.

naught (nôt) *n.* **1.** nothing. **2.** zero.

naugh′ty (nô′tē) *adj.,* **-tier, -tiest. 1.** disobedient; bad. **2.** improper.

nau·sea (nô′zē ə, -zhə, -sē ə, -shə) *n.* **1.** a feeling of impending vomiting. **2.** disgust. —**nau′se·ate′** (-zē-āt′, -zhē-, -sē-, -shē-) *v.t.*

nau′seous (-shəs, -zē əs) *adj.* **1.** causing nausea. **2.** affected with nausea.

nau′ti·cal (nô′ti kəl) *adj.* of ships, sailors, or navigation.

nau′tical mile′ *n.* a unit of distance equal to 1.852 kilometers.

nau′ti·lus (nôt′l əs) *n.* a deep-sea mollusk having a pearly shell.

na′val (nā′vəl) *adj.* of or for ships or a navy.

nave (nāv) *n.* the main lengthwise part of a church.

na′vel (nā′vəl) *n.* the depression in the center surface of the belly where the umbilical cord was connected.

nav′i·gate′ (nav′i gāt′) *v.,* **-gated, -gating.** —*v.t.* **1.** to traverse (water or air). **2.** to direct (a ship or aircraft) on a course. —*v.i.* **3.** to walk or find one's way. —**nav′i·ga′tor,** *n.* —**nav′i·ga·ble,** *adj.*

na′vy (nā′vē) *n., pl.* **-vies.** a nation's warships and crews.

na′vy bean′ *n.* a small white bean.

na′vy blue′ *n.* dark blue.

nay (nā) *adv., n.* no.

nay′say′er *n.* a person who is habitually negative.

Na′zi (nät′sē, nat′-) *n.* a member of the National Socialist party in Germany, headed by Adolf Hitler. —**Na′zism,** *n.*

NB nota bene.

NC North Carolina. Also, **N.C.**

ND North Dakota. Also, **N.D.**

N.Dak. North Dakota.

NE 1. Nebraska. **2.** northeast.

Ne·an′der·thal′ man (nē an′dər-thôl′) *n.* a member of the subspecies of humans that lived in the Stone Age.

neap′ tide′ (nēp) *n.* the tide with the lowest high point, midway between spring tides.

near (nēr) *adv.* **1.** close by. —*adj.* **2.** close. **3.** intimate. —*v.t., v.i.* **4.** to approach. —**near′ness,** *n.*

near′by′ *adj., adv.* close by.

near′ly *adv.* almost.

near′-sight′ed (-sī′tid, -sī′-) *adj.* seeing distinctly only at short distances. —**near′-sight′ed·ness,** *n.*

neat (nēt) *adj.* **1.** orderly. **2.** skillful. **3.** undiluted. —**neat′ly,** *adv.*

Neb. Nebraska.

neb′u·la (neb′yə lə) *n., pl.* **-lae** (-lē′), **-las.** a luminous mass of gas or stars. —**neb′u·lar,** *adj.*

neb′u·lous (neb′yə ləs) *adj.* **1.** hazy or vague. **2.** cloudlike.

nec′es·sar′y (nes′ə ser′ē) *adj., n., pl.* **-saries.** —*adj.* **1.** essential. **2.** required by facts or reason. —*n.* **3.** something necessary.

ne·ces′si·tate′ (nə ses′i tāt′) *v.t.,* **-tated, -tating.** to make necessary or unavoidable.

ne·ces′si·ty *n., pl.* **-ties. 1.** something necessary. **2.** the state or fact of being necessary. **3.** poverty.

neck (nek) *n.* **1.** the part of the body connecting the head and trunk. —*v.i.* **2.** *Slang.* to kiss and embrace amorously.

neck′lace (-lis) *n.* a piece of jewelry worn around the neck.

neck′tie′ *n.* a decorative fabric strip worn under the collar and tied in front.

ne·crol′o·gy (nə krol′ə jē, ne-) *n., pl.* **-gies.** a list of individuals who have died.

nec′ro·man′cy (nek′rə man′sē) *n.* magic. —**nec′ro·manc′er,** *n.*

ne·cro·sis (nə krō′sis) *n.* the death of a tissue or of an organ.

nec′tar (nek′tər) *n.* **1.** the sweet secretion of flowers. **2.** (in Greek myth) the drink of the gods.

nec′tar·ine (nek′tə rēn′) *n.* a variety of peach having a smooth skin.

nee (nā) *adj.* (of a woman) born; having as a maiden name. Also, **née.**

need (nēd) *n.* **1.** a requirement. **2.** a condition marked by necessity. —*v.t.* **3.** to have need of. —*v.i.* **4.** to be in need. —*aux.v.* **5.** to be obliged. —*Idiom.* **6.** if need be, if necessary.

nee′dle (nēd′l) *n., v.,* **-dled, -dling.** —*n.* **1.** a slender pointed implement for sewing, knitting, etc. **2.** anything similar, as for an indicator or gauge. **3.** a hypodermic syringe. —*v.t.* **4.** to prod or goad.

nee′dle·point′ *n.* embroidery on canvas.

need′less *adj.* not needed; unnecessary. —**need′less·ly,** *adv.*

nee′dle·work′ *n.* the art or product of working with a needle.

needs (nēdz) *adv.* necessarily.

need′y *adj.,* **-ier, -iest.** very poor.

ne′er-do-well′ (nâr′-) *n.* an idle, worthless person.

ne·far′i·ous (ni fâr′ē əs) *adj.* wicked.

ne·gate′ (ni gāt′, neg′āt) *v.t.,* **-gated, -gating.** to deny; nullify.

neg′a·tive (neg′ə tiv) *adj.* **1.** expressing denial or refusal. **2.** lacking positive attributes. **3.** *Math.* minus. **4.** *Photog.* having light and shade reversed. —*n.* **5.** a negative statement. **6.** *Photog.* a negative image.

ne·glect′ (ni glekt′) *v.t.* **1.** to disregard or fail to do. —*n.* **2.** disregard; negligence. —**ne·glect′ful,** *adj.*

neg·li·gee′ (neg′li zhā′, neg′li-zhā′) *n.* a woman's sheer dressing gown.

neg′li·gent (neg′li jənt) *adj.* guilty of or characterized by neglect. —**neg′li·gence,** *n.*

neg′li·gi·ble (-jə bəl) *adj.* very small; unimportant.

ne·go′ti·a·ble (ni gō′shē ə bəl, -shə bəl) *adj.* **1.** capable of being negotiated. **2.** transferable, as securities. —**ne·go′ti·a·bil′i·ty,** *n.*

ne·go′ti·ate (-shē āt′) *v.,* **-ated, -ating.** —*v.i.* **1.** to deal or bargain with another. —*v.t.* **2.** to arrange for by discussion. —**ne·go′ti·a′tion,** *n.* —**ne·go′ti·a′tor,** *n.*

neigh (nā) *n.* **1.** the cry of a horse. —*v.i.* **2.** to make such a sound.

neigh′bor (nā′bər) *n.* **1.** a person or thing near another. —*v.t., v.i.* **2.** to be near.

neigh′bor·hood *n.* **1.** a surrounding area. **2.** a district having a separate identity.

nei′ther (nē′thər, nī′-) *conj., adj.*

—**Pronunciation.** See EITHER.

nem′a·tode (nem′ə tōd′) *n.* a long, cylindrical, unsegmented worm.

nem·e·sis (nem′ə sis) *n., pl.* **-ses. 1.** a source of harm or failure. **2.** an unconquerable opponent.

neo- a prefix meaning new.

Ne′o·lith′ic (nē′ə lith′ik) *adj.* of the later Stone Age.

ne·ol′o·gism (nē ol′ə jiz′əm) *n.* a new word or phrase.

ne′on (nē′on) *n.* a gas used in some electrical signs.

ne′o·na′tal (nē′ō nāt′l) *adj.* referring to the care of newborn babies.

ne′o·nate′ (nē′ə nāt′) *n.* a newborn child.

ne′o·phyte′ (-fīt′) *n.* a beginner.

ne′o·plasm (-plaz′əm) *n.* a growth of abnormal tissue; a tumor.

ne·pen′the (ni pen′thē) *n.* anything inducing a pleasurable sensation of forgetfulness.

neph′ew (nef′yōō) *n.* a son of one's brother or sister.

ne·phri′tis (nə frī′tis) *n.* inflammation of the kidneys.

Nev. Nevada.

ne′ plus′ ul′tra (nē′ plus′ ul′trə, nā′) *n.* the highest point.

nep′o·tism (nep′ə tiz′əm) *n.* favoritism based on family relationship.

Nep′tune (nep′tōōn, -tyōōn) *n.* **1.** the planet eighth from the sun. **2.** the Roman god of the sea.

nerd (nûrd) *n. Slang.* **1.** a dull or unattractive person. **2.** a person devoted to a nonsocial pursuit.

nerve (nûrv) *n., v.,* **nerved, nerving.** —*n.* **1.** a bundle of fiber that conveys impulses between the brain and other parts of the body. **2.** courage. **3.** *Informal.* presumption.

4. nerves, anxiety; unease. —*v.t.* **5.** to give courage to.

nerve′ gas′ *n.* a poison gas that interferes with nerve functions.

nerv′ous *adj.* **1.** uneasy or anxious. **2.** having or caused by disordered nerves. **3.** of nerves. —**nerv′ous·ly,** *adv.*

nerv′y *adj.,* **-ier, -iest.** *Informal.* brashly bold; presumptuous.

-ness a suffix meaning quality or state.

nest (nest) *n.* **1.** a structure of grass, twigs, etc., prepared by a bird for its eggs. **2.** any place used by an animal for rearing its young. **3.** a group of things fitting tightly together. —*v.i.* **4.** to settle in a nest. —*v.t.* **5.** to fit one within another.

nest′ egg′ *n.* money saved for emergencies, retirement, etc.

nes′tle (nes′əl) *v.,* **-tled, -tling.** to lie close and snug.

net¹ (net) *n., v.,* **netted, netting.** —*n.* **1.** Also, **net′ting.** a lacelike fabric of uniform mesh. **2.** anything serving to catch or ensnare. **3.** a computer or telecommunications network. —*v.t.* **4.** to cover with a net. **5.** to ensnare.

net² (net) *adj., v.,* **-, netted, netting.** —*adj.* **1.** exclusive of loss or remaining after deductions. —*n.* **2.** the net income, profit, etc. —*v.t.* **3.** to gain as clear profit.

neth′er (neth′ər) *adj.* lower.

net′i·quette (net′i kit, -ket′) *n.* the etiquette of computer networks, esp. the Internet.

net′tle (net′l) *n., v.,* **-tled, -tling.** —*n.* **1.** a plant with stinging hairs. —*v.t.* **2.** to irritate; sting.

net′tle·some (-səm) *adj.* **1.** causing irritation. **2.** easily provoked.

net′work′ *n.* **1.** a netlike combination of intersecting elements. **2.** a group of associated radio or television stations. **3.** a computer or telecommunications system linked to permit information exchanges. —*v.i.* **4.** to engage in networking.

net′work compu′ter *n.* a computer with minimal processing power, designed primarily to provide access to networks.

net′work·ing *n.* the informal sharing of information among people who have common interests.

neu′ral (nŏor′əl, nyŏor′-) *adj.* of nerves or the nervous system.

neu·ral′gia (nŏo ral′jə, nyŏo-) *n.* a sharp pain along a nerve.

neur′as·the′ni·a (nŏor əs thē′nē ə, nyŏor′-) *n.* a pattern of symptoms often linked with depression.

neu·ri′tis (nŏo rī′tis, nyŏo-) *n.* inflammation of a nerve.

neu·rol′o·gy (-rol′ə jē) *n.* the branch of medicine dealing with the nervous system. —**neu·rol′o·gist,** *n.* —**neu′ro·log′i·cal** (nŏor′ə loj′i kəl) *adj.*

neu′ron (nŏor′on, nyŏor′-) *n.* a cell that is the basic unit of the nervous system.

neu·ro′sis (nŏo rō′sis, nyŏo-) *n., pl.* **-ses.** an emotional disorder characterized by anxiety, obsessional thoughts, compulsive acts, etc.

neu′ro·sur′ger·y (nŏor′ō sûr′jə rē, nyŏor′-) *n.* surgery of the brain and other nerve tissue.

neu·rot′ic (-rot′ik) *adj.* **1.** of or marked by neurosis. —*n.* **2.** a neurotic person.

neu′ro·trans′mit·ter *n.* a chemical substance that transmits nerve impulses across a synapse.

neu′ter (nŏo′tər, nyŏo′-) *adj.* **1.** neither male nor female. —*v.t.* **2.** to spay or castrate (a dog, cat, etc.).

neu′tral (nŏo′trəl, nyŏo′-) *adj.* **1.** taking no side in a controversy. **2.** not emphatic or positive. —*n.* **3.** a neutral person or state. —**neu′tral′i·ty** (-tral′i tē) *n.* —**neu′tral·ize′,** *v.t.,* —**neu′tral·ly,** *adv.*

neu′tron (nŏo′tron, nyŏo′-) *n.* an elementary particle having no charge, found in the nucleus of an atom.

Nev. Nevada.

nev′er (nev′ər) *adv.* not ever.

nev′er·the·less′ *adv.* in spite of that.

new (nŏo, nyŏo) *adj.* **1.** of recent origin or existence. **2.** unfamiliar. —*adv.* **3.** recently; freshly.

new′el (nŏo′əl, nyŏo′-) *n.* the post supporting the handrail at the head or foot of a flight of stairs.

new′fan′gled (-fang′gəld) *adj.* of a new kind or fashion.

new′ly *adv.* **1.** recently. **2.** anew.

new′ly·wed′ *n.* a person who has recently married.

news (nŏoz, nyŏoz) *n.* **1.** a report of a recent event. **2.** a report of recent

events in a newspaper, on the radio, or on television.

news′cast′ *n.* a broadcast of the news on radio or television. —**news′cast′er,** *n.*

news′group′ *n.* an on-line discussion group on a specific topic.

news′let′ter *n.* a periodic informational report for a specialized group.

news′pa·per (nŏoz′-, nyŏoz′-) *n.* a periodical containing news, comment, features, advertising, etc.

news′print′ *n.* the paper on which newspapers are printed.

news′reel′ *n.* a short motion picture of recent news events.

news′stand′ *n.* a sales booth for newspapers, periodicals, etc.

news′wor′thy *adj.* interesting enough to warrant press coverage.

newt (nŏot, nyŏot) *n.* a salamander.

New′ Tes′tament *n.* the portion of the Christian Bible recording the life and teachings of Christ and His disciples.

new′ton (nŏot′n, nyŏot′n) *n.* a unit of force.

new′ wave′ *n.* a movement that breaks with traditional values, techniques, etc.

new′ year′ *n.* **1.** New Year, the first day of the year. **2.** the year approaching.

next (nekst) *adj.* **1.** immediately following in time, order, etc. —*adv.* **2.** in the nearest place after. **3.** at the first subsequent time.

next′-door′ *adj.* in the next house, apartment, etc.

nex′us (nek′səs) *n., pl.* **nexus.** a link or connection.

NH New Hampshire. Also, **N.H.**

ni′a·cin (nī′ə sin) *n.* nicotinic acid.

nib (nib) *n.* a pen point.

nib′ble *v.,* **-bled, -bling,** *n.* —*v.t., v.i.* **1.** to bite off in small bits. —*n.* **2.** a small morsel.

nice (nīs) *adj.,* **nicer, nicest. 1.** agreeable. **2.** fastidious.

ni′ce·ty (nī′si tē) *n., pl.* **-ties. 1.** a subtle point. **2.** a refinement.

niche (nich) *n.* **1.** a recess in a wall. **2.** a suitable role or position.

nick (nik) *n.* **1.** a notch or hollow place in a surface. **2.** a precise or opportune moment. —*v.t.* **3.** to injure slightly. **4.** to make a nick in. —*Idiom.* **5.** in the nick of time, at the last possible moment.

nick′el (nik′əl) *n.* a hard silver-white metal. **2.** a five-cent coin.

nick′el·o′de·on (-ə lō′dē ən) *n.* **1.** an early motion-picture house. **2.** a coin-operated automatic piano.

nick′name′ *n., v.,* **-named, -naming.** —*n.* **1.** an informal name. —*v.t.* **2.** to give a nickname to.

nic′o·tine′ (nik′ə tēn′) *n.* a toxic liquid alkaloid found in tobacco.

niece (nēs) *n.* a daughter of one's brother or sister.

nif′ty (nif′tē) *adj.,* **-tier, -tiest.** *Informal.* smart; fine.

nig′gard·ly (nig′ərd lē) *adj.* stingy.

nig′gling (nig′ling) *adj.* trivial.

nigh (nī) *adv., adj.* near.

night (nīt) *n.* the period between sunset and sunrise.

night′cap′ *n.* **1.** an alcoholic drink taken before bed. **2.** a cap worn while sleeping.

night′club′ *n.* an establishment open at night, offering food, drink, and entertainment.

night′ crawl′er *n.* an earthworm.

night′fall′ *n.* the coming of night.

night′gown′ *n.* a gown for sleeping.

night′hawk′ *n.* a nocturnal American bird.

night′in·gale′ (nīt′n gāl′, nī′ting-) *n.* a small European thrush that sings at night.

night′ly *adj., adv.* occurring every night.

night′mare′ (-mâr′) *n.* **1.** a bad dream. **2.** a harrowing event.

night′ owl′ *n.* a person who often stays up late at night.

night′shade′ *n.* a plant sometimes used in medicine.

night′shirt′ *n.* a loose shirtlike garment worn in bed.

night′ stick′ *n.* a club carried by police officers.

ni′hil·ism (nī′ə liz′əm, nē′-) *n.* **1.** a belief that existence has no meaning. **2.** total rejection of established laws and institutions. —**ni′hil·ist,** *n.* —**ni′hil·is′tic,** *adj.*

nil (nil) *n.* nothing.

nim′ble (nim′bəl) *adj.,* **-bler, -blest.** agile; quick. —**nim′bly,** *adv.*

nim′bus (nim′bəs) *n., pl.* **-bi** (-bī) **-buses. 1.** a halo. **2.** a rain cloud.

nim′rod (nim′rod) *n.* a skilled hunter.

nin′com·poop′ (nin′kəm pŏop′, ning′-) *n.* a fool.

nine (nīn) *n., adj.* eight plus one. —**ninth,** *adj., n.*

nine′pins′ *n.pl.* a bowling game played with nine wooden pins.

nine′teen′ *n., adj.* ten plus nine. —**nine′teenth′,** *n., adj.*

nine′ty *n., adj.* ten times nine. —**nine′ti·eth,** *adj., n.*

nin′ny (nin′ē) *n., pl.* **-nies.** a fool.

ni·o′bi·um (nī ō′bē əm) *n.* a steel-gray metallic element.

nip¹ (nip) *v.,* **nipped, nipping.** —*v.t.* **1.** to pinch or bite. **2.** to check the growth of. **3.** to affect sharply. —*n.* **4.** a pinch. **5.** a biting quality.

nip² (nip) *v.,* **nipped, nipping.** —*v.i.* **1.** to drink an alcoholic liquor in small sips. —*n.* **2.** a small drink of alcoholic liquor.

nip′ple *n.* **1.** a milk-discharging protuberance on the female breast. **2.** a nipple-shaped object.

nip′py *adj.,* **-pier, -piest. 1.** chilly. **2.** pungent.

nir·va′na (nir vä′nə, -van′ə, nər-) *n.* **1.** (in Buddhism) freedom from all passion. **2.** a state of bliss.

nit (nit) *n.* the egg of a louse.

ni′ter (nī′tər) *n.* the white salt used in gunpowder, fertilizer, etc. Also, **ni′tre.**

nit′-pick′ *v.i. Informal.* to argue or find fault pettily.

ni′trate (nī′trāt, -trit) *n.* the salt of nitric acid.

ni′tric ac′id (nī′trik) *n.* a caustic liquid used in the manufacture of explosives, fertilizers, etc.

ni′tro·gen (nī′trə jən) *n.* a colorless, odorless, tasteless gas.

ni′tro·glyc′er·in (nī′trə glis′ər in) *n.* a colorless, highly explosive oil.

ni′trous (nī′trəs) *adj.* of niter. **2.** Also, **ni′tric.** containing nitrogen.

ni′trous ox′ide *n.* a colorless, sweet-smelling gas.

nit′ty-grit′ty (nit′ē grit′ē) *n. Slang.* the crux of a matter.

nit′wit′ *n.* a foolish person.

nix (niks) *n.* **1.** nothing. —*adv.* **2.** no. —*v.t.* **3.** to veto.

NJ New Jersey. Also, **N.J.**

NM New Mexico.

N. Mex. New Mexico.

no¹ (nō) *adv., n., pl.* **noes, nos.** —*adv.* **1.** a word used to express dissent, denial, or refusal. —*n.* **2.** a negative vote.

no² (nō) *adj.* not any.

no. 1. north. **2.** number.

no·bel′i·um (nō bel′ē əm, -bēl′ē-) *n.* a synthetic radioactive element.

no·bil′i·ty (nō bil′i tē) *n., pl.* **-ties. 1.** the noble class. **2.** the state or quality of being noble.

no′ble (nō′bal) *adj.,* **-bler, -blest,** *n.* —*adj.* **1.** of high rank by birth. **2.** admirable or magnificent. —*n.* **3.** a person of noble rank. —**no′ble·man,** *n.* —**no′ble·wom′an,** *n.fem.*

no·blesse′ o·blige′ (nō bles′ ō-blēzh′) *n.* the moral obligation of the rich to show generosity to the less fortunate.

no′bod·y (nō′bod′ē, -bud′ē, -bə dē) *pron., n., pl.* **-bodies.** —*pron.* **1.** no person. —*n.* **2.** a person of no importance.

no′-brain′er *n. Informal.* something requiring little thought.

noc·tur′nal (nok tûr′nl) *adj.* **1.** of the night. **2.** occurring or active by night.

noc′turne (-tûrn) *n.* a dreamy or pensive musical composition.

nod (nod) *v.,* **nodded, nodding,** *n.* —*v.t.* **1.** to incline (the head) briefly. —*v.i.* **2.** to become sleepy. **3.** to sway gently. —*n.* **4.** a brief inclination of the head.

node (nōd) *n.* **1.** a protuberance. **2.** a joint in a plant stem.

nod′ule (noj′ōol) *n.* a small knob or lump. —**nod′u·lar,** *adj.*

No·el′ (nō el′) *n.* Christmas.

no′-fault′ *adj.* (of auto accident insurance, divorces, etc.) effective without establishing fault.

nog′gin (nog′ən) *n.* **1.** a small mug. **2.** *Informal.* the head.

noise (noiz) *n., v.,* **noised, noising.** —*n.* **1.** a sound, esp. loud or harsh. —*v.t.* **2.** to spread, as rumors. —**nois′y,** *adj.* —**nois′i·ly,** *adv.*

noi′some (noi′səm) *adj.* **1.** offensive. **2.** harmful.

no′mad (nō′mad) *n.* a wanderer. —**no·mad′ic,** *adj.*

no′ man's′ land′ *n.* the area between warring armies.

nom de plume (nom′ də plōom′) *n.* the name used by a writer.

no′men·cla′ture (nō′mən klā′chər) *n.* a set or system of names.

nom′i·nal (nom′ə nl) *adj.* **1.** in name only; so-called. **2.** trifling.

nom′i·nate′ (-nāt′) *v.t.,* **-nated, -nating. 1.** to propose as a candidate. **2.** to appoint. —**nom′i·na′tion,** *n.*

nom′i·na·tive (nom′ə nə tiv) *adj.* **1.** denoting the grammatical case of a noun or pronoun used as the subject of a verb. —*n.* **2.** the nominative case.

nom′i·nee′ *n.* a person nominated.

non- a prefix meaning not.

non′age (non′ij, nō′nij) *n.* the period of legal minority.

non′a·ge·nar′i·an (non′ə jə när′ē-ən, nō′nə-) *n.* a person between 90 and 99 years old.

nonce (nons) *n.* the present occasion.

non′cha·lant′ (non′shə länt′) *adj.* coolly unconcerned. —**non′cha·lance′,** *n.* —**non′cha·lant′ly,** *adv.*

non′com·bat′ant (non′kəm-bat′nt, non kom′bə tnt) *n.* **1.** a member of a military force who is not a fighter. **2.** a civilian in wartime.

non′commis′sioned of′ficer *n.* an enlisted person ranking below a commissioned or warrant officer in the armed forces.

non′com·mit′tal *adj.* giving no particular view, feeling, etc.

non′ com′pos men′tis (non′ kom′pəs men′tis) *adj. Law.* not of sound mind.

non′con·duc′tor *n.* a substance that does not readily conduct heat, electricity, etc.

non′con·form′ist *n.* a person who refuses to conform.

non′de·script′ (non′di skript′) *adj.* of no particular kind.

none (nun) *pron. sing. and pl.* **1.** not one; not any. —*adv.* **2.** in no way.

non·en′ti·ty *n., pl.* **-ties.** an unimportant person or thing.

none′such′ *n.* a person or thing without equal.

none′the·less′ *adv.* nevertheless.

non·met′al *n.* an element not having the character of a metal, as carbon or nitrogen.

no′-no′ *n. Informal.* a forbidden thing.

non′pa·reil′ (non′pə rel′) *adj.* **1.** having no equal. —*n.* **2.** a person or thing without equal.

non·par′ti·san *adj.* **1.** not taking sides. **2.** belonging to no party.

non·plus′ (non plus′, non′plus) *v.t.* **-plussed** *or* **-plused, -plussing** *or* **-plusing.** to confuse.

non·prof′it *adj.* not profit motivated.

non′rep·re·sen·ta′tion·al *adj.* not resembling any object in nature.

non′re·stric′tive *adj.* noting a word, phrase, or clause describing a modified element but not essential to its meaning.

non′sec·tar′i·an *adj.* not affiliated with a religious denomination.

non′sense (non′sens, -səns) *n.* senseless or absurd words or actions. —**non·sen′si·cal,** *adj.*

non se′qui·tur (non sek′wi tər, -tōor′) *n.* a statement unrelated to the preceding one.

non′stand′ard *adj.* not conforming to usage considered acceptable by educated native speakers.

non′stop′ *adj., adv.* without intermediate stops. Also, **non-stop.**

non′sup·port′ *n.* failure to provide financial support.

non·un′ion *adj.* **1.** not belonging to a labor union. **2.** not produced by union workers.

non·vi′o·lence *n.* the policy of refraining from using violence. —**non·vi′o·lent,** *adj.*

noo′dle (nŏod′l) *n.* a thin strip of dough, cooked in soup, casseroles, etc.

nook (nŏok) *n.* a corner of a room.

noon (nŏon) *n.* twelve o'clock in the daytime. —**noon′time′,** *n.*

no′ one′ *pron.* not anyone.

noon′tide′ *n.* midday.

noose (nŏos) *n.* a loop with a running knot that pulls tight.

nor (nôr; *unstressed* nər) *conj.* or not: used with **neither.**

Nor′dic (nôr′dik) *adj.* of the physical type of the peoples of northern Europe, typically tall stature, blond hair, and blue eyes.

norm (nôrm) *n.* a standard or model.

nor′mal (nôr′məl) *adj.* **1.** of standard type; usual. —*n.* **2.** the standard or average. —**nor′mal·cy, nor·mal′i·ty** (-mal′i tē) n. —**nor′mal·ize′,** v.t., v.i.

nor′mal school′ n. a school for training teachers.

nor′ma·tive (nôr′mə tiv) adj. establishing a norm.

Norse (nôrs) n. the inhabitants or speech of medieval Scandinavia.

north (nôrth) n. **1.** a cardinal point of the compass, lying to the left of a person facing the rising sun. **2.** **the North,** a region in this direction. —adj. **3.** toward, in, or from the north. —**north′ern,** adj. —**north′ern·er,** n. —**north′ward,** adv., adj.

north′east′ n. **1.** a point or direction midway between north and east. **2.** **the Northeast,** a region in this direction. —adj., adv. **3.** toward, in, or from the northeast. —**north′east′ern,** adj.

north′er·ly adj., adv. toward or blowing from the north.

North′ern Hem′isphere n. the half of the earth between the North Pole and the equator.

North′ Pole′ n. the end of the earth's axis of rotation, marking the northernmost point on earth.

North′ Star′ n. the bright star close to the north pole of the heavens; Polaris.

north′west′ n. **1.** a point or direction midway between north and west. **2.** **the Northwest,** a region in this direction. —adj., adv. **3.** toward, in, or from the northwest. —**north′west′ern,** adj.

Nor·we′gian (-wē′jən) adj. **1.** of Norway or its inhabitants. —n. **2.** a native of Norway. **3.** the language of Norway.

nose (nōz) n., v., nosed, nosing. —n. **1.** the part of the head containing the nostrils. **2.** the sense of smell. **3.** the projecting part of any object. —v.t. **4.** to perceive by smell. **5.** to push forward with the nose. —v.i. **6.** to pry. **7.** to head cautiously. —**Idiom.** **8.** **on the nose,** precisely.

nose′cone′ n. the forward section of a rocket.

nose′dive′ n., v., -dived or -dove, -dived, -diving. —n. **1.** a downward plunge. —v.i. **2.** to go into a nosedive.

nose′gay′ n. a small bouquet.

nosh (nosh) Informal. —v.i., v.t. to snack (on). —n. **2.** a snack.

no′-show′ n. a person who neither uses nor cancels a reservation.

nos·tal′gia (no stal′jə) n. a sentimental yearning for the past.

nos′tril (nos′trəl) n. either of the two external openings of the nose for breathing.

nos′trum (nos′trəm) n. **1.** a quack remedy. **2.** a pet solution.

nos′y (nō′zē) adj., -ier, -iest. Informal. unduly inquisitive.

not (not) adv. a word expressing negation, denial, or refusal.

no′ta be′ne (nō′tə ben′ē) Latin. note well.

no′ta·ble (nō′tə bəl) adj. **1.** worthy of note; important. —n. **2.** a prominent person. —**no′ta·bly,** adv.

no′ta·rize′ (nō′tə rīz′) v.t., -rized, -rizing. to authenticate through a notary.

no′ta·ry (nō′tə rē) n., pl. -ries. an official authorized to verify documents. Also, **notary public.**

no·ta′tion (nō tā′shən) n. **1.** a short note. **2.** a special symbol. —**no·ta′tion·al,** adj.

notch (noch) n. **1.** an angular cut. —v.t. **2.** to make a notch in.

note (nōt) n., v., noted, noting. —n. **1.** a brief record, comment, etc. **2.** a short letter. **3.** a distinction. **4.** an observation. **5.** a paper promising payment. **6.** a musical sound or written symbol. —v.t. **7.** to write down. **8.** to notice.

note′book′ n. **1.** a book with blank pages for writing notes. **2.** a lightweight laptop computer.

not′ed adj. famous.

note′wor′thy adj. worthy of attention.

noth′ing (nuth′ing) n. **1.** not anything. **2.** a trivial action, thing, etc. —adv. **3.** not at all.

noth′ing·ness n. **1.** lack of being. **2.** unconsciousness.

no′tice (nō′tis) n., v., -ticed, -ticing. —n. **1.** information; warning. **2.** a note, sign, etc., that informs or warns. **3.** attention; heed. —v.t. **4.** to pay attention to or perceive. **5.** to mention.

no′tice·a·ble adj. attracting notice or attention. —**no′tice·a·bly,** adv.

---

no′ti·fy′ v.t., -fied, -fying. to give notice to. —**no′ti·fi·ca′tion,** n.

no′tion (nō′shən) n. **1.** an idea. **2.** an opinion. **3.** a whim. **4.** notions, small items, as pins or trim.

no·to′ri·ous (nō tôr′ē əs, nə-) adj. widely known, esp. unfavorably. —**no′to·ri′e·ty** (-tə rī′i tē) n.

not′with·stand′ing prep. **1.** in spite of. —adv. **2.** nevertheless. —conj. **3.** although.

nou′gat (nōō′gət) n. a pastelike candy with nuts.

nought (nôt) n. naught.

noun (noun) n. a word denoting a person, place, or thing.

nour′ish (nûr′ish, nur′-) v.t. to sustain with food. —**nour′ish·ment,** n.

nou′veau riche′ (nōō′vō rēsh′) n., pl. **nou·veaux riches** (nōō′vō rēsh′). a newly rich person.

Nov. November.

no′va (nō′və) n., pl. -vas, -vae (-vē). a star that suddenly becomes much brighter, then gradually fades.

nov′el¹ (nov′əl) n. a long fictional narrative. —**nov′el·ist,** n.

nov′el² (nov′əl) adj. new or strange.

nov′el·ty n., pl. -ties. **1.** unfamiliarity. **2.** a new or amusing thing.

No·vem′ber (nō vem′bər) n. the eleventh month of the year.

no·ve′na (nō vē′nə, nə-) n., pl. -nae (-nē) -nas. a Roman Catholic devotion occurring on nine consecutive days.

nov′ice (nov′is) n. **1.** a beginner. **2.** a person just received into a religious order.

no·vi′ti·ate (nō vish′ē it, -āt′) n. the period of being a novice.

No′vo·caine′ (nō′və kān′) Trademark. a local anesthetic.

now (nou) adv. **1.** at the present time. **2.** immediately. —conj. **3.** since. —n. **4.** the present.

now′a·days′ (-ə dāz′) adv. in these times.

no′where adv. not anywhere.

nox′ious (nok′shəs) adj. harmful.

noz′zle (noz′əl) n. a projecting spout.

nth (enth) adj. utmost.

nu (nōō, nyōō) n., pl. **nus.** the 13th letter of the Greek alphabet.

nu′ance (nōō′äns, nyōō′-) n. a shade of expression, color, or meaning.

nub (nub) n. **1.** the gist. **2.** a knob or lump.

nu′bile (nōō′bil, -bīl, nyōō′-) adj. **1.** (of a young woman) marriageable. **2.** (of a young woman) sexually attractive.

nu′cle·ar (nōō′klē ər, nyōō′-) adj. **1.** of or involving atomic weapons. **2.** powered by nuclear energy. **3.** of or forming a nucleus.

nu′clear en′ergy n. energy released by reactions within atomic nuclei, as in nuclear fission or fusion.

nu′clear fam′ily n. a social unit composed of a father, a mother, and children.

nu′clear phys′ics n. the branch of physics dealing with atoms.

nu′clear win′ter n. the devastation, darkness, and cold that could result from a nuclear war.

nu′cle·on (nōō′klē on′, nyōō′-) n. a proton or neutron.

nu′cle·us (-klē əs) n., pl. -cle·i (-klē ī) -cleuses. **1.** a central part. **2.** the central body of a living cell. **3.** the core of an atom.

nude (nōōd, nyōōd) adj. **1.** naked. —n. **2.** a naked human figure.

nudge (nuj) v., nudged, nudging, n. —v.t. **1.** to push slightly. —n. **2.** a slight push.

nud′ism (nōō′diz əm, nyōō′-) n. the practice of going nude. —**nud′ist,** n.

nu′ga·to′ry (nōō′gə tôr′ē, nyōō′-) adj. **1.** trifling. **2.** futile.

nug′get (nug′it) n. a lump (esp. of gold).

nui′sance (nōō′səns, nyōō′-) n. an annoying thing or person.

nuke (nōōk, nyōōk) n., v., nuked, nuking. Informal. —n. **1.** a nuclear weapon or power plant. —v.t. **2.** to attack with nuclear weapons.

null (nul) adj. of no effect.

null′i·fy′ v.t., -fied, -fying. **1.** to make null. **2.** to make legally void.

numb (num) adj. **1.** deprived of feeling. —v.t. **2.** to make numb.

num′ber (num′bər) n. **1.** the sum of a group of units. **2.** a numeral. **3.** one of a series or group. **4.** a large quantity. —v.t. **5.** to mark with numbers. **6.** to count. —v.i. **7.** to amount to in numbers.
—**Usage.** See AMOUNT.

num′ber·less adj. too many to count.

---

nu′mer·al (nōō′mər əl, nyōō′-) n. **1.** a word or sign representing a number. —adj. **2.** of numbers.

nu′mer·ate′ (-mə rāt′) v.t., -ated, -ating. to count.

nu′mer·a′tor n. the part of a fraction written above the line.

nu·mer′i·cal (nōō mer′i kəl, nyōō-) adj. of or denoting numbers.

nu′mer·ol′o·gy (nōō′mə rol′ə jē, nyōō′-) n. the study of numbers to determine their supernatural meaning.

nu′mer·ous (-mər əs) adj. very many.

nu′mi·nous (nōō′mə nəs, nyōō′-) adj. supernatural.

nu′mis·mat′ics (nōō′miz mat′iks, -mis-, nyōō′-) n. the science of coins and medals.

num′skull′ (num′skul′) n. Informal. a stupid person. Also, **numb′skull′.**

nun (nun) n. a woman living with a religious group under vows.

nun′ci·o′ (nun′shē ō′, -sē ō′, nōōn′-) n., pl. -cios. a papal representative in a foreign capital.

nun′ner·y (nun′ə rē) n., pl. -neries. a convent.

nup′tial (nup′shəl, -chəl) adj. **1.** of marriage. —n. **2.** nuptials, the marriage ceremony.

nurse (nûrs) n., v., nursed, nursing. —n. **1.** a person who cares for sick people or children. —v.t. **2.** to minister to in sickness. **3.** to look after carefully. **4.** to suckle.

nurs′er·y n., pl. -eries. **1.** a room set apart for young children. **2.** a place where young plants are grown.

nurs′ery school′ n. a prekindergarten school for children.

nurs′ing home′ n. a residential institution caring for the aged or infirm.

nurs′ling (-ling) n. a nursing infant or young animal.

nur′ture (nûr′chər) v., -tured, -turing, n. —v.t. **1.** to feed and care for during growth. —n. **2.** upbringing. **3.** something that nourishes.

nut (nut) n. **1.** a dry fruit consisting of an edible kernel in a shell. **2.** the kernel. **3.** a perforated, threaded metal block used to screw on the end of a bolt. **4.** Slang. an insane or eccentric person. —**nut′crack′er,** n. —**nut′shell′,** n.

nut′hatch′ n. a small songbird that seeks food along tree trunks.

nut′meg (-meg) n. the aromatic seed of an East Indian tree.

nu′tri·a (nōō′trē ə,nyōō′-) n. **1.** a South American aquatic rodent. **2.** its fur.

nu′tri·ent (nōō′trē ənt, nyōō′-) adj. **1.** nourishing. —n. **2.** a nutrient substance.

nu′tri·ment (-trə mənt) n. nourishment.

nu·tri′tion (-trish′ən) n. **1.** the process of nourishing or being nourished. **2.** the study of dietary requirements. —**nu·tri′tious, nu′tri·tive,** adj. —**nu·tri′tion·ist,** n.

nuts (nuts) adj. Slang. crazy.

nut′ty adj., -tier, -tiest. **1.** tasting of or like nuts. **2.** Slang. insane; senseless. —**nut′ti·ness,** n.

nuz′zle (nuz′əl) v.t., v.i., -zled, -zling. **1.** to touch or rub with the nose, snout, etc. **2.** to cuddle.

NV Nevada.

NW northwest. Also, **N.W.**

NY New York. Also, **N.Y.**

ny′lon (nī′lon) n. **1.** a tough, elastic synthetic substance used for yarn, bristles, etc. **2.** nylons, stockings of nylon.

nymph (nimf) n. **1.** any of a class of female water or forest deities. **2.** a beautiful girl.

nym′pho·ma′ni·a (nim′fə mā′nē ə) n. uncontrollable sexual desire in women. —**nym′pho·ma′ni·ac′,** n.

O

O, o (ō) n. the fifteenth letter of the English alphabet.

O (ō) interj. (an expression of surprise, gladness, pain, etc.)

o' (ə, ō) prep. a shortened form of of.

oaf (ōf) n. a clumsy, rude person. —**oaf′ish,** adj.

oak (ōk) n. a hardwood tree bearing acorns.

oa′kum (ō′kəm) n. loose fiber used in calking.

---

oar (ôr) n. a flat-bladed shaft for rowing a boat. —**oars′man,** n.

oar′lock′ n. a device providing a pivot for an oar.

o·a′sis (ō ā′sis) n., pl. -ses. a fertile place in the desert.

oat (ōt) n. a cereal grass grown for its edible grain.

oath (ōth) n. **1.** a solemn affirmation; vow. **2.** a curse.

oat′meal′ n. **1.** ground oats. **2.** a cooked breakfast food.

ob′bli·ga′to (ob′li gä′tō) n., pl. -tos, -ti (-tē). a musical line performed by a single instrument accompanying a solo part.

ob′du·rate (ob′dŏŏ rit, -dyŏŏ-) adj. stubborn. —**ob′du·ra·cy,** n.

o·be·di·ent (ō bē′dē ənt) adj. obeying or willing to obey. —**o·be′di·ence,** n.

o·bei′sance (ō bā′səns, ō bē′-) n. **1.** a bow or curtsy. **2.** homage.

ob′e·lisk (ob′ə lisk) n. a tapering, four-sided shaft of stone.

o·bese′ (ō bēs′) adj. very fat. —**o·bes′i·ty,** n.

o·bey′ (ō bā′) v.t. **1.** to do as ordered by. **2.** to comply with.

ob·fus′cate (ob′fə skāt′, ob fus′kāt) v.t., -cated, -cating. to confuse. —**ob′fus·ca′tion,** n.

o·bit·er dic′tum (ob′i tər dik′təm) n., pl. **obiter dicta** (-tə). an incidental remark.

o·bit′u·ar′y (ō bich′ŏŏ er′ē) n., pl. -aries. a notice of a person's death, as in a newspaper.

obj. **1.** object. **2.** objective.

ob·ject′ n. (ob′jikt, -jekt) **1.** something solid. **2.** a thing or person to which attention is directed. **3.** an end; motive. **4.** a noun or pronoun that represents the goal of an action. —v.i. (əb jekt′) **5.** to say that one is opposed. —**ob·jec′tor,** n.

ob·jec′tion (əb jek′shən) n. **1.** an argument against. **2.** the act of objecting.

ob·jec′tion·a·ble (əb jek′shə nə bəl) adj. causing disapproval; offensive.

ob·jec′tive n. **1.** a purpose; goal. —adj. **2.** not influenced by personal feelings. **3.** of the grammatical case indicating the object of a verb or preposition. —**ob·jec·tiv′i·ty** (ob′jik tiv′i tē) n.

ob′ject les′son n. a practical illustration of a principle.

ob·jet d'art′ (ob′zhā där′) n., pl. **objets d'art** (ob′zhā där′). an object of artistic worth.

ob·late′ (ob′lāt, o blāt′) adj. flattened at the poles, as a spheroid.

ob·la′tion (o blā′shən) n. an offering; sacrifice.

ob′li·gate′ (ob′li gāt′) v.t., -gated, -gating. to bind morally or legally. —**ob′li·ga′tion,** n.

ob·lig′a·to′ry (ə blig′ə tôr′ē) adj. compulsory; required.

o·blige′ (ə blīj′) v.t., obliged, obliging. **1.** to require. **2.** to do a favor for.

o·blig′ing adj. willing to help.

ob·lique′ (ə blēk′, ō blēk′) adj. **1.** slanting. **2.** indirect. —**ob·lique′ly,** adv.

ob·lit′er·ate′ (ə blit′ə rāt′) v.t., -ated, -ating. to remove all traces of.

ob·liv′i·on (ə bliv′ē ən) n. **1.** the state of being forgotten. **2.** the state of forgetting.

ob·liv′i·ous (ə bliv′ē əs) adj. unmindful or unaware.

ob′long (ob′lông′) adj. **1.** of a rectangular shape that is longer than it is broad. —n. **2.** an oblong figure.

ob′lo·quy (ob′lə kwē) n., pl. -quies. public disgrace.

ob·nox′ious (əb nok′shəs) adj. very offensive.

o′boe (ō′bō) n. a woodwind instrument with a double-reed mouthpiece. —**o′bo·ist,** n.

obs. obsolete.

ob·scene′ (əb sēn′) adj. **1.** offensive to decency or morality. **2.** disgusting. —**ob·scen′i·ty** (-sen′i tē, -sē′ni-) n.

ob·scure′ adj., v., -scured, -scuring. —adj. **1.** not clear to the understanding. **2.** not easily noticed. **3.** not famous. —v.t. **4.** to make obscure. —**ob·scu′ri·ty,** n. —**ob·scure′ly,** adv.

ob·se′qui·ous (əb sē′kwē əs) adj. excessively deferential.

ob′se·quy (ob′si kwē) n., pl. -quies. a funeral rite.

ob·serv′ance (əb zûr′vəns) n. **1.** the act of observing a law, custom, etc. **2.** the celebration of a holiday.

ob·serv′ant adj. **1.** quick to notice.

---

2. careful in the observing of a law, ritual, etc.

ob′ser·va′tion (ob′zûr vā′shən) n. **1.** an observing or being observed. **2.** a remark.

ob·serv′a·to′ry (əb zûr′və tôr′ē) n., pl. -ries. a place equipped for observing astronomical phenomena.

ob·serve′ v.t., -served, -serving. **1.** to see; notice; watch. **2.** to remark. **3.** to obey, as a law. **4.** to celebrate, as a holiday.

ob·sess′ (əb ses′) v.t. **1.** to preoccupy the thoughts of constantly. —v.i. **2.** to think about something constantly. —**ob·ses′sive,** adj.

ob·ses′sion (əb sesh′ən) n. **1.** the domination of one's thoughts or feelings by a persistent idea, desire, etc. **2.** the idea or desire itself.

ob·sid′i·an (əb sid′ē ən) n. a dark volcanic glass.

ob′so·les′cent (ob′sə les′ənt) adj. becoming obsolete. —**ob′so·les′cence,** n.

ob′so·lete′ (-lēt′) adj. no longer in use.

ob′sta·cle (ob′stə kəl) n. something that is in the way.

ob·stet′rics (əb ste′triks) n. the branch of medicine concerned with pregnancy and childbirth. —**ob′ste·tri′cian** (ob′sti trish′ən) n. —**ob·stet′ric,** adj.

ob′sti·nate (ob′stə nit) adj. **1.** stubborn. **2.** not yielding to treatment. —**ob′sti·na·cy** (-nə sē) n. —**ob′sti·nate·ly,** adv.

ob·strep′er·ous (əb strep′ər əs) adj. unruly.

ob·struct′ (əb strukt′) v.t. **1.** to block. **2.** to hinder the passage, progress, etc., of. —**ob·struc′tion,** n. —**ob·struc′tive,** adj.

ob·tain′ (əb tān′) v.t. **1.** to get or acquire. —v.i. **2.** to be customary.

ob·trude′ (əb trōōd′) v., -truded, -truding. **1.** to thrust forward. —v.i. **2.** to intrude. —**ob·tru′sive** (-trōō′siv) adj.

ob·tuse′ (əb tōōs′, -tyōōs′) adj. **1.** not perceptive. **2.** not sharp. **3.** (of an angle) between 90° and 180°.

ob′verse n. (ob′vûrs) **1.** the side, as of a coin, bearing the principal design. **2.** a counterpart. —adj. (ob′vûrs, ob′vûrs) **3.** facing the observer.

ob′vi·ate′ (ob′vē āt′) v.t., -ated, -ating. to make unnecessary.

ob′vi·ous (ob′vē əs) adj. easily seen or understood. —**ob′vi·ous·ly,** adv.

oc·ca′sion (ə kā′zhən) n. **1.** a particular time. **2.** a special time or event. **3.** an opportunity. **4.** the immediate cause. —v.t. **5.** to cause.

oc·ca′sion·al adj. **1.** not occurring frequently. **2.** of a special occasion. —**oc·ca′sion·al·ly,** adv.

oc′ci·dent (ok′si dənt) n. the west.

oc·clude′ (ə klōōd′) v.t., -cluded, -cluding. to close or stop up. —**oc·clu′sion** (-klōō′zhən) n.

oc·cult′ (ə kult′, ok′ult) adj. **1.** supernatural. **2.** secret. —n. **3.** occult matters.

oc′cu·pa′tion (ok′yə pā′shən) n. **1.** a person's work. **2.** an activity. **3.** taking control of a place by force. —**oc′cu·pa′tion·al,** adj.

occupa′tional ther′apy n. therapy utilizing useful activities for psychological or physical rehabilitation.

oc′cu·py v.t., -pied, -pying. **1.** to fill (time, space, etc.). **2.** to inhabit. **3.** to take possession of (an area) by force. **4.** to keep busy. —**oc′cu·pan·cy,** n. —**oc′cu·pant,** n.

oc·cur′ (ə kûr′) v.i., -curred, -curring. **1.** to happen. **2.** to appear. **3.** to come to mind. —**oc·cur′rence,** n.

o′cean (ō′shən) n. **1.** the large body of salt water covering much of the earth. **2.** any of its five main parts. —**o′ce·an′ic** (ō′shē an′ik) adj.

o′cea·nog′ra·phy (ō′shə nog′rə-fē, ō′shē ə-) n. the study of oceans and the life in them.

oc′e·lot′ (os′ə lot′, ō′sə-) n. a small, spotted American wildcat.

o′cher (ō′kər) n. a yellow-to-red earthy material used as a pigment. Also, **o′chre.**

o′clock′ (ə klok′) adv. by the clock.

Oct. October.

oc′ta·gon′ (ok′tə gon′, -gən) n. a plane figure with eight sides.

oc′tane (ok′tān) n. a colorless liquid hydrocarbon in petroleum.

oc′tane num′ber n. a designation of the quality of gasoline.

oc′tave (ok′tiv, -tāv) n. **1.** a tone on the eighth degree from a given musical tone. **2.** the interval between such tones.

oc•ta′vo (ok tä′vō,-tä′-) n., pl. **-vos.** a book size formed by printing on sheets folded to form 8 leaves or 16 pages.

oc•tet′ (ok tet′) n. **1.** a group of eight musicians. **2.** music composed for such a group.

Oc•to′ber (ok tō′bər) n. the tenth month of the year.

oc′to•ge•nar′i•an (ok′tə jə när′ē-ən) n. a person between 80 and 89 years old.

oc′to•pus (ok′tə pəs) n., pl. **-puses, -pi** (-pī). an eight-armed sea mollusk.

oc′u•lar (ok′yə lər) adj. of the eyes.

OD (ō′dē′) n., pl. **ODs** or **OD′s**, v., **OD′d** or **ODed, OD′ing.** Slang. —n. **1.** an overdose of a drug, esp. a fatal one. —v.i. **2.** to take a drug overdose.

odd (od) adj. **1.** unusual; eccentric. **2.** not part of a set. **3.** (of a number) not exactly divisible by two.

odd′ball′ n. Informal. a peculiar person or thing.

odd′i•ty n., pl. **-ties. 1.** strangeness. **2.** a strange thing or person.

odds (odz) n. **1.** the probability that something is more or less likely to occur than something else. **2.** this probability expressed as a ratio. —Idiom. **3. at odds,** in disagreement.

odds′ and ends′ n.pl. **1.** miscellaneous items. **2.** scraps.

odds′-on′ adj. most likely.

ode (ōd) n. a poem of praise.

o′di•ous (ō′dē əs) adj. hateful.

o′di•um n. intense disgust.

o•dom′e•ter (ō dom′i tər) n. an instrument that measures the distance traveled.

o′dor (ō′dər) n. a smell or scent. —**o′dor•ous,** adj.

o′dor•if•er•ous (ō′də rif′ər əs) adj. having an odor, esp. a bad one.

od′ys•sey (od′ə sē) n. a long, adventurous journey.

o′er (ōr) prep., adv. Poetic. over.

oeu′vre (Fr. œ′vrə) n., pl. **oeu•vres** (Fr. œ′vrə). all the works of a writer, painter, etc.

of (uv, ov; unstressed əv or, esp. before consonants, ə) prep. **1.** from. **2.** belonging to. **3.** by. **4.** containing. **5.** about. —aux. v. **6.** Nonstandard. have.

—**Usage.** Because the preposition OF, when unstressed (a piece of cake), and the unstressed or contracted auxiliary verb HAVE (could have gone; could've gone) are both pronounced (əv) or (ə) in connected speech, inexperienced writers commonly confuse the two words, spelling HAVE as OF (I would of handed in my book report, but the dog ate it). Professional writers use this spelling deliberately, especially in fiction, to represent the speech of the uneducated: If he could of went home, he would of.

off (ôf) adv. **1.** away. **2.** no longer attached or covering. **3.** not operating or in effect. —prep. **4.** away from. —adj. **5.** not in effect. **6.** in error. **7.** free from duty. **8.** of less than the ordinary activity. **9.** unlikely. —Idiom. **10. off and on,** intermittently; at intervals.

off′al (ô′fəl) n. **1.** the viscera and remains of a butchered animal. **2.** garbage.

off′beat′ adj. unconventional.

off′-col′or adj. of questionable taste.

of•fend′ (ə fend′) v.t. **1.** to irritate, annoy, or anger. **2.** to affect disagreeably. —v.i. **3.** to commit an offense.

of•fend′er n. **1.** a person who offends. **2.** a criminal.

of•fense′ n. **1.** (ə fens′) a breaking of a rule or law. **2.** (ə fens′) a feeling of resentment and displeasure. **3.** (ə fens′) an attack. **4.** (ô′fens) the attacking side. Also, **of•fence′.**

of•fen′sive adj. **1.** causing resentful displeasure. **2.** unpleasant; disagreeable. —n. **3.** an attack.

of′fer (ô′fər) v.t. **1.** to present for acceptance or refusal. **2.** to propose; suggest. **3.** to bid as a price. —n. **4.** a proposal; bid.

of′fer•ing n. **1.** something offered. **2.** the act of one who offers.

of′fer•to′ry (-tôr′ē) n., pl. **-ries. 1.** the offering to God of bread and wine in the Eucharistic service. **2.** the collection of money at a religious service. **3.** the music accompanying such an offering.

off′hand′ adj. **1.** done without previous thought. **2.** casual or curt. —adv. **3.** in an offhand way.

of′fice (ô′fis) n. **1.** a place of business. **2.** a position of authority or trust. **3.** a duty or function. **4.** a religious service.

of′fice-hold′er n. a public official.

of•fi′cer n. **1.** a person of authority in an organization. **2.** a person holding a commission in the armed services. **3.** a member of a police department.

of•fi′cial (ə fish′əl) n. **1.** a person who holds office. —adj. **2.** authorized. **3.** pertaining to public office.

of•fi′ci•ant (ə fish′ē ənt) n. a person who officiates at a religious service.

of•fi′ci•ate′ (-āt′) v.i., **-ated, -at•ing.** to perform official duties.

of•fi′cious adj. too aggressive in offering unwanted help or advice.

off′ing (ô′fing) n. —Idiom. **in the offing,** in the near future.

off′-key′ adj. not in tune.

off′-lim′its adj. forbidden.

off′-put′ting adj. provoking uneasiness, annoyance, etc.

off′set′ v.t., **-set, -set•ting.** to compensate for.

off′shoot′ n. a branch.

off′shore′ adj., adv. in the water and away from shore.

off′spring′ n. children.

off′stage′ adv., adj. out of sight of the audience.

off′-the-cuff′ adj. impromptu.

off′-the-rec′ord adj. not to be quoted.

off′-the-wall′ adj. Informal. bizarre.

off′track′ adj. occurring away from the racetrack.

off′ year′ n. **1.** a year without a major election. **2.** a year marked by reduced production.

oft (ôft) adv. Poetic. often.

of′ten (ô′fən, ôf′tən) adv. many times; frequently.

o′gle (ō′gəl) v., **ogled, ogling,** n. —v.t., v.i. **1.** to look (at) amorously or flirtatiously. —n. **2.** an ogling glance.

o′gre (ō′gər) n. **1.** in fairy tales, a hideous giant who eats human flesh. **2.** a cruel person.

oh (ō) interj. (an exclamation of surprise, pain, sympathy, etc.)

OH Ohio.

ohm (ōm) n. a unit of electrical resistance.

-oid a suffix meaning like.

oil (oil) n. **1.** a greasy combustible liquid used for lubricating, heating, etc. —v.t. **2.** to smear or supply with oil. —adj. **3.** of oil. —**oil′y,** adj.

oil′cloth′ n. a cotton fabric made waterproof with oil.

oil′skin′ n. **1.** a fabric made waterproof with oil. **2.** (often pl.) a garment made of this, as a raincoat.

oint′ment (oint′mənt) n. a soft, oily preparation, often medicated, for applying to the skin.

OK Oklahoma.

OK (ō′kā′) adj., adv., v., **OK′d, OK′ing,** n., pl. **OK′s.** —adj., adv. **1.** all right. —v.t. **2.** to approve. —n. **3.** approval. Also, **O.K., o′kay′.**

Okla. Oklahoma.

o′kra (ō′krə) n. a leafy vegetable with sticky, edible pods.

old (ōld) adj. **1.** having lived or existed for a long time. **2.** having lived or existed for a specified time. **3.** shabby through age or use. **4.** of long standing. **5.** Also, **old′en.** former; ancient. —n. **6.** time long past.

Old′ Eng′lish n. the English language before c1150.

old′-fash′ioned adj. having the style, ideas, etc., of an earlier time.

Old′ Guard′ n. (sometimes l.c.) the conservative members of a group.

old′ hand′ n. a person with long experience.

old′ hat′ adj. old-fashioned; dated.

old′ school′ n. supporters of established custom.

old′ster n. Informal. an elderly person.

Old′ Tes′ta•ment n. the complete Bible of the Jews, being the first division of the Christian Bible.

old′-tim′er n. Informal. an elderly person.

Old′ World′ n. Europe, Asia, and Africa.

old′-world′ adj. old-fashioned; traditional.

o′le•ag′i•nous (ō′lē aj′ə nəs) adj. **1.** oily. **2.** unctuous; fawning.

o′le•an′der (ō′lē an′dər) n. a poisonous evergreen shrub with pink, red, or white flowers.

o′le•o•mar′ga•rine (ō′lē ō′-) n. margarine. Also, **o′le•o′.**

ol•fac′to•ry (ol fak′tə rē, ôl-) adj. pertaining to the sense of smell.

ol′i•gar′chy (-gär′kē) n., pl. **-chies.** government by a small group. —**ol′i•garch′,** n.

ol′ive (ol′iv) n. **1.** a small, oval fruit eaten as a relish and used as a source of oil. **2.** a yellowish green color.

om′buds•man′ (om′bədz mən, om bōōdz′-) n., pl. **-men.** an official who investigates individuals' complaints against an institution or an employer.

o•me′ga (ō mē′gə, ō meg′ə) n. the last letter of the Greek alphabet.

om′e•let (om′lit, om′ə-) n. a dish of beaten eggs cooked and folded. Also, **om′e•lette.**

o′men (ō′mən) n. an event believed to predict good or evil.

om′i•cron (om′i kron′, ō′mi-) n. the 15th letter of the Greek alphabet.

om′i•nous (om′ə nəs) adj. threatening evil. —**om′i•nous•ly,** adv.

o•mit′ (ō mit′) v.t., **omitted, omitting. 1.** to leave out. **2.** to fail (to do, make, use, etc.). —**o•mis′sion** (ō mish′ən) n.

omni- a prefix meaning all.

om′ni•bus′ (om′nə bus′, -bəs) n., pl. **-buses. 1.** a bus. **2.** an anthology.

om•nip′o•tent (om nip′ə tənt) adj. having unlimited power. —**om•nip′o•tence,** n.

om′ni•pres′ent (om′nə prez′ənt) adj. present everywhere at once.

om•nis′cient (om nish′ənt) adj. knowing all things.

om•niv′o•rous (om niv′ər əs) adj. eating all kinds of foods.

on (on) prep. **1.** attached to, supported by, or suspended from. **2.** in contact with. **3.** near to. **4.** toward. **5.** at the time of. **6.** concerning. —adv. **7.** in, into, or onto a thing, place, or person. **8.** forward. **9.** into or in operation. —adj. **10.** in use. —Idiom. **11. on and off,** intermittently. **12. on and on,** at great length.

—**Usage.** See ABOUT.

once (wuns) adv. **1.** formerly. **2.** a single time. **3.** at any time. —conj. **4.** as soon as. —Idiom. **5. at once, a.** at the same time. **b.** immediately. **6. once and for all,** decisively. **7. once in a while,** occasionally.

once′-o′ver n. a quick look.

on′co•gene′ (ong′kə jēn′) n. any gene causing the beginning of cancerous growth.

on•col′o•gy (-kol′ə jē) n. the branch of medicine dealing with tumors and cancer. —**on•col′o•gist,** n.

on′com′ing adj. approaching.

one (wun) adj. **1.** single. **2.** individual. **3.** common to all. —n. **4.** the first and lowest whole number. **5.** a single person or thing. —pron. **6.** a person or thing. **7.** any person or thing.

one′ness n. unity.

on′er•ous (on′ər əs, ō′nər-) adj. burdensome.

one•self′ (wun self′, wunz-) pron. a person's self. Also, **one′s self.**

one′-sid′ed adj. **1.** with all advantage on one side. **2.** biased.

one′-time′ adj. former.

one′-track′ adj. obsessed with one subject.

one′-way′ adj. moving or allowing movement in one direction only.

on′go′ing adj. continuing.

on′ion (un′yən) n. a common plant having an edible, pungent bulb.

on′-line′ adj. operating under the direct control of, or connected to, a main computer.

on′look′er n. a spectator; witness.

on′ly (ōn′lē) adv. **1.** alone; solely. **2.** merely. —adj. **3.** being the single one of the kind. —conj. **4.** but.

on′o•mat′o•poe′ia (on′ə mat′ə-pē′ə, -mä′tə-) n. the formation of a word by the imitation of a sound.

on′rush′ n. a rapid advance.

on′set′ n. **1.** a beginning. **2.** an attack.

on′slaught′ (on′slôt′) n. an attack.

on′to prep. upon; on.

on•tog′e•ny (on tog′ə nē) n. the development of an individual organism.

on•tol′o•gy (on tol′ə jē) n. the branch of metaphysics studying existence or being.

o′nus (ō′nəs) n. **1.** an unfair burden. **2.** responsibility.

on′ward (-wərd) adv. **1.** forward. —adj. **2.** directed or moving forward.

on′yx (on′iks, ō′niks) n. a kind of varicolored quartz.

oo′dles (ōōd′lz) n.pl. Informal. a large quantity.

ooze (ōōz) v., **oozed, oozing.** —v.i. **1.** to leak out slowly. —n. **2.** something that oozes. **3.** soft mud.

o•pac′i•ty (ō pas′i tē) n., pl. **-ties.** the state of being opaque.

o′pal (ō′pəl) n. a precious iridescent stone.

o′pa•les′cent (ō′pə les′ənt) adj. with a play of colors like that of the opal.

o•paque′ (ō pāk′) adj. **1.** not allowing light to pass through. **2.** dark; dull. **3.** not clear.

op. cit. (op′ sit′) in the work cited.

OPEC (ō′pek) n. Organization of Petroleum Exporting Countries.

Op′-Ed′ (op′ed′) n. a newspaper section devoted to articles by commentators, essayists, etc.

o′pen (ō′pən) adj. **1.** not closed, locked, or covered. **2.** not restricted. **3.** available or accessible. **4.** frank. **5.** unfolded. **6.** undecided. —v.t., v.i. **7.** to make or become open. **8.** to begin. **9.** to come apart. —n. **10.** any open space.

o′pen-and-shut′ adj. easily solved or decided; obvious.

o′pen-end′ed adj. unrestricted.

o′pen-hand′ed adj. generous.

o′pen•ing n. **1.** an unobstructed or unoccupied place. **2.** a gap or hole. **3.** a beginning. **4.** an opportunity.

o′pen-mind′ed adj. without prejudice.

op′er•a (op′ər ə, op′rə) n. a drama in which the words are sung to music. —**op•er•at′ic** (-ə rat′ik) adj.

op′era glass′es n.pl. small, low-power binoculars.

op′er•ate′ (-ə rāt′) v., **-ated, -ating.** —v.i. **1.** to work or function. **2.** to exert force or influence. **3.** to perform surgery. —v.t. **4.** to manage or use (a machine). —**op′er•a′tion,** n.

op′er•at′ing sys′tem n. software that directs a computer's operations.

op′er•a′tion n. **1.** the act or manner of operating. **2.** a practical or mechanical process. **3.** a surgical procedure. —**op′er•a′tion•al,** adj.

op′er•a′tion•al adj. able to function.

op′er•a•tive (-ər ə tiv, -ə rā′tiv) n. **1.** a worker. **2.** a spy. —adj. **3.** in operation.

op′er•et′ta (op′ə ret′ə) n. a light opera.

oph′thal•mol′o•gy (of′thal mol′ə-jē, -tha-, -thal-, op′-) n. the branch of medicine dealing with the eye. —**oph′thal•mol′o•gist,** n.

o′pi•ate (ō′pē it, -āt′) n. a drug containing opium.

o•pine′ (ō pīn′) v.t., v.i., **-pined, -pining.** to express an opinion.

o•pin′ion (ə pin′yən) n. a belief or judgment.

o•pin′ion•at′ed (-yə nā′tid) adj. stubborn regarding one's own opinions.

o′pi•um (ō′pē əm) n. a narcotic made from the juice of certain poppies.

o•pos′sum (ə pos′əm, pos′əm) n. a marsupial of the eastern U.S.

op•po′nent (ə pō′nənt) n. **1.** a person on the opposite side, as in a contest. **2.** a person opposed to something.

op′por•tune′ (op′ər tōōn′, -tyōōn′) adj. appropriate; timely. —**op′por•tune′ly,** adv.

op′por•tun′ism n. the grasping of opportunities without regard for consequences or ethical considerations. —**op′por•tun′ist,** n. —**op′por•tun•is′tic,** adj.

op′por•tu′ni•ty n., pl. **-ties.** a favorable time or condition for doing something.

op•pose′ (ə pōz′) v.t., **-posed, -posing. 1.** to resist. **2.** to be hostile to. **3.** to set (something) opposite something else.

op′po•site (op′ə zit, -sit) adj. **1.** in the corresponding position on the other side. **2.** completely different. —n. **3.** one that is opposite.

op′po•si′tion (-zish′ən) n. **1.** the action of opposing. **2.** hostility. **3.** one that opposes, protests, etc.

op•press′ (ə pres′) v.t. **1.** to exercise harsh authority over. **2.** to lie heavily on. —**op•pres′sor,** n.

op•pro′bri•um (ə prō′brē əm) n. disgrace and reproach.

opt (opt) v.i. to make a choice.

on′yx (on′iks, ō′niks) n. a kind of

op′tic (op′tik) adj. of the eye or sight.

op′ti•cal adj. **1.** made to assist sight. **2.** visual. **3.** of optics.

op′tical disc′ n. a disk on which digital data is stored and read by a laser.

op′tical scan′ner n. a device for scanning and digitizing printed material.

op•ti′cian (op tish′ən) n. a person who makes or sells eyeglasses.

op′tics n. the branch of science dealing with light and vision.

op′ti•mal adj. most favorable; best.

op′ti•mism (op′tə miz′əm) n. **1.** a tendency to have a favorable view of things. **2.** the belief that good will prevail. —**op′ti•mist,** n. —**op′ti•mis′tic,** adj.

op′ti•mum (-məm) n. **1.** the best (point, degree, amount, etc.). —adj. **2.** most favorable; best.

op′tion (op′shən) n. **1.** the power or right to choose. **2.** a choice. —**op′tion•al,** adj.

op•tom′e•try (op tom′i trē) n. the profession of examining the eyes for defects. —**op•tom′e•trist,** n.

op′u•lent (op′yə lənt) adj. **1.** wealthy. **2.** richly supplied. —**op′u•lence,** n.

o′pus (ō′pəs) n., pl. **op•er•a** (op′-ər ə, op′rə). a musical or literary work.

or (ôr; unstressed ər) conj. (used to connect alternatives.)

OR 1. operating room. **2.** Oregon.

-or¹ a suffix meaning condition or quality.

-or² a suffix meaning a person or thing that does something.

or′a•cle (ôr′ə kəl) n. **1.** (in the ancient world) one believed to give answers from the gods. **2.** a wise person. —**o•rac′u•lar,** adj.

o′ral (ôr′əl) adj. **1.** spoken. **2.** of the mouth.

or′ange (ôr′inj) n. **1.** a round, reddish-yellow citrus fruit. **2.** a reddish yellow.

o•rang′u•tan′ (ō rang′ōō tan′, ə rang′-) n. a large, long-armed ape.

o•ra′tion (ō rā′shən) n. a speech.

or′a•tor (ôr′ə tər) n. an eloquent public speaker.

or′a•to′ri•o′ (-tôr′ē ō′) n., pl. **-rios.** a musical work for voices and orchestra, usu. on a religious theme.

or′a•to′ry n. **1.** eloquent public speaking. **2.** the art of public speaking. —**or′a•tor′i•cal** (ôr′ə tôr′-), adj.

orb (ôrb) n. a sphere or globe.

or′bit (ôr′bit) n. **1.** the curved path of a planet, satellite, etc., around a celestial body. **2.** a sphere of influence. —v.t., v.i. **3.** to travel in or send into an orbit. —**or′bit•al,** adj.

or′chard (ôr′chərd) n. a group of cultivated fruit trees.

or′ches•tra (ôr′kə strə, -kes trə) n. **1.** a large company of instrumental performers. **2.** the main floor of a theater. —**or•ches′tral,** adj.

or′ches•trate′ (ôr′kə strāt′) v.t., **-trated, -trating. 1.** to arrange (music) for an orchestra. **2.** to arrange the elements of to produce a certain effect. —**or′ches•tra′tion,** n.

or′chid (ôr′kid) n. a tropical plant with showy flowers having three petals.

or•dain′ (ôr dān′) v.t. **1.** to invest as a member of the clergy. **2.** to give orders for; decree.

or•deal′ (ôr dēl′, ôr′dēl) n. any severely difficult experience.

or′der (ôr′dər) n. **1.** an authoritative command. **2.** a methodical arrangement; sequence. **3.** obedience to authority. **4.** goods bought or sold. **5.** a group bound by common religious rules. —v.t., v.i. **6.** to give an order (to). **7.** to put in order. —Idiom. **8. in order, a.** appropriate. **b.** properly arranged. **c.** according to the rules. **9. in short order,** quickly. **10. out of order, a.** inappropriate. **b.** improperly arranged. **c.** not according to the rules. **d.** not operating.

or′der•ly adj., adv., n., pl. **-lies.** —adj. **1.** arranged in a tidy manner. **2.** well-behaved. —adv. **3.** methodically. **4.** according to established order. —n. **5.** a hospital attendant.

or′di•nal (ôr′dn əl) adj. **1.** showing a position in a series, as first or second. —n. **2.** an ordinal number.

or′dinal num′ber n. any of the numbers that express position in a series, as first and second.

or′di•nance (ôr′dn əns) n. a law.

or′di•nar′y (-dn er′ē) adj. **1.** commonplace. **2.** usual; normal. —Idiom. **3. out of the ordinary,** unusual. —**or′di•nar′i•ly,** adv.

or·di·na·tion (ôr/dn ā/shən) *n.* the act or ceremony of ordaining.

ord/nance (ôrd/nəns) *n.* military weapons of all kinds.

or/dure (ôr/jər, -dyŏŏr) *n.* dung.

ore (ôr) *n.* a rock or mineral containing metal.

Ore. Oregon.

o·reg/a·no (ə reg/ə nō/) *n.* an aromatic plant whose leaves are used as seasoning.

or/gan (ôr/gən) *n.* **1.** a musical instrument having pipes activated by keyboard and foot pedals and sounded by compressed air. **2.** a part of an animal or plant having a specific function. **3.** a periodical. —**or/gan·ist,** *n.*

or/gan·dy (ôr/gən dē) *n., pl.* **-dies.** a thin stiff cotton fabric.

or/gan·elle/ (ôr/gə nel/) *n.* a specialized cell structure having a specific function.

or·gan/ic (ôr gan/ik) *adj.* **1.** of carbon compounds. **2.** of living organisms. **3.** grown without synthetic fertilizers, pesticides, etc.

or/gan·ism (-gə niz/əm) *n.* any individual life form.

or·gan·i·za/tion (ôr/gə nə zā/shən) *n.* **1.** an organizing or being organized. **2.** something organized. **3.** a group organized for some purpose. —**or/gan·i·za/tion·al,** *adj.*

or/gan·ize/ (-gə nīz/) *v.,* **-ized, -izing.** —*v.t.* **1.** to put in order. **2.** to form into a whole. **3.** to gather (people) into a group for a common purpose. —*v.i.* **4.** to become organized.

or·gan/za (ôr gan/zə) *n.* a sheer fabric with a crisp finish.

or/gasm (ôr/gaz əm) *n.* a sexual climax.

or/gy (ôr/jē) *n., pl.* **-gies. 1.** any unrestrained indulgence. **2.** a wild party.

o/ri·el (ôr/ē əl) *n.* a bay window.

o/ri·ent *n.* (ôr/ē ənt, -ē ent/) **1.** the Orient, the countries of Asia, the east. —*v.t.* (ôr/ē ent/) **3.** to make familiar with new surroundings. **4.** to place facing in a certain direction. —**o/ri·en·ta/tion,** *n.*

o/ri·en·teer/ing (-tēr/ing) *n.* the sport of navigating unknown terrain.

or/i·fice (ôr/ə fis) *n.* an opening.

o/ri·ga/mi (ôr/i gä/mē) *n.* the Japanese art of folding paper into decorative forms.

or/i·gin (ôr/i jin) *n.* **1.** the source from which something arises. **2.** the beginning of something. **3.** a person's birth or ancestry.

o·rig/i·nal (ə rij/ə nl) *adj.* **1.** first. **2.** not copied from something else. **3.** inventive; creative. —*n.* **4.** a first type from which others are made. **5.** an original work, document, etc. —**o·rig/i·nal/i·ty** (-nal/i tē) *n.* —**o·rig/i·nal·ly,** *adv.*

o·rig/i·nate/ *v.t., v.i.,* **-nated, -nating.** to bring or come into being.

o/ri·ole/ (ôr/ē ōl/) *n.* a brightcolored songbird.

or/i·son (ôr/i zən) *n.* a prayer.

Or/lon (ôr/lon) *Trademark.* a synthetic fabric resembling nylon.

or/mo·lu/ (ôr/mə lōō/) *n., pl.* **-lus.** a copper-zinc alloy used to imitate gold.

or/na·ment *n.* (-nə mənt) **1.** something added to beautify; decoration. —*v.t.* (-ment/, -mənt) **2.** to decorate. —**or/na·men/tal,** *adj.*

or·nate/ (ôr nāt/) *adj.* elaborately decorated. —**or·nate/ly,** *adv.*

or/ner·y (ôr/nə rē) *adj.* illtempered.

or/ni·thol/o·gy (ôr/nə thol/ə jē) *n.* the study of birds. —**or/ni·thol/o·gist,** *n.*

o/ro·tund/ (ôr/ə tund/) *adj.* **1.** (of the voice or speech) rich and clear. **2.** (of speech or writing) pompous.

or/phan (ôr/fən) *n.* **1.** a child whose parents are both dead. —*adj.* **2.** of or for orphans. —*v.t.* **3.** to cause to become an orphan.

or/phan·age (-fə nij) *n.* a home for orphans.

or/ris (ôr/is) *n.* a kind of iris.

or/tho·don/tics (ôr/thə don/tiks) *n.* the branch of dentistry dealing with the correction of irregular teeth. —**or/tho·don/tic,** *adj.* —**or/tho·don/tist,** *n.*

or/tho·dox/ (ôr/thə doks/) *adj.* **1.** conforming to the approved form of any doctrine, philosophy, etc. **2.** conventional. **3. Orthodox,** of the Eastern Christian Church. **4. Orthodox,** of Orthodox Judaism.

or·thog/ra·phy (ôr thog/rə fē) *n., pl.* **-phies.** spelling. —**or/tho·graph/ic** (ôr/thə graf/ik) *adj.*

or/tho·pe/dics (ôr/thə pē/diks) *n.*

the branch of medicine dealing with the skeletal system. —**or/tho·pe/dist,** *n.*

-ory a suffix meaning: **1.** of, characterized by, or serving to. **2.** a place or instrument for.

os/cil·late/ (os/ə lāt/) *v.i.,* **-lated, -lating.** to swing to and fro. —**os/cil·la/tion,** *n.* —**os/cil·la/tor,** *n.*

os·cil/lo·scope (ə sil/ə skōp/) *n.* a device that uses a cathode-ray tube to show changes in electric quantity.

os/cu·late/ (os/kyə lāt/) *v.t., v.i.,* **-lated, -lating.** to kiss.

o/sier (ō/zhər) *n.* a tough, flexible willow twig used in wickerwork.

-osis a suffix meaning: **1.** action or condition. **2.** an abnormal state.

os/mi·um (oz/mē əm) *n.* a hard, heavy metallic element used in alloys.

os·mo/sis (oz mō/sis, os-) *n.* the diffusion of a liquid through a membrane into another liquid.

os/prey (os/prē, -prā) *n.* a large bird of prey that feeds on fish.

os/se·ous (os/ē əs) *adj.* of, like, or containing bone.

os/si·fy/ (os/ə fī/) *v.t., v.i.,* **-fied, -fying.** to convert into bone.

os·ten/si·ble (o sten/sə bəl) *adj.* outwardly appearing as such. —**os·ten/si·bly,** *adv.*

os/ten·ta/tion (os/ten tā/shən, -tən-) *n.* pretentious display. —**os/ten·ta/tious,** *adj.*

os/te·o·ar·thri/tis (os/tē ō är thrī/tis) *n.* arthritis marked by breakdown of cartilage in the joints.

os/te·op/a·thy (os/tē op/ə thē) *n.* the treatment of disease by manipulating the affected part. —**os/te·o·path/** (-ə path/) *n.* —**os/te·o·path/ic,** *adj.*

os/te·o·po·ro/sis (os/tē ō pə rō/sis) *n.* a disorder in which the bones become increasingly brittle, porous, and prone to fracture.

os/tra·cize/ (os/tra sīz/) *v.t.,* **-cized, -cizing.** to exclude from society; banish. —**os/tra·cism** (-siz/əm) *n.*

os/trich (ô/strich) *n.* a large, swiftfooted, flightless bird.

oth/er (uth/ər) *adj.* **1.** additional. **2.** different. **3.** remaining. **4.** not long past. —*pron.* **5.** Usu., **others.** other persons or things.

oth/er·wise/ *adv.* **1.** under other circumstances. **2.** in a different way. **3.** in other respects.

oth/er·world/ly *adj.* concerned with a spiritual or imaginary world.

o/ti·ose/ (ō/shē ōs/, ō/tē-) *adj.* **1.** idle. **2.** useless.

ot/ter (ot/ər) *n.* a furbearing aquatic mammal.

ot/to·man (ot/ə mən) *n.* a low, cushioned seat.

ought (ôt) *aux. v.* **1.** (used to express obligation or advisability). **2.** (used to express probability).

ounce (ouns) *n.* a unit of weight equal to $\frac{1}{16}$ lb. avoirdupois or $\frac{1}{12}$ lb. troy.

our (ou^r, ou/ər; *unstressed* är) *pron.* the possessive form of **we,** used before a noun.

ours *pron.* the possessive form of **we,** used as a predicate adjective.

our·selves/ *pron.* **1.** a reflexive substitute for **us. 2.** an intensive with or substitute for **we** or **us.**

-ous a suffix meaning full of.

oust (oust) *v.t.* to expel or force out from a place or position.

oust/er *n.* expulsion.

out (out) *adv.* **1.** not in the usual place, position, etc. **2.** in or into the outdoors. **3.** so as to project or extend. **4.** known to the public. **5.** not in effective use or operation. **6.** to a state of nonexistence, exhaustion, etc. —*adj.* **7.** not at one's home or place of work. **8.** not operating. —*prep.* **9.** out from or through. **10.** out along or on. —*n.* **11.** a means of evasion. —*Idiom.* **12.** on the outs, quarreling.

out- a prefix meaning: **1.** outward. **2.** outside. **3.** to surpass.

out/age (ou/tij) *n.* an interruption or failure in a supply of power.

out/-and-out/ *adj.* complete; absolute.

out/back/ *n.* a remote area.

out/board/ *adj.* located on the exterior of a ship or boat.

out/bound/ *adj.* headed for the open sea.

out/break/ *n.* **1.** a sudden occurrence. **2.** a riot.

out/build/ing *n.* a detached building smaller than a main building.

out/burst/ *n.* a violent outpouring.

out/cast/ *n.* an exiled person.

out/class/ *v.t.* to outdo in style or excellence.

out/come/ *n.* a final result.

out/crop/ *n.* an underlying layer of rock that emerges on the earth's surface.

out·dat/ed *adj.* out-of-date.

out·dis/tance *v.t.,* **-tanced, -tancing.** to leave behind, as in racing.

out·do/ *v.t.,* **-did, -done, -doing.** to do better than.

out/door/ *adj.* done or occurring in the open air.

out/doors/ *adv.* **1.** in the open air. —*n.* **2.** the world away from buildings; open air.

out/er *adj.* **1.** situated farther out. **2.** situated on the outside.

out/er·most/ *adj.* situated farthest out.

out/er space/ *n.* **1.** space beyond the earth's atmosphere. **2.** space beyond the solar system.

out/field/ *n.* the area of a baseball field beyond the diamond. —**out/field/er,** *n.*

out/fit/ *n., v.,* **-fitted, -fitting.** —*n.* **1.** a set of articles for any purpose. **2.** a set of clothes. **3.** an organized group of persons. —*v.t.* **4.** to equip.

out/flank/ *v.t.* **1.** to go beyond the flank of (an enemy force). **2.** to outmaneuver.

out/flow/ *n.* **1.** a flowing out. **2.** something that flows out.

out/fox/ *v.t.* to outsmart.

out/go/ *n., pl.* **-goes.** money paid out.

out/go/ing *adj.* **1.** departing. **2.** retiring from a position or office. **3.** friendly; sociable.

out/grow/ *v.t.,* **-grew, -grown, -growing.** to grow too large or mature for.

out/growth/ *n.* an additional result.

out/house/ *n.* an outbuilding serving as a toilet.

out/ing *n.* a pleasure trip.

out·land/ish (-lan/dish) *adj.* strange or odd.

out/last/ *v.t.* to last longer than.

out/law/ *n.* **1.** a habitual criminal. —*v.t.* **2.** to declare illegal.

out/lay/ *n.* a sum of money spent.

out/let/ (-let, -lit) *n.* **1.** an opening or passage out. **2.** a market for goods. **3.** a means of expression.

out/line/ *n., v.,* **-lined, -lining.** —*n.* **1.** the line by which an object is bounded. **2.** a drawing showing only an outer contour. **3.** a general description. —*v.t.* **4.** to draw or represent in outline.

out/live/ (-liv/) *v.t.,* **-lived, -living.** to live longer than.

out/look/ *n.* **1.** the view from a place. **2.** one's mental attitude. **3.** prospect for the future.

out/ly/ing *adj.* remote.

out/mod/ed (-mō/did) *adj.* **1.** no longer fashionable. **2.** obsolete.

out·num/ber *v.t.* to exceed in number.

out/-of-bod/y *adj.* characterized by the sensation that the mind has left the body.

out/-of-date/ *adj.* outmoded.

out/-of-doors/ *n.* outdoors.

out/-of-the-way/ *adj.* **1.** isolated; remote. **2.** unusual.

out/pa/tient *n.* a patient who receives treatment at a hospital without being admitted.

out/place/ment *n.* assistance in finding a new job, provided by a company from an employee being let go.

out/post/ *n.* an outlying military post.

out/put/ *n.* **1.** the quantity produced in a certain period. **2.** the power produced by an electrical device. **3.** information made available by computer.

out/rage/ *n., v.,* **-raged, -raging.** —*n.* **1.** an act of wanton violence. **2.** great anger. —*v.t.* **3.** to subject to outrage.

out·ra/geous (-rā/jəs) *adj.* **1.** grossly offensive. **2.** beyond reasonable limits.

ou·tré/ (ōō trā/) *adj.* bizarre.

out/reach/ *n.* **1.** an act of reaching out. —*adj.* **2.** concerned with extending community services.

out/rig/ger (-rig/ər) *n.* a framework supporting a float extended from the side of a boat.

out/right/ *adj.* (-rīt/) **1.** complete; thorough. —*adv.* (-rīt/, -rīt/) **2.** completely. **3.** openly.

out/run/ *v.t.,* **-ran, -run, -running. 1.** to run faster or farther than. **2.** to exceed.

out/sell/ *v.t.,* **-sold, -selling.** to sell more than.

out/set/ *n.* beginning.

out/shine/ *v.t.,* **-shone** or **-shined, -shining. 1.** to shine more brightly than. **2.** to surpass in excellence.

out/side/ *n.* (out/sīd/, -sīd/) **1.** the outer surface, appearance, etc. **2.** the space beyond an enclosure or boundary. —*adj.* (out/sīd/, out/-) **3.** of, being, done, etc., on the outside. **4.** remote. **5.** not belonging to a group. —*adv.* (out/sīd/) **6.** on or to the outside. —*prep.* (out/sīd/, out/sīd/) **7.** on the outside of.

out·sid/er *n.* a person who doesn't belong to a group.

out/skirts/ *n.pl.* the outlying district.

out·smart/ *v.t.* to outwit.

out/spo/ken *adj.* candid.

out/spread/ *adj.* extended.

out/stand/ing *adj.* **1.** excellent. **2.** prominent. **3.** not yet paid.

out/strip/ *v.t.,* **-stripped, -stripping. 1.** to exceed. **2.** to get ahead of.

out/take/ *n.* a segment of film edited out of the published version.

out/ward (-wərd) *adj.* **1.** on the outside. —*adv.* **2.** Also, **out/wards.** toward the outside. —**out/ward·ly,** *adv.*

out/weigh/ *v.t.* to exceed in importance.

out/wit/ *v.t.,* **-witted, -witting.** to get the better of by superior cleverness.

o/va (ō/və) *n.* pl. of **ovum.**

o/val (ō/vəl) *adj.* egg-shaped.

o/va·ry (ō/və rē) *n., pl.* **-ries.** the female reproductive gland. —**o·var/i·an** (ō vâr/ē ən) *adj.*

o/vate (ō/vāt) *adj.* egg-shaped.

o·va/tion (ō vā/shən) *n.* enthusiastic applause.

ov/en (uv/ən) *n.* a chamber for baking or drying.

o/ver (ō/vər) *prep.* **1.** above in position, authority, etc. **2.** on or to the other side of; across. **3.** so as to cover. **4.** in excess of. **5.** concerning. **6.** during. —*adv.* **7.** so as to affect the whole surface. **8.** from one side to another. **9.** from an upright position. **10.** once more. **11.** in addition. —*adj.* **12.** upper. **13.** surplus. **14.** too great. **15.** past.

o/ver·a·chieve/ *v.i.,* **-chieved, -chieving.** to perform better than expected, esp. in school.

o/ver·act/ *v.i.* to perform in an exaggerated manner.

o/ver·age/ (ō/vər āj/) *adj.* beyond the acceptable or desirable age.

o/ver·all/ (ō/vər ôl/) *adv., adj.* **1.** from one end to the other. **2.** including everything. —*n.* **3. overalls,** loose, stout trousers.

o/ver·awe/ *v.t.,* **-awed, -awing.** to subdue by inspiring awe.

o/ver·bear/ing *adj.* domineering.

o/ver·blown/ *adj.* **1.** excessive. **2.** pretentious.

o/ver·board/ *adv.* over the side of a ship into the water.

o/ver·cast/ (-kast/, -kast/) *adj.* **1.** cloudy. **2.** gloomy.

o/ver·charge/ *v.,* **-charged, -charging.** —*v.t., v.i.* **1.** to charge too high a price. **2.** to overload. —*n.* (ō/var chärj/) **3.** a charge exceeding a fair price. **4.** an excessive load.

o/ver·coat/ *n.* a coat worn over ordinary clothing.

o/ver·come/ *v.,* **-came, -come, -coming.** —*v.t.* **1.** to prevail over (opposition, temptations, etc.). **2.** to overpower. —*v.i.* **3.** to win.

o/ver·do/ *v.,* **-did, -done, -doing.** —*v.t.* **1.** to do to excess. —*v.i.* **2.** to do too much.

o/ver·dose/ *n., v.,* **-dosed, -dosing.** —*n.* **1.** an excessive dose of a drug. —*v.i.* **2.** to take such a dose.

o/ver·draft/ *n.* **1.** the act of overdrawing a checking account. **2.** the amount overdrawn.

o/ver·draw/ *v.t.,* **-drew, -drawn, -drawing.** to draw upon (an account) in excess of the balance.

o/ver·drive/ *n.* a mechanism that reduces the power required to maintain speed by lowering the gear ratio.

o/ver·due/ *adj.* past due.

o/ver·flow/ *v.,* **-flowed, -flown, -flowing.** —*v.t., v.i.* (ō/vər flō/) **1.** to flow or run over; flood. —*n.* (ō/vər flō/) **2.** an instance of flooding. **3.** something that runs over.

o/ver·grow/ *v.t.,* **-grew, -grown, -growing.** to cover with growth.

o/ver·hand/ *adv.* with hand and arm raised above the shoulder.

o/ver·hang/ *v.,* **-hung, -hanging,** *n.* —*v.t., v.i.* (ō/vər hang/) **1.** to project over (something). —*n.* (ō/vər hang/) **2.** something that extends over.

o/ver·haul/ *v.t.* (ō/vər hôl/) **1.** to investigate thoroughly, as for repair. **2.** to catch up with. —*n.* (ō/vər hôl/) **3.** a complete examination and repair.

o/ver·head/ *adv.* (ō/vər hed/) **1.** above one's head. —*n.* (ō/vər hed/) **2.** general business expenses, as rent and lighting.

o/ver·hear/ *v.t.,* **-heard, -hearing.** to hear (words or a speaker) without the speaker's knowledge.

o/ver·joyed/ (-joid/) *adj.* very happy.

o/ver·kill/ *n.* any greatly excessive amount.

o/ver·land/ (-land/, -lənd) *adv., adj.* across open country.

o/ver·lap/ *v.,* **-lapped, -lapping,** *n.* —*v.t., v.i.* (ō/vər lap/) **1.** to extend over and beyond. —*n.* (ō/vər lap/) **2.** an overlapping part.

o/ver·lay/ *v.t.,* **-laid, -laying. 1.** to lay or place (one thing) over another. **2.** to finish with a decorative layer.

o/ver·lie/ *v.i.,* **-lay, -lain, -lying.** to lie over or on.

o/ver·look/ *v.t.* **1.** to fail to notice. **2.** to excuse. **3.** to give a view over.

o/ver·ly *adv.* excessively.

o/ver·night/ *adv.* (-nīt/) **1.** during the night. **2.** suddenly. —*adj.* (-nīt/) **3.** done, made, etc., during the night. **4.** staying for one night.

o/ver·pass/ *n.* a bridge crossing over traffic.

o/ver·play/ *v.t.* to exaggerate.

o/ver·pow/er *v.t.* **1.** to overwhelm in feeling. **2.** to subdue.

o/ver·rate/ *v.t.,* **-rated, -rating.** to rate too highly.

o/ver·reach/ *v.t.* **1.** to reach over or beyond. **2.** to defeat (oneself) by trying too hard.

o/ver·re·act/ *v.i.* to react too emotionally. —**o/ver·re·ac/tion,** *n.*

o/ver·ride/ *v.t.,* **-rode, -ridden, -riding.** to prevail over; overrule.

o/ver·rule/ *v.t.,* **-ruled, -ruling.** to rule against.

o/ver·run/ *v.t.,* **-ran, -run, -running.** to swarm over.

o/ver·seas/ *adv.* across the sea.

o/ver·see/ *v.t.,* **-saw, -seen, -seeing.** to supervise. —**o/ver·se/er,** *n.*

o/ver·shad/ow *v.t.* to be more important than.

o/ver·shoot/ *v.t.,* **-shot, -shooting.** to shoot or go beyond so as to miss.

o/ver·sight/ *n.* **1.** an error of neglect. **2.** supervision.

o/ver·sleep/ *v.i.,* **-slept, -sleeping.** to sleep beyond a desired time.

o/ver·state/ *v.t.,* **-stated, -stating.** to exaggerate in describing. —**o/ver·state/ment,** *n.*

o/ver·stay/ *v.i.* to stay too long.

o/ver·step/ *v.t.,* **-stepped, -stepping.** to go beyond.

o·vert/ (ō vûrt/, ō/vûrt) *adj.* not concealed.

o/ver·take/ *v.t.,* **-took, -taken, -taking.** to catch up with or pass.

o/ver-the-count/er *adj.* **1.** sold legally without a prescription. **2.** not listed on or traded through an organized securities exchange.

o/ver·throw/ *v.,* **-threw, -thrown, -throwing,** *n.* —*v.t.* (ō/vər thrō/) **1.** to defeat; depose. —*n.* (ō/vər thrō/) **2.** an act or instance of overthrowing or being overthrown.

o/ver·time/ *n.* time worked in addition to regular hours.

o/ver·tone/ *n.* an additional meaning or implication.

o/ver·ture (ō/vər chər, -chŏŏr/) *n.* **1.** an orchestral prelude, as to an opera. **2.** a first move in a relationship, negotiation, etc.

o/ver·turn/ *v.t.* **1.** to cause to turn over. **2.** to defeat. —*v.i.* **3.** to turn over.

o/ver·view/ *n.* a general perception or description.

o/ver·ween/ing (-wē/ning) *adj.* **1.** conceited. **2.** excessive.

o/ver·weight/ (ō/vər wāt/) *adj.* weighing more than is normal.

o/ver·whelm/ (-hwelm/, -welm/) *v.t.* **1.** to overpower emotionally. **2.** to overcome completely. **3.** to bury beneath a mass of something.

o/ver·work/ *v.i., v.t.* **-worked** or **-wrought, -working.** (ō/ver wûrk/) to work or cause to work too hard.

o/ver·wrought/ (ō/vər rôt/, ō/vər-) *adj.* extremely excited.

o/vi·duct/ (ō/vi dukt/) *n.* a tube

through which ova are transported from the ovary to the uterus.

o·vip′a·rous (ō vip′ər əs) *adj.* producing eggs that hatch outside the body.

ov′u·late (ov′yə lāt′, ō′vyə-) *v.i.*, **-lated, -lating.** to produce and discharge eggs from an ovary.

ov′ule (ov′yōōl, ō′vyōōl) *n.* **1.** the structure that develops into a seed after fertilization. **2.** a small egg.

o′vum (ō′vəm) *n.*, *pl.* **ova** (ō′və). a female reproductive cell.

owe (ō) *v.t.*, **owed, owing. 1.** to be obligated to pay or give to another. **2.** to be indebted to or for.

owl (oul) *n.* a nocturnal bird of prey.

owl′et *n.* a small owl.

own (ōn) *adj.* **1.** of or belonging to. —*v.t.* **2.** to possess. **3.** to acknowledge. —**own′er,** *n.* —**own′er·ship′,** *n.*

ox (oks) *n.*, *pl.* **oxen.** a bovine animal, esp. a castrated adult bull.

ox′blood′ *n.* a deep, dull red color.

ox′ bow′ (-bō′) *n.* the U-shaped part of a yoke placed under and around the neck of an ox.

ox′ford (oks′fərd) *n.* a low shoe laced over the instep.

ox′i·dant (ok′si dənt) *n.* a chemical agent that oxidizes.

ox′ide (ok′sīd, -sid) *n.* a compound of oxygen and another element.

ox′i·dize (ok′si dīz′) *v.*, **-dized, -dizing.** —*v.t.* **1.** to combine chemically with oxygen. —*v.i.* **2.** to become oxidized. —**ox′i·da′tion,** *n.*

ox′y·a·cet′y·lene′ (ok′sē ə set′l ēn′, -in) *n.* a mixture of oxygen and acetylene used for cutting and welding steel.

ox′y·gen (ok′si jən) *n.* a colorless, odorless gas necessary to life.

ox′y·gen·ate (-jə nāt′) *v.t.*, **-ated, -ating.** to enrich with oxygen.

ox′y·mo·ron (ok′si môr′on) *n.*, *pl.* **-mora.** a figure of speech that uses seeming contradictions.

oys′ter (oi′stər) *n.* an edible mollusk having an irregularly shaped shell.

oz. ounce.

o′zone (ō′zōn, ō zōn′) *n.* a form of oxygen in the upper atmosphere.

o′zone hole′ *n.* any part of the ozone layer depleted by atmospheric pollution.

o′zone lay′er *n.* the layer of the upper atmosphere where most ozone is concentrated.

P

P, p (pē) *n.* the sixteenth letter of the English alphabet.

PA 1. Also, **Pa.** Pennsylvania. **2.** public-address system.

PAC (pak) *n.*, *pl.* **PACs, PAC's.** political action committee.

pace (pās) *n.*, *v.*, **paced, pacing.** —*n.* **1.** a rate of movement or progress. **2.** a single step. —*v.t.* **3.** to set the pace for. **4.** to measure by pacing. —*v.i.* **5.** to take slow, regular steps. —**pac′er,** *n.*

pace′mak′er *n.* an electronic device for controlling the heartbeat.

pace′set′ter *n.* a person who sets a pace for others to follow.

pach′y·derm′ (pak′i dûrm′) *n.* a large thick-skinned mammal, as the elephant.

pach′y·san′dra (pak′ə san′drə) *n.*, *pl.* **-dras.** a low plant used as ground cover.

pa·cif′ic (pə sif′ik) *adj.* peaceful.

pac′i·fi′er (pas′ə fī′ər) *n.* **1.** a nipple-shaped device for a baby to suck on. **2.** one that pacifies.

pac′i·fism (pas′ə fiz′əm) *n.* opposition to war or violence. —**pac′i·fist,** *n.*

pac′i·fy′ *v.t.*, **-fied, -fying. 1.** to calm. **2.** to appease.

pack (pak) *n.* **1.** a group of items wrapped together for easy handling or selling. **2.** a group of people or things. **3.** a group of wolves, dogs, etc. —*v.t.* **4.** to make into a pack. **5.** to fill with anything. **6.** to crowd together within. —*v.i.* **7.** to fill luggage with belongings for travel. **8.** to press together. —**Idiom. 9. pack it in,** to abandon one's efforts. —**pack′er,** *n.*

pack′age (-ij) *n.*, *v.*, **-aged, -aging.** —*n.* **1.** a bundle; parcel. **2.** a container in which something is packed. **3.** a group of related things

offered as a unit. —*v.t.* **4.** to put into a package.

pack′et *n.* **1.** a small package. **2.** a small ship carrying mail, passengers, etc., on a fixed route.

pack′ rat′ *n.* **1.** a rat that carries off shiny articles to its nest. **2.** *Informal.* a person who saves useless items.

pact (pakt) *n.* an agreement.

pad¹ (pad) *n.*, *v.*, **padded, padding.** —*n.* **1.** a cushionlike mass of soft material. **2.** a bound package of writing paper. **3.** a soft part under an animal's paw. —*v.t.* **4.** to furnish with soft material. **5.** to expand with false or useless matter.

pad² (pad) *n.*, *v.*, **padded, padding.** —*n.* **1.** a dull sound, as of footsteps. —*v.i.* **2.** to walk with a dull sound.

pad′dle¹ (pad′l) *n.*, *v.*, **-dled, -dling.** —*n.* **1.** a short oar for two hands. —*v.i.*, *v.t.* **2.** to propel (a canoe) with a paddle.

pad′dle² (pad′l) *v.i.*, **-dled, -dling.** to move the feet and hands in shallow water.

pad′dle wheel′ *n.* a wheel with projecting paddles for propelling a ship.

pad′dock (pad′ək) *n.* a fenced area for horses.

pad′dy (pad′ē) *n.*, *pl.* **-dies.** a rice field.

pad′dy wag′on *n.* a van for transporting prisoners.

pad′lock′ *n.* **1.** a detachable lock with a sliding U-shaped shackle. —*v.t.* **2.** to fasten with a padlock.

pa′dre (pä′drā) *n.*, *pl.* **-dres.** a clergyman.

pae′an (pē′ən) *n.* a song of praise.

pa′gan (pā′gən) *n.* **1.** a person who does not believe in an established religion; heathen. —*adj.* **2.** of pagans; heathen. —**pa′gan·ism,** *n.*

page¹ (pāj) *n.*, *v.*, **paged, paging.** —*n.* **1.** a written or printed surface, as in a book. —*v.* **2. page through,** to turn pages.

page² (pāj) *n.*, *v.*, **paged, paging.** —*n.* **1.** a boy servant. **2.** an employee who carries messages, runs errands, etc. —*v.t.* **3.** to summon (a person) in a public place by calling his or her name.

pag′eant (paj′ənt) *n.* an elaborate show or parade with people in costume. —**pag′eant·ry,** *n.*

pag′i·nate (-ə nāt′) *v.t.*, **-nated, -nating.** to number the pages of. —**pag′i·na′tion,** *n.*

pa·go′da (pə gō′də) *n.* a Far Eastern temple tower having a series of upward-curving roofs.

paid (pād) *v.* a pt. and pp. of **pay.**

pail (pāl) *n.* a bucket.

pain (pān) *n.* **1.** physical or mental suffering. **2.** pains, effort. —*v.t.* **3.** to hurt. —**pain′ful,** *adj.* —**pain′less,** *adj.*

pain′kil′ler *n.* something that relieves pain.

pains′tak′ing *adj.* careful.

paint (pānt) *n.* **1.** a liquid coloring matter used as a decorative or protective coating. —*v.t.* **2.** to represent in paint. **3.** to apply paint to. —*v.i.* **4.** to engage in painting. —**paint′er,** *n.* —**paint′ing,** *n.*

pair (pâr) *n.*, *pl.* **pairs, pair,** *v.* —*n.* **1.** a combination of two things matched for use together. **2.** an object consisting of two joined parts. **3.** two associated persons or things. —*v.t.*, *v.i.* **4.** to form (into) a pair. —**Usage.** See COUPLE.

pais′ley (pāz′lē) *adj.* having a colorful, detailed pattern of curved figures.

pa·ja′mas (pə jä′məz, -jam′əz) *n.pl.* a jacket and trousers for sleeping in.

pal (pal) *n. Informal.* a close friend.

pal′ace (pal′is) *n.* the official residence of a sovereign.

pal′a·din (pal′ə din) *n.* a heroic champion.

pal′an·quin′ (pal′ən kēn′) *n.* an enclosed chair or bed carried on men's shoulders.

pal′at·a·ble (pal′ə tə bəl) *adj.* acceptable to the taste.

pal′ate (-it) *n.* **1.** the roof of the mouth. **2.** the sense of taste.

pa·la′tial (pə lā′shəl) *adj.* splendidly built or furnished.

pal′a·ver (pə lav′ər, -lä′vər) *n.* idle talk.

pale¹ (pāl) *adj.*, **paler, palest,** *v.*, **paled, paling.** —*adj.* **1.** without much color; near-white. —*v.t.*, *v.i.* **2.** to make or become pale.

pale² (pāl) *n.* a stake. **2.** limits.

Pa′le·o·lith′ic (pā′lē ə lith′ik) *adj.* of the early Stone Age.

pa′le·on·tol′o·gy (-ən tol′ə jē) *n.*

the science of early life forms, as represented by their fossils.

Pa′le·o·zo′ic (-ə zō′ik) *adj.* pertaining to a geologic era 570 to 230 million years ago.

Pal′es·tin′i·an (pal′ə stin′ē ən) *n.* **1.** a native or inhabitant of ancient or modern Palestine. —*adj.* **2.** of Palestine or Palestinians.

pal′ette (pal′it) *n.* a thin board on which a painter lays and mixes colors.

pal′frey (pôl′frē) *n.*, *pl.* **-freys.** a riding horse.

pal′i·mo·ny (pal′ə mō′nē) *n.* alimony awarded to a member of an unmarried couple.

pal′imp·sest (pal′imp sest′) *n.* a manuscript with text erased to make room for another text.

pal′in·drome (pal′in drōm′) *n.* a word or verse reading the same backward as forward.

pal′ing (pā′ling) *n.* a fence of stakes.

pal′i·sade′ (pal′ə sād′) *n.* **1.** a fence of stakes. **2. palisades,** a line of cliffs.

pall (pôl) *n.* **1.** a cloth spread on a coffin. **2.** something that covers with darkness. —*v.i.* **3.** to become wearisome or distasteful.

pall′bear′er *n.* one of the persons who carries the coffin at a funeral.

pal′let¹ (pal′it) *n.* **1.** a straw mattress. **2.** a small bed.

pal′let² (pal′it) *n.* a low platform on which goods are placed.

pal′li·ate (pal′ē āt′) *v.t.*, **-ated, -ating. 1.** to relieve without curing. **2.** to try to reduce the seriousness of (an offense).

pal′li·a·tive (-ā′tiv, -ə tiv) *n.* a drug that relieves symptoms without curing.

pal′lid (pal′id) *adj.* pale.

pal′lor (pal′ər) *n.* paleness.

palm¹ (päm) *n.* **1.** the inner surface of the hand. —*v.t.* **2.** to conceal in the hand. **3. palm off,** to get someone to accept (something) by fraudulent means.

palm² (päm) *n.* a tall, unbranched tropical tree with a crown of large leaves.

pal·met′to (pal met′ō, päl-, pä-) *n.*, *pl.* **-tos, -toes.** a species of palm.

palm′is·try (pä′mə strē) *n.* the art of telling fortunes from the lines on the palms of the hands. —**palm′ist,** *n.*

palm′y *adj.*, **-ier, -iest.** thriving.

pal′o·mi′no (pal′ə mē′nō) *n.*, *pl.* **-nos.** a light tan or golden horse.

pal′pa·ble (pal′pə bəl) *adj.* **1.** able to be touched. **2.** obvious. —**pal′pa·bly,** *adv.*

pal′pate (pal′pāt) *v.t.*, **-pated, -pating.** to examine by touch. —**pal·pa′tion,** *n.*

pal′pi·tate (pal′pi tāt′) *v.i.*, **-tated, -tating. 1.** to throb with unnatural rapidity. **2.** to quiver, as with excitement. —**pal′pi·ta′tion,** *n.*

pal′sy (pôl′zē) *n.*, *pl.* **-sies.** paralysis and tremors.

pal′try (pôl′trē) *adj.*, **-trier, -triest.** worthless. —**pal′tri·ness,** *n.*

pam′pas (pam′pəz; *attributively* -pəs) *n.* the vast plains of South America.

pam′per (pam′pər) *v.t.* to treat with excessive indulgence.

pam′phlet (pam′flit) *n.* a thin booklet.

pam′phlet·eer′ *n.* a writer of pamphlets.

pan¹ (pan) *n.*, *v.*, **panned, panning.** —*n.* **1.** a broad, shallow container for cooking, washing, etc. —*v.t.* **2.** *Informal.* to criticize. —*v.i.* **3.** to wash gravel, sand, etc., in a pan to search for gold. **4. pan out,** *Informal.* to have a successful outcome.

pan² (pan) *v.*, **panned, panning.** —*v.i.*, *v.t.* **1.** to swivel (a camera) in filming. —*n.* **2.** the act of panning a camera.

pan- a prefix meaning all.

pan′a·ce′a (pan′ə sē′ə) *n.* a cure-all.

pa·nache′ (pə nash′, -näsh′) *n.* a grand or flamboyant manner; flair.

pan′cake′ *n.* a flat fried batter cake.

pan′chro·mat′ic (pan′krō mat′ik) *adj.* sensitive to all visible colors.

pan′cre·as (pan′krē əs, pang′-) *n.* a large gland near the stomach that secretes insulin into the blood. —**pan′cre·at′ic,** *adj.*

pan′da (pan′də) *n.* a black-and-white bearlike animal of China.

pan·dem′ic (pan dem′ik) *adj.* (of a disease) epidemic over a large area.

pan′de·mo′ni·um (pan′də mō′nē-əm) *n.* wild disorder or uproar.

pan′der (-dər) *v.i.* to cater to the desires of others. —**pan′der,** *n.*

pane (pān) *n.* a glass section of a window or door.

pan′e·gyr′ic (pan′i jir′ik, -jī′rik) *n.* speech or writing in praise of a person or thing.

pan′el (pan′l) *n.*, *v.*, **-eled, -eling.** —*n.* **1.** a bordered section of a wall, door, etc. **2.** a public discussion group. **3.** a list of persons called for jury duty. —*v.t.* **4.** to arrange in or ornament with panels. —**pan′el·ing,** *n.*

pan′el·ist *n.* a member of a panel.

pang (pang) *n.* a sudden feeling of distress or pain.

pan′han′dle¹ *n.* a long, narrow strip of a larger territory.

pan′han′dle² *v.i.*, **-dled, -dling.** *Informal.* to beg from passersby.

pan′ic (pan′ik) *n.*, *v.*, **-icked, -icking.** —*n.* **1.** sudden overwhelming fear. —*v.t.*, *v.i.* **2.** to affect or be affected with panic. —**pan′ick·y,** *adj.* —**pan′ic-strick′en,** *adj.*

pan′i·cle (pan′i kəl) *n.* a loose flower cluster.

pan′nier (pan′yər, -ē ər) *n.* a large basket for carrying goods.

pan′o·ply (pan′ə plē) *n.*, *pl.* **-plies.** an impressive display.

pan′o·ram′a (pan′ə ram′ə, -rä′mə) *n.* a view over a wide area or of changing events. —**pan′o·ram′ic,** *adj.*

pan′sy (pan′zē) *n.*, *pl.* **-sies.** a kind of violet with bright, variously colored flowers.

pant (pant) *v.i.* **1.** to breathe hard and quickly. **2.** to long eagerly.

pan′ta·loons′ (pan′tl ōōnz′) *n.pl.* a man's close-fitting trousers.

pan′the·ism (pan′thē iz′əm) *n.* a religious belief or philosophical doctrine that identifies God with the universe. —**pan′the·is′tic,** *adj.*

pan′the·on (pan′thē on′) *n.* **1.** a building with tombs or memorials of a nation's famous dead. **2.** the heroes of a nation, movement, etc., as a group.

pan′ther (pan′thər) *n.* a cougar or leopard, usu. black.

pan′ties (pan′tēz) *n.pl.* women's underpants. Also, **pan′ty.**

pan′to·graph′ (pan′tə graf′) *n.* an instrument for copying traced figures.

pan′to·mime′ (pan′tə mīm′) *n.*, *v.*, **-mimed, -miming.** —*n.* **1.** gesture without speech. **2.** a play in which the performers express themselves by gesture only. —*v.t.*, *v.i.* **3.** to express (oneself) in pantomime. —**pan′to·mim′ist,** *n.*

pan′try (pan′trē) *n.*, *pl.* **-tries.** a room or closet in which food and kitchen supplies are kept.

pants (pants) *n.pl.* trousers.

pant′y·hose′ *n.* (*used with a pl. v.*) one-piece stockings plus panties.

pan′zer (pan′zər) *adj.* **1.** armored. —*n.* **2.** a tank or armored vehicle.

pap (pap) *n.* soft food.

pa′pa (pä′pə, pə pä′) *n.* father.

pa′pa·cy (pā′pə sē) *n.*, *pl.* **-cies. 1.** the office of the pope. **2.** the period during which a pope is in office.

pa′pal (pā′pəl) *adj.* of the pope or the papacy.

pa·pa′ya (pə pä′yə) *n.* a yellow, melonlike tropical American fruit.

pa′per (pā′pər) *n.* **1.** a substance made in thin sheets from wood pulp, rags, etc., for writing on, wrapping, etc. **2.** a document. **3.** a newspaper. **4.** a scholarly essay, article, etc. **5.** wallpaper. —*v.t.* **6.** to cover with wallpaper. —*adj.* **7.** of paper. —**pa′per·y,** *adj.*

pa′per·back′ *n.* a book bound in a paper cover.

pa′per ti′ger *n.* a person or nation that seems strong but is actually weak.

pa′per trail′ *n.* a written record, as of transactions.

pa′per·weight′ *n.* a small, heavy object placed on papers to keep them from scattering.

pa′pier-mâ·ché′ (pā′pər mə shā′) *n.* dampened paper pulp mixed with glue and molded to form objects.

pa·pil′la (pə pil′ə) *n.*, *pl.* **-pil·lae** (-pil′ē). any small nipplelike projection, as on the tongue. —**pap′il·lar′y** (pap′ə ler′ē) *adj.*

pa·poose′ (pa pōōs′) *n.* a North American Indian baby.

pap·ri′ka (pa prē′kə) *n.* a red spice made from dried sweet peppers.

Pap′ test′ (pap) *n.* a test for cancer of the cervix.

pa·py′rus (pə pī′rəs) *n.*, *pl.* **-ri. 1.** a tall aquatic plant made into a kind

of paper by the ancient Egyptians. **2.** the paper made from this.

par (pär) *n.* **1.** an equality in value or standing. **2.** an average amount, degree, etc. **3.** in golf, a standard number of strokes for a hole or a course.

para- a prefix meaning: **1.** beside. **2.** beyond. **3.** auxiliary.

par′a·ble (par′ə bəl) *n.* a short allegory to teach a moral.

pa·rab′o·la (pə rab′ə lə) *n.* a U-shaped curve, surface, object, etc.

par′a·chute′ (par′ə shōōt′) *n.*, *v.*, **-chuted, -chuting.** —*n.* **1.** a folding, umbrellalike apparatus used to descend slowly and safely through the air. —*v.t.*, *v.i.* **2.** to drop by parachute. —**par′a·chut′ist,** *n.*

pa·rade′ (pə rād′) *n.*, *v.*, **-raded, -rading.** —*n.* **1.** a public procession in honor of a holiday, person, etc. **2.** a military ceremony involving a formal assembly of troops. —*v.t.* **3.** to display ostentatiously. —*v.i.* **4.** to march in a procession. **5.** to assemble in military order.

par′a·digm (par′ə dīm′, -dim) *n.* an example or model.

par′a·dise′ (-dīs′, -dīz′) *n.* **1.** heaven. **2.** a place of perfect happiness. —**par′a·di·sa′i·cal,** *adj.*

par′a·dox′ (-doks′) *n.* a statement that seems self-contradictory. —**par′a·dox′i·cal,** *adj.*

par′af·fin (-fin) *n.* a waxy, solid substance.

par′a·gon′ (-gon′, -gən) *n.* a model of excellence.

par′a·graph′ (-graf′) *n.* **1.** a unit of written or printed matter, beginning on a new line that is usu. indented. —*v.t.* **2.** to divide into paragraphs.

par′a·keet′ (-kēt′) *n.* a small parrot with a long tail.

par′a·le′gal *n.* a lawyer's assistant.

par′al·lax′ (-ə laks′) *n.* the apparent displacement of an observed object due to the changed position of the viewer.

par′al·lel′ (-ə lel′, -ləl) *adj.*, *n.*, *v.*, **-leled, -leling.** —*adj.* **1.** (of lines or planes) going in the same direction and being the same distance apart at all points. **2.** having the same direction, nature, etc.; similar. —*n.* **3.** a parallel line or plane. **4.** anything parallel or similar to something else. —*v.t.* **5.** to be parallel to. —**par′al·lel·ism,** *n.*

par′al·lel′o·gram (-lel′ə gram′) *n.* a four-sided figure whose opposite sides are parallel.

pa·ral′y·sis (pə ral′ə sis) *n.*, *pl.* **-ses.** a loss or impairment of the ability to move. —**par′a·lyt′ic** (par′ə lit′ik) *n.*, *adj.* —**par′a·lyze′,** *v.t.*

par′a·me′ci·um (par′ə mē′shē-əm,-sē əm) *n.*, *pl.* **-cia** (-shē-ə,-sē ə). an oval, freshwater protozoan.

par′a·med′ic *n.* a person trained to give emergency medical care.

pa·ram′e·ter (pə ram′i tər) *n.* **1.** a determining characteristic. **2.** parameters, limits or boundaries.

par′a·mil′i·ta·ry (par′ə mil′i ter′ē) *adj.* of organizations operating in place of or in addition to a regular military force.

par′a·mount′ (par′ə mount′) *adj.* greatest; utmost.

par′a·mour′ (par′ə mōōr′) *n.* a lover.

par′a·noi′a (par′ə noi′ə) *n.* a mental disorder marked by delusions of persecution. —**par′a·noid′,** *adj.*, *n.*

par′a·pet (par′ə pit, -pet′) *n.* a wall at the edge of a roof or terrace.

par′a·pher·na′lia (-fər nāl′yə, -fə-) *n.pl.* **1.** equipment for a particular activity. **2.** personal belongings.

par′a·phrase′ (par′ə frāz′) *n.*, *v.*, **-phrased, -phrasing.** —*v.t.*, *v.i.* **1.** to express in different words. —*n.* **2.** such a rephrasing.

par′a·ple′gi·a (-plē′jē ə, -jə) *n.* paralysis of both lower limbs. —**par′a·ple′gic,** *n.*, *adj.*

par′a·pro·fes′sion·al *adj.* engaged in a profession in a partial or secondary capacity.

par′a·psy·chol′o·gy *n.* the branch of psychology that studies the power of perceiving things beyond the range of the senses.

par′a·site′ (par′ə sīt′) *n.* an animal or plant that lives on another organism. —**par′a·sit′ic** (-sit′ik) *adj.*

par′a·sol′ (par′ə sôl′) *n.* a light umbrella used as a sunshade.

par′a·thy′roid gland′ *n.* one of the small glands near the thyroid.

par′a·troop′er *n.* a soldier trained to land in combat areas by parachuting from airplanes.

par'boil' (pär'boil') *v.t.* to boil partially.

par'cel (pär'səl) *n., v.,* **-celed, -celing.** —*n.* **1.** a package. **2.** a part. —*v.* **3. parcel out,** to divide in portions.

parch (pärch) *v.t., v.i.* to make or become very dry by heat.

par•chee'si (pär chē'zē) *n.* a game resembling backgammon.

parch'ment (pärch'mənt) *n.* the skin of sheep, goats, etc., prepared for writing on.

par'don (pär'dn) *n.* **1.** a legal release from a penalty. **2.** forgiveness. —*v.t.* **3.** to excuse; forgive. —**par'don•a•ble,** *adj.*

pare (pâr) *v.t.,* **pared, paring.** to cut off the outer part of.

par•e•gor'ic (par'i gôr'ik) *n.* a mild sedative obtained from opium.

par'ent (pâr'ənt, par'-) *n.* **1.** a father or mother. **2.** a source or cause. —**pa•ren'tal** (pə ren'tl) *adj.* —**par'ent•hood',** *n.*

par'ent•age (-ən tij) *n.* ancestry.

pa•ren'the•sis (pə ren'thə sis) *n., pl.* **-ses** (-sēz). **1.** one of the upright curves ( ) used to mark off an inserted word or phrase. **2.** material so inserted. —**par'en•thet'i•cal** (par'ən thet'i kəl) *adj.*

pa•re'sis (pə rē'sis, par'ə sis) *n.* partial paralysis.

par ex'cel•lence' (pär ek'sə läns') *adj.* superior.

par•fait' (pär fā') *n.* a layered ice cream dessert.

pa•ri'ah (pə rī'ə) *n.* an outcast.

par•i•mu'tu•el (par'i myŏŏ'chŏŏ əl) *n.* a form of betting on races.

par'ish (par'ish) *n.* **1.** a district having its own church and clergy. **2.** a local church and its activities. —**pa•rish'ion•er,** *n.*

par'i•ty (par'i tē) *n.* equality.

park (pärk) *n.* **1.** a tract of land set apart for public use. —*v.t., v.i.* **2.** to put (a car) in a place temporarily.

par'ka (pär'kə) *n.* a warm hooded jacket.

Par'kin•son's disease' (pär'kin-səns) *n.* a neurological disease characterized by tremors and a shuffling walk.

park'way' *n.* a broad thoroughfare with a dividing strip or side strips planted with grass, trees, etc.

par'lance (pär'ləns) *n.* a way of speaking.

par'lay (pär'lā, -lē) *v.t.* to make use of (assets) for a large gain.

par'ley (pär'lē) *n.* **1.** a discussion. —*v.i.* **2.** to hold a parley.

par'lia•ment (pär'lə mənt) *n.* a national legislature.

par'lia•men•tar'i•an (-men târ'ē-ən, -mən-) *n.* an expert in parliamentary rules.

par'lia•men'ta•ry (-men'tə rē) *adj.* **1.** of, by, or having a parliament. **2.** in accordance with the rules of debate.

par'lor (pär'lər) *n.* a room for receiving guests.

Par'me•san' (pär'mə zän', -zən) *n.* a hard, dry Italian cheese.

par'mi•gia'na (pär'mə zhä'nə, -zhän') *adj.* cooked with Parmesan cheese.

pa•ro'chi•al (pə rō'kē əl) *adj.* **1.** of a parish. **2.** of very limited scope; provincial.

paro'chial school' *n.* a school run by a religious organization.

par'o•dy (par'ə dē) *n., pl.* **-dies,** *v.,* **-died, -dying.** —*n.* **1.** a comic imitation of a literary or musical work. —*v.t.* **2.** to make a parody of.

pa•role' (pə rōl') *n., v.,* **-roled, -roling.** —*n.* **1.** a conditional release from prison. —*v.t.* **2.** to put on parole. —**pa•rol•ee'** (-rō lē') *n.*

par•ox'ysm (par'ək siz'əm) *n.* a sudden, violent outburst. —**par'ox•ys'mal,** *adj.*

par'quet' (pär kā') *n.* a floor made of wood pieces laid in a pattern.

par'que•try (-ki trē) *n.* wooden mosaic work.

par'ri•cide' (par'ə sīd') *n.* the crime of killing one's mother, father, or other close relative.

par'rot (par'ət) *n.* **1.** a hook-billed, bright-colored bird that can be taught to mimic speech. —*v.t.* **2.** to repeat without understanding.

par'ry (par'ē) *v.,* **-ried, -rying,** *n., pl.* **-ries.** —*v.t.* **1.** to ward off; evade. —*n.* **2.** an act of parrying.

parse (pärs) *v.,* **parsed, parsing.** —*v.t.* **1.** to analyze (a word or sentence) grammatically. —*v.i.* **2.** to admit of being parsed.

par'si•mo'ny (pär'sə mō'nē) *n.* stinginess. —**par'si•mo'ni•ous,** *adj.*

pars'ley (pärs'lē) *n.* a garden herb with either curled leaf clusters or flat compound leaves.

pars'nip (pär'snip) *n.* a plant with a large, white edible root.

par'son (pär'sən) *n.* a member of the Protestant clergy.

par'son•age (-sə nij) *n.* the house provided for a parson.

part (pärt) *n.* **1.** a distinct portion of a whole. **2.** some but not all. **3.** a share. **4.** a role. —*v.t., v.i.* **5.** to separate; divide.

par•take' (pär tāk') *v.i.,* **-took, -taken, -taking. 1.** to participate. **2.** to take or have a portion.

par•terre' (pär târ') *n.* the rear section of theater seats under the balcony.

par•the•no•gen'e•sis (pär'thə nō-jen'ə sis) *n.* the development of an egg without fertilization.

par'tial (pär'shəl) *adj.* **1.** being part; incomplete. **2.** favoring one group over another. —*Idiom.* **3. partial to,** especially fond of. —**par•tial'i•ty,** *n.*

par•tic'i•pate' (pär tis'ə pāt') *v.i.,* **-pated, -pating.** to take part or have a share. —**par•tic'i•pant,** *n.* —**par•tic'i•pa'tion,** *n.*

par'ti•ci•ple (pär'tə sip'əl) *n.* a verbal form that can be used as an adjective or to form certain tenses with an auxiliary verb.

par'ti•cle (pär'ti kəl) *n.* a tiny piece.

par'ti•col'ored (pär'tē kul'ərd) *adj.* having areas of different colors.

par•tic'u•lar (pər tik'yə lər, pə-) *adj.* **1.** pertaining to a specific person, thing, etc. **2.** special; unusual. **3.** exacting; fussy. —*n.* **4.** a distinct part; detail.

par•tic'u•lar•ize' *v.,* **-ized, -izing.** —*v.t.* **1.** to state in detail. —*v.i.* **2.** to give details.

par•tic'u•lar•ly *adv.* **1.** especially. **2.** specifically.

par•tic'u•late (-lit, -lāt', pär-) *adj.* of or composed of particles.

part'ing *n.* a departure or separation.

par'ti•san (pär'tə zən, -sən) *n.* **1.** a supporter of a person, cause, etc. **2.** a guerrilla.

par•ti'tion (pär tish'ən) *n.* **1.** a division into parts. **2.** something that separates. —*v.t.* **3.** to divide into parts.

part'ly *adv.* not wholly.

part'ner (pärt'nər) *n.* **1.** a person who is associated with another; associate. **2.** a spouse or lover. —**part'ner•ship',** *n.*

par'tridge (pär'trij) *n.* a game bird of the pheasant family.

part'-song' *n.* a song with parts for several voices.

part'-time' *adj.* (-tīm') **1.** involving or working less than the usual or full time. —*adv.* (-tīm') **2.** on a part-time basis.

par'tu•ri'tion (pär'tŏŏ rish'ən, -tyŏŏ-) *n.* childbirth.

par'ty (pär'tē) *n., pl.* **-ties. 1.** a social gathering. **2.** a group working or traveling together. **3.** a group supporting a common cause or policy. **4.** a specific individual.

par'ty line' (pär'tē līn' for 1; līn' for 2) *n.* **1.** the guiding policy of a political party. **2.** a telephone line connecting the telephones of several subscribers.

par've•nu' (pär'və nŏŏ', -nyŏŏ') *n., pl.* **-nus.** a person who has new wealth but not social acceptance.

pas'chal (pas'kəl) *adj.* of Passover or Easter.

pa•sha' (pä'shə, pə shä') *n.* (formerly) a Turkish official.

pass (pas) *v.,* **passed, passed or past, passing,** *n.* —*v.t.* **1.** to move past, by, across, or through. **2.** to undergo successfully. **3.** to go beyond. **4.** to approve. **5.** to transfer (a ball) to a teammate. —*v.i.* **6.** to go or move onward. **7.** to go by; elapse. **8.** to be accepted, allowed, or approved. **9.** to get through successfully. **10.** to refuse one's turn. **11. pass away** or **on,** to die. **12. ~ out,** to faint. **13. ~ over,** to disregard. **14. ~ up,** to refuse to accept. —*n.* **15.** the act of passing. **16.** a route through the mountains. **17.** permission to come or go. **18.** a free ticket. **19.** a state of affairs. —*Idiom.* **20. make a pass,** to do or say something intended to be sexually inviting.

pas'sa•ble *adj.* adequate.

pas'sage (pas'ij) *n.* **1.** a passing from one place or condition to another. **2.** the right to pass. **3.** the route by which one passes. **4.** a corridor. **5.** a section of a written work or a musical composition. —**pas'sage•way',** *n.*

pass'book' *n.* a record of a depositor's bank balance.

pas•sé' (pa sā') *adj.* out-of-date.

pas'sel (pas'əl) *n.* a large group.

pas'sen•ger (pas'ən jər) *n.* a traveler on a bus, train, ship, etc.

pass'er•by' *n., pl.* **passersby.** a person who passes by.

pas'sim (pas'im) *adv.* here and there.

pass'ing *adj.* brief; transitory.

pas'sion (pash'ən) *n.* **1.** any very strong emotion. **2.** sexual desire. **3.** enthusiasm. **4.** the object of one's passion. **5. Passion,** the sufferings of Christ. —**pas'sion•ate,** *adj.*

pas'sive (pas'iv) *adj.* **1.** acted upon by an external force. **2.** submitting without resistance. **3.** designating a voice, verb form, or construction indicating a subject acted upon by the verb. —**pas'sive•ly,** *adv.* —**pas•siv'i•ty,** *n.*

pas'sive resist'ance *n.* nonviolent opposition.

pas'sive smok'ing *n.* the inhaling of others' smoke.

pass'key' *n.* a master key or skeleton key.

Pass'o'ver (pas'ō'vər) *n.* a Jewish festival commemorating the Israelites' Exodus from Egypt.

pass'port *n.* an official document proving a person's identity and used when traveling abroad.

pass'word' *n.* a secret word used to gain access.

past (past) *adj.* **1.** gone by or elapsed in time. **2.** of an earlier time. **3.** designating a verb tense referring to times gone by. —*n.* **4.** past time or events. **5.** the history of a person, nation, etc. —*adv.* **6.** so as to pass by or beyond. —*prep.* **7.** after. **8.** beyond.

pas'ta (pä'stə) *n.* a dried flour-and-egg dough made into various shapes, as spaghetti.

paste (pāst) *n., v.,* **pasted, pasting.** —*n.* **1.** a soft, sticky mixture used as an adhesive. **2.** dough. **3.** heavy glass used for making artificial gems. —*v.t.* **4.** to fasten with paste.

paste'board' *n.* a firm board made of layers of paper.

pas•tel' (pa stel') *n.* **1.** a soft, delicate color. **2.** a crayon made of ground pigment. **3.** a drawing made with such crayons.

pas'teur•ize' (pas'chə rīz') *v.t.,* **-ized, -izing.** to heat (a food) to a high temperature to destroy bacteria.

pas•tiche' (pa stēsh') *n.* an artistic work made up of selections from borrowed sources.

pas•tille' (pa stēl') *n.* a lozenge.

pas'time' (pas'tīm') *n.* something that makes time pass pleasantly.

past' mas'ter *n.* an expert.

pas'tor (pas'tər) *n.* a minister or priest.

pas'to•ral *adj.* **1.** having rural charm. **2.** of shepherds. **3.** of pastors or spiritual guidance.

pas'to•rale' (-räl') *n.* a dreamy musical composition.

pas•tra'mi (pə strä'mē) *n.* beef brisket cured and smoked before cooking.

pas'try (pā'strē) *n., pl.* **-tries. 1.** dough, esp. when prepared with shortening. **2.** a sweet baked food with a crust of dough.

pas'tur•age (pas'chər ij) *n.* grazing ground.

pas'ture *n., v.,* **-tured, -turing.** —*n.* **1.** grassy land for the grazing of livestock. —*v.t.* **2.** to put out (livestock) to graze on pasture.

past'y (pā'stē) *adj.,* **-ier, -iest.** like paste in texture or color.

pat¹ (pat) *v.,* **patted, patting,** *n.* —*v.t.* **1.** to strike or tap gently. —*n.* **2.** a light stroke. **3.** a small mass of something soft, as butter.

pat² (pat) *adj.* **1.** exactly to the point. —*Idiom.* **2. stand pat,** to cling firmly to one's decision.

patch (pach) *n.* **1.** a small piece of material used to mend a tear. **2.** a piece of material used to cover an injured part or to administer medication through the skin. **3.** a small area or a plot of land. —*v.t.* **4.** to mend or cover with a patch. **5. patch up, a.** to repair in a hasty way. **b.** to settle, as a quarrel.

patch' test' *n.* an allergy test in which a patch of material with an allergen is applied to the skin.

patch'y *adj.,* **-ier, -iest.** irregular in surface or quality.

pate (pāt) *n.* the top of the head.

pâ•té' (pä tā', pa-) *n.* a paste of pureed or chopped meat, liver, etc.

pa•tel'la (pə tel'ə) *n., pl.* **-tellae** (tel'ē). the kneecap.

pat'ent (pat'nt) *n.* **1.** the exclusive right to be the only maker or seller of an invention for a specified number of years. **2.** an invention protected by this right. —*adj.* **3.** protected by a patent. **4.** obvious. —*v.t.* **5.** to obtain a patent on.

pat'ent leath'er *n.* a hard, glossy, smooth leather.

pat'ent med'icine *n.* a drug protected by a trademark.

pa•ter'nal (pə tûr'nl) *adj.* **1.** fatherly. **2.** related through or inherited from one's father.

pa•ter'nal•ism *n.* the practice of managing people in the way a father deals with his children. —**pa•ter'nal•is'tic,** *adj.*

pa•ter'ni•ty (-ni tē) *n.* fatherhood.

pa'ter•nos'ter (pä'tər nos'tər) *n.* the Lord's Prayer.

path (path) *n.* **1.** Also, **path'way'.** a way by which people or animals pass on foot. **2.** a route along which something moves. **3.** a course of action.

pa•thet'ic (pə thet'ik) *adj.* arousing pity. —**pa•thet'i•cal•ly,** *adv.*

path'o•gen (path'ə jən, -jen') *n.* a disease-producing agent.

path'o•log'i•cal (-loj'i kəl) *adj.* **1.** of pathology. **2.** caused by disease; sick. **3.** characterized by an unhealthy compulsion.

pa•thol'o•gy (pə thol'ə jē) *n.* the study of the origin, nature, and cause of diseases. —**pa•thol'o•gist,** *n.*

pa'thos (pā'thos, -thōs) *n.* the quality or power of arousing pity.

-pathy a suffix meaning: **1.** feeling. **2.** method of treatment.

pa'tient (pā'shənt) *n.* **1.** a person under medical care. —*adj.* **2.** enduring delay, annoyance, etc., without complaint. —**pa'tience,** *n.*

pat'i•na (pat'n ə, pə tē'nə) *n.* a green film on old bronze.

pa'ti•o' (pat'ē ō', n., pl. **-tios. 1.** an inner open courtyard. **2.** a paved recreational area adjoining a house.

pat'ois (pat'wä) *n.* a regional form of a language.

pa'tri•arch' (pā'trē ärk') *n.* **1.** the male head of a family. **2.** a venerable old man. —**pa'tri•ar'chal,** *adj.*

pa'tri•ar'chy (-är'kē) *n., pl.* **-chies.** a form of social organization in which a male is head of the family.

pa•tri'cian (pə trish'ən) *n.* **1.** a member of the aristocracy. —*adj.* **2.** aristocratic.

pat'ri•cide' (pa'trə sīd') *n.* **1.** the act of killing one's father. **2.** a person who commits such an act. —**pat'ri•cid'al,** *adj.*

pat'ri•mo'ny (-mō'nē) *n., pl.* **-nies.** an inherited estate.

pa'tri•ot (pā'trē ət, -ot') *n.* a person who supports his or her country. —**pa'tri•ot'ic,** *adj.* —**pa'tri•ot•ism** (-ə tiz'əm) *n.*

pa•trol' (pə trōl') *v.,* **-trolled, -trolling,** *n.* —*v.t., v.i.* **1.** to pass regularly through or around (an area) in guarding. —*n.* **2.** a person or group assigned to patrol.

pa•trol'man *n., pl.* **-men.** a police officer who patrols a given route.

pa'tron (pā'trən) *n.* **1.** a person who supports an artist, charity, etc. **2.** a regular customer or client.

pa'tron•age (pā'trə nij, pa'-) *n.* **1.** business provided by customers, clients, etc. **2.** political control of appointments to office. **3.** a patron's support of an artist, charity, etc.

pa'tron•ize' *v.t.,* **-ized, -izing. 1.** to give a store, restaurant, etc., one's regular patronage. **2.** to treat condescendingly.

pa'tron saint' *n.* a saint regarded as a special guardian.

pat'ro•nym'ic (pa'trə nim'ik) *n.* a name derived from the name of a father or ancestor.

pat'sy (pat'sē) *n., pl.* **-sies.** *Slang.* a person who is easily fooled or manipulated.

pat'ter¹ (pat'ər) *v.i.* **1.** to make a series of light tapping sounds. —*n.* **2.** a light tapping sound.

pat'ter² (pat'ər) *n.* **1.** rapid, glib talk. —*v.i., v.t.* **2.** to speak glibly or rapidly.

pat'tern (pat'ərn) *n.* **1.** a decorative design. **2.** a set of qualities, acts, etc., forming a characteristic arrangement. **3.** a model to be imitated. —*v.t.* **4.** to make after a pattern.

pat'ty (pat'ē) *n., pl.* **-ties.** a flat cake of ground or minced food.

pau'ci•ty (pô'si tē) *n.* smallness of quantity.

paunch (pônch) *n.* a large belly. —**paunch'y,** *adj.*

pau'per (pô'pər) *n.* a very poor person.

pause (pôz) *n., v.,* **paused, pausing.** —*n.* **1.** a temporary stop or rest. —*v.i.* **2.** to make a pause.

pave (pāv) *v.t.,* **paved, paving. 1.** to cover (a road, walk, etc.) with concrete, stones, or asphalt. —*Idiom.* **2. pave the way,** to prepare the way. —**pave'ment,** *n.*

pa•vil'ion (pə vil'yən) *n.* **1.** a light open building used for concerts, exhibits, etc. **2.** a large tent.

paw (pô) *n.* **1.** the foot of an animal. —*v.t., v.i.* **2.** to scrape or strike with the paws. **3.** to touch clumsily.

pawl (pôl) *n.* a pivoted bar engaging with the teeth of a ratchet wheel.

pawn¹ (pôn) *v.t.* **1.** to deposit as security for money borrowed. —*n.* **2.** the state of being pawned. **3.** something pawned. —**pawn'shop',** *n.*

pawn² (pôn) *n.* a chess piece of the lowest value. **2.** someone who is controlled by others.

pawn'bro'ker *n.* a person who lends money at interest on personal property deposited until redeemed.

paw'paw' (pô'pô', pə pô') *n.* a tree bearing purple flowers and a fleshy edible fruit.

pay (pā) *v.,* **paid, paying,** *n.* —*v.t.* **1.** to give (money) in exchange for goods or services. **2.** to settle (a debt). **3.** to transfer money to (a person) for goods or services. **4.** be profitable to. **5.** to give (attention, a compliment, etc.) as due. **6.** to let out (rope). —*v.i.* **7.** to transfer money as in making a purchase or settling a debt. **8.** to be worthwhile. —*n.* **9.** wages, salary, etc. —**pay'a•ble,** *adj.* —**pay'ee',** *n.* —**pay'er,** *n.* —**pay'ment,** *n.*

pay' dirt' *n.* **1.** profitable soil to mine. **2.** *Informal.* any source of wealth.

pay'load' *n.* **1.** revenue-producing cargo. **2.** explosives, passengers, or cargo carried by an aircraft.

pay'mas'ter *n.* a person in charge of paying out wages.

pay'off' *n.* **1.** the payment of a salary, debt, etc. **2.** the final result. **3.** *Informal.* a bribe.

pay•o'la (pā ō'lə) *n.* a bribe in return for the dishonest use of one's position.

pay'roll' *n.* **1.** a list of employees to be paid, with the amount due to each. **2.** the total of these amounts.

PC 1. *pl.* **PCs** or **PC's.** personal computer. **2.** politically correct.

PCB *pl.* **PCBs, PCB's.** a highly toxic compound, formerly used in industry.

PCP, phencyclidine: a drug used as a tranquilizer.

PCS Personal Communications Service: a system of digital wireless communications, used esp. for mobile phones.

PE physical education.

pea (pē) *n.* the round edible seed of a cultivated legume.

peace (pēs) *n.* **1.** freedom from war, trouble, or disturbance. **2.** a treaty ending a war. —**peace'mak'er,** *n.* —**peace'time',** *n.*

peace'ful *adj.* **1.** at peace. **2.** desiring peace. Also, **peace'a•ble.**

peach (pēch) *n.* a round, pinkish-yellow, fuzzy-skinned fruit.

pea'cock' (pē'kok') *n.* the male peafowl, having fanlike iridescent tail feathers.

pea'fowl' *n.* a large Asiatic bird of the pheasant family.

pea'hen' *n.* the female peafowl.

pea' jack'et *n.* a short, heavy coat of navy-blue wool.

peak (pēk) *n.* **1.** the pointed top of something, esp. a mountain. **2.** the highest or most important point. —*v.i.* **3.** to reach a peak of activity, popularity, etc.

peaked (pē'kid) *adj.* sickly; haggard.

peal (pēl) *n.* **1.** a loud, prolonged sound, as of bells or thunder. **2.** a set of bells. —*v.t., v.i.* **3.** to sound or burst forth in a peal.

pea'nut' *n.* the pod or edible seed of a plant of the legume family.

pear (pâr) *n.* an edible fruit with rounded shape that grows smaller toward the stem.

pearl (pûrl) *n.* **1.** a hard, smooth, near-white gem formed within the shell of an oyster. **2.** something similar. —**pearl'y,** *adj.*

peas'ant (pez'ənt) n. a person who works on the land.

peat (pēt) n. decomposed vegetable matter found in bogs, cut and dried for fuel. —**peat'y,** adj.

peat' moss' n. any moss from which peat may form, used as mulch.

peb'ble (peb'əl) n. a small, rounded stone. —**peb'bly,** adj.

pe·can' (pi kän', -kan') n. the smooth-shelled edible nut of a tree of the hickory family, cultivated in the southern U.S. and Mexico.

pec'ca·dil'lo (pekʹə dilʹō) n., pl. -loes, -los. a trifling sin.

pec'ca·ry (pekʹə rē) n., pl. -ries. a small wild pig of Central and South America.

peck[1] (pek) v.t. 1. to strike with the beak or with something pointed. —v.i. 2. to make strokes with the beak or with something pointed. —n. 3. a quick stroke. 4. a quick kiss.

peck[2] (pek) n. a dry measure of 8 quarts.

peck'ing or'der n. a hierarchy within a group.

pec'tin (pekʹtin) n. a substance in ripe fruit that causes jelly to set.

pec'to·ral (pekʹtər əl) adj. of, in, or on the chest.

pec'u·late' (pekʹyə lātʹ) v.t., v.i., -lated, -lating. to embezzle (money). —**pec'u·la'tion,** n.

pe·cul'iar (pi kyōōlʹyər) adj. 1. odd; strange. 2. uncommon. 3. belonging exclusively to some person, group, or thing. —**pe·cu'li·ar'i·ty** (-lē ar'i tē) n., pl. -ties. —**pe·cul'iar·ly,** adv.

pe·cu'ni·ar'y (pi kyōōʹnē er'ē) adj. of money.

ped'a·gogue' (pedʹə gogʹ) n. a teacher. —**ped'a·go·gy** (-gōʹjē, -gojʹē) n. —**ped'a·gog'ic, ped'a·gog'i·cal,** adj.

ped'al (pedʹl) n., v., -aled, -aling, adj. —n. 1. a foot-operated lever. —v.t., v.i. 2. to work the pedals (of).

ped'ant (pedʹnt) n. 1. a person who overemphasizes rules and details. 2. a person who makes an excessive display of learning. —**pe·dan'tic,** adj. —**ped'ant·ry,** n.

ped'dle (pedʹl) v.t., v.i., -dled, -dling. to carry (small articles) about for sale. —**ped'dler,** n.

ped'es·tal (pedʹə stl) n. a base for a column, statue, etc.

pe·des'tri·an (pə desʹtrē ən) n. 1. a person who is walking. —adj. 2. walking. 3. dull.

pe'di·at'rics (pēʹdē aʹtriks) n. the branch of medicine dealing with the care and diseases of children. —**pe'di·a·tri'cian** (-ə trishʹən) n. —**pe'di·at'ric,** adj.

ped'i·cab' (pedʹi kabʹ) n. a three-wheeled conveyance operated by pedals.

ped'i·cure' (pedʹi kyŏorʹ) n. professional care of the feet.

ped'i·gree' (pedʹi grēʹ) n. 1. ancestry. 2. a certificate of ancestry, esp. of a purebred animal.

ped'i·ment (pedʹə mənt) n. a low triangular gable above an end wall, colonnade, etc.

pe·dom'e·ter (pə domʹi tər) n. a device that measures the distance walked.

pe·dun'cle (pi dungʹkəl, pēʹdungʹ) n. the stalk that supports a flower cluster.

peek (pēk) v.i. 1. to look quickly or furtively. —n. 2. a quick, furtive look.

peel (pēl) v.t. 1. to remove the skin or rind of. 2. to strip away from something. —v.i. 3. (of skin, paint, etc.) to come off in pieces. 4. to lose the skin, paint, etc. —n. 5. the skin or rind of a fruit or vegetable.

peen (pēn) n. the end of a hammer head opposite the striking surface.

peep[1] (pēp) v.i. 1. to look through a small opening or from a hidden location. 2. to show slightly. —n. 3. a quick look.

peep[2] (pēp) n. 1. a short, shrill cry. —v.i. 2. to utter a short, shrill cry.

peer[1] (pēr) n. 1. a person who is the equal of another. 2. a member of the British nobility. —**peer'age,** n.

peer[2] (pēr) v.i. to look searchingly or with difficulty.

peer'less adj. without equal.

peeve (pēv) v., n., peeved, peeving. —n. 1. a source of annoyance. —v.t. 2. to make peevish; vex.

peev'ish (pēʹvish) adj. cross.

peg (peg) n., v., pegged, pegging. —n. 1. a pin of wood, metal, etc. —v.t. 2. to fasten with pegs.

peg' leg' n. a wooden leg.

peign·oir' (pān wär', pen-) n. a woman's loose dressing gown.

pe·jo'ra·tive (pi jôrʹə tiv) adj. disparaging; negative.

Pe'king·ese' (pēʹkə nēzʹ, -nēsʹ) n., pl. Pekingese. a small, long-haired Chinese dog with a flat muzzle.

pe'koe (pēʹkō) n. black tea.

pe·lag'ic (pə lajʹik) adj. of the open seas.

pel'i·can (pelʹi kən) n. a large fish-eating bird with a throat pouch.

pel·la'gra (pə lagʹrə, -lāʹgrə, -läʹ-) n. a disease caused by a lack of niacin in the diet.

pel'let (pelʹit) n. a small, round mass, as of food.

pell'-mell' (pelʹmelʹ) adv. in disorderly haste.

pel·lu'cid (pə lōōʹsid) adj. very clear.

pelt[1] (pelt) v.t. 1. to attack with repeated blows. —v.i. 2. (of rain) to come down hard and fast.

pelt[2] (pelt) n. the skin of an animal.

pel'vis (pelʹvis) n. 1. the cavity in the lower trunk of the body. 2. the bones forming this. —**pel'vic,** adj.

pem'mi·can (pemʹi kən) n. dried food.

pen[1] (pen) n., v., penned, penning. —n. 1. an instrument for writing or drawing with ink. —v.t. 2. to write or draw with a pen.

pen[2] (pen) n., v., penned, penning. —n. 1. a small enclosure for animals. —v.t. 2. to confine in a pen.

pe'nal (pēnʹl) adj. of or prescribing punishment. —**pe'nal·ize',** v.t.

pen'al·ty (penʹl tē) n., pl. -ties. a punishment for violating a law.

pen'ance (-əns) n. a punishment as penitence for sin.

pence (pens) n. Brit. pl. of **penny.**

pen'chant (penʹchənt) n. a liking.

pen'cil (penʹsəl) n. a slender stick of graphite or crayon enclosed in wood, metal, etc., used for writing or drawing.

pen'dant (penʹdənt) n. an ornament hanging from a chain around the neck.

pend'ent (penʹdənt) adj. hanging.

pend'ing prep. 1. until. 2. during. —adj. 3. awaiting decision.

pen'du·lous (penʹji ləs, penʹdyə-) adj. hanging loosely.

pen'du·lum (-ləm) n. a body suspended from a fixed point and swinging freely.

pen'e·trate' (penʹi trātʹ) v.t., v.i., -trated, -trating. 1. to pierce or pass into or through (something). 2. to understand; have insight. —**pen'e·tra'tion,** n.

pen'guin (pengʹgwin, penʹ-) n. a flightless aquatic bird of Antarctic regions.

pen'i·cil'lin (penʹə silʹin) n. an antibiotic produced in certain molds.

pen·in'su·la (pə ninʹsə lə) n. land almost completely surrounded by water. —**pen·in'su·lar,** adj.

pe'nis (pēʹnis) n. the male organ of copulation and urination. —**pe'nile** (pēnʹl) adj.

pen'i·tent (penʹi tənt) adj. 1. sorry for a sin or fault. —n. 2. a penitent person. —**pen'i·tence,** n.

pen'i·ten'tia·ry (-tenʹshə rē) n., pl. -ries. a prison.

pen'knife' n. a small pocketknife.

pen'light' n. a flashlight shaped like a fountain pen.

Penn. Pennsylvania. Also, **Penna.**

pen' name' n. a writer's pseudonym.

pen'nant (penʹənt) n. 1. a long, tapering flag. 2. a flag symbolizing a championship.

pen'ny (penʹē) n., pl. pennies, Brit. pence. a small coin, equal to one cent in the U.S. and Canada, and to $\frac{1}{100}$ pound in the United Kingdom.

pen'ny pinch'er n. a stingy person. —**pen'ny-pinch'ing,** adj.

pen'ny·weight' n. (in troy weight) 24 grains, or $\frac{1}{20}$ of an ounce.

pe·nol'o·gy (pē nolʹə jē) n. the study of the punishment of crime and the management of prisons. —**pe·nol'o·gist,** n.

pen' pal' n. a person with whom one exchanges letters regularly.

pen'sion (penʹshən) n. 1. a fixed periodic payment for past service, injury sustained, etc. 2. (pän sēʹ ōnʹ) (in Europe) a boardinghouse or small hotel. —v.t. 3. to give a pension to.

pen'sion·er n. a person receiving a pension.

pen'sive (penʹsiv) adj. gravely thoughtful. —**pen'sive·ly,** adv.

penta- a prefix meaning five.

pen'ta·gon' (penʹtə gonʹ) n. a plane figure having five sides.

pen'ta·gram' (-gramʹ) n. a five-pointed, star-shaped symbol.

pen·tam'e·ter (pen tamʹi tər) n. a verse of five feet.

Pen'ta·teuch' (penʹtə tōōk, -tyōōkʹ) n. the first five books of the Old Testament.

pen·tath'lon (pen tathʹlən, -lon) n. an athletic contest consisting of five events.

Pen'te·cost' (penʹti kôstʹ) n. the seventh Sunday after Easter, commemorating the descent of the Holy Spirit upon the Apostles.

Pen'te·cos'tal adj. of Christian groups that emphasize the Holy Spirit.

pent'house' (pentʹhousʹ) n. a rooftop apartment.

pent'-up' adj. restrained; confined.

pe·nu'che (pə nōōʹchē) n. a brown-sugar fudge.

pe·nul'ti·mate (pi nulʹtə mit) adj. being or occurring next to last.

pe·num'bra (pə numʹbrə) n., pl. -brae (-brē) -bras. the partial shadow outside the complete shadow of a celestial body in eclipse. —**pe·num'bral,** adj.

pe·nu'ri·ous (pə nŏŏrʹē əs, -nyŏŏrʹ-) adj. 1. stingy. 2. very poor.

pen'u·ry (penʹyə rē) n. poverty.

pe'on (pēʹən, -on) n. an unskilled worker.

pe'o·ny (pēʹə nē) n., pl. -nies. a plant with large, showy red, white, or pink flowers.

peo'ple (pēʹpəl) n., v., -pled, -pling. —n. 1. persons in general. 2. the body of persons constituting a nation or ethnic group. —v.t. 3. to populate.

pep (pep) n., v., pepped, pepping. —n. 1. energy or liveliness. —v. pep up, to make or become vigorous. —**pep'py,** adj.

pep'per (pepʹər) n. 1. a condiment made from the pungent dried berries of a tropical shrub. 2. the usu. red or green edible fruit of certain plants, ranging from mild to hot in flavor. —v.t. 3. to season with pepper. 4. to pelt with missiles. —**pep'per·y,** adj.

pep'per·corn' n. the dried berry of the pepper plant.

pep'per mill' n. a device for grinding peppercorns.

pep'per·mint' n. an aromatic herb of the mint family.

pep'per·o'ni (pepʹə rōʹnē) n., pl. -nis. a highly seasoned hard sausage.

pep'sin (pepʹsin) n. an enzyme, produced in the stomach, that digests proteins.

pep'tic (pepʹtik) adj. of or aiding digestion.

per (pûr; unstressed pər) prep. for; by means of.

per'ad·ven'ture adv. Archaic. maybe.

per·am'bu·late' (pər amʹbyə lātʹ) v., -lated, -lating. —v.t. 1. to walk about or through. —v.i. 2. to stroll.

per·am'bu·la'tor n. a baby carriage.

per an'num (pər anʹəm) adv. yearly.

per·cale' (pər kālʹ) n. a smooth, closely woven cotton fabric.

per cap'i·ta (pər kapʹi tə) adj., adv. by or for each person.

per·ceive' (pər sēvʹ) v.t., -ceived, -ceiving. 1. to become aware of by seeing, hearing, etc. 2. to understand. —**per·ceiv'a·ble,** adj.

per·cent' (pər sentʹ) n. one one-hundredth part.

per·cent'age (-senʹtij) n. 1. a rate or proportion per hundred. 2. a proportion.

per·cen'tile (-tīl, -til) n. one of the values of a statistical variable that divides the distribution of the variable into 100 equal parts.

per'cept (pûrʹsept) n. the result of perceiving.

per·cep'ti·ble (-sepʹtə bəl) adj. capable of being perceived.

per·cep'tion n. 1. the act or faculty of perceiving. 2. insight. 3. the result of perceiving.

per·cep'tive adj. showing insight.

per·cep'tu·al (-chōō əl) adj. involving perception.

perch[1] (pûrch) n. 1. a horizontal rod serving as a roosting place for birds. 2. a high position, resting place, etc. —v.i., v.t. 3. to rest or set on a perch.

perch[2] (pûrch) n. a small freshwater fish with a spiny fin.

per·chance' (pər chansʹ) adv. Poetic. maybe; by chance.

per'co·late' (pûrʹkə lātʹ) v., -lated, -lating. —v.t. 1. to cause (a liquid) to filter through something porous. —v.i. 2. to filter.

per'co·la'tor n. a coffee pot in which boiling water is forced up through a hollow stem and filters down through ground coffee.

per·cus'sion (pər kushʹən) n. the striking of one body against another.

percus'sion in'strument n. a musical instrument, as the drum or cymbal, that is struck to produce a sound.

per di'em (pər dēʹəm) adv. 1. by the day. —n. 2. a daily allowance for expenses.

per·di'tion (pər dishʹən) n. eternal damnation; hell.

per·dur'a·ble (-dŏŏrʹə bəl,-dyŏŏrʹ-) adj. very durable.

per'e·gri·nate' (perʹi grə nātʹ) v.i., v.t., -nated, -nating. to travel (over or through), esp. on foot. —**per'e·gri·na'tion,** n.

per'e·grine fal'con (perʹi grin, -grēnʹ) n. a kind of falcon that feeds on birds taken in flight.

per·emp'to·ry (pə rempʹtə rē) adj. permitting no denial or refusal. —**per·emp'to·ri·ly,** adv.

per·en'ni·al (pə renʹē əl) adj. 1. lasting indefinitely. 2. (of plants) living more than two years. 3. continuing. —n. 4. a perennial plant. —**per·en'ni·al·ly,** adv.

per'fect (pûrʹfikt) adj. 1. without flaws. 2. excellent. 3. complete; thorough. 4. designating a verb tense that indicates an action already completed. —v.t. (pər fektʹ) 5. to make faultless.

per·fec'tion n. 1. a perfecting or being perfect. 2. something perfect. 3. the highest degree of excellence.

per·fec'tion·ism n. insistence on perfection. —**per·fec'tion·ist,** n.

per'fi·dy (pûrʹfi dē) n., pl. -dies. treachery. —**per·fid'i·ous,** adj.

per'fo·rate' (pûrʹfə rātʹ) v.t., -rated, -rating. to make holes through. —**per'fo·ra'tion,** n.

per·force' (pər fôrsʹ) adv. of necessity.

per·form' (-fôrmʹ) v.t. 1. to carry out; do. 2. to present (a play, musical work, etc.) before an audience. —v.i. 3. to do something. 4. to give a performance. —**per·form'er,** n.

per·form'ance (-fôrʹməns) n. 1. an entertainment presented before an audience. 2. the act of performing. 3. a specific action, deed, etc.

perform'ing arts' n. arts requiring public performance.

per·fume n. (pûrʹfyōōm, pər fyōōmʹ) 1. a sweet-smelling liquid for applying to the body. 2. a pleasant fragrance. —v.t. (pər fyōōmʹ, pûrʹfyōōm) 3. to fill with a pleasant fragrance. —**per·fum'er·y,** n.

per·func'to·ry (pər fungkʹtə rē) adj. done without care or attention. —**per·func'to·ri·ly,** adv.

per·haps' (pər hapsʹ) adv. maybe.

peri- a prefix meaning aroun, surrounding, or near.

per'i·car'di·um (perʹi kärʹdē əm) n. the sac enclosing the heart.

per'i·gee' (-jēʹ) n. the point nearest the earth in the orbit of a moon or satellite.

per'i·he'li·on (perʹə hēʹlē ən) n. the point nearest the sun in the orbit of a planet or comet.

per'il (perʹəl) n. 1. danger. —v.t. 2. to endanger. —**per'il·ous,** adj.

pe·rim'e·ter (pə rimʹi tər) n. 1. the outer boundary of a two-dimensional figure. 2. the length of such a boundary.

per'i·ne'um (perʹə nēʹəm) n., pl. -nea. the area between the genitals and the anus.

pe'ri·od (pērʹē əd) n. 1. a portion of time. 2. the mark (.) indicating the end of a sentence. 3. an occurrence of menstruation.

pe'ri·od'ic (-odʹik) adj. recurring regularly or intermittently. —**pe·ri·od'i·cal·ly,** adv.

pe'ri·od'i·cal n. a publication issued at regular intervals. —adj. 2. of such publications. 3. periodic.

pe'ri·od'ic ta'ble n. a table showing the chemical elements in related groups, arranged by atomic number.

per'i·o·don'tal (perʹē ə donʹtl) adj. of or concerning bone, tissue, and gums surrounding and supporting the teeth.

per'i·pa·tet'ic (perʹə pə tetʹik) adj. walking or traveling about.

pe·riph'er·al (pə rifʹər əl) adj. 1. located on the periphery. 2. only partly relevant. —n. 3. an external hardware device connected to a computer's CPU.

pe·riph'er·y n., pl. -eries. 1. the boundary of a surface or area. 2. a surrounding region or area.

pe·riph'ra·sis (pə rifʹrə sis) n., pl. -ses (-sēzʹ). the use of a roundabout form of expression.

per'i·scope' (perʹə skōpʹ) n. an optical instrument consisting of a tube in which mirrors or prisms reflect to give a view from below or behind an obstacle.

per'ish (perʹish) v.i. 1. to die. 2. to decay.

per'ish·a·ble adj. 1. subject to decay or destruction. —n. 2. Usu. **perishables.** something perishable, esp. food.

per'i·stal'sis (perʹə stôlʹsis, -stalʹ-) n., pl. -ses (-sēz). the muscle contractions and relaxations that move food along the alimentary canal.

per'i·to·ne'um (perʹi tn ēʹəm, -tōʹ-) n. the lining of the abdominal cavity.

per'i·to·ni'tis (-tn īʹtis) n. inflammation of the peritoneum.

per'i·win'kle[1] (perʹi wingʹkəl) n. an edible marine snail.

per'i·win'kle[2] (perʹi wingʹkəl) n. a trailing evergreen plant with blue flowers.

per'jure (pûrʹjər) v.t., -jured, -juring. to make (oneself) guilty of perjury.

per'ju·ry (pûrʹjə rē) n., pl. -ries. giving false testimony under oath.

perk[1] (pûrk) v. **perk up,** to become or make lively or cheerful.

perk[2] (pûrk) n. a perquisite.

perk'y adj., -ier, -iest. cheerful.

per'ma·frost' (pûrʹmə frôstʹ) n. permanently frozen subsoil.

per'ma·nent (-nənt) adj. 1. lasting indefinitely. 2. a curl set in the hair by chemicals. —**per'ma·nence,** n. —**per'ma·nent·ly,** adv.

per'me·a·ble (pûrʹmē ə bəl) adj. letting fluids through.

per'me·ate' (-āt') v.t., v.i., -ated, -ating. to penetrate or spread through all parts (of).

per·mis'si·ble (pər misʹə bəl) adj. allowable.

per·mis'sion (-mishʹən) n. authorization or consent to do something.

per·mis'sive (-misʹiv) adj. 1. loose or lax in discipline. 2. giving permission.

per·mit' v., -mitted, -mitting, n. —v.t. (pər mitʹ) 1. to allow to do something. 2. to allow to occur. —v.i. 3. to afford opportunity. —n. (pûrʹmit, pər mitʹ) 4. a written order giving permission.

per'mu·ta'tion (pûrʹmyŏō tāʹshən) n. alteration or transformation.

per·ni'cious (pər nishʹəs) adj. causing serious harm.

per'o·ra'tion (perʹə rāʹshən) n. 1. a very lengthy speech. 2. the concluding part of a speech.

per·ox'ide (pə rokʹsīd) n., pl. -ided, -iding. —n. 1. hydrogen peroxide. 2. an oxide with two bonded oxygen atoms. —v.t. 3. to bleach with peroxide.

per'pen·dic'u·lar (pûrʹpən dikʹyə lər) adj. 1. vertical. 2. meeting a given line at right angles. —n. 3. a perpendicular line or position.

per'pe·trate' (pûrʹpi trātʹ) v.t., -trated, -trating. to carry out; commit. —**per'pe·tra'tion,** n. —**per'pe·tra'tor,** n.

per·pet'u·al (pər pechʹōō əl) adj. 1. continuing or lasting forever. 2. not ceasing. —**per·pet'u·ate',** v.t.

per·pe·tu'i·ty (pûrʹpi tōōʹi tē, -tyōōʹ-) n. in perpetuity, forever.

per·plex' (pər pleksʹ) v.t. to cause to be confused. —**per·plex'i·ty,** n.

per'qui·site (pûrʹkwə zit) n. a benefit beyond one's regular income.

per se' (pûr sāʹ, sēʹ, pər) adv. by, of, for, or in itself; intrinsically.

per'se·cute' (pûrʹsi kyōōtʹ) v.t., -cuted, -cuting. to subject to cruel treatment, esp. because of religion or race. —**per'se·cu'tion,** n. —**per'se·cu'tor,** n.

per'se·vere' (pûrʹsə vērʹ) v.i., -vered, -vering. to continue steadfastly. —**per'se·ver'ance,** n.

per'si·flage' (pûrʹsə fläzhʹ) n. light, bantering talk.

per·sim'mon (pər simʹən) n. a plumlike orange fruit.

per·sist' (pər sistʹ, -zistʹ) v.i. 1. to continue firmly in spite of opposition. 2. to endure. —**per·sist'ence,** n. —**per·sist'ent,** adj.

per·snick'et·y (pər snikʹi tē) adj. Informal. fussy.

per'son (pûrʹsən) n. 1. a human

being. **2.** the individual personality of a human being. **3.** the body of a living human being. **4.** a grammatical category applied to pronouns and verbs, used to distinguish the one speaking, the one spoken to, and the one or thing spoken about. —*Idiom.* **5. in person,** in one's own presence.

per'son·a·ble *adj.* attractive in appearance and manner.

per'son·age (-sə nij) *n.* a distinguished person.

per'son·al (-sə nl) *adj.* **1.** of, by, or relating to a certain person. **2.** done in person. **3.** of the body, clothing, or appearance. **4.** of grammatical person. **5.** *Law.* of property that is movable.

per'sonal comput'er *n.* a microcomputer for individual use.

per'sonal effects' *n.pl.* belongings.

per'son·al'i·ty (-sə nal'ə tē) *n., pl.* **-ties. 1.** distinctive personal character. **2.** a famous person.

per'son·al·ize' *v.t.,* **-ized, -izing. 1.** to have marked with one's name. **2.** to make personal.

per'son·al·ly *adv.* **1.** in person. **2.** as if directed at oneself. **3.** as regards oneself. **4.** as a person.

per'son·al·ty (-sə nəl tē) *n.,pl.* **-ties.** personal property.

per·so'na non gra'ta (pər sō'nə non grä'tə) *n.* a person who is not welcome.

per·son·i·fy' (pər son'ə fī') *v.t.,* **-fied, -fying. 1.** to embody; typify. **2.** to attribute a human character to. —**per·son·i·fi·ca'tion,** *n.*

per'son·nel' (pûr'sə nel') *n.* employees.

per·spec'tive (pər spek'tiv) *n.* **1.** a technique of depicting space relationships on a flat surface. **2.** the way objects appear from their relative distance and positions. **3.** a mental view or prospect.

per'spi·ca'cious (pûr'spi kā'shəs) *adj.* having keen insight. —**per'spi·cac'i·ty** (-kas'i tē) *n.*

per·spic'u·ous (pər spik'yōō əs) *adj.* clearly expressed or presented. —**per'spi·cu'i·ty** (pûr'-) *n.*

per·spire' (pər spī°r') *v.i.,* **-spired, -spiring.** to sweat. —**per·spi·ra'tion** (pûr'spə rā'shən) *n.*

per·suade' (pər swād') *v.t.,* **-suaded, -suading. 1.** to prevail upon (a person) to act as suggested. **2.** to convince. —**per·sua'sive,** *adj.* —**per·sua'sive·ly,** *adv.*

per·sua'sion (-swā'zhən) *n.* **1.** the act or power of persuading. **2.** a belief. **3.** a religious opinion.

pert (pûrt) *adj.* **1.** impertinent; saucy. **2.** lively.

per·tain' (pər tān') *v.i.* **1.** to relate. **2.** to belong as a part.

per'ti·na'cious (pûr'tn ā'shəs) *adj.* holding stubbornly to a purpose, opinion, etc.

per'ti·nent (-tn ənt) *adj.* relevant. —**per'ti·nence,** *n.*

per·turb' (pər tûrb') *v.t.* to disturb greatly. —**per'tur·ba'tion,** *n.*

pe·ruke' (pə rōōk') *n.* a man's wig of the 17th and 18th centuries.

pe·ruse' (pə rōōz') *v.t.,* **-rused, -rusing.** to read carefully. —**pe·ru'sal,** *n.*

per·vade' (pər vād') *v.t.,* **-vaded, -vading.** to become spread throughout all parts of. —**per·va'sive,** *adj.*

per·verse' (pər vûrs') *adj.* stubbornly determined not to do what is expected. —**per·ver'si·ty,** *n.*

per·vert' *v.t.* (pər·vûrt') **1.** to corrupt. **2.** to turn to an improper use. **3.** to distort. —*n.* (pûr'vûrt) **4.** a perverted person. —**per·ver'sion,** *n.*

pes'ky (pes'kē) *adj.,* **-kier, -kiest.** annoying; troublesome.

pe'so (pā'sō) *n.* the basic monetary unit of many Latin American countries.

pes'si·mism (pes'ə miz'əm) *n.* the tendency to expect the worst. —**pes'si·mist,** *n.* —**pes'si·mis'tic,** *adj.* —**pes'si·mis'ti·cal·ly,** *adv.*

pest (pest) *n.* a troublesome person, animal, or thing.

pes'ter (pes'tər) *v.t.* to annoy continually, as with requests.

pes'ti·cide' (pes'tə sīd') *n.* a poison used to kill harmful insects or weeds.

pes·tif'er·ous (pe stif'ər əs) *adj.* **1.** bearing disease. **2.** dangerous **3.** troublesome.

pes'ti·lence (pes'tl əns) *n.* a deadly epidemic disease.

pes'tle (pes'əl, pes'tl) *n.* a tool for pounding or crushing.

pes'to (pes'tō) *n.* a sauce of basil, nuts, garlic, olive oil, and cheese.

pet (pet) *n., adj., v.,* **petted, petting.** —*n.* **1.** a tame animal that is cared for affectionately. **2.** a favorite. —*adj.* **3.** treated as a pet. **4.** favorite. —*v.t.* **5.** to present with affection. —*v.i* **6.** to engage in amorous caressing.

pet'al (pet'l) *n.* one of the colored outer parts of a flower.

pe·tard' (pi tärd') *n.* an explosive device.

pe'ter (pē'tər) *v.* **peter out,** to diminish gradually.

pet'i·ole' (pet'ē ōl') *n.* the stalk that attaches a leaf to a stem.

pet'it (pet'ē) *adj. Law.* petty.

pe·tite' (pə tēt') *adj.* small.

pe·ti'tion (pə tish'ən) *n.* **1.** a formal request signed by those submitting it and addressed to a person in authority. —*v.t.* **2.** to present a petition to. —**pe·ti'tion·er,** *n.*

pet'rel (pe'trəl) *n.* a small sea bird.

pet'ri·fy' (pe'trə fī') *v.t.,* **-fied, -fying. 1.** to turn into stone. **2.** to paralyze with fear.

pet'ro·chem'i·cal (pe'trō kem'i·kəl) *n.* a chemical obtained from petroleum.

pet'ro·dol'lars *n.pl.* revenues in dollars accumulated by petroleum-exporting countries.

pet'rol (pe'trəl) *n. Brit.* gasoline.

pet'ro·la'tum (pe'trə lā'təm) *n.* a gelatinous mass obtained from petroleum, used as a lubricant.

pe·tro'le·um (pə trō'lē əm) *n.* an oily liquid found underground that yields gasoline, kerosene, etc.

pe·trol'o·gy (-trol'ə jē) *n.* the study of rocks.

pet'ti·coat' (pet'ē kōt') *n.* an underskirt.

pet'ti·fog' (pet'ē fog') *v.i.,* **-fogged, -fogging.** to quibble over trifles.

pet'tish (pet'ish) *adj.* petulant.

pet'ty (pet'ē) *adj.,* **-tier, -tiest. 1.** small or trivial. **2.** small-minded. —**pet'ti·ness,** *n.*

pet'ty cash' *n.* a fund for paying minor expenses.

pet'ty ju'ry *n.* a jury impaneled in a civil or criminal trial.

pet'ty of'ficer *n.* a noncommissioned officer in the navy.

pet'u·lant (pech'ə lənt) *adj.* showing impatient irritation. —**pet'u·lance,** *n.*

pe·tu'ni·a (pi tōō'nyə, -tyōō'-) *n.* a garden plant with colorful funnel-shaped flowers.

pew (pyōō) *n.* one of the fixed benches with backs in a church.

pe'wee (pē'wē) *n.* any of several New World flycatchers.

pew'ter (pyōō'tər) *n.* an alloy of tin and another metal.

pg. page.

pH a symbol describing the acidity or alkalinity of a chemical solution.

pha·e'ton (fā'i tn, fā'ə tən) *n.* an open carriage or automobile.

phag'o·cyte' (fag'ə sīt') *n.* any cell that ingests foreign particles.

pha·lan'ger (fə lan'jər) *n.* a tree-dwelling Australian marsupial.

pha'lanx (fā'langks, fal'angks) *n., pl.* **-lanxes, -langes** (fə lan'jēz). **1.** a compact mass of persons, animals, or things. **2.** a bone of a finger or toe.

phal'lus (fal'əs) *n., pl.* **phalli** (fal'ī). **1.** the penis. **2.** an image of the penis as a symbol of male generative powers. —**phal'lic,** *adj.*

phan'tasm (fan'taz əm) *n.* an apparition; phantom.

phan·tas'ma·go'ri·a (-mə gôr'ē ə) *n.* a shifting series of phantasms or illusions, as in a dream.

phan'tom (-təm) *n.* **1.** a ghostlike image. —*adj.* **2.** unreal; illusory.

Phar'aoh (fâr'ō) *n.* a title of an ancient Egyptian king.

Phar'i·see' (far'ə sē') *n.* **1.** a member of an ancient Jewish sect. **2.** **pharisee,** a self-righteous person.

phar'ma·ceu'ti·cal (fär'mə sōō'ti·kəl) *adj.* pertaining to pharmacy.

phar'ma·col'o·gy (-kol'ə jē) *n.* the study of the uses and effects of drugs.

phar'ma·co·poe'ia (-kə pē'ə) *n.* a book that lists drugs, their formulas, etc.

phar'ma·cy (-sē) *n., pl.* **-cies. 1.** a drugstore. **2.** the art and science of preparing and dispensing drugs. —**phar'ma·cist,** *n.*

phar'ynx (far'ingks) *n., pl.* **pharynges** (fə rin'jēz), **pharynxes.** the tube connecting the mouth and the nasal passages with the esophagus. —**pha·ryn'ge·al,** *adj.* —**phar'yn·gi'tis** (far'ən jī'tis) *n.*

phase (fāz) *n.* **1.** a stage in a process of change or development. —*v.* **2. phase in,** to put into use gradually. **3. ~ out,** to bring to an end gradually.

phase'out' *n.* a gradual dismissal or termination.

phat (fat) *adj. Slang.* great; terrific.

Ph.D. Doctor of Philosophy.

pheas'ant (fez'ənt) *n.* a large, long-tailed game bird.

phe'no·bar'bi·tal' (fē'nō bär'bi·tôl', -tal') *n.* a white powder used as a sedative.

phe'nol (fē'nôl) *n.* a poisonous substance used as a disinfectant and antiseptic.

phe·nom'e·non' (fi nom'ə non', -nən) *n., pl.* **-ena** (-ə nə). **1.** a fact, occurrence, or circumstance that can be observed. **2.** an extraordinary thing or person. —**phe·nom'e·nal,** *adj.* —**phe·nom'e·nal·ly,** *adv.*

pher'o·mone' (fer'ə mōn') *n.* a chemical substance released by an animal that influences the behavior of other members of the species.

phi (fī) *n., pl.* **phis.** the 21st letter of the Greek alphabet.

phi'al (fī'əl) *n.* a vial.

phil- a prefix meaning loving.

phi·lan'der·er (fi lan'dər ər) *n.* a man who has many love affairs. —**phi·lan'der,** *v.i.*

phi·lan'thro·py (fi lan'thrə pē) *n., pl.* **-pies.** love of humanity, as shown in charitable acts. **2.** a benevolent act, work, or institution. —**phil'an·throp'ic** (fil'ən throp'ik) *adj.* —**phi·lan'thro·pist,** *n.*

phi·lat'e·ly (fi lat'l ē) *n.* the collection and study of postage stamps. —**phi·lat'e·list,** *n.*

-phile a suffix meaning one that loves or has strong enthusiasm for, as *bibliophile.*

phil'har·mon'ic (fil'här mon'ik) *adj.* **1.** music-loving. —*n.* **2.** a symphony orchestra.

phil·is·tine' (fil'ə stēn', -stīn') *n.* a person who is indifferent to culture.

phi·lo·den'dron (fil'ə den'drən) *n., pl.* **-drons, -dra.** a tropical climbing plant, grown as a houseplant.

phi·lol'o·gy (fi lol'ə jē) *n.* the study of languages. —**phi·lol'o·gist,** *n.*

phi·los'o·pher (fi los'ə fər) *n.* **1.** a person trained in philosophy. **2.** a person guided by reason.

phi·los'o·phy (-fē) *n., pl.* **-phies. 1.** the study of the truths and principles of being and knowledge. **2.** a system of philosophical belief. **3.** the principles of a particular field of knowledge or action. —**phil'o·soph'i·cal** (fil'ə sof'i kəl) *adj.* —**phi·los'o·phize',** *v.i.*

phil'ter (fil'tər) *n.* a magic potion.

phle·bi'tis (flə bī'tis) *n.* inflammation of a vein.

phle·bot'o·my (-bot'ə mē) *n., pl.* **-mies.** the practice of opening a vein to let blood.

phlegm (flem) *n.* **1.** thick mucus in the respiratory passages. **2.** apathy.

phleg·mat'ic (fleg mat'ik) *adj.* unemotional or unenthusiastic.

phlo'em (flō'em) *n.* the tissue in a plant through which food passes.

phlox (floks) *n.* a garden plant with showy white or purple flowers.

-phobe a suffix meaning one who hates or fears.

pho'bi·a (fō'bē ə) *n.* a morbid fear.

-phobia a suffix meaning fear.

phoe'be (fē'bē) *n.* a small American flycatcher.

phoe'nix (fē'niks) *n.* a mythical bird that burns, then rises from its ashes.

phone (fōn) *n., v.t., v.i.,* **phoned, phoning.** *Informal.* telephone.

phone' card' *n.* a prepaid card used to make calls from any telephone.

pho'neme (fō'nēm) *n.* any minimal unit of speech sound that distinguishes one word from another.

pho·net'ics (fə net'iks) *n.* the study of speech sounds and their written representation. —**pho·net'ic,** *adj.*

phon'ics (fon'iks) *n.* a method of teaching reading and spelling based on phonetics.

phono- a prefix meaning sound.

pho'no·graph' (fō'nə graf') *n.* a sound-producing machine using records in the form of grooved disks. —**pho'no·graph'ic,** *adj.*

pho·nol'o·gy (fə nol'ə jē) *n., pl.* **-gies. 1.** the system of sounds in a language. **2.** the study of sounds in a language.

pho'ny (fō'nē) *adj.,* **-nier, -niest,** *n., pl.* **-nies.** —*adj.* **1.** false; fake. **2.** not sincere. —*n.* **3.** a phony person or thing. —**pho'ni·ness,** *n.*

phos'gene (fos'jēn) *n.* a poisonous, colorless liquid or gas.

phos'phate (fos'fāt) *n.* **1.** a salt of phosphoric acid. **2.** a fertilizer containing phosphorus.

phos'phor (fos'fər) *n.* a substance that is luminous when struck by certain kinds of light.

phos'pho·res'cent (-fə res'ənt) *adj.* luminous. —**phos'pho·res'cence,** *n.*

phos'pho·rus (-fər əs) *n.* a non-metallic element used in matches and fertilizer.

pho'to (fō'tō) *n., pl.* **-tos.** *Informal.* a photograph.

photo- a prefix meaning light.

pho'to·cop'y *n., pl.* **-ies,** *v.,* **-ied, -ying.** —*n.* **1.** a photographic copy of a document. —*v.t.* **2.** to make a photocopy of.

pho'to·e·lec'tric *adj.* of or using electrical effects produced by light.

pho'to·en·grav'ing *n.* a photographic process of preparing printing plates for letterpress printing.

pho'to fin'ish *n.* a finish of a race so close as to require a photograph to determine the winner.

pho'to·gen'ic (fō'tə jen'ik) *adj.* looking attractive in photos.

pho'to·graph' (fō'tə graf') *n.* **1.** a picture produced by photography. —*v.t.***2.** to take a photograph of.

pho·tog'ra·phy (fə tog'rə fē) *n.* the process of producing images on a sensitized surface by the action of light. —**pho·tog'ra·pher,** *n.* —**pho'to·graph'ic** (fō'tə graf'ik) *adj.*

pho'ton (fō'ton) *n.* a quantum of electromagnetic radiation.

pho'to·sen'si·tive *adj.* sensitive to light.

Pho'to·stat' (fō'tə stat') *n.* **1.** *Trademark.* a camera for photographing documents, drawings, etc. **2.** (*often l.c.*) the photograph so made. —*v.t.* **3. photostat,** to copy with this camera.

pho'to·syn'the·sis *n.* the conversion by plants of carbon dioxide and water into carbohydrates, aided by light and chlorophyll.

phrase (frāz) *n., v.,* **phrased, phrasing.** —*n.* **1.** a sequence of words forming a unit within a sentence or clause. **2.** a passage of four to eight measures of music. —*v.t.* **3.** to express in a particular way.

phra'se·ol'o·gy (frā'zē ol'ə jē) *n.* manner of verbal expression.

phy·lac'ter·y (fi lak'tə rē) *n., pl.* **-teries.** one of two leather cubes containing Biblical verses, worn by Jewish men during morning prayers.

phy·log'e·ny (fī loj'ə nē) *n.* the development of a particular group of organisms.

phy'lum (fī'ləm) *n., pl.* **-la.** the primary classification of plants or animals.

phys'ic (fiz'ik) *n.* a medicine that purges.

phys'i·cal *adj.* **1.** of the body. **2.** of matter as opposed to spirit. **3.** of physics. —*n.* **4.** a full medical examination.

phys'ical anthropol'ogy *n.* the study of the evolutionary changes in human body structure.

phys'ical sci'ence *n.* a science that deals with inanimate matter or energy, as physics or chemistry.

phys'ical ther'a·py *n.* the treatment of physical disability or pain by techniques such as exercise or massage.

phy·si'cian (fi zish'ən) *n.* a medical doctor.

phys'ics (fiz'iks) *n.* the science that deals with matter, motion, energy, and force. —**phys'i·cist,** *n.*

phys'i·og'no·my (fiz'ē og'nə mē, -on'ə-) *n., pl.* **-mies.** the face.

phys'i·og'ra·phy (-og'rə fē) *n.* the branch of geography concerned with features of the earth's surface.

phys'i·ol'o·gy (-ol'ə jē) *n.* the science dealing with the functions of living organisms. —**phys'i·o·log'i·cal** (-ə loj'i kəl) *adj.* —**phys'i·ol'o·gist,** *n.*

phys'i·o·ther'a·py (fiz'ē ō-) *n.* physical therapy.

phy·sique' (fi zēk') *n.* bodily structure.

pi (pī) *n., pl.* **pis.** the Greek letter π, used as the symbol for the ratio of the circumference of a circle to its diameter (3.14159+).

pi·a·nis'si·mo (pē'ə nis'ə mō', pyä-) *adv. Music.* very softly.

pi·an'o (pē an'ō) *n., pl.* **-anos,** *adv.* —*n.* **1.** a musical instrument in which felt-covered hammers, operated from a keyboard, strike metal strings. —*adv.* (pē ä'nō) **2.** *Music.* softly. —**pi·an'ist** (pē an'ist, pē'ə·nist) *n.*

pi·az'za (pē az'ə) *n.* an open public square, esp. in Italy.

pi'ca (pī'kə) *n.* a unit of measure in printing.

pic'a·resque' (pik'ə resk') *adj.* a form of fiction that describes the adventures of a roguish hero.

pic'a·yune' (pik'ē yōōn', pik'ə-) *adj.* insignificant; petty.

pic'ca·lil'li (pik'ə lil'ē) *n.* a spiced vegetable relish.

pic'co·lo' (pik'ə lō') *n., pl.* **-los.** a small flute.

pick[1] (pik) *v.t.* **1.** to choose. **2.** to pluck one by one. **3.** to dig or break into, esp. with a pointed instrument. **4. pick at,** to eat sparingly. **5. ~ on,** to criticize or tease. **6. ~ out,** to select. **~** *n.* **7.** the act of choosing. **8.** something chosen. **9.** the best part.

pick[2] (pik) *n.* **1.** Also, **pick'ax', pick'axe'.** a sharp-pointed tool for breaking up soil, rock, etc. **2.** a pointed tool.

pick'er·el (pik'ər əl) *n.* a small pike.

pick'et (pik'it) *n.* **1.** a pointed stake driven into the ground. **2.** a person who demonstrates in front of a workplace. **3.** troops posted to warn of an enemy attack. —*v.t.* **4.** to enclose with pickets. **5.** to place pickets at (a building). —*v.i.* **6.** to demonstrate as a picket.

pick'et line' *n.* a line of strikers or other pickets.

pick'le (pik'əl) *n., v.,* **-led, -ling.** —*n.* **1.** a cucumber or other vegetable preserved in vinegar and spices. **2.** a predicament. —*v.t.* **3.** to preserve in vinegar or brine.

pick'pock'et *n.* a person who steals from others' pockets.

pick'up' *n.* **1.** a small open-body truck. **2.** the ability to accelerate rapidly. **3.** an improvement.

pick'y *adj.,* **-ier, -iest.** extremely fussy or finicky.

pic'nic (pik'nik) *n., v.,* **-nicked, -nicking.** —*n.* **1.** an outing and outdoor meal. —*v.i.* **2.** to have a picnic. —**pic'nick·er,** *n.*

pi'cot (pē'kō) *n.* decorative loops along the edge of lace, ribbon, etc.

pic·to'ri·al (pik tôr'ē əl) *adj.* of, like, or expressed in pictures.

pic'ture (pik'chər) *n., v.,* **-tured, -turing.** —*n.* **1.** a representation of a person, object, or scene, as a painting or photograph. **2.** a description. **3.** the embodiment of some quality. —*v.t.* **4.** to represent in a picture. **5.** to imagine.

pic'tur·esque' (-chə resk') *adj.* visually charming or quaint.

pid'dle (pid'l) *v.i.,* **-dled, -dling.** to waste time.

pid'dling *adj.* trivial; negligible.

pidg'in (pij'ən) *n.* a language developed to allow speakers of different languages to communicate.

pie (pī) *n.* a baked dish of fruit, meat, etc., in a pastry crust.

pie'bald' (pī'bôld') *adj.* having patches of different colors.

piece (pēs) *n., v.,* **pieced, piecing.** —*n.* **1.** one part or portion of a whole. **2.** a quantity of something forming a unit. **3.** an artistic work. **4.** an example of something. —*v.t.* **5.** to make by joining pieces.

pièce de ré·sis'tance' (pyes də Rā zē stäns') *n., pl.* **pièces de résistance** (pyes-). **1.** the principal dish of a meal. **2.** the principal item of a series.

piece' goods' *n.pl.* goods sold at retail by linear measure.

piece'meal' *adv.* gradually.

piece'work' *n.* work done and paid for by the piece.

pie' chart' *n.* a graph in which sectors of a circle represent quantities.

pied (pīd) *adj.* many-colored.

pied'-à-terre' (pyā'də târ') *n., pl.* **pieds'-à-terre'** (pyā'-). an apartment for part-time use.

pier (pēr) *n.* **1.** a structure built out over the water, used as an entertainment area, a landing place for ships, etc. **2.** a vertical support for masonry, steel, etc.

pierce (pērs) *v.,* **pierced, piercing.** —*v.t.* **1.** to penetrate, as a pointed object does. **2.** to make a hole in. **3.** to force a way through. **4.** to sound sharply through. —v.i. **5.** to force a way through something.

pi•e•ty (pī′i tē) n. **1.** reverence for God or devotion to religious duties. **2.** a pious act, belief, etc.

pif′fle (pif′əl) n. Informal. nonsense. —**pif′fling**, adj.

pig (pig) n. **1.** a swine. **2.** a gluttonous or sloppy person. **3.** a bar of metal. —**pig′gish**, adj.

pi′geon (pij′ən) n. a short-legged bird with a small head and compact body.

pi′geon•hole′ n., v., -**holed**, -**holing**. —n. **1.** a small compartment, as in a desk. —v.t. **2.** to classify. **3.** to put aside indefinitely.

pi′geon-toed′ adj. having toes or feet turned inward.

pig′gy•back′ adv. **1.** on the back. —adj. **2.** astride the back. **3.** attached to something else.

pig′head′ed adj. stubborn.

pig′ i′ron n. crude iron cast in pigs or blocks.

pig′let n. a baby pig.

pig′ment n. coloring matter.

pig′men•ta′tion n. coloration.

pig′pen′ n. **1.** a stall for pigs. **2.** a filthy or untidy place.

pig′tail′ n. a braid of hair.

pike[1] (pīk) n. a large, slender freshwater fish.

pike[2] (pīk) n. a long, heavy spear.

pike[3] (pīk) n. a turnpike.

pik′er n. Slang. a stingy person.

pi′laf (pē′läf, pi läf′) n. a Middle Eastern rice dish.

pi•las′ter (pi las′tər) n. a shallow decorative feature projecting from a wall and imitating the form of a column.

pil′chard (pil′chərd) n. a marine fish, related to the herring.

pile[1] (pīl) n., v., **piled, piling.** —n. **1.** a group of things lying one upon the other. **2.** a large amount of anything. —v.t. **3.** to lay or place in a pile. **4. pile up,** to accumulate.

pile[2] (pīl) n. Also, **pil′ing.** a long beam driven into the ground as part of a foundation or retaining wall.

pile[3] (pīl) n. a soft surface on cloth or rugs, formed by upright threads.

piles (pīlz) n.pl. hemorrhoids.

pil′fer (pil′fər) v.i., v.t. to steal, esp. in small amounts. —**pil′fer•age**, n.

pil′grim (pil′grim, -grəm) n. **1.** a traveler to a sacred place. **2. Pilgrim,** one of the early Puritan settlers in America. —**pil′grim•age**, n.

pill (pil) n. a small tablet or capsule of medicine.

pil′lage (pil′ij) v., -**laged, -laging,** n. —v.t., v.i. **1.** to loot and plunder. —n. **2.** booty or spoils.

pil′lar (pil′ər) n. **1.** a slender vertical structure used as a support or ornament. **2.** a chief supporter of a community, organization, etc.

pill′box′ n. **1.** a box for pills. **2.** a small boxlike fortification for machine guns or antitank weapons.

pil′lo•ry (pil′ə rē) n., pl. -**ries,** v., -**ried, -rying.** —n. **1.** a wooden framework used to confine and expose offenders. —v.t. **2.** to put in the pillory. **3.** to expose to public contempt.

pil′low (pil′ō) n. a cloth case filled with soft material, used to cushion the head. —**pil′low•case′**, n.

pi′lot (pī′lət) n. **1.** a person qualified to operate an aircraft. **2.** a person who steers a ship. **3.** a guide. —v.t. **4.** to act as pilot of. **5.** to steer. —adj. **6.** experimental.

pi′lot•house′ n. an enclosed structure on the deck of a ship.

pi′lot light′ n. a small flame used to relight the main burners.

pi•men′to (pi men′tō) n., pl. -**tos.** the red fruit of a sweet pepper.

pimp (pimp) n. **1.** a person who solicits customers for prostitutes. —v.i. **2.** to act as a pimp.

pim•per′nel (pim′pər nel′, -nl) n. a plant with red, blue, or white flowers.

pim′ple (pim′pəl) n. a small swelling of skin. —**pim′ply**, adj.

pin (pin) n., v., **pinned, pinning.** —n. **1.** a slender pointed piece of metal, wood, etc., for fastening or support. —v.t. **2.** to fasten with a pin. **3.** to hold fast. **4. pin down,** to force (someone) to make a decision.

PIN (pin) n. a personal identification number.

pin′a•fore′ (pin′ə fôr′) n. a sleeveless, apronlike garment worn over a dress or blouse.

pin′ball′ n. a game in which a spring-driven ball rolls against pins on a sloping board.

pince′-nez′ (pans′nā′, pins′-) n., pl. **pince-nez.** eyeglasses held on by a spring that pinches the nose.

pin′cers (pin′sərz) n.pl. **1.** a gripping tool with a pair of pivoted jaws. **2.** a grasping organ, as the claws of a lobster.

pinch (pinch) v.t. **1.** to squeeze tightly between the finger and thumb. **2.** to constrict. **3.** Slang. to steal. —v.i. **4.** to economize. —n. **5.** a pinching. **6.** a tiny amount. **7.** an emergency. —**Idiom. 8. pinch pennies,** to be very frugal.

pinch′-hit′ v.i., -**hit, -hitting.** to substitute for someone.

pine[1] (pīn) n. an evergreen tree with needle-shaped leaves and woody cones containing seeds.

pine[2] (pīn) v.i., **pined, pining. 1.** to yearn painfully. **2.** to fail in health from grief, regret, etc.

pin′e•al gland′ (pin′ē əl) n. a gland in the brain that is involved in biorhythms and gonadal development.

pine′ap•ple (pīn′ap′əl) n. a juicy tropical fruit with spiny-edged leaves.

pin′feath′er n. an undeveloped feather.

ping (ping) v.i. **1.** to produce a sharp sound like a bullet striking metal. —n. **2.** a pinging sound.

Ping′-Pong′ (ping′pong′) Trademark. table tennis.

pin′head′ n. **1.** the head of a pin. **2.** a stupid person.

pin′ion[1] (pin′yən) n. **1.** the wing of a bird. —v.t. **2.** to bind (a person's arms or hands) so they cannot be used.

pin′ion[2] (pin′yən) n. a small cogwheel.

pink (pingk) n. **1.** a pale red. **2.** a fragrant garden plant having pink, white, or red flowers. **3.** the highest degree.

pink′eye′ n. a contagious inflammation of the membrane that covers the eye and lines the eyelid.

pink′ing shears′ n. shears with notched blades.

pin′ mon′ey n. any small sum set aside.

pin′na•cle (pin′ə kəl) n. a lofty peak or position.

pin′nate (pin′āt, -it) adj. (of a leaf) having leaflets on each side of a common stalk.

pi′noch•le (pē′nuk əl, -nok-) n. a game using 48 cards.

pin′point′ v.t. to locate exactly.

pin′stripe′ n. a very thin stripe in fabrics. —**pin′striped′**, adj.

pint (pīnt) n. a liquid and dry measure equal to one-half of a quart.

pin′tle (pin′tl) n. a pin or bolt.

pin′to (pin′tō, pēn′-) adj., n., pl. -**tos.** —adj. **1.** marked with spots of white and other colors. —n. **2.** a pinto horse.

pin′to bean′ n. a bean with pinkish mottled seeds.

pin′wheel′ n. a windmill-like toy that spins on a stick.

pin′yin′ (pin′yin′) n. a system for transliterating Chinese into the Latin alphabet.

pi•o•neer′ (pī′ə nēr′) n. **1.** an early arrival in new territory. **2.** the first one in any effort. —v.i. **3.** to act as a pioneer.

pi′ous (pī′əs) adj. **1.** devout. **2.** hypocritically virtuous. —**pi′ous•ly**, adv.

pip[1] (pip) n. a spot on a playing card, domino, etc.

pip[2] (pip) n. a small fruit seed.

pipe (pīp) n., v., **piped, piping.** —n. **1.** a hollow cylinder for conveying fluid. **2.** a tube with a small bowl at one end for smoking tobacco. **3.** a tube used as a musical instrument. —v.i. **4.** to play on a pipe. —v.t. **5.** to convey by pipe. **6.** to play (music) on a pipe. **7.** to utter in a shrill tone.

pipe′ dream′ n. an unrealistic hope.

pipe′line′ n. **1.** linked pipes for transporting oil, water, etc. **2.** a route for supplies. **3.** a channel of information.

pip′ing n. **1.** pipes. **2.** the sound of pipes. **3.** a kind of trimming for clothing, upholstery, etc.

pip′pin (pip′in) n. a kind of apple.

pip′squeak′ (pip′skwēk′) n. Informal. an unimportant person.

pi′quant (pē′kənt, -känt) adj. **1.** agreeably sharp in taste. **2.** mentally stimulating. —**pi′quan•cy**, n.

pique (pēk) v., **piqued, piquing,** n. —v.t. **1.** to arouse resentment in. **2.** to excite (interest, curiosity, etc.). —n. **3.** an irritated feeling.

pi•qué′ (pi kā′) n. a corded cotton fabric.

pi′ra•cy (pī′rə sē) n., pl. -**cies. 1.** robbery at sea. **2.** the illegal use of copyrighted material.

pi•ra′nha (pi rän′yə, -ran′-, -rä′nə, -ran′ə) n., pl. -**nhas, -nha.** a small predatory South American fish.

pi′rate (pī′rət) n., v., -**rated, -rating.** —n. **1.** a person who practices piracy. —v.t. **2.** to take by piracy. **3.** to reproduce (a book, invention, etc.) without authorization.

pir′ou•ette′ (pir′ŏ̄ et′) n., -**etted, -etting.** —v.i. **1.** to spin on the toes in dancing. —n. **2.** such spinning.

pis′ca•to′ri•al (pis′kə tôr′ē əl) adj. of fishing.

pis′mire (pis′mīr′, piz′-) n. an ant.

pis•ta′chi•o′ (pi stash′ē ō′) n., pl. -**chios.** a nut containing an edible, greenish kernel.

pis′til (pis′tl) n. the seed-bearing organ of a flower. —**pis′til•late** (-t il, -āt′) adj.

pis′tol (pis′tl) n. a short gun fired with one hand.

pis′tol-whip′ v.t., -**whipped, -whipping.** to beat with a pistol.

pis′ton (pis′tən) n. a disk or cylinder sliding within a longer cylinder, as in an engine or pump.

pit[1] (pit) n., v., **pitted, pitting.** —n. **1.** a hole in the ground. **2.** a hollow in a surface. **3. the pits,** Slang. an unpleasant place or situation. **4.** the space in the front of a theater in which the musicians sit. —v.t. **5.** to mark with pits. **6.** to set in opposition.

pit[2] (pit) n., v., **pitted, pitting.** —n. **1.** the stone of a fruit. —v.t. **2.** to remove the pit from.

pi′ta (pē′tə) n. a round, flat bread with a pocket.

pitch[1] (pich) v.t. **1.** to throw. **2.** to set up, as a tent. **3.** to set at a certain point. —v.i. **4.** to fall forward. **5.** to plunge and rise, as a ship. **6. pitch in,** Informal. to contribute to a common cause. —n. **7.** a throw. **8.** relative point or degree. **9.** the degree of height or depth of a musical tone. **10.** the degree of slope. **11.** Informal. a sales talk.

pitch[2] (pich) n. a sticky dark substance from coal tar.

pitch′-black′ adj. extremely black.

pitch′blende′ (-blend′) n. a black mineral that is the principal ore of uranium and radium.

pitch′-dark′ adj. very dark.

pitch′er[1] (pich′ər) n. a container with a handle and spout, for pouring liquids.

pitch′er[2] (pich′ər) n. Baseball. the person who throws the ball to the batter.

pitch′fork′ n. a large, long-handled fork for lifting and pitching hay.

pitch′man n., pl. -**men.** a person who makes a sales pitch.

pitch′ pipe′ n. a small pipe producing pitches when blown into.

pit′e•ous (pit′ē əs) adj. pathetic.

pit′fall′ n. a trap; hazard.

pith (pith) n. **1.** the spongy central tissue in a plant stem. **2.** the important part.

pith′y adj., -**ier, -iest.** brief and forceful in expression.

pit′i•a•ble (pit′ē ə bəl) adj. **1.** deserving pity. **2.** contemptible. —**pit′i•a•bly**, adv.

pit′i•ful (-i fəl) adj. **1.** deserving pity. **2.** arousing contempt. —**pit′i•ful•ly**, adv.

pit′tance (pit′ns) n. a very small amount, esp. of money.

pi•tu′i•tar•y gland′ (pi tŏō′i ter′ē, -tyŏŏ′-) n. a gland at the base of the brain that affects all of the body's hormonal functions.

pit′y (pit′ē) n., pl. -**ies,** v., -**ied, -ying.** —n. **1.** sympathetic sorrow for another's suffering. **2.** cause for regret. —v.t. **3.** to feel pity for. —**pit′i•less**, adj.

piv′ot (piv′ət) n. **1.** a shaft on which something turns. —v.i. **2.** to turn on a pivot. —v.t. **3.** to place on a pivot. —**piv′ot•al**, adj.

pix′el (pik′sal, -sel) n. the smallest element of an image in a video display system.

pi•zazz′ (pə zaz′) n. Informal. **1.** energy. **2.** flair. Also, **pi•zzazz′.**

piz′za (pēt′sə) n. a baked, open-faced pie topped with cheese, tomato sauce, etc.

piz•ze•ri•a (pēt′sə rē′ə) n. a restaurant serving mainly pizza.

piz′zi•ca′to (pit′si kä′tō) adj. Music. played by plucking the strings with the finger.

pkg. package.

pkwy. parkway.

pl. 1. place. **2.** plural.

plac′ard (plak′ärd, -ərd) n. a public sign or notice.

pla′cate (plā′kāt, plak′āt) v.t., -**cated, -cating.** to appease.

place (plās) n., v., **placed, placing.** —n. **1.** a particular portion of space. **2.** any part of a body or surface. **3.** position or situation. **4.** a region. **5.** a building, location, residence, etc. —v.t. **6.** to put in a particular position or situation. **7.** to identify. **8.** to make (a bet, phone call, etc.). —**place′ment**, n.

pla•ce′bo (plə sē′bō) n., pl. -**bos, -boes.** a pill containing no medication, given to reassure a patient or as a control in testing a drug.

pla•cen′ta (plə sen′tə) n. the structure in the uterus which attaches to and nourishes the fetus.

plac′er (plas′ər) n. surface gravel containing gold particles.

plac′id (plas′id) adj. calm; serene. —**pla•cid′i•ty**, n. —**plac′id•ly**, adv.

plack′et (plak′it) n. a slit at the neck, waist, or wrist of a garment.

pla′gia•rize′ (plā′jə rīz′) v.t., v.i., -**rized, -rizing.** to copy and claim as one's own work. —**pla′gia•rism**, n.

plague (plāg) n., v., **plagued, plaguing.** —n. **1.** an often fatal epidemic disease. **2.** any affliction or vexation. —v.t. **3.** to trouble.

plaid (plad) n. a fabric woven in a cross-barred pattern of different colors.

plain (plān) adj. **1.** clear or distinct. **2.** easily understood. **3.** straightforward. **4.** ordinary. **5.** unadorned; simple. **6.** not beautiful. —adv. **7.** clearly and simply. —n. **8.** a level area of land. —**plain′ly**, adv.

plain′clothes′man n., pl. -**men.** a police officer who wears civilian clothes on duty.

plain′song′ n. the music of the early Christian Church, chanted in unison.

plaint (plānt) n. a complaint.

plain′tiff (plān′tif) n. one who brings a suit in a court.

plain′tive (plān′tiv) adj. mournful. —**plain′tive•ly**, adv.

plait (plāt, plat) n. **1.** a braid. **2.** a pleat. —v.t. **3.** to braid. **4.** to pleat.

plan (plan) n., v., **planned, planning.** —n. **1.** a scheme or method of action or arrangement, developed in advance. **2.** an outline, diagram, or sketch. —v.t., v.i. **3.** to make a plan (for). —**plan′ner**, n.

plane[1] (plān) n. **1.** a flat or level surface. **2.** a level of character. **3.** an airplane. —adj. **4.** flat or level.

plane[2] (plān) n., v., **planed, planing.** —n. **1.** a tool for smoothing wood or metal. —v.t. **2.** to smooth with a plane.

plan′et (plan′it) n. any of the nine heavenly bodies revolving around the sun. —**plan′e•tar′y**, adj.

plan′e•tar′i•um (-i târ′ē əm) n., pl. -**iums, -ia.** a building or room with an optical device that projects a representation of the stars and planets on a domed ceiling.

plane′ tree′ n. a large, spreading shade tree, esp. the North American sycamore.

plan′gent (plan′jənt) adj. resounding loudly.

plank (plangk) n. **1.** a long flat piece of timber. **2.** one of the principles in a political platform. —**plank′ing**, n.

plank′ton (plangk′tən) n. microscopic organisms floating in water.

plant (plant) n. **1.** a living organism that has no sense organs and cannot move about. **2.** the buildings, equipment, etc., necessary for an industrial business; factory. —v.t. **3.** to set in the ground for growth. **4.** to place firmly.

plan′tain (plan′tin) n. **1.** a tropical bananalike plant. **2.** a common flat-leaved weed.

plan′tar (plan′tər) adj. of the soles of the feet.

plan•ta′tion (plan tā′shən) n. **1.** a large estate on which crops are cultivated. **2.** a group of planted trees.

plant′er n. **1.** a container for growing plants. **2.** a tool for planting seeds. **3.** a plantation owner.

plaque (plak) n. **1.** a metal plate or tablet attached to a wall as a memorial or an ornament. **2.** a sticky, whitish film formed on tooth surfaces.

plash (plash) n. **1.** a gentle splash. —v.t., v.i. **2.** to splash gently.

plas′ma (plaz′mə) n. the clear liquid part of blood or lymph.

plas′ter (plas′tər) n. **1.** a pasty mix-

ture of lime, sand, and water for covering walls. **2.** a medicinal preparation spread on cloth and applied to the body. —v.t. **3.** to cover or treat with plaster.

plas′ter•board′ n. a material for insulating or covering walls.

plas′ter of Par′is (par′is) n. a powdery form of gypsum used in making plasters and casts.

plas′tic (plas′tik) n. **1.** a synthetic or natural material that is hardened after shaping. **2.** a credit card. —adj. **3.** made of plastic. **4.** able to be molded. —**plas•tic′i•ty** (-tis′ə tē) n.

plas′tic sur′gery n. the branch of surgery dealing with the repair, replacement, or reshaping of parts of the body.

plate (plāt) n., v., **plated, plating.** —n. **1.** a shallow round dish for food. **2.** gold or silver ware. **3.** a thin sheet of metal, plastic, glass, etc. —v.t. **4.** to coat (metal) with a film of gold or silver. **5.** to cover with protective metal plates.

pla•teau′ (pla tō′) n., pl. -**teaus, -teaux** (-tōz′). **1.** an area of high, level land. **2.** a period of little growth.

plate′ glass′ n. thick, smooth glass, as used for windows.

plat′en (plat′n) n. a plate in a printing press that presses the paper against an inked surface.

plat′form (plat′fôrm) n. **1.** a raised flooring or structure. **2.** a set of announced political principles.

plat′i•num (plat′n əm) n. a grayish white metallic element that is resistant to most chemicals.

plat′i•tude′ (plat′i tōōd′, -tyōōd′) n. a trite remark.

pla•ton′ic (plə ton′ik) adj. spiritual, not sexual.

pla•toon′ (plə tōōn′) n. a small military unit.

plat′ter (plat′ər) n. a large, shallow serving dish.

plat′y•fish′ (plat′ē-) n., pl. -**fish, -fishes.** a freshwater fish common in aquariums.

plat′y•pus (plat′i pəs) n., pl. -**puses, -pi** (-pī′). an aquatic, egg-laying Australian mammal having webbed feet and a ducklike bill.

plau′dits (plô′dits) n.pl. an expression of approval; applause.

plau′si•ble (plô′zə bəl) adj. credible; believable. —**plau′si•bil′i•ty**, n.

play (plā) n. **1.** a dramatic work or performance. **2.** recreation. **3.** fun or jest. **4.** freedom of movement. —v.t. **5.** to act the part of. **6.** to engage in (a game). **7.** to employ in a game. **8.** to perform on (a musical instrument). **9.** to perform (music). —v.i. **10.** to amuse oneself. **11.** to take part in a game. **12.** to perform on a musical instrument. **13.** to move about lightly. **14. play down,** to treat as unimportant. **15. ~ out,** to exhaust. **16. ~ up,** to emphasize. —**play′er**, n.

play′back′ n. **1.** a reproduction of a recording. **2.** the apparatus used in producing playbacks.

play′bill′ n. a program or announcement of a play.

play′boy′ n. a man who pursues a life of pleasure without responsibilities or attachments.

play′ date′ n. an appointment made by parents from separate families to have their young children play together.

play′ful (-fəl) adj. **1.** full of fun. **2.** pleasantly humorous. —**play′ful•ly**, adv. —**play′ful•ness**, n.

play′go′er n. a person who goes to the theater.

play′ground′ n. an area used by children for outdoor recreation.

play′house′ n. **1.** a theater. **2.** a small house for children to play in.

play′mate′ n. a companion in play.

play′-off′ n. a series of games played to decide a championship.

play′ on words′ n. a pun.

play′pen′ n. a small enclosure in which a baby can play.

play′thing′ n. a toy.

play′wright′ (-rīt′) n. a writer of plays.

pla′za (plä′zə, plaz′ə) n. **1.** a public square. **2.** a shopping center.

plea (plē) n. **1.** an appeal or entreaty. **2.** a defendant's answer to a charge in a court of law.

plea′ bar′gain n. an agreement in which a criminal defendant pleads guilty to a lesser charge.

plead (plēd) v., **pleaded** or **pled** (pled), **pleading.** —v.i. **1.** to entreat earnestly. **2.** to put forward a plea in a law court. —v.t. **3.** to offer as an excuse. **4.** to argue (a case) in a law court. **5.** to make a plea of. —**plead′er,** *n.*

pleas′ant (plez′ənt) *adj.* agreeable; pleasing. —**pleas′ant·ly,** *adv.*

pleas′ant·ry *n., pl.* **-ries.** a good-humored remark.

please (plēz) *adv., v.,* **pleased, pleasing.** —*adv.* **1.** (used in polite requests) be so kind as to. —*v.t., v.i.* **2.** to give pleasure or satisfaction (to).

pleas′ur·a·ble (plezh′ər ə bəl) *adj.* enjoyable.

pleas′ure *n.* **1.** enjoyment or a source of enjoyment. **2.** one's will or desire.

pleat (plēt) *n.* **1.** a double fold of cloth. —*v.t.* **2.** to fold in pleats.

ple·be′ian (pli bē′ən) *adj.* of the common people.

pleb′i·scite (pleb′ə sīt′) *n.* a direct vote by citizens on a question.

plec′trum (plek′trəm) *n., pl.* **-tra** (-trə), **-trums.** a small piece of metal or plastic for plucking the strings of a musical instrument.

pledge (plej) *n., v.,* **pledged, pledging.** —*n.* **1.** a solemn promise. **2.** something delivered as security on a loan. —*v.t.* **3.** to bind by pledge. **4.** to promise. **5.** to give as a pledge.

Pleis′to·cene′ (plī′stə sēn′) *adj.* pertaining to the geologic epoch forming the earlier half of the Quaternary Period, during which modern humans first appeared.

ple′na·ry (plē′nə rē, plen′ə-) *adj.* full; complete.

plen′i·po·ten′ti·ar′y (plen′ə pə ten′shē er′ē, -shə rē) *n., pl.* **-aries,** *adj.* —*n.* **1.** a diplomat with full authority. —*adj.* **2.** having full authority.

plen′i·tude (plen′i tōōd′, -tyōōd′) *n.* abundance.

plen′ty (plen′tē) *n.* an abundant supply. —*adv.* *Informal.* **2.** very.

pleth′o·ra (pleth′ər ə) *n.* an overabundance.

pleu′ra (plōōr′ə) *n., pl.* **pleur·ae** (plōōr′ē). one of a pair of membranes that cover the lungs and line the chest wall.

pleu′ri·sy (plōōr′ə sē) *n.* inflammation of the pleura.

Plex′i·glas (plek′si glas′) *Trademark.* a light, durable transparent plastic.

plex′us (plek′səs) *n., pl.* **-uses, -us.** a network, as of nerves or blood vessels.

pli′a·ble (plī′ə bəl) *adj.* easily bent or influenced; flexible. —**pli′a·bil′i·ty,** *n.*

pli′ant (-ənt) *adj.* pliable.

pli′ers (plī′ərz) *n.pl.* small pincers for bending wire, holding objects, etc.

plight¹ (plīt) *n.* a distressing condition.

plight² (plīt) *v.t.* to pledge.

PLO Palestine Liberation Organization.

plod (plod) *v.i.,* **plodded, plodding.** **1.** to walk heavily. **2.** to work slowly and steadily. —**plod′der,** *n.*

plop (plop) *v.,* **plopped, plopping.** *n.* —*v.t., v.i.* **1.** to drop with a sound like that of an object hitting water. **2.** to drop with direct impact. —*n.* **3.** a plopping sound or fall.

plot (plot) *n., v.,* **plotted, plotting.** —*n.* **1.** a secret plan. **2.** the main story of a novel, play, etc. **3.** a small piece of ground. —*v.t.* **4.** to plan secretly. **5.** to mark on a map. —*v.i.* **6.** to conspire. —**plot′ter,** *n.*

plov′er (pluv′ər, plō′vər) *n.* a kind of shore bird.

plow (plou) *n.* **1.** an implement for turning soil or for removing snow. —*v.t.* **2.** to turn or remove with a plow. —*v.i.* **3.** to work with a plow. **4.** to make one's way laboriously. Also, **plough.** —**plow′man,** *n.*

plow′share′ *n.* the blade of a plow.

ploy (ploi) *n.* a clever maneuver.

pluck (pluk) *v.t.* **1.** to pull out (feathers, flowers, etc.) from a fixed position. **2.** to sound (the strings of a musical instrument). —*n.* **3.** a pull or tug. **4.** courage.

pluck′y *adj.,* **-ier, -iest.** courageous.

plug (plug) *n., v.,* **plugged, plugging.** —*n.* **1.** an object for stopping a hole. **2.** an attachment for an electrical cord that establishes contact in a socket. **3.** favorable mention. —*v.t.* **4.** to stop with a plug. **5.** to mention favorably. —*v.i.* **6.** to work steadily. **7. plug in,** to connect to a power source.

plum (plum) *n.* **1.** a juicy round

fruit with a smooth skin. **2.** a deep purple. **3.** a desirable thing.

plum′age (plōō′mij) *n.* the feathers of a bird.

plumb (plum) *n.* **1.** a small weight suspended by a line (**plumb′ line′**) and used to measure depth or to ascertain a vertical line. —*adj.* **2.** perpendicular. —*adv.* **3.** vertically. **4.** exactly. **5.** completely. —*v.t.* **6.** to test by a plumb line. **7.** to examine closely.

plumb′er *n.* a person who installs and repairs plumbing.

plumb′ing *n.* the system of water pipes and drains in a building.

plume (plōōm) *n., v.,* **plumed, pluming.** —*n.* **1.** a large feather. **2.** an ornamental tuft. —*v.t.* **3.** to preen. **4.** to adorn with plumes.

plum′met (plum′it) *n.* **1.** the weight on a plumb line. —*v.i.* **2.** to plunge.

plump¹ (plump) *adj.* having a full, rounded form. —**plump′ness,** *n.*

plump² (plump) *v.i., v.t.* **1.** to drop heavily. —*n.* **2.** a heavy fall. —*adv.* **3.** heavily. **4.** directly.

plun′der (plun′dər) *v.t.* **1.** to rob by force, as in war. —*n.* **2.** a plundering. **3.** something taken in plundering.

plunge (plunj) *v.,* **plunged, plunging,** *n.* —*v.t., v.i.* **1.** to thrust suddenly into something. —*v.i.* **2.** to fall or cast oneself into water from a height. **3.** to rush or dash. —*n.* **4.** an act or instance of plunging.

plung′er *n.* **1.** a pistonlike part moving within the cylinder of certain machines. **2.** a device with a handle and suction cup, used to unclog drains.

plunk (plungk) *v.t.* **1.** to throw or drop heavily. —*v.i.* **2.** to give forth a twanging sound. —*n.* **3.** the sound of plunking.

plu′ral (plōōr′əl) *adj.* **1.** of, being, or containing more than one. —*n.* **2.** a plural form. —**plur′al·ize′,** *v.t., v.i.*

plu′ral·ism *n.* a condition in which minority groups participate in society, yet maintain their distinctions.

plu·ral′i·ty (plōō ral′i tē) *n., pl.* **-ties.** **1.** in an election with three or more candidates, the excess of votes received by the leading candidate over those received by the next candidate. **2.** a majority.

plus (plus) *prep.* **1.** increased by. —*adj.* **2.** involving addition. **3.** positive. —*n.* **4.** something additional.

plush (plush) *n.* **1.** a velvetlike fabric having a deep pile. —*adj.* **2.** luxurious.

Plu′to (plōō′tō) *n.* **1.** the planet ninth from the sun. **2.** the Roman god of the underworld.

plu′to·crat′ (plōō′tə krat′) *n.* **1.** a wealthy person. **2.** a member of a wealthy governing class. —**plu·toc′ra·cy** (-tok′rə sē) *n.*

plu·to′ni·um (plōō tō′nē əm) *n.* a radioactive metallic element.

plu′vi·al (plōō′vē əl) *adj.* of rain.

ply¹ (plī) *v.,* **plied, plying.** —*v.t.* **1.** to work with busily. **2.** to carry on, as a trade. **3.** to offer something pressingly to. **4.** to travel along regularly. —*v.i.* **5.** to travel regularly between certain places. **6.** to perform one's work busily.

ply² (plī) *n., pl.* **plies.** a thickness.

ply′wood′ *n.* a building material consisting of sheets of wood glued over each other.

p.m. after noon. Also, **P.M.**

PMS premenstrual syndrome.

pneu·mat′ic (nōō mat′ik, nyōō-) *adj.* **1.** of gases. **2.** operated by air.

pneu·mo′nia (nōō mōn′yə, nyōō-) *n.* inflammation of the lungs.

P.O. post office.

poach¹ (pōch) *v.i., v.t.* to take (game or fish) illegally. —**poach′er,** *n.*

poach² (pōch) *v.t.* to cook (eggs, fish, etc.) in a small amount of simmering liquid.

pock′et (pok′it) *n.* **1.** a small pouch sewed on or into a garment. **2.** a pouchlike receptacle or cavity. **3.** an isolated group or area. —*adj.* **4.** small. —*v.t.* **5.** to put into one's pocket. **6.** to take as one's own, usu. dishonestly.

pock′et·book′ *n.* a purse.

pock′et·knife′ *n.* a small folding knife.

pock′mark′ (pok′märk′) *n.* a scar from acne, chickenpox, etc.

pod (pod) *n.* a long, narrow seed vessel.

po·di′a·try (pə dī′ə trē) *n.* the diagnosis and treatment of foot disorders. —**po·di′a·trist,** *n.*

po′di·um (pō′dē əm) *n., pl.* **-diums, -dia** (-dē ə). a small raised platform.

po′em (pō′əm) *n.* a composition in verse.

po·e·sy (-ə sē) *n.* poetry.

po′et (pō′it) *n.* one who writes poetry.

po′et·as·ter (-as′tər) *n.* an inferior poet.

poet′ic jus′tice *n.* a fitting distribution of rewards and punishments.

poet′ic li′cense *n.* liberty taken by a writer in deviating from fact to produce a desired effect.

po′et·ry (-i trē) *n.* **1.** poems collectively. **2.** the art of writing poems. **3.** poetic qualities. —**po·et′ic** (pō-et′ik), **po·et′i·cal,** *adj.*

po·grom′ (pə grum′, -grom′) *n.* an organized massacre.

poign′ant (poin′yənt) *adj.* **1.** keenly distressing. **2.** affecting the emotions. —**poign′an·cy,** *n.*

poin·ci·an′a (poin′sē an′ə) *n., pl.* **-as.** a tropical tree with showy red, orange, or yellow flowers.

poin·set′ti·a (poin set′ē ə, -set′ə) *n., pl.* **-as.** a tropical plant with scarlet, white, or pink flowers.

point (point) *n.* **1.** a sharp end. **2.** a projecting part. **3.** a dot. **4.** a definite position or time. **5.** a compass direction. **6.** a basic reason, purpose, etc. **7.** a detail. **8.** a unit in accounting, scoring, etc. —*v.t.* **9.** to indicate. **10.** to direct (the finger, a weapon, etc.). —*v.i.* **11.** to indicate position or direction. **12.** to be directed. —*Idiom.* **13. beside the point,** irrelevant. **14. to the point,** relevant.

point′-blank′ *adj.* **1.** direct; plain. —*adv.* **2.** directly.

point′ed *adj.* **1.** having a point. **2.** sharp. **3.** aimed at a particular person. **4.** emphasized.

point′er *n.* **1.** one that points. **2.** a long stick for pointing. **3.** a breed of hunting dog.

poin′til·lism (pwan′tl iz′əm) *n.* the technique in painting of using dots of pure color that are optically mixed into the resulting hue by the viewer.

point′less *adj.* futile.

poise (poiz) *n., v.,* **poised, poising.** —*n.* **1.** balance. **2.** a dignified, self-confident manner. —*v.t., v.i.* **3.** to balance or be balanced.

poi′son (poi′zən) *n.* **1.** a substance that kills or harms seriously. —*v.t.* **2.** to kill or injure with poison. **3.** to put poison in or on. —**poi′son·er,** *n.* —**poi′son·ous,** *adj.*

poi′son i′vy *n.* **1.** a vine or shrub having shiny leaves with three leaflets. **2.** a rash caused by touching poison ivy.

poke (pōk) *v.,* **poked, poking,** *n.* —*v.t.* **1.** to prod with something pointed. **2.** to thrust. —*v.i.* **3.** to make a thrusting movement. **4.** to pry. —*n.* **5.** a thrust or push.

pok′er¹ (pō′kər) *n.* a rod for stirring a fire.

pok′er² (pō′kər) *n.* a gambling card game.

pok′er-faced′ *adj.* showing no emotion or intention.

pok′y (pō′kē) *adj.,* **pokier, pokiest.** slow; dull. Also, **poke′y.**

po′lar (pō′lər) *adj.* **1.** of the North or South Pole. **2.** of magnetic poles. —**po·lar′i·ty,** *n.*

po′lar bear′ *n.* a white arctic bear.

Po·lar′is (pō lâr′is, -lar′-, pə-) *n.* the bright star close to the north pole of the heavens.

po·lar·i·za′tion (-lər ə zā′shən) *n.* **1.** the division of a group into opposing factions. **2.** a state in which rays of light exhibit different properties in different directions. —**po′lar·ize′,** *v.t., v.i.*

pole¹ (pōl) *n., v.,* **poled, poling.** —*n.* **1.** a long slender rod. —*v.t.* **2.** to propel with a pole.

pole² (pōl) *n.* **1.** each end of the axis of a sphere, esp. the earth. **2.** one of two opposite principles.

pole′cat′ *n.* **1.** a European mammal that ejects a bad-smelling fluid. **2.** a skunk.

po·lem′ics (pə lem′iks) *n.* the art or practice of debate. —**po·lem′ic,** *n., adj.* —**po·lem′i·cist,** *n.*

pole′ vault′ *n.* an athletic event in which a vault over a horizontal bar is performed with a long pole.

po·lice′ (pə lēs′) *n., v.,* **-liced, -licing.** —*n.* **1.** an organized civil force for keeping order and enforcing the law. —*v.t.* **2.** to keep in order. —**po·lice′man, po·lice′wom·an,** *n.*

pol′i·cy¹ (pol′ə sē) *n., pl.* **-cies.** a definite course of action.

pol′i·cy² (pol′ə sē) *n., pl.* **-cies.** an insurance contract.

po·li·o·my′e·li′tis (pō′lē ō mī′ə-

lī′tis) *n.* an infectious viral disease of the spinal cord, often resulting in paralysis. Also called **po′li·o′.**

pol′ish (pol′ish) *v.t.* **1.** to make glossy. **2.** to make refined. —*n.* **3.** a polishing substance. **4.** a gloss. **5.** refinement.

Pol′ish (pō′lish) *n.* **1.** the language or people of Poland. —*adj.* **2.** of Poland, its inhabitants, or their language.

po·lite′ (pə līt′) *adj.* showing good manners. —**po·lite′ly,** *adv.*

pol′i·tesse′ (pol′i tes′, pô′lē-) *n.* politeness.

pol′i·tic (pol′i tik) *adj.* **1.** prudent; expedient. **2.** political.

po·lit′i·cal (pə lit′i kal) *adj.* of government or politics. —**po·lit′i·cal·ly,** *adv.*

polit′ically correct′ *adj.* marked by a progressive attitude on issues of race, gender, etc. —**polit′ical correct′ness,** *n.*

polit′ical sci′ence *n.* the social science dealing with political institutions and government.

pol·i·ti′cian (pol′i tish′ən) *n.* a person who is active in politics, esp. as a career.

po·lit′i·cize′ (pə lit′ə sīz′) *v.t.,* **-cized, -cizing.** to give a political character to.

pol′i·tick′ing (pol′i tik′ing) *n.* political campaigning.

pol′i·tics (pol′i tiks) *n.* **1.** the science or conduct of government. **2.** political affairs, methods, or principles.

pol′ka (pōl′kə, pō′kə) *n.* a lively dance for couples.

pol′ka dot′ *n.* a pattern of dots.

poll (pōl) *n.* **1.** a sampling of public opinion. **2. polls,** the place where people vote. **3.** the act of voting or the votes cast in an election. **4.** a list of individuals, as for voting. —*v.t.* **5.** to take a sampling of the opinions of. **6.** to receive at the polls, as votes.

pol′len (pol′ən) *n.* the powdery fertilizing element of flowers.

pol′li·nate′ (-ə nāt′) *v.t.,* **-nated, -nating.** to convey pollen to the stigma of (a flower). —**pol′li·na′tion,** *n.*

pol′li·wog′ (pol′ē wog′) *n.* a tadpole.

poll′ster (pōl′stər) *n.* a person who takes public-opinion polls.

pol·lute′ (pə lōōt′) *v.t.,* **-luted, -luting.** to contaminate or make foul, as with chemicals or waste products. —**pol·lu′tion,** *n.* —**pol·lut′ant,** *n.*

po′lo (pō′lō) *n., pl.* **-los.** a game played on horseback by two teams who drive a ball with long-handled mallets.

pol′o·naise′ (pol′ə nāz′,pō′lə-) *n.* a slow dance or music for this.

pol′troon′ (pol trōōn′) *n.* a coward.

pol·ter·geist′ (pōl′tər gīst′) *n.* a noisy spirit that throws things about.

pol·troon′ (pol trōōn′) *n.* a coward.

poly- a prefix meaning many.

pol′y·an′dry (pol′ē an′drē) *n.* the practice of having more than one husband at a time.

pol′y·es′ter (pol′ē es′tər) *n.* a polymer used to make plastics, textiles, etc.

pol′y·eth′yl·ene′ (-eth′ə lēn′) *n.* a plastic polymer used esp. for containers and packaging.

po·lyg′a·my (pə lig′ə mē) *n.* the practice of having more than one spouse, esp. a wife, at one time. —**po·lyg′a·mist,** *n.* —**po·lyg′a·mous,** *adj.*

pol′y·glot′ (pol′ē glot′) *adj.* able to speak, read, or write several languages.

pol′y·gon′ (pol′ē gon′) *n.* a figure having three or more straight sides.

pol′y·graph′ (pol′i graf′) *n.* a lie detector.

pol′y·he′dron (pol′ē hē′drən) *n., pl.* **-drons, -dra** (-drə). a solid figure having four or more sides.

pol′y·math′ (pol′ē math′) *n.* a person of great learning in several fields.

pol′y·mer (pol′ə mər) *n.* a compound formed by the combination of many smaller molecules. —**pol′y·mer·i·za′tion,** *n.*

pol′y·no′mi·al (pol′ə nō′mē əl) *n.* an algebraic expression consisting of two or more terms.

pol′yp (pol′ip) *n.* **1.** a projecting growth from a mucous surface. **2.** a cylindrical water animal with tentacles.

same time. —**pol′y·phon′ic** (pol′ē-fon′ik) *adj.*

pol′y·sty′rene (pol′ē stī′rēn, -stēr′ēn) *n.* a polymer used in molded objects and as an insulator.

pol′y·syl·lab′ic *adj.* consisting of many syllables.

pol′y·tech′nic (-tek′nik) *adj.* offering instruction in many applied sciences, technical subjects, etc.

pol′y·the·ism *n.* belief in more than one god.

pol′y·un·sat′u·rat′ed *adj.* of a class of fats associated with low cholesterol content.

po·made′ (po mād′, -mäd′) *n.* a hair ointment.

pome′gran′ate (pom′gran′it, pom′i-) *n.* a round, red fruit with many seeds.

pom′mel (pum′əl, pom′-) *n., v.,* **-meled, -meling.** —*n.* **1.** a knob on the hilt of a sword or the front of a saddle. —*v.t.* **2.** to pummel.

pomp (pomp) *n.* stately display.

pom′pa·dour′ (pom′pə dôr′, -dōr′) *n.* an arrangement of hair in which it is brushed up high from the forehead.

pom·pa·no′ (pom′pə nō′) *n., pl.* **-nos, -no.** a fish inhabiting waters off the S Atlantic and Gulf states.

pom′pom′ (pom′pom′) *n.* an ornamental tuft.

pomp′ous (pom′pəs) *adj.* full of ostentatious self-importance or dignity. —**pom·pos′i·ty** (-pos′i tē) *n.* —**pomp′ous·ly,** *adv.*

pon′cho (pon′chō) *n., pl.* **-chos.** a blanketlike cloak.

pond (pond) *n.* a small lake.

pon′der (pon′dər) *v.i., v.t.* to consider (something) thoughtfully.

pon′der·ous *adj.* not graceful.

pone (pōn) *n.* unleavened corn bread.

pon·gee′ (pon jē′) *n.* a silk fabric.

pon′iard (pon′yərd) *n.* a dagger.

pon′tiff (pon′tif) *n.* **1.** the pope. **2.** any chief priest; bishop. —**pon·tif′i·cal,** *adj.*

pon·tif′i·cate′ (pon tif′i kāt′) *v.i.,* **-cated, -cating.** to speak with an affected air of authority.

pon·toon′ (pon tōōn′) *n.* a floating support.

po′ny (pō′nē) *n., pl.* **-nies.** a small horse.

po′ny·tail′ *n.* hair gathered and fastened at the back of the head so as to hang freely.

poo′dle (pōōd′l) *n.* a kind of dog with thick, curly hair.

pool¹ (pōōl) *n.* **1.** a small pond. **2.** a collection of liquid on a surface. **3.** a large basin filled with water for swimming.

pool² (pōōl) *n.* **1.** a game resembling billiards. **2.** a combination of resources, funds, etc., available for sharing. **3.** a shared facility or resource. —*v.t.* **4.** to put into a common fund or supply.

poop (pōōp) *n.* the upper deck on the stern of a ship.

poor (pōōr) *adj.* **1.** having little money. **2.** not very good. **3.** unfortunate.

pop¹ (pop) *v.,* **popped, popping.** —*v.i.* **1.** to make or burst with a quick, explosive sound. **2.** to come or go suddenly. —*v.t.* **3.** to burst quickly. —*n.* **4.** a quick, explosive sound. **5.** a fizzy soft drink.

pop² (pop) *adj.* **1.** of popular songs or art. **2.** reflecting the tastes of the general public. —*n.* **3.** popular music.

pop′corn′ *n.* a kind of corn whose kernels burst in dry heat.

pope (pōp) *n.* (*often cap.*) the bishop of Rome as the head of the Roman Catholic Church.

pop′in·jay′ (pop′in jā′) *n.* a vain, shallow person.

pop′lar (pop′lar) *n.* any of several tall, slender, fast-growing trees.

pop′lin (pop′lin) *n.* a plain, usu. cotton fabric.

pop′o·ver *n.* a puffy, hollow muffin.

pop′py (pop′ē) *n., pl.* **-pies.** a plant with showy, usu. red flowers.

pop′py·cock′ *n.* nonsense.

pop′u·lace (pop′yə ləs) *n.* the general public.

pop′u·lar (-lər) *adj.* **1.** generally liked and approved. **2.** of the people. **3.** prevalent. —**pop′u·lar′i·ty** (-lar′i tē) *n.* —**pop′u·lar·ize′,** *v.t.* —**pop′u·lar·ly,** *adv.*

pop′u·late′ (-lāt′) *v.t.,* **-lated, -lating.**

pop′u·la′tion *n.* the total number of persons inhabiting a given area.

pop′u·lism *n.* a political philosophy or movement promoting the interests of the common people. —**pop′u·list,** n.

pop′u·lous adj. with many inhabitants.

por′ce·lain (pôr′sə lin, pôrs′lin) n. glassy ceramic ware; china.

porch (pôrch) n. **1.** an open or enclosed room attached to the outside of a house. **2.** a covered entrance to a building.

por·cine (pôr′sīn) adj. of or like swine.

por′cu·pine′ (pôr′kyə pīn′) n. a large rodent with stiff, sharp quills.

pore[1] (pôr) v., pored, poring. pore over, to ponder or study intently.

pore[2] (pôr) n. a minute opening, as in the skin.

pork (pôrk) n. the flesh of hogs as food.

pork′ bar′rel n. government money for local improvements intended to ingratiate legislators with their constituents.

por·nog′ra·phy (pôr nog′rə fē) n. writings, photographs, etc., intended to cause sexual excitement. —**por′no·graph′ic** (-nə graf′ik) adj. —**por·nog′ra·pher,** n.

po′rous (pôr′əs) adj. permeable by water, air, etc. —**po′rous·ness,** n.

por′phy·ry (pôr′fə rē) n., pl. -ries. a hard purplish red rock.

por′poise (pôr′pəs) n. an aquatic mammal with a blunt, rounded snout.

por′ridge (pôr′ij, por′-) n. a thick cereal made of boiled oatmeal.

por′rin·ger (pôr′in jər, por′-) n. a small dish for soup, porridge, etc.

port[1] (pôrt) n. **1.** a place where ships load or unload. **2.** a harbor.

port[2] (pôrt) n. **1.** the left side of a vessel, facing forward. —adj. **2.** of or on the left side.

port[3] (pôrt) n. a sweet, dark red wine.

port[4] (pôrt) n. **1.** an opening in a ship's side. **2.** a data connection in a computer to which a peripheral device can be attached.

port′a·ble adj. readily carried.

por′tage (pôr′tij, pôr täzh′) n. **1.** an overland route between navigable streams. **2.** the carrying of boats, supplies, etc., over such a route.

por′tal (pôr′tl) n. a door or gate, esp. a large one.

port·cul′lis (pôrt kul′is) n. a heavy iron grating at the gateway of a castle.

por·tend′ (pôr tend′) v.t. to indicate in advance.

por′tent (-tent) n. **1.** an omen. **2.** threatening or disquieting significance. —**por·ten′tous,** adj.

por′ter (pôr′tər) n. **1.** a railroad attendant. **2.** a baggage carrier. **3.** a person who cleans or maintains a building, store, etc.

por′ter·house′ n. a choice cut of beefsteak.

port·fo′li·o′ (pôrt fō′lē ō′) n., pl. -lios. **1.** a flat, portable case for carrying loose sheets of paper. **2.** a collection of one's work, as drawings, photographs, etc. **3.** the investments held by one person.

port′hole′ n. a small, round window in a ship's side.

por′ti·co′ (pôr′ti kō′) n., pl. -coes, -cos. a structure with a roof supported by columns.

por·tiere′ (pôr tyâr′, -tēr′) n. a curtain hung in a doorway. Also, **por·tière.′**

por′tion (pôr′shən) n. **1.** a part of a whole. **2.** a share. —v.t. **3.** to divide into shares.

port′ly (pôrt′lē) adj., -lier, -liest. rather heavy and dignified. —**port′li·ness,** n.

port·man′teau (pôrt man′tō) n., pl. -teaus, -teaux (-tōz, tō). a leather trunk opening into two halves.

por′trait (pôr′trit, -trāt) n. a picture, sculpture, etc., showing a specific person. —**por′trai·ture** (-tri chər) n.

por·tray′ (pôr trā′) v.t. **1.** to make a picture of. **2.** to depict in words. **3.** to represent on the stage. —**por·tray′al,** n.

Por′tu·guese′ (-chə gēz′, -gēs′) adj., n., pl. -guese. —adj. **1.** of Portugal, its inhabitants, or their language. —n. **2.** a native of Portugal. **3.** the language of Portugal and Brazil.

Por′tuguese man′-of-war′ n. a poisonous marine animal.

por′tu·la′ca (pôr′chə lak′ə) n., pl. -as. a low-growing garden plant with showy flowers.

pose (pōz) v., posed, posing, n. —v.i. **1.** to assume or hold a physi-

cal position, attitude, or character. **2.** to pretend to be what one is not. —v.t. **3.** to place in a specific position. **4.** to ask (a question). —n. **5.** a position or character assumed.

po′ser n. **1.** a person who poses, as for an artist. **2.** a difficult question.

po·seur′ (pō zûr′) n. an affected person.

posh (posh) adj. elegant; luxurious.

pos′it (poz′it) v.t. to lay down or assume as a fact or principle.

po·si′tion (pə zish′ən) n. **1.** the place occupied by a person or thing. **2.** an opinion on a question. **3.** situation. **4.** rank. **5.** a job. —v.t. **6.** to place.

pos′i·tive (poz′i tiv) adj. **1.** definite; certain. **2.** affirmative. **3.** confident. **4.** constructive. **5.** (of a quantity) greater than zero. **6.** deficient in electrons. **7.** revealing the presence of the thing tested for. **8.** denoting the first degree of comparison of an adjective or adverb. —n. **9.** something positive. **10.** a photographic image. —**pos′i·tive·ly,** adv.

pos′i·tron′ (poz′i tron′) n. a particle with the same mass as an electron but a positive charge.

posse (pos′ē) n. a body of persons assisting a sheriff.

pos·sess′ (pə zes′) v.t. **1.** to have under ownership or domination. **2.** to have as a quality. **3.** to control or dominate. —**pos·ses′sor,** n.

pos·sessed′ adj. controlled by a strong feeling or by the supernatural.

pos·ses′sion n. **1.** a possessing or being possessed. **2.** a thing possessed. **3.** possessions, property. **4.** a territory governed by a state.

pos·ses′sive adj. **1.** desiring to dominate another. **2.** of the grammatical case indicating ownership. —n. **3.** the possessive case.

pos′si·ble (pos′ə bəl) adj. that may be, happen, be done, etc. —**pos′si·bil′i·ty,** n. —**pos′si·bly,** adv.

pos′sum (pos′əm) n. an opossum.

post[1] (pōst) n. **1.** an upright support of timber or metal. **2.** a message sent to a newsgroup. —v.t. **3.** to attach (a notice) to a wall. **4.** to make publicly known, as by a poster. **5.** to send (a message) to a newsgroup.

post[2] (pōst) n. **1.** a position of duty, trust, etc. **2.** a station for soldiers or traders. —v.t. **3.** to station at a post. **4.** to provide, as bail.

post[3] (pōst) n. **1.** Chiefly Brit. mail. —v.t. **2.** to inform. **3.** to enter in a ledger. **4.** Chiefly Brit. to mail.

post- a prefix meaning: after or behind.

post′age (pō′stij) n. the charge for mailing.

post′al (pōs′tl) adj. concerning mail.

post·bel′lum (-bel′əm) adj. after a war, esp. the U.S. Civil War.

post′card′ n. a small notecard usu. having a picture on one side and space for a stamp, address, and message on the other.

post·date′ (pōst dāt′, pōst′-) v.t., -dated, -dating. **1.** to mark with a date later than the actual date. **2.** to follow in time.

post′er (pō′stər) n. a large sign, notice, or picture announcing something.

pos·te′ri·or (po stēr′ē ər, pō-) adj. **1.** situated behind. **2.** coming after. —n. **3.** the buttocks.

pos·ter′i·ty (po ster′i tē) n. one's descendants.

post′ exchange′ n. a retail store on a military base.

post·grad′u·ate (pōst graj′ŏŏ it, -āt′) n. **1.** a student taking advanced work after graduation. —adj. **2.** of postgraduates.

post′haste′ adv. speedily.

post′hu·mous (pos′chə məs, -chŏŏ-) adj. occurring after a person's death.

pos·til′ion (pō stil′yən, po)- n. a person who rides the leading left horse of those pulling a carriage.

post′mark′ n. **1.** an official mark on a piece of mail showing the place and time of mailing. —v.t. **2.** to stamp with a postmark.

post′mas′ter n. the official in charge of a post office.

post me·rid′i·em′ (mə rid′ē əm, -em′) adj. after noon.

post′mis′tress n. a woman in charge of a post office.

post·mod′ern adj. pertaining to late-20th-century artistic movements that developed in reaction to modernism.

post·mor′tem (-môr′təm) adj. **1.**

of or occurring in the time after death. —n. **2.** an examination of the body after death; autopsy.

post·na′tal (-nāt′l) adj. after childbirth.

post′ of′fice n. a place where mail is handled, stamps are sold, etc.

post′paid′ adv., adj. with the postage paid in advance.

post·par′tum (-pär′təm) adj. following childbirth.

post·pone′ (pōst pōn′, pōs-) v.t., -poned, -poning. to put off to a later time. —**post·pone′ment,** n.

post·pran′di·al (-pran′dē əl) adj. after a meal.

post′script′ n. a note added to a letter that has already been signed.

pos′tu·late′ v., -lated, -lating, n. —v.t. (pos′chə lāt′) **1.** to assume the truth of as a basis for reasoning. —n. (-lit) **2.** something postulated.

pos′ture (pos′chər) n., v., -tured, -turing. —n. **1.** the position or carriage of the body. —v.i. **2.** to strike a pose.

post′war′ adj. after a war.

po′sy (pō′zē) n., pl. -sies. a flower or bouquet.

pot[1] (pot) n., v., potted, potting. —n. **1.** a round deep container for cooking, serving, etc. **2.** a flowerpot. —v.t. **3.** to put into a pot. —**Idiom. 4. go to pot,** to become ruined.

pot[2] (pot) n. Slang. marijuana.

po′ta·ble (pō′tə bəl) adj. drinkable.

pot′ash′ (pot′ash′) n. potassium carbonate, esp. from wood ashes.

po·tas′si·um (pə tas′ē əm) n. a silvery white metallic element.

po·ta′tion (pō tā′shən) n. a drink.

po·ta′to (pə tā′tō, -tə) n., pl. -toes. the edible tuber of a cultivated plant.

pot′bel′ly n., pl. -lies. a belly that sticks out. —**pot′bel′lied,** adj.

pot′boil′er n. a mediocre work of literature or art produced merely for financial gain.

po′tent (pōt′nt) adj. **1.** powerful. **2.** (of a male) capable of sexual intercourse. —**po′ten·cy,** n.

po′ten·tate′ (-tāt′) n. a powerful person, as a monarch.

po·ten′tial (pə ten′shəl) adj. **1.** capable of being developed. —n. **2.** possibility. **3.** a latent ability that may or may not be developed. —**po·ten′tial·ly,** adv.

poth′er (poth′ər) n. **1.** commotion. —v.t., v.i. **2.** to bother.

pot′hole′ n. a hole formed in pavement.

po′tion (pō′shən) n. a medicinal or magical drink.

pot′luck′ n. **1.** a meal to which people bring food to be shared. **2.** whatever is available.

pot·pour′ri′ (pō′pŏŏ rē′) n. **1.** a fragrant mixture of dried flowers and spices. **2.** any miscellaneous grouping.

pot′sherd′ (pot′shûrd′) n. a pottery fragment.

pot′shot′ n. **1.** a casual or aimless shot. **2.** a random or incidental criticism.

pot′tage (pot′ij) n. a thick soup.

pot′ter (pot′ər) n. a person who makes earthen pots.

pot′ter's field′ n. a burial ground for the poor.

pot′ter·y n., pl. -teries. **1.** earthenware. **2.** a place where earthen vessels are made.

pouch (pouch) n. a small bag or sack or something shaped like this.

poul′tice (pōl′tis) n. a soft moist mass applied as medicine.

poul′try (pōl′trē) n. domestic fowl.

pounce (pouns) v., pounced, pouncing, n. —v.i. **1.** to swoop down or spring suddenly. **2.** to seize eagerly. —n. **3.** a sudden swoop.

pound[1] (pound) v.t. **1.** to strike repeatedly and heavily. **2.** to crush by pounding. —v.i. **3.** to beat heavily, as the heart. **4.** to run heavily.

pound[2] (pound) n., pl. pounds, pound. **1.** a unit of weight: in the U.S., **pound avoirdupois** (16 ounces) and **pound troy** (12 ounces). **2.** the British monetary unit.

pound[3] (pound) n. an enclosure for stray animals or for impounded vehicles.

pound′ cake′ n. a rich, sweet cake.

pour (pôr) v.t. **1.** to send (a liquid) flowing. **2.** to emit or utter continuously. —v.i. **3.** to flow along. **4.** to rain heavily.

pout (pout) v.i. **1.** to thrust out the

lips in displeasure or sullenness. —n. **2.** a sullen look or mood.

pov′er·ty (pov′ər tē) n. **1.** the state of being poor. **2.** a lack.

POW pl. **POWs, POW's.** prisoner of war.

pow′der (pou′dər) n. **1.** a solid substance crushed to fine loose particles. —v.t. **2.** to reduce to powder. **3.** to apply powder to. —**pow′der·y,** adj.

pow′der keg′ n. **1.** a container for gunpowder. **2.** an explosive situation.

pow′er (pou′ər) n. **1.** ability to act. **2.** strength. **3.** authority. **4.** a person, nation, etc., having great influence. **5.** mechanical energy. **6.** the product of repeated multiplications of a number by itself. **7.** the magnifying capacity of an optical instrument. —v.t. **8.** to supply with power. —**pow′er·ful,** adj.

pow′er·house′ n. **1.** a building where electricity is generated. **2.** a dynamic person.

pow′er of attor′ney n. a written legal authorization for another person to act in one's place.

pox (poks) n. a disease marked by skin eruptions.

pp. 1. pages. **2.** past participle.

ppd. 1. postpaid. **2.** prepaid.

P.P.S. an additional postscript.

PR public relations.

prac′ti·ca·ble (prak′ti kə bəl) adj. able to be put into practice.

prac′ti·cal adj. **1.** of or resulting from practice or action as opposed to theory. **2.** suitable for use. **3.** levelheaded. **4.** virtual. —**prac′ti·cal′i·ty,** n.

prac′ti·cal·ly adv. **1.** almost. **2.** in a practical way.

prac′tice (-tis) n., v., -ticed, -ticing. —n. **1.** a habitual or customary way of doing something. **2.** the action of doing something. **3.** repeated performance to acquire skill. **4.** the exercise of a profession. —v.t. **5.** to do habitually or repeatedly or as a profession. —v.i. **6.** to do something repeatedly to acquire skill. Also, Brit., **prac′tise** (for defs. 5–6).

prac′ti·cum (-ti kəm) n. a course of study devoted to practical experience in a field.

prac·ti′tion·er (-tish′ə nər) n. a person engaged in a profession.

prag·mat′ic (prag mat′ik) adj. concerned with practical values and results. —**prag′ma·tism,** n. —**prag′ma·tist,** n.

prai′rie (prâr′ē) n. a broad, flat, treeless grassland.

prai′rie dog′ n. a burrowing squirrel of W North America.

prai′rie schoon′er n. a covered wagon used by the pioneers crossing North America.

praise (prāz) n., v., praised, praising. —n. **1.** words of strong approval. **2.** worship of God. —v.t. **3.** to express approval of. **4.** to worship. —**praise′wor′thy,** adj.

pra′line (prā′lēn, prä′-) n. a confection of caramelized nuts and sugar.

pram (pram) n. Chiefly Brit. a baby carriage.

prance (prans) v., pranced, prancing, n. —v.i. **1.** to step about gaily or proudly. —n. **2.** the act of prancing.

prank (prangk) n. a playful trick. —**prank′ster,** n.

prate (prāt) v.i., v.t., prated, prating. to talk foolishly.

prat′fall′ (prat′fôl′) n. a fall on the buttocks.

prat′tle (prat′l) v., -tled, -tling, n. —v.i., v.t. **1.** to talk in a foolish or childish way. —n. **2.** chatter.

prawn (prôn) n. a large shrimplike shellfish.

pray (prā) v.i. **1.** to say prayers. —v.t. **2.** to entreat earnestly.

prayer (prâr) n. **1.** a devout petition to or spiritual communication with God. **2.** a petition.

pre- a prefix meaning before or in front of.

preach (prēch) v.t. **1.** to deliver (a sermon). **2.** to advocate. —v.i. **3.** to preach a sermon. **4.** to advise in a tedious or moralizing way. —**preach′er,** n. —**preach′y,** adj.

pre·am′ble (prē′am′bəl, prē am′-) n. an introductory declaration.

Pre·cam′bri·an (prē kam′brē ən, -kām′-) adj. pertaining to the earliest era of earth history.

pre·can′cer·ous adj. showing pathological changes that may be preliminary to malignancy.

pre·car′i·ous (pri kâr′ ēs) adj. uncertain; dangerous.

pre·cau′tion (pri kô′shən) n. a pru-

dent advance measure. —**pre·cau′tion·ar′y,** adj.

pre·cede′ (pri sēd′) v.t., v.i., -ceded, -ceding. to go or come before.

prec′e·dence (pres′i dəns) n. the act, fact, or right of preceding.

prec′e·dent (pres′i dənt) n. a past case used as an example or guide.

pre′cept (prē′sept) n. a rule of conduct.

pre·cep′tor (pri sep′tər, prē′sep-) n. a teacher.

pre′cinct (prē′singkt) n. a bounded or defined area.

pre′ci·os′i·ty (presh′ē os′i tē) n., pl. -ties. fastidious refinement.

pre′cious (presh′əs) adj. **1.** valuable. **2.** beloved. **3.** affectedly refined. —**pre′cious·ly,** adv.

prec′i·pice (pres′ə pis) n. a cliff.

pre·cip′i·tate′ v., -tated, -tating, adj., n. —v.t. (pri sip′i tāt′) **1.** to hasten the occurrence of. **2.** to separate (a solid) from a solution. **3.** to fling down. —v.i. **4.** to condense from vapor and fall to the earth's surface as rain, snow, etc. **5.** to separate from a solution as a precipitate. —adj. (-tit) **6.** rash or impetuous; hasty. —n. (-tit) **7.** a substance precipitated from a solution. **8.** condensed moisture. —**pre·cip′i·tate·ly,** adv.

pre·cip′i·ta′tion n. **1.** rain, snow, etc., or the amount that has fallen at a place in a given period. **2.** the act or result of precipitating. **3.** sudden haste.

pre·cip′i·tous adj. **1.** extremely steep. **2.** precipitate.

pré·cis′ (prā sē′, prā′sē) n. a summary.

pre·cise′ (pri sīs′) adj. **1.** definitely stated, defined, or fixed. **2.** exact. —**pre·ci′sion** (-sizh′ən) n.

pre·clude′ (pri klŏŏd′) v.t., -cluded, -cluding. to prevent or exclude the possibility of. —**pre·clu′sion** (-klŏŏ′zhən) n. —**pre·clu′sive,** adj.

pre·co′cious (pri kō′shəs) adj. unusually advanced in mental development or talent. —**pre·coc′i·ty** (-kos′ə tē) n.

pre·cog·ni′tion (prē′kog nish′ən) n. knowledge of a future event through extrasensory means.

pre′-Co·lum′bi·an, adj. of the period before the arrival of Columbus in the Americas.

pre·con·ceive′ (prē′kən sēv′) v.t., -ceived, -ceiving. to form (an opinion) beforehand. —**pre′con·cep′tion,** n.

pre′con·di′tion n. something necessary for a subsequent result.

pre·cur′sor (pri kûr′sər, prē′kûr-) n. **1.** a predecessor. **2.** a harbinger.

pred′a·tor (pred′ə tər) n. one that preys on others.

pred′a·to·ry adj. preying on others.

pred′e·ces′sor (-ses′ər) n. one who precedes another.

pre·des′ti·na′tion (pri des′tə nā′shən) n. **1.** fate; destiny. **2.** the doctrine that everything has been determined in advance by God. —**pre·des′ti·na′tion,** v.t.

pre·de·ter′mine (prē′di tûr′min) v.t., -mined, -mining. to decide in advance. —**pre′de·ter′mi·na′tion,** n.

pre·dic′a·ment (pri dik′ə mənt) n. a difficult situation.

pred′i·cate v., -cated, -cating, n. —v.t. (pred′i kit) **1.** the part of a sentence that expresses the action performed by or the state of the subject. —adj. (-kit) **2.** belonging to the predicate of a sentence. —v.t. (-kāt′) **3.** to declare. **4.** to find a basis for.

pre·dict′ (pri dikt′) v.t., v.i. to tell (what will happen) in advance. —**pre·dict′a·ble,** adj. —**pre·dic′tion,** n. —**pre·dic′tor,** n.

pre·di·lec′tion (pred′l ek′shən, prēd′-) n. a preference.

pre·dis·pose′ (prē′di spōz′) v.t., -posed, -posing. **1.** to make susceptible. **2.** to incline. —**pre·dis′po·si′tion,** n.

pre·dom′i·nate′ (pri dom′ə nāt′) v.i., -nated, -nating. to be more powerful or common. —**pre·dom′i·nance,** n. —**pre·dom′i·nant,** adj.

pre·em′i·nent (prē em′ə nənt) adj. superior; outstanding. —**pre·em′i·nence,** n. —**pre·em′i·nent·ly,** adv.

pre·empt′ (prē empt′) v.t. **1.** to take the place of. **2.** to replace before others can. **3.** to occupy (land) to establish a prior right to buy. —**pre·emp′tive,** adj.

preen (prēn) v.t. **1.** to trim or clean (feathers or fur) with the beak or tongue. **2.** to dress (oneself) carefully. **3.** to pride (oneself) on something.

pre·fab·ri·cate' v.t., **-cated**, **-cating.** to build in parts for quick assembly. —**pre'fab·ri·ca'tion**, n.

pref'ace (pref'is) n., v., **-aced**, **-acing.** —n. **1.** an introductory statement. —v.t. **2.** to provide with or introduce by a preface. —**pref'a·to'ry** (-ə tôr'ē) adj.

pre'fect (prē'fekt) n. a chief magistrate. —**pre'fec·ture** (-fek shər) n.

pre·fer' (pri fûr') v.t., **-ferred, -ferring. 1.** to like better. —**Idiom. 2. prefer charges,** to make an accusation of wrongdoing against another.

pref'er·a·ble (pref'ər ə bəl) adj. more desirable.

pref'er·ence (-əns) n. **1.** a preferring or being preferred. **2.** something preferred. **3.** an advantage given to one over others. —**pref'er·en'tial** (-ə ren'shəl) adj.

pre·fer'ment (pri fûr'mənt) n. advancement or promotion.

pre·fig'ure (prē fig'yər) v.t., **-ured, -uring.** to foreshadow.

pre'fix n. (-fiks) **1.** a syllable or syllables put before a word to qualify its meaning. —v.t. (also prē fiks') **2.** to put before.

preg'nant (preg'nənt) adj. **1.** having a child developing in the body. **2.** full of meaning. —**preg'nan·cy**, n.

pre·hen'sile (pri hen'sil, -sīl) adj. adapted for grasping.

pre'his·tor'ic adj. of the time before recorded history.

pre·judge' v.t., **-judged, -judging.** to judge prematurely.

prej'u·dice (prej'ə dis) n., v., **-diced, -dicing.** —n. **1.** an opinion formed beforehand or without knowledge. **2.** unreasonable, hostile attitudes regarding a group. —v.t. **3.** to affect with a prejudice. —**prej'u·di'cial** (-dish'əl) adj.

prel'ate (prel'it) n. a high church official.

pre·lim'i·nar'y (pri lim'ə ner'ē) adj., n., pl. **-naries.** —adj. **1.** leading up to the main action or event. —n. **2.** a preliminary action.

pre·lit'er·ate (prē lit'ər it) adj. lacking a written language.

prel'ude (prel'yōōd, prā'lōōd) n. **1.** a preliminary to a major event. **2.** an introductory piece of music.

pre·mar'i·tal (prē mar'i tl) adj. before marriage.

pre·ma·ture' adj. born, coming, done, or occurring too soon. —**pre'ma·ture'ly**, adv.

pre·med'i·tate' v.t., v.i., **-tated, -tating.** to plan in advance.

pre·mier' (pri mēr', -myēr') n. **1.** a prime minister. —adj. **2.** chief.

pre·miere' (pri mēr', -myâr') n. the first public performance.

prem'ise (prem'is) n. **1.** a statement from which a conclusion is drawn. **2. premises**, a building with its grounds.

pre'mi·um (prē'mē əm) n. **1.** a periodic payment for an insurance policy. **2.** a bonus. **3.** an extra charge. **4.** great value.

pre'mo·ni'tion (prem'ə nish'ən, prē'mə-) n. a foreboding.

pre·na'tal (prē nāt'l) adj. before birth or before giving birth.

pre·oc'cu·py' v.t., **-pied, -pying.** to engross completely.

pre'or·dain' v.t. to decree in advance.

prep (prep) v.t., v.i., **prepped, prepping.** to prepare.

prep'a·ra'tion (prep'ə rā'shən) n. **1.** a means by which one prepares for something. **2.** a preparing or being prepared. **3.** a substance prepared for use.

pre·par'a·to'ry (pri par'ə tôr'ē) adj. **1.** preparing. **2.** introductory.

preparatory school n. a private secondary school preparing students for college. Also, **prep school.**

pre·pare' (pri pâr') v.t., v.i., **-pared, -paring.** to make or get ready.

pre·par'ed·ness (-pâr'id nis, -pârd'nis) n. the state of being prepared, esp. for war.

pre·pay' (prē pā') v.t., **-paid, -paying.** to pay beforehand.

pre·pon'der·ant (pri pon'dər ənt) adj. superior in force or numbers. —**pre·pon'der·ance**, n.

prep'o·si'tion (prep'ə zish'ən) n. a word placed before a noun or pronoun to indicate space, time, means, etc.

pre·pos·sess'ing (prē'-) adj. impressing favorably.

pre·pos'ter·ous (pri pos'tər əs) adj. absurd.

pre'puce (prē'pyōōs) n. the skin covering the head of the penis.

pre'quel (prē'kwəl) n. a sequel to a film, play, etc., that prefigures the original.

pre·req'ui·site (pri rek'wə zit, prē-) adj. **1.** required in advance. —n. **2.** something prerequisite.

pre·rog'a·tive (pri rog'ə tiv, pə-rog'-) n. a special right or privilege.

pres. 1. present. **2.** president.

pres'age (pres'ij) v.t., **-aged, -aging. 1.** to foreshadow. **2.** to predict.

pres·by·o'pi·a (prez'bē ō'pē ə, pres'-) n. farsightedness, usu. associated with aging.

pres'by·ter (prez'bi tər, pres'-) n. **1.** a priest. **2.** an elder.

Pres·by·te'ri·an (prez'bi tēr'ē ən, pres'-) adj. **1.** of various churches governed by elders or presbyters of equal rank. —n. **2.** a member of a Presbyterian church.

pres'by·ter·y n., pl. **-teries.** the body of church elders and ministers.

pre'school' (prē'skōōl') adj. **1.** of or for children between infancy and kindergarten age. —n. (-skōōl') **2.** a school for preschool children.

pre'sci·ence (presh'əns, -ē əns) n. foresight. —**pre'sci·ent**, adj.

pre·scribe' (pri skrīb') v.t., **-scribed, -scribing. 1.** to order for use, as medicine. **2.** to lay down as a rule to be followed. —**pre·scrip'tion** (-skrip'shən) n. —**pre·scrip'tive** (-skrip'tiv) adj.

pres'ence (prez'əns) n. **1.** the fact of being present. **2.** immediate vicinity. **3.** impressive personal appearance or bearing.

presence of mind n. the ability to think clearly and act appropriately, as during a crisis.

pres'ent' (prez'ənt) adj. **1.** being or occurring now. **2.** being at a particular place. **3.** designating a verb tense referring to an action or state existing now. —n. **4.** the present time. **5.** the present tense.

pre·sent' v.t. (pri zent') **1.** to give, bring, or offer. **2.** to bring before the public. —n. (prez'ənt) **3.** a gift.

pre·sent'a·ble (pri zen'tə bəl) adj. suitable in looks, dress, etc.

pres·en·ta'tion (prez'ən tā'shən, prē'zen-) n. **1.** a presenting or being presented. **2.** a performance. **3.** a demonstration, lecture, etc.

pre·sen'ti·ment (-mənt) n. a feeling of something impending.

pres'ent·ly (prez'ənt lē) adv. **1.** soon. **2.** at the present time.

pres·er·va'tion·ist (prez'ər vā'shə nist) n. one who advocates preservation, esp. of wildlife, historical places, etc.

pre·serv'a·tive (pri zûr'və tiv) n. **1.** a substance used to preserve foods from spoilage. —adj. **2.** tending to preserve.

pre·serve' (pri zûrv') v., **-served, -serving**, n. —v.t. **1.** to keep alive or safe. **2.** to maintain. **3.** to treat (food) to prevent spoilage. —n. **4.** preserves, preserved fruit. **5.** a place where animals are protected. —**pres'er·va'tion** (prez'ər vā'shən) n.

pre·side' (pri zīd') v.i., **-sided, -siding.** to have charge of a meeting.

pres'i·dent (prez'i dənt) n. **1.** the chief of state of a republic. **2.** the chief officer of a corporation, college, etc. —**pres'i·den·cy**, n.

pre·sid'i·um (pri sid'ē əm) n., pl. **-iums, -ia.** an executive committee.

press (pres) v.t. **1.** to act upon with steady weight or force. **2.** to squeeze. **3.** to make smooth by ironing. **4.** to urge to hurry or comply. —v.i. **5.** to exert force. **6.** to push forward. **7.** to crowd. —n. **8.** newspapers, magazines, etc., collectively. **9.** a device for printing. **10.** a device for stamping, crushing, etc. **11.** a crowd. **12.** urgency.

press' a'gent n. a person employed to obtain favorable publicity for a client.

press' con'ference n. an interview with reporters held by an official.

press'ing adj. urgent.

press' release' n. a statement distributed to the press.

pres'sure (presh'ər) n., v., **-sured, -suring.** —n. **1.** the exertion of force by one body upon another. **2.** stress. **3.** urgency, as of business. —v.t. **4.** to put pressure on.

pres'sure cook'er n. a pot for cooking by steam under pressure.

pres'sure group' n. a group that tries to influence legislation.

pres'sur·ize' v.t., **-ized, -izing.** to produce normal air pressure in (an airplane, spacesuit, etc.) at high altitudes. —**pres'sur·i·za'tion**, n.

pres·ti·dig·i·ta'tion (pres'ti dij'i-tā'shən) n. sleight of hand.

pres·tige' (pre stēzh', -stēj') n. reputation as a result of success, rank, etc. —**pres·ti'gious** (-stij'əs) adj.

pres'to (pres'tō) adv. very quickly.

pre·sume' (pri zōōm') v., **-sumed, -suming. 1.** to take for granted or suppose to be true. —v.i. **2.** to act with unjustified boldness. —**pre·sum'a·bly**, adv.

pre·sump'tion (-zump'shən) n. **1.** something presumed; assumption. **2.** impertinent boldness.

pre·sump'tu·ous (-chōō əs) adj. behaving with impertinent or unwarranted boldness.

pre'sup·pose' (prē'sə pōz') v.t., **-posed, -posing. 1.** to assume beforehand. **2.** to assume the prior existence of. —**pre'sup·po·si'tion** (-sup əzish'ən) n.

pre·teen' n. **1.** a child between 10 and 13 years old. —adj. **2.** of or for preteens.

pre·tend' (pri tend') v.t. **1.** to feign. **2.** to make believe. **3.** to claim falsely. —**pre·tend'er**, n.

pre·ten'sion (pri ten'shən) n. **1.** a claim to something. **2.** Often, **pretensions.** an unwarranted claim, as to importance.

pre·ten'tious adj. **1.** overly self-important. **2.** ostentatious. —**pre·ten'tious·ly**, adv.

pre'ter·nat'u·ral (prē'tər nach'-ər əl) adj. exceptional.

pre'text (prē'tekst) n. something put forward to conceal a true reason.

pret'ty (prit'ē) adj., **-tier, -tiest**, adv. —adj. **1.** pleasingly attractive in a delicate way. —adv. **2.** moderately. **3.** very. —**pret'ti·ly**, adv. —**pret'ti·ly**, adv.

pret'zel (pret'səl) n. a crisp knotted or elongated biscuit, usu. salted.

pre·vail' (pri vāl') v.i. **1.** to be widespread. **2.** to exercise persuasion. **3.** to gain victory.

pre·vail'ing adj. **1.** most common. **2.** having superior influence.

prev'a·lent (prev'ə lənt) adj. widespread; general. —**prev'a·lence**, n.

pre·var'i·cate' (pri var'i kāt') v.i., **-cated, -cating.** to speak evasively; lie. —**pre·var'i·ca'tion**, n.

pre·vent' (pri vent') v.t. **1.** to keep from happening. **2.** to stop from doing something. —**pre·vent'a·ble**, adj. —**pre·ven'tion**, n.

pre·ven'tive (-tiv) adj. **1.** serving to prevent. —n. **2.** a preventive agent. Also, **pre·vent'a·tive.**

pre'view' (prē'vyōō') n. **1.** an earlier view or showing. —v.t. **2.** to view or show beforehand.

pre'vi·ous (prē'vē əs) adj. coming or occurring before something else. —**pre'vi·ous·ly**, adv.

prey (prā) n. **1.** an animal hunted as food by another animal. **2.** any victim. —v. **3. prey on, a.** to seize prey. **b.** to victimize another.

price (prīs) n., v., **priced, pricing.** —n. **1.** the amount for which a thing is bought or sold. **2.** what must be given, done, etc., to obtain something. —v.t. **3.** to fix the price of. **4.** to ask the price of.

price'less adj. too valuable to set a price on.

pric'ey adj., **-ier, -iest.** Informal. expensive.

prick (prik) n. **1.** a slight puncture by a pointed object. **2.** a sharp pain. —v.t. **3.** to pierce slightly with a sharp point. **4.** to cause sharp pain to. **5.** to point (the ears).

prick'le n., v., **-led, -ling.** —n. **1.** a small, sharp point. **2.** a pricking feeling. —v.t. **3.** to cause a tingling sensation in. —v.i. **4.** to tingle. —**prick'ly**, adj.

prick'ly heat' n. an itching rash caused by an inflammation of the sweat glands.

pride (prīd) n., v., **prided, priding.** —n. **1.** self-respect. **2.** something causing one to be proud. **3.** conceit. **4.** a group of lions. —v. **5. pride oneself on,** to be proud of. —**pride'ful**, adj.

priest (prēst) n. **1.** a member of the clergy. **2.** a person authorized to perform religious rites. —**priest'-hood**, n.

priest'ess (prē'stis) n. a woman who officiates in sacred rites.

prig (prig) n. a self-righteous person. —**prig'gish**, adj.

prim (prim) adj. stiffly proper.

pri·ma·cy (prī'mə sē) n., pl. **-cies.** the state of being first in rank, importance, etc.

pri'ma don'na (prē'mə don'ə, prim'ə) n. **1.** a principal female opera singer. **2.** a temperamental person.

pri·ma fa·ci·e (prī'mə fā'shē ē', fā'shē) adj. sufficient to establish a fact unless rebutted.

pri'mal (prī'məl) adj. **1.** first; original. **2.** most important.

pri·ma·ri·ly (prī mâr'ə lē, -mer'-) adv. **1.** chiefly. **2.** originally.

pri'ma·ry (prī'mer ē, -mə rē) adj., n., pl. **-ries.** —adj. **1.** first in importance, order, or time. —n. **2.** a preliminary election for choosing party candidates.

pri'mate (-māt or, esp. for 2, -mit) n. **1.** a mammal of the order including humans, apes, and monkeys. **2.** a high church official.

prime (prīm) adj., n., v., **primed, priming.** —adj. **1.** first in importance or quality. **2.** basic. —n. **3.** the best stage or part. —v.t. **4.** to prepare for a special purpose or function.

prime' merid'ian n. the meridian running through Greenwich, England, from which longitude east and west is reckoned.

prime' min'ister n. the head of government and of the cabinet in a parliamentary system.

prim'er' (prim'ər; esp. Brit. prī'mər) n. an elementary book, esp. for reading.

prim'er' (prī'mər) n. a first coat of paint.

prime' rate' n. the minimum interest rate charged by banks to their best-rated customers.

prime' time' n. the hours having the largest television audience.

pri·me'val (prī mē'vəl) adj. of the first ages of the world.

prim'i·tive (prim'i tiv) adj. **1.** of early ages or an early state of development. **2.** simple or crude.

pri'mo·gen'i·ture (prī'mə jen'i-chər) n. the right of inheritance by the eldest son.

pri·mor'di·al (prī môr'dē əl) adj. existing from the very beginning.

primp (primp) v.t., v.i. to dress (oneself) with care.

prim'rose' (prim'rōz') n. a plant with colorful, five-lobed flowers.

prince (prins) n. **1.** the son of a king or queen. **2.** a ruler.

prince'ly adj. **1.** lavish. **2.** of a prince.

prin'cess (prin'sis, -ses) n. **1.** the daughter of a king or queen. **2.** the consort of a prince.

prin'ci·pal (prin'sə pəl) adj. **1.** chief. —n. **2.** a chief, head, or leader. **3.** the head of a school. **4.** a person authorizing another to act for him or her. **5.** a capital sum, distinguished from interest.

prin'ci·pal'i·ty (-pal'i tē) n., pl. **-ties.** a state ruled by a prince.

prin'ci·ple (prin'sə pəl) n. **1.** a rule of conduct or action. **2.** a fundamental truth or cause.

print (print) v.t., v.i. **1.** to reproduce from inked types, plates, etc. **2.** to write in letters like those of print. **3.** to produce (a photograph) from a negative. —n. **4.** printed lettering or material. **5.** a cloth having a design or pattern. **6.** a mark made by the pressure of one thing on another. **7.** a photograph.

print'out' n. printed output of a computer.

pri'or' (prī'ər) adj. preceding in time, order, importance, etc.

pri'or' (prī'ər) n. an officer in a religious house. —**pri'o·ry**, n.

pri'or·ess (-is) n. a woman who is an officer in a religious house.

pri'or·i·tize' (prī ôr'i tīz') v.t., **-tized, -tizing.** to arrange in order of priority.

pri·or'i·ty n., pl. **-ties. 1.** the right to take precedence over others. **2.** something given special or prior attention.

prism (priz'əm) n. a transparent body for dispersing light into a spectrum.

pris'on (priz'ən) n. a place where criminals are confined. —**pris'on·er**, n.

pris'sy (pris'ē) adj., **-sier, -siest.** excessively or affectedly proper.

pris'tine (pris'tēn, pri stēn') adj. pure.

pri'vate (prī'vit) adj. **1.** of, belonging to, or confined to a particular person or group. **2.** not provided or maintained by public funds. **3.** personal; secret. —n. **4.** a soldier of one of the three lowest ranks. —**pri'va·cy**, n. —**pri'vate·ly**, adv.

pri'va·teer' (prī'və tēr') n. a pri-

vately owned vessel commissioned to fight. —**pri'va·teer'ing**, n.

pri'vate eye' n. Informal. a private detective.

pri·va'tion (prī vā'shən) n. hardship.

priv'et (priv'it) n. an evergreen shrub often grown as a hedge.

priv'i·lege (priv'ə lij, priv'lij) n., v., **-leged, -leging.** —n. **1.** a special advantage enjoyed by a particular group. —v.t. **2.** to grant a privilege to.

priv'y (priv'ē) adj., n., pl. **privies.** —adj. **1.** having knowledge of something private. —n. **2.** an outdoor toilet.

priv'y coun'cil n. a board of personal advisors, as of a sovereign.

prize' (prīz) n. **1.** a reward for victory, superiority, etc. **2.** a thing worth striving for. —adj. **3.** worthy of a prize.

prize' (prīz) v.t., **prized, prizing. 1.** to esteem highly.

pro' (prō) adv., adj., n., pl. **pros.** —adv. **1.** in favor of a plan, opinion, etc. —n. **2.** a vote in favor of something. **3.** a person upholding the affirmative in a debate.

pro' (prō) adj., n., pl. **pros.** professional.

pro- a prefix meaning: **1.** favoring. **2.** before or in front of.

prob'a·ble (prob'ə bəl) adj. **1.** likely to occur or prove true. **2.** affording ground for belief. —**prob'a·bil'i·ty**, n. —**prob'a·bly**, adv.

pro'bate (prō'bāt) n., adj., v., **-bated, -bating.** —n. **1.** the official authentication of a will. —adj. **2.** of probate. —v.t. **3.** to establish a will's validity.

pro·ba'tion n. **1.** the testing of a person's conduct or character. **2.** the period of such testing. **3.** the conditional release of a prisoner.

probe (prōb) v., **probed, probing**, n. —v.t. **1.** to examine thoroughly. —n. **2.** an investigation. **3.** an instrument for exploring a wound.

pro'bi·ty (prō'bi tē, prob'i-) n. honesty.

prob'lem (prob'ləm) n. **1.** a matter involving uncertainty or difficulty. **2.** a question proposed for solution. —**prob'lem·at'ic**, adj.

pro·bos'cis (prō bos'is, -kis) n., pl. **-cises.** a flexible snout.

pro·ced'ure (prə sē'jər) n. the act or manner of proceeding to accomplish something. —**pro·ced'ur·al**, adj.

pro·ceed' v.i. (-sēd') **1.** to go forward. **2.** to carry on an action. **3.** to issue forth. —n. (-prō'sēd) **4. proceeds,** the sum derived from a sale or other transaction.

pro·ceed'ing n. **1.** an action or course of action. **2. proceedings, a.** a record of the business discussed at a meeting. **b.** legal action.

proc'ess (pros'es; esp. Brit. prō'ses) n. **1.** a series of actions directed to some end. **2.** a continuous action or series of changes. **3.** a legal summons. —v.t. **4.** to treat by a particular process. **5.** to handle according to a routine procedure.

pro·ces'sion (prə sesh'ən) n. a line of persons, vehicles, etc., moving along in a ceremonious manner.

pro·ces'sion·al n. a piece of music for accompanying a procession, as at the beginning of a church service.

pro-choice' (prō chois') adj. supporting the right to legalized abortion.

pro·claim' (prō klām', prə-) v.t. to announce formally. —**proc'la·ma'tion** (prok'lə mā'shən) n.

pro·cliv'i·ty (prō kliv'i tē) n., pl. **-ties.** a natural tendency.

pro·cras'ti·nate' (prō kras'tə nāt', prə-) v.i., v.t., **-nated, -nating.** to delay (action). —**pro·cras'ti·na'tion**, n.

pro·cre·ate' (prō'krē āt') v.t., v.i., **-ated, -ating.** to produce (offspring). —**pro'cre·a'tion**, n.

proc·tol'o·gy (prok tol'ə jē) n. the branch of medicine dealing with the rectum. —**proc·tol'o·gist**, n.

proc'tor (prok'tər) n. **1.** a person who supervises students at examinations. —v.t., v.i. **2.** to supervise or monitor.

pro·cure' (prō kyoor', prə-) v.t., **-cured, -curing. 1.** to obtain by effort. **2.** to obtain (a person) for prostitution. —**pro·cur'a·ble**, adj. —**pro·cure'ment**, n.

prod (prod) v., **prodded, prodding**, n. —v.t. **1.** to jab or poke. **2.** to incite; goad. —n. **3.** a poke. **4.** a pointed instrument used to goad.

prod'i·gal (prod'i gəl) adj. **1.**

wastefully extravagant. **2.** lavishly abundant. —n. **3.** a spendthrift. —**prod′i•gal′i•ty,** n.

pro•di′gious (prə dij′əs) adj. extraordinary in size, amount, etc. —**pro•di′gious•ly,** adv.

prod′i•gy (prod′i jē) n., pl. **-gies.** a very gifted person, esp. a child.

pro•duce′ v., **-duced, -ducing,** —v.t. (prə dōōs′, -dyōōs′) **1.** to bring into existence; create. **2.** to bear, as young, fruit, etc. **3.** to present; exhibit. —v.i. **4.** to yield products, offspring, etc. —n. (prod′-ōōs, -yōōs, prō′dōōs, -dyōōs) **5.** agricultural products collectively.

prod′uct (prod′əkt) n. **1.** a thing produced by labor. **2.** a person or thing resulting from a process. **3.** the result obtained by multiplying.

pro•duc′tion (prə duk′shən) n. **1.** the act of producing. **2.** something produced. **3.** the amount produced. —**pro•duc′tive,** adj.

pro′duc•tiv′i•ty (prō′duk tiv′i tē, prod′ək), n. **1.** the quality of being productive. **2.** the rate at which things are produced.

pro•fane′ (prə fān′, prō-) adj., v., **-faned, -faning.** —adj. **1.** disrespectful toward sacred things. **2.** secular. —v.t. **3.** to defile. **4.** to treat (a sacred thing) with contempt. —**prof′a•na′tion** (prof′ə nā′shən) n.

pro•fan′i•ty (-fan′i tē) n., pl. **-ties. 1.** the quality of being profane. **2.** blasphemous or vulgar language.

pro•fess′ (prə fes′) v.t. **1.** to pretend to. **2.** to declare. **3.** to affirm one's faith in.

pro•fes′sion n. **1.** an occupation requiring advanced education. **2.** the persons engaged in such an occupation. **3.** a declaration.

pro•fes′sion•al adj. **1.** of or engaged in a profession. **2.** following an occupation for payment. —n. **3.** a professional person.

pro•fes′sor (prə fes′ər) n. a college teacher of the highest rank.

prof′fer (prof′ər) v.t. to offer.

pro•fi′cient (prə fish′ənt) adj. expert; skilled. —**pro•fi′cien•cy,** n.

pro′file (prō′fīl) n. **1.** a side view. **2.** a biographical sketch.

prof′it (prof′it) n. **1.** the monetary gain from a business transaction after expenses have been met. **2.** gain; benefit. —v.i., v.t. **3.** to gain or cause to gain a profit. —**prof′it•a•ble,** adj.

prof′it•eer′ n. **1.** a person who makes an unfair profit. —v.i. **2.** to act as a profiteer.

prof′li•gate (-li git, -gāt′) adj. **1.** immoral. **2.** extravagant. —n. **3.** a profligate person. —**prof′li•ga•cy,** n.

pro for′ma (prə fôr′mə) adj. done as a matter of form or for the sake of form.

pro•found′ (prə found′) adj. **1.** showing deep thought or insight. **2.** intense. **3.** deep. —**pro•fun′di•ty** (-fun′di tē) n.

pro•fuse′ (-fyōōs′) adj. extravagant; abundant. —**pro•fuse′ly,** adv. —**pro•fu′sion** (-fyōō′zhən) n.

pro•gen′i•tor (prō jen′i tər) n. an ancestor.

prog′e•ny (proj′ə nē) n. offspring collectively.

pro•ges′ter•one (prō jes′tə rōn′) n. a female hormone that prepares the uterus for the fertilized egg.

prog•na′thous (prog′nə thəs) adj. having protrusive jaws.

prog•no′sis (prog nō′sis) n., pl. **-noses** (-nō′sēz). a forecast, esp. of the course of a disease.

prog•nos′ti•cate′ (-nos′ti kāt′) v.t., **-cated, -cating.** to predict.

pro′gram (prō′gram, -grəm) n., v., **-grammed, -gramming.** —n. **1.** a plan of things to do. **2.** a schedule of entertainments. **3.** a television or radio show. **4.** a series of instructions enabling a computer to perform a task. —v.t. **5.** to make a program for or including. —**pro′gram•ma•ble,** adj. —**pro′gram•mer,** n.

prog′ress n. (prog′res, -rəs; esp. Brit. prō′gres) **1.** advancement toward a goal. **2.** permanent improvement. **3.** forward movement. —v.i. (prə gres′) **4.** to go forward. **5.** to develop.

pro•gres′sion n. **1.** the act of progressing. **2.** a series.

pro•gres′sive adj. **1.** advocating reform. **2.** advancing step by step.

pro•hib′it (prō hib′it) v.t. to forbid; prevent.

pro′hi•bi′tion (prō′ə bish′ən) n. **1.** the act of prohibiting. **2. Prohibition,** the period, 1920–33, when the manufacture and sale of alcoholic drinks was forbidden in the U.S. —**pro′hi•bi′tion•ist,** n.

pro•hib′i•tive (-hib′ə tiv) adj. **1.** prohibiting. **2.** too expensive.

proj′ect n. (proj′ekt, -ikt; esp. Brit. prō′jekt) **1.** a plan. **2.** a large and important undertaking. —v.t. (prə jekt′) **3.** to plan. **4.** to impel forward. **5.** to cast upon a surface, as a shadow. **6.** to cause to protrude. —**pro•jec′tion,** n.

pro•jec′tile (prə jek′til, -tīl) n. an object fired with explosive force.

pro•jec′tion•ist (-shə nist) n. an operator of a motion-picture projector.

pro•jec′tor n. an apparatus for casting an image onto a screen.

pro′le•tar′i•at (prō′li târ′ē ət) n. the working class. —**pro′le•tar′i•an,** adj., n.

pro-life′ adj. opposed to legalized abortion.

pro•lif′er•ate′ (prə lif′ə rāt′) v.i., v.t., **-ated, -ating.** to increase or spread rapidly.

pro•lif′ic (-ik) adj. highly productive.

pro•lix′ (prō liks′, prō′liks) adj. tediously long and wordy.

pro′logue (prō′lôg) n. the introductory part of a novel, play, etc.

pro•long′ (prə lông′) v.t. to extend the duration or length of. —**pro′lon•ga′tion** (prō′-) n.

prom (prom) n. a formal dance at a high school or college.

prom′e•nade′ (prom′ə nād′, -näd′) n., v., **-naded, -nading.** —n. **1.** a leisurely walk. **2.** a space for such a walk. —v.t., v.i. **3.** to stroll (through or about).

prom′i•nent (prom′ə nənt) adj. **1.** conspicuous. **2.** projecting. **3.** well-known. —**prom′i•nence,** n.

pro•mis′cu•ous (prə mis′kyōō əs) adj. having numerous casual sexual partners. —**prom′is•cu′i•ty** (prom′i-skyōō′i tē) n.

prom•ise (prom′is) n., v., **-ised, -is-ing.** —n. **1.** an assurance that one will act as specified. **2.** indication of future excellence. —v.t., v.i. **3.** to assure by a promise. **4.** to afford ground for expecting. —**prom′is•ing,** adj.

prom′is•so′ry (prom′ə sôr′ē) adj. containing a promise of payment.

prom′on•to′ry (prom′ən tôr′ē) n., pl. **-ries.** a high peak projecting into the sea or overlooking low land.

pro•mote′ (prə mōt′) v.t., **-moted, -moting. 1.** to further the progress of. **2.** to advance. **3.** to encourage the sales or acceptance of. —**pro•mot′er,** n. —**pro•mo′tion,** n.

prompt (prompt) adj. **1.** done without delay. **2.** quick to act. —v.t. **3.** to induce to action; inspire. **4.** to give a cue to; remind. —**prompt′-ness,** n.

prom′ul•gate (prom′əl gāt′, prō-mul′gāt) v.t., **-gated, -gating.** to proclaim formally.

prone (prōn) adj. **1.** likely; inclined. **2.** lying flat, esp. face downward.

prong (prông) n. a point.

pro′noun′ (prō′noun′) n. a word used as a substitute for a noun.

pro•nounce′ (prə nouns′) v.t., **-nounced, -nouncing. 1.** to enunciate or articulate (sounds, words, etc.). **2.** to utter formally. —**pro-nounce′ment,** n.

pro•nounced′ adj. **1.** strongly marked. **2.** decided.

pron′to (pron′tō) adv. quickly.

pro•nun′ci•a′tion (prə nun′sē ā′-shən) n. the production of the sounds of speech.

proof (prōōf) n. **1.** evidence establishing a truth or fact. **2.** a copy of printed matter for correcting errors. —adj. **3.** invulnerable.

-proof a suffix meaning resistant.

proof′read′ (-rēd′) v.t., v.i., **-read** (red′), **-reading.** to read (printers′ proofs, copy, etc.) to detect and mark errors. —**proof′read′er,** n.

prop (prop) n., v., **propped, prop-ping.** —n. **1.** a rigid support. **2.** a person serving as a support. —v.t. **3.** to support with a prop.

prop′a•gan′da (prop′ə gan′də) n. **1.** ideas or information spread to promote or injure a cause, nation, etc. **2.** the spreading of such ideas. —**prop′a•gan′dist,** n. —**prop′a•gan′dize,** v.t., v.i.

prop′a•gate′ (prop′ə gāt′) v., **-gated, -gating.** —v.t. **1.** to cause (an organism) to reproduce. **2.** to spread or disseminate. —v.i. **3.** to multiply by natural reproduction. —**prop′a•ga′tion,** n.

pro′pane (prō′pān) n. a colorless flammable gas, used esp. as a fuel.

pro•pel′ (prə pel′) v.t., **-pelled, -pelling.** to drive forward.

pro•pel′lant (prə pel′ənt) n. a propelling agent. Also, **pro•pel•lent.**

pro•pel′ler n. a screwlike device for propelling an airplane, ship, etc.

pro•pen′si•ty (prə pen′si tē) n., pl. **-ties.** an inclination or tendency.

prop′er (prop′ər) adj. **1.** suitable; fitting. **2.** conforming to social conventions, manners, or good taste. **3.** correct. **4.** in the strict sense.

prop′er noun′ n. a noun that is the name of a particular person, place, or thing and is usu. capitalized.

prop′er•ty n., pl. **-ties. 1.** that which one owns. **2.** land or real estate. **3.** an attribute or quality.

proph′e•sy′ (prof′ə sī′) v.t., v.i., **-sied, -sying.** to predict (future events). —**proph′e•cy** (-sē) n.

proph′et (-it) n. **1.** a person who speaks for God. **2.** an inspired leader. **3.** a person who predicts. —**pro•phet′ic** (prə fet′ik) adj.

pro′phy•lac′tic (prō′fə lak′tik) adj. **1.** preventing disease or infection. —n. **2.** a prophylactic medicine, measure, or device.

pro′phy•lax′is (prō′fə lak′sis) n. the prevention of disease, as by protective measures.

pro•pin′qui•ty (prō ping′kwi tē) n. nearness.

pro•pi′ti•ate′ (prə pish′ē āt′) v.t., **-ated, -ating.** to make less angry.

pro•pi′tious (-pish′əs) adj. favorable. —**pro•pi′tious•ly,** adv.

pro•po′nent (prə pō′nənt) n. an advocate; supporter.

pro•por′tion (prə pôr′shən) n. **1.** comparative or proper relation of dimensions or quantities. **2.** symmetry. **3.** proportions, dimensions. —v.t. **4.** to adjust in proper relation. —**pro•por′tion•al,** adj.

pro•por′tion•ate (-shə nit) adj. being in due proportion.

pro•pos′al (prə pō′zəl) n. **1.** proposing something. **2.** something proposed. **3.** an offer of marriage.

pro•pose′ (prə pōz′) v.t., **-posed, -posing.** —v.t. **1.** to suggest. **2.** to plan; intend. —v.i. **3.** to make an offer of marriage.

prop′o•si′tion (prop′ə zish′ən) n. **1.** the act of proposing or a plan proposed. **2.** a statement. **3.** a proposal of sexual relations. —v.t. **4.** to propose sexual relations to.

pro•pound′ (prə pound′) v.t. to offer for consideration.

pro•pri′e•tar′y (prə prī′i ter′ē) adj. **1.** made and sold only by the owner of the patent, trademark, etc. **2.** of a proprietor.

pro•pri′e•tor (prə prī′ə tər) n. the owner of a business, property, etc.

pro•pri′e•ty n., pl. **-ties.** conformity to established standards of behavior, manners, etc.

pro•pul′sion (prə pul′shən) n. a propelling force.

pro•rate′ (prō rāt′, prō′rāt′) v.t., v.i., **-rated, -rating.** to divide or calculate proportionally.

pro•sa′ic (prō zā′ik) adj. commonplace. —**pro•sa′i•cal•ly,** adv.

pro•sce′ni•um (prō sē′nē əm, prə-) n., pl. **-niums,** -nia (-nē ə). the arch separating a stage from the auditorium. Also, **proscenium arch.**

pro•scribe′ (prō skrīb′) v.t., **-scribed, -scribing.** to prohibit.

prose (prōz) n. ordinary language as distinguished from verse.

pros′e•cute′ (pros′i kyōōt′) v.t., **-cuted, -cuting. 1.** to begin legal proceedings against. **2.** to go on with (an undertaking) to the end. —**pros′e•cu′tion,** n. —**pros′e•cu′-tor,** n.

pros′e•lyt•ize′ (pros′ə li tīz′) v.t., v.i., **-ized, -izing.** to try to convert (someone) to another opinion, belief, etc. —**pros′e•lyte′** (-līt′), n.

pros′o•dy (pros′ə dē) n., pl. **-dies.** the study of poetic meters and versification.

pros′pect (pros′pekt) n. **1.** Usu., **prospects, a.** the likelihood of success. **b.** the outlook for the future. **2.** expectation. **3.** a potential customer. —v.t., v.i. **4.** to search (an area), as for gold. —**pros′pec•tor,** n.

pro•spec′tive (prə spek′tiv) adj. potential or likely.

pro•spec′tus (prə spek′təs) n. a description of a new investment or purchase.

pros′per (pros′pər) v.i. to be successful, esp. financially. —**pros-per′i•ty** (-per′ə tē) n. —**pros′per-ous,** adj.

pros′tate (pros′tāt) n. a gland surrounding the neck of the bladder in males.

pros•the′sis (pros thē′sis) n., pl. **-ses** (-sēz). a device that substitutes for or supplements a missing or defective body part. —**pros•thet′ic** (-thet′ik) adj.

pros′ti•tute′ (pros′ti tōōt′, -tyōōt′) n., v., **-tuted, -tuting.** —n. **1.** a person who engages in sexual intercourse for money. —v.t. **2.** to put to an unworthy use. —**pros′ti•tu′tion,** n.

pros′trate (pros′trāt) v., **-trated, -trating,** adj. —v.t. **1.** to cast (oneself) facedown, as in humility. **2.** to overcome or exhaust. —adj. **3.** lying flat. **4.** helpless, weak, or exhausted.

pros′y (prō′zē) adj., **-ier, -iest.** dull.

pro•tag′o•nist (prō tag′ə nist) n. the main character in a novel, play, etc.

pro′te•an (prō′tē ən, prō tē′-) adj. assuming different forms.

pro•tect′ (prə tekt′) v.t. to defend from injury, attack, etc. —**pro•tec′-tion,** n. —**pro•tec′tive,** adj.

pro•tec′tion•ism (-shə niz′əm) n. the practice of protecting industries from foreign competition by imposing import duties.

pro•tec′tor•ate (-tər it) n. a weak state that is protected and partly controlled by a stronger one.

pro′té•gé′ (prō′tə zhā′) n. a person under the friendly patronage of someone interested in his or her welfare.

pro′tein (prō′tēn, -tē in) n. an organic compound forming a large portion of the mass of all life forms.

pro′ tem′por•e′ (prō′ tem′pə rē′, -rā′) adv. **1.** temporarily. —adj. **2.** temporary.

pro′test n. (prō′test) **1.** an objection. —v.i., v.t. (prə test′, prō′test) **2.** to make a protest (against). —**pro′tes•ta′tion,** n. —**pro•test′er,** n.

Prot′es•tant (prot′ə stənt) n. **1.** a Christian who belongs to a church that began by breaking away from the Roman Catholic Church in the 16th century. —adj. **2.** of Protestants or their religion. —**Prot•es•tant•ism′,** n.

proto- a prefix meaning earliest.

pro′to•col′ (prō′tə kôl′) n. **1.** the customs dealing with diplomatic precedence, etiquette, etc. **2.** an original draft of a treaty. **3.** a set of rules for exchanging messages between computers.

pro′ton (prō′ton) n. the part of an atom bearing a positive charge.

pro′to•plasm′ (prō′tə plaz′əm) n. the substance of which cells are formed.

pro′to•type′ n. the model on which something is based. —**pro′-to•typ′i•cal,** adj.

pro′to•zo′an (-zō′ən) n., pl. **-zo-ans,** -zoa (-zō′ə). a one-celled organism that obtains nourishment by ingesting food rather than by photosynthesis.

pro•tract′ (prō trakt′, prə-) v.t. to draw out, esp. in time. —**pro•trac′-tion,** n.

pro•trac′tor n. an instrument for measuring angles.

pro•trude′ (prō trōōd′, prə-) v.i., v.t., **-truded, -truding.** to jut out or cause to jut out. —**pro•tru′sion** (-trōō′zhən) n. —**pro•tru′sive** (-trōō′siv) adj.

pro•tu′ber•ant (prō tōō′bər ənt) adj. bulging out. —**pro•tu′ber-ance,** n.

proud (proud) adj. **1.** full of pride. **2.** highly creditable. **3.** arrogant. —**proud′ly,** adv.

prove (prōōv) v., **proved, proving.** —v.t. **1.** to establish the truth, validity, or worth of. —v.i. **2.** to turn out. **3.** to be found to be.

prov′e•nance (prov′ə nəns, -nänz′) n. a place or source of origin.

prov′en•der (prov′ən dər) n. food, esp. dry food for livestock.

prov′erb (prov′ərb) n. a popular saying expressing some commonplace truth. —**pro•ver′bi•al** (prə-vûr′bē əl) adj.

pro•vide′ (prə vīd′) v., **-vided, vid-ing.** —v.t. **1.** to make available; supply. **2.** to stipulate beforehand. —v.i. **3.** to supply means of support. —**pro•vid′er,** n.

pro•vid′ed conj. on the condition that.

prov′i•dence (prov′i dəns) n. **1.** God's care. **2.** foresight.

prov′i•dent (-dənt) adj. showing foresight; prudent.

prov′i•den′tial (-den′shəl) adj. fortunate or lucky.

prov′ince (prov′ins) n. **1.** an administrative unit of a country. **2.** a sphere of activity.

pro•vin′cial (prə vin′shəl) adj. **1.** of a particular province. **2.** narrow-minded; unsophisticated.

pro•vi′sion (prə vizh′ən) n. **1.** something stated as necessary or binding. **2.** the act of providing. **3.** what is provided. **4.** an arrangement made beforehand. **5.** provisions, supplies of food.

pro•vi′sion•al adj. temporary.

pro•vi′so (prə vī′zō) n., pl. **-sos, -soes.** something required in an agreement; stipulation.

pro•vo•ca•teur′ (prə vok′ə-tûr′,-tōōr′) n. a person who provokes trouble, esp. as an agent for the police or a foreign power.

pro•voc′a•tive (prə vok′ə tiv) adj. stimulating; exciting.

pro•voke′ (-vōk′) v.t., **-voked, -vok-ing. 1.** to anger or vex. **2.** to arouse. —**prov′o•ca′tion** (prov′ə kā′shən) n.

pro′vost (prō′vōst) n. **1.** a superintendent. **2.** a high-ranking university administrator.

prow (prou) n. the front part of a ship.

prow′ess (prou′is) n. **1.** exceptional ability. **2.** bravery.

prowl (proul) v.i., v.t. to roam or search stealthily. —**prowl′er,** n.

prox•im′i•ty (prok sim′i tē) n. nearness.

prox′y (prok′sē) n., pl. **proxies.** a person authorized to act for another or the power to do so.

Pro′zac (prō′zak) Trademark. a drug used as an antidepressant.

prude (prōōd) n. a person who is excessively proper or modest, esp. in sexual matters. —**prud′er•y,** n. —**prud′ish,** adj.

pru′dence n. practical wisdom; caution. —**pru′dent,** adj. —**pru′-dent•ly,** adv.

prune[1] (prōōn) n. a dried plum.

prune[2] (prōōn) v.t., **pruned, prun-ing. 1.** to cut off undesirable twigs, branches, etc., from. **2.** to remove (anything undesirable).

pru′ri•ent (prōōr′ē ənt) adj. having or causing lewd thoughts. —**pru′ri-ence,** n.

pry[1] (prī) v.i., **pried, prying.** to inquire or look too closely.

pry[2] (prī) v.t., **pried, prying. 1.** to move or open with a lever. **2.** to obtain with difficulty.

P.S. 1. postscript. **2.** Public School.

psalm (säm) n. a sacred song.

pseu′do (sōō′dō) adj. false.

pseu′do•nym (sōōd′n im) n. a false name used by a writer.

psi (sī, psī) n., pl. **psis.** the 23rd letter of the Greek alphabet.

psit′ta•co′sis (sit′ə kō′sis) n. a disease affecting birds and transmissible to humans.

pso•ri′a•sis (sə rī′ə sis) n. a chronic, inflammatory skin disease.

psych (sīk) v.t. Informal. **1.** to intimidate. **2.** to prepare psychologically.

psy′che (sī′kē) n. the human soul or mind.

psy′che•del′ic (sī′ki del′ik) adj. of or causing a mental state of distorted sense perceptions and hallucinations.

psy•chi′a•try (si kī′ə trē, sī-) n. the branch of medicine concerned with mental diseases. —**psy•chi•at′ric** (sī′kē a′trik) adj. —**psy•chi′a•trist,** n.

psy′chic (sī′kik) adj. **1.** of the psyche. **2.** pertaining to an apparently nonphysical force or agency. —n. **3.** a person sensitive to psychic influences.

psy•cho•a•nal′y•sis n. a professional technique for investigating conscious and unconscious psychological processes and treating mental illness. —**psy′cho•an′a•lyst,** n. —**psy′cho•an′a•lyze′,** v.t.

psy•chol′o•gy (sī kol′ə jē) n. the science of mental states and behavior. —**psy′cho•log′i•cal** (-kə loj′i-kəl) adj. —**psy•chol′o•gist,** n.

psy′cho•path′ (sī′kə path′) n. a person having a disorder marked by amoral or antisocial behavior. —**psy′cho•path′ic,** adj. —**psy′-chop•a•thy** (-kop′ə thē), n.

psy•cho′sis (sī kō′sis) n., pl. **-ses** (-sēz). a severe mental disorder marked by delusions. —**psy•chot′ic** (sī kot′ik) adj.

psy′cho•so•mat′ic (-sə mat′ik) adj. (of a physical disorder) caused by one's emotional state.

psy′cho•ther′a•py n., pl. **-pies.**

the treatment of mental disorders. —psy/cho·ther/a·pist, n.

pt. 1. part. 2. pint. 3. point.

ptar/mi·gan (tär/mi gən) n. a species of mountain grouse.

pter/o·dac/tyl (ter/ə dak/til) n. an extinct flying reptile.

pto/maine (tō/mān) n. a substance produced during the decay of plant and animal matter.

pub (pub) n. a tavern.

pu/ber·ty (pyōō/bər tē) n. the period of life when a person reaches sexual maturity. —pu/ber·tal, adj.

pu·bes/cent (-bes/ənt) adj. arriving at puberty. —pu·bes/cence, n.

pu/bic (pyōō/bik) adj. of or near the genitals.

pub/lic (pub/lik) adj. 1. of or for people generally. 2. open to the view or knowledge of all. —n. 3. people.

pub/li·ca/tion n. 1. the act of publishing a book, piece of music, etc. 2. something published.

pub/lic defend/er n. a lawyer who represents impoverished clients at public expense.

pub/lic domain/ n. the legal status of material no longer protected by copyright or patent.

pub·lic/i·ty (pu blis/i tē) n. 1. public attention directed to someone or something. 2. material promoting this.

pub/li·cize/ v.t., -cized, -cizing. to bring to public notice.

pub/lic rela/tions n.pl. the actions of an organization in promoting goodwill with the public.

pub/lish (pub/lish) v.t. 1. to issue (printed matter) for general distribution. 2. to make publicly known. —v.i. 3. to issue newspapers, books, etc. —pub/lish·er, n.

puck (puk) n. a black rubber disk hit into the goal in hockey.

puck/er (puk/ər) v.t., v.i. 1. to draw or gather into wrinkles. —n. 2. a wrinkle.

puck/ish (puk/ish) adj. mischievous.

pud/ding (pŏŏd/ing) n. a soft, creamy dessert.

pud/dle (pud/l) n. a small pool of water.

pudg/y (puj/ē) adj., -ier, -iest. short and fat. —pudg/i·ness, n.

pueb/lo (pweb/lō) n., pl. -los. a communal dwelling of certain Indians in the southwestern U.S.

pu/er·ile (pyōō/ər il, -ə rīl/) adj. childish. —pu/er·il/i·ty, n.

puff (puf) n. 1. a short, light blowing of air, smoke, etc. 2. a ball or pad of light, soft material. 3. an overenthusiastic review of a book, performance, etc. —v.i. 4. to blow with puffs. 5. to breathe hard and fast. —v.t. 6. to send forth in puffs. 7. to inflate. —puff/i·ness, n. —puff/y, adj.

puf/fin (puf/in) n. a sea bird with a short neck and a colorful bill.

pug (pug) n. a kind of small dog with a wrinkled face.

pu/gil·ism (pyōō/jə liz/əm) n. boxing. —pu/gil·ist, n.

pug·na/cious (pug nā/shəs) adj. always ready to fight. —pug·nac/i·ty (-nas/ə tē) n.

pug/ nose/ n. a short, broad, somewhat turned-up nose.

puke (pyōōk) v., puked, puking, n. Slang. —v.i., v.t. 1. to vomit. —n. 2. vomit.

pul/chri·tude/ (pul/kri tōōd/, -tyōōd/) n. beauty.

pule (pyōōl) v.i., puled, puling. to whine.

pull (pŏŏl) v.t. 1. to draw; haul. 2. to move (something) toward oneself with force. 3. to strain (a muscle). 4. to tear. —v.i. 5. to exert a drawing or hauling force. 6. to move or go. 7. **pull for,** to support actively. 8. **~ off,** Informal. to perform successfully. 9. **~ through,** to come through safely. —n. 10. the act of pulling. 11. force. 12. a handle. 13. influence.

pul/let (pŏŏl/it) n. a young hen.

pul/ley (pŏŏl/ē) n. a wheel for guiding a rope.

Pull/man (pŏŏl/mən) Trademark. a railroad sleeping car.

pull/out/ n. 1. a withdrawal. 2. a section of a publication that can be pulled out.

pull/o/ver adj. 1. put on by being drawn over the head. —n. 2. a pullover garment.

pul/mo·nar/y (pul/mə ner/ē, pŏŏl/-) adj. of the lungs.

pulp (pulp) n. 1. the soft fleshy part of fruit. 2. the inner substance of

the tooth. 3. any soft, moist mass. —v.t. 4. to reduce to pulp.

pul/pit (pŏŏl/pit, pul/-) n. a raised structure in a church from which a sermon is preached.

pul/sar (pul/sär) n. a celestial object that emits regular pulses of radiation.

pul/sate (pul/sāt) v.i., -sated, -sating. to expand and contract rhythmically. —pul·sa/tion, n.

pulse (puls) n., v., pulsed, pulsing. —n. 1. the heartbeat. —v.i. 2. to beat or throb.

pul/ver·ize/ (pul/və rīz/) v.t., v.i., -ized, -izing. to reduce to or be reduced to powder.

pu/ma (pyōō/mə, pōō/-) n. a cougar.

pum/ice (pum/is) n. a porous volcanic glass used as an abrasive.

pum/mel (pum/əl) v.t., -meled, -meling. to strike or beat with the fists.

pump (pump) n. 1. a device for raising or driving fluids. —v.t. 2. to raise or drive with a pump. 3. to move by an up and down action. 4. to try to get information from.

pum/per·nick/el (pum/pər nik/əl) n. a coarse, dark rye bread.

pump/kin (pump/kin or, commonly, pung/kin) n. a large, edible orange fruit of a garden vine.

pun (pun) n., v., punned, punning. —n. 1. a humorous use of words alike in sound but different in meaning. —v.i. 2. to make puns. —pun/ster, n.

punch¹ (punch) n. 1. a thrusting blow with the fist. —v.t. 2. to hit with the fist. 3. to strike or hit in operating.

punch² (punch) n. 1. a tool or machine for making holes, driving nails, etc. —v.t. 2. to make (a hole) with a punch.

punch³ (punch) n. a beverage of fruit juice, sugar, soda, and sometimes alcohol.

punch/ card/ n. a card on which data is stored in a pattern of small holes.

pun/cheon (pun/chən) n. a large cask.

punch/ line/ n. the climactic phrase in a joke.

punch/y adj., -ier, -iest. 1. befuddled; dazed. 2. forceful.

punc·til/i·ous (pungk til/ē əs) adj. exact in the observance of the formalities of conduct.

punc/tu·al (pungk/chōō əl) adj. arriving on time; prompt. —punc/tu·al/i·ty, n.

punc/tu·ate/ (-āt/) v.t., -ated, -ating. 1. to mark with punctuation. 2. to interrupt periodically.

punc/tu·a/tion n. the use of commas, semicolons, etc.

punc/ture (pungk/chər) n., v., -tured, -turing. —n. 1. the act of piercing with a pointed object. 2. a hole so made. —v.t., v.i. 3. to pierce with a pointed object.

pun/dit (pun/dit) n. an expert.

pun/gent (pun/jənt) adj. 1. sharp in taste; biting. 2. forceful and sharp. —pun/gen·cy, n.

pun/ish (pun/ish) v.t. to subject to pain, confinement, loss, etc., for an offense. —pun/ish·ment, n.

pu/ni·tive (pyōō/ni tiv) adj. punishing.

punk (pungk) n. 1. Slang. something or someone worthless or unimportant. 2. Slang. a young hoodlum. 3. Also, **punk rock.** rock music marked by aggressive lyrics. 4. a style marked by bizarre clothing, hairstyles, etc., suggesting defiance of social norms. —adj. 5. Informal. poor in quality. 6. of punk rock or the punk style.

punt¹ (punt) n. 1. a kick in football. —v.t., v.i. 2. to kick (a dropped ball) before it touches the ground.

punt² (punt) n. 1. a small, flat-bottomed boat. —v.t., v.i. 2. to propel (a punt) with a pole.

pu/ny (pyōō/nē) adj., -nier, -niest. small and weak.

pup (pup) n. a young dog.

pu/pa (pyōō/pə) n., pl. -pae (-pē) -pas. an insect in the stage between the larva and the winged adult. —pu/pal, adj.

pu/pil¹ (pyōō/pəl) n. a person being taught.

pu/pil² (pyōō/pəl) n. the opening in the iris of the eye.

pup/pet (pup/it) n. 1. a doll or figure manipulated by the hand or by strings. 2. a person, government, etc., whose actions are controlled by another. —pup/pet·ry, n.

pup/pet·eer/ (pup/i tēr/) n. a person who manipulates puppets.

pup/py (pup/ē) n., pl. -pies. a young dog.

pup/ tent/ n. a small tent.

pur/blind (pûr/blīnd/) adj. 1. partially blind. 2. lacking understanding.

pur/chase (pûr/chəs) v., -chased, -chasing, n. —v.t. 1. to buy. —n. 2. acquisition by payment. 3. something bought. 4. leverage.

pure (pyŏŏr) adj., purer, purest. 1. free of pollutants. 2. being that and nothing else. 3. absolute. 4. theoretical, as science or mathematics. 5. chaste. —pure/ly, adv.

pure/bred (adj. -bred/) 1. having ancestors over many generations from a recognized breed. —n. 2. (pyōōr/bred/) a purebred animal.

pu·rée/ (pyŏŏ rā/, -rē/) n., v., -réed, -réeing. —n. 1. cooked food that has been sieved or blended. —v.t. 2. to make a purée of.

pur/ga·to/ry (pûr/gə tôr/ē) n., pl. -ries. (esp. in Roman Catholic belief) a place or state in which penitent souls are purified after death. 2. any condition or place of temporary punishment.

purge (pûrj) v., purged, purging. —v.t. 1. to cleanse; purify. 2. to eliminate (undesirable members) from an organization. 3. to clear (the stomach or intestines) by causing evacuation. —n. 4. the act or means of purging. —pur/ga·tive (-gə tiv) adj., n.

pu/ri·fy/ (pyōōr/ə fī/) v.t., v.i., -fied, -fying. to make or become pure.

Pu/rim (pŏŏr/im) n. a Jewish festival commemorating the saving of the Jews in Persia from destruction.

pur/ism (pyŏŏr/iz əm) n. insistence on purity in language, style, etc.

Pu/ri·tan (pyōōr/i tn) n. 1. a member of a strict Protestant group originating in 16th-century England. 2. **puritan,** a person of strict moral views. —pu/ri·tan/i·cal, adj.

pu/ri·ty (pyōōr/i tē) n. the condition of being pure.

purl (pûrl) v.t., v.i. to knit with an inverted stitch.

pur/lieu (pûr/lōō, pûrl/yōō) n., pl. -lieus. 1. purlieus, neighborhood. 2. an outlying district.

pur/loin/ (pər loin/, pûr/loin) v.t., v.i. to steal.

pur/ple (pûr/pəl) n. a color blended of red and blue.

pur/port v.t. (pər pôrt/) 1. to claim. 2. to imply. —n. (pûr/pôrt) 3. meaning.

pur/pose (pûr/pəs) n., v., -posed, -posing. —n. 1. the reason for which something is done, made, etc. 2. intention. —v.t., v.i. 3. to intend. —Idiom. 4. **on purpose,** intentionally. —pur/pose·ful, adj. —pur/pose·less, adj.

purr (pûr) n. 1. the low, continuous vibrating sound made by a cat. —v.i. 2. to make this sound.

purse (pûrs) n., v., pursed, pursing. —n. 1. a bag for money and small things. 2. a sum of money offered as a prize or gift. —v.t. 3. to pucker, as the lips.

purs/er n. a financial officer on a ship.

pur·su/ant (pər sōō/ənt) adv. **pursuant to,** according to.

pur·sue/ v.t., -sued, -suing. 1. to follow in order to catch. 2. to carry on or engage in.

pur·suit/ (-sōōt/) n. 1. the act of pursuing. 2. an occupation or pastime.

pu/ru·lent (pyōōr/ə lənt, pyōōr/yə-) adj. full of pus. —pu/ru·lence, n.

pur·vey/ (pər vā/) v.t. to provide; supply. —pur·vey/or, n.

pur/view (pûr/vyōō) n. the range of operation, authority, or concern.

pus (pus) n. the liquid matter found in sores, abscesses, etc.

push (pŏŏsh) v.t. 1. to press against with force to move forward. 2. to put demands on. 3. to urge. 4. Slang. to peddle (illicit drugs). —v.i. 5. to exert a thrusting force on something. 6. to proceed by strong effort. —n. 7. the act of pushing. 8. a strong effort.

push/o/ver n. one easily victimized or overcome.

push/y adj., -ier, -iest. obnoxiously self-assertive. —push/i·ness, n.

pu/sil·lan/i·mous (pyōō/sə lan/ə-məs) adj. cowardly.

puss/y (pŏŏs/ē) n., pl. **pussies.** a cat. Also, **puss.**

puss/y·foot/ v.i. 1. to move stealthily. 2. to act irresolutely.

puss/y wil/low n. a small willow with silky catkins.

pus/tule (pus/chōōl) n. a pimple containing pus.

put (pŏŏt) v., put, putting. n. —v.t. 1. to cause to be in a specific place, condition, relation, etc. 2. to set to a task. 3. to express. 4. to apply to a purpose. 5. to impose. 6. to throw. 7. **put across,** to cause to be understood or accepted. 8. **put off, a.** to postpone. **b.** to evade. 9. **~ up with,** to tolerate.

put/-down/ n. Informal. a snubbing remark.

pu/tre·fy/ (pyōō/trə fī/) v.t., v.i., -fied, -fying. to rot. —pu/tre·fac/tion (-fak/shən) n.

pu·tres/cent (-tres/ənt) adj. becoming putrid. —pu·tres/cence, n.

pu/trid (-trid) adj. rotten.

putsch (pŏŏch) n. a sudden political revolt or uprising.

putt (put) v.t., v.i. 1. to strike (a golf ball) gently. —n. 2. such a stroke.

put/ter¹ (put/ər) v.i. to busy oneself in a leisurely manner.

put/ter² (put/ər) n. a club for putting.

put/ty (put/ē) n., v., -tied, -tying. —n. 1. a compound of whiting and oil used to secure windowpanes, fill holes, etc. —v.t. 2. to secure with putty.

puz/zle (puz/əl) n., v., -zled, -zling. —n. 1. a toy, game, or problem to be solved for amusement. 2. a difficult question or matter. —v.t. 3. to mystify. —v.i. 4. to ponder a perplexing problem.

Pvt. Private.

PX post exchange.

pyg/my (pig/mē) n., pl. -mies. a dwarf.

py/lon (pī/lon) n. a tall thin metal structure used as a support.

py·lo/rus (pī lôr/əs, pi-) n., pl. -lori (-lôr/ī). the opening between the stomach and the start of the intestine. —py·lor/ic, adj.

py/or·rhe/a (pī/ə rē/ə) n. a gum disease.

pyr/a·mid (pir/ə mid) n. a solid with triangular sides meeting in a point at the top. —py·ram/i·dal (pə ram/ə dl) adj.

pyre (pī³r) n. a heap of wood, esp. for burning a corpse.

py/rite (pī/rīt) n. a common yellow mineral containing sulfur and iron.

py/ro·ma/ni·a (pī/rə mā/nē ə) n. a compulsion for setting fires. —py/-ro·ma/ni·ac/, n.

py/ro·tech/nics (-tek/niks) n. a firework display. —py/ro·tech/nic, adj.

py/thon (pī/thon) n. a large snake that kills by crushing its prey.

pyx (piks) n. the container in which the reserved Eucharist is kept.

Q

Q, q (kyōō) n. the seventeenth letter of the English alphabet.

Q.E.D. which was to be shown or demonstrated.

qt. pl. qt., qts. quart.

qty. quantity.

quack¹ (kwak) n. 1. the harsh cry of a duck. —v.i. 2. to utter a quack.

quack² (kwak) n. a fraudulent pretender to medical or other skill. —quack/er·y, n.

quad¹ (kwod) n. a quadrangle.

quad² (kwod) n. a quadruplet.

quad/ran/gle (-rang/gəl) n. 1. a plane figure with four angles and four sides. 2. a four-sided area surrounded by buildings. —quad·ran/gu·lar (kwo drang/gyə lər) adj.

quad/rant (-rənt) n. 1. an arc of 90°. 2. an instrument for measuring altitudes.

quad/ra·phon/ic (-rə fon/ik) adj. of sound reproduced through four recording tracks.

quad·ren/ni·al (kwo dren/ē əl) adj. 1. occurring every four years. 2. of or lasting for four years.

quad/ri·lat/er·al (-lat/ər əl) adj. 1. four-sided. —n. 2. a four-sided plane figure.

qua·drille/ (kwo dril/, kwə-) n. a square dance for four couples.

quad/ri·ple/gi·a (kwod/rə plē/jē ə, -jə) n. paralysis of the entire body below the neck. —quad/ri·ple/gic, n., adj.

quad/ru·ped/ (-rŏŏ ped/) n. a four-footed animal.

quad·ru/ple (kwo drŏŏ/pəl, -drup/əl) adj., n., v., -pled, -pling. —adj. 1. of four parts. 2. four times as great. —n. 3. a number or

amount four times as great as another. —v.t., v.i. 4. to make or become four times as great.

quad·ru/plet (-drup/lit, -drōō/plit) n. one of four children born at one birth.

quad·ru/pli·cate (-drōō/pli kit) n. a group of four copies.

quaff (kwof, kwaf) v.i., v.t. 1. to drink heartily. —n. 2. a beverage quaffed.

quag/mire/ (kwag/mī³r/, kwog/-) n. boggy ground.

qua/hog (kwô/hog, kō/-) n. an edible American clam.

quail¹ (kwāl) n., pl. **quails, quail.** a game bird resembling domestic fowls.

quail² (kwāl) v.i. to shrink in fear.

quaint (kwānt) adj. pleasingly old-fashioned or odd. —quaint/ly, adv.

quake (kwāk) v.i., quaked, quaking. to tremble.

Quak/er (kwā/kər) n. a member of the Society of Friends.

qual/i·fy/ (kwol/ə fī/) v., -fied, -fying. —v.t 1. to make proper or fit, as for a job. 2. to modify or limit. 3. to moderate. —v.i. 4. to show oneself fit, competent, or eligible. —qual·i·fi·ca/tion, n.

qual/i·ty (-i tē) n., pl. -ties. 1. a characteristic or property. 2. relative merit. 3. excellence.

qual/ity time/ n. time devoted exclusively to nurturing a cherished person or activity.

qualm (kwäm), n. a pang of conscience; misgiving.

quan/da·ry (kwon/də rē, -drē) n., pl. -ries. a dilemma.

quan/ti·fy/ (kwon/tə fī/) v.t., -fied, -fying. to determine or express the quantity of.

quan/ti·ty (-ti tē) n., pl. -ties. 1. a definite or indefinite amount or measure. 2. a large amount.

quan/tum (-təm) n., pl. **-ta,** adj. —n. 1. quantity or amount. 2. Physics. a very small, indivisible quantity of energy. —adj. 3. sudden and significant.

quar/an·tine/ (kwôr/ən tēn/) n., v., -tined, -tining. —n. 1. strict isolation to prevent spread of disease. —v.t. 2. to put in quarantine.

quark (kwôrk, kwärk) n. a subatomic particle thought to form the basis of all matter.

quar/rel (kwôr/əl) n., v., -reled, -reling. —n. 1. an angry dispute. —v.i. 2. to disagree angrily. —quar/rel·some, adj.

quar/ry (kwôr/ē) n., pl. -ries, v., -ried, -rying. —n. 1. a pit from which stone is taken. 2. an object of pursuit. —v.t. 3. to get from a quarry.

quart (kwôrt) n. a measure of capacity: in liquid measure, $\frac{1}{4}$ gallon; in dry measure, $\frac{1}{8}$ peck.

quar/ter n. 1. one of four equal parts. 2. a coin worth 25 cents. 3. quarters, lodgings; accommodations. 4. mercy. —v.t. 5. to divide into quarters. 6. to lodge.

quar/ter·deck/ n. the rear part of a ship's upper deck.

quar/ter horse/ n. a horse capable of great sprints of speed.

quar/ter·ly adj., n., pl. -lies, adv. —adj. 1. occurring, done, etc., each quarter year. 2. a quarterly publication. —adv. 3. once each quarter year.

quar/ter·mas/ter n. 1. a military officer in charge of quarters, supplies, etc. 2. a naval officer in charge of signals.

quar/ter note/ n. a musical note equal in time value to one quarter of a whole note.

quar·tet/ (kwôr tet/) n. 1. a group of four singers or players. 2. a musical composition for four performers.

quar/to (kwôr/tō) n., pl. -tos. a book page of sheets folded twice.

quartz (kwôrts) n. a hard crystalline mineral.

qua/sar (kwā/zär, -zər) n. an astronomical source of powerful radio energy.

quash (kwosh) v.t. to subdue; suppress.

qua/si (kwā/zī, -sī, kwä/sē, -zē) adj. resembling; seeming to be.

quasi- a prefix meaning somewhat.

Quat/er·nar/y (kwot/ər ner/ē, kwə-tûr/nə rē) adj. pertaining to the present geologic period forming the latter part of the Cenozoic Era.

quat/rain (kwo/trān) n. a four-line stanza.

qua/ver (kwā/vər) v.i. 1. to quiver. 2. to speak in a trembling tone. —n. 3. a quavering tone.

quay (kē) *n.* a landing place beside water; wharf.

quea'sy (kwē'zē) *adj.* **-sier, -siest.** 1. nauseated. 2. uneasy.

queen (kwēn) *n.* 1. a female sovereign. 2. the wife of a king. 3. the fertile female of bees, ants, etc. —*v.t.* 4. to crown as queen.

queer (kwēr) *adj.* 1. strange; odd. —*n.* 2. *Slang: Disparaging and Offensive.* (a contemptuous term used to refer to a homosexual.)

quell (kwel) *v.t.* to suppress.

quench (kwench) *v.t.* 1. to satisfy or slake. 2. to extinguish.

quer'u·lous (kwer'ə ləs, kwer'yə-) *adj.* complaining; whining.

que'ry (kwēr'ē) *n., pl.* **-ries,** *v.,* **-ried, -rying.** —*n.* 1. a question. —*v.t.* 2. to question.

quest (kwest) *n.* a search.

ques'tion (kwes'chən) *n.* 1. a sentence in a form intended to elicit information. 2. a matter for discussion or dispute. —*v.t.* 3. to ask questions of. 4. to doubt or dispute. —**ques'tion·er,** *n.*

ques'tion·a·ble *adj.* 1. of doubtful honesty or morality. 2. uncertain.

ques'tion mark' *n.* a punctuation mark (?) indicating a question.

ques'tion·naire' (-chə när') *n.* a list of questions.

queue (kyōō) *n., v.,* **queued, queuing.** —*n.* 1. a line of persons. 2. a single braid of hair. —*v.t.* 3. **queue up,** to form a line while waiting.

quib'ble (kwib'əl) *v.,* **-bled, -bling,** *n.* —*v.i.* 1. to speak ambiguously in evasion. 2. to make petty objections. —*n.* 3. the act of quibbling.

quiche (kēsh) *n.* a pie of unsweetened custard and cheese, onion, etc.

quick (kwik) *adj.* 1. prompt; done promptly. 2. swift. 3. alert. —*n.* 4. living persons. 5. sensitive flesh under the nails. —*adv.* 6. in a quick manner. —**quick'ly,** *adv.*

quick' bread' *n.* bread made with leavening that permits immediate baking.

quick'en *v.t.* 1. to hasten. —*v.i.* 2. to become livelier or more rapid.

quick'ie *n.* something done or enjoyed in only a short time.

quick'lime' *n.* untreated lime.

quick'sand' *n.* soft sand yielding easily to weight.

quick'sil'ver *n.* mercury.

quid pro quo (kwid' prō kwō') *n., pl.* **quid pro quos, quids pro quo.** something given or taken in return for something else.

qui·es'cent (kwē es'ənt, kwī-) *adj.* inactive. —**qui·es'cence,** *n.*

qui'et (kwī'it) *adj.* 1. being at rest. 2. peaceful. 3. silent. 4. restrained. —*v.t., v.i.* 5. to make or become quiet. —*n.* 6. tranquillity. 7. silence. —**qui'et·ly,** *adv.*

qui·e'tus (kwī ē'təs) *n.* 1. a final settlement. 2. release from life.

quill (kwil) *n.* 1. a large feather. 2. a spine of a porcupine.

quilt (kwilt) *n.* a padded and lined bed covering. —**quilt'ed,** *adj.*

quince (kwins) *n.* a yellowish acid fruit.

qui'nine (kwī'nīn) *n.* a bitter substance used esp. to treat malaria.

quin·tes'sence (kwin tes'əns) *n.* the pure essence or most perfect example of something. —**quin'tes·sen'tial** (-tə sen'shəl) *adj.*

quin·tet' (kwin tet') *n.* 1. a group of five singers or players. 2. a musical composition for a quintet.

quin·tu'plet (-tup'lit, -tōō'plit, -tyōō'-) *n.* one of five children born at one birth.

quip (kwip) *n., v.,* **quipped, quipping.** —*n.* 1. a witty or sarcastic remark. —*v.i.* 2. to make a quip.

quire (kwīⁱr) *n.* a set of 24 uniform sheets of paper.

quirk (kwûrk) *n.* a peculiarity. —**quirk'y,** *adj.*

quirt (kwûrt) *n.* a short riding whip.

quis'ling (kwiz'ling) *n.* a traitor.

quit (kwit) *v.,* **quit** or **quitted, quitting.** —*v.t.* 1. to stop. 2. to give up or leave. —*v.i.* 3. to give up a job or position.

quit'claim' *n.* a transfer of one's interest.

quite (kwīt) *adv.* 1. completely. 2. really.

quits (kwits) *adj.* 1. being on equal terms. —*Idiom.* 2. **call it quits,** to end something.

quit'tance (kwit'ns) *n.* 1. recompense. 2. discharge from debt.

quiv'er¹ (kwiv'ər) *v.i.* 1. to tremble. —*n.* 2. the act of quivering.

quiv·er² (kwiv'ər) *n.* a case for arrows.

quix·ot'ic (kwik sot'ik) *adj.* extravagantly idealistic; impractical.

quiz (kwiz) *v.,* **quizzed, quizzing,** *n., pl.* **quizzes.** —*v.t.* 1. to question. —*n.* 2. a short test.

quiz'zi·cal *adj.* 1. comical. 2. puzzled. —**quiz'zi·cal·ly,** *adv.*

quoin (koin, kwoin) *n.* 1. an external solid angle. 2. a cornerstone.

quoit (kwoit, koit) *n.* a flat ring thrown to encircle a peg in the game of **quoits.**

quon'dam (kwon'dəm, -dam) *adj.* former.

Quon'set hut' (kwon'sit) *Trademark.* a semicylindrical metal shelter with end walls.

quo'rum (kwôr'əm) *n.* the number of members needed to transact business legally.

quo'ta (kwō'tə) *n.* 1. the proportional share due. 2. the number or amount officially allowed.

quo·ta'tion (kwō tā'shən) *n.* 1. the act of quoting. 2. the words quoted. 3. a stated price.

quota'tion mark' *n.* one of a pair of punctuation marks enclosing a quotation, shown as (") at the beginning and (") at the end.

quote (kwōt) *v.,* **quoted, quoting,** *n.* —*v.t.* 1. to repeat verbatim. 2. to cite. 3. to state (a price). —*n.* 4. *Informal.* a quotation.

quoth (kwōth) *v. Archaic.* said.

quo·tid'i·an (kwō tid'ē ən) *adj.* 1. daily; everyday. 2. ordinary.

quo'tient (kwō'shənt) *n.* the number of times one number is contained in another.

R

R, r (är) *n.* the eighteenth letter of the English alphabet.

rab'bi (rab'ī) *n.* a Jewish religious leader. —**rab·bin'ic** (rə bin'ik), **rab·bin'i·cal,** *adj.*

rab'bin·ate (rab'ə nit, -nāt') *n.* 1. the office of a rabbi. 2. rabbis collectively.

rab'bit (rab'it) *n.* a long-eared hopping mammal.

rab'ble (rab'əl) *n.* 1. a mob. 2. the common people.

rab'ble-rous'er (-rou'zər) *n.* a person who stirs up the public.

rab'id (rab'id) *adj.* 1. irrationally intense. 2. having rabies.

ra'bies (rā'bēz) *n.* a fatal disease transmitted by the bite of an infected animal.

rac·coon' (ra kōōn') *n.* a small nocturnal carnivorous mammal.

race¹ (rās) *n., v.,* **raced, racing.** —*n.* 1. a contest of speed. 2. a competition. 3. onward flow or course. —*v.i., v.t.* 4. to run a race (against). 5. to (cause to) run or go swiftly. —**rac'er,** *n.*

race² (rās) *n.* 1. a group of people related by common descent, language, etc. 2. a classification of humans based on physical characteristics. —**ra'cial** (rā'shəl) *adj.*

ra·ceme' (rā sēm', rə-) *n.* a flower cluster with flowers borne on stalks along the main stem.

rac'ism (rā'siz əm) *n.* hatred of or prejudice against another race.

rack¹ (rak) *n.* 1. a structure for storage. 2. a toothed bar engaging with the teeth of a pinion. 3. a torture device.

rack² (rak) *n.* rack and ruin, decline or destruction.

rack·et¹ (rak'it) *n.* 1. loud noise. 2. a dishonest or illegal activity.

rack·et² (rak'it) *n.* a bat with a netted frame, used in tennis, badminton, etc. Also, **rac'quet.**

rack'e·teer' *n.* a criminal engaged in a racket.

rac'on·teur' (rak'on tûr', -tōōr', -ən-) *n.* a skilled storyteller.

rac'quet·ball (rak'it-) *n.* a game like handball, played with rackets.

rac'y (rā'sē) *adj.,* **-ier, -iest.** 1. lively. 2. risqué. —**rac'i·ly,** *adv.*

ra'dar (rā'där) *n.* an electronic device that locates unseen objects by measuring radio waves.

ra'di·al (-dē əl) *adj.* of rays or radii.

ra'di·ant (-ənt) *adj.* 1. emitting rays of light. 2. bright; exultant. 3. emitted in rays. —**ra'di·ance,** *n.* —**ra'di·ant·ly,** *adv.*

ra'di·ate (-āt') *v.,* **-ated, -ating.** —*v.i.* 1. to spread like rays from a center. 2. to emit rays. —*v.t.* 3. to emit in rays.

ra'di·a'tion *n.* 1. the process in which energy is emitted as particles or waves, transmitted, and absorbed. 2. the process of radiating. 3. something radiated.

ra'di·a'tor *n.* 1. a heating device. 2. an engine-cooling device.

rad'i·cal (rad'i kəl) *adj.* 1. favoring drastic reforms. 2. basic. —*n.* 3. a person with radical ideas. 4. an atom or group of atoms behaving as a unit. —**rad'i·cal·ism,** *n.* —**rad'i·cal·ly,** *adv.*

ra'di·o (rā'dē ō') *n., pl.* **-dios.** 1. a way of transmitting sound by electromagnetic waves, without wires. 2. an apparatus for sending or receiving such waves.

ra'di·o·ac'tive *adj.* emitting radiation from the atomic nucleus. —**ra'di·o·ac·tiv'i·ty,** *n.*

ra'di·o·car'bon *n.* a radioactive isotope of carbon, used in dating organic materials.

ra'di·ol'o·gy (-ol'ə jē) *n.* the use of radiation, as x-rays, for medical diagnosis and treatment.

rad'ish (rad'ish) *n.* the crisp root of a garden plant, eaten raw.

ra'di·um (rā'dē əm) *n.* a radioactive metallic element.

ra'di·us (-əs) *n., pl.* **-dii** (-dē ī) **-diuses.** 1. a straight line from the center of a circle to the circumference. 2. a bone of the forearm.

ra'don (rā'don) *n.* an inert radioactive gaseous element produced by the decay of radium.

RAF Royal Air Force.

raf'fi·a (raf'ē ə) *n.* a fiber made from the leafstalks of a palm.

raff'ish (raf'ish) *adj.* 1. jaunty; rakish. 2. gaudily vulgar or cheap.

raf'fle (raf'əl) *n., v.,* **-fled, -fling.** —*n.* 1. a lottery in which people buy chances to win a prize. —*v.t.* 2. to dispose of by raffle.

raft (raft) *n.* a floating platform of logs or planks.

raft'er (raf'tər) *n.* a framing timber of a roof.

rag (rag) *n.* a torn or worn scrap of cloth.

rag·a·muf'fin (rag'ə muf'in) *n.* a ragged child.

rage (rāj) *n., v.,* **raged, raging.** —*n.* 1. violent anger. 2. an object of popular enthusiasm. —*v.i.* 3. to be violently angry. 4. to move or act violently.

rag'ged (rag'id) *adj.* 1. clothed in torn garments. 2. torn or tattered. 3. rough or uneven.

rag'lan sleeve' *n.* a set-in sleeve with a slanting seam from neckline to armhole.

ra·gout' (ra gōō') *n.* a stew.

rag'time' *n.* syncopated jazz.

rag'weed' *n.* a plant whose pollen causes hay fever.

raid (rād) *n.* 1. a sudden assault or attack. —*v.t., v.i.* 2. to attack suddenly.

rail¹ (rāl) *n.* 1. a horizontal bar forming a support or barrier. 2. one of a pair of steel bars forming a railroad track. 3. railroad.

rail² (rāl) *v.i.* to complain bitterly.

rail'ing *n.* a barrier of rails and posts.

rail'ler·y (rā'lə rē) *n.* good-humored kidding; banter.

rail'road' *n.* 1. a road with fixed rails on which trains run. 2. a system of such roads and trains. —*v.t.* 3. to push through hastily.

rail'way' *n. Chiefly Brit.* a railroad.

rai'ment (rā'mənt) *n.* clothing.

rain (rān) *n.* 1. water falling from the sky in drops. 2. a heavy, continuous fall. —*v.i., v.t.* 3. to fall or send down as rain. —**rain'y,** *adj.*

rain'bow' (-bō') *n.* an arc of colors sometimes seen in the sky opposite the sun during rain.

rain' check' *n.* 1. a postponement of an invitation. 2. a ticket for future admission to an event postponed by rain.

rain'coat' *n.* a waterproof coat.

rain'fall' *n.* the amount of rain falling in an area in a given time.

rain'for'est *n.* a tropical forest in an area of high annual rainfall.

raise (rāz) *v.,* **raised, raising,** *n.* —*v.t.* 1. to lift up. 2. to set upright. 3. to cause to appear or arise. 4. to grow. 5. to increase, as in amount. 6. to collect. 7. to rear. —*n.* 8. an increase in pay.

rai'sin (rā'zin) *n.* a dried grape.

rai·son d'être (rā'zōn de'trə) *n., pl.* **raisons d'être.** reason for existence.

ra'jah (rä'jə) *n.* (formerly) an Indian king or prince.

rake¹ (rāk) *n., v.,* **raked, raking.** —*n.* 1. an agricultural tool with a handle and row of teeth. —*v.t.* 2. to gather or smooth with a rake. 3. to gather in abundance. 4. to sweep with gunfire. —*v.i.* 5. to use a rake.

rake² (rāk) *n.* a dissolute man.

rake'-off' *n.* an amount received, esp. illicitly.

rak'ish (rā'kish) *adj.* jaunty.

ral'ly (ral'ē) *v.,* **-lied, -lying,** *n., pl.* **-lies.** —*v.t., v.i.* 1. to bring or come into order. 2. to call or come together. 3. to (cause to) recover. —*n.* 4. a sharp rise. 5. a renewal of strength. 6. a mass meeting.

ram (ram) *n., v.,* **rammed, ramming.** —*n.* 1. a male sheep. 2. a device for battering, forcing, etc. —*v.t.* 3. to strike forcibly.

RAM (ram) *n.* random-access memory: computer memory for running programs and temporarily storing data.

ram'ble *v.,* **-bled, -bling,** *n.* —*v.i.* 1. to stroll idly. 2. to talk vaguely. —*n.* 3. a stroll. —**ram'bler,** *n.*

ram·bunc'tious (-bungk'shəs) *adj.* difficult to control or handle.

ram'i·fi·ca'tion (ram'ə fi kā'shən) *n.* a consequence.

ram'i·fy' (-ə fī') *v.t., v.i.,* **-fied, -fying.** to divide into branches.

ramp (ramp) *n.* a sloping surface between two levels.

ram'page (ram'pāj) *n., v.,* **-paged, -paging.** —*n.* 1. an eruption of violent behavior. —*v.i.* 2. to move furiously about.

ramp'ant (ram'pənt) *adj.* vigorous; unrestrained.

ram'part (-pärt, -pərt) *n.* a mound of earth raised for defense.

ram'rod' *n.* a rod for cleaning or loading a gun.

ram'shack'le *adj.* rickety.

ranch (ranch) *n.* a large farm, esp. for raising livestock. —**ranch'er,** *n.*

ran'cid (ran'sid) *adj.* smelling or tasting spoiled.

ran'cor (rang'kər) *n.* lasting resentment. —**ran'cor·ous,** *adj.*

ran'dom (ran'dəm) *adj.* occurring or done without aim or pattern.

rand'y (ran'dē) *adj.,* **-ier, -iest.** sexually aroused; lustful.

rang (rang) *v.* pt. of **ring.**

range (rānj) *n., v.,* **ranged, ranging.** —*n.* 1. limits; extent. 2. a row or series. 3. a mountain chain. 4. a grazing area. 5. a cooking stove. 6. a place for target shooting. 7. the distance between gun and target. —*v.t.* 8. to arrange in a line. 9. to pass over (an area). —*v.i.* 10. to vary within limits.

rang'er (rān'jər) *n.* 1. the warden of a forest tract. 2. a civil officer who patrols a large area.

rang'y (rān'jē) *adj.,* **-ier, -iest.** slender and long-limbed.

rank¹ (rangk) *n.* 1. a social or official position or standing. 2. high position. 3. a row or series. 4. **ranks,** enlisted soldiers. —*v.t., v.i.* 5. to put or be in a particular rank.

rank² (rangk) *adj.* 1. growing excessively. 2. smelling bad. 3. utter. —**rank'ness,** *n.*

rank' and file' *n.* 1. members apart from leaders. 2. enlisted soldiers.

rank'ing *adj.* 1. senior. 2. renowned.

ran·kle (rang'kəl) *v.i., v.t.,* **-kled, -kling.** to cause resentment (in).

ran'sack (ran'sak) *v.t.* 1. to search thoroughly. 2. to plunder; pillage.

ran'som (ran'səm) *n.* 1. a sum demanded for the release of a captive. —*v.t.* 2. to pay ransom for.

rant (rant) *v.i.* 1. to speak wildly. —*n.* 2. violent speech. —**rant'er,** *n.*

rap (rap) *n., v.,* **rapped, rapping.** —*v.t., v.i.* 1. to hit quickly and sharply. —*n.* 2. a sharp blow. 3. popular music marked by rhythmical intoning of rhymed verses over a repetitive beat. —**rap'per,** *n.*

ra·pa'cious (rə pā'shəs) *adj.* predatory; greedy.

rape (rāp) *n., v.,* **raped, rap·ing.** —*n.* 1. the act of forcing a person to have sexual intercourse. 2. an act of plunder. —*v.t., v.i.* 3. to commit rape (on). —**rap'ist,** *n.*

rap'id (rap'id) *adj.* 1. swift. —*n.* 2. **rapids,** the swift-moving part of a river. —**ra·pid'i·ty,** *n.* —**rap'id·ly,** *adv.*

ra'pi·er (rā'pē ər) *n.* a slender sword.

rap'ine (rap'in) *n.* plunder.

rap·port' (ra pôr') *n.* a sympathetic relationship.

rap'proche·ment' (rap'rōsh mäN') *n.* an establishment of harmonious relations.

rap·scal'lion (rap skal'yən) *n.* a rascal.

rap' sheet' *n. Slang.* a record of a person's arrests and convictions.

rapt (rapt) *adj.* engrossed.

rap'ture (rap'chər) *n.* ecstatic joy. —**rap'tur·ous,** *adj.*

ra'ra a'vis (râr'ə ā'vis) *n., pl.* **ra'rae a'ves** (râr'ē ē'vēz). a rare person or thing.

rare¹ (râr) *adj.* 1. uncommon. 2. not dense, as a gas. —**rare'ly,** *adv.* —**rare'ness,** *n.* —**rar'i·ty,** *n.*

rare² (râr) *adj.,* **rarer, rarest.** (of meat) cooked just slightly. —**rare'ness,** *n.*

rare'bit (râr'bit) *n.* a dish of melted cheese.

rar·e·fy' (râr'ə fī') *v.t., v.i.,* **-fied, -fying.** to make or become thin, as air.

rar'ing *adj.* very eager or anxious.

ras'cal (ras'kəl) *n.* a dishonest or mischievous person.

rash¹ (rash) *adj.* recklessly hasty. —**rash'ly,** *adv.* —**rash'ness,** *n.*

rash² (rash) *n.* a skin eruption.

rash'er *n.* a serving of bacon.

rasp (rasp) *v.t.* 1. to scrape, as with a file. 2. to irritate. —*v.i.* 3. to speak gratingly. —*n.* 4. a coarse file. 5. a rasping sound.

rasp'ber'ry (raz'ber'ē, -bə rē) *n., pl.* **-ries.** a small, juicy red or black fruit.

rat (rat) *n.* a rodent larger than a mouse.

ratch'et (rach'it) *n.* a wheel or bar with teeth.

rate (rāt) *n., v.,* **rated, rating.** —*n.* 1. a charge in proportion to something that varies. 2. degree of speed or progress. —*v.t.* 3. to estimate the value of. 4. to consider; judge.

rath'er (rath'ər) *adv.* 1. somewhat. 2. in preference. 3. on the contrary.

raths'kel·ler (rät'skel'ər, rat'-) *n.* a restaurant or bar below street level.

rat'i·fy' (rat'ə fī') *v.t.,* **-fied, -fying.** to confirm formally.

ra'tio (rā'shō, -shē ō') *n., pl.* **-tios.** relative number or extent; proportion.

ra'ti·oc'i·na'tion (rash'ē os'ə nā'shən) *n.* reasoning.

ra'tion (rash'ən, rā'shən) *n.* 1. a fixed allowance. —*v.t.* 2. to apportion. 3. to put on a ration.

ra'tion·al (rash'ə nəl) *adj.* 1. sensible. 2. sane. —**ra'tion·al'i·ty,** *n.*

ra'tion·ale' (-nal') *n.* a reasonable basis for action.

ra'tion·al·ism *n.* advocacy of precise reasoning as the source of truth. —**ra'tion·al·ist,** *n.*

ra'tion·al·ize' *v.t., v.i.,* **-ized, -izing.** to find a plausible reason for (one's behavior or attitude).

rat' race' *n.* an exhausting, competitive routine activity.

rat·tan' (ra tan', rə-) *n.* the hollow stem of a climbing palm used for wickerwork.

rat'tle (rat'l) *v.,* **-tled, -tling,** *n.* —*v.i.* 1. to make a series of short, sharp sounds. 2. to chatter. —*v.t.* 3. to cause to make a rattling noise. 4. to disconcert; confuse. —*n.* 5. a rattling sound. 6. a baby's toy that rattles.

rat'tle·snake' *n.* a venomous American snake.

rat'ty *adj.,* **-tier, -tiest.** shabby.

rau'cous (rô'kəs) *adj.* 1. hoarse; harsh. 2. rowdy; disorderly.

raun'chy (rôn'chē, rän'-) *adj.,* **-chier, -chiest.** 1. vulgar; smutty. 2. lecherous. 3. dirty; slovenly.

rav'age (rav'ij) *v.,* **-aged, -aging,** *n.* —*v.t., v.i.* 1. to do ruinous damage (to). —*n.* 2. ruinous damage. —**rav'ag·er,** *n.*

rave (rāv) *v.i.,* **raved, raving.** to talk wildly.

rav'el (rav'əl) *v.t.* 1. to disentangle the threads of. 2. to entangle. 3. to make clear. —*v.i.* 4. to fray.

ra'ven (rā'vən) *n.* a large shiny black bird.

rav'en·ing (rav'ə ning) *adj.* greedy for prey.

rav'en·ous *adj.* very hungry; greedy. —**rav'en·ous·ly,** *adv.*

ra·vine' (rə vēn') *n.* a deep, narrow valley.

ra'vi·o'li (rav'ē ō'lē) *n.* small pockets of pasta filled with cheese or meat.

rav'ish (rav'ish) *v.t.* 1. to seize and carry off. 2. to rape. 3. to fill with strong emotion.

rav'ish·ing *adj.* extremely beautiful.

raw (rô) *adj.* 1. in the natural state. 2. uncooked. 3. damp and chilly. 4. untrained.

raw'boned' *adj.* lean and bony.

raw′hide′ n. the untanned hide of cattle.

ray¹ (rā) n. **1.** a narrow beam of light. **2.** a trace. **3.** a line outward from the center.

ray² (rā) n. a flat-bodied deep-sea fish.

ray′on (rā′on) n. a silklike synthetic fabric.

raze (rāz) v.t., **razed, razing.** to tear down; demolish.

ra′zor (rā′zər) n. a sharp-edged instrument for shaving.

razz (raz) v.t. to make fun of; mock.

R.C. Roman Catholic.

rd. road.

re¹ (rā) n. the musical syllable used for the second note of a scale.

re² (rē, rā) prep. with reference to.

re- **1.** a prefix meaning: back or backward. **2.** again.

reach (rēch) v.t. **1.** to come to. **2.** to be able to touch. **3.** to stretch. **4.** to extend as far as. —v.i. **5.** to stretch with the hand. **6.** to extend. —n. **7.** the act of reaching. **8.** extent.

re·act′ (rē akt′) v.i. **1.** to act upon each other. **2.** to respond.

re·ac′tant (-ak′tənt) n. a substance that undergoes change in a chemical reaction.

re·ac′tion n. **1.** a responsive act. **2.** a reverse movement or tendency. **3.** a chemical change.

re·ac·tion·ar·y adj., n., pl. **-ar·ies.** —adj. **1.** extremely conservative politically. —n. **2.** a reactionary person.

re·ac′tor n. an apparatus for producing useful nuclear energy.

read (rēd) v., **read** (red) **reading.** —v.t. **1.** to understand or utter aloud (something printed or written). **2.** to register. **3.** to access (computer data). —v.i. **4.** to read printed matter. —**Idiom. 5. read between the lines,** to understand by means of implications. —**read′er,** n.

read′er·ship′ n. (rē′dər ship′) n. the people who read a publication.

read′ing (rē′ding) n. **1.** something read. **2.** an interpretation of a written or musical work. **3.** data indicated on an instrument.

read′-on′ly (rēd) adj. noting computer data that can be read but not changed.

read′y (red′ē) adj., **-ier, -iest,** v., **-ied, -ying,** n. —adj. **1.** fully prepared. **2.** willing. **3.** apt. —v.t. **4.** to make ready. —n. **5.** the state of being ready. —**read′i·ly,** adv. —**read′i·ness,** n.

read′y-made′ adj. ready for use when bought.

re·a′gent (rē ā′jənt) n. a chemical used in analysis and synthesis.

re′al (rē′əl, rēl) adj. **1.** actual. **2.** genuine. **3.** denoting immovable property. —**re′al·ness,** n.

re′al estate′ n. property in land and buildings. Also, **re′al·ty** (rē′əl tē, rēl′-).

re·al·ism n. **1.** a tendency to see things as they really are. **2.** the representation of things as they really are. —**re′al·ist,** n. —**re′al·is′tic,** adj. —**re′al·is′ti·cal·ly,** adv.

re·al′i·ty (rē al′i tē) n., pl. **-ties.** **1.** the state or quality of being real. **2.** a real thing or fact.

re′al·ize′ v.t., **-ized, -izing. 1.** to understand clearly. **2.** to make real. **3.** to get as profit. —**re′al·i·za′tion,** n.

re′al·ly adv. **1.** actually. **2.** genuinely; truly. **3.** indeed.

realm (relm) n. **1.** a kingdom. **2.** a special field.

ream (rēm) n. a standard quantity of paper, usu. 500 sheets.

reap (rēp) v.t. to harvest. —**reap′er,** n.

rear (rēr) n. **1.** the back part. —adj. **2.** of or at the rear. —v.t. **3.** to care for to maturity. **4.** to raise; erect. —v.i. **5.** to rise on the hind legs.

rear′ ad′mi·ral n. a naval officer above a captain.

rear′most′ adj. farthest back.

rear′ward (-wərd) adv. **1.** Also, **rear′wards.** toward the rear. —adj. **2.** located in the rear.

rea′son (rē′zən) n. **1.** a cause for a belief, act, etc. **2.** sound judgment. **3.** sanity. —v.i. **4.** to think or argue logically. —v.t. **5.** to infer. —**Idiom. 6. within reason,** justifiable. —**rea′son·ing,** n.

rea′son·a·ble (rē′zə nə bəl, rēz′nə-) adj. **1.** logical. **2.** moderate. **3.** not expensive. **4.** rational.

re′as·sure′ (rē′ə shŏŏr′, -shûr′) v.t., **-sured, -suring.** to restore the confidence of. —**re′as·sur′ance,** n.

re·bate (rē′bāt) n., v., **-bated, -bating.** —n. **1.** a return of part of the amount paid. —v.t. **2.** to return (part of a payment).

re·bel′ v., **-belled, -belling.** —v.i. (ri bel′) **1.** to rise in arms against one's government. **2.** to resist any authority. —n. (reb′əl) **3.** one who rebels. —**re·bel′lion,** n. —**re·bel′lious,** adj. —**re·bel′lious·ly,** adv.

re·bound′ v.i. (ri bound′) **1.** to spring back after impact. —n. (rē′bound′) **2.** the act of rebounding.

re·buff′ (ri buf′) n. **1.** a blunt repulse or refusal. —v.t. **2.** to refuse or repel.

re′bus (rē′bəs) n. a puzzle in which pictures and symbols combine to represent a word.

re·but′ (ri but′) v.t., **-butted, -butting.** to prove wrong; refute. —**re·but′tal,** n.

re·cal′ci·trant (ri kal′si trənt) adj. resisting control.

re·call′ v. (ri kôl′) **1.** to remember. **2.** to call back. **3.** to withdraw. —n. (rē′kôl) **4.** the act of recalling.

re·cant′ (ri kant′) v.t. to retract (a statement, opinion, etc.).

re′cap′ (rē′kap′) v., **-capped, -capping,** n. —v.t. **1.** to recapitulate. **2.** to recondition (a tire) by adding a rubber strip. —n. **3.** a recapitulation. **4.** a recapped tire.

re′ca·pit′u·late (rē′kə pich′ə lāt′) v.t., v.i., **-lated, -lating.** to summarize; sum up.

re′cap′ture v., **-tured, -turing,** n. —v.t. **1.** to capture again. **2.** to experience again. —n. **3.** a recovery by capture.

recd. or **rec′d.** received.

re·cede′ (ri sēd′) v.i., **-ceded, -ceding. 1.** to move or appear to move back.

re·ceipt′ (ri sēt′) n. **1.** a written acknowledgment of receiving. **2.** receipts, an amount received. **3.** the act of receiving.

re·ceive′ v.t., **-ceived, -ceiving. 1.** to take (something offered or delivered). **2.** to experience. **3.** to welcome (guests). **4.** to accept.

re·ceiv′er n. **1.** one that receives. **2.** a device that receives electrical signals and converts them. **3.** a person put in charge of property in litigation. —**re·ceiv′er·ship′,** n.

re′cent (rē′sənt) adj. happening, done, or made lately. —**re′cent·ly,** adv.

re·cep′ta·cle (ri sep′tə kəl) n. a container.

re·cep′tion (ri sep′shən) n. **1.** the act of receiving. **2.** the fact or manner of being received. **3.** a social function.

re·cep′tion·ist n. a person who receives callers in an office.

re·cep′tive (-tiv) adj. quick to understand and consider ideas.

re·cep′tor (-tər) n. a nerve ending that is sensitive to stimuli.

re·cess′ (ri ses′, rē′ses) n. **1.** a temporary cessation of work. **2.** an alcove. **3.** recesses, an inner part. —v.i. **4.** to take a recess. —v.t. **5.** to make a recess in.

re·ces′sion (-sesh′ən) n. **1.** an economic decline. **2.** a withdrawing procession.

re·ces′sion·al n. music played at the end of a church service.

re·ces′sive (-ses′iv) adj. receding.

re·cher·ché (rə shâr′shā, rə shâr shā′) adj. **1.** very rare or choice. **2.** affectedly refined.

re·cid′i·vism (ri sid′ə viz′əm) n. repeated or habitual relapse, as into crime. —**re·cid′i·vist,** n., adj.

rec′i·pe (res′ə pē) n. instructions for preparing food or drink.

re·cip′i·ent (ri sip′ē ənt) n. **1.** one who receives. —adj. **2.** receiving.

re·cip′ro·cal (ri sip′rə kəl) adj. given and received in return; mutual. —**re·cip′ro·cal·ly,** adv.

re·cip′ro·cate′ (-kāt′) v.i., v.t., **-cated, -cating. 1.** to give, feel, etc., in return. **2.** to move alternately backward and forward. —**re·cip′ro·ca′tion,** n.

rec′i·proc′i·ty (res′ə pros′i tē) n. mutual exchange.

re·cit′al (ri sīt′l) n. a musical or dance performance.

rec′i·ta·tive′ (res′i tə tēv′) n. a style of vocal music intermediate between speaking and singing.

re·cite′ (ri sīt′) v.t., v.i., **-cited, -citing. 1.** to repeat (something) from memory. **2.** to narrate (something) in detail.

reck′less (rek′lis) adj. heedless of danger or consequences; careless.

reck′on (rek′ən) v.t. **1.** to calculate. **2.** to regard as; esteem. **3.** Informal. to suppose. **4. reckon with,** to deal with.

reck′on·ing n. **1.** a settling of accounts. **2.** navigational calculation.

re·claim′ (ri klām′) v.t. **1.** to make usable, as land. **2.** to extract reusable material. **3.** to use again with minimal change.

re·cline′ (ri klīn′) v.i., v.t., **-clined, -clining.** to lean or cause to lean back.

re·clin′er n. a chair with an adjustable back and footrest.

rec·luse (rek′lōōs, ri klōōs′) n. a person living in seclusion.

re·cog′ni·zance (ri kog′nə zəns, -kon′ə-) n. a bond pledging one to do a particular act.

rec′og·nize′ (rek′əg nīz′) v.t., **-nized, -nizing. 1.** to identify from previous knowledge. **2.** to acknowledge formally. **3.** to greet. —**rec′og·ni′tion** (-nish′ən) n.

re·coil′ (rē koil′) v.i. **1.** to shrink back. **2.** to spring back. —n. **3.** the act of recoiling.

rec′ol·lect′ (rek′ə lekt′) v.t., v.i. to remember. —**rec′ol·lec′tion,** n.

rec′om·mend′ (rek′ə mend′) v.t. **1.** to present as worthy. **2.** to advise. —**rec′om·men·da′tion,** n.

rec′om·pense′ (rek′əm pens′) v., **-pensed, -pensing.** —v.t. **1.** to repay or reward for services, injury, etc. —n. **2.** such compensation.

rec′on·cile′ (rek′ən sīl′) v.t., **-ciled, -ciling. 1.** to bring into agreement. **2.** to restore to friendliness. —**rec′on·cil·i·a′tion** (-sil′ē ā′shən) n.

rec′on·dite (rek′ən dīt′) adj. **1.** very profound or difficult; abstruse. **2.** known by a few; esoteric.

re′con·nais′sance (ri kon′ə səns, -zəns) n. a survey of enemy territory.

re′con·noi′ter (rē′kə noi′tər, rek′ə-) v.t., v.i. to make a reconnaissance (of).

re·cord′ v.t. (ri kôrd′) **1.** to set down in writing. **2.** to register for mechanical reproduction. —n. (rek′ərd) **3.** what is recorded. **4.** a disk on which sound is recorded. **5.** the best yet attained. —adj. (rek′ərd) **6.** best. —**Idiom. 7. off the record,** not for publication. **8. on record,** publicly declared. —**re·cord′ing,** n.

re·cord′er n. **1.** a person who records. **2.** a recording device. **3.** a flute with a mouthpiece like a whistle and eight finger holes.

re·count′ (ri kount′) v.t. **1.** to count again. —n. (rē′kount′) **2.** a second count. Also, **re-count.**

re·count′ (ri kount′) v.t. to narrate.

re·coup′ (ri kōōp′) v.t. to recover; make up.

re′course (rē′kôrs, ri kôrs′) n. a source of help.

re·cov′er (ri kuv′ər) v.t. **1.** to get back. **2.** to reclaim. —v.i. **3.** to regain health. —**re·cov′er·a·ble,** adj. —**re·cov′er·y,** n.

rec′re·ant (rek′rē ənt) adj. **1.** cowardly. **2.** disloyal. —n. **3.** a cowardly or disloyal person.

re′-cre·ate′ (rē′krē āt′) v.t., **-created, -creating.** to create anew.

rec′re·a′tion (rek′rē ā′shən) n. **1.** mental or physical refreshment after work. **2.** a means of enjoyable relaxation. —**rec′re·a′tion·al,** adj.

re·crim′i·nate′ (ri krim′ə nāt′) v.t., **-nated, -nating.** to accuse in return. —**re·crim′i·na′tion,** n.

re′cru·des′cence (rē′krōō des′əns) n. a breaking out again after inactivity. —**re′cru·des′cent,** adj.

re·cruit′ (ri krōōt′) n. **1.** a new member, esp. of the armed forces. —v.t. **2.** to enlist. —**re·cruit′ment,** n.

rec′tan′gle (rek′tang′gəl) n. a parallelogram with four right angles. —**rec·tan′gu·lar** (-tang′gyə lər) adj.

rec′ti·fy′ (rek′tə fī′) v.t., **-fied, -fying. 1.** to correct. —**rec′ti·fi′a·ble,** adj. —**rec′ti·fi·ca′tion,** n.

rec′ti·lin′e·ar (rek′tl in′ē ər) adj. **1.** forming a straight line. **2.** formed by straight lines.

rec′ti·tude′ (rek′ti tōōd′, -tyōōd′) n. moral rightness.

rec′to (rek′tō) n., pl. **-tos.** the right-hand page of a book.

rec′tor (rek′tər) n. **1.** a member of the clergy in charge of a parish. **2.** the head of some universities or schools.

rec′to·ry n., pl. **-ries.** a rector's house.

rec′tum (rek′təm) n. the lowest part of the intestine. —**rec′tal,** adj.

re·cum′bent (ri kum′bənt) adj. lying down. —**re·cum′ben·cy,** n.

re·cu′per·ate′ (ri kōō′pə rāt′) v.i., **-ated, -ating.** to regain health. —**re·cu′per·a′tion,** n.

re·cur′ (ri kûr′) v.i., **-curred, -curring. 1.** to occur again. **2.** to return in thought. —**re·cur′rence,** n. —**re·cur′rent,** adj.

re·cy′cle (rē sī′kəl) v.t., v.i., **-cled, -cling. 1.** to treat (refuse) to extract reusable material. **2.** to use again with minimal change.

red (red) n., adj., **redder, reddest.** —n. **1.** the color of blood. **2.** (often cap.) a communist. —adj. **3.** of or like red. **4.** (often cap.) communist. —**red′den,** v.t., v.i. —**red′dish,** adj.

re·dact′ (ri dakt′) v.t. to edit.

red′ blood′ cell′ n. a blood cell that contains hemoglobin and carries oxygen.

red′cap′ n. a baggage porter.

re·deem′ (ri dēm′) v.t. **1.** to pay off. **2.** to recover. **3.** to fulfill. **4.** to deliver from sin by sacrifice. —**re·deem′er,** n. —**re·demp′tion** (-demp′shən) n.

red′-hand′ed adj., adv. in the act of wrongdoing.

red′head′ n. a person with red hair. —**red′head′ed,** adj.

red′ her′ring n. something intended to distract attention from the real problem or issue.

red′-hot′ adj. **1.** red with heat. **2.** furious. **3.** very fresh or new.

re·di′al v.t. (rē′dī′əl, -dīl′) **1.** to dial again. —n. (rē′dī′əl, -dīl′) **2.** a telephone function that automatically redials the last number called. **3.** a button that performs this function.

red′-let′ter adj. memorable.

red′lin′ing n. refusal by banks to grant mortgages in specified urban areas.

red′o·lent (red′l ənt) adj. **1.** odorous. **2.** suggestive.

re·doubt′ (ri dout′) n. a small isolated fort.

re·doubt′a·ble adj. evoking fear or respect.

re·dound′ (ri dound′) v.i. **1.** to have an effect. **2.** to result. **3.** to reflect upon a person.

re·dress′ v.t. (ri dress′) **1.** to set right (a wrong). —n. (rē′dres) **2.** the act of redressing.

red′ tape′ n. bureaucratic routine.

re·duce′ (ri dōōs′, -dyōōs′) v.t., **-duced, -ducing. 1.** to make less in size, rank, etc. **2.** to put into a simpler form or state. —v.i. **3.** to lose weight. —**re·duc′i·ble,** adj. —**re·duc′tion** (-duk′shən) n.

re·dun′dant (ri dun′dənt) adj. **1.** excessive; superfluous. **2.** wordy. —**re·dun′dance, re·dun′dan·cy,** n.

red′wood′ (red′wŏŏd′) n. a huge evergreen tree of California.

reed (rēd) n. **1.** a tall marsh grass. **2.** a small piece of cane or metal at the mouth of a wind instrument. —**reed′y,** adj.

reef (rēf) n. a narrow ridge near the surface of water.

reek (rēk) v.i. **1.** to smell strongly and unpleasantly. —n. **2.** such a smell.

reel¹ (rēl) n. **1.** a turning device for winding up cord or film. —v.t. **2.** to wind on a reel. **3. reel off,** to say fluently and quickly.

reel² (rēl) v.i. **1.** to sway or stagger. **2.** to whirl.

reel³ (rēl) n. a lively Scottish dance.

re·en′try (rē en′trē) n., pl. **-tries. 1.** a second entry. **2.** a return into the earth's atmosphere.

ref (ref) n., v.t., v.i., **reffed, reffing.** referee.

re·fec′to·ry (ri fek′tə rē) n., pl. **-ries.** a dining hall.

re·fer′ (ri fûr′) v., **-ferred, -ferring.** —v.t. **1.** to direct for information or aid. —v.i. **2.** to direct attention. **3.** to have recourse, as for information. **4.** to make reference. —**re·fer′ral,** n.

ref′er·ee′ (ref′ə rē′) n., **-ees,** v., **-eed, -eeing.** —n. **1.** a judge. —v.t., v.i. **2.** to preside over or act as referee.

ref′er·ence (ref′ər əns) n. **1.** the act or fact of referring. **2.** something referred to. **3.** a person from whom one seeks a recommendation. **4.** a statement regarding a person's character or abilities.

ref′er·en′dum (ref′ə ren′dəm) n., pl. **-dums, -da.** the referring of a legislative measure to the vote of the electorate.

ref′er·ent (ref′ər ənt) n. something referred to.

re·fill′ v.t., v.i. (rē fil′) **1.** to fill again. —n. (rē′fil′) **2.** a second filling.

re·fine′ (ri fīn′) v.t., **-fined, -fining. 1.** to free from impurities or error. **2.** to teach good manners, taste, etc. —**re·fin′er,** n. —**re·fine′ment,** n.

re·fin′er·y n., pl. **-eries.** an establishment for refining.

re·flect′ (ri flekt′) v.t. **1.** to cast back. **2.** to show; mirror. **3.** to bring (credit or discredit) on one. —v.i. **4.** to think. —**re·flec′tion,** n. —**re·flec′tor,** n.

re′flex (rē′fleks) adj. **1.** denoting involuntary action. **2.** bent. —n. **3.** an involuntary movement.

re·flex′ive adj. **1.** (of a verb) having the same subject and object. **2.** (of a pronoun) showing identity with the subject.

re·form′ (ri fôrm′) n. **1.** the improvement of what is wrong. —v.t., v.i. **2.** to change for the better. —**re·form′er,** n. —**ref′or·ma′tion** (ref′ər mā′shən) n.

re·form′a·to·ry (ri fôr′mə tôr′ē) n., pl. **-ries.** a prison for young offenders.

re·frac′tion (ri frak′shən) n. the change of direction of light or heat rays in passing to another medium. —**re·fract′,** v.t. —**re·frac′tive,** adj.

re·frac′to·ry adj. stubborn.

re·frain′¹ (ri frān′) v.i. to keep oneself from doing or saying something.

re·frain′² (ri frān′) n. a recurring passage in a song or poem.

re·fresh′ (ri fresh′) v.t. **1.** to give new vigor and energy to. **2.** to stimulate. —**re·fresh′ing,** adj.

re·fresh′ment n. **1.** something that refreshes. **2.** refreshments, food and drink for a light meal. **3.** a refreshing or being refreshed.

re·frig′er·ate′ (ri frij′ə rāt′) v.t., **-ated, -ating.** to make or keep cold. —**re·frig′er·ant** (-ə rənt) adj., n. —**re·frig′er·a′tion,** n.

re·frig′er·a′tor n. a cabinet for keeping food cold.

ref′uge (ref′yōōj) n. (a place giving) shelter from danger.

ref′u·gee′ (ref′yŏŏ jē′) n. a person who flees for safety.

re·ful′gent (ri ful′jənt) adj. shining brightly. —**re·ful′gence,** n.

re·fund′ v.t. (ri fund′) **1.** to give back (money). —n. (rē′fund) **2.** the act of refunding. **3.** an amount refunded. —**re·fund′a·ble,** adj.

re·fur′bish (rē fûr′bish) v.t. to renovate.

re·fuse′¹ (ri fyōōz′) v.t., v.i., **-fused, -fusing.** to decline to accept, give, or do (something). —**re·fus′al,** n.

ref′use² (ref′yōōs) n. rubbish.

re·fute′ (ri fyōōt′) v.t., **-futed, -futing.** to prove wrong. —**ref′u·ta′tion,** n.

re·gain′ (rē gān′) v.t. to get again.

re′gal (rē′gəl) adj. royal.

re·gale′ (ri gāl′) v.t., **-galed, -galing.** to entertain grandly.

re·ga′lia (ri gāl′yə) n.pl. emblems of royalty, office, etc.

re·gard′ (ri gärd′) v.t. **1.** to look upon in a particular way. **2.** to respect. **3.** to look at. **4.** to concern. —n. **5.** reference; relation. **6.** attention. **7.** respect and liking.

re·gard′ing prep. concerning.

re·gard′less adv. **1.** despite everything. —adj. **2.** unmindful.

re·gat′ta (ri gat′ə, -gä′tə) n. an organized series of boat races.

re·gen′er·ate′ (ri jen′ə rāt′) v.t., **-ated, -ating.** —v.t. **1.** to give new life or spiritual vigor to. —v.i. **2.** to form anew. —**re·gen′er·a′tive,** adj.

re′gent (rē′jənt) n. **1.** a person ruling in place of a monarch. **2.** a university governor. —**re′gen·cy,** n.

reg′i·cide′ (rej′ə sīd′) n. **1.** the act of killing a king. **2.** a person who kills a king.

re·gime′ (rə zhēm′, rā-) n. a system of rule.

reg′i·men (rej′ə mən) n. a regulated course of diet, exercise, etc., for health.

reg′i·ment n. (rej′ə mənt) **1.** an infantry unit. —v.t. (rej′ə ment′) **2.** to subject to strict, uniform discipline. —**reg′i·men′tal,** adj.

re′gion (rē′jən) n. an area; district. —**re′gion·al,** adj.

re′gion·al·ism n. a feature peculiar to a geographical region.

reg′is·ter (rej′ə stər) n. **1.** a written list; record. **2.** the range of a voice or instrument. **3.** a device for controlling the passage of warm air. —v.t. **4.** to enter in a register. **5.** to show. —v.i. **6.** to enter oneself on a list of voters. —**reg′is·tra′tion** (-strā′shən) n.

reg′is·trar′ (-strär′) n. an official recorder.

reg′is·try n., pl. **-tries. 1.** registration. 2. a place where a register is kept. 3. an official record.

reg′nant (reg′nənt) *adj.* 1. ruling. 2. widespread.

re•gress′ (ri gres′) *v.i.* to return to a previous, inferior state. —**re•gres′sion,** *n.* —**re•gres′sive,** *adj.*

re•gret′ (ri gret′) *v.,* **-gretted, -gret-ting,** *—v.t.* 1. to feel sorry about. —*n.* 2. a feeling of loss or sorrow. —**re•gret′ta•ble,** *adj.* —**re•gret′ful,** *adj.*

reg′u•lar (reg′yə lər) *adj.* 1. usual. 2. evenly or uniformly arranged. 3. recurring at fixed times. 4. orderly. 5. (of verbs) having normal inflections. 6. denoting a permanent army. —*n.* 7. a regular soldier. 8. a long-standing customer. —**reg′u•lar′i•ty,** *n.* —**reg′u•lar•ize′,** *v.t.*

reg′u•late′ (-lāt′) *v.t.,* **-lated, -lating.** 1. to control by rule, method, etc. 2. to adjust. —**reg′u•la•to•ry** (-lə tôr′ē) *adj.*

reg′u•la′tion *n.* 1. the act of regulating. 2. a rule.

re•gur′gi•tate′ (ri gûr′ji tāt′) *v.t.,* **-tated, -tating.** to bring up from the stomach. —**re•gur′gi•ta′tion,** *n.*

re•ha•bil′i•tate′ (rē′hə bil′i tāt′, rē′ə-) *v.t.,* **-tated, -tating.** to restore to health or good condition. —**re•ha•bil′i•ta′tion,** *n.*

re•hash′ *v.t.* (rē hash′) 1. to rework or reuse in a new form without significant change. —*n.* (rē′hash′) 2. the act of rehashing. 3. something rehashed.

re•hearse′ (ri hûrs′) *v.t., v.i.,* **-hearsed, -hearsing.** to practice (a play, music, etc.) before performance. —**re•hears′al,** *n.*

reign (rān) *n.* 1. (the period of) royal rule. —*v.i.* 2. to have sovereign power or title.

re•im•burse′ (rē′im bûrs′) *v.t.,* **-bursed, -bursing.** to repay, as for expenses. —**re•im•burse′ment,** *n.*

rein (rān) *n.* 1. a narrow strap fastened to the bridle for controlling an animal. —*Idiom.* 2. **give (free) rein to,** to give freedom to.

re′in•car•na′tion (rē′in kär nā′shən) *n.* the continuation of the soul after death in a new body.

rein′deer′ (rān′dēr′) *n.* a large arctic deer.

re′in•force′ (rē′in fôrs′) *v.t.,* **-forced, -forcing.** to strengthen with support, troops, etc. —**re′in•force′ment,** *n.*

re′in•state′ (rē′in stāt′) *v.t.,* **-stated, -stating.** to put back into a former position or state. —**re′in•state′ment,** *n.*

re•it′er•ate′ (rē it′ə rāt′) *v.t.,* **-ating.** to repeat. —**re•it′er•a′tion,** *n.*

re•ject′ *v.t.* (ri jekt′) 1. to refuse or discard. —*n.* (rē′jekt) 2. something rejected. —**re•jec′tion,** *n.*

re•joice′ (ri jois′) *v.i.,* **-joiced, -joic-ing.** to be glad.

re•join′ (-join′) *v.t.* 1. to answer. 2. to join again.

re•join′der (-dər) *n.* a response.

re•ju′ve•nate′ (ri jōō′və nāt′) *v.t.,* **-nated, -nating.** to make young again.

re•lapse′ *v.,* **-lapsed, -lapsing,** *n.* —*v.i.* 1. to fall back into a former state or practice. 2. to fall back into illness after apparent recovery. —*n.* (ri laps′, rē′laps) 3. an act or instance of relapsing.

re•late′ (ri lāt′) *v.,* **-lated, -lating.** —*v.t.* 1. to tell. 2. to connect in thought or meaning. —*v.i.* 3. to have relation. 4. to establish a sympathetic relationship.

re•lat′ed *adj.* 1. associated. 2. connected by blood or marriage.

re•la′tion *n.* 1. connection. 2. a relative. 3. the act of relating. —**re•la′tion•ship′,** *n.*

rel′a•tive (rel′ə tiv) *n.* 1. a person connected with another by blood or marriage. —*adj.* 2. comparative.

rel′ative humid′ity *n.* the ratio of water vapor in the air at a given temperature to the amount the air could hold.

rel′a•tiv′i•ty *n.* the principle that time, mass, etc., are relative, not absolute, concepts.

re•lax′ (ri laks′) *v.t., v.i.* 1. to make or become less tense, firm, etc. 2. to rest from work. —**re•lax•a′tion** *n.*

re′lay (rē′lā) *n.* 1. a fresh supply of persons, animals, etc., to relieve others. —*v.t.* 2. to receive and carry forward.

re•lease′ (ri lēs′) *v.,* **-leased, -leas-ing,** *n.* —*v.t.* 1. to let go. —*n.* 2. an act or instance of releasing.

rel′e•gate′ (rel′i gāt′) *v.t.,* **-gated,**

-gating. 1. to consign to an inferior position. 2. to turn over.

re•lent′ (ri lent′) *v.i.* to become more mild or forgiving. —**re•lent′-less,** *adj.*

rel′e•vant (rel′ə vənt) *adj.* having to do with the matter in question.

re•li′a•ble (ri lī′ə bəl) *adj.* trustworthy. —**re•li′a•bil′i•ty,** *n.*

re•li′ance (-əns) *n.* 1. trust; dependence. 2. confidence. —**re•li′-ant,** *adj.*

rel′ic (rel′ik) *n.* 1. an object surviving from the past. 2. a personal memorial of a sacred person.

re•lief′[1] (ri lēf′) *n.* 1. alleviation of pain or distress. 2. help given to poor people. 3. a pleasing change.

re•lief′[2] (ri lēf′) *n.* projection of a figure from its background, as in sculpture.

re•lieve′ (ri lēv′) *v.t.,* **-lieved, -liev-ing.** 1. to ease. 2. to break the sameness of. 3. to discharge from duty.

re•li′gion (ri lij′ən) *n.* 1. belief in and worship of a God or other superhuman agency. 2. a particular system of these beliefs.

re•li′gious (-əs) *adj.* 1. of religion. 2. pious; devout. 3. conscientious. —**re•li′gious•ly,** *adv.*

re•lin′quish (ri ling′kwish) *v.t.* to give up; surrender.

rel′i•quar′y (rel′i kwer′ē) *n., pl.* **-ies.** a receptacle for religious relics.

rel′ish (rel′ish) *n.* 1. enjoyment or liking. 2. something savory. —*v.t.* 3. to take enjoyment in.

re•live′ (rē liv′) *v.t.,* **-lived, -living.** to experience again.

re•lo′cate (rē lō′kāt, -lō kāt′) *v.t., v.i.,* **-cated, -cating.** to move. —**re′lo•ca′tion,** *n.*

re•luc′tant (ri luk′tənt) *adj.* unwilling. —**re•luc′tance,** *n.*

re•ly′ (ri lī′) *v.i.,* **-lied, -lying.** to depend confidently.

REM (rem) *n.* quick, darting movement of the eyes during sleep.

re•main′ (ri mān′) *v.i.* 1. to continue to be. 2. to stay; be left. —*n.* **remains,** 3. that which remains. 4. a corpse.

re•main′der (-dər) *n.* that which is left over.

re•mand′ (ri mand′) *v.t.* to send back, as to a lower court of law.

re•mark′ (ri märk′) *v.t.* 1. to say casually. 2. to note; observe. —*v.i.* 3. to make a comment. —*n.* 4. notice or mention. 5. a casual comment.

re•mark′a•ble *adj.* extraordinary.

rem′e•dy (rem′i dē) *v.,* **-died, -dy-ing,** *n., pl.* **-dies.** —*v.t.* 1. to cure or alleviate. 2. to correct. —*n.* 3. something that remedies. —**re•me′di•al,** *adj.*

re•mem′ber (ri mem′bər) *v.t.* 1. to recall or retain in memory. 2. to mention (a person) to another as sending greetings. —*v.i.* 3. to recall something to memory. —**re•mem′-brance** (-brəns) *n.*

re•mind′ (ri mīnd′) *v.t.* to cause to remember. —**re•mind′er,** *n.*

rem′i•nisce′ (rem′ə nis′) *v.i.,* **-nisced, -niscing.** to recall past experiences. —**rem′i•nis′cence,** *n.* —**rem′i•nis′cent,** *adj.*

re•miss′ (ri mis′) *adj.* negligent.

re•mis′sion *n.* 1. the act of forgiving. 2. a period when symptoms of disease subside.

re•mit′ (-mit′) *v.t.,* **-mitted, -mitting.** 1. to send (money), usu. in payment. 2. to pardon. 3. to slacken; abate.

re•mit′tance *n.* money sent.

re•mit′tent *adj.* (of illness) less severe at times.

rem′nant (rem′nənt) *n.* 1. a small remaining part. 2. a trace.

re•mod′el (rē mod′l) *v.t.,* **-eled, -el-ing.** to alter in structure or form.

re•mon′strate (ri mon′strāt) *v.i.,* **-strated, -strating.** to protest; plead in protest.

re•morse′ (ri môrs′) *n.* regret for wrongdoing. —**re•morse′ful,** *adj.* —**re•morse′less,** *adj.*

re•mote′ (ri mōt′) *adj.* 1. far distant. 2. faint. —*n.* 3. a remote control (def. 2). —**re•mote′ly,** *adv.*

remote′ control′ *n.* 1. control of an apparatus from a distance, as by radio signals. 2. a device used for such control.

re•move′ (ri mōōv′) *v.,* **-moved, -moving.** —*v.t.* 1. to take away or off. 2. to move to another place. —*n.* 3. a distance of separation. —**re•mov′al,** *n.* —**re•mov′a•ble,** *adj.*

re•mu′ner•ate′ (ri myōō′nə rāt′) *v.t.,* **-ated, -ating.** to pay for work,

---

services, etc. —**re•mu′ner•a′tion,** *n.*

ren•ais•sance′ (ren′ə säns′) *n.* 1. a revival. 2. **Renaissance,** a cultural period of the 14th-17th centuries marked by a great revival of interest in art, literature, and learning.

re•nas′cent (ri nā′sənt) *adj.* being reborn; springing again into being or vigor.

rend (rend) *v.t.* 1. to tear apart. 2. to disturb with noise. 3. to distress.

ren′der (ren′dər) *v.t.* 1. to cause to be. 2. to do, show, or furnish. 3. to perform. 4. to give back. 5. to melt (fat).

ren′dez•vous (rän′də vōō′, -dā-) *n., pl.* **-vous.** an appointment or place to meet.

ren•di′tion (ren dish′ən) *n.* 1. the act of rendering. 2. a translation or interpretation, as of a role.

ren′e•gade′ (ren′i gād′) *n.* a deserter.

re•nege′ (ri nig′, -neg′) *v.i.,* **-neged, -neging.** to break a promise.

re•new′ (ri nōō′, -nyōō′) *v.t.* 1. to begin or do again. 2. to make like new; replenish. 3. to extend for an additional period. —**re•new′al,** *n.*

ren′net (ren′it) *n.* 1. a membrane lining the stomach of a calf or other animal. 2. a preparation of this used in making cheese.

re•nounce′ (ri nouns′) *v.t.,* **-nounced, -nouncing.** to give up voluntarily.

ren′o•vate′ (ren′ə vāt′) *v.t.,* **-vated, -vating.** to restore to good condition.

re•nown′ (ri noun′) *n.* fame. —**re•nowned′,** *adj.*

rent[1] (rent) *n.* 1. a payment for the use of property. —*v.t.* 2. to grant or have use of in return for rent. —*v.i.* 3. to be leased for rent. —**rent′er,** *n.*

rent[2] (rent) *n.* a tear made by rending.

rent′al *n.* 1. an amount given or received as rent. 2. the act of renting. 3. property rented.

re•nun′ci•a′tion (ri nun′sē ā′shən, -shē-) *n.* the act of renouncing.

Rep. 1. Representative. 2. Republic. 3. Republican.

re•pair′[1] (ri pâr′) *v.t.* 1. to restore to sound condition. 2. to remedy. —*n.* 3. an act or instance of repairing. 4. condition with respect to soundness.

re•pair′[2] (ri pâr′) *v.i.* to go.

rep′a•ra′tion (rep′ə rā′shən) *n.* amends for injury or damage.

rep′ar•tee′ (rep′ər tē′, -tā′, -är-) *n.* an exchange of wit; banter.

re•past′ (ri past′) *n.* a meal.

re•pa′tri•ate′ (rē pā′trē āt′) *v.t.,* **-ated, -ating.** to send back to one's native country.

re•pay′ (ri pā′) *v.t.,* **-paid, -paying.** to pay back. —**re•pay′ment,** *n.*

re•peal′ (ri pēl′) *v.t.* 1. to revoke officially. —*n.* 2. the act of repealing.

re•peat′ (ri pēt′) *v.t.* 1. to say, tell, or do again. —*n.* 2. the act of repeating. 3. something repeated.

re•peat′ed *adj.* said or done again and again. —**re•peat′ed•ly,** *adv.*

re•peat′er *n.* 1. one that repeats. 2. a gun firing several shots in rapid succession.

re•pel′ (ri pel′) *v.t.,* **-pelled, -pelling.** 1. to drive back; thrust away. 2. to arouse disgust or aversion in. —**re•pel′lent,** *adj., n.*

re•pent′ (ri pent′) *v.i., v.t.* to feel contrite or penitent (for). —**re•pent′ance,** *n.* —**re•pent′ant,** *adj.* —**re•pent′ant•ly,** *adv.*

re′per•cus′sion (rē′pər kush′ən) *n.* 1. an indirect result. 2. an echo.

rep′er•toire′ (rep′ər twär′, -twôr′, rep′ə-) *n.* a group of works that a performer or company can perform. Also, **rep′er•to•ry.**

rep′e•ti′tion (rep′ə tish′ən) *n.* 1. the act of repeating. 2. something repeated. —**rep′e•ti′tious,** *adj.* —**re•pet′i•tive** (ri pet′i tiv) *adj.*

repet′itive strain′ in′jury *n.* a debilitating disorder, esp. of the hand or arm, caused by the stress of repeated movements. Also, **repet′itive strain′ disor′der.**

re•pine′ (ri pīn′) *v.i.,* **-pined, -pin-ing.** 1. to complain. 2. to yearn.

re•place′ (ri plās′) *v.t.,* **-placed, -placing.** 1. to take the place of. 2. to provide a substitute for. 3. to put back.

re•play *v.t.* (rē plā′) 1. to play again. —*n.* (rē′plā) 2. the act of replaying. 3. something replayed.

re•plen′ish (ri plen′ish) *v.t.* to

---

make full again. —**re•plen′ish-ment,** *n.*

re•plete′ (ri plēt′) *adj.* abundantly filled. —**re•ple′tion,** *n.*

rep′li•ca (rep′li kə) *n.* a copy.

rep′li•cate′ (-kāt′) *v.t.,* **-cated, -cat-ing.** to duplicate or reproduce.

rep′li•ca′tion *n.* 1. a reply. 2. a replica. 3. the act of replicating.

re•ply′ (ri plī′) *v.,* **-plied, -plying,** *n., pl.* **-plies.** —*v.i., v.t.* 1. to give or return as an answer. —*n.* 2. an answer.

re•port′ (ri pôrt′) *n.* 1. a statement of events or findings. 2. rumor. 3. a loud noise. 4. to tell of. 5. to inform against. —*v.i.* 6. to present oneself.

re•port′age (ri pôr′tij, rep′ôr täzh′) *n.* 1. the act of reporting news. 2. reported news.

re•port′er *n.* 1. one who reports. 2. a person employed to gather and report news.

re•pose′ (ri pōz′) *n., v.,* **-posed, -posing.** —*n.* 1. rest or sleep. 2. tranquility. —*v.i.* 3. to rest or sleep. —**re•pose′ful,** *adj.*

re•pos′i•to•ry (ri poz′i tôr′ē) *n., pl.* **-tories.** a place where things are stored.

re′pos•sess′ (rē′pə zes′) *v.t.* to take back.

rep′re•hen′si•ble (rep′rə hen′sə-bəl) *adj.* blameworthy.

rep′re•sent′ (rep′ri zent′) *v.t.* 1. to act or speak for. 2. to portray. 3. to express. —**rep′re•sen•ta′tion,** *n.*

rep′re•sent′a•tive (-zen′tə tiv) *n.* 1. one that represents another. 2. a member of a legislative body. —*adj.* 3. representing. 4. typical.

re•press′ (ri pres′) *v.t.* 1. to inhibit. 2. to suppress. —**re•pres′sive,** *adj.* —**re•pres′sion,** *n.*

re•prieve′ (ri prēv′) *v.,* **-prieved, -prieving,** *n.* —*v.t.* 1. to delay the punishment of. —*n.* 2. a delay in punishment. 3. a respite.

rep′ri•mand′ (rep′rə mand′) *n.* 1. severe criticism. —*v.t.* 2. to scold or criticize severely.

re•pris′al (ri prī′zal) *n.* infliction of injuries in retaliation.

re•proach′ (ri prōch′) *v.t.* 1. to blame or censure. —*n.* 2. blame; discredit. —**re•proach′ful,** *adj.*

rep′ro•bate′ (rep′rə bāt′) *n.* 1. a hopelessly bad person. —*adj.* 2. morally corrupt.

re′pro•duce′ (rē′prə dōōs′, -dyōōs′) *v.,* **-duced, -ducing.** —*v.t.* 1. to copy or duplicate. 2. to produce (new individuals). —*v.i.* 3. to bear offspring. —**re′pro•duc′tion** (-duk′-shən) *n.* —**re′pro•duc′tive,** *adj.*

re•proof′ (ri prōōf′) *n.* an act of reproving.

re•prove′ (-prōōv′) *v.t.,* **-proved, -proving.** to criticize or censure.

rep′tile (rep′til, -tīl) *n.* a scaly, air-breathing animal, as a snake.

re•pub′lic (ri pub′lik) *n.* a state governed by representatives elected by citizens.

re•pub′li•can (ri pub′li kən) *adj.* 1. of or favoring a republic. 2. **Republican,** of the Republican Party, one of two major political parties in the U.S. —*n.* 3. **Republican,** a member of the Republican Party.

re•pu′di•ate′ (ri pyōō′dē āt′) *v.t.,* **-ated, -ating.** to reject as worthless, not binding, or false.

re•pug′nant (ri pug′nənt) *adj.* objectionable; offensive. —**re•pug′-nance,** *n.*

re•pulse′ (ri puls′) *v.,* **-pulsed, -pulsing,** *n.* —*v.t.* 1. to drive back with force. —*n.* 2. the act of repulsing. 3. a rejection. —**re•pul′sion,** *n.*

re•pul′sive *adj.* disgusting.

rep′u•ta•ble (rep′yə tə bəl) *adj.* of good reputation.

rep′u•ta′tion (-tā′shən) *n.* 1. a public estimation of character. 2. good name.

re•pute′ (ri pyōōt′) *n., v.,* **-puted, -puting.** —*n.* 1. reputation. —*v.t.* 2. to consider; believe.

re•quest′ (ri kwest′) *v.t.* 1. to ask for. —*n.* 2. the act of requesting. 3. what is requested.

req′ui•em (rek′wē əm) *n.* a mass for the dead or a musical setting of this.

re•quire′ (ri kwī′r′) *v.t.,* **-quired, -quiring.** 1. to need. 2. to demand. —**re•quire′ment,** *n.*

req′ui•site (rek′wə zit) *adj.* 1. necessary. —*n.* 2. a necessary thing.

req′ui•si′tion (-zish′ən) *n.* 1. a formal order or demand. —*v.t.* 2. to take for official use.

re•quite′ (ri kwīt′) *v.t.,* **-quited, -quiting.** to give or do in return. —**re•quit′al** (-kwīt′l) *n.*

---

re•run′ (rē′run′) *n.* 1. the showing of a motion picture or television program after its initial run. 2. the program shown.

re•scind′ (ri sind′) *v.t.* to repeal.

res′cue (res′kyōō) *v.t.,* **-cued, -cuing,** *n.* —*v.t.* 1. to free from danger, capture, etc. —*n.* 2. the act of rescuing.

re•search′ (ri sûrch′, rē′sûrch) *n.* 1. diligent investigation. —*v.i., v.t.* 2. to investigate carefully. —**re•search′er,** *n.*

re•sec′tion (ri sek′shən) *n.* surgical removal of part of an organ.

re•sem′ble (ri zem′bəl) *v.t.,* **-bled, -bling.** to be similar to. —**re•sem′blance,** *n.*

re•sent′ (ri zent′) *v.t.* to feel indignation or displeasure at. —**re•sent′ful,** *adj.* —**re•sent′ment,** *n.*

res′er•va′tion (rez′ər vā′shən) *n.* 1. the act of withholding or setting apart. 2. a particular doubt or misgiving. 3. an advance assurance of accommodations. 4. land for the use of an American Indian tribe.

re•serve′ (ri zûrv′) *v.,* **-served, -serving,** *n.* —*v.t.* 1. to keep back or set aside. —*n.* 2. something reserved. 3. part of a military force held in readiness to support active forces. 4. reticence. —*adj.* 5. kept in reserve.

re•served′ *adj.* 1. held for future use. 2. self-restrained.

re•serv′ist *n.* a member of the military reserves.

res′er•voir′ (rez′ər vwär′, -vwôr′, rez′ə-) *n.* 1. a place where water is stored for use. 2. a supply.

re•side′ (ri zīd′) *v.i.,* **-sided, -siding.** 1. to dwell. 2. to be vested, as powers.

res′i•dence (rez′i dəns) *n.* 1. a dwelling place. 2. the act or fact of residing. —**res′i•dent,** *n.* —**res′i•den′tial** (-den′shəl) *adj.*

res′i•den•cy *n., pl.* **-cies.** 1. residence (def. 2). 2. a period of advanced medical training.

res′i•due′ (-dōō′, -dyōō′) *n.* a part remaining. —**re•sid′u•al** (ri zij′ōō-əl) *adj.*

re•sign′ (ri zīn′) *v.t., v.i.* 1. to give up (a job, right, etc.), esp. formally. 2. to submit, as to fate or force.

re•signed′ *adj.* submissive or acquiescent.

re•sil′i•ent (ri zil′yənt) *adj.* 1. springing back. 2. recovering readily from adversity. —**re•sil′i•ence,** *n.*

res′in (rez′in) *n.* a substance exuded from some plants, used in medicines, plastics, etc.

re•sist′ (ri zist′) *v.t., v.i.* to withstand; offer opposition (to). —**re•sist′ant,** *adj.*

re•sist′ance *n.* 1. the act of resisting. 2. the ability to resist disease. 3. opposition to electric current.

re•sis′tor *n.* a device that introduces resistance into an electrical circuit.

res′o•lute′ (rez′ə lōōt′) *adj.* determined on an action or result.

res′o•lu′tion *n.* 1. a formal expression of group opinion. 2. determination. 3. a solution of a problem.

re•solve′ (ri zolv′) *v.,* **-solved, -solving,** *n.* —*v.t.* 1. to decide firmly. 2. to state formally. 3. to dispel. 4. to solve. —*n.* 5. resolution; determination.

res′o•nant (rez′ə nənt) *adj.* 1. resounding. 2. rich in sound.

res′o•nate′ (-nāt′) *v.i.,* **-nated, -nat-ing.** to resound.

re•sort′ (ri zôrt′) *v.i.* 1. to apply or turn (to) for use, help, etc. 2. to go often. —*n.* 3. a place much frequented, esp. for recreation. 4. a source of help.

re•sound′ (ri zound′) *v.i.* to ring with sound; sound loudly.

re•sound′ing *adj.* impressively complete. —**re•sound′ing•ly,** *adv.*

re′source (rē′sôrs, ri sôrs′) *n.* 1. a source of aid or supply. 2. **resources,** sources of wealth.

re•source′ful *adj.* able to deal with new situations or difficulties.

re•spect′ (ri spekt′) *n.* 1. a detail; point. 2. reference. 3. esteem. —*v.t.* 4. to hold in esteem.

re•spect′a•ble *adj.* 1. worthy of respect. 2. decent.

re•spect′ful *adj.* showing respect. —**re•spect′ful•ly,** *adv.*

re•spect′ing *prep.* concerning.

re•spec′tive *adj.* in the order previously named.

res′pi•ra′tion (res′pə rā′shən) *n.* the act or process of breathing. —**res′pi•ra•to′ry** (-pər ə tôr′ē) *adj.*

res′pi•ra′tor (res′pə rā′tər) *n.* an apparatus to produce artificial breathing.

res'pite (res'pit) *n.* a temporary relief or delay.

re•splend'ent (ri splen'dənt) *adj.* gleaming. —**re•splend'ence,** *n.*

re•spond' (ri spond') *v.i., v.t.* to answer or react.

re•spond'ent *n.* a defendant.

re•sponse' (-spons') *n.* a reply.

re•spon'si•bil'i•ty *n., pl.* -ties. 1. the state of being responsible. 2. an obligation. 3. initiative.

re•spon'si•ble *adj.* 1. causing or allowing things to happen. 2. capable of rational thought. 3. reliable.

re•spon'sive *adj.* responding readily. —**re•spon'sive•ly,** *adv.*

rest¹ (rest) *n.* 1. (a period of) quiet or sleep. 2. inactivity after work or motion. 3. *Music.* an interval of silence. 4. a supporting device. —*v.i.* 5. to refresh oneself. 6. to cease from motion. 7. to lie or lean. 8. to be based or found. —*v.t.* 9. to give rest to. 10. to place for rest or support. —**rest'ful,** *adj.* —**rest'ful•ly,** *adv.*

rest² (rest) *n.* 1. the remaining part. —*v.i.* 2. to continue to be.

res'tau•rant (res'tər ənt, -tə ränt') *n.* a public eating place.

res'tau•ra•teur' (-tər ə tûr') *n.* a restaurant owner.

res'ti•tu'tion (res'ti tōō'shən, -tyōō'-) *n.* 1. amends for damage. 2. the return of rights, property, etc.

res'tive (res'tiv) *adj.* restless.

rest'less *adj.* 1. lacking rest. 2. uneasy. 3. always moving. —**rest'less•ly,** *adv.* —**rest'less•ness,** *n.*

re•store' (ri stôr') *v.t.,* -stored, -storing. 1. to bring back, as to use or good condition. 2. to give back. —**res'to•ra'tion,** *n.* —**re•stor'a•tive,** *adj., n.*

re•strain' (ri strān') *v.t.* 1. to hold back. 2. to confine.

re•straint' (-strānt') *n.* 1. a restraining influence. 2. confinement. 3. constraint.

re•strict' (ri strikt') *v.t.* to confine; limit. —**re•stric'tion,** *n.* —**re•stric'tive,** *adj.*

rest' room' a room in a public building with toilets and basins.

re•sult' (ri zult') *n.* 1. an outcome; consequence. —*v.i.* 2. to occur as a result. 3. to end. —**re•sult'ant,** *adj., n.*

re•sume' (ri zōōm') *v.t., v.i.,* -sumed, -suming. to begin again after interruption. —**re•sump'tion** (-zump'shən) *n.*

ré'su•mé' (rez'ŏŏ mā') *n.* a summary, esp. of a person's education and work.

re•sur'face (rē sûr'fis) *v.t.,* -faced, -facing. 1. to give a new surface to. 2. to come to the surface again.

re•sur'gent (ri sûr'jənt) *adj.* rising again. —**re•sur'gence,** *n.*

res'ur•rect' (rez'ə rekt') *v.t.* to bring to life again. —**res'ur•rec'tion,** *n.*

re•sus'ci•tate' (ri sus'i tāt') *v.t.* to revive. —**re•sus'ci•ta'tion,** *n.*

re'tail (rē'tāl) *n.* 1. the sale of goods to consumers. —*v.t., v.i.* 2. to sell or be sold at a retail price. —**re'tail•er,** *n.*

re•tain' (ri tān') *v.t.* 1. to keep or hold. 2. to engage the services of.

re•tain'er *n.* 1. a fee paid to secure services. 2. an old servant.

re•take' *v.,* -took, -taken, -taking, *n.* —*v.t.* (rē tāk') 1. to take again. 2. to photograph again. —*n.* (rē' tāk) 3. a picture photographed again.

re•tal'i•ate' (ri tal'ē āt') *v.i.,* -ated, -ating. to return like for like, esp. evil. —**re•tal'i•a'tion,** *n.* —**re•tal'i•a•to'ry** (-ə tôr'ē) *adj.*

re•tard' (ri tärd') *v.t.* to delay.

re•tard'ant *n.* a substance slowing a chemical reaction.

re•tard'ed *adj.* slow or weak in mental development.

retch (rech) *v.i.* to try to vomit.

re•ten'tion (ri ten'shən) *n.* 1. the act or power of retaining. 2. memory. —**re•ten'tive,** *adj.*

ret'i•cent (ret'ə sənt) *adj.* saying little. —**ret'i•cence,** *n.*

ret'i•na (ret'n ə) *n.* a coating on the back part of the eyeball that receives images.

ret'i•nue (ret'n ōō', -yōō') *n.* a train of attendants.

re•tire' (ri tī°r') *v.i.,* -tired, -tiring. —*v.i.* 1. to end one's working life. 2. to withdraw. 3. to go to bed. —*v.t.* 4. to cause to retire. —**re•tire'ment,** *n.*

re•tired' *adj.* withdrawn from office, occupation, etc.

re•tir'er *n.* a person who has retired from work.

re•tir'ing *adj.* shy.

re•tool' (rē tōōl') *v.t., v.i.* to replace the tools and machinery of (a factory).

re•tort'¹ (ri tôrt') *v.t.* 1. to reply smartly. —*n.* 2. a sharp or witty reply.

re•tort'² (ri tôrt') *n.* a long-necked vessel used in distilling.

re•touch' (rē tuch') *v.t.* to touch up.

re•trace' (rē trās') *v.t.,* -traced, -tracing. to go back over.

re•tract' (ri trakt') *v.t.* to withdraw. —**re•trac'tion,** *n.* —**re•tract'a•ble,** *adj.*

re'tread' (rē tred') *n.* a tire that has had new tread added.

re•treat' (ri trēt') *n.* 1. a forced withdrawal. 2. a private place. —*v.i.* 3. to withdraw.

re•trench' (ri trench') *v.i.* to reduce expenses. —**re•trench'ment,** *n.*

ret'ri•bu'tion (re'trə byōō'shən) *n.* deserved punishment; retaliation.

re•trieve' (ri trēv') *v.t.,* -trieved, -trieving. 1. to regain or restore. 2. to access in a computer. —**re•triev'er,** *n.*

ret'ro•ac'tive (re'trō ak'tiv) *adj.* applying also to the past.

ret'ro•fit' *v.t.,* -fitted, -fitting. to furnish with newly developed equipment.

ret'ro•grade' *adj.* moving backward.

ret'ro•gress' (re'trə gres') *v.i.* to return to an earlier or more primitive condition. —**ret'ro•gres'sion,** *n.* —**ret'ro•gres'sive,** *adj.*

ret'ro•nym (re'trə nim) *n.* a term, such as *manual typewriter,* coined to distinguish an original referent from a later development.

ret'ro•spect' (re'trə spekt') *n.* an occasion of looking back. —**ret'ro•spec'tive,** *adj., n.*

re•turn' (ri tûrn') *v.i.* 1. to go or come back. —*v.t.* 2. to repay. 3. to put, bring, or give back. —*n.* 4. the act or fact of returning. 5. a recurrence. 6. a repayment or requital. 7. Often, **returns.** profit. 8. an official report.

re•turn•ee' (ri tûr nē', -tûr'nē) *n.* a person who has returned.

re•u•nite' (rē'yə nīt') *v.t., v.i.,* -nited, -niting. to unite after separation. —**re•un'ion,** *n.*

rev (rev) *n., v.,* revved, revving. —*n.* 1. a revolution of a machine part. —*v.t.* 2. to increase the speed of (a motor).

Rev. Reverend.

re•vamp' (rē vamp') *v.t.* to renovate or revise.

re•veal' (ri vēl') *v.t.* to disclose.

rev•eil•le (rev'ə lē) *n.* a signal to awaken military personnel.

rev'el (rev'əl) *v.i.,* -eled, -eling. 1. to enjoy greatly. 2. to make merry. —*n.* 3. **revels,** lively festivities; merrymaking. —**rev'el•ry,** *n.*

rev'e•la'tion *n.* an often surprising disclosure.

re•venge' (ri venj') *v.,* -venged, -venging, *n.* —*v.t.* 1. to inflict harm in return for. —*n.* 2. the act of revenging. 3. vindictiveness. —**re•venge'ful,** *adj.*

rev'e•nue' (rev'ən yōō', -ə nōō') *n.* income, esp. of a government or business.

re•ver'ber•ate' (ri vûr'bə rāt') *v.i.,* -ated, -ating. 1. to echo again and again. 2. to reflect. —**re•ver'ber•a'tion,** *n.*

re•vere' (ri vēr') *v.t.,* -vered, -vering. to hold in deep respect.

rev'er•ence (rev'ər əns) *n., v.,* -enced, -encing. —*n.* 1. deep respect and awe. —*v.t.* 2. to regard with reverence. —**rev'er•ent, rev'er•en'tial** (-ə ren'shəl) *adj.*

Rev'er•end *adj.* a title used with the name of a member of the clergy.

rev'er•ie (rev'ə rē) *n.* a daydream.

re•verse' (ri vûrs') *adj., n., v.,* -versed, -versing. —*adj.* 1. opposite in position, action, etc. 2. of or for backward motion. —*n.* 3. a reverse part, position, etc. 4. a misfortune. —*v.t.* 5. to turn in an opposite direction or position. —**re•ver'sal,** *n.* —**re•vers'i•ble,** *adj.*

re•vert' (-vûrt') *v.i.* to go back to an earlier state, topic, etc.

re•view' *n.* 1. a critical report, as on a book or film. 2. a repeated viewing. 3. a general survey. 4. a formal inspection. —*v.t.* 5. to go over or examine again. 6. to inspect formally. 7. to write a review of. —**re•view'er,** *n.*

re•vile' (ri vīl') *v.t.,* -viled, -viling. to speak abusively to or about.

re•vise' (ri vīz') *v.t.,* -vised, -vising.

to change or amend the content of. —**re•vi'sion** (-vizh'ən) *n., adj.*

re•vi'sion•ism (ri vizh'ə niz'əm) *n.* departure from an accepted doctrine. —**re•vi'sion•ist,** *n., adj.*

re•vi'tal•ize' (rē vīt'l īz') *v.t.,* -ized, -izing. to bring new vitality to.

re•viv'al (ri vī'vəl) *n.* 1. restoration to life, use, etc. 2. a religious awakening. —**re•viv'al•ist,** *n.*

re•vive' *v.t., v.i.,* -vived, -viving. to bring or come back to life or use.

re•voke' (ri vōk') *v.t.,* -voked, -voking. to annul or repeal. —**rev'o•ca•ble** (rev'ə kə bəl) *adj.*

re•volt' (ri vōlt') *v.i.* 1. to rebel. —*v.t.* 2. to fill with disgust. —*n.* 3. a rebellion. —**re•volt'ing,** *adj.*

rev'o•lu'tion (rev'ə lōō'shən) *n.* 1. the overthrow of a government. 2. a fundamental change. 3. an act or instance of revolving. —**rev'o•lu'tion•ar'y,** *adj., n.*

rev'o•lu'tion•ize' *v.t.,* -ized, -izing. to cause fundamental change in.

re•volve' (ri volv') *v.i.,* -volved, -volving. 1. to move in a circular course. 2. to rotate.

re•volv'er *n.* a pistol with a revolving cylinder holding cartridges.

re•vue' (ri vyōō') *n.* a theatrical show.

re•vul'sion (ri vul'shən) *n.* a strong feeling of disgust.

re•ward' (ri wôrd') *n.* 1. recompense for merit, service, etc. —*v.t.* 2. to give a reward (for).

re•ward'ing *adj.* giving satisfaction.

re•word' (rē wûrd') *v.t.* to put into other words.

re•write' *v.t.,* -wrote, -written, -writing. 1. to revise. 2. to write again.

RFD rural free delivery.

rhap'so•dize' (rap'sə dīz') *v.i.,* -dized, -dizing. to talk with extravagant enthusiasm.

rhap'so•dy (-sə dē) *n., pl.* -dies. 1. an exaggerated expression of enthusiasm. 2. a free-form musical composition.

rhe'o•stat' (rē'ə stat') *n.* a device for regulating electric current.

rhe'sus (rē'səs) *n.* a type of monkey used in research.

rhet'o•ric (ret'ər ik) *n.* 1. the skillful use of language. 2. exaggerated speech.

rhetor'ical ques'tion *n.* a question asked for effect, not an answer.

rheum (rōōm) *n.* a thin discharge of mucous membranes.

rheu'ma•tism (rōō'mə tiz'əm) *n.* a disease causing pain and stiffness in the joints or muscles. —**rheu•mat'ic** (rōō mat'ik) *adj., n.*

Rh factor an antigen in blood that may cause a severe reaction in an individual lacking it.

rhine'stone' (rīn'stōn') *n.* an artificial diamondlike gem.

rhi•ni'tis (rī nī'tis) *n.* inflammation of the nose.

rhi•noc'er•os (rī nos'ər əs) *n.* a large thick-skinned mammal with a horned snout.

rhi'zome (rī'zōm) *n.* a rootlike stem.

rho (rō) *n., pl.* rhos. the 17th letter of the Greek alphabet.

rho'do•den'dron (rō'də den'drən) *n.* a flowering evergreen shrub.

rhom'boid (rom'boid) *n.* an oblique-angled parallelogram with only the opposite sides equal.

rhom'bus (-bəs) *n., pl.* -buses, -bi (-bī). an oblique-angled parallelogram with all sides equal.

rhu'barb (rōō'bärb) *n.* a garden plant with edible stalks.

rhyme (rīm) *n., v.,* rhymed, rhyming. —*n.* 1. agreement in the end sounds of lines or words. 2. a verse with such correspondence. —*v.i.* 3. to make or form a rhyme.

rhythm (rith'əm) *n.* 1. movement with a uniformly recurring element. 2. a pattern of pulses in music resulting from strong and weak beats. —**rhyth'mic, rhyth'mi•cal,** *adj.*

RI Rhode Island. Also, **R.I.**

rib¹ (rib) *n., v.,* ribbed, ribbing. —*n.* 1. one of the curved bones enclosing the chest. 2. a riblike part. —*v.t.* 3. to furnish with ribs.

rib² (rib) *v.t.,* ribbed, ribbing. to tease.

rib'ald (rib'əld; *spelling pron.* rī'bəld) *adj.* bawdy in speech. —**rib'ald•ry,** *n.*

rib'bon (rib'ən) *n.* a strip of silk, rayon, etc.

ri'bo•fla'vin (rī'bō flā'vin, -bə-) *n.*

an important vitamin in milk, fresh meat, eggs, and leafy vegetables.

rice (rīs) *n.* an edible starchy grain.

rich (rich) *adj.* 1. having abundant and costly possessions. 2. abounding. 3. costly. 4. containing butter, eggs, cream, etc. 5. strong; vivid. 6. mellow. 7. **the rich,** rich people.

rich'es *n.pl.* abundant and valuable possessions.

Rich'ter scale (rik'tər) *n.* a scale for indicating the intensity of an earthquake.

rick (rik) *n.* a stack of hay, straw, etc.

rick'ets (rik'its) *n.* a childhood bone disease caused by lack of vitamin D.

rick'et•y (rik'i tē) *adj.,* -ier, -iest. likely to fall or collapse.

rick'shaw (rik'shô, -shä) *n.* a two-wheeled passenger vehicle pulled by a person.

ric'o•chet' (rik'ə shā') *v.i.,* -cheted (-shād'), -cheting (-shā'ing), *n.* —*v.i.* 1. to rebound from a flat surface. —*n.* 2. such a movement.

ri•cot'ta (ri kot'ə, -kô'tə) *n.* a soft Italian cheese.

rid (rid) *v.t.,* rid or ridded, ridding. to clear or free of. —**rid'dance,** *n.*

rid'dle¹ (rid'l) *n.* 1. a question requiring ingenuity to answer. 2. a puzzling thing or person.

rid'dle² (rid'l) *v.t.,* -dled, -dling. to pierce with many holes.

ride (rid) *v.,* rode (rōd) ridden, riding, *n.* —*v.i.* 1. to be carried in traveling. 2. to rest on something. —*v.t.* 3. to sit on and manage (a horse, bicycle, etc.). —*n.* 4. a journey on a horse, camel, etc., or in a vehicle. 5. a vehicle in which people ride for amusement.

rid'er *n.* 1. a person who rides. 2. a clause attached to a legislative bill before passage.

ridge (rij) *n., v.,* ridged, ridging. —*n.* 1. a long narrow elevation. —*v.t.* 2. to provide with ridges.

ridge'pole' *n.* a horizontal beam on a roof to which rafters are attached.

rid'i•cule' (rid'i kyōōl') *n., v.,* -culed, -culing. —*n.* 1. speech or action intended to make fun of someone. —*v.t.* 2. to make fun of; mock.

ri•dic'u•lous (ri dik'yə ləs) *adj.* very foolish; absurd. —**ri•dic'u•lous•ly,** *adv.*

rife (rīf) *adj.* 1. widespread. 2. abounding.

riff (rif) *n.* a repeated phrase in jazz or rock music.

riff'raff' (rif'raf') *n.* the lowest classes; rabble.

ri'fle¹ (rī'fəl) *n.* a shoulder firearm with a spirally grooved barrel.

ri'fle² (rī'fəl) *v.t.,* -fled, -fling. to ransack and rob.

rift (rift) *n.* 1. a split or crack. 2. a disagreement.

rig (rig) *v.,* rigged, rigging, *n.* —*v.t.* 1. to fit with tackle and other parts. 2. to put together as makeshift. 3. to manipulate fraudulently. —*n.* 4. an arrangement of masts, booms, tackle, etc. 5. equipment.

rig'ging *n.* the ropes and chains that support and work masts, sails, etc.

right (rīt) *adj.* 1. just or good. 2. correct. 3. in good condition. 4. on the side that is toward the east when one faces north. 5. straight. —*n.* 6. that which is right. 7. the right side. 8. something to which a person is entitled. 9. **the Right,** people holding conservative political views. —*adv.* 10. directly; completely. 11. set correctly. 12. in the right position. 13. correct. —**right'ly,** *adv.* —**right'ist,** *adj., n.*

right' an'gle a 90-degree angle.

right'eous (rī'chəs) *adj.* acting in a moral way.

right'ful *adj.* belonging by or having a just claim. —**right'ful•ly,** *adv.*

right'-hand'ed *adj.* 1. using the right hand more easily. 2. for the right hand.

right' of way' *n.* 1. the right of one vehicle to proceed before another. 2. a path that may lawfully be used.

right'size' *v.t.,* -sized, -sizing. to adjust to an appropriate size, as a work force.

right'-to-life' *adj.* advocating laws making abortion illegal. —**right'-to-life'er,** *n.*

right' wing' *n.* the conservative element in an organization. —**right'-wing',** *adj.*

rig'id (rij'id) *adj.* 1. stiff; inflexible. 2. strict; severe. —**ri•gid'i•ty,** *n.*

confused talk. 2. a complicated procedure.

rig'or (rig'ər) *n.* 1. strictness. 2. hardship. —**rig'or•ous,** *adj.*

ri'gor mor'tis (rig'ər môr'tis) *n.* stiffening of the body after death.

rile (rīl) *v.t.,* riled, riling. to irritate.

rill (ril) *n.* a small brook.

rim (rim) *n., v.,* rimmed, rimming. —*n.* 1. an outer edge. —*v.t.* 2. to furnish with a rim.

rime¹ (rīm) *n.* rough white frost.

rime² (rīm) *n., v.i.,* rimed, rim•ing. rhyme.

rind (rind) *n.* a firm outer layer.

ring¹ (ring) *n.* 1. a circular band worn on the finger. 2. something shaped like a ring. 3. a circular enclosed area. 4. a group cooperating for unethical purposes. —*v.t.* 5. to surround with a ring.

ring² (ring) *v.,* rang (rang) rung (rung) ringing. —*v.i.* 1. to sound clearly and resonantly. 2. to cause a bell to sound. 3. to resound; re-echo. 4. to seem; appear. —*v.t.* 5. to cause to ring. 6. to announce by a bell. 7. to telephone. —*n.* 8. a ringing sound. 9. a telephone call. 10. a characteristic quality.

ring'er *n.* 1. one that rings. 2. a person or thing that closely resembles another. 3. an athlete entered in competition in violation of eligibility rules.

ring'lead'er *n.* a leader in mischief.

ring'let (-lit) *n.* a curled lock of hair.

ring'mas'ter *n.* a person in charge of performances in a circus ring.

ring'worm' *n.* a contagious skin disease.

rink (ringk) *n.* a floor or sheet of ice for skating on.

rinse (rins) *v.,* rinsed, rinsing, *n.* —*v.t.* 1. to wash in clean water. 2. to remove soap, dirt, etc., by rinsing. —*n.* 3. the act of rinsing. 4. liquid for rinsing.

ri'ot (rī'ət) *n.* 1. a disturbance by a mob. 2. wild disorder. —*v.i.* 3. to take part in a riot. —**ri'ot•ous,** *adj.*

rip (rip) *v.,* ripped, ripping, *n.* —*v.t.* 1. to cut, tear apart, or tear off roughly. —*v.i.* 2. to become torn apart. —*n.* 3. a tear made by ripping. —**rip'per,** *n.*

R.I.P. may he, she, or they rest in peace.

rip'cord' *n.* a cord that opens a parachute.

ripe (rīp) *adj.,* riper, ripest. 1. fully developed; mature. 2. ready. —**rip'en,** *v.i., v.t.* —**ripe'ness,** *n.*

rip'off' *n. Slang.* a theft or exploitation.

ri•poste' (ri pōst') *n.* a quick, sharp reply or reaction.

rip'ple (rip'əl) *v.,* -pled, -pling, *n.* —*v.i.* 1. to form small waves. —*n.* 2. a pattern of small waves.

rip'ple effect' *n.* a spreading effect.

rip'-roar'ing *adj.* boisterously exciting.

rip'saw' *n.* a saw for cutting wood with the grain.

rip'tide' *n.* a tide that opposes other tides.

rise (rīz) *v.,* rose (rōz) risen (riz'ən) rising, *n.* —*v.i.* 1. to get up. 2. to revolt. 3. to appear. 4. to originate. 5. to move upward. 6. to increase. 7. (of dough) to expand. —*n.* 8. an upward movement or slope. 9. origin. 10. upward slope. —**ris'er,** *n.*

ris'i•ble (riz'ə bəl) *adj.* causing laughter.

risk (risk) *n.* 1. a chance of injury or loss. —*v.t.* 2. to expose to risk. 3. to take the chance of. —**risk'y,** *adj.*

ris•qué' (ri skā') *adj.* bawdy; indecent.

rite (rīt) *n.* a ceremonial act.

rite' of pas'sage *n.* an event marking a passage from one stage of life to another.

rit'u•al (rich'ōō əl) *n.* a procedure for religious or other rites.

ri'val (rī'vəl) *n., adj., v.,* -valed, -valing. —*n.* 1. a competitor. 2. an equal. —*adj.* 3. being a rival. —*v.t.* 4. to compete with. 5. to match. —**ri'val•ry,** *n.*

rive (rīv) *v.t., v.i.,* rived, rived or riven (riv'ən) riving. to tear apart; split.

riv'er (riv'ər) *n.* a large natural stream.

riv'et (riv'it) *n.* 1. a metal bolt hammered after insertion. —*v.t.* 2. to fasten with or as if with rivets.

riv'u•let (riv'yə lit) *n.* a small stream.

RN registered nurse.

roach (rōch) *n.* a cockroach.

road (rōd) *n.* an open way for travel.

road/block/ *n.* an obstruction placed across a road to halt traffic.

road/kill/ *n.* the body of an animal killed on a road by a vehicle.

road/run/ner *n.* a terrestrial cuckoo of the western U.S.

road/ show/ *n.* a show, as a play, performed by touring actors.

road/ war/rior *n. Slang.* a person who travels extensively on business.

roam (rōm) *v.i., v.t.* to wander; rove.

roan (rōn) *adj.* **1.** of a dark color with gray or white spots. —*n.* **2.** a roan horse.

roar (rôr) *v.i.* **1.** to make a loud, deep sound. —*v.t.* **2.** to express in a roar. —*n.* **3.** a loud, deep sound.

roast (rōst) *v.t.* **1.** to cook by dry heat. —*n.* **2.** roasted meat. —*roast/er, n.*

rob (rob) *v.t.,* **robbed, robbing.** to steal from. —*rob/ber, n.* —*rob/ber·y, n.*

robe (rōb) *n.* a long loose garment.

rob/in (rob/in) *n.* a red-breasted songbird.

ro/bot (rō/bət, -bot) *n.* **1.** a humanlike machine that performs tasks. **2.** a person who acts mechanically.

ro·bot/ics *n.* the technology of computer-controlled robots.

ro·bust/ (rō bust/, rō/bust) *adj.* healthy.

rock (rok) *n.* **1.** a mass of stone. **2.** Also, **rock-'n'-roll.** popular music with a steady, insistent rhythm. —*v.t., v.i.* **3.** to move back and forth. —*rock/y, adj.*

rock/ bot/tom *n.* the lowest level.

rock/er *n.* **1.** the curved support of a cradle or rocking chair. **2.** a rocking chair.

rock/et (rok/it) *n.* a tube propelled by discharge of gases from it.

rock/et·ry *n.* the science of rocket design.

rock/ing chair/ *n.* a chair mounted on rockers.

rock/-ribbed/ *adj.* **1.** having ridges of rock. **2.** unyielding.

rock/ salt/ *n.* salt occurring in rocklike masses.

ro·co/co (rə kō/kō, rō/kə kō/) *adj., n.* (of or in) an elaborate decorative style of many curves.

rod (rod) *n.* **1.** a slender shaft. **2.** a linear measure of 5½ yards.

ro/dent (rōd/nt) *n.* a small gnawing or nibbling mammal.

ro/de·o (rō/dē ō/, rō dā/ō) *n., pl.* **-deos.** an exhibition of cowboy skills.

roe¹ (rō) *n.* fish eggs.

roe² (rō) *n., pl.* **roes, roe.** a small deer.

roent·gen (rent/gən, -jən) *n.* a unit for measuring radiation dosage.

rog/er (roj/ər) *interj.* (message) received.

rogue (rōg) *n.* **1.** a dishonest person; scoundrel. **2.** a playfully mischievous person. —*ro/guer·y, n.* —*ro/guish, adj.*

roil (roil) *v.t.* **1.** to make muddy. **2.** to vex.

roist/er (roi/stər) *v.i.* **1.** to swagger. **2.** to carouse. —*roist/er·er, n.*

role (rōl) *n.* a part or function, as of a character in a play.

role/ mod/el *n.* a person imitated by others.

roll (rōl) *v.i.* **1.** to move by turning over and over. **2.** to move on wheels. **3.** to have a deep long sound. **4.** to rock from side to side. —*v.t.* **5.** to flatten, as with a rolling pin. **6.** to form into a roll or ball. —*n.* **7.** a list; register. **8.** anything cylindrical. **9.** a small cake of bread. **10.** a deep long sound. —*roll/er, n.*

roll/back/ *n.* a return to a lower level.

roll/ call/ *n.* the calling of names for checking attendance.

Roll/er·blade/ *n., v.,* **-bladed, -blading.** *1. Trademark.* a brand of in-line skates. —*v.i.* **2.** (*often l.c.*) to skate on in-line skates.

roll/er coast/er *n.* an amusementpark railroad with a winding route and steep inclines.

roll/er skate/ *n.* a skate with four wheels. —**roll/er-skate/,** *v.i.* —**roll/er skat/er, n.**

rol/lick·ing (rol/i king) *adj.* jolly.

roll/ing pin/ *n.* a cylinder for rolling out dough.

roll/o/ver *n.* a reinvestment of funds.

ro/ly-po/ly (rō/lē pō/lē, -pō/lē) *adj.* short and round.

ROM (rom) *n.* read-only memory: nonmodifiable computer memory containing instructions to the system.

ro·maine/ (rō mān/, rə-) *n.* a kind of lettuce with a cylindrical head of long leaves.

ro/man (rō/mən) *n.* **1.** a native or citizen of Rome or the Roman Empire. **2.** an upright style of printing type. **3.** of ancient or modern Rome.

Ro/man Cath/olic *adj.* **1.** of the Roman Catholic Church. —*n.* **2.** a member of the Roman Catholic Church.

Ro/man Cath/olic Church/ *n.* the Christian church of which the pope is the supreme head.

ro·mance/ (rō mans/) *n., v.,* **-manced, -mancing.** —*n.* **1.** a tale of heroic or marvelous exploits. **2.** a colorful, fanciful quality. **3.** a love affair. —*v.t.* **4.** to woo passionately.

Ro/man nu/merals *n.pl.* numbers using letters as symbols: I = 1, V = 5, X = 10, L = 50, C = 100, D = 500, M = 1,000.

ro·man/tic (rō man/tik) *adj.* **1.** of romance. **2.** impractical or unrealistic. **3.** imbued with idealism. **4.** preoccupied with love. **5.** passionate; fervent. **6.** of a style of art stressing imagination and emotion. —*n.* **7.** a romantic person.

ro·man/ti·cism (-tə siz/əm) *n.* **1.** romantic spirit. **2.** (*often cap.*) an artistic style emphasizing imagination and emotion.

ro·man/ti·cize/ *v.t.,* **-cized, -cizing.** to invest with romantic character.

romp (romp) *v.i.* **1.** to play in a lively or boisterous manner. —*n.* **2.** a lively frolic.

romp/ers *n.pl.* a child's loose outer garment.

rood (rōōd) *n.* **1.** a crucifix. **2.** one-quarter of an acre.

roof (rōōf, rōf) *n., pl.* **roofs. 1.** the upper covering of a building. —*v.t.* **2.** to provide with a roof. —*roof/er, n.*

rook¹ (rōōk) *n.* **1.** a European crow. —*v.t.* **2.** to cheat.

rook² (rōōk) *n.* a chess piece moving horizontally or vertically.

rook/ie *n.* a beginner.

room (rōōm, rōōm) *n.* **1.** a separate space within a building. **2.** space available for something. —*v.i.* **3.** to lodge. —*room/er, n.* —*room/mate/, n.* —*room/y, adj.*

roost (rōōst) *n.* **1.** a perch where fowls rest. —*v.i.* **2.** to sit on a roost.

roost/er *n.* a male chicken.

root¹ (rōōt, rōōt) *n.* **1.** a plant part that grows downward into the soil. **2.** the embedded portion of a hair, tooth, etc. **3.** a source. **4.** a quantity that when multiplied by itself a certain number of times produces a given quantity. —*v.i.* **5.** to become fixed. —*v.t.* **6.** to fix by or as if by roots. **7.** to dig up by the roots. **8. root out,** to remove completely.

root² (rōōt, rōōt) *v.i.* to turn up the soil with the snout.

root³ (rōōt) *v.i.* to encourage a team by cheering enthusiastically.

root/ beer/ *n.* a soft drink flavored with extracts of roots, barks, and herbs.

root/ canal/ *n.* the root portion of the pulp cavity of a tooth.

rope (rōp) *n., v.,* **roped, roping.** —*n.* **1.** a strong twisted cord. —*v.t.* **2.** to fasten or catch with a rope.

Roque/fort (rōk/fərt) *Trademark.* a strong-flavored cheese, veined with mold.

Ror/schach test/ (rôr/shäk) *n.* a diagnostic personality test based on interpretations of inkblot designs.

ro/sa·ry (rō/zə rē) *n., pl.* **-ries. 1.** a series of prayers recited by Roman Catholics. **2.** a string of beads counted in saying the rosary.

rose¹ (rōz) *n.* a thorny plant with showy, fragrant flowers.

rose² (rōz) *v.* pt. of **rise.**

ro·sé/ (rō zā/) *n.* a pink wine.

ro/se·ate (rō/zē it, -āt/) *adj.* rosy.

rose/mar/y (rōz/mâr/ē, -mə rē) *n.* an aromatic shrub used for seasoning.

ro·sette/ (rō zet/) *n.* a rose-shaped ornament.

ros/in (roz/in) *n.* the solid left after distilling pine resin.

ros/ter (ros/tər) *n.* a list of persons, events, etc.

ros/trum (ros/trəm) *n., pl.* **-trums, -tra** (-trə). a speakers' platform.

ros/y (rō/zē) *adj.,* **-ier, -iest. 1.** pink or pinkish-red. **2.** bright or promising. —*ros/i·ly, adv.*

rot (rot) *v.,* **rotted, rotting,** *n.* —*v.i., v.t.* **1.** to decay. —*n.* **2.** decay. **3.** a disease characterized by decay of tissue.

ro/tate (rō/tāt) *v.i., v.t.,* **-tated, -tating. 1.** to turn on or as on an axis. **2.** to proceed or cause to proceed in a fixed succession. —*ro/ta·ry* (-tə rē) *adj.* —*ro·ta/tion, n.*

ROTC (är/ō tē sē/, rot/sē) Reserve Officers Training Corps.

rote (rōt) *n.* **by rote,** from memory, in a mechanical way.

ro·tis/ser·ie (rō tis/ə rē) *n.* a machine with a revolving spit for roasting.

ro/tor (rō/tər) *n.* a rotating part.

ro/to·till/er (rō/tə til/ər) *n.* a motorized device with spinning blades for tilling soil.

rot/ten (rot/n) *adj.* **1.** decaying. **2.** corrupt. —*rot/ten·ness, n.*

ro·tund/ (rō tund/) *adj.* rounded; plump.

ro·tun/da (rō tun/də) *n.* a round room.

rou·é/ (rōō ā/) *n.* a dissolute man.

rouge (rōōzh) *n., v.,* **rouged, rouging.** —*n.* **1.** a red cosmetic for cheeks. —*v.t.* **2.** to color with rouge.

rough (ruf) *adj.* **1.** not smooth. **2.** violent in action or motion. **3.** harsh. **4.** crude. **5.** approximate. —*n.* **6.** a rough thing or part.

rough/age (-ij) *n.* coarse or fibrous material in food.

rough/en *v.t., v.i.* to make or become rough.

rou·lette/ (rōō let/) *n.* a gambling game based on a spinning disk.

round (round) *adj.* **1.** circular, curved, or spherical. **2.** complete. **3.** expressed as an approximate number. **4.** sonorous. —*n.* **5.** something round. **6.** a complete course, series, etc. **7.** a cut of beef between the rump and leg. **8.** a song in which voices enter at intervals. **9.** a stage of competition, as in a tournament. —*adv.* **10.** throughout. **11.** around. —*prep.* **12.** around. —*v.t.* **13.** to make round. **14.** to travel around. **15.** to express as a round number. —*v.i.* **16.** to become round. **16. round up,** to bring together. —*round/ness, n.*

round/a·bout/ *adj.* indirect.

roun/de·lay/ (roun/dl ā/) *n.* a song in which a phrase is continually repeated.

round/house/ *n.* a building for servicing locomotives.

round/ly *adv.* unsparingly.

round/ ta/ble *n.* a group gathered for a conference.

round/ trip/ *n.* a trip to a place and back.

round/up/ *n.* **1.** a bringing together. **2.** a summary.

round/worm/ *n.* a nematode that infests the intestines of mammals.

rouse (rouz) *v.t., v.i.,* **roused, rousing.** to stir up; arouse.

roust/a·bout/ (roust/ə bout/) *n.* a laborer, as at a circus.

rout (rout) *n.* **1.** a defeat ending in disorderly flight. —*v.t.* **2.** to force to flee in disorder.

route (rōōt, rout) *n., v.,* **routed, routing.** —*n.* **1.** a course of travel. —*v.t.* **2.** to send by a particular route.

rou·tine/ (rōō tēn/) *n.* **1.** a regular order of action. —*adj.* **2.** like or by routine. **3.** ordinary.

rove (rōv) *v.i., v.t.,* **roved, roving.** to wander (over or through) aimlessly. —*rov/er, n.*

row¹ (rō) *n.* a number of persons or things in a line.

row² (rō) *v.t., v.i.* **1.** to propel (a boat) with oars. **2.** to convey in a rowboat. —*row/boat/, n.*

row³ (rou) *n.* a noisy dispute.

row/dy (rou/dē) *adj.,* **-dier, -diest,** *n., pl.* **-dies.** —*adj.* **1.** rough and disorderly. —*n.* **2.** a rowdy person.

roy/al (roi/əl) *adj.* of kings or queens. —*roy/al·ly, adv.*

roy/al·ist *n.* a person favoring rule by a king or queen.

roy/al·ty (- tē) *n., pl.* **-ties. 1.** royal persons. **2.** royal power. **3.** an agreed share of proceeds paid to an author, inventor, etc.

rpm revolutions per minute.

RR 1. railroad. **2.** rural route.

RSVP please reply.

rub (rub) *v.,* **rubbed, rubbing,** *n.* —*v.t.* **1.** to apply pressure to in cleaning, smoothing, etc. **2.** to move or apply with pressure. **3.** to press against with friction. —*v.i.* **4.** to rub something. —*n.* **5.** the act of rubbing. **6.** a difficulty. —*Idiom.* **7. rub the wrong way,** to irritate.

rub/ber (rub/ər) *n.* **1.** elastic material from a tropical tree. **2.** rubbers, rubber overshoes. —*rub/ber·y, adj.*

rub/ber band/ *n.* a band of rubber used for holding things together.

rub/ber ce·ment/ *n.* a liquid adhesive.

rub/ber·neck/ *Informal.* —*v.i.* **1.** to stare curiously. —*n.* **2.** a curious onlooker. **3.** a sightseer.

rub/ber stamp/ *n.* a stamp with a rubber printing surface.

rub/bish (rub/ish) *n.* **1.** waste or trash. **2.** nonsense.

rub/ble (rub/əl) *n.* broken stone.

rub/down/ *n.* a massage.

ru·bel/la (rōō bel/ə) *n.* a usu. mild viral infection that may cause fetal damage if contracted during pregnancy. Also, **German measles.**

ru/bi·cund (rōō/bi kund/) *adj.* red.

ru/ble (rōō/bəl) *n.* a monetary unit of Russia and of some former Soviet states.

ru/bric (rōō/brik) *n.* **1.** a title or heading. **2.** a class or category.

ru/by (rōō/bē) *n., pl.* **-bies.** a red gem.

ruck/sack/ (ruk/sak/, rōōk/-) *n.* a knapsack.

ruck/us (ruk/əs) *n.* a noisy commotion.

rud/der (rud/ər) *n.* a flat vertical piece for steering a ship, aircraft, etc.

rud/dy (rud/ē) *adj.,* **-dier, -diest.** having a healthy red color.

rude (rōōd) *adj.,* **ruder, rudest. 1.** not polite. **2.** rough or crude.

ru/di·ment (rōō/də mənt) *n.* a basic thing to learn. —*ru/di·men/ta·ry* (-men/tə rē) *adj.*

rue (rōō) *v.t.,* **rued, ruing.** to regret. —*rue/ful, adj.*

ruff (ruf) *n.* **1.** a gathered or pleated collar. **2.** a collar of hairs or feathers on an animal's neck.

ruf/fi·an (ruf/ē ən) *n.* a rough or lawless person.

ruf/fle (ruf/əl) *v.,* **-fled, -fling,** *n.* —*v.t.* **1.** to make uneven. **2.** to disturb. **3.** to gather in folds. —*n.* **4.** a break in evenness. **5.** a strip of fabric gathered on one edge.

rug (rug) *n.* a floor covering.

Rug/by (rug/bē) *n.* a British form of football.

rug/ged (rug/id) *adj.* **1.** roughly irregular. **2.** severe. **3.** strong.

ru/in (rōō/in) *n.* **1.** complete loss or destruction. **2.** ruins, the remains of fallen buildings, monuments, etc. —*v.t., v.i.* **3.** to bring or come to ruin or ruins. —*ru/in·a/tion, n.* —*ru/in·ous, adj.*

rule (rōōl) *n., v.,* **ruled, ruling.** —*n.* **1.** a principle; regulation. **2.** control or government. **3.** a ruler (def. 2). —*v.t., v.i.* **4.** to exercise control (over); govern. **5.** to decide in the manner of a judge. **6.** to mark with a ruler. —*rul/ing, n., adj.*

rul/er *n.* **1.** a person who rules. **2.** a straight-edged strip for measuring and drawing lines.

rum (rum) *n.* an alcoholic liquor made from sugarcane or molasses.

rum/ba (rum/bə, rōōm/-) *n.* a Cuban dance.

rum/ble (rum/bəl) *v.,* **-bled, -bling,** *n.* —*v.i.* **1.** to make a long, deep, heavy sound. —*n.* **2.** such a sound.

ru/mi·nant (rōō/mə nənt) *n.* **1.** a cud-chewing mammal, as a cow. —*adj.* **2.** cud-chewing.

-nating. 1. to chew cud. **2.** to meditate.

rum/mage (rum/ij) *v.i., v.t.,* **-maged, -maging.** to search thoroughly (through).

rum/my (rum/ē) *n.* a card game in which cards are matched in sets and sequences.

ru/mor (rōō/mər) *n.* **1.** an unconfirmed but widely repeated story. —*v.t.* **2.** to tell as a rumor.

rump (rump) *n.* **1.** the rear part of an animal's body. **2.** the buttocks.

rum/pus (rum/pəs) *n.* a noisy disturbance.

run (run) *v.,* **ran** (ran) **run, running,** *n.* —*v.i.* **1.** to go, move, or depart quickly. **2.** to take part in a race. **3.** to be a candidate. **4.** to flow. **5.** to extend or continue. **6.** to operate. **7.** to total. **8.** to recur persistently. —*v.t.* **9.** to manage. **10.** to operate. **11.** to compete in. **12. run across,** to meet accidentally. **13. ~ down,** to knock down with a vehicle. **14. ~ out of,** to use up the supply of. **15. ~ over,** to hit and drive over with a vehicle. —*n.* **16.** an act or period of running. **17.** a raveled line in knitting. **18.** freedom of action. **19.** a scoring unit in baseball. —*Idiom.* **20. in the long run,** over a long period.

run/a·round/ *n.* an evasive action or response.

run/a·way/ *n.* **1.** a fugitive. **2.** something that has broken away from control. —*adj.* **3.** escaped. **4.** uncontrolled.

run/-down/ *adj.* **1.** weary. **2.** fallen into disrepair. **3.** (of a clock or watch) not running because not wound.

run/down/ *n.* a short summary.

rune (rōōn) *n.* an ancient Germanic alphabet character. —*ru/nic, adj.*

rung¹ (rung) *v.* pt. and pp. of **ring.**

rung² (rung) *n.* **1.** a ladder step. **2.** a bar between chair legs.

run/-in/ *n.* a confrontation.

run/ner *n.* **1.** one that runs. **2.** a messenger. **3.** a blade of a skate. **4.** a strip of fabric, carpet, etc.

run/ner-up/ *n.* a competitor finishing in second place.

run/off/ *n.* a final contest held to break a tie.

run/-of-the-mill/ *adj.* mediocre.

runt (runt) *n.* an undersized thing.

run/way/ *n.* a strip where airplanes take off and land.

rup/ture (rup/chər) *n., v.,* **-tured, -turing.** —*n.* **1.** the act of breaking or state of being broken. **2.** a hernia. —*v.i., v.t.* **3.** to suffer or cause to suffer a rupture.

ru/ral (rōōr/əl) *adj.* of or in the country.

ruse (rōōz) *n.* a deception or trick.

rush¹ (rush) *v.i., v.t.* **1.** to move or cause to move with speed. —*n.* **2.** the act of rushing. **3.** hurried activity. **4.** a hurried state. —*adj.* **5.** requiring or done in haste.

rush² (rush) *n.* a grasslike marsh plant.

rusk (rusk) *n.* a sweet raised bread that has been dried and baked again.

rus/set (rus/it) *n.* a reddish brown.

Rus/sian (rush/ən) *adj.* **1.** of Russia, its inhabitants, or its language. —*n.* **2.** a native of Russia. **3.** the language of Russia.

rust (rust) *n.* **1.** a red-orange coating that forms on iron and steel exposed to air and moisture. —*v.t., v.i.* **2.** to form rust (on). —*rust/y, adj.*

rus/tic (rus/tik) *adj.* **1.** rural. **2.** simple. —*n.* **3.** a country person.

rus/tle (rus/əl) *v.i., v.t.,* **-tled, -tling,** *n.* **1.** to make or cause to make small soft sounds. **2.** to steal (livestock). —*n.* **3.** a rustling sound.

rut¹ (rut) *n.* **1.** a groove worn in the ground. **2.** a fixed, dull way of proceeding.

rut² (rut) *n.* a period of sexual excitement in male deer, goats, etc.

ru/ta·ba/ga (rōō/tə bā/gə) *n.* a yellow turnip.

ruth/less (rōōth/lis) *adj.* without pity or mercy. —*ruth/less·ness, n.*

RV recreational vehicle.

Rx prescription.

rye (rī) *n.* a cereal grass used for flour, feed, and whiskey.

S

S, s (es) n. the nineteenth letter of the English alphabet.

S south, southern.

Sab·bath (sab′əth) n. a day of religious observance and rest, observed on Saturday by Jews and on Sunday by most Christians.

sab·bat·i·cal (sə bat′i kəl) n. a paid leave of absence for study, writing, or travel, granted to teachers.

sa·ber (sā′bər) n. a one-edged sword. Also, **sa·bre.**

sa·ble (sā′bəl) n. a small mammal with dark-brown fur.

sab·o·tage (sab′ə täzh′) n., v., **-taged, -taging.** —n. 1. deliberate injury to equipment or interference with production. —v.t. 2. to injure or attack by sabotage.

sab·o·teur (-tûr′) n. a person who sabotages.

sac (sak) n. a baglike part.

sac·cha·rin (sak′ər in) n. a synthetic, noncaloric sugar substitute.

sac·cha·rine (-ər in, -ə rēn′) adj. overly sweet or sentimental.

sac·er·do·tal (sas′ər dōt′l) adj. priestly.

sa·chet (sa shā′) n. a small bag of perfumed powder.

sack¹ (sak) n. 1. a large stout bag. 2. a bag. 3. Slang. dismissal from a job. —v.t. 4. Slang. to dismiss from a job.

sack² (sak) v.t 1. to loot (a place) after capture; plunder. —n. 2. the plundering of a captured place.

sack·cloth′ n. a coarse cloth worn for penance or mourning.

sac·ra·ment (sak′rə mənt) n. 1. a symbolic rite, as baptism, in the Christian church. 2. Sacrament, the Eucharist.

sa·cred (sā′krid) adj. 1. holy. 2. connected with religion. 3. dedicated to some person or purpose. 4. regarded with reverence.

sac·ri·fice (sak′rə fīs′) n., v., **-ficed, -ficing.** —n. 1. the offering of something to a deity. 2. something so offered. 3. the giving up of something valued for the sake of something else. —v.t., v.i. 4. to make a sacrifice (of). —**sac·ri·fi·cial** (-fish′əl) adj.

sac·ri·lege (-lij) n. violation or profanation of anything sacred. —**sac·ri·le·gious** (-lij′əs, -lē′jəs) adj.

sac·ris·ty (-ri stē) n., pl. **-ties.** a room in a church where sacred objects are kept.

sac·ro·il·i·ac (sak′rō il′ē ak′, sā′krō-) n. a joint in the lower back.

sac·ro·sanct (sak′rō sangkt′) adj. sacred.

sac·rum (sak′rəm, sā′krəm) n., pl. **sacra.** a bone forming the rear wall of the pelvis.

sad (sad) adj., **sadder, saddest.** affected by, marked by, or causing sorrow. —**sad′den,** v.t., v.i.

sad·dle (sad′l) n., v., **-dled, -dling.** —n. 1. a seat for a rider on a horse. 2. anything resembling a saddle. —v.t. 3. to put a saddle on. 4. to burden.

sad·dle·bag′ n. a pouch laid over the back of a horse or mounted over the rear wheel of a bicycle or motorcycle.

sad·ism (sā′diz əm, sad′iz-) n. pleasure in causing pain. —**sad′ist,** n. —**sa·dis′tic** (sə dis′tik) adj.

sa·fa·ri (sə fär′ē) n. 1. a hunting expedition, esp. in E Africa. 2. a long journey.

safe (sāf) adj., **safer, safest.** —adj. 1. offering security from danger. 2. free from injury or risk. 3. dependable. —n. 4. a steel or iron box for valuables. —**safe′ly,** adv.

safe′-con·duct a document authorizing safe passage.

safe′-de·pos′it providing safekeeping for valuables.

safe·guard′ n. 1. something that ensures safety. —v.t. 2. to protect.

safe′ sex′ n. sexual activity in which precautions are taken to avoid sexually transmitted diseases.

safe·ty n. 1. the state of being safe. 2. freedom from injury, danger, or loss. 3. a device to prevent injury.

safe·ty glass′ n. shatter-resistant glass.

safe·ty pin′ n. a pin bent back on itself with a guard covering the point.

safe·ty ra·zor n. a razor with a blade guard.

saf·flow·er (saf′lou′ər) n. a thistle-like plant whose seeds yield oil.

saf·fron (saf′rən) n. the orange-colored stigmas of a crocus, used to color and flavor foods.

sag (sag) v., **sagged, sagging,** n. —v.i. 1. to bend, esp. in the middle, from weight or pressure. 2. to hang loosely. —n. 3. a sagging place.

sa·ga (sä′gə) n. a heroic tale.

sa·ga·cious (sə gā′shəs) adj. shrewd. —**sa·gac′i·ty** (-gas′ə tē) n.

sage¹ (sāj) n., adj., **sager, sagest.** —n. 1. a wise person. —adj. 2. wise.

sage² (sāj) n. a plant of the mint family, used in cooking.

sage·brush′ n. a bushy plant of the dry plains of the western U.S.

sa·go (sā′gō) n. a starchy substance from some palms.

said (sed) v. pt. and pp. of **say.**

sail (sāl) n. 1. a sheet of fabric spread to catch the wind to propel a vessel or a windmill. 2. a trip in a sailing vessel. —v.i. 3. to travel over water. 4. to control a sailboat. 5. to move smoothly and effortlessly. —v.t. 6. to sail upon or over. 7. to navigate (a ship). —**sail′or,** n.

sail·cloth′ n. fabric used for boat sails or tents.

sail·fish′ n. a large fish with an upright fin.

saint (sānt) n. 1. a holy person, esp. one formally recognized by the Christian Church. 2. an especially good or kind person. —**saint′hood,** n. —**saint′ly,** adj.

sake (sāk) n. 1. benefit. 2. purpose.

sa·laam (sə läm′) n. 1. a salutation used in Islamic countries. 2. a low bow with one hand on the forehead.

sa·la·cious (sə lā′shəs) adj. lewd; indecent.

sal·ad (sal′əd) n. a cold dish of raw vegetables or fruit.

sal·a·man·der (sal′ə man′dər) n. a small, tailed amphibian.

sa·la·mi (sə lä′mē) n. a spicy, garlic-flavored sausage.

sal·a·ry (sal′ə rē) n., pl. **-ries.** fixed payment for regular work.

sale (sāl) n. 1. the act of selling. 2. a special offering of goods at reduced prices. 3. a transfer of property for money. —**sales′man,** n. —**sales′wom·an,** n.fem. —**sales′per·son,** n. —**sales′peo·ple,** n.pl.

sales·man·ship′ n. the skill of selling a product or idea.

sal·i·cyl·ic acid (sal′ə sil′ik) n. a white crystalline substance used in aspirin.

sa·li·ent (sā′lē ənt) adj. 1. prominent. 2. pointing outward. —n. 3. a projecting part. —**sa′li·ence,** n.

sa·line (sā′lēn, -līn) adj. salty.

sa·li·va (sə lī′və) n. a colorless fluid that forms in the mouth. —**sal′i·var·y** (sal′ə ver′ē) adj. —**sal′i·vate** (-vāt′) v.i. —**sal′i·va′tion,** n.

Salk′ vaccine′ (sôk) n. a vaccine against poliomyelitis.

sal·low (sal′ō) adj. having a sickly complexion.

sal·ly (sal′ē) n., pl. **-lies.** 1. a sudden attack. 2. a witty remark.

salm·on (sam′ən) n. a pink-fleshed food fish of northern waters.

sal·mo·nel·la (sal′mə nel′ə) n., pl. **-nellae** (-nel′ē) **-nellas.** a rod-shaped bacterium that causes food poisoning.

sa·lon′ (sə lon′; Fr. sa lôn′) n. 1. an elegant drawing room. 2. a gathering of leaders in the arts, politics, etc. 3. a shop offering a special service to a fashionable clientele.

sa·loon′ (sə lōōn′) n. a place where liquor is sold and drunk.

sal·sa (säl′sə, -sä) n. 1. a hot sauce containing chilies. 2. a type of Latin-American music with elements of jazz, rock, and soul.

salt (sôlt) n. 1. sodium chloride, used for seasoning and preserving food. 2. a chemical compound derived from an acid and a base. 3. a sailor. —v.t. 4. to season or preserve with salt. —**Idiom.** 5. **take with a grain of salt,** to be skeptical about. —**salt′y,** adj.

salt·cel·lar n. a shaker or dish for salt.

sal·tine′ (sôl tēn′) n. a crisp, salted cracker.

salt′ lick′ n. a place where animals go to lick salt deposits.

salt·pe·ter (-pē′tər) n. potassium nitrate.

sa·lu·bri·ous (sə lōō′brē əs) adj. good for the health.

sal·u·tar·y (sal′yə ter′ē) adj. healthful; beneficial.

sal·u·ta·tion (sal′yə tā′shən) n. 1. a greeting. 2. the opening of a letter.

sa·lute (sə lōōt′) v., **-luted, -luting,** n. —v. 1. a gesture of greeting or respect. —v.t., v.i. 2. to give a salute (to).

sal·vage (sal′vij) n., v., **-vaged, -vaging.** —v.t. 1. to save from destruction. 2. the act of saving a ship or cargo at sea. 3. the property saved.

sal·va·tion (-vā′shən) n. 1. the act of saving or the means of being saved. 2. deliverance from the consequences of sin.

salve (sav) n., v., **salved, salving.** —n. 1. an ointment for sores. —v.t. 2. to soothe with salve.

sal·ver (sal′vər) n. a tray.

sal·vo (sal′vō) n., pl. **-vos, -voes.** a simultaneous discharge of guns.

same (sām) adj. 1. identical with what has just been mentioned. 2. corresponding. 3. unchanged. —pron. 4. the same person or thing. —**same′ness,** n.

sam·o·var (sam′ə vär′) n. a metal urn used esp. in Russia to make tea.

sam·pan (sam′pan) n. a small boat of the Far East.

sam·ple (sam′pəl) n., adj., v., **-pled, -pling.** —n. 1. a small part that shows the nature or quality of the whole. —adj. 2. serving as a sample. —v.t. 3. to take a sample of.

sam·pler n. a piece of needlework done to show a beginner's skill.

sam·u·rai (sam′ŏŏ rī′) n., pl. **-rai.** a member of a hereditary warrior class in feudal Japan.

san·a·to·ri·um (san′ə tôr′ē əm) n., pl. **-toriums, -toria** (-tôr′ē ə). 1. a hospital for treating chronic diseases. 2. a sanitarium.

sanc·ti·fy (sangk′tə fī′) v.t., **-fied, -fying.** to make holy. —**sanc′ti·fi·ca′tion,** n.

sanc·ti·mo·ni·ous (-mō′nē əs), adj. hypocritically devout.

sanc·tion (sangk′shən) n. 1. permission or approval. 2. action by one state against another to force compliance with an obligation. —v.t. 3. to authorize; approve.

sanc·ti·ty (sangk′ti tē) n. holiness; sacredness.

sanc·tu·ar·y (-chŏŏ er′ē) n. **-ies.** 1. a holy place, as the chancel of a church. 2. a place of refuge.

sanc·tum (-təm) n., pl. **-tums, -ta.** a private place; retreat.

sand (sand) n. 1. fine, loose grains of rock. 2. **sands,** a sandy region. —v.t. 3. to smooth or polish with sandpaper.

san·dal (san′dl) n. a shoe consisting of a sole fastened to the foot with straps.

san·dal·wood′ n. a fragrant wood.

sand·bag′ n. a sand-filled bag used as fortification, ballast, etc.

sand·bank′ n. a large mass of sand.

sand′ bar′ n. a bar of sand formed by tidal action in a river or sea.

sand·blast′ v.t. to clean with a blast of air laden with sand.

sand·box′ n. a receptacle holding sand for children to play in.

sand′ dol′lar n. a disklike sea animal.

sand·lot′ n. 1. a vacant lot used by youngsters for games. —adj. 2. played in a sandlot.

sand·man′ n. a figure in folklore who puts sand in children's eyes to make them sleepy.

sand·pa′per n. 1. paper coated with sand for smoothing. —v.t. 2. to smooth with sandpaper.

sand·pip′er (-pī′pər) n. a thin-billed shore bird.

sand·stone′ n. rock formed chiefly of sand.

sand·storm′ n. a windstorm with clouds of sand.

sand·wich (sand′wich, san′-) n. 1. two slices of bread with a filling between them. —v.t. 2. to insert between two other things.

sand·wich genera′tion n. the generation of people still raising their children while caring for their aging parents.

sane (sān) adj., **saner, sanest.** free from mental disorder; rational.

sang-froid (Fr. sän frwA′) n. coolness of mind; composure.

san·gui·nar·y (sang′gwə ner′ē) adj. 1. bloody. 2. bloodthirsty.

san·guine (-gwin) adj. optimistic.

san·i·tar·i·um (san′i târ′ē əm) n., pl. **-iums, -ia** (-ē ə). a place for the treatment of invalids and convalescents.

san·i·tar·y (-ter′ē) adj. 1. of health. 2. free from dirt and germs.

san·i·tary nap′kin n. a pad worn to absorb menstrual flow.

san·i·tize v.t. **-tized, -tizing.** 1. to make free from dirt. 2. to make less offensive by removing objectionable elements.

san·i·ty n. soundness of mind.

San·skrit (san′skrit) n. an ancient language of India.

sap¹ (sap) n. 1. the fluid that carries mineral salts and sugar through a woody plant. 2. a fool.

sap² (sap) v.t., **sapped, sapping.** to weaken or undermine gradually.

sa·pi·ent (sā′pē ənt) adj. wise.

sap·ling (sap′ling) n. a young tree.

sap·phire (saf′ī°r) n. a deep-blue gem.

sar·casm (sär′kaz əm) n. scornful, ironic language. —**sar·cas′tic,** adj.

sar·co·ma (sär kō′mə) n., pl. **-mas, -mata** (-mə tə). a malignant tumor.

sar·coph·a·gus (sär kof′ə gəs) n., pl. **-gi** (-jī′, -gī′). a stone coffin.

sar·dine (sär dēn′) n. a small fish of the herring family.

sar·don·ic (sär don′ik) adj. scornfully mocking. —**sar·don′i·cal·ly,** adv.

sa·ri (sär′ē) n. a long cloth wrapped around the body, worn as a woman's garment in India.

sa·rong (sə rông′) n. a skirtlike garment worn in Malaysia.

sar·sa·pa·ril·la (sas′pə ril′ə) n. 1. a tropical American vine. 2. a soft drink flavored with roots of this plant.

sar·to·ri·al (sär tôr′ē əl) adj. of tailors or tailoring.

SASE self-addressed stamped envelope.

sash¹ (sash) n. a band of cloth worn over the shoulder or around the waist.

sash² (sash) n. a framework in which the panes of a window are set.

sass (sas) Informal. —n. 1. impudent back talk. —v.t. 2. to answer back impudently. —**sas′sy,** adj.

sas·sa·fras′ (sas′ə fras′) n. an American tree with an aromatic root bark.

sat (sat) v. pt. and pp. of **sit.**

Sat. Saturday.

Sa′tan (sāt′n) n. the devil. —**sa·tan′ic** (sə tan′ik) adj.

satch·el (sach′əl) n. a small bag with a handle.

sate (sāt) v.t., **sated, sating.** to satisfy fully.

sat·el·lite (sat′l īt′) n. 1. a natural or artificial body that revolves around a planet. 2. a country under the influence of another.

sat·ellite dish′ n. a dish-shaped reflector, used esp. for receiving satellite and microwave signals.

sa·ti·ate (sā′shē āt′) v.t., **-ated, -ating.** to supply to excess.

sat·in (sat′n) n. a glossy silk or rayon fabric. —**sat′in·y,** adj.

sat·ire (sat′ī°r) n. the use of irony or ridicule in exposing vice, folly, etc. —**sa·tir′i·cal** (sə tir′i kəl), **sa·tir′ic,** adj. —**sat′i·rist** (sat′ər ist) n.

sat·i·rize (sat′ə rīz′) v.t., **-rized, -rizing.** to ridicule with satire.

sat·is·fac′tory (sat′is fak′tə rē) adj. serving to satisfy; adequate. —**sat·is·fac·to·ri·ly,** adv.

sat·is·fy′ (-fī′) v.t., **-fied, -fying.** 1. to fulfill the desire, needs, or demands of. 2. to fulfill the requirements of. 3. to convince. —**sat·is·fac′tion** (-fak′shən) n.

sa′trap (sā′trap, sa′-) n. a petty tyrant.

sat′u·rate′ (sach′ə rāt′) v.t., **-rated, -rating.** 1. to soak completely. 2. to load or fill to the utmost.

Sat′ur·day′ (sat′ər dā′, -dē) n. the seventh day of the week.

Sat·urn (sat′ərn) n. 1. the planet sixth from the sun. 2. a Roman god of agriculture.

sat′ur·nine′ (-ər nīn′) adj. gloomy.

sa′tyr (sā′tər, sat′ər) n. 1. a deity of ancient Greece, part man and part goat. 2. a lecherous man.

sauce (sôs) n. 1. a liquid dressing for food. 2. stewed fruit.

sauce·pan′ n. a cooking pot with a handle.

sau·cer n. a small shallow dish.

sau′cy (-sē) adj. **-cier, -ciest.** 1. impertinent. 2. jaunty. —**sau′ci·ly,** adv.

sauer·kraut′ (sou°r′krout′, sou′ər-) n. shredded salted and fermented cabbage.

sau′na (sô′nə) n. a bath heated by steam.

saun′ter (sôn′tər) v.i. 1. to stroll. —n. 2. a stroll.

sau′ri·an (sôr′ē ən) adj. of or resembling a lizard.

sau·ro·pod′ (sôr′ə pod′) n. a huge dinosaur with a small head and a long neck and tail.

sau′sage (sô′sij) n. minced seasoned meat, often in a casing.

sau·té′ (sō tā′, sô-) v.t., **-téed, -téeing.** to fry in a small amount of fat.

sau·terne′ (sō tûrn′) n. a sweet white wine.

sav·age (sav′ij) adj. 1. wild; uncivilized. 2. brutal; cruel. —n. 3. an uncivilized person. 4. a brutal or cruel person. —**sav′age·ly,** adv. —**sav′age·ry,** n.

sa·van·na (sə van′ə) n. a grassy plain with scattered trees. Also, **sa·van′nah.**

sa·vant′ (sa vänt′) n. a learned person.

save¹ (sāv) v., **saved, saving** —v.t. 1. to rescue from danger or harm. 2. to keep safe or unhurt. 3. to set aside in reserve. —v.i. 4. to set aside money.

save² (sāv) prep. 1. with the exception of. —conj. 2. except.

sav·ing n. 1. a reduction in spending. 2. **savings,** money put aside.

sav·ior (sāv′yər) n. 1. one who rescues. 2. **Savior,** Jesus Christ. Also, **saviour.**

sa′voir-faire′ (sav′wär fâr′) n. knowledge of how to behave in any situation.

sa′vor (sā′vər) v.t. to taste, smell, or experience with enjoyment.

sa′vor·y adj. 1. pleasing in taste or smell. 2. an aromatic herb of the mint family.

sav′vy (sav′ē) n. 1. practical understanding. —adj. 2. shrewd and well-informed.

saw¹ (sô) v. pt. of **see.**

saw² (sô) n., v., **sawed, sawed** or **sawn, sawing.** —n. 1. a cutting tool with a toothed metal blade. —v.t., v.i. 2. to cut with a saw. —**saw′yer** (sô′yər) n.

saw′dust′ n. fine particles of wood produced in sawing.

saw·horse′ n. a frame for supporting wood while it is being sawed.

saw·mill′ n. a mill where timber is sawed.

sax (saks) n. a saxophone.

Sax′on (sak′sən) n. a member of a Germanic people who invaded Britain in the 5th-6th centuries.

sax′o·phone′ (sak′sə fōn′) n. a wind instrument with a conical tube and a reed mouthpiece.

say (sā) v., **said** (sed) **saying,** —v.t. 1. to speak; utter; recite. 2. to express in words; state. 3. to state as an opinion. —n. 4. the right to speak or choose.

say′ing n. a proverb.

say′-so′ n., pl. **say-sos.** one's personal assurance; word.

SC South Carolina. Also, **S.C.**

scab (skab) n., v., **scabbed, scabbing.** —n. 1. a crust forming over a sore. 2. a worker who takes a striker's place on the job. —v.i. 3. to form a scab. 4. to work as a scab. —**scab′by,** adj.

scab·bard (skab′ərd) n. a sheath for a sword, dagger, etc.

scab·rous (skab′rəs) adj. 1. having a rough surface. 2. indecent; obscene.

scad (skad) n. **scads,** a great quantity.

scaf·fold (skaf′əld, -ōld) n. 1. Also, **scaf′fold·ing.** a raised platform for workers and materials, used in construction. 2. a platform on which a criminal is executed.

scal·a·wag′ (skal′ə wag′) n. a rascal.

scald (skôld) v.t. 1. to burn with hot liquid or steam. 2. to heat to just below boiling. —n. 3. a burn caused by scalding.

scale¹ (skāl) n., v., **scaled, scaling.** —n. 1. one of the flat hard plates covering fish, snakes, etc. 2. a thin flake or coating. —v.t. 3. to remove the scales from. —v.i. 4. to come off in scales. —**scal′y,** adj.

scale² (skāl) n. Often, **scales.** a device for weighing.

scale³ (skāl) n., v., **scaled, scaling.** —n. 1. an ordered series of steps or degrees. 2. a series of marks at regular intervals for measuring. 3. relative size or extent. 4. a succession of musical tones. —v.t. 5. to climb. 6. to make according to a scale.

scal·lion (skal′yən) n. a small green onion.

scal·lop (skol′əp, skal′-) n. 1. a bivalve mollusk with a fluted shell. 2. one of a series of curves on a border. —v.t. 3. to finish (an edge) with scallops.

scalp (skalp) *n.* **1.** the skin and hair of the top of the head. —*v.t.* **2.** to cut the scalp from. **3.** to resell at an inflated price.

scal′pel (skal′pəl) *n.* a small surgical knife.

scamp (skamp) *n.* a rascal.

scam (skam) *n., v.,* **scammed, scamming.** —*n.* **1.** a fraudulent scheme; swindle. —*v.t.* **2.** to cheat.

scam′per *v.i.* **1.** to run quickly. —*n.* **2.** a quick run.

scam′pi (skam′pē, skäm′-) *n., pl.* **-pi.** **1.** a large shrimp. **2.** a dish of scampi cooked in butter and garlic.

scan (skan) *v.,* **scanned, scanning.** —*v.t.* **1.** to examine closely. **2.** to glance at hastily. **3.** to read (data) for use by a computer. —*v.i.* **4.** (of verse) to conform to metrical rules.

scan′dal (skan′dl) *n.* **1.** a disgraceful action or circumstance. **2.** disgrace. **3.** malicious gossip. —**scan′dal·ous,** *adj.*

scan′dal·ize′ *v.t.,* **-ized, -izing.** to outrage; shock.

scan′dal·mon′ger *n.* a person who spreads scandal.

scan′ner *n.* **1.** a person or thing that scans. **2.** a device that monitors selected radio frequencies and reproduces any signal detected. **3.** an optical scanner.

scan′sion (skan′shən) *n.* the metrical analysis of verse.

scant (skant) *adj.* barely adequate. Also, **scant′y.** —**scant′i·ly,** *adv.*

scape′goat (skāp′gōt′) *n.* one who is made to bear the blame for others.

scape′grace *n.* a scamp; rascal.

scap′u·la (skap′yə lə) *n., pl.* **-las, -lae** (-lē′). either of two flat triangular bones forming the back part of the shoulder; the shoulder blade.

scar (skär) *n., v.,* **scarred, scarring.** —*n.* **1.** a mark left by a healed wound. —*v.t., v.i.* **2.** to mark with or form a scar.

scar′ab (skar′əb) *n.* **1.** a large beetle, sacred in ancient Egypt. **2.** a representation of a scarab.

scarce (skârs) *adj.,* **scarcer, scarcest.** **1.** insufficient to fill a need. **2.** rare. —**scar′ci·ty, scarce′ness,** *n.*

scarce′ly *adv.* **1.** barely. **2.** probably not.

scare (skâr) *v.,* **scared, scaring,** *n.* —*v.t., v.i.* **1.** to frighten or become frightened. —*n.* **2.** a sudden fright.

scare′crow′ *n.* an object, usu. a figure of a person, set up to frighten birds away from crops.

scarf (skärf) *n., pl.* **scarfs, scarves** (skärvz). a strip or square of cloth worn about the neck, shoulders, or head.

scar′i·fy′ (skar′ə fī′) *v.t.,* **-fied, -fying.** **1.** to make scratches or slight cuts in. **2.** to criticize harshly.

scar′let (skär′lit) *n.* a bright red.

scar′let fe′ver *n.* a contagious disease marked by a red rash.

scar′y (skâr′ē) *adj.,* **-ier, -iest.** causing fear.

scat (skat) *v.i.,* **scatted, scatting.** to run off.

scath′ing (skā′thing) *adj.* bitterly severe.

scat·o·log′i·cal (skat′l ōj′i kəl) *adj.* concerned with obscenity.

scat′ter (skat′ər) *v.t.* **1.** to throw loosely about. —*v.i.* **2.** to separate and disperse.

scat′ter·brain′ *n.* a person incapable of serious, connected thought.

scat′ter rug′ *n.* a small rug.

scav′enge (skav′inj) *v.,* **-enged, -enging.** —*v.t.* **1.** to search for (usable objects) among discarded material. —*v.i.* **2.** to act as a scavenger. —**scav′eng·er,** *n.*

sce·nar′i·o′ (si nâr′ē ō′, -när′-) *n., pl.* **-ios.** **1.** a plot outline. **2.** an imagined sequence of events.

scene (sēn) *n.* **1.** the place where something occurs. **2.** a view. **3.** a division of a play, film, etc. **4.** a public display of emotion. **5.** a sphere of activity or interest. —**sce′nic,** *adj.*

scen′er·y (sē′nə rē) *n.* **1.** the features of a landscape. **2.** a stage set.

scent (sent) *n.* **1.** a distinctive odor, esp. an agreeable one. **2.** a trail marked by this. **3.** the sense of smell. —*v.t.* **4.** to perceive by the sense of smell. **5.** to perfume.

scep′ter (sep′tər) *n.* a rod carried as an emblem of royal power. Also, **scep′tre.**

scep′tic (skep′tik) *n.* a skeptic.

sched′ule (skej′ŏŏl, -ŏŏl; *Brit.* shed′yŏŏl, shej′ŏŏl) *n., v.,* **-uled, -uling.** —*n.* **1.** a list of things to be done with the time allotted for each. **2.** a

---

timetable. —*v.t.* **3.** to enter in a schedule. **4.** to plan for a certain date.

scheme (skēm) *n., v.,* **schemed, scheming.** —*n.* **1.** a plan of action. **2.** an intrigue; plot. —*v.t., v.i.* **3.** to plan or plot. —**sche·mat′ic** (ski-mat′ik) *adj.*

scher′zo (skert′sō) *n., pl.* **-zos, -zi** (-sē). a playful musical movement.

Schick′ test′ (shik) *n.* a diphtheria immunity test.

schil′ling (shil′ing) *n.* the monetary unit of Austria.

schism (siz′əm, skiz′-) *n.* a division within a group, as a church.

schist (shist) *n.* a layered crystalline rock.

schiz·o·phre′ni·a (skit′sə frē′nē ə) *n.* a severe mental disorder marked by delusions and hallucinations. —**schiz·o·phren′ic** (-fren′ik) *adj., n.*

schle·miel′ (shlə mēl′) *n. Slang.* an awkward and unlucky person.

schlep (shlep) *v.,* **schlepped, schlepping,** *n. Slang.* —*v.t., v.i.* **1.** to carry or move with great effort. —*n.* **2.** a slow or awkward person. **3.** a tedious journey.

schlock (shlok) *n. Slang.* something of cheap or inferior quality.

schmaltz (shmälts, shmôlts) *n. Informal.* excessive sentimentality, esp. in music. —**schmaltz′y,** *adj.*

schnapps (shnäps, shnaps) *n.* a strong alcoholic liquor.

schol′ar (skol′ər) *n.* **1.** a learned person. **2.** a student. —**schol′ar·ly,** *adj.*

schol′ar·ship′ *n.* **1.** the qualities or knowledge of scholars. **2.** financial aid granted to a promising student.

scho·las′tic (skə las′tik) *adj.* of schools or scholars.

school[1] (skŏŏl) *n.* **1.** an institution for teaching and learning. **2.** the students and teachers at such an institution. **3.** a group of persons following the same principles or beliefs. —*v.t.* **4.** to educate; train.

school[2] (skŏŏl) *n.* a group of fish.

schoon′er (skŏŏ′nər) *n.* a sailing ship with fore and aft sails.

schuss (shŏŏs, shŏŏs) *n.* a straight downhill ski run at high speed.

schwa (shwä) *n.* the vowel sound in certain unstressed syllables, as *a* in *sofa;* usually represented by ə.

sci·at′i·ca (sī at′i kə) *n.* pain in the lower back and thigh. —**sci·at′ic,** *adj.*

sci′ence (sī′əns) *n.* systematic knowledge, esp. of the physical world, gained through observation and experimentation. —**sci·en·tif′ic** (-tif′ik) *adj.* —**sci·en·tif′i·cal·ly,** *adv.* —**sci′en·tist,** *n.*

sci′ence fic′tion *n.* fiction dealing with space travel, robots, etc.

sci-fi (sī′fī′) *n., adj. Informal.* science fiction.

scim′i·tar (sim′i tər) *n.* a curved sword.

scin·til′la (sin til′ə) *n.* a tiny particle.

scin′til·late′ (-tl āt′) *v.i.,* **-lated, -lating.** to sparkle.

sci′on (sī′ən) *n.* **1.** a descendant. **2.** a plant shoot cut for grafting.

scis′sors (siz′ərz) *n.pl.* a cutting instrument with two pivoted blades that work against each other.

scle·ro′sis (skli rō′sis) *n.* a hardening of a body tissue or part.

scoff (skôf) *v.i.* to express mockery or scorn.

scoff′law′ *n.* a person who flouts the law, as by ignoring traffic tickets.

scold (skōld) *v.t., v.i.* **1.** to find fault (with) angrily. —*n.* **2.** a person who is constantly scolding.

sco·li·o′sis (skō′lē ō′sis) *n.* lateral curvature of the spine.

sconce (skons) *n.* a wall bracket for candles or electric lights.

scone (skōn, skon) *n.* a soft, flat biscuitlike cake.

scoop (skŏŏp) *n.* **1.** a small deep shovel for food. **2.** the bucket of a steam shovel. **3.** the act of scooping. **4.** the quantity taken up. **5.** news published by one newspaper before its rivals. —*v.t.* **6.** to take up with a scoop. **7.** to publish news before (one's rivals).

scoot (skŏŏt) *v.i.* to go swiftly.

scoot′er *n.* **1.** a child's two-wheeled vehicle. **2.** a two-wheeled motor vehicle.

scope (skōp) *n.* extent or range.

scorch (skôrch) *v.t., v.i.* **1.** to burn or become burnt slightly. —*n.* **2.** a superficial burn.

score (skôr) *n., pl.* **scores,** (for 3) **score,** *v.,* **scored, scoring.** —*n.* **1.** a

---

record of points made, as in a game. **2.** a notch, scratch, or mark. **3.** a group of twenty. **4.** the written or printed music for a movie, play, etc. —*v.t.* **5.** to earn in a game. **6.** to make notches, cuts, or marks in or on. **7.** to compose a score for. **8.** to earn points, as in a game. **9.** to keep score, as of a game. **10.** to achieve success. —**scor′er,** *n.*

scorn (skôrn) *n.* **1.** contempt. **2.** mockery. —*v.t.* **3.** to treat, regard, or reject with scorn. —**scorn′ful,** *adj.*

scor′pi·on (skôr′pē ən) *n.* a small animal of the spider family with a poisonous stinger in the end of its long tail.

Scot (skot) *n.* a native or inhabitant of Scotland. —**Scot′tish,** *adj., n.pl.*

scotch (skoch) *v.t.* to put an end to.

Scotch (skoch) *n.* a whiskey made in Scotland.

scot′-free′ *adj.* free from punishment or obligation.

Scots (skots) *n.* the English spoken in Scotland.

Scot′tish Gael′ic *n.* a Celtic language spoken in parts of Scotland. Also, **Scots Gaelic.**

scoun′drel (skoun′drəl) *n.* a dishonorable person.

scour[1] (skouər) *v.t., v.i.* **1.** to cleanse by rubbing. **2.** to clear out by the force of water.

scour[2] (skouər) *v.t.* to search (a place) thoroughly.

scourge (skûrj) *n., v.,* **scourged, scourging.** —*n.* **1.** a whip. **2.** a cause of affliction. —*v.t.* **3.** to whip.

scout (skout) *n.* **1.** a person sent ahead to obtain information. **2.** a person employed to find new talent. —*v.i., v.t.* **3.** to search as a scout. **4.** to search (for).

scow (skou) *n.* a flat-bottomed, flat-ended boat.

scowl (skoul) *v.i.* **1.** to frown in a sullen or angry manner. —*n.* **2.** a scowling expression.

scrab′ble (skrab′əl) *v.i., v.t.,* **-bled, -bling.** **1.** to scratch frantically with the hands or paws. **2.** to scribble.

scrag′gly *adj.,* **-glier, -gliest.** **1.** uneven. **2.** shaggy.

scram (skram) *v.i.,* **scrammed, scramming.** *Informal.* to go away quickly.

scram′ble (skram′bəl) *v.,* **-bled, -bling,** *n.* —*v.i.* **1.** to move quickly, esp. on the hands and knees. —*v.t.* **2.** to mix together confusedly. **3.** to cook (eggs) while stirring. **4.** to make (a radio or television signal) unintelligible. —*n.* **5.** a quick climb. **6.** a disorderly struggle for possession.

scrap (skrap) *n., v.,* **scrapped, scrapping.** —*n.* **1.** a small piece. **2.** discarded material. —*v.t.* **3.** to discard as useless. —**scrap′py,** *adj.*

scrap′book′ *n.* a blank book for mounting keepsakes.

scrape (skrāp) *v.,* **scraped, scraping,** *n.* —*v.t.* **1.** to draw something rough or sharp over (a surface) so as to smooth it. **2.** to remove by scraping. **3.** to injure by rubbing against something rough or sharp. **4.** to collect with difficulty. —*v.i.* **5.** to rub against something gratingly. **6.** to make a grating sound. **7.** to get by with difficulty; economize. —*n.* **8.** an act or sound of scraping. **9.** a scraped place. **10.** a distressing situation. —**scrap′er,** *n.*

scratch (skrach) *v.t.* **1.** to mark, tear, or rub with something sharp. **2.** to strike out or cancel. **3.** to use nails or claws. —*n.* **4.** a mark or injury from scratching. **5.** the act or sound of scratching. —*adj.* **6.** gathered hastily and carelessly. —*Idiom.* **7. from scratch,** from the beginning or from nothing. **8. up to scratch,** satisfactory.

scrawl (skrôl) *v.i., v.t.* **1.** to write carelessly or awkwardly. —*n.* **2.** such handwriting.

scraw′ny (skrô′nē) *adj.,* **-nier, -niest.** excessively thin. —**scraw′ni·ness,** *n.*

scream (skrēm) *n.* **1.** a loud sharp cry. —*v.i., v.t.* **2.** to utter (with) a loud, sharp cry.

screech (skrēch) *n.* **1.** a harsh, shrill sound. —*v.t., v.i.* **2.** to utter with or make a harsh, shrill sound.

screen (skrēn) *n.* **1.** a movable or fixed device that protects or conceals. **2.** a frame holding a wire mesh, used in a window or doorway. **3.** a surface on which motion pictures are flashed. **4.** anything that shelters or conceals. **5.** a sieve. —*v.t.* **6.** to shelter, protect, or conceal with a screen. **7.** to sift, sort,

---

or separate through a screen. **8.** to project on a screen.

screen′play′ *n.* the outline or full script of a motion picture.

screw (skrŏŏ) *n.* **1.** a metal fastener with a spirally threaded shank, driven by twisting. **2.** something having a spiral form. **3.** a propeller. —*v.t.* **4.** to fasten with a screw. **5.** to attach, detach, or adjust by twisting. —*v.i.* **6.** to become attached, detached, or adjusted by being twisted.

screw′ball′ *Slang.* —*n.* **1.** an eccentric person. —*adj.* **2.** eccentric.

screw′driv′er *n.* a tool for turning screws.

scrib′ble (skrib′əl) *v.,* **-bled, -bling,** *n.* —*v.t., v.i.* **1.** to write or draw hastily or carelessly. —*n.* **2.** hasty, careless writing or drawing.

scribe (skrīb) *n.* a person who writes or copies manuscripts.

scrim (skrim) *n.* a fabric of open weave.

scrim′mage (skrim′ij) *n., v.,* **-maged, -maging.** —*n.* **1.** in football, the action while the ball is in play. **2.** a practice game. —*v.i.* **3.** to engage in a scrimmage.

scrimp (skrimp) *v.i., v.t.* to be frugal (with).

scrim′shaw′ (skrim′shô′) *n.* carved articles of whalebone.

scrip (skrip) *n.* **1.** paper money issued for temporary use. **2.** a certificate worth a fraction of a share of stock.

script (skript) *n.* **1.** the written text of a play, film, etc. **2.** handwriting.

scrip′ture (skrip′chər) *n.* **1.** sacred writing. **2. Scriptures,** the Bible. —**scrip′tur·al,** *adj.*

scriv′ner (skriv′nər) *n.* a scribe.

scrod (skrod) *n.* a young codfish or haddock.

scrof·u·la (skrof′yə lə) *n.* tuberculosis of the lymphatic glands. —**scrof′u·lous,** *adj.*

scroll (skrōl) *n.* **1.** a roll of parchment, paper, etc., with writing on it. —*v.i.* **2.** to move a cursor smoothly, causing new data to appear on a computer screen.

scro′tum (skrō′təm) *n., pl.* **-ta** (-tə) **-tums.** the pouch of skin containing the testicles. —**scro′tal,** *adj.*

scrounge (skrounj) *v.,* **scrounged, scrounging.** —*v.t.* **1.** to take without intending to repay. **2.** to get by or as if by foraging. —*v.i.* **3.** to look around for what is needed. —**scroung′er,** *n.*

scrub[1] (skrub) *v.,* **scrubbed, scrubbing,** *n.* —*v.t.* **1.** to rub hard, esp. in washing. —*v.i.* **2.** to clean something by rubbing hard. —*n.* **3.** an act of scrubbing.

scrub[2] (skrub) *n.* **1.** low trees or shrubs. **2.** anything small or poor. —**scrub′by,** *adj.*

scruff (skruf) *n.* the back of the neck; nape.

scruff′y (skruf′ē) *adj.,* **-ier, -iest.** untidy; shabby.

scrump′tious (skrump′shəs) *adj.* extremely pleasing; delicious.

scru′ple (skrŏŏ′pəl) *n.* a moral or ethical consideration that affects one's actions.

scru′pu·lous (-pyə ləs) *adj.* **1.** having scruples. **2.** exact.

scru′ti·nize′ (skrŏŏt′n īz′) *v.t.,* **-nized, -nizing.** to examine closely. —**scru′ti·ny,** *n.*

scu′ba (skŏŏ′bə) *n.* a portable breathing device for swimmers.

scud (skud) *v.i.,* **scudded, scudding.** to move quickly.

scuff (skuf) *v.t., v.i.* to mar or become marred by hard use.

scuf′fle *n., v.,* **-fled, -fling.** —*n.* **1.** a rough, confused struggle. —*v.i.* **2.** to engage in a scuffle.

scull (skul) *n.* **1.** a light racing boat. **2.** an oar mounted on the stern of a boat. —*v.t., v.i.* **3.** to propel (a boat) with sculls.

scul′ler·y (skul′ə rē) *n., pl.* **-leries.** a workroom off a kitchen.

scul′lion (-yən) *n.* a kitchen servant.

sculp′ture (skulp′chər) *n., v.,* **-tured, -turing.** **1.** the art of carving or modeling wood, stone, etc., to make three-dimensional works of art. **2.** a work or works made in this way. —*v.t.* **3.** to carve or model (a piece of sculpture). **4.** to work as a sculptor. —**sculp′tor** (-tər) *n.*

scum (skum) *n.* **1.** a film on top of a liquid. **2.** low, worthless persons.

scup′per (skup′ər) *n.* an opening in a ship's side to drain off water.

scurf (skûrf) *n.* **1.** loose scales of skin. **2.** scaly matter on a surface.

---

scur′ril·ous (skûr′ə ləs) *adj.* coarsely or obscenely abusive.

scur′ry (skûr′ē, skur′ē) *v.i.,* **-ried, -rying.** to move with haste; hurry.

scur′vy (skûr′vē) *n., adj.,* **-vier, -viest.** —*n.* **1.** a disease caused by lack of vitamin C. —*adj.* **2.** contemptible.

scut′tle[1] (skut′l) *n.* a coal bucket.

scut′tle[2] (skut′l) *v.i.,* **-tled, -tling.** to run with short, quick steps.

scut′tle[3] (skut′l) *v.t.,* **-tled, -tling.** to sink (a ship) by making holes in the bottom.

scut′tle·butt′ (-but′) *n. Informal.* rumor; gossip.

scythe (sīth) *n.* a tool with a long handle and a curved blade for cutting grass by hand.

SD South Dakota. Also, **S.D.**

S. Dak. South Dakota.

SE southeast.

sea (sē) *n.* **1.** the salt water covering much of the earth. **2.** an ocean. **3.** a large wave. **4.** a great quantity. —*Idiom.* **5. at sea,** uncertain. —**sea′coast′,** *n.* —**sea′shore′,** *n.*

sea′ anem′o·ne *n.* a solitary marine polyp with flowerlike tentacles.

sea′ bass′ (bas) *n.* a marine food fish.

sea′bed′ *n.* the ocean floor.

sea′ cow′ *n.* a manatee.

sea′far·ing *adj.* traveling by or working at sea. —**sea′far′er,** *n.*

sea′food′ *n.* edible marine fish or shellfish.

sea′go·ing *adj.* fit for going to sea.

sea′ gull′ *n.* a gull.

sea′ horse′ *n.* a small fish with a head like that of a horse.

seal[1] (sēl) *n.* **1.** an emblem or symbol used to indicate that something is authentic. **2.** a means of closing something tightly. **3.** a stamplike label. —*v.t.* **4.** to affix a seal to. **5.** to fasten with a seal. **6.** to decide or settle. —**seal′ant,** *n.*

seal[2] (sēl) *n., pl.* **seals, seal.** a marine animal with large flippers.

sea′ lev′el *n.* the position of the sea's surface at mean level between low and high tide.

sea′ li′on *n.* a large seal.

seam (sēm) *n.* **1.** the line formed when two edges meet. **2.** a thin layer in the ground, as of coal. **3.** a wrinkle or scar. —*v.t.* **4.** to join together in a seam.

sea′man *n., pl.* **-men.** a sailor.

seam′stress (-stris) *n.* a woman whose occupation is sewing.

seam′y *adj.,* **-ier, -iest.** sordid.

sé′ance (sā′äns) *n.* a meeting to attempt communication with the spirits of the dead.

sea′plane′ *n.* an airplane equipped with floats.

sea′port′ *n.* a port for seagoing vessels.

sear (sēr) *v.t.* to burn the surface of.

search (sûrch) *v.t.* **1.** to look or feel through carefully in order to find something. —*n.* **2.** an act of searching.

search′light′ *n.* a device for projecting a strong beam of light.

sea′shell′ *n.* the shell of a marine mollusk.

sea′sick·ness *n.* nausea from the motion of a ship. —**sea′sick′,** *adj.*

sea′son (sē′zən) *n.* **1.** any of four periods of the year. **2.** the usual time when something takes place or flourishes. —*v.t.* **3.** to flavor (food) with salt, spices, etc. **4.** to prepare for use. —**sea′son·al,** *adj.*

sea′son·a·ble *adj.* appropriate to the time of year.

sea′son·ing *n.* flavoring, as salt, spices, or herbs.

seat (sēt) *n.* **1.** something for sitting on. **2.** the part of something on which a person sits. **3.** a right to sit, as in Congress. **4.** a place in which something is established. —*v.t.* **5.** to place in or on a seat. **6.** to find seats for.

seat′ belt′ *n.* straps to keep a passenger secure in a vehicle.

seat′ing *n.* **1.** the arrangement of seats. **2.** an act of furnishing with a seat.

sea′ ur′chin *n.* a small, round sea animal with a spiny shell.

sea′weed′ *n.* a plant growing in the sea.

sea′wor′thy *adj.,* **-thier, -thiest.** fit for sea travel.

se·ba′ceous (si bā′shəs) *adj.* of or secreting a fatty substance.

se·cede′ (si sēd′) *v.i.,* **-ceded, -ceding.** to withdraw from membership in a nation, alliance, etc. —**se·ces′sion** (-sesh′ən) *n.*

se·clude′ (si klŏŏd′) *v.t.,* **-cluded,**

-**clud·ing.** to remove from contact with others. —**se·clu'sion,** n.

sec'ond[1] (sek'ənd) adj. **1.** next after the first. **2.** other; another. —n. **3.** a second part or the second one of a series. **4.** a person who aids or supports another. **5. seconds, a.** an additional helping of food. **b.** imperfect goods. —v.t. **6.** to support. —adv. **7.** in the second place. —**sec'ond·ly,** adv.

sec'ond[2] (sek'ənd) n. the sixtieth part of a minute.

sec'ond·ar·y (-ən der'ē) adj. **1.** second in order, rank, or time. **2.** not primary. **3.** less important.

sec'ond-guess' v.t. to use hindsight in criticizing or correcting.

sec'ond·hand' adj. **1.** not new. **2.** not directly known or experienced.

sec'ond na'ture n. a deeply ingrained habit or tendency.

sec'ond-rate' adj. inferior.

sec'ond string' n. a squad of players available to replace those who start a game.

sec'ond wind' n. (wind) energy for a renewed effort.

se'cret (sē'krit) adj. **1.** kept from the knowledge of others. —n. **2.** something secret. **3.** a mystery. —**se'cre·cy,** n.

sec're·tar·i·at (sek'ri tār'ē ət) n. a group of administrative officials.

sec're·tar·y (-ter'ē) n., pl. **-taries. 1.** an office assistant. **2.** the head of a governmental department. **3.** a tall writing desk. —**sec're·tar'i·al,** adj.

se·crete[1] (si krēt') v.t., **-creted, -creting.** to discharge or release by secretion.

se·crete[2] (si krēt') v.t., **-creted, -creting.** to hide.

se·cre'tion (-krē'shən) n. **1.** the process of producing a substance within the body, as in a gland or cell. **2.** the product secreted.

se'cre·tive (sē'kri tiv, si krē'-) adj. tending to keep things secret. —**se'cre·tive·ly,** adv.

sect (sekt) n. a group with a common religious faith.

sec·tar·i·an (sek târ'ē ən) adj. **1.** of a sect. **2.** limited in scope. —n. **3.** a sectarian person.

sec'tion (sek'shən) n. **1.** a separate or distinct part. —v.t. **2.** to cut or divide into sections.

sec'tor (sek'tər) n. **1.** a plane figure bounded by two radii and an arc. **2.** a distinct part.

sec'u·lar (sek'yə lər) adj. worldly; not religious. —**sec'u·lar·ism,** n. —**sec'u·lar·ize',** v.t.

se·cure' (si kyoor') adj., v., **-cured, -curing. 1.** safe. **2.** firmly in place. **3.** certain. —v.t. **4.** to get hold of. **5.** to make secure. —**se·cure'ly,** adv.

se·cu'ri·ty (-kyoor'i tē) n., pl. **-ties. 1.** safety. **2.** freedom from care. **3.** protection against crime, attack, etc. **4.** something given as a pledge. **5.** securities, stocks or bonds.

secu'rity blan'ket n. something that gives a feeling of safety.

se·dan' (si dan') n. an enclosed automobile for four or more.

se·date' (si dāt') adj., v. **-dated, -dating.** —adj. **1.** calm, dignified, and composed. —v.t. **2.** to give a sedative to. —**se·date'ly,** adv. —**se·da'tion,** n.

sed'a·tive (sed'ə tiv) adj. **1.** tending to soothe or relieve pain or agitation. —n. **2.** a sedative drug.

sed'en·tar·y (sed'n ter'ē) adj. characterized by or requiring sitting.

Se'der (sā'dər) n. a ceremonial dinner on the first or first two nights of Passover.

sedge (sej) n. a grassy marsh plant.

sed'i·ment (sed'ə mənt) n. matter settling to the bottom of a liquid. —**sed'i·men·ta·ry,** adj.

se·di'tion (si dish'ən) n. incitement to rebellion. —**se·di'tious,** adj.

se·duce' (si dōōs', -dyōōs') v.t., **-duced, -ducing. 1.** to lead astray. **2.** to induce to have sexual intercourse. —**se·duc'er,** n. —**se·duc'tion** (-duk'shən) n. —**se·duc'tive,** adj.

sed'u·lous (sej'ə ləs) adj. diligent.

see[1] (sē) v., **saw** (sô) **seen, seeing.** —v.t. **1.** to perceive with the eyes; look at. **2.** to understand. **3.** to visualize. **4.** to recognize. **5.** to find out. **6.** to make sure. **7.** to escort. **8.** to visit. —v.i. **9.** to have the power of sight. **10.** to understand.

see[2] (sē) n. a bishop's jurisdiction.

seed (sēd) n. **1.** a fertilized plant ovule from which a new plant will grow. **2.** sperm; semen. **3.** the

source of something. **4.** offspring. —v.t. **5.** to sow with seed. **6.** to remove the seeds from. —v.i. **7.** to produce seed. —**Idiom. 8. go to seed, a.** to stop growing as seed develops. **b.** to become shabby.

seed'ling n. a plant grown from seed.

seed' mon'ey n. money for beginning an enterprise.

seed'y adj., **-ier, -iest. 1.** shabby. **2.** having many seeds.

see'ing conj. inasmuch as.

seek (sēk) v.t., **sought, seeking. 1.** to search for. **2.** to try; attempt.

seem (sēm) v.i. to appear to be.

seem'ing adj. apparent.

seem'ly adj., **-lier, -liest.** proper.

seen (sēn) v. pp. of **see.**

seep (sēp) v.i. to pass, flow, or ooze gradually. —**seep'age,** n.

seer (sēr) n. a prophet.

seer'suck·er (sēr'suk'ər) n. a striped cotton fabric.

see'saw' (sē'sô') n. **1.** a balanced plank on which two children ride up and down while seated at opposite ends. **2.** going up and down or back and forth. —v.i., v.t. **3.** to move on or as if on a seesaw.

seethe (sēth) v.i., **seethed, seething. 1.** to boil; foam. **2.** to be agitated or excited.

see'-through' adj. transparent.

seg'ment (seg'mənt) n. **1.** a part; section. —v.t., v.i. **2.** to divide into segments. —**seg'men·ta'tion,** n.

seg're·gate' (seg'ri gāt') v.t., **-gated, -gating.** to separate from others. —**seg're·ga'tion,** n.

se'gue (sā'gwā, seg'wā) v.i., **segued, segueing,** n. —v.i. **1.** to continue at once with the next section. **2.** to make a smooth transition. —n. **3.** a smooth transition.

sei'gnior (sēn'yər, sān'-) n. a lord. —**sei·gnio'ri·al, sei·gno'ri·al** (sēn·yôr'ē əl) adj.

seine (sān) n. a fishing net.

seis'mic (sīz'mik, sīs'-) adj. of or caused by earthquakes.

seis'mo·graph' (-mə graf') n. an instrument for recording the intensity of earthquakes. —**seis·mog'ra·phy,** n.

seis·mol'o·gy (-mol'ə jē) n. the science of earthquakes. —**seis'mo·log'i·cal,** adj. —**seis·mol'o·gist,** n.

seize (sēz) v.t., **seized, seizing. 1.** to take hold of suddenly or forcibly. **2.** to take possession of.

seiz'ure (sē'zhər) n. **1.** an act of seizing. **2.** a sudden attack of illness.

sel'dom (sel'dəm) adv. not often.

se·lect' (si lekt') v.t., v.i. **1.** to choose. —adj. **2.** chosen carefully; choice. **3.** careful in choosing. —**se·lec'tion,** n. —**se·lec'tive,** adj.

se·lect'man n., pl. **-men.** a town officer in New England.

self (self) n., pl. **selves** (selvz) **1.** a person referred to as an individual. **2.** a person's own nature. **3.** personal advantage or interests.

self'-ad·dressed' adj. addressed for return to the sender.

self'-as·ser'tion n. an expression of one's own importance, opinions, etc. —**self'-as·ser'tive,** adj.

self'-as·sur'ance n. confidence in one's ability. —**self'-as·sured',** adj.

self'-cen'tered adj. interested only in oneself.

self'-con'fi·dence n. faith in one's own judgment, ability, etc. —**self'-con'fi·dent,** adj.

self'-con'scious adj. embarrassed or uneasy.

self'-con·tained' adj. **1.** containing within itself all that is necessary. **2.** reserved in behavior.

self'-con·trol' n. restraint of one's actions. —**self'-con·trolled',** adj.

self'-de·fense' n. **1.** the act of defending oneself or one's property. **2.** a plea that use of force was necessary in defending one's person.

self'-de·ni'al n. the sacrifice of one's desires.

self'-de·ter'mi·na'tion n. **1.** the freedom to act as one chooses. **2.** freedom of a nation to choose its own form of government.

self'-ef·fac'ing adj. keeping oneself in the background.

self'-ev'i·dent adj. obvious.

self'-im·por'tant adj. having or showing an exaggerated sense of one's own importance.

self'-in'ter·est n. one's personal benefit.

self'ish (sel'fish) adj. caring only for oneself. —**self'ish·ly,** adv.

self'less adj. having little concern for oneself; unselfish.

self'-made' adj. owing one's success entirely to one's own efforts.

self'-pos·sessed' adj. calm; poised.

self'-pres·er·va'tion n. the instinctive desire to guard one's safety.

self'-re·spect' n. proper regard for oneself. —**self'-re·spect'ing,** adj.

self'-re·straint' n. self-control.

self'-right'eous adj. smugly convinced that one is morally right.

self'same' adj. identical.

self'-sat·is·fied' adj. feeling or showing a smug satisfaction with oneself or one's achievements.

self'-seek'ing n. **1.** the selfish seeking of one's own interests or ends. —adj. **2.** given to or characterized by self-seeking.

self'-serv'ice adj. **1.** of a commercial establishment in which customers serve themselves. **2.** designed to be used without the aid of an attendant.

self'-serv'ing adj. serving to further one's own interests.

self'-styled' adj. so called only by oneself.

self'-suf·fi'cient adj. able to supply one's own needs without external assistance.

self'-willed' adj. stubborn; obstinate.

sell (sel) v., **sold** (sōld) **selling.** —v.t. **1.** to exchange (goods, property, or services) for money. **2.** to offer for sale. **3.** to promote the sale, acceptance, or approval of. —v.i. **4.** to engage in selling. **5.** to be offered for sale. **6. sell out, a.** to dispose of all of one's stock by selling. **b.** to betray. —**sell'er,** n.

selt'zer (selt'sər) n. effervescent mineral water.

sel'vage (sel'vij) n. a finished edge on fabric.

se·man'tics (si man'tiks) n. the study of meaning in language.

sem'a·phore' (sem'ə fôr') n. an apparatus for visual signaling.

sem'blance (sem'bləns) n. **1.** outward appearance. **2.** a likeness.

se'men (sē'mən) n. the male reproductive fluid.

se·mes'ter (si mes'tər) n. half of a school year.

semi- a prefix meaning half.

sem'i·cir'cle n. a half circle. —**sem'i·cir'cu·lar,** adj.

sem'i·co'lon n. a punctuation mark (;) between parts of a sentence.

sem'i·con·duc'tor n. a substance, as silicon, with electrical conductivity between that of an insulator and a conductor.

sem'i·fi'nal adj. **1.** of the next to last round in a tournament. —n. **2.** a semifinal round or bout.

sem'i·nal (sem'ə nl) adj. **1.** of or consisting of semen. **2.** influencing future development.

sem'i·nar' (-när') n. a class in which advanced students discuss their research.

sem'i·nar'y (-ner'ē) n., pl. **-ies.** a school that prepares students for the priesthood, ministry, or rabbinate.

sem'i·pre'cious (sem'ē-, sem'ī-) adj. having value as a gem, but not classified as precious.

Se·mit'ic (sə mit'ik) n. **1.** a language family of Africa and Asia, including Hebrew and Arabic. —adj. **2.** of Semitic languages or their speakers.

sem'i·tone' n. a musical pitch halfway between two whole tones.

sem'o·li'na (sem'ə lē'nə) n. ground durum wheat.

sen'ate (sen'it) n. a legislative body, esp. (cap.) the upper house of the legislatures of the United States, Canada, etc. —**sen'a·tor** (-i-tər) n.

send (send) v.t., **sent, sending. 1.** to cause or enable to go. **2.** to cause to be taken to a destination. **3.** to emit. —**send'er,** n.

send'-off' n. a farewell demonstration of good wishes.

se·nes'cent (si nes'ənt) adj. growing old. —**se·nes'cence,** n.

se'nile (sē'nīl) adj. showing mental weakness because of old age. —**se·nil'i·ty** (si nil'ə tē) n.

sen'ior (sēn'yər) adj. **1.** older. **2.** of higher rank or longer service. **3.** denoting the final year in high school or college. —n. **4.** a senior person. **5.** a student in the final year of high school or college.

sen'ior cit'izen n. an older person.

sen·ior'i·ty (sēn yôr'i tē) n. the

status conferred by length of service.

se'nior mo'ment n. Often Facetious. a brief lapse in memory, esp. in an older person.

sen·sa'tion (sen sā'shən) n. **1.** perception through the senses. **2.** a feeling produced by stimulation of the senses or the mind. **3.** excited interest. **4.** the person or thing causing this.

sen·sa'tion·al adj. startling; shocking. —**sen·sa'tion·al·ism,** n.

sense (sens) n., v., **sensed, sensing.** —n. **1.** one of the faculties, sight, hearing, smell, taste, or touch, by which humans and animals perceive the environment. **2.** a feeling based on one of the senses. **3.** a special ability for perception or appreciation. **4.** practical intelligence. **5.** meaning. —v.t. **6.** to perceive by the senses.

sen·si·bil'i·ty (sen'sə bil'i tē) n., pl. **-ties.** capacity for feeling.

sen'si·ble adj. **1.** having, using, or showing good sense. **2.** aware. **3.** capable of feeling or perceiving. —**sen'si·bly,** adv.

sen'si·tive adj. **1.** readily affected by outside stimuli. **2.** responsive to the feelings of others. **3.** easily offended. —**sen'si·tiv'i·ty,** n.

sen'si·tize' (-tīz') v.t., v.i., **-tized, -tizing.** to make or become sensitive.

sen'sor (sen'sôr, -sər) n. a device sensitive to light, temperature, or radiation level that transmits a signal to another instrument.

sen'so·ry (-sə rē) adj. of sensation or the senses.

sen'su·al (sen'shōō əl) adj. **1.** pleasing the senses. **2.** indulging in physical pleasures. —**sen·su·al'i·ty** (-al'i tē) n. —**sen'su·al·ly,** adv.

sen'su·ous adj. of or affecting the senses.

sen'tence (sen'tns) n., v., **-tenced, -tencing.** —n. **1.** a group of words expressing a complete thought. **2.** a punishment ordered by a court of law. —v.t. **3.** to pronounce sentence upon.

sen·ten'tious (sen ten'shəs) adj. **1.** using maxims or pompous words. **2.** moralizing.

sen'tient (sen'shənt) adj. capable of perceiving through the senses.

sen'ti·ment (-tə mənt) n. **1.** an opinion or attitude. **2.** tender feelings. **3.** a thought influenced by emotion.

sen'ti·men'tal (-men'tl) adj. expressing or appealing to tender or romantic feelings. **2.** nostalgic.

sen'ti·nel (sen'tn l, -tə nl) n. one that stands watch.

sen'try (sen'trē) n., pl. **-tries.** a guard.

se'pal (sē'pəl) n. one of the leaflike parts of a flower calyx.

sep'a·rate' v., **-rated, -rating,** adj. —v.t. (sep'ə rāt') **1.** to put or keep apart; divide. —v.i. **2.** to move or come apart. **3.** to stop living together as a married couple. —adj. (-rit) **4.** not connected. —**sep'a·ra'tion,** n. —**sep'a·ra·ble,** adj.

sep'a·ra·tist (-ər ə tist, -ə rā'-) n. an advocate of separation.

sep'a·ra·tor n. an apparatus for separating ingredients.

se'pi·a (sē'pē ə) n. **1.** a brown pigment. **2.** a dark brown.

sep'sis (sep'sis) n. invasion of the body by harmful microorganisms. —**sep'tic** (-tik) adj.

Sept. September.

Sep·tem'ber (sep tem'bər) n. the ninth month of the year.

sep·tet' (sep tet') n. a group of seven.

sep'ti·ce'mi·a (sep'tə sē'mē ə) n. blood poisoning.

sep'tic tank' n. a tank in which sewage is decomposed.

sep'tu·a·ge·nar'i·an (sep'chōō ə jə när'ē ən) n. a person 70 to 79 years old.

Sep'tu·a·gint (-jint) n. the oldest Greek version of the Old Testament.

sep'tum (sep'təm) n., pl. **-ta.** a dividing wall in a plant or animal structure.

sep'ul·cher (sep'əl kər) n. a burial place. Also, **sep'ul·chre.**

seq. **1.** sequel. **2.** the following.

se'quel (sē'kwəl) n. **1.** a literary work, film, etc., continuing the narrative of an earlier one. **2.** a subsequent development.

se'quence (-kwəns) n. **1.** the following of one thing after another. **2.** a continuous connected series.

se·ques'ter (si kwes'tər) v.t. **1.** to

remove or withdraw into solitude. **2.** to set apart.

se'quin (sē'kwin) n. a small shiny disk used as ornamentation.

se·quoi'a (si kwoi'ə) n. a large coniferous tree of California.

se·ra'glio (si ral'yō, -räl'-) n., pl. **-glios.** a harem.

se·ra'pe (sə rä'pē) n. a brightly colored shawl worn esp. in Mexico.

ser'aph (ser'əf) n., pl. **-aphs, -aphim** (-ə fim) a member of the highest order of angels. —**se·raph'ic** (sə raf'ik) adj.

sere (sēr) adj. dry; withered.

ser·e·nade' (ser'ə nād') n., v., **-naded, -nading.** —n. **1.** music performed in the open air at night, as by a lover to his lady. —v.t., v.i. **2.** to perform a serenade (for).

ser'en·dip'i·ty (ser'ən dip'i tē) n. luck in making desirable discoveries by accident. —**ser'en·dip'i·tous,** adj.

se·rene' (sə rēn') adj. **1.** peaceful; calm. **2.** clear; fair. —**se·ren'i·ty** (-ren'ə tē) n.

serf (sûrf) n. a person in feudal servitude. —**serf'dom,** n.

serge (sûrj) n. a strong twilled fabric.

ser'geant (sär'jənt) n. **1.** a noncommissioned officer above a corporal. **2.** a police officer below a captain or lieutenant.

ser'geant at arms' n. an officer whose chief duty is to preserve order.

se'ri·al (sēr'ē əl) n. **1.** something appearing in installments at regular intervals. —adj. **2.** of a serial. **3.** of or in a series.

se'ries (sēr'ēz) n. a number of related things arranged or occurring in succession.

ser'if (ser'if) n. a smaller line used to finish off a main stroke of a printed letter.

ser'i·graph' (ser'i graf') n. a silk-screen print.

se'ri·ous (sēr'ē əs) adj. **1.** of, requiring, or marked by deep thought. **2.** somber. **3.** important. **4.** critical or threatening.

ser'mon (sûr'mən) n. a religious speech delivered by a cleric.

ser'pent (sûr'pənt) n. a snake.

ser'pen·tine' (-pən tēn', -tīn') adj. winding like a snake.

ser'rat·ed (ser'ā tid) adj. notched or toothed on the edge. Also, **ser'rate** (ser'it).

se'rum (sēr'əm) n., pl. **serums, sera** (sēr'ə). **1.** the clear, pale yellow liquid that separates from the clot in blood. **2.** such liquid used as an inoculation against a certain disease. **3.** a watery animal fluid.

serv'ant (sûr'vənt) n. a person employed by another, esp. to do domestic work.

serve (sûrv) v., **served, serving.** —v.i. **1.** to act as a servant. **2.** to present food or drink. **3.** to do one's official duty. **4.** to suffice. **5.** (in tennis, volleyball, etc.) to put the ball into play. —v.t. **6.** to offer food or drink to. **7.** to present (food or drink) to someone. **8.** to work for as a servant. **9.** to undergo (a term of imprisonment, service, etc.). **10.** (in tennis, volleyball, etc.) to put (the ball) into play. **11.** to render homage to. **12.** to make legal delivery of (a process or writ).

serv'ice (sûr'vis) n., v., **-iced, -icing.** —n. **1.** an act of helpful activity. **2.** the providing or a provider of maintenance or repair. **3.** the performance of duties or duties performed. **4.** an act of public worship. **5.** a set of dishes or utensils. **6.** domestic employment. **7.** (a branch of) the armed forces. **8.** (in tennis, volleyball, etc.) the act or manner of serving the ball. —v.t. **9.** to maintain, repair, or restore. **10.** to supply with services.

serv'ice·a·ble adj. usable.

serv'ice·man, n., pl. **-men. 1.** a person in the armed forces. **2.** a gasoline station attendant.

ser'vile (sûr'vil, -vīl) adj. slavishly submissive. —**ser·vil'i·ty** (-vil'ə tē) n.

ser'vi·tor (sûr'vi tər) n. a servant or attendant.

ser'vi·tude' (-tōōd', -tyōōd') n. bondage.

ses'a·me (ses'ə mē) n. the small edible seed of a tropical plant.

ses'qui·cen·ten'ni·al (ses'kwi-sen ten'ē əl) n. **1.** a 150th anniversary. —adj. **2.** of or marking the completion of 150 years.

ses'sion (sesh'ən) n. a meeting, as of a court or class.

set (set) v., **set, setting,** n., adj.

—*v.t.* **1.** to put or place. **2.** to fix definitely. **3.** to put (a broken bone) in position. **4.** to arrange (type) for printing. —*v.i.* **5.** to sink below the horizon. **6.** to become firm. **7. set forth, a.** to state. **b.** to begin a trip. **8. ~ off, a.** to cause to explode. **b.** to begin. **9. ~ up, a.** to raise. **b.** to establish. —*n.* **10.** a group; complete collection. **11.** a radio or television receiver. **12.** a construction representing the setting of the action in a play. —*adj.* **13.** prearranged. **14.** resolved.

set′back′ *n.* a return to a worse condition.

set·tee′ (se tē′) *n.* a small sofa.

set′ter (set′ər) *n.* a long-haired hunting dog.

set′ting *n.* **1.** the position of something that has been set. **2.** surroundings. **3.** the locale and period of a story, play, etc. **4.** a mounting for a jewel. **5.** the music composed for certain words.

set·tle (set′l) *v.*, **-tled, -tling.** —*v.t.* **1.** to put in order. **2.** to pay. **3.** to colonize. **4.** to quiet or calm. **5.** to resolve. —*v.i.* **6.** to come to an agreement or decision. **7.** to take up residence. **8.** to come to rest. **9.** to sink gradually. —**set′tle·ment,** *n.* —**set′tler,** *n.*

set′-to′ (-tōō′) *n., pl.* **set-tos.** a brief, sharp fight.

set′up′ *n.* organization; arrangement.

sev′en (sev′ən) *n., adj.* six plus one. —**sev′enth,** *adj., n.*

sev′en·teen′ (-tēn′) *adj., n.* sixteen plus one. —**sev′en·teenth′,** *adj., n.*

sev′enth heav′en *n.* bliss.

sev′en·ty *n., adj.* ten times seven. —**sev′en·ti·eth,** *adj., n.*

sev′er (sev′ər) *v.t., v.i.* to separate; break off. —**sev′er·ance,** *n.*

sev′er·al (sev′ər əl) *adj.* **1.** some, but not many. **2.** respective; individual. **3.** various. —*n.* **4.** several persons or things.

se·vere′ (sə vēr′) *adj.*, **-verer, -verest. 1.** harsh. **2.** serious or stern. **3.** austere. **4.** intense; violent. —**se·ver′i·ty** (-ver′i tē) *n.* —**se·vere′ly,** *adv.*

sew (sō) *v.*, **sewed, sewed or sewn, sewing.** —*v.t.* **1.** to make, repair, or attach by stitches. —*v.i.* **2.** to work with a needle and thread.

sew′age (sōō′ij) *n.* wastes that pass through sewers.

sew′er (sōō′ər) *n.* an underground passage for waste water, refuse, etc.

sex (seks) *n.* **1.** either the male or female division of a species. **2.** the differences by which the male and female are distinguished. **3.** the attraction drawing one individual sexually toward another. **4.** sexual intercourse. —**sex′u·al** (sek′shōō əl) *adj.* —**sex′u·al·i·ty,** *n.*

sex·a·ge·nar′i·an (sek′sə jə nâr′ē ən) *n.* a person 60 to 69 years old.

sex′ chro′mosome *n.* a chromosome that determines an individual′s sex.

sex′ism *n.* discrimination because of sex, esp. against women. —**sex′ist,** *n., adj.*

sex′tant (sek′stənt) *n.* an instrument for finding one′s position at sea.

sex·tet′ (seks tet′) *n.* a group of six musicians or a composition for such a group.

sex′ton (sek′stən) *n.* a church caretaker.

sex′ual harass′ment *n.* unwelcome sexual advances, esp. by a superior.

sex′ual in′tercourse *n.* genital contact between individuals, esp. penetration of the penis into the vagina.

sex′ually transmit′ted disease′ *n.* any disease transmitted by sexual contact.

sex′y *adj.*, **-ier, -iest.** sexually interesting or exciting; erotic.

SGML Standard Generalized Markup Language: a set of standards enabling a user to create a markup scheme for tagging the elements of an electronic document.

Sgt. Sergeant.

shab′by (shab′ē) *adj.*, **-bier -biest. 1.** worn out or run-down. **2.** mean. —**shab′bi·ness,** *n.*

shack (shak) *n.* a rough cabin.

shack·le (shak′əl) *n., v.,* **-led, -ling.** —*n.* **1.** an iron bond for the wrist, ankle, etc. —*v.t.* **2.** to put shackles on. **3.** to restrain; inhibit.

shad (shad) *n.* an edible marine fish that spawns in rivers upstream from the sea.

shade (shād) *n., v.,* **shaded, shading.** —*n.* **1.** a slightly dark, cool

place. **2.** a place sheltered from the sun. **3.** something used to shut out light. **4.** the degree of darkness of a color. **5.** a slight amount. —*v.t.* **6.** to dim or darken. **7.** to protect from light or heat. —*v.i.* **8.** to change by degrees.

shad′ow (shad′ō) *n.* **1.** a dark image cast on a surface by a body intercepting a light. **2.** comparative darkness. **3.** a trace. **4.** a cause of gloom. —*v.t.* **5.** to cast a shadow over. **6.** to follow secretly. —**shad′ow·y,** *adj.*

shad′ow·box′ *v.i.* to go through the motions of boxing without an opponent, as in training.

shad′y *adj.*, **-ier, -iest. 1.** giving or located in shade. **2.** dishonest.

shaft (shaft) *n.* **1.** a long slender rod. **2.** a ray or beam. **3.** a revolving bar in an engine. **4.** a vertical underground space, as in a mine. **5.** *Slang.* unfair treatment. —*v.t.* **6.** *Slang.* to treat unfairly.

shag (shag) *n.* **1.** matted wool, hair, etc. **2.** a long, thick pile or nap.

shah (shä) *n.* (formerly, in Iran) a king.

shake (shāk) *v.*, **shook** (shŏŏk), **shaken, shaking.** —*v.i., v.t.* **1.** to move up and down or back and forth with short, quick movements. **2.** to come or force off or out by quick movements. **3.** to tremble or cause to tremble. **4.** to clasp (a person′s hand) in greeting. **5.** to disturb greatly. —*n.* **6.** an act of shaking. **7.** shakes, a spell of trembling.

shake′down′ *n.* **1.** extortion, as by blackmail. **2.** a thorough search.

shake′up′ *n.* a thorough organizational reform.

shak′y *adj.*, **-ier, -iest.** not firm.

shale (shāl) *n.* layered rock.

shall (shal; *unstressed* shəl) *auxiliary v., pres.* **shall;** *past* **should. 1.** plan to or intend to. **2.** will have to or is determined to. **3.** (in laws, directives, etc.) must. **4.** (used in questions).

—**Usage.** Today, WILL is used in place of SHALL to indicate future time in all three persons and in all types of speech and writing. SHALL has some use, chiefly in formal contexts, to express determination: *I shall return. We shall overcome.* SHALL also occurs in the language of law and in directives: *All visitors shall observe posted regulations.*

shal′lot (shal′ət) *n.* an onionlike plant with a bulb used in cooking.

shal′low (shal′ō) *adj.* **1.** not deep. **2.** superficial. —*n.* **3.** shallows, a shallow part of a body of water.

sham (sham) *n., adj., v.,* **shammed, shamming.** —*n.* **1.** a pretense or imitation. —*adj.* **2.** pretended. —*v.t., v.i.* **3.** to pretend.

sham·ble (sham′bəl) *v.*, **-bled, -bling,** —*v.i.* **1.** to walk awkwardly. —*n.* **2.** a shambling gait. **3. shambles,** a scene of confusion.

shame (shām) *n., v.,* **shamed, shaming.** —*n.* **1.** distress and guilt over a wrong or foolish act. **2.** disgrace. —*v.t.* **3.** to cause to feel shame. **4.** to motivate by shame. —**shame′ful, adj.** —**shame′less, adj.**

sham·poo (sham pōō′) *n.* **1.** a liquid soap for washing the hair. **2.** a cleansing agent for rugs, upholstery, etc. —*v.t.* **4.** to wash or cleanse with shampoo.

sham′rock (sham′rok) *n.* a small clover with a three-part leaf.

shang·hai (shang′hī) *v.t.*, **-haied, -haiing.** to force (a sailor) to join the crew of a ship.

shank (shangk) *n.* the part of the leg between the knee and the ankle.

shan′tung (shan′tung′) *n.* a kind of silk.

shan′ty (shan′tē) *n., pl.* **-ties.** a crudely built hut or cabin.

shape (shāp) *n., v.,* **shaped, shaping.** —*n.* **1.** the outline or form of something. **2.** condition. **3.** orderly arrangement. —*v.t.* **4.** to give shape to. **5.** to adjust to a certain condition. —**shape′less,** *adj.*

shape′ly *adj.*, **-lier, -liest.** having a pleasing shape. —**shape′li·ness,** *n.*

shard (shärd) *n.* a fragment, esp. of broken earthenware.

share (shâr) *n., v.,* **shared, sharing.** —*n.* **1.** a portion allotted to one person. **2.** one of the equal parts into which a company′s stock is divided. —*v.t.* **3.** to divide and distribute in shares. **4.** to use, enjoy, etc., jointly. —*v.i.* **5.** to have a share.

share′crop′per *n.* a tenant farmer who pays part of the crop as rent.

share′hold′er *n.* one that owns shares of stock.

shark (shärk) *n.* **1.** a large marine fish, often ferocious. **2.** one who preys greedily on others.

shark′skin′ *n.* a smooth, silky fabric with a dull surface.

sharp (shärp) *adj.* **1.** having a thin cutting edge or fine point. **2.** abrupt. **3.** clearly defined. **4.** (of taste) pungent. **5.** (of sound) piercing. **6.** felt acutely, as cold. **7.** mentally acute. **8.** shrewd. **9.** *Music.* above the true pitch. **10.** keenly or acutely. **11.** punctually. —*n.* **12.** a musical tone one half step above a given tone or the symbol indicating this. —**sharp′en·er,** *v.t., v.i.* —**sharp′en·er,** *n.* —**sharp′ly,** *adv.* —**sharp′ness,** *n.*

sharp′er *n.* a swindler.

sharp′-eyed′ *adj.* having keen sight.

sharp′shoot′er *n.* a skilled shooter.

sharp′-tongued′ *adj.* harsh or critical in speech.

shat′ter (shat′ər) *v.i., v.t.* to break or cause to break in pieces.

shat′ter·proof′ *adj.* made to resist shattering.

shave (shāv) *v.*, **shaved, shaved or shaven, shaving.** —*v.i.* **1.** to remove hair with a razor. —*v.t.* **2.** to remove hair from (face, legs, etc.) close to the skin. **3.** to cut thin slices from. —*n.* **4.** the act or result of shaving.

shav′ings *n.pl.* thin slices of wood.

shawl (shôl) *n.* a long covering for the head and shoulders.

she (shē) *pron.* **1.** the female last mentioned. —*n.* **2.** a female.

sheaf (shēf) *n., pl.* **sheaves.** a bundle.

shear (shēr) *v.t.*, **sheared, sheared or shorn, shearing. 1.** to cut (something). **2.** to clip the hair, fleece, etc., from.

shears *n.pl.* large scissors.

sheath (shēth) *n.* **1.** a case for a blade. **2.** any similar covering.

sheathe (shēth) *v.t.*, **sheathed, sheathing.** to put into a sheath.

she·bang′ (shə bang′) *n. Informal.* a thing, contrivance, or affair.

shed¹ (shed) *n.* a simple shelter.

shed² (shed) *v.*, **shed, shedding.** —*v.t.* **1.** to pour or give forth. **2.** to lose (leaves, skin, etc.) by a natural process. **3.** to throw off. —*v.i.* **4.** to cast off a natural covering.

sheen (shēn) *n.* brightness.

sheep (shēp) *n., pl.* **sheep.** a mammal bred for wool and meat.

sheep′ dog′ *n.* a dog trained to herd sheep.

sheep′fold′ *n.* an enclosure for sheep.

sheep′ish *adj.* embarrassed.

sheer¹ (shēr) *adj.* **1.** transparent and thin. **2.** complete; utter. **3.** very steep.

sheer² (shēr) *v.t., v.i.* to turn from a course.

sheet¹ (shēt) *n.* **1.** a large piece of cloth used as bedding. **2.** a broad thin layer or covering. **3.** a thin piece, as of glass, metal, etc.

sheet² (shēt) *n.* a rope or wire used to control a ship′s sail.

sheik (shēk) *n.* (in Arab countries) a ruler.

shek′el (shek′əl) *n.* an ancient Hebrew and modern Israeli monetary unit.

shelf (shelf) *n., pl.* **shelves** (shelvz). **1.** a horizontal slab attached to a wall for holding objects. **2.** something resembling this, as a ledge.

shelf′ life′ *n.* the period during which a product is fit for use.

shell (shel) *n.* **1.** a hard outer covering of an animal or a seed, egg, nut, etc. **2.** a metal case filled with an explosive charge. **3.** a light racing boat. —*v.t.* **4.** to remove the shell of. **5.** to fire shells at.

shel·lac′ (shə lak′) *n., v.,* **-lacked, -lacking.** —*n.* **1.** a substance used in varnish. —*v.t.* **2.** to coat with shellac. **3.** *Slang.* to defeat.

shell′fish′ *n.* an aquatic animal having a shell.

shell′ shock′ *n.* combat fatigue.

shel′ter (shel′tər) *n.* **1.** a structure that offers protection against rain, cold, etc. **2.** the protection provided by a shelter. —*v.t.* **3.** to provide with or take shelter.

shelve (shelv) *v.t.,* **shelved, shelving. 1.** to put on a shelf. **2.** to put off or aside. **3.** to remove from active use.

she·nan′i·gans (shə nan′i gənz) *n.pl. Informal.* mischief.

shep′herd (shep′ərd) *n.* **1.** a person who tends sheep. —*v.t.* **2.** to guide.

sher′bet (shûr′bit) *n.* a frozen, fruit-flavored dessert.

sher′iff (sher′if) *n.* a county law-enforcement officer.

sher′ry (sher′ē) *n., pl.* **-ries.** a fortified wine served as a cocktail.

shib′bo·leth (shib′ə lith) *n.* a common saying; slogan.

shield (shēld) *n.* **1.** a plate of armor carried on the arm. **2.** something or someone that protects. —*v.t.* **3.** to protect.

shift (shift) *v.t., v.i.* **1.** to move from one place or direction to another. —*n.* **2.** a change from one place or direction to another. **3.** a scheduled period of work.

shift′less *adj.* lacking ambition.

shift′y *adj.*, **-ier, -iest.** devious.

shill (shil) *n.* a person who poses as a customer to lure others.

shil·le·lagh (shə lā′lē, -lə) *n.* a rough Irish walking stick or cudgel.

shil′ling (shil′ing) *n.* a former British coin, the 20th part of a pound.

shil·ly-shal·ly (shil′ē shal′ē) *v.i.,* **shilly-shallied, shilly-shallying.** to be unable to make up one′s mind.

shim′mer (shim′ər) *v.i.* **1.** to glow faintly; flicker. —*n.* **2.** a faint glow.

shim′my (shim′ē) *n., pl.* **-mies,** *v.,* **-mied, -mying.** *Informal.* —*n.* **1.** a shaking or wobbling. —*v.i.* **2.** to shake or wobble.

shin (shin) *n.* the front of the leg from the knee to the ankle.

shin′dig′ (shin′dig′) *n. Informal.* an elaborate and usu. large party.

shine (shīn) *v.,* **shone** (shōn) or (for 6) **shined, shining.** —*v.i.* **1.** to give forth or glow with light. **2.** to sparkle. **3.** to excel. —*v.t.* **4.** to cause to shine. **5.** to direct the light of. **6.** to polish. —*n.* **7.** brightness. **8.** a polish. —**shin′y,** *adj.*

shin′er *n. Informal.* a black eye.

shin′gle¹ (shing′gəl) *n., v.,* **-gled, -gling.** —*n.* **1.** a thin slab of wood, asbestos, etc., used in overlapping rows as covering for a roof or outside wall. **2.** a small signboard. —*v.t.* **3.** to cover with shingles.

shin′gle² (shing′gəl) *n.* **1.** smooth pebbles lying loose on a beach. **2.** an area of these.

shin′gles *n.* a viral disease marked by skin eruptions and pain in the involved nerves.

shin′ splints′ *n.pl.* a painful condition of the shins associated with strenuous activity.

Shin′to (shin′tō) *n.* a native religion of Japan.

ship (ship) *n., v.,* **shipped, shipping.** —*n.* **1.** a large vessel for navigating in water. —*v.t.* **2.** to transport by ship, rail, truck, etc. **3.** to put (as oars) in place for use on a ship or boat. **4.** to send away. —**ship′board′,** *n.* —**ship′mate′,** *n.*

-ship a suffix meaning: **1.** state or quality. **2.** position or rank. **3.** skill or art.

ship′ment *n.* **1.** the act of shipping. **2.** something that is shipped.

ship′shape′ *adj., adv.* in good order.

ship′wreck′ *n.* **1.** the destruction of a ship. —*v.i., v.t.* **2.** to suffer or cause to suffer shipwreck.

ship′wright′ *n.* a carpenter who repairs or builds ships.

ship′yard′ *n.* a place where ships are built or repaired.

shire (shī°r) *n.* a county in Great Britain.

shirk (shûrk) *v.t., v.i.* to evade (work or duty).

shirr (shûr) *v.t.* **1.** to gather (cloth) on parallel threads. **2.** to bake (eggs).

shirt (shûrt) *n.* a garment for the upper part of the body.

shirt′ing *n.* fabric used to make shirts.

shirt′tail′ *n.* the part of a shirt below the waistline.

shirt′waist′ *n.* a tailored blouse.

shish′ ke·bab′ (shish′ kə bob′) *n.* cubes of meat broiled on a skewer.

shiv′er (shiv′ər) *v.i.* **1.** to tremble, as with cold. —*n.* **2.** a tremble or quiver. —**shiv′er·y,** *adj.*

shoal¹ (shōl) *n.* a shallow place in a body of water.

shoal² (shōl) *n.* a large number, esp. of fish.

shoat (shōt) *n.* a young pig.

shock (shok) *n.* **1.** a sudden, violent emotional upset. **2.** a sudden and violent blow, impact, etc. **3.** severely diminished blood circulation caused by trauma. **4.** the effect of an electric charge on the body. —*v.t.* **5.** to affect with horror, sur-

prise, etc. **6.** to subject to electric shock.

shock′ absorb′er *n.* a device for damping sudden, rapid motion.

shock′ ther′apy *n.* a treatment for mental disorders using a drug or electricity.

shod′dy (shod′ē) *adj.*, **-dier, -diest.** of poor quality. —**shod′di·ly,** *adv.*

shoe (shōō) *n., v.,* **shod** (shod) **shoeing.** —*n.* **1.** an external covering for the foot. **2.** a horseshoe. **3.** the part of a brake that presses against a rotating wheel. —*v.t.* **4.** to provide with shoes.

shoe′horn′ *n.* a curved device to assist in slipping on a shoe.

shoe′lace′ *n.* a lace for fastening a shoe.

shoe′mak′er *n.* a person who makes or mends shoes.

shoe′string′ *n.* **1.** a shoelace. **2.** a very small amount of money.

shoe′tree′ *n.* a device placed inside a shoe to hold its shape.

sho′gun (shō′gən) *n.* one of the chief military commanders of Japan from the 8th to 12th centuries.

shoo (shōō) *interj., v.,* **shooed, shooing.** —*interj.* **1.** (used to drive away animals). —*v.t.* **2.** to drive away by shouting "shoo."

shoo′-in′ *n.* one regarded as certain to win.

shook (shŏŏk) *v.* pt. of **shake.**

shoot (shōōt) *v.,* **shot, shooting,** *n.* —*v.t.* **1.** to hit, wound, or kill with a missile. **2.** to discharge (a weapon). **3.** to send forth swiftly or suddenly. **4.** to photograph. —*v.i.* **5.** to move or pass swiftly or suddenly. **6.** to hunt with a gun. **7.** to put forth buds or shoots. —*n.* **8.** new growth from a plant. **9.** a shooting contest. —**shoot′er,** *n.*

shoot′ing star′ *n.* a meteor.

shop (shop) *n., v.,* **shopped, shopping.** —*n.* **1.** a store. **2.** a workshop. **3.** a factory, office, or business. —*v.i.* **4.** to look at or purchase goods.

shop′lift′er *n.* one who steals from shops while posing as a customer.

shop′talk′ *n.* conversation about one′s work or occupation.

shop′worn′ *adj.* worn from being handled.

shore¹ (shōr) *n.* the land along the edge of a body of water.

shore² (shōr) *v.t.,* **shored, shoring.** to prop or support with a post or beam.

shorn (shōrn) *v.* a pp. of **shear.**

short (shôrt) *adj.* **1.** not long or tall. **2.** rudely brief. **3.** not sufficient. **4.** not reaching a target or standard. **5.** (of pastry) crisp and flaky. —*adv.* **6.** abruptly. —*n.* **7.** anything short. **8. shorts,** short trousers. **9.** a short circuit. —*v.i., v.t.* **10.** to form a short circuit (on). —*Idiom.* **11. in short,** briefly. —**short′en,** *v.t., v.i.*

short′age (shôr′tij) *n.* scarcity.

short′bread′ *n.* a rich butter cookie.

short′cake′ *n.* a rich biscuit topped with fruit and cream.

short′change′ *v.t.,* **-changed, -changing. 1.** to give less than the correct change to. **2.** to cheat.

short′ cir′cuit *n.* an abnormal connection between two points in a circuit.

short′com′ing *n.* a deficiency.

short′cut′ *n.* a shorter way to get somewhere or to accomplish something.

short′en·ing (shôrt′ning) *n.* butter or another fat used to make pastry.

short′hand′ *n.* a system of rapid handwriting.

short′-hand′ed *adj.* not having enough workers.

short′-lived′ (-līvd, -livd) *adj.* lasting only a short time.

short′ly *adv.* **1.** in a short time. **2.** briefly.

short′ shrift′ *n.* little attention or consideration.

short′-sight′ed *adj.* lacking foresight.

short′stop′ *n. Baseball.* the player or position covering the area between second and third base.

short′-tem′pered *adj.* very irritable.

short′wave′ *n.* a radio wave of frequencies over 1600 kilohertz, used for long-distance transmission.

shot¹ (shot) *v.* pt. and pp. of **shoot.**

shot² (shot) *n.* **1.** the discharge of a weapon. **2.** the sound of this. **3.** an act or instance of shooting. **4.** a person who shoots. **5.** a missile for discharge from a firearm. **6.** an attempt or try. **7.** a photograph. **8.** a stroke or throw in a game. **9.** an injection. **10.** a heavy metal ball used in the shot put.

shot'gun' *n.* a smoothbore gun.

shot' put' *n.* a competition in which a heavy metal ball is thrown for distance. —**shot'-put'ter,** *n.*

should (shŏŏd) *v.* pt. of **shall.**

shoul'der (shōl'dər) *n.* **1.** the part of the body from the neck to the upper joint of the arm in humans or the foreleg in animals. **2.** a border along a highway. —*v.t.* **3.** to push with or as if with the shoulder. **4.** to take up, as a burden.

shoul'der blade' *n.* the scapula.

shout (shout) *v.i., v.t.* **1.** to call or cry out loudly. —*n.* **2.** a loud call or cry.

shove (shuv) *v.,* **shoved, shoving,** *n.* —*v.t.* **1.** to push roughly. —*n.* **2.** a rough push.

shov'el (shuv'əl) *n., v.,* **-eled, -eling.** —*n.* **1.** a tool with a broad scoop and handle. —*v.t.* **2.** to dig or move with a shovel.

show (shō) *v.,* **showed, shown** or **showed, showing,** *n.* —*v.t.* **1.** to cause or allow to be seen. **2.** to point out. **3.** to explain. **4.** to guide. —*v.i.* **5.** to be visible. **6. show off, a.** to display proudly. **b.** to act in a way that attracts attention. —*n.* **7.** an exhibition. **8.** a performance. **9.** appearance.

show'boat' *n.* a boat used as a traveling theater.

show'case' *n., v.,* **-cased, -casing.** —*n.* **1.** a setting for displaying something. —*v.t.* **2.** to exhibit to best advantage.

show'down' *n.* a decisive confrontation.

show'er (shou'ər) *n.* **1.** a brief fall of rain, snow, etc. **2.** a bath in which water is sprayed on the body. **3.** a party at which gifts are given. —*v.t.* **4.** to give abundantly. —*v.i.* **5.** to bathe in a shower. **6.** to rain in a shower.

show'-off' (shō'-) *n.* a person who seeks attention.

show'piece' *n.* something worthy of being exhibited.

show'place' *n.* a place, as a large house, notable for its beauty.

show'y *adj.,* **-ier, -iest.** making an impressive display; ostentatious.

shrank (shrangk) *v.* a pt. of **shrink.**

shrap'nel (shrap'nl) *n.* fragments from an exploding shell.

shred (shred) *n., v.,* **shredded** or **shred, shredding.** —*n.* **1.** a torn piece or strip. **2.** a bit. —*v.t.* **3.** to reduce to shreds.

shrew (shrōō) *n.* **1.** a quarrelsome woman. **2.** a small mouselike mammal. —**shrew'ish,** *adj.*

shrewd (shrōōd) *adj.* clever.

shriek (shrēk) *n.* **1.** a loud shrill cry. —*v.i., v.t.* **2.** to utter (with) a shriek.

shrike (shrīk) *n.* a predatory bird with a sharply hooked bill.

shrill (shril) *adj.* **1.** high-pitched and piercing. —*v.t., v.i.* **2.** to cry shrilly.

shrimp (shrimp) *n.* a small, long-tailed edible shellfish.

shrine (shrīn) *n.* a sacred place.

shrink (shringk) *v.,* **shrank** (shrangk) or **shrunk** (shrungk), **shrunk** or **shrunken, shrinking.** —*v.i.* **1.** to become smaller. **2.** to draw back. —*v.t.* **3.** to make smaller.

shrink'age (shring'kij) *n.* the process or amount of shrinking.

shrink'ing vi'olet *n.* a shy person.

shrink'-wrap' *v.,* **shrink-wrapped, shrink-wrapping,** —*v.t.* **1.** to seal in plastic film that when exposed to heat shrinks tightly around the object it covers. —*n.* **2.** the plastic used to shrink-wrap.

shrive (shrīv) *v.t.,* **shrove** (shrōv) or **shrived, shriven** (shriv'ən) or **shrived, shriving.** **1.** to impose penance on. **2.** to grant absolution to.

shriv'el (shriv'əl) *v.t., v.i.,* **-eled, -eling.** to shrink and wrinkle, as from dryness.

shroud (shroud) *n.* **1.** a burial cloth. **2.** something that conceals. **3.** one of the ropes supporting the masts of a ship. —*v.t.* **4.** to hide from view.

shrub (shrub) *n.* a woody perennial plant smaller than a tree. —**shrub'ber•y,** *n.*

shrug (shrug) *v.,* **shrugged, shrugging,** *n.* —*v.t., v.i.* **1.** to move (the shoulders) to show ignorance, indifference, etc. —*n.* **2.** this movement.

shrunk (shrungk) *v.* a pp. and pt. of **shrink.**

shtick (shtik) *n. Slang.* a show-business routine.

shuck (shuk) *n.* **1.** a husk, as of

corn, or shell, as of an oyster. —*v.t.* **2.** to remove the shucks from. **3.** to remove.

shud'der (shud'ər) *v.i.* **1.** to tremble, as from horror. —*n.* **2.** this movement.

shuf'fle (shuf'əl) *v.,* **-fled, -fling,** *n.* —*v.i.* **1.** to drag the feet in walking. —*v.t.* **2.** to move (the feet) along the ground without lifting. **3.** to intermix (playing cards). —*n.* **4.** a shuffling gait. **5.** an act of shuffling cards.

shuf'fle•board' *n.* a game in which disks are pushed with cues on a marked floor surface.

shun (shun) *v.t.,* **shunned, shunning.** to avoid.

shunt (shunt) *v.t., v.i.* **1.** to divert. **2.** to switch (a train) to a side track.

shut (shut) *v.,* **shut, shutting,** *adj.* —*v.t.* **1.** to move into a closed position. **2.** to close by bringing together the parts of. **3.** to confine. —*v.i.* **4.** to become shut. **5. shut down,** to cease operations. **6. — out, a.** to exclude. **b.** to prevent (an opponent) from scoring. **7. — up,** to stop or cause to stop talking. —*adj.* **8.** closed.

shut'-in' *n.* a person confined, as by illness, to the house, a hospital, etc.

shut'out' *n.* a game in which one side does not score.

shut'ter *n.* **1.** a solid or louvered movable cover for a window. **2.** a device for opening and closing a camera lens.

shut'ter•bug' *n.* an amateur photographer.

shut'tle (shut'l) *n., v.,* **-tled, -tling.** —*n.* **1.** a bus, plane, etc., moving back and forth between two destinations. **2.** a device for moving thread back and forth in weaving. —*v.i., v.t.* **3.** to move or cause to move quickly back and forth.

shut'tle•cock' *n.* the feathered object hit in badminton.

shy (shī) *adj.,* **shyer** or **shier, shyest** or **shiest,** *v.,* **shied, shying.** —*adj.* **1.** bashful. **2.** easily frightened. **3.** lacking. —*v.i.* **4.** to start back or aside, as in fear.

shy'ster (shī'stər) *n.* an unscrupulous lawyer.

Si'a•mese' twins' (sī'ə mēz', -mēs') *n.pl.* twins joined together by a body part.

sib'i•lant (sib'ə lənt) *adj.* **1.** hissing. —*n.* **2.** a hissing sound.

sib'ling (sib'ling) *n.* a brother or sister.

sib'yl (sib'əl) *n.* a female prophet.

sic (sik) *v.t.,* **sicked, sicking.** to urge to attack.

sic (sik) *adv. Latin.* so; thus: used in brackets to indicate that something has been used or spelled as quoted.

sick (sik) *adj.* **1.** not healthy; ill. **2.** nauseated. **3.** deeply distressed. **4.** gruesome. —**sick'en,** *v.t., v.i.*

sick'le (sik'əl) *n.* a tool with a curved blade and a short handle, used for cutting grass, grain, etc.

sick'ly *adj.,* **-lier, -liest. 1.** not well. **2.** faint; weak.

side (sīd) *n., adj., v.,* **sided, siding.** —*n.* **1.** the surface of something, esp. a part other than the front, back, top, or bottom. **2.** the right or left half of the body. **3.** an aspect. **4.** region or position with reference to a central point. **5.** a contesting team or group. **6.** a faction. —*adj.* **7.** at, on, from, or toward one side. —*v.i.* **8. side with** (or **against**), to support (or oppose). —*Idiom.* **9. take sides,** to support one party in a dispute.

side'bar' *n.* a short news feature highlighting a longer story.

side'board' *n.* a piece of dining-room furniture for holding china.

side'burns' *n.pl.* short whiskers in front of the ears.

side' effect' *n.* an often bad secondary effect, as of a drug.

side'kick' *n.* **1.** a close friend. **2.** a confederate or assistant.

side'light' *n.* an item of incidental information.

side'line' *n., pl.* **-lines. 1.** a business or activity in addition to one's primary business. **2.** an additional line of goods. **3.** a line defining the side of an athletic field.

side'long' *adj., adv.* to or toward the side.

si•de're•al (sī dēr'ē əl) *adj.* of or determined by the stars.

side'sad'dle *n.* **1.** a saddle on which a woman rides with both legs on one side of the horse. —*adv.* **2.** on a sidesaddle.

side'show' *n.* a minor show connected with a principal one.

side'split'ting *adj.* very funny.

side'-step' *v.i., v.t.,* **-stepped, -stepping.** to avoid, as by stepping aside.

side'swipe' *v.t.,* **-swiped, -swiping.** to strike with a glancing blow along the side.

side'track' *v.t., v.i.* to divert.

side'walk' *n.* a paved walk along a street.

side'ways' *adj., adv.* **1.** with one side forward. **2.** toward or from one side. Also, **side'wise'.**

sid'ing *n.* **1.** weatherproof facing for frame buildings. **2.** a short railroad track for halted cars.

si'dle (sīd'l) *v.i.,* **-dled, -dling.** to move sideways, esp. furtively.

SIDS (sidz) *n.* sudden infant death syndrome.

siege (sēj) *n.* **1.** the surrounding of a fortified place to force its surrender. **2.** a prolonged period of troubles.

si•en'na (sē en'ə) *n.* a yellowish- or reddish-brown pigment.

si•er'ra (sē er'ə) *n.* a jagged chain of hills or mountains.

si•es'ta (sē es'tə) *n.* a midday rest.

sieve (siv) *n.* a utensil with a meshed surface for straining.

sift (sift) *v.t.* **1.** to pass through a sieve. **2.** to separate by or as if by a sieve.

sigh (sī) *v.i.* **1.** to exhale audibly in grief, weariness, etc. **2.** to yearn. —*n.* **3.** the act or sound of sighing.

sight (sīt) *n.* **1.** the power of seeing. **2.** a glimpse. **3.** one's range of vision. **4.** a device, as on a firearm, for guiding one's aim. **5.** something worth seeing. —*v.t.* **6.** to see. **7.** to aim by a sight. —*Idiom.* **8. sight unseen,** without previous examination. —**sight'less,** *adj.*

sight'ed *adj.* not blind.

sight'ly *adj.,* **-lier, -liest.** pleasing to the sight.

sight'read' (rēd) *v.t., v.i.,* **-read** (-red') **-reading.** to perform without previous practice or study.

sight'see'ing *n.* visiting new places and things of interest. —**sight'se'er,** *n.*

sig'ma (sig'mə) *n., pl.* **-mas.** the 18th letter of the Greek alphabet.

sign (sīn) *n.* **1.** an indication. **2.** a conventional mark, figure, etc., used instead of a word. **3.** a board, placard, etc., bearing an advertisement, warning, or instruction. **4.** a gesture. **5.** a trace. **6.** an omen. —*v.t.* **7.** to put one's signature to. **8.** to engage by written agreement. **9.** to convey (a message) in sign language. —*v.i.* **10.** to write one's signature. **11.** to employ sign language. **12. sign in** or **out,** to record one's arrival or departure. **13. ~ up,** to enlist.

sig'nal (sig'nl) *n., adj., v.,* **-naled, -naling.** —*n.* **1.** a sign or gesture that indicates, warns, or commands. —*adj.* **2.** serving as a signal. **3.** notable. —*v.t., v.i.* **4.** to communicate by symbols.

sig'nal•ly *adv.* notably.

sig'na•to'ry (sig'nə tôr'ē) *n., pl.* **-ries.** a signer.

sig'na•ture (-nə chər) *n.* **1.** a person's name in his or her own handwriting. **2.** *Music.* a sign indicating the key or meter of a piece.

sig'net (sig'nit) *n.* a small seal.

sig•nif'i•cance (sig nif'i kəns) *n.* **1.** importance. **2.** meaning. —**sig•nif'i•cant,** *adj.*

signif'icant oth'er *n.* a spouse or cohabiting lover.

sig'ni•fy' *v.,* **-fied, -fying.** —*v.t.* **1.** to make known. **2.** to mean. —*v.i.* **3.** to be of importance. —**sig'ni•fi•ca'tion,** *n.*

sign' lan'guage *n.* a visual-gestural language, used by deaf people.

Sikh (sēk) *n.* a member of a religion of India that rejects the Hindu caste system. —**Sikh'ism,** *n.*

si'lage (sī'lij) *n.* fodder preserved in a silo.

si'lence (sī'ləns) *n., v.,* **-lenced, -lencing.** —*n.* **1.** absence of sound or noise. —*v.t.* **2.** to make silent.

si'lenc•er *n.* a device for deadening the report of a firearm.

si'lent *adj.* **1.** making no sound. **2.** not speaking. **3.** unspoken. **4.** (of a letter) not pronounced.

sil'hou•ette' (sil'ōō et') *n., v.,* **-etted, -etting.** —*n.* **1.** a dark filled-in outline of an object against a light background. —*v.t.* **2.** to show in silhouette.

sil'i•ca (sil'i kə) *n.* silicon dioxide, appearing as quartz, sand, flint, etc.

sil'i•cate (-kit, -kāt') *n.* a mineral,

as quartz, consisting of silicon and oxygen with a metal.

sil'i•con (-kən, -kon') *n.* a nonmetallic element that constitutes more than one fourth of the earth's crust in its combined forms.

sil'i•cone' (-kōn') *n.* a polymer with silicon and oxygen atoms, used in adhesives, lubricants, etc.

sil'i•co'sis (-kō'sis) *n.* a lung disease caused by inhaling silica particles.

silk (silk) *n.* **1.** the fine soft fiber from the cocoon of the silkworm. **2.** thread or cloth made from it. —*adj.* **3.** Also, **silk'en, silk'y.** of silk.

silk'screen' *n.* a printmaking technique in which color is forced through the pores of a mesh cloth. —*v.t.* **2.** to print by silkscreen.

silk'worm' *n.* a moth caterpillar that spins silk to make its cocoon.

sill (sil) *n.* a horizontal piece beneath a window or door.

sil'ly (sil'ē) *adj.,* **-lier, -liest. 1.** foolish. **2.** ridiculous. —**sil'li•ness,** *n.*

si'lo (sī'lō) *n., pl.* **-los. 1.** a tower for storing fodder. **2.** an underground housing for a missile.

silt (silt) *n.* **1.** earth or sand carried and deposited by a stream. —*v.t., v.i.* **2.** to fill up with silt.

Si•lu'ri•an (si lŏŏr'ē ən) *adj.* of the third period of the Paleozoic Era.

sil'ver (sil'vər) *n.* **1.** a white metallic element used for making coins, jewelry, etc. **2.** coins, utensils, etc., of silver. **3.** a shiny grayish white. —*adj.* **4.** of or plated with silver.

sil'ver bul'let *n.* a quick solution to a difficult problem.

sil'ver•fish' *n.* a wingless, silvery-gray insect that damages paper.

sil'ver lin'ing *n.* a prospect of hope or comfort.

sil'ver ni'trate *n.* a poisonous powder used in photography.

sil'ver-tongued' *adj.* eloquent.

sil'ver•ware' *n.* eating and serving utensils of silver or other metal.

sim'i•an (sim'ē ən) *n.* **1.** an ape or monkey. —*adj.* **2.** of or resembling apes or monkeys.

sim'i•lar (sim'ə lər) *adj.* having a general likeness or resemblance. —**sim•i•lar'i•ty** (-lar'i tē) *n.* —**sim'i•lar•ly,** *adv.*

sim'i•le' (-ə lē) *n.* a phrase comparing two things using "like" or "as."

si•mil'i•tude' (si mil'i tōōd', -tyōōd') *n.* likeness; resemblance.

sim'mer (sim'ər) *v.i., v.t.* to remain or keep near the boiling point.

si'mo•ny (sī'mə nē) *n.* the buying or selling of ecclesiastical preferments.

sim•pa'ti•co' (sim pä'ti kō') *adj.* like-minded.

sim'per (sim'pər) *v.i.* **1.** to smile in a silly way. —*n.* **2.** such a smile.

sim'ple (sim'pəl) *adj.,* **-pler, -plest. 1.** not difficult; easy. **2.** not complicated; plain. **3.** mentally weak. —**sim•plic'i•ty** (-plis'i tē) *n.*

sim'ple in'terest *n.* interest payable only on the principal.

sim'ple•ton (-tən) *n.* a fool.

sim'pli•fy' (-plə fī') *v.t.,* **-fied, -fying.** to make simpler.

sim•plis'tic (-plis'tik) *adj.* foolishly or naïvely simple.

sim'u•late' (sim'yə lāt') *v.t.,* **-lated, -lating.** to imitate the appearance or characteristics of.

si'mul•cast' (sī'məl kast') *n., v.,* **-cast, -casted, -casting.** —*n.* **1.** a program broadcast simultaneously on radio and television. —*v.t., v.i.* **2.** to broadcast (in) a simulcast.

si•mul•ta'ne•ous (-tā'nē əs) *adj.* occurring at the same time.

sin (sin) *n., v.,* **sinned, sinning.** —*n.* **1.** an offense against a religious or moral law. —*v.i.* **2.** to commit a sin. —**sin'ner,** *n.* —**sin'ful,** *adj.*

since (sins) *prep.* **1.** continuously from. **2.** in the period after. —*conj.* **3.** from the time when. **4.** because. —*adv.* **5.** from then till now. **6.** subsequently.

si•ncere' (sin sēr') *adj.,* **-cerer, -cerest. 1.** honest. **2.** genuine. —**sin•cer'i•ty** (-ser'i tē) *n.* —**sin•cere'ly,** *adv.*

si'ne•cure' (sī'ni kyŏŏr') *n.* a well-paying job requiring little work.

si'ne di'e (sī'nē dī'ē) without fixing a day for future action.

si'ne qua non' (sī' nē kwä nōn') *n.* an indispensable condition.

sin'ew (sin'yōō) *n.* **1.** a tendon. **2.** strength. —**sin'ew•y,** *adj.*

sing (sing) *v.,* **sang** (sang) or **sung** (sung) **sung, singing.** —*v.i.* **1.** to

use the voice to make musical sounds. **2.** to make a whistling or humming sound. **3.** to perform (a song). **4.** to proclaim in song. —**sing'er,** *n.*

singe (sinj) *v.t.,* **singed, singeing,** *n.* —*v.t.* **1.** to burn superficially. —*n.* **2.** singeing.

sin'gle (sing'gəl) *adj., v.,* **-gled, -gling,** *n.* —*adj.* **1.** one only. **2.** intended for one person. **3.** unmarried. —*v.t.* **4.** to select (one) from others. —*n.* **5.** a single thing. **6.** an unmarried person.

sin'gle file' *n.* a line of persons or things one behind the other.

sin'gle-hand'ed *adj.* **1.** by one's own effort; unaided. —*adv.* **2.** by one person alone.

sin'gle-mind'ed *adj.* having or showing a single aim or purpose.

sin'gly *adv.* **1.** separately. **2.** one at a time. **3.** single-handed.

sing'song' *n.* a monotonous, rhythmical rise and fall of the voice.

sin'gu•lar (sing'gyə lər) *adj.* **1.** extraordinary. **2.** strange. **3.** of the grammatical category denoting one person or thing. —*n.* **4.** the singular number or form.

sin'is•ter (sin'ə stər) *adj.* threatening evil.

sink (singk) *v.,* **sank** (sangk) or **sunk** (sungk), **sunk** or **sunken, sinking,** *n.* —*v.i.* **1.** to fall, drop, or descend to a lower level or state. **2.** to fail in health. **3.** to decrease in amount or intensity. —*v.t.* **4.** to cause to sink. **5.** to dig, as a shaft. —*n.* **6.** a basin connected with a water supply and a drain.

sink'hole' *n.* a hole in rock through which surface water drains into an underground passage.

sink'ing fund' *n.* a fund for paying off a debt.

sin'u•ous (sin'yōō əs) *adj.* winding.

si'nus (sī'nəs) *n.* one of the cavities in the skull connecting with the nasal cavities.

sip (sip) *v.,* **sipped, sipping,** *n.* —*v.t., v.i.* **1.** to drink a little at a time. —*n.* **2.** an act of sipping. **3.** the amount taken in a sip.

si'phon (sī'fən) *n.* **1.** a tube for drawing liquids by gravity and suction to another container. —*v.t., v.i.* **2.** to draw or pass through a siphon.

sir (sûr) *n.* **1.** a formal term of address for a man. **2. Sir,** the title of a knight or baronet.

sire (sīər) *n., v.,* **sired, siring.** —*n.* **1.** a male parent. —*v.t.* **2.** to beget.

si'ren (sī'rən) *n.* **1.** a noise-making device used on emergency vehicles. **2.** a mythical creature whose seductive singing lured sailors to destruction. **3.** a seductively beautiful woman.

sir'loin' (sûr'loin) *n.* a cut of beef from the loin.

si•roc'co (sə rok'ō) *n., pl.* **-cos.** a hot, dusty wind from N Africa.

si'sal (sī'səl, sis'əl) *n.* a fiber used in making ropes.

sis'sy (sis'ē) *n., pl.* **-sies.** a weak or timid person.

sis'ter (sis'tər) *n.* **1.** a female child of the same parents as another person. **2.** a woman connected, as by race, to another. **3.** a female member of a religious order. —*adj.* **4.** being in close relationship with another. —**sis'ter•ly,** *adj.*

sis'ter-in-law' *n., pl.* **sisters-in-law. 1.** the sister of one's spouse. **2.** the wife of one's brother.

sit (sit) *v.,* **sat** (sat) **sitting.** —*v.i.* **1.** to rest with the body supported on the buttocks. **2.** to be located. **3.** to pose, as for an artist. **4.** to be in session. **5.** (of a bird) to cover eggs for hatching. —*v.t.* **6.** to cause to sit. **7. sit in on,** to be an observer at. **8. ~ out,** to fail to take part in.

si•tar' (si tär') *n.* an Indian lute.

site (sīt) *n.* a position or location.

sit'-in' *n.* a protest by demonstrators who occupy and refuse to leave a place.

sit'ting duck' *n.* an easy target or victim.

sit'u•ate' (sich'ōō āt') *v.t.,* **-ated, -ating.** to locate.

sit'u•a'tion (-ā'shən) *n.* **1.** location. **2.** circumstances. **3.** a job.

sitz' bath' (sits) *n.* a bath in which only the thighs and hips are immersed.

six (siks) *n., adj.* five plus one. —**sixth,** *adj., n.*

six'teen' *n., adj.* ten plus six. —**six•teenth',** *adj., n.*

sixth' sense' *n.* intuition.

six'ty *n., adj.* ten times six. —**six'ti•eth,** *adj., n.*

siz·a·ble (sī′zə bəl) *adj.* fairly large. Also, **size′a·ble.**

size[1] (sīz) *n., v.,* **sized, sizing.** —*n.* **1.** dimensions, magnitude, or extent. **2.** one of a series of standard measures for manufactured articles. —*v.t.* **3.** to sort according to size. **4. size up,** to judge.

size[2] (sīz) *n., v.,* **sized, sizing.** Also, **sizing.** *n.* a gluey coating for paper, cloth, etc. —*v.t.* **2.** to coat with size.

siz′zle (siz′əl) *v.,* **-zled, -zling.** —*v.i.* **1.** to make a hissing sound, as in frying. —*n.* **2.** a sizzling sound.

skate[1] (skāt) *n., pl.* **skates,** *v.,* **skated, skating.** —*n.* **1.** an ice skate. **2.** a roller skate. —*v.i.* **3.** to glide on skates. —**skat′er,** *n.*

skate[2] (skāt) *n., pl.* **skates, skate.** a flat-bodied marine fish; ray.

skate′board′ *n.* an oblong board on roller-skate wheels.

ske·dad′dle (ski dad′l) *v.i.,* **-dled, -dling.** *Informal.* to run away quickly.

skeet (skēt) *n.* the sport of shooting at clay targets hurled to simulate the flight of game birds.

skein (skān) *n.* a coil of yarn.

skel′e·ton (skel′i tn) *n.* the bones that form the body's framework. —**skel′e·tal,** *adj.*

skel′eton key′ *n.* a key that opens various simple locks.

skep′tic (skep′tik) *n.* a person who doubts or questions. —**skep′ti·cal,** *adj.* —**skep′ti·cism** (-siz′əm) *n.*

sketch (skech) *n.* **1.** a simple hasty drawing. **2.** a rough plan. —*v.i., v.t.* **3.** to make a sketch (of).

sketch′y *adj.,* **-ier, -iest.** vague; approximate. —**sketch′i·ly,** *adv.*

skew (skyōō) *v.i., v.t.* to turn aside.

skew′er *n.* **1.** a pin for holding together pieces of meat while cooking. —*v.t.* **2.** to fasten with or as if with a skewer.

ski (skē) *n.* **1.** one of a pair of slender runners for gliding over snow. —*v.i., v.t.* **2.** to travel on skis (over).

skid (skid) *n., v.,* **skidded, skidding.** —*n.* **1.** an uncontrollable sideways slide on a surface. **2.** a surface on which to slide a heavy object. —*v.i.* **3.** to slip or slide sideways.

skid′ row′ (rō) *n.* a run-down urban area frequented by vagrants.

skiff (skif) *n.* a small boat.

skill (skil) *n.* **1.** the ability to do something well. **2.** a craft or trade. —**skilled,** *adj.* —**skill′ful,** *adj.*

skil′let (skil′it) *n.* a frying pan.

skim (skim) *v.,* **skimmed, skimming.** —*v.t.* **1.** to remove (floating matter) from the surface of a liquid. **2.** to move lightly over. **3.** to read superficially. —*v.i.* **4.** to move lightly over a surface. **5.** to read something superficially.

skim′ milk′ *n.* milk with the cream removed.

skimp (skimp) *v.i., v.t.* to scrimp.

skimp′y *adj.,* **-ier, -iest.** lacking in size or fullness.

skin (skin) *n., v.,* **skinned, skinning.** —*n.* **1.** the outer covering of an animal body. **2.** an outer layer, as the rind of fruit. —*v.t.* **3.** to remove the skin of.

skin′ div′ing *n.* underwater swimming with flippers and a face mask and sometimes with scuba gear.

skin′flint′ *n.* a stingy person.

skin′ny *adj.,* **-nier, -niest.** very thin.

skin′ny-dip′ *v.i.,* **skinny-dipped, skinny-dipping.** *Informal.* to swim in the nude.

skip (skip) *v.,* **skipped, skipping,** *n.* —*v.i.* **1.** to spring; leap. —*v.t.* **2.** to omit. —*n.* **3.** a light jump.

skip′per *n.* the master of a ship.

skir′mish (skûr′mish) *n.* **1.** a brief fight between small forces. —*v.i.* **2.** to engage in a skirmish.

skirt (skûrt) *n.* **1.** the part of a dress or coat below the waist. **2.** a woman's garment extending down from the waist. —*v.t.* **3.** to lie or pass along the edge of. **4.** to avoid.

skit (skit) *n.* a short, usu. amusing play.

skit′ter (skit′ər) *v.i.* to go or glide rapidly.

skit′tish *adj.* **1.** easily frightened. **2.** frisky.

skiv′vy (skiv′ē) *n., pl.* **-vies. 1.** a man's cotton T-shirt. **2. skivvies,** men's underwear consisting of a T-shirt and shorts.

skul·dug′ger·y (skul dug′ə rē) *n.* dishonorable or deceitful behavior.

skulk (skulk) *v.i.* to sneak about.

skull (skul) *n.* the bony framework of the head.

skull′cap′ *n.* a small, brimless, close-fitting cap.

skunk (skungk) *n.* **1.** a small mammal with black-and-white fur that sprays a bad-smelling fluid as defense. **2.** a contemptible person.

sky (skī) *n., pl.* **skies.** the upper atmosphere of the earth.

sky′cap′ *n.* an airport porter.

sky′jack′ *v.t.* to hijack (an airliner).

sky′light′ *n.* a window in a roof.

sky′line′ *n.* an outline of buildings against the sky.

sky′rock′et *n.* **1.** a firework that rises into the air before exploding. —*v.i., v.t.* **2.** to rise or cause to rise rapidly.

sky′scrap′er *n.* a building with many stories.

sky′writ′ing *n.* writing in the sky by smoke released from an airplane.

slab (slab) *n.* a broad, flat, thick piece of material.

slack (slak) *adj.* **1.** loose. **2.** careless. **3.** slow or sluggish. **4.** inactive. —*n.* **5.** a slack condition. **6.** an inactive period. —*v.t., v.i.* **7.** to slacken. —**slack′ly,** *adv.*

slack′en *v.t., v.i.* to make or become slack.

slack′er *n.* one who evades work.

slacks *n.pl.* trousers for casual wear.

slag (slag) *n.* refuse matter separated during the smelting of a metal from its ore.

slake (slāk) *v.t.,* **slaked, slaking.** to quench (thirst, desire, etc.).

sla′lom (slä′ləm) *n.* a downhill ski race over a winding, zigzag course.

slam (slam) *v., n.,* **slammed, slamming,** *n.* —*v.t., v.i.* **1.** to shut forcefully and noisily. —*n.* **2.** the act or sound of slamming.

slam′ dunk′ *n.* a forceful, often dramatic dunk shot in basketball.

slam′mer *n. Slang.* a prison.

slan′der (slan′dər) *n.* **1.** a false, malicious statement that damages a person's reputation. —*v.t.* **2.** to utter slander against.

slang (slang) *n.* very informal, colorful language. —**slang′y,** *adj.*

slant (slant) *v.i.* **1.** to slope. —*v.t.* **2.** to cause to slant. **3.** to present (news) with a particular point of view. —*n.* **4.** a slope. **5.** a particular point of view.

slap (slap) *v., n.,* **slapped, slapping,** *n.* —*v.t.* **1.** to strike sharply with the open hand. —*n.* **2.** a blow.

slap′dash′ *adj.* hasty and careless.

slap′hap′py *adj.,* **-pier, -piest. 1.** befuddled. **2.** agreeably foolish.

slap′stick′ *n.* boisterous comedy with broad farce and horseplay.

slash (slash) *v.t.* **1.** to cut violently. **2.** to reduce sharply. —*n.* **3.** a violent sweeping stroke or cut. **4.** a stroke (/) used as a dividing line.

slat (slat) *n.* a thin narrow strip of wood or metal.

slate (slāt) *n., v.,* **slated, slating.** —*n.* **1.** a kind of rock that splits horizontally. **2.** a thin piece of slate. **3.** a list of candidates. —*v.t.* **4.** to cover with slates.

slath′er (slath′ər) *v.t.* to spread (on) thickly.

slat′tern (slat′ərn) *n.* an untidy woman. —**slat′tern·ly,** *adj.*

slaugh′ter (slô′tər) *n.* **1.** the killing of animals, esp. for food. **2.** the brutal killing of people, esp. in great numbers. —*v.t.* **3.** to butcher for food. **4.** to massacre.

Slav (släv, slav) *n.* a member of a Slavic-speaking people.

slave (slāv) *n., v.,* **slaved, slaving.** —*n.* **1.** a person owned by another. **2.** a person under the domination of another. —*v.i.* **3.** to work like a slave. —**slav′er·y,** *n.*

slav′er (sla′vər) *v.i.* to drool.

Slav′ic (slä′vik, slav′ik) *n.* **1.** the Indo-European language family that includes Russian, Polish, Czech, etc. —*adj.* **2.** of these languages or their speakers.

slav′ish (slā′vish) *adj.* **1.** of or resembling a slave. **2.** deliberately imitating.

slay (slā) *v.t.,* **slew** (slōō) **slain, slaying.** to kill. —**slay′er,** *n.*

slea′zy (slē′zē) *adj.,* **-zier, -ziest.** disreputable or squalid.

sled (sled) *n., v.,* **sledded, sledding.** —*n.* **1.** a platform on runners for gliding over snow. —*v.i.* **2.** to ride on or transport by sled.

sledge (slej) *n.* **1.** a heavy sledlike vehicle. **2.** Also, **sledge′ham′mer.** a large heavy hammer.

sleek (slēk) *adj.* **1.** smooth and glossy. **2.** streamlined. —*v.t.* **3.** to make sleek. —**sleek′ly,** *adv.*

sleep (slēp) *v.,* **slept** (slept) **sleeping,** *n.* —*v.i.* **1.** to rest during the natural suspension of consciousness. —*n.* **2.** the state or period of sleeping. —**sleep′less,** *adj.* —**sleep′y,** *adj.*

sleep′er *n.* **1.** a person who sleeps. **2.** a railroad car equipped for sleeping. **3.** an unexpected success.

sleep′ing bag′ *n.* a warmly lined bag in which a person can sleep.

sleep′ing car′ *n.* a railroad car with sleeping accommodations.

sleep′ing sick′ness *n.* an infectious disease of Africa, characterized by wasting and lethargy.

sleep′walk′ing *n.* the act of walking while asleep. —**sleep′walk′,** *v.i.* —**sleep′walk′er,** *n.*

sleet (slēt) *n.* **1.** rain that freezes as it falls. —*v.i.* **2.** to fall as sleet.

sleeve (slēv) *n.* **1.** the part of a garment covering the arm. **2.** a tubular piece fitting over another part. —**sleeve′less,** *adj.*

sleigh (slā) *n.* a horse-drawn vehicle on runners, used for traveling over snow.

sleight′ of hand′ (slīt) *n.* skill in conjuring or juggling.

slen′der (slen′dər) *adj.* **1.** thin. **2.** not adequate.

sleuth (slōōth) *n.* a detective.

slew (slōō) *v.* pt. of **slay.**

slice (slīs) *n., v.,* **sliced, slicing.** —*n.* **1.** a thin, flat piece cut from something. —*v.t.* **2.** to cut into slices. —**slic′er,** *n.*

slick (slik) *adj.* **1.** slippery. **2.** sly. **3.** clever. —*n.* **4.** an oil-covered area. **5.** a slippery place. —*v.t.* **6.** to make sleek or smooth.

slick′er *n.* a loose oilskin raincoat.

slide (slīd) *v.,* **slid, sliding,** —*v.t.* **1.** to move or cause to move easily. —*n.* **2.** an act of sliding. **3.** a smooth surface for sliding. **4.** a glass plate used to examine objects with a microscope. **5.** a transparent picture, mounted for projection on a screen.

slid′ing scale′ *n.* a scale, as of prices, that varies with such conditions as ability to pay.

slight (slīt) *adj.* **1.** trifling; small. **2.** slim. —*v.t.* **3.** to treat as unimportant. —*n.* **4.** such treatment; a snub.

slight′ly *adv.* barely; partly.

slim (slim) *adj.,* **slimmer, slimmest. 1.** slender. **2.** scanty. —*v.t., v.i.* **3.** to make or become slim. —**slim′ness,** *n.*

slime (slīm) *n.* **1.** thin sticky mud. **2.** a sticky secretion. —**slim′y,** *adj.*

sling (sling) *n., v.,* **slung** (slung) **slinging.** —*n.* **1.** a looped rope, bandage, etc., used to support or carry something. **2.** a straplike device for hurling stones. —*v.t.* **3.** to throw. **4.** to place in or move by a sling.

sling′shot′ *n.* a Y-shaped stick with an elastic strip between two prongs, for shooting small missiles.

slink (slingk) *v.i.,* **slunk** (slungk) **slinking.** to go furtively. —**slink′y,** *adj.*

slip (slip) *v.,* **slipped, slipping,** *n.* —*v.i.* **1.** to move easily. **2.** to slide suddenly and accidentally. **3.** to make a mistake. **4.** to decline in quality. —*v.t.* **5.** to cause to move smoothly. **6.** to put, pass, or insert quickly or stealthily. **7.** to escape (the memory). —*n.* **8.** a slipping. **9.** a mistake. **10.** a woman's garment worn under a dress. **11.** a space for a ship in a dock.

slip′cov′er *n.* an easily removable cloth cover for a piece of furniture.

slip′knot′ *n.* a knot that slips easily along a cord.

slipped′ disk′ *n.* an abnormal protrusion of a spinal disk between vertebrae.

slip′per *n.* a light shoe.

slip′per·y *adj.* **1.** causing slipping. **2.** tending to slip.

slip′shod′ (-shod′) *adj.* careless.

slip′-up′ *n.* a mistake.

slit (slit) *v.,* **slit, slitting,** *n.* —*v.t.* **1.** to make a long cut in. —*n.* **2.** a narrow cut or opening.

slith′er (slith′ər) *v.i.* to slide.

sliv′er (sliv′ər) *n.* **1.** a small, thin piece. —*v.t., v.i.* **2.** to cut into slivers.

slob (slob) *n.* a slovenly person.

slob′ber *v.i.* **1.** to let saliva dribble from the mouth. **2.** saliva dribbling from the mouth.

sloe (slō) *n.* the small sour fruit of the blackthorn.

sloe′-eyed′ *adj.* **1.** having very dark eyes. **2.** having slanted eyes.

slog (slog) *v.i.,* **slogged, slogging. 1.** to plod heavily. **2.** to work hard.

slo′gan (slō′gən) *n.* a motto.

sloop (slōōp) *n.* a single-masted sailboat.

slop (slop) *v.,* **slopped, slopping,** *n.* —*v.t., v.i.* **1.** to spill or splash (liquid). —*n.* **2.** kitchen waste fed to swine. **3.** unappetizing food or drink.

slope (slōp) *v.,* **sloped, sloping,** —*v.i., v.t.* **1.** to incline or cause to incline; slant. —*n.* **2.** a sloping surface. **3.** the amount by which a thing slopes.

slop′py *adj.,* **-pier, -piest. 1.** untidy. **2.** careless. —**slop′pi·ly,** *adv.*

slosh (slosh) *v.i.* **1.** to splash through water, mud, etc. **2.** (of a liquid) to move noisily within a container.

slot (slot) *n.* **1.** a long, narrow opening. **2.** a place in a series.

sloth (slôth) *n.* **1.** laziness. **2.** a slow-moving South American mammal. —**sloth′ful,** *adj.*

slot′ machine′ *n.* a gambling machine.

slouch (slouch) *v.i.* **1.** to sit, stand, or walk with a drooping posture. —*n.* **2.** a drooping posture or gait. —**slouch′y,** *adj.*

slough[1] (slou) *n.* **1.** a muddy area or swamp. **2.** a state of despair.

slough[2] (sluf) *v.t.* to shed.

slov′en (sluv′ən) *n.* an untidy or careless person.

slov′en·ly *adj.,* **-lier, -liest. 1.** untidy or unclean. **2.** slipshod; negligent. —**slov′en·li·ness,** *n.*

slow (slō) *adj.* **1.** not fast or quick. **2.** not intelligent or perceptive. **3.** running behind time. —*adv.* **4.** in a slow manner. —*v.t., v.i.* **5.** to make or become slow.

slow′ burn′ *n. Informal.* a gradual building up of anger.

slow′down′ *n.* a slackening of pace or speed.

slow′ mo′tion *n.* the process of projecting a film or television sequence so that action appears to be slowed down.

slow′poke′ *n. Informal.* a person who moves, works, or acts very slowly.

slow′-wit′ted *adj.* slow to understand.

sludge (sluj) *n.* mud, mire, or ooze.

slue (slōō) *v.i., v.t.,* **slued, sluing.** to turn around.

slug[1] (slug) *n.* **1.** a slimy, crawling mollusk having no shell. **2.** a bullet. **3.** a metal disk used as a coin or token.

slug[2] (slug) *v.,* **slugged, slugging,** *n.* —*v.t.* **1.** to hit hard, esp. with the fist. —*n.* **2.** a hard blow, esp. with the fist. —**slug′ger,** *n.*

slug′gard (slug′ərd) *n.* a lazy person.

slug′gish *adj.* inactive; slow.

sluice (slōōs) *n., v.,* **sluiced, sluicing.** —*n.* **1.** a channel with a gate to control the flow of water. —*v.t.* **2.** to cleanse with flowing water.

slum (slum) *n.* a squalid, crowded residence or neighborhood.

slum′ber (slum′bər) *v.i.* **1.** to sleep. —*n.* **2.** a sleep.

slum′lord′ *n.* a landlord of slum dwellings who charges exorbitant rents.

slump (slump) *v.i.* **1.** to drop heavily or suddenly. —*n.* **2.** a slumping.

slur[1] (slûr) *v.,* **slurred, slurring,** —*v.t.* **1.** to pronounce indistinctly. **2.** to sing or play (two notes) without a break. —*n.* **3.** a slurred sound.

slur[2] (slûr) *n.* a disparaging remark.

slurp (slûrp) *v.t., v.i.* **1.** to eat or drink with loud sucking noises. —*n.* **2.** a slurping sound.

slush (slush) *n.* partly melted snow.

slush′ fund′ *n.* money used for illicit political purposes.

slut (slut) *n.* a slovenly or immoral woman.

sly (slī) *adj.,* **slyer, slyest** or **slier, sli-est. 1.** cunning. **2.** stealthy.

smack[1] (smak) *v.t.* **1.** to open and close (the lips) noisily. **2.** to strike or kiss loudly. —*n.* **3.** a loud slap or kiss. **4.** a smacking of the lips. —*adv.* **5.** directly.

smack[2] (smak) *n.* **1.** a slight flavor. **2.** a trace. —*v.i.* **3.** to have a slight flavor or trace.

smack[3] (smak) *n.* a small fishing boat.

small (smôl) *adj.* **1.** not big; little. **2.** not very important. **3.** mean-spirited. —*adv.* **4.** in a small way. **5.** in small pieces. —*n.* **6.** a small or narrow part, as of the back.

small′ fry′ *n.pl.* **1.** young children. **2.** unimportant people.

small′-mind′ed *adj.* petty or selfish.

small′pox′ *n.* a contagious disease marked by fever and pustules.

small′-scale′ *adj.* **1.** of limited scope. **2.** being a small version of an original.

small′ talk′ *n.* light conversation.

small′-time′ *adj.* not important.

smarm′y (smär′mē) *adj.,* **-ier, -iest.** excessively flattering or servile.

smart (smärt) *v.i.* **1.** to cause or feel a sharp stinging pain. —*adj.* **2.** clever; intelligent. **3.** sharp. **4.** stylish. —*n.* **5.** a sharp local pain.

smart al′eck (al′ik) *n. Informal.* an obnoxiously conceited and impertinent person. Also, **smart al′ec.**

smart′ bomb′ *n.* an air-to-surface missile guided by a laser beam.

smart′en *v.t., v.i.* **1.** to improve in appearance.

smash (smash) *v.t., v.i.* **1.** to break into pieces violently. **2.** to hit, collide, or strike with force. **3.** to destroy or be destroyed. —*n.* **4.** the act or sound of smashing. **5.** a collision or crash. **6.** ruin. **7.** *Informal.* a great success.

smat′ter·ing (smat′ər ing) *n.* slight knowledge.

smear (smēr) *v.t.* **1.** to spread or apply (an oily or dirty substance). **2.** to slander. —*n.* **3.** a stain or spot. **4.** a slanderous attack.

smell (smel) *v.,* **smelled** or **smelt, smelling,** —*v.t.* **1.** to perceive the odor of with the nose. —*v.i.* **2.** to have an odor. —*n.* **3.** the faculty of smelling. **4.** odor. —**smell′y,** *adj.*

smelt[1] (smelt) *v.t.* **1.** to melt (ore) in order to separate the metal. **2.** to refine (metal) by smelting.

smelt[2] (smelt) *n., pl.* **smelts, smelt.** a small, silvery food fish.

smid′gen (smij′ən) *n.* a very small amount.

smi′lax (smī′laks) *n.* a delicate twining plant.

smile (smīl) *v.,* **smiled, smiling,** *n.* —*v.i.* **1.** to look pleased, amused, etc. —*n.* **2.** a smiling facial expression.

smirk (smûrk) *v.i.* **1.** to smile smugly, affectedly, or offensively. —*n.* **2.** such a smile.

smite (smīt) *v.t.,* **smote** (smōt) **smitten** (smit′n) or **smote, smiting. 1.** to strike hard. **2.** to affect strongly.

smith (smith) *n.* a worker in metal.

smith′er·eens′ (smith′ə rēnz′) *n.pl.* small pieces.

smith′y (smith′ē, smith′ē) *n., pl.* **-ies.** a blacksmith's shop.

smit′ten (smit′n) *adj.* infatuated.

smock (smok) *n.* a long, loose garment worn to protect the clothing while working.

smog (smog) *n.* smoke and fog.

smoke (smōk) *n., v.,* **smoked, smoking.** —*n.* **1.** the visible vapor and gases from a burning substance. —*v.i.* **2.** to give off smoke. **3.** to inhale and puff out tobacco smoke. —*v.t.* **4.** to inhale and puff out the smoke of. **5.** to cure (meat, fish, etc.) by exposure to smoke. —**smok′er,** *n.* —**smoke′less,** *adj.* —**smok′y,** *adj.*

smoke′ detec′tor *n.* an alarm activated by the presence of smoke.

smoke′house′ *n.* a building in which meat or fish is cured with smoke.

smoke′ screen′ *n.* **1.** a mass of dense smoke for concealment. **2.** something intended to deceive.

smoke′stack′ *n.* a pipe for the escape of smoke, gases, etc.

smol′der (smōl′dər) *v.i.* **1.** to burn without flame. **2.** to exist in a suppressed state. Also, **smoul′der.**

smooch (smōōch) *Informal.* —*v.i.* **1.** to kiss. —*n.* **2.** a kiss.

smooth (smōōth) *adj.* **1.** having an even surface; not rough. **2.** not lumpy. **3.** moving or flowing freely. **4.** tranquil. —*v.t.* **5.** to make smooth.

smooth′bore′ *adj.* (of a gun) not rifled.

smor′gas·bord′ (smôr′gəs bôrd′; *often* shmôr′-) *n.* a buffet meal of assorted foods.

smoth′er (smuth′ər) *v.t.* **1.** to suffocate or stifle. **2.** to cover closely. **3.** to suppress.

smudge (smuj) *n., v.,* **smudged, smudging.** —*n.* **1.** a dirty mark or smear. —*v.t., v.i.* **2.** to make or become smudged.

smug (smug) *adj.* self-satisfied; complacent.

smug′gle *v.t.,* **-gled, -gling. 1.** to import or export secretly and illegally. **2.** to bring or take secretly.

smut (smut) *n.* **1.** soot. **2.** a dirty mark. **3.** obscenity. **4.** a fungous disease of plants. —**smut′ty,** *adj.*

snack (snak) *n.* **1.** a light meal. —*v.i.* **2.** to eat a snack.

snaf•fle (snaf′əl) *n.* a horse's bit without a curb.

snag (snag) *n.,* *v.,* **snagged, snagging.** —*n.* **1.** a sharp projection. **2.** an obstacle. **3.** a tear or pull in a fabric. —*v.t.* **4.** to catch on a snag.

snail (snāl) *n.* a slow-moving, spiral-shelled mollusk.

snail′ mail′ *n.* physical delivery of mail, as contrasted with e-mail.

snake (snāk) *n.,* *v.,* **snaked, snaking.** —*n.* **1.** a long, limbless, scaly reptile. —*v.i.* **2.** to wind like a snake.

snap (snap) *v.,* **snapped, snapping,** *n.,* *adj.* —*v.i.,* *v.t.* **1.** to make or cause to make a sudden sharp sound. **2.** to break abruptly. **3.** to grasp with a quick bite. **4.** to say or speak quickly and sharply. **5.** to take a snapshot (of). —*n.* **6.** a snapping sound. **7.** a kind of fastener. **8.** *Informal.* an easy task. —*adj.* **9.** made or done suddenly.

snap′drag•on *n.* a plant with spikes of two-lipped flowers.

snap′pish *adj.* cross or irritable.

snap′py *adj.,* **-pier, -piest.** *Informal.* **1.** quick. **2.** smart; stylish.

snap′shot′ *n.* an unposed photograph.

snare (snâr) *n.,* *v.,* **snared, snaring.** —*n.* **1.** a trap with a noose. —*v.t.* **2.** to trap with a snare.

snarl[1] (snärl) *v.i.* **1.** to growl. —*n.* **2.** an act or sound of snarling.

snarl[2] (snärl) *n.* **1.** a tangle, as of thread. —*v.i.,* *v.t.* **2.** to become or cause to become tangled.

snatch (snach) *v.t.* **1.** to grab suddenly. —*n.* **2.** a grabbing motion. **3.** a bit or fragment.

sneak (snēk) *v.i.,* *v.t.* **1.** to go, act, or take furtively. —*n.* **2.** a person who sneaks.

sneak′er *n.* a rubber-soled shoe.

sneak′ pre′view *n.* a preview of a motion picture, often shown in addition to an announced film.

sneer (snēr) *v.i.* **1.** to smile or laugh contemptuously. —*n.* **2.** a contemptuous look.

sneeze (snēz) *v.,* **sneezed, sneezing,** *n.* —*v.i.* **1.** to expel the breath suddenly and audibly through the nose. —*n.* **2.** an act of sneezing.

snick′er (snik′ər) *v.i.* **1.** to laugh in a half-suppressed or disrespectful manner. —*n.* **2.** a snickering laugh.

snide (snīd) *adj.,* **snider, snidest.** derogatory in a nasty, insinuating way.

sniff (snif) *v.i.,* *v.t.* **1.** to inhale quickly and audibly. **2.** to draw in by sniffing. —*n.* **3.** the act or sound of sniffing.

snif′ter (snif′tər) *n.* a pear-shaped glass for brandy.

snip (snip) *v.,* **snipped, snipping,** *n.* —*v.i.,* *v.t.* **1.** to cut with small, quick strokes. —*n.* **2.** a small piece cut off. **3.** the act of snipping.

snipe (snīp) *n.,* *v.,* **sniped, sniping.** —*n.* **1.** a long-billed sandpiper. —*v.i.* **2.** to shoot from a hidden position. **3.** to make snide remarks. —**snip′er,** *n.*

snip′pet (snip′it) *n.* a small bit, scrap, or fragment.

snip′py *adj.,* **-pier, -piest.** sharp or curt, esp. in a haughty way.

snit (snit) *n.* an agitated state.

snitch[1] (snich) *v.t. Informal.* to steal; pilfer.

snitch[2] (snich) *Informal.* —*v.i.* **1.** to turn informer; tattle. —*n.* **2.** an informer.

sniv•el (sniv′əl) *v.i.* **1.** to weep weakly. **2.** to have a runny nose.

snob (snob) *n.* a person overconcerned with position, wealth, etc. —**snob′bish,** *adj.* —**snob′ber•y,** *n.*

snoop (snōōp) *Informal.* —*v.i.* **1.** to prowl or pry. —*n.* **2.** Also, **snoop′er.** a person who snoops.

snoot′y (snōō′tē) *adj.,* **-ier, -iest.** *Informal.* snobbish; condescending.

snooze (snōōz) *v.,* **snoozed, snoozing,** *n.* —*v.i.* **1.** to sleep for a short time. —*n.* **2.** a short sleep.

snore (snôr) *v.,* **snored, snoring,** *n.* —*v.i.* **1.** to breathe with hoarse or harsh sounds in sleep. —*n.* **2.** an act or sound of snoring.

snor′kel (snôr′kəl) *n.* **1.** a tube through which a swimmer can breathe while underwater. —*v.i.* **2.** to swim while using a snorkel.

snort (snôrt) *v.i.* **1.** to exhale loudly and harshly. **2.** to express contempt by snorting. —*n.* **3.** an act or sound of snorting.

snot (snot) *n.* **1.** *Vulgar.* nasal mucus. **2.** *Informal.* an impudently disagreeable young person. —**snot′ty,** *adj.*

snout (snout) *n.* the projecting nose and jaw of an animal.

snow (snō) *n.* **1.** white crystalline ice flakes that fall to earth. —*v.i.,* *v.t.* **2.** to fall or let fall as or like snow. —**snow′y,** *adj.* —**snow′storm,** *n.*

snow′ball′ *n.* **1.** a ball of snow. —*v.i.,* *v.t.* **2.** to increase or cause to increase rapidly.

snow′board′ *n.* a board for gliding on snow, resembling a wide ski ridden in a standing position.

snow′drift′ *n.* a mound or bank of snow driven together by the wind.

snow′drop′ *n.* an early-blooming plant with white flowers.

snow′fall′ *n.* **1.** a fall of snow. **2.** the amount of snow at a particular place or in a given time.

snow′flake′ *n.* a small crystal or flake of snow.

snow′man′ *n.* a figure of a person made of packed snow.

snow′mo•bile′ (-mə bēl′) *n.* a motor vehicle for travel on snow.

snow′shoe′ *n.* a racketlike shoe for walking on snow.

snow′suit′ *n.* a child's warmly insulated outer garment.

snow′ tire′ *n.* a tire with a deep tread for increased traction on snow.

snub (snub) *v.,* **snubbed, snubbing,** *n.* —*v.t.* **1.** to treat with scorn. —*n.* **2.** an affront or slight.

snuff[1] (snuf) *v.t.,* *v.i.* **1.** to inhale noisily. **2.** to smell. —*n.* **3.** powdered tobacco that is inhaled.

snuff[2] (snuf) *v.t.* to extinguish (a candle).

snuf•fle *v.,* **-fled, -fling,** *n.* —*v.i.* **1.** to sniff or snuff. —*n.* **2.** an act or sound of snuffling.

snug (snug) *adj.,* **snugger, snuggest.** **1.** cozy. **2.** trim; neat.

snug′gle *v.i.,* *v.t.,* **-gled, -gling.** to nestle or cuddle.

so (sō) *adv.* **1.** in this or that way. **2.** to such a degree. **3.** as stated. —*conj.* **4.** with the result that. **5.** in order that.

soak (sōk) *v.i.* **1.** to lie in a liquid and become thoroughly wet. —*v.t.* **2.** to wet thoroughly. **3.** to absorb.

so′-and-so′ *n.,* *pl.* **so-and-sos.** a person or thing not definitely named.

soap (sōp) *n.* **1.** a substance used for washing. —*v.t.* **2.** to rub with soap.

soap′box′ *n.* an improvised platform on which a speaker stands.

soap′stone′ *n.* a variety of talc.

soar (sôr) *v.i.* to fly upward.

sob (sob) *v.,* **sobbed, sobbing,** *n.* —*v.i.,* *v.t.* **1.** to weep with uneven catching of the breath. —*n.* **2.** an act or sound of sobbing.

so′ber (sō′bər) *adj.* **1.** not drunk. **2.** serious. **3.** restrained. —*v.t.,* *v.i.* **4.** to make or become sober. —**so•bri′e•ty,** *n.*

so′bri•quet′ (sō′bri kā′, -ket′) *n.* a nickname.

so′-called′ *adj.* called thus.

soc′cer (sok′ər) *n.* a form of football played by kicking a large, round ball.

so′cia•ble (sō′shə bəl) *adj.* friendly. —**so′cia•bil′i•ty,** *n.*

so′cial (sō′shəl) *adj.* **1.** of or marked by friendly relations. **2.** living with others in a community. **3.** of or based on status in a society. —**so′cial•ly,** *adv.*

so′cial•ism (-shə liz′əm) *n.* a theory or system of social organization based on government or community ownership of the means of production and distribution of goods. —**so′cial•ist,** *n.*

so′cial•ite′ (-shə līt′) *n.* a socially prominent person.

so′cial•ize′ *v.,* **-ized, -izing.** —*v.t.* **1.** to make fit for life in society. **2.** to establish according to the theories of socialism. —*v.i.* **3.** to mingle with others in a friendly way.

so′cial secu′rity *n.* (*often caps.*) a federal program of old age, unemployment, health, disability, and survivors' insurance.

so′cial work′ *n.* services or activities designed to improve social conditions among poor, sick, or troubled persons.

so•ci′e•ty (sə sī′i tē) *n.,* *pl.* **-ties.** **1.** an organized group of people living together. **2.** a group of persons united by common interests. **3.** companionship; company. **4.** the class of fashionable people.

Soci′ety of Friends′ *n.* a Christian sect founded in England that is opposed to oath-taking and war.

so•ci•o•ec•o•nom′ic (sō′sē ō-, sō′shē ō-) *adj.* pertaining to a combi-

nation of social and economic factors.

so•ci•ol′o•gy (sō′sē ol′ə jē, sō′shē-) *n.* the study of human social relations and institutions. —**so•ci•ol′o•gist,** *n.*

sock[1] *n.* a short stocking.

sock[2] (sok) *v.t.* to hit hard.

sock′et (sok′it) *n.* a hollow part for holding another part.

sod (sod) *n.* grass with its roots.

so′da (sō′də) *n.* **1.** a carbonated, flavored sweet soft drink. **2.** a drink made with soda water, flavored syrup, and ice cream. **3.** a preparation containing sodium.

so′da crack′er *n.* a crisp cracker.

so′da foun′tain *n.* a counter at which ice cream, sodas, etc., are served.

so•dal′i•ty (-dal′i tē) *n.,* *pl.* **-ties.** an association.

so′da wa′ter *n.* water charged with carbon dioxide.

sod′den (sod′n) *adj.* soaked.

so′di•um (sō′dē əm) *n.* a soft, silver-white metallic element.

so′dium bicar′bonate *n.* baking soda.

so′dium chlo′ride *n.* salt.

sod′o•my (sod′ə mē) *n.* anal or oral copulation.

so′fa (sō′fə) *n.* a couch with a back and arms.

soft (sôft) *adj.* **1.** yielding readily to touch or pressure. **2.** not rough or harsh. **3.** gentle; pleasant. **4.** not hard. **5.** (of water) free from mineral salts. —**sof′ten,** *v.t.,* *v.i.*

soft′ball′ *n.* **1.** a form of baseball played with a larger, softer ball. **2.** the ball used.

soft′-boiled′ *adj.* (of an egg) boiled only until the yolk is partially set.

soft′ drink′ *n.* a nonalcoholic drink.

soft′-heart′ed *adj.* very sympathetic.

soft′ mon′ey *n.* money contributed to a political candidate or party that is not subject to federal regulations.

soft′-ped′al *v.t.,* **soft-pedaled, soft-pedaling.** to make less obvious; play down.

soft′ sell′ *n.* a quietly persuasive method of selling.

soft′ soap′ *n.* persuasive talk.

soft′ware′ *n.* programs for use with a computer.

sog′gy (sog′ē) *adj.,* **-gier, -giest.** **1.** soaked. **2.** damp and heavy.

soi•gné (swän yā′; *Fr.* swA nyā′) *adj.* elegant. Also, **soi•gnée′.**

soil[1] (soil) *n.* **1.** the loose surface layer of the earth. **2.** ground. **3.** dirt. **4.** a land.

soil[2] (soil) *v.t.,* *v.i.* to make or become dirty.

soi•rée′ (swä rā′) *n.* an evening party.

so′journ *v.i.* (sō′jûrn, sō jûrn′) **1.** to dwell briefly. —*n.* (sō′jûrn) **2.** a short stay.

sol′ace (sol′is) *n.,* *v.,* **-aced, -acing.** —*n.* **1.** comfort in sorrow. —*v.t.* **2.** to comfort.

so′lar (sō′lər) *adj.* of the sun.

so′lar cell′ *n.* a cell that converts sunlight into electricity.

so•lar′i•um (sə lâr′ē əm, sō-) *n.,* *pl.* **-iums, -ia** (-ē ə). a glass-enclosed room for enjoying sunlight.

so′lar plex′us *n.* a point on the stomach wall just below the sternum.

so′lar sys′tem *n.* the sun and all the celestial bodies revolving around it.

sol′der (sod′ər) *n.* **1.** an alloy that can be fused for joining metal. —*v.t.,* *v.i.* **2.** to join with solder.

sol′dier (sōl′jər) *n.* **1.** a person in military service. —*v.i.* **2.** to serve as a soldier.

sole[1] (sōl) *adj.* being the only one. —**sole′ly,** *adv.*

sole[2] (sōl) *n.,* *v.,* **soled, soling.** —*n.* **1.** the bottom of a foot or shoe. —*v.t.* **2.** to put a sole on (a shoe).

sole[3] (sōl) *n.* an edible marine flatfish.

sol′emn (sol′əm) *adj.* **1.** grave; serious. **2.** formal or ceremonious. —**so•lem′ni•ty** (sə lem′ni tē) *n.* —**sol′emn•ly,** *adv.*

sol′em•nize′ (-nīz′) *v.t.,* **-nized, -nizing.** **1.** to observe with formality. **2.** to perform the ceremony of (marriage).

so•lic′it (sə lis′it) *v.t.* **1.** to try to obtain by asking for. —*v.i.* **2.** to solicit something desired. —**so•lic′i•ta′tion,** *n.*

so•lic′i•tor (-i tər) *n.* **1.** a person who solicits. **2.** *Brit.* a lawyer.

so•lic′i•tous *adj.* anxious; concerned. —**so•lic′i•tude′,** *n.*

sol′id (sol′id) *adj.* **1.** having length, breadth, and thickness. **2.** not hollow. **3.** not liquid or gaseous. **4.** substantial. **5.** consisting entirely of one material. —*n.* **6.** a solid body or substance. —**so•lid′i•fy′,** *v.t.,* *v.i.* —**so•lid′i•ty,** *n.* —**sol′id•ly,** *adv.*

sol•i•dar′i•ty (-i dar′i tē) *n.* unity of attitude or purpose.

sol′id•ly *adv.* **1.** firmly. **2.** wholeheartedly; fully.

so•lil′o•quy (sə lil′ə kwē) *n.,* *pl.* **-quies.** **1.** a speech in a play in which a character speaks as if alone. **2.** the act of talking to oneself. —**so•lil′o•quize′,** *v.i.,* *v.t.*

sol′i•taire′ (sol′i târ′) *n.* **1.** a card game for one person. **2.** a gem set by itself.

sol′i•tar′y (sol′i ter′ē) *adj.* **1.** alone. **2.** single. **3.** remote. —**sol′i•tude′,** *n.*

so′lo (sō′lō) *n.,* *pl.* **-los,** *adj.,* *adv.* —*n.* **1.** a performance by one person. —*adj.,* *adv.* **2.** (performed) alone. —**so′lo•ist,** *n.*

sol′stice (sol′stis, sōl′-) *n.* the time in summer (June 21) or winter (Dec. 21) when the sun is at its greatest distance from the celestial equator.

sol′u•ble (sol′yə bəl) *adj.* able to be dissolved. —**sol′u•bil′i•ty,** *n.*

so•lu′tion (sə lōō′shən) *n.* **1.** the process of solving a problem. **2.** an explanation or answer. **3.** the process of dissolving one substance in another. **4.** the resulting liquid.

solve (solv) *v.t.,* **solved, solving.** to find the answer for.

sol′vent (sol′vənt) *adj.* **1.** able to pay one's debts. **2.** causing dissolving. —*n.* **3.** an agent that dissolves.

som′ber (som′bər) *adj.* **1.** gloomy; dark. **2.** very serious. —**som′ber•ly,** *adv.*

som•bre′ro (som brâr′ō) *n.,* *pl.* **-ros.** a tall, wide-brimmed hat.

some (sum; *unstressed* səm) *adj.* **1.** being an unknown or unnamed one. **2.** unspecified in number, amount, etc. —*pron.* **3.** an unspecified number or amount. —*adv.* **4.** approximately.

—Usage. SOME is used in sentences that are affirmative: *I'd like some milk.* ANY is used instead of SOME with negative phrases or in questions: *I don't want any milk. I never see any of my friends these days. Do you have any milk?* But SOME can be used in questions when the answer is expected to be "yes": *Can I have some milk, please?*

some′bod′y (sum′bod′ē, -bud′ē, -bə dē) *pron.* some person. Also, **some′one′.**

some′day′ *adv.* at some distant time.

some′how′ *adv.* in some way.

som′er•sault′ (sum′ər sôlt′) *n.* **1.** a heels-over-head roll of the body. —*v.i.* **2.** to perform a somersault.

some′thing′ *n.* an unspecified thing.

some′time′ *adv.* **1.** at an indefinite time. —*adj.* **2.** former.

some′times′ *adv.* now and then.

some′what′ *adv.* to some extent.

some′where′ *adv.* in, at, or to an unspecified place.

som•nam′bu•lism (som nam′byə liz′əm, səm-) *n.* sleepwalking.

som′no•lent (som′nə lənt) *adj.* sleepy. —**som′no•lence,** *n.*

son (sun) *n.* a male offspring.

so′nar (sō′när) *n.* a method or apparatus for detecting objects in water by means of sound waves.

so•na′ta (sə nä′tə) *n.* an instrumental composition, usu. in several movements.

song (sông) *n.* **1.** music for singing. **2.** the art or act of singing. —**song′ster,** *n.*

song′bird′ *n.* a bird that sings.

son′ic (son′ik) *adj.* of sound.

son′ic boom′ *n.* a loud noise caused by an aircraft moving at supersonic speed.

son′-in-law′ *n.,* *pl.* **sons-in-law.** the husband of one's daughter.

son′net (son′it) *n.* a poem of 14 lines.

son′o•gram (son′ə gram′, sō′nə-) *n.* the visual image made by reflected sound waves in an ultrasound examination.

so•no′rous (sə nôr′əs, son′ər əs) *adj.* resonant, with a rich, full sound. —**so•nor′i•ty,** *n.*

soon (sōōn) *adv.* in a short time.

soot (sŏŏt, sōōt) *n.* a black powdery substance in smoke. —**soot′y,** *adj.*

soothe (sōōth) *v.t.,* **soothed, soothing.** **1.** to calm. **2.** to ease or allay.

sooth′say′er (sōōth′sā′ər) *n.* a person who predicts events.

sop (sop) *n.,* *v.,* **sopped, sopping.** —*n.* **1.** something given to pacify. —*v.t.* **2.** to soak or dip in liquid. **3.** to absorb (liquid).

soph′ism (sof′iz əm) *n.* a false but plausible argument. —**soph′ist,** *n.*

so•phis′ti•cat•ed (sə fis′ti kā′tid) *adj.* **1.** worldly; not naive. **2.** complex; intricate. —**so•phis′ti•cate** (-kit) *n.* —**so•phis′ti•ca′tion,** *n.*

soph′ist•ry (sof′ə strē) *n.,* *pl.* **-ries.** clever but unsound reasoning.

soph′o•more′ (sof′ə môr′) *n.* a second-year high school or college student.

soph′o•mor′ic (-môr′ik) *adj.* intellectually immature.

so•po•rif′ic (sop′ə rif′ik, sō′pə-) *adj.* **1.** causing sleep. —*n.* **2.** a soporific agent.

sop′py (sop′ē) *adj.,* **-pier, -piest.** **1.** very wet. **2.** sentimental.

so•pran′o (sə pran′ō) *n.,* *pl.* **-pranos.** **1.** the highest singing voice in women and boys. **2.** a singer with such a voice. —*adj.* **3.** of the highest pitch in music.

sor•bet′ (sôr bā′, sôr′bit) *n.* a fruit or vegetable ice.

sor′cer•y (sôr′sə rē) *n.,* *pl.* **-cer•ies.** the exercise of supernatural powers granted by evil spirits. —**sor′cer•er,** *n.* —**sor′cer•ess,** *n.*

sor′did (sôr′did) *adj.* **1.** morally base. **2.** filthy.

sore (sôr) *adj.,* **sorer, sorest,** *n.* —*adj.* **1.** painful or tender. **2.** causing or suffering pain or distress. **3.** annoyed. —*n.* **4.** a sore spot.

sore′head′ *n. Informal.* a person who is easily annoyed.

sor′ghum (sôr′gəm) *n.* a cereal grass used in making syrup.

so•ror′i•ty (sə rôr′i tē) *n.,* *pl.* **-ties.** a club of women or girls.

sor′rel[1] (sôr′əl) *n.* **1.** a reddish brown. **2.** a horse of this color.

sor′rel[2] (sôr′əl) *n.* a salad plant with acid leaves.

sor′row (sor′ō) *n.* **1.** grief or the cause or expression of grief. —*v.i.* **2.** to feel or express sorrow. —**sor′row•ful,** *adj.*

sor′ry (sor′ē) *adj.,* **-rier, -riest.** **1.** feeling regret or pity. **2.** wretched.

sort (sôrt) *n.* **1.** a particular kind or class. **2.** character or quality. —*v.t.* **3.** to arrange by kind. —*Idiom.* **4.** **out of sorts,** irritable.

sor′tie (sôr′tē) *n.* **1.** an attack by defending troops. **2.** a combat mission.

SOS (es′ō′es′) *n.* a call for help.

so′-so′ *adj.* **1.** neither good nor bad. —*adv.* **2.** tolerably.

sot′to vo′ce (sot′ō vō′chē) *adv.* in a low voice; softly.

sou•brette′ (sōō bret′) *n.* a coquettish maidservant in a play or opera.

souf•flé′ (sōō flā′) *n.* a light, puffy baked dish made with egg whites.

sough (sou, suf) *v.i.* **1.** to rustle or murmur, as wind. —*n.* **2.** a soughing sound.

sought (sôt) *v.* pt. and pp. of seek.

soul (sōl) *n.* **1.** the spiritual part of a human being. **2.** an essential part. **3.** a person. **4.** shared ethnic awareness and pride among black Americans. —*adj.* **5.** of black American customs and culture. —**soul′ful,** *adj.*

sound[1] (sound) *n.* **1.** the sensation affecting the organs of hearing. **2.** vibrations that can be perceived by the ear. **3.** something heard. —*v.i.* **4.** to make a sound. **5.** to give a certain impression. —*v.t.* **6.** to cause to sound. **7.** to pronounce.

sound[2] (sound) *adj.* **1.** healthy; strong. **2.** secure; reliable. **3.** valid. —**sound′ly,** *adv.*

sound[3] (sound) *v.t.* **1.** to measure the depth of (water). **2.** to try to find out the views of.

sound[4] (sound) *n.* a strait or inlet of the sea.

sound′ bar′rier *n.* an abrupt increase in drag experienced by an aircraft approaching the speed of sound.

sound′ bite′ *n.* a brief statement excerpted for broadcast news.

sound′ing board′ *n.* **1.** a thin board placed in a musical instrument to enhance resonance. **2.** a person whose reactions reveal the acceptability of an idea.

sound′proof′ *adj.* **1.** not able to be penetrated by sound. —*v.t.* **2.** to make soundproof.

sound'track' *n.* the band on a strip of motion-picture film on which sound is recorded.

soup (sōōp) *n.* a liquid food of vegetables, seasonings, meat, etc.

soup•con' (sōōp sôn') *n.* a slight trace.

soup'y *adj.*, **-ier, -iest. 1.** resembling soup in consistency. **2.** very thick. **3.** overly sentimental.

sour (sou°r) *adj.* **1.** acid in taste; tart. **2.** spoiled. **3.** disagreeable. —*v.t., v.i.* **4.** to make or become sour. —**sour'ly,** *adv.*

source (sôrs) *n.* **1.** any thing or place from which something comes. **2.** the place where a river begins. **3.** something or someone that supplies information.

sour' grapes' pretended scorn for something one cannot have.

souse (sous) *v.,* **soused, sousing,** *n.* —*v.t., v.i.* **1.** to immerse in liquid. **2.** to pickle. —*n.* **3.** a pickled food. **4.** *Slang.* a drunkard.

south (south) *n.* **1.** a cardinal point of the compass lying directly opposite north. **2. the South,** a region in this direction. —*adj., adv.* **3.** toward, in, or from the south. —**south'ern,** *adj.* —**south'ern•er,** *n.* —**south'ward,** *adv., adj.*

south'east' *n.* **1.** the point or direction midway between south and east. **2. the Southeast,** a region in this direction. —*adj., adv.* **3.** toward, in, or from the southeast. —**south'east'ern,** *adj.*

south'er•ly (suth'ər lē) *adj., adv.* toward or blowing from the south.

South'ern Hem'isphere *n.* the half of the earth between the South Pole and the equator.

south'paw' *n. Informal.* a left-handed person.

South' Pole' *n.* the southern end of the earth's axis, the southernmost point on earth.

south'west' *n.* **1.** the point or direction midway between south and west. **2. the Southwest,** a region in this direction. —*adj., adv.* **3.** toward, in, or from the southwest. —**south'west'ern,** *adj.*

sou•ve•nir' (sōō'və nēr') *n.* a memento.

sov'er•eign (sov'rin, -ər in) *n.* **1.** a supreme ruler. **2.** a former British gold coin worth one pound. —*adj.* **3.** supreme in power. **4.** independent. —**sov'er•eign•ty,** *n.*

so'vi•et' (sō'vē et', -it) *n.* **1.** (in the former USSR) a governing body. —*adj.* **2. Soviet,** of the former USSR.

sow¹ (sō) *v.t.* **1.** to scatter (seed) for growth. **2.** to scatter seed over. **3.** to implant or introduce. —*v.i.* **4.** to sow seed. —**sow'er,** *n.*

sow² (sou) *n.* an adult female swine.

soy'bean' (soi'-) *n.* the seed of a plant of the legume family.

soy' sauce' *n.* a salty sauce made from fermented soybeans.

spa (spä) *n.* a resort with a mineral spring.

space (spās) *n., v.,* **spaced, spacing.** —*n.* **1.** the unlimited expanse in which all objects are located. **2.** a particular part of this. **3.** space beyond the earth's atmosphere. **4.** an empty area. **5.** an interval of time. —*v.t.* **6.** to separate by spaces.

space'craft' *n., pl.* **-craft.** a vehicle for traveling in outer space.

space' heat'er *n.* a device for heating a small area.

space'ship' *n.* a spacecraft.

space' shut'tle *n.* a reusable spacecraft.

space' sta'tion *n.* a manned spacecraft orbiting the earth and serving as a base for research.

spa'cious (spā'shəs) *adj.* roomy.

Spack'le (spak'əl) *Trademark.* a brand of plasterlike material for patching cracks.

spade¹ (spād) *n., v.,* **spaded, spading.** —*n.* **1.** a tool with a flat blade for digging. —*v.t.* **2.** to dig with a spade.

spade² (spād) *n.* a playing card with a black figure shaped like an inverted heart with a short stem.

spa•ghet'ti (spə get'ē) *n.* pasta in the form of long strings.

spam (spam) *n., v.,* **spammed, spamming.** —*n.* **1.** a disruptive message posted on a computer network. —*v.t.* **2.** to send spam.

span¹ (span) *n., v.,* **spanned, spanning.** —*n.* **1.** the full extent of something. **2.** the space between two supports. **3.** a short period of time. —*v.t.* **4.** to extend across.

span² (span) *n.* a pair of animals driven together.

span'dex *n.* an elastic synthetic fiber.

span'gle (spang'gəl) *n., v.,* **-gled, -gling.** —*n.* **1.** a small, thin piece of glittering metal, used to decorate a garment. —*v.t.* **2.** to decorate with spangles.

Span'iard (span'yərd) *n.* a native of Spain.

span'iel (span'yəl) *n.* a kind of dog having droopy ears and a silky coat.

Span'ish (span'ish) *adj.* **1.** of Spain, its inhabitants, or their language. —*n.* **2.** the language of Spain and much of Latin America.

Span'ish moss' *n.* a plant that grows in long strands over trees.

spank (spangk) *v.t.* **1.** to slap on the buttocks. —*n.* **2.** such a blow.

spank'ing *n.* **1.** a series of spanks on the buttocks, esp. in punishment. —*adj.* **2.** brisk; vigorous.

spar¹ (spär) *n.* a stout pole, as a mast, for supporting sails.

spar² (spär) *v.i.,* **sparred, sparring. 1.** to box with light blows. **2.** to engage in a dispute.

spare (spâr) *v.,* **spared, sparing,** *adj.,* **sparer, sparest.** —*v.t.* **1.** to refrain from harming or punishing. **2.** to do without. —*adj.* **3.** kept in reserve. **4.** extra. **5.** thin.

spare'rib' *n.* a cut of meat from the ribs, esp. of pork.

spark (spärk) *n.* **1.** a burning particle. **2.** a flash of electricity. **3.** something that stimulates. **4.** a small amount.

spar'kle *v.,* **-kled, -kling,** *n.* —*v.i.* **1.** to shine with flashes of light; glitter. **2.** to be vivacious. **3.** to produce little bubbles. —*n.* **4.** a sparkling light.

spark' plug' *n.* a device in an internal-combustion engine that ignites the fuel.

spar'row (spar'ō) *n.* a small, common, gray-brown songbird.

sparse *adj.,* **sparser, sparsest.** thinly distributed. —**sparse'ness,** *n.*

spar'tan *adj.* austere.

spasm (spaz'əm) *n.* **1.** a sudden involuntary muscular contraction. **2.** a sudden burst of activity.

spas•mod'ic (spaz mod'ik) *adj.* **1.** of or marked by spasms. **2.** intermittent.

spas'tic (spas'tik) *adj.* of or marked by spasms.

spat (spat) *n.* a petty quarrel.

spate (spāt) *n.* a sudden outpouring.

spa'tial (spā'shəl) *adj.* of or in space.

spat'ter (spat'ər) *v.t., v.i.* **1.** to sprinkle in many fine drops. —*n.* **2.** an act or sound of spattering.

spat'u•la (spach'ə lə) *n.* an implement with a broad flexible blade.

spawn (spôn) *n.* **1.** the eggs of fish, frogs, etc. —*v.i., v.t.* **2.** to deposit (spawn). **3.** to bring forth.

spay (spā) *v.t.* to remove the ovaries of (a female dog, cat, etc.).

speak (spēk) *v.,* **spoke** (spōk) **spoken, speaking.** —*v.i.* **1.** to utter words; talk. **2.** to deliver a speech. —*v.t.* **3.** to utter or express with the voice. —**speak'er,** *n.*

speak'eas'y *n., pl.* **-easies.** a place selling alcoholic beverages illegally.

spear (spēr) *n.* **1.** a long staff with a sharp-pointed head. —*v.t.* **2.** to pierce with a spear.

spear'head' *n.* **1.** the head of a spear. **2.** a leader. —*v.t.* **3.** to lead.

spear'mint' *n.* an aromatic herb.

spe'cial (spesh'əl) *adj.* **1.** particular in nature or purpose. **2.** unusual or unique. **3.** exceptional. —*n.* **4.** a special thing or person.

spe'cial•ize' *v.i.,* **-ized, -izing.** to study or work in a special field. —**spe'cial•ist,** *n.* —**spe'cial•i•za'tion,** *n.*

spe'cial•ty *n., pl.* **-ties. 1.** a person's field of special interest or competence. **2.** a special article, service, feature, etc.

spe'cie (spē'shē, -sē) *n.* coined money.

spe'cies (spē'shēz, -sēz) *n.* a group of related animals or plants that can breed among themselves.

spe•cif'ic (spi sif'ik) *adj.* **1.** precise or explicit. **2.** peculiar or limited to someone or something. —**spe•cif'i•cal•ly,** *adv.*

spec'i•fi•ca'tion (spes'ə fi kā'shən) *n.* **1.** something specified. **2.** a detailed statement of requirements.

specif'ic grav'ity *n.* the ratio of the density of a substance to the density of a standard substance, water being the standard.

spec'i•fy' *v.t.,* **-fied, -fying.** to mention or require explicitly.

spec'i•men (spes'ə mən) *n.* a part or an individual taken as an example or a sample to be tested.

spe'cious (spē'shəs) *adj.* apparently true or good but lacking real merit.

speck (spek) *n.* a small spot or bit.

speck'le (-əl) *n., v.,* **-led, -ling.** —*n.* **1.** a small speck. —*v.t.* **2.** to mark with speckles.

specs (speks) *n.pl. Informal.* **1.** spectacles; eyeglasses. **2.** specifications.

spec'ta•cle (spek'tə kəl) *n.* **1.** anything presented to view. **2.** a public display. **3. spectacles,** eyeglasses.

spec•tac'u•lar (-tak'yə lər) *adj.* dramatic; thrilling.

spec'ta•tor (spek'tā tər) *n.* an observer.

spec'ter (spek'tər) *n.* a ghost. Also, **spec'tre.**

spec'tral (-trəl) *adj.* of a specter or a spectrum.

spec'trum (-trəm) *n., pl.* **-tra** (-trə), **-trums. 1.** a band of colors formed when a light ray is dispersed. **2.** a broad range.

spec'u•late' (spek'yə lāt') *v.i.,* **-lated, -lating. 1.** to think; conjecture. **2.** to invest at some risk in the hope of making a large profit. —**spec'u•la'tion,** *n.* —**spec'u•la'tive** (-lā'tiv, -lə tiv) *adj.* —**spec'u•la'tor,** *n.*

speech (spēch) *n.* **1.** the power of speaking. **2.** the act or manner of speaking. **3.** something spoken. **4.** a talk before an audience. —**speech'less,** *adj.*

speed (spēd) *n., v.,* **sped** (sped) or **speeded, speeding.** —*n.* **1.** swiftness. **2.** relative rate of motion. —*v.t.* **3.** to increase the rate of speed of. —*v.i.* **4.** to go fast. **5.** to drive at an illegal rate of speed. —**speed'y,** *adj.* —**speed'i•ly,** *adv.*

speed•om'e•ter (spē dom'i tər, spi-) *n.* an instrument for indicating speed.

speed'well' *n.* a plant having spikes of small flowers.

spe•le•ol'o•gy (spē'lē ol'ə jē) *n.* the exploration and study of caves.

spell¹ (spel) *v.,* **spelled** or **spelt, spelling. 1.** to give the letters of in order. **2.** (of letters) to form (a word). **3.** to mean. —*v.i.* **4.** to spell words.

spell² (spel) *n.* **1.** words believed to have magic power. **2.** a fascination.

spell³ (spel) *n.* **1.** a period of activity, time, or weather. **2.** a bout or attack. —*v.t.* **3.** to take the place of for a time.

spell'bound' *adj.* fascinated.

spe•lunk'er (spi lung'kər) *n.* a person who explores caves.

spend (spend) *v.,* **spent, spending.** —*v.t.* **1.** to pay out (money). **2.** to pass (time). **3.** to use up. —**spend'er,** *n.*

spend'thrift' *n.* a person who spends extravagantly.

spent (spent) *v.* pt. and pp. of **spend.**

sperm (spûrm) *n.* **1.** a male reproductive cell. **2.** semen. —**sper•mat'ic** (-mat'ik) *adj.*

sper•mat'o•zo'on (spûr mat'ə zō'ən, -on) *n., pl.* **-zoa** (-zō'ə). a mature male reproductive cell.

sper'mi•cide' (-mə sīd') *n.* a sperm-killing agent.

spew (spyōō) *v.i., v.t.* **1.** to gush or pour out. **2.** to vomit.

sphere (sfēr) *n.* **1.** a round solid geometric figure. **2.** a field of activity. —**spher'i•cal,** *adj.*

sphe'roid (sfēr'oid) *n.* a solid figure similar to a sphere in shape.

sphinc'ter (sfingk'tər) *n.* a circular band of muscle that closes a body opening.

sphinx (sfingks) *n.* an ancient Egyptian figure with a human head and a lion's body.

spice (spīs) *n., v.,* **spiced, spicing.** —*n.* **1.** an aromatic plant substance used to season food. —*v.t.* **2.** something that gives zest. **3.** to season with spice. **4.** to give zest to. —**spic'y,** *adj.*

spick'-and-span' (spik'ən span') *adj.* spotlessly clean.

spi'der (spī'dər) *n.* a web-spinning insectlike animal with eight legs.

spiel (spēl, shpēl) *n. Slang.* a glib speech intended to persuade.

spiff'y (spif'ē) *adj.,* **-ier, -iest.** *Informal.* smart; fine.

spig'ot (spig'ət) *n.* a faucet.

spike¹ (spīk) *n., v.,* **spiked, spiking.** —*n.* **1.** a long thick nail. **2.** a stiff, pointed part. —*v.t.* **3.** to fasten with spikes. **4.** to suppress or stop. —**spik'y,** *adj.*

spike² (spīk) *n.* **1.** an ear of grain. **2.** a stalk of flowers.

spill (spil) *v.,* **spilled** or **spilt, spilling.** —*v.t.* **1.** to cause to run or flow from a container, esp. accidentally. **2.** to shed (blood). —*v.i.* **3.** to run or flow from a container. —**spill'age,** *n.*

spill'way' *n.* a passage through which excess water escapes.

spin (spin) *v.,* **spun** (spun) **spinning,** *n.* —*v.t.* **1.** to make (yarn) by drawing out and twisting fibers. **2.** to form (fibers) into yarn. **3.** to cause to rotate rapidly. —*v.i.* **4.** to rotate rapidly. **5.** to spin yarn or thread. —*n.* **6.** a spinning motion. **7.** a short ride. **8.** *Slang.* a viewpoint or bias.

spin'ach (spin'ich) *n.* a plant with edible, dark green leaves.

spi'nal (spīn'l) *adj.* of the spine or spinal cord.

spi'nal col'umn *n.* the series of vertebrae forming the axis of the skeleton.

spi'nal cord' *n.* the cord of nerve tissue extending through the spinal column.

spin' con'trol *n. Slang.* an attempt to give a bias to news coverage.

spin'dle (spin'dl) *n.* **1.** a tapered rod on which thread is wound in spinning. **2.** any shaft or axis.

spin'dly, *adj.,* **-dli•er, -dli•est.** tall and thin.

spin' doc'tor *n. Slang.* a press agent or spokesperson skilled at spin control.

spine (spīn) *n.* **1.** the backbone. **2.** the back of a book binding. **3.** a stiff bristle or thorn. —**spin'y,** *adj.*

spine'less *adj.* weak in character.

spin'et (spin'it) *n.* a small piano.

spin'na•ker (spin'ə kər) *n.* a large sail on a yacht.

spin'ning wheel' *n.* a device for spinning yarn or thread.

spin'-off' *n.* a by-product or secondary development.

spin'ster (spin'stər) *n. Usu. Disparaging.* an unmarried woman, esp. elderly.

spi'ral (spī'rəl) *n., adj., v.,* **-raled, -raling.** —*n.* **1.** a curve made by circling a fixed point while approaching or receding from it. —*adj.* **2.** of or like a spiral. —*v.i., v.t.* **3.** to move or cause to move on a spiral course.

spire (spīr) *n.* a tall, sharply pointed roof forming the top of a tower or steeple.

spi•re'a (spī rē'ə) *n.* a garden shrub with white or pink flowers.

spir'it (spir'it) *n.* **1.** the vital force in humans; mind or soul. **2.** a ghost. **3. spirits,** mood or feelings. **4.** vigor. **5.** general meaning. **6. spirits,** alcoholic liquor. —*v.t.* **7.** to carry off mysteriously.

spir'it•u•al (-chōō əl) *adj.* **1.** of the spirit or the soul. **2.** religious. —*n.* **3.** a religious song originating among blacks in the southern U.S. —**spir'it•u•al•ly,** *adv.* —**spir'it•u•al'i•ty** (-al'i tē) *n.*

spir'it•u•al•ism *n.* the belief that spirits of the dead communicate with the living. —**spir'it•u•al•ist,** *n., adj.*

spi'ro•chete' (spī'rə kēt') *n.* any of various mobile, spiral bacteria.

spit¹ (spit) *v.,* **spat** (spat) or **spit, spitting.** —*v.i., v.t.* **1.** to eject (saliva) from the mouth. —*n.* **2.** saliva. **3.** the act of spitting.

spit² (spit) *n.* **1.** a pointed rod for roasting meat. **2.** a narrow point of land. —*v.t.* **3.** to pierce with a spit.

spite (spīt) *n., v.,* **spited, spiting.** —*n.* **1.** a malicious desire to harm or annoy someone. —*v.t.* **2.** to treat with spite. —**Idiom. 3. in spite of,** not being hindered by. —**spite'ful,** *adj.*

spit'fire' *n.* a person with a fiery temper.

spit'tle *n.* saliva.

spit•toon' (spi tōōn') *n.* a large bowl serving as a receptacle for spit, esp. from chewing tobacco.

splash (splash) *v.t.* **1.** to dash (water, mud, etc.) about in drops. **2.** to wet or soil with such drops. —*v.i.* **3.** to fall or move with a splash. —*n.* **4.** an act or sound of splashing. **5.** a spot. **6.** a striking impression. —**splash'y,** *adj.*

splash'down' *n.* the landing of a space vehicle in the ocean.

splat (splat) *n.* a sound made by splattering or slapping.

splat'ter *v.t., v.i.* to splash widely.

splay (splā) *v.t., v.i.* **1.** to spread out. **2.** to slant.

spleen (splēn) *n.* **1.** an abdominal organ that helps maintain the

proper condition of the blood. 2. ill humor.

splen'did (splen'did) *adj.* gorgeous; superb; fine. —**splen'dor,** *n.*

sple•net'ic (spli net'ik) *adj.* **1.** of the spleen. **2.** irritable or spiteful.

splice (splīs) *v.,* **spliced, splicing,** *n.* —*v.t.* **1.** to join by interweaving or overlapping, as ropes, film, etc. —*n.* **2.** a union made by splicing.

splint (splint) *n.* **1.** a piece of rigid material for immobilizing a broken part of the body while it heals. —*v.t.* **2.** to brace with a splint.

splin'ter *n.* **1.** a thin sharp fragment, as of wood or glass. —*v.t., v.i.* **2.** to break into splinters.

split (split) *v.,* **split, splitting,** *n., adj.* —*v.t., v.i.* **1.** to separate or divide, esp. lengthwise. **2.** to burst. —*n.* **3.** the act of splitting. **4.** a breach. —*adj.* **5.** cleft; divided.

split'-lev'el *adj.* **1.** (of a house) having rooms on levels a half story apart. —*n.* **2.** a split-level house.

split' pea' *n.* a dried green pea.

split' person'ality *n.* a mental disorder in which a person acquires several personalities.

splotch (sploch) *n.* **1.** a large spot. —*v.t.* **2.** to mark with splotches.

splurge (splûrj) *n., v.,* **splurged, splurging.** —*n.* **1.** a big expenditure. —*v.i.* **2.** to be extravagant.

splut'ter (splut'ər) *v.i.* **1.** to talk rapidly and confusedly. —*n.* **2.** spluttering talk.

spoil (spoil) *v.,* **spoiled** or **spoilt, spoiling,** *n.* —*v.t.* **1.** to damage. **2.** to harm the character of (esp. a child) by excessive indulgence. —*v.i.* **3.** to become unfit for use. —*n.* **4. spoils,** plunder. —**spoil'age,** *n.*

spoil'sport' *n.* a person who spoils the pleasure of others.

spoils' sys'tem *n.* the practice of filling nonelective public offices with supporters of the victor.

spoke¹ (spōk) *v.* a pt. of **speak.**

spoke² (spōk) *n.* a bar between the hub and the rim of a wheel.

spokes'man or **spokes'wom'an** or **spokes'per'son** *n., pl.* **-men** or **-wom•en** or **-per•sons.** a person who speaks for another or for a group.

sponge (spunj) *n., v.,* **sponged, sponging.** —*n.* **1.** a marine animal with a porous skeleton. **2.** its absorbent skeleton or an imitation, used for cleaning. —*v.t.* **3.** to clean with a sponge. **4.** to get by imposing on another. —*v.i.* **5.** to impose or live on another. —**spong'er,** *n.*

sponge' cake' *n.* a light cake without shortening.

spon'sor (spon'sər) *n.* **1.** one who recommends or supports. **2.** an advertiser on radio or television. **3.** a godparent. —*v.t.* **4.** to act as sponsor for. —**spon'sor•ship,** *n.*

spon•ta'ne•ous (spon tā'nē əs) *adj.* **1.** occurring naturally or without planning. **2.** impulsive. —**spon'ta•ne'i•ty** (-tə nē'i tē, -nā'-) *n.*

sponta'neous combus'tion *n.* the ignition of a substance without heat from an external source.

spoof (spōōf) *n.* **1.** a parody. —*v.t., v.i.* **2.** to make fun (of) lightly.

spook (spōōk) *n.* **1.** a ghost. —*v.t., v.i.* **2.** to frighten or become frightened. —**spook'y,** *adj.*

spool (spōōl) *n.* a cylinder on which something is wound.

spoon (spōōn) *n.* **1.** a utensil for stirring or taking up food. —*v.t.* **2.** to eat with or lift in a spoon. —**spoon'ful,** *n.*

spoon'bill' *n.* a large wading bird.

spoon'er•ism (spōō'nə riz'əm) *n.* the inadvertent transposition of the initial sounds of words.

spoon'-feed' *v.t.* **1.** to feed with a spoon. **2.** to provide with information in a simplified way.

spoor (spōōr) *n.* a track or scent of a wild animal.

spo•rad'ic (spə rad'ik) *adj.* occasional; scattered.

spore (spôr) *n.* the asexual reproductive cell of a fungus, fern, etc.

sport (spôrt) *n.* **1.** a competitive athletic activity. **2.** recreation. **3.** a sportsmanlike person. **4.** mockery. **5.** an object of sport. —*v.t.* **6.** to amuse oneself. —*v.t.* **7.** to wear or display.

spor'tive *adj.* playful.

sports' car' *n.* a small, high-powered car.

sports'man *n., pl.* **-men. 1.** a person who engages in sports, esp. hunting and fishing. **2.** a person who shows fairness and grace in winning and defeat. —**sports′man·like′,** adj. —**sports′man·ship′** n.

sport′-util′ity ve′hicle n. a rugged vehicle with a trucklike chassis, designed for occasional off-road use.

sport′y adj., **-ier, -iest.** flashy.

spot n., v., **spotted, spotting.** —n. **1.** a discolored mark; stain. **2.** a small part. **3.** a place. —v.t. **4.** to stain with spots. **5.** to notice. —v.i. **6.** to make a spot. —adj. **7.** made, done, etc., at once. —**spot′less,** adj. —**spot′ty,** adj.

spot′ check′ n. a random sampling or investigation. —**spot′-check′,** v.t., v.i.

spot′light′ n. **1.** an intense light focused on a person or thing. **2.** intense public attention.

spouse (spous) n. a husband or wife.

spout (spout) v.t., v.i. **1.** to discharge or issue with force. **2.** to say or speak insincerely. —n. **3.** a pipe or lip on a container.

sprain (sprān) v.t. **1.** to injure by wrenching. **2.** such an injury.

sprang (sprang) v. a pt. of **spring.**

sprat (sprat) n. a herringlike fish.

sprawl (sprôl) v.i. **1.** to stretch out ungracefully. —n. **2.** a sprawling position.

spray¹ (sprā) n. **1.** liquid falling through the air in fine droplets. **2.** a device for producing a spray. —v.t., v.i. **3.** to scatter as spray. **4.** to apply in a spray. —**spray′er,** n.

spray² (sprā) n. an arrangement of flowers, leaves, etc.

spread (spred) v., **spread, spreading,** n. —v.t., v.i. **1.** to stretch or open out. **2.** to force or move apart. **3.** to distribute over an area. **4.** to apply in a layer. **5.** to become or make widely known. —n. **6.** the act of spreading. **7.** expanse; range. **8.** a cloth cover for a bed. **9.** a food for spreading.

spread′-ea′gle adj., v., **-gled, -gling.** —adj. **1.** suggestive of an eagle with outstretched wings. —v.t. **2.** to stretch out in this way.

spread′sheet′ n. **1.** an outsize ledger sheet. **2.** such a sheet simulated by computer software.

spree (sprē) n. a spell or bout of indulgence.

sprig (sprig) n. a twig or shoot.

spright′ly (sprīt′lē) adj., **-lier, -liest.** lively. —**spright′li·ness,** n.

spring (spring) v., **sprang** (sprang) or **sprung** (sprung) **sprung, springing,** n. —v.i. **1.** to rise or leap suddenly. **2.** to come into being; arise. —v.t. **3.** to cause to spring. **5.** to cause to operate suddenly. **5.** to develop. —n. **6.** the season after winter. **7.** a jump. **8.** a place where water issues from the ground. **9.** an elastic device that recovers its shape after being bent, stretched, etc. —**spring′time′,** n. —**spring′y,** adj.

spring′board′ n. **1.** a flexible board used in diving and gymnastics. **2.** a starting point.

spring′ fe′ver n. a restless feeling associated with spring.

spring′ tide′ n. the large rise and fall of the tide at the time of the new or the full moon.

sprin′kle (spring′kəl) v., **-kled, -kling,** n. —v.t., v.i. **1.** to scatter in drops. **2.** to rain slightly in scattered drops. —n. **3.** an instance of sprinkling. **4.** something sprinkled.

sprint (sprint) v.i. **1.** to run fast for a short distance. —n. **2.** a short fast run. —**sprint′er,** n.

sprite (sprīt) n. an elf; fairy.

sprock′et (sprok′it) n. a tooth on a wheel engaging with a chain.

sprout (sprout) v.i. **1.** to begin to grow; bud. —n. **2.** a plant shoot.

spruce¹ (sproos) n. a cone-bearing evergreen tree.

spruce² (sproos) adj., **sprucer, sprucest,** v., **spruced, sprucing.** —adj. **1.** trim; neat. —v.t., v.i. **2.** to make or become spruce.

sprung (sprung) v. a pt. and pp. of **spring.**

spry (sprī) adj., **spryer** or **sprier, spryest** or **spriest.** nimbly energetic.

spud (spud) n. **1.** Informal. a potato. **2.** a spadelike digging tool.

spume (spyoom) n. foam.

spunk (spungk) n. Informal. courage; spirit. —**spunk′y,** adj.

spur (spûr) n., v., **spurred, spurring.** —n. **1.** a sharp device worn on a boot heel to goad a horse. **2.** a spurlike part. —v.t. **3.** to urge on.

—**Idiom. 4. on the spur of the moment,** suddenly.

spu′ri·ous (spyŏŏr′ē əs) adj. not genuine. —**spu′ri·ous·ly,** adv.

spurn (spûrn) v.t. to scorn; reject.

spurt (spûrt) n. **1.** a sudden, forceful gush. **2.** a brief increase of effort. —v.i., v.t. **3.** to gush, expel in, or make a spurt.

sput′ter (sput′ər) v.i. **1.** to make rapid popping sounds. **2.** to talk incoherently. —n. **3.** an act or sound of sputtering.

spu′tum (spyoo′təm) n. spittle.

spy (spī) n., pl. **spies,** v., **spied, spying.** —n. **1.** a person employed by a government to gather information about another country. **2.** a person who keeps secret watch on others. —v.i. **3.** to act as a spy. —v.t. **4.** to catch sight of.

spy′ glass′ n. a small telescope.

squab (skwob) n. a young pigeon.

squab′ble (skwob′əl) n., v., **-bled, -bling.** —n. **1.** a petty quarrel. —v.i. **2.** to engage in a petty quarrel.

squad (skwod) n. a small group, esp. of soldiers or police officers.

squad′ car′ n. a police car.

squad′ron (-rən) n. a unit in the Navy, Air Force, etc.

squal′id (skwol′id) adj. filthy and repulsive.

squall¹ (skwôl) n. a sudden, strong gust of wind, often with rain or snow.

squall² (skwôl) v.i. **1.** to cry out loudly. —n. **2.** a loud cry.

squal′or (skwol′ər) n. a squalid condition.

squan′der (skwon′dər) v.t. to use or spend wastefully.

square (skwâr) n., v., **squared, squaring,** adj., **squarer, squarest,** adv. —n. **1.** a rectangle with four equal sides and four right angles. **2.** anything shaped like a square. **3.** an open area formed by intersecting streets. **4.** the product of a number multiplied by itself. **5.** Slang. a conventional, unimaginative person. —v.t. **6.** to make square in form. **7.** to multiply (a number) by itself. **8.** to make even. **9.** to adjust. —v.i. **10.** to agree. —adj. **11.** forming a right angle. **12.** of square shape. **13.** having all accounts settled. **14.** honest. **15.** Slang. conventional. —adv. **16.** honestly. —**square′ly,** adv.

square′ dance′ n. a dance by four couples arranged in a square.

square′ root′ n. the quantity of which a given quantity is the square.

squash¹ (skwosh) v.t. **1.** to crush into a pulplike mass. **2.** to suppress. —n. **3.** a squashed mass. **4.** a game resembling tennis.

squash² (skwosh) n. the edible fruit of plants of the gourd family.

squat (skwot) v., **squatted** or **squat, squatting,** adj., n. —v.i. **1.** to sit on the haunches or heels. **2.** to occupy another's property illegally. —adj. **3.** stocky. —n. **4.** a squatting position.

squawk (skwôk) n. **1.** a loud harsh cry. —v.i. **2.** to utter squawks. **3.** to complain.

squeak (skwēk) n. **1.** a small shrill sound. —v.i., v.t. **2.** to utter (with) a squeak. —**squeak′y,** adj.

squeal (skwēl) n. **1.** a long shrill cry. —v.i., v.t. **2.** to utter (with) a squeal.

squeam′ish (skwē′mish) adj. easily nauseated or disgusted.

squee′gee (skwē′jē) n. an implement for cleaning glass surfaces.

squeeze (skwēz) v., **squeezed, squeezing,** n. —v.t. **1.** to press forcibly together. **2.** to extract by pressing. —v.i. **3.** to exert pressure. **4.** to force one's way. —n. **5.** an act of squeezing. **6.** a hug.

squelch (skwelch) v.t. **1.** to silence, as with a crushing retort. —n. **2.** a crushing retort.

squib (skwib) n. **1.** a short witty item. **2.** a hissing firecracker.

squid (skwid) n. a 10-armed marine animal with a long, slender body.

squig′gle (skwig′əl) n. a short, irregular twist. —**squig′gly,** adj.

squint (skwint) v.i. **1.** to look with the eyes partly closed. **2.** to be cross-eyed. —n. **3.** a squinting look. **4.** a cross-eyed condition.

squire (skwīⁱr) n., v., **squired, squiring.** —n. **1.** an English country gentleman. **2.** an escort. —v.t. **3.** to escort.

squirm (skwûrm) v.i. to wriggle or writhe.

squir′rel (skwûr′əl) n. a bushy-tailed, tree-living rodent.

squirt (skwûrt) v.t. **1.** to eject liquid in a thin stream. **2.** to cause to squirt. **3.** to wet in this way. —n. **4.** a jet of liquid.

squish (skwish) v.t. **1.** to squash. —v.i. **2.** to make a gushing sound when walked in. —n. **3.** a squishing sound.

Sr. 1. Senior. **2.** Sister.

SRO 1. single-room occupancy. **2.** standing room only.

SS social security.

SST supersonic transport.

St. 1. Saint. **2.** Street.

stab (stab) v., **stabbed, stabbing,** n. —v.t., v.i. **1.** to pierce with a pointed weapon. —n. **2.** a thrust with a pointed weapon.

sta′bi·lize′ (stā′bə līz′) v.t., v.i., **-lized, -lizing.** to make, keep, or become stable.

sta′ble¹ (stā′bal) n., v., **-bled, -bling,** adj. —n. **1.** a building for horses. —v.t., v.i. **2.** to put or stay in a stable.

sta′ble² (stā′bal) adj. steady. —**sta·bil′i·ty,** n.

stac·ca′to (stə kä′tō) adj. Music. shortened and detached when played or sung.

stack (stak) n. **1.** an orderly pile or heap. **2.** stacks, a book storage area. **3.** a great quantity. —v.t. **4.** to pile in a stack.

sta′di·um (stā′dē əm) n., pl. **-diums, -dia.** an open structure for games, surrounded by rows of tiered seats.

staff (staf) n., pl. **staves** (stāvz) or **staffs** (for 1, 3); **staffs** (for 2); v. —n. **1.** a stick carried as a support, weapon, etc. **2.** a body of administrators or assistants. **3.** a set of five lines on which music is written. —v.t. **4.** to provide with a staff.

staff′er n. a member of a staff.

stag (stag) n. **1.** an adult male deer. —adj. **2.** for men only. —adv. **3.** without a date.

stage (stāj) n., v., **staged, staging.** —n. **1.** a single step in a process or series. **2.** a raised platform, esp. one on which actors perform. **3. the stage,** the theater as a profession. —v.t. **4.** to present on stage.

stage′coach′ n. a horse-drawn public coach that traveled over a fixed route.

stage′hand′ n. a theater worker who deals with props and scenery.

stage′struck′ adj. obsessed with the theater.

stag′ger (stag′ər) v.i. **1.** to move unsteadily. —v.t. **2.** to astonish. **3.** to arrange in an alternating pattern. —n. **4.** a staggering movement.

stag′ger·ing adj. amazing.

stag′nant (stag′nənt) adj. **1.** not flowing; foul; stale. **2.** inactive. —**stag′nate** (-nāt) v.i.

staid (stād) adj. sedate or solemn.

stain (stān) n. **1.** a discolored patch; blemish. **2.** a kind of dye. —v.t. **3.** to discolor. **4.** to color with a stain. —v.i. **5.** to become stained.

stain′less adj. **1.** unstained. **2.** not liable to rusting.

stain′less steel′ n. steel allied with chromium to resist rust.

stair (stâr) n. **1.** one of a series of steps between levels. **2. stairs,** a flight of steps. —**stair′case′, stair′way′,** n.

stair′well′ n. a vertical shaft containing stairs.

stake¹ (stāk) n., v., **staked, staking.** —n. **1.** a pointed stick. —v.t. **2.** to mark off with stakes. **3.** to support with a stake.

stake² (stāk) n., v., **staked, staking.** —n. **1.** something wagered. **2.** a share. **3. stakes,** a prize. —v.t. **4.** to risk. **5.** to provide money for. —Idiom. **6. at stake,** at risk.

stake′out′ n. surveillance by the police.

sta·lac′tite (stə lak′tīt) n. an icicle-shaped formation hanging from a cave roof.

sta·lag′mite (stə lag′mīt) n. a cone-shaped deposit on a cave floor.

stale (stāl) adj., **staler, stalest.** not fresh.

stale′mate′ (-māt′) n. a deadlocked position.

stalk¹ (stôk) n. a plant stem.

stalk² (stôk) v.i. **1.** to walk stiffly. —v.t. **2.** to pursue (a person or animal) stealthily. —**stalk′er,** n.

stall¹ (stôl) n. **1.** a compartment in a stable for one animal. **2.** a sales booth. **3.** a condition in which an engine stops. —v.t., v.i. **4.** to put or keep in a stall. **5.** to stop, esp. unintentionally.

stall² (stôl) v.i., v.t. **1.** to delay. —n. **2.** a pretext for delay.

stal′lion (stal′yən) n. a male horse.

stal′wart (stôl′wərt) adj. **1.** robust. **2.** brave. **3.** steadfast. —n. **4.** a stalwart person.

sta′men (stā′mən) n. the pollen-bearing organ of a flower.

stam′i·na (stam′ə nə) n. endurance.

stam′mer (stam′ər) v.i., v.t. **1.** to speak or say with involuntary breaks or repetitions. —n. **2.** such speech.

stamp (stamp) v.t. **1.** to bring (the foot) down forcibly. **2.** to pound with the foot. **3.** to impress (something) with a mark. **4.** to impress (a mark) on something. —v.i. **5.** to bring the foot down forcibly. —n. **6.** a gummed printed label showing that postage has been paid. **7.** a marking device. **8.** an official mark.

stam·pede′ (stam pēd′) n., v., **-peded, -peding.** —n. **1.** a panicky rush or flight. —v.i., v.t. **2.** to flee or cause to flee in a stampede.

stamp′ing ground′ n. a favorite haunt.

stance (stans) n. a way of standing.

stanch (stônch, stanch) v.t. **1.** to stop the flow of, esp. blood. —v.i. **2.** to stop flowing.

stan′chion (stan′shən) n. an upright post.

stand (stand) v., **stood** (stŏŏd) **standing,** n. —v.i. **1.** to rise to, be in, or remain in an upright position. **2.** to remain firm. **3.** to be located. **4.** to remain unchanged. —v.t. **5.** to set upright. **6.** to endure. **7. stand by, a.** to abide by. **b.** to be loyal to. **c.** to be ready to act. **8. ~ for, a.** to represent. **b.** to tolerate. **9. ~ out,** to be prominent. **10. ~ up, a.** to be convincing. **b.** to be lasting. **c.** to fail to keep an appointment with. —n. **11.** a position or attitude. **12.** the place occupied by a witness giving testimony in court. **13.** a raised platform. **14. stands,** a section of seats for spectators. **15.** a support for small articles. **16.** an outdoor salesplace. **17.** an area of trees.

stand′ard (stan′dərd) n. **1.** something serving as a basis for comparison or judgment. **2.** a flag. **3.** an upright support. —adj. **4.** being a model or basis for comparison.

stand′ard-bear′er n. the leader of a cause.

stand′ard·ize′ v.t., **-ized, -izing.** to make conform with a standard.

stand′ard time′ n. the civil time officially adopted for a region.

stand′by′ n., pl. **-bys. 1.** a person or thing that can be depended on. **2.** one ready to be a substitute.

stand′-in′ n. a substitute.

stand′ing n. **1.** status or reputation. **2.** duration. —adj. **3.** upright. **4.** not flowing. **5.** lasting; fixed.

stand′off′ n. a tie or draw.

stand′off′ish adj. aloof.

stand′out′ n. one that is conspicuously superior.

stand′pipe′ n. a vertical pipe into which water is pumped to obtain a required pressure.

stand′point′ n. a viewpoint.

stand′still′ n. a complete halt.

stand′-up′ adj. **1.** erect. **2.** performing a comic monologue while standing alone before an audience.

stan′za (stan′zə) n. a division of a poem.

staph′y·lo·coc′cus (staf′ə lə kok′-əs) n., pl. **-ci** (-sī, -sē). any of several spherical bacteria occurring in clusters.

sta′ple¹ (stā′pəl) n., v., **-pled, -pling.** —n. **1.** a thin, bracket-shaped wire fastener. —v.t. **2.** to fasten with a staple. —**sta′pler,** n.

sta·ple² (stā′pəl) n. **1.** a basic item, as of food. —adj. **2.** basic or chief.

star (stär) n., adj., v., **starred, starring.** —n. **1.** a heavenly body that appears as a fixed point of light at night. **2.** a figure with five or six points. **3.** a principal or famous performer. **4.** an asterisk. —adj. **5.** principal. —v.i. **6.** to be outstanding. **7.** to perform as a star. —**star′ry,** adj. —**star′dom,** n.

star′board′ (-bərd, -bôrd′) n. **1.** the right side of a ship, facing forward. —adj. **2.** of or on the right side.

starch (stärch) n. **1.** a white tasteless substance found in rice, corn, wheat, potatoes, etc. **2.** a preparation of starch used to stiffen fabrics. —v.t. **3.** to stiffen with starch.

stare (stâr) v., **stared, staring,** n. —v.i. **1.** to gaze fixedly. —n. **2.** a fixed look.

star′fish′ n. a star-shaped sea animal.

star′gaze′ v.i., **-gazed, -gazing. 1.** to gaze at the stars. **2.** to daydream.

stark (stärk) adj. **1.** complete; utter. **2.** bleak. —adv. **3.** completely.

star′let (-lit) n. a young movie actress.

star′light′ n. light emanating from the stars. —**star′lit′,** adj.

star′ling n. a songbird with speckled black plumage.

star′ry-eyed′ adj. overly romantic or idealistic.

start (stärt) v.i. **1.** to begin to move, go, or act. **2.** to give a sudden jerk, as from shock. —v.t. **3.** to set moving or acting. **4.** to establish. —n. **5.** a beginning. **6.** a startled movement. **7.** a lead. —**start′er,** n.

star′tle v.t., v.i., **-tled, -tling.** to surprise or be surprised.

starve (stärv) v., **starved, starving.** —v.i. **1.** to die or suffer from hunger. —v.t. **2.** to kill or weaken by hunger. —**star·va′tion,** n.

stash (stash) v.t. **1.** to hide away. —n. **2.** something hidden away. **3.** a hiding place.

stat (stat) n. a statistic.

state (stāt) n., adj., v., **stated, stating.** —n. **1.** the condition of a person or thing. **2.** a nation. **3.** a political unit of a federal union. **4.** formality. —adj. **5.** of a state or government. **6.** ceremonial. —v.t. **7.** to declare. —**state′hood,** n.

state′craft′ n. the art of government.

state′house′ n. the building in which a state legislature sits.

state′less adj. lacking nationality.

state′ly adj., **-lier, -liest.** dignified.

state′ment n. **1.** a declaration. **2.** a report on a business account.

state′ of the art′ n. the most advanced stage of a science, art, etc.

state′room′ n. a private room on a ship.

states′man n. a highly respected and influential political leader who is devoted to public service. —**states′man·ship′,** n.

stat′ic (stat′ik) adj. **1.** fixed; at rest; showing no change. —n. **2.** atmospheric electricity. **3.** interference caused by such electricity.

sta′tion (stā′shən) n. **1.** a regular stopping place for trains or buses. **2.** a place from which broadcasts are sent. **3.** an assigned place or office. **4.** status. —v.t. **5.** to assign a place to.

sta′tion·ar′y (-shə ner′ē) adj. not moving; not movable; fixed.

sta′tion·er′y (-shə ner′ē) n. writing materials.

sta·tis′tics (stə tis′tiks) n. the science of collecting, classifying, and using numerical data. —**stat′is·ti′cian** (stat′ə stish′ən) n.

stat′u·ar′y (stach′oo er′ē) n. statues.

stat′ue (stach′oo) n. a carved, molded, or cast figure.

stat′u·esque′ (-esk′) adj. tall and dignified.

stat′u·ette′ (-et′) n. a little statue.

stat′ure (-ər) n. **1.** height. **2.** status from achievement.

sta′tus (stā′təs, stat′əs) n. **1.** present condition. **2.** social standing.

sta′tus quo′ (kwō) n. the existing state.

sta′tus sym′bol n. a possession believed to indicate high social status.

stat′ute (stach′oot) n. a law. —**stat′u·to′ry** (-oo tôr′ē) adj.

stat′ute of limita′tions n. a law defining the period within which legal action may be taken.

staunch (stônch) adj. firm; steadfast; strong.

stave (stāv) n., v., **staved** or (for 3) **stove** (stōv), **staving.** —n. **1.** a narrow strip of wood. **2.** a stick or rod. —v.t. **3.** to break a hole in. **4. stave off,** to prevent.

stay (stā) v.i. **1.** to remain in a place or condition; continue. **2.** to dwell. —v.t. **3.** to stop or restrain. —n. **4.** a period of time spent at one place. **5.** a stop; pause.

stay′ing pow′er n. endurance.

STD sexually transmitted disease.

stead (sted) n. **1.** the place of a person taken by another. —Idiom. **2. stand in good stead,** to prove useful to.

stead′fast′ adj. **1.** fixed in place. **2.** firm in purpose or loyalty.

stead′y adj., **-ier, -iest,** v., **-ied, -ying.** —adj. **1.** firmly fixed. **2.** regular. **3.** calm; not excitable. **4.** unwavering. —v.t., v.i. **5.** to make or become steady. —**stead′i·ly,** adv.

steak (stāk) n. a slice of meat or fish.

steal (stēl) v., **stole** (stōl), **stolen**, **stealing.** —v.t. **1.** to take wrongfully. —v.i. **2.** to commit theft. **3.** to move very quietly.

stealth (stelth) n. secret action. —**stealth′y,** adj.

steam (stēm) n. **1.** water in the form of gas or vapor. **2.** power or energy. —v.i. **3.** to pass off as or give off steam. —v.t. **4.** to treat with steam, as in cooking. —adj. **5.** operated by steam. **6.** conducting steam. —**steam′boat′, steam′ship′,** n.

steam′er n. **1.** a vessel moved by steam. **2.** a device for cooking, treating, etc., with steam.

steam′roll′er n. **1.** a heavy vehicle with a roller used for paving roads. —v.t. **2.** to crush, flatten, or overwhelm as if with a steamroller.

steam′ shov′el n. a machine for excavating.

steed (stēd) n. a horse.

steel (stēl) n. **1.** an alloy of iron with carbon. —adj. **2.** of or like steel. —v.t. **3.** to make resolute.

steel′ wool′ n. a mass of steel shavings, used for scouring and smoothing.

steep[1] (stēp) adj. **1.** sloping sharply. **2.** exorbitant. —**steep′ly,** adv.

steep[2] (stēp) v.t. **1.** to soak in a liquid. **2.** to saturate. —v.i. **3.** to lie soaking in a liquid.

stee′ple (stē′pəl) n. a structure topped with a spire, as on a church.

stee′ple•chase′ n. a horse race with artificial obstacles.

stee′ple•jack′ n. a person who builds or repairs steeples.

steer[1] (stēr) v.t. **1.** to guide the course of. **2.** to direct; guide. —v.i. **3.** to steer a vessel or vehicle.

steer[2] (stēr) n. a castrated ox.

steer′age (-ij) n. the part of a ship for passengers paying the least.

steg′o•saur′ (steg′ə sôr′) n. a plant-eating dinosaur with bony plates along the back.

stein (stīn) n. a mug, esp. for beer.

stel′lar (stel′ər) adj. **1.** of stars. **2.** outstanding.

stem[1] (stem) n., v., **stemmed, stemming.** —n. **1.** the supporting stalk of a plant. **2.** something resembling this. **3.** a family's line of descent. **4.** the part of a word that does not change. —v.t. **5.** to remove the stem of. —v.i. **6.** to originate.

stem[2] (stem) v.t., **stemmed, stemming.** to stop or check.

stem[3] (stem) n., v., **stemmed, stemming.** —n. **1.** the front of a ship. —v.t. **2.** to advance against.

stem′ware′ n. glassware with footed stems.

stench (stench) n. a bad odor.

sten′cil (sten′səl) n., v., **-ciled, -ciling.** —n. **1.** a sheet with a cut-out design to color over and reproduce on an underlying surface. —v.t. **2.** to make with a stencil.

ste•nog′ra•phy (-rə fē) n. shorthand writing. —**ste•nog′ra•pher,** n.

sten•to′ri•an (sten tôr′ē ən) adj. very loud.

step (step) n., v., **stepped, stepping.** —n. **1.** the movement of the foot in walking. **2.** the distance of such movement. **3.** a pace. **4.** a footprint. **5.** a stage in a process. **6.** a level on a stair. —v.i. **7.** to move in steps. **8.** to walk a short way. **9.** to press with the foot.

step- a prefix showing a relation created by the remarriage of a parent. —**step′broth′er,** n. —**step′child,** n. —**step′daugh′ter,** n. —**step′fath′er,** n. —**step′moth′er,** n. —**step′par′ent,** n. —**step′sis′ter,** n. —**step′son′,** n.

step′lad′der n. a ladder with a hinged supporting frame.

steppe (step) n. a vast plain.

-ster a suffix meaning one who is; one who is associated with; or one who makes or does.

ster′e•o (ster′ē ō′, stēr′-) n., pl. **-eos.** stereophonic sound or equipment.

ster′e•o•phon′ic (ster′ē ə fon′ik, stēr′-) adj. (of recorded sound) played through two or more speakers.

ster′e•o•type′ n., v., **-typed, -typing.** —n. **1.** a simplified image of a person, group, etc. **2.** an idea, expression, etc., without originality. —v.t. **3.** to regard as a stereotype.

ster′ile (ster′il; esp. Brit. -īl) adj. **1.** free from living germs. **2.** unable to produce offspring; barren. —**ste•ril′i•ty** (stə ril′i tē) n.

ster′i•lize′ v.t., **-lized, -lizing.** to make sterile. —**ster′i•li•za′tion,** n. —**ster′i•liz′er,** n.

ster′ling (stûr′ling) adj. **1.** containing 92.5% silver. **2.** of British money. **3.** excellent.

stern[1] (stûrn) adj. strict; grim.

stern[2] (stûrn) n. the rear part of a ship or boat.

ster′num (stûr′nəm) n., pl. **-na, -nums.** the bony plate to which the ribs are attached.

ste′roid (stēr′oid, ster′-) n. a fat-soluble organic compound.

stet (stet) v., **stetted, stetting.** —v.i. **1.** let it stand (a direction to retain printed material previously deleted). —v.t. **2.** to mark with the word "stet."

steth′o•scope′ (steth′ə skōp′) n. a medical instrument for listening to sounds in the body.

ste′ve•dore′ (stē′vi dôr′) n. a person who loads and unloads ships.

stew (stōō, styōō) v.t. **1.** to cook by simmering. —v.i. **2.** to worry. —n. **3.** a stewed dish of vegetables, meat, etc. **4.** a state of worry.

stew′ard (stōō′ərd, styōō′-) n. **1.** a person who manages another's affairs, property, etc. **2.** a person in charge of food, supplies, etc., for a ship, club, etc. **3.** a domestic employee on a ship or airplane. —**stew′ard•ship,** n.

stick[1] (stik) n. **1.** a cut or broken branch. **2.** a long, slender piece.

stick[2] (stik) v., **stuck** (stuk) **sticking,** n. **1.** to pierce; stab. **2.** to thrust (into or through). **3.** to fasten or attach. —v.i. **4.** to be fastened or attached. **5.** to become jammed. **6.** to protrude. **7.** stick up for, to defend. —n. **8.** an adhesive label.

stick′-in-the-mud′ n. a person who avoids change.

stick′ler n. someone who insists on something difficult.

stick′pin′ n. an ornamental pin.

stick′ shift′ n. a manual transmission.

stick′y adj. **-ier, -iest,** n. —adj. **1.** adhesive. **2.** humid. —**stick′i•ness,** n.

stiff (stif) adj. **1.** rigid. **2.** not moving easily. **3.** very formal in manner. —**stiff′en,** v.t., v.i.

stiff′-necked′ adj. stubborn.

sti′fle (stī′fəl) v., **-fled, -fling.** —v.t. **1.** to smother. **2.** to repress. —v.i. **3.** to suffocate.

stig′ma (stig′mə) n., pl. **stig•ma•ta** (stig mä′tə, -mə-) **-mas. 1.** a mark of disgrace. **2.** the pollen-receiving part of a pistil. **3. stigmata,** marks resembling the wounds of Christ.

stig′ma•tize′ (-tīz′) v.t., **-tized, -tizing.** to set a mark of disgrace or discredit upon.

stile (stīl) n. a set of steps over a fence, wall, etc.

sti•let′to (sti let′ō) n., pl. **-tos, -toes.** a thin-bladed dagger.

still[1] (stil) adj. **1.** motionless. **2.** silent. **3.** tranquil. —adv. **4.** until now. **5.** yet. **6.** even then. —conj. **7.** and yet. —v.t., v.i. **8.** to make or become still. —n. **9.** silence. —**still′ness,** n.

still[2] (stil) n. a distilling apparatus.

still′born′ adj. born dead.

still′ life′ n. a picture of inanimate objects, as flowers, fruit, etc.

stilt (stilt) n. one of two poles with foot supports enabling the user to walk above the ground.

stilt′ed adj. stiffly dignified.

stim′u•lant (stim′yə lənt) n. a drug or drink that temporarily stimulates the body or mind.

stim′u•late′ (-lāt′) v.t., **-lated, -lating. 1.** to rouse to action. **2.** to excite. —**stim′u•la′tion,** n.

stim′u•lus (-ləs) n., pl. **-li.** something that stimulates.

sting (sting) v., **stung** (stung) **stinging,** n. —v.t. **1.** to wound with a sharp-pointed organ, as bees do. **2.** to cause to feel a sharp pain. —v.i. **3.** to feel a sharp pain. —n. **4.** a wound or pain caused by stinging. —**sting′er,** n.

sting′ray′ n. a ray with a flexible tail armed with a bony, usu. poisonous, spine.

stin′gy (stin′jē) adj., **-gier, -giest. 1.** not wanting to give or spend. **2.** scanty.

stink (stingk) v., **stank** (stangk) or **stunk** (stungk), **stunk, stinking,** n. —v.i. **1.** to emit a bad odor. —n. **2.** a bad odor.

stint (stint) v.i. **1.** to be frugal. —v.t. **2.** to limit unduly. —n. **3.** a period of time spent on a task. **4.** a limitation.

sti′pend (stī′pend) n. a periodic fixed payment.

stip′ple (stip′əl) v.t., **-pled, -pling.** to paint or cover with tiny dots.

stip′u•late′ (stip′yə lāt′) v.t., **-lated, -lating.** to require as a condition.

stir (stûr) v., **stirred, stirring,** n. —v.t., v.i. **1.** to mix or agitate (a substance) by moving a spoon around in it. **2.** to move. **3.** to affect or be moved strongly. **4.** to incite, rouse, or be roused. —n. **5.** movement. **6.** excitement.

stir′-cra′zy adj. Slang. restless from long confinement.

stir′-fry′ v.t., **stir-fried, stir-frying.** to fry quickly while stirring constantly over high heat.

stir′rup (stûr′əp, stir′-) n. a loop-like support for the foot, suspended from a saddle.

stitch (stich) n. **1.** one complete movement of a needle in sewing, knitting, etc. **2.** a sudden pain, esp. in the side. —v.t. **3.** to join with stitches. —v.i. **4.** to sew.

stock (stok) n. **1.** a supply of goods on hand. **2.** the shares of a company. **3.** livestock. **4.** a line of descent. **5.** meat broth. **6. stocks,** a framework in which prisoners were publicly confined. **7.** the wooden piece to which the barrel of a rifle is attached. —adj. **8.** standard; common. **9.** kept on hand. —v.t. **10.** to supply. **11.** to store for future use. —v.i. **12.** to lay in a stock of something. —Idiom. **13.** take stock, **a.** to make an inventory of stock. **b.** to appraise prospects.

stock•ade′ (sto kād′) n. an enclosure built of upright posts driven into the ground.

stock′brok′er n. a broker who buys and sells securities for customers.

stock′ com′pany n. a theatrical company acting a repertoire of plays.

stock′ exchange′ n. a place where securities are bought and sold. Also, **stock market.**

stock′hold′er n. an owner of stock in a corporation.

stock′ing n. a close-fitting covering for the foot and leg.

stock′pile′ n., v., **-piled, -piling.** —n. **1.** a supply of something kept in reserve. —v.t., v.i. **2.** to accumulate for eventual use.

stock′-still′ adj. motionless.

stock′y adj., **-ier, -iest.** sturdy and short.

stock′yard′ n. an enclosure for livestock about to be slaughtered.

stodg′y (stoj′ē) adj., **-ier, -iest. 1.** dull; boring. **2.** old-fashioned.

sto′ic (stō′ik) adj. **1.** Also, **sto′i•cal.** not reacting to pain or stress. —n. **2.** a person who represses emotion.

stoke (stōk) v.t., v.i., **stoked, stoking.** to stir up and feed (a fire).

stole[1] (stōl) v. pt. of **steal.**

stole[2] (stōl) n. a long scarf or narrow strip worn over the shoulders.

sto′len (stō′lən) v. pp. of **steal.**

stol′id (stol′id) adj. unemotional; not easily moved. —**sto•lid′i•ty,** n.

stom′ach (stum′ək) n. **1.** the organ in which food is stored and partly digested. **2.** appetite; desire. —v.t. **3.** to endure; tolerate.

stomp (stomp) v.t., v.i. to tread (on) heavily.

stone (stōn) n., pl. **stones** (or for 4) **stone,** adj., v., **stoned, stoning.** —n. **1.** a hard, mineral substance. **2.** a small rock. **3.** a gem. **4.** Brit. a unit of weight equal to 14 pounds. **5.** a stonelike seed. **6.** a hard substance formed in the body, as in the kidney. —adj. **7.** of stone. —v.t. **8.** to throw stones at. **9.** to remove stones from. —**ston′y,** adj.

Stone′ Age′ n. the prehistoric period before the use of metals.

stone′wall′ v.i. to be evasive or uncooperative.

stood (stŏŏd) v. pt. and pp. of **stand.**

stooge (stōōj) n. **1.** a person who feeds lines to a comedian. **2.** an underling or assistant.

stool (stōōl) n. **1.** a seat without arms or back. **2.** fecal matter.

stool′ pi′geon n. Slang. a decoy or informer.

stoop[1] (stōōp) v.i. **1.** to bend the body forward and downward. **2.** to condescend. —n. **3.** a stooping posture.

stoop[2] (stōōp) n. a small doorway or porch.

stop (stop) v., **stopped, stopping,** n. —v.t. **1.** to put an end to the progress, movement, or operation of. **2.** to prevent. **3.** to block (an opening). —v.i. **4.** to cease moving, acting, or operating. **5.** to halt for a stay or visit. —n. **6.** an act, instance, or place of stopping. **7.** a hindrance. **8.** a set of organ pipes

stop′gap′ n. a temporary substitute.

stop′o′ver n. a temporary stop on a journey.

stop′per n. a plug.

stop′watch′ n. a watch that can be stopped or started at any instant, used for timing.

stor′age (stôr′ij) n. **1.** a storing or being stored. **2.** capacity for storing.

store (stôr) n., v., **stored, storing.** —n. **1.** a place where merchandise is sold. **2.** a supply or quantity. —v.t. **3.** to put away for future use. —Idiom. **4.** set store by. **5.** to value. —**store′keep′er,** n.

store′front′ n. **1.** a small street-level store. —adj. **2.** located in a storefront.

store′house′ n. a building for storage.

store′room′ n. a room in which supplies or goods are stored.

stork (stôrk) n. a wading bird with long legs and a long neck and bill.

storm (stôrm) n. **1.** heavy rain, snow, etc., with wind. **2.** a violent assault. —v.i. **3.** to blow, rain, etc., strongly. **4.** to rage. —v.t. **5.** to attack. —**storm′y,** adj. —**storm′i•ly,** adv.

sto′ry[1] (stôr′ē) n., pl. **-ries. 1.** a written or spoken account of something. **2.** a fictitious tale. **3.** a news report. **4.** a lie.

sto′ry[2] (stôr′ē) n., pl. **-ries.** a horizontal section of a building.

stoup (stōōp) n. a basin for holy water.

stout (stout) adj. **1.** solidly built. **2.** strong; sturdy. **3.** firm. —n. **4.** a dark ale.

stout′-heart′ed adj. brave and resolute.

stove (stōv) n. an apparatus for giving heat for warmth or cooking.

stow (stō) v.t. **1.** to put away, as cargo. **2. stow away,** to hide on a ship or airplane to get free passage. —**stow′age,** n. —**stow′a•way′,** n.

stra•bis′mus (strə biz′məs) n. a visual defect; cross-eye.

strad′dle (strad′l) v., **-dled, -dling,** n. —v.i., v.t. **1.** to have one leg on either side (of). —n. **2.** an act of straddling.

strafe (strāf, sträf) v.t., **strafed, strafing.** to shoot from airplanes.

strag′gle (strag′əl) v.i., **-gled, -gling.** to stray from the course; ramble. —**strag′gler,** n.

straight (strāt) adj. **1.** without a bend or curve. **2.** direct. **3.** honest. **4.** right. **5.** in order. **6.** undiluted. **7.** Informal. heterosexual. —adv. **8.** directly. **9.** in a straight line. **10.** honestly. —n. **11.** a straight part. **12.** a five-card sequence in poker.

straight′-arm′ v.t. to deflect (an opponent) by pushing away with the arm held straight.

straight′ ar′row n. an often righteously conventional person.

straight′a•way′ adv. **1.** at once. —n. **2.** a straight stretch.

straight′edge′ n. a bar with a straight edge for use in drawing lines.

straight′en v.t., v.i. **1.** to make or become straight. **2. straighten out, a.** to free or become free of confusion or difficulties. **b.** to improve in conduct or character. —**straight′en•er,** n.

straight′ face′ n. an expression that conceals one's feelings.

straight′for′ward adj. direct; frank.

straight′ man′ n. an entertainer who acts as a foil for a comedian.

strain[1] (strān) v.t. **1.** to exert to the utmost. **2.** to draw tight. **3.** to injure by stretching. **4.** to filter. —v.i. **5.** to make a great effort. —n. **6.** great effort. **7.** an injury from overexertion. **8.** severe pressure.

strain[2] (strān) n. **1.** the descendants of a common ancestor. **2.** ancestry. **3.** hereditary trait. **4.** a trace.

strain[3] (strān) n. a melody.

strained adj. not natural.

strait (strāt) n. **1.** a narrow waterway connecting two large bodies of water. **2. straits,** distress.

strait′en v.t. **1.** to put into financial difficulties. **2.** to restrict.

strait′jack′et n. **1.** a garment of strong material designed to restrain a violent person. **2.** anything that severely confines or hinders.

strait′-laced′ adj. excessively strict in conduct or morality.

strand[1] (strand) v.t. **1.** to run aground. **2.** to leave helpless. —n. **3.** a shore.

strand[2] (strand) n. **1.** one of the fi-

bers twisted to form a rope, cable, etc. 2. a lock of hair. **3.** a string, as of beads.

strange (strānj) adj., **stranger, strangest. 1.** unusual; odd. **2.** unfamiliar. —**strange′ly,** adv.

stran′ger (strān′jər) n. **1.** a person who is not known. **2.** a newcomer.

stran′gle (strang′gəl) v., **-gled, -gling.** —v.t. **1.** to kill by choking. **2.** to stifle. —v.i. **3.** to become strangled. —**stran′gu•la′tion** (-gyə lā′shən) n.

stran′gle•hold′ n. a restrictive force.

stran′gu•late′ (-gyə lāt′) v.t., **-lated, -lating.** to constrict.

strap (strap) n., v., **strapped, strapping.** —n. **1.** a narrow strip or band of leather for fastening or holding things together. —v.t. **2.** to fasten with a strap.

strapped adj. needing money.

strat′a•gem (strat′ə jəm) n. a plan; trick.

strat′e•gy (strat′i jē) n., pl. **-gies. 1.** a plan for achieving a goal. **2.** the planning and direction of military operations. —**stra•te′gic** (strə tē′jik) adj. —**strat′e•gist,** n.

strat′i•fy′ (strat′ə fī′) v.t., v.i., **-fied, -fying.** to form into or become arranged in layers. —**strat′i•fi•ca′tion,** n.

strat′o•sphere′ (-ə sfēr′) n. the upper region of the atmosphere.

stra′tum (strā′təm, strat′əm) n., pl. **-ta** (-tə), **-tums.** a layer of material.

straw (strô) n. **1.** a stalk of cereal grass. **2.** a mass of dried stalks. **3.** a tube for sucking up a liquid.

straw′ber′ry (-ber′ē, -bə rē) n., pl. **-ries.** a red, juicy fruit having seeds on the surface.

straw′ boss′ n. an assistant foreman.

straw′ vote′ n. an unofficial vote taken to determine the general trend of opinion.

stray (strā) v.i. **1.** to go from one's course or rightful place. —adj. **2.** straying or having strayed. **3.** isolated. —n. **4.** a lost or homeless creature.

streak (strēk) n. **1.** a long, narrow mark or smear. **2.** a vein; stratum. **3.** a series. —v.t. **4.** to mark with streaks. —v.i. **5.** to flash rapidly.

stream (strēm) n. **1.** a flowing body of water. **2.** a steady flow. —v.i. **3.** to flow in or as if in a stream.

stream′er n. a long narrow flag.

stream′lined′ adj. **1.** shaped to offer the least resistance to a current. **2.** designed for greatest efficiency. —**stream′line′,** v.t.

street (strēt) n. a paved public road in a town or city.

street′car′ n. a public conveyance running on rails along city streets.

street′ smarts′ n.pl. shrewd awareness of how to survive in an urban environment. —**street′-smart′,** adj.

street′wise′ adj. possessing street smarts.

strength (strengkth, strength, strenth) n. **1.** the quality or state of being strong. **2.** intensity. **3.** force in numbers. **4.** a strong or valuable quality.

strength′en v.t., v.i. to make or grow stronger.

stren′u•ous (stren′yōō əs) adj. vigorous; active.

strep′ throat′ (strep) n. an acute sore throat caused by streptococci.

strep′to•coc′cus (strep′tə kok′əs) n., pl. **-ci** (-sī, -sē). one of a group of bacteria causing serious diseases.

stress (stres) v.t. **1.** to emphasize. **2.** to subject to strain. —n. **3.** physical, mental, or emotional strain or tension. **4.** emphasis.

stretch (strech) v.t. **1.** to spread out. **2.** to extend. **3.** to draw tight. —v.i. **4.** to extend one's limbs or body. **5.** to extend over a time or distance. —n. **6.** a stretching or being stretched. **7.** an extension; expansion. **8.** a continuous length.

stretch′er n. **1.** a canvas-covered frame for carrying the sick and injured. **2.** a device for stretching.

strew (strōō) v.t., **strewed, strewed** or **strewn, strewing.** to scatter.

stri′at•ed (strī′ā tid) adj. furrowed; streaked. —**stri•a′tion** (-ā′shən) n.

strick′en (strik′ən) adj. afflicted, as by disease or sorrow.

strict (strikt) adj. **1.** narrowly limited; exact; precise. **2.** severe; exacting. —**strict′ly,** adv.

stric′ture (strik′chər) n. **1.** an ab-

normal contraction of a body passage. **2.** an adverse criticism.
stride (strīd) *v.*, **strode** (strōd), **strid-den** (strid′n), **striding**. *n.* —*v.i., v.t.* **1.** to walk (over or along) with long steps. **2.** a long step. **3.** a step forward, as in development.
stri′dent (strīd′nt) *adj.* harsh in sound. —**stri′den•cy**, *n.*
strife (strīf) *n.* bitter conflict.
strike (strīk) *v.*, **struck** (struk), **struck** or **strick•en** (strik′ən), **striking**, *n.* —*v.t.* **1.** to hit forcibly. **2.** to ignite (a match). **3.** to impress. **4.** to cancel. **5.** to afflict or affect. **6.** to find, as gold or oil. **7.** to mark by chimes, as the hour. —*v.i.* **8.** to deal a blow. **9.** to make an attack. **10.** to stop work to compel an employer's agreement to workers' demands. **11.** to sound by percussion. **12. strike out,** *Baseball.* to put or be put out on three strikes. —*n.* **13.** an act of striking. **14.** a group work stoppage to compel agreement to workers' demands. **15.** *Baseball.* the failure of a batter to hit a pitched ball. **16.** *Bowling.* the knocking-down of all the pins at once.
strik′ing *adj.* conspicuously attractive or impressive.
string (string) *n., v.,* **strung** (strung) **stringing.** —*n.* **1.** a thin cord or thread for tying. **2.** a series or set. **3.** a tightly stretched cord or wire on a musical instrument. **4.** a plant fiber. **5. strings,** conditions. —*v.t.* **6.** to supply with strings. **7.** to arrange in a row. **8.** to thread on a string. —**string′y,** *adj.*
string′ bean′ *n.* a bean with an edible pod.
stringed *adj.* fitted with strings.
strin′gent (strin′jənt) *adj.* very strict. —**strin′gen•cy,** *n.*
string′er (string′-) *n.* **1.** a part-time news reporter. **2.** a horizontal timber connecting upright posts.
strip¹ (strip) *v.,* **stripped, stripping.** —*v.t.* **1.** to remove covering or clothing from. **2.** to take away. **3.** to clear out; empty. —*v.i.* **4.** to remove one's clothes.
strip² (strip) *n.* a long narrow piece.
stripe (strīp) *n., v.,* **striped, striping.** —*n.* **1.** a band differing in color, material, or texture from the background. **2.** a strip of braid or fabric worn on a sleeve to indicate military rank. —*v.t.* **3.** to mark with stripes.
strip′ling (strip′ling) *n.* a youth.
strip′ mall′ *n.* stores or restaurants in adjacent spaces in one long building.
strip′ mine′ *n.* a mine in an open pit. —**strip′-mine′,** *v.t., v.i.*
strive (strīv) *v.i.,* **strove** (strōv), **striven** (striv′ən), **striving.** to try hard; struggle.
strobe (strōb) *n.* an electronic flash producing rapid bursts of light.
stroke¹ (strōk) *n.* **1.** an act of striking. **2.** a blockage or hemorrhage of a blood vessel leading to the brain. **3.** a single complete movement, as in swimming. **4.** a single mark made by a pen, brush, etc. **5.** a sudden happening.
stroke² (strōk) *v.,* **stroked, stroking,** *n.* —*v.t.* **1.** to rub gently; caress. —*n.* **2.** an act or instance of stroking.
stroll (strōl) *v.i., v.t.* **1.** to walk idly (along or through). —*n.* **2.** a walk.
stroll′er *n.* a chairlike carriage in which young children are pushed.
strong (strông) *adj.* **1.** powerful; vigorous. **2.** not weak; intense. **3.** able to resist strain or force.
strong′-arm′ *adj.* **1.** involving force. —*v.t.* **2.** to use force on.
strong′box′ *n.* a strongly made box for money.
strong′hold′ *n.* a fortress.
stron′ti•um (stron′shē əm, -shəm, -tē əm) *n.* a metallic chemical element whose compounds are used in fireworks.
strop (strop) *n., v.,* **stropped, stropping.** —*n.* **1.** a flexible strap for sharpening razors. —*v.t.* **2.** to sharpen on a strop.
stro′phe (strō′fē) *n., pl.* **-phes.** a section of a poem.
struck (struk) *v.* pt. and a pp. of **strike.**
struc′ture (struk′chər) *n.* **1.** the manner in which something is built or arranged. **2.** something constructed. —**struc′tur•al,** *adj.*
stru′del (strōōd′l; *Ger.* shtrōōd′l) *n.* a fruit-filled pastry.
strug′gle (strug′əl) *v.,* **-gled, -gling,** *n.* —*v.i.* **1.** to contend; strive. —*n.* **2.** a strong effort. **3.** a conflict.
strum (strum) *v.,* **strummed,**

strumming. to play lightly on (a stringed instrument).
strum′pet (strum′pit) *n.* a prostitute.
strut¹ (strut) *v.,* **strutted, strutting,** *n.* —*v.i.* **1.** to walk in a vain, pompous manner. —*n.* **2.** a strutting walk.
strut² (strut) *n.* a prop; truss.
strych′nine (strik′nin, -nēn, -nīn) *n.* a colorless poison that affects the central nervous system.
stub (stub) *n., v.,* **stubbed, stubbing.** —*n.* **1.** a short remaining piece. —*v.t.* **2.** to strike (one's toe) against something. —**stub′by,** *adj.*
stub′ble (stub′əl) *n.* **1.** short stumps, as of grain stalks. **2.** a short growth of beard. —**stub′bly,** *adj.*
stub′born (stub′ərn) *adj.* **1.** unreasonably obstinate. **2.** persistent.
stuc′co (stuk′ō) *n., pl.* **-coes, -cos,** *v.,* **-coed, -coing.** —*n.* **1.** a plaster finish for exterior walls. —*v.t.* **2.** to cover with stucco.
stuck′-up′ *adj. Informal.* snobbishly conceited.
stud¹ (stud) *n., v.,* **studded, studding.** —*n.* **1.** a projecting knob, pin, etc. **2.** one of the upright posts forming the frame of a wall. **3.** a detachable button. —*v.t.* **4.** to set with studs. **5.** to be scattered over the surface of.
stud² (stud) *n.* a male animal kept for breeding.
stu′dent (stōōd′nt, styōōd′-) *n.* a person who studies.
stud′ied (stud′ēd) *adj.* deliberate.
stu′di•o′ (stōō′dē ō′, styōō′-) *n., pl.* **-dios. 1.** an artist's workroom. **2.** a place equipped for radio or television broadcasting.
stud′y (stud′ē) *n., pl.* **-ies,** *v.,* **-ied, -ying.** —*n.* **1.** applying the mind in an effort to learn. **2.** the object of study. **3.** a detailed analysis. **4.** deep thought. **5.** a room for studying, writing, etc. —*v.i.* **6.** to apply the mind to acquiring knowledge. —*v.t.* **7.** to make a study of.
stuff (stuf) *n.* **1.** material used to make something. **2.** personal belongings. **3.** unspecified matter or objects. **4.** worthless ideas or talk. —*v.t.* **5.** to cram full; pack.
stuffed′ shirt′ *n.* a pompous, self-satisfied person.
stuff′ing *n.* **1.** material stuffed in something. **2.** a filling for poultry, vegetables, etc.
stuff′y *adj.,* **-ier, -iest. 1.** lacking fresh air. **2.** pompous; pedantic.
stul′ti•fy′ (stul′tə fī′) *v.t.,* **-fied, -fying. 1.** to cause to look foolish **2.** to make futile or ineffectual.
stum′ble (stum′bəl) *v.,* **-bled, -bling,** *n.* —*v.i.* **1.** to lose one's balance. **2. stumble upon,** to discover by chance. —*n.* **3.** a stumbling.
stum′bling block′ *n.* an obstacle.
stump (stump) *n.* **1.** the lower part of a tree after the top is gone. **2.** any short remaining part. —*v.t.* **3.** to baffle. —*v.i.* **4.** to campaign politically. **5.** to walk heavily.
stun (stun) *v.t.,* **stunned, stunning. 1.** to render unconscious. **2.** to amaze.
stun′ning *adj.* strikingly attractive.
stunt¹ (stunt) *v.t.* to stop or slow the growth of.
stunt² (stunt) *n.* a feat showing skill or daring.
stu′pe•fy′ (stōō′pə fī′, styōō′-) *v.t.,* **-fied, -fying. 1.** to put into a stupor. **2.** to astonish.
stu•pen′dous (stōō pen′dəs, styōō-) *adj.* **1.** amazing. **2.** immense.
stu′pid (stōō′pid, styōō′-) *adj.* lacking intelligence. —**stu•pid′i•ty,** *n.*
stu′por (-pər) *n.* a dazed or insensible state.
stur′dy (stûr′dē) *adj.,* **-dier, -diest. 1.** strongly built. **2.** firm.
stur′geon (stûr′jən) *n.* a large fish of fresh and salt water, valued as a source of caviar.
stut′ter (stut′ər) *v.i., v.t.* **1.** to speak or say with repetitions, prolongations, etc. —*n.* **2.** stuttering or a speech defect marked by stuttering. —**stut′ter•er,** *n.*
sty¹ (stī) *n., pl.* **sties.** a pigpen.
sty² (stī) *n., pl.* **sties.** an inflamed swelling on the eyelid.
style (stīl) *n., v.,* **styled, styling.** —*n.* **1.** a distinct way of acting, speaking, or writing. **2.** the current fashion. **3.** elegance. —*v.t.* **4.** to design in accordance with a particular style. **5.** to name.
styl′ish *adj.* fashionable.
styl′ist *n.* a person who cultivates a distinctive style. —**sty•lis′tic,** *adj.*
styl′ize *v.t.,* **-ized, -izing.** to cause

to conform to a conventionalized style.
sty′lus (stī′ləs) *n.* a pointed tool used in artwork.
sty′mie (stī′mē) *v.t.,* **-mied, -mying.** to hinder or obstruct.
styp′tic (stip′tik) *adj.* checking bleeding.
Sty′ro•foam′ (stī′rə fōm′) *Trademark.* a lightweight plastic.
sua′sion (swā′zhən) *n.* persuasion.
suave (swäv) *adj.* smoothly polite and agreeable. —**suav′i•ty,** *n.*
sub- a prefix meaning under, below, or beneath; secondary.
sub′a•tom′ic *adj.* of particles within an atom.
sub•com•mit′tee *n.* a committee appointed out of a main committee.
sub•con′scious *adj.* **1.** existing beneath one's consciousness. —*n.* **2.** ideas, feelings, etc., of which one is unaware. —**sub•con′scious•ly,** *adv.*
sub•con′ti•nent *n.* a large subdivision of a continent.
sub′cul′ture *n.* a group with social, economic, or other traits distinguishing it from others within the larger society.
sub•cu•ta′ne•ous *adj.* beneath the skin.
sub′di•vide′ (sub′di vīd′, sub′di-vīd′) *v.t., v.i.,* **-vided, -viding.** to divide into smaller parts. —**sub′di•vi′sion,** *n.*
sub•due′ (səb dōō′, -dyōō′) *v.t.,* **-dued, -duing. 1.** to overcome. **2.** to reduce the force or intensity of. **3.** to bring under control.
sub•fam′i•ly (sub fam′ə lē, sub′-fam′ə lē) *n., pl.* **-lies. 1.** a category of related organisms within a family. **2.** a group of related languages within a family.
sub′head′ *n.* **1.** a heading of a subdivision. **2.** a subordinate division of a title.
sub′ject *n.* (sub′jikt) **1.** a matter of thought, concern, etc. **2.** a person under the rule of a government. **3.** a noun or pronoun that performs the action or is in the state of the predicate. **4.** something or someone represented in a work of art. —*adj.* (sub′jikt) **5.** being a subject. **6.** liable; exposed. —*v.t.* (səb jekt′) **7.** to cause to experience. **8.** to make liable. —**sub•jec′tion,** *n.*
sub•jec′tive *adj.* dependent on personal views. —**sub•jec•tiv′i•ty,** *n.*
sub•join′ (səb join′) *v.t.* to append.
sub′ju•gate′ (sub′jə gāt′) *v.t.,* **-gated, -gating.** to subdue; conquer. —**sub′ju•ga′tion,** *n.*
sub•junc′tive (səb jungk′tiv) *adj.* **1.** designating a verb mood used for doubtful or hypothetical statements or questions. —*n.* **2.** the subjunctive mood or a verb in this mood.
sub′lease′ *n., v.,* **-leased, -leasing.** —*n.* (sub′lēs′) **1.** a lease granted to another by the tenant of a property. —*v.t., v.i.* (sub lēs′) **2.** to rent by sublease (of).
sub•let′ (sub let′, sub′let′) *v.t., v.i.,* **-let, -letting.** to sublease.
sub•li′mate (sub′lə māt′) *v.t.,* **-mated, -mating.** to divert (biological impulses) to other channels.
sub•lime′ (sə blīm′) *adj.* **1.** lofty; noble. —*n.* **2.** that which is sublime. —**sub•lim′i•ty** (-blim′i tē) *n.*
sub•lim′i•nal (sub lim′ə nl) *adj.* below the threshold of consciousness.
sub′ma•chine′ gun′ *n.* an automatic weapon.
sub′ma•rine′ *n.* (sub′mə rēn′, sub′mə rēn′) **1.** a vessel that can navigate under water. —*adj.* (sub′-mə rēn′) **2.** of submarines. **3.** being under the sea.
sub•merge′ (səb mûrj′) *v.t., v.i.,* **-merged, -merging.** to put or sink under water. —**sub•mer′gence,** *n.*
sub•merse′ (-mûrs′) *v.t.,* **-mersed, -mersing.** to submerge. —**sub•mer′sion,** *n.* —**sub•mers′i•ble,** *adj.*
sub•mis′sive *adj.* yielding or obeying readily. —**sub•mis′sive•ly,** *adv.*
sub•mit′ (səb mit′) *v.,* **-mitted, -mitting.** —*v.t.* **1.** to yield; surrender. **2.** to offer for consideration. —*v.i.* **3.** to yield oneself to another's authority. —**sub•mis′sion** (-mish′ən) *n.*
sub•nor′mal (sub nôr′məl) *adj.* of less than normal intelligence.
sub•or′bit•al *adj.* making less than a complete orbit.
sub•ze′ro *adj.* indicating lower than zero on some scale.
suc•ceed′ (sək sēd′) *v.i.* **1.** to turn out successfully. **2.** to come next. —*v.t.* **3.** to come after.

or treat as subordinate. —**sub•or′di•na′tion,** *n.*
sub•orn′ (sə bôrn′) *v.t.* to bribe or incite to crime, esp. to perjury.
sub′plot′ (sub′plot′) *n.* a secondary plot.
sub•poe′na (sə pē′nə, səb-) *n., v.,* **-naed, -naing.** —*n.* **1.** a summons to appear in court. —*v.t.* **2.** to serve with a subpoena.
sub ro′sa (sub rō′zə) *adv.* secretly.
sub•scribe′ (səb skrīb′) *v.t., v.i.,* **-scribed, -scribing. 1.** to pay or pledge (money) as a contribution. **2.** to obtain a subscription, as to a publication. **3.** to give one's consent (to). —**sub•scrib′er,** *n.*
sub′script (sub′skript) *n.* a letter, number, etc., written low on a line of text.
sub•scrip′tion *n.* the right to receive a publication or to attend a series of performances for a sum paid.
sub′se•quent (sub′si kwənt) *adj.* later; following.
sub•ser′vi•ent (səb sûr′vē ənt) *adj.* **1.** servile; submissive. **2.** subordinate. —**sub•ser′vi•ence,** *n.*
sub•side′ *v.i.,* **-sided, -siding. 1.** to sink; settle. **2.** to become less active or violent. —**sub•sid′ence,** *n.*
sub•sid′i•ar′y (-sid′ē er′ē) *adj.,* *pl.* **-aries.** —*adj.* **1.** auxiliary. **2.** subordinate. —*n.* **3.** anything subsidiary.
sub′si•dy (-si dē) *n., pl.* **-dies.** direct financial aid, esp. by a government. —**sub′si•dize′,** *v.t.*
sub•sist′ (səb sist′) *v.i.* to continue to exist.
sub′soil′ *n.* the layer of earth immediately under the surface soil.
sub•son′ic *adj.* of a speed below the speed of sound.
sub′stance (sub′stəns) *n.* **1.** physical matter or material. **2.** solid quality. **3.** the essential part. **4.** wealth.
sub•stand′ard *adj.* below standard.
sub•stan′tial (səb stan′shəl) *adj.* **1.** of real worth or effect. **2.** fairly large. **3.** strong. **4.** real. **5.** wealthy.
sub•stan′ti•ate′ (-shē āt′) *v.t.,* **-ated, -ating.** to support with evidence.
sub•stan′tive (sub′stən tiv) *adj.* **1.** essential. **2.** real. —*n.* **3.** a noun, pronoun, or word used as a noun.
sub′sti•tute′ (sub′sti tōōt′, -tyōōt′) *v.,* **-tuted, -tuting.** —*n.* **1.** a person or thing serving in place of another. —*v.t.* **2.** to put in place of another. —*v.i.* **3.** to serve as a substitute.
sub′struc′ture *n.* a structure forming a foundation.
sub•sume′ (səb sōōm′) *v.t.,* **-sumed, -suming.** to consider or include as part of something larger.
sub′ter•fuge′ (sub′tər fyōōj′) *n.* a means used to evade or conceal.
sub′ter•ra′ne•an (-tə rā′nē ən) *adj.* underground.
sub′text *n.* an underlying or implicit meaning.
sub′ti•tle *n., v.,* **-tled, -tling.** —*n.* **1.** a secondary or subordinate title, as of a book. **2.** a translation of dialogue, appearing at the bottom of a motion-picture screen. —*v.t.* **3.** to give subtitles to.
sub′tle (sut′l) *adj.,* **-tler, -tlest. 1.** difficult to perceive; delicate or fine. **2.** discerning. **3.** clever. —**sub′tle•ty,** *n.*
sub•to′tal (sub′tōt′l, sub tōt′-) *n., v.,* **-totaled, -totaling.** —*n.* **1.** the total of a part of a group of figures. —*v.t., v.i.* **2.** to determine a subtotal (for).
sub•tract′ *v.t., v.i.* to take (one number) from another. —**sub•trac′tion,** *n.*
sub′tra•hend′ (sub′trə hend′) *n.* a number subtracted from another number.
sub•trop′i•cal *adj.* bordering on the tropics.
sub′urb (sub′ûrb) *n.* a residential district just outside a city. —**sub•ur′ban,** *adj.* —**sub•ur′ban•ite′,** *n.*
sub•ur′bi•a (-bē ə) *n.* **1.** suburbs or suburbanites collectively. **2.** life in the suburbs.
sub•ven′tion (səb ven′shən) *n.* a grant of money.
sub•vert′ (-vûrt′) *v.t.* to overthrow. —**sub•ver′sion,** *n.* —**sub•ver′sive,** *adj., n.*
sub′way′ *n.* an underground electric railway.

suc•cess′ (-ses′) *n.* **1.** a favorable outcome. **2.** good fortune. **3.** a successful thing or person. —**suc•cess′ful.**
suc•ces′sion (-sesh′ən) *n.* **1.** the act of following in sequence. **2.** a sequence of persons or things. **3.** the right or process of succeeding another. —**suc•ces′sive,** *adj.*
suc•ces′sor *n.* one that succeeds another.
suc•cinct′ (sək singkt′) *adj.* without useless words; concise.
suc′cor (suk′ər) *n.* **1.** help; aid. —*v.t.* **2.** to help.
suc′co•tash′ (suk′ə tash′) *n.* corn and beans cooked together.
suc′cu•lent (suk′yə lənt) *adj.* juicy.
suc•cumb′ (sə kum′) *v.i.* **1.** to yield. **2.** to die.
such (such) *adj.* **1.** of that kind, extent, etc. —*n.* **2.** such a person or thing.
suck (suk) *v.t.* **1.** to draw into the mouth by using the lips and tongue. **2.** to draw (liquid) from. **3.** to draw upon in the mouth. **4.** to draw something in by sucking. —*n.* **5.** the act of sucking.
suck′er *n.* **1.** one that sucks. **2.** *Informal.* a gullible person. **3.** a lollipop. **4.** a shoot from an underground stem or root. **5.** a freshwater fish.
suck′le *v.t., v.i.,* **-led, -ling.** to nurse at the breast.
suck′ling (-ling) *n.* **1.** an infant. **2.** an unweaned animal.
su′crose (sōō′krōs) *n.* sugar.
suc′tion (suk′shən) *n.* **1.** sucking. **2.** the force that draws a substance into a vacuum.
sud′den (sud′n) *adj.* abrupt; quick; unexpected. —**sud′den•ly,** *adv.*
suds (sudz) *n.pl.* **1.** soapy water. **2.** foam; lather. —**suds′y,** *adj.*
sue (sōō) *v.t., v.i.,* **sued, suing.** to bring a civil action (against).
suede (swād) *n.* soft, napped leather.
su′et (sōō′it) *n.* the hard fat around the kidneys of cattle and sheep.
suf′fer (suf′ər) *v.i., v.t.* **1.** to undergo (pain, loss, etc.) **2.** to tolerate.
suf′fer•ance (-əns) *n.* **1.** tolerance. **2.** endurance.
suf•fice′ (sə fīs′) *v.i., v.t.,* **-ficed, -ficing.** to be enough (for).
suf•fi′cient (-fish′ənt) *adj.* enough. —**suf•fi′cien•cy,** *n.*
suf′fix (suf′iks) *n.* an element added to the end of a word to form another word.
suf′fo•cate′ (suf′ə kāt′) *v.,* **-cated, -cating.** —*v.t.* **1.** to kill or choke by cutting off air to the lungs. —*v.i.* **2.** to become suffocated. —**suf′fo•ca′tion,** *n.*
suf′fra•gan (suf′rə gən) *n.* an assistant bishop.
suf′frage (suf′rij) *n.* the right to vote.
suf•fuse′ (sə fyōōz′) *v.t.* to overspread; pervade.
sug′ar (shŏŏg′ər) *n.* **1.** a sweet substance obtained from sugar cane or sugar beet. —*v.t.* **2.** to sweeten with sugar. —**sug′ar•less,** *adj.* —**sug′ar•y,** *adj.*
sug′ar beet′ *n.* a beet with a white root having a high sugar content.
sug′ar cane′ *n.* a tall grass that is the chief source of sugar.
sug′ar-coat′ *v.t.* to make more pleasant or acceptable.
sug′ar ma′ple *n.* a maple with a sweet sap.
sug′ar•plum′ *n.* a candy.
sug•gest′ (sag jest′, sə-) *v.t.* **1.** to mention or propose for consideration or action. **2.** to call to mind.
sug•gest′i•ble *adj.* easily led or influenced. —**sug•gest′i•bil′i•ty,** *n.*
sug•ges′tion *n.* **1.** the act of suggesting. **2.** something suggested. **3.** a slight trace.
sug•ges′tive *adj.* suggesting.
su′i•cide′ (sōō′ə sīd′) *n.* **1.** the intentional killing of oneself. **2.** a person who commits suicide. —**su′i•cid′al,** *adj.*
su′i ge′ne•ris (sōō′ē jen′ər is, sōō′ī) *adj.* being one of a kind.
suit (sōōt) *n.* **1.** a set of clothes. **2.** a legal action. **3.** a class of playing cards. —*v.t.* **4.** to be becoming to. **5.** to please. —*v.i.* **6.** to be appropriate.
suit′a•ble *adj.* appropriate; fitting.
suit′case′ *n.* a rectangular piece of luggage.
suite (swēt) *n.* **1.** a series or set, as of rooms or furniture. **2.** a retinue.
suit′or (sōō′tər) *n.* a man who courts a woman.

sul'fa drug' (sul'fə), n. a group of drugs used in the treatment of wounds, burns, and infections.

sul'fate (-fāt) n. a salt of sulfuric acid.

sul'fide (-fīd, -fid) n. a sulfur compound.

sul'fur (-fər) n. a yellow nonmetallic element. —**sul·fur'ic**, **sul'fur'ous**, adj.

sulfu'ric ac'id n. a corrosive liquid used in chemicals and explosives.

sulk (sulk) v.i. **1.** to be sullen and aloof. —n. **2.** a fit of sulking.

sulk'y adj., **-ier**, **-iest**, n., pl. **-ies**. —adj. **1.** sullen; ill-humored. —n. **2.** a two-wheeled racing carriage for one person. —**sulk'i·ly**, adv.

sul'len (sul'ən) adj. **1.** silently ill-humored. **2.** gloomy.

sul'ly (sul'ē) v.t., **-lied**, **-lying**. to soil; defile.

sul'phur (-fər) n. sulfur.

sul'tan (sul'tn) n. a ruler of an Islamic country. —**sul'tan·ate**, n.

sul·ta'na (-tan'ə) n. a small raisin.

sul'try adj., **-trier**, **-triest**. **1.** hot and humid. **2.** (of a woman) passionate. —**sul'tri·ness**, n.

sum (sum) n., v., **summed**, **summing**. —n. **1.** the result obtained by adding two or more numbers. **2.** an amount. —v.t. **3.** to total. **4. sum up**, to summarize.

su'mac (sōō'mak, shōō'-) n. a small tree with long pinnate leaves.

sum'ma·rize (sum'ə rīz') v.t., **-rized**, **-rizing**. to make or be a summary of.

sum'ma·ry (-rē) n., pl. **-ries**, adj. —n. **1.** a brief presentation of the main points. —adj. **2.** concise. **3.** prompt.

sum·ma'tion (sə mā'shən) n. the act or result of summing up.

sum'mer (sum'ər) n. **1.** the season between spring and fall. —adj. **2.** of, like, or for summer. —v.i. **3.** to spend or pass the summer. —**sum'mer·y**, adj.

sum'mer·house' n. a structure in a garden that provides shade.

sum'mit (sum'it) n. the highest point, part, or degree.

sum'mon (sum'ən) v.t. **1.** to order to appear. **2.** to gather together.

sum'mons n. **1.** an order to appear before a court. **2.** a command ordering someone to appear somewhere.

su'mo (sōō'mō) n. a Japanese form of wrestling featuring extremely heavy contestants.

sump (sump) n. a pit, basin, or reservoir into which liquid drains.

sump'tu·ous (sump'chōō əs) adj. revealing great expense; luxurious.

sun (sun) n., v., **sunned**, **sunning**. —n. **1.** the star that is the heat- and light-giving body of the solar system. **2.** sunshine. —v.t. **3.** to expose to sunshine.

Sun. Sunday.

sun'bathe' v.i., **-bathed**, **-bathing**. to expose the body to sunlight.

Sun'belt' n. the southern and southwestern U.S.

sun'block' n. a substance that protects against sunburn and prevents most tanning.

sun'burn' n., v., **-burned** or **-burnt**, **-burning**. —n. **1.** a superficial burn from the sun's rays. —v.i., v.t. **2.** to suffer or cause to suffer from sunburn.

sun'dae (sun'dā, -dē) n. ice cream topped with syrup, nuts, fruit, etc.

Sun'day (sun'dā, -dē) n. the first day of the week.

sun'der (sun'dər) v.t., v.i. to separate.

sun'di'al n. an outdoor instrument for telling time by the shadow of a pointer cast by the sun on a dial.

sun'dries (-drēz) n.pl. small, miscellaneous items.

sun'dry (sun'drē) adj. various.

sun'fish' n. a freshwater fish.

sun'flow'er n. a tall plant with yellow flowers and edible seeds.

sung (sung) v. a pt. and pp. of **sing**.

sun'glass·es n.pl. eyeglasses with tinted lenses to protect the eyes from the sun.

sun'light' n. the light of the sun.

sun'lit' adj. lighted by the sun.

sun'ny adj., **-nier**, **-niest**. **1.** full of sunshine. **2.** cheerful; jolly.

sun'rise' n. the rise of the sun above the horizon. Also, **sun'up'**.

sun'roof' n. a section of an automobile roof that can be opened.

sun'screen' n. a substance that protects skin from ultraviolet light.

sun'set' n. the setting of the sun below the horizon. Also, **sun'down'**.

sun'shine' n. the direct light of the sun.

sun'spot' n. a dark spot on the sun.

sun'stroke' n. illness from overexposure to the sun's rays.

sun'tan' n. a darkening of the skin caused by exposure to the sun.

sup (sup) v.i. **1.** supped, supping. to eat supper.

su'per (sōō'pər) n. **1.** a superintendent, esp. of an apartment building. —adj. **2.** first-rate.

super- a prefix meaning above or over; exceeding; larger or more.

su'per·a·bun'dant adj. exceedingly abundant.

su·perb' (sōō pûrb', sə-) adj. very fine. —**su·perb'ly**, adv.

su'per·charge' (sōō'pər charj') v.t., **-charged**, **-charging**. **1.** to charge with abundant energy. **2.** to supply air to (an engine) at high pressure.

su'per·cil'i·ous (sōō'pər sil'ē əs) adj. haughtily disdainful.

su'per·con·duc·tiv'i·ty n. the disappearance of electrical resistance in certain metals at extremely low temperatures. —**su'per·con'duct'or**, n.

su'per·e'go n. the part of the personality representing the conscience.

su'per·fi'cial (-fish'əl) adj. **1.** of, on, or near the surface. **2.** shallow, obvious, or insignificant. —**su'per·fi'ci·al'i·ty** (-fish'ē al'i tē) n.

su·per'flu·ous (sōō pûr'flōō əs) adj. being more than is necessary. —**su'per·flu'i·ty** (-flōō'i tē) n.

su'per·high'way (sōō'pər hī'wā, sōō'pər hī'wā') n. a highway for travel at high speeds.

su'per·hu'man adj. **1.** beyond what is human. **2.** exceeding human strength.

su'per·im·pose' v.t., **-posed**, **-posing**. to place over something else.

su'per·in·tend' (sōō'pər in tend', sōō'prin-) v.t. to oversee and direct.

su'per·in·tend'ent (sōō'pər in ten'dənt, sōō'prin-) n. **1.** a person who oversees a department, district, etc. **2.** a custodian in an apartment building.

su·pe'ri·or (sə pēr'ē ər, sōō-) adj. **1.** higher in rank, degree, grade, or quality. **2.** above average; better. **3.** arrogant. —n. **4.** a superior person. **5.** the head of a convent or monastery. —**su·pe'ri·or'i·ty**, n.

su·per'la·tive (sə pûr'lə tiv, sōō-) adj. **1.** of the highest kind; best. **2.** designating the highest degree of comparison of adjectives and adverbs. —n. **3.** anything superlative.

su'per·man' (sōō'pər-) n., pl. **-men**. a person of extraordinary powers.

su'per·mar'ket n. a large self-service store that sells food and household goods.

su'per·nat'u·ral adj. **1.** being beyond what can be explained by the laws of nature; ghostly. —n. **2.** the realm of supernatural beings or things.

su'per·no'va n., pl. **-vas**, **-vae** (-vē). a nova millions of times brighter than the sun.

su'per·nu'mer·ar'y (-nōō'mə rer'ē, -nyōō'-) adj., n., pl. **-aries**. —adj. **1.** extra. —n. **2.** an extra person or thing. **3.** a performer with no speaking lines.

su'per·pow'er n. a large, powerful nation greatly influencing world affairs.

su'per·script' n. a number, symbol, etc., written high on a line of text.

su'per·sede' (-sēd') v.t., **-seded**, **-seding**. to take the place of.

su'per·son'ic adj. faster than the speed of sound.

su'per·star' n. an entertainer or sports figure of world renown.

su'per·sti'tion (-stish'ən) n. an irrational belief in the ominous significance of a particular thing, event, etc. —**su'per·sti'tious**, adj.

su'per·store' n. a very large store that stocks a wide variety of merchandise.

su'per·struc'ture n. the upper part of a building or vessel.

su'per·vene' (-vēn') v.i., **-vened**, **-vening**. to occur as something extraneous. —**su'per·ven'tion** (-ven'-) n.

su'per·vise (-vīz') v.t., **-vised**, **-vising**. to watch over and direct. —**su'per·vi'sion** (-vizh'ən) n. —**su'per·vi'sor**, n. —**su'per·vi'so·ry**, adj.

su'per·wom'an n., pl. **-women. 1.** a woman of extraordinary powers. **2.** a woman who copes successfully with the demands of career, marriage, and motherhood.

su·pine' (sōō pīn') adj. **1.** lying on the back. **2.** passive.

sup'per (sup'ər) n. the evening meal.

sup·plant' (sə plant') v.t. to take the place of, esp. by force.

sup'ple (sup'əl) adj., **-pler**, **-plest**. flexible; limber.

sup'ple·ment n. (sup'lə mənt) **1.** something added to complete or improve a thing. —v.t. (-ment') **2.** to add to or complete. —**sup'ple·men'tal** (-men'tl), **sup'ple·men'ta·ry**, adj.

sup'pli·cate' (sup'li kāt') v.t., v.i., **-cated**, **-cating**. to beg (for) humbly. —**sup'pli·ant** (sup'lē ənt), **sup'pli·cant**, n., adj.

sup·ply' (sə plī') v., **-plied**, **-plying**, n., pl. **-plies**. —v.t. **1.** to furnish; provide. **2.** to fill (a need). —n. **3.** the act of supplying. **4.** something supplied. **5.** a stock of items. —**sup·pli'er**, n.

supply'-side' adj. of the economic theory that reduced taxes will stimulate economic growth.

sup·port' (sə pôrt') v.t. **1.** to hold up; bear. **2.** to provide a living for. **3.** to uphold or advocate (a cause). **4.** to corroborate (a statement). —n. **5.** a supporting or being supported. **6.** a thing or person that supports. —**sup·port'a·ble**, adj. —**sup·port'ive**, adj.

support' group' n. a group of people who meet regularly to discuss shared problems.

sup·pose' (sə pōz') v., **-posed**, **-posing**. —v.t. **1.** to assume to be true. **2.** to think. —v.i. **3.** to assume something. **4. to be supposed to**, to be expected to. —**sup·pos'ed·ly** (-pō'zid lē), adv. —**sup·po·si'tion** (sup'ə zish'ən) n.

sup·pos'i·to'ry (sə poz'i tôr'ē) n., pl. **-ries**. a solid mass of medication that melts on insertion into the rectum or vagina.

sup·press' (sə pres') v.t. **1.** to put an end to by force. **2.** to restrain. **3.** to withhold from circulation. —**sup·pres'sion** (-presh'ən) n.

sup'pu·rate' (sup'yə rāt') v.i., **-rated**, **-rating**. to form or discharge pus. —**sup'pu·ra'tion**, n.

su'pra (sōō'prə) adv. above, esp. in a text.

su·prem'a·cist (sə prem'ə sist, sōō-) n. a person who advocates the supremacy of a particular group.

su·preme' (sə prēm', sōō-) adj. highest in rank, authority, quality, or importance. —**su·prem'a·cy** (-prem'ə sē) n. —**su·preme'ly**, adv.

Supreme' Be'ing n. God.

Supreme' Court' n. **1.** the highest court of the U.S. **2.** supreme court, the highest court of a state.

sur·cease' (sûr sēs') n. ceasing; end.

sur·charge' n., v., **-charged**, **-charging**. —n. (sûr'chärj') **1.** an extra charge. —v.t. (sûr chärj', sûr'chärj') **2.** to put a surcharge on.

sure (shoor, shûr) adj., **surer**, **surest**. **1.** certain; positive. **2.** reliable. —adv. **3.** certainly. —**sure'ly**, adv.

sure'fire' adj. Informal. sure to work.

sure'foot'ed adj. not likely to stumble.

sure'ty (shoor'i tē, shoor'tē, shûr'-) n., pl. **-ties. 1.** security against loss or damage. **2.** a person who accepts responsibility for another.

surf (sûrf) n. **1.** waves breaking on a shore. —v.i. **2.** to ride on the crest of a wave while standing or lying on a **surfboard**. **3.** to search randomly, as for information on the Internet or a program on TV. —v.t. **4.** to search through (a computer network or TV channels). —**surf'er**, n.

sur'face (sûr'fis) n., adj., v., **-faced**, **-facing**. —n. **1.** the outermost layer of something; outside. **2.** outward appearance. —adj. **3.** of or on a surface. —v.t. **4.** to finish the surface of. —v.i. **5.** to come to the surface.

sur'feit (sûr'fit) n. **1.** an excess, esp. of food or drink. —v.t. **2.** to supply or feed to excess.

surf'ing n. the sport of riding the surf, usu. on a **surf'board'**.

surge (sûrj) n., v., **surged**, **surging**. —n. **1.** a wavelike forward movement. **2.** a sudden strong rush. —v.i. **3.** to move in a surge.

sur'geon (sûr'jən) n. a physician who specializes in surgery.

surge' protec'tor n. a device to protect a computer, telephone, etc., from damage by high-voltage electrical surges.

sur'ger·y (-jə rē) n., pl. **-geries. 1.** the treatment of disease, injuries, etc., by operating on the body with instruments. **2.** treatment by a surgeon. —**sur'gi·cal** (-ji kəl) adj.

sur'ly (sûr'lē) adj., **-lier**, **-liest**. rude and sullen. —**sur'li·ness**, n.

sur·mise' (sər mīz') v., **-mised**, **-mising**. —v.t., v.i. **1.** to guess. —n. (sər mīz', sûr'mīz) **2.** a guess or conjecture.

sur·mount' (sər mount') v.t. **1.** to get over or on top of. **2.** to overcome.

sur'name' (sûr'nām') n. a family name.

sur·pass' (sər pas') v.t. **1.** to exceed. **2.** to excel. **3.** to transcend. —**sur·pass'ing**, adj.

sur'plice (sûr'plis) n. a loose white robe worn over a cassock.

sur'plus (sûr'plus, -pləs) n. **1.** an amount beyond that needed; excess. —adj. **2.** being a surplus.

sur·prise' (sər prīz', sə-) v., **-prised**, **-prising**. —v.t. **1.** to strike with astonishment. **2.** to come upon unexpectedly. —n. **3.** something that surprises. **4.** the feeling of being surprised. **5.** the act of surprising.

sur·re'al·ism (sə rē'ə liz'əm) n. a 20th-century style of art and literature that attempts to express the subconscious meaning of images. —**sur·re'al·ist**, n., adj.

sur·ren'der (sə ren'dər) v.t. **1.** to yield to the power or control of another. **2.** to abandon. —v.i. **3.** to give oneself up. —n. **4.** a surrendering.

sur'rep·ti'tious (sûr'əp tish'əs) adj. stealthy; secret.

sur'ro·gate (sûr'ə gāt', -git, sur'-) n. a substitute. **2.** a judge concerned with wills, estates, etc.

sur'rogate moth'er n. a woman who bears a child for another.

sur·round' (sə round') v.t. to encircle; enclose.

sur·round'ings n.pl. environment.

sur'tax' (sûr'taks') n. an additional tax, esp. on high incomes.

sur·veil'lance (sər vā'ləns) n. a close watch kept over someone or something.

sur·vey' v.t. (sər vā') **1.** to view or study. **2.** to measure or determine the dimensions or nature of. —n. (sûr'vā) **3.** a comprehensive view. **4.** the act of surveying land or a description that results.

sur·vey'ing n. the science of making land surveys. —**sur·vey'or**, n.

sur·vive' (sər vīv') v., **-vived**, **-viving**. —v.i. **1.** to remain alive. —v.t. **2.** to outlive. **3.** to live through. —**sur·vi'val**, n. —**sur·vi'vor**, n.

sus·cep'ti·ble (sə sep'tə bəl) adj. likely to be affected or influenced. —**sus·cep'ti·bil'i·ty**, n.

su'shi (sōō'shē) n. a Japanese dish of cakes of cold rice with raw fish, vegetables, etc.

sus·pect' v.t. (sə spekt') **1.** to believe to be guilty, false, etc. **2.** to mistrust. **3.** to think likely. —n. (sus'pekt) **4.** one suspected of a crime. —adj. (sus'pekt) **5.** liable to doubt.

sus·pend' (sə spend') v.t. **1.** to hang. **2.** to keep from falling by hanging. **3.** to make temporarily inactive. **4.** to postpone.

sus·pend'ers n.pl. straps for holding up trousers.

sus·pense' (sə spens') n. uncertainty; anxiety.

sus·pen'sion n. **1.** a suspending or being suspended. **2.** temporary inactivity. **3.** a state in which undissolved particles are dispersed in a fluid.

suspen'sion bridge' n. a bridge with a deck suspended from cables.

sus·pi'cion (sə spish'ən) n. **1.** a suspecting or being suspected. **2.** a trace.

sus·pi'cious (sə spish'əs) adj. **1.** having suspicions. **2.** causing suspicion.

sus·tain' (sə stān') v.t. **1.** to support. **2.** to keep going; maintain. **3.** to uphold as valid.

sus'te·nance (sus'tə nəns) n. food; nourishment.

su'ture (sōō'chər) n., v., **-tured**, **-turing**. —n. **1.** the joining of the edges of a wound. **2.** a stitch used to close a wound. —v.t. **2.** to join by suture.

SUV pl. **SUVs**. a sport-utility vehicle.

su'ze·rain (sōō'zə rin, -rān') n. **1.** a state having control over a dependent state. **2.** a feudal overlord. —**su'ze·rain·ty**, n.

svelte (svelt, sfelt) adj. gracefully slender.

swab (swob) n., v., **swabbed**, **swabbing**. —n. **1.** a bit of cloth, cotton, etc., esp. on a stick, used for cleaning or applying medicine. —v.t. **2.** to clean with a swab.

swad'dle (swod'l) v.t., **-dled**, **-dling**. to bind (a newborn infant) with strips of cloth.

swag (swag) n. something fastened at each end and hanging down in the middle.

swag'ger v.i. **1.** to walk with an insolent air. —n. **2.** such a gait.

Swa·hi'li (swä hē'lē) n. a Bantu language of Africa.

swain (swān) n. **1.** a male admirer. **2.** a country lad.

swal'low[1] (swol'ō) v.t. **1.** to take into the stomach through the throat. **2.** to take in and envelop. **3.** to accept without question. —v.i. **4.** to perform the act of swallowing. —n. **5.** the act of swallowing. **6.** an amount swallowed.

swal'low[2] (swol'ō) n. a graceful songbird with long wings and a forked tail.

swal'low·tail' n. **1.** a deeply forked tail like that of a swallow. **2.** a butterfly with long hind wings.

swam (swam) v. pt. of **swim**.

swa'mi (swä'mē) n. a Hindu religious teacher.

swamp (swomp) n. **1.** an area of wet, spongy ground. —v.t. **2.** to flood with water. **3.** to overwhelm. —**swamp'y**, adj.

swan (swon) n. a large, usu. white long-necked swimming bird.

swank (swangk) adj. **1.** stylish or elegant. **2.** pretentiously stylish. Also, **swank'y**.

swan' song' n. a final act or farewell appearance.

swap (swop) v., **swapped**, **swapping**, n. —v.t., v.i. **1.** to trade. —n. **2.** a trade or exchange.

swarm (swôrm) n. **1.** a group of honeybees. **2.** a large moving mass of people, insects, etc. —v.i. **3.** to move in a swarm.

swarth'y (swôr'thē, -thē) adj., **-ier**, **-iest**. dark in skin color.

swash'buck'ler (swosh'buk'lər) n. a swaggering fellow. —**swash'buck'ling**, adj., n.

swas'ti·ka (swos'ti kə) n. a figure of a cross with the arms bent at right angles: the emblem of the Nazi Party.

swat (swot) v., **swatted**, **swatting**, n. —v.t. **1.** to hit sharply. —n. **2.** a sharp blow. —**swat'ter**, n.

swatch (swoch) n. a sample, as of cloth.

swath (swoth) n. a long cut made by a scythe or mowing machine.

swathe (swoth, swäth) v., **swathed**, **swathing**. —v.t. **1.** to wrap or bind closely. —n. **2.** a bandage.

sway (swā) v.i. **1.** to swing or move to and fro. —v.t. **2.** to influence. —n. **3.** a swaying movement. **4.** controlling influence.

sway'back' n. an excessive downward curvature of the back, esp. of horses. —**sway'backed'**, adj.

swear (swâr) v., **swore** (swôr), **sworn**, **swearing**. —v.i. **1.** to make a solemn declaration by something sacred. **2.** to bind oneself by an oath; vow. **3.** to use profane language. —v.t. **4.** to state on oath. **5. swear in**, to admit to office by administering an oath of office.

sweat (swet) v., **sweat** or **sweated**, **sweating**, n. —v.i. **1.** to excrete moisture through the pores; perspire. **2.** to gather moisture from the surrounding air. **3.** Informal. to work hard. —v.t. **4.** to excrete (moisture) through the pores. —n. **5.** moisture given off by the body through the pores; perspiration. **6.** Informal. a state of anxiety. —**sweat'y**, adj.

sweat'er n. a knitted jacket.

sweat' gland' n. a tubular gland in the skin that secretes sweat.

sweat'pants' n. loose pants of absorbent fabric.

sweat'shirt' n. a loose pullover of absorbent fabric.

sweat'shop' n. a shop employing workers at low wages, for long hours.

Swede (swēd) n. a native of Sweden.

Swed'ish (swē'dish) adj. **1.** of Sweden, its inhabitants, or their language. —n. **2.** the language of Sweden.

sweep (swēp) v., **swept** (swept), **sweeping**, n. —v.t. **1.** to move or clear with a broom or brush. **2.** to pass or draw over a surface with a smooth, rapid movement. —v.i. **3.**

to sweep a floor or room with a broom. **4.** to move swiftly and smoothly. —n. **5.** the act of sweeping. **6.** extent.

sweep'ing adj. of wide scope.

sweep'stakes' n. **1.** a contest in which the prize consists of stakes put up by the competitors. **2.** a lottery.

sweet (swēt) adj. **1.** having the taste of sugar. **2.** fragrant. **3.** fresh. **4.** pleasant in sound. **5.** amiable. —n. **6.** anything sweet. —**sweet'en,** v.t., v.i.

sweet'bread' n. the thymus or pancreas, esp. of a calf or lamb, used for food.

sweet'bri'er n. a wild rose.

sweet'en·er n. a substance, esp. a substitute for sugar, used to sweeten food or drink.

sweet'heart' n. a beloved person.

sweet'meat' n. a candy.

sweet' pea' n. an annual vine with fragrant blooms.

sweet' pep'per n. a mild-flavored bell-shaped pepper.

sweet' pota'to n. a plant with a sweet edible root.

sweet'-talk' v.t., v.i. to cajole.

sweet' tooth' n. a liking or craving for sweets.

sweet' wil'liam (wil'yəm) n. a low plant with dense clusters of pink, red, and white flowers.

swell (swel) v., **swelled, swelled** or **swollen, swelling,** n., adj. —v.i., v.t. **1.** to grow or cause to grow in size, degree, force, etc. —n. **2.** an act or state of swelling. **3.** a long, unbroken wave. **4.** an increase in amount, intensity, etc. —adj. **5.** Informal. excellent.

swel'ter (swel'tər) v.i. to suffer from oppressive heat.

swel'ter·ing adj. very hot.

swept (swept) v. pt. and pp. of sweep.

swerve (swûrv) v., **swerved, swerving,** n. —v.i., v.t. **1.** to turn or cause to turn aside. —n. **2.** the act of swerving.

swift (swift) adj. **1.** moving with great speed. **2.** prompt or quick. —n. **3.** a swallowlike bird known for its swift flight. —**swift'ly,** adv.

swig (swig) n., v., **swigged, swigging.** Informal. —n. **1.** a swallow of liquid. —v.t., v.i. **2.** to drink heartily.

swill (swil) n. **1.** moist garbage fed to hogs. —v.i., v.t. **2.** to guzzle.

swim (swim) v., **swam** (swam), **swum,** (swum), **swimming.** —v.i. **1.** to move in water by the action of the limbs, fins, etc. **2.** to be immersed. **3.** to be dizzy. —v.t. **4.** to move in or across by swimming. —n. **5.** an act or period of swimming.

swim'suit' n. a bathing suit.

swin'dle (swin'dl) v., **-dled, -dling,** n. —v.t., v.i. **1.** to cheat; defraud. —n. **2.** an act of swindling; fraud.

swine (swīn) n. pl. **swine. 1.** an animal with short legs, a disklike snout, and cloven hooves; pig or hog. **2.** a contemptible person.

swing (swing) v., **swung** (swung) **swinging,** n., —v.i., v.t. **1.** to move or cause to move to and fro. **2.** to move or cause to move on a fixed axis. **3.** to hang or cause to hang freely. —n. **4.** the act, way, or extent of swinging. **5.** a suspended seat for swinging. **6.** a style of jazz marked by a smooth beat and flowing phrasing. —adj. **7.** capable of determining an outcome.

swing' shift' n. a work shift from midafternoon until midnight.

swipe (swīp) n., v., **swiped, swiping.** —n. **1.** a strong, sweeping blow. —v.t. **2.** to strike with a swipe. **3.** to slide (a magnetic card) quickly through an electronic device. **4.** Informal. to steal.

swirl (swûrl) v.i., v.t. **1.** to move or cause to move with a whirling motion. —n. **2.** a swirling movement.

swish (swish) v.i., v.t. **1.** to rustle. —n. **2.** a swishing sound.

Swiss (swis) adj., n., pl. **Swiss.** —adj. **1.** of Switzerland. —n. **2.** a native of Switzerland.

Swiss' cheese' (swis) n. a firm, pale yellow cheese with holes.

switch (swich) n. **1.** a device for turning electric current on or off. **2.** a change. **3.** a flexible rod. —v.t. **4.** to whip with a switch. **5.** to change or exchange. **6.** to change (electric current) on or off. —v.i. **7.** to change or shift. **8.** to make an exchange. **9.** to lash.

switch'back' n. a zigzag highway or railroad track arrangement for climbing a steep grade.

switch'blade' n. a pocketknife with a blade released by a spring.

switch'board' n. a panel for controlling electric circuits.

swiv'el (swiv'əl) v., **-eled, -eling,** n. —v.t., v.i. **1.** to rotate. —n. **2.** a device permitting the rotation of the thing mounted on it.

swiz'zle stick' (swiz'əl) n. a small wand for stirring mixed drinks.

swol'len (swō'lən) v. pp. of swell.

swoon (swōōn) v.i. **1.** to faint. —n. **2.** a faint.

swoop (swōōp) v.i. **1.** to sweep down through the air. —n. **2.** a sweeping descent.

sword (sôrd) n. a weapon with a blade fixed in a hilt or handle.

sword'fish' n. a marine fish with a swordlike upper jaw.

swore (swôr) v. pt. of swear.

sworn (swôrn) v. **1.** pp. of swear. —adj. **2.** bound by an oath.

swum (swum) v. pp. of swim.

syb'a·rite' (sib'ə rīt') n. a person devoted to pleasure.

syc'a·more' (sik'ə môr') n. a plane tree with lobed leaves.

syc'o·phant (sik'ə fənt, -fant', sī'kə-) n. a servile flatterer.

syl·lab'i·cate' (si lab'i kāt') v.t., **-cat·ed, -cat·ing.** to divide into syllables; syllabify. —**syl·lab'i·ca'tion,** n.

syl·lab'i·fy' (-fī') v.t., **-fied, -fying.** to divide into syllables. —**syl·lab'i·fi·ca'tion,** n.

syl'la·ble (sil'ə bəl) n. a single unit of speech or the letters representing this.

syl'la·bus (sil'ə bəs) n., pl. **-buses, -bi** (-bī') an outline of a course of study.

syl'lo·gism (sil'ə jiz'əm) n. a form of logical reasoning that contains two statements which lead to a conclusion.

sylph (silf) n. **1.** a graceful woman. **2.** an imaginary being supposed to inhabit the air.

syl'van (sil'vən) adj. of forests.

sym'bi·o'sis (sim'bē ō'sis, -bī-) n., pl. **-ses** (-sēz). the living together of two dissimilar organisms. —**sym·bi·ot'ic** (-ot'ik) adj.

sym'bol (sim'bəl) n. **1.** an emblem; token; sign. **2.** a thing that represents something else. —**sym·bol'ic** (-bol'ik), adj. —**sym'bol·ize',** v.t.

sym'bol·ism n. **1.** representing things by symbols. **2.** symbolic meaning.

sym'me·try (sim'i trē) n. pleasing balance or proportion. —**sym·met'ri·cal** (si me'tri kəl) adj.

sym'pa·thize' (-thīz') v.i., **-thized, -thizing. 1.** to share in a feeling. **2.** to feel or express sympathy.

sym'pa·thy (-thē) n., pl. **-thies. 1.** sharing or the ability to share the feelings of another. **2.** a feeling or expression of compassion. —**sym·pa·thet'ic** (-thet'ik) adj.

sym'pho·ny (sim'fə nē) n., pl. **-nies. 1.** a long composition for a large orchestra. **2.** harmony of sounds. —**sym·phon'ic** (-fon'ik) adj.

sym·po'si·um (sim pō'zē əm) n., pl. **-siums, -sia** (-zē ə) a meeting for discussion of one topic.

symp'tom (simp'təm) n. a sign or indication, esp. of disease. —**symp·to·mat'ic** (-tə mat'ik) adj.

syn'a·gogue' (sin'ə gog') n. **1.** a Jewish house of worship. **2.** a congregation of Jews.

syn'apse' (sin'aps, si naps') n. a region where nerve impulses are transmitted from an axon terminal to an adjacent structure. —**syn·ap'tic,** adj.

sync (singk) n., v., **synced, syncing.** —n. **1.** synchronization. **2.** harmonious relationship. —v.t., v.i. **3.** to synchronize.

syn'chro·nize' (sing'krə nīz') v., **-nized, -nizing. 1.** to cause to show the same time. **2.** to cause to move or work exactly together. —v.i. **3.** to occur at the same time. —**syn'chro·ni·za'tion,** n. —**syn'chro·nous,** adj.

syn'co·pate' (sing'kə pāt', sin'-) v.t., **-pated, -pating.** to shift (a musical accent) to a beat that is normally unaccented. —**syn'co·pa'tion,** n.

syn'di·cate n., v., **-cated, -cating.** —n. (sin'də kit) **1.** a combination of persons or companies for a large joint enterprise. **2.** an agency selling news stories to a number of publications at the same time. —v.t. (sin'di kāt') **3.** to combine into a syndicate. **4.** to publish through a syndicate. —v.i. **5.** to combine to form a syndicate.

syn'drome (sin'drōm, -drəm) n. a group of symptoms characteristic of a disease.

syn'er·gism (sin'ər jiz'əm) n. the joint action of agents so that their combined effect is greater than the sum of their individual effects. Also, **synergy.**

syn'od (sin'əd) n. an assembly of church delegates.

syn'o·nym (sin'ə nim) n. a word meaning the same as another. —**syn·on'y·mous** (si non'ə məs) adj.

syn·op'sis (si nop'sis) n., pl. **-ses** (-sēz). a brief summary.

syn'tax (sin'taks) n. the arrangement of words into sentences and phrases.

syn'the·sis (sin'thə sis) n., pl. **-ses** (-sēz). the combining of parts into a whole.

syn'the·size' v., **-sized, -sizing.** —v.t. **1.** to form by combining parts or elements. —v.i. **2.** to make or form a synthesis.

syn'the·siz'er n. an electronic, usu. computerized device for creating or modifying musical sounds.

syn·thet'ic (sin thet'ik) adj. **1.** produced artificially rather than by nature. **2.** of synthesis.

synthet'ic fu'el n. fuel made esp. from coal or shale.

syph'i·lis (sif'ə lis) n. an infectious venereal disease.

syr·inge' (sə rinj', sir'inj) n. a tube with a piston or rubber bulb for drawing in and ejecting fluids.

syr'up (sir'əp, sûr'-) n. a sweet thick liquid. —**syr'up·y,** adj.

sys'tem (sis'təm) n. **1.** an orderly assemblage of facts, parts, etc., forming a whole. **2.** a method. **3.** a group of bodily organs concerned with the same function. **4.** the body as a whole functioning unit. —**sys'tem·at'ic** (-tə mat'ik) adj.

sys'tem·a·tize' (-tə mə tīz') v.t., **-tized, -tizing.** to arrange according to a system.

sys·tem'ic (si stem'ik) adj. affecting the entire body.

sys'tems anal'ysis n. the study of the data-processing needs of a project.

sys'to·le' (sis'tə lē) n. the normal rhythmic contraction of the heart. —**sys·tol'ic** (si stol'ik) adj.

T

T, t (tē) n. the twentieth letter of the English alphabet.

tab (tab) n. **1.** a small projecting flap. —Idiom. **2. keep tabs on,** keep watch over.

Ta·bas'co (tə bas'kō) n. Trademark. a pungent condiment sauce.

tab'by (tab'ē) n., pl. **-bies.** a striped or brindled cat.

tab'er·nac'le (tab'ər nak'əl) n. **1.** a large church. **2.** (often cap.) a portable place of worship used by the Israelites in the wilderness. **3.** a receptacle for the reserved Eucharist.

ta'ble (tā'bəl) n., v., **-bled, -bling.** —n. **1.** a piece of furniture consisting of a flat part resting on legs. **2.** the food served at a table. **3.** a compact arrangement of information in parallel columns. —v.t. **4.** to postpone discussion of.

tab·leau' (ta blō', tab'lō) n., pl. **-leaux** (ta blōz'). a representation of a scene by silent, posed, costumed people.

ta'ble d'hôte' (tä'bəl dōt', tab'əl) n. a restaurant meal of fixed courses and price.

ta'ble·land' n. an elevated level land area; plateau.

ta'ble·spoon' n. a large spoon. **2.** a measuring spoon holding ½ fluid ounce. —**ta'ble·spoon·ful',** n.

tab'let (tab'lit) n. **1.** a pad of writing paper. **2.** a small slab of stone. **3.** a pill.

ta'ble ten'nis n. a game resembling tennis, played on a table with paddles and a small hollow ball.

ta'ble·ware' n. the dishes, utensils, etc., used at the table.

tab'loid (tab'loid) n. a newspaper with small pages, usu. concentrating on sensational news.

ta·boo' (ta bōō', tə-) n., pl. **-boos.** —adj. **1.** forbidden by religion or custom. —n. **2.** a social prohibition.

ta'bor (tā'bər) n. a small drum.

tab'u·lar (tab'yə lər) adj. arranged in a table.

tab'u·late' (tab'yə lāt') v.t., **-lated,** **-lating.** to arrange in a table. —**tab'u·la'tion,** n.

ta·chom'e·ter (ta kom'i tər, tə-) n. an instrument measuring the speed of rotation of a vehicle's engine.

tach'y·car'di·a (tak'i kär'dē ə) n. excessively rapid heartbeat.

tac'it (tas'it) adj. understood or implied without being expressed in words. —**tac'it·ly,** adv.

tac'i·turn' (tas'i tûrn') adj. silent. —**tac'i·tur·ni·ty,** n.

tack (tak) n. **1.** a short nail with a flat head. **2.** a ship's direction relative to the direction of the wind. **3.** a long temporary stitch. —v.t. **4.** to fasten with a tack. **5.** to add on. —v.i. **6.** to change course.

tack'le v., **-led, -ling,** n. —v.t. **1.** to undertake to handle or solve. —n. **2.** fishing equipment. **3.** hoisting apparatus.

tack'y¹ adj., **-ier, -iest.** slightly sticky. —**tack'i·ness,** n.

tack'y² adj., **-ier, -iest.** in poor taste. —**tack'i·ness,** n.

ta'co (tä'kō) n. a fried tortilla folded and filled with chopped meat, cheese, lettuce, etc.

tact (takt) n. skill in handling delicate situations. —**tact'ful,** adj.

tac·ti'cian (tak tish'ən) n. a person skilled in tactics.

tac'tics (tak'tiks) n. **1.** the maneuvering of armed forces. **2.** (used with a pl. v.) methods for attaining success. —**tac'ti·cal,** adj.

tac'tile (tak'til, -tīl) adj. of the sense of touch.

tad (tad) n. Informal. **1.** a small amount or degree. **2.** a small child.

tad'pole (tad'pōl) n. the larval form of frogs and toads.

taf'fe·ta (taf'i tə) n. a lustrous silk or rayon fabric.

taf'fy (taf'ē) n., pl. **-fies.** a chewy candy made from boiled sugar or molasses.

tag¹ (tag) n., v., **tagged, tagging.** —n. **1.** a small piece of paper, plastic, etc., attached as a marker or label. —v.t. **2.** to furnish with a tag. **3. tag along,** to follow closely.

tag² (tag) n., v., **tagged, tagging. 1.** a children's game in which one player chases the others. —v.t. **2.** to touch in a game of tag.

t'ai chi ch'uan (tī' jē' chwän', chē') n. a Chinese system of meditative exercises. Also, **tai' chi'.**

tail (tāl) n. **1.** the rear part of an animal, esp. that forming an appendage. **2.** something resembling this. **3.** the reverse of a coin. **4.** the bottom or end part. —v.t. **5.** to follow closely.

tail'bone' n. the coccyx.

tail'gate' n., v., **-gated, -gating.** —n. **1.** the hinged board or gate at the back of a vehicle. —v.i., v.t. **2.** to drive too closely behind (another vehicle).

tail'light' n. a red light at the rear of a vehicle.

tai'lor (tā'lər) n. **1.** a person who makes, mends, or alters clothes. —v.t. **2.** to fashion to a particular style or purpose.

tail'piece' n. a piece, design, etc., added at the end; appendage.

tail'pipe' n. an exhaust pipe at the rear of a motor vehicle.

tail'spin' n. the descent of an airplane in a steep spiral dive.

tail'wind' (-wind') n. a wind coming from directly behind.

taint (tānt) v.t. **1.** to affect with something bad; contaminate. —n. **2.** a trace of something bad.

take (tāk) v., **took** (tōōk) **taken, taking,** n. —v.t. **1.** to get possession of; seize. **2.** to receive. **3.** to choose. **4.** to react to. **5.** to remove. **6.** to absorb. **7.** to travel by. **8.** to occupy. **9.** to endure. **10.** to require. **11. take after,** to resemble. **12. ~ off, a.** to remove. **b.** to leave the ground. **c.** to depart. **d.** to achieve sudden success. **13. ~ over,** to assume possession of. —n. **14.** something taken.

take'off' n. **1.** the leaving of the ground in leaping or flying. **2.** a humorous imitation.

take'out' adj. **1.** intended to be taken from a restaurant and eaten elsewhere. —n. **2.** food taken out from a restaurant.

take'o'ver n. **1.** a seizing of authority or control. **2.** the acquisition of a corporation through the purchase of stock.

talc (talk) n. a soft green-to-gray mineral. Also, **tal'cum.**

tal'cum pow'der (tal'kəm) n. a powder for the skin made of purified talc.

tale (tāl) n. **1.** a story. **2.** a lie.

tale'bear'er n. a gossip.

tal'ent (tal'ənt) n. a special natural ability.

tal'is·man (tal'is mən, -iz-) n. an object worn or carried to bring good luck.

talk (tôk) v.i. **1.** to exchange ideas by speaking. —v.t. **2.** to express in words. **3.** to discuss. —n. **4.** the act of talking. **5.** an informal speech. **6.** a conference. **7.** gossip. —**talk'a·tive,** adj. —**talk'er,** n.

talk'ing-to' n., pl. **talking-tos.** a scolding.

talk'y adj., **-ier, -iest. 1.** containing too much talk, dialogue, etc. **2.** talkative.

tall (tôl) adj. **1.** of great height. **2.** of a specified height.

tal'low (tal'ō) n. the hard fat of sheep and cattle, used to make candles and soap.

tal'ly (tal'ē) n., pl. **-lies,** v., **-lied, -lying.** —n. **1.** a record of amounts. —v.t. **2.** to record or count. —v.i. **3.** to match.

Tal'mud (täl'mōōd, tal'məd) n. a collection of Jewish law and tradition. —**Tal·mud'ic,** adj.

tal'on (tal'ən) n. a claw.

tal'us (tal'əs) n., pl. **-li.** the anklebone.

ta·ma'le (tə mä'lē) n. a Mexican dish of cornmeal and meat wrapped in corn husks.

tam'a·rack' (tam'ə rak') n. a N American larch.

tam'a·rind (-ə rind) n. a tropical fruit containing seeds in a juicy acid pulp.

tam'bou·rine' (-bə rēn') n. a small drum with metal jingles in a frame.

tame (tām) adj., **tamer, tamest,** v., **tamed, taming.** —adj. **1.** not wild; domesticated. **2.** dull. —v.t. **3.** to make tame. —**tame'ly,** adv. —**tam'er,** n.

tamp (tamp) v.t. to pack in tightly.

tam'per v. **tamper with,** to meddle or interfere with.

tam'pon (tam'pon) n. a plug of cotton or the like inserted into a wound or body cavity to absorb blood.

tan (tan) v., **tanned, tanning,** n. —v.t. **1.** to make or become brown by exposure to sun. **2.** to convert (a hide) into leather. —n. **3.** the light brown color of skin that has been exposed to the sun. **4.** a yellowish brown. —**tan'ner,** n. —**tan'ner·y,** n.

tan'a·ger (tan'ə jər) n. a small, brightly colored songbird.

tan'dem (tan'dəm) adv. **1.** one behind the other. —n. **2.** a bicycle for two persons.

tang (tang) n. a strong flavor or odor.

tan'ge·lo' (tan'jə lō') n., pl. **-los.** a fruit that is a cross between a grapefruit and a tangerine.

tan'gent (tan'jənt) adj. **1.** touching. —n. **2.** a tangent line, plane, etc. —Idiom. **3. off on a tangent,** changing suddenly from one course or thought to another.

tan·gen'tial (-jen'shəl) adj. **1.** touching. **2.** not relevant.

tan'ge·rine' (tan'jə rēn') n. a loose-skinned fruit similar to an orange.

tan'gi·ble (tan'jə bəl) adj. **1.** able to be touched. **2.** real. —**tan'gi·bil'i·ty,** n.

tan'gle (tang'gəl) v., **-gled, -gling,** n. —v.t. **1.** to bring together into a confused mass. **2.** to catch in a snare. —v.i. **3.** to become tangled. **4.** to come into conflict. —n. **5.** a tangled state or mass.

tan'go (tang'gō) n., pl. **-gos,** v., **-goed, -going.** —n. **1.** a Latin-American ballroom dance. —v.i. **2.** to dance the tango.

tank (tangk) n. **1.** a large receptacle for liquid or gas. **2.** an armored combat vehicle.

tank'ard (tang'kərd) n. a large cup with a handle.

tank'er n. a ship, truck, or airplane for transporting liquid bulk cargo.

tan'nin (tan'in) n. an astringent compound used in tanning.

tan'sy (tan'zē) n., pl. **-sies.** a strong-scented herb with yellow flowers.

tan'ta·lize' (tan'tl īz') v.t., **-lized, -lizing.** to torment with something desired but out of reach.

tan'ta·mount' (tan'tə mount') adj. equivalent.

tan'trum (tan'trəm) n. a noisy outburst of bad temper.

tap¹ (tap) n., v., **tapped, tapping.** —v.t., v.i. **1.** to strike lightly. —n. **2.** a light blow or the sound of this.

tap[2] (tap) *n.*, *v.*, **tapped, tapping.** —*n.* **1.** a plug or faucet through which liquid is drawn. **2.** a connection on an electrical circuit. **3.** an act of wiretapping. —*v.t.* **4.** to draw liquid from. **5.** to draw upon. **6.** to furnish with a tap. **7.** to wiretap.

tap′ dance′ *n.* a dance in which the rhythm is audibly tapped out by the foot. —**tap′-dance**, *v.i.*

tape (tāp) *n.*, *v.*, **taped, taping.** —*n.* **1.** a narrow strip of fabric, paper, etc., sometimes with an adhesive surface. **2.** a magnetic tape. —*v.t.* **3.** to tie, bind, or attach with tape. **4.** to record on tape.

tape′ deck′ *n.* an audio system component for playing tapes.

tape′ meas′ure *n.* a tape marked for measuring.

ta′per (tā′pər) *v.t.*, *v.i.* **1.** to make or become narrower toward one end. **2.** taper off, to decrease gradually. —*n.* **3.** a gradual decrease. **4.** a slender candle.

tape′ record′er *n.* an electrical device for recording or playing back sound recorded on magnetic tape.

tap′es·try (tap′ə strē) *n.*, *pl.* **-tries.** a heavy, decorative, woven fabric used esp. for wall hangings.

tape′worm′ *n.* a long, flat parasitic worm found in the digestive tract.

tap·i·o·ca (tap′ē ō′kə) *n.* a starchy preparation from the cassava, used as a thickener.

ta′pir (tā′pər, tə pēr′) *n.* a tropical piglike animal.

tap′root′ *n.* a main, central root pointing downward and giving off small lateral roots.

taps *n.* a bugle signal sounded at night as an order to extinguish lights, and sometimes at military funerals.

tar[1] (tär) *n.*, *v.*, **tarred, tarring.** —*n.* **1.** a dark, sticky product from coal, wood, etc. **2.** smoke components. —*v.t.* **3.** to cover with tar.

tar′an·tel′la (tar′ən tel′ə) *n.* a rapid, whirling southern Italian dance.

ta·ran′tu·la (tə ran′chə lə) *n.* a large, hairy spider.

tar′dy (tär′dē) *adj.*, **-dier, -diest.** late. —**tar′di·ness**, *n.*

tare[1] (târ) *n.* a kind of vetch.

tare[2] (târ) *n.* the weight of a wrapping or receptacle.

tar′get (tär′git) *n.* **1.** an object aimed at, as in shooting. **2.** a goal. **3.** an object of abuse. —*v.t.* **4.** to make a target of.

tar′iff (tar′if) *n.* **1.** a list of export or import duties. **2.** one such duty.

tar′nish (tär′nish) *v.t.* **1.** to dull the luster of. **2.** to disgrace. —*v.i.* **3.** to become tarnished. —*n.* **4.** a tarnished coating or state.

ta′ro (tär′ō, tar′ō, târ′ō) *n.* a tropical plant with an edible tuber.

ta′rot (tar′ō, ta rō′) *n.* any of a set of 22 playing cards used for fortune-telling.

tar·pau′lin (tär pô′lin, tär′pə lin) *n.* a waterproofed covering.

tar′ra·gon (tar′ə gon′, -gən) *n.* a plant with aromatic leaves used as seasoning.

tar′ry (tar′ē) *v.i.*, **-ried, -rying. 1.** to stay. **2.** to delay.

tar′sus (tär′səs) *n.*, *pl.* **-si.** the bones forming the ankle joint. —**tar′sal,** *adj.*

tart[1] (tärt) *adj.* **1.** sour; acid. **2.** sharp in manner or expression. —**tart′ly,** *adv.*

tart[2] (tärt) *n.* a pastry shell filled with fruit or custard.

tar′tan (tär′tn) *n.* a woolen cloth with a crisscross pattern, originally worn in Scotland.

tar′tar (tär′tər) *n.* a hard deposit on the teeth. —**tar·tar′ic** (-tar′ik, -tär′-) *adj.*

tar′tar sauce′ *n.* a mayonnaise sauce containing chopped pickles, onions, etc.

task (task) *n.* **1.** a piece of work, esp. one that is difficult. —*v.t.* **2.** to put a strain on. —*Idiom.* **3.** take to task, to reprimand.

task′ force′ *n.* a group for carrying out a specific task.

task′mas′ter *n.* a person who assigns burdensome tasks.

tas′sel (tas′əl) *n.* a fringed ornament hanging from a roundish knob.

taste (tāst) *v.*, **tasted, tasting.** —*v.t.* **1.** to test the flavor of by taking into the mouth. **2.** to eat or drink a little of. **3.** to perceive the flavor of. —*v.i.* **4.** to have a particular flavor. —*n.* **5.** the sense by which flavor is perceived. **6.** the act of tasting. **7.** flavor. **8.** a sense of

what is harmonious or beautiful. —**taste′ful,** *adj.* —**taste′less,** *adj.*

taste′ bud′ *n.* one of numerous small bodies that are organs for the sense of taste.

tast′y *adj.*, **-ier, -iest.** good-tasting; savory. —**tast′i·ness,** *n.*

tat′ting *n.* **1.** the making of a kind of knotted lace with a shuttle. **2.** such lace.

tat′tle (tat′l) *v.*, **-tled, -tling.** *n.* —*v.i.* **1.** to tell something secret about another person. —*n.* **2.** gossip. —**tat′tler, tat′tle·tale′,** *n.*

tat·too′ (ta tōō′) *n.* **1.** an indelible marking on the skin made by puncturing and dyeing. —*v.t.* **2.** to mark by tattoo. **3.** to put (tattoos) on the skin.

tau (tou, tô) *n.*, *pl.* **taus.** the 19th letter of the Greek alphabet.

taunt (tônt, tänt) *v.t.* to reproach scornfully. —*n.* a scornful remark.

taupe (tōp) *n.* a brownish gray.

taut (tôt) *adj.* tight; tense.

tau·tol′o·gy (tô tol′ə jē) *n.* needless repetition of an idea in different words. —**tau′to·log′i·cal** (-tl-oj′i kəl) *adj.*

tav′ern (tav′ərn) *n.* a saloon.

taw′dry (tô′drē) *adj.*, **-drier, -driest.** gaudy; cheap.

taw′ny (tô′nē) *adj.* yellow-brown.

tax (taks) *n.* **1.** a sum of money paid to a government. **2.** a burdensome duty. —*v.t.* **3.** to impose a tax. **4.** to burden. **5.** to accuse. —**tax′a·ble,** *adj.* —**tax·a′tion,** *n.*

tax′i (tak′sē) *n.*, *v.*, **taxied, taxiing.** —*n.* **1.** a taxicab. —*v.i.* **2.** to ride in a taxicab. **3.** (of an airplane) to move on the ground under its own power.

tax′i·cab′ *n.* an automobile carrying paying passengers.

tax′i·der′my (tak′si dûr′mē) *n.* the art of preserving, stuffing, and mounting the skins of animals. —**tax′i·der′mist,** *n.*

tax·on′o·my (tak son′ə mē) *n.*, *pl.* **-mies.** the scientific classification of organisms.

tax′pay′er *n.* a person who pays a tax.

tax′ shel′ter *n.* a financial arrangement that reduces or eliminates the taxes due.

TB tuberculosis. Also, **T.B.**

tbs. tablespoon. Also, **tbsp.**

T cell *n.* a cell involved in regulating the immune system's response to infected or malignant cells.

tea (tē) *n.* **1.** the dried aromatic leaves of an Asian shrub. **2.** a beverage made by the infusion of these leaves in hot water. **3.** a similar beverage made by steeping the leaves or flowers of other plants. **4.** a light afternoon meal.

teach (tēch) *v.*, **taught, teaching.** —*v.t.*, *v.i.* to give instruction (to or about). —**teach′er,** *n.*

tea′cup′ *n.* a cup in which tea is served.

teak (tēk) *n.* an East Indian tree with hard wood.

tea′ket′tle *n.* a kettle with a cover, spout, and handle, used for boiling water.

teal (tēl) *n.* **1.** any of several small freshwater ducks. **2.** a greenish blue.

team (tēm) *n.* **1.** the persons forming a side in a contest. **2.** persons or animals working together. —*v.i.* **3.** to join in a team. —**team′mate′,** *n.* —**team′work′,** *n.*

team′ster (-stər) *n.* a person who drives a team or a truck.

tea′pot′ *n.* a container with a spout, in which tea is made.

tear[1] (târ) *v.*, **tore** (tôr), **torn, tearing,** *n.* —*v.t.* **1.** to pull apart by force. **2.** to divide. **3.** to produce by tearing. **4.** to injure by tearing. —*v.i.* **5.** to become torn. **6.** to move hastily. —*n.* **7.** the act of tearing. **8.** a rip or hole.

tear[2] (tēr) *n.* **1.** a drop of the saline fluid that lubricates and flows from the eye. —*v.i.* **2.** (of the eyes) to fill with tears. —**tear′ful** (tēr′-) *adj.*

tear′ gas′ (tēr) *n.* a gas that makes the eyes smart and water.

tear′jerk′er (tēr′jûr′kər) *n.* Informal. a sentimental story, play, etc.

tease (tēz) *v.*, **teased, teasing,** *n.* —*v.t.* **1.** to annoy with taunts, mockery, etc. —*v.i.* **2.** to tease a person or animal. —*n.* **3.** a person who teases. —**teas′er,** *n.*

tea′spoon′ *n.* **1.** a small spoon. **2.** a measuring spoon holding ⅓ fluid ounce. —**tea′spoon·ful′,** *n.*

teat (tēt, tit) *n.* a nipple.

tech′ni·cal (tek′ni kəl) *adj.* **1.** of

the mechanical or industrial arts and applied sciences. **2.** of an art, science, or trade. **3.** considered in a strict sense.

tech·ni·cal′i·ty (-kal′i tē) *n.*, *pl.* **-ties. 1.** a technical point or detail. **2.** technical character.

Tech′ni·col′or *Trademark.* the system of making color motion pictures.

tech·nique′ (-nēk′) *n.* a method used to accomplish something.

tech′no (tek′nō) *n.* a style of disco music characterized by very fast synthesizer rhythms.

tech·noc′ra·cy (-nok′rə sē) *n.*, *pl.* **-cies.** government by technological experts.

tech·nol′o·gy (-nol′ə jē) *n.*, *pl.* **-gies. 1.** the study of the applied sciences, engineering, etc. **2.** the practical application of knowledge. —**tech·no·log′i·cal** (-nə loj′i kəl) *adj.* —**tech·nol′o·gist,** *n.*

tec·ton′ic (tek ton′ik) *adj.* **1.** of the structure and movements of the earth's crust. **2.** of building or construction.

tec·ton′ics (-ton′iks) *n.* the branch of geology that studies the forces that cause the earth's crust to be deformed.

ted′dy bear′ (ted′ē) *n.* a stuffed toy bear.

Te De′um (tā dā′əm) *n.* a hymn of praise and thanksgiving.

te′di·ous (tē′dē əs, tē′jəs) *adj.* long and tiresome. —**te′di·um,** *n.*

tee (tē) *n.*, *v.*, **teed, teeing. 1.** a mound of earth or a peg from which a golf ball is driven. —*v.t.* **2.** to place (a ball) on a tee. **3. tee off,** to strike a ball from a tee.

teem (tēm) *v.i.* to abound; swarm.

teens (tēnz) *n.pl.* **1.** the numbers 13 through 19. **2.** the ages 13 through 19. —**teen′ag′er,** *n.*

tee′ter (tē′tər) *v.i.* **1.** to move unsteadily. **2.** to waver.

teethe (tēth) *v.i.*, **teethed, teething.** to grow or cut teeth.

tee·to′tal·er (tē tōt′l ər, tē′tōt′-) *n.* a person who does not drink alcoholic beverages.

Tef′lon (tef′lon) *Trademark.* a polymer with nonsticking properties, used to coat cookware. —*adj.* **2.** impervious to blame or criticisms.

tel. **1.** telegram. **2.** telegraph. **3.** telephone.

tel′e·cast′ (tel′i kast′) *v.*, **-cast** or **-casted, -casting,** *n.* —*v.t.*, *v.i.* **1.** to broadcast by television. —*n.* **2.** a television broadcast.

tel′e·com·mu′ni·ca′tions *n.* the science and technology of transmitting information in the form of electromagnetic signals.

tel′e·con′fer·ence *n.* a conference of participants in different locations via telecommunications equipment.

tel′e·gen′ic (-jen′ik) *adj.* having qualities that televise well.

tel′e·graph′ (-graf′) *n.* **1.** an electrical apparatus or process for sending a message (**tel′e·gram′**). —*v.t.* **2.** to send by telegraph. —**te·leg′raph′ic,** *adj.* —**te·leg′ra·phy** (tə-leg′rə fē) *n.*

tel′e·mar′ket·ing *n.* selling or advertising by telephone.

te·lep′a·thy (tə lep′ə thē) *n.* communication between minds without sensory means. —**tel′e·path′ic** (tel′ə path′ik) *adj.*

tel′e·phone′ (tel′ə fōn′) *n.*, *v.*, **-phoned, -phoning.** —*n.* **1.** an electrical apparatus or process for transmitting speech. —*v.t.*, *v.i.* **2.** to send (a message) to (a person) by telephone.

tel′e·phone tag′ *n.* repeated unsuccessful attempts by two persons to reach each other by telephone.

tel′e·pho′to *adj.* of a lens producing a large image of a small or distant object.

tel′e·scope′ *n.*, *v.*, **-scoped, -scoping.** —*n.* **1.** an optical instrument for enlarging an image of distant objects. —*v.t.*, *v.i.* **2.** to force or slide (one section) into another. **3.** to condense or become condensed. —**tel′e·scop′ic** (-skop′ik) *adj.*

tel′e·thon′ (-thon′) *n.* a television broadcast to raise money for charity.

tel′e·van′ge·list (-i van′jə list) *n.* an evangelist who conducts religious services on television. —**tel′e·van′ge·lism** (-liz′əm) *n.*

tel′e·vise′ (-vīz′) *v.t.*, *v.i.*, **-vised, -vising.** to broadcast by television.

tel′e·vi′sion *n.* **1.** the broadcasting of images via radio waves to receiv-

ers that project them on screens. **2.** a set for receiving such broadcasts.

tell (tel) *v.*, **told** (tōld) **telling.** —*v.t.* **1.** to narrate. **2.** to communicate in words. **3.** to reveal. **4.** to recognize. **5.** to inform. **6.** to order. **7.** to give an account. **8.** to produce a marked effect. —**tell′ing,** *adj.*

tell′-all′ *adj.* thoroughly revealing.

tell′er *n.* a bank cashier.

tell′tale′ *adj.* revealing.

te·mer′i·ty (tə mer′i tē) *n.* rash boldness.

temp (temp) *n.* a temporary worker.

tem′per *n.* **1.** a state of mind or feelings. **2.** heat of mind or passion. **3.** calmness when provoked. —*v.t.* **4.** to moderate. **5.** to heat and cool (metal) to obtain the proper hardness and strength.

tem′per·a (tem′pər ə) *n.* a technique of painting using a medium containing egg and water or oil.

tem′per·a·ment (tem′pər ə mənt, -prə mənt) *n.* mental disposition.

tem′per·a·men′tal (-men′tl) *adj.* moody or sensitive.

tem′per·ance (tem′pər əns) *n.* **1.** moderation. **2.** total abstinence from alcohol.

tem′per·ate (-pər it) *adj.* moderate.

Tem′perate Zone′ *n.* the part of the earth's surface lying between either tropic and the nearest polar circle.

tem′per·a·ture (-pər ə chər, -prə-) *n.* the degree of warmth or coldness.

tem′pest (tem′pist) *n.* a violent storm or disturbance. —**tem·pes′tu·ous** (-pes′chōō əs) *adj.* —**tem·pes′tu·ous·ly,** *adv.*

tem′plate (tem′plit) *n.* a pattern, mold, etc., serving as a gauge or guide in mechanical work.

tem′ple[1] (tem′pəl) *n.* a building dedicated to worship.

tem′ple[2] (tem′pəl) *n.* the flat area at the side of the forehead.

tem′po (tem′pō) *n.*, *pl.* **-pos, -pi** (-pē). the rate of speed of a musical passage.

tem′po·ral (tem′pər əl) *adj.* **1.** of time. **2.** worldly.

tem′po·rar′y (-pə rer′ē) *adj.* not permanent. —**tem′po·rar′i·ly,** *adv.*

tem′po·rize′ (-rīz′) *v.i.*, **-rized, -rizing.** to delay by evasion.

tempt (tempt) *v.t.* **1.** to entice to do something wrong. **2.** to appeal strongly to. —**temp·ta′tion,** *n.*

tem·pu′ra (tem pŏŏr′ə) *n.* a Japanese deep-fried dish of vegetables or seafood.

ten (ten) *n.*, *adj.* nine plus one. —**tenth,** *n.*, *adj.*

ten′a·ble (ten′ə bəl) *adj.* able to be held, maintained, or defended. —**ten′a·bil′i·ty,** *n.*

te·na′cious (tə nā′shəs) *adj.* **1.** holding fast. **2.** highly retentive. —**te·na′cious·ly,** *adv.* —**te·nac′i·ty** (-nas′i tē) *n.*

ten′an·cy (ten′ən sē) *n.*, *pl.* **-cies.** occupancy of land, a house, a position, etc.; tenure.

ten′ant (-ənt) *n.* **1.** one renting from a landlord. **2.** an occupant.

Ten′ Command′ments *n.* the laws given to Moses by God on Mount Sinai.

tend[1] (tend) *v.i.* **1.** to be inclined to do something. **2.** to lead in a certain direction.

tend[2] (tend) *v.t.* to take care of.

tend′en·cy (ten′dən sē) *n.*, *pl.* **-cies.** a disposition to behave or act in a certain way.

ten·den′tious (-den′shəs) *adj.* having or showing bias.

ten′der[1] *adj.* **1.** soft; delicate; weak. **2.** young. **3.** soft-hearted. **4.** affectionate. **5.** very sensitive. —**ten′der·ness,** *n.* —**ten′der·ize′,** *v.t.*

ten′der[2] *v.t.* **1.** to present or offer formally. —*n.* **2.** something offered.

ten′der[3] *n.* **1.** a person who tends. **2.** a ship carrying provisions to other ships. **3.** a car carrying fuel and water for a locomotive.

ten′der·foot′ *n.*, *pl.* **-foots, -feet.** *Informal.* an inexperienced person.

ten′der·heart′ed *adj.* soft-hearted.

ten′der·loin′ *n.* **1.** tender meat on a loin of beef, pork, etc. **2.** the brothel district of a city.

ten′don (-dən) *n.* a band of dense tissue connecting a muscle to a bone or part.

ten′dril (-dril) *n.* a clinging threadlike organ of a climbing plant.

ten′e·ment (-ə mənt) *n.* a run-down apartment house.

ten′et (-it) *n.* a principle, doctrine, dogma, etc.

Tenn. Tennessee.

ten′nis *n.* a game played with a ball and rackets (**tennis rackets**) on a rectangular court (**tennis court**).

ten′on (-ən) *n.* a projection inserted into a cavity (**mortise**) to form a joint.

ten′or (-ər) *n.* **1.** the highest ordinary adult male singing voice. **2.** a singer with this voice. **3.** general sense. **4.** continuous course or progress. —*adj.* **5.** of the pitch between alto and bass.

ten′pins′ *n.* a bowling game played with ten wooden pins.

tense[1] (tens) *adj.*, **tenser, tensest,** *v.*, **tensed, tensing.** —*adj.* **1.** taut; rigid. **2.** emotionally strained. —*v.t.*, *v.i.* **3.** to make or become tense. —**tense′ly,** *adv.*

tense[2] (tens) *n.* the inflected form of a verb indicating time of an action or state.

ten′sile (ten′səl, -sil, -sīl) *adj.* **1.** of tension. **2.** able to be stretched.

ten′sion (-shən) *n.* **1.** a stretching or being stretched. **2.** mental or emotional strain.

tent (tent) *n.* a portable shelter, usu. of fabric supported by poles.

ten′ta·cle (ten′tə kəl) *n.* a long, flexible part of certain animals, used for touching, grasping, etc.

ten′ta·tive (-tə tiv) *adj.* **1.** experimental. **2.** unsure. —**ten′ta·tive·ly,** *adv.*

ten′ter·hook′ (-tər hŏŏk′) *n.* —*Idiom.* **on tenterhooks,** in suspense.

ten′u·ous (ten′yōō əs) *adj.* **1.** lacking a sound basis. **2.** thin or slender. **3.** rare. —**ten′u·ous·ly,** *adv.*

ten′ure (-yər) *n.* the holding of property or a position.

te′pee (tē′pē) *n.* a cone-shaped tent used by the Plains Indians.

tep′id (tep′id) *adj.* lukewarm. —**te·pid′i·ty,** **tep′id·ness,** *n.*

te·qui′la (tə kē′lə) *n.* a strong Mexican liquor.

ter′cen·ten′ni·al (tûr′-) *n.* a 300th anniversary or its celebration. Also, **ter′cen·ten′a·ry.**

term (tûrm) *n.* **1.** a name for something. **2.** the time through which something lasts. **3.** an appointed time. **4. terms,** the conditions of an agreement or bargain. —*v.t.* **5.** to name; designate.

ter′ma·gant (tûr′mə gənt) *n.* a violent, quarrelsome woman.

ter′mi·nal (-mə nl) *adj.* **1.** situated at the end; concluding. **2.** leading to death. —*n.* **3.** an end or extremity. **4.** the terminating point for trains, buses, etc. **5.** a point of electrical connection. **6.** a device for entering information into or receiving information from a computer. —**ter′mi·nal·ly,** *adv.*

ter′mi·nate′ (-nāt′) *v.*, **-nated, -nating.** —*v.i.*, *v.t.* to come or bring to an end. —**ter′mi·na′tion,** *n.*

ter′mi·nol′o·gy (-nol′ə jē) *n.*, *pl.* **-gies.** the terms of a specialized subject.

ter′mi·nus (-nəs) *n.* **1.** the end of anything. **2.** the end of the line for buses, trains, etc.

ter′mite (tûr′mīt) *n.* a destructive wood-eating insect.

tern (tûrn) *n.* a gull-like aquatic bird.

terp′si·cho·re′an (tûrp′si kə-rē′ən,-kôr′ē ən) *adj.* of dancing.

ter′race (ter′əs) *n.*, *v.*, **-raced, -racing.** —*n.* **1.** a raised level of earth with vertical or sloping sides. **2.** an open area connected with a house. **3.** a porch or balcony. —*v.t.* **4.** to make into a terrace.

ter′ra cot′ta (ter′ə kot′ə) *n.* a hard, brownish-red clay used for making pottery.

ter′ra fir′ma (fûr′mə) *n.* solid land.

ter·rain′ (tə rān′) *n.* an area of land or a specified nature.

ter′ra·pin (ter′ə pin) *n.* an edible North American turtle.

ter·rar′i·um (tə râr′ē əm) *n.*, *pl.* **-iums, -ia** (-ē ə). a glass tank for raising plants or land animals.

ter·raz′zo (tə rä′tsō, -raz′ō) *n.* mosaic flooring composed of stone chips and cement.

ter·res′tri·al (tə res′trē əl) *adj.* **1.** of or living on earth. **2.** of land as distinct from water.

ter′ri·ble (ter′ə bəl) *adj.* dreadful; horrible. —**ter′ri·bly,** *adv.*

ter′ri·er (ter′ē ər) *n.* a small lively dog.

ter·rif′ic (tə rif′ik) *adj.* **1.** extremely great or intense. **2.** excellent. —**ter·rif′i·cal·ly,** *adv.*

ter·ri·fy (ter'ə fī') v.t., -fied, -fy-ing. to fill with terror.

ter·ri·to·ry (ter'i tôr'ē) n., pl. -ries. 1. any large area of land. 2. the land and waters under a state's control. 3. a field of action, thought, etc. —**ter·ri·to·ri·al**, adj.

ter·ror (ter'ər) n. intense fear.

ter·ror·ism n. the use of violence and threats to obtain political demands. —**ter·ror·ist**, n., adj.

ter·ror·ize v.t., -ized, -izing. to fill with terror. —**ter·ror·i·za'tion**, n.

ter·ry (ter'ē) n., pl. -ries. a pile fabric with uncut loops, used for towels. Also, **terry cloth**.

terse (tûrs) adj. 1. concise. 2. curt; brusque. —**terse·ly**, adv.

ter·ti·ar·y (tûr'shē er'ē) adj. of the third rank or stage.

tes·sel·late (tes'ə lāt') v.t., -lated, -lating. to form in a mosaic pattern of small squares.

test (test) n. 1. the means used to determine the quality, content, etc., of something. 2. an examination to evaluate a student or class. —v.t. 3. to subject to a test.

tes·ta·ment (tes'tə mənt) n. 1. either of two sections of the Bible. 2. a legal will. —**tes'ta·men'ta·ry** (-men'tə rē) adj.

tes·tate (-tāt) adj. having left a valid will. —**tes'ta·tor**, n.

tes·ti·cle (-ti kəl) n. either of two male sex glands located in the scrotum. Also, **tes'tis** (tes'tis).

tes·ti·fy (-tə fī') v.i., -fied, -fying. 1. to serve as evidence. 2. to give testimony.

tes·ti·mo·ni·al (-mō'nē al) n. 1. a recommendation of a person or thing. 2. a tribute.

tes·ti·mo·ny n., pl. -nies. 1. the statement of a witness under oath. 2. proof.

tes·tos·ter·one (tes tos'tə rōn') n. a male sex hormone.

test' tube' n. a slender glass tube used in laboratories.

tes·ty (tes'tē) adj., -tier, -tiest. irritable. —**tes'ti·ly**, adv.

tet·a·nus (tet'n əs) n. a bacterial disease marked by muscular rigidity.

tête·-à·-tête (tāt'ə tāt', tet'ə tet') n. a private conversation.

teth·er (teth'ər) n. 1. a rope, chain, etc., for fastening an animal to a stake. —v.t. 2. to fasten with a tether. —*Idiom.* 3. **at the end of one's tether**, having reached the end of one's ability or resources.

tet·ra (te'trə) n., pl. -ras. a small, brightly colored fish of tropical American waters.

tetra- a prefix meaning four.

tet·ra·he·dron (-hē'drən) n., pl. -drons, -dra. a solid contained by four plane faces.

te·tram·e·ter (te tram'i tər) n. a verse of four feet.

Tex. Texas.

text (tekst) n. 1. the main body of matter in a book or manuscript. 2. the actual words spoken or written. 3. a quotation from Scripture. —**tex'tu·al** (-chō əl) adj.

text'book' n. a book used by students in a course.

tex·tile (teks'tīl, -til) n. 1. any woven material. —adj. 2. of textiles or weaving.

tex·ture (teks'chər) n. the physical structure or composition of a material, object, etc. —**tex'tur·al**, adj.

thal·a·mus (thal'ə məs) n. the part of the brain that transmits and integrates sensory impulses.

tha·lid·o·mide (thə lid'ə mīd') n. a drug formerly used as a sedative, found to cause fetal abnormalities when taken during pregnancy.

thal·li·um (thal'ē əm) n. a rare metallic element.

than (than, then; unstressed thən, ən) conj. 1. (used to introduce the second member of a comparison). 2. (used to indicate a difference in kind, place, etc.).

thank (thangk) v.t. 1. to express gratitude to. —n. 2. thanks, an expression of gratitude. —**thank'ful**, adj.

thank'less adj. not likely to be appreciated.

thanks·giv·ing n. 1. an expression of thanks, esp. to God. 2. **Thanksgiving**, a U.S. holiday observed on the fourth Thursday of November.

that (that; unstressed that) pron., pl. those (thōz), adv., adj., conj. —pron., adj. 1. a demonstrative word indicating a. the person, thing, etc., more remote. b. one of two persons, things, etc., pointed out or mentioned before (opposed to **this**). 2. a relative pronoun used as: a.

the subject or object of a relative clause. b. the object of a preposition. —adv. 3. to that extent. —conj. 4. a word used to introduce a dependent clause or one expressing reason, result, etc.

thatch (thach) n. 1. rushes, straw, etc., woven together for covering roofs. —v.t. 2. to cover with thatch.

thaw (thô) v.i. 1. to melt. —v.t. 2. to remove ice or frost from. —n. 3. an act or instance of thawing.

the (stressed thē; unstressed before a consonant thə, unstressed before a vowel thē) def. article. 1. (used to indicate a particular person or thing). 2. (used to mark a noun indicating the best, most important, etc.). 3. (used to mark a noun standing for one or all of a kind). 4. (used before adjectives that are used as nouns).

the·a·ter (thē'ə tar, thē'-) n. 1. a building for the presentation of plays, movies, etc. 2. **the theater**, dramatic art. 3. a place of action. Also, **the'a·tre**. —**the·at'ri·cal** (-ə'tri kəl) adj.

the·at·rics n. 1. (used with a sing. v.) the art of staging plays. 2. (used with a pl. v.) exaggerated actions.

thee (thē) pron. Archaic. the objective case of **thou**.

theft (theft) n. an act or instance of stealing.

their (thâr; unstressed thər) pron. 1. the possessive form of **they** used before a noun. 2. **theirs**, that which belongs to them.

the·ism (thē'iz əm) n. belief in the existence of a god or gods. —**the'ist**, n.

them (them; unstressed thəm, əm) pron. the objective case of **they**.

theme (thēm) n. 1. the central subject of a work of art. 2. a subject of discussion. 3. a short essay. 4. a principal melody in a musical composition. —**the·mat'ic** (-mat'ik) adj.

them·selves (tham selvz', them'-) pron. an emphatic or reflexive form of them.

then (then) adv. 1. at that time. 2. soon afterward. 3. at another time. 4. besides. 5. in that case. —adj. 6. being such at that time.

thence (thens) adv. 1. from that place or time. 2. therefore.

thence·forth' (thens'fôrth', thens'-fôrth') adv. from that place or time on.

the·oc·ra·cy (thē ok'rə sē) n.,pl. -cies. 1. a form of government in which the rulers claim to carry out divine law. 2. government by priests. —**the'o·crat'ic** (-ə krat'ik) adj.

the·ol·o·gy (-ol'ə jē) n. 1. the study of religious truth. 2. a particular form, system, or branch of this study. —**the'o·lo'gian** (-ə lō'jən, -jē ən) n. —**the'o·log'i·cal** (-loj'i kəl) adj.

the·o·rem (thē'ər əm, thēr'əm) n. Math. a proposition or formula containing something to be proved.

the·o·ret·i·cal (thē'ə ret'i kəl) adj. of, consisting in, or existing only in theory.

the·o·ry (thē'ə rē, thēr'ē) n., pl. -ries. 1. a group of propositions used as principles to explain a class of phenomena. 2. a proposed explanation. 3. the branch of a field of knowledge that deals with its principles rather than its practice. —**the'o·rist**, n. —**the'o·rize**, v.i.

ther·a·peu·tic (ther'ə pyōo'tik) adj. curing, healing, or maintaining health. —**ther'a·peu·ti·cal·ly**, adv. —**ther'a·peu'tics**, n.

ther·a·py (ther'ə pē) n., pl. -pies. the treatment of disease or disorders. —**ther'a·pist** (-pist) n.

there (thâr; unstressed thər) adv. 1. in, at, or to that place. 2. at that point; in that matter. —n. 3. that place or point. —interj. 4. an exclamation of relief or satisfaction.

there·a·bout' or **there'a·bouts'** adv. near that place, time, number, amount, etc.

there·af'ter adv. after that.

there·by' (thâr'bī') adv. by means of that.

there'fore' adv. as a result.

there·in' adv. in that place.

there·of' adv. of or from that.

there·on' adv. 1. on that. 2. immediately after that.

there·up·on' adv. 1. immediately after that. 2. because of that. 3. upon that.

there·with' adv. with or in addition to that.

ther'mal (thûr'məl) adj. of or retaining heat.

ther·mo·dy·nam·ics (thûr'mō dī-nam'iks) n. the science concerned with the relations between heat and mechanical energy or work.

ther·mom'e·ter (thər mom'i tər) n. an instrument for measuring temperature.

ther·mo·nu·cle·ar (thûr'mō-) adj. of nuclear-fusion reactions at extremely high temperatures.

Ther'mos (thûr'məs) Trademark. a container with a vacuum between double walls for heat insulation.

ther'mo·sphere' n. the region of the upper atmosphere in which temperature increases continually with altitude.

ther'mo·stat' (-mə stat') n. a device that automatically sets and maintains a desired temperature. —**ther'mo·stat'ic**, adj.

the·sau·rus (thi sôr'əs) n., pl. -sauruses, -sauri (-sôr'ī). a dictionary of synonyms and antonyms.

these (thēz) pron. pl. of **this**.

the·sis (thē'sis) n., pl. -ses (-sēz). 1. a proposition to be proved. 2. a lengthy essay presented for a university degree.

thes·pi·an (thes'pē ən) adj. 1. of dramatic art. —n. 2. an actor or actress.

the·ta (thā'tə) n., pl. -tas. the eighth letter of the Greek alphabet.

they (thā) pron.pl. the nominative plural of **he, she**, and **it**.

thi·a·mine (thī'ə min, -mēn') n. vitamin B₁. Also, **thi'a·min**.

thick (thik) adj. 1. not thin. 2. measured between opposite surfaces. 3. dense. 4. heavy. —n. 5. the thickest part. —**thick'en**, v.t., v.i. —**thick'en·er**, n.

thick'et n. a thick growth of shrubs, bushes, etc.

thick'set' adj. 1. set closely; dense. 2. heavily or solidly built.

thick'-skinned' adj. not sensitive to criticism or contempt.

thief (thēf) n., pl. **thieves** (thēvz). a person who steals. —**thieve**, v.t., v.i. —**thiev'er·y** (thē'və rē) n.

thigh (thī) n. the part of the leg between the hip and the knee.

thim·ble (thim'bəl) n. a cap to protect the finger while sewing.

thin (thin) adj., **thinner, thinnest**, v., **thinned, thinning**. —adj.1. having little extent between opposite sides; slender. 2. lean. 3. widely separated. 4. rarefied; diluted. 5. flimsy. 6. weak. —v.t., v.i. 7. to make or become thin.

thing (thing) n. 1. an inanimate object. 2. a matter. 3. an action. 4. an event. 5. a thought or idea. 6. **things**, personal possessions.

think (thingk) v., **thought** (thôt), **thinking**. —v.i. 1. to use one's mind rationally. 2. to have something as the subject of one's thoughts. 3. to form an idea. 4. to have a belief or opinion. —v.t. 5. to have in the mind. 6. to believe. —**think'er**, n.

think' tank' n. a research organization employed to analyze problems and plan future developments.

thin'ner n. a liquid used to dilute paint.

thin'-skinned' adj. sensitive to criticism or contempt.

third (thûrd) adj. 1. next after the second. 2. being one of three equal parts. —n. 3. a third part or the third one of a series.

third'-class' adj. of the lowest class or quality.

third' degree' n. the use of brutal measures by police (or others) in obtaining information.

third' dimen'sion n. 1. thickness or depth. 2. an aspect that heightens reality.

third' par'ty n. 1. any party to a case or quarrel who is incidentally involved. 2. in a two-party political system, a usu. temporary party composed of independents.

third'-rate' adj. of poor quality.

Third' World' n. the developing countries of Asia, Africa, and Latin America.

thirst (thûrst) n. 1. the sensation caused by the need of drink. —v.i. 2. to be thirsty. —**thirst'y**, adj. —**thirst'i·ly**, adv.

thir·teen' (thûr'tēn') n., adj. ten plus three. —**thir·teenth'**, adj., n.

thir'ty (thûr'tē) n., adj. ten times three. —**thir'ti·eth**, adj., n.

this (this) pron., adj. **these** (thēz), adv. —pron., adj. 1. a demonstrative word indicating something as just mentioned, present, near, etc. —adv. 2. to the indicated extent.

this'tle (this'əl) n. a prickly plant.

thith'er (thith'ər, thith'-) adv. to that place, point, etc.

tho (thō) conj., adv. a simplified spelling of **though**.

thong (thông) n. 1. a strip of leather. 2. a sandal with a strip of leather, plastic, etc., passing between the first two toes.

tho'rax (thôr'aks) n., pl. **thoraxes, thoraces** (thôr'ə sēz'). the part of the body between the neck and the abdomen. —**tho·rac'ic** (thô ras'ik) adj.

thor'i·um (thôr'ē əm) n. a grayish-white radioactive metallic element.

thorn (thôrn) n. a sharp spine on a plant. —**thorn'y**, adj.

thor'ough (thûr'ō, thur'ō) adj. 1. complete. 2. having or done with great attention to detail. —**thor'ough·ly**, adv.

thor'ough·bred' (-ō bred', -ə bred') adj. 1. of pure breed or stock. —n. 2. a thoroughbred animal, esp. a horse.

thor'ough·fare' n. a road, street, etc., that is open at both ends.

thor'ough·go'ing adj. extremely thorough.

those (thōz) pron., adj. pl. of **that**.

thou (thou) pron. Archaic (except in elevated prose or in addressing God). you (the second person singular in the nominative case).

though (thō) conj. 1. in spite of the fact that. 2. even if. —adv. 3. however.

thought¹ (thôt) n. 1. the result of mental activity. 2. an idea. 3. the act, process, or capacity of thinking. 4. an opinion.

thought² (thôt) v. pt. and pp. of **think**.

thought'ful adj. 1. occupied with thought. 2. careful. 3. considerate. —**thought'ful·ly**, adv.

thought'less adj. 1. showing lack of thought. 2. careless; inconsiderate. —**thought'less·ly**, adv.

thou'sand (thou'zənd) n., adj. ten times one hundred. —**thou'sandth**, adj., n.

thrall (thrôl) n. 1. slavery; bondage. 2. a person in bondage; slave.

thrash (thrash) v.t. 1. to beat thoroughly. —v.i. 2. to toss about wildly.

thread (thred) n. 1. a fine spun cord of flax, cotton, etc., used for sewing. 2. the ridge of a screw. —v.t. 3. to pass thread through. 4. to make (one's way) through obstacles.

thread'bare' adj. shabby.

threat (thret) n. 1. an expression of intent to harm. 2. an indication of possible trouble.

threat'en v.t., v.i. 1. to utter threats (against). 2. to be a threat (to).

three (thrē) n., adj. two plus one.

three'-di·men'sion·al adj. having or seeming to have depth as well as width and height.

three'fold' adj. 1. having three parts. 2. three times as great.

three'score' adj. sixty.

thren'o·dy (thren'ə dē) n., pl. -dies. a song of lamentation.

thresh (thresh) v.t., v.i. to separate (grain or seeds) from (a plant). —**thresh'er**, n.

thresh'old (thresh'ōld, -hōld) n. 1. a doorway sill. 2. an entrance or beginning.

thrice (thrīs) adv. three times.

thrift (thrift) n. economical management.

thrift' shop' n. a store that sells secondhand goods, often to benefit a charity.

thrift'y adj., -ier, -iest. saving; frugal.

thrill (thril) v.t. 1. to affect with sudden emotion or excitement. —v.i. 2. to vibrate. —n. 3. a sudden wave of emotion or excitement.

thrill'er n. a suspenseful story.

thrive (thrīv) v.i., **thrived, thriving**. to prosper or flourish.

throat (thrōt) n. the passage from the mouth to the lungs or esophagus.

throat'y adj., -ier, -iest. (of a sound) husky; hoarse.

throb (throb) v., **throbbed, throbbing**, n. —v.i. 1. to beat violently or rapidly. 2. to vibrate. —n. 3. an act of throbbing.

throe (thrō) n. 1. a violent spasm. —*Idiom.* 2. **in the throes of**, in a violent struggle with.

throm·bo'sis (throm bō'sis) n. clotting of blood in the blood vessels or heart.

throm'bus (-bəs) n., pl. **-bi** (-bī). a clot formed in thrombosis.

throne (thrōn) n. the official chair of a sovereign, bishop, etc.

throng (thrông) n. 1. a crowd. —v.i. 2. to gather in large numbers.

throt·tle (throt'l) n., v., -tled, -tling. —n. 1. a device controlling the flow of fuel. —v.t. 2. to choke. 3. to silence or check.

through (thrōō) prep. 1. in one side and out the other side of. 2. past; beyond. 3. between or among. 4. done with. 5. by the means or reason of. —adv. 6. in at one side and out at the other. 7. all the way. 8. to the end. 9. finished. 10. extending from one side to the other.

through·out' prep. 1. in every part of. —adv. 2. in or during every part.

throw (thrō) v., **threw** (thrōō), **thrown, throwing**, n. —v.t. 1. to propel or cast forth. 2. to cause to fall. 3. to move (a lever or switch). 4. to confuse. 5. **throw away, a.** to discard. **b.** to waste. 6. to add as a bonus. 7. **~ up**, to vomit. —n. 8. an act of throwing. 9. the distance something is thrown. 10. a light blanket. —**throw'er**, n.

throw'a·way' adj. 1. to be discarded after use. —n. 2. a notice distributed free.

throw'back' n. a reversion to an earlier type.

thru (thrōō) prep., adv., adj. an informal spelling of **through**.

thrush (thrush) n. 1. a migratory songbird with dull feathers. 2. a fungal infection.

thrust (thrust) v., **thrust, thrusting**, n. —v.t. 1. to push. —v.i. 2. to make a lunge or stab. 3. to force one's way. —n. 4. a thrusting movement. 5. a force propelling a missile, ship, etc. 6. the main point.

thru'way' (thrōō'wā') n. an expressway providing a direct route between distant areas.

thud (thud) n., v., **thudded, thudding**. —n. 1. a dull striking sound. —v.i. 2. to make a thudding sound.

thug (thug) n. a violent criminal.

thumb (thum) n. 1. the short, thick finger next to the forefinger. —v.t. 2. to manipulate with the thumb.

thumb'nail' n. 1. the nail of the thumb. —adj. 2. brief and concise.

thumb'screw' n. a screw turned by the thumb and forefinger.

thumb'tack' n. 1. a tack with a large, flat head. —v.t. 2. to secure with a thumbtack.

thump (thump) n. 1. a heavy blow. —v.t., v.i. 2. to strike heavily.

thump'ing adj. 1. exceptional. 2. of or like a thump.

thun'der (thun'dər) n. 1. the loud noise accompanying lightning. 2. any loud noise. —v.i. 3. to give forth thunder. 4. to make a noise like thunder. 5. to speak loudly. —**thun'der·ous**, adj.

thun'der·bolt' n. a flash of lightning with thunder.

thun'der·clap' n. a crash of thunder.

thun'der·cloud' n. an electrically charged cloud producing lightning and thunder.

thun'der·head' n. a mass of clouds warning of thunderstorms.

thun'der·struck' adj. astonished.

Thurs. Thursday.

Thurs'day (thûrz'dā, -dē) n. the fifth day of the week.

thus (thus) adv. 1. in this way. 2. as a result. 3. to this extent.

thwack (thwak) v.t. 1. to strike hard with something flat. —n. 2. a sharp blow with something flat.

thwart (thwôrt) v.t. to oppose or frustrate.

thy (thī) pron. Archaic. the possessive case of **thou**.

thyme (tīm; spelling pron. thīm) n. an aromatic plant of the mint family used as seasoning.

thy'mus (thī'məs) n. a gland at the base of the neck that helps produce T cells.

thy'roid (thī'roid) n. 1. a ductless gland near the windpipe, involved in controlling metabolism and growth. —adj. 2. of this gland.

thy·self' (thī self') pron. a reflexive and intensive form of **thou** or **thee**.

ti·ar·a (tē ar'ə, -är'ə, -âr'ə) n. a woman's ornamental coronet.

tib·i·a (tib'ē ə) n., pl. **-iae** (-ē ē') **-ias**. the bone from the knee to the ankle.

tic (tik) n. a sudden twitch.

tick¹ (tik) n. 1. a slight, sharp, recurring click. —v.i. 2. to make a ticking sound.

tick² (tik) n. a bloodsucking mite.

tick'er n. **1.** one that ticks. **2.** a telegraphic instrument that prints stock prices, market reports, etc., on tape (**ticker tape**). **3.** Slang. the heart.

tick'et (-it) n. **1.** a printed slip indicating the right to admission, transportation, etc. **2.** a tag. **3.** a summons for a traffic or parking violation. —v.t. **4.** to attach a ticket to.

tick'ing n. a cotton fabric used to cover mattresses and pillows.

tick'le v., **-led**, **-ling.** —v.t. **1.** to touch lightly so as to make tingle or itch. **2.** to gratify. —v.i. **3.** to have or produce a tingling sensation. —n. **4.** a tickling sensation. —**tick'lish,** adj.

tick'ler file' n. a file for reminding the user at appropriate times of matters needing attention.

tick'-tack-toe' (tik'tak tō') n. a game for two players, each trying to complete a row of three X's or three O's on a nine-square grid.

tid'al wave' n. a large, destructive ocean wave.

tid'bit' (tid'bit') n. a choice bit, as of food.

tid'dly-winks' (tid'lē wingks') n. a game in which small disks are snapped with larger disks into a cup.

tide (tīd) n., v., **tided, tiding.** —n. **1.** the periodic rise and fall of the ocean. **2.** a tendency. —v. **3. tide over,** to help to get through a difficult period. —**tid'al,** adj.

tide'land' n. land alternately exposed and covered by the tide.

ti'dings (tī'dingz) n.pl. news.

ti'dy (tī'dē) adj., **-dier, -diest**, v., **-died, -dying.** —adj. **1.** neat and orderly. **2.** fairly large. —v.t. **3.** to make tidy. —**ti'di·ly,** adv.

tie (tī) v., **tied, tying.** —v.t. **1.** to fasten with a cord, string, etc. **2.** to make into a bow. **3.** to bind. **4.** to make the same score as. —v.i. **5.** to make the same score. —n. **6.** something used to tie or join. **7.** a necktie. **8.** equality in scores, votes, etc. **9.** a contest in which this occurs. **10.** a bond of kinship, affection, etc.

tie'-dye'ing n. a method of dyeing with sections of garment bound so as not to receive dye.

tie'-in' n. a link or association.

tier (tēr) n. a row or rank.

tie'-up' n. a temporary stoppage of business, traffic, etc.

tiff (tif) n. a petty quarrel.

ti'ger (tī'gər) n. a large striped Asian cat.

ti'ger lil'y n. a lily with flowers of a dull-orange color spotted with black.

tight (tīt) adj. **1.** firmly fixed in place. **2.** stretched so as to be tense. **3.** fitting closely. **4.** firm; rigid. **5.** scarce. **6.** stingy. —**tight'en,** v.t., v.i. —**tight'ly,** adv. —**tight'ness,** n.

tight'-fist'ed adj. stingy.

tight'-lipped' adj. reluctant to speak.

tight'rope' n. a taut wire or cable on which acrobats perform.

tights n.pl. a skintight garment covering the hips, legs, and feet.

tight'wad' n. a stingy person.

til'de (til'də) n. a diacritical mark (~) placed over a letter.

tile (tīl) n., v., **tiled, tiling.** —n. **1.** a thin piece of baked clay or stone, used for covering roofs, floors, etc. —v.t. **2.** to cover with tiles.

til'ing n. **1.** the process of covering with tiles. **2.** tiles collectively.

till¹ (til) prep., conj. until.

  —**Usage.** TILL and UNTIL are used interchangeably in speech and writing: *It rained till/until nearly midnight.* TILL is not a shortened form of UNTIL and is not spelled *'till.* 'TIL is usually considered a spelling error, though commonly used in business and advertising: *open 'til ten.*

till² (til) v.t., v.i. **1.** to prepare (land) for raising crops. —**till'age,** n.

till³ (til) n. a drawer in which money is kept in a shop.

till'er n. a handle for turning the rudder in steering.

tilt (tilt) v.t. **1.** to cause to slope. —v.i. **2.** to slope. **3.** to charge with a lance. —n. **4.** a slope. **5.** a tournament.

tim'bale (tim'bəl) n. **1.** a preparation of minced meat, seafood, etc., cooked in a mold. **2.** this mold, usually of paste, and sometimes fried.

tim'ber (tim'bər) n. **1.** wood suitable for building. **2.** trees. **3.** a wooden beam.

tim'ber·line' n. the altitude above sea level at which timber ceases to grow.

tim'ber wolf' n. a large brindled wolf of northern North America.

tim'bre (tam'bər, tim'-) n. the characteristic quality of a sound.

time (tīm) n., v., **timed, timing.** —n. **1.** the length of all existence, past, present, and future. **2.** a limited or particular period of time. **3.** a definite point in time. **4.** an occasion. **5.** an appointed or proper time. **6.** a system of measuring time. **7.** times, an era. **8.** rhythm in music. —v.t. **9.** to determine, record, or schedule the time of. —**Idiom. 10.** ahead of time, early. **11.** at the same time, nevertheless. **12.** for the time being, temporarily. **13.** from time to time, occasionally. **14.** time after time, again and again. —**Idiom. 10.** of the highest quality.

time' clock' n. a clock with an attachment that records the times of arrival and departure of employees.

time'-hon'ored adj. long valued or used; traditional.

time'keep'er n. an official who times, regulates, and records the length of a contest.

time'less adj. restricted to no particular time.

time' line' n. **1.** a linear representation of events in the order in which they occurred. **2.** a schedule.

time'ly adj., **-lier, -liest.** occurring at a suitable time.

time'-out' n. a brief suspension of activity, as in a sports contest.

time'piece' n. a clock or watch.

times prep. multiplied by.

time'-shar'ing n. **1.** a plan in which several people share the cost of a vacation home. **2.** a system in which users at different terminals simultaneously use a single computer.

time'ta·ble n. a schedule of times of arrivals, departures, etc.

time'worn' adj. showing the effects of long use. **2.** trite.

time' zone' n. one of 24 divisions of the globe coinciding with meridians at successive hours from the observatory at Greenwich, England.

tim'id (tim'id) adj. easily alarmed; shy. —**ti·mid'i·ty,** n.

tim'ing (tī'ming) n. the control of the time or speed of an action, event, etc., so that it occurs at the proper moment.

tim'or·ous (tim'ər əs) adj. fearful or timid. —**tim'or·ous·ly,** adv.

tim'o·thy (tim'ə thē) n., pl. **-thies.** a coarse fodder grass.

tim'pa·ni (tim'pə nē) n.pl. a set of kettledrums. —**tim'pa·nist,** n.

tin (tin) n., v., **tinned, tinning.** —n. **1.** a malleable metallic element. —v.t. **2.** to cover with tin.

tinc'ture (tingk'chər) n. a medicinal solution in alcohol.

tin'der (tin'dər) n. any dry substance that ignites easily.

tin'der·box' n. **1.** a box for tinder. **2.** a potential source of violence.

tine (tīn) n. a prong of a fork.

tin'foil' n. tin or a tin and lead alloy in a thin sheet.

tinge (tinj) v., **tinged, tingeing** or **tinging,** n. —v.t. **1.** to impart a trace of color, taste, etc., to. —n. **2.** a slight trace.

tin'gle (ting'gəl) v., **-gled, -gling,** n. —v.i., v.t. **1.** to feel or cause slight stings. —n. **2.** a tingling sensation.

tink'er (ting'kər) n. a mender of pots, kettles, pans, etc. —v.i. **2.** to putter. **3.** to work clumsily.

tin'kle (ting'kəl) v., **-kled, -kling,** —v.i., v.t. **1.** to make or cause light ringing sounds. —n. **2.** a tinkling sound.

tin' plate' n. a thin iron or steel sheet coated with tin.

tin'sel (tin'səl) n. **1.** thin strips of glittering metal, paper, etc. **2.** anything showy and worthless.

tint (tint) n. **1.** a shade of a color. **2.** a delicate color. —v.t. **3.** to give a tint to.

tin'tin·nab·u·la'tion (tin'ti nab'-yə lā'shən) n. the ringing or sound of bells.

tin'type' n. an old type of positive photograph made on a sensitized sheet of iron or tin.

ti'ny (tī'nē) adj., **-nier, -niest.** very small.

-tion a suffix meaning action or process; result of action; or state or condition.

tip¹ (tip) n., v., **tipped, tipping.** —n.

1. a slender or pointed end of something. **2.** a small piece covering the end of something. —v.t. **3.** to furnish with a tip. **4.** to form or adorn the tip of.

tip² (tip) v., **tipped, tipping,** n. —v.t. **1.** to overturn. —v.i. **2.** to tilt. —n. **3.** a tipping or being tipped.

tip³ (tip) n., v., **tipped, tipping.** —n. **1.** a gift of money for service provided; gratuity. **2.** a piece of confidential information. **3.** a useful hint. —v.t., v.i. **4.** to give a tip (to).

tip'-off' n. a hint or warning.

tip'ster (-star) n. a person who sells tips, as for betting.

tip'sy adj., **-sier, -siest.** slightly drunk.

tip'toe' (-tō') n., v., **-toed, -toeing.** —n. **1.** the tip of the toe. —v.i. **2.** to move on tiptoes.

tip'top' (-top', -top') n. **1.** the extreme top. —adj. **2.** situated at the very top. **3.** of the highest quality.

ti'rade (tī'rād, tī rād') n. a long, angry outburst.

tire¹ (tīⁱr) v.t., v.i., **tired, tiring.** to make or become exhausted or bored. —**tire'less,** adj.

tire² (tīⁱr) n. a ring of rubber, metal, etc., around a wheel.

tired (tīⁱrd) adj. **1.** exhausted; fatigued. **2.** weary. —**tired'ly,** adv.

tire'some adj. causing annoyance or boredom.

tis'sue (tish'ōō) n. **1.** a substance forming the body of an animal or plant. **2.** a soft, absorbent paper. **3.** a light, gauzy fabric.

tis'sue pa'per n. very thin paper for wrapping.

ti'tan (tīt'n) n. a person or thing of great size or power. —**ti·tan'ic** (tī-tan'ik) adj.

ti·tan'i·um (tī tā'nē əm) n. a corrosion-resistant metallic element.

tit for tat (tit' fər tat') n. an equivalent given in retaliation.

tithe (tīth) n., v., **tithed, tithing.** —n. **1.** a tenth part of goods or income, paid to support a church. —v.t., v.i. **2.** to give or pay a tithe (of).

tit'ian (tish'ən) n. a bright golden brown.

tit'il·late' (tit'l āt') v.t., **-lated, -lating.** to excite agreeably.

tit'i·vate' (-ə vāt') v.t., v.i., **-vated, -vating.** to make (oneself) smart or spruce.

ti'tle (tīt'l) n., v., **-tled, -tling.** —n. **1.** the name of a book, picture, etc. **2.** a caption. **3.** a word indicating rank or office. **4.** a championship. **5.** the right to something. **6.** a document showing this. —v.t. **7.** to furnish with a title.

tit'mouse' (tit'mous') n., pl. **-mice.** a small bird with a crest and a conical bill.

tit'ter (tit'ər) n. a giggle. —v.i **2.** to giggle.

tit'tle (tit'l) n. a very small thing.

tit'u·lar (tich'ə lər, tit'yə-) adj. **1.** being such in title only. **2.** of or having a title.

tiz'zy (tiz'ē) n., pl. **-zies.** Slang. a nervous, distracted state.

TN Tennessee.

TNT trinitrotoluene.

to (tōō; unstressed tōō, tə) prep. **1.** as far as. **2.** in the direction of; toward. **3.** to the limit of. **4.** before; until. **5.** as compared with. —adv. **6.** toward a closed position. **7.** toward action or work. —**Idiom. 8. to and fro,** back and forth.

toad (tōd) n. a froglike animal living mostly on land.

toad'stool' n. a fungus with an umbrellalike cap.

toad'y n., pl. **-ies,** v., **-ied, -ying.** —n. **1.** a person who flatters to gain favors. —v.i. **2.** to behave in this way.

toast¹ (tōst) n. **1.** sliced bread browned by dry heat. —v.t. **2.** to brown (bread, cheese, etc.) by heat. —v.i. **3.** to become toasted.

toast² (tōst) n. **1.** words of welcome or congratulations said before drinking to a person or event. —v.t., v.i. **2.** to propose or drink a toast (to).

toast'er n. an appliance for toasting bread.

toast'mas'ter n. a person who introduces after-dinner speakers or proposes toasts.

toast'y adj., **-ier, -iest.** cozily warm.

to·bac'co (tə bak'ō) n., pl. **-cos, -coes. 1.** a plant with leaves prepared for smoking or chewing. **2.** a product made from such leaves.

to·bog'gan (tə bog'ən) n. **1.** a

long, narrow, flat-bottomed sled. —v.i. **2.** to coast on a toboggan.

toc·ca'ta (tə kä'tə) n. Music. a keyboard composition in the style of an improvisation.

toc'sin (tok'sin) n. a bell sounded as an alarm.

to·day' (tə dā') n. **1.** this day, time, or period. —adv. **2.** on this day. **3.** at the present time.

tod'dle (tod'l) v.i., **-dled, -dling.** to move with short, unsteady steps, like a young child. —**tod'dler,** n.

tod'dy (tod'ē) n., pl. **-dies.** a drink made of liquor, hot water, and sugar.

to-do' n., pl. **to-dos.** a fuss.

toe (tō) n. **1.** one of the five parts on the front of the foot. **2.** the part of a shoe or sock covering the toes. —**toe'nail',** n.

toe'hold' n. **1.** a small niche that supports the toes. **2.** any slight advantage.

tof'fee (tô'fē) n. a candy made of brown sugar, butter, and vinegar.

to'fu (tō'fōō) n. a soft cheeselike food made from soybean milk.

to'ga (tō'gə) n. (in ancient Rome) a man's formal outer garment.

to·geth'er (tə geth'ər) adv. **1.** into or in one gathering, association, or single mass. **2.** at the same time. **3.** in cooperation.

to·geth'er·ness n. warm fellowship.

togs n.pl. Informal. clothes.

toil (toil) n. **1.** hard, exhausting work. —v.i. **2.** to work hard.

toi'let (toi'lit) n. **1.** a bathroom fixture for urination and defecation. **2.** a bathroom; lavatory. **3.** Also, **toi·lette'.** the act or process of dressing or grooming oneself.

toi'let·ry n., pl. **-ries.** an article or preparation used in grooming.

toi'let wa'ter n. a scented liquid used as a light perfume.

toil'some (-səm) adj. laborious or fatiguing.

to·kay' (tō kā') n. **1.** a rich, sweet wine. **2.** the variety of grape from which it is made.

to'ken (tō'kən) n. **1.** something expressing or representing a feeling, fact, etc.; sign or symbol. **2.** a metal disk used in place of money. —adj. **3.** being merely a token.

to'ken·ism n. making a minimal effort to conform to a law or social pressure.

tole (tōl) n. enameled or lacquered metal.

tol'er·a·ble (tol'ər ə bəl) adj. **1.** capable of being tolerated. **2.** fairly good.

tol'er·ance (-əns) n. **1.** fairness toward those whose race, religion, etc., differ from one's own. **2.** the capacity to endure something. —**tol'er·ant,** adj. —**tol'er·ant·ly,** adv.

tol'er·ate' (-ə rāt') v.t., **-ated, -ating. 1.** to allow; permit. **2.** to put up with. —**tol'er·a'tion,** n.

toll¹ (tōl) n. **1.** a payment, as for driving on a highway or crossing a bridge. **2.** a payment for a long-distance telephone call.

toll² (tōl) v.t. **1.** to ring (a bell) with slow, repeated strokes. —v.i. **2.** (of a bell) to ring slowly.

toll'booth' n. a booth where a toll is collected.

tol'u·ene' (tol'yōō ēn') n. a flammable liquid used in the making of TNT.

tom (tom) n. the male of various animals.

tom'a·hawk' (tom'ə hôk') n. a light ax used by North American Indians.

to·ma'to (tə mā'tō) n., pl. **-toes.** a pulpy, juicy red fruit used as a vegetable.

tomb (tōōm) n. a burial chamber for a dead body; grave.

tom'boy' (tom'-) n. an energetic, boisterous girl whose behavior is considered boyish.

tomb'stone' n. a stone marker on a grave.

tom'cat' n. a male cat.

tome (tōm) n. a large, heavy book.

tom'fool'er·y (tom'fōō'lə rē) n. foolish or silly behavior.

tom'my·rot' n. Slang. nonsense.

to·mor'row (tə môr'ō) n. **1.** the day after today. —adv. **2.** on the day after today.

tom'-tom' n. a primitive drum played with the hands.

ton (tun) n. a unit of weight, equal to 2000 pounds (**short ton**) in the U.S. and 2240 pounds (**long ton**) in Great Britain.

to·nal'i·ty (tō nal'i tē) n., pl. **-ties.**

the sum of relations between the tones of a musical scale.

tone (tōn) n., v., **toned, toning.** —n. **1.** any sound with reference to its quality, pitch, etc. **2.** quality of sound. **3.** a vocal sound. **4.** a particular style or manner. **5.** firmness. **6.** elegance. —v.t. **7.** to give a certain tone to. —**ton'al,** adj.

tone'-deaf' adj. unable to distinguish differences in musical pitch.

tongs (tôngz) n.pl. a two-armed implement for picking up an object.

tongue (tung) n. **1.** an organ in the mouth, used for tasting, eating, and speaking. **2.** a language. **3.** anything resembling a tongue.

tongue'-lash'ing n. a severe scolding.

tongue'-tied' adj. unable to speak, as from shyness.

tongue' twist'er n. a sequence of words that is difficult to pronounce rapidly.

ton'ic (ton'ik) n. **1.** an invigorating medicine. —adj. **2.** invigorating.

to·night' (tə nīt') n. **1.** this night. —adv. **2.** on this night.

ton'nage (tun'ij) n. **1.** the carrying capacity or total volume of a ship. **2.** ships collectively.

ton'sil (ton'səl) n. an oval mass of lymphoid tissue in the throat.

ton'sil·lec·to·my (-sə lek'tə mē) n., pl. **-mies.** the surgical removal of the tonsils.

ton'sil·li'tis (-lī'tis) n. inflammation of the tonsils.

ton·so'ri·al (ton sôr'ē əl) adj. of barbers.

ton'sure (ton'shər) n. the shaved part of the head of a monk.

too (tōō) adv. **1.** in addition. **2.** excessively; extremely.

tool (tōōl) n. **1.** a hand implement, as a hammer or saw. **2.** the working part of a machine. **3.** anything used for accomplishing a purpose. **4.** a person exploited by another; dupe. —v.t. **5.** to shape, work, or decorate with a tool.

toot (tōōt) v.i., v.t. to sound (a horn or whistle) in quick blasts.

tooth (tōōth) n., pl. **teeth** (tēth). **1.** one of the hard white structures attached to the jaw, used for biting and chewing. **2.** a toothlike projection, as on a comb or saw.

tooth'ache' n. a pain in a tooth.

tooth' and nail' adv. with all one's resources and energy.

tooth'brush' n. a brush for cleaning the teeth.

tooth'paste' n. a paste for cleaning the teeth.

tooth'pick' n. a small pointed stick for removing bits of food from between the teeth.

tooth'some (-səm) adj. tasty.

tooth'y (tōō'thē, -thē) adj., **-ier, -iest.** having or displaying conspicuous teeth.

top¹ (top) n., v., **topped, topping.** —n. **1.** the highest or uppermost point, surface, rank, etc. **2.** a lid. **3.** a garment for the upper part of the body. —adj. **4.** highest. —v.t. **5.** to put a top on. **6.** to reach or be at the top of. **7.** to outdo.

top² (top) n. a child's spinning toy.

to'paz (tō'paz) n. a yellowish or brownish crystalline gem.

top' brass' n. high-ranking officials.

top'coat' n. a light overcoat.

top'flight' (top'-) adj. excellent.

top' hat' n. a man's tall silk hat.

top'-heav'y adj. heavier at the top than at the bottom.

top'ic (top'ik) n. a subject of discussion or writing.

top'i·cal adj. of or dealing with matters of current interest.

top'mast' n. the mast next above a lower mast on a sailing ship.

top'most adj. highest.

top'-notch' adj. first-rate.

to·pog'ra·phy (tə pog'rə fē) n. **1.** the surface features of an area. **2.** the detailed mapping of such features.

top'ping n. a sauce or garnish placed on food.

top'ple v.i., v.t., **-pled, -pling.** to fall or cause to fall over.

top'-se'cret adj. extremely secret.

top'soil' n. fertile upper soil.

top'sy-tur'vy (top'sē tûr'vē) adv., adj. **1.** upside down. **2.** in confusion.

toque (tōk) n. a woman's hat with little or no brim.

tor (tôr) n. a hill.

To'rah (tôr'ə, tōr'ə) n. (sometimes l.c.). **1.** the five books of Moses. **2.** the whole Jewish scripture, law, and teaching.

torch (tôrch) *n.* a burning stick used for light.

torch′bear′er *n.* **1.** a person who carries a torch. **2.** a leader in a movement.

tor′e·a·dor′ (tôr′ē ə dôr′) *n.* a bullfighter.

tor·ment′ *v.t.* (tôr ment′) **1.** to cause great suffering to. —*n.* (tôr′ment) **2.** great suffering or its cause. —**tor·men′tor,** *n.*

tor·na′do (tôr nā′dō) *n., pl.* **-does, -dos.** a violent windstorm with a funnel-shaped cloud.

tor·pe′do (tôr pē′dō) *n., pl.* **-does,** *v.,* **-doed, -doing.** —*n.* **1.** a self-propelled missile launched in water and exploding on impact. —*v.t.* **2.** to strike with a torpedo.

tor′pid (tôr′pid) *adj.* **1.** inactive. **2.** dull or lethargic.

tor′por (-pər) *n.* **1.** inactivity. **2.** indifference; apathy.

torque (tôrk) *n.* a force producing rotation.

tor′rent (tôr′ənt) *n.* a rapid, violent stream. —**tor·ren′tial** (tô ren′shəl, tə-) *adj.*

tor′rid (tôr′id) *adj.* **1.** very hot. **2.** passionate.

Tor′rid Zone′ *n.* the part of the earth between the Tropic of Cancer and the Tropic of Capricorn.

tor′sion (tôr′shən) *n.* **1.** a twisting or being twisted. **2.** the twisting of an object by two equal opposing torques.

tor′so (tôr′sō) *n., pl.* **-sos, -si.** the trunk of the body.

tort (tôrt) *n. Law.* a civil wrong (other than breach of contract or trust) for which the law requires that damages be paid.

torte (tôrt) *n., pl.* **tortes.** a rich cake.

tor·tel·li·ni (tôr′tl ē′nē) *n.* (*used with a sing. or pl. v.*) small ring-shaped pieces of pasta filled with meat, cheese, or vegetables.

tor·til′la (tôr tē′ə) *n.* a flat, round Mexican bread, made from cornmeal or wheat flour.

tor′toise (tôr′təs) *n.* a turtle, esp. one living on land.

tor′toise·shell′ *n.* **1.** the horny brown and yellow shell of certain turtles, used for combs and ornaments. **2.** synthetic tortoiseshell.

tor′tu·ous (tôr′chŏŏ əs) *adj.* **1.** twisting. **2.** indirect; devious.

tor′ture (tôr′chər) *n., v.,* **-tured, -turing.** —*n.* **1.** extreme pain. **2.** the infliction of great pain, esp. for punishment or coercion. —*v.t.* **3.** to subject to torture.

tor′tur·ous *adj.* involving or causing torture or suffering.

toss (tôs) *v.t.* **1.** to throw lightly. **2.** to fling about. **3.** to jerk upward. —*v.i.* **4.** to move irregularly or restlessly. —*n.* **5.** a throw or pitch.

toss′up′ *n.* **1.** the tossing of a coin to decide something. **2.** an even chance.

tot (tot) *n.* a small child.

to′tal (tōt′l) *adj., n., v.,* **-taled, -taling.** —*adj.* **1.** entire. **2.** complete. —*n.* **3.** the total amount. —*v.t.* **4.** to add together. **5.** to add up to. **6.** to damage beyond repair. —*v.i.* **7.** to amount. —**to·tal′i·ty** (-tal′i tē) *n.* —**to′tal·ly,** *adv.*

to·tal·i·tar′i·an (tō tal′i târ′ē ən) *adj.* of a government in which one party has dictatorial control. —**to·tal′i·tar′i·an·ism,** *n.*

tote (tōt) *v.,* **toted, toting.** —*v.t.* **1.** to carry. —*n.* **2.** an open handbag or shopping bag; tote bag.

tote′ bag′ *n.* a large open handbag.

to′tem (tō′təm) *n.* an object in nature assumed as the emblem of a clan, family, or related group.

to′tem pole′ *n.* a pole with carved and painted figures, erected by Indians of the NW coast of North America.

tot′ter (tot′ər) *v.i.* **1.** to walk unsteadily. **2.** to sway as if about to fall.

tou′can (tōō′kan, -kän) *n.* a brightly colored tropical American bird with a large bill.

touch (tuch) *v.t.* **1.** to put the hand, finger, etc., into contact with. **2.** to bring or come into contact with. **3.** to reach. **4.** to affect with tenderness or sympathy. —*v.i.* **5.** to touch someone or something. **6.** to come into or be in contact. —*n.* **7.** a touching or being touched. **8.** the sense by which a thing is perceived by physical contact. **9.** ability. **10.** a slight trace.

touch′ and go′ *n.* an uncertain state of affairs.

touch′down′ *n.* **1.** the act of scor-

ing in football by touching the ball to the ground behind the opponent's goal line. **2.** the act of landing, as of an airplane.

tou·ché (tōō shā′) *interj.* (used to acknowledge a touch in fencing or a telling remark or rejoinder).

touch′-me-not′ *n.* a yellow-flowered plant whose ripe seed vessels burst open when touched.

touch′screen′ or **touch′ screen′** *n.* a computer display that can respond to the presence of a finger on its surface.

touch′stone′ *n.* a test for the qualities of a thing.

touch′y *adj.,* **-ier, -iest.** easily offended. —**touch′i·ness,** *n.*

tough (tuf) *adj.* **1.** not easily broken, cut, or chewed. **2.** sturdy. **3.** unyielding. **4.** difficult. **5.** unruly or rough. —*n.* **6.** a brutal, lawless person. —**tough′en,** *v.t., v.i.*

tou·pee′ (tōō pā′) *n.* a patch of false hair worn to cover a bald spot.

tour (tōŏr) *n.* **1.** a long journey, visiting places of interest or giving performances. **2.** a period of duty in one place. —*v.i., v.t.* **3.** to go on a tour (through).

tour′ de force′ (tōŏr′ də fôrs′) *n., pl.* **tours de force.** an exceptional achievement.

tour′ism *n.* **1.** the occupation of providing various services to tourists. **2.** the promotion of tourist travel.

tour′ist *n.* a person who makes a tour, as for sightseeing.

tour′ma·line (tōŏr′mə lin, -lēn′) *n.* a mineral occurring in various transparent gems.

tour′na·ment (tōŏr′nə mənt, tûr′-) *n.* **1.** a contest involving a series of matches between competitors. **2.** a medieval contest between knights on horseback.

tour′ni·quet (tûr′ni kit, tōŏr′-) *n.* a bandlike device for stopping bleeding.

tou′sle (tou′zəl, -səl) *v.t.,* **-sled, -sling.** to disorder or dishevel, as hair.

tout (tout) *Informal.* —*v.i.* **1.** to solicit business, votes, etc., in a persistent and annoying way. —*v.t.* **2.** to solicit in a persistent and annoying way. **3.** to praise highly.

tow (tō) *v.t.* **1.** to pull or haul (a car, barge, etc.) by rope or chain. —*n.* **2.** an act of towing. **3.** something towed.

to·ward (tôrd, twôrd) *prep.* Also, **to·wards′. 1.** in the direction of. **2.** with respect to. **3.** shortly before.

tow′el (tou′əl, toul) *n.* an absorbent cloth or paper for wiping.

tow′er (tou′ər) *n.* **1.** a tall structure, either standing alone or forming part of another building. —*v.i.* **2.** to stand high.

tow′er·ing *adj.* **1.** very high or tall. **2.** extreme or intense.

tow′head′ (tō′hed′) *n.* a person with very light-colored hair.

tow′line′ (tō′līn′) *n.* a cable for towing.

town (toun) *n.* **1.** a small city. **2.** the central business area of a city. **3.** the people who live in a town. —**towns′folk′, towns′peo′ple,** *n.pl.* —**towns′man,** —**towns′wom′an,** *n.fem.*

town′ house′ *n.* one of a group of similar houses joined by common side walls.

town′ meet′ing *n.* a meeting of the voters of a town.

town′ship *n.* a division of a county.

tow′path′ (tō′path′) *n.* a path along the bank of a canal or river, for use in towing boats.

tox·e′mi·a (tok sē′mē ə) *n.* blood poisoning resulting from the presence of toxins in the blood. —**tox·e′mic,** *adj.*

tox′ic (tok′sik) *adj.* **1.** of or caused by a toxin. **2.** poisonous. —**tox·ic′i·ty,** *n.*

tox′i·col′o·gy (-si kol′ə jē) *n.* the study of poisons.

tox′ic shock′ syn′drome *n.* a rapidly developing toxemia.

tox′in (tok′sin) *n.* a poison produced by an animal, plant, or bacterium.

toy (toi) *n.* **1.** a thing to play with. —*v.* **2. toy with,** to play or trifle with.

trace (trās) *n., v.,* **traced, tracing.** —*n.* **1.** a mark or sign left by something. **2.** a very small amount. —*v.t.* **3.** to follow the course of. **4.** to find out by investigating. **5.** to copy (a drawing) by following its

lines on a transparent sheet placed over it.

trac′er·y *n., pl.* **-eries.** an ornamental pattern of interlacing lines.

tra′che·a (trā′kē ə) *n., pl.* **-cheae** (-kē ē′). the windpipe.

tra·che·ot′o·my (-ot′ə mē) *n., pl.* **-mies.** the operation of cutting into the trachea to help a person breathe.

track (trak) *n.* **1.** a pair of parallel rails on which a train runs. **2.** marks left by an animal, person, or vehicle. **3.** a path. **4.** a course for running. **5.** a band of recorded sound, as on a compact disc. —*v.t.* **6.** to follow; pursue.

track′ball′ *n.* a computer input device for controlling the pointer on a screen by rotating a ball set inside a case.

track′ rec′ord *n.* a record of achievements or performance.

tract (trakt) *n.* **1.** an area of land. **2.** a specific area of the body.

tract[2] (trakt) *n.* a brief pamphlet, esp. on religion or politics.

trac′ta·ble (trak′tə bəl) *adj.* easily managed or controlled.

trac′tion (-shən) *n.* **1.** the adhesive friction of a body on a surface. **2.** a pulling or being pulled.

trac′tor (-tər) *n.* a powerful vehicle for pulling farm machinery.

trade (trād) *n., v.,* **traded, trading.** —*n.* **1.** the buying, selling, or exchange of goods; commerce. **2.** an exchange. **3.** an occupation. —*v.t.* **4.** to buy and sell. **5.** to exchange. —*v.i.* **6.** to carry on trade. **7.** to make an exchange. —**trad′er,** *n.* —**trades′man,** *n.*

trade′-in′ *n.* goods given in whole or part payment for a purchase.

trade′mark′ *n.* any registered name, symbol, etc., used by a manufacturer to identify its goods.

trade′ name′ *n.* a word or phrase by which a particular class of goods is designated.

trade′-off′ *n.* the exchange of one thing for another.

trade′ un′ion *n.* a labor union.

trade′ wind′ (wind) *n.* any sea wind blowing from the northeast in the Northern Hemisphere and from the southeast in the Southern Hemisphere.

tra·di′tion (trə dish′ən) *n.* **1.** the handing down of beliefs, customs, etc., through generations. **2.** something so handed down. —**tra·di′tion·al,** *adj.* —**tra·di′tion·al·ist,** *n.*

tra·duce′ (trə dōōs′, -dyōōs′) *v.t.,* **-duced, -ducing.** to slander.

traf′fic (traf′ik) *n., v.,* **-ficked, -ficking.** —*n.* **1.** vehicles, persons, etc., moving over a route. **2.** trade. —*v.i.* **3.** to trade.

traf′fic cir′cle *n.* a circular roadway at a multiple intersection.

traf′fic light′ *n.* a set of signal lights at an intersection.

tra·ge′di·an (trə jē′dē ən) *n.* an actor in or writer of tragedy.

trag′e·dy (traj′i dē) *n., pl.* **-dies. 1.** a serious drama with an unhappy ending. **2.** a sad event. —**trag′ic,** *adj.*

trail (trāl) *n.* **1.** a path, as in a forest. **2.** the track, scent, etc., left by an animal or person. —*v.t.* **3.** to draw or drag along behind. **4.** to follow the track of. **5.** to follow behind, as in a race. —*v.i.* **6.** to drag, esp. along the ground. **7.** to lag behind. **8. trail off,** to gradually become weaker.

trail′blaz′er *n.* a pioneer.

trail′er *n.* **1.** a vehicle drawn by a truck for hauling freight. **2.** a vehicle with accommodations for living, attached to a car.

train *n.* **1.** connected railroad cars pulled by a locomotive. **2.** a moving line of persons, vehicles, etc. **3.** part of a long skirt that trails behind. **4.** a series of events, ideas, etc. —*v.t.* **5.** to form the behavior of by discipline and instruction. **6.** to make fit. **7.** to aim, as a gun. —*v.i.* **8.** to become trained. —**train·ee′,** *n.* —**train′er,** *n.*

traipse (trāps) *v.i.,* **traipsed, traipsing.** to walk aimlessly.

trait (trāt) *n.* a characteristic.

trai′tor (trā′tər) *n.* a person who betrays another or any trust. —**trai′tor·ous,** *adj.*

tra·jec′to·ry (trə jek′tə rē) *n., pl.* **-ries.** the curve described by a projectile in flight.

tram (tram) *n. Brit.* a streetcar.

tram′mel (tram′əl) *n., v.,* **-meled, -meling.** —*n.* **1.** something that hinders action; restraint. —*v.t.* **2.** to hinder or restrain.

tramp (tramp) *v.i.* **1.** to walk with a

firm, heavy step. **2.** to hike. —*n.* **3.** a vagrant; vagabond. **4.** a firm, heavy tread or the sound of this. **5.** a hike.

tram′ple *v.t., v.i.,* **-pled, -pling.** to step roughly (on).

tram′po·line′ (tram′pə lēn′, -lin) *n.* a canvas sheet attached by springs to a frame, used for tumbling.

trance (trans) *n.* a half-conscious or hypnotic state.

tran′quil (trang′kwil) *adj.* peaceful; calm. —**tran′quil·ly,** *adv.* —**tran·quil′li·ty,** *n.* —**tran′quil·ize′,** *v.t., v.i.*

tran′quil·iz′er (-kwi lī′zər) *n.* a drug that has a calming effect.

trans- a prefix meaning across, through, or on the other side; changing thoroughly; beyond or surpassing.

trans·act′ (tran sakt′, -zakt′) *v.t.* to carry on (business, negotiations, etc.). —**trans·ac′tion,** *n.*

trans·at·lan′tic (trans′at lan′tik, tranz′-) *adj.* **1.** crossing the Atlantic. **2.** on the other side of the Atlantic.

trans·ceiv′er (tran sē′vər) *n.* a radio transmitter and receiver combined.

tran·scend′ (tran send′) *v.t.* **1.** to go beyond the ordinary limits of. **2.** to surpass; exceed.

tran·scend′ent *adj.* **1.** going beyond ordinary limits. **2.** superior; supreme.

tran′scen·den′tal (tran′sen den′tl, -sən-) *adj.* beyond ordinary human experience.

trans′con·ti·nen′tal (trans′kon tnen′tl) *adj.* **1.** extending across a continent. **2.** on the other side of a continent.

tran·scribe′ (tran skrīb′) *v.t.,* **-scribed, -scribing. 1.** to make a written or typed copy of (spoken material). **2.** to arrange (music) for a different instrument. —**tran′script,** *n.* —**tran·scrip′tion** (-skrip′shən) *n.*

trans·duc′er (trans dōō′sər, -dyōō′, tranz-) *n.* a device, as a microphone, that converts a signal from one form of energy to another.

tran′sept (tran′sept) *n.* the part of a church crossing the nave at right angles.

trans·fer′ *v.,* **-ferred, -ferring,** *n.* —*v.t.* (trans fûr′, trans′fər) **1.** to convey or hand over. —*v.i.* **2.** to transfer oneself or be transferred. **3.** to change from one bus, train, etc., to another. —*n.* (trans′fər) **4.** the means or act of transferring. —**trans·fer′a·ble,** *adj.* —**trans·fer′al,** *n.* —**trans·fer′ence,** *n.*

trans·fig′ure *v.t.,* **-ured, -uring. 1.** to transform. **2.** to change in appearance to something more beautiful or glorious. —**trans′fig·u·ra′tion,** *n.*

trans·fix′ *v.t.* **1.** to make motionless, as with awe. **2.** to pierce.

trans·form′ *v.t.* to change in form, appearance, condition, nature, etc. —**trans·for·ma′tion,** *n.*

trans·form′er *n.* a device for converting electrical currents.

trans·fuse′ (-fyōōz′) *v.t.,* **-fused, -fusing. 1.** to transfer (blood) by injecting into a blood vessel. **2.** to diffuse into or through. —**trans·fu′sion,** *n.*

trans·gen′dered (trans jen′dərd, tranz-) *adj.* **1.** appearing or attempting to be a member of the opposite sex, as a transsexual. **2.** pertaining to transgendered persons.

trans·gress′ (trans gres′, tranz-) *v.i.* **1.** to violate a law, moral code, etc. —*v.t.* **2.** to go beyond (a limit). —**trans·gres′sion** (-gresh′ən) —**trans·gres′sor,** *n.*

tran′sient (tran′shənt, -zhənt, -zē ənt) *adj.* lasting or staying only a short time.

tran·sis′tor (tran zis′tər) *n.* a small electronic device that controls the flow of an electric current.

trans′it (tran′sit, -zit) *n.* the act or fact of passing across, over, or through.

tran·si′tion (tran zish′ən, -sish′-) *n.* passage from one position, condition, etc., to another. —**tran·si′tion·al,** *adj.*

tran′si·tive (tran′si tiv, -zi-) *adj.* (of a verb) taking a direct object.

tran′si·to·ry (tran′si tôr′ē, -zi-) *adj.* lasting only a short time.

trans·late′ (trans lāt′, tranz-, -lāt, tranz′-) *v.t.,* **-lated, -lating. 1.** to turn from one language into another. **2.** to change the form or condition of. —**trans·la′tion,** *n.* —**trans·lat′a·ble,** *adj.* —**trans·lat′or,** *n.*

trans·lit′er·ate′ (-lit′ə rāt′) *v.t.,*

-ated, -ating. to change (letters or words) into the corresponding characters of another alphabet.

trans·lu′cent (-lōō′sənt) *adj.* not transparent but allowing light to pass through.

trans·mi·gra′tion *n.* the passage of a soul into another body.

trans·mis′sion (-mish′ən) *n.* **1.** the act or process of transmitting. **2.** something transmitted. **3.** a set of gears to transfer force between mechanisms, as in an automobile. **4.** a broadcast.

trans·mit′ (-mit′) *v.t.,* **-mitted, -mitting. 1.** to send from one person or place to another. **2.** to pass on by heredity. **3.** to cause (light, heat, etc.,) to pass through a medium. **4.** to emit (radio or television signals). —**trans·mit′ter,** *n.*

trans·mog′ri·fy′ (-mog′rə fī′) *v.t.,* **-fied, -fying.** to change in appearance or form; transform.

trans·mute′ (-myōōt′) *v.t., v.i.,* **-muted, -muting.** to change from one nature or form into another. —**trans·mut′a·ble,** *adj.* —**trans·mu·ta′tion,** *n.*

trans·na′tion·al *adj.* going beyond national boundaries or interests.

trans·o·ce·an′ic *adj.* crossing the ocean.

tran′som (tran′səm) *n.* **1.** a crosspiece separating a door or window from a window above it. **2.** a window above such a crosspiece.

trans·pa·cif′ic (trans′-) *adj.* **1.** crossing the Pacific. **2.** on the other side of the Pacific.

trans·par′ent (-pâr′ənt) *adj.* **1.** able to be seen clearly through. **2.** easily understood; obvious. —**trans·par′en·cy,** *n.*

tran·spire′ (tran spī²r′) *v.i.,* **-spired, -spiring. 1.** to occur. **2.** to give off waste matter, watery vapor, etc., through the surface.

trans·plant′ *v.t.* (trans plant′) **1.** to remove and put or plant in another place. —*n.* (trans′plant′) **2.** the act of transplanting. **3.** something transplanted. —**trans′plan·ta′tion,** *n.*

trans·port′ *v.t.* (trans pôrt′) **1.** to convey from one place to another. **2.** to carry away by strong emotion. —*n.* (trans′pôrt) **3.** the act of transporting. **4.** something that transports. —**trans·port′er,** *n.*

trans·pose′ (-pōz′) *v.t.,* **-posed, -posing. 1.** to reverse the position or order of. **2.** to put (a musical composition) into a different key. —**trans′po·si′tion,** *n.*

trans·sex′u·al *n.* **1.** a person feeling an identity with the opposite sex. **2.** a person whose sex has been surgically altered.

trans·sub·stan′ti·a′tion *n.* (in the Eucharist) the conversion of the whole substance of bread and wine into the body and blood of Christ.

trans·verse′ (trans vûrs′, tranz-; trans′vûrs, tranz′-) *adj.* **1.** lying or reaching across. —*n.* **2.** something transverse. —**trans·verse′ly,** *adv.*

trans·ves′tite (trans ves′tīt, tranz-) *n.* a person who dresses in clothing of the opposite sex.

trap (trap) *n., v.,* **trapped, trapping.** —*n.* **1.** a device for catching animals. **2.** a scheme for catching a person unawares. **3.** a U-shaped section in a pipe to prevent the escape of air or gases. —*v.t.* **4.** to catch in a trap. —*v.i.* **5.** to trap animals for their fur.

tra·peze′ (tra pēz′, trə-) *n.* a suspended bar used in acrobatics.

trap′e·zoid′ (trap′ə zoid′) *n.* a four-sided figure with two parallel sides.

trap′pings *n.pl.* **1.** ornamental articles of equipment or dress. **2.** conventional outward forms.

trash (trash) *n.* **1.** anything worthless. —*v.t.* **2.** to vandalize.

trau′ma (trou′mə, trô′-) *n., pl.* **-mata, -mas. 1.** a bodily injury. **2.** an experience causing lasting psychological harm. —**trau·mat′ic** (trə -mat′ik) *adj.*

tra·vail′ (trə vāl′, trav′āl) *n.* painfully difficult work.

trav′el (trav′əl) *v.,* **-eled, -eling,** *n.* —*v.i.* **1.** to go from one place to another. **2.** to pass or be transmitted. —*n.* **3.** the act of traveling, esp. to faraway places. —**trav′el·er,** *n.*

trav′e·logue′ (-lôg′) *n.* a lecture, film, etc., describing travel. Also, **trav′e·log′.**

trav·erse′ *v.,* **-ersed, -ersing,** *n.* —*v.t.* (trə vûrs′, trav′ərs) **1.** to pass over, through, or along. —*n.* (trav′-

ərs, trə vûrs/) 2. something that crosses.

trav′es·ty (trav′ə stē) n., pl. **-ties,** v., **-tied, -tying.** —n. 1. a grotesque imitation. —v.t. 2. to make a travesty of.

trawl (trôl) n. 1. a fishing net dragged along the sea bottom. —v.i., v.t. 2. to fish with a trawl. —**trawl′er,** n.

tray (trā) n. a flat, shallow receptacle with raised edges.

treach′er·y (trech′ə rē) n. betrayal of trust. —**treach′er·ous,** adj.

tread (tred) v., **trod** (trod), **trodden** or **trod, treading,** n. —v.t. 1. to step or walk. —v.i. 2. to walk on, in, or along. 3. to trample underfoot. —n. 4. the act, sound, or manner of walking. 5. something on which one walks or stands. 6. the raised pattern on a rubber tire.

trea′dle (tred′l) n. a lever worked by the foot to drive a machine.

tread′mill′ n. a device worked by treading on moving steps or an endless moving belt.

trea′son (trē′zən) n. a violation of allegiance to one's sovereign or state.

treas·ure (trezh′ər) n., v., **-ured, -uring.** —n. 1. accumulated wealth. 2. anything greatly valued. —v.t. 3. to prize. 4. to put away for future use.

treas′ure-trove′ (-trōv′) n. 1. anything valuable that one finds. 2. treasure of unknown ownership, found hidden.

treas′ur·y n., pl. **-uries.** 1. a place for keeping public or private funds. 2. funds. 3. **Treasury,** the government department that handles funds. —**treas′ur·er,** n.

treat (trēt) v. 1. to act, behave toward, or regard in a certain way. 2. to buy food, gifts, etc., for. 3. to give medical care to. 4. to subject to some agent or action. 5. to deal with in speech, writing, etc. —n. 6. entertainment, food, etc., paid for by someone else. 7. something special and enjoyable.

trea′tise (trē′tis) n. formal writing on a particular subject.

trea′ty (trē′tē) n., pl. **-ties.** a formal agreement between nations.

tre′ble (treb′əl) adj., n., v., **-bled, -bling.** —adj. 1. triple. 2. of the highest musical pitch or range. —n. 3. the treble part, voice, or instrument. —v.t., v.i. 4. to triple.

tree (trē) n., v., **treed, treeing.** —n. 1. a large plant with a woody trunk and branches. 2. something shaped like this. —v.t. 3. to drive up a tree, as one pursued.

tre′foil (trē′foil, tref′oil) n. 1. a plant having leaves with three leaflets. 2. something shaped like this.

trek (trek) n., v., **trekked, trekking.** —n. 1. a slow and difficult journey. —v.i. 2. to make a trek.

trel′lis (trel′is) n. a lattice supporting vines.

trem′ble (trem′bəl) v., **-bled, -bling,** n. —v.i. 1. to quiver; shake. 2. to be afraid. —n. 3. the act or state of trembling.

tre·men′dous (tri men′dəs) adj. extraordinarily great.

trem′o·lo (trem′ə lō′) n., pl. **-los.** a vibrating effect produced on an instrument or in the voice.

trem′or (trem′ər, trē′mər) n. 1. involuntary shaking. 2. any vibration.

trem′u·lous (trem′yə ləs) adj. trembling. 2. fearful.

trench (trench) n. 1. a long, narrow ditch dug by soldiers for defense. 2. a deep furrow or ditch.

trench′ant (tren′chənt) adj. incisive; keen. 2. vigorous.

trench′ coat′ n. a belted, double-breasted raincoat with epaulets.

trench′er n. a flat piece of wood on which meat is served or carved.

trench′er·man n., pl. **-men.** a person with a hearty appetite.

trench′ foot′ n. a disease of the feet caused by prolonged exposure to cold and wet.

trench′ mouth′ n. an ulcerating infection of the gums and teeth.

trend (trend) n. 1. the general tendency. 2. style.

trend′y adj., **-ier, -iest.** following the latest fad.

trep·i·da′tion (trep′i dā′shən) n. fearful anxiety.

tres′pass (tres′pəs, -pas) v.i. 1. to enter property or land unlawfully. 2. to commit an offense. —n. 3. the act of trespassing. —**tres′pass·er,** n.

tress (tres) n. Usu., **tresses.** long locks of hair.

tres′tle (tres′əl) n. a supporting frame composed of a bar on two pairs of spreading legs.

trey (trā) n. (in cards or dice) three.

tri- a prefix meaning three.

tri′ad (trī′ad, -əd) n. a group of three.

tri·age′ (trē äzh′) n. the process of sorting victims to determine priority of medical treatment.

tri′al (trī′əl) n. 1. the hearing and deciding of a case in a court of law. 2. a test. 3. an attempt. 4. something annoying. 5. a source of suffering.

tri′an·gle (trī′ang′gəl) n. a figure with three straight sides and three angles. —**tri·an′gu·lar,** adj.

Tri·as′sic (trī as′ik), adj. of a period of the Mesozoic Era when dinosaurs first appeared.

tribe (trīb) n. a group of people united by common descent and sharing common customs. —**trib′al,** adj.

tribes′man n., pl. **-men.** a member of a tribe.

trib′u·la′tion (trib′yə lā′shən) n. severe trial or suffering or an instance of this.

tri·bu′nal (trī byoon′l, tri-) n. 1. a court of justice. 2. a place of judgment.

trib′une (trib′yoon, tri byoon′) n. a person who defends the rights of the people.

trib′u·tar·y (trib′yə ter′ē) n., pl. **-taries,** adj. —n. 1. a stream flowing into a larger body of water. —adj. 2. flowing into a larger body of water.

trib′ute (trib′yoot) n. 1. a speech or gift expressing gratitude or respect. 2. (formerly) a tax paid by one state to acknowledge subjugation to another.

trice (trīs) n. an instant.

tri′cen·ten′ni·al (trī′sen ten′ē əl) n. a tercentennial.

tri′ceps (trī′seps) n. the muscle at the back of the upper arm.

trich′i·no′sis (trik′ə nō′sis) n. infestation of the intestines and muscle tissue by a parasitic worm.

trick (trik) n. 1. something intended to deceive or cheat. 2. a practical joke. 3. a knack. 4. the set of cards played and won in one round. —v.t. 5. to deceive or cheat. —**trick′er·y,** n. —**trick′ster,** n. —**trick′y,** adj.

trick′le (trik′əl) v., **-led, -ling,** n. —v.i. 1. to flow in a small, gentle stream. 2. to move slowly. —n. 3. a trickling flow.

tri′col′or (trī′kul′ər) n. 1. three colors. —n. 2. a three-colored flag, esp. that of France.

tri·cus′pid adj. having three cusps or points, as a tooth.

tri′cy·cle (trī′si kəl, -sik′əl) n. a child's vehicle with one large front wheel and two smaller rear wheels.

tri′dent (trīd′nt) n. a three-pronged spear.

tried (trīd) adj. tested; proved.

tri·en′ni·al (trī en′ē əl) adj. 1. lasting three years. 2. occurring every three years. —n. 3. a period of three years. 4. a third anniversary.

tri′fle (trī′fəl) n., v., **-fled, -fling.** —n. 1. an article of small value. 2. a trivial matter or amount. —v. 3. **trifle with,** to deal lightly with; play or toy with. —**tri′fling,** adj.

tri·fo′li·ate (trī fō′lē it,-āt) adj. having three leaves or leaflike parts.

trig′ger (trig′ər) n. 1. a projecting tongue pressed to fire a gun. 2. a device pressed to release a spring. —v.t. 3. to cause (a reaction, process, etc.).

tri·glyc′er·ide′ (trī glis′ə rīd′, -ər id) n. an ester obtained from glycerol, forming much of the fats and oils stored in tissues.

trig·o·nom′e·try (trig′ə nom′i trē) n. the mathematical study of the relations between the sides and angles of triangles.

trill (tril) n. 1. a rapid alternation of two nearby musical tones. 2. a similar sound, as that made by a bird. —v.t., v.i. 3. to sing or play with a trill.

tril′lion (tril′yən) n., adj. a number represented by 1 followed by 12 zeroes.

tril′li·um (tril′ē əm) n. a plant of the lily family, having three leaves and one flower.

tril′o·gy (tril′ə jē) n., pl. **-gies.** a group of three works on a related theme.

trim (trim) v., **trimmed, trimming,** n., adj., **trimmer, trimmest.** —v.t. 1. to make neat or to reduce by cut-

ting, clipping, etc. 2. to decorate with ornaments. 3. to adjust (a ship's sails) to the direction of the wind. —n. 4. ornamentation. 5. a trimming by cutting, as of hair. —adj. 6. neat. 7. in good condition. —**trim′mer,** n.

tri′ma·ran′ (trī′mə ran′) n. a boat similar to a catamaran but having three hulls.

tri·mes′ter (trī mes′tər, trī′mes-) n. 1. a period of three months. 2. one of three terms of the academic year.

trim′ming (trim′ing) n. 1. something used to decorate. 2. **trimmings,** something accompanying a main dish. 3. pieces cut off in trimming.

tri·ni′tro·tol′u·ene′ (trī nī′trō tol′yoo ēn′) n. a high explosive, known as TNT.

Trin′i·ty (trin′i tē) n. the union of Father, Son, and Holy Spirit.

trin′ket (tring′kit) n. a small ornament of little value.

tri′o (trē′ō) n., pl. **trios.** 1. a group of three. 2. music for three voices or instruments.

trip (trip) n., v., **tripped, tripping.** —n. 1. a journey. 2. a stumble. 3. Slang. a drug-induced event. —v.i., v.t. 4. to stumble or cause to stumble. 5. to make or cause to make a mistake. 6. to release suddenly, as a switch. 7. to move lightly and quickly. —**trip′per,** n.

tri·par′tite (trī pär′tīt) adj. 1. consisting of three parts. 2. involving three parties.

tripe (trīp) n. 1. the stomach of a ruminant, as an ox, used as food. 2. Slang. worthless statements or writing.

tri′ple (trip′əl) adj., n., v., **-pled, -pling.** —adj. 1. consisting of three parts. 2. three times as great. —n. 3. Baseball. a hit allowing a batter to reach third base. —v.t., v.i. 4. to make or become triple.

tri′plet (trip′lit) n. one of three children born at a single birth.

trip′li·cate (-li kit, -kāt′) adj. 1. consisting of three identical parts. —n. 2. one of a set of three copies.

tri′pod (trī′pod) n. a three-legged stand or support.

trip′tych (trip′tik) n. a set of three panels side by side, with pictures or carvings.

trite (trīt) adj., **triter, tritest.** commonplace; hackneyed.

tri′umph (trī′əmf, -umf) n. 1. victory; success. 2. joy over victory or success. —v.i. 3. to be victorious or successful. 4. to rejoice over victory or success. —**tri·um′phal,** adj. —**tri·um′phant,** adj.

tri·um′vi·rate (-vər it, -və rāt′) n. a group of three officials governing jointly, as in ancient Rome.

triv′et (triv′it) n. a device protecting a table top from hot objects.

triv′i·a (triv′ē ə) n. (used with a sing. or pl. v.) things that are very unimportant.

triv′i·al adj. of very little importance. —**triv·i·al′i·ty,** n.

tro·chee′ (trō′kē) n. a verse foot of two syllables, the first stressed and the second unstressed. —**tro·cha′ic** (-kā′ik) adj.

trog′lo·dyte′ (trog′lə dīt′) n. 1. a prehistoric cave dweller. 2. a hermit.

troi′ka (troi′kə) n. 1. a Russian vehicle drawn by three horses. 2. a ruling group of three.

troll¹ (trōl) n. in folklore, a supernatural being living underground or in caves.

troll² (trōl) v.t., v.i. 1. to sing in a rolling voice. 2. to fish (in) with a line trailing behind a slow-moving boat.

trol′ley (trol′ē) n. 1. Also **trolley car.** an electric streetcar receiving current from an overhead wire. 2. a small cart or table on wheels. 3. a carriage or truck traveling on an overhead track.

trol′lop (trol′əp) n. 1. an untidy or slovenly woman. 2. a prostitute.

trom·bone′ (trom bōn′, trom′bōn) n. a brass wind instrument with a U-shaped metal tube and a slide. —**trom·bon′ist,** n.

troop (troop) n. 1. an assemblage of persons or things. 2. a cavalry unit. —v.i. 3. to gather or move in great numbers. 4. to walk, as if in a march.

troop′ship′ n. a ship for conveying military troops; transport.

tro′phy (trō′fē) n., pl. **-phies.** 1. anything taken in competition, war, etc., and preserved as a me-

mento. 2. something given as a prize.

tro′phy wife′ n. the young, often second, wife of a rich middle-aged man.

trop′ic (trop′ik) n. 1. either of two lines of latitude, one **(tropic of Can′cer)** 23 ½° N, and the other **(tropic of Cap′ricorn)** 23 ½° S of the equator. 2. **the tropics,** the regions lying between these latitudes, having a hot climate.

trop′o·sphere′ (trop′ə sfēr′, trō′pə-) n. the lowest layer of the atmosphere.

trot (trot) v., **trotted, trotting,** n. —v.i., v.t. 1. (of a horse) to go or cause to go at a gait in which the legs move in diagonal pairs. 2. to hurry. —n. 3. a trotting gait. —**trot′ter,** n.

troth (trôth, trōth) n. Archaic. 1. faithfulness. 2. one's promise.

trou′ba·dour′ (troo′bə dôr′) n. a medieval lyric poet of S France.

trou′ble (trub′əl) v., **-bled, -bling,** n. —v.t. 1. to distress. 2. to inconvenience. 3. to cause pain or discomfort to. —n. 4. difficulty, annoyance, or disturbance. 5. physical or mental distress. 6. inconvenience. —**trou′ble·some,** adj.

trou′bled adj. 1. emotionally or mentally distressed. 2. economically or socially distressed.

trou′ble·mak′er n. a person who causes trouble.

trou′ble·shoot′er n. an expert in eliminating causes of trouble.

trough (trôf) n. 1. a long, narrow open container out of which animals eat or drink. 2. a long depression, as between two waves. 3. an area of low atmospheric pressure.

trounce (trouns) v.t., **trounced, trouncing.** to defeat decisively.

troupe (troop) n. a company of performers. —**troup′er,** n.

trou′sers (trou′zərz) n.pl. a two-legged outer garment covering the lower part of the body.

trous′seau (troo′sō, troo sō′) n., pl. **-seaux, -seaus** (-sōz). an outfit of clothing, linen, etc., for a bride.

trout (trout) n. a freshwater game fish of the salmon family.

trow′el (trou′əl) n. 1. a flat-bladed tool for spreading or smoothing. 2. a small digging tool.

troy (troi) n. expressed in troy weight.

troy′ weight′ (troi), n. a system of weights for precious metals and gems.

tru′ant (troo′ənt) n. 1. a student absent from school without permission. —adj. 2. absent from school without permission. —**tru′an·cy,** n.

truce (troos) n. a temporary suspension of military hostilities.

truck¹ (truk) n. 1. a large motor vehicle for carrying goods. 2. a wheeled cart for moving heavy objects. —v.t. 3. to transport by truck. —**truck′er,** n.

truck² (truk) n. 1. vegetables raised for the market. 2. dealings.

truck′ farm′ n. a farm on which vegetables are grown for market.

truck′le v.i., **-led, -ling.** to submit humbly.

truc′u·lent (truk′yə lənt, troo′kyə-) adj. aggressively hostile. —**truc′u·lence,** n.

trudge (truj) v., **trudged, trudging,** n. —v.i. 1. to walk, esp. wearily. —n. 2. a tiring walk.

true (troo) adj., **truer, truest.** 1. conforming to reality or fact. 2. real. 3. loyal. 4. legitimate. 5. correct. —**tru′ly,** adv.

true′-blue′ adj. totally loyal.

truf′fle (truf′əl) n. 1. a kind of edible fungus that grows under the ground. 2. a chocolate confection resembling a truffle in shape.

tru′ism (troo′iz əm) n. an obvious truth.

trump (trump) n. 1. any playing card of a suit outranking other suits. 2. the suit itself. —v.t., v.i. 3. to take (a trick) with a trump. 4. **trump up,** to invent deceitfully.

trump′er·y n., pl. **-eries.** 1. something without use or value. 2. nonsense.

trum′pet (trum′pit) n. 1. a brass wind instrument with a curved tube and a flaring bell. 2. something shaped like a trumpet. —v.i. 3. to make a loud, trumpetlike sound. —v.t. 4. to proclaim loudly. —**trum′pet·er,** n.

trun′cate (trung′kāt) v.t., **-cated, -cating.** to shorten by cutting off a part.

trun′cheon (trun′chən) n. a short club carried as a weapon.

trun′dle (trun′dl) v.i., v.t., **-dled, -dling.** to roll along.

trun′dle bed′ n. a low bed on casters.

trunk (trungk) n. 1. the main stem of a tree. 2. a large, heavy box for carrying or storing clothes, personal items, etc. 3. a large storage compartment in a car. 4. the body of a person or animal excluding the head and limbs. 5. an elephant's long, flexible nasal appendage. 6. **trunks,** shorts worn for athletics.

trunk′ line′ n. 1. a major long-distance transportation line. 2. a telephone line between two switching devices.

truss (trus) v.t. 1. to bind or tie. 2. to fasten the legs and wings of (a fowl) before cooking. 3. to support with a truss. —n. 4. a rigid supporting framework. 5. a device worn for supporting a hernia.

trust (trust) n. 1. firm reliance on the integrity, ability, etc., of a person or thing. 2. confident expectation. 3. responsibility; care. 4. something entrusted to one's care. 5. the holding of legal title for another's benefit. —v.t. 6. to have confidence in. 7. to hope. —v.i. 8. to have confidence. —**trust′wor·thy,** adj.

trus·tee′ n. 1. a person appointed to administer the affairs of a company, institution, etc. 2. a person who holds title to property for another's benefit.

trus·tee′ship n. 1. the office of a trustee. 2. the control of a territory granted by the United Nations. 3. the territory.

trust′ fund′ n. money, stocks, etc., held in trust.

trust′ ter′ritory n. a territory which the United Nations has placed under the administrative control of a country.

trust′y adj., **-ier, -iest.** able to be trusted.

truth (trooth) n. 1. something true. 2. the quality of being true. —**truth′ful,** adj.

try (trī) v., **tried, trying,** v.t. 1. to make an effort to do. 2. to test or sample. 3. to examine and determine judicially. 4. to strain the endurance, patience, etc., of. —v.i. 5. to make an effort. 6. **try on,** to put on (clothing) to judge its fit. 7. **try out,** a. to experiment with. b. to take part in a test for a job, role, etc.

try′ing adj. annoying; irksome.

try′out′ n. a trial or test of fitness, ability, etc.

tryst (trist, trīst) n. 1. an appointment, as of lovers, to meet. 2. the meeting or place of meeting.

tsar (zär, tsär) n. a czar.

tset′se fly (tset′sē, tsē′tsē) n. an African fly that can transmit sleeping sickness.

T′-shirt′ n. a short-sleeved pullover shirt.

tsp. teaspoon.

T square n. a T-shaped ruler used in mechanical drawing.

tsu·na′mi (tsoo nä′mē) n. a huge wave caused by an undersea earthquake or volcano.

tub (tub) n. 1. a bathtub. 2. a deep, round, open container.

tu′ba (too′bə, tyoo′-) n. a low-pitched brass wind instrument.

tub′by (tub′ē) adj., **-bier, -biest.** short and fat.

tube (toob, tyoob) n. 1. a hollow pipe for conveying fluids. 2. a compressible container from which paste may be squeezed. 3. a railroad or vehicular tunnel. 4. **the tube,** Informal. television. 5. Brit. the subway. —**tu·bu·lar** (-byə lər) adj. —**tub′ing,** n.

tu′ber (too′bər, tyoo′-) n. a fleshy thickening of an underground stem or shoot. —**tu′ber·ous,** adj.

tu′ber·cle (-kəl) n. a small roundish projection, nodule, or swelling.

tu·ber′cu·lin (too bûr′kyə lin,tyoo-) n. a liquid prepared from the tuberculosis bacillus, used in a test for tuberculosis.

tu·ber′cu·lo′sis (-lō′sis) n. an infectious disease marked by the formation of tubercles, esp. in the lungs. —**tu·ber′cu·lar,** adj.

tube′rose′ (toob′-, tyoob′-) n. a cultivated plant with a sweet-smelling flower.

tu′bule (-byool) n. a small tube.

tuck (tuk) v.t. 1. to put into a small or concealing space. 2. to push in the edge of (a sheet, shirt, etc.) so as to hold in place. 3. to draw up in folds. **4.** to cover snugly. —*n.* **5.** a flat fold sewn into cloth.

tuck′er *v.* **tucker out,** *Informal.* to tire; exhaust.

Tues. Tuesday. Also, **Tue.**

Tues′day (tōōz′dā, -dē, tyōōz′-) *n.* the third day of the week.

tuft (tuft) *n.* **1.** a bunch of feathers, hairs, grass, etc., growing or fastened together. **2.** a cluster of threads tied together at the base. —*v.t.* **3.** to furnish or decorate with tufts. —**tuft′ed,** *adj.*

tug (tug) *v.,* **tugged, tugging,** *n.* —*v.t., v.i.* **1.** to pull (at) with force or effort. —*n.* **2.** an act of tugging. **3.** a tugboat.

tug′boat′ *n.* a small, powerful boat used for towing.

tug′ of war′ *n.* **1.** a contest between teams pulling on the opposite ends of a rope. **2.** a struggle for supremacy.

tu·i′tion (tōō ish′ən, tyōō-) *n.* the fee for instruction, as at a college.

tu′lip (tōō′lip, tyōō′-) *n.* a plant bearing cup-shaped flowers of various colors.

tulle (tōōl) *n.* a thin silk or rayon net.

tum′ble (tum′bəl) *v.,* **-bled, -bling,** *n.* —*v.i.* **1.** to fall over or down. **2.** to perform gymnastic feats. **3.** to roll about; toss. —*n.* **4.** the act of tumbling.

tum′ble-down′ *adj.* dilapidated.

tum′bler *n.* **1.** a drinking glass. **2.** a part of a lock that engages a bolt. **3.** a performer of tumbling feats.

tum′ble-weed′ *n.* a plant whose upper part becomes detached and is driven about by the wind.

tum′brel (tum′brəl) *n.* a farmer's cart that can be tilted to discharge its load. Also, **tum′bril.**

tu′mid (tōō′mid, tyōō-) *adj.* **1.** swollen. **2.** pompous.

tum′my (tum′ē) *n., pl.* **-mies.** *Informal.* the stomach or abdomen.

tu′mor (tōō′mər, tyōō′-) *n.* an uncontrolled, abnormal growth of cells in a part of the body.

tu′mult (tōō′mult, -malt, tyōō′-) *n.* violent disturbance, commotion, or uproar. —**tu·mul′tu·ous** (-mul′-chōō əs) *adj.*

tun (tun) *n.* a large cask.

tu′na (tōō′na, tyōō′-) *n.* a large marine fish, used as food.

tun′dra (tun′drə, tōōn′-) *n.* a vast, treeless, arctic plain.

tune (tōōn, tyōōn) *n., v.,* **tuned, tuning.** —*n.* **1.** a melody. **2.** the state of proper pitch, frequency, or condition. **3.** agreement. —*v.t.* **4.** to adjust (a musical instrument) to the correct pitch. **5.** to adjust (a radio or television) to receive a broadcast. **6.** to adjust (a motor) to run smoothly. —**tun′er,** *n.* —**tune′ful,** *adj.* —**tune′less,** *adj.*

tune′-up′ *n.* an adjustment, as of a motor, to improve working condition.

tung′sten (tung′stən) *n.* a metallic element used for electric-lamp filaments.

tu′nic (tōō′nik, tyōō′-) *n.* **1.** a gownlike garment worn by the ancient Greeks and Romans. **2.** a woman's straight upper garment. **3.** the coat of a uniform.

tun′ing fork′ *n.* a two-pronged steel instrument producing a tone of constant pitch when struck.

tunnel (tun′l) *n., v.,* **-neled, -neling.** —*n.* **1.** an underground passage. —*v.t., v.i.* **2.** to make a tunnel (through or under).

tur′ban (tûr′bən) *n.* a head covering made of a long cloth wound around the head.

tur′bid (tûr′bid) *adj.* **1.** (of liquids) muddy or unclear. **2.** confused.

tur′bine (tûr′bin, -bīn) *n.* a motor driven by a wheel turned by the pressure of a moving fluid or gas.

tur·bo·jet′ (tûr′bō-) *n.* **1.** a jet engine that compresses air for combustion by a turbine-driven compressor. **2.** an airplane with such engines.

tur·bo·prop′ *n.* **1.** a turbojet engine with a turbine-driven propeller. **2.** an airplane with such engines.

tur′bot (tûr′bət) *n.* a kind of flatfish.

tur′bu·lent (tûr′byə lənt) *adj.* **1.** being in a state of agitation. **2.** marked by disturbance or disorder.

tu·reen′ (tōō rēn′, tyōō-) *n.* a large covered dish for soup, stew, etc.

turf (tûrf) *n.* **1.** a layer of matted earth formed by grass and roots. **2.** a familiar area, as of residence or expertise. **3. the turf,** horse racing.

tur′gid (tûr′jid) *adj.* **1.** swollen. **2.**

pompous. —**tur·gid′i·ty,** *n.* —**tur′gid·ly,** *adv.*

tur′key (tûr′kē) *n.* a large, edible N American bird with brown feathers.

tur′key vul′ture *n.* a blackish brown New World vulture.

tur′mer·ic (tûr′mər ik) *n.* an aromatic spice from an Asian plant.

tur′moil (tûr′moil) *n.* great excitement or disturbance.

turn (tûrn) *v.t.* **1.** to rotate. **2.** to move around. **3.** to reverse. **4.** to change the course or position of. **5.** to change or alter. **6.** to put to some use. **7.** to reach or pass (a certain age, amount, etc.). **8.** to shape on a lathe. —*v.i.* **9.** to rotate. **10.** to move around. **11.** to change position or course. **12.** to change in form or appearance. **13.** to become spoiled. **14.** to become. **15. turn down,** to reject. **16.** ~ **in, a.** to go to bed. **17.** ~ **off, a.** to stop the flow of. **b.** to extinguish. **c.** *Slang.* to alienate. **18.** ~ **on, a.** to cause to flow. **b.** to switch on. **c.** *Slang.* to arouse the interest of. **d.** to become hostile to. **19.** ~ **over,** to give. —*n.* **20.** a rotation. **21.** a change or point of change. **22.** one's due time or opportunity. **23.** a trend. **24.** a short walk, ride, etc. **25.** an inclination or aptitude. **26.** a service or disservice.

turn′a·bout′ *n.* a change of opinion, loyalty, etc.

turn′coat′ *n.* a person who changes to the opposite faction.

turn′ing point′ *n.* the point at which a decisive change takes place.

tur′nip (tûr′nip) *n.* the fleshy, edible root of either of two plants of the mustard family.

turn′key *n.* the keeper of a prison's keys.

turn′off′ *n.* a small road that branches off from a larger one.

turn′out′ *n.* the attendance at a meeting, show, etc.

turn′o′ver *n.* **1.** the rate at which workers are replaced. **2.** the amount of business done in a given time. **3.** a small folded pastry with a filling.

turn′pike′ (-pīk′) *n.* an express highway on which tolls are charged.

turn′stile′ *n.* a gate with revolving arms to allow people through one by one.

turn′ta·ble *n.* a rotating platform.

tur′pen·tine′ (tûr′pən tīn′) *n.* a strong-smelling oil derived from coniferous trees, used as a paint thinner and solvent.

tur′pi·tude′ (tûr′pi tōōd′, -tyōōd′) *n.* vile character; depravity.

tur′quoise (tûr′koiz, -kwoiz) *n.* **1.** a greenish-blue mineral used as a gem. **2.** a greenish blue.

tur′ret (tûr′it, tur′-) *n.* **1.** a small tower. **2.** a revolving structure for mounting a gun on a tank or ship.

tur′tle (tûr′tl) *n.* a water- or land-dwelling reptile with a shell-encased body.

tur′tle·dove′ (-duv′) *n.* a small dove noted for its soft cooing.

tur′tle·neck′ *n.* **1.** a high, close-fitting collar. **2.** a garment with a turtleneck.

tusk (tusk) *n.* a very long tooth, as of an elephant or walrus.

tus′sle (tus′əl) *v.,* **-sled, -sling,** *n.* —*v.i.* **1.** to struggle or fight. —*n.* **2.** a vigorous struggle.

tus′sock (tus′ək) *n.* a tuft of growing grass.

tu′te·lage (tōōt′l ij, tyōōt′-) *n.* **1.** guardianship. **2.** instruction.

tu′tor (tōō′tər, tyōō′-) *n.* **1.** a private instructor. —*v.t., v.i.* **2.** to act as a tutor (to). —**tu·to′ri·al** (-tôr′ē əl) *adj.*

tut′ti-frut′ti (tōō′tē frōō′tē) *n.* a sweet, esp. ice cream, flavored with a variety of fruits.

tu·tu′ (tōō′tōō′) *n.* a short, full skirt worn by a ballerina.

tux (tuks) *n. Informal.* a tuxedo.

tux·e′do (tuk sē′dō) *n., pl.* **-dos.** a man's semiformal suit.

TV television.

twad′dle (twod′l) *n.* nonsense.

twain (twān) *adj., n.* two.

twang (twang) *v.i., v.t.* **1.** to make or cause a sharp, vibrating sound. **2.** to speak or utter with a nasal tone. —*n.* **3.** a twanging sound.

tweak (twēk) *v.t.* **1.** to seize and pull or twist. **2.** to make a minor adjustment to. —*n.* **3.** a sharp pull and twist.

tweed (twēd) *n.* a thick, coarse woolen cloth.

tweet (twēt) *n.* **1.** a chirping sound. —*v.i.* **2.** to chirp.

tweet′er *n.* a small loudspeaker for reproducing high-frequency sounds.

tweez′ers (twē′zərz) *n.pl.* small pincers.

twelve (twelv) *n., adj.* ten plus two. —**twelfth,** *adj., n.*

Twelve′ Step′ *adj.* of or based on a program for recovery from addiction that provides 12 progressive levels toward attainment.

twen′ty (twen′tē) *n., adj.* ten times two. —**twen′ti·eth,** *adj., n.*

24-7 (twen′tē fôr′ sev′ən) *adv. Slang.* continually; constantly (alluding to twenty-four hours a day, seven days a week).

twerp (twûrp) *n. Slang.* an insignificant or despicable person.

twice (twīs) *adv.* **1.** two times. **2.** doubly.

twid′dle (twid′l) *v.t., v.i.,* **-dled, -dling. 1.** to turn about or play with (something). —*Idiom.* **2. twiddle one's thumbs,** to be idle.

twig (twig) *n.* a small offshoot of a branch or tree.

twi′light′ (twī′līt′) *n.* **1.** light from the sky after sunset. **2.** the period of this light.

twill (twil) *n.* a fabric woven in parallel diagonal lines. —**twilled,** *adj.*

twin (twin) *n.* **1.** either of two children born at a single birth.

twine (twīn) *n., v.,* **twined, twining.** —*n.* **1.** a strong thread or string of twisted strands. —*v.t.* **2.** to twist together. **3.** to wind or coil. —*v.i.* **4.** to wind around something.

twinge (twinj) *n., v.,* **twinged, twinging.** —*n.* **1.** a sudden, sharp pain. —*v.t., v.i.* **2.** to affect with or have a twinge.

twin′kle (twing′kəl) *v.,* **-kled, -kling,** *n.* —*v.i.* **1.** to shine with a flickering gleam. —*n.* **2.** a flickering gleam.

twin′kling *n.* an instant.

twirl (twûrl) *v.i., v.t.* **1.** to spin; whirl. —*n.* **2.** a twirling.

twist (twist) *v.t.* **1.** to turn by rotating. **2.** to combine (strands) by winding together. **3.** to form into a coil by winding, rolling, etc. **4.** to distort. **5.** to wrench. —*v.i.* **6.** to become twisted. **7.** to writhe or squirm. **8.** to turn to face another direction. —*n.* **9.** a curve or turn. **10.** a spin. **11.** distortion, as of meaning. **12.** a wrench. **13.** a sudden, unexpected change.

twist′er *n. Informal.* a tornado.

twit (twit) *v.,* **twitted, twitting,** *n.* —*v.t.* **1.** to taunt; tease. —*n.* **2.** *Informal.* a fool.

twitch (twich) *v.t., v.i.* **1.** to pull (at) or move with a jerk. —*n.* **2.** a quick jerky movement.

twit′ter (twit′ər) *v.i.* **1.** to utter small, tremulous sounds, as a bird. **2.** to tremble with excitement. —*n.* **3.** a twittering sound. **4.** a state of excitement.

two (tōō) *n., adj.* one plus one.

two′-bit′ *adj. Informal.* inferior or unimportant.

two′ bits′ *n. Informal.* 25 cents.

two′-faced′ *adj.* hypocritical.

two′-fist′ed *adj.* strong and vigorous.

two′fold′ *adj.* (-fōld′) **1.** having two parts. **2.** twice as great. —*adv.* (fōld′) **3.** in two-fold measure.

two′-ply′ *adj.* consisting of two layers, strands, etc.

two′some (-səm) *n.* a pair.

two′-time′ *v.t., v.i.,* **-timed, -timing.** *Informal.* to be unfaithful to.

two′-way′ *adj.* **1.** allowing movement in two directions. **2.** involving two participants.

twp. township.

TX Texas.

-ty a suffix meaning state or condition.

ty·coon′ (tī kōōn′) *n.* a businessperson having great wealth and power.

tyke (tīk) *n.* a small child.

tym·pan′ic mem′brane (tim-pan′ik) *n.* a membrane separating the middle from the external ear.

tym′pa·num (tim′pə nəm) *n.* **1.** the middle ear. **2.** the tympanic membrane.

type (tīp) *n., v.,* **typed, typing.** —*n.* **1.** a kind or class. **2.** a thing or person that is typical of a class or group. **3.** a set of characters used in printing. —*v.t.* **4.** to write on a typewriter, computer keyboard, etc. —*v.i.* **5.** to write using a typewriter, computer keyboard, etc. —**typ′ist,** *n.*

type′cast′ *v.t.,* **-cast, -casting.** to cast (an actor) exclusively in the same kind of role.

type′script′ *n.* typewritten matter.

type′set′ter *n.* **1.** a person who sets type. **2.** a machine for setting type. —**type′set′,** *v.t.*

type′writ′er *n.* a machine for writing mechanically.

ty′phoid (tī′foid) *n.* an infectious disease marked by fever and intestinal inflammation. Also, **ty′phoid fe′ver.**

ty·phoon′ (tī fōōn′) *n.* a tropical hurricane of the W Pacific.

ty′phus (tī′fəs) *n.* an infectious disease transmitted by lice and fleas and characterized by reddish spots on the skin.

typ′i·cal (tip′i kəl) *adj.* having the essential characteristics of a particular type or group.

typ′i·fy′ *v.t.,* **-fied, -fying.** to serve as a typical example or symbol of.

ty′po (tī′pō) *n., pl.* **-pos.** an error in typography or typing.

ty·pog′ra·phy (tī pog′rə fē) *n.* the art, process, or style of printing.

ty·ran′no·saur′ (ti ran′ə sôr′, tī-) *n.* a large dinosaur that walked upright.

tyr′an·ny (tir′ə nē) *n., pl.* **-nies. 1.** arbitrary or unrestrained exercise of power. **2.** the government of a tyrant. —**ty·ran′ni·cal** (ti ran′i kəl, tī-) *adj.* —**tyr′an·nize′,** *v.t., v.i.*

ty′rant (tī′rənt) *n.* an oppressive, unjust, or absolute ruler.

ty′ro (tī′rō) *n., pl.* **-ros.** a beginner.

tzar (zär, tsär) *n.* czar.

U

U, u (yōō) *n.* the twenty-first letter of the English alphabet.

u·biq′ui·tous (yōō bik′wi təs) *adj.* present everywhere at the same time.

U′-boat′ *n.* a German submarine.

ud′der (ud′ər) *n.* a baggy mammary gland, esp. of a cow.

UFO (yōō′ef′ō′; *sometimes* yōō′fō) *n., pl.* **UFOs, UFO's.** an unidentified flying object.

ug′ly (ug′lē) *adj.,* **-lier, -liest. 1.** very unattractive; repulsive. **2.** threatening; dangerous. **3.** quarrelsome.

u·kase′ (yōō kās′, -kāz′) *n.* an order by an absolute authority.

u·ku·le′le (yōō′kə lā′lē) *n.* a small guitar.

ul′cer (ul′sər) *n.* an open sore, as on the stomach lining. —**ul′cer·ous,** *adj.* —**ul′cer·ate′,** *v.i., v.t.*

ul′na (ul′nə) *n.* the larger bone of the forearm. —**ul′nar,** *adj.*

ul·te′ri·or (ul tēr′ē ər) *adj.* not acknowledged; concealed.

ul′ti·mate (-mit) *adj.* **1.** farthest. **2.** basic. **3.** final. —**ul′ti·mate·ly,** *adv.*

ul′ti·ma′tum (-mā′təm, -mä′-) *n., pl.* **-tums, -ta** (-tə). a final demand.

ultra- a prefix meaning beyond; extremely.

ul′tra·high′ fre′quency (ul′trə-hī′) *n.* a radio frequency between 300 and 3000 megahertz.

ul′tra·ma·rine′ *n.* a deep blue.

ul′tra·sound′ *n.* the application of sound above human hearing to medical diagnosis and therapy.

ul′tra·vi′o·let *adj.* of or producing invisible rays beyond violet in the spectrum.

um′ber (um′bər) *n.* a reddish brown.

um·bil′i·cal cord′ (um bil′i kəl) *n.* a cordlike structure connecting the fetus with the placenta, conveying nourishment and removing wastes.

um·bil′i·cus (-kəs) *n., pl.* **-ci** (-sī). the navel. —**um·bil′i·cal,** *adj.*

um′brage (um′brij) *n.* offense.

um·brel′la (um brel′ə) *n.* a cloth-covered folding metal framework on a carrying stick, used for protection from rain or sun.

um′laut (ōōm′lout) *n.* **1.** (in Germanic languages) assimilation in which a vowel is influenced by a following vowel. **2.** a diacritical mark (¨) used over a vowel to indicate umlaut.

ump (ump) *n., v.t., v.i.* umpire.

um′pire (um′pīᵊr) *n., v.,* **-pired, -piring.** —*n.* **1.** a rules official in certain sports. —*v.t., v.i.* **2.** to decide or act as umpire.

ump′teen′ (ump′tēn′) *adj. Informal.* innumerable. —**ump′teenth′,** *adj.*

UN United Nations.

un- a prefix indicating negative or opposite sense.

un·a′ble (un ā′bəl) *adj.* lacking the necessary power, skill, or resources.

un·ac·count′a·ble *adj.* **1.** impossible to account for. **2.** not responsible.

un·af·fect′ed *adj.* **1.** without affectation. **2.** not concerned.

u·nan′i·mous (yōō nan′ə məs) *adj.* being in complete agreement. —**u·na·nim′i·ty** (-nə nim′i tē) *n.*

un·as·sum′ing (un′-) *adj.* modest; without vanity.

un·at·tached′ *adj.* **1.** not attached. **2.** not engaged or married.

un·a·vail′ing *adj.* futile.

un·a·wares′ *adv.* not knowingly.

un·bal′anced *adj.* **1.** out of balance. **2.** irrational; deranged.

un·bear′a·ble *adj.* intolerable.

un·be·com′ing *adj.* unattractive or unseemly.

un·bend *v.t., v.i.,* **-bent, -bending. 1.** to straighten. **2.** to relax.

un·bend′ing *adj.* rigidly formal or unyielding.

un·bid′den *adj.* **1.** not commanded. **2.** not asked.

un·blush′ing *adj.* showing no remorse; shameless.

un·bos′om *v.t.* to disclose (a confidence, secret, etc.).

un·bowed′ (-boud′) *adj.* **1.** not bent. **2.** not subjugated.

un·bri′dled *adj.* unrestrained.

un·bro′ken *adj.* **1.** not broken. **2.** undisturbed. **3.** not tamed.

un·bur′den *v.t.* **1.** to free from a burden. **2.** to relieve (one's mind, conscience, etc.) by confessing.

un·called′-for′ *adj.* not warranted.

un·can′ny *adj.* strange; mysterious.

un·cer′e·mo′ni·ous *adj.* **1.** informal. **2.** rudely abrupt.

un·chart′ed *adj.* unexplored.

un′ci·al (un′shē əl, -shəl) *adj.* a form of writing with a rounded shape used esp. in early Greek and Latin manuscripts.

un·clad′ *adj.* naked.

un′cle (ung′kəl) *n.* **1.** the brother of one's father or mother. **2.** the husband of one's aunt.

Un′cle Sam′ (sam) *n.* the United States government personified as a tall man with white whiskers.

un·com′pro·mis′ing *adj.* rigid.

un·con·cern′ *n.* indifference.

un·con·di′tion·al *adj.* absolute; without conditions or reservations.

un·con′scion·a·ble (-shən-) *adj.* not restrained by conscience; unscrupulous.

un·con′scious *adj.* **1.** lacking awareness, sensation, or cognition. **2.** not perceived at the level of awareness. **3.** done without intent. —*n.* **4. the unconscious,** the part of the mind rarely accessible to awareness but influencing behavior.

un·couth′ (un kōōth′) *adj.* rude; boorish.

unc′tion (ungk′shən) *n.* **1.** anointment with oil. **2.** excessive earnestness of manner.

unc′tu·ous (ungk′chōō əs) *adj.* **1.** overly suave or smug. **2.** oily.

un·cut′ (un-) *adj.* **1.** not shortened or unabridged. **2.** not yet given shape as a gemstone.

un·daunt′ed *adj.* not discouraged.

un·de·mon′stra·tive *adj.* not expressing emotion; reserved.

un·der (un′dər) *prep.* **1.** beneath; below. **2.** less than. **3.** below in rank. **4.** subject to the authority of. **5.** within the category of. —*adv.* **6.** below or beneath something. **7.** in or into a lower degree, amount, position, or condition. —*adj.* **8.** lower.

under- a prefix meaning: **1.** below. **2.** lower in grade. **3.** of lesser degree or amount.

un′der·a·chieve′ *v.i.,* **-achieved, -achieving.** to perform below one's potential.

un′der·age′ *adj.* being below the legal or required age.

un′der·bel′ly *n., pl.* **-ies. 1.** the lower abdomen. **2.** a vulnerable area.

un′der·brush′ *n.* low shrubs, vines, etc., in a forest.

un′der·car′riage *n.* the supporting framework underneath a vehicle.

un′der·clothes′ *n.pl.* underwear.

un′der·cov′er *adj.* secret.

un′der·cur′rent *n.* a hidden tendency or feeling.

un′der·cut′ *v.t.,* **-cut, -cutting.** to sell at a lower price than.

un′der·de·vel′oped *adj.* insufficiently developed.

un′der·dog′ *n.* **1.** a person expected to lose a contest or conflict. **2.** a victim of injustice.

un·der·done' *adj.* not cooked enough.

un·der·es'ti·mate' (-māt') *v.t.,* **-mated, -mating.** to estimate too low.

un·der·ex·pose' *v.t.,* **-posed, -pos·ing.** to expose (film) to insufficient light or for too short a period.

un·der·gar'ment *n.* an item of underwear.

un·der·go' *v.t.,* **-went, -gone, -go·ing.** to experience; endure.

un·der·grad'u·ate (-it) *n.* a college student who has not received a first degree.

un·der·ground' (un'dər ground') *adv.* **1.** under the ground. **2.** in secrecy. —*adj.* (-ground') **3.** existing underground. **4.** secret. **5.** reflecting nonconformist views. —*n.* (-ground') **6.** a secret resistance army.

un·der·growth' *n.* underbrush.

un·der·hand' *adj.* sly; secret.

un·der·line' *v.t.,* **-lined, -lining. 1.** to draw a line under. **2.** to stress.

un·der·ling' (-ling) *n.* a subordinate.

un·der·mine' (un'dər mīn', un'dər mīn') *v.t.,* **-mined, -mining.** to weaken or destroy, esp. secretly.

un·der·neath' (-nēth', -nēth') *prep.* **1.** beneath; under. —*adv.* **2.** below.

un·der·pass' *n.* a passage running underneath.

un·der·pin'ning *n.* **1.** a system of supports. **2. underpinnings,** a foundation; basis.

un·der·priv'i·leged *adj.* denied the normal privileges of a society.

un·der·score' *v.t.,* **-scored, -scoring.** to underline; stress.

un·der·sec're·tar'y *n., pl.* **-taries.** a government official subordinate to a principal secretary.

un·der·signed' *n.* **the undersigned,** the person or persons signing a document.

un·der·staffed' *adj.* not having enough workers.

un·der·stand' *v.,* **-stood, -standing.** —*v.t.* **1.** to see the meaning of. **2.** to have a thorough knowledge of. **3.** to regard as settled. **4.** to infer. —*v.i.* **5.** to perceive what is meant. **6.** to accept sympathetically.

un·der·stand'ing *n.* **1.** comprehension. **2.** personal interpretation. **3.** intellectual ability; intelligence. **4.** a mutual agreement. —*adj.* **5.** marked by tolerance or sympathy.

un·der·state' *v.t.,* **-stated, -stating. 1.** to state less strongly than the facts warrant. **2.** to set forth in restrained terms. —**un·der·state'ment,** *n.*

un·der·stud'y *n., pl.* **-studies,** *v.,* **-ied, -ying.** —*n.* **1.** an actor who learns another's part in order to serve as a substitute if necessary. —*v.t., v.i.* **2.** to learn (a role) as an understudy (for).

un·der·take' *v.t.,* **-took, -taken, -taking. 1.** to take upon oneself, as a task. **2.** to promise.

un·der·tak'er *n.* a funeral director; mortician.

un·der·tak'ing (un'dər tā'king, un'dər tā'-) *n.* **1.** something undertaken. **2.** a promise.

un·der-the-coun'ter *adj.* illegal; unauthorized.

un·der·tone' *n.* **1.** a low tone. **2.** an underlying quality. **3.** a subdued color.

un·der·tow' (-tō') *n.* a strong current under the surface that is moving in a direction opposite that of the surface current.

un·der·wear' *n.* garments worn under outer clothing.

un·der·world' *n.* **1.** the criminal element of a society. **2.** the realm of the spirits of the dead.

un·der·write' (un'dər rīt', un'dər rīt') *v.t.,* **-wrote, -written, -writing. 1.** to agree to finance. **2.** to guarantee the security of.

un·do' (un dōō') *v.t.,* **-did, -done, -doing. 1.** to reverse or annul. **2.** to unfasten. **3.** to destroy.

un·do'ing *n.* **1.** a reversing. **2.** ruin. **3.** a cause of ruin.

un'du·late' (un'jə lāt', -dyə-) *v.i., v.t.,* **-lated, -lating.** to move or cause to move with a wavy motion. —**un'du·la'tion,** *n.*

un·dy'ing *adj.* eternal; unending.

un·earned' *adj.* **1.** not earned by service. **2.** not deserved. **3.** (of income) derived from investments.

un·earth' *v.t.* to discover.

un·earth'ly *adj.* **1.** supernatural; weird. **2.** unreasonable; absurd.

un·eas'y *adj.,* **-ier, -iest.** anxious.

un'e·quiv'o·cal *adj.* definite.

un'e·vent'ful *adj.* routine.

un'ex·cep'tion·al *adj.* ordinary.

un·feel'ing *adj.* lacking sympathy. —**un·feel'ing·ly,** *adv.*

un·flap'pa·ble (un flap'ə bəl) *adj.* not easily upset or panicked.

un·fledged' (-flejd') *adj.* **1.** lacking sufficient feathers for flight. **2.** immature.

un·found'ed *adj.* not supported by evidence.

un·frock' *v.t.* to deprive of ecclesiastical rank, authority, etc.

un·gain'ly (-gān'lē) *adj.* clumsy.

un'guent (ung'gwənt) *n.* an ointment.

un'gu·late (ung'gyə lit, -lāt') *adj.* **1.** having hoofs. —*n.* **2.** a hoofed mammal.

un·hand' *v.t.* to release.

un·hinge' *v.t.,* **-hinged, -hinging. 1.** to remove from hinges. **2.** to make mentally unstable.

uni- a prefix meaning one.

u'ni·corn' (yōō'ni kôrn') *n.* a mythical horselike animal with one horn.

u'ni·form' (yōō'nə fôrm') *adj.* **1.** exactly like others. **2.** constant. —*n.* **3.** the distinctive clothing of a specific group. —*v.t.* **4.** to clothe in a uniform. —**u'ni·form'i·ty,** *n.*

u'ni·fy' (-fī') *v.t., v.i.,* **-fied, -fying.** to make or become a single unit. —**u'ni·fi·ca'tion,** *n.*

u'ni·lat'er·al *adj.* one-sided.

un·im·peach'a·ble (un'im pē'chə bəl) *adj.* above reproach.

un'in·hib'it·ed *adj.* unrestrained by convention.

un·in'ter·est·ed *adj.* not interested; indifferent.
    —**Usage.** See DISINTERESTED.

un'ion (yōōn'yən) *n.* **1.** a uniting or being united. **2.** a combination. **3.** a group joined for a common purpose. **4.** a labor union.

un'ion·ize' *v.t., v.i.,* **-ized, -iz·ing.** to organize into a labor union.

Un'ion Jack' the British flag.

u·nique' (yōō nēk') *adj.* **1.** only. **2.** most unusual or rare.
    —**Usage.** UNIQUE is an adjective representing an absolute state that cannot exist in degrees. Therefore, it cannot be sensibly used with a limiting or comparative adverb such as "very," "most," or "extremely": *She has a unique* (not "*very unique*" or "*most unique*") *style of singing.*

u'ni·sex' (yōō'nə seks') *adj.* suitable for both sexes.

u'ni·son (-sən, -zən) *n.* **1.** perfect agreement. **2.** *Music.* identity in pitch.

u'nit (yōō'nit) *n.* **1.** a single entity. **2.** one of a number of identical or similar parts within a whole.

u·nite' (yōō nīt') *v.t., v.i.,* **united, uniting. 1.** to bring or come together in a single unit. **2.** to join in a common goal.

u'ni·ty (yōō'ni tē) *n., pl.* **-ties. 1.** the state of being united; oneness. **2.** agreement.

u'ni·va'lent (yōō'nə vā'lənt,yōō niv'ə-) *adj.* having a chemical valence of one.

u'ni·ver'sal (yōō'nə vûr'səl) *adj.* **1.** of, affecting, or understood by all. **2.** applicable or existing everywhere. —**u'ni·ver·sal'i·ty** (-sal'i tē) *n.*

U'niver'sal Prod'uct Code' a standardized bar code used in ringing up purchases in a store.

u'ni·verse' (-vûrs') *n.* all things that exist, including heavenly bodies.

u'ni·ver'si·ty (-vûr'si tē) *n., pl.* **-ties.** an institution of higher learning composed of various specialized colleges and at least one graduate school.

un·kempt' (un kempt') *adj.* untidy.

un·lead'ed (-led'id) *adj.* (of gasoline) free of pollution-causing lead.

un·less' (un les', ən-) *conj.* except when.

un·let'tered *adj.* illiterate.

un·mit'i·gat'ed *adj.* **1.** not lessened. **2.** absolute.

un·nerve' *v.t.,* **-nerved, -nerving.** to deprive of courage, strength, or determination.

un·par'al·leled' *adj.* without equal.

un·plumbed' *adj.* not explored in depth.

un·prin'ci·pled *adj.* without principles or ethics.

un·print'a·ble *adj.* unfit for print, esp. because obscene.

un·rav'el *v.,* **-eled, -eling.** —*v.t.* **1.** to separate the threads of. **2.** to

solve. —*v.i.* **3.** to become unraveled.

un·read' (-red') *adj.* **1.** not read. **2.** lacking in knowledge gained by reading.

un're·con·struct'ed *adj.* stubbornly maintaining beliefs considered out of date.

un·re·mit'ting *adj.* not ceasing.

un·rest' *n.* disturbance or turmoil.

un·ruf'fled *adj.* calm.

un·ru'ly (un rōō'lē) *adj.,* **-lier, -liest.** difficult to control.

un·sa'vo·ry *adj.* **1.** unpleasant in taste or smell. **2.** morally objectionable.

un·scru'pu·lous *adj.* not scrupulous; unprincipled. —**un·scru'pu·lous·ly,** *adv.*

un·sea'son·a·ble *adj.* **1.** being out of season. **2.** not timely.

un·seat' *v.t.* **1.** to dislodge from a seat. **2.** to remove from political office.

un·seem'ly *adj.,* **-lier, -liest.** improper.

un·set'tle *v.t.,* **-tled, -tling. 1.** to cause to be unstable; disturb. **2.** to agitate the mind or emotions of.

un·sound' *adj.* **1.** unhealthy. **2.** not solid or secure. **3.** not valid.

un·spar'ing *adj.* **1.** profuse. **2.** unmerciful.

un·speak'a·ble *adj.* **1.** exceeding the power of speech. **2.** inexpressibly bad or objectionable.

un·sta'ble *adj.* **1.** unsteady. **2.** emotionally unbalanced.

un·strung' *adj.* nervously upset; unnerved.

un·sung' *adj.* unappreciated.

un·ten'a·ble *adj.* indefensible.

un·think'a·ble *adj.* not to be imagined; impossible.

un·ti'dy *adj.,* **-dier, -diest.** not tidy or neat. —**un·tid'i·ly,** *adv.*

un·tie' *v.,* **-tied, -tying.** —*v.t.* **1.** to loosen or open (something tied). —*v.i.* **2.** to become untied.

un·til' (un til') *conj.* **1.** up to the time when. **2.** before. —*prep.* **3.** onward to the time of. **4.** before.
    —**Usage.** See TILL.

un'to (un'tōō; *unstressed* -tə) *prep.* **1.** to. **2.** until.

un·told' *adj.* countless.

un·touch'a·ble *adj.* **1.** not allowed to be touched. **2.** beyond control or criticism. **3.** a member of the lowest caste in India.

un·to·ward' *adj.* **1.** unfortunate. **2.** not proper.

un·well' *adj.* ill or ailing.

un·wield'y *adj.,* **-ier, -iest.** awkward to handle.

un·wit'ting *adj.* not aware.

un·wont'ed (un wōn'tid, -wōn'-, -wun'-) *adj.* not habitual or usual.

up (up) *adv., prep., adj., v.,* **upped, upping.** —*adv.* **1.** to, toward, in, or on a higher place or level. **2.** to or in an erect position. **3.** out of bed. **4.** to or at an equal point. **5.** into existence or view. —*prep.* **6.** to, toward, or at a higher place or farther point on or in. —*adj.* **7.** moving or facing upward. —*v.t.* **8.** to increase or raise. —**Idiom. 9. ups and downs,** alternating good and bad fortune. **10. up to, a.** as far as. **b.** as many as. **c.** capable of. **d.** dependent upon. **e.** doing.

up'-and-com'ing *adj.* likely to succeed; promising.

up'beat' *adj.* optimistic; happy.

up·braid' (up brād') *v.t.* to reproach severely.

up'bring'ing *n.* the care and training of children.

UPC Universal Product Code.

up'com'ing *adj.* about to take place or appear.

up'coun'try *adj., adv.* of, toward, or in the interior of a region.

up·date' (up'dāt', up dāt') *v.t.,* **-dated, -dating.** —*v.t.* **1.** to bring up to date. —*n.* **2.** new information. **3.** an updated version.

up'draft' *n.* an upward movement of air.

up·end' *v.t., v.i.* to set on end.

up'front' *adj.* **1.** invested or paid in advance. **2.** honest; candid.

up'grade' *n., v.,* **-graded, -grading.** —*n.* (up'grād') **1.** an improved or enhanced version. **2.** an increase, rise, or improvement. **3.** an upward incline. —*v.t.* (up grād', up'grād') **4.** to raise in rank, quality, value, etc.

up·heav'al (up hē'vəl) *n.* a sudden and great movement or change.

up'hill' *adv.* up a slope or incline.

up·hold' *v.t.,* **-held, -holding.** to defend or support.

up·hol'ster (up hōl'stər, ə pōl'-) *v.t.* to provide (furniture) with

coverings, stuffing, etc. —**up·hol'ster·er,** *n.* —**up·hol'ster·y,** *n.*

up'keep' *n.* **1.** maintaining something in good condition. **2.** the cost of upkeep.

up'land (up'lənd, -land') *n.* an elevated region.

up·lift' *v.t.* (up lift') **1.** to lift up. **2.** to improve. —*n.* (up'lift') **3.** a lifting up. **4.** improvement.

up·on' (ə pon', ə pôn') *prep.* on.

up'per *adj.* higher.

up'per·case' *adj.* **1.** (of a letter) capital. —*n.* **2.** a capital letter.

up'per hand' *n.* the controlling position; advantage.

up·pi'ty (up'i tē) *adj. Informal.* haughty, snobbish, or arrogant.

up'right' (up'rīt', up rīt') *adj.* **1.** in a vertical position; erect. **2.** righteous or honest. —*n.* **3.** something standing upright.

up·ris'ing (up'rī'zing, up rī'-) *n.* a revolt.

up'roar' *n.* tumult; noise; din.

up·roar'i·ous (-ē əs) *adj.* **1.** characterized by uproar. **2.** very funny. —**up·roar'i·ous·ly,** *adv.*

up·root' *v.t.* **1.** to tear up by the roots. **2.** to remove to a new place.

up'scale' *adj.* for people at the upper end of the economic scale.

up·set' *v.,* **-set, -setting,** *n., adj.* —*v.t.* (up set') **1.** to knock over. **2.** to distress emotionally or physically. **3.** to defeat. —*n.* (up'set') **4.** upsetting or being upset. **5.** a defeat. —*adj.* (up set') **6.** overturned. **7.** disturbed.

up'shot' *n.* the final result.

up'side down' *adv.* **1.** with the upper part undermost. **2.** in or into complete disorder. —**up'·side-down',** *adj.*

up·si'lon (yōōp sə'lon, up-) *n.* the 20th letter of the Greek alphabet.

up'stage' *adv., adj., v.,* **-staged, -staging.** —*adv.* **1.** at or toward the back of a stage. —*adj.* **2.** of the back of a stage. —*v.t.* **3.** to draw attention away from, as by moving upstage. **4.** to outdo professionally or socially.

up'stairs' *adv., adj.* on or to an upper floor.

up'start' *n.* a person newly risen to wealth or importance.

up'-to-date' *adj.* modern.

up'ward (up'wərd) *adv.* **1.** toward a higher place. —*adj.* **2.** moving upward. Also, **up'wards.**

u·ra'ni·um (yōō rā'nē əm) *n.* a white, radioactive metallic element, important in the development of atomic energy.

U'ra·nus (yōōr'ə nəs, yōō rā'-) *n.* **1.** the planet seventh from the sun. **2.** in Greek myth, a personification of the sky.

ur'ban (ûr'bən) *adj.* of a city.

ur·bane' (ûr bān') *adj.* suave and sophisticated. —**ur·ban'i·ty** (-ban'i tē) *n.*

ur'chin (ûr'chin) *n.* a ragged child.

u·re'a (yōō rē'ə, yōōr'ē ə) *n.* a compound occurring in body fluids, esp. urine.

u·re'mi·a (yōō rē'mē ə) *n.* the presence in the blood of products normally excreted in urine.

u·re'ter (yōō rē'tər) *n.* a duct that conveys urine from a kidney to the bladder.

u·re'thra (yōō rē'thrə) *n., pl.* **-thrae** (-thrē) **-thras.** a duct that conveys urine and, in males, semen.

urge (ûrj) *v.,* **urged, urging.** —*v.t.* **1.** to push along, encourage, or incite. **2.** to insist on. —*n.* **3.** a desire; impulse.

ur'gent (ûr'jənt) *adj.* requiring immediate attention. —**ur'gen·cy,** *n.*

u·ri'nal (yōōr'ə nl) *n.* a wall fixture used by men for urinating. **2.** a receptacle for urine.

u'ri·nal'y·sis (-nal'ə sis) *n., pl.* **-ses.** a diagnostic analysis of urine.

u'ri·nar'y (-ner'ē) *adj.* of urine or of the organs that secrete and discharge urine.

u'ri·nate' (-nāt') *v.i.,* **-nated, -nating.** to pass urine. —**u'ri·na'tion,** *n.*

u'rine (yōōr'in) *n.* the yellowish liquid secreted by the kidneys. —**u'ric** (yōōr'ik) *adj.*

urn (ûrn) *n.* **1.** a container with a faucet for serving coffee or tea. **2.** a container for the ashes of a cremated person. **3.** a vase with a pedestal.

u·rol'o·gy (yōō rol'ə jē) *n.* the branch of medicine dealing with the urinary or genitourinary tract. —**u·rol'o·gist,** *n.*

us (us) *pron.* the objective case of we.

us'age (yōō'sij, -zij) *n.* **1.** a custom

or practice. **2.** the way in which something is used.

use *v.,* **used, using,** *n.* —*v.t.* (yōōz or, for pt. form of 5, yōōst) **1.** to put into service. **2.** to consume. **3.** to treat. **4.** to take unfair advantage of. —*v.i.* **5.** to be accustomed. —*n.* (yōōs) **6.** a using or being used. **7.** the purpose for which something is used. **8.** the power of using something. —**use'ful,** *adj.* —**use'less,** *adj.* —**us'er,** *n.*

us·er-friend'ly *adj.* easy to operate.

ush'er (ush'ər) *n.* **1.** a person who escorts others to their seats. —*v.t.* **2.** to act as an usher to.

u'su·al (yōō'zhōō əl) *adj.* customary; common. —**u·su·al·ly,** *adv.*

u·surp' (yōō sûrp', -zûrp') *v.t.* to seize (a position, power, etc.) by force or without legal right. —**u·surp'er,** *n.*

u'su·ry (yōō'zhə rē) *n.* lending money at exorbitant rates of interest. —**u'sur·er,** *n.*

UT Utah. Also, **Ut.**

u·ten'sil (yōō ten'səl) *n.* a tool or instrument, esp. for the kitchen.

u'ter·us (yōō'tər əs) *n., pl.* **-teri** (-tə rī'). a hollow organ in female mammals in which the fertilized egg develops. —**u'ter·ine** (-in) *adj.*

u·til·i·tar'i·an (yōō til'i târ'ē ən) *adj.* of practical use.

u·til'i·ty *n., pl.* **-ties. 1.** usefulness. **2.** a public service, as the providing of electricity.

u'ti·lize' (yōōt'l īz') *v.t.,* **-lized, -lizing.** to put to practical use. —**u'ti·li·za'tion,** *n.*

ut'most' (ut'mōst') *adj.* **1.** greatest. **2.** furthest.

U·to'pi·an (yōō tō'pē ən) *adj.* impossibly perfect.

ut'ter[1] (ut'ər) *v.t.* to speak; say.

ut'ter[2] (ut'ər) *adj.* complete; total.

ut'ter·ly *adv.* completely; absolutely.

u'vu·la (yōō'vyə lə) *n., pl.* **-las, -lae.** the small, fleshy part on the soft palate.

ux·o'ri·ous (uk sôr'ē əs,ug zôr'-) *adj.* foolishly or excessively fond of one's wife.

V

V, v (vē) *n.* the twenty-second letter of the English alphabet.

VA Virginia. Also, **Va.**

va'can·cy (vā'kən sē) *n., pl.* **-cies. 1.** the state of being vacant. **2.** a vacant space or position.

va'cant (-kənt) *adj.* **1.** empty. **2.** unoccupied.

va'cate (vā'kāt) *v.t.,* **-cated, -cating.** to cause to be vacant.

va·ca'tion (vā kā'shən, və-) *n.* **1.** a period of rest or freedom from duty, business, etc. —*v.i.* **2.** to take a vacation.

vac'ci·nate' (vak'sə nāt') *v.t.,* **-nated, -nating.** to inoculate against disease. —**vac'ci·na'tion,** *n.*

vac·cine' (vak sēn') *n.* a substance injected into the bloodstream to give immunity from infection.

vac'il·late' (vas'ə lāt') *v.i.,* **-lated, -lating. 1.** to be indecisive. **2.** to waver. —**vac'il·la'tion,** *n.*

va·cu'i·ty (va kyōō'i tē, və-) *n., pl.* **-ties. 1.** the state of being vacuous. **2.** absence of intelligence.

vac'u·ous (vak'yōō əs) *adj.* **1.** empty. **2.** showing a lack of intelligence. —**vac'u·ous·ly,** *adv.*

vac'u·um (vak'yōōm, -yōō əm, -yəm) *n.* **1.** a space from which all matter has been removed. —*v.t., v.i.* **2.** to clean with a vacuum cleaner.

vac'uum bot'tle *n.* a bottle with a double wall enclosing a vacuum, used to keep liquids hot or cold.

vac'uum clean'er *n.* an electrical appliance for cleaning by suction.

vac'uum-packed' *adj.* packed with as much air as possible evacuated before sealing.

vag'a·bond' (vag'ə bond') *adj.* **1.** wandering. —*n.* **2.** a wanderer. **3.** a vagrant.

va·gar'y (və gâr'ē, vā'gə rē) *n., pl.* **-garies.** a capricious act or idea.

va·gi'na (və jī'nə) *n., pl.* **-nas, -nae.** the passage from the uterus to the vulva. —**vag'i·nal** (vaj'ə nl) *adj.*

va'grant (vā'grənt) *n.* **1.** a person who has no home. —*adj.* **2.** wandering. —**va'gran·cy,** *n.*

vague (vāg) *adj.,* **vaguer, vaguest.**

1. not clearly expressed. **2.** indistinct.

vain (vān) *adj.* **1.** conceited. **2.** futile. —*Idiom.* **3. in vain,** without effect. —**vain′ly,** *adv.*

vain·glo′ry *n.* excessive vanity. —**vain·glo′ri·ous,** *adj.*

val′ance (val′əns, vā′ləns) *n.* a drapery across the top of a window.

vale (vāl) *n.* a valley.

val′e·dic·to′ri·an (val′i dik tôr′ē ən) *n.* a graduating student who delivers the valedictory.

val′e·dic′to·ry (-tə rē) *n., pl.* **-ries.** a farewell address, esp. one delivered at commencement.

va′lence (vā′ləns) *n.* the relative combining capacity of an atom compared with that of the hydrogen atom.

val′en·tine′ (val′ən tīn′) *n.* **1.** an affectionate card or gift sent on February 14 (**St. Valentine's Day**). **2.** a sweetheart greeted on that day.

val′et (va lā′, val′it, val′ā) *n.* a personal manservant.

val′iant (val′yənt) *adj.* brave.

val′id (val′id) *adj.* **1.** sound; logical. **2.** legally binding. —**va·lid′i·ty** (və lid′i tē) *n.*

val′i·date′ (-i dāt′) *v.t.,* **-dated, -dating.** to make valid; confirm. —**val′i·da′tion,** *n.*

va·lise′ (və lēs′) *n.* a traveling bag.

val′ley (val′ē) *n.* a long depression between uplands or mountains.

val′or (val′ər) *n.* bravery.

val′u·a·ble (-yॉo ə bəl, -yə bəl) *adj.* **1.** of great worth, importance, etc. —*n.* **2. valuables,** articles of great value.

val′u·a′tion (val′yॉo ā′shən) *n.* an estimate of a thing's value.

val′ue *n., v.,* **-ued, -uing.** —*n.* **1.** worth or importance. **2.** equivalent worth in money, goods, etc. **3. values,** the abstract concepts of what is right or good. —*v.t.* **4.** to estimate the worth of. **5.** to regard highly. —**val′ue·less,** *adj.*

valve (valv) *n.* **1.** a device for controlling the flow of a liquid or gas. **2.** a structure allowing a body fluid to flow in one direction only.

va·moose′ (va mॉos′) *v.i.,* **-moosed, -moosing.** *Slang.* to leave hurriedly.

vamp (vamp) *n.* **1.** the upper front part of a shoe or boot. **2.** *Slang.* a seductive woman. —*v.t., v.i.* **3.** to seduce (a man)

vam′pire (vam′pīr′) *n.* (in folklore) a corpse that is said to be reanimated and to suck the blood of living persons.

van (van) *n.* **1.** a covered truck for moving furniture, animals, etc. **2.** a small closed trucklike vehicle.

van′dal (van′dl) *n.* a person who willfully damages or destroys another's property.

van′dal·ize′ *v.t.,* **-ized, -izing.** to destroy or deface deliberately. —**van′dal·ism,** *n.*

vane (vān) *n.* **1.** a weathervane. **2.** one of a set of blades on a rotor to be moved by fluid or air.

van′guard′ (van′gärd′-) *n.* the foremost part of an advancing army, a movement, etc.

va·nil′la (və nil′ə; *often* -nel′ə) *n.* **1.** a tropical orchid, whose fruit (**vanilla bean**) yields a flavoring extract. **2.** this flavoring.

van′ish (van′ish) *v.i.* to disappear.

van′i·ty (van′i tē) *n., pl.* **-ties. 1.** excessive pride in oneself, esp. in one's appearance. **2.** futility.

van′quish (vang′kwish, van′-) *v.t* to conquer; defeat.

van′tage (van′tij) *n.* **1.** a place or condition offering some advantage. **2.** an advantage.

vap′id (vap′id) *adj.* insipid; dull.

va′por (vā′pər) *n.* **1.** visible matter, as mist, suspended in air. **2.** a gas.

va′por·ize′ (-pə rīz′) *v.t., v.i.,* **-ized, -izing.** to change into vapor. —**va′por·i·za′tion,** *n.* —**va′por·iz′er,** *n.*

var′i·a·ble (vâr′ē ə bəl) *adj.* **1.** changeable. **2.** inconstant. —*n.* **3.** something variable. —**var′i·a·bil′i·ty,** *n.*

var′i·ance (-əns) *n.* **1.** the state of being variable. **2.** disagreement.

var′i·ant *adj.* **1.** varying. **2.** differing. —*n.* **3.** a variant form, spelling, etc.

var′i·a′tion (-ā′shən) *n.* **1.** a change. **2.** amount of change. **3.** a different form of something. **4.** the transformation of a melody with changes in harmony, rhythm, etc.

var′i·col′ored (vâr′i kul′ərd) *adj.* having various colors.

var′i·cose′ (var′i kōs′) *adj.* abnormally swollen, as veins.

var′i·e·gate′ (vâr′ē i gāt′, vâr′i-)

v.t., **-gated, -gating. 1.** to make varied in appearance. **2.** to give variety to.

va·ri′e·ty (və rī′i tē) *n., pl.* **-ties. 1.** diversity. **2.** a number of different things. **3.** a kind or sort.

va·ri′o·la (və rī′ə lə) *n.* smallpox.

var′i·ous (vâr′ē əs) *adj.* **1.** of different kinds. **2.** several.

var′mint (vär′mənt) *n.* an undesirable, usu. verminous animal.

var′nish (vär′nish) *n.* **1.** a resinous solution that dries to form a hard, glossy coat. **2.** a gloss. —*v.t.* **3.** to coat with varnish.

var′y (vâr′ē) *v.t.,* **varied, varying. 1.** to change. **2.** to cause to be different. —*v.i.* **3.** to differ.

vas′cu·lar (vas′kyə lər) *adj.* of vessels that convey fluids, as blood.

vase (vās, vāz, väz) *n.* a tall container, esp. for flowers.

vas·ec′to·my (va sek′tə mē, və-) *n., pl.* **-mies.** surgical removal of part of the sperm-carrying duct of the testis, resulting in sterility.

vas′sal (vas′əl) *n.* **1.** a feudal holder of land who renders service to a lord. **2.** a subject, servant, etc.

vast (vast) *adj.* immense; huge.

vat (vat) *n.* a large container, as a tank, for liquids.

vaude′ville (vôd′vil, vōd′-, vô′də-) *n.* a form of popular entertainment made up of separate acts.

vault[1] (vôlt) *n.* **1.** an arched ceiling or roof. **2.** an arched space, chamber, etc. **3.** a room for the safekeeping of valuables. —*v.t., v.i.* **4.** to build or cover with a vault. —**vault′ed,** *adj.*

vault[2] (vôlt) *v.i., v.t.* to leap (over).

vault′ing *adj.* **1.** leaping. **2.** excessive.

vaunt (vônt, vänt) *v.t., v.i.* **1.** to boast (of). —*n.* **2.** a boast.

VCR videocassette recorder.

VD venereal disease.

V′-Day′ *n.* a day of military victory.

VDT video display terminal.

veal (vēl) *n.* the flesh of a calf as used for food.

vec′tor (vek′tər) *n.* a quantity possessing both magnitude and direction.

veep (vēp) *n. Informal.* a vice president.

veer (vēr) *v.i.* to change direction.

veg′e·ta·ble (vej′tə bəl, vej′i tə-) *n.* **1.** a plant grown for food. —*adj.* **2.** of vegetables.

veg′e·tar′i·an (vej′i târ′ē ən) *n.* **1.** a person who does not eat meat, fish, or fowl. —*adj.* **2.** of vegetarians. **3.** consisting solely of vegetables. —**veg′e·tar′i·an·ism,** *n.*

veg′e·tate′ (-tāt′) *v.i.,* **-tated, -tating. 1.** to grow as plants do. **2.** to live a dull, inactive life. —**veg′e·ta′tive,** *adj.*

veg′e·ta′tion *n.* plants collectively.

ve′he·ment (vē′ə mənt) *adj.* showing strong feeling. —**ve′he·mence, ve′he·men′cy,** *n.*

ve′hi·cle (vē′i kəl) *n.* **1.** a conveyance for passengers or goods, as a car, truck, etc. **2.** a means by which something is transmitted. —**ve·hic′u·lar** (-hik′yə lər) *adj.*

veil (vāl) *n.* **1.** a piece of material concealing the face. **2.** a part of a headdress, as of a nun or a bride. **3.** a cover; screen. **4.** a pretense. —*v.t.* **5.** to cover with a veil.

vein (vān) *n.* **1.** one of the vessels conveying blood to the heart. **2.** a tubular riblike thickening, as in a leaf or insect wing. **3.** a layer of ore, coal, etc., in rock. **4.** a quality. —*v.t.* **5.** to furnish or mark with veins.

Vel·cro (vel′krō) *Trademark.* a fastening tape with opposing pieces of nylon that interlock.

veld (velt, felt) *n.* the open grassy country in South Africa. Also, **veldt.**

vel′lum (vel′əm) *n.* parchment.

ve·loc′i·ty (və los′i tē) *n., pl.* **-ties.** speed.

ve′lo·drome′ (vē′lə drōm′) *n.* an indoor arena with a banked track for cycling.

ve·lour′ (və lॉor′) *n.* a velvetlike fabric used for clothing and upholstery.

vel′vet (vel′vit) *n.* a woven fabric with a thick, soft pile. —**vel′vet·y,** *adj.*

vel′vet·een′ (-vi tēn′) *n.* a cotton fabric resembling velvet.

ve′nal (vēn′l) *adj.* corrupt.

vend (vend) *v.t.* to sell.

ven·det′ta (ven det′ə) *n.* a long, bitter feud.

vend′ing machine′ *n.* a coin-

operated machine for selling small articles.

ven′dor *n.* one that sells.

ve·neer′ (və nēr′) *n.* **1.** a thin layer of material for covering wood. **2.** a superficial appearance. —*v.t.* **3.** to cover with a veneer.

ven′er·a·ble (ven′ər ə bəl) *adj.* worthy of reverence.

ven′er·ate′ (-ə rāt′) *v.t.,* **-ated, -ating.** to revere. —**ven′er·a′tion,** *n.*

ve·ne′re·al (və nēr′ē əl) *adj.* of or transmitted by sexual intercourse.

ve·ne′tian blind′ (və nē′shən) *n.* a window blind with horizontal slats.

venge′ance (ven′jəns) *n.* **1.** infliction of harm in retaliation for a wrong. —*Idiom.* **2. with a vengeance,** to an extreme degree.

venge′ful *adj.* seeking vengeance.

ve′ni·al (vē′nē əl, vēn′yəl) *adj.* (of a sin) pardonable.

ven′i·son (ven′ə sən, -zən) *n.* the flesh of a deer used for food.

ven′om (ven′əm) *n.* **1.** a poisonous fluid secreted by some snakes, spiders, etc. **2.** spite; malice. —**ven′om·ous,** *adj.*

ve′nous (vē′nəs) *adj.* **1.** of or having veins. **2.** of or being the blood carried back to the heart by veins.

vent (vent) *n.* **1.** an opening serving as an outlet, as for fluid or fumes. **2.** expression; utterance. —*v.t.* **3.** to express freely. **4.** to release or discharge through a vent.

ven′ti·late′ (ven′tl āt′) *v.t.,* **-lated, -lating.** to provide with fresh air. —**ven′ti·la′tion,** *n.* —**ven′ti·la′tor,** *n.*

ven′tral (ven′trəl) *adj.* of or near the belly; abdominal.

ven′tri·cle (ven′tri kəl) *n.* either of two lower chambers of the heart.

ven·tril′o·quism′ (ven tril′ə kwiz′əm) *n.* the art of speaking so that the voice seems to come from another source. —**ven·tril′o·quist,** *n.*

ven′ture (ven′chər) *n., v.,* **-tured, -turing.** —*n.* **1.** an undertaking involving risk. —*v.t.* **2.** to risk; dare. —*v.i.* **3.** to undertake a venture. —**ven′ture·some** (-səm), *adj.*

ven′ue (ven′yॉo) *n.* the scene or locale of an action or event.

Ve′nus (vē′nəs) *n.* **1.** the second planet from the sun. **2.** the Roman goddess of love.

Ve′nus's-fly′trap′ *n.* a plant with hinged leaves that trap insects.

ve·rac′i·ty (və ras′ə tē) *n.* truthfulness or accuracy. —**ve·ra′cious** (-rā′shəs) *adj.*

ve·ran′da (-ran′də) *n.* an open porch. Also, **ve·ran′dah.**

verb (vûrb) *n.* a part of speech expressing action, state, or occurrence.

ver′bal (vûr′bəl) *adj.* **1.** of or in the form of words. **2.** oral. —**ver′bal·ly,** *adv.*

ver′bal·ize′ *v.t., v.i.,* **-ized, -izing.** to express (something) in words.

ver·ba′tim (vər bā′tim) *adv.* word for word.

ver·be′na (vər bē′nə) *n.* a plant with long spikes of flowers.

ver′bi·age (vûr′bē ij) *n.* an overabundance of words.

ver·bose′ (vər bōs′) *adj.* excessively wordy. —**ver·bos′i·ty** (-bos′i tē) *n.*

ver·bo′ten (vər bōt′n, fər-) *adj.* forbidden.

ver′dant (vûr′dnt) *adj.* green with vegetation. —**ver′dan·cy,** *n.*

ver′dict (vûr′dikt) *n.* a judgment or decision.

ver′di·gris′ (vûr′di grēs′, -gris) *n.* a green or bluish patina on some metals.

ver′dure (vûr′jər) *n.* **1.** greenness. **2.** green vegetation.

verge (vûrj) *n., v.,* **verged, verging.** —*n.* **1.** an edge or margin. —*v.i.* **2.** to border.

ver′i·fy′ (ver′ə fī′) *v.t.,* **-fied, -fying. 1.** to prove to be true. **2.** to ascertain the correctness of. —**ver′i·fi′a·ble,** *adj.* —**ver′i·fi·ca′tion,** *n.*

ver′i·ly (-lē) *adv. Archaic.* truly.

ver′i·si·mil′i·tude′ (-si mil′i tॉod′, -tyॉod′) *n.* the appearance of truth.

ver′i·ta·ble (-tə bəl) *adj.* genuine.

ver′i·ty (-tē) *n.* truth.

ver′mi·cel′li (vûr′mi chel′ē, -sel′ē) *n.* pasta in the form of long threads.

ver·mil′ion (vər mil′yən) *n.* a bright red.

ver′min (vûr′min) *n.pl.* small, objectionable animals or insects. —**ver′min·ous,** *adj.*

ver·mouth′ (vər mॉoth′) *n.* a white wine flavored with herbs.

ver·nac′u·lar (vər nak′yə lər, va-nak′-) *n.* **1.** the native speech of an

area. **2.** the language of a particular group. —*adj.* **3.** (of language) used locally or in everyday speech.

ver′nal (vûr′nl) *adj.* of spring.

ve·ron′i·ca (və ron′i kə) *n.* a plant with opposite leaves and clusters of small flowers.

ver′sa·tile (vûr′sə tl; *esp. Brit.* -tīl′) *adj.* capable of doing a variety of things well. —**ver′sa·til′i·ty,** *n.*

verse (vûrs) *n.* **1.** a line of a poem. **2.** a type of metrical composition. **3.** a poem. **4.** poetry. **5.** a division of a Biblical chapter.

versed *adj.* expert; skilled.

ver′si·fy′ (vûr′sə fī′) *v.,* **-fied, -fying.** —*v.t.* **1.** to treat in or turn into verse. —*v.t.* **2.** to compose verses. —**ver′si·fi·ca′tion,** *n.*

ver′sion (vûr′zhən, -shən) *n.* **1.** a particular account of something. **2.** a special form. **3.** a translation.

ver′so (vûr′sō) *n., pl.* **-sos.** the left-hand page of a book.

ver′sus (vûr′səs, -saz) *prep.* in opposition or contrast to.

ver′te·bra (vûr′tə brə) *n., pl.* **-brae, -bras.** one of the bones of the spinal column. —**ver′te·bral,** *adj.*

ver′te·brate′ (-brit, -brāt′) *adj.* **1.** having vertebrae. —*n.* **2.** a vertebrate animal.

ver′tex (vûr′teks) *n., pl.* **-texes, -tices** (-tə sēz′). the highest point.

ver′ti·cal (vûr′ti kəl) *adj.* **1.** perpendicular to level ground; upright. —*n.* **2.** something vertical.

ver·tig′i·nous (vər tij′ə nəs) *adj.* **1.** whirling. **2.** affected with or liable to cause vertigo.

ver′ti·go′ (vûr′ti gō′) *n., pl.* **-goes.** dizziness.

verve (vûrv) *n.* vivaciousness.

ver′y (ver′ē) *adv., adj.,* **-ier, -iest.** —*adv.* **1.** extremely. **2.** absolutely. —*adj.* **3.** precise. **4.** mere **5.** sheer; utter. **6.** actual.

ves′i·cle (ves′i kəl) *n.* a small sac in the body.

ves′pers (-parz) *n.* an evening religious service.

ves′sel (ves′əl) *n.* **1.** a ship or boat. **2.** a container, esp. one for liquids. **3.** a tube or duct that conveys a bodily fluid.

vest (vest) *n.* **1.** a waist-length sleeveless garment. —*v.t.* **2.** to clothe. **3.** to endow with powers, rights, etc.

ves′tal (ves′tl) *adj.* **1.** chaste; pure. —*n.* **2.** a chaste woman.

vest′ed *adj.* held completely and permanently.

vest′ed in′terest *n.* a special interest in a system, arrangement, or institution for personal reasons.

ves′ti·bule (ves′tə byॉol′) *n.* a small room between the outer door and the interior of a building.

ves′tige (ves′tij) *n.* **1.** a trace of something extinct. **2.** a very small amount of something. —**ves·tig′i·al** (ve stij′ē əl, -stij′əl) *adj.*

vest′ing *n.* the granting to an employee of the right to pension benefits despite early retirement.

vest′ment *n.* a ceremonial garment, esp. that worn by clergy during a religious service.

vest′-pock′et (-pok′it) *adj.* very small.

ves′try (ves′trē) *n., pl.* **-tries. 1.** a room in a church for vestments or for meetings. **2.** a committee managing temporal affairs in the Episcopal church.

vet (vet) *n.* **1.** a veterinarian. **2.** a veteran.

vetch (vech) *n.* a climbing plant cultivated esp. for forage.

vet′er·an (vet′ər ən) *n.* **1.** a person who has served in the armed forces. **2.** an experienced person. —*adj.* **3.** experienced.

vet′er·i·nar′i·an (-ə nâr′ē ən) *n.* a doctor qualified to treat the diseases and injuries of animals.

vet′er·i·nar′y (-ner′ē) *n., pl.* **-naries.** —*adj.* **1.** a veterinarian. —*adj.* **2.** of or for the medical and surgical treatment of animals.

ve′to (vē′tō) *n., pl.* **-toes,** *v.,* **-toed, -toing.** —*n.* **1.** the power of the executive branch of government to reject an action of the legislative branch. **2.** a strong prohibition. —*v.t.* **3.** to reject (a bill) by veto.

vex (veks) *v.t.* **1.** to irritate. **2.** to worry. —**vex·a′tion,** *n.* —**vex·a′tious,** *adj.* —**vexed,** *adj.*

vi′a (vī′ə, vē′ə) *prep.* by way of.

vi′a·ble (vī′ə bəl) *adj.* **1.** capable of living. **2.** practicable; workable.

vi′a·duct′ (-ə dukt′) *n.* a bridge carrying a road or railroad.

Vi·ag′ra (-ag′rə) *Trademark.* a drug used to treat impotence.

vi′al (vī′əl, vīl) *n.* a small glass container.

vi′and (vī′ənd) *n.* an article of food.

vibes (vībz) *n.pl. Slang.* something, esp. an emotional aura, emitted as if by vibration.

vi′brant (vī′brənt) *adj.* **1.** vibrating. **2.** energetic; vital. —**vi′bran·cy,** *n.*

vi′bra·phone′ (vī′brə fōn′) *n.* an instrument like a metal xylophone, with electrically enhanced resonance.

vi′brate (vī′brāt) *v.i.,* **-brated, -brating. 1.** to move to and fro very rapidly and continuously. **2.** to resonate. —**vi·bra′tion,** *n.* —**vi′bra·tor,** *n.*

vi·bra′to (vi brä′tō) *n., pl.* **-tos.** a pulsating effect produced by rapid but slight alterations in pitch.

vi·bur′num (vī bûr′nəm) *n.* a shrub bearing white flower clusters.

vic′ar (vik′ər) *n.* **1.** a parish priest in the Anglican church. **2.** a representative of a bishop in the Roman Catholic church.

vic′ar·age (-ij) *n.* the residence of a vicar.

vi·car′i·ous (vī kâr′ē əs, vi-) *adj.* **1.** done or suffered in place of another. **2.** felt through imagined participation in the experience of another. —**vi·car′i·ous·ly,** *adv.*

vice (vīs) *n.* **1.** an evil habit or practice. **2.** immoral conduct. **3.** a personal fault.

vice- a prefix meaning deputy.

vice′-ad′mi·ral (vīs′-) *n.* a commissioned officer ranking above a rear admiral.

vice·ge′rent (-jēr′ənt) *n.* a deputy to a sovereign or magistrate.

vice′ pres′i·dent *n.* an officer next in rank to a president. —**vice′ pres′i·den·cy,** *n.*

vice′roy′ (vīs′roi) *n.* a person who rules an area as the deputy of the sovereign.

vi′ce ver′sa (vī′sə vûr′sə, vīs′, vī′sē) *adv.* in reverse order.

vi·cin′i·ty (vi sin′i tē) *n., pl.* **-ties.** the neighborhood; nearby area.

vi′cious (vish′əs) *adj.* **1.** evil. **2.** malicious. **3.** savage.

vi·cis′si·tude′ (vi sis′i tॉod′, -tyॉod′) *n.* change or variation.

vic′tim (vik′təm) *n.* **1.** a person who suffers from an injurious action or event. **2.** a person who is cheated. **3.** a creature sacrificed in a religious rite. —**vic′tim·ize′,** *v.t.*

vic′tor (vik′tər) *n.* a winner. —**vic·to′ri·ous** (-tôr′ē əs) *adj.*

vic′to·ry (-tə rē) *n., pl.* **-ries.** success in winning a contest, battle, etc.

vict′uals (vit′lz) *n.pl.* food.

vid′e·o′ (vid′ē ō′) *n., pl.* **-eos,** *adj.* —*n.* **1.** the visual elements of a telecast. **2.** a videotape or videocassette. —*adj.* **3.** of television.

vid′e·o·cas·sette′ *n.* a cassette containing videotape.

vid′eocassette′ record′er *n.* an electronic device for recording and playing videocassettes.

vid′e·o·disc′ *n.* a disc on which pictures and sound are recorded for playback on a TV set.

vid′eo game′ *n.* an electronic game played on a screen.

vid′e·o·tape′ *n., v.,* **-taped, -taping.** —*n.* **1.** magnetic tape on which a TV program, motion picture, etc., can be recorded. —*v.t.* **2.** to record on videotape.

vie (vī) *v.i.,* **vied, vying.** to contend for superiority.

view (vyॉo) *n.* **1.** seeing or beholding. **2.** a range of vision. **3.** a sight, as of a landscape. **4.** a picture of a scene. **5.** a manner of looking at something. **6.** a personal opinion. —*v.t.* **7.** to see; look at. **8.** to consider. —**view′er,** *n.*

view′find′er *n.* a camera part for viewing what will appear in a picture.

view′point′ *n.* **1.** a point of view. **2.** a place from which there is a good view.

vig′il (vij′əl) *n.* a period of staying awake to watch or pray.

vig′i·lant (-lənt) *adj.* **1.** watchful. **2.** wary. —**vig′i·lance,** *n.*

vig′i·lan′te (-lan′tē) *n.* a person who takes the law into his or her own hands.

vi·gnette′ (vin yet′) *n.* a literary sketch.

vig′or (vig′ər) *n.* **1.** active strength. **2.** vitality. —**vig′or·ous,** *adj.*

Vik′ing (vī′king) *n.* a medieval Scandinavian raider.

vile (vīl) *adj.,* **viler, vilest. 1.** very bad. **2.** highly offensive. **3.** evil. —**vile′ly,** *adv.* —**vile′ness,** *n.*

vil′i·fy′ (vil′ə fī′) *v.t.,* **-fied, -fying.** to speak ill of. —**vil′i·fi·ca′tion,** *n.*

vil′la (vil′ə) *n.* a country residence.

vil′lage (vil′ij) *n.* a small town. —**vil′lag·er,** *n.*

vil′lain (vil′ən) *n.* a wicked person. —**vil′lain·ous,** *adj.* —**vil′lain·y,** *n.*

vil′lein (vil′ən, -ān) *n.* a feudal tenant.

vim (vim) *n.* vitality.

vin′ai·grette′ (vin′ə gret′) *n.* a dressing, esp. for salad, of oil and vinegar usu. with herbs.

vin′di·cate′ (vin′di kāt′) *v.t.,* **-cated, -cating. 1.** to clear, as from a suspicion. **2.** to uphold or justify. —**vin′di·ca′tion,** *n.*

vin·dic′tive (vin dik′tiv) *adj.* holding a grudge; vengeful.

vine (vīn) *n.* a creeping or climbing plant with a slender stem.

vin′e·gar (vin′i gər) *n.* a sour liquid obtained by fermentation of wine or cider. —**vin′e·gar·y,** *adj.*

vine′yard (vin′yərd) *n.* a plantation of grapevines.

vin′tage (vin′tij) *n.* **1.** the wine or grapes from one harvest. **2.** the output of a particular time. —*adj.* **3.** of a specified vintage. **4.** being the best of a kind. **5.** of a style of the past.

vint′ner (vint′nər) *n.* a person who makes wine.

vi′nyl (vīn′l) *n.* a type of plastic.

vi·o′la (vē ō′lə) *n.* a stringed instrument resembling the violin but slightly larger and deeper in tone.

vi′o·late′ (vī′ə lāt′) *v.t.,* **-lated, -lating. 1.** to break or transgress. **2.** to break through or into. **3.** to desecrate. **4.** to rape. —**vi′o·la′tor,** *n.*

vi′o·lent *adj.* **1.** uncontrolled, strong, or rough. **2.** caused by destructive force. **3.** intense; severe. —**vi′o·lence,** *n.* —**vi′o·lent·ly,** *adv.*

vi′o·let (vī′ə lit) *n.* **1.** a low plant bearing bluish purple flowers. **2.** a bluish purple.

vi′o·lin′ (vī′ə lin′) *n.* a stringed instrument of treble pitch, played with a bow. —**vi′o·lin′ist,** *n.*

vi·o·lon·cel′lo (vē′ə lən chel′ō, vī′-) *n., pl.* **-los.** a cello.

VIP (vē′ī′pē′) *Informal.* very important person.

vi′per (vī′pər) *n.* **1.** a kind of venomous snake. **2.** a treacherous person. —**vi′per·ous,** *adj.*

vi·ra′go (vi rä′gō, -rā′-) *n., pl.* **-goes, -gos.** a shrewish woman.

vi′ral (vī′rəl) *adj.* of or caused by a virus.

vir′gin (vûr′jin) *n.* **1.** a person who has not had sexual intercourse. **2. the Virgin,** Mary, the mother of Jesus. —*adj.* **3.** of or like a virgin. **4.** untouched; unused. —**vir′gin·al, adj.** —**vir·gin′i·ty,** *n.*

vir′gule (vûr′gyōōl) *n.* an oblique stroke (/) used as a dividing line.

vir′ile (vir′əl) *adj.* **1.** manly. **2.** vigorous. **3.** capable of procreating. —**vi·ril′i·ty,** *n.*

vi·rol′o·gy (vī rol′ə jē, vi-) *n.* the study of viruses. —**vi·rol′o·gist,** *n.*

vir′tu·al (vûr′chōō əl) *adj.* **1.** being such in effect, though not actually. **2.** simulated by a computer.

virtual real′ity *n.* realistic simulation of an environment by a computer system.

vir′tue (vûr′chōō) *n.* **1.** moral excellence. **2.** chastity. **3.** an admirable quality.

vir·tu·o′so (vûr′chōō ō′sō) *n., pl.* **-sos, -si.** a person of special skill, esp. in music. —**vir′tu·os′i·ty** (-os′i tē) *n.*

vir′tu·ous (-əs) *adj.* **1.** conforming to moral principles. **2.** chaste. —**vir′tu·ous·ly,** *adv.*

vir′u·lent (vir′yə lənt, vir′ə-) *adj.* **1.** very poisonous or infectious. **2.** violently hostile. —**vir′u·lence,** *n.*

vi′rus (vī′rəs) *n.* **1.** a tiny infectious agent that causes disease. **2.** a self-replicating code planted illegally in a computer program.

vi′sa (vē′zə) *n.* a passport endorsement permitting the bearer to enter a foreign country.

vis′age (viz′ij) *n.* **1.** the face. **2.** aspect.

vis′-à-vis′ (vē′zä vē′) *prep.* **1.** in relation to. **2.** opposite. —*adv., adj.* **3.** face to face.

vis′cer·a (vis′ər ə) *n.pl.* the internal organs of the body.

vis′cer·al *adj.* **1.** proceeding from instinct rather than intellect. **2.** of the viscera. —**vis′cer·al·ly,** *adv.*

vis′count (vī′kount′) *n.* a nobleman ranking below an earl or count. —**vis′count·ess,** *n.fem.*

vis′cous (vis′kəs) *adj.* sticky; gluey. Also, **vis′cid** (vis′id).

vise (vīs) *n.* a device, usu. with two jaws, for holding an object firmly.

vis′i·bil′i·ty (viz′ə bil′i tē) *n.* the range of vision under given conditions.

vis′i·ble (viz′ə bəl) *adj.* **1.** capable of being seen. **2.** perceptible.

vi′sion (vizh′ən) *n.* **1.** the power or sense of sight. **2.** imagination or unusually keen perception. **3.** a mental image of something imaginary.

vi′sion·ar′y (vizh′ə ner′ē) *adj., pl.* **-ies.** —*adj.* **1.** given to or marked by fanciful or impractical ideas. **2.** seen in a vision. —*n.* **3.** a person of unusual foresight. **4.** a seer of visions. **5.** a dreamer.

vis′it (viz′it) *v.t.* **1.** to go or come to see. **2.** to stay temporarily at. **3.** to afflict. **4.** to access (a Web site). —*v.i.* **5.** to make a visit. —*n.* **6.** an act of visiting. **7.** a stay as a guest. —**vis′i·tor,** *n.*

vis′i·tant, *n.*

vis′it·a′tion (-i tā′shən) *n.* **1.** a formal visit. **2.** a punishment, as from God.

vi′sor (vī′zər) *n.* the projecting front part of a cap, helmet, etc.

vis′ta (vis′tə) *n.* an extended view in one direction.

vis′u·al (vizh′ōō əl) *adj.* **1.** of or used in seeing. **2.** visible.

vis′u·al·ize′ *v.i., v.t.,* **-ized, -izing.** to form a mental image (of). —**vis′u·al·i·za′tion,** *n.*

vi′tal (vīt′l) *adj.* **1.** of or necessary to life. **2.** essential. **3.** energetic.

vi·tal′i·ty (-tal′i tē) *n., pl.* **-ties. 1.** physical or mental vigor. **2.** power to live or grow.

vi′tal signs′ *n.pl.* essential body functions, comprising pulse rate, body temperature, and respiration.

vi′tal statis′tics *n.pl.* statistics concerning deaths, births, and marriages.

vi′ta·min (vī′tə min) *n.* an organic substance found in food and essential to maintain life.

vi′ti·ate′ (vish′ē āt′) *v.t.,* **-ated, -ating. 1.** to impair the quality or effectiveness of. **2.** to make legally invalid.

vit′i·cul′ture (vit′i kul′chər, vī′ti-) *n.* the cultivation of grapes.

vit′re·ous (vi′trē əs) *adj.* of or like glass.

vit′reous hu′mor *n.* the transparent gelatinous substance that fills the eyeball.

vit′ri·fy′ *v.t., v.i.,* **-fied, -fying.** to change into glass.

vi·trine′ (vi trēn′) *n.* a glass cabinet.

vit′ri·ol (vi′trē əl) *n.* **1.** a glassy metallic compound. **2.** sulfuric acid. **3.** savagely caustic criticism. —**vit′ri·ol′ic** (-ol′ik) *adj.*

vi·tu′per·ate′ (vī tōō′pə rāt′, -tyōō′-, vi-) *v.t.,* **-ated, -ating.** to criticize harshly. —**vi·tu′per·a′tion,** *n.* —**vi·tu′per·a′tive,** *adj.*

vi·va′cious (vi vā′shəs, vī-) *adj.* lively. —**vi·vac′i·ty** (-vas′i tē) *n.*

viv′id (viv′id) *adj.* **1.** strikingly bright or intense, as color or an image. **2.** clearly perceptible. **3.** full of life. —**viv′id·ly,** *adv.*

vi·vip′ar·ous (vī vip′ər əs, vi-) *adj.* bringing forth living young rather than eggs.

viv′i·sec′tion (viv′ə sek′shən) *n.* the dissection of a live animal.

vix′en (vik′sən) *n.* **1.** a female fox. **2.** an ill-tempered woman.

vi·zier′ (vi zēr′, viz′yər) *n.* a high official in some Muslim countries.

vo·cab′u·lar′y (vō kab′yə ler′ē) *n., pl.* **-laries. 1.** all the words used by a person or group. **2.** an alphabetical list of defined words.

vo′cal (vō′kəl) *adj.* **1.** of the voice. **2.** of or for singing. **3.** outspoken.

vo′cal cords′ *n.pl.* membranes in the larynx that vibrate to produce sound.

vo′cal·ist (-kə list) *n.* a singer.

vo′cal·ize′ *v.,* **-ized, -iz·ing.** —*v.t.* **1.** to articulate. —*v.i.* **2.** to utter sounds with the vocal cords. —**vo′cal·i·za′tion,** *n.*

vo·ca′tion (vō kā′shən) *n.* an occupation, business, or profession. —**vo·ca′tion·al,** *adj.*

voc′a·tive (vok′ə tiv) *adj.* of or being a grammatical case used to indicate the one being addressed.

vo·cif′er·ate′ (vō sif′ə rāt′) *v.i.,*

v.t., **-ated, -ating.** to cry noisily; shout.

vo·cif′er·ous, *adj.* making a loud or vehement outcry. —**vo·cif′er·ous·ly,** *adv.*

vod′ka (vod′kə) *n.* a colorless distilled liquor made from rye or wheat.

vogue (vōg) *n.* **1.** the current fashion. **2.** popularity.

voice (vois) *n., v.,* **voiced, voicing.** —*n.* **1.** sound uttered through the mouth. **2.** an expressed will or desire. **3.** the right to express an opinion. **4.** a verb form indicating whether the subject is acting or acted upon. —*v.t.* **5.** to express or declare. —**voice′less,** *adj.*

voice′ mail′ *n.* an electronic system that routes voice messages to appropriate recipients.

voice′-o′ver *n.* the voice of an off-screen narrator or announcer.

void (void) *adj.* **1.** without legal force. **2.** useless. **3.** empty. —*n.* **4.** emptiness. —*v.t.* **5.** to invalidate. **6.** to empty. —**void′a·ble,** *adj.*

voile (voil) *n.* a lightweight, semi-sheer fabric.

vol. volume.

vol′a·tile (vol′ə tl) *adj.* **1.** evaporating rapidly. **2.** explosive. **3.** unstable.

vol·ca′no (vol kā′nō) *n., pl.* **-noes, -nos. 1.** a vent in the earth's crust from which lava, steam, and ashes are expelled. **2.** a mountain formed from this lava and ash. —**vol·can′ic** (-kan′ik) *adj.*

vole (vōl) *n.* a short-tailed, stocky rodent.

vo·li′tion (vō lish′ən, və-) *n.* will.

vol′ley (vol′ē) *n.* **1.** a discharge of many missiles together. **2.** a burst of many things at once. **3.** the return of a ball before it hits the ground, as in tennis. —*v.t., v.i.* **4.** to discharge or be discharged in a volley. **5.** to return (a ball) before it hits the ground.

vol′ley·ball′ *n.* **1.** a game in which a large ball is volleyed back and forth over a net. **2.** the ball used in this game.

volt (vōlt) *n.* a unit of electromotive force.

volt′age (vōl′tij) *n.* electromotive force expressed in volts.

volt′me′ter *n.* an instrument for measuring the voltage between two points.

vol′u·ble (vol′yə bəl) *adj.* fluent; talkative. —**vol·u·bil′i·ty,** *n.*

vol′ume (vol′yōōm, -yəm) *n.* **1.** a book. **2.** the amount of space occupied by or contained in an object. **3.** a quantity; mass. **4.** loudness of sound.

vo·lu′mi·nous (və lōō′mə nəs) *adj.* **1.** filling volumes. **2.** of great size.

vol′un·tar′y (vol′ən ter′ē) *adj.* **1.** done, made, given, etc., by free choice and without expecting compensation. **2.** depending on voluntary action. **3.** done by or consisting of volunteers. **4.** controlled by the will. —**vol′un·tar′i·ly,** *adv.*

vol′un·teer′ *n.* **1.** a person who offers to serve or work without expecting payment. —*v.i.* **2.** to offer oneself as a volunteer. —*v.t.* **3.** to offer or perform voluntarily.

vo·lup′tu·ous (və lup′chōō əs) *adj.* **1.** luxurious; sensuous. **2.** full and shapely. —**vo·lup′tu·ous·ly,** *adv.*

vo·lute′ (və lōōt′) *n.* a spiral object.

vom′it (vom′it) *v.i., v.t.* **1.** to eject (the contents of the stomach) through the mouth. **2.** to eject or be ejected with force. —*n.* **3.** vomited matter.

voo′doo (vōō′dōō) *n.* a polytheistic religion deriving chiefly from African cult worship.

vo·ra′cious (vô rā′shəs) *adj.* greedy; ravenous. —**vo·ra′cious·ly,** *adv.* —**vo·rac′i·ty** (-ras′i tē) *n.*

vor′tex (vôr′teks) *n., pl.* **-texes, -tices** (-tə sēz′). a whirling mass or movement.

vo′ta·ry (vō′tə rē) *n., pl.* **-ries.** a worshiper; devotee.

vote (vōt) *n., v.,* **voted, voting.** —*n.* **1.** a formal expression of opinion or choice, as in an election. **2.** the right to this; suffrage. **3.** the number of votes cast. —*v.i.* **4.** to cast one's vote. —*v.t.* **5.** to establish or determine by vote. —**vot′er,** *n.*

vouch (vouch) *v.* **vouch for,** to give a guarantee of the dependability or accuracy of.

vouch′er *n.* a document, receipt, etc., proving an expenditure.

vouch·safe′ *v.t.,* **-safed, -safing.** to grant or give.

vow (vou) *n.* **1.** a solemn promise

or pledge. —*v.t.* **2.** to promise solemnly. —*v.i.* **3.** to make a vow.

vow′el (vou′əl) *n.* **1.** a speech sound made without obstructing the flow of air. **2.** a letter representing a vowel.

voy′age (voi′ij) *n., v.,* **-aged, -aging.** —*n.* **1.** a journey. —*v.i.* **2.** to make a voyage.

vo·yeur′ (vwä yûr′, voi ûr′) *n.* a person who obtains sexual gratification by looking at sexual objects or acts. —**vo·yeur′ism,** *n.*

V.P. Vice President. Also, **VP.**

vs. versus.

VT Vermont. Also, **Vt.**

vul′can·ize′ (vul′kə nīz′) *v.t.,* **-ized, -izing.** to treat (rubber) with sulfur and heat to strengthen it. —**vul′can·i·za′tion,** *n.*

vul′gar (vul′gər) *adj.* **1.** lacking good breeding or taste. **2.** obscene. **3.** of the ordinary people in a society. **4.** expressed in their language. —**vul·gar′i·ty** (-gar′i tē) *n.*

vul′gar·ism *n.* **1.** vulgarity. **2.** a vulgar word.

vul′ner·a·ble (vul′nər ə bəl) *adj.* **1.** liable to physical or emotional hurt. **2.** open to attack.

vul′ture (vul′chər) *n.* a large, carrion-eating bird.

vul′va (vul′və) *n., pl.* **-vae, -vas.** the external female genitalia.

vy′ing (vī′ing) *n.* pres. part. of **vie.**

W

W, w (dub′əl yōō′, -yōō) *n.* the twenty-third letter of the English alphabet.

W west, western.

WA Washington.

wack′y (wak′ē) *adj.,* **-ier, -iest.** *Slang.* odd or irrational.

wad (wod) *n., v.,* **wadded, wadding.** —*n.* **1.** a small soft mass. **2.** a large quantity. —*v.t.* **3.** to form into a wad. **4.** to stuff with a wad.

wad′dle (wod′l) *v.,* **-dled, -dling,** *n.* —*v.i.* **1.** to sway in walking, as a duck. —*n.* **2.** a waddling gait.

wade (wād) *v.i.,* **waded, wading. 1.** to walk through water, mud, snow, etc. **2.** to walk laboriously.

wa′fer (wā′fər) *n.* **1.** a thin crisp biscuit. **2.** a small disk of unleavened bread used in the Eucharist.

waf′fle¹ (wof′əl) *n.* a batter cake baked in a double griddle (**waffle iron**).

waf′fle² (wof′əl) *v.i.,* **-fled, -fling.** to speak or write equivocally.

waft (wäft, waft) *v.t., v.i.* **1.** to float lightly and smoothly through the air. —*n.* **2.** the sound, odor, etc., wafted.

wag (wag) *v.,* **wagged, wagging.** —*v.t., v.i.* **1.** to move rapidly back and forth. —*n.* **2.** the act of wagging. **3.** a witty person. —**wag′gish,** *adj.*

wage (wāj) *n., v.,* **waged, waging.** —*n.* **1.** Often, **wages.** money for work done. **2. wages,** recompense. —*v.t.* **3.** to carry on (an argument, war, etc.).

wa′ger (wā′jər) *n.* **1.** a bet. —*v.t., v.i.* **2.** to bet.

wag′on (wag′ən) *n.* a four-wheeled vehicle for moving heavy loads.

wag′on train′ *n.* a train of wagons and horses.

waif (wāf) *n.* a homeless child.

wail (wāl) *n.* **1.** a long mournful cry. **2.** a sound like this. —*v.i.* **3.** to express sorrow with a long mournful cry.

wain′scot (wān′skət, -skot, -skōt) *n.* wood paneling lining an interior wall.

waist (wāst) *n.* **1.** the narrow part of the body between the ribs and the hips. **2.** the part of a garment covering the waist.

waist′band′ *n.* a band, as on a skirt, encircling the waist.

waist′coat′ (wes′kət, wāst′kōt′) *n. Brit.* a vest.

waist′line′ (wāst′līn′) *n.* the circumference of the body at the waist.

wait (wāt) *v.i.* **1.** to remain inactive until a specified time or until an event occurs. **2.** to be ready. **3.** to await. **4.** to postpone. **5. wait on,** to serve. —*n.* **6.** an act or period of waiting. —*Idiom.* **7. lie in wait,** to lie in ambush.

wait′er *n.* a man who waits on tables. —**wait′ress,** *n.fem.*

wait′ing list′ *n.* a list of persons waiting, as for reservations.

waive (wāv) *v.t.,* **waived, waiving.** to refrain from claiming (a right).

waiv′er *n.* a statement relinquishing a right.

wake¹ (wāk) *v.,* **waked** or **woke** (wōk), **waked, waking.** —*v.i.* **1.** to become roused from sleep. **2.** to become aware of something. —*v.t.* **3.** to rouse from sleep. —*n.* **4.** a vigil beside a corpse awaiting burial.

wake² (wāk) *n.* the track of waves left by a vessel.

wake′ful *adj.* awake; alert.

wak′en *v.t., v.i.* to awake; awaken.

wale (wāl) *n., v.,* **waled, waling.** —*n.* **1.** a mark left on the skin by a rod or whip. **2.** a vertical cord in fabric. —*v.t.* **3.** to mark with wales.

walk (wôk) *v.i.* **1.** to move on foot at a moderate pace. —*v.t.* **2.** to go along, through, or over on foot. **3.** to cause or help to walk. —*n.* **4.** an act, course, or manner of walking. **5.** a distance walked. **6.** a sidewalk or path. **7.** a line of work or position in society.

walk′a·way′ *n.* an easy victory.

walk′ie-talk′ie (wô′kē tô′kē) *n.* a portable radio transmitter and receiver.

walk′ing stick′ *n.* **1.** a stick used for support in walking. **2.** an insect with a long twiglike body.

walk′out′ *n.* a strike in which workers leave their place of work.

wall (wôl) *n.* **1.** an upright structure that divides, encloses, etc. **2.** a barrier or obstruction. —*v.t.* **3.** to enclose, divide, etc., with a wall.

wall′board′ *n.* artificial material used to make or cover walls.

wal′let (wol′it) *n.* a small flat case for paper money, cards, etc.

wall′eye′ (wôl′-) *n.* **1.** a N American freshwater food fish. **2.** a condition in which the eye or eyes are turned outward.

wall′flow′er *n.* **1.** a shy person who remains at the side at a party. **2.** a plant with fragrant yellow or orange flowers.

Wal·loon′ (wo lōōn′) *n.* a member of the French-speaking population of S and E Belgium.

wal′lop (wol′əp) *Informal.* —*v.t.* **1.** to thrash or defeat. —*n.* **2.** a hard blow.

wal′lop·ing *adj. Informal.* **1.** very large. **2.** impressive.

wal′low (wol′ō) *v.i.* **1.** to roll around, as in mud. **2.** to indulge oneself.

wall′pa′per *n.* decorative paper for covering walls and ceilings.

wal′nut′ (wôl′nut′, -nət) *n.* a meaty edible nut with a wrinkled shell.

wal′rus (wôl′rəs) *n.* a large tusked mammal of Arctic seas.

waltz (wôlts) *n.* **1.** a ballroom dance in triple rhythm. —*v.i., v.t.* **2.** to dance a waltz (with).

wam′pum (wom′pəm) *n.* shell beads, formerly used by North American Indians as money.

wan (won) *adj.,* **wanner, wannest.** pale; worn-looking. —**wan′ly,** *adv.*

wand (wond) *n.* a slender rod, as one used by a magician.

wan′der (won′dər) *v.i.* **1.** to roam from one place to another without a definite purpose. **2.** to go astray. —*v.t.* **3.** to travel about, on, or through. —**wan′der·er,** *n.*

wan′der·lust′ *n.* a strong desire to travel.

wane (wān) *v.,* **waned, waning,** *n.* —*v.i.* **1.** to decline or decrease. —*n.* **2.** a decline or decrease.

wan′gle (wang′gəl) *v.t.,* **-gled, -gling.** to bring out or obtain by scheming or underhand methods.

Wan′kel engine (wäng′kəl) *n.* an internal-combustion rotary engine with a triangular motor that revolves in a chamber.

wan′na·be′ (won′ə bē′) *n. Informal.* one who aspires, often vainly, to emulate another's success or status.

want (wont) *v.t.* **1.** to feel a need or desire for. **2.** to lack; be deficient in. —*v.i.* **3.** to have a need. —*n.* **4.** lack. **5.** poverty.

want′ing *adj., prep.* lacking.

wan′ton (won′tn) *adj.* **1.** malicious or unjustifiable. **2.** unrestrained. —*n.* **3.** a wanton person.

war (wôr) *n., v.,* **warred, warring.** —*n.* **1.** armed conflict. —*v.t.* **2.** to make or carry on war.

war′ble (wôr′bəl) *v.,* **-bled, -bling,** *n.* —*v.i., v.t.* **1.** to sing with trills, as birds. —*n.* **2.** a warbled song.

war′bler *n.* a small songbird, often brightly colored.

ward (wôrd) n. 1. a division of a city. 2. a division of a hospital. 3. a person under the legal care of a guardian or court. 4. custody. —v. 5. **ward off**, to repel or avert.

ward'en (wôr'dn) n. 1. a keeper. 2. the head of a prison.

ward'er n. a guard.

ward'robe' n. 1. a collection of clothes. 2. a clothes closet.

ward'room' n. the living quarters for all ship's officers other than the captain.

ware (wâr) n. 1. **wares**, goods for sale. 2. a particular kind of merchandise.

ware'house' n., v., -housed, -housing. —n. (wâr'hous') 1. a storehouse for goods or merchandise. —v.t. (-houz', -hous') 2. to place or store in a warehouse.

war'fare' n. the waging of war.

war'head' n. the section of a missile containing the explosive.

war'-horse' n. Informal. a veteran of many conflicts.

war'like' adj. fond of or threatening war.

war'lock' n. a male witch.

warm (wôrm) adj. 1. having, giving, or feeling moderate heat. 2. friendly; affectionate. 3. heated or angry. —v.t., v.i. 4. to make or become warm. —**warmth**, n.

warm'-blood'ed adj. (of an animal) having a relatively constant body temperature that is independent of the environment.

warmed'-o'ver adj. 1. reheated. 2. stale; not new.

warm'heart'ed adj. having emotional warmth.

war'mong'er (wôr'mung'ər, -mong'-) n. a person who advocates war.

warn (wôrn) v.t. 1. to give advance notice of danger, evil, etc. 2. to advise to be careful. —**warn'ing**, n., adj.

warp (wôrp) v.t. 1. to bend out of shape; distort. —v.i. 2. to become warped. —n. 3. a bend or twist. 4. the lengthwise threads in a loom.

war'rant (wôr'ənt) n. 1. justification or authorization. 2. a guarantee. 3. a document authorizing something. —v.t. 4. to authorize or justify. 5. to guarantee.

war'rant of'ficer n. a military officer ranking below a commissioned officer.

war'ran•ty n., pl. -ties. a written guarantee.

war'ren (wôr'ən) n. a place where rabbits live.

war'ri•or (wôr'ē ər) n. a soldier.

war'ship' n. a ship armed for combat.

wart (wôrt) n. a small hard growth on the skin. —**wart'y**, adj.

war'y (wâr'ē) adj., -ier, -iest. 1. watchful. 2. careful. —**war'i•ly**, adv.

was (wuz, woz; unstressed wəz) v. the first and third pers. sing., past indicative of **be**.

wash (wosh) v.t. 1. to cleanse with liquid, esp. water. 2. to flow through or over. 3. to carry in flowing. 4. to overlay with a thin coating, as of paint. —v.i. 5. to wash oneself, clothes, etc. 6. to be carried by water. —n. 7. the act of washing. 8. Also, **wash'ing.** items to be washed. 9. a liquid covering. 10. rough water or air behind a moving ship or plane. —**wash'a•ble**, adj.

Wash. Washington.

wash'board' n. a board to scrub clothes on.

wash'bowl' n. a large bowl for washing the hands and face. Also, **wash'ba•sin.**

wash'cloth' n. a cloth for washing the face or body.

washed'-out' adj. 1. faded. 2. Informal. weary or tired-looking.

washed'-up' adj. Informal. done for; having failed.

wash'er n. 1. a machine for washing. 2. a flat ring of rubber, metal, etc., used under a bolt to give tightness.

wash'out' n. 1. a washing out of earth by water. 2. Slang. a failure.

wash'room' n. a room with washbowls and toilets.

wasn't (wuz'ənt, woz'-) a contraction of **was not.**

wasp (wosp) n. a slender winged stinging insect.

WASP (wosp) n. a white Anglo-Saxon Protestant. Also, **Wasp.**

wasp'ish adj. irritable; snappish.

was'sail (wos'əl, wo säl') n. 1. a toast to a person's health. 2. a festivity with much drinking.

waste (wāst) v., wasted, wasting, n., adj. —v.t. 1. to spend or consume uselessly or carelessly. 2. to fail to use. 3. to make weak. —v.i. 4. to be consumed or spent uselessly or carelessly. 5. to become gradually used up. 6. to become weak. —n. 7. useless expenditure. 8. neglect. 9. gradual decay. 10. devastation or a devastated area. 11. anything left over. —adj. 12. not used. 13. left over or worthless. 14. desolate. —**waste'ful**, adj.

waste'land' n. barren land.

wast'rel (wā'strəl) n. 1. a spendthrift. 2. an idler.

watch (woch) v.i. 1. to look attentively. 2. to be careful. 3. to remain vigilant. —v.t. 4. to view attentively. 5. to guard. 6. **watch out**, to be on one's guard. —n. 7. close, constant observation. 8. a guard. 9. a period of watching. 10. a small timepiece. —**watch'ful**, adj.

watch'band' n. a band for holding a wristwatch on the wrist.

watch'dog' n. 1. a dog that guards property. 2. a guardian, as against illegal conduct.

watch'man n. a person who keeps watch.

watch'tow'er n. a tower for a guard.

watch'word' n. 1. a password. 2. a slogan.

wa'ter (wô'tər) n. 1. an odorless, tasteless liquid composed of hydrogen and oxygen that forms rivers, seas, lakes, rain, etc. 2. a body of water. 3. **waters**, the sea that borders and is controlled by a country. 4. a liquid organic secretion. —v.t. 5. to sprinkle or supply with water. 6. to dilute. —v.i. 7. to fill with or secrete water. —adj. 8. of, for, or powered by water.

wa'ter•bed' n. a bed with a liquid-filled mattress.

wa'ter buf'falo n. a domesticated Asian buffalo with curved horns.

wa'ter chest'nut n. an aquatic plant with an edible, nutlike fruit.

wa'ter clos'et n. a room containing a flush toilet.

wa'ter•col'or n. 1. a pigment mixed with water. 2. a painting using such pigments.

wa'ter•course' n. 1. a stream of water. 2. the bed of a stream.

wa'ter•cress' n. a plant that grows in streams and bears pungent leaves used in salad.

wa'ter•fall' n. a steep fall of water from a height.

wa'ter•fowl' n., pl. -fowl, -fowls. an aquatic bird.

wa'ter•front' n. a part of a city on the edge of a body of water.

wa'ter gap' n. a transverse gap in a mountain ridge.

wa'tering place' n. a resort by the water or having mineral springs.

wa'ter lil'y n. an aquatic plant with showy flowers.

wa'ter line' n. one of a series of lines on a ship's hull indicating the level to which it is immersed.

wa'ter•logged' adj. filled or soaked with water.

wa'ter•mark' n. 1. a design impressed on paper that is visible when light shines through it. 2. a mark showing the height to which water has risen. —v.t. 3. to put a watermark in (paper).

wa'ter•mel'on n. a large melon with sweet red pulp.

wa'ter moc'casin n. the cottonmouth.

wa'ter•proof' adj. 1. impervious to water. —v.t. 2. to make waterproof.

wa'ter rat' n. an aquatic rodent, as the muskrat.

wa'ter-repel'lent adj. repelling water but not entirely waterproof.

wa'ter•shed' n. 1. an area drained by a river or stream. 2. a ridge dividing such areas. 3. an important point of division or transition.

wa'ter ski' n. a short, broad ski for gliding over water while being towed by a boat. —**wa'ter-ski'**, v.i. —**wa'ter-ski'er**, n.

wa'ter•spout' n. a tornadolike storm over a lake or ocean.

wa'ter ta'ble n. the underground level beneath which soil and rock are saturated with water.

wa'ter•tight' adj. 1. constructed or fitted to be impervious to water. 2. allowing no doubt.

wa'ter•way' n. a body of water as a route of travel.

wa'ter wheel' n. a wheel turned by water to provide power for machinery.

wa'ter•works' n.pl. a system by which water is collected, stored, purified, and pumped for a city.

wa'ter•y adj. of, like, or full of water.

watt (wot) n. a unit of electric power.

wat'tle¹ (wot'l) n. flesh hanging from the throat or chin of certain birds, as the turkey.

wat'tle² (wot'l) n. interwoven rods and twigs, used for making walls and fences.

wave (wāv) n., v., waved, waving. —n. 1. a moving ridge on the surface of water. 2. a surge; rush. 3. an outward curve. 4. a wavelike vibration, as in the transmission of sound or light. 5. a sign with a moving hand, flag, etc. —v.i. 6. to move back and forth or up and down. 7. to curve. 8. to signal by moving the hand. —v.t. 9. to cause to wave. 10. to express by a waving movement. —Idiom. 11. **make waves**, Informal. to disturb the status quo. —**wav'y**, adj.

wave'length' n. the distance between two successive points in a wave, as of light or sound.

wa'ver (wā'vər) v.i. 1. to be unsteady. 2. to flicker or quiver. 3. to feel or show indecision.

wax¹ (waks) n. 1. a solid, yellowish substance secreted by bees. 2. any similar substance. —v.t. 3. to rub or polish with wax. —**wax'en**, adj. —**wax'y**, adj.

wax² (waks) v.i. 1. to increase. 2. to become.

wax' bean' n. a variety of string bean bearing yellowish, waxy pods.

wax' muse'um n. a museum displaying wax effigies of famous persons.

wax' myr'tle n. a bayberry of the southeastern U.S.

wax' pa'per n. paper made moisture-resistant by a paraffin coating.

wax'wing' n. a small crested songbird with red-tipped wing feathers.

way (wā) n. 1. a method or means. 2. manner. 3. a direction. 4. a road or route. 5. space for passing. 6. condition. —Idiom. 7. **by the way**, incidentally. 8. **by way of**, by the route of; through. 9. **give way**, a. to yield. b. to collapse.

way'bill' n. a list of goods with shipping directions.

way'far'er n. a traveler.

way'lay' (wā'lā', wā lā') v.t., -laid, -laying. to lie in wait for.

way'-out' adj. Informal. very unconventional.

ways' and means' n.pl. methods of raising revenue.

way'side' n. land next to a road.

way'ward (-wərd) adj. stubbornly willful.

we (wē) pron. the nominative plural of **I**.

weak (wēk) adj. 1. not strong; frail. 2. lacking in strength, force, intensity, etc. 3. deficient. —**weak'en**, v.t., v.i. —**weak'ly**, adv. —**weak'ness**, n.

weak'-kneed' adj. yielding readily to opposition or intimidation.

weak'ling (-ling) n. a weak creature.

weal (wēl) n. well-being.

wealth (welth) n. 1. abundance of possessions or riches. 2. plentiful amount. —**wealth'y**, adj.

wean (wēn) v.t. 1. to accustom (a child or young animal) to food other than the mother's milk. 2. to rid of an undesirable object or habit.

weap'on (wep'ən) n. 1. a device for attack or defense. 2. something used against an adversary.

weap'on•ry n. weapons collectively.

wear (wâr) v., wore (wôr), worn, wearing, n. —v.t. 1. to have on the body for covering or ornament. 2. to cause to deteriorate gradually through use. 3. to fatigue. —v.i. 4. to deteriorate from use. 5. to withstand continued use. 6. **wear down**, to overcome by persistence. 7. **~ off**, to diminish gradually. —n. 8. a wearing or being worn. 9. clothing of a specific kind. 10. gradual deterioration. 11. durability. —**wear'a•ble**, adj.

wea'ri•some (wēr'ē səm) adj. tiring or tedious.

wea'ry (wēr'ē) adj., -rier, -riest, v., -ried, -rying. —adj. 1. tired. 2. dissatisfied. —v.t., v.i. 3. to make or become tired. —**wea'ri•ly**, adv.

wea'sel (wē'zəl) n. a small flesh-eating animal with a long, slender body.

weath'er (weth'ər) n. 1. the state of the atmosphere with respect to moisture, temperature, etc. —v.t. 2. to expose to weather. 3. to withstand. —v.i. 4. to endure exposure to the weather.

weath'er-beat'en adj. worn or marked by weather.

weath'er•ing n. the action of wind and water on exposed rock.

weath'er•ize' v.t., -ized, -izing. to make secure against cold weather.

weath'er•proof' adj. 1. able to withstand all kinds of weather. —v.t. 2. to make weatherproof.

weath'er•vane' n. a device to show the direction of the wind.

weave (wēv) v., wove (wōv), woven or wove, weaving, n. —v.t. 1. to interlace (threads, strands, etc.) so as to form cloth. 2. to form by weaving. 3. to combine into a connected whole. —v.i. 4. to make something by weaving. 5. to move in a winding course. —n. 6. a pattern or method of weaving. —**weav'er**, n.

web (web) n., v., webbed, webbing. —n. 1. something woven. 2. a cobweb. 3. something that entangles. 4. a membrane between the toes of ducks, geese, etc. 5. **the Web**, the World Wide Web. —v.t. 6. to cover with a web.

web'foot' n. a foot with webbed toes. —**web'foot'ed**, adj.

Web'mas'ter (web'mas'tər, -mä-stər) n. a person who designs or maintains a Web site.

Web' site' n. a group of pages on the World Wide Web devoted to one topic or several related topics. Also, **web'site/.**

Web'ster (web'stər) n. a dictionary of the English language. Also, **Web'ster's.**

wed (wed) v.t., v.i., wedded, wedded or wed, wedding. 1. to marry. 2. to unite.

Wed. Wednesday.

wed'ding n. a marriage ceremony.

wedge (wej) n., v., wedged, wedging. —n. 1. a tapered triangular piece of hard material. 2. something that splits or divides. —v.t. 3. to split with a wedge. 4. to pack tightly into a space. —v.i. 5. to force a way like a wedge.

wed'lock n. the state of being married.

Wednes'day (wenz'dā, -dē) n. the fourth day of the week.

wee (wē) adj. tiny.

weed (wēd) n. 1. an undesirable plant growing in cultivated ground. —v.t. 2. to free from weeds. 3. to remove as undesirable. —v.i. 4. to remove weeds. —**weed'y**, adj.

weeds (wēdz) n.pl. black clothes for mourning.

week (wēk) n. 1. a period of seven successive days. 2. the working part of a week.

week'day' n. any day except Sunday, or, often, Saturday and Sunday.

week'end' (-end', -end') n. the period between Friday evening and Monday morning.

week'ly adj., adv., n., pl. -lies. —adj. 1. happening, appearing, etc., once a week. 2. lasting a week. —adv. 3. once a week. —n. 4. a weekly periodical.

weep (wēp) v.i., wept (wept), weeping. to shed tears.

wee'vil (wē'vəl) n. a beetle destructive to grain, fruit, etc.

weft (weft) n. (in weaving) the woof.

weigh (wā) v.t. 1. to measure the heaviness of. 2. to consider. —v.i. 3. to have weight or importance. 4. to bear down as a burden.

weight (wāt) n. 1. amount of heaviness. 2. a system of units for expressing weight. 3. a unit of heaviness or mass. 4. a solid mass. 5. a burden. 6. importance. —v.t. 7. to add weight to. —**weight'y**, adj. —**weight'less**, adj.

weir (wēr) n. 1. a dam in a stream. 2. a fence set in a stream to catch fish.

weird (wērd) adj. 1. supernatural. 2. strange; peculiar.

weird'o (wēr'dō) n., pl. -os. Slang. an odd or eccentric person.

wel'come (wel'kəm) n., v., -comed, -coming, adj. —n. 1. a friendly reception. —v.t. 2. to receive or greet with pleasure. —adj. 3. gladly received. 4. given permission or consent.

weld (weld) v.t. to unite, esp. by heating and pressing. —n. 2. a welded joint. —**weld'er**, n.

wel'fare' (wel'fâr') n. 1. well being. 2. assistance given, esp. by the government, to those in need.

well¹ (wel) adv., compar. **better**, superl. **best**, adj. —adv. 1. in a good or satisfactory manner. 2. excellently; properly. 3. thoroughly. 4. with approval. 5. with good reason. —adj. 6. in good health. 7. satisfactory or good.

well² (wel) n. 1. a hole drilled in the earth to reach water, oil, etc. 2. a natural or abundant source. 3. a vertical shaft for air, stairs, or an elevator. —v.i. 4. to rise or gush.

well'-ad•vised' adj. prudent.

well'-ap•point'ed adj. attractively furnished.

well'-be'ing n. a good or prosperous condition.

well'-born' adj. of good family.

well'-bred' adj. showing good manners.

well'-dis•posed' adj. feeling favorable, sympathetic, or kind.

well'-done' adj. 1. done accurately and skillfully. 2. thoroughly cooked.

well'-found'ed adj. based on good reasons, sound information, etc.

well'-ground'ed adj. having good basic knowledge of a subject.

well'-heeled' adj. prosperous.

well'-in•formed' adj. having extensive knowledge.

well'man'nered adj. polite.

well'-mean'ing adj. having good intentions. —**well'-meant'**, adj.

well'-nigh' adv. very nearly.

well'-off' adj. 1. prosperous. 2. in a good or favorable condition.

well'-round'ed adj. desirably varied.

well'spring' n. a source.

well'-to-do' adj. wealthy.

well'-worn' adj. 1. showing the effects of extensive use. 2. trite.

Welsh (welsh, welch) adj. 1. of Wales, its people, or its language. —n. 2. the people or language of Wales.

welt (welt) n. 1. a ridge on the skin, as from a blow. 2. a strip around the edge of a shoe. 3. a strip or cord sewn along a seam.

wel'ter (wel'tər) v.i. 1. to toss or roll, as waves. 2. to wallow. —n. 3. a confused mass.

wen (wen) n. a small cyst.

wench (wench) n. a girl or young woman.

wend (wend) v. **wend one's way**, to go.

went (went) v. pt. of **go**.

were (wûr; unstressed wər) v. plural and pres. subjunctive of **be**.

weren't (wûrnt, wûr'ənt) a contraction of **were not**.

were'wolf' (wâr'wŏŏlf', wēr'wŏŏlf', wûr'-) n., pl. -wolves. (in folklore) a human turned into a wolf.

west (west) n. 1. a cardinal point of the compass, the direction in which the sun sets. 2. **the West**, a region in this direction. —adj., adv. 3. toward, in, or from the west.

West'ern Hem'isphere n. the half of the globe that includes North and South America.

west'ern•ize' (wes'tər nīz') v.t., -ized, -izing. to influence with western ideas and customs.

west'ward (-wərd) adv. 1. toward the west. —adj. 2. moving or facing toward the west.

wet (wet) adj., wetter, wettest, n., v., wet or wetted, wetting. —adj. 1. covered or soaked with water. 2. rainy. —n. 3. moisture. 4. wet weather. —v.t., v.i. 5. to make or become wet.

wet' blan'ket n. one that dampens enthusiasm.

wet' nurse' n. a woman hired to suckle another's infant.

wet' suit' n. a close-fitting rubber suit worn for body warmth, as by scuba divers.

whack (hwak, wak) Informal. —v.t., v.i. 1. to strike sharply. —n. 2. a smart blow.

whale (hwāl, wāl) n., pl. **whales**, **whale**, v., whaled, whaling. —n. 1. a large marine mammal with a fishlike body. —v.i. 2. to hunt and kill whales.

whale'bone' n. an elastic horny substance in the upper jaw of some whales.

wharf (hwôrf, wôrf) n., pl. **wharves**. a structure where ships moor to load and unload.

wharf'age n. 1. the use of a wharf. 2. a charge for such use.

what (hwut, hwot, wut, wot; *unstressed* hwət, wət) *pron.* **1.** (used as a request for information). **2.** (used to ask about the character, identity, or worth of a person or thing). **3.** how much? **4.** that which. **5.** as much or as many. **6.** (used interrogatively before nouns). **7.** whatever or whichever. —*adv.* **8.** to what extent or degree?

what·ev'er *pron.* **1.** anything that. **2.** no matter what. —*adj.* **3.** no matter what. —*interj.* **4.** (used to indicate indifference).

what'not' *n.* a small open cupboard for knickknacks.

what'so·ev'er *pron., adj.* whatever.

wheat (hwēt, wēt) *n.* the grain of a common cereal grass, used esp. for flour.

whee'dle (hwēd'l, wēd'l) *v.t., v.i.,* **-dled, -dling.** to influence (a person) by flattery.

wheel (hwēl, wēl) *n.* **1.** a circular frame or disk turning on an axis. —*v.t., v.i.* **2.** to turn, rotate, or revolve. **3.** to move on wheels.

wheel'bar'row *n.* a one-wheeled cart for conveying small loads.

wheel'base' *n.* the distance between the front and rear axles.

wheel'chair' *n.* a chair mounted on wheels for use by persons who cannot walk.

wheeze (hwēz, wēz) *v.,* **wheezed, wheezing,** *n.* —*v.i.* **1.** to breathe with difficulty and with a whistling sound. —*n.* **2.** a wheezing breath.

whelp (hwelp, welp) *n.* **1.** the young of a dog, wolf, bear, etc. —*v.t., v.i.* **2.** to give birth to (whelps).

when (hwen, wen; *unstressed* hwən, wən) *adv.* **1.** at what time? —*conj.* **2.** at what time. **3.** at the time that. —*pron.* **4.** what or which time.

whence (hwens, wens) *adv., conj.* from what place, source, or cause?

when·ev'er *adv.* at whatever time.

where (hwâr, wâr) *adv.* **1.** in, at, or to what place? **2.** in what respect? —*conj.* **3.** in, at, or to what place or situation. —*pron.* **4.** what place? **5.** the place in or point at which.

where'a·bouts' *adv.* **1.** about where? —*n.* **2.** the place where someone or something is.

where·as' *conj.* **1.** while on the contrary. **2.** considering that.

where·by' *conj.* by what or which; under the terms of which.

where'fore' *adv., conj.* **1.** for that cause or reason. **2.** *Archaic.* why? —*n.* **3.** a reason.

where·in' *conj.* **1.** in what or in which. —*adv.* **2.** in what way or respect?

where·of' *adv., conj.* of what.

where'up·on' *conj.* **1.** upon which. **2.** at or after which.

wher·ev'er *conj.* in, at, or to whatever place or circumstance.

where'with·al' (-with ôl', -with-) *n.* means with which to do something.

wher'ry (hwer'ē, wer'ē) *n., pl.* **-ries.** a light rowboat for one person.

whet (hwet, wet) *v.t.,* **whetted, whetting. 1.** to sharpen. **2.** to stimulate (appetite, interest, etc.).

wheth'er (hweth'ər, weth'-) *conj.* (used to introduce an alternative).

whet'stone' *n.* a stone for sharpening blades by friction.

whey (hwā, wā) *n.* the watery part of curdled milk.

which (hwich, wich) *pron.* **1.** what one or ones? **2.** the one that. —*adj.* **3.** what one or ones of (those mentioned).

which·ev'er *pron.* any that.

whiff (hwif, wif) *n.* a slight puff or trace.

while (hwīl, wīl) *n., conj., v.,* **whiled, whiling.** —*n.* **1.** an interval of time. —*conj.* **2.** during the time that. **3.** even though. —*v.* **4.** while away, to cause (time) to pass pleasantly.

whim (hwim, wim) *n.* an irrational or fanciful decision or idea.

whim'per (hwim'pər, wim'-) *v.i., v.t.* **1.** to cry softly and plaintively. —*n.* **2.** a whimpering cry.

whim'sy (hwim'zē, wim'-) *n., pl.* **-sies.** a fanciful idea; whim. —**whim'si·cal,** *adj.*

whine (hwīn, wīn) *v.,* **whined, whining,** *n.* —*v.i., v.t.* **1.** to utter (with) a low, nasal complaining sound. —*n.* **2.** a whining sound or complaint.

whin'ny (hwin'ē, win'ē) *n., pl.* **-nies,** *v.,* **-nied, -nying.** —*n.* **1.** a gentle neigh. —*v.i.* **2.** to utter a whinny.

whip (hwip, wip) *v.,* **whipped,**

whipping, *n.* —*v.t.* **1.** to strike repeatedly or flog as punishment. **2.** to move, pull, or seize suddenly. **3.** to defeat. **4.** to beat to a froth. —*v.i.* **5.** to move quickly and suddenly; lash about. —*n.* **6.** an instrument with a lash and a handle for striking a person or animal. **7.** a party manager in a legislature.

whip'cord' *n.* a fabric with diagonal ribs.

whip'lash' *n.* **1.** the lash of a whip. **2.** a neck injury caused by a sudden jerking of the head.

whip'per·snap'per (hwip'ər-snap'ər, wip'-) *n.* an insignificant but presumptuous person.

whip'pet (hwip'it, wip'-) *n.* a type of slender swift dog.

whip'poor·will' (hwip'ər wil', wip'-) *n.* a nocturnal American bird.

whir (hwûr, wûr) *v.,* **whirred, whirring,** *n.* —*v.i., v.t.* **1.** to move quickly with a humming sound. —*n.* **2.** such a sound.

whirl (hwûrl, wûrl) *v.i.* **1.** to spin or turn rapidly. **2.** to move quickly. —*v.t.* **3.** to cause to whirl. —*n.* **4.** a whirling movement. **5.** a rapid round of events. **6.** an attempt.

whirl'i·gig' (hwûr'lē gig', wûr'-) *n.* a toy that spins in the wind.

whirl'pool' *n.* water in a swift circular downward motion.

whirl'wind' (-wind') *n.* a whirling mass of air.

whisk (hwisk, wisk) *v.t.* **1.** to move with a rapid sweeping stroke. **2.** to move or carry lightly. **3.** to whip or blend with a whisk. —*n.* **4.** the act of whisking. **5.** a wire implement for beating food.

whisk'er *n.* **1.** one of the long bristly hairs growing near the mouth of some animals, as the cat. **2. whiskers,** the hair on a man's face.

whis'key (hwis'kē, wis'-) *n.* a distilled alcoholic liquor made from grain or corn. Also, **whis'ky.**

whis'per (hwis'pər, wis'pər) *v.i., v.t.* **1.** to speak or utter very softly. —*n.* **2.** the sound of whispering. **3.** something whispered.

whist (hwist, wist) *n.* a card game that is an early form of bridge.

whis'tle (hwis'əl, wis'-) *v.,* **-tled, -tling,** *n.* —*v.i.* **1.** to make a high clear sound with breath, air, or steam. —*n.* **2.** a device for making such sounds. **3.** the sound of whistling.

whis'tle-blow'er *n.* a person who publicly discloses wrongdoing.

whis'tle stop' *n.* a small town.

whit (hwit, wit) *n.* a particle; bit.

white (hwīt, wīt) *adj.* **1.** of the color of pure snow. **2.** having light skin. **3.** pale. —*n.* **4.** a color without hue that is the opposite of black. **5.** a light-skinned person. **6.** a white or light material or part. —**whit'en,** *v.t., v.i.*

white' blood' cell' *n.* a nearly colorless blood cell of the immune system.

white'-bread' *adj.* bland; conventional.

white'cap' *n.* a wave with a foaming white crest.

white'-col'lar *adj.* of professional or office workers whose jobs usu. do not involve manual labor.

white' el'ephant *n.* a possession of no use to the owner but of use to another.

white'fish' *n.* a small freshwater food fish.

white' flag' *n.* an all-white flag used to signal surrender or truce.

white' gold' *n.* a gold alloy colored white esp. by the presence of nickel.

white' goods' *n.pl.* household linens.

white' lie' *n.* a small, harmless lie.

white'wash' *n.* **1.** a substance for whitening walls, woodwork, etc. —*v.t.* **2.** to cover with whitewash. **3.** to cover the faults or errors of.

white' wa'ter *n.* frothy water, as in rapids.

whith'er (hwith'ər, with'-) *adv., conj.* **1.** to what place, point, end, or action? —*conj.* **2.** to which or whatever place.

whit'ing¹ (hwī'ting, wī'-) *n.* a small Atlantic food fish.

whit'ing² (hwī'ting, wī'-) *n.* pure-white chalk powder.

whit'low (hwit'lō, wit'-) *n.* an inflammation on a finger or toe.

Whit'sun·day (hwit'sun dā', -dē, -sən dā', wit'-) *n.* Pentecost.

whit'tle (hwit'l, wit'-) *v.t.,* **-tled, -tling.** —*v.t.* **1.** to cut, trim, or shape (wood) bit by bit with a knife. **2.** to

reduce. —*v.i.* **3.** to whittle wood. —**whit'tler,** *n.*

whiz (hwiz, wiz) *v.,* **whizzed, whizzing,** *n.* —*v.i.* **1.** to move with a humming, buzzing, or hissing sound. —*n.* **2.** a whizzing sound. **3.** *Informal.* a person who is very good at something. Also, **whizz.**

who (hōō) *pron.* **1.** what person? **2.** the person that.

whoa (hwō, wō) *interj.* (a command to stop).

who·dun'it (-dun'it) *n.* a detective story.

who·ev'er *pron.* anyone that.

whole (hōl) *adj.* **1.** entire; total; complete; undivided. **2.** not damaged or injured. **3.** *Math.* not fractional. —*n.* **4.** the entire amount or extent. **5.** a complete thing. —**whol'ly,** *adv.* —**whole'ness,** *n.*

whole'-heart'ed *adj.* sincere.

whole' note' *n. Music.* a note equal in time value to four quarter notes.

whole'sale' *n., adj., v.,* **-saled, -saling.** —*n.* **1.** the sale of goods in quantity, as to retailers. —*adj.* **2.** of or engaged in sale by wholesale. —*v.t., v.i.* **3.** to sell by wholesale. —**whole'sal'er,** *n.*

whole'some (-səm) *adj.* healthful.

whole'-wheat' *adj.* prepared with the complete wheat kernel.

whom (hōōm) *pron.* the objective case of **who.**

whom·ev'er *pron.* the objective case of **whoever.**

whoop (hwōōp, hwŏŏp, wōōp, wŏŏp; *esp. for 2* hōŏp, hŏŏp) *n.* **1.** a loud shout or cry. **2.** a gasping sound characteristic of whooping cough. —*v.i., v.t.* **3.** to utter (with) a loud cry.

whoop'ing cough' (hōō'ping, hŏŏp'ing) *n.* an infectious disease characterized by short, convulsive coughs followed by whoops.

whop'per (hwop'ər, wop'-) *n. Informal.* **1.** something very large. **2.** a big lie.

whop'ping *adj. Informal.* very large.

whore (hôr; *often* hŏŏr) *n.* a prostitute.

whorl (hwûrl, hwôrl, wûrl, wôrl) *n.* a circular arrangement; spiral.

whose (hōōz) *pron.* the possessive case of **who.**

who'so·ev'er *pron.* whoever.

why (hwī, wī) *adv., conj., n., pl.* **whys.** —*adv.* **1.** for what reason or purpose? **2.** for what cause. **3.** the reason for which. —*n.* **4.** the cause or reason.

WI Wisconsin.

wick (wik) *n.* a twist of soft threads that absorb fuel and burn in a candle, lamp, etc.

wick'ed (wik'id) *adj.* **1.** morally bad; evil; sinful. **2.** harmful. **3.** very unpleasant. —**wick'ed·ly,** *adv.*

wick'er *n.* **1.** a slender, pliant twig. **2.** things made of wicker. —*adj.* **3.** made of wicker. —**wick'er·work',** *n.*

wick'et (wik'it) *n.* **1.** a small gate or opening. **2.** a hoop in croquet. **3.** a framework in cricket.

wide (wīd) *adj.,* **wider, widest,** *adv.* —*adj.* **1.** of great size from side to side; broad. **2.** having a specified width. **3.** of great range. **4.** far from an objective. —*adv.* **5.** to the utmost. **6.** away from an objective. **7.** over a large area. —**wide'ly,** *adv.* —**wid'en,** *v.t., v.i.*

wide'-awake' *adj.* **1.** fully awake. **2.** alert or observant.

wide'-eyed' *adj.* with the eyes open wide, in amazement or innocence.

wide'spread' *adj.* occurring or distributed over a wide area.

wid'ow (wid'ō) *n.* **1.** a woman whose husband has died. —*v.t.* **2.** to make a widow of. —**wid'ow·er,** *n.masc.* —**wid'ow·hood,** *n.*

width (width, witth) *n.* **1.** extent from side to side; breadth. **2.** something of a specific width.

wield (wēld) *v.t.* **1.** to exercise (power, influence, etc.). **2.** to handle.

wie'ner (wē'nər) *n.* a small sausage; frankfurter.

wife (wīf) *n., pl.* **wives** (wīvz) a married woman. —**wife'ly,** *adj.*

wig (wig) *n.* a covering of natural or artificial hair for the head.

wi'geon (wij'ən) *n., pl.* **-eons,-eon.** a freshwater duck.

wig'gle (wig'əl) *v.,* **-gled, -gling,** *n.* —*v.i., v.t.* **1.** to move with quick, irregular side-to-side movements. —*n.* **2.** a wiggling movement. —**wig'gly,** *adj.* —**wig'gler,** *n.*

wig'wag' (wig'wag') *v.,* **-wagged, -wagging,** *n.* —*v.t., v.i.* **1.** to signal in code with a flag or lantern. —*n.* **2.** such signaling. **3.** a message so sent.

wig'wam (-wom) *n.* an American Indian dwelling of rounded shape.

wild (wīld) *adj.* **1.** not cultivated. **2.** not civilized. **3.** violent. **4.** not inhabited or developed. **5.** disorderly. —*adv.* **6.** in a wild manner. —*n.* **7.** a wilderness. —**wild'ly,** *adv.*

wild'cat' *n., v.,* **-catted, -catting.** —*n.* **1.** a medium-sized cat, as the bobcat. —*v.i., v.t.* **2.** to search (an unknown area) for oil, gas, or ore. —*adj.* **3.** not sanctioned by a labor union.

wil'de·beest (wil'də bēst', vil'-) *n.* a gnu.

wil'der·ness (wil'dər nis) *n.* a wild or desolate region.

wild'-eyed' *adj.* **1.** having a wild expression in the eyes. **2.** extreme or radical.

wild'fire' *n.* an outdoor fire that spreads rapidly and is hard to extinguish.

wild'flow'er *n.* the flower of a plant that grows wild.

wild'-goose' chase' *n.* a senseless search for something unobtainable.

wild'life' *n.* animals living in the wild.

wile (wīl) *n.* a trick to fool, trap, or entice.

will¹ (wil) *auxiliary v.* and *v., pres.* **will;** *past* **would.** —*auxiliary verb.* **1.** (used to express a future tense). **2.** (used to express willingness or determination). **3.** (used to express capability). —*v.t., v.i.* **4.** to wish; like.

—Usage. See SHALL.

will² (wil) *n.* **1.** the power of conscious action or choice. **2.** wish; pleasure. **3.** attitude toward another. **4.** a legal document declaring one's wishes for the disposition of one's property after death. —*v.t.* **5.** to decide upon or bring about by an act of the will. **6.** to give by will; bequeath. **7.** to influence by the power of the will.

will'ful (wil'-) *adj.* **1.** intentional. **2.** headstrong; stubborn. Also, **wil'ful.**

wil'lies (wil'ēz) *n.pl. Slang.* nervousness.

will'ing *adj.* **1.** inclined. **2.** cheerfully done, given, etc. —**will'ing·ly,** *adv.* —**will'ing·ness,** *n.*

will'-o'-the-wisp' (wil'ə the wisp') *n.* **1.** a flitting, elusive light. **2.** something that fascinates and deludes.

wil'low (wil'ō) *n.* a slender tree or shrub with tough, pliant branches.

wil'low·y *adj.* **-ier, -iest.** tall and slender.

wil'ly-nil'ly (wil'ē nil'ē) *adv.* whether one wishes or not.

wilt (wilt) *v.i.* **1.** to wither or droop. —*v.t.* **2.** to cause to wilt.

wil'y (wī'lē) *adj.,* **-ier, -iest.** crafty; cunning.

wimp (wimp) *n. Informal.* a weak, ineffectual person. —**wimp'y,** *adj.*

win (win) *v.,* **won** (wun), **winning,** *n.* —*v.i.* **1.** to finish first in a competition. **2.** to succeed by effort. —*v.t.* **3.** to succeed in reaching. **4.** to get by effort. **5.** to be victorious in. —*n.* **6.** a victory.

wince (wins) *v.,* **winced, wincing,** *n.* —*v.i.* **1.** to shrink back, as from pain or a blow. —*n.* **2.** a wincing movement.

winch (winch) *n.* **1.** the crank or handle of a machine. **2.** a windlass for hoisting.

wind¹ (wind) *n.* **1.** air in motion. **2.** breath or breathing. **3. winds,** the wind instruments in an orchestra. **4.** a hint or intimation. **5.** gas in the stomach or intestines. —*v.t.* **6.** to make short of breath. **7.** to follow by scent. —*Idiom.* **8.** in the wind, about to occur. —**wind'y** (win'dē) *adj.*

wind² (wīnd) *v.,* **wound** (wound) **winding.** —*v.i.* **1.** to have or take a curving or spiral course. —*v.t.* **2.** to wrap around. **3.** to roll (thread, yarn, etc.) into a ball or on a spool. **4.** to tighten the spring of (a clock, toy, etc.). **5. wind up, a.** to bring or come to an end. **b.** to excite. —*n.* **6.** a turn.

wind'bag' (wind'-) *n.* a pompous talker.

wind'break' (wind'-) *n.* something that shelters from the wind.

wind'chill fac'tor (wind'chil') *n.* the apparent temperature felt on exposed skin owing to the combination of temperature and wind speed.

wind'ed (win'did) *adj.* breathless.

wind'fall' (wind'-) *n.* **1.** an unexpected piece of good fortune. **2.** something, as fruit, blown down.

wind'ing sheet' (wīn'ding) *n.* a shroud.

wind' in'strument (wind) *n.* a musical instrument sounded by an air current, esp. the breath.

wind'jam·mer (wind'jam'ər, win'-) *n.* a large sailing ship.

wind'lass (wind'ləs) *n.* a device for hoisting, consisting of a horizontal drum around which a rope is wound.

wind'mill' (wind'-) *n.* a mill that is driven by the wind acting on vanes or sails.

win'dow (win'dō) *n.* **1.** an opening in a building, vehicle, etc., for air and light, usu. fitted with glass in a frame. **2.** the glass in a window frame. **3.** a period of time for doing something. **4.** a portion of a computer screen, surrounded by borders, on which data is displayed.

win'dow dress'ing *n.* **1.** the art, act, or technique of decorating store display windows. **2.** something done solely to create a favorable impression.

win'dow·pane' *n.* a pane of glass for a window.

win'dow-shop' *v.i.,* **-shopped, -shopping.** to look at articles in store windows without making purchases. —**win'dow shop'per,** *n.*

wind'pipe' (wind'-) *n.* the trachea.

wind'shield' (wind'-, win'-) *n.* a glass shield above the dashboard of an automobile.

wind'sock' (wind'-) *n.* a mounted cloth cone that catches the wind to indicate wind direction.

wind'storm' (wind'-) *n.* a storm with heavy wind but little or no precipitation.

wind'surf'ing (wind'-) *n.* the sport of riding on a surfboard mounted with a sail. —**wind'surf',** *v.i.*

wind'-swept' (wind'-) *adj.* exposed to or blown by the wind.

wind'up' (wīnd'-) *n.* the conclusion of an action or activity.

wind'ward (wind'wərd) *adv.* **1.** toward the wind. —*adj.* **2.** of, in, or toward the direction from which the wind blows. —*n.* **3.** the direction from which the wind blows.

wine (wīn) *n., v.,* **wined, wining.** —*n.* **1.** the fermented juice of grapes. **2.** a dark purplish red. —*v.t., v.i.* **3.** to supply with or drink wine. —*Idiom.* **4. wine and dine,** to entertain lavishly.

win'er·y *n., pl.* **-eries.** a place where wine is made.

wing (wing) *n.* **1.** either of two forelimbs or appendages by which birds, insects, and bats are able to fly. **2.** any winglike or projecting structure. **3.** flight. **4.** one of the winglike structures on an airplane. **5. wings,** the space at the side of a stage. **6.** an extreme faction within an organization. —*v.i.* **7.** to travel on wings. —*v.t.* **8.** to transport on wings. **9.** to wound in the wing or arm. **10. wing it,** to improvise. —*Idiom.* **11. under one's wing,** under one's protection. —**wing'ed,** *adj.*

wing'ding' *n. Slang.* a noisy, exciting party.

wink (wingk) *v.i.* **1.** to close and open an eye quickly. **2.** to signal by winking. **3.** to twinkle. —*v.t.* **4.** to make (an eye) wink. **5. wink at,** to ignore (wrongdoing). —*n.* **6.** the act of winking.

win'ner (win'ər) *n.* one that wins.

win'ning *n.* **1. winnings,** that which is won. —*adj.* **2.** charming.

win'now (win'ō) *v.t.* **1.** to free (grain) of chaff by a forced current of air. **2.** to separate.

win'some (win'səm) *adj.* sweetly or innocently charming.

win'ter (win'tər) *n.* **1.** the cold season between autumn and spring. —*adj.* **2.** of, like, or for winter. —*v.i.* **3.** to spend the winter. —**win'try,** *adj.*

win'ter·green' *n.* a creeping aromatic evergreen shrub bearing white flowers and red berries.

win-win *adj.* advantageous to both sides, as in a negotiation.

wipe (wīp) *v.,* **wiped, wiping,** *n.* —*v.t.* **1.** to clean or dry by rubbing lightly. **2.** to rub (something) over a surface. —*n.* **3.** the act of wiping. —**wip'er,** *n.*

wire (wī°r) *n., adj., v.,* **wired, wiring.** —*n.* **1.** a slender, flexible piece of metal. **2.** a length of wire used as a conductor of current. **3.** a telegram or telegraph. —*adj.* **4.** made of wire. —*v.t.* **5.** to equip, furnish, or connect with wire. **6.** to send by telegraph.

wire′less *adj.* **1.** activated by electromagnetic waves rather than wires. —*n.* **2.** *Brit.* a radio.

wire′ serv′ice *n.* an agency that sends syndicated news by wire to its subscribers.

wire′tap′ *n.*, *v.*, **-tapped, -tapping.** —*n.* **1.** an act or instance of connecting secretly into a telephone. —*v.t.* **2.** to listen in on by means of a wiretap. —*v.i.* **3.** to tap a telephone wire.

wir′ing *n.* a system of electric wires.

wir′y *adj.*, **-ier, -iest.** like wire; lean and strong. —**wir′i•ness,** *n.*

Wis. Wisconsin.

wis′dom (wiz′dəm) *n.* **1.** the quality of being wise. **2.** wise sayings.

wis′dom tooth′ *n.* the third molar on each side of the upper and lower jaws.

wise¹ (wīz) *adj.* **1.** having good judgment and understanding. **2.** having scholarly knowledge. **3.** informed. —**wise′ly,** *adv.*

wise² (wīz) *n.* way; manner.

wise′a•cre (-ā′kər) *n.* a conceited, often insolent person.

wise′crack′ *n.* **1.** a smart or facetious remark. —*v.i.*, *v.t.* **2.** to make or say as a wisecrack.

wish (wish) *v.t.* **1.** to want; desire. **2.** to express a hope or desire for. —*v.i.* **3.** to yearn. **4.** to make a wish. —*n.* **5.** a desire or an expression of a desire. **6.** the thing desired. —**wish′ful,** *adj.* —**wish′ful•ly,** *adv.*

wish′bone′ *n.* a forked bone in front of the breastbone in most birds.

wish′y-wash′y (wish′ē wosh′ē) *adj.* weak.

wisp (wisp) *n.* **1.** a thin tuft, lock, or mass. **2.** a thin puff or streak. —**wisp′y,** *adj.*

wis•te′ri•a (wi stēr′ē ə) *n.* a climbing shrub with long clusters of pale purple flowers.

wist′ful (wist′fəl) *adj.* marked by pensive longing. —**wist′ful•ly,** *adv.*

wit¹ (wit) *n.* **1.** the power of combining perception with clever expression. **2.** a person having this. **3.** wits, mental faculties.

wit² (wit) —*Idiom.* **to wit,** namely.

witch (wich) *n.* a woman thought to practice magic.

witch′craft′ *n.* the practices of witches; sorcery.

witch′ doc′tor *n.* a person in some cultures who uses magic esp. to cure illness.

witch′er•y *n.* witchcraft; magic. **2.** charm.

witch ha′zel (hā′zəl) *n.* **1.** a shrub bearing small yellow flowers. **2.** an astringent lotion made from its leaves and bark.

with (with, with) *prep.* **1.** accompanied by. **2.** by means of. **3.** having. **4.** owing to. **5.** at the same time as. **6.** in a manner showing.

with•draw′ (with drô′, with-) *v.*, **-drew, -drawn, -drawing.** —*v.t.* **1.** to draw back, away, or aside. **2.** to retract. —*v.i.* **3.** to remove oneself from a place or activity.

with•draw′al *n.* **1.** a withdrawing or being withdrawn. **2.** ceasing to use an addictive drug.

with′er (with′ər) *v.i.*, *v.t.* to (cause to) shrivel or fade.

with′ers *n.pl.* the high part of a horse's back at the base of the neck.

with•hold′ (with hōld′, with-) *v.t.*, **-held, -holding.** to hold or keep back.

withhold′ing tax′ *n.* that part of an employee's tax liability withheld by an employer from wages.

with•in′ (with in′, with-) *adv.* **1.** inside; inwardly. —*prep.* **2.** in or into the interior or compass of. **3.** in the scope of.

with•out′ *prep.* **1.** not having. **2.** not accompanied by. **3.** at or to the outside of. —*adv.* **4.** outside. **5.** lacking something.

with•stand′ (with stand′, with-) *v.t.*, **-stood, -standing.** to resist.

wit′less *adj.* stupid.

wit′ness (wit′nis) *v.t.* **1.** to see, hear, or know by personal experience. **2.** to testify. **3.** to attest by one's signature. —*n.* **4.** a person who has witnessed something. **5.** one who gives testimony. **6.** testimony.

wit′ti•cism′ (wit′ə siz′əm) *n.* a witty remark.

wit′ting *adj.* knowing; aware.

wit′ty *adj.*, **-tier, -tiest.** having or showing wit. —**wit′ti•ly,** *adv.*

wiz′ard (wiz′ərd) *n.* a magician or sorcerer. —**wiz′ard•ry,** *n.*

wiz′ened (wiz′ənd, wē′zənd) *adj.* shriveled.

wk. week.

w/o without.

wob′ble (wob′əl) *v.i.*, **-bled, -bling.** to move unsteadily from side to side. —**wob′bly,** *adj.*

woe (wō) *n.* grief, trouble, or affliction. —**woe′ful,** *adj.* —**woe′ful•ly,** *adv.*

woe′be•gone′ (-bi gôn′) *adj.* showing woe; forlorn.

wok (wok) *n.* a bowl-shaped Chinese cooking pan.

wolf (wŏŏlf) *n.*, *pl.* **wolves** (wŏŏlvz). —*n.* **1.** a wild carnivorous animal of the dog family. **2.** a cruelly greedy person. **3.** a man who makes amorous advances to women. —*v.t.* **4.** to eat ravenously. —**wolf′ish,** *adj.*

wolf′hound′ *n.* a kind of large dog.

wol′ver•ine′ (wŏŏl′və rēn′) *n.* a North American mammal of the weasel family.

wom′an (wŏŏm′ən) *n.*, *pl.* **women** (wim′in). an adult female person.

womb (wŏŏm) *n.* the uterus.

wom′bat (wom′bat) *n.* a burrowing, herbivorous Australian marsupial.

won′der (wun′dər) *v.i.* **1.** to think or speculate curiously. **2.** to marvel. —*n.* **3.** a cause of amazement, admiration, etc. **4.** Also, **won′der•ment.** a feeling of amazement, puzzlement, etc.

won′der•ful *adj.* **1.** excellent. **2.** exciting wonder.

won′drous *adj.* remarkable.

wont (wônt, wōnt, wunt) *adj.* accustomed. —*n.* **2.** habit. —**wont′ed,** *adj.*

won′t (wōnt) a contraction of **will not.**

woo (wŏŏ) *v.t.* to seek to win, esp. in marriage. —**woo′er,** *n.*

wood (wŏŏd) *n.* **1.** the hard, fibrous substance under the bark of trees. **2.** timber or firewood. **3.** **woods,** forest. —*adj.* **4.** made of wood. **5.** living in the woods. —*v.t.* **6.** to plant with trees. —**wood′craft′,** *n.* —**wood′y,** *adj.*

wood′bine′ (-bīn′) *n.* any of various vines, as the honeysuckle.

wood′chuck′ *n.* a bushy-tailed burrowing rodent. Also called **ground′hog′.**

wood′cut′ *n.* a print made from a carved block of wood.

wood′ed *adj.* covered with trees.

wood′en *adj.* **1.** made of wood. **2.** without feeling or expression.

wood′land (-land′, -land) *n.* land covered with trees.

wood′peck′er *n.* a bird with a hard bill for boring into wood in search of insects.

wood′pile′ *n.* a stack of firewood.

wood′ruff (-rəf, -ruf′) *n.* a fragrant plant with small white flowers.

wood′shed′ *n.* a shed for storing firewood.

woods′man *n.* a person who works in the woods.

woods′y *adj.*, **-ier, -iest.** of or resembling woods.

wood′wind′ (-wind′) *n.* a musical instrument of the group including the flute, clarinet, oboe, and bassoon.

wood′work′ *n.* the wooden fittings inside a building. —**wood′work′er,** *n.*

woof (wŏŏf, wŏŏf) *n.* the threads running from side to side in a loom.

woof′er (wŏŏf′ər) *n.* a loudspeaker to reproduce low-frequency sounds.

wool (wŏŏl) *n.* **1.** the soft curly hair of sheep, goats, etc. **2.** a garment, yarn, or fabric of wool. **3.** a substance resembling the wool of sheep. —**wool′en** or (*esp. Brit.*) **wool′len,** *adj.*, *n.*

wool′gath′er•ing *n.* daydreaming.

wool′ly *adj.* **1.** of or resembling wool. **2.** confused or disorganized.

wool′ly bear′ *n.* a caterpillar with woolly hairs.

word (wûrd) *n.* **1.** one or more spoken sounds carrying meaning and forming a basic unit of speech. **2.** the written representation of this. **3.** **words, a.** the text of a song. **b.** a quarrel. **4.** something said. **5.** a promise. **6.** a command. —*v.t.* **7.** to express in words. —**word′less,** *adj.*

word′age (wûr′dij) *n.* **1.** words collectively. **2.** a number of words.

word′ing *n.* the way of expressing something.

word′ of mouth′ *n.* oral communication.

word′play′ *n.* witty repartee.

word′ proc′essing *n.* the production and storage of documents using computers. —**word′ proc′essor,** *n.*

word′y *adj.*, **-ier, -iest.** using too many words; verbose. —**word′i•ness,** *n.*

work (wûrk) *n.* **1.** exertion; labor. **2.** a task. **3.** employment. **4.** a place of employment. **5.** the materials on which one works. **6.** the result of exertion, labor, etc. **7.** **works,** an industrial plant. —*adj.* **8.** of or for work. —*v.i.* **9.** to do work. **10.** to function. **11.** to prove effective. —*v.t.* **12.** to use or operate. **13.** to bring about. **14.** to cause to work. **15.** to solve (a puzzle, problem, etc.). **16.** to cause a strong emotion in. —*Idiom.* **17. in the works,** in preparation. —**work′a•ble,** *adj.* —**work′er,** *n.*

work′a•day′ (wûr′kə dā′) *adj.* commonplace; uneventful.

work′a•hol′ic (-hô′lik) *n.* a person who works compulsively.

work′horse′ *n.* a person who works tirelessly.

work′house′ *n.* a penal institution for minor offenders.

work′load′ *n.* the amount of work that a machine or employee is expected to perform.

work′man *n.*, *pl.* **-men.** a man skilled in manual, mechanical, or industrial work.

work′man•like′ *adj.* skillful.

work′man•ship′ *n.* **1.** the skill of a workman. **2.** the quality of work.

work′out′ *n.* **1.** practice or a test to maintain or determine physical ability or endurance. **2.** a structured regimen of physical exercise.

work′shop′ *n.* **1.** a place where work is done. **2.** a seminar to develop a skill or technique.

work′sta′tion *n.* a work area for one person, as in an office, usu. with electronic equipment.

world (wûrld) *n.* **1.** the earth. **2.** a particular part of the earth. **3.** a realm or domain. **4.** humanity. **5.** the universe. **6.** Often, **worlds,** a great quantity. —*Idiom.* **7. out of this world,** extraordinary.

world′-class′ *adj.* of the highest caliber.

world′ly *adj.*, **-lier, -liest. 1.** of this world. **2.** sophisticated; experienced. —**world′li•ness,** *n.*

world′ly-wise′ *adj.* wise as to the affairs of this world.

world′-wea′ry *adj.* blasé.

World′ Wide′ Web′ *n.* a system of extensively interlinked hypertext documents: a branch of the Internet.

worm (wûrm) *n.* **1.** a long, softbodied creeping animal. **2.** something resembling a worm. **3.** **worms,** an intestinal disorder caused by parasites. —*v.i.* **4.** to creep or crawl slowly and stealthily. —*v.t.* **5.** to extract (a secret) craftily. **6.** to insinuate. **7.** to free from intestinal worms.

worm′wood′ *n.* a bitter aromatic herb.

worn (wôrn) *v.* **1.** pp. of **wear.** —*adj.* **2.** exhausted; spent.

worn′-out′ *adj.* **1.** exhausted. **2.** destroyed by wear.

wor′ry (wûr′ē, wur′ē) *v.*, **-ried, -rying,** *n.*, *pl.* **-ries.** —*v.i.* **1.** to feel anxious. —*v.t.* **2.** to make anxious. **3.** to seize with the teeth and shake. —*n.* **4.** anxiety. **5.** a cause of anxiety. —**wor′ri•some,** *adj.*

worse (wûrs) *adj.* **1.** less good; less favorable. —*n.* **2.** that which is worse. —*adv.* **3.** in a worse way. —**wors′en,** *v.t.*, *v.i.*

wor′ship (wûr′ship) *n.*, *v.*, **-shiped, -shiping** or **-shipped, -shipping.** —*n.* **1.** reverence for a god. **2.** adoring reverence. **3.** a formal expression of reverence. —*v.t.* **4.** to render religious reverence to. **5.** to feel adoring regard for. —*v.i.* **6.** to engage in religious worship. —**wor′shiper,** *n.* —**wor′ship•ful,** *adj.*

worst (wûrst) *adj.* **1.** least satisfactory; least well. **2.** in the poorest condition. —*n.* **3.** that which is worst. —*adv.* **4.** in the worst way. —*v.t.* **5.** to defeat.

wor′sted (wŏŏs′tid, wûr′stid) *n.* **1.** firmly twisted wool yarn or thread. **2.** fabric made of it.

worth (wûrth) *adj.* **1.** good enough to justify. **2.** having a value of. —*n.* **3.** excellence; importance. **4.** wealth. **5.** a quantity of something of a specified value. —**worth′less,** *adj.*

worth′while′ *adj.* repaying time and effort spent.

wor′thy (wûr′thē) *adj.*, **-thier, -thiest. 1.** having merit or value. **2.** deserving. —**wor′thi•ly,** *adv.*

would (wŏŏd; *unstressed* wəd) *v.* pt. of **will.**

would′-be′ *adj.* wishing, pretending, or intended to be.

wound (wŏŏnd) *n.* **1.** an injury from external violence. —*v.t.* **2.** to inflict a wound upon. **3.** to grieve with an insult or reproach.

wrack (rak) *n.* damage or destruction.

wraith (rāth) *n.* a ghost.

wran′gle (rang′gəl) *v.*, **-gled, -gling,** *n.* —*v.i.* **1.** to argue noisily. —*v.t.* **2.** to round up (livestock). —*n.* **3.** a noisy argument.

wrap (rap) *v.*, **wrapped** or **wrapt, wrapping,** *n.* —*v.t.* **1.** to enclose or envelop. **2.** to wind or fold about. —*v.i.* **3.** to become wrapped. **4. wrap up,** to conclude. —*n.* **5.** a shawl. **6.** a piece of flat bread wrapped around a filling.

wrap′per *n.* **1.** one that wraps. **2.** Also, **wrapping.** an outer cover. **3.** a long loose garment.

wrath (rath) *n.* fierce anger.

wreak (rēk) *v.t.* to inflict (punishment, vengeance, etc.).

wreath (rēth) *n.* a circular band of leaves, flowers, etc.

wreathe (rēth) *v.t.*, **wreathed, wreathing. 1.** to encircle with a wreath. **2.** to envelop.

wreck (rek) *n.* **1.** anything reduced to ruins. **2.** destruction. **3.** a person in ruined health. —*v.t.* **4.** to damage or destroy.

wreck′age *n.* **1.** wrecking or being wrecked. **2.** the remains of something wrecked.

wreck′er *n.* **1.** a vehicle for towing wrecked automobiles. **2.** one that demolishes buildings.

wren (ren) *n.* a small brown-gray songbird.

wrench (rench) *v.t.* **1.** to twist or pull forcibly. **2.** to injure by wrenching. —*n.* **3.** a wrenching movement. **4.** a tool for turning bolts, nuts, etc.

wrest (rest) *v.t.* **1.** to take away by force. **2.** to get by effort. —*n.* **3.** a twist or wrench.

wres′tle (res′əl) *v.*, **-tled, -tling,** *n.* —*v.t.* **1.** to contend with by trying to force another person down. —*v.i.* **2.** to engage in wrestling. **3.** to struggle. —*n.* **4.** a struggle.

wretch (rech) *n.* a pitiable person.

wretch′ed *adj.* **1.** miserable or pitiable. **2.** contemptible. **3.** worthless.

wrig′gle (rig′əl) *v.*, **-gled, -gling,** *n.* —*v.i.* **1.** to twist to and fro; squirm. —*v.t.* **2.** to cause to wriggle. —*n.* **3.** the act of wriggling.

wring (ring) *v.*, **wrung** (rung) **wringing,** *n.* —*v.t.* **1.** to twist or compress forcibly. **2.** to clasp tightly. —*n.* **3.** a twist or squeeze. —**wring′er,** *n.*

wrin′kle (ring′kəl) *n.*, *v.*, **-kled, -kling.** —*n.* **1.** a small crease in the skin, in fabric, etc. **2.** a problem. —*v.t.*, *v.i.* **3.** to form wrinkles (in). —**wrin′kly,** *adj.*

wrist (rist) *n.* the joint between the hand and the arm.

writ (rit) *n.* a court order directing a person to do or not to do something.

write (rīt) *v.*, **wrote** (rōt) **written** (rit′n) **writing.** —*v.t.* **1.** to form (letters, words, etc.) by hand on paper. **2.** to express in writing. **3.** to be the author or composer of. —*v.i.* **4.** to express ideas in writing. **5.** to write a letter.

write′-in′ *n.* a candidate or vote for a candidate not listed on a ballot but written in by the voter.

write′-off′ *n.* something cancelled, as a debt.

writ′er *n.* a person engaged in writing, esp. as an occupation.

writhe (rīth) *v.*, **writhed, writhing,** *n.* —*v.i.* **1.** to twist and turn, as in pain. —*n.* **2.** a writhing movement.

wrong (rông) *adj.* **1.** not morally good. **2.** deviating from truth or fact; incorrect. **3.** not proper or suitable. —*n.* **4.** evil; injury; error. —*adv.* **5.** in a wrong manner. —*v.t.* **6.** to do wrong to. **7.** to misjudge. —*Idiom.* **8. in the wrong,** in error. —**wrong′ly,** *adv.*

wrong′do′er *n.* a person who does wrong, esp. a sinner or transgressor. —**wrong′do′ing,** *n.*

wrong′ful *adj.* not fair or legal. —**wrong′ful•ly,** *adv.*

wrong′head′ed *adj.* misguided and stubborn.

wroth (rôth) *adj.* angry.

wrought (rôt) *adj.* **1.** worked. **2.** shaped by beating.

wrought′-up′ *adj.* excited or disturbed.

wry (rī) *adj.*, **wrier, wriest. 1.** contorted; twisted. **2.** ironic. —**wry′ly,** *adv.* —**wry′ness,** *n.*

wuss (wŏŏs) *n.* *Slang.* a weakling; wimp.

WV West Virginia. Also, **W. Va.**

WWW World Wide Web.

WY Wyoming. Also, **Wyo.**

WYSIWYG (wiz′ē wig′) *adj.* of or being a computer display screen that shows text exactly as it will appear when printed.

X

X, x (eks) *n.* the twenty-fourth letter of the English alphabet.

X′ chro′mosome *n.* a sex chromosome that determines femaleness when paired with another X chromosome and that occurs singly in males.

xen•o•pho′bi•a (zen′ə fō′bē ə, zē′nə-) *n.* an unreasonable fear or hatred of foreigners. —**xen′o•pho′bic,** *adj.*

xe•rog′ra•phy (zi rog′rə fē) *n.* a copying process in which resins are fused to paper electrically.

Xe′rox (zēr′oks) *n.* **1.** *Trademark.* a brand name for a copying machine using xerography. **2.** (*sometimes l.c.*) a copy made on a Xerox. —*v.t.*, *v.i.* **3.** (*sometimes l.c.*) to print or reproduce by Xerox.

xi (zī, sī; *Gk.* ksē) *n.*, *pl.* **xis.** the 14th letter of the Greek alphabet.

Xmas (kris′məs; *often* eks′məs) *n.* Christmas.

X-rat•ed (eks′rā′tid) *adj.* sexually explicit; obscene.

x′-ray′ *n.* **1.** a highly penetrating type of electromagnetic ray, used esp. in medicine. **2.** a photograph made by x-rays. —*v.t.* **3.** to photograph or examine with x-rays.

xy′lem (zī′ləm, -lem) *n.* a woody tissue of plants.

xy′lo•phone′ (zī′lə fōn′) *n.* a musical instrument of wooden bars struck with small wooden hammers. —**xy′lo•phon′ist,** *n.*

Y

Y, y (wī) *n.* the twenty-fifth letter of the English alphabet.

-y a suffix meaning: **1.** full of or like. **2.** inclined to. **3.** dear or little. **4.** action of. **5.** quality or state.

yacht (yot) *n.* **1.** a boat or ship used for private cruising or racing. —*v.i.* **2.** to sail in a yacht. —**yacht′ing,** *n.* —**yachts′man,** *n.*

ya′da-ya•da-ya′da (yä′də yä′də yä′də) *adv.* *Slang.* and so on; and so forth. Also, **yad′da-yad′da-yad′da.**

ya′hoo (yä′hōō) *n.* an uncultivated or boorish person.

yak¹ (yak) *n.* a long-haired Tibetan ox.

yak² (yak) *v.*, **yakked, yakking,** *n.* *Slang.* —*v.i.* **1.** to gab; chatter. —*n.* **2.** incessant idle or gossipy talk.

yam (yam) *n.* the edible potatolike root of an African climbing vine.

yam′mer (yam′ər) *v.i.* *Informal.* **1.** to whine or complain. **2.** to talk loudly and constantly.

yank (yangk) *v.i.*, *v.t.* **1.** to pull sharply; jerk. —*n.* **2.** a sudden, sharp pull; jerk.

Yan′kee (yang′kē) *n.* a native or inhabitant of the United States, northern U.S., or New England.

yap (yap) *v.*, **yapped, yapping,** *n.* —*v.i.* **1.** to bark sharply; yelp. **2.** *Slang.* to talk noisily or foolishly. —*n.* **3.** a sharp bark. **4.** *Slang.* noisy, foolish talk.

yard¹ (yärd) *n.* **1.** a linear unit equal to 3 feet or 36 inches. **2.** a long spar supporting the head of a sail.

yard² (yärd) *n.* **1.** the ground adjoining or surrounding a building. **2.** an enclosed outdoor area for a specific purpose.

yard′age (yär′dij) *n.* an amount in yards.

yard′arm′ *n.* either of the yards of a square sail.

yard/stick/ *n.* **1.** a measuring stick one yard long. **2.** a criterion.

yar/mul•ke (yär/məl kə, -mə-, yä/-) *n.* a skullcap worn by Jewish males.

yarn (yärn) *n.* **1.** a strand or thread used for knitting or weaving. **2.** a tale.

yar/row (yar/ō) *n.* a plant with flat-topped clusters of white-to-yellow flowers.

yaw (yô) *v.i.* **1.** to deviate from a straight course, as a ship. —*n.* **2.** the movement of yawing.

yawl (yôl) *n.* a small sailboat.

yawn (yôn) *v.i.* **1.** to open the mouth wide involuntarily, as from sleepiness or boredom. —*n.* **2.** the act of yawning.

Y/ chro/mosome *n.* a sex chromosome present only in males and paired with an X chromosome.

ye (yē) *pron. Archaic.* you.

yea (yā) *adv.* **1.** yes. —*n.* **2.** an affirmative vote.

year (yēr) *n.* **1.** a period of 365 or 366 days. **2. years, a.** age. **b.** a long time. —**year/ly,** *adv., adj.*

year/book/ *n.* **1.** a book published annually with information on the past year. **2.** a commemorative book published by a graduating class.

year/ling (-ling) *n.* an animal in its second year.

yearn (yûrn) *v.i.* to have a strong desire; long.

year/-round/ *adj.* **1.** continuing, available, or used throughout the year. —*adv.* **2.** throughout the year.

yeast (yēst) *n.* a fungus causing fermentation, used in brewing alcoholic beverages and as a leaven in baking bread.

yell (yel) *v.i., v.t.* **1.** to shout loudly. —*n.* **2.** such a shout.

yel/low (yel/ō) *n.* **1.** the color of butter, lemons, etc. —*adj.* **2.** of or like yellow. **3.** cowardly. —*v.t., v.i.* **4.** to make or become yellow.

yel/low fe/ver *n.* an infectious tropical disease transmitted by mosquitoes.

yel/low jack/et *n.* a small yellow and black wasp.

yelp (yelp) *v.i., v.t.* **1.** to give a sharp, shrill cry. —*n.* **2.** such a cry.

yen (yen) *n.* a desire or craving.

yeo/man (yō/mən) *n.* **1.** a petty officer in the navy. **2.** an independent farmer.

yes (yes) *adv.* **1.** (used to express affirmation or agreement). —*n.* **2.** an affirmative reply.

ye•shi/va (yə shē/və) *n.* an Orthodox Jewish school.

yes/-man/ *n., pl.* **yes-men.** a person who always agrees with superiors.

yes/ter•day (yes/tar dā/, -dē) *adv., n.* **1.** (on) the day before today. **2.** (in) the recent past.

yet (yet) *adv.* **1.** up to this (or that) time; still. **2.** besides; in addition. **3.** even. **4.** nevertheless. —*conj.* **5.** still; nevertheless.

yew (yōō) *n.* an evergreen tree with needlelike foliage.

Yid•dish (yid/ish) *n.* a language of central and E European Jews that is based on German and written in the Hebrew alphabet.

yield (yēld) *v.t.* **1.** to produce; give forth. **2.** to surrender or relinquish. **3.** to give as required. —*v.i.* **4.** to give way. **5.** to give a return. —*n.* **6.** a quantity yielded or produced.

yip (yip) *v.,* **yipped, yipping,** *n.* —*v.i.* **1.** to bark sharply. —*n.* **2.** a sharp bark.

yo/del (yōd/l) *v.,* **-deled, -deling.** —*v.t., v.i.* **1.** to sing with quick changes to and from falsetto. —*n.* **2.** a yodeled song.

yo/ga (yō/gə) *n.* a series of postures and breathing exercises practiced to attain physical and mental control and tranquillity.

yo/gurt (yō/gərt) *n.* a custardlike food made from milk curdled by bacterial action. Also, **yo/ghurt.**

yoke (yōk) *n., v.,* **yoked, yoking.** —*n.* **1.** a wooden piece put across the necks of oxen pulling a cart, plow, etc. **2.** a frame resting on a person's shoulders to carry two loads. **3.** the fitted upper part of a garment. **4.** oppression or servitude. —*v.t.* **5.** to put a yoke on. **6.** to join or unite.

yo/kel (yō/kəl) *n.* a country bumpkin.

yolk (yōk) *n.* the yellow part of an egg.

Yom Kip•pur (yom kip/ər; *Heb.* yōm/ kē pōōr/) *n.* the holiest Jewish holiday, observed by fasting and prayers of repentance.

yon/der (yon/dər) *adj., adv.* over there. Also, **yon.**

yore (yôr) *n.* time past.

you (yōō; *unstressed* yŏŏ, yə) *pron.* the person or persons addressed.

young (yung) *adj.* **1.** in the early stages of life, operation, etc. **2.** of youth. —*n.* **3.** young persons. **4.** young offspring. —**young/ish,** *adj.*

young/ster (-stər) *n.* a child.

your (yŏŏr, yôr; *unstressed* yər) *pron., adj.* a possessive form of **you;** (without noun following) **yours.**
—**Usage.** Do not confuse YOUR and YOU'RE. YOUR is the possessive form of "you": *Your book is overdue at the library.* YOU'RE is the contraction of "you are": *You're just the person we need for this job.*

you're (yŏŏr; *unstressed* yər) a contraction of **you are.**
—**Usage.** See YOUR.

your•self/ *pron.* an emphatic or reflexive form of **you.**

youth (yōōth) *n.* **1.** the state or time of being young. **2.** young persons. **3.** a young person, esp. a young man. —**youth/ful,** *adj.*

yowl (youl) *v.i.* **1.** to howl. —*n.* **2.** a yowling cry.

yo-yo (yō/yō) *n., pl.* **yo-yos,** *v.,* **yo-yoed, yo-yoing.** —*n.* **1.** a spoollike toy that is spun out and reeled in by a string looped on the player's finger. —*v.i.* **2.** to move up and down or back and forth.

yr. year.

yuc/ca (yuk/ə) *n.* an American plant with sword-shaped leaves and white flowers.

yule (yōōl) *n.* Christmas.

yule/tide/ *n.* the Christmas season.

yum/my (yum/ē) *adj.,* **-mier, -miest.** very pleasing, esp. to the taste.

yup/pie (yup/ē) *n.* a young, ambitious, and affluent professional who lives in or near a city.

Z

Z, z (zē; *esp. Brit.* zed) *n.* the twenty-sixth letter of the English alphabet.

zaf/tig (zäf/tik, -tig), *adj. Slang.* (of a woman) pleasantly plump.

za/ny (zā/nē) *adj.,* **-nier, -niest.** crazily funny. —**za/ni•ness,** *n.*

zap (zap) *v.t.,* **zapped, zapping.** *Informal.* to kill or defeat.

zeal (zēl) *n.* intense ardor or eagerness. —**zeal/ous** (zel/əs) *adj.*

zeal/ot (zel/ət) *n.* an excessively zealous person; fanatic. —**zeal/ot•ry,** *n.*

ze/bra (zē/brə) *n.* a wild, striped horselike animal.

Zen (zen) *n.* a Buddhist movement emphasizing enlightenment by meditation and direct, intuitive insight. Also, **Zen/ Budd/hism.**

ze/nith (zē/nith) *n.* the highest point.

zeph/yr (zef/ər) *n.* a mild breeze.

zep/pe•lin (zep/ə lin) *n.* a large dirigible of the early 20th century.

ze/ro (zēr/ō) *n., pl.* **-ros, -roes. 1.** the figure or numerical symbol 0. **2.** nothing. **3.** the lowest point or degree.

ze/ro hour/ *n.* the starting time for an event or action.

zest (zest) *n.* something adding flavor, interest, etc. —**zest/ful,** *adj.*

ze/ta (zā/tə), *n., pl.* **-tas.** the sixth letter of the Greek alphabet.

zig/zag/ (zig/zag/) *n., adj., adv., v.,* **-zagged, -zagging.** —*n.* **1.** a line going sharply from side to side. —*adj.* **2.** having sharp turns back and forth. —*adv.* **3.** in a zigzag manner. —*v.t., v.i.* **4.** to make into or go in a zigzag.

zilch (zilch) *n. Slang.* zero; nothing.

zil/lion (zil/yən) *n. Informal.* an extremely large, indeterminate number.

zinc (zingk) *n.* a bluish white metallic element.

zinc/ ox/ide *n.* a white powder used in pigments and ointments.

zing (zing) *n.* **1.** a sharp singing sound. —*v.i., v.t.* **2.** to move or cause to move with a zing. —*interj.* **3.** (descriptive of such a sound.)

zin/ni•a (zin/ē ə) *n.* a plant with dense, colorful flowers.

Zi/on (zī/ən) *n.* **1.** the Jewish people. **2.** Palestine as the Jewish homeland. **3.** heaven as the final gathering place of true believers.

zip¹ (zip) *v.,* **zipped, zipping.** —*v.i.* **1.** to act or go with great energy. —*n.* **2.** energy.

zip² (zip) *v.t., v.i.,* **zipped, zipping.** to fasten (with) a zipper.

ZIP (zip) *n.* a way of compressing electronic files for storage and transfer.

ZIP/ code/ *Trademark.* a system to expedite mail delivery by assigning a numerical code to every postal area in the U.S.

zip/per *n.* a fastener with tracks of teeth that can be interlocked by pulling a sliding piece.

zip/py *adj.,* **-pier, -piest.** lively; smart.

zir/con (zûr/kon) *n.* a mineral that is used as a gem when transparent.

zir•co/ni•um (zûr kō/nē əm) *n.* a metallic element used in metallurgy and ceramics.

zit (zit) *n. Slang.* a pimple.

zith/er (zith/ər, zith/-) *n.* a stringed musical instrument that is played with a plectrum and the fingertips.

zi/ti (zē/tē) *n.* short, tubular pasta.

zo/di•ac/ (zō/dē ak/) *n.* an imaginary belt in the heavens containing paths of the sun, moon, and the major planets, divided into 12 signs, each named after a constellation.

zom/bie (zom/bē) *n.* **1.** (in voodoo) a reanimated corpse. **2.** a person whose behavior is listless or mechanical.

zone (zōn) *n., v.,* **zoned, zoning.** —*n.* **1.** a special area. **2.** one of five divisions of the earth's surface based on climate and latitude. —*v.t.* **3.** to divide into or mark with zones. —**zon/al,** *adj.*

zoo (zōō) *n.* a parklike area where live animals are exhibited.

zo•ol/o•gy (zō ol/ə jē) *n.* the scientific study of animals. —**zo/o•log/i•cal** (-ə loj/i kəl) *adj.* —**zo•ol/o•gist,** *n.*

zoom (zōōm) *v.i.* **1.** to move with a loud hum or buzz. **2.** to move suddenly and sharply.

zoom/ lens/ *n.* a camera lens allowing continual change of magnification without loss of focus.

zo/o•pho/bi•a (zō/ə-) *n.* fear of animals.

zo/o•phyte/ (-fīt/) *n.* an invertebrate animal resembling a plant, as a coral.

zuc•chi/ni (zōō kē/nē) *n.* a cucumber-shaped summer squash.

zwie/back/ (zwī/bak/, -bäk/, swē/-) *n.* a biscuit of dried, twice-baked bread.

zy/gote (zī/gōt) *n.* a cell produced by the union of two gametes. —**zy•got/ic** (-got/ik) *adj.*

zy/mur•gy (zī/mûr jē) *n.* the branch of applied chemistry dealing with fermentation.

Rules of Punctuation

1. **Period (.):** Ends a sentence that makes a statement or expresses a request, order, or command. It is also used after most abbreviations.
2. **Question Mark (?):** Ends a sentence that asks a question.
3. **Exclamation Point (!):** Ends a sentence that expresses strong emotion or feeling.
4. **Colon (:):** Used (a) to introduce a formal or long direct quotation; (b) to introduce a long series of items or illustrations; (c) in the salutation of a formal letter.
5. **Semicolon (;):** Used (a) to separate long clauses of a compound sentence; (b) to separate independent clauses if the conjunction is omitted; (c) to separate long items in a series.
6. **Comma (,):** Used (a) to separate independent clauses connected by conjunctions *and, but, or, nor, for, yet, so*; (b) to separate a nonrestrictive clause from the rest of the sentence; (c) to separate three or more words, phrases, or clauses in a series; (d) to set off appositives and nouns in direct address; (e) to set off mild interjections; (f) to separate words in dates and addresses; (g) to introduce a direct quotation.
7. **Dash (—):** Used (a) to show a definite interruption or change of thought; (b) to indicate the omission of words, letters, or numbers.
8. **Apostrophe (’):** Used (a) in the possessive forms of nouns and indefinite pronouns; (b) to indicate the omission of one or more letters in contractions; (c) to form plurals of numbers or letters.
9. **Hyphen (-):** Used (a) to mark the break in an unfinished word at the end of a line; (b) between a prefix and a proper name or when the emphasis is on the prefix; (c) in fractions and in compound numerals from twenty-one to ninety-nine; (d) between the parts of certain compound words.
10. **Parentheses ( ):** Used to set off words, phrases, or clauses that are not basic to the main point of the sentence.
11. **Brackets ([ ]):** Used to indicate editorial explanation.
12. **Quotation Marks (“ ”):** Used (a) to enclose direct quotations; (b) to set off titles.

Rules of Spelling

No spelling rule should be followed blindly, for every rule has exceptions, and words analogous in some forms may differ in others.

1. **Silent E Dropped.** Silent *e* at the end of a word is usually dropped before a suffix beginning with a vowel: *abide, abiding; recite, recital.* Exceptions: Words ending in *ce* or *ge* retain the *e* before a suffix beginning with *a* or *o* to keep the soft sound of the consonant: *notice, noticeable; courage, courageous.*
2. **Silent E Kept.** A silent *e* following a consonant (or another *e*) is usually retained before a suffix beginning with a consonant: *late, lateness; spite, spiteful.* Exceptions: *fledgling, acknowledgment, judgment, wholly,* and a few similar words.
3. **Final Consonant Doubled.** A final consonant following a single vowel in one-syllable words or in a syllable that will take the main accent when combined with a suffix is doubled before a suffix beginning with a vowel: *begin, beginning; occur, occurred.* **Exceptions:** *h* and *x (ks)* in final position; *transferable, gaseous,* and a few others.
4. **Final Consonant Single.** A final consonant following another consonant or a double vowel or diphthong or not in a stressed syllable is not doubled before a suffix beginning with a vowel: *part, parting; remark, remarkable.* **Exceptions:** an unaccented syllable does not prevent doubling of the final consonant, especially in British usage: *traveller* beside *traveler,* etc.
5. **Double Consonants Remain.** Double consonants are usually retained before a suffix except when a final *l* is to be followed by *ly* or *less.* To avoid a triple *lll*, one *l* is usually dropped: *full, fully.* **Exceptions:** Usage is divided, with *skilful* beside *skillful, instalment* beside *installment,* etc.
6. **Final Y.** If the y follows a consonant, change *y* to *i* before all endings except *ing.* Do not change it before *ing* or if it follows a vowel: *bury, buried, burying; try, tries;* but *attorney, attorneys.* **Exceptions:** *day, daily; gay, gaily; lay, laid; say, said.*
7. **Final IE to Y.** Words ending in *ie* change to *y* before *ing: die, dying; lie, lying.*
8. **Double and Triple E Reduced.** Words ending in double *e* drop one *e* before an ending beginning in *e,* to avoid a triple *e.* Words ending in silent *e* usually drop the *e* before endings beginning in *e* to avoid forming a syllable. Other words ending in a vowel sound commonly retain the letters indicating the sound. *Free-ed = freed.*
9. **EI or IE.** Words having the sound of *U* are commonly spelled *ie* following all letters but *c*; with a preceding *c,* the common spelling is *ei.* Examples: *believe, achieve, besiege* but *conceit, ceiling, receive, conceive.* When the sound is *j,* the common spelling is *ei* regardless of the preceding letter. Examples: *eight, weight, deign.* **Exceptions:** *either, neither, seize, financier;* some words in which *e* and *i* are pronounced separately, such as *notoriety.*
10. **Words Ending in C.** Before an ending beginning with *e, i,* or *y,* words ending in *c* commonly add *k* to keep the *c* hard: *panic, panicky.*
11. **Compounds.** Some compounds written as a unit bring together unusual combinations of letters. They are seldom changed on this account. *Bookkeeper, roommate.* **Exceptions:** A few words are regularly clipped when compounded, such as *full* in *awful, cupful,* etc.

WORDS OFTEN MISSPELLED

accept
accessible
accommodate
acquaint
adequate
adherent
adjournment
aisle
all right
already
always
analyze
answer
appreciate
argument
bachelor
bankruptcy
basis
beggar
beginning
believe
beneficial
brilliant
brutality
bulletin
buoyant
bureau
calendar
camouflage
candidate
carriage
category
cavalry
ceiling
cemetery
cite
committee
competition
complement
compliment
conscious
corps
courteous
curiosity
deceive
descendant
desert
dessert
disappoint
discipline

dissatisfy
ecstasy
effect
efficient
eighth
embarrass
endurance
enough
environment
erroneous
exaggerate
excel
existence
extraordinary
fallacy
fascinate
fascism
foreign
formally
formerly
friend
furniture
gauge
grievous
guarantee
guard
handkerchief
height
hereditary
humorous
hygiene
hypocrisy
incident
indigestible
initiative
intercede
irrelevant
irresistible
its (vs. *it's*)
judgment
knowledge
laboratory
lead
led
leisure
liable
license
literature
livelihood
loose

lose
magazine
maneuver
marriage
material
medicine
minute
mischievous
misspelled
mortgage
muscle
mysterious
naive
necessary
neither
niece
noticeable
notoriety
occasion
occurred
omission
oneself
optimism
pageant
parallel
parliament
particularly
peasant
perceive
perspiration
piece
precede
proceed
prescription
principal
principle
privilege
pronunciation
psychology
quiet
quite
receipt
receive
recommend
reference
referred
reign
restaurant
rhythm
sacrifice

sacrilegious
salary
scarcity
schedule
scheme
scholarly
seize
sergeant
siege
stationary
stationery
subtle
successful
sufficient
superintendent
surprise
syllable
sympathize
systematically
tear
their
thorough
tonight
tournament
tragedy
truly
twelfth
typical
tyranny
unanimous
until
usually
valuable
variety
vegetable
vengeance
village
villain
weather
weird
wherever
whether
whim
wholly
whose
woolen
written
wrote
yacht
zealous

a-[1], *prefix.* from Old English, used **1.** before some nouns to make them into adverbs showing "place where": *a-* + *shore* → *ashore* = *on (or into) the shore.* **2.** before some verbs to make them into words showing a state or process: *a-* + *sleep* → *asleep* (= *sleeping*); *a-* + *blaze* → *ablaze* (= *blazing*).

a-[2], *prefix.* a variant spelling of **an-**. It comes from Latin and is used before some adjectives to mean "not"; *a-* + *moral* → *amoral* (= *without morals*); *a-* + *tonal* → *atonal* (= *without tone*).

ab-, *prefix.* from Latin, used before some words and roots to mean "off, away": *abnormal* (= *away from what is normal*). Compare A-[2].

ad-, *prefix.* from Latin, meaning "toward" and indicating direction or tendency: *ad-* + *join* → *adjoin* (= join toward, attack).

ambi-, *prefix.* from Latin, meaning "both" and "around." These meanings are found in such words as: *ambiguous, ambivalence, ambiance.*

amphi- *prefix.* from Greek, meaning "both; on two sides." This meaning is found in such words as: *amphibian, amphibious, amphitheater.*

an-, *prefix.* from Greek, used before roots or stems beginning with a vowel or *h*, meaning "not; without; lacking": *anaerobic* (= *without oxygen*); *anonymous* (= *without name*). Compare A-[2].

ante-, *prefix.* from Latin, used before roots, meaning **1.** "happening before": *antebellum* (= *before the war*). **2.** "located in front of": *anteroom* (= *room located in front of another*).

anti-, *prefix.* from Greek, used before nouns and adjectives, meaning **1.** against, opposed to: *anti-Semitic, antislavery.* **2.** preventing, counteracting, or working against: *anticoagulant, antifreeze.* **3.** destroying or disabling: *antiaircraft, antipersonnel.* **4.** identical to in form or function, but lacking in some important ways: *anticlimax, antihero, antiparticle.* **5.** an antagonist or rival of: *Antichrist, antipope.* **6.** situated opposite: *Anti-Lebanon.* Also, *before a vowel,* **ant-**.

apo-, *prefix.* from Greek, meaning "away, off, apart": *apo-* + *strophe* → *apostrophe* (= *a turn away, digression*).

aqua-, *prefix.* from Latin, meaning "water." This meaning is found in such words as: *aquaculture, aqualung, aquarium, aquatic, aqueduct, aqueous, aquifer.*

auto-, *prefix.* from Greek, meaning "self." This meaning is found in such words as: *autocrat, autograph, autonomous, autonomy, autopsy.* Also, *esp. before a vowel,* **aut-**.

baro-, *prefix.* from Greek, meaning "weight." This meaning is found in such words as: *barograph, barometer, baroreceptor.*

be-, *prefix.* from Old English, used **1.** to make verbs meaning "to make, become, treat as": *be-* + *cloud* → *becloud* (= *make like a cloud, hard to see*); *be-* + *friend* → *befriend* (= *treat someone as a friend*). **2.** before adjectives and verbs ending in *-ed* to mean "covered all over; completely; all around": *be-* + *decked* → *bedecked* (= *decked or covered all over*); *be-* + *jeweled* → *bejeweled* (= *covered with jewels*).

bi-, *prefix.* from Latin, meaning "twice, two." This meaning is found in such words as: *biennial, bisect, bicentennial, bigamy, biped, binoculars, bilateral, bipartisan,* *biweekly.* —**Usage.** In some words, especially words referring to time periods, the prefix *bi-* has two meanings: "twice a + ~ " and "every two + ~ -s". Thus, *biannual* means both "twice a year" and "every two years." Be careful; check many of these words.

bio-, *prefix.* from Greek, meaning "life." This meaning is found in such words as: *biodegradable, biology, biosphere.*

centi-, *prefix.* from Latin, used before roots to mean "hundredth" or "hundred": *centiliter* (= *one hundredth of a liter*); *centipede* (= *(creature having) one hundred feet*).

chiro-, *prefix.* from Greek, meaning "hand." This meaning is found in such words as: *chirography, chiropodist, chiropractor, chiromancy.*

circum-, *prefix.* from Latin, meaning "round, around." This meaning is found in such words as *circuit, circuitous, circumcise, circumference, circumnavigate, circumstance, circumvent, circumlocution, circus.*

co-, *prefix.* from Latin, meaning **1.** "joint, jointly, together." This meaning is found in such words as: *cochair, costar, coworker.* **2.** "auxiliary, helping." This meaning is found in such words as: *copilot.*

col-[1], var. of COM- before *l: collateral.*

col-[2], var. of COLO- before a vowel: *colectomy.*

com-, *prefix.* from Latin, meaning "with, together with." This meaning is found in such words as: *combine, compare, commingle.* For variants before other sounds, see CO-, COL-[1], CON-, COR-.

con-, *prefix.* a variant spelling of COM-. It comes from Latin, meaning "together, with." This meaning is found in such words as: *convene, condone, connection.*

contra-, *prefix.* from Latin, meaning "against, opposite, opposing." This meaning is found in such words as: *contraband, contraception, contradict, contrary.*

cor-, *prefix.* another form of COM- that is used before roots beginning with *r: correlate.*

counter-, *prefix.* from Middle English, meaning "against, counter to, opposed to." This meaning is found in such words as: *counterattack, counteroffer, counterclockwise.*

de-, *prefix.* from Latin, used to form verbs and some adjectives meaning **1.** motion or being carried down from, away, or off: *deplane* (= *move down or off an airplane*); *descend* (= *move or go down*); **2.** reversing or undoing the effects of an action: *deflate* (= *reverse the flow of air out of something*); *dehumanize* (= *reverse the positive, humanizing effects of something*); **3.** taking out or removal of a thing: *decaffeinate* (= *take out the caffeine from something*); *declaw* (= *remove the claws of an animal*); **4.** finishing or completeness of an action: *defunct* (= *completely non-functioning*); *despoil* (= *completely spoil*).

deci-, *prefix.* from Latin, meaning "ten." This meaning now appears in the names of units of measurement that are one tenth the size of the unit named by the second element of the compound: *decibel* (= *one tenth of a bel*); *deciliter* (= *one-tenth of a liter*). See the root -DEC-.

dem-, *prefix.* from Greek, meaning "people." This meaning is found in such words as: *demagogue, democracy, demography.*

demi-, *prefix.* from French, meaning "half." This meaning is found in such words as: *demigod, demitasse.*

demo-, *prefix.* like DEM-, from Greek, meaning "people, population." This meaning is found in such words as: *democracy, demography.*

di-, *prefix.* from Greek, meaning "two, double." This meaning is found in such words as: *diptych, dioxide.*

dia-, *prefix.* from Greek, meaning "through, across, from point to point; completely." These meanings are found in such words as: *diachronic, diagnosis, dialogue, dialysis, diameter, diaphanous, diarrhea, diathermy.*

dis-, *prefix.* from Latin, meaning "apart." It now has the following meanings: **1.** opposite of: *disagreement* (= opposite of agreement). **2.** not: *disapprove:* (= not to approve); *dishonest* (= not honest); *disobey* (= not obey). **3.** reverse; remove: *disconnect* (= to remove the connection of); *discontinue* (= to stop continuing); *dissolve* (= remove the solidness of; make liquid).

dys-, *prefix.* from Greek, meaning "ill, bad." This meaning is found in such words as: *dysentery, dyslexia, dyspepsia.*

electro-, *prefix.* from New Latin, meaning "electric" or "electricity": *electro- + magnetic → electromagnetic.*

em-, *prefix.* a form of EN- used before roots beginning with *b, p,* and sometimes *m: embalm.* Compare IM-1.

en-, *prefix.* ultimately from Latin, used before adjectives or nouns to form verbs meaning **1.** to cause (a person or thing) to be in (the place, condition, or state mentioned); to keep in or place in: *en- + rich → enrich* (= to cause to be rich); *en- + tomb → entomb* (= to cause to be in a tomb); **2.** to restrict on all sides, completely: *en- + circle → encircle* (= to restrict on all sides within a circle).

epi-, *prefix.* from Greek, meaning "on, upon, at" (*epicenter*), "outer, exterior" (*epidermis*), "accompanying, additional" (*epiphenomenon*).

eu-, *prefix.* from Greek, meaning "good, well"; it now sometimes means "true, genuine." This meaning is found in such words as: *eugenics, eulogize, eulogy, euphemism, euphoria, euthanasia.*

Euro-, *prefix.* contraction of "Europe," used with roots and means "Europe," "Western Europe," or "the European Community": *Euro- + -centric → Eurocentric* (= centered on Europe); *Euro- + -crat → Eurocrat* (= bureaucrat in the European Community). Also, *esp. before a vowel,* **Eur-.**

ex-, *prefix.* from Latin, meaning **1.** "out, out of, away, forth." It is found in such words as: *exclude, exhale, exit, export, extract.* **2.** "former; formerly having been": *ex-member* (= former member).

exo-, *prefix.* from Greek, meaning "outside, outer, external": *exocentric.* Also, *before a vowel,* **ex-.**

extra-, *prefix.* from Latin, meaning "outside of; beyond": *extra- + galactic → extragalactic* (= outside the galaxy); *extra- + sensory → extrasensory* (= beyond the senses).

fore-, *prefix.* from Old English, used before nouns, meaning **1.** before (in space, time, condition, etc.): *fore- + -cast → forecast* (= prediction before weather comes); *fore- + taste → foretaste* (= a taste before the event takes place); *fore- + warn → forewarn* (= to warn ahead of time). **2.** front: *fore- + head → forehead* (= front of the head). **3.** preceding: *fore- + father → forefather* (= father that came before). **4.** superior: *fore- + man → foreman* (= superior to the other workers).

hemo- (or **hema-**), *prefix.* from Greek, meaning "blood." This meaning is found in such words as: *hemoglobin,* *hemophilia, hemorrhage, hemorrhoid.* Also, *esp. before a vowel,* **hem-.**

hyper-, *prefix.* from Greek, used **1.** before nouns and adjectives meaning "excessive; overly; too much; unusual": *hyper- + critical → hypercritical* (= overly critical); *hyper- + inflation → hyperinflation* (= inflation that is unusual or too high). Compare SUPER-. **2.** in computer words to refer to anything not rigidly connected in a step-by-step manner: *hyper- + text → hypertext* (= text or information that the user can gain access to in the order he or she chooses).

hypo-, *prefix.* from Greek, used before roots, meaning "under, below": *hypo- + dermic → hypodermic* (= under the skin); *hypo- + thermia → hypothermia* (= heat or temperature below what it should be). Also, *esp. before a vowel,* **hyp-.**

il-1, *prefix.* another form of IN-2 that is used before roots beginning with *l;* it means "not": *il- + legible → illegible* (= that cannot be easily read).

il-2, *prefix.* another form of IN-1 that is used before roots beginning with *l;* it means "in, into": *il- + -luminate* (= light) *→ illuminate* (= shine on or into).

im-1, *prefix.* another form of IN-2 that is used before roots beginning with *p, b,* and *m;* it means "not": *im- + possible → impossible* (= that is not possible).

im-2, *prefix.* another form of IN-1 that is used before roots beginning with *p, b,* and *m;* it means "in, into": *im- + -migrate → immigrate* (= travel in or into).

in-1, *prefix.* from Old English, used before verbs and nouns and means "in; into; on": *in- + come → income* (= money coming in); *in- + corporate* (= body) *→ incorporate* (= make into one body); *in- + land → inland* (= in the land).

in-2, *prefix.* from Latin, used before adjectives, meaning "not": *in- + accurate → inaccurate* (= not accurate); *in- + capable → incapable* (= not capable); *in- + direct → indirect* (= not direct). For variants before other sounds, see IM-, IL-, IR-.

inter-, *prefix.* from Latin, meaning "between, among": *intercity* (= between cities); *interdepartmental* (= between or among departments).

intra-, *prefix.* from Latin, meaning "within": *intraspecies* (= within species). Compare INTRO-, INTER-.

intro-, *prefix.* from Latin, meaning "inside, within": *intro- + -duce* (= lead) *→ introduce* (= bring inside or within to meet someone); *intro- + -version* (= a turning) *→ introversion* (= a turning inside or within). Compare INTRA-.

ir-1, *prefix.* another form of IN-1 that is used before roots beginning with *r: ir- + radiate → irradiate.*

ir-2, *prefix.* another form of IN-2 that is used before roots beginning with *r: ir- + reducible → irreducible.*

iso-, *prefix.* from Greek, meaning "equal." This meaning is found in such scientific and chemical words as: *isochromatic.*

kilo-, *prefix.* from Greek, used before quantities, meaning "thousand": *kilo- + liter → kiloliter* (= one thousand liters); *kilo- + watt → kilowatt* (= one thousand watts).

mal-, *prefix.* from Latin, meaning "bad; wrongful; ill." This meaning is found in such words as: *maladroit, malcontent, malfunction.*

maxi-, *prefix.* contraction of the word *maximum,* meaning "very large or long in comparison with others of its kind." This meaning is found in such words as: *maxiskirt.*

mega-, *prefix.* from Greek, meaning **1.** extremely large, huge: *megalith (= extremely large stone or rock); meagstructure (= a huge structure).* **2.** one million of the units of (the base root or word): *megahertz (= one million hertz); megaton (= one million tons).* **3.** very large quantities or amounts: *megabucks (= a great deal of money); megadose (= a large dose of medicine)* **4.** things that are extraordinary examples of their kind: *megahit (= a smash movie or stage hit); megatrend (= important, very popular trend).*

meta-, *prefix.* from Greek, meaning "after, along with, beyond, among, behind." These meanings are found in such words as: *metabolism, metamorphosis, metaphor, metaphysics.*

micro-, *prefix.* from Latin, meaning **1.** small or very small in comparison with others of its kind: *micro- + organism → microorganism (= very small living creature).* **2.** restricted in scope: *micro- + habitat → microhabitat; micro- + economics → microeconomics.* **3.** containing or dealing with texts that require enlargement to be read: *micro- + film → microfilm.* **4.** one millionth: *micro- + gram → microgram.* Also, *esp. before a vowel,* **micr-.**

mid-, *prefix.* from Old English, meaning "being at or near the middle point of": *midday; mid-Victorian; mid-twentieth century.*

milli-, *prefix.* from Latin, meaning **1.** one thousand: *milli- + -pede (= foot) → millipede (= a small creature with very many legs).* **2.** (in the metric system) equal to 1/1000 of the unit mentioned: *milli- + meter → millimeter (= 1/1000 of a meter).*

mini-, *prefix.* contraction of the word *minimum,* meaning **1.** of a small or reduced size in comparison with others of its kind: *mini- + car → minicar; mini- + gun → minigun.* **2.** limited in scope, intensity, or duration: *mini- + boom (= economic upturn) → miniboom (= short-lived economic boom); mini- + course → minicourse (= short course of study).* **3.** (of clothing) short; not reaching the knee: *mini- + dress → minidress; mini- + skirt → miniskirt.* See -MIN-, -MICRO-.

mis-, *prefix.* from Old English, used before nouns, verbs, and adjectives meaning **1.** mistaken; wrong; wrongly; incorrectly: *mis- + trial → mistrial (= a trial conducted improperly); mis- + print → misprint (= something incorrectly printed); misfire: (= fail to fire properly).* **2.** the opposite of: *mis- + trust → mistrust (= the opposite of trust).*

mono-, *prefix.* from Greek, meaning "one, single, lone." This meaning is found in such words as: *monarch, monastery, monochrome, monocle, monogamy, monogram, monograph, monolingual, monolith, monologue, mononucleosis, monopoly, monopterous, monorail, monosyllable, monotonous.*

multi-, *prefix.* from Latin, meaning "many, much, multiple, many times, more than one, composed of many like parts, in many respects": *multi- + colored → multicolored (= having many colors); multi- + vitamin → multivitamin (= composed of many vitamins).*

neo-, *prefix.* from Greek, meaning "new." It has come to mean "new, recent, revived, changed": *neo- + colonialism → neocolonialism (= colonialism that has been revived); neo- + -lithic → neolithic (= of a recent Stone Age).* Also, *esp. before a vowel,* **ne-.**

neuro-, *prefix.* from Greek, meaning "nerve, nerves." Its meaning now includes "nervous system," and this meaning is found in such words as: *neurology, neurosurgery.*

non-, *prefix.* from Latin, usually meaning "not," used **1.** before adjectives and adverbs and means a simple negative or absence of something: *non- + violent → nonviolent.* **2.** before a noun of action and means the failure of such action: *non- + payment → nonpayment (= failure to pay).* **3.** before a noun to suggest that the thing mentioned is not true, real, or worthy of the name, as in *nonbook, noncandidate, non-event.*

ob-, *prefix.* from Latin, used before roots, meaning "toward," "to," "on," "over," "against": *ob- + -jec- → object.*

octa-, *prefix.* from Greek, meaning "eight": *octa- + -gon → octagon (= eight-sided figure).*

omni-, *prefix.* from Latin, meaning "all": *omni- + directional → omnidirectional (= in all directions).*

ortho-, *prefix.* from Greek, meaning "straight, upright, right, correct": *ortho- + graph → orthography (= correct writing); ortho- + dontics → orthodontics (= dentistry dealing with straightening teeth); ortho- + pedic → orthopedic (= correction of improper bone structure from childhood).*

out-, *prefix.* from Old English, used **1.** before verbs, meaning "going beyond, surpassing, or outdoing (the action of the verb)": *out- + bid → outbid; out- + do → outdo; out- + last → outlast.* **2.** before nouns to form certain compounds meaning "outside; out": *out- + cast → outcast; out- + come → outcome; out- + side → outside.*

over-, *prefix.* from Old English, meaning **1.** the same as the adverb or adjective OVER, as in: *overboard; overcoat; overhang; overlord; overthrow.* **2.** "over the limit; to excess; too much; too": *overact (= to act too much); overcrowd (= to crowd too many people or things into); overaggressive (= too aggressive); overfull; overweight.* **3.** "outer," as when referring to an outer covering: *overskirt (= a skirt worn over something, such as a gown).*

pan-, *prefix.* from Greek, meaning "all." This meaning is found in such words as: *panorama; pantheism.* It is also used esp. in terms that imply or suggest the union of all branches of a group: *Pan-American; Pan- + hellenic (Greek) → Panhellenic (= all Greeks united in one group); Pan-Slavism (= all the people of Slavic background united).*

para-¹, *prefix.* from Greek, meaning 1. "at or to one side of, beside, side by side." This meaning is found in such words as: *parabola; paragraph.* 2. "beyond, past, by": *paradox.* 3. "abnormal, defective": *paranoia.* 4. (before names of jobs or occupations) "ancillary, subsidiary, assisting." This meaning is found in such words as: *paralegal; paraprofessional.* Also, *esp. before a vowel,* **par-.**

para-², *prefix.* taken from PARACHUTE, and is used to form compounds that refer to persons or things that use parachutes or that are landed by parachute: *paratrooper.*

penta-, *prefix.* from Greek, meaning "five": *penta- + -gon → pentagon (= five-sided figure).*

per-, *prefix.* from Latin, used before roots, meaning "through, thoroughly, completely, very": *per- + -vert → pervert (= a person completely turned away from the normal); per- + -fect → perfect (= thoroughly or completely done).*

peri-, *prefix.* from Greek, used before roots, meaning **1.** "about, around": *peri- + meter → perimeter (= distance around an area); peri- + -scope → periscope (= instru-*

ment for looking around oneself). **2.** "enclosing, surrounding": peri- + cardium → pericardium (= a sac surrounding the heart). **3.** "near": peri- + helion → perihelion (= point of an orbit nearest to the sun).

petro-¹, prefix. from Greek, meaning "rock, stone": petro- + -ology → petrology (= the study of rocks or stone).

petro-², prefix. taken from PETROLEUM and used to form compounds: petro- + chemistry → petrochemistry; petro- + power → petropower (= power derived from petroleum).

photo-, prefix. from Greek, meaning "light": photo- + biology → photobiology; photo- + -on → photon (= elementary "particle" of light). Also means "photographic" or "photograph": photo- + copy → photocopy.

poly-, prefix. from Greek, meaning "much, many": polyandry (= the custom of having many husbands); polyglot (= speaking many languages).

post-, prefix. from Latin, meaning "after (in time), following (some event)"; "behind, at the rear or end of": post- + industrial → postindustrial (= after the industrial age); post- + war → postwar (= after the war).

pre-, prefix. from Latin, **1.** meaning "before, in front of," "prior to, in advance of," "being more than, surpassing": pre- + -dict → predict (= say in advance of something); pre- + eminent → preeminent (= surpassing or being more than eminent); pre- + face → preface (= something written in front of a book, etc.) **2.** used before verbs to form new verbs that refer to an activity taking place before or instead of the usual occurrence of the same activity: pre- + board → preboard (= to board an airplane before the other passengers); pre- + cook → precook (= cook before regular cooking). **3.** used in forming adjectives that refer to a period of time before the event, period, person, etc., mentioned in the root: pre- + school → preschool (= before the age of starting school); pre- + war → prewar (= before the war started).

pro-¹, prefix. from Latin, **1.** meaning "forward, forward movement or location; advancement": proceed; progress; prominent; promote; propose. **2.** used before roots and words, meaning "bringing into existence": procreate; produce. **3.** used before roots and words, meaning "in place of": pronoun. **4.** used to form adjectives, meaning "favoring the group, interests, course of action, etc., named by the noun; calling for the interests named by the noun": pro- + choice → pro-choice (= in favor of allowing a choice to be made regarding abortions); pro- + war → prowar (= in favor of fighting a war).

pro-², prefix. from Greek, meaning **1.** "before, beforehand, in front of": prognosis; prophylactic; prothesis; proboscis. **2.** "primitive or early form": prodrug; prosimian.

proto-, prefix. from Greek, meaning "first, foremost, earliest form of": proto- + lithic → protolithic; protoplasm. Also, esp. before a vowel, **prot-.**

pseudo-, prefix. from Greek, meaning **1.** "false; pretended; unreal": pseudo- + intellectual → pseudointellectual (= a person pretending to be an intellectual). **2.** "closely or deceptively resembling": pseudo- + carp → pseudocarp (= a fish closely resembling a carp); pseudo- + -pod → pseudopod (= a part of an animal that closely resembles a foot). Also, esp. before a vowel, **pseud-.**

psycho-, prefix. from Greek, meaning "soul; mind." This meaning is found in such words as: parapsychology, psychedelic, psychiatry, psychic, psychological, psychology, psychopath, psychosis, psychotic.

pyro-, prefix. from Greek, meaning "fire, heat, high temperature": pyromaniac, pyrotechnics.

quasi-, prefix. from Latin, meaning "as if, as though." It is used before adjectives and nouns and means "having some of the features but not all; resembling; almost the same as": quasi-scientific, quasiparticle, quasi-stellar.

radio-, prefix. ultimately from Latin radius, meaning "beam, ray." It is used before roots and nouns and means "radiant energy": radiometer. It is also used to mean "radio waves": radiolocation; radiotelephone. Other meanings are: **1.** the giving off of rays as a result of the breakup of atomic nuclei: radioactivity; radiocarbon. **2.** x-rays: radiograph; radiotherapy.

re-, prefix. from Latin, used **1.** before roots and sometimes words to form verbs and nouns meaning or referring to action in a backward direction: re- + -cede- → recede (= fall back); re- + -vert- → revert (= turn back). **2.** to form verbs or nouns showing action in answer to or intended to undo or reverse a situation: rebel; remove; respond; restore; revoke. **3.** to form verbs or nouns showing action that is done over, often with the meaning that the outcome of the original action was in some way not enough or not long lasting, or that the performance of the new action brings back an earlier state of affairs: recapture; reoccur; repossess; resole (= put another sole on a shoe); retype.

retro-, prefix. from Latin, meaning "back, backward": retro- + -gress → retrogress (= proceed backward); retro- + rocket → retrorocket.

self-, prefix. from Old English, used **1.** before nouns to refer to something that one does by oneself or to oneself: self-control (= control of oneself); self-government; self-help; self-portrait. **2.** before adjectives and nouns to refer to an action that is done without assistance: self-adhesive; a self-loading gun; self-study.

semi-, prefix. from Latin, meaning **1.** "half": semiannual; semicircle. **2.** "partially; partly; somewhat": semiautomatic; semidetached; semiformal. **3.** "happening or occurring twice in (a certain length of time)": semiannual.

sex-, prefix. from Latin, meaning "six": sexpartite (= having six parts or divisions).

socio-, prefix. from Latin, used before roots and sometimes words, meaning "social; sociological; society": socio- + economic → socioeconomic; socio- + -metry → sociometry (= social statistics).

step-, prefix. from Old English, used before words to name a member of a family related by the remarriage of a parent and not by blood: When my father married his second wife, she already had a son who became my stepbrother.

sub-, prefix. from Latin, meaning **1.** "under, below, beneath": subsoil; subway. **2.** "just outside of, near": subalpine; subtropical. **3.** "less than, not quite": subhuman; subteen. **4.** "secondary, at a lower point in a hierarchy": subcommittee; subplot. Sometimes this prefix is spelled as **su-, suc-, suf-, sug-, sum-, sup-, sur-, sus-.**

super-, prefix. from Latin, meaning **1.** "above, beyond; above or over (another); situated or located over": superimpose, superstructure, superficial. **2.** "an individual, thing, or property that surpasses customary or normal amounts or levels, as being larger, more powerful, or having something to a great degree or to too great a degree": superconductivity, superman, supercomputer, superhighway, superhuman, supercritical, supercool.

supra-, prefix. from Latin, meaning "above, over; beyond the limits of": supraorbital; supranational. Compare SUPER-.

sur-, *prefix.* from French, meaning "over, above, in addition": *surcharge; surname; surrender.*

sym-, *prefix.* another form of the prefix SYN-. It appears before roots beginning with *b, p, m: symbol; symphony; symmetry.*

syn-, *prefix.* from Greek, meaning "with; together." This meaning is found in such words as: *synchronous, idiosyncrasy, photosynthesis, synagogue, synchronize, synonym, synthesis.* See SYM-.

tele-, *prefix.* **1.** from Greek, meaning "far." It is used before roots and sometimes words and means "reaching over a distance, carried out between two remote points, performed or operating through electronic transmissions": *telegraph; telekinesis; teletypewriter.* **2.** *tele-* is also used to mean "television:" *telegenic; telethon.* Also, *esp. before a vowel,* **tel-**.

trans-, *prefix.* from Latin, used **1.** before verb roots that refer to movement or carrying from one place to another; it means "across; through": *transfer; transmit; transplant.* **2.** to mean "complete change": *transform; transmute.* **3.** before roots to form adjectives that mean "crossing, going beyond, on the other side of (the place or thing named)": *transnational; trans-Siberian.*

tri-, *prefix.* from Latin, meaning "three": *triatomic; trilateral.*

ultra-, *prefix.* from Latin, meaning **1.** "located beyond, on the far side of": *ultraviolet.* **2.** "carrying to the furthest degree possible, on the fringe of": *ultraleft; ultramodern.* **3.** "extremely": *ultralight.* **4.** "going beyond normal or customary bounds or limits": *ultramicroscope; ultrasound; ultrastructure.*

un-[1], *prefix.* from Old English, used very freely to form adjectives and the adverbs and nouns formed from these adjectives. It means "not," and it brings negative or opposite force: *unfair, unfairly, unfairness; unfelt; unseen; unfitting; unformed; unheard-of; unrest; unemployment.*

un-[2], *prefix.* from Old English, used **1.** before verbs, meaning "a reversal of some action or state, or a removal, a taking away, or a release": *unbend; uncork; unfasten.* **2.** before some verbs to intensify the meaning: *unloose (= let loose with force).*

under-, *prefix.* from Old English, meaning **1.** "a place or situation below or beneath": *underbrush; undertow.* **2.** "lower in grade, rank or dignity": *undersheriff; understudy.* **3.** before adjectives to mean "of lesser degree, extent, or amount": *undersized.* **4.** "not showing enough; too little": *underfed.*

vice-, *prefix.* from Latin, meaning "in place of, instead of." It is used before roots and sometimes words and means "deputy"; it is used esp. in the titles of officials who serve in the absence of the official named by the base word: *viceroy (→ vice- + roy, "king"); vice-chancellor; vice-chairman.*

COMMON SUFFIXES

-ability, *suffix.* ultimately from Latin, a combination of -ABLE and -ITY, used to form nouns from adjectives that end in *-able: capable (adjective) → capability (noun); reliable (adjective) → reliability (noun).*

-able, *suffix.* ultimately from Latin, added to verbs to form adjectives meaning "capable of, fit for, tending to": *teach + -able → teachable (= capable of being taught); photograph + -able → photographable = (fit for photographing).* Compare -IBLE.

-aceous, *suffix.* from Latin, meaning "having the nature of, made of." This meaning is found in such words as *herbaceous, cretaceous.*

-acious, *suffix.* from Latin, used after some roots to form adjectives meaning "tending to; abounding in": *tenacious* (from *ten-* "hold on" + *-acious*) = *tending to hold on; loquacious* (from *loq(u)-* "talk" + *-acious*) = *tending to talk.* Compare -OUS.

-acity, *suffix.* from Middle English, used after some roots to form nouns with the meaning "tendency toward; abundance in": *tenacity* (from- *ten-* "hold on" + *-acity*) = *tendency toward holding on.*

-age, *suffix.* ultimately from Latin, used to form noncount mass or abstract nouns **1.** from other nouns, with meanings such as "collection" (*coinage = a collection or group of coins*) and "quantity or measure" (*footage = quantity of feet in measurement*). **2.** from verbs, with meanings such as "process" (*coverage = the act or process of covering*), "the outcome of, the fact of" or "the physical effect or remains of" (*spoilage = the result of spoiling; wreckage = the remains of wrecking*), and "amount charged" (*towage = charge for towing; postage = amount charged for posting, that is, sending through the mail*).

-aholic, *suffix.* (originally taken from the word ALCOHOLIC) used to form new words with the general meaning "a person who is addicted to or strongly desires" the activity being shown by the initial part of the word. Thus, a *chargeaholic* is someone who uses a charge card a lot; a *foodaholic* is someone who always wants food. Compare -HOLIC.

-al[1], *suffix.* from Latin, added to nouns to form adjectives meaning "relating to, of the kind of, having the form or character of": *autumn + -al → autumnal (= relating to the season autumn); nature + -al → natural (= having the character of nature).*

-al[2], *suffix.* from Latin, added to verbs to form nouns meaning "the act of": *deny + -al → denial (= the act of denying); refuse + -al → refusal (= the act of refusing).*

-ally, *suffix.* form from **-al**[1] + **-ly,** used to form adverbs from certain adjectives ending in -IC: *terrific (adj.) + -ally → terrifically (adverb).*

-an, *suffix.* from Latin, meaning "of, pertaining to, having qualities of," **1.** added to names of places or people to form adjectives and nouns meaning **a.** being connected with a place: *Chicago + -an → Chicagoan;* **b.** having membership in a group of: *Episcopal + -(i)an → Episcopalian;* **2.** used to form adjectives meaning "of or like (someone); supporter or believer of": *Christ + -(i)an → Christian; Freud + -(i)an → Freudian (= supporter of or believer in the theories of Sigmund Freud).* **3.** used to form nouns from words ending in *-ic* or *-y* meaning "one who works with": *electric + -(i)an → electrician; comedy + -an → comedian.*

-ance, *suffix.* ultimately from Latin, used **1.** after some adjectives ending in -ANT to form nouns meaning "quality or state of": *brilliant + -ance → brilliance.* **2.** *after some* verb roots to form nouns: *appear* + *-ance* → *appearance*; *resemble* + *-ance* → *resemblance*. See -ANT, -ENCE.

-ant, *suffix.* from Latin, used **1.** after some verbs to form adjectives meaning "doing or performing (the action of the verb)": *please* + *-ant* → *pleasant* (= *doing the pleasing*). **2.** after some verbs to form nouns meaning "one who does or performs (the action of the verb, often a formal action)": *serve* + *-ant* → *servant* (= *one who serves*); *apply* (+ *ic*) + *-ant* → *applicant* (= *one who formally applies, as for a job*). **3.** after some verbs to form nouns meaning: "substance that does or performs (the action of the verb)": *cool* (verb = "to make cool") + *-ant* → *coolant* (= *substance to keep engines cool*). See -ENT.

-ar, *suffix.* from Latin, used **1.** after some nouns (many of which have an *l* before the end) to form adjectives: *circle* + *-ar* → *circular*; *single* + *-ar* → *singular*. **2.** after some verbs to form nouns meaning "one who does or performs an act of": *beg* + *-ar* → *beggar*; *lie* + *-ar* → *liar*.

-ard, *suffix.* from French, used after some verbs and nouns to form nouns that refer to persons who regularly do an activity, or who are characterized in a certain way, as indicated by the stem: *dullard* (= *one who is dull*); *drunkard* (= *one who is drunk*).

-arian, *suffix.* from Latin, used **1.** after some nouns and adjectives that end in -ARY to form personal nouns: *library* + *-arian* → *librarian*; *seminary* + *-arian* → *seminarian*; *veterinary* + *-arian* → *veterinarian*. **2.** after some roots to form nouns meaning "a person who supports, calls for, or practices the principles of (the root noun)": *authority* + *-arian* → *authoritarian* (= *one who believes in central authority*); *totality* + *-arian* → *totalitarian* (= *one who believes in total governmental rule*).

-art, *suffix.* variant form of -ARD, found in such words as: *braggart*.

-ary, *suffix.* from Latin, used **1.** after some nouns to form adjectives meaning: "relating to, connected with": *element* + *-ary* → *elementary*; *honor* + *-ary* → *honorary*. **2.** after some roots to form personal nouns, or nouns that refer to objects that hold or contain things: *secretary;* *-libr-* (= root meaning "book") + *-ary* → *library* (= *place for holding books*); *glossary* (= *place containing specialized words and their meanings*). **3.** after some nouns to form adjectives meaning "contributing to; for the purpose of": *inflation* + *-ary* → *inflationary* (= *contributing to inflation*); *compliment* + *-ary* → *complimentary* (= *for the purpose of complimenting*).

-ate, *suffix.* **1.** from Latin, used to form adjectives meaning "showing; full of": *passion* + *-ate* → *passionate* (= *showing passion*); *consider* + *-ate* → *considerate* (= *showing the action of considering*); *literate*. **2.** used to form verbs meaning "cause to become (like); act as": *regular* + *-ate* → *regulate* (= *make regular, act by rule*); *active* + *-ate* → *activate* (= *cause to become active*); *hyphenate; calibrate*. **3.** used to form nouns meaning **a.** a group of people: *elector* + *-ate* → *electorate* (= *group who elect*). **b.** an area ruled by: *caliph* (a kind of ruler) + *-ate* → *caliphate* (= *area ruled by a caliph*); *protector* + *-ate* → *protectorate* (= *area ruled by a protecting nation*). **c.** the office, institution, or function of: *consul* + *-ate* → *consulate; magistrate; potentate.*

-ation, *suffix.* from Latin, used after some verbs or adjectives (some of which end in -ATE) to form nouns meaning "state or process of": *starve* + *-ation* → *starvation* (= *condition of starving*); *separate* + *-ation* → *separation* (= *state of being separate*).

-ative, *suffix.* from Latin, used after some verbs (some of which end in -ATE) and nouns to form adjectives: *regulate* + *-ative* → *regulative* (= *with the power to regulate*); *norm* (= *rule*) + *-ative* → *normative* (= *having rules*).

-ator, *suffix.* from Latin, used after verbs ending in -ATE to form nouns meaning "person or thing that does or performs (the action of the verb)": *agitate* + *-ator* → *agitator* (= *person who agitates; machine that agitates*); *vibrate* + *-ator* → *vibrator* (= *thing that vibrates*); *narrator; generator; mediator; incubator.*

-based, *suffix.* from the word *base*, used **1.** after nouns to form adjectives. **2.** after nouns of place to form adjectives meaning "operating or working from": *ground* + *-based* → *ground-based* (= *operating from the ground*); *New York* + *-based* → *New York-based* (= *working from New York*). **3.** after nouns to form adjectives meaning "making use of": *computer* + *based* → *computer-based* (= *making use of computers; "as in "computer-based instruction"*); *logic* + *-based* → *logic-based* (= *making use of logic*).

-burger, *suffix.* (originally taken from the word *hamburger*) used after roots and some words to form nouns that mean "the food added to, or substituted for, a basic hamburger": *cheese* + *-burger* → *cheeseburger* (= *a hamburger with cheese added on top*); *fish* + *-burger* → *fishburger* (= *fish substituted for the meat of a hamburger*).

-cracy, *suffix.* ultimately from Greek, meaning "power; rule; government," used after roots to form nouns meaning "rule; government": *auto-* + *-cracy* → *autocracy* (-*government by one ruler*); *theo-* ("God") + *-cracy* → *theocracy* (-*a country governed by the rule of God or a god*). Compare -CRAT.

-crat, *suffix.* ultimately from Greek, meaning "ruler; person having power," used after roots to form nouns meaning "ruler; member of a ruling body": *auto-* + *-crat* → *autocrat* (= *a ruler governing alone*). Compare -CRACY.

-cy, *suffix.* from French and Latin, used **1.** to form nouns from adjectives that have stems that end in *-t, -te, -tic,* and esp. *-nt* **a.** to form abstract nouns: *democrat* + *-cy* → *democracy; accurate* + *-cy* → *accuracy; expedient* + *-cy* → *expediency; lunatic* + *-cy* → *lunacy.* **b.** to form action nouns: *vacant* + *-cy* → *vacancy; occupant* + *-cy* → *occupancy.* **2.** to form nouns meaning "rank or office of": *captain* + *-cy* → *captaincy* (= *rank or office of a captain*); *magistra(te)* + *-cy* → *magistracy* (= *office of a magistrate*).

-dom, *suffix.* from Old English, used after some nouns and adjectives to form nouns meaning **1.** domain or area ruled: *king* + *-dom* → *kingdom* (= *area a king rules*). **2.** collection of persons: *official* + *-dom* → *officialdom* (= *a collection of officials*). **3.** rank: *earl* + *-dom* → *earldom* (= *the rank or position of an earl*). **4.** general condition: *free* + *-dom* → *freedom* (= *general condition of being free*).

-ed, *suffix.* from Old English, **1.** added to words with the following rules of form: **a.** For most regular verbs that end in a consonant, *-ed* is added directly afterwards: *cross* + *-ed* → *crossed*. When the verb ends in *-y,* the *-y* changes to *-i* and *-ed* is added: *ready* + *-ed* → *readied*. If the root ends in *-e,* an *e* is dropped: *save* + *-ed* → *saved*. **b.** The pronunciation of the suffix *-ed* depends on the *sound* that appears before it. After the sounds *p, k, f, th, s, sh,* and *ch* the suffix is pronounced (t): *cross* + *-ed* → *crossed* (krôst); after the sounds *t, d* it is pronounced *(id): edit + -ed → edited (ed'i tid); after all other sounds it is pronounced (d): budge + -ed → budged (bujd).* **2.** carries a number of different meanings. It is used **a.** to form the past tense and past participle of regular verbs: *He crossed the river. He had crossed the river when we got there.* **b.** to form an adjective indicating a condition or quality due to action of the verb: *inflated balloons (= balloons that have been inflated).* **c.** after nouns to form adjectives meaning "possessing, having, or characterized by (whatever the noun base is)": *beard + -ed → bearded (= possessing or having a beard).*

-ee, *suffix.* from French, used **1.** after verbs that take an object to form nouns meaning "the person who is the object of the action of the verb": *address + -ee → addressee (= the person whom someone else addresses).* **2.** after verbs that do not take an object to form nouns meaning "the one doing or performing the act of the verb": *escape + -ee → escapee (= one performing the act of escaping).* **3.** after other words to form nouns meaning "the one who is or does": *absent + -ee → absentee (= one who is absent).*

-eer, *suffix.* from French, used to form nouns meaning "the person who produces, handles, or is associated with" the base word: *engine + -eer → engineer (= person handling an engine).*

-en, *suffix.* from Old English, used **1. a.** after some adjectives to form verbs meaning "to be or make": *hard + -en → harden (= to be or make hard).* **b.** after some nouns to form verbs meaning "to add to, cause to be, or have": *length + -en → lengthen (= to add length to; make long).* **2.** after some nouns that are materials or sources of something to form adjectives that describe the source or material: *gold + -en → golden (= like gold).*

-ence, *suffix.* from Latin, used **1.** after some adjectives ending in -ENT to form nouns meaning "quality or state of": *abstin(ent) + -ence → abstinence.* **2.** after some verb roots to form nouns: *depend + -ence → dependence.* See -ANCE, -ENT.

-ent, *suffix.* from Latin, used **1.** after some verbs to form adjectives meaning "doing or performing (the action of the verb)": *differ + -ent → different.* **2.** after some verbs to form nouns meaning "one who does or performs (the action)": *stud(y) + -ent → student (= one who studies).* See -ANT, -ENCE.

-er¹, *suffix.* from Old English, used **1.** after verbs to form nouns meaning "a person, animal or thing that performs the action of the verb" or "the person, animal or thing used in performing the action of the verb": *bake + -er → baker (= a person who bakes); teach + -er → teacher (= a person who teaches); fertilize + -er → fertilizer (= a thing that is used to fertilize)* **2.** after nouns to form new nouns that refer to the occupation, work, or labor of the root noun: *hat + -er → hatter (= one whose work is making hats); roof + -er → roofer (= one whose occupation is repairing roofs).* **3.** after nouns to form new nouns that refer to the place of origin, or the dwelling place, of the root noun: *Iceland + -er → Icelander (= person who originally comes from Iceland); southern + -er → southerner (= a person who originally comes from, or lives in, the south).* Compare -IER, -OR.

-er², *suffix.* from Middle English, regularly used to form the comparative form of short adjectives and adverbs: *hard + -er → harder; small + -er → smaller; fast + -er → faster.*

-ery (or **-ry**), *suffix.* from French, used **1.** to form nouns that refer to **a.** things in a collection: *green + -ery → greenery* (= green plants as a group); *machine + -ery → machinery (= a group or collection of machines)* **b.** people in a collection: *Jew + -ry → Jewry (= Jews as a group); peasant + -ry → peasantry (= peasants as a group)* **c.** an occupation, activity, or condition: *dentist + -ry → dentistry (= occupation of a dentist); rival + -ry → rivalry (= condition of being a rival); rob + -ery → robbery (= activity of robbing or being robbed).* **2.** to form nouns that refer to a place where the activity of the root is done: *bake + -ery → bakery (= place where baking is done); wine + -ery → winery (= place where wine is made).*

-ese, *suffix.* ultimately from Latin, used **1.** after nouns that refer to place names: **a.** to form adjectives to describe things made in or relating to the place: *Japan + -ese → Japanese (= of or relating to Japan or its people); Vienna + -ese → Viennese (= of or relating to Vienna or its people)* **b.** to form nouns with the meanings "the people living in (the place)" or "the language of (the place)": *Vietnam + -ese → Vietnamese (= the people living in/the language spoken in Vietnam).* **2.** to form nouns that describe in an insulting or humorous way the language characteristic of or typical of the base word: *Brooklyn + -ese → Brooklynese (= the language characteristic of Brooklyn); journal + -ese → journalese (= the language typical of journalists).*

-esque, *suffix.* from French, used after nouns and proper names to form adjectives meaning "resembling," "in the style or manner of," "suggesting the work of" the person or thing denoted by the base word: *Kafka + -esque → Kafkaesque (= in the style or manner of Franz Kafka); Lincoln + -esque → Lincolnesque (= in the style of Abraham Lincoln); picture + -esque → picturesque (= resembling or suggesting a picture).*

-ess, *suffix.* from French, used to form a feminine noun: *count + -ess → countess; god + -ess → goddess; lion + -ess → lioness.* —**Usage.** *The use of words ending in -ESS has declined sharply in the latter half of the 20th century, but some are still current: actress (but some women prefer actor); adventuress; enchantress; governess (only in its child-care sense); heiress (largely in journalistic writing); hostess (but women who conduct radio and television programs are hosts); seamstress; seductress; temptress; and waitress.*

-est, *suffix.* from Old English, regularly used to form the superlative form of short adjectives and adverbs: *fast + -est → fastest; soon + -est → soonest; warm + -est → warmest.*

-ette, *suffix.* from French, used **1.** after nouns to form nouns that refer to a smaller version of the original noun or root: *kitchen + -ette → kitchenette (= small kitchen); novel + -ette → novelette (= smaller novel).* **2.** after nouns to form nouns that refer specifically to a female: *major + -ette → majorette (= female leader of a band, or baton twirler); usher + -ette → usherette (= female usher in a movie theater).* **3.** after nouns to form nouns that refer to a name that is an imitation product of the root: *leather + -ette → leatherette (= imitation leather product).* —**Usage.** *English nouns in which -ETTE signifies a feminine role or identity have been thought of as implying inferiority or unimportance and are now generally avoided. Only (drum) majorette is still widely used, usually indicating a young woman who twirls a baton with a marching band.*

-ferous, *suffix.* from the root *-fer* + the suffix *-ous.* This suffix is found in such words as: *coniferous, pestiferous.*

-fest, *suffix.* from German, added to nouns to form nouns meaning "an assembly of people engaged in a common activity" named by the first element of the compound: *gab + -fest → gabfest (= group of people gabbing or talking a lot); song + -fest → songfest (= assembly of people singing together)*.

-fold, *suffix.* from Old English, used after words that refer to a number or quantity to form adjectives meaning "having the number of kinds or parts" or "multiplied the number of times": *four + -fold → fourfold (= multiplied four times); many + -fold → manyfold (= having many parts or kinds)*.

-footed, *suffix.* from the word *foot*, added to nouns to form adjectives meaning "having (the kind of, number of, etc.) a foot or feet indicated": *a four-footed animal (= an animal having four feet)*.

-free, *suffix.* from Old English, used after nouns to form adjectives meaning "not containing (the noun mentioned); without": *sugar + -free → sugar-free (= not containing sugar); trouble + -free → trouble-free (= without trouble)*.

-ful, *suffix.* from Old English, used **1.** after nouns to form adjectives meaning "full of; characterized by": *beauty + -ful → beautiful (= full of beauty); care + -ful → careful (= characterized by care)*. **2.** after verbs to form adjectives meaning "tending to; able to": *harm + -ful → harmful (= tending to harm); wake + -ful → wakeful (= tending to stay awake)*. **3.** after nouns to form nouns meaning "as much as will fill": *spoon + -ful → spoonful (= as much as will fill a spoon); cup + -ful → cupful (= as much as will fill a cup)*.

-fy, *suffix.* ultimately from Latin, used **1.** after roots to form verbs meaning "to make; cause to be; render": *pure + -fy → purify (= to make pure); simple + -fy → simplify (= make simple); liquid + -fy → liquefy (= to make into a liquid)*. **2.** to mean "cause to conform to": *citify (= cause to conform to city ways)*. Compare -IFY.

-gate, *suffix.* derived from *Watergate*, originally the name of a hotel complex where officials of the Republican party were caught trying to burglarize Democratic party headquarters. *Watergate* then came to be associated with "a political cover-up and scandal." The suffix is used after some nouns to form nouns that refer to scandals resulting from concealed crime in government or business: *Iran + -gate → Irangate (= a scandal involving arms sales to Iran)*.

-gon, *suffix.* from Greek, meaning "side; angle." This suffix is used after roots to form nouns that refer to plane figures having the number of sides mentioned: *poly- (= many) + -gon → polygon (= a many-sided figure)*.

-gram, *suffix.* from Greek, meaning "what is written." It is used after roots to form nouns that refer to something written or drawn, either by hand or machine: *cardio- (= of or relating to the heart) + -gram → cardiogram (= a recording and diagram of a heartbeat, drawn by a machine)*. Compare -GRAPH-.

-hearted, *suffix.* from Middle English, used after adjectives to form adjectives meaning "having the character or personality of (the adjective mentioned)": *cold + -hearted → coldhearted (= having a cold heart; unkind or mean); light + -hearted → lighthearted (= feeling light and happy)*.

-holic, *suffix.* another form of -AHOLIC: *choco(late) + -holic → chocoholic (= person addicted to chocolate)*.

-hood, *suffix.* from Old English, used to form nouns meaning **1.** "the state or condition of": *likely + -hood → likelihood (= the state or condition of being likely); child + -hood → childhood (= the state or period of time of being a child)*. **2.** "a body or group of persons of a particular character or class": *priest + -hood → priesthood (= a body of priests)*.

-ian, *suffix.* from Latin, used to form nouns and adjectives with the meanings of -AN: *Orwell + -ian → Orwellian (= interested in, or relating to, the writing of George Orwell); Washington + -ian → Washingtonian (= a person who lives in Washington)*.

-iatrics, *suffix.* from Greek, used after some roots to form nouns meaning "healing; the medical practice of": *ger- (= old people) + -iatrics → geriatrics (= the healing of older people); ped- (= child) + -iatrics → pediatrics (= medical practice involving children)*.

-iatry, *suffix.* from Greek, used after some roots to form nouns meaning "healing; the medical practice of": *pod- (= foot) + -iatry → podiatry (= the healing of the foot); psych- (= the mind) + -iatry → psychiatry (= the medical practice dealing with the mind)*.

-ibility, *suffix.* from Latin, used to form nouns from adjectives that end in -ible: *reducible (adjective) → reducibility (= the state or condition of being reducible, of being able to be reduced); flexible (adjective) → flexibility (= the state or condition of being able to move smoothly)* See -ABILITY, -ABLE, -IBLE.

-ible, *suffix.* a variant form of -ABLE, used after roots, mostly of verbs, to form adjectives meaning "capable of, fit for, tending to": *cred- (= believe) + -ible → credible (= that can be believed); vis- (= see) + -ible → visible (= that can be seen); reduce + -ible → reducible (= that can be reduced)*. See -ABILITY, -ABLE, -IBILITY.

-ic, *suffix.* from Middle English, used after nouns to form adjectives meaning "of or relating to": *metal + -ic → metallic; poet + -ic → poetic*. This suffix is also used after nouns to form adjectives meaning "having some characteristics of; in the style of": *ballet + -ic → balletic; sophomore + -ic → sophomoric; Byron + -ic → Byronic (= in the style of the writer Byron)*.

-ical, *suffix.* a combination of -IC and -AL[1], used after roots to form adjectives meaning "of or relating to": *rhetor- + -ical → rhetorical*. This suffix originally provided synonyms to adjectives that ended in -IC: *poet + -ic → poetic; poet + -ical → poetical*. But some of these pairs of words or formations are now different in meaning: *econom- + -ic → economic (= of or relating to economics); econom- + -ical → economical (= being careful in spending money); histor- + -ic → historic (= having a long history; important); histor- + -ical → historical (= happening in the past)*.

-ician, *suffix.* extracted from *physician, musician,* etc., used after nouns or roots to form nouns meaning "the person having the occupation or work of": *beauty + -ician → beautician (= person who works in a beauty shop); mort- (= death) + -ician → mortician (= person working to prepare dead people for burial)*.

-ics, *suffix.* from Latin, used after roots to form nouns meaning "a body of facts, knowledge, or principles." Such nouns usually correspond to adjectives ending in IC or -ICAL: *eth- (= custom; character) + -ics → ethics (= the principles of good character); phys- (= body) + -ics → physics (= the principles of bodies in motion and at rest)*.

-ier, *suffix.* from French, used after nouns or roots to form nouns meaning "person or thing that does (the action of the word mentioned); person or thing in charge of (the word mentioned)": *finance* + *-ier* → *financier* (= *person doing finance*); *cour-* (= *run*) + *-ier* → *courier* (= *messenger*); *hotel* + *-ier* → *hotelier* (= *person in charge of hotels*). Compare -ER[1].

-ify, *suffix*. from French, used to form verbs meaning "cause to be in (a stated condition); to make or cause to become (a certain condition)": *intense* + *-ify* → *intensify* (= *cause to be intense*); *speechify* (= *make speeches*). See -FY.

-in, *suffix*. extracted from *sit-in*, used after some verbs to form nouns that refer to organized protests through, using, or in support of the named activity: *pray* + *-in* → *pray-in* (= *a protest in which participants engage in passive resistance and prayer*).

-ine[1], *suffix*. from Latin, used after some roots or nouns to form adjectives meaning "of, relating to, or characteristic of; of the nature of; made of": *crystal* + *-ine* → *crystalline* (= *of, like, or made of crystal*); *equ-* (= *horse*) + *-ine* → *equine* (= *of or relating to horses*).

-ine[2], *suffix*. from French, used after some roots to form nouns that name chemical substances and elements: *caffe-* (= *coffee*) + *-ine* → *caffeine* (= *a chemical substance found in coffee*); *chlor-* + *-ine* → *chlorine*.

-ing[1], *suffix*. **1.** from Old English, used after verbs to form nouns that express the action of the verb or its result, product, material, etc.: *build* + *-ing* → *building: the art of building; a new building*. **2.** after roots (other than verb roots) to form nouns: *off* + *-ing* → *offing*.

-ing[2], *suffix*. from Middle English, used after verbs to form the present participle of verbs: *walk* + *-ing* → *walking: Is the baby walking yet?* These participles are often used as adjectives: *war* + *-ing* → *warring: warring factions*. Some adjectives ending in *-ing* are formed by combining a prefix with a verb. Thus *outgoing* is formed from *out-* + the present participle form of the verb *go* (= *going*). Other examples: *uplifting, outstanding, incoming*.

-ion, *suffix*. ultimately from Latin, used after some roots to form nouns that refer to action or condition: *uni-* (= *one*) + *-ion* → *union* (= *condition of being one*). Compare -TION.

-ious, *suffix*. from Latin, a variant form of -OUS, used after roots to form adjectives: *hilar-* (= *cheerful*) + *-ious* → *hilarious* (= *very funny*).

-ise, *suffix*. *Chiefly British*. See -IZE.

-ish, *suffix*. from Old English, used **1.** after nouns or roots to form adjectives meaning **a.** relating to; in the same manner of; having the characteristics of: *brute* + *-ish* → *brutish*. **b.** of or relating to the people or language of: *Brit-* + *-ish* → *British*; *Swede* + *-ish* → *Swedish*. **c.** like; similar to: *baby* + *-ish* → *babyish*; *mule* + *-ish* → *mulish*; *girl* + *-ish* → *girlish*. **d.** addicted to; inclined or tending to: *book* + *-ish* → *bookish* (= *tending to read books a great deal*). **e.** near or about: *fifty* + *-ish* → *fiftyish* (*nearly fifty years old*). **2.** after adjectives to form adjectives meaning "somewhat, rather": *old* + *-ish* → *oldish* (= *somewhat old*); *red* + *-ish* → *reddish* (= *somewhat red*); *sweet* + *-ish* → *sweetish*.

-ism, *suffix*. from Greek, used **1.** after verb roots to form action nouns: *baptize* → *bapt-* + *-ism* → *baptism*. **2.** to form nouns showing action or practice: *adventure* + *-ism* → *adventurism* (= *the action or practice of taking risks in intervening in international affairs*). **3.** used to form nouns showing state or condition: *alcoholism* (= *disease or condition in which alcohol is involved*). **4.** after roots to form nouns showing the names of principles or doctrines: *Darwinism* (= *principles of Darwin's theory of evolution*); *despotism*. **5.** to form nouns showing an example of a use: *witticism* (= *example of something witty*); *Africanism* (= *word from Africa or from an African language*). Compare -IST, -IZE.

-ist, *suffix*. from French and Latin, forms nouns usually corresponding to verbs ending in *-ize* and nouns ending in *-ism*, and referring to a person who practices or is concerned with something: *novel* + *-ist* → *novelist* (= *someone writing a novel*); *terrorist* (= *one who practices terrorism, one who terrorizes*).

-ite, *suffix*. from Latin, used after nouns and roots to form nouns meaning: **1.** a person associated with or living in a place; a person connected with a tribe, leader, set of beliefs, system, etc.: *Manhattan* + *-ite* → *Manhattanite*; *Israel* + *-ite* → *Israelite*; *Labor* + *-ite* → *Laborite* (= *someone following the Labor Party*). **2.** mineral or fossil; explosive; chemical compound or drug product: *anthracite; cordite; dynamite; sulfite*.

-itis, *suffix*. ultimately from Greek, used **1.** after roots that refer to an inflammation or disease affecting a certain part of the body: *appendix* + *-itis* → *appendicitis; bronchi* (= *part of the lungs*) + *-itis* → *bronchitis*. **2.** to form nouns made up for a particular occasion to refer to something comparable in a funny way to a disease: *The teenagers seem to be suffering from telephonitis* (= *excessive use of the telephone, as if using it were a disease*).

-ive, *suffix*. from French and Latin, used after roots or nouns to form adjectives meaning "having a tendency or connection with; like": *act(ion)* + *-ive* → *active* (= *tending to be full of action or activity*); *sport* + *-ive* → *sportive* (= *like sports*).

-ize, *suffix*. ultimately from Greek, used to form verbs meaning **1.** "to make; cause to become": *fossil* + *-ize* → *fossilize* (= *to make something into a fossil*); *sterile* + *-ize* → *sterilize* (= *to make something sterile*). **2.** "to convert into, give a specified character or form to; change to a state of": *computer* + *-ize* → *computerize* (= *make an office use computers*); *dramat-* + *-ize* → *dramatize* (= *give the form of a drama to some other piece of work*); *American* + *-ize* → *Americanize* (= *convert to an American character*). **3.** "to subject to; cause to undergo or suffer from (an emotion or a process, sometimes named after its originator)": *hospital* + *-ize* → *hospitalize* (= *cause to undergo treatment in a hospital*); *terror* + *-ize* → *terrorize* (= *cause to suffer terror*); *galvan-* + *-ize* → *galvanize* (= *to coat metal or stimulate electrically, as by the experiments of L. Galvani, Italian physicist*). Also, *chiefly British*, **-ise**.

-less, *suffix*. from Old English, used **1.** after nouns to form adjectives meaning "without, not having (the thing or quality named by the noun)": *care* + *-less* → *careless*; *shame* + *-less* → *shameless* **2.** after verbs to form adjectives meaning "that cannot be" plus the *-ed/en* form of the verb; or "that never" plus the *-s* form of the verb: *tire* + *-less* → *tireless* (= *that never tires*); *count* + *-less* → *countless* (= *that cannot be counted*).

-let, *suffix*. from Middle English, used **1.** after a noun to form a noun that is a smaller version of the original noun or root: *book* + *-let* → *booklet* (= *a smaller book*); *pig* + *-let* → *piglet* (= *a smaller pig*). **2.** after a noun to form a noun that is a band, ornament, or article of clothing worn on the part of the body mentioned: *ankle* + *-let* → *anklet* (= *piece of clothing like a sock worn on the ankle*); *wrist* + *-let* → *wristlet* (= *ornament like a bracelet worn on the wrist*).

-like, *suffix.* from Middle English, used after nouns to form adjectives meaning "of or resembling (the noun base)": *child + -like → childlike; life + -like → lifelike.*

-ling, *suffix.* from Old English, used **1.** to form a noun that indicates a feeling of distaste or disgust for the person or thing named: *hire + -ling → hireling (= someone hired to do menial or distasteful tasks); under + -ling → underling.* **2.** to form a noun that is a smaller version or example of the base word: *prince + -ling; duck + -ling → duckling.*

-logy, *suffix.* from Greek, meaning "word." It is used after roots to form nouns meaning "field of study, discipline; list of": *astro- (= star) + -logy → astrology (= study of the influence of stars or events); bio- (= life) + -logy → biology (= study of living things).*

-ly, *suffix.* from Middle English, used **1.** after adjectives to form adverbs: *glad + -ly → gladly; gradual + -ly → gradually.* **2.** after nouns that refer to units of time, to form adjectives and adverbs meaning "at or for every (such unit of time)": *hour + -ly → hourly (= at every hour); day + -ly → daily (= on or for every day).* **3.** after nouns to form adjectives meaning "like (the noun mentioned):" *saint + -ly → saintly; coward + -ly → cowardly.*

-man, *suffix.* from Old English, used to form nouns meaning "person, or man, who is or does (something connected with the noun base)": *mail + -man → mailman (= person who delivers mail).*

-mania, *suffix.* from Greek, used after roots to form nouns meaning "great or strong enthusiasm for (the element of the root)": *biblio- (= book) + -mania → bibliomania (= excessive or strong interest or enthusiasm for books).*

-ment, *suffix.* from French and Latin, used **1.** after verbs to form nouns that refer to the action of the verb: *govern + -ment → government.* **2.** after verbs to form nouns that refer to a state or condition resulting from the action of a verb: *refresh + -ment → refreshment.* **3.** after verbs to form nouns that refer to a product resulting from the action of a verb: *frag- + -ment → fragment (= a piece resulting from the breaking off of something).*

-ness, *suffix.* from Old English, used after adjectives and verbs ending in *-ing* or *-ed/-en* to form nouns that refer to the quality or state of the adjective or verb: *dark + -ness → darkness; prepared + -ness → preparedness (= a state of being prepared).*

-o, *suffix.* derived from Romance nouns ending in *-o,* used **1.** as the final element in certain nouns that are shortened from longer nouns: *ammo (from "ammunition"); combo (from "combination"); promo (from "promotion").* **2.** after certain adjectives and nouns to form nouns that have an unfavorable or insulting meaning: *weird + -o → weirdo (= a very weird person); wine + -o → wino (= someone who drinks too much wine).* **3.** after certain nouns and adjectives to form informal nouns or adjectives; these are often used when speaking directly to another: *kid + -o → kiddo (= a kid or person); neat + -o → neato (= an informal use of "neat"); right + -o → righto (= an informal use of "right").*

-off, *suffix.* from Old English, used to form nouns that name or refer to a competition or contest, esp. between finalists or to break a tie: *cook + -off → cookoff (= a cooking contest); runoff (= a deciding final contest).*

-oid, *suffix.* from Greek, used to form adjectives and nouns meaning "resembling, like," with the suggestion of an incomplete or imperfect similarity to the root element: *human + -oid → humanoid (= resembling a human, but not quite the same).*

-onym, *suffix.* from Greek, meaning "word, name." This meaning is found in such words as: *pseudonym, homonym.*

-or, *suffix.* from French, used to form nouns that are agents, or that do or perform a function: *debtor; tailor; traitor; projector; repressor; sensor; tractor.*

-ory¹, *suffix.* **1.** from Middle English, used after nouns and verbs that end in *-e* to form adjectives meaning "of or relating to (the noun or verb mentioned)": *excrete + -ory → excretory (= of or relating to excreting); sense + -ory → sensory (= of or relating to the senses).* **2.** after certain roots to form adjectives meaning "providing or giving": *satisfact- + -ory → satisfactory (= giving satisfaction).*

-ory², *suffix.* from Latin, used after roots to form nouns that refer to places or things that hold (the root), or places that are used for (the root): *cremat- + -ory → crematory (= a place where bodies are cremated); observat(ion) + -ory → observatory (= place where observations of the heavens are made).*

-ose¹, *suffix.* from Latin, used after roots to form adjectives meaning "full of, abounding in, given to, or like (the root)": *verb- (= word) + -ose → verbose (= full of words); bellic- (= war) + -ose → bellicose (= eager for fighting or war).*

-ose², *suffix.* extracted from *glucose,* used after roots to form nouns that name sugars, carbohydrates, and substances that are formed from proteins: *fruct- + -ose → fructose (= a fruit sugar); lact- + -ose → lactose (= a milk sugar); prote- + ose → proteose (= a compound made from protein).*

-ous, *suffix.* from French, used **1.** after roots to form adjectives meaning "possessing, full of (a given quality)": *glory + -ous → glorious; wonder + ous → wondrous; covet + -ous → covetous; nerve + -ous → nervous.* **2.** after roots to form adjectives referring to the names of chemical elements: *stannous chloride,* $SnCl_2$.

-person, *suffix.* from Latin, used to replace some paired, sex-specific suffixes such as -MAN and -WOMAN or -ER¹ and -ESS: *salesman/saleswoman* are replaced by *sales + -person → salesperson; waiter/waitress* are replaced by *wait + -person → waitperson.*

-phile, *suffix.* from Greek, used **1.** after roots and sometimes words to form nouns meaning "lover of, enthusiast for (a given object)": *biblio- + -phile → bibliophile (= lover of books); Franco- + -phile → Francophile (= lover of France or French things).* **2.** after roots to form nouns meaning "a person sexually attracted to or overly interested in (a given object)": *pedo- + -phile → pedophile (= someone with a sexual attraction for children).*

-phobe, *suffix.* from Greek, used after roots and sometimes words to form nouns that refer to persons who have a fear of something named by the root or preceding word: *Anglo- + phobe → Anglophobe (= fear of English-speakers or of England).*

-phobia, *suffix.* from Greek, used after roots and sometimes words to form nouns with the meaning "dread of, unreasonable hatred toward (a given object)": *agora- (= open space) + phobia → agoraphobia (= fear of open spaces); xeno- (= foreign) + -phobia → xenophobia (= hatred toward foreigners).*

-phobic, *suffix.* from Greek, used after roots and words to form adjectives or nouns meaning "(a person) having a continuous, irrational fear or hatred toward" the object named in the root or preceding word: *xeno- (= foreign) + -phobic → xenophobic (= (a person) having a fear or hatred of foreigners)*.

-proof, *suffix.* ultimately from Latin, used to form adjectives meaning "resistant; not allowing through" the word mentioned: *child + -proof → childproof (= resistant to a child's opening it); water + proof → waterproof (= not allowing water through)*.

-ry, *suffix.* See -ERY.

-s¹ (or **-es**), (s, z, iz), *suffix.* from Old English, used after the root form of verbs and marks the third person singular present indicative form, agreeing with a subject that is singular: *He walks. She runs. The wind rushes through the trees*.

-s² (or **-es**), *suffix.* from Old English, used after count nouns and marks the plural form: *weeks; days; bushes; taxes; ladies; pianos; potatoes*.

-ship, *suffix.* from Old English, used to form nouns meaning **1.** "state or condition of": *friend + -ship → friendship; kin + -ship → kinship*. **2.** "the skill or ability of": *statesman + -ship → statesmanship; apprentice + -ship → apprenticeship*. **3.** "the relation of": *fellow + -ship → fellowship*.

-sick, *suffix.* from Old English, used to form adjectives meaning "sick or ill of or from (the noun of the root)": *car + -sick → carsick (= sick from traveling in a car); air + -sick → airsick (= sick from flying in a plane)*.

-some¹, *suffix.* from Old English, used to form adjectives meaning "like; tending to": *burden + -some → burdensome (= like a burden); quarrel + -some → quarrelsome (= tending to quarrel)*.

-some², *suffix.* from Old English, used to form nouns meaning "a collection (of the number mentioned) of objects": *threesome (= a group of three)*.

-speak, *suffix.* from Old English, used after the ends of words and sometimes roots to form compound nouns that name the style or vocabulary of a certain field of work, interest, time period, etc., that is mentioned in the first word or root: *ad(vertising) + -speak → adspeak (= the jargon of advertising); art + -speak → artspeak (= the language used in discussing art); future + -speak → futurespeak*.

-ster, *suffix.* from Old English, used at the ends of words to form nouns, often implying a bad or negative sense, and referring esp. to one's occupation, habit, or association: *game + ster → gamester (= one greatly interested in games); trick + -ster → trickster (= one who uses or enjoys dishonest tricks)*.

-th, *suffix.* ultimately from Greek, used after words that refer to numbers to form adjectives referring to the number mentioned: *(four + -th →) fourth; tenth*.

-tion, *suffix.* from Latin, used after verbs to form nouns that refer to actions or states of the verb: *relate + -tion → relation; sect- + -tion → section; abbreviate + -tion → abbreviation*. Compare -ION.

-tious, *suffix.* from Latin, used after roots to form adjectives, some of which are related to nouns: *fiction: fictitious; ambition: ambitious; caution: cautious; rambunctious, propitious*.

-tude, *suffix.* from Latin, used after roots, especially adjectives, to form nouns that refer to abstract ideas: *exact + -tude → exactitude; apt + -tude → aptitude; gratitude; altitude*.

-ty, *suffix.* from French, used after adjectives to form nouns that name or refer to a state or condition: *able + -ty → ability; certain + -ty → certainty; chaste + -ty → chastity*.

-ure, *suffix.* from French, used after roots and verbs to form abstract nouns that refer to action, result, and instrument or use: *press- + -ure → pressure; legislate + -ure → legislature; fract- + ure → fracture*.

-ville, *suffix.* from French, used **1.** in place names, where it meant "city, town": *Charlottesville*. **2.** after roots or words to form informal words, not all of them long-lasting, that characterize a condition, place, person, group, or situation: *dulls + -ville (= a dull, boring situation); gloomsville*.

-ward, *suffix.* from Old English, used to form adjectives or adverbs meaning "in or toward a certain direction in space or time": *backward*. Also, **-wards**.

-ways, *suffix.* from Middle English, used to form adjectives or adverbs meaning "in a certain direction, manner, or position": *sideways*.

-wide, *suffix.* from Old English, used to form adjectives meaning "extending or applying throughout a certain, given space," as mentioned by the noun: *community + -wide → communitywide (= applying to or throughout the community); countrywide; worldwide*.

-wise, *suffix.* from Old English, used **1.** to form adjectives and adverbs meaning "in a particular manner, position, or direction": *clockwise (= moving in a direction like the hands of a clock)*. **2.** to form adverbs meaning "with reference to": *Timewise we can finish the work, but qualitywise, I'm not so sure*.

-woman, *suffix.* from Middle English, used to form nouns meaning "involving a woman; a woman in the role of": *chairwoman; spokeswoman*.

-worthy, *suffix.* from Old English, used to form adjectives meaning **1.** "deserving of, fit for": *news + -worthy → newsworthy (= fit for the news); trust + -worthy → trustworthy*. **2.** "capable of travel in or on": *road + -worthy → roadworthy (= capable of traveling on the road); seaworthy*.

-y¹, *suffix.* from Old English, used to form adjectives meaning "having, showing, or similar to (the substance or action of the word or stem)": *blood + -y → bloody; cloud + -y → cloudy; sexy; squeaky*.

-y² (or **-ie**), *suffix.* from Middle English, used **1.a.** to form nouns that bring or add a meaning of dearness or familiarity to the noun or adjective root, such as proper names, names of pets, or in baby talk: *Bill + -y → Billy; Susan + -ie → Susie; bird + -ie → birdie; sweetie*. **b.** to form nouns that are informal, new, or intended to be new; sometimes these have slightly unpleasant meanings or associations: *boondocks → boon- + -ies → boonies; group + -ie → groupie; Okie (a person from Oklahoma); preemie (= a premature baby); rookie*. **2.** after adjectives to form nouns, often with the meaning that the noun is an extreme (good or bad) example of the adjective or quality: *bad + -ie → baddie; big + -ie → biggie; toughie; sharpie; sickie; whitey*. Compare -O.

-y,³ *suffix.* from Latin, used after verbs to form nouns of action, and certain other abstract nouns: *inquire + -y → inquiry; in + fame + -y → infamy*.

Writing a Research Paper

Writing a research paper requires you to focus on an assigned or chosen topic; gather and interpret research materials; formulate arguments; and organize, document, and express ideas. A research paper may be informative, argumentative, or narrative. It should always be (1) clear in purpose, (2) unbiased, (3) concise, and (4) well documented, with sources acknowledged within the text and in the reference list.

The Topic

The subject of a research paper should raise a question that is not easily answered. The more complex the research question, the easier it is to meet minimum page requirements. It is important, however, not to choose a subject that is so difficult or obscure that no one has written about it. Before settling on a topic, reassure yourself that a paper about this subject is feasible in the time allotted.

Preliminary Research

Think about the thesis of your paper, which will establish the point of your writing. Ask yourself how you are going to communicate your point. What kind of research do you need to argue your thesis? Before you make a commitment to a topic, do some preliminary research to assure yourself that you will be able to locate enough information to write a paper.

Brainstorming

Many writers find prewriting activities helpful when they are developing the subject of their paper. Brainstorming, listmaking, and clustering are some of the creative thinking activities that help writers explore the subjects related to their topic. When you brainstorm, jot down both good and bad ideas along with any examples or tidbits that come to mind. Don't censor or structure your ideas. Instead, you should let your thoughts wander freely. You may want to sit down with friends and think out loud. Let go. Have fun and be silly. Some of the ideas that are funny in a brainstorming session can be restructured into serious arguments. You will find that exploring all of your options at an early stage will help you establish the limits of your arguments as you continue writing.

Choose a topic that is interesting to you. If you are bored with your subject, your audience will be, too. It is easier to spend time researching and writing a paper if you are genuinely interested in the topic.

Creating a Thesis Argument

Remember that a research paper has a thesis as well as a subject. This means that your thoughts and conclusions, not those of other writers, are the essence of the paper. Your research serves only to inform, organize, and support your analysis and conclusions.

The thesis is the "so what" content of the paper. While the topic is what you want to talk about, the thesis is the argument you want to make. Some examples of topics and theses are:

Topic

The Big Bang Theory

Toni Morrison's Novel *Beloved*

Second Language Acquisition

The Emancipation Proclamation

Thesis

The big bang theory explains the expanding of the universe as recorded by telescopes tracking stars.

Toni Morrison's *Beloved* comments on the conservative political movements of the 1980s which encouraged African-Americans to assimilate, effectively denying their cultural history.

The critical period as it is presented in the research of Johnson and Newport does not explain the negative correlation of age and second language learning after puberty.

The Emancipation Proclamation did not address the issue of social inequality in the nineteenth century.

The thesis should capture the essence of your argument in one sentence. Remember that assertions alone do not constitute your argument. You must support each assertion with solid evidence and logical reasoning. You may find at some point later in the writing process that your thesis does not agree with the arguments made in your paper. If this happens, you need to evaluate your thesis and your arguments. Have you discovered something new while writing your paper that makes you rethink your thesis? In this case you should revise your thesis. Has the paper drifted from the point you wanted to make when you wrote your thesis? In that case, you can back up and revise your arguments to get your paper back on track.

Research

The method of research depends on the topic of the paper. You may find journal articles, books, Web pages or interviews to be helpful, depending on your topic. For the accuracy of your own research, you must evaluate the reliability of every source and discard unreliable or false material.

Evaluating Sources

When evaluating the reliability of a source, you should ask three critical questions: (1) is the source well documented? (2) is the source up-to-date? and (3) does the source represent scholarly and professional information?

Documentation in your source materials is as important as the documentation in your own paper. If a source cites previous research in a professional manner and documents new research so that it may be cited by other papers and studies, it can contribute respected information to your paper.

Even respected sources can become outdated. In some fields, like the sciences, findings from ten years ago now might have been proven false and may sound ridiculous next to more recent research. In other studies, like literature, older sources do not lose respectability as quickly. Even for research in the humanities, however, it is important to address both established research and newer theories in your paper.

Finally, it is important to determine the level of academic research presented in the source. Some materials are written based on studies that are funded by businesses with marketing interests. Other materials may be written by interested but uninformed individuals who are presenting nothing more than their personal opinions. Some sources may be filled with the writing of academics padding their tenure portfolios.

The best guard against being taken in by biased, unprofessional writing is a broad base of research. If a work is respected in a field, it will be cited in other sources. Beyond informing yourself through extensive reading, you must, as a writer, think critically about the materials you are reading. Do they seem reasonable? Well researched? Well documented? Current? Unbiased? You must answer all of these questions about a source's reliability before you can agree or disagree with its content.

LIBRARY RESEARCH

In spite of the wealth of information on-line, the library continues to be the best resource for most research. Library research may include books, journals, abstracts, and newspapers.

Books

Most libraries have electronic catalogs that you can search by author, title, or keyword. Some libraries still have card catalogs with note cards organized alphabetically by author and title. Think about the brainstorming you have already done for your paper. What kind of research do you need to make your point? Search the catalog for keywords. Take careful notes with both the call numbers and the bibliographic information of books that look promising. The call numbers will help you find the book. The bibliographic information will help you document your sources in the final paper. Books about a particular subject are often shelved together, so after you have a few call numbers, go into the stacks to find those books. A library map should help you locate the book in the stacks based on its call number. When a book looks promising, look at the titles shelved around it. If a book is relevant to your research, look at its bibliography. The sources used in writing that work may also be useful to you.

Journals

Journals are excellent sources; they often have more specialized information and more recent research than books contain. Journals are usually shelved in a separate area of the library and are often cataloged in a separate database. Some libraries may have bound volumes of indexes for journals. Individual journals often have printed indexes for each year. These indexes may be arranged by subject or paper title. Indexes will typically contain information about the author and title of the article along with a brief description, or abstract, about the research questions and findings.

In many fields of research, indexes are published that cover publications in all of the journals related to that field. The library help desk should be able to answer your questions about which journals are available in your area of interest. You may need to search the following indexes to find articles published about your topic.

Anthropology	Anthropological Literature
Arts	Arts and Humanities Citation Index
Business	Business Periodicals Index
Education	ERIC
Engineering	Engineering Index
Life Sciences	BIOSIS
Linguistics	Linguistics and Language Behavior Abstracts (LLBA)
Literature	Modern Language Association (MLA) Bibliography; Contemporary Literary Criticism (CLC) Select
Performing Arts	International Index to the Performing Arts (IIPA)
Politics	PAIS Bulletin
Social Sciences	Social Science Citation Index (SSCI)
Dissertations from all subject areas	Dissertation Abstracts

INTERNET RESEARCH

Internet research can help you direct your inquiry and formulate your theories when you are brainstorming. One of the best ways to use the Internet is for a "fishing expedition." This is the kind of research that you do when you feel you have an interesting topic, but you don't yet have a thesis and you don't know which direction you will want to take in developing your paper. Set a time limit for Internet browsing; you can follow links for hours and very easily lose sight of your research goal or waste time. Visit more than one search engine and search all of the keywords related to your topic. Follow the links that look interesting. Open promising links in new windows so you don't have to keep moving backward and forward. If you are working on your personal computer, bookmark the URLs you want to come back to. Take notes and carefully document the sources of your information. Don't assume that you will easily find a page again simply because you stumbled across it the first time. If a URL looks helpful, write it down.

Be aware of the limitations of Internet research to answer specific questions or find precise facts. Before you spend time looking for specific information, ask yourself if searching the Net is the easiest way to find what you are looking for. Could you glean the same information from your textbook, your instructor, or a phone call to a company or organization? If you don't find the answer to your question on the Internet, don't waste time following unlikely links. You are probably right to think that the information exists on the Web, but it may be buried so deeply that it cannot be found. Know when to disconnect and look somewhere else.

Evaluating Sources

While it is a good idea to evaluate the reliability of all your sources, it is especially important to verify the reliability of information from the Internet, because the World Wide Web is not regulated as many other published sources are. As with traditional sources, an Internet source should be (1) well documented, (2) up-to-date, and (3) professionally written. When using information from a Web site, writers need to consider (1) who published the page (a company or an individual), (2) the purpose of the publication (personal, professional, scholarly, or commercial), (3) how old the page is, and (4) how well the information is documented.

Many Web pages that look professional and scholarly may not be. The domain name may help establish whether the page is an official, licensed publication of a respected group; however, even these domain names can be deceptive. Look carefully for some indication that the page is official and that the information is licensed. Be aware that the Web is often used for advertising. Commercial pages by pharmaceutical companies, for instance, may have biased medical information intended to promote their product. Traditional books and journals always show a date of publication. This information is not always available on Web pages. If the site has information about the last time it was updated, make a note for your citation information. If no such date is available, be aware that you have no guarantee that the information you are reading is current. Good Web pages will also have documentation for information that comes from other sources and for data from research. Don't use undocumented data; without documentation, you will not be able to defend its inclusion in your research paper.

Documenting Sources

The major style guides have guidelines for citations from the Internet in the text of a paper and in the reference list. Because there is no standard that requires Web page authors to give their names or document the date a page was created or updated, you may not be able to fill in all of the fields of bibliographic information. If the information is not given on the page, simply leave out the empty fields in your documentation.

INTERVIEWS AND STUDIES

Both interviews and studies require time and effort to plan and execute. The payoff for this work is often small, with your results filling only a fraction of the final paper. Nonetheless, interviews and studies often contribute fresh material and make your research more original.

Interviews are appropriate for both small informal papers about your community, your school, or your family and formal studies about industries and corporations. Interviews can be conducted by phone or in person. Prepare your questions well in advance, but be willing to follow lines of inquiry that are presented by the interviewee as well. If you decide to use quotations or other specific information from the interview in your final paper, it is best to first check with the interviewee, allowing him or her to make corrections or adjustments.

Studies may take the form of experiments or surveys. When giving a survey, it is important to construct your questionnaire in an unbiased manner. Leading questions will invalidate your results. Try to limit the number of open-ended questions in a written questionnaire. They are difficult to quantify, and people may leave them blank because they are more time-consuming and less structured than other questions. Experiments are usually based on the measurable differences between a control group and a test group. Work out the details of the experiment and then speak with an instructor or mentor about the design for your study. The structure of your experiment and the number of variables you study will affect the kind of analyses that can be performed on your data. If you need people to participate in your experiment, you may have to get approval from a board at your school or another agency. Make sure you have permission from any supervising committee and from the participants in your study to use the data you are gathering in a paper.

TAKING RESEARCH NOTES

When you read, take systematic notes, organizing and explaining various aspects of the topic. Don't photocopy large sections of books or print every page of Internet research you find. This wastes the time you spend doing it and the time you will need to spend later to sift through the information and find what is relevant. Think while you read about what kind of information you will need to prove your point. Taking notes on index cards will help you sort and rearrange information. If you are taking notes on a computer, attach bibliographic information and page numbers to each note so that you don't risk separating the note from its source when cutting and pasting.

While taking notes, record not only factual information but also relevant quotations, questions that come to mind, and personal observations and ideas. Write both the source and the page number of direct quotations and information that is the unique idea of another person. You may find it helpful to summarize various points as you go—in your own words, not those of the authors consulted. This will make the actual writing of the paper easier and lessen the risk of inadvertent plagiarism.

WRITING

PREWRITING

Before you begin writing, take inventory of your research. Brainstorm for arguments as you did for topics. Some people find it helpful to explain their research to a friend. Ask your friend to point out problems in your argument or ask questions if he or she doesn't understand your point. This exercise allows you to work out your opinions and arguments before you start writing. Make some kind of a rough outline to organize your approach to the topic. Outlines can be traditional linear representations of your points or a less structured grouping of thoughts in tree or web form. Preparing an outline or diagram will also help you decide how to organize the material.

ORGANIZING PARAGRAPHS

Some traditional ways to organize a paper are:

> chronologically
> by category
> in order of importance
> from the concrete to the abstract.

Organize your arguments based on the evidence you have gathered in your research. Each argument should be presented in a separate paragraph. In general, the length of a paragraph in a double-spaced format should range from one-third to one-half of the page. This is only a rule of thumb. However, if a paragraph is shorter than one-third of the page, consider fleshing out the point further. If a paragraph is longer than half of the page, you may be grouping two or more points together. Break separate arguments out into separate paragraphs for clarity.

The typical paragraph begins with a topic sentence. The body of the paragraph follows and contains the bulk of the content. The concluding sentence brings closure to the paragraph and transitions to the next paragraph. Transitions between paragraphs are important for clarity. Even if your arguments are well supported and your organization is logical, your paper will be confusing without transition sentences. The last sentence of each paragraph should show the reader how the next paragraph relates to the current point. Sequential paragraphs without transition sentences are disorienting, like two participants in a conversation talking about different things.

Conversation without Transition:

A: "I am a fan of the Chicago Bears."

B: "I like hot dogs."

Paragraph without Transition:

People who went to football games as children feel nostalgic about the sport.

People like hot dogs and soda.

Conversation with Transition:

A: "I am a fan of the Chicago Bears."

B: "*I love going to football games and ordering food. I love hot dogs.*"

Paragraph with Transition:

People who went to football games as children feel nostalgic about the sport. *Their nostalgia may be sparked by the game or any number of other factors.*

Some fans may love hot dogs and soda *because of the memories they associate with these tastes.*

The first paragraph of a paper is the introduction. In this paragraph, introduce both your topic, the "what," and your thesis, the "so what." Your introduction should be catchy, making the reader want to read the rest of the paper. The introduction also tells the reader what to expect in the rest of the paper. Think of this as a preview, not a statement of purpose. Avoid announcing your intentions to your audience.

A Statement of Purpose (avoid this)

In this paper I will show that requests are like complaints; they can be seen as rude and require politeness.

A Preview (better)

Requesting behavior resembles complaining behavior and meets all of the criteria for a face-threatening act outlined in the research of Brown and Levinson.

Your preview of coming arguments need not be very detailed, but it should prepare the reader for the kind of material that will be found in the paper. The introduction should also build the reader's confidence in your writing and research. It is important to write as a voice of authority from the beginning of your paper. If you express doubts about your research or knowledge, your audience won't feel motivated to read what you have written.

The introduction and the conclusion are often the most difficult sections to compose. If beginning the paper is difficult, you may want to freewrite, without structuring or censoring your thoughts. Don't just sit looking at the blank page and trying to think of a title. Start getting your ideas on paper. Once you have warmed up and found your voice, you can go back and rewrite your introduction. Some people skip the introduction entirely when they begin writing. You can start with a section of the paper that is easier to write and come back later to the introduction and title sections.

The body of your paper is where you make your argument. Your research should determine how you organize the content of this section. It is important, however, to do more than simply report your findings. Do not wait until the conclusion to add your analysis of the data. As each part of your research is presented, add your original ideas and critiques. Integrate quotations and paraphrases of established research with your own thoughts. Be sure to carefully document information that you have taken from other sources. Then add to the research based on your understanding of the facts. Your synthesis of the material will show how well you understand the research you have gathered.

Every argument has a weak point. It is often important to use one of the paragraphs in the body of your paper to acknowledge the limitations in your argument. Do not ignore important arguments against your position or your research findings. A paragraph that discusses the weakness in your argument should both concede limits and show how your main argument is strong in spite of these flaws.

The conclusion of your paper should revisit the promises made in the introduction and show how they were fulfilled. Show how the claims made by your thesis have been supported in the body of your paper. Do not simply recopy material from other sections of your paper into your conclusion. Your conclusion should leave the reader feeling that something was accomplished or proven in the body of the paper. Finally, the conclusion should leave the reader with a sense of closure, a feeling that your research and your analysis form a complete whole and the discussion has come to an end.

VOICE AND TONE

Your voice and tone should be appropriate to your audience. Use vocabulary and style that are based on your knowledge of your audience and your relationship with your audience. Before you begin writing your paper, ask your instructor what level of formality is expected. Traditionally, research papers required a detached, formal style. In this style, all first-person references were avoided. If a first-person reference was unavoidable, the plural was preferred, *we* in place of *I*. In many cases the passive voice was preferred over the active voice. This style has been criticized by some readers and writers as being too vague and encouraging convoluted prose. Writers are now often encouraged to use the active voice and to include first-person references when necessary. These style constraints are a matter of personal preference. Find out which style is expected of you before you begin writing. Regardless of the level of formality you choose to exhibit in your paper, you should always (1) follow the rules of grammar, (2) eliminate colloquial expressions, including contractions (*a lot, really, stuff; can't, won't*) and (3) avoid judgmental adjectives (*fabulous, awesome, horrific*).

Do not expect to write a good research paper in just one draft. A second and third draft will almost always be necessary. In the first draft, concentrate on substance and organization. Grammar, sentence construction, and spelling can be corrected later.

REVISING, EDITING, AND PROOFREADING

After the first draft has been read and reread, it should be rewritten and reorganized as much as necessary. If you compose your original draft on the computer, save subsequent drafts as separate documents so that you can go back to an earlier draft if necessary. Save frequently, and print copies of various drafts for easy reference in the revision process.

Computerized spell checkers and grammar checkers are useful tools, but they do not replace proofreading. A spell checker is most reliable in finding misspellings that produce "nonwords"—words with transposed, wrong, or missing letters. For example, it will reject *ther* (for *there*) and *teh* (for *the*). However, it cannot distinguish between words that sound or look alike but differ in meaning. It will accept *to* or *too* regardless of context. A grammar checker will look for some of these errors but will not find all of them, and it may even tell you something is an error when it is not. For instance, in the sentence *This wastes the time you spend sifting through your research notes*, the grammar checker suggests the corrections: *This waste* or *These wastes.* It believes that *waste* is a noun, and *This* is a determiner. In fact, *This* is a pronoun and *wastes* is a verb. In addition, a grammar checker often talks about errors in a way that is difficult to under-

stand. The computerized checkers are helpful as long as you do not rely too heavily on them. Proofread your work to see if your sentences are complete, your spelling is correct, and your writing is clear and concise. Some errors are easy to miss on the monitor, so print a hard copy to use for editing.

It is often useful to read your paper out loud. This helps you notice errors that your eyes might otherwise skim over. Reading aloud also helps you hear the rhythm of your prose. Have you balanced long and short sentences to avoid a monotonous rhythm? Think about what you are saying. Does your argument make sense? Do you need more information to make any of your points clearer?

Proofread with a pencil in hand and expect to find mistakes. You have finished the hard part and are in the home stretch. It is only natural to want to rush through this last stage and get your paper printed out and handed in. Fight the urge to skip the proofreading and editing steps. Do your paper justice by making it as perfect as it can be.

FINISHING AND POLISHING

Make sure your final draft is in the correct format. The specifics of this format will depend on the instructions you received with your assignment. Is the paper typed in an accepted style with standard margins, the requested spacing, and an approved font? Does your instructor want the paper turned in with a title page? A typical title page includes the title of the paper, your name, the name of the course and instructor, and the date. Are the pages numbered? Some instructors prefer that the pages be marked with the student's last name and page number. This information is usually put in the header of a document created with a word processor.

The final manuscript should be as professional looking as possible. Eliminating errors allows the reader to focus on the essence of the term paper: your research, reasoning, insights, and writing.

Documentation of sources is usually presented in in-text citations, though it may also be given in footnotes or endnotes. In-text citations take two forms: (1) the author-page system, which is widely used in the humanities; and (2) the author-date system, which has been adopted in social and natural science writing. The recognized standard for author-page notation is *The MLA Style Manual*, which is published by the Modern Language Association. *The Manual of the American Psychological Association* (APA) presents the accepted standards of the author-date system. Each of these styles of in-text citation is presented briefly here. For a more comprehensive explanation, you can refer to the style guides themselves.

The basic technique in both systems is to include just enough information in the text to enable the reader to find the relevant item in the reference list. A list of works cited must always be included at the end of the text. If this list includes all of the sources related to the paper, rather than only those sources cited in the text, the list is called a bibliography. The lists are organized in alphabetical order by the first element in the entry, usually the author. For examples, see the sample bibliography entries on the inside covers of this guide.

AUTHOR-PAGE IN-TEXT DOCUMENTATION (MLA) FOR WRITING IN THE HUMANITIES

This system includes the author of the work and the relevant page number. There is no punctuation between these elements. The period that ends the sentence follows an in-text citation.

> American novelists have always had a difficult relationship with their public (Brooks 247).

If the author is mentioned in the text, then just the page number is needed in the parentheses.

> As Brooks has observed, American novelists have always had a difficult relationship with their public (247).

If the reference is to a work as a whole rather than to a specific part, then no additional citation is needed.

> In *Gilded Twilight*, Brooks establishes himself as the most thoughtful of the poststructuralist critics.

If your paper uses more than one source by the same author, the title of the work referred to is included in the parentheses, usually in a shortened form.

> Brooks's comments on Melville are surprisingly negative (*Gilded* 83).

If you are referring to more than one work, all of the references should be included in the same parentheses.

> Recently critics have had surprisingly negative things to say about Melville (Brooks, *Gilded* 83; Adams and Rubens 432; Leibinz 239).

In a citation from the World Wide Web, include page numbers only if they are fixed. Pages from printouts should not be included. You may substitute paragraph numbers for page numbers, in which case a comma follows the author's name. If there is no author for the Web page, list the title.

> New criticism fails to explain the imagery of Billy Budd (Darnell, par. 14).

AUTHOR-DATE IN-TEXT DOCUMENTATION (APA) FOR WRITING IN THE SCIENCES

In the author-date system, a comma follows the author's name. As in the MLA style, the period that ends the sentence follows the parentheses.

You can work the author and date information into the text itself.

> McBain (1991) demonstrates that there is at least one alternative to the accepted view.

> In a 1991 study, McBain demonstrates that there is at least one alternative to the accepted view.

You may also present the reference to a study as in-text documentation.

> A recent study carried out at McGill came to the opposite conclusion (McBain, 1991).

When the reference list contains more than one work by an author, they are distinguished by the year of publication. If you use more than one work published by a single author in the same year, letters are used to distinguish them.

> Several innovative studies in the last few years have demonstrated that this matter is not as settled as was once thought (Brewer, 1989; Fischer & Rivera, 1988; McBain, 1989a, 1989b, 1991; Silvano, Blomstedt, & Meigs, 1987).

Ordinarily, page numbers are included only when there is a direct quotation.

> One respected researcher notes that little notice has been taken of "the substantial number of counterexamples that have not been either questioned or explained" (McBain, 1991, p. 238).

Web sites should be cited with author and date information. If no author information is available, the title can be used.

> The film exploits the imagery of the commedia dell'arte and the kabuki theater (Bonikowski, 1998).

FOOTNOTES AND ENDNOTES

Footnotes and endnotes can be used for additional material that does not fit conveniently into the text. The super-scripted numbers refer the reader to additional material at the bottom of the page or to the end of the text. Traditionally, footnotes have been used to cite sources of information, ideas, and quotations included in the text. With this method of citation, the author, title, place of publication, publisher, date of publication and page number are used in the first citation of the work. Subsequently, only the author and page number are needed. In older works, *ibid* is used for sequential citations from a single source. The use of *ibid* is no longer recommended. The major style manuals now recommend in-text citations. Footnotes are still commonly used in such published materials as books and journals. Whether you choose to document sources with in-text citations or footnotes, complete information about your sources should be included in a reference list at the end of the work.

MLA Reference List

This table shows how the items in the reference list would be treated in the author-page (MLA) system. Information about the author-date (APA) system is found on the following page.

Type of Document	(MLA) Works Cited
Book	David, Ron. *Toni Morrison Explained: A Reader's Road Map to the Novels.* New York: Random House, 2000.
Book two authors	Liftin, Hilary, and Kate Montgomery. *Dear Exile.* New York: Vintage, 1999.
Book more than three authors	King, Dean et al. *Harbors and High Seas: An Atlas and Geographical Guide to the Aubrey-Maturin Novels of Patrick O'Brian.* New York: Owl Books, 1996.
Book revised edition	Titelman, Gregory. *Random House Dictionary of America's Popular Proverbs and Sayings.* 2nd ed. New York: Random House, 2000.
Edited book	Phillips, Louis, ed. *The Random House Treasury of Best-Loved Poems.* 2nd ed. New York: Random House, 1995.
Book no author	*The Literate Life: Exploring Language Arts Standards Within a Cycle of Learning.* Urbana: National Council of Teachers of English, 1997.
Book corporate author	College Board. *The College Board College Cost & Financial Aid Handbook 2000.* New York: College Entrance Examination Board, 1999.
Book in volumes	Cassidy, Frederic G., and Joan Houston Hall, eds. *Dictionary of American Regional English.* Vol. 3. Cambridge: Belknap Press of Harvard UP, 1996.
Book translated	Eco, Umberto. *Kant and the Platypus: Essays on Language and Cognition.* Trans. Alastair McEwen. New York: Harcourt Brace, 1999.
Work from a collection or anthology	Tarone, Elaine. "Some thoughts on the notion of communication strategy." *Strategies in Interlanguage Communication.* Eds. Faerch and Kasper. New York: Longman, 1983. 61–74.
Journal article	Burridge, Kate. "Euphemism with Attitude." *English Today* 47, 12 (July 1996): 42–43, 49.
Journal article two authors	Arndt, Horst, and Richard W. Janney. "Verbal, prosodic, and kinesic emotive contrasts in speech." *Journal of Pragmatics* 15, 6 (1991): 521–549.
Journal article more than two authors	Mascia-Lees, Frances E., Pat Sharpe, and Colleen B. Cohen. "Double Liminality and the Black Woman Writer." *American Behavioral Scientist* 31 (1987): 101–14.
Journal article on-line	Williams, S. H. "Truth, Speech, and Ethics: A Feminist Revision of Free Speech Theory." *Genders* 30 (1999). 31 Jan. 2000 < http://www.genders.org /g30/g30_williams.html > .
Magazine article	King, Stephen. "The Reel Stephen King." *Entertainment Weekly* 10 Dec. 1999: 38–40.
Newspaper article	Simon, Clea. "The Web Catches and Reshapes Radio." *The New York Times* 10 Jan. 2000: 1,15.
Dissertation or Thesis	Ragone, Agnes C. "An exploratory study of thanking in French and Spanish: native norms vs. non-native production." Diss. University of Texas, 1998.
Web site professional	Nichols, Wendalyn. "Sensitive Language." *Words@Random.* 11 Jan. 2000. < http://www.randomhouse.com/words/language > .
Web site personal	Guerrero, Donna. *La Profesoressa: Travel, Tips and Tidbits of Italy.* 14 Jan. 2000. < http://www.geocitites.com/TheTropics/Cabana/2939 > .
Discussion list or list server posting	Kulbrandstad, Lars. "Am.E pronunciation of 'semi' – summary." On-line posting. 17 Jan. 2000. American Dialect Society Listserve 14 Feb. 2000 < http:// listserv.linguistlist.org/cgi-bin/wa?A2 = ind0001C&L = ads-l&P = R1347 > .
E-mail	Braham, Carol. "Latin-American Spanish." E-mail to Heather G. Bonikowski. 21 March 2000.
Two or more works by one author	Costello, Elaine. *Random House Webster's American Sign Language Dictionary.* New York: Random House, 1994.
	---. *Signing: How to Speak with Your Hands.* New York: Bantam, 1995.

Titles may be italicized or underlined. Italics and underlining are equivalent.
Choose one of the two treatments and use it consistently.

APA REFERENCE LIST

This table shows how the items in the reference list would be treated in the author-date (APA) system. Information about the author-page (MLA) system is found on the previous page. For more details, you should consult these style guides.

Type of Document	(APA) References
Book	Goldhammer, John D. (1996). *Under the Influence: The Destructive Effects of Group Dynamics*. Amherst, MA: Prometheus Books.
Book two authors	Perron, P., & Danesi, M. (1999). *Analyzing Cultures: An Introduction and Handbook*. Bloomington, IN: Indiana University Press.
Book more than three authors	Weaver, W., Timoshenko, S.P., Yound, D. H., & Young, D. (1990). *Vibration Problems in Engineering*. New York: John Wiley & Sons.
Book revised edition	Brown, P., & Levinson, S. (1987). *Politeness: Some Universals in Language Use*. (Rev. ed.) Cambridge: Cambridge University Press.
Edited book	Birdsong, David, (Ed.). (1999). *Second Language Acquisition and the Critical Period Hypothesis*. New York: Lawrence Erlbaum Associates.
Book no author	*Publication Manual of the American Psychological Association*. (4th ed.) (1994). Washington, D.C.: American Psychological Association.
Book corporate author	American Psychiatric Association. (1996). *American Psychiatric Association Practice Guidelines*. Washington, D.C.: American Psychiatric Association.
Book in volumes	Lighter, J.E. (1997). *The Random House Historical Dictionary of American Slang, Vol. 2. H-O*. New York: Random House.
Book translated	Eliade, M. (1991). *The Myth of the Eternal Return: Or, Cosmos and History*. (W.R. Trask, Trans.). Princeton: Princeton University Press.
Work from a collection or anthology	Nikula, T. (1997). Interlanguage view on hedging. In Markkenan and Schroder (Eds.), *Hedging and Discourse: Approaches to the Analysis of a Pragmatic Phenomenon in Academic Texts* (pp. 188–207). Berlin: Walter de Gruyter.
Journal article	Andrews, Edna. (1996). Cultural Sensitivity and Political Correctness: The Linguistic Problem of Naming. *American Speech, 71-4*, 389-404.
Journal article two authors	Nespor, M., & Vogel, I. (1986). On clashes and lapses. *Phonology, 6*, 69-116.
Journal article more than two authors	Barringer, H. R., Takeuchi, D. T., & Xenos, P.C. (1990). Education, occupational prestige, and income of Asian-Americans: Evidence from the 1980 Census. *Sociology of Education, 63*, 27–43.
Journal article on-line	Hart, W. B. (1999). The Intercultural Sojourn as the Hero's Journey. *The Edge: The E-Journal of Intercultural Relations 2 (1)*. Retrieved January 31, 2000, from the World Wide Web: http://www.kumo.swcp.com/biz/theedge/hero.htm.
Magazine article	Maryles, D. (2000, January 10). Connecting the Numbers. *Publishers Weekly*, 25–27.
Newspaper article	Mossberg, W. (2000, January 20). Will the New AOL Still Serve User Needs?. *Wall Street Journal*, p. B1.
Dissertation or Thesis	Blyth, C. (1990). *Evaluation in Oral Quebecois Narrative: The Function of Non-referential Meaning in Discourse*. Unpublished doctoral dissertation, Cornell University, Ithaca, NY.
Web site professional	Land, T. [a.k.a Beads] (1998, October 15). Web Extension to American Psychological Association Style (WEAPAS) (Rev. 1.6) [WWW document]. URL http://www.beadsland.com/weapas/
Web site personal	Bonikowski, Derek. *Venus Films*. Retrieved February 10, 2000, from the World Wide Web: http://www.geocities.com/Hollywood/Studio/4110/main.html
Discussion list or list server posting	Newmeyer, F. (January 18, 2000). Grammatical elements and discourse functions. [On-line posting]. Retrieved February 14, 2000 from LINGUIST Discussion List, list archives, on the World Wide Web: http://listserv .linguistlist.org/cgi-bin/wa?A2 = ind0001C&L = linguist&P = R8845
E-mail	Pearsons, E. (June 17, 2000). RHWUD CD-ROM patch. [E-mail].
Two or more works by one author	Lagatree, K. (1998). *Feng Shui at Work*. New York: Villard.
	Lagatree, K. (2000). *Checklists for Life: 104 Lists to Help You Get Organized, Save Time, and Unclutter Your Life*. New York: Random House.

U.S. AND METRIC EQUIVALENTS

LINEAR MEASURE

U.S. Customary	Metric
1 inch	25.4 millimeters (mm)
	2.54 centimeters (cm)
1 foot (12 in.)	304.8 millimeters (mm)
	30.48 centimeters (cm)
	0.3048 meter (m)
1 yard (36 in.; 3 ft.)	0.9144 meter (m)
1 rod (16.5 ft.; 5.5 yds.)	5.029 meters (m)
1 statute mile (5280 ft.; 1760 yds.)	1609.3 meters (m)
	1.6093 kilometers (km)

Metric	U.S. Customary
1 millimeter (mm)	0.03937 in.
1 centimeter (cm)	0.3937 in.
1 meter (m)	39.37 in.
	3.2808 ft.
	1.0936 yds.
1 kilometer (km)	3280.8 ft.
	1093.6 yds.
	0.62137 mi.

LIQUID MEASURE

U.S. Customary	Metric
1 fluid ounce (fl. oz.)	29.573 milliliters (ml)
1 pint (16 fl. oz.)	0.473 (liter) (l)
1 quart (2 pints; 32 fl. oz.)	9.4635 deciliters (dl)
	0.94635 liter (l)
1 gallon (4 quarts; 128 fl. oz.)	3.7854 liters (l)

Metric	U.S. Customary
1 milliliter (ml)	0.033814 fl. oz.
1 deciliter (dl)	3.3814 fl. oz.
1 liter (l)	33.814 fl. oz.
	1.0567 qts.
	0.26417 gal.

AREA MEASURE

U.S. Customary	Metric
square inch (0.007 sq. ft.)	6.452 square centimeters (cm²)
	645.16 square millimeters (mm²)
square foot (144 sq. in.)	929.03 square centimeters (cm²)
	0.092903 square meter (m²)
square yard (9 sq. ft.)	0.83613 square meter (m²)
square rod (30.25 sq. yd.)	
square mile (640 acres)	2.59 square kilometers (km²)

Metric	U.S. Customary
1 square millimeter (mm²)	0.00155 square inch (sq. in.)
1 square centimeter (cm²)	0.155 square inch (sq. in.)
1 centiare	10.764 square feet (sq. ft.)
1 square kilometer (km²)	0.38608 square mile (sq. mi.)

CAPACITY

U.S. Customary	Metric
cubic inch (0.00058 cu. ft.)	16.387 cubic centimeters (cc; cm³)
	0.016387 liter (l)
cubic foot (1728 cu. in.)	0.028317 cubic meter (m³)
cubic yard (27 cu. ft.)	0.76455 cubic meter (m³)
cubic mile (cu. mi.)	4.16818 cubic kilometers (k³)

Metric	U.S. Customary
1 cubic centimeter (cc; cm³)	0.061023 cubic inch (cu. in.)
1 cubic meter (m³)	35.135 cubic feet (1.3079 cu. yd.)
1 cubic kilometer (km³)	0.23990 cubic mile

AVOIRDUPOIS WEIGHTS

U.S. Customary	Metric
1 grain	0.064799 gram (g)
1 ounce (437.5 grains)	28.350 grams (g)
1 pound (16 oz.)	0.45359 kilograms (kg)
1 short ton (2000 lb.)	907.18 kilograms (kg)
	0.90718 metric ton
1 long ton (2240 lb.)	1016 kilograms (kg)
	1.016 metric tons

METRIC UNITS

EASY ESTIMATION GUIDE (rounded off for rule-of-thumb estimations).

Prefix		Metric Unit		U.S. Equivalents			
milli-	= 1/1000	1 millimeter	=	0.039 inch			
centi-	= 1/100	1 centimeter	=	0.39 inch			
deci-	= 1/10	1 decimeter	=	3.937 inches =	0.32 foot		
		1 meter	=	39.37 inches	= 3.2 feet =	1.1 yard	
deka-	= 10	1 dekameter	=	393.7 inches	= 32 feet	= 10 yards	
hecto-	= 100	1 hectometer	=	3937 inches	= 328 feet	= 109 yards	
kilo-	= 1000	1 kilometer	= 39300 inches	= 3280 feet	= 1090 yards		

METRIC CONVERSION TABLES

Metric to U.S.	U.S. to Metric

Length

Metric to U.S.	U.S. to Metric
millimeters × 0.04 = inches	inches × 25.4 = millimeters
centimeters × 0.39 = inches	inches × 2.54 = centimeters
meters × 3.28 = feet	feet × .304 = meters
meters × 1.09 = yards	yards × 0.91 = meters
kilometers × 0.6 = miles	miles × 1.6 = kilometers

Volume

Metric to U.S.	U.S. to Metric
milliliters × 0.03 = fluid ounces	teaspoons × 5 = milliliters
milliliters × 0.06 = cubic inches	tablespoons × 15 = milliliters
liters × 2.1 = pints	cubic inches × 16 = milliliters
liters × 1.06 = quarts	fluid ounces × 30 = milliliters
liters × 0.26 = gallons	cups × 0.24 = liters
cubic meters × 35.3 = cubic feet	pints × 0.47 = liters
cubic meters × 1.3 = cubic yards	quarts × 0.95 = liters
	gallons × 3.8 = liters
	cubic feet × 0.03 = cubic meters
	cubic yards × 0.76 = cubic meters

Mass

Metric to U.S.	U.S. to Metric
grams × 0.035 = ounces	ounces × 28 = grams
kilograms × 2.2 = pounds	pounds × 0.45 = kilograms
short tons × 0.9 = metric tons	metric tons × 1.1 = short tons

Area

Metric to U.S.
square centimeters × 0.16 = square inches
square meters × 1.2 = square yards
square kilometers × 0.4 = square miles
hectares (ha) × 2.5 = acres

U.S. to Metric
square inches × 6.5 = square centimeters
square feet × 0.09 = square meters
square yards × 0.8 = square meters
square miles × 2.6 = square kilometers
acres × 0.4 = hectares

Temperature

degrees Fahrenheit − 32 × 5/9 = degrees Celsius
degrees Celsius × 9/5 + 32 = degrees Fahrenheit

MATH AND SCIENCE FORMULAS

Mathematics

Arithmetic

Order of Operations
1. Within Parentheses
2. Exponents and Roots
3. Multiplication and Division
4. Addition and Subtraction

Logarithms

Definition $\qquad \log_b n = x \leftrightarrow b^x = n$

Product Rule $\qquad \log_b(xy) = \log_b x + \log_b y$

Quotient Rule $\qquad \log_b\left(\dfrac{x}{y}\right) = \log_b x - \log_b y$

Power Rule $\qquad \log_b\left(x^r\right) = r\log_b x$

Algebra

$$(x+y)^2 = x^2 + 2xy + y^2$$

$$(x-y)^2 = x^2 - 2xy + y^2$$

Quadratic Equation $\qquad ax^2 + bx + c = 0$

$$x = \frac{-b \pm \sqrt{b^2 - 4ac}}{2a}$$

Plane Geometry

Pythagorean Theorem $\qquad a^2 + b^2 = c^2$

Areas

Triangle $\qquad A = \frac{1}{2}bh = \frac{1}{2} \times$ base $\times$ height

Rectangle $\qquad A = bh =$ base $\times$ height

Square $\qquad A = S^2 = \dfrac{d^2}{2} = (\text{side})^2 = \dfrac{(\text{diagonal})^2}{2}$

Parallelogram $\qquad A = bh =$ base $\times$ height

Trapezoid $\qquad A = \left(\dfrac{b_1 + b_2}{2}\right)h = \left(\dfrac{\text{base}1 + \text{base}2}{2}\right) \times$ height

Sum of angles $\qquad$ Sum of Angles $= (n-2) \cdot 180°$

n = number of sides of a convex polygon

Circumference of a circle $\qquad C = 2\pi r = 2 \times \pi \times$ radius

Area of a circle $\qquad A = \pi r^2 = \pi \times (\text{radius})^2$

Solid Geometry

Rectangular Solid

Volume $\qquad V = lwh =$ length $\times$ width $\times$ height

Surface area $\qquad SA = 2lw + 2wh + 2lh$

Cube

Volume $\qquad V = s^3 = (\text{side})^3$

Surface area $\qquad SA = 6s^2 = 6 \times (\text{side})^2$

Cylinder

Volume $\qquad V = \pi r^2 h = \pi \times (\text{radius})^2 \times$ height

Surface Area $\qquad SA = 2\pi r^2 + 2\pi rh$

r = radius $\qquad$ h = height

Trigonometry

$$\sin = \frac{\text{opposite}}{\text{hypotenuse}}$$

$$\cos = \frac{\text{adjacent}}{\text{hypotenuse}}$$

$$\tan = \frac{\text{opposite}}{\text{adjacent}}$$

$$\tan x = \frac{\sin x}{\cos x}$$

$$\sin^2 x + \cos^2 x = 1$$

Law of Sines $\qquad \dfrac{\sin A}{a} = \dfrac{\sin B}{b} = \dfrac{\sin C}{c}$

Law of Cosines $\qquad c^2 = a^2 + b^2 - 2ab \cos c$

Science

Chemistry

$$q = mc\Delta T$$

heat (loss or gain) = mass × specific heat × the difference between final and initial temperatures

$$PV = nRT$$

pressure (in atm) × volume (in liters) = number of moles of gas particles × ideal gas constant × temperature in Kelvin

$$\text{Density} = \frac{\text{mass}}{\text{volume}}$$

To convert Celsius to Kelvin $\quad K = C° + 273$

MATH AND SCIENCE FORMULAS (CONT.)

Diatomic molecules
hydrogen (H_2)
nitrogen (N_2)
fluorine (F_2)
oxygen (O_2)
iodine (I_2)
chlorine (Cl_2)
bromine (Br_2)

Exothermic: H (enthalpy) is negative, enthalpy decreases
Endothermic: H (enthalpy) is positive, enthalpy decreases

molarity (M) $\qquad M = \dfrac{\text{number of moles solute}}{\text{number of liters solution}}$

molality (m) $\qquad m = \dfrac{\text{number of moles solute}}{\text{number of kilograms solvent}}$

hydrogen ion
concentration $\qquad pH = -\log[H^+]$

ionization
of water $\qquad H_2O(\ell) \rightleftharpoons H^+(aq) + OH^-(aq)$

Biology

DNA (double helix)
A:T
T:A
C:G
G:C

RNA (single strand)
A:U
U:A
C:G
G:C

A = adenine; T = thymine; C = cytosine; G = guanine;
U = uracil

Physics

Acceleration

$$a = \frac{\Delta v}{\Delta t}$$

a = average acceleration
Δv = changes in velocity
Δt = change in time

Displacement

$$x = v_0 t + \frac{1}{2}at^2$$

x = displacement
v_0 = initial velocity
t = time
a = acceleration

Force
$F = ma$ = mass × acceleration

Force of gravity

$$F = \frac{Gm_1 m_2}{r^2}$$

G = gravitational constant
m_1 = mass 1

m_2 = mass 2
r = distance between objects

Force of a Spring

$$F = -kx$$

F = force
k = spring constant
x = displacement

Momentum
momentum = mass × velocity

Torque
torque = force × lever arm

Centripetal Force

$$F = \frac{mv^2}{r}$$

m = mass
v = speed
r = radius

Force of Friction

$$f = F_N \mu$$

f = force of friction
F_N = normal force
μ = coefficient of friction

Work

$$W = Fd$$

W = work done by applied force
F = force in direction of displacement
d = displacement

Kinetic Energy

$$KE = \frac{1}{2}mv^2$$

KE = kinetic energy
m = mass
v = velocity

Potential Energy

$$V = mgh$$

V = gravitational potential energy
m = mass
g = gravitational acceleration
h = height

Power

$$P = \frac{W}{t}$$

P = power
W = work
t = time

$$P = Fv$$

P = power
F = force
v = velocity

Waves

$$f = \frac{1}{T}$$

f = frequency
T = period

Periodic Table of the Elements

Legend:

Group Number	1
Atomic Number	1
Symbol	H
Name	hydrogen
Atomic Mass	1.00797
Date of Discovery	1766

1	2	3	4	5	6	7	8	9	10	11	12	13	14	15	16	17	18
1 H hydrogen 1.00797 1766																	2 He helium 4.0026 1895
3 Li lithium 6.939 1817	4 Be beryllium 9.0122 1798											5 B boron 10.811 1808	6 C carbon 12.011 †	7 N nitrogen 14.0067 1772	8 O oxygen 15.9994 1774	9 F fluorine 18.9984 1886	10 Ne neon 20.183 1898
11 Na sodium 22.9898 1807	12 Mg magnesium 24.312 1808											13 Al aluminum 26.9815 1825	14 Si silicon 28.086 1823	15 P phosphorus 30.9738 1669	16 S sulfur 32.064 †	17 Cl chlorine 35.453 1774	18 Ar argon 39.948 1894
19 K potassium 39.102 1807	20 Ca calcium 40.08 1808	21 Sc scandium 44.956 1879	22 Ti titanium 47.90 1791	23 V vanadium 50.942 1830	24 Cr chromium 51.996 1797	25 Mn manganese 54.938 1774	26 Fe iron 55.847 †	27 Co cobalt 58.933 1737	28 Ni nickel 58.71 1751	29 Cu copper 63.54 †	30 Zn zinc 65.37 1746	31 Ga gallium 69.72 1875	32 Ge germanium 72.59 1886	33 As arsenic 74.922 †	34 Se selenium 78.96 1817	35 Br bromine 79.909 1826	36 Kr krypton 83.80 1898
37 Rb rubidium 85.47 1861	38 Sr strontium 87.62 1790	39 Y yttrium 88.905 1794	40 Zr zirconium 91.22 1789	41 Nb niobium 92.906 1801	42 Mo molybdenum 95.94 1778	43 Tc technetium (98) 1937	44 Ru ruthenium 101.07 1844	45 Rh rhodium 102.905 1803	46 Pd palladium 106.4 1803	47 Ag silver 107.870 †	48 Cd cadmium 112.40 1817	49 In indium 114.82 1863	50 Sn tin 118.69 †	51 Sb antimony 121.75 †	52 Te tellurium 127.60 1782	53 I iodine 126.904 1804	54 Xe xenon 131.30 1898
55 Cs cesium 132.905 1860	56 Ba barium 137.34 1808	57 La lanthanum 138.91 1839	72 Hf hafnium 178.49 1923	73 Ta tantalum 180.948 1802	74 W tungsten 183.85 1783	75 Re rhenium 186.2 1925	76 Os osmium 190.2 1804	77 Ir iridium 192.2 1804	78 Pt platinum 195.09 1735	79 Au gold 196.967 †	80 Hg mercury 200.59 †	81 Tl thallium 204.37 1861	82 Pb lead 207.19 †	83 Bi bismuth 208.980 †	84 Po polonium (210) 1898	85 At astatine (210) 1940	86 Rn radon (222) 1898
87 Fr francium (223) 1939	88 Ra radium (226) 1898	89 Ac actinium (227) 1899	104 Unq unnilquadium (257) 1969	105 Unp unnilpentium (260) 1970	106 Unh unnilhexium (263) 1974	107 Uns unnilseptium (262) 1976	108 Uno unniloctium (265) Disputed	109 Une unnilennium (266) 1982	110 Uun ununnilium (269) 1987	111 Uuu unununium (272) 1994	112 Uub ununbium (277) 1996						

Lanthanides

57 La lanthanum 138.91 1839	58 Ce cerium 140.12 1803	59 Pr praseodymium 140.907 1885	60 Nd neodymium 144.24 1925	61 Pm promethium (147) 1945	62 Sm samarium 150.35 1879	63 Eu europium 151.96 1901	64 Gd gadolinium 157.25 1880	65 Tb terbium 158.924 1843	66 Dy dysprosium 162.50 1886	67 Ho holmium 164.930 1878	68 Er erbium 167.26 1843	69 Tm thulium 168.934 1879	70 Yb ytterbium 173.04 1878	71 Lu lutetium 174.97 1907

Actinides

89 Ac actinium (227) 1899	90 Th thorium 232.038 1828	91 Pa protactinium (231) 1917	92 U uranium 238.03 1798	93 Np neptunium (237) 1940	94 Pu plutonium (242) 1940	95 Am americium (243) 1945	96 Cm curium (247) 1944	97 Bk berkelium (247) 1949	98 Cf californium (249) 1950	99 Es einsteinium (254) 1952	100 Fm fermium (253) 1953	101 Md mendelevium (256) 1955	102 No nobelium (254) 1957	103 Lr lawrencium (257) 1961

Notes:
Numbers in parentheses indicate mass of the most stable isotope.
† The element was discovered in ancient times and no recorded date is known.

HISTORIC SITES OF THE UNITED STATES

STATES OF THE UNITED STATES

State	Postal Abbr.	Capital	State Nickname
Alabama	AL	Montgomery	Cotton State
Alaska	AK	Juneau	Last Frontier
Arizona	AZ	Phoenix	Grand Canyon State
Arkansas	AR	Little Rock	Land of Opportunity
California	CA	Sacramento	Golden State
Colorado	CO	Denver	Centennial State
Connecticut	CT	Hartford	Constitution State
Delaware	DE	Dover	First State
Florida	FL	Tallahassee	Sunshine State
Georgia	GA	Atlanta	Empire State of the South
Hawaii	HI	Honolulu	Aloha State
Idaho	ID	Boise	Gem State
Illinois	IL	Springfield	Land of Lincoln
Indiana	IN	Indianapolis	Hoosier State
Iowa	IA	Des Moines	Hawkeye State
Kansas	KS	Topeka	Sunflower State
Kentucky	KY	Frankfort	Bluegrass State
Louisiana	LA	Baton Rouge	Pelican State
Maine	ME	Augusta	Pine Tree State
Maryland	MD	Annapolis	Old Line State
Massachusetts	MA	Boston	Bay State
Michigan	MI	Lansing	Wolverine State
Minnesota	MN	St. Paul	Gopher State
Mississippi	MS	Jackson	Magnolia State
Missouri	MO	Jefferson City	Show Me State
Montana	MT	Helena	Treasure State
Nebraska	NE	Lincoln	Cornhusker State
Nevada	NV	Carson City	Silver State
New Hampshire	NH	Concord	Granite State
New Jersey	NJ	Trenton	Garden State
New Mexico	NM	Santa Fe	Land of Enchantment
New York	NY	Albany	Empire State
North Carolina	NC	Raleigh	Tarheel State
North Dakota	ND	Bismarck	Flickertail State
Ohio	OH	Columbus	Buckeye State
Oklahoma	OK	Oklahoma City	Sooner State
Oregon	OR	Salem	Beaver State
Pennsylvania	PA	Harrisburg	Keystone State
Rhode Island	RI	Providence	Ocean State
South Carolina	SC	Columbia	Palmetto State
South Dakota	SD	Pierre	Mount Rushmore State
Tennessee	TN	Nashville	Volunteer State
Texas	TX	Austin	Lone Star State
Utah	UT	Salt Lake City	Beehive State
Vermont	VT	Montpelier	Green Mountain State
Virginia	VA	Richmond	Old Dominion State
Washington	WA	Olympia	Evergreen State
West Virginia	WV	Charleston	Mountain State
Wisconsin	WI	Madison	Badger State
Wyoming	WY	Cheyenne	Equality State

PRESIDENTS AND VICE PRESIDENTS OF THE UNITED STATES

President	Born	Died	Birthplace	Residence	Party	Dates in office	Vice President	Dates in Office
1. George Washington	Feb. 22, 1732	Dec. 14, 1799	Westmoreland Co., Va.	Va.	Fed.	1789-1797	John Adams	1789-1797
2. John Adams	Oct. 30, 1735	July 4, 1826	Quincy, Mass.	Mass.	Fed.	1797-1801	Thomas Jefferson	1797-1801
3. Thomas Jefferson	Apr. 13, 1743	July 4, 1826	Shadwell, Va.	Va.	Rep*	1801-1809	Aaron Burr George Clinton	1801-1805 1805-1809
4. James Madison	Mar. 16, 1751	June 28, 1836	Port Conway, Va.	Va.	Rep.*	1809-1817	George Clinton** Elbridge Gerry	1809-1812 1813-1814
5. James Monroe	Apr. 28, 1758	July 4, 1831	Westmoreland Co., Va.	Va.	Rep*	1817-1825	Daniel Tompkins	1817-1825
6. John Quincy Adams	July 11, 1767	Feb. 23, 1848	Quincy, Mass.		Rep*	1825-1829	John C. Calhoun	1825-1829
7. Andrew Jackson	Mar. 15, 1767	June 8, 1845	New Lancaster Co., S.C.	Tenn.	Dem.	1829-1837	John C. Calhoun Martin Van Buren (4*)	1829-1832 1833-1837
8. Martin Van Buren	Dec. 5, 1782	July 24, 1862	Kinderhook, N.Y.	N.Y.	Dem.	1837-1841	Richard M. Johnson	1837-1841
9. William Henry Harrison**	Feb. 9, 1773	Apr. 4, 1841	Berkeley, Va.	Ohio	Whig	1841	John Tyler (4*)	1841
10. John Tyler	Mar. 29, 1790	Jan. 18, 1862	Greenway, Va.	Va.	Whig	1841-1845		
11. James Knox Polk	Nov. 2, 1795	June 15, 1849	Mecklenburg Co., N.C.	Tenn.	Dem.	1845-1849	George M. Dallas	1845-1849
12. Zachary Taylor**	Nov. 24, 1784	July 9, 1850	Orange Co., Va.	La.	Whig	1849-1850	Millard Fillmore (4*)	1849-1850
13. Millard Fillmore	Jan. 7, 1800	Mar. 8, 1874	Cayuga Co., N. Y.	N.Y.	Whig	1850-1853		
14. Franklin Pierce	Nov. 23, 1804	Oct. 8, 1869	Hillsboro, N.H.	N.H.	Dem.	1853-1857	William R. King**	1853
15. James Buchanan	Apr. 23, 1791	June 1, 1868	Mercersburg, Pa.	Pa.	Dem.	1857-1861	John C. Breckinridge	1857-1861
16. Abraham Lincoln**	Feb. 12, 1809	Apr. 15, 1865	Hardin Co., Ky.	Ill.	Rep.***	1861-1865	Hannibal Hamlin Andrew Johnson (4*)	1861-1865 1865
17. Andrew Johnson	Dec. 29, 1808	July 31, 1875	Raleigh, N.C.	Tenn.	Dem***	1865-1869		
18. Ulysses Simpson Grant	Apr. 27, 1822	July 23, 1885	Point Pleasant, Ohio	Ill.	Rep.	1869-1877	Schuyler Colfax Henry Wilson**	1869-1873 1873-1875
19. Rutherford Birchard Hayes	Oct. 4, 1822	Jan. 17, 1893	Delaware, Ohio	Ohio	Rep.	1877-1881	William A. Wheeler	1877-1881
20. James Abram Garfield**	Nov. 19, 1831	Sept. 19, 1881	Orange, Ohio	Ohio	Rep.	1881	Chester A. Arthur (4*)	1881
21. Chester Alan Arthur	Oct. 5, 1830	Nov. 18, 1886	Fairfield, Vt.	N.Y.	Rep.	1881-1885		
22. Grover Cleveland	Mar. 18, 1837	June 24, 1908	Caldwell, N.J.	N.Y.	Dem.	1885-1889	Thomas A. Hendricks**	1885
23. Benjamin Harrison	Aug. 20, 1833	Mar. 13, 1901	North Bend, Ohio	Ind.	Rep.	1889-1893	Levi P. Morton	1889-1893
24. Grover Cleveland	See number 22					1893-1897	Adlai E. Stevenson	1893-1897
25. William McKinley**	Jan. 29, 1843	Sept. 14, 1901	Niles, Ohio	Ohio	Rep.	1897-1901	Garret A. Hobart** Theodore Roosevelt (4*)	1897-1899 1901
26. Theodore Roosevelt	Oct. 27, 1858	Jan. 6, 1919	New York, N.Y.	N.Y.	Rep.	1901-1909	Charles W. Fairbanks	1905-1909
27. William Howard Taft	Sept. 15, 1857	Mar. 8, 1930	Cincinnati, Ohio	Ohio	Rep.	1909-1913	James S. Sherman	1909-1912
28. Woodrow Wilson	Dec. 28, 1856	Feb. 3, 1924	Staunton, Va.	N.J.	Dem.	1913-1921	Thomas R. Marshall	1913-1921
29. Warren Gamaliel Harding**	Nov. 2, 1865	Aug. 2, 1923	Bloomington Grove, Ohio	Ohio	Rep.	1921-1923	Calvin Coolidge (4*)	1921-1923
30. Calvin Coolidge	July 4, 1872	Jan. 5, 1933	Plymouth, Vt.	Mass.	Rep.	1923-1929	Charles G. Dawes	1925-1929
31. Herbert Clark Hoover	Aug. 10, 1874	Oct. 20, 1964	West Branch, Iowa	Calif.	Rep.	1929-1933	Charles Curtis	1929-1933
32. Franklin Delano Roosevelt**	Jan. 30, 1882	Apr. 12, 1945	Hyde Park, N.Y.	N.Y.	Dem.	1933-1945	John Nance Garner Henry Agard Wallace Harry S Truman (4*)	1933-1941 1941-1945 1945
33. Harry S Truman	May 8, 1884	Dec. 26, 1972	Lamar, Mo.	Mo.	Dem.	1945-1953	Alben W. Barkley	1949-1953
34. Dwight David Eisenhower	Oct. 14, 1890	Mar. 28, 1969	Denison, Tex.	N.Y.	Rep.	1953-1961	Richard M. Nixon	1953-1961
35. John Fitzgerald Kennedy**	May 29, 1917	Nov. 22, 1963	Brookline, Mass.	Mass.	Dem.	1961-1963	Lyndon B. Johnson (4*)	1961-1963
36. Lyndon Baines Johnson	Aug. 27, 1908	Jan. 22, 1973	Johnson City, Tex.	Tex.	Dem.	1963-1969	Hubert H. Humphrey	1965-1969
37. Richard Milhous Nixon (5*)	Jan. 9, 1913	Apr. 22, 1994	Yorba Linda, Calif.	Calif.	Rep.	1969-1974	Spiro T. Agnew Gerald R. Ford (4*)	1969-1973 1973-1974
38. Gerald Rudolph Ford	July 14, 1913		Omaha, Nebr.	Mich.	Rep.	1974-1977	Nelson A. Rockefeller	1974-1977
39. James Earl Carter, Jr.	Oct. 1, 1924		Plains, Ga.	Ga.	Dem.	1977-1981	Walter F. Mondale	1977-1981
40. Ronald Wilson Reagan	Feb. 6, 1911	June 5, 2004	Tampico, Ill.	Calif.	Rep.	1981-1989	George H. W. Bush	1981-1989
41. George Herbert Walker Bush	June 12, 1924		Milton, Mass.	Tex.	Rep.	1989-1993	James Danforth Quayle	1989-1993
42. William Jefferson Clinton	Aug. 19, 1946		Hope, Ark.	Ark.	Dem.	1993-2001	Albert A. Gore, Jr.	1993-2001
43. George Walker Bush	July 6, 1946		New Haven, Conn.	Tex.	Rep.	2001-	Richard Bruce Cheney	2001-

*Now the Democratic Party
**Died in Office
***Elected on the Union party ticket
(4*)Succeeded to Presidency
(5*)Resigned

Nation	Capital	Nation	Capital
Afghanistan	Kabul	Gambia	Banjul
Albania	Tirana	Georgia	Tbilisi
Algeria	Algiers	Germany	Berlin
Andorra	Andorra la Vella	Ghana	Accra
Angola	Luanda	Greece	Athens
Antigua and Barbuda	Saint Johns	Grenada	St. Georges
Argentina	Buenos Aires	Guatemala	Guatemala City
Armenia	Yerevan	Guinea	Conakry
Australia	Canberra	Guinea-Bissau	Bissau
Austria	Vienna	Guyana	Georgetown
Azerbaijan	Baku	Haiti	Port-au-Prince
Bahamas	Nassau	Honduras	Tegucigalpa
Bahrain	Manama	Hungary	Budapest
Bangladesh	Dhaka	Iceland	Reykjavik
Barbados	Bridgetown	India	New Delhi
Belarus	Minsk	Indonesia	Jakarta
Belgium	Brussels	Iran	Tehran
Belize	Belmopan	Iraq	Baghdad
Benin	Porto Novo	Ireland	Dublin
Bhutan	Thimphu	Israel	Jerusalem
Bolivia	La Paz	Italy	Rome
Bosnia and Herzegovina	Sarajevo	Ivory Coast	Abidjan
Botswana	Gabarone	Jamaica	Kingston
Brazil	Brasilia	Japan	Tokyo
Brunei	Bandar Seri Begawan	Jordan	Amman
Bulgaria	Sofia	Kazakhstan	Akmola
Burkina Faso	Ouagadougou	Kenya	Nairobi
Burundi	Bujumbura	Kiribati	Tarawa
Cambodia	Phnon Penh	Korea, North	Pyongyang
Cameroon	Yaoundé	Korea, South	Seoul
Canada	Ottawa	Kuwait	Kuwait
Cape Verde	Praia	Kyrgyzstan	Bishkek
Central African Republic	Bangui	Laos	Vientiane
Chad	N'Djamena	Latvia	Riga
Chile	Santiago	Lebanon	Beirut
China	Beijing	Lesotho	Maseru
Colombia	Bagota	Liberia	Monrovia
Comoros	Moroni	Libya	Tripoli
Congo, Democratic Republic of	Kinshasa	Liechtenstein	Vaduz
Congo, Republic of	Brazzaville	Lithuania	Vilnius
Costa Rica	San José	Macedonia	Skopje
Croatia	Zagreb	Madagascar	Antananarivo
Cuba	Havana	Malawi	Lilongwe
Cyprus	Nicosia	Malaysia	Kuala Lumpur
Czech Republic	Prague	Maldives	Malé
Denmark	Copenhagen	Mali	Bamako
Djibouti	Djibouti	Malta	Valletta
Dominica	Roseau	Marshall Islands	Majuro
Dominican Republic	Santo Domingo	Mauritania	Nouakchott
Ecuador	Quito	Mauritius	Port Louis
Egypt	Cairo	Mexico	Mexico City
El Salvador	San Salvador	Micronesia	Kolonia
Equatorial Guinea	Malabo	Moldova	Kishinev
Eritrea	Asmara	Monaco	Monaco
Estonia	Tallinn	Mongolia	Ulan Bator
Ethiopia	Addis Ababa	Morocco	Rabat
Fiji	Suva	Mozambique	Maputo
Finland	Helsinki	Myanmar (Burma)	Yangon
France	Paris	Namibia	Windhoek
Gabon	Libreville	Naura	—

Nation	Capital	Nation	Capital
Nepal	Katmandu	Somalia	Mogadishu
Netherlands	Amsterdam	South Africa	Pretoria & Cape Town
New Zealand	Wellington	Spain	Madrid
Nicaragua	Managua	Sri Lanka	Colombo
Niger	Niamey	Sudan	Khartoum
Nigeria	Abuja	Suriname	Paramaribo
Norway	Oslo	Swaziland	Mbabane
Oman	Muscat	Sweden	Stockholm
Pakistan	Islamabad	Switzerland	Bern
Palau	Koror	Syria	Damascus
Panama	Panama City	Taiwan	Taipei
Papua New Guinea	Port Moresby	Tajikistan	Dushanbe
Paraguay	Asunción	Tanzania	Dodoma
Peru	Lima	Thailand	Bangkok
Philippines	Manila	Togo	Lomé
Poland	Warsaw	Tonga	Nukualofa
Portugal	Lisbon	Trinidad and Tobago	Port-of-Spain
Qatar	Doha	Tunisia	Tunis
Romania	Bucharest	Turkey	Ankara
Russia	Moscow	Tuvalu	Funafuti
Rwanda	Kigali	Turkmenistan	Ashgabat
St. Kitts and Nevis	Basseterre	Uganda	Kampala
St. Lucia	Castries	Ukraine	Kiev
St. Vincent and the Grenadines	Kingstown	United Arab Emirates	Abu Dhabi
Samoa	Apia	United Kingdom	London
San Marino	San Marino	United States	Washington, D.C.
São Tomé and Principe	São Tomé	Uruguay	Montevideo
Saudi Arabia	Riyadh	Uzbekistan	Tashkent
Senegal	Dakar	Vanuatu	Vila
Seychelles	Victoria	Venezuela	Caracas
Sierra Leone	Freetown	Vietnam	Hanoi
Singapore	Singapore	Yemen	Sanaa
Slovakia	Bratislava	Yugoslavia	Belgrade
Slovenia	Ljubljana	Zambia	Lusaka
Solomon Islands	Honiara	Zimbabwe	Harare

HOW TO THINK ABOUT THE SAT

The Educational Testing Service (ETS) is the company that writes the SAT. Close your eyes for a moment and try to picture what goes on at ETS headquarters during a question-writing session. What images popped into your mind? If you imagined a room full of distinguished Nobel Prize-winning mathematicians and literary professors, you'd be way off base. If you saw some stuffy-yet-brilliant college professors, working hand-in-hand with the Department of Education, keep dreaming. How about a group of noble teachers and educators? Not even close.

The truth is that the SAT is written by a bunch of regular Joes whose jobs just happen to involve writing test questions. Why does this matter? Because you should always remember that the SAT is nothing special. It is simply a test. And with our help, you can master it.

WHAT ETS IS GOOD AT

The folks at ETS are quite good at writing standardized tests (it is their job, after all). They've been doing it for more than 80 years, and they write tests for all sorts of programs. They have administered the test so many times that they know exactly how you will approach it. They know how you'll attack certain questions, what sort of mistakes you'll probably make, and even what answer you'll be most likely to pick.

Kinda freaky, isn't it?

However, ETS's strength is also a weakness. Because the test is standardized, the SAT has to ask the same type of questions over and over again. Sure, the numbers or the words might change, but the basics don't. With enough practice, you can learn to think like ETS.

LEARN TO THINK LIKE ETS

ETS uses the same tricks over and over again; once you become aware of them, you won't fall for them. ETS also likes certain types of answers. If you notice, you aren't asked to pick the *correct* answer choice for each question on the SAT; instead, you are asked to select the *best* answer. What is the best answer? The best answer is simply what ETS says is the best answer. But don't worry, we'll tell you how to find it.

THE SAT ISN'T SCHOOL

Our job isn't to teach you math or English—leave that to your most knowledgeable and beloved school teachers. Instead, we're going to teach you the SAT. You'll soon see that the SAT involves a very different skill set.

Be forewarned that some of the approaches we're going to show you will seem weird or unnatural. In fact, if you tried to pull off some of this stuff in school, your teacher wouldn't be amused. But you must trust us. Try tackling the problems using our techniques, and keep practicing until they become easier. You'll see a real improvement in your score.

Now let's take a look at those techniques and get down to business.

CRACKING MULTIPLE-CHOICE QUESTIONS

What's the capital of Malawi?

Give up?

Unless you spend your spare time studying an atlas, you may not even know that Malawi is a tiny country in Africa, much less what its capital is. If this question came up on a test, you'd have to skip it, wouldn't you? Well, maybe not. Let's turn this question into a multiple-choice question—just like all the questions on the SAT Critical Reading and Grammar sections, and the majority of questions you'll find on the SAT Math section—and see if you can figure out the answer anyway.

    1. The capital of Malawi is

       (A) Washington, D.C.

       (B) Paris

       (C) Tokyo

       (D) London

       (E) Lilongwe

The question doesn't seem that hard anymore, does it? Of course, we made our example extremely easy. (By the way, there won't actually be any questions about geography on the SAT.) But you'd be surprised by how many people give up on SAT questions that aren't much more difficult than this one just because they don't know the correct answer right off the top of their heads. "Capital of Malawi? Oh, no! I've never heard of Malawi!" These students don't stop to think that they might be able to find the correct answer simply by eliminating all of the answer choices they know are wrong.

YOU ALREADY KNOW ALMOST ALL OF THE ANSWERS

All but a handful of the questions on the SAT are multiple-choice questions, and every multiple-choice question is followed by five answer choices. On every single multiple-choice question, one of those choices, and only one, will be the correct answer to the question. You won't have to come up with the answer from scratch. You only have to identify it.

How will you do that?

LOOK FOR THE WRONG ANSWERS INSTEAD OF THE RIGHT ONES

Why? Because wrong answers are usually easier to find. Remember the question about Malawi? Even though you didn't know the answer off the top of your head, you easily figured it out by eliminating the four obviously incorrect choices. You looked for wrong answers first.

In other words, you used the Process of Elimination, which we'll call POE for short. This is an extremely important concept. It's one of the keys to improving your SAT score.

The great artist Michelangelo once said that when he looked at a block of marble, he could see a statue inside it. All he had to do to make a sculpture, he said, was to chip away everything that wasn't part of it. You should approach difficult SAT multiple-choice questions in the same way, by chipping away everything that's not correct. By first eliminating the most obviously incorrect choices on difficult questions, you will be able to focus your attention on the few choices that remain.

THIS ISN'T THE WAY YOU'RE TAUGHT TO THINK IN SCHOOL

In school, your teachers expect you to work carefully and thoroughly, spending as long as it takes to understand whatever it is you're working on. They want you to prove not only that you know the answer to a question, but also that you know how to derive it. When your algebra teacher gives you a test in class, he or she wants you to work through every problem, logical step by logical step. You probably even have to show your work. If you don't know all the steps required to arrive at the solution, you may not receive full credit, even if you somehow manage to come up with the correct answer.

But the SAT is different. It isn't like school. You don't have to prove that you know why your answer is correct. The only thing ETS's scoring machine cares about is the answer you come up with. If you darken the right space on your answer sheet, you'll get credit, even if you didn't quite understand the question.

PROCESS OF ELIMINATION (POE)

There won't be many questions on the SAT in which incorrect choices will be as easy to eliminate as they were on the Malawi question. But if you read this book carefully, you'll learn how to eliminate at least one choice on virtually any SAT multiple-choice question, if not two, three, or even four choices.

What good is it to eliminate just one or two choices on a five-choice SAT question? Plenty. In fact, for most students, it's an important key to earning higher scores. Here's another example:

2. The capital of Qatar is
(A) Paris
(B) Dukhan
(C) Tokyo
(D) Doha
(E) London

On this question you'll almost certainly be able to eliminate three of the five choices by using POE. That means you're still not sure of the answer. You know that the capital of Qatar has to be either Doha or Dukhan, but you don't know which.

Should you skip the question and go on? Or should you guess?

CLOSE YOUR EYES AND POINT

You've probably heard a lot of different advice about guessing on multiple-choice questions on the SAT. Some teachers and guidance counselors tell their students never to guess and to mark an answer only if they're absolutely certain that it's correct. Others tell their students not to guess unless they are able to eliminate two or three of the choices.

Both of these pieces of advice are incorrect.

Even ETS is misleading about guessing. Although it tells you that you *can* guess, it doesn't tell you that you *should*. In fact, if you can eliminate even one incorrect choice on an SAT multiple-choice question, guessing blindly from among the remaining choices will most likely improve your score. And if you can eliminate two or three choices, you'll be even more likely to improve your score by guessing.

THE BIG BAD GUESSING PENALTY

Your raw score on the SAT is the number of questions you got right, minus a fraction of the number you got wrong (except on the grid-ins, which are scored a little differently). Every time you answer an SAT question correctly, you get one raw point. Every time you leave an SAT question blank, you get zero raw points. Every time you answer an SAT question incorrectly, ETS subtracts one-fourth of a raw point if the question has five answer choices, or nothing if it is a grid-in.

ETS refers to the subtracted fraction as the "guessing penalty." The penalty is supposed to discourage students from guessing on multiple-choice questions (and getting the right answer out of sheer luck). However, let's take a closer look at how the penalty works.

Raw scores can be a little confusing, so let's think in terms of money instead. For every question you answer correctly on the SAT, ETS will give you a dollar. For every multiple-choice question you leave blank, ETS will give you nothing. For every multiple-choice question you get wrong, you will have to give 25 cents back to ETS. That's exactly the way raw scores work.

What happens to your score if you select the correct answer on one question and incorrect choices on four questions? Remember what we said about money: ETS gives you a dollar for the one answer you got right; you give ETS a quarter for each of the four questions you missed. Four quarters equal a dollar, so you end up exactly where you started, with nothing—which is the same thing that would have happened if you had left all five questions blank. Now, what happens if you guess on four questions, but—for each of those questions—you can eliminate one incorrect answer choice? Random odds say you will get one question right—get a dollar—and miss the other three questions—give back 75 cents. You've just gained a quarter! So, in some cases, guessing can work in your favor.

To Guess or Not to Guess: That Is the Question

When it comes to guessing, the most important thing to remember is that it's all about the money. Or in this case, the points. Remember, you're not trying to show someone how smart you are. You're trying to get as many raw points as you can without losing fractions of a point in the process.

So here's how guessing should fit into your overall test-taking strategy. First, answer all of the questions you know you can get right away. Avoid making quick guesses early in a section, since you probably won't need to answer every question to get your target score, and there will be more questions later that you'll know how to do. Plus, you can always come back to a question.

Then, determine how many more questions—if any—you need to attempt in order to reach your target score. If you find that you need to attempt more questions, then guess—using the tools we're going to give you in this book. The test writers create wrong answers in fairly predictable ways. We'll show you the traps they've laid out for you throughout the test, so you can eliminate answer choices if you need to guess.

Finally, only guess if you've eliminated *at least one* answer choice. If you can't eliminate one, leave that question blank.

Credit for Partial Information

Earning points for a guess probably seems a little bit like cheating or stealing: You get something you want, but you didn't do anything to earn it.

This is not a useful way to think about the SAT. It's also not true. Look at the following example:

3. The Sun is a

(A) main-sequence star

(B) meteor

(C) asteroid

(D) white dwarf star

(E) planet

If you've paid any attention at all in school for the past ten years or so, you probably know that the Sun is a star. You can easily tell, therefore, that the answer to this question must be either A or D. You can tell this not only because it seems clear from the context that "white dwarf" and "main-sequence" are kinds of stars—as they are—but also because you know for a fact that the Sun is not a planet, a meteor, or an asteroid. Still, you aren't sure which of the two possible choices is correct.

Heads, You Win a Dollar; Tails, You Lose a Quarter

By using POE you've narrowed down your choice to two possibilities. If you guess randomly you'll have a fifty-fifty chance of being correct, like flipping a coin—heads you win a dollar, tails you lose a quarter. Those are extremely good odds on the SAT. But let's say that, in spite of everything we've told you, you just can't bring yourself to guess. You decide to leave the question blank.

Now, let's say there is a guy sitting next to you who is, to put it politely, no rocket scientist. When it comes to this question, he has no idea what the Sun is: planet, asteroid, meteor—he's clueless. So he leaves the question blank, too.

Even though you know more about the Sun than this guy, you both earn exactly the same score: zero. According to the SAT, you don't know any more about the Sun than he does. (The answer, by the way, is A. And don't worry, there won't be any questions about astronomy on the SAT.)

If you were in class, this probably wouldn't happen. Your teacher might give you credit for knowing that the Sun is some kind of star. In math class, your teacher probably gives you partial credit on a difficult problem if you set it up correctly, even if you make a silly mistake and get the wrong answer.

Guessing Intelligently: The Balancing Act

Guessing makes it possible to earn points for knowing partial information on the SAT. You may not know the information that leads you directly to the answer, but you could know information that tells you what the answer definitely is not. You probably won't know everything about every question on the test, but there could be a lot of questions about which you know something. Doesn't it seem fair that you should be able to earn some credit for what you *do* know?

Remember, because it's all about the points, there will be times that you should absolutely not guess. But by combining your aggressive POE skills with knowing how many questions you need to attempt, you will increase your score.

TEXTBOOK GRAFFITI

At school you probably aren't allowed to write in your textbooks, unless your school requires you to buy them. You probably even feel a little peculiar about writing in the books you own. Books are supposed to be read, you've been told, and you're not supposed to scrawl all over them.

Because you've been told this so many times, you may be reluctant to write in your test booklet when you take the SAT. Your proctor will tell you that you are supposed to write in it—the booklet is the only scratch paper you'll be allowed to use; it says so right in the instructions from ETS—but you may still feel bad about marking it up.

DON'T BE RIDICULOUS!

Your test booklet is just going to be thrown away when you're finished with it. No one is going to read what you wrote in it and decide that you're stupid because you couldn't remember what 2 + 2 was without writing it down. Your SAT score won't be any higher if you don't make any marks in your booklet. In fact, if you don't take advantage of it, your score will probably be lower than it should be.

OWN YOUR TEST BOOKLET

You paid for your test booklet; act as though you own it. Scratch work is extremely important on the SAT. Don't be embarrassed about it. After all, writing in your test booklet will help you keep your mind on what you're doing.

- When you work on a geometry problem that provides a diagram, don't hesitate to write all over it. What if there's no diagram? Draw one yourself—don't simply try to imagine it. Keep track of your work directly on the diagram to help you avoid making careless mistakes.
- On sentence completion questions, you will often need to come up with your own word or two to help you answer a question. Write it down! Trying to retain information in your head leads to confusion and errors. Your test booklet is your scratch paper—use it.
- When you use POE to eliminate a wrong answer choice, physically cross off the answer choice in your test booklet. Don't leave it there to confuse you. You may often need to carefully consider two remaining answer choices. You want to be clear about which answer choices are left in the running.
- When you answer a question but don't feel entirely certain of your answer, circle the question or put a big question mark in the margin beside it. That way, if

you have time later on, you can get back to it without having to search through the entire section.

You probably think of scratch paper as something that is useful only in arithmetic. But you'll need scratch paper on the SAT Critical Reading and Writing sections, too. The Critical Reading sections of your booklet should be just as marked up as the Math ones.

TRANSFER YOUR ANSWERS AT THE END OF EACH GROUP

Scratch work isn't the only thing we want you to do in your test booklet. We also want you to mark your answers there. For each group of sentence completions, you should transfer your answers to the answer sheet when you come to the end of the group of questions. For all other questions (except grid-ins), you should transfer your answers one page at a time.

Doing this will save you a great deal of time, because you won't have to look back and forth between your test booklet and your answer sheet every few seconds. You will also be less likely to make mistakes in marking your answers on the answer sheet. However, be sure to give yourself enough time to transfer your answers. Don't wait until the last five minutes.

The only exception to this are the grid-ins, the ten non–multiple-choice math questions. You will need to grid each answer as you find it.

BASIC PRINCIPLES SUMMARY

1. When you don't know the right answer to a multiple-choice question, look for wrong answers instead. They're usually easier to find.
2. When you find a wrong answer choice, eliminate it. In other words, use POE, the Process of Elimination.
3. ETS doesn't care if you understand the questions on the SAT. All it cares about is whether or not you darken the correct space on your answer sheet.
4. When deciding whether to guess on a question, consider how many questions you need to attempt to reach your target score.
5. Intelligent guessing on multiple-choice questions enables you to earn credit for partial information.
6. Use your test booklet for scratch paper.
7. Transfer your answers to your answer sheet all at once when you reach the end of each group of sentence completions, or one page at a time for all other questions (except for the grid-ins). And remember, give yourself enough time to transfer your answers; don't wait until the last five minutes.

Excerpted from *Cracking the SAT 2007*, ISBN 978-0-375-76545-2, Random House, June 2006

The Princeton Review Helps You Navigate the College Admissions Process.

Find the Right School

Best 361 Colleges, 2008 Edition
978-0-375-76621-3 • $21.95/C$27.95
Previous Edition: 978-0-375-76558-2

Complete Book of Colleges, 2008 Edition
978-0-375-76620-6 • $26.95/C$34.95
Previous Edition: 978-0-375-76557-5

America's Best Value Colleges, 2008 Edition
978-0-375-76601-5 • $18.95/C$24.95

Guide to College Visits
978-0-375-76600-8 • $20.00/C$25.00

Get In

Cracking the SAT, 2008 Edition
978-0-375-76606-0 • $19.95/C$24.95

Cracking the SAT with DVD, 2008 Edition
978-0-375-76607-7 • $33.95/C$42.00

Math Workout for the NEW SAT
978-0-375-76433-2 • $16.00/C$23.00

**Reading and Writing Workout
for the NEW SAT**
978-0-375-76431-8 • $16.00/C$23.00

**11 Practice Tests for the SAT and PSAT,
2008 Edition**
978-0-375-76614-5 • $19.95/C$26.95
Previous Edition: 978-0-375-76544-5

Cracking the ACT, 2007 Edition
978-0-375-76585-8 • $19.95/C$24.95

Cracking the ACT with DVD, 2007 Edition
978-0-375-76586-5 • $31.95/C$39.95

Crash Course for the ACT, 3rd Edition
978-0-375-76587-2 • $9.95/C$12.95

Crash Course for the New SAT
978-0-375-76461-5 • $9.95/C$13.95

Get Help Paying for It

How to Save for College
978-0-375-76425-7 • $14.95/C$21.00

**Paying for College Without Going Broke,
2007 Edition**
978-0-375-76567-4 • $20.00/C$27.00

NOTES